ATLANTIC OCEAN

Portsmouth
An attractive and graceful historic harbor town known for its excellent selection of restaurants

The Berkshires
Rolling countryside, the Tanglewood Music Festival, country inns and lots of relaxed summer culture

Boston
The lively and cultured hub of New England, marked by Old World charm and New World sophistication

Cape Cod National Seashore
Sandy dunes, exquisite bay-long Atlantic beaches, and abundant clams, oysters and lobsters

Martha's Vineyard & Nantucket Island
Hiking, biking, boating, swimming and sunbathing – island living at its finest

Newport
Palatial mansions from a bygone era gracing a picturesque shoreline

Block Island
A sleepy little island with Victorian inns, beaches, nature trails and an excellent harbor

Mystic Seaport Museum
Historic re-creation of a 19th-century working coastal town, where much of the movie Amistad was filmed

Litchfield Hills
Quintessential New England towns, beautiful lakes and great hiking and biking

Boothbay Harbor

Portland
Kennebunk
Kennebunkport
Ogunquit
Portsmouth

White Mountain National Forest
Lakes Region
Lake Winnipesaukee

Gloucester
Rockport
Cape Ann
Salem
Marblehead
BOSTON
Cambridge

Hanover

New Hampshire

CONCORD
Manchester

Vermont

Connecticut River

Manchester
Bennington
Brattleboro

Appalachian Trail

Williamstown
Lenox
Berkshire Hills

ALBANY

New York

New York

Long Island

Long Island Sound

Litchfield Hills
New Haven

New London
Groton
Mystic

Connecticut
HARTFORD
Pioneer Valley
Springfield
Worcester
Concord
Quabbin Reservoir
Massachusetts

Rhode Island
PROVIDENCE
South County
Narragansett
Newport
Block Island

Plymouth
Provincetown
Cape Cod National Seashore
Cape Cod
Hyannis
Falmouth
Woods Hole
Edgartown
Martha's Vineyard
Nantucket
Nantucket Island

68°W
69°W
70°W
71°W
72°W

41°N
42°N
43°N

New England
3rd edition – July 2002
First published – September 1996

Published by
Lonely Planet Publications Pty Ltd ABN 36 005 607 983
90 Maribyrnong St, Footscray, Victoria 3011, Australia

Lonely Planet Offices
Australia Locked Bag 1, Footscray, Victoria 3011
USA 150 Linden St, Oakland, CA 94607
UK 10a Spring Place, London NW5 3BH
France 1 rue du Dahomey, 75011 Paris

Photographs
Many of the images in this guide are available for licensing from
Lonely Planet Images.
W www.lonelyplanetimages.com

Front cover photograph
Marlow, New Hampshire (Mark Newma

ISBN 1 74059 025 2

text & maps © Lonely Planet Publications Pty Ltd 2002
photos © photographers as indicated 2002

Printed by SNP SPrint (M) Sdn Bhd
Printed in Malaysia

Contents

2 Contents

AROUND BOSTON
161

CAPE COD
206

MARTHA'S VINEYARD & NANTUCKET ISLAND
254

CENTRAL MASSACHUSETTS & THE BERKSHIRES
286

RHODE ISLAND
333

CONNECTICUT
368

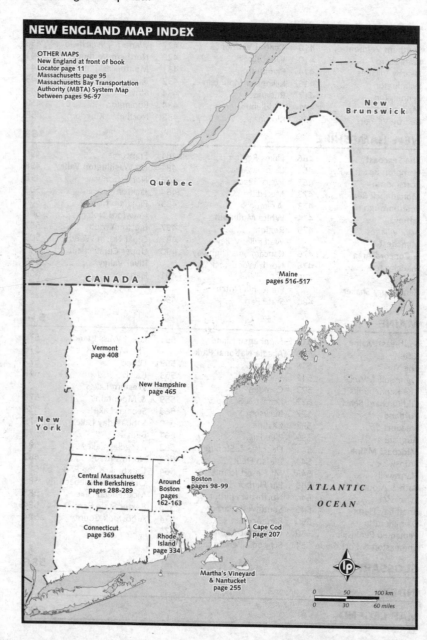

NEW ENGLAND MAP INDEX

OTHER MAPS
New England at front of book
Locator page 11
Massachusetts page 95
Massachusetts Bay Transportation
Authority (MBTA) System Map
between pages 96-97

Québec

New
Brunswick

CANADA

Maine
pages 516-517

Vermont
page 408

New Hampshire
page 465

New
York

Central Massachusetts
& the Berkshires
pages 288-289

Around
Boston
pages
162-163

Boston
pages 98-99

ATLANTIC
OCEAN

Connecticut
page 369

Rhode
Island
page 334

Cape Cod
page 207

Martha's Vineyard
& Nantucket
page 255

0   50   100 km
0   30   60 miles

The Authors

Randall Peffer
As a boy, Randy hopped a freight train out of Pittsburgh, PA, in search of the King of the Hoboes. His mother claims he's still looking. A widely published feature writer, Randy has contributed to *National Geographic*, *Smithsonian, Islands, Travel Holiday, Sail, Reader's Digest* and most US major metro dailies. He is author of Lonely Planet's *Puerto Rico* and *Virgin Islands*, coordinating author of *Virginia & the Capital Region* and contributor to LP's two *Unpacked* volumes. He wrote National Geographic's *Driving Guide – New York, New Jersey and Pennsylvania* and two nautical memoirs, *Watermen* and *Logs of the Dead Pirates Society*. Randy captains a research schooner and teaches literature and writing at Phillips Academy in Andover, MA.

Kim Grant
Kim grew up in the Boston area and graduated from Mt Holyoke College in 1984. After two years of traveling around Europe on $10 a day, she was determined to make a living traveling, writing and photographing. Almost 20 years later, she is author or co-author of LP's *Boston, Miami, Florida* and *USA*, as well as *Cape Cod, Martha's Vineyard & Nantucket: An Explorer's Guide*, *Best Places to Stay in Hawaii* (someone's gotta do it) and *Best Places to Stay in New England*. Represented by Lonely Planet Images, Kim's photography is also published under the Bindu Press imprint. Her shooting exploits recently took her across Vermont backroads to photograph sheep, cows and goats for *The Cheeses of Vermont*. Kim lives with her partner in a circa-1900 Victorian in Dorchester, Boston's largest, oldest and most diverse neighborhood.

Andrew Rebold
Andrew grew up in New Jersey but always looked forward to summers in Maine. After studying in Dijon, France, and backpacking much of Western Europe, he was addicted to travel. He earned a BA in Geography from Clark University, then joined the Peace Corps in Mali, West Africa. He next came to LP as a cartographer. Andrew co-authored *Africa on a Shoestring* and contributed to *West Africa*. His passions include cycling, keeping his fingers crossed for the Red Sox, and sipping Moxie on the verandah while looking forward to a world with less complicated women. Andrew is pursuing a Masters of Public Health at Columbia University.

John Spelman
Martyn Bowden and David Venturo taught John to write during his sophomore year of college. Nineteen years earlier, moments after his birth in Providence, RI, he had been transported 5 miles across the border to Rehoboth, MA, before he was old enough to protest. Ever since, he's lied pathetically and often, claiming to be a Rhode Islander to people who don't even care. After 21 years of cushy New England living, John moved to San Francisco to be a nameless face in Lonely Planet's cartography department. In his spare time, John dreams about the preservation of New England's material landscape while trying to develop an understanding of urban design theory.

FROM THE AUTHORS

Randall Peffer First of all, thanks to my co-authors for their enthusiasm in uncovering fresh corners of New England. Their wit kept me emotionally afloat while I was adrift in a sea of computer files. Senior editor Maria Donohoe and project editors Rachel Bernstein, Kathryn Ettinger and Michael Johnson offered many suggestions to enrich the text. Cartographer Kat Smith produced excellent maps, and illustrator Justin Marler and designers Henia Miedzinski and Shelley Firth are wizards at their crafts. Tammy Fortin, the tattooed muse, ministered to all our souls with sushi, suds and girl-band rock. Thanks also to the research librarians at Phillips Academy's Oliver Wendell Holmes Library for their magical ability to unearth rare sources at lightning speed.

Most importantly, thanks to Jackie, Jacob and Noah, for giving me the time, space and support to finish this project. The adventure of travel writing would be hollow indeed without having my family to share it.

Kim Grant If sports are a metaphor for life, then let the games begin. The 2001-02 New England Patriots, Super Bowl XXXVI champs, redefined the word T-E-A-M. No individual rose above the others, but each stepped up to do their part when it was time. That's how championship teams are made, and this guidebook has been created with the same spirit. From the cast of fellow authors and cartos to the editors, ably directed by Maria Donohoe and Rachel Bernstein, this book epitomizes T-E-A-M effort. Now, if only the Boston Red Sox could forget about the so-called curse and put their egos aside…Go Pats! Go Sox!

Andrew Rebold I'd like to give a bear hug of thanks to Josh and Carmel Howe for their endless wisdom, support and kindness (and Portland apartment). Merci buckets to Anita Keller for joining me on the first leg of the trip. Thanks to Randy Peffer for being such a fabulous mentor, though we never got to hoist that pint (er, uh, sail…) on his boat. It was a pleasure to work on the 'other side of the fence' with my old friend John Spelman. Hats off to senior editor Maria Donohoe, editor Rachel Bernstein, and lead cartographer Kat Smith who helped make the Maine chapter wicked good. Lastly, I'd like to dedicate my chunk of this book to my Aunt Esther and Uncle Paul Abramson, who are responsible/guilty for opening my eyes to Maine at a young age.

John Spelman This book's smallest state probably owes more thanks than it's due. My mother provided heaps of advice and free lodging. My cultural understanding of Rhode Island and its relationship with ice cream could not exist without my grandparents, who wisely elected to raise their family there. Many thanks go to my aunt, and to Catherine and the other Sisters of Mercy. Stuart McNaught's Newport insights were particularly numerous. Thanks to Maria Donohoe for giving me this gig, to Alex Guilbert for releasing me from my day job and to Rachel Bernstein for putting up with my shit. Kat Smith knows why she's mentioned here. Randy Peffer deserves cred for stellar guidance. Honorable mentions go to Robert Reid and Andy Rebold. Lisa, my domestic pal, not only provided technical support, but also dealt with our rat-infested apartment during my absence.

This Book

Randall Peffer was the coordinating author of this 3rd edition of *New England*. He updated the introductory chapters, wrote Central Massachusetts & the Berkshires and Connecticut and co-authored the Around Boston chapter. Kim Grant co-authored Around Boston with Randy and wrote Boston, Cape Cod, Martha's Vineyard & Nantucket Island, Vermont and New Hampshire. John Spelman wrote the Rhode Island chapter and Andrew Rebold wrote Maine.

Earlier editions of *New England* were written by Tom Brosnahan, Steve Jermanok and Kim Grant.

FROM THE PUBLISHER

New England 3 was edited and proofed by Rachel Bernstein, Michael Johnson and Kathryn Ettinger in LP's Oakland office, with special guest-star appearances by editors Elaine Merrill and Susan Shook Molloy. Over-the-top proofing was also done by Ben Greensfelder and Elaine. Senior editor Maria Donohoe oversaw the project with steady support, and Wade Fox lent a helpful hand. Ken DellaPenta created the index.

Kat Smith headed up the cartographic team, with senior cartographers Tracey Croom and Bart Wright at her side. Marji Hamm, Graham Neale, David Ryder, Brad Lodge, Gina Gillich, Sara Nelson, Herman So and Sherry Veverka drew the maps with the help of Narinder Bansal, Buck Cantwell, Justin Colgan, Dion Good, Patrick Huerta, Rachel Jereb, Don Patterson, Terence Philippe, Eric Thomsen and Rudie Watzig. Cartographic data specialist John Spelman did his thing, and the cartographers received technical assistance from Chris Howard and ongoing support from cartographic manager Alex Guilbert.

Henia Miedzinski and Shelley Firth laid out the book with skill and style. Emily Douglas designed the cover and Gerilyn Attebury handled the production of the cover and designed the lovely color wraps, all with the support of senior designer (and multitasker) Tracey Croom. Justin Marler coordinated the illustrations; his work, plus that of illustrators Mark Butler, Hugh D'Andrade, Shelley Firth, Hayden Foell, Jennifer Steffey, Jim Swanson and Wendy Yanagihara, bring the text to life. Design manager Susan Rimerman kept everything on track.

Many thanks to authors Randy, Kim, Andy and S-P-E, for being simply delightful to work with, and to the New England Patriots for providing last-minute, but lasting, inspiration.

ACKNOWLEDGMENTS

Grateful acknowledgment is made to the Massachusetts Bay Transportation Authority for reproduction permission for the MBTA map.

Foreword

ABOUT LONELY PLANET GUIDEBOOKS

The story begins with a classic travel adventure: Tony and Maureen Wheeler's 1972 journey across Europe and Asia to Australia. Useful information about the overland trail did not exist at that time, so Tony and Maureen published the first Lonely Planet guidebook to meet a growing need.

From a kitchen table, then from a tiny office in Melbourne (Australia), Lonely Planet has become the largest independent travel publisher in the world, an international company with offices in Melbourne, Oakland (USA), London (UK) and Paris (France).

Today Lonely Planet guidebooks cover the globe. There is an ever-growing list of books, and there's information in a variety of forms and media. Some things haven't changed. The main aim is still to help make it possible for adventurous travelers to get out there – to explore and better understand the world.

At Lonely Planet we believe travelers can make a positive contribution to the countries they visit – if they respect their host communities and spend their money wisely. Since 1986 a percentage of the income from each book has been donated to aid projects and human-rights campaigns.

Updates Lonely Planet thoroughly updates each guidebook as often as possible. This usually means there are around two years between editions, although for more unusual or more stable destinations the gap can be longer. Check the imprint page (following the color map at the beginning of the book) for publication dates.

Between editions, up-to-date information is available in two free newsletters – the paper *Planet Talk* and email *Comet* (to subscribe, contact any Lonely Planet office) – and on our website at www.lonelyplanet.com. The *Upgrades* section of the website covers a number of important and volatile destinations and is regularly updated by Lonely Planet authors. *Scoop* covers news and current affairs relevant to travelers. And, lastly, the *Thorn Tree* bulletin board and *Postcards* section of the site carry unverified, but fascinating, reports from travelers.

Correspondence The process of creating new editions begins with the letters, postcards and emails received from travelers. This correspondence often includes suggestions, criticisms and comments about the current editions. Interesting excerpts are immediately passed on via newsletters and the website, and everything goes to our authors to be verified when they're researching on the road. We're keen to get more feedback from organizations or individuals who represent communities visited by travelers.

Lonely Planet gathers information for everyone who's curious about the planet – and especially for those who explore it firsthand. Through guidebooks, phrasebooks, activity guides, maps, literature, newsletters, image library, TV series and Web site, we act as an information exchange for a worldwide community of travelers.

Research Authors aim to gather sufficient practical information to enable travelers to make informed choices and to make the mechanics of a journey run smoothly. They also research historical and cultural background to help enrich the travel experience and allow travelers to understand and respond appropriately to cultural and environmental issues.

Authors don't stay in every hotel because that would mean spending a couple of months in each medium-size city and, no, they don't eat at every restaurant because that would mean stretching belts beyond capacity. They do visit hotels and restaurants to check standards and prices, but feedback based on readers' direct experiences can be very helpful.

Many of our authors work undercover; others aren't so secretive. None of them accept freebies in exchange for positive write-ups. And none of our guidebooks contain any advertising.

Production Authors submit their manuscripts and maps to offices in Australia, the USA, the UK or France. Editors and cartographers – all experienced travelers themselves – then begin the process of assembling the pieces. When the book finally hits the shops, some things are already out of date, we start getting feedback from readers and the process begins again....

WARNING & REQUEST

Things change – prices go up, schedules change, good places go bad and bad places go bankrupt – nothing stays the same. So, if you find things better or worse, recently opened or long since closed, please tell us and help make the next edition even more accurate and useful. We genuinely value all the feedback we receive. Julie Young coordinates a well-traveled team that reads and acknowledges every letter, postcard and email and ensures that every morsel of information finds its way to the appropriate authors, editors and cartographers for verification.

Everyone who writes to us will find their name in the next edition of the appropriate guidebook. They will also receive the latest issue of *Planet Talk*, our quarterly printed newsletter, or *Comet*, our monthly email newsletter. Subscriptions to both newsletters are free. The very best contributions will be rewarded with a free guidebook.

Excerpts from your correspondence may appear in new editions of Lonely Planet guidebooks, the Lonely Planet website, *Planet Talk* or *Comet*, so please let us know if you *don't* want your letter published or your name acknowledged.

Send all correspondence to the Lonely Planet office closest to you:

Australia: Locked Bag 1, Footscray, Victoria 3011
USA: 150 Linden St, Oakland, CA 94607
UK: 10A Spring Place, London NW5 3BH
France: 1 rue du Dahomey, 75011 Paris

Or email us at: talk2us@lonelyplanet.com.au

For news, views and updates, see our website: www.lonelyplanet.com

HOW TO USE A LONELY PLANET GUIDEBOOK

The best way to use a Lonely Planet guidebook is any way you choose. At Lonely Planet, we believe the most memorable travel experiences are often those that are unexpected, and the finest discoveries are those you make yourself. Guidebooks are not intended to be used as if they provided a detailed set of infallible instructions!

Contents All Lonely Planet guidebooks follow the same format. The Facts about the Country chapters or sections give background information ranging from history to weather. Facts for the Visitor gives practical information on issues like visas and health. Getting There & Away gives a brief starting point for researching travel to and from the destination. Getting Around gives an overview of the transport options available when you arrive.

The peculiar demands of each destination determine how subsequent chapters are broken up, but some things remain constant. We always start with background, then proceed to sights, places to stay, places to eat, entertainment, getting there and away, and getting around information – in that order.

Heading Hierarchy Lonely Planet headings are used in a strict hierarchical structure that can be visualized as a set of Russian dolls. Each heading (and its following text) is encompassed by any preceding heading that is higher on the hierarchical ladder.

Entry Points We do not assume guidebooks will be read from beginning to end, but that people will dip into them. The traditional entry points are the list of contents and the index. In addition, however, some books have a complete list of maps and an index map illustrating map coverage.

There may also be a color map that shows highlights. These highlights are dealt with in greater detail later in the book, along with planning questions. Each chapter covering a geographical region usually begins with a locator map and another list of highlights. Once you find something of interest in a list of highlights, turn to the index.

Maps Maps play a crucial role in Lonely Planet guidebooks and include a huge amount of information. A legend is printed on the back page. We seek to have complete consistency between maps and text, and to have every important place in the text captured on a map. Map key numbers usually start in the top left corner.

Although inclusion in a guidebook usually implies a recommendation, we cannot list every good place. Exclusion does not necessarily imply criticism. In fact, there are a number of reasons why we might exclude a place – sometimes it is simply inappropriate to encourage an influx of travelers.

Introduction

New England. The very words conjure up images that seduce travelers. Some people picture a North American Oxford, with the ivory towers of Harvard and the parapets of Yale among the ivy-covered walls of the world's highest concentration of colleges and universities. Others imagine white clapboard churches on village greens, granite mountains for hiking and skiing, glacial lakes for boating and fishing and 6000 miles of rockbound coast for seafaring and dreaming.

The 'Early America' of Indians, Pilgrims, Salem witches and revolutionary 'tea parties' is alive and well here in the northeast corner of the United States, side-by-side with the edgy, contemporary New England seen through the camera lenses of *Ally McBeal, Providence, The Practice* and *Good Will Hunting*.

New England's dark woods, rocky coast and dusty corners are the settings for the gothic novels of Hawthorne, Melville, John Irving and Stephen King. Old mill towns like Lowell, MA, sport fresh faces since the arrival of immigrants from the Spanish Caribbean and Southeast Asia. In today's New England, the scents of traditional steamed lobster, cod fish and clam 'chowdah' mix with those of Puerto Rican mofongo and Bangkok-style pad thai.

While cruising the coast of North America in 1614, English explorer Capt John Smith christened the region 'New England.' Early settlers and cartographers first used the term to refer to the four British colonies of Massachusetts, Rhode Island, Connecticut and New Hampshire. But by the 18th century, the current states of

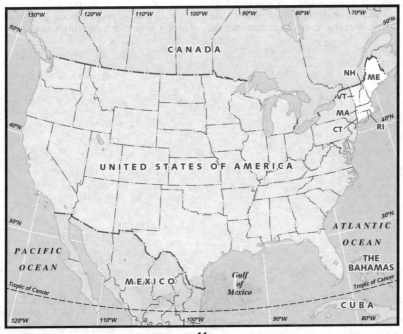

Maine and Vermont had become part of New England, and the residents of the entire area were known far and wide as 'Yankees.' Since then, the six states and their citizens have made a self-conscious effort to preserve the independent spirit, love of learning and classic colonial architecture established here by generations of Puritan and Quaker religious dissidents who fled persecution in 17th-century England.

Though New Englanders feel a common regional identity, the six states are quite different in character. Massachusetts is the powerhouse, with the lion's share of vacation resorts and with Boston as the 'hub' of the region's commerce and industry.

Rhode Island, the smallest state in the Union, is like Switzerland – it's enhanced rather than diminished by its size. It is a land of coastal mansions, sailboats, Italian restaurants and recent immigrants.

Connecticut's cosmopolitan feel comes from its several important coastal cities as well as from its proximity to New York City.

Vermont has unspoiled peaks and forests, lakes and towns. Here there are far more cows than people. It's little wonder why 'flatlanders' (non-Vermonters) flock to the state's Green Mountains for summer hiking and winter skiing.

New Hampshire, the Granite State, is famous for its right-wing, less-government, pro-commerce policies, and for the majesty of the White Mountain National Forest. The highest peak in the eastern US is here, Mt Washington (6288 feet), along with a short, but dramatic, seacoast.

Maine is New England's last frontier and the largest of the states in the region. There are vast forests in Maine as well as 3500 miles of indented coastline, remote island communities, Acadia National Park and innumerable potato fields.

A traveler setting out to see most regions of the US must think of distances in continental terms. Not so in New England. Like its European namesake, New England packs history, culture and character into a relatively small space. From Boston, you can reach most points in the region in a morning's drive, and no point in the six states is more than a day's drive away.

Facts about New England

HISTORY
Early Times
Scholars believe that a Mongolian race crossed the Bering Strait, over a land bridge from east Asia to Alaska, sometime between 12,000 and 25,000 years ago. These people were the first human inhabitants of the Americas. They reached present-day New England in about 10,000 or 9000 BC. Their history has been lost, and archaeologists are not certain if they were the ancestors of the Algonquian peoples who inhabited the region when the first European settlers arrived.

The first peoples of New England developed an agrarian tradition, raising corn, beans, pumpkins and tobacco. They also hunted turkey, deer, moose, beaver, squirrel and rabbit, and harvested clams, lobsters and fish from coastal waters. These tribes were not allied as a single power. Intertribal warfare wasn't uncommon here, making a united defense against the European settlers impossible. In eastern North America, the Algonquian-speaking groups (Iroquois, Delaware, Micmac and Lenape, for example) fought each other for fertile lands and rights to hunting and fishing grounds, particularly after the climate began growing colder and less hospitable in about 1000 BC.

See Native Americans under Population & People, later in this chapter, for additional information.

The Explorers
Most historians believe the Vikings were the first European arrivals, exploring New England in around AD 1000 and calling it Vinland. But the Spaniards, Irish and Portuguese all claim the honor as well, some pointing to inscriptions on Dighton Rock, near the Taunton River in Berkeley, MA, as proof.

Even assuming the Norse came first, their colonies failed, leaving it to subsequent explorers to put down permanent roots in the New World. The next Europeans who stumbled across the continent were the Spaniards; Christopher Columbus, an Italian mariner in the service of the Spanish Crown, reached landfall in the Caribbean in 1492.

Upon Columbus' return to Europe, his supposed confirmation of the tales of 'western islands,' or 'Indies,' sent explorers from many nations racing across the ocean in search of adventure and glory. John Cabot (actually Giovanni Caboto, another Italian mariner) claimed the land of New England for his patron, King Henry VII of England, in 1497. In 1534, Jacques Cartier claimed the land for France by setting a cross on the Gaspé Peninsula in eastern Canada on the Gulf of St Lawrence.

Despite these claims, actual European colonization of North America did not occur until the 17th century. The French sent settlers to the North American continent, first to Quebec in 1604 and then to Nova Scotia in 1608. The English followed with the settlement at Jamestown, Virginia, in 1607. In 1621, the Dutch West India Company received a huge but ill-defined land grant from the government of Holland and soon sent settlers to the Hudson River Valley.

But it was the English explorers and settlers who most successfully colonized New England. In 1602, British mariner Bartholomew Gosnold, in command of the *Concord*, explored the New England coast from Maine to Rhode Island. Three years later, George Weymouth took a Pawtuxet man named Tisquantum (Squanto) prisoner and sailed back to England to show him at court.

These earliest explorers had only one lasting effect on the region that would become New England – smallpox. After initial contact with the Europeans, the local Native Americans suffered a plague they called 'The Great Sadness' in 1617. The Native American population of south coastal Massachusetts declined from about 40,000 to about 4000 in three short years.

Pilgrim Founders

English captain John Smith – the man whom Pocahontas saved from execution near the Jamestown colony – arrived in the region in 1614 and coined the name 'New England' for the area. Upon his return to London, Smith praised New England's possibilities for settlement. His recommendation soon attracted a group of religious dissenters in search of a place where they could practice their Congregationalist beliefs unhindered by government.

The small ship *Mayflower* set sail from Plymouth, England, in the late summer of 1620. The boat carried 102 passengers, some animals, tools, seed, household goods and foodstuffs, all bound for New England. After a tedious two-month voyage, these English 'Pilgrims' made landfall at Provincetown, on the tip of Cape Cod, in November, when the winds of winter had already begun to blow.

Having left England in disagreement with their financial backers, the Virginia Company, the Pilgrims now found themselves without a governing charter. While still aboard ship, they composed the Mayflower Compact, defining 'majority rule' as their fundamental law. After skirmishes with local Native Americans, the Pilgrims finally moved to Plymouth, MA, arriving there in December. Though the local people were not bitterly hostile, the New England winter was. The Pilgrims hastily built shelters, but about half of them perished of scurvy, exposure and other privations during the winter of 1620–21.

In the spring of 1621, things began to improve for the people of the 'Plimoth Plantation.' Squanto, the Pawtuxet who had been taken to England in 1605 by George Weymouth, had returned to the New World in 1615. Hearing of the new English settlement, he sought out the Pilgrims. Speaking both languages, Squanto facilitated a 50-year treaty of peace between the Pilgrims and Massasoit, the *sachem* (chief) of the Wampanoag people in whose territory the Pilgrims had settled. Though the Narragansett (who lived farther inland) remained hostile, the Pilgrim-Wampanoag alliance

secured basic peace. Squanto also taught the new arrivals essential survival skills: how to plant corn, and how and where to hunt deer and other game. The colonists elected William Bradford governor. He proved to be a born leader of strong character and great resourcefulness and led the colony's development until his death in 1657.

In the summer of 1621, the new colony grew its first modest corn crop, but this had to be shared with a boatload of new arrivals from England. Even so, at harvest time that autumn, the colonists celebrated their survival with a three-day feast of Thanksgiving, inviting their Wampanoag neighbors to join them.

Following this first English toehold at Plymouth, the Massachusetts Bay Colony began its settlement at what would become Boston (1628). Soon the region boasted several thousand English settlers, with more coming every year.

Growth of a Nation

From the mid-1600s to the mid-1700s, both the population and wealth of the New England colonies grew rapidly. The region's forests and fields produced food and natural resources in abundance, and New England's numerous natural ports provided a springboard for the lucrative maritime trade.

As colonists flooded into New England, the indigenous peoples retreated and died – victims of war, smallpox, typhoid and alcoholism, to which they were genetically susceptible. Within only three generations, the native peoples of the region were reduced to small, relatively powerless groups of survivors.

Though New Englanders still considered themselves subjects of the English Crown, they had no representation in Parliament. Nor did they think they needed it. From the first days of settlement in New England, the colonists had governed themselves by majority rule in their own legislative councils, with oversight by governors appointed from London. The colonists saw their affairs as largely separate from the concerns of the old country.

But after the Restoration of 1660, English monarchs began to assert more control. The wars fought between 1689 and 1763, including the French & Indian War, were echoes in the New World of continental French and English rivalries, and the conflicts cost the colonists dearly. Besides the local battles and Native American depredations brought on by the wars, the expenses of colonial defense provided a rationale for direct taxation of the colonies from London: If the English government was going to spend money defending the colonists, then the colonists could help to pay the bill for their defense.

The problem the colonists saw in this reasoning was that they had no voice in the deliberations over these new taxes. Parliament decided taxes, which meant taxation without representation.

King George III (reigned 1760–1820) and Great Britain's Prime Minister Lord North pursued taxation of the colonies vigorously. In 1764, Parliament passed the Sugar Act, requiring colonial subjects to pay duties on sugar. And in 1765, the Stamp Act imposed a tax on all public and legal documents, such as newspapers, licenses and leases.

War & Independence

Tensions mounted between the colonists and British authority, resulting in several confrontations. An angry crowd in Boston taunted and threatened a small number of Royal Army sentries in March 1770. The English sentries, afraid for their lives, fired into the crowd and killed five colonists, including freed slave Crispus Attucks. The nascent revolution thus had its first martyrs in this 'Boston Massacre.'

In response to the massacre, Parliament repealed a number of the repressive Townshend Acts, passed in 1767, but England retained a tax on tea as a symbol of London's right to tax the colonists directly. The colonists' response was the Boston Tea Party: In the dead of night on December 16, 1773, a band of colonials masquerading as Africans and Native Americans (to play into racial stereotypes of mischievous non-

whites) forcibly boarded HMS *Dartmouth* and two other ships and dumped the cargoes of taxable tea into Boston Harbor.

In response, Parliament passed what were known in the colonies as the 'Intolerable Acts.' The colonists, who had traditionally maintained militias against the possibility of Native American attack, began arming and training for war with their erstwhile motherland.

Battles of Lexington & Concord In April 1775, a British spy posing as a carpenter from Maine in search of work discovered that the colonials were stockpiling arms and munitions at Concord, about 18 miles west of Boston. On the night of April 18, secret orders sent a British expeditionary force to Concord under cover of darkness to make a surprise search of the town at dawn.

American spies learned of the plan, and three riders – Paul Revere, William Dawes and Samuel Prescott – sped to the countryside to spread the word: 'The British are coming!' Members of the local militias, called 'minutemen' because of their ability to be ready for battle at a moment's notice, proved true to their name, turning out, matchlocks in hand, to face the 'aggressors.'

The small local militia, with little training and no experience, was about to face a sizable force of the world's best professional soldiers, and no one knew what might happen. Word went out beyond Lexington and Concord for minuteman reinforcements.

The crunch of 700 British soldiers' boots in the streets of Lexington must have terrified the 70 minutemen lined up in defensive formation on Lexington Green at dawn, but they did not disperse when ordered to do so by Major Pitcairn, the British commander. Tension mounted, and finally a shot rang out. Many followed as the redcoats overwhelmed the colonial force. Eight minutemen died in the melee.

If the Lexington minutemen had been apprehensive, those assembled at Concord had reason to be scared stiff. Joined by the minutemen from surrounding towns, the Concord group mustered on a hill with a view of the town across the Concord River.

Having been warned well in advance by spies in Boston of the British expedition, the colonists had spirited away their Concord arms caches and hidden them elsewhere. The British search for arms turned up only a few wooden gun carriages, which the redcoats set afire.

Seeing smoke rising from the town, the minutemen assumed their town was being put to the torch. 'Will you let them burn the town down?' shouted one. Emboldened, they advanced down the hill and engaged the British at the North Bridge. The British, having marched to the far side of the bridge to disperse the minutemen, retreated back across it when met with salvos from colonial muskets. The ranks of the minutemen swelled as reinforcements poured in from distant towns. By noon, now seriously outnumbered, the British force began its retreat from Concord to Boston. Minutemen sniped at them all along the way, inflicting a shocking number of casualties.

News of the battles of Lexington and Concord spread through the colonies, inflaming revolutionary fervor among most colonists, and terrifying those loyalists who still supported the Crown.

Ticonderoga & Bunker Hill The battles of Lexington and Concord provoked the gathering of the Second Continental Congress in Philadelphia on May 10, 1775, to decide on defensive measures. On the same day, Ethan Allen led his Green Mountain Boys from Vermont in a successful assault against the British outpost at Fort Ticonderoga (for details, see the boxed text 'Ethan Allen & Vermont'). The Revolutionary War was well under way.

The British held Boston. But the Americans fortified Breed's Hill, next to Bunker Hill, right across Boston Harbor. The British threw wave after wave of troops up the hill, only to see them mowed down by American fire. With his troops' ammunition running low, Colonel Prescott, the American commander, shouted the famous order, 'Don't fire until you see the whites of their eyes!' His troops obeyed, leaving more than 1000 royal soldiers wounded or dying on the slopes of Breed's Hill before retreating for lack of ammunition.

Meanwhile, the Continental Congress selected George Washington to lead American forces against those of the Crown. Divided loyalties cleft colonial society.

Ethan Allen & Vermont

Far from Boston, New York and Hartford, rural Vermont was the last corner of New England to be settled. In 1749, Benning Wentworth, royal governor of New Hampshire, issued land grants to Vermont territory for the settlement of towns. This infuriated New York, which also claimed the land (as did the French Crown).

In 1764, King George III upheld New York's claim, and in 1770, Vermont farmer Ethan Allen organized the Green Mountain Boys to carry out attacks against New York claimants. His exploits became so well known that the governor of New York offered a reward of £100 for Allen's capture.

At the beginning of the Revolutionary War, Allen's Green Mountain Boys and a small force from Connecticut made a surprise attack on Fort Ticonderoga on Lake Champlain, forcing the fort's astonished British commander to surrender in a bloodless victory.

During the war, the residents of the 'New Hampshire Grants' organized a constituent assembly and, in 1777, declared Vermont an independent state. The new state petitioned Congress for admission to the US, but was refused (because of competing land grants), whereupon Ethan Allen and others plotted to have Vermont come under the aegis of the British Crown as an independent state. In 1791, however, Vermont was admitted to the Union.

Many colonists remained loyal to the British monarchy despite its injustice; others saw independence as the only solution.

Declaration of Independence On May 4, 1776, the colony of Rhode Island and Providence Plantations formally renounced allegiance to King George III, provoking the British to occupy the area. By this time it was clear to the colonists what needed to be done, and on July 4, 1776, colonial leaders met in Philadelphia to sign the Declaration of Independence.

The Revolutionary War raged throughout the colonies. Although many decisive battles, such as Valley Forge and Yorktown, did not take place in New England, this is where the war began. April 19 (Patriots' Day), the date of the battles at Lexington and Concord in 1775, is a holiday in Massachusetts, and reenactments of the battles occur each year.

Early USA
The Revolutionary War freed the American colonies from British governance, but it did not guarantee America's survival as an independent nation. Americans had no strong, effective central government. It took most of the 1780s to work out the details, but by 1789 the US lawmakers had written, amended and ratified the basic law of the land, the Constitution. Freed at last from the restrictions imposed by Great Britain, New England's mariners and merchants built up the young nation's trade in fishing and commerce, to be followed soon after by manufacturing.

19th Century
New England prospered from another sort of 'water power.' Smugglers brought designs from Britain to New England for water-powered textile machinery. And soon New England's rivers featured thickets of mills turning out clothing, shoes and machinery.

Only the War of 1812 got in the way of New England's progress. While most of the US saw the war as a chance to grab Canada from the British, New Englanders saw it as an interruption of their very profitable maritime trade. There was even talk of New England concluding a separate peace with Great Britain.

After the war, local prosperity returned quickly. Wealth from the Industrial Revolution, added to that from the fishing, whaling and maritime trades, made up for the region's relatively modest agricultural endowments and allowed 19th-century Boston to become the country's most highly educated and literary-minded city, earning it the nickname 'Athens of America.' The boom in textile weaving turned Vermont into one huge sheep farm, as farmers felled the state's forests to make grazing land.

Perhaps because of their strong traditions of self-reliance, self-government and religious morals, New Englanders were in the vanguard of numerous 19th-century reform movements, including temperance (abstinence from the use of alcoholic beverages), improvements in prisons and insane asylums, the prohibition of child labor and the abolition of slavery.

The notable flowering of literature that took place in mid-19th-century New England (see Literature under Arts, later in this chapter) included many important abolitionist works, such as Harriet Beecher Stowe's *Uncle Tom's Cabin*. The Underground Railroad (see the boxed text) had many overnight 'stations' in New England, and during the Civil War (1861–65), the Union army's 54th Massachusetts Regiment (depicted in the film *Glory*) distinguished itself as the first body of African American troops from a free state.

As the century drew to a close, New England saw its prosperity threatened on all sides. With the advent of steam engines, the great textile factories no longer needed river power. And laborers were organizing and agitating for better pay and working conditions. In response, factories moved to the South where the wages were lower. Steel-hulled, steam-powered ships replaced New England's renowned wooden, wind-powered clipper ships. Petroleum, natural gas and electricity did away with the need for whale oil.

The Underground Railroad

Before the Civil War (1861–65), those in favor of abolishing slavery formed a secret network of guides and safe houses to escort runaway slaves to the 'free' (nonslavery) states of the American Union. Called the Underground Railroad, it stretched as far as Canada after 1851 and the passage of the Fugitive Slave Act, which required escaped slaves to be returned to their owners even from free states.

The Underground Railroad had important 'stations' in many New England towns, including Farmington, CT; Burlington, VT; Canaan, NH; Portland, ME; and New Bedford, MA, to name a few. Many abolitionists risked imprisonment for guiding and sheltering escaped slaves on their way to freedom.

Among the more prominent abolitionists was orator William Lloyd Garrison (1805–79), of Newburyport, MA, who published the antislavery newspaper *The Liberator* and introduced Frederick Douglass (1817–95) to the world. Born into slavery in Maryland, Douglass became a spokesperson for abolitionism throughout New England. He wrote three autobiographies, was the country's first African American publisher, and served as government minister to Haiti.

Harriet Beecher Stowe (1811–96), of Litchfield, CT, was from a family of abolitionists that included her brother, the Reverend Henry Ward Beecher. Stowe's novel *Uncle Tom's Cabin*, published in the early 1850s, told the story of a slave family's flight and quest for freedom along the Underground Railroad. It sold an astounding 500,000 copies in the US and abroad and scholars count it among the factors leading to the Civil War and the abolition of slavery.

Harriet Tubman (circa 1820–1913), known as 'Moses the deliverer,' escaped from slavery in Maryland, only to risk recapture by returning to the slave state to rescue her brethren and parents, whom she brought to Boston. Her motto was 'I can't die but once.' When she finally did, many years later, she was a free woman.

Charles L Blockson's book *The Underground Railroad: Dramatic Firsthand Accounts of Daring Escapes to Freedom* has more information.

Millions of immigrants who had come from abroad to share in New England's commercial boom – many fleeing Ireland's potato famine – had only minimal skills in a diminishing job market. As new settlers moved westward across North America, they opened up vast farming and grazing lands, producing far greater agricultural riches than the rocky soil and northerly climate of New England would allow.

20th Century

WWI gave a boost to the New England economy, but the stock market crash of 1929 drove the region and the nation into the Great Depression.

The labor needs of WWII (1941–45) benefited New England's economy in some ways. The shipyards in Maine and Massachusetts, the firearms factories of Connecticut and the naval ports of all the coastal states redoubled their business as the Allies required additional labor and materials. The brainpower of New England's universities also contributed to the war effort.

But recession followed as New England's defense-related businesses found themselves with far fewer orders for their goods. During the 1960s, when John F Kennedy of Massachusetts was president of the US and John McCormack of Massachusetts was Speaker of the House of Representatives (to be succeeded in that office by Thomas P O'Neill, also of Massachusetts), money from government defense contracts began flowing into New England. Youth from the postwar baby boom began crowding the region's hundreds of colleges and universities. Enchanted by New England's historic towns, seacoast and livable cities, many college graduates remained in the region to pursue careers in high technology, medical research and finance, which became the basis for prosperity that continues to this day.

During the 1980s Boston housing prices soared as well-educated engineers and technicians were recruited nationally and internationally to join the region's fast-growing companies. Waves of immigrants from Southeast Asia, Puerto Rico, the Dominican Republic, Haiti and Brazil arrived to fill entry-level service and manufacturing jobs. Meanwhile, the 'clean' industry of tourism (with no industrial pollutants) brought wealth to parts of rural Vermont, New Hampshire and Maine.

When recession hit the computer industry in the late 1980s, New England's fortunes dipped, but not for long. The subsequent continuation of the country's longest stock-market boom poured money into the coffers of Boston's banks and money-management firms, and venture capital produced a bumper crop of successful high-tech startup companies that flourished into the 1990s.

21st Century

At the outset of the new century, New England's fundamental strengths in education, finance, high technology, health care, tourism and sophisticated manufacturing remain intact.

The 21st century finds New England a more liberal and diverse society than ever before. Not only will you hear a medley of languages spoken in the streets of most cities, large towns and resorts, but you will also see a rainbow of people of different races and ethnic backgrounds as well as out and proud gay couples sharing their lives together. Meanwhile, New England women like New Hampshire governor Jeanne Shaheen, Massachusetts governor Jane Swift and Maine senator Olympia Snow are rising to prominence.

The downside to New England's prosperity is that housing prices here are among the highest in the country. A simple three-bedroom home can cost well over $500,000, and high real-estate prices are turning formerly diverse neighborhoods and small towns into bastions of the gentry. Meanwhile, developers are eyeing New England's traditional family farms for housing developments (see Ecology & Environment, later in this chapter).

GEOGRAPHY

New England's topography is glacial, but its geology dates from long before the glaciers covered this part of North America. Several billion years ago, as the earth's crust shrank and wrinkled, towering mountain ranges rose here. Friction and pressure from the clash of rock masses turned sand to marble and formed the distinctive gneiss and schist, flecked with shiny mica, seen throughout the region.

Magma (molten rock) from the earth's core crept into crevasses and cracks in the earth's crust and filled huge air bubbles hidden beneath the surface. Magma that cooled quickly near the surface became fine-grained stone called trap. Rock that cooled slowly deep within the earth became New England's distinctive granite, which was later thrust to the surface, or exposed by erosion. You can readily 'read' New England's geology in the dikes (rock veins) and batholiths (huge granite mounds) found here.

Beginning several hundred million years ago, the earth thrust up the bedrock of New England into a spine of craggy mountains, running roughly from northeast to southwest. Over the ages, erosion and geologic pressures reduced these early alps to lower heights, so that eight million years ago they looked much as they do today.

A million years ago, the earth's temperature dropped and the polar ice caps built and spread toward the equator. This last ice age blanketed New England with a river of ice a half-mile thick.

Pushed slowly southward by the pressure of ice buildup at the North Pole, these glaciers dredged up millions of tons of soil and rock and carried them southward. At the glaciers' southernmost extent, deposits of the soil and rock formed the islands of Nantucket and Martha's Vineyard.

Throughout New England is evidence of the ice's retreat 10,000 to 20,000 years ago. It scooped out holes that became glacial ponds (Thoreau's Walden Pond, for example; see Concord in the Around Boston chapter); deposited rock and debris in oblong hills called drumlins (Bunker Hill); and left huge granite boulders called erratics in fields and streams.

The resulting landscape has verdant, winding valleys; abundant forests; and a rocky coastline sculpted into coves and sprinkled with sandy beaches. The mountains lack dramatic height, but that makes them all the more accessible. Farmers may complain that New England's rock-strewn soil 'grows boulders' (they're actually pushed up by the succession of freezing winters), but outdoors enthusiasts find the New England topography a perfect place for bicycling, hiking, canoeing, kayaking and boating.

CLIMATE

In 1838, the author Harriet Martineau wrote, 'I believe no one attempts to praise the climate of New England.'

New England's weather conforms to that humorous dictum, 'If you don't like the weather, just wait a minute.' It is not at all impossible to have hot, muggy 90°F days in July followed by a day or two of cool 65°F weather. And the January thaw – when the temperature rises from below freezing to 50°, 60° or even 70°F – is a fervently awaited (if not always dependable) anomaly.

The most predictable weather is in spring and autumn, when the days are warm and the nights are cool.

Spring

Spring can be very short: 'Last year it was on a Tuesday' is the typical joke. If the spring weather, usually occurring at some point between late April and early June, lasts awhile, the season can be glorious, with apple and cherry trees in bloom and farmers out tapping maple trees for sap. If spring is short, it may just come on a Tuesday, to be followed on Wednesday by the heat and humidity of summer.

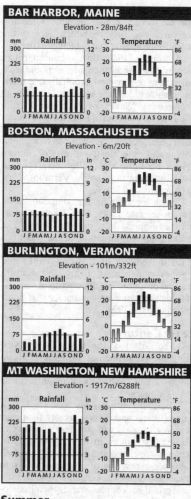

Summer

Depending on the year, June can be late spring, with some cool, rainy days, or early summer, with balmy temperatures. July and August are warm to hot, with temperatures above 90°F – occasionally above 100°F – and high humidity. Sea temperatures, however, never get really high even in the dog days of summer, keeping the temperatures in coastal locations in the comfortable

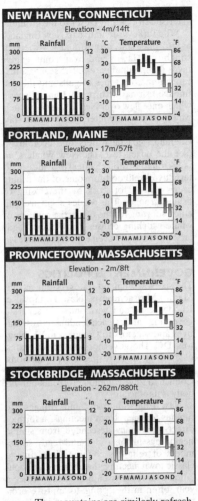

NEW HAVEN, CONNECTICUT
Elevation - 4m/14ft

PORTLAND, MAINE
Elevation - 17m/57ft

PROVINCETOWN, MASSACHUSETTS
Elevation - 2m/8ft

STOCKBRIDGE, MASSACHUSETTS
Elevation - 262m/880ft

range. The mountains are similarly refreshing. Fair weather typically lasts into late September.

Autumn

This is New England's finest season, a pleasant period with daytime temperatures above 60° or 70°F, and cool, sometimes chilly, nights. As the weather gets steadily cooler in late September, the foliage begins to change color, and by early October the color of the maples and beeches reaches its peak in northern New England. The wave of color spreads south through mid-October, and the Columbus Day (the second Monday in October) holiday weekend is a time when everyone goes 'leaf-peeping.'

The color depends upon rainfall and temperature patterns, however, and its timing is not predictable until a few weeks before it happens. It is also uneven; you may travel in late October through country that's bare of foliage, only to turn into a valley where the trees are ablaze with color.

Harvest time includes fresh cranberries on sale in the markets and 'pick-your-own fruit' days and cider making at orchards throughout the region.

By November most of the leaves have fallen from the trees, but a brief period of 'Indian Summer' often brings back a week or so of warm daytime temperatures. By the end of November it's clear that winter is approaching, and by mid-December icy winds begin to blow.

Winter

Winter can be severe or moderate; it is rarely mild. Though the snow can start in November, this is considered early. It's expected in December. Total snowfall is anywhere from a few inches to the 9 feet recorded in the winter of 1995–96. Winter weather is generally most moderate along the south coast of Massachusetts, Rhode Island and Connecticut. Almost all of interior New England, not just the mountains, features harsh weather with lakes 'iced in' until April. When it's not snowing, however, you'll find winter in New England likely to be bright and sunny, with temperatures between 15°F and freezing (32°F), with occasional days below 0°F in severe winters.

ECOLOGY & ENVIRONMENT

The 1990s were a time of remarkable steps to reclaim New England's environment from centuries of neglect as well as urban, industrial and agricultural pollution. A new sewage treatment facility for Boston at Deer Island has been a major step in improving the water quality of Boston Harbor. The work of Save the Bay in Rhode Island has stifled industrial and sewage pollution in the estuary and similar improvements have occurred in Massachusetts' Buzzards Bay. In Maine, environmental legislation has greatly limited paper-mill pollution of rivers and bays. The establishment of Stellwagen Bank Marine Sanctuary in Massachusetts Bay ensures a protected feeding area for whales, dolphins and fish.

But environmental problems persist for New England largely because of urban sprawl, which threatens remaining coastal wilderness as well as inland farms and forests. Environmental groups are currently challenging commercial coastal development proposals in Boston, Rhode Island, Connecticut and Maine. Environmentalists are also lobbying for support of a farm bill that will protect New England countryside and traditional family farms from development. Fisheries-management biologists and lawyers are still trying to solve the problem with overfishing on Georges Banks and in the Gulf of Maine. The concept of 'ocean zoning,' restricting sectors of the coastal waters for special uses, is now a hot topic among state legislators and environmentalists. Groundwater pollution is a significant problem from military firing ranges like the Massachusetts Military Reservation on Cape Cod.

For current information on New England environmental issues, visit [W] www.clf.org, the website of the Conservation Law Foundation (62 Summer St, Boston 02110).

FLORA & FAUNA

For the last 10,000 to 20,000 years, the region has been covered in thick forests of beech, birch, hemlock, maple, oak, pine and spruce. The forest floor harbors flowers and mushrooms suited to the northerly climate.

White-tailed deer, moose, black bears, coyotes, raccoons, beavers, woodchucks (groundhogs), rabbits and porcupines populate the forests. Visitors comment on the legions of squirrels (mostly gray, but some smaller red) that hop about on the lawns and paths and leap from tree to tree in the forest

canopy. Chipmunks, smaller and with characteristic stripes, stay closer to the ground.

Wild turkeys are native to New England, as are pheasant, grouse and a variety of songbirds. Hawks and even some eagles favor the mountain areas. The seacoast features numerous types of gulls and the distinctive fish hawk (osprey). Canada geese, which once flew over New England on their way south for the winter, have come to stay.

Whales, dolphins and seals play in New England's coastal waters, and ecotourism (see the boxed text 'The New Whalers,' in the Around Boston chapter) provides an alternative livelihood for some of the fishing crews put out of work by the closing of fishing grounds. The whales seem truly to enjoy sporting for the boats; the captains of whale-watching cruises know their 'regulars' by name, and even expect the whales at certain maritime rendezvous.

GOVERNMENT & POLITICS

The six New England states – Connecticut, Maine, Massachusetts, New Hampshire, Rhode Island and Vermont – are separate governing entities, each sending representatives and senators to Congress in Washington, DC. The governors of the six states, elected by their respective populations, meet as the New England Governors' Council to solve common problems, but this body is unofficial.

New England towns and villages are famous for their 'town meetings,' a form of direct democracy descended from simple beginnings in the rough-and-ready settlements of religious congregations. In the classic town meeting, the entire adult population of a town assembles once or twice a year, often in the spring, to approve ordinances and budgets. Anyone can speak, and many do. Most towns have made practical modifications to the town meeting scheme so that for most of the year, an elected council and a professional town manager carry out municipal business. But important, and especially budgetary, questions are decided at town meetings.

New England is the ancestral home of formidable political dynasties in American politics. Most people associate the Kennedy family with Massachusetts. But far fewer realize that former president George HW Bush and his son President George W Bush descend from a Connecticut senator and trace their education to Phillips Academy (Andover, MA) and Yale. George HW Bush maintains his family residence in Kennebunkport, ME.

ECONOMY

Electronic and medical technology, light industry, fishing, tourism, farming and the service sector all fuel the New England economy.

New England Yankees have always been famous for their technical prowess. In the 19th century, Connecticut achieved prominence for the gadgets, watches, clocks and firearms turned out in its shops and its factories. Today, MA 128, Boston's ring road, is the East Coast counterpart to California's Silicon Valley. Research, computer programming and electronics manufacturing thrive here.

Though the region has a long history of shipbuilding, much of the industry's business has moved to northern Europe and Asia. Sophisticated ships (including nuclear submarines), however, are still built in Connecticut's Groton–New London area and in Bath, ME.

Farming New England's rocky land has never been easy, but the soil itself can be rich. Some native crops introduced by Native Americans to the first European settlers still have an important role in New England's commercial agricultural economy. Tart, sour, ruby-red cranberries are still a major cash crop grown in the bogs and wetlands of Massachusetts and Rhode Island for juice, sauces, jellies and pies. Blueberries are an important crop in Maine and several other states.

New England farmers grow apples, cherries, grapes, lettuce, peaches, pears, plums, rhubarb, strawberries, sweet corn, tomatoes and many other vegetables and fruits.

Though Vermont is famous for its maple syrup, all of the New England states produce excellent maple syrup from the sap of

Maple Sugaring

During New England's spring thaw (late March to early April), when nights are still cold but days are warm, the sap of the sugar maple tree (Acer saccharum) rises. Farmers go out to the sugar bush (grove of sugar maples), tap little metal pipes into the tree trunks, and collect the sap in buckets or through a network of plastic tubing.

The collected sap is transferred to big vats, where it is simmered for hours and reduced to a thick, amber-colored syrup with a distinctive flavor. Grade A Light Amber and Medium Amber are the finest grades, traditionally used on pancakes or waffles, or crystallized and molded into maple sugar candy. Dark Amber has a heartier, stronger flavor good for cooking. Grade B, very dark and coarse, is used in some baking recipes and in commercial food preparation.

Because of the time and labor required for harvesting and preparation, maple sugar is not cheap. Nevertheless, for its devotees there is no substitute.

If you're interested in learning more about maple sugaring, check out the website for the Massachusetts Maple Producers Association (W www.massmaple.org), a nonprofit organization dedicated to the preservation and promotion of maple sugaring.

the sugar maple tree (see the boxed text 'Maple Sugaring').

Dairy and sheep farming are important throughout the region, but especially in Vermont, which is well known for its cheese and premium ice cream.

The legendary New England fishing industry is not what it used to be. Overfishing threatens the once-inexhaustible fishing grounds, and the lobster industry may be in for a similar fate. During the 1980s, easy bank loans encouraged by government programs led to investment in more efficient boats and equipment, which in turn led to larger seafood harvests. In 1994, the government belatedly changed its policies and temporarily closed the fishing grounds of Georges Bank, a mainstay of the New England economy since colonial times. At the outset of the 21st century, some fish stocks have bounced back, and boats are once again fishing Georges under stiff restrictions. But the future of the fishery remains a question.

POPULATION & PEOPLE

New England is home to almost 14,000,000 people, or about 5% of the US population. The following figures from the 2000 census represent the states' approximate populations, ranked by size from largest to smallest:

Connecticut	3,500,000
Maine	1,200,000
Massachusetts	6,300,000
New Hampshire	1,200,000
Rhode Island	1,000,000
Vermont	600,000

Native Americans

New England landscapes echo with long Native American names such as Connecticut, Massachusetts, Narragansett, Pemigewasset, Penobscot and Winnipesaukee, testifying to the peoples who lived here before the arrival of the Europeans.

Reporting on his discoveries along the New England coast, Captain John Smith wrote of 'large fields of corn (maize), and great troops of well-proportioned people.'

The Native American population at the time might have been somewhere between 25,000 and 75,000, but no one took a census. Scholars believe that about 10 major tribes of the Algonquian linguistic group, often divided into clans, inhabited the present New England region when the Pilgrims arrived. Among these tribes were the Abenaki, Malecite, Micmac, Narragansett, Passamaquoddie, Penobscot, Pequot and Wampanoag. They lived in villages of about 100 people each under the leadership of a *sachem,* migrating between summer fishing camps on the coast (where sea breezes kept away black flies and mosquitoes) and winter camps in the interior. The groups lived an agrarian lifestyle, with corn crops central. Although corn was their dietary staple, the Native Americans gathered raspberries, blueberries, strawberries, grapes and cranberries in season. On the coast they gathered shellfish like quahog clams, mussels and oysters and fished for lobster, scup, mackerel, bluefish, striped bass and herring. They also used spears to harpoon pilot whales. During the winter they hunted deer, turkey, pheasant and quails in the forest. Inevitably, conflicts over hunting and fishing grounds brought short-lived armed conflicts between clans like the Wampanoags and Narragansetts, and those old grievances helped the English to divide and conquer the Native Americans during events like King Philip's War (1675–76).

Today, New England is home to about 36,000 Native Americans, some of whom live on reservations of ancestral land such as those on Martha's Vineyard and in Mashpee, MA, and on Indian Island, ME. During the 1990s some groups of New England Native Americans won the right to erect gambling casinos (see the boxed text 'Foxwoods,' in the Connecticut chapter) as compensation for treaty violations by the federal government. Other Native American groups are following suit.

Immigrants

The British and French made the first European claims to this land, and they have left their mark throughout New England. The French presence is most obvious in northern and eastern Maine and in the northern reaches of Vermont and New Hampshire, where many residents are bilingual. But colonies of French speakers exist in some Massachusetts industrial towns, where French Canadians went in search of work.

In the mid-19th century, many Africans and Caribbean islanders ended up in New England after fleeing Southern slavery on the Underground Railroad (see the boxed text 'The Underground Railroad').

In the 19th and early 20th centuries, Armenian, Greek, Irish, Italian, Jewish and Portuguese immigrants flooded into the region to provide labor for its factories and fishing boats. Many neighborhoods in the region's cities still hold fast to these century-old European ties.

Recently, immigrants have come from around the world to study at New England's universities, work in its factories or manage its high-tech firms. You can hear Caribbean rhythms in Hartford and Springfield, smell Vietnamese and Cambodian cookery in Cambridge and Lowell and see signs in Brazilian Portuguese in Somerville, MA.

EDUCATION

New England is an education mecca. Students from all over the USA and the world come to New England to take advantage of its hundreds of excellent schools, colleges and universities. The Boston area alone claims in excess of 225,000 college students.

New Englanders' desire for religious education inspired the founding of many of the great colleges, universities and graduate schools in the region. Although today secular in outlook, Amherst, Bowdoin, Brown, Dartmouth, Harvard, Tufts, Williams and Yale were all founded to train candidates for the ministry.

The Boston Latin School, the country's oldest school (founded in 1635), has always been supported by public taxes and has accepted applicants from all social classes. Not surprisingly, New England also has many highly regarded private preparatory schools, including Phillips Academy (in Andover, MA), Phillips Exeter Academy (in Exeter, NH), Groton Preparatory School (Groton, MA), Deerfield Academy (Greenfield, MA) and Choate Rosemary Hall School (Wallingford, CT).

ARTS

New England looks upon itself as the birthplace of North American culture, and it has a lot of evidence to prove the point. Many of the best-known early US architects, painters, silversmiths and other artisans came from New England.

Crafts

In colonial times, popular arts like sewing, quilting, glassblowing and ironmongery thrived in New England. Furniture making, painting and other more sophisticated artistic pursuits developed as well.

Perhaps the region's most famous early artisan was Paul Revere. Remembered mostly for his midnight ride to warn the minutemen that the redcoats were coming, Revere was in fact a master silversmith. His famous design for the Revere bowl is still followed today.

The best-loved New England art from past centuries is scrimshaw, the carving and engraving of ivory. Ivory teeth and whalebone were readily available byproducts of the whaling trade, and whaling voyages often allowed for long hours of inactivity for sailors. Many sailors became expert scrimshanders, turning out remarkably fine, delicate carvings. Some objects were utilitarian, such as kitchen utensils, buttons, letter openers and corset stays. Other objects, like cameos, brooches and pins, were made for gifts and to exhibit the artisan's abilities. The scenes etched on scrimshaw pieces were often of ships and other nautical subjects. Though scrimshaw is still done, most pieces are replicas on imitation ivory (plastic). Authentic antique pieces are very valuable.

The Shakers produced furniture of such high quality that they're among the finest New England artisans of the 19th century (see the Religion section, later in this chapter). At their communal settlements in Maine, New Hampshire and western Massachusetts, the Shakers equated work with prayer, and each object was made as a tribute to the Almighty. The Shakers worked hard, carefully and well, and their harmonious, pleasant designs continue to be reproduced by artisans today.

Painting

For all its wealth, 19th-century New England society could not fully nurture its renowned artists, most of whom sought training and artistic fulfillment abroad. These included Henry Sargent (1770–1845), of Gloucester, MA, who was a student of Benjamin West's, and James Abbott McNeill Whistler (1834–1903), of Lowell, MA,

Puritan Gravestones

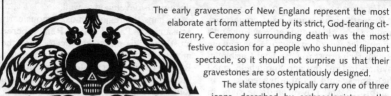

The early gravestones of New England represent the most elaborate art form attempted by its strict, God-fearing citizenry. Ceremony surrounding death was the most festive occasion for a people who shunned flippant spectacle, so it should not surprise us that their gravestones are so ostentatiously designed.

The slate stones typically carry one of three icons, described by archaeologists as the Death's Head, Cherub, and Urn and Willow. Each style reflects popular cultural beliefs. Generally, Death's Heads (they look like winged skulls) represent a severe reverence for death, while the human-faced Cherub implies a relaxing of religious and moral ideals. The classical revival images of the Urn and Willow signify a growing national culture following the successful Revolutionary War.

Some of the best stones rest in Boston's Old Granary Burying Ground and Copp's Hill Burying Ground. These not only contain good representatives of the different iconographic styles, but are also the final resting places of notable colonial figures, such as John Hancock, Samuel Adams, Paul Revere and Cotton Mather.

If early graves really interest you, stay at the **Putnam House** (☎ 508-865-9094, *211 Putnam Hill Rd, Sutton, MA*), where singles/doubles are $55/75. One of the owners, a British professor, might know more about colonial cemeteries than anyone else in New England. The 18th-century interior of this B&B has been preserved with academic attention to detail. Call for directions.

–John Spelman

who challenged the tradition of representational painting by blurring lines and emphasizing the play of light in his work.

An exception was Winslow Homer (1836–1910), who pursued a career as an illustrator for the popular press but later dedicated his talents to painting. Though a Bostonian, Homer is most famous for his accurately depicted scenes of the New England coast.

By the 20th century, however, New England – Boston in particular – was capable of supporting world-class artists. John Singer Sargent (1856–1925) painted his telling portraits of Boston's upper class, and Childe Hassam (1859–1935) used Boston Common and other New England cityscapes and landscapes as subjects for his impressionist works.

Norman Rockwell (1894–1978), perhaps New England's most famous artist, reached his public mainly through his magazine illustrations, particularly the covers he painted for the *Saturday Evening Post*. His evocative, realistic pictures of common men, women and children involved in the small triumphs, tragedies and comedies of daily life cemented US popular culture and helped define the nation's concept of what it meant to be an American. Rockwell lived and worked in Arlington, Vermont, and Stockbridge, MA, both of which now have major museums of his work.

Highly regarded for her 'American primitive' paintings of rural life, Anna Mary Robertson Moses (1860–1961) didn't begin painting until in her late 70s. See Bennington in the Vermont chapter for information on 'Grandma Moses.'

Sculpture

New England has produced its share of sculptors. Daniel Chester French (1850–1931) designed the minuteman memorial in

Concord, MA, and the seated Lincoln in Washington, DC's Lincoln Memorial. Augustus Saint-Gaudens (1848–1907) was born in Ireland and worked in New York, London and Rome, but he finished his career in Cornish, NH. His evocative memorial statue of Colonel Robert Gould Shaw stands in Boston's Public Garden. Alexander Calder (1898–1976) made many of his world-famous mobiles and stabiles at his studio in Roxbury, CT.

Architecture

Though not as eager to break with architectural tradition as are some US regions, New England has its share of dramatic modern structures. These include the glass-sheathed, airfoil skyscrapers of Boston and of Hartford, CT, and the radical IM Pei–designed John F Kennedy Library & Museum, just outside of Boston (see the Boston chapter for details).

During the final decades of the 20th century, historic preservation became a Yankee obsession, and the well-protected and restored historic cores of towns and cities are examples of the many architectural styles that flourished here. At the time of settlement, the Pilgrims in Plymouth built simple thatched-roof log huts – and were glad to have them. As the Pilgrims prospered, wood-frame clapboard houses followed. By the 18th century, Yankees were building elaborate Georgian structures inspired by the Palladian architecture of Inigo Jones and the English baroque style of Christopher Wren. Called Georgian after the reigning British monarchs, the style was – and still is – used extensively: Harvard, Dartmouth and many other New England schools boast a riot of red-brick and white cornices in Georgian style. The typical tall-steepled New England meetinghouse (church) is a variation on the Palladian design.

When European taste moved on to the classical revival aesthetic in the late 18th and early 19th centuries, American taste followed. The updated Roman temple design that Thomas Jefferson used for Monticello influenced New Englanders as well, and soon

Greek- and Roman-style temples appeared as college halls, courthouses and bank buildings. Boston's Quincy Market echoes the neoclassicism of London's Haymarket.

State capitols built in the 19th century typically featured neoclassical domes, colonnades and arcades. Perhaps the best example of this style is the Massachusetts State House, designed by Charles Bulfinch (1763–1844). Even when the rest of New England and the nation had succumbed to a fascination with Gothic Revival, Boston architect Henry Hobson Richardson (1838–86) continued to build romantic Romanesque structures like Trinity Church (erected between 1872 and 1877), in Copley Square, Boston.

New England's fascination with European styles continued into the 20th century, but was diluted by a blossoming of local creativity. While modified Cape Cod–cottage styles migrated to the Midwest and California, ranch-style houses started popping up in New England.

The lyrical art nouveau style of the early 20th century left little impression on the region, and most modern art deco buildings have fallen to the wrecker's ball. However, one exceptional example, the Fleet Bank Building, still stands in Providence, RI.

In the 1950s and '60s, the international style reigned, producing huge glass and steel towers such as Boston's Prudential Center. Also during this era, preservationists reclaimed the sturdy granite warehouses along Boston's waterfront for apartments, offices, shops and restaurants.

During the prosperity of the 1990s, Boston, Hartford, Providence and Portland reeled under the construction of office towers. But the economic slowdown at the outset of the 21st century has put temporary breaks on development, giving governments, environmentalists and citizens a chance to think carefully about future construction and the need for green zones in towns, cities and suburbs alike.

Literature

Early Works The lifeblood of New England culture has always been literature.

The region's traditional reverence for literature comes from the Puritans, who believed that through religious education one came to know God. American literature, therefore, was initially ecclesiastical.

The New Englanders' passion for literacy showed itself as early as 1828, when Noah Webster (1758–1843) published his *American Dictionary of the English Language.* It sold hundreds of thousands of copies in edition after edition – an astounding achievement considering the country's small and mostly rural population at the time.

New England produced the first African American female poet of note, Phillis Wheatley (1753–1784). Sold from a slave ship in Boston, she began writing poetry at the age of 14 and her later work was celebrated in both North America and Europe.

By the late 19th century, New England's colleges had become magnets for literati of all beliefs and opinions. Some New England towns – most notably Concord, MA – nurtured the seeds of 19th-century America's literary and philosophical flowering. Ralph Waldo Emerson (1803–82), a founder of Transcendentalism (see the Religion section, later in this chapter), believed in the mystical unity of all creation. His essays gained a nationwide – even worldwide – audience for the teachings he promulgated from his home in Concord.

Emerson's friend and fellow Concordian Henry David Thoreau (1817–62) was among the first Americans to advocate a life of simplicity, lived in harmony with nature. Such beliefs were a radical departure from the prevailing industrial and commercial Protestantism of the time, but they gained a wide and impassioned following. Thoreau is best remembered for *Walden,* his journal of observations written during his solitary sojourn from 1845 to 1847 in a log cabin at Walden Pond, on the outskirts of Concord. Less well known but equally engaging are

Thoreau's travelogues, *The Maine Woods* and *Cape Cod.*

Another Concord author, Nathaniel Hawthorne (1804–64) was America's first great short-story writer and author of *The Scarlet Letter, Twice-Told Tales* and *The House of the Seven Gables.*

Louisa May Alcott (1832–88), although born in Pennsylvania, lived much of her life in Concord, too, and wrote in order to contribute to the family income. She knew Emerson and Thoreau well. Her largely autobiographical novel *Little Women* is her best-known work, but its several sequels – *Little Men* and *Jo's Boys* – are also still read with pleasure by many Americans.

Among New England's classics are many dealing with its maritime past, including *Moby Dick,* by Herman Melville (1819–91), and *Two Years Before the Mast,* by Richard Henry Dana (1815–82).

Altogether different are Henry James' *The Bostonians* and John P Marquand's *The Late George Apley,* novels of Boston parlor society.

Few New England authors were more prominent than Mark Twain (born Samuel Clemens, 1835–1910), who reached a worldwide audience. Born in Missouri, Twain settled in Hartford, CT, and there wrote *The Adventures of Tom Sawyer* as well as *The Adventures of Huckleberry Finn.* He also wrote *A Connecticut Yankee in King Arthur's Court.*

Several New England writers were instrumental in the battle against slavery preceding and during the Civil War. Among them were John Greenleaf Whittier (1807–92) and Harriet Beecher Stowe (1811–96). Stowe's best-selling fictionalization of life on a slave-holding plantation, *Uncle Tom's Cabin,* received acclaim both in the USA and abroad and helped to hasten the end of American

Abolitionist Harriet Beecher Stowe

slavery. More information on Stowe is given in the boxed text 'The Underground Railroad.'

In 1903, Harvard graduate and sociologist Dr WEB DuBois (1868–1963), of Great Barrington, MA, wrote *The Souls of Black Folk*, an influential book that sought to change the way blacks dealt with segregation, urging pride in African heritage.

The Last Puritan, by George Santayana (1863–1952), explores what it might be like for someone with 17th-century Puritan ideals to be attending Harvard in the 20th century.

Henry Wadsworth Longfellow (1807–82) wrote *The Song of Hiawatha, Paul Revere's Ride*, 'The Village Blacksmith,' 'Excelsior' and 'The Wreck of the Hesperus.' Emily Dickinson (1830–86), called 'the Belle of Amherst,' crafted beautiful poems, mostly published following her death. Edna St Vincent Millay (1892–1950) wrote poetry that reflects her native Maine.

New England's signature poet is, of course, Robert Frost (1874–1963). Born in California, Frost returned to his New England roots and attended Dartmouth and Harvard. He tried farming at various places in Vermont and New Hampshire (with very limited success). His many books of poetry use New England themes to explore the depths of human emotion and experience.

Stephen Vincent Benét (1898–1943), the author of *John Brown's Body*, about the abolitionist, lived in Stonington, CT.

Pulitzer Prize–winning novelist Edith Wharton (1862–1937) was born in New York, but she married a Boston banker. Her best-known novel, *Ethan Frome*, gives a grim but accurate picture of emotional entanglements on a New England farm. It's based on observations that Wharton made at her grand summer mansion at Lenox, in Massachusetts' Berkshire hills.

Playwrights from New England include Eugene O'Neill (1888–1953), author of *Long Day's Journey into Night*. O'Neill's house in New London, CT, has become a museum. Arthur Miller (born 1915), though from New York, wrote *The Crucible*, successfully dramatizing the Salem, MA, witch trials.

Modern Prose For up-to-date action set in Boston and elsewhere in New England, pick up any of the 'Spenser' thrillers written by Robert B Parker. Maine resident Stephen King, author of horror novels such as *Carrie* and *The Shining*, owes an artistic debt to pioneering gothic/sci-fi novelist HP Lovecraft (1890–1937) of Rhode Island.

Jaws, by Peter Benchley, set on Martha's Vineyard, is the novel from which the popular motion picture (1975) grew. Benchley's grandfather was humorist Robert Benchley (1889–1945), born in Worcester, MA, and a member of New York's famous Algonquin Round Table.

Among New England's contemporary voices is Annie Proulx, award-winning author of *The Shipping News*. She describes rural Vermont in her novel *Postcards*. John Irving, a New Hampshire native, wrote *Hotel New Hampshire, The World According to Garp, Cider House Rules* and *A Prayer for Owen Meany*, all of which are set in New England. Donna Tartt wrote *The Secret History*, in which characters commit murder at a college modeled on her alma mater, Vermont's Bennington College. Jay McInerney of Connecticut attended nearby Williams College. His novel *Last of the Savages* is about two very different students who become friends at a New England prep school. Sebastian Junger's *The Perfect Storm* is the dramatic account of a Gloucester fishing boat in its fight for survival in a North Atlantic gale.

Today, New England's universities host a flock of famous writers in residence who offer seminars and appear for readings. Kurt Vonnegut, Carlos Fuentes and Derek Walcott ply their trade here.

SOCIETY & CONDUCT

Generalizing about regional character is dangerous and reductive. This is particularly true when it comes to New England, which is a diverse assemblage of ethnic and racial communities. But from the outset of European colonialism, New England has been a clannish place, and while the first colonists preached tolerance and respected diversity, dissent and freedom of belief, they preferred to live among their own kind. To some extent this clannishness persists today in New England with people living in Yankee (white Protestant), Irish, Italian, African American, Jewish, Latino, French, Asian or gay enclaves that are side by side, but only modestly integrated, with communities of people with different races, ethnicity or beliefs. Integration occurs in the workplace and schools, but not so much in social venues like restaurants, pubs and clubs.

If New Englanders from a multitude of backgrounds share common traits, one of those traits must be a diligent work ethic. A powerful work ethic was at the heart of Puritan beliefs and has been a hallmark of the so-called New England Yankee since the days of the first colonists. It was also an essential quality for surviving New England's challenging climate and rugged geography. Even today, visitors remark at the sense of purpose they feel among New Englanders. 'It's as is everybody thinks they are on important missions,' observed a traveler from France, who noted that pedestrians rarely seem to stroll. By some accounts, Boston's citizens are the fastest walkers of any city population in the world.

Another touchstone of the Yankee character is independence: 'Live Free or Die' is the motto stamped on New Hampshire license plates, and plenty of New Englanders cherish the sentiment. Such rugged individualism cloaks itself in conservative clothing in New England, where women have been voted the worst dressed females in America by fashion magazines. Except in the boardroom, New England fashion tends toward 'crunchy' chamois shirts, jeans and hiking boots or artsy black sweaters, scarves and dresses worn over purple or orange leggings. Of course, the preppie crowd got their start here: Khaki slacks, button-down shirts and loafers are still the uniform du jour for the upper middle class.

So what's to like about us? Where's the fun? Well, an awful lot of us are culture vultures. We love making and consuming art of every variety, from the Boston Symphony to a drag-queen beauty pageant. And many of us are addicts of education. In fact, one of the best ways to get to know New Englanders is to enroll in a class at a school or community center. There are tens of thousands of these 'continuing ed' courses, lasting a couple of days or a couple of months, with a class to meet your interest – whether it's belly dancing or astrophysics. After class, we'll show you the pubs, discos and jazz caves. Then we'll introduce you to our other addiction: outdoor recreation. If you like hiking, biking, skiing, sailing, kayaking, jogging or fishing, we're here for you.

But watch out for us on the highway, especially around Boston. For many of us, driving is a contact sport.

RELIGION

New England began its modern history as a haven for religious dissenters, and the tradition of religious freedom and pluralism continues today. Today, the region is home to large numbers of Christian Protestants and Roman Catholics, and smaller numbers of Jews, Muslims, Hindus and Buddhists. Although relatively few in number (peaking at around 40,000 in the 1930s), Eastern European Jews put their cultural stamp on Boston neighborhoods. Their descendants have created a notable Jewish cultural enclave in the Boston suburb of Brookline and an internationally recognized educational facility, Brandeis University, in Waltham, MA.

The Pilgrims who arrived at Plymouth in 1620 were 'Puritans,' believers in a strict form of Calvinism that sought to 'purify' the church of the 'excesses' of ceremony acquired over the centuries. The Bible was to be interpreted closely, not to be subjected to elaborate theological interpretation.

The Pilgrims disagreed early and often on the details of religious belief and church governance. A common solution to theological disagreements was for the minority group to shove off into the wilderness and establish a new community where they could worship as they wished. Thomas Hooker and his followers abandoned Cambridge, MA, to found Hartford, CT; and Roger Williams and his flock split to found Providence, RI. In many cases the new colonial towns, having more recently suffered intolerance, were more tolerant themselves. Newport, RI, although founded by Puritans, soon had a Quaker meetinghouse and a Jewish synagogue.

Shakerism

Shakerism originated among members of the Society of Friends ('Quakers') in Manchester, England, in the mid-1700s. One of the sect's early leaders was Ann Lee (1736–84). 'Mother Ann,' as she came to be known, had a religious epiphany in 1770 and came to believe that she was the manifestation of Christ's 'female nature.' Mother Ann emigrated to the New World in 1775 and established a community with her followers in Watervliet, New York. In later years, Shaker communities were founded throughout New England. At its height, New England Shakerism boasted some 6000 members.

The name 'Shakers' derives from the sect's religious ceremonies, which involved a trembling dance to symbolize being possessed of the Holy Spirit. The tenets of Shakerism called for closed communities, set apart from the world, in which men and women lived in separate quarters, coming together only for prayer, dining and work. Work was looked upon as an act of worship, and the result an offering to God. The Shakers' craft items such as quilts and furniture possess a timeless beauty and flawless quality.

But cut off from the world there could be no proselytizing, and cut off from the opposite sex there could be no procreation, so Shakerism has pretty much died out. Their crafts survive, however, in museums throughout the USA and in the four former Shaker communities that are now museums in Hancock and Harvard, MA; Sabbathday Lake, ME; and Canterbury, NH.

Christian Science

In 1866, Mary Baker Eddy of New Hampshire experienced a miraculously speedy recovery from an accident. She attributed her cure to the healing powers of God as lived and taught by Christ. After a thorough study of the Bible and its teachings on the matter of medical science and health, she formulated the tenets of Christian Science. Today, her findings and beliefs are embodied in the Church of Christ, Scientist, headquartered in Boston, with churches now spread throughout the world in 70 countries. The sect's fame has spread through its respected daily newspaper, the *Christian Science Monitor.* See the boxed text 'Mary Baker Eddy.'

Congregationalism

The basic belief of Congregationalists is that each Protestant Christian community should have full control of its own affairs. When the movement began in England in the 1500s, the Church of England prosecuted early proponents, called Independents. Congregationalism flourished in colonial New England. New England's noted early preachers, including Jonathan Edwards, were all Congregationalists. And Congregationalists founded the region's most prominent colleges, including Amherst, Harvard, Williams and Yale, though the colleges were nonsectarian.

Unitarianism

In its earliest forms, Unitarianism declared the unity of God, which was blasphemy to Christians who believed that God was made up of God the Father, Jesus Christ the Son, and the Holy Spirit. In its American incarnation, Unitarianism became a religion based on reason, compassion, self-government and community service. It has no doctrine; members declare only that 'in the love of truth and in the spirit of Jesus, we unite for worship of God and service to Man.' Unitarian beliefs were advocated most forcefully by William Ellery Channing (1780–1842), by Ralph Waldo Emerson (1803–82) and by Theodore Parker (1810–60).

Universalism

John Murray (1741–1815) arrived in New Jersey from England in 1770 to preach the Universalist belief that God's purpose was to save every person from sin through the divine grace of Jesus. John Murray settled in

Mary Baker Eddy

The Women's National Book Association recently named Mary Baker Eddy's *Science and Health* as one of the 75 books by women 'whose words have changed the world.'

Mary Baker Eddy (1821–1910), the founder of Christian Science, was born in Bow, NH. Sickly as a child, she grew into a pious young woman noted for her stubbornness and love of study. She married in 1843, but her husband died four months before the birth of their son. Left with no resources and in poor health, she had no choice but to allow her son to be raised by others. She married again in 1853 and, preoccupied with questions of health, studied alternative therapeutic methods such as homeopathy, arriving finally at the belief that the roots of physical illness were mental and spiritual.

According to her own account, as she lay bedridden and alone one day in 1866, she opened the Bible and began to read an account of how Jesus had healed the sick. By the time Eddy put down the book, she herself was healed. For three years thereafter, Eddy retreated from society to contemplate her miraculous cure and to formulate the principles of Christian Science, a system of belief based less on traditional faith than on a rational understanding that the mind is an inalienable part of the goodness that is God.

Mary Baker Eddy taught that by consciously working to gain 'the mind of Christ,' normal humans can enter into a state in which spirit is more powerful than – and in command of – material things, including the human body. *Science and Health,* which details her philosophy, appeared in 1875. 'Critics took pleasure in saying that the book was wholly original, but would never be read,' Eddy noted wryly. To date, the book has sold more than 9 million copies.

In 1879, Eddy and a small group of adherents founded the Church of Christ, Scientist, which, unusual among sects at the time, encouraged the full equality of men and women. In 1881, Eddy founded the Massachusetts Metaphysical College in Boston to train practitioners in Christian Science healing arts. Men and women were equally welcome, and the training provided hundreds of women with careers, allowing them a measure of financial self-sufficiency – something Eddy prized. Even as she discussed retirement, Eddy continued to write and publish, founding the respected *Christian Science Monitor* newspaper at the age of 88.

–Paige R Penland

Gloucester, MA, and here he founded the first Universalist church in America.

Universalism spread throughout New England, with each congregation being independent, though all accepted a common doctrine. Early on, it had a Calvinist cast, but Universalism distanced itself from strict Calvinism in the 19th century and later allied itself closely with Unitarianism. The Universalist Church merged into the Unitarian Universalist Association in 1961.

Transcendentalism

Emerson, Thoreau, Bronson Alcott and other prominent thinkers in Concord, MA, during the mid-1800s refined the tenets of Unitarianism into a belief called Transcendentalism. They believed not just that God was inherent in all people, but that each person could 'listen' to that Godlike part for ethical, moral and spiritual guidance. Further, they believed that humans must seek to understand nature and to live in harmony with it. This was no doubt the inspiration for Thoreau's retreat at Walden Pond from 1845 to 1847.

Other Transcendentalist thinkers went even further. In 1841, they purchased Brook Farm in West Roxbury, MA (now an affluent Boston suburb), as a living laboratory for their beliefs. Hawthorne, Melville and other Transcendentalists both famous and unknown lived together at Brook Farm until 1847, when the experiment came to an end. Though it must be counted a failure, the Brook Farm experiment identified an ideal that is perhaps more meaningful today than it was a century and a half ago.

LANGUAGE

Though the principal language of New England is English, other languages thrive as well. Northern Maine is home to communities of French-speakers descended from the *voyageurs* (early explorers) of Quebec. Gloucester, New Bedford and other coastal towns harbor significant communities of Portuguese-speakers from Portugal, the Azores and the Cape Verde Islands who came to New England to work the fishing grounds. In Boston's North End, many older people still speak only Italian, and in Hartford you may hear the musical patois of the West Indies. Legal notices in the Boston area are frequently printed in English, Portuguese, Spanish, Vietnamese and Cambodian in recognition of immigrants who arrived during the last decades of the 20th century.

New Englanders, and especially Bostonians, are well known for abbreviating many words. Massachusetts Avenue becomes 'Mass Ave'; the Harvard Business School becomes 'the B School'; Cape Cod is 'the Cape' and Martha's Vineyard is 'the Vineyard.' Boston's subway system, officially the MBTA Rapid Transit System, becomes 'the T' in local parlance.

But the region is most famous for the broad-voweled English that's commonly called the Boston accent. 'Pahk the cah in Hahvahd Yahd' (Park the car in Harvard Yard) is the common joke sentence satirizing the peculiar 'r' that is also common to some dialects in England. During John F Kennedy's presidency, comedians satirized his speech for the 'r's that would disappear in some places ('cah' for car) and pop up in others ('Cuber,' pronounced **Kyoo**-berr,' for Cuba).

To the north, the people of Maine and New Hampshire often punctuate their speech with the meaningless sound 'ayuh' (uh-**yuh**).

See the Glossary at the end of this book for the meanings of some additional regional colloquialisms.

Facts for the Visitor

HIGHLIGHTS
Boston
Rich in history, architecture, universities and culture, Boston is compact enough for strolling. You can explore much of the city on foot: the Freedom Trail, the waterfront, historic and lively neighborhoods (like the North End and Back Bay), museums, parks and neighboring Cambridge (home of Harvard University and its museums). Close enough for great day trips are historic Lexington and Concord, Salem, Marblehead, Gloucester, Rockport and Plymouth.

Cape Cod & the Islands
From April to November, Cape Cod and the islands of Nantucket and Martha's Vineyard offer historic villages, hundreds of inns and B&Bs, a host of restaurants and pubs, hiking, biking, sailing and beachcombing 'til ya drop.

Central Massachusetts & the Berkshires
In central Massachusetts, the most visited attraction is Old Sturbridge Village, a re-created 17th-century town. The college towns and surrounding hills of the Pioneer Valley offer culture, history and outdoor adventures. In western Massachusetts, visit one of the Berkshires' fine old summer vacation resorts or attend a performance at the Tanglewood Music Festival, the Jacob's Pillow Dance Festival or the Williamstown Theater Festival.

Connecticut
Mystic Seaport Museum is a re-created maritime town of the 19th century. New Haven features Yale University, excellent museums and a hip cultural district. Visit Hartford to see Mark Twain's mansion at Nook Farm. For pristine rural scenery, go to the well-preserved towns of Essex, Old Lyme and Ivoryton at the mouth of the Connecticut River, or to the scenic Litchfield Hills in the northwestern corner of the state.

Maine
Enjoy the beach resort towns along the southern coast and then head to Portland. Go 'Downeast,' stopping in several of the traditional coastal towns (Blue Hill, Boothbay Harbor, Camden, Castine, Pemaquid Point) before reaching Bar Harbor and Acadia National Park. You'll find an abundance of outdoor adventure in the spectacular lakes and mountains of north-central Maine.

New Hampshire
In New Hampshire, you should see Portsmouth and historic Strawbery Banke on the coast. Also make stops at Manchester (for the Currier Gallery of Art) and at Concord (the state capital) on your way to Lake Winnipesaukee for water sports and the White Mountain National Forest for hiking, camping and river running. Check out mountainous Franconia Notch State Park, north of Lincoln, and don't miss the scenic drive along the Kancamagus Hwy (NH 112) between Lincoln and Conway. North Conway is the outdoor-activity center of the region.

Rhode Island
In Rhode Island, Newport rules. Tour the mansions of America's 'Robber Barons'; scout out the shops and restaurants on Thames St; spend an afternoon on one of the beaches, or take a day trip on the ferry to Block Island.

Vermont
Drive – and walk – in the Green Mountains here in northern New England, preferably along VT 100, which threads its way from south to north through the center of one of the most rural states in the union. Take time to explore the cosmopolitan towns of Bennington, Dorset, Grafton, Manchester, Middlebury, Stowe and Woodstock. Be sure to see the vast Shelburne Museum south of Burlington.

SUGGESTED ITINERARIES

There's no 'right' way to see New England, but it can help to have sample itineraries. Try to visit cities on weekends and country towns and resorts on weekdays, especially in summer or the foliage season. This gets you lower prices and fewer crowds.

Less than a Week

If you have only three to five days, use **Boston** as your base. Plan to spend half a day walking the Freedom Trail (you may spend most of a day, though) and another half-day at the Museum of Fine Arts and the Gardner Museum. The Museum of Science, the New England Aquarium and the Children's Museum are also top picks.

If you're a shopper, schedule a half-day at Downtown Crossing or spend the time strolling past the boutiques on Newbury St. Harvard Square requires a half-day for an amble through Harvard Yard with some shopping, or a full day if you include a visit to Harvard's excellent museums.

For excursions, go west to Lexington (by car) and Concord (car or train), or north to Salem (car, bus or train) and Marblehead (car or bus). You could even do a day trip to Plymouth (preferably by car or bus tour). In summer, excursion boats sail from Boston to Provincetown and back in a day, and these boats are the best way to go to the tip of Cape Cod on a day trip.

A Week or More

If you have a week or 10 days, you can (after spending several days in Boston) really get a taste of New England. Your itinerary will change depending upon the season, but consider these high points.

Stay at least one night in an old **Cape Cod** town. If you can stay two or three nights, or even more, spend one day on an excursion to one of the islands, Martha's Vineyard or Nantucket, or better yet, overnight there. Stop in Plymouth on the way to or from the Cape.

If it's summer or autumn, drive to the **Berkshires** and stay at least one night, perhaps stopping midway to tour Old Sturbridge Village. If you have two nights to spend, take in Williamstown or the Litchfield Hills of northwestern Connecticut.

In **Rhode Island**, spend a long half-day in Providence, and at least one night in Newport touring the mansions and strolling the Cliff Walk. With another night to spend, you can take in some sun on the Rhode Island beaches. Block Island requires at least a day of its own.

Drive north to New Hampshire's **White Mountains** for a few days of sightseeing, hiking, canoeing, white-water rafting or skiing, spending the nights in campgrounds or country inns. Two nights is the minimum you'll need to see central New Hampshire. With three, you can tour Lake Winnipesaukee as well.

Portsmouth, NH, **Portland**, ME, and the towns of the southern Maine coast are only a few hours' drive or bus ride from Boston, making them accessible for an overnight excursion. If you have two nights to spend here, you can take in Boothbay Harbor and even Camden, though you'll want at least a full day, and preferably three or five days, for a windjammer (sailing) cruise along the Maine coast.

Two Weeks

With two weeks to spend, you'll have the time to see Boston and other top sights as well as venture to some of the more remote parts of New England, which are of interest to outdoor enthusiasts.

In **Downeast Maine**, spend two nights on Mt Desert Island exploring Acadia National Park, a night (or more) on a windjammer and the rest of your time in any of the coastal towns.

Spend three or four days in the wilds of **northern Maine** on a canoe or kayak excursion, on a white-water rafting expedition, or hiking and camping. Rafting is most exciting in the springtime when the rivers rage.

Though southern **Vermont** is only a few hours' drive from Boston, it takes several more hours to get to the northern part of the state. With four or five days to devote to Vermont, spend a day and a half exploring Bennington, Brattleboro and classic Yankee farm towns such as Newfane and Grafton.

Then drive north along VT 100 through the center of the state, camping or staying at inns. In winter Killington offers downhill skiing, snowboarding and cross-country skiing; in summer, hiking and mountain biking.

Make a detour to hip Woodstock and then continue north via Waitsfield to Stowe for a hike on the Long Trail or for skiing in winter. Finish with a visit to Burlington and the Shelburne Museum.

Take a day or two to visit New Haven and the historic towns of the **Connecticut** coast. After at least a day at Mystic Seaport Museum, head up the Connecticut River Valley. Stop at Hartford for a half-day on your way to Lake Waramaug and the Litchfield Hills.

PLANNING

Many travelers think of New England as a summer destination, with another busy season when the fall foliage reaches its full color. But if you are prepared to roll with the region's abrupt and dramatic changes in weather, you can explore and enjoy New England year-round.

When to Go

From mid-July through August, the summer resort areas are very busy, accommodations are fully booked and restaurants are crowded. One good time to travel here is between mid-May and mid-June, before the local schools close and families hit the road. But avoid Boston at the end of May when the city is packed for college graduations. The early part of September, after the big summer rush but before the 'leaf-peepers' (foliage tourists) arrive, is another great time. The weather in these shoulder seasons is generally warm and sunny. Early November is a serene, almost haunting, time in New England before the snows hit. December to March is ski season in the mountains. Cape Cod, Rhode Island and the Connecticut coast can have fine warm days in April and May (you can also get buckets of rain).

Maps

Lonely Planet publishes a thorough, annotated map of Boston. Local chambers of commerce usually hand out simple maps of their towns.

The most detailed state highway maps are those distributed free by state governments. You can call or write state tourism offices in advance (see Tourist Offices, later in this chapter) and have the maps sent to you, or you can pick up the maps at highway tourism information offices ('welcome centers') when you enter a state on a major highway (see Tourist Offices for details).

Other highway maps with sufficient detail to be useful are for sale in gas stations, bookstores, newsstands and lodging places.

US Dept of the Interior Geological Survey (USGS) topographical maps cover the USA at a scale of 1:24,000, showing every road, path and building (though some of these may be out of date). They are superb close-up maps for hiking or intensive exploration by car. USGS also publishes a variety of other maps, including metropolitan and resort-destination maps at scales between 1:24,000 and 1:100,000, and state topographical maps at 1:500,000.

Information on ordering USGS maps is now available on the USGS website W www.usgs.gov or by writing to USGS Information Services, Box 25286, Denver, CO 80225. When you order maps, also request the folder describing topographic maps and the symbols used on them. For faster, easier service, you may order maps from Boston's Globe Corner Bookstore (☎ 617-497-6277, 800-358-6013, W www.globecorner.com).

See the boxed text 'Bookstores,' in the Boston chapter, for information on other bookstores.

Hiking trail maps are available from outdoors organizations (see Guidebooks, later in this chapter).

Atlases

If you plan to do a lot of traveling – especially hiking or biking – in a particular state, you may want to get a state atlas.

The Delorme Mapping Company (☎ 207-846-7100, W www.delorme.com, PO Box 298, Yarmouth, ME 04096) sells atlases for all New England states, except Connecticut and

Rhode Island, for $17. The Massachusetts atlas is done at an impressive 1:80,000 scale.

Arrow Map Company (☎ 508-279-1177, 800-343-7500, ⓦ www.arrowmap.com, 50 Scotland Blvd, Bridgewater, MA 02324) has atlases covering all the New England states and many individual cities and towns as well.

What to Bring

If you take prescription medicines regularly, bring a supply of the medicine. You can bring a prescription to be filled as well, as long as the prescription was written in the US. Local pharmacies won't fill foreign prescriptions.

From mid-June through early September in southern New England, have cool summer clothing plus a sweater or jacket for evenings. A windbreaker and sweater will be necessary for the mountains of northern New England and the windy coast. If you plan to dine in fancy restaurants in Newport, Boston or other cosmopolitan centers, you'll need to dress up (skirt, dress, or coat and tie). An umbrella or raincoat and hat are good to have any time of year.

In spring (April to May) and autumn (mid-September to late October or mid-November), mornings and afternoons can be chilly, and nights can approach freezing, so have warmer clothes.

For the winter (mid-November through March), have cold-weather gear: fleece, woolens, waterproof footwear, a warm hat, scarf and gloves. From mid-December through February, Boston can have several weeks when the temperature does not go above freezing and even a few days when it does not reach 10°F. In northern New England, the cold lasts even longer and is more bitter.

TOURIST OFFICES
Local Tourist Offices

State tourism offices will send you excellent detailed road maps, lists of lodgings, festivals and special events, and other materials before your trip.

They also maintain 'welcome centers' at major highway entrances to their states.

Typically, you drive across the state line into a new state, and one of the next exits will have a welcome center with toilets, a picnic area, vending machines for hot and cold drinks and snacks, and an information desk dispensing maps and brochures as well as camping, lodging and restaurant lists.

Here are the main addresses for state-run tourist offices:

Connecticut Office of Tourism
(☎ 860-270-8080, 800-282-6863, fax 860-563-4877, ⓦ www.ctbound.org) 505 Hudson St, Hartford, CT 06106

Maine Office of Tourism
(☎ 207-287-5711, 888-624-6345, fax 207-623-0388, ⓦ www.visitmaine.com) 59 State House Station, Augusta, ME 04330

Massachusetts Office of Travel & Tourism
(☎ 617-973-8500, 800-227-MASS from US & Canada, fax 617-973-8525, ⓦ www.massvacations.com) 10 Park Plaza, Suite 4510, Boston, MA 02116

New Hampshire Office of Travel & Tourism Development
(☎ 603-271-2666, 800-386-4664, fax 603-271-6870, ⓦ www.visitnh.com) 172 Pembroke Rd, PO Box 1856, Concord, NH 03302-0856

Rhode Island Tourism Division
(☎ 401-222-2601, 800-556-2484, fax 401-222-2102, ⓦ www.visitrhodeisland.com) 1 West Exchange St, Providence, RI 02903

Vermont Dept of Tourism and Marketing
(☎ 802-828-3236, 800-837-6668, fax 802-828-3233, ⓦ www.1-800-vermont.com) 6 Baldwin St, Montpelier, VT 05633-1301

Chambers of Commerce

Often associated with convention and visitors' bureaus (CVBs), these are membership organizations for local businesses including hotels, restaurants and shops. Although they often provide maps and other useful information, they usually don't tell you about establishments that are not chamber members, and these nonmembers are often the cheapest or most independent establishments.

A local chamber of commerce usually maintains an information booth at the entrance to the town or in the town center, often open only during tourist seasons (summer, foliage season, ski season). It might also have a separate business office (ie, not an information office) elsewhere. Some chamber information offices will help you make reservations at member lodgings.

In this book, the addresses and telephone numbers of local chambers of commerce and tourist offices are given in the Information sections under town headings.

Tourist Offices Abroad

US embassies and consulates abroad may have some tourist information (see Embassies & Consulates, later in this chapter).

In Montreal, Quebec, contact the New England Tourism Centre (☎ 514-731-4898, W www.ne-tc.com, 4270 Sere St, Laurent).

In the UK try Chelsea Travel (☎ 020-7351-4466, fax 020-7376-3123, W www.absite.com/chelseatravel, 292 Fulham Rd, London).

VISAS & DOCUMENTS
Passport & Visas

To enter the USA, Canadians must have proof of Canadian citizenship, such as a passport or a citizenship card with photo ID. Visitors from other countries must have a valid passport, and most visitors also require a US visa. Check out the US State Dept website (W www.travel.state.gov/visa_services.html) for visa information.

A reciprocal visa-waiver program allows citizens of some countries to enter the USA without a US visa for stays of 90 days or less. These countries include Andorra, Argentina, Australia, Austria, Belgium, Brunei, Denmark, Finland, France, Germany, Iceland, Ireland, Italy, Japan, Liechtenstein, Luxembourg, Monaco, the Netherlands, New Zealand, Norway, San Marino, Slovenia, Spain, Sweden, Switzerland and the UK. Under this program you must have a roundtrip ticket that is nonrefundable in the USA, and you are not allowed to extend your stay beyond 90 days.

Other travelers need to obtain a visa from a US consulate or embassy. In most countries the process can be done by mail.

Your passport should be valid for at least six months longer than your intended stay in the USA, and you'll need to submit a recent photo (37mm by 37mm) with the application. Documents of financial stability and/or guarantees from a US resident are sometimes required, particularly for those from developing countries.

Visa applicants may be required to 'demonstrate binding obligations' that will ensure their return home. Because of this requirement, those planning to travel through other countries before arriving in the USA are generally better off applying for their US visa while they are still in their home countries rather than while on the road.

The most common type of visa is a Non-Immigrant Visitors Visa: B1 for business purposes, B2 for tourism or visits to friends and relatives. A visitor's visa is good for one or five years with multiple entries, and it specifically prohibits the visitor from taking paid employment in the USA. If you're coming to the USA to work or study, you will probably need a different type of visa, and the company or institution to which you're going should make the arrangements. Allow six months in advance for processing the application. For information on work visas and employment in the US, see the Work section, later in this chapter.

The validity period of your US Visitors Visa depends on your citizenship. The length of time you are allowed to stay in the USA is ultimately determined by US immigration authorities at the port of entry.

If you want to extend your visa – to stay in the USA past the date stamped in your passport – contact the Justice Dept's Immigration & Naturalization Service (INS) before the stamped date. The INS has ceased listing their local telephone numbers. Contact ☎ 800-375-5283 or W www.ins.usdoj.gov for all information or forms. The Boston office is in the John F Kennedy Federal Office Building, 5th floor, Government Center, Boston, MA 02203; take the subway to the Government Center station. It's a good idea to bring a US citizen with you to vouch for your character, and to bring some sort of proof that you have enough currency to support yourself.

Travel Insurance

No matter how you're traveling, make sure you purchase travel insurance. This should cover you not only for medical expenses and luggage theft or loss, but also for cancellations or delays in your travel arrangements. You should be covered for the worst possible case, such as an accident that requires hospital treatment and a flight home. Coverage depends on your insurance and type of ticket, so ask both your insurer and your ticket-issuing agency to explain the finer points. Both STA Travel (☎ 800-777-0112) and Council Travel (☎ 800-226-8624) offer travel insurance options at reasonable prices. In the UK, apply for insurance to Europ Assistance (☎ 0181-680-1234, Ⓦ www.europassistance.com, 252 High St, Croydon, Surrey CR0 1NF).

Travel insurance also covers lost tickets. Make sure you have a separate record of all your ticket details – or better still, a photocopy of the tickets. Also make a copy of your policy in case the original is lost.

Buy travel insurance as early as possible. If you buy it the week before you fly, you may discover that you're not covered for delays to your flight caused by strikes or other industrial action that started before you took out the insurance.

Insurance may seem very expensive – but it's nowhere near the cost of a medical emergency in the United States. (See the Health section, later in this chapter, for more information.)

International Driving Permit

An International Driving Permit is a useful accessory for foreign visitors in the USA. Local traffic police are more likely to accept it as valid identification than an unfamiliar document from another country. Your national automobile association can provide one for a nominal fee. It's usually valid for one year.

Automobile Association Card

If you plan on doing a lot of driving in the USA, it might be beneficial to join your national automobile association. Members of clubs affiliated with the American Automobile Association (AAA) can get roadside assistance as well as discounts on lodging, car rental and sightseeing admission with membership cards. See the Useful Organizations section later in this chapter for more information.

Hostel Card

Most hostels in the USA are members of Hostelling International–American Youth Hostels (HI-AYH). For more information on HI-AYH, see the Useful Organizations and Hostels sections, later in this chapter.

Student & Youth Cards

In college towns such as Amherst, Boston, Cambridge, Hanover or New Haven, your student ID card sometimes can get you discounts. Museums and attractions outside these cities may also give small discounts to students. You'll need a card to prove that you are one.

Photocopies

It's a good idea to make photocopies of your important travel documents (passport data page and visa page, credit cards, travel insurance policy, air/bus/train tickets, driver's license, etc). Keep the copies in a different, safe place from the documents themselves. If your documents are lost or stolen, replacing them will be much easier.

EMBASSIES & CONSULATES
US Embassies & Consulates Abroad

US diplomatic offices abroad include the following:

Australia

Embassy: (☎ 02-6214-5600, Ⓦ www.usis-australia.gov/embassy.html) 21 Moonah Place, Yaralumla, ACT 2600

Consulate: (☎ 02-9373-9200, Ⓦ www.usconsydney.org) Level 59 MLC Center, 19-29 Martin Place, Sydney, NSW 2000

Consulate: (☎ 03-9526-5900, Ⓦ www.usis-australia.gov/melbourne) Level 6, 553 St Kilda Rd (PO Box 6722), Melbourne, VIC 3004

Consulate: (☎ 08-9231-9400, Ⓦ www.usis-australia.gov/perth) St George's Court, 13th floor, 16 St George's Terrace, Perth, WA 6000

Austria
Embassy: (☎ 1-31339-0, Ⓦ www.usembassy
vienna.at) Boltzmanngasse 16, A-1090, Vienna

Canada
Embassy: (☎ 613-238-5335, Ⓦ www.usembassy
canada.gov) 290 Sussex Dr, Ottawa, ON K1N
5G8
Consulate: (☎ 902-429-2485) 2000 Barrington St,
Cogswell Tower, Suite 910, Halifax, NS B3J 3K1
Consulate: ☎ 514-398-9695) 1155 rue St-
Alexandre, Montreal, Quebec H2Z 1Z2
Consulate: (☎ 416-595-1700) 360 University Ave,
Toronto, ON M5G 1S4
There are also consulates in Calgary, Quebec
City and Vancouver.

Denmark
Embassy: (☎ 35-55-31-44, Ⓦ www.usembassy.dk)
Dag Hammarskjölds Allé 24, 2100 Copenhagen

Finland
Embassy: (☎ 9-171-931, Ⓦ www.usembassy.fi)
Itäinen Puistotie 14, 00140 Helsinki

France
Embassy: (☎ 08 36 70 14 88, Ⓦ www.amb-usa.fr)
2 rue Saint-Florentin, 75382 Paris Cedex 08

Germany
Embassy: (☎ 030-832-9233, Ⓦ www.usembassy
.de) Clayallee 170, 14195 Berlin
There are consulates in Dusseldorf, Frankfurt,
Hamburg, Leipzig and Munich.

Greece
Embassy: (☎ 1-721-2951, Ⓦ www.usisathens.gr)
91 Vasilissis Sophias Blvd, 10160 Athens
There is a consulate general in Thessaloniki.

Ireland
Embassy: (☎ 01-688-7122, Ⓦ www.indigo.ie/
usembassy-usis) 42 Elgin Rd, Ballsbridge,
Dublin 4

Israel
Embassy: (☎ 3-519-7327, Ⓦ www.usis-israel
.org.il) 71 Hayarkon St, Tel Aviv
There is a consulate in Jerusalem.

Italy
Embassy: (☎ 6-46-741, Ⓦ www.usis.it) Via Vittorio
Veneto 119/A, 00187 Rome

Japan
Embassy: (☎ 3-224-5000) 1-10-5 Akasaka Chome,
Minato-ku, Tokyo

Mexico
Embassy: (☎ 5-209-9100, Ⓦ www.usembassy
.org.mx) Paseo de la Reforma 305, Colonia
Cuauhtémoc, 06500 México, DF
There are consulates in Ciudad Juárez, Gua-
dalajara, Hermosillo, Matamoros, Mérida, Mon-
terrey, Nuevo Laredo and Tijuana.

Netherlands
Embassy: (☎ 70-310-9209, Ⓦ www.usemb.nl)
Lange Voorhout 102, 2514 EJ The Hague
Consulate: (☎ 20-575-5309) Museumplein 19,
1071 DJ Amsterdam

New Zealand
Embassy: (☎ 9-303-2724) General Bldg, 29
Shortland St, Auckland

Spain
Embassy: (☎ 1-906-421431 from Spain only, fee
payable; US passport holders call ☎ 91587-2251)
Calle Serrano 75, 28006 Madrid

Sweden
Embassy: (☎ 08 783 53 00, fax 660 58 79,
Ⓦ www.usis.usemb.se) Dag Hammarskjölds Väg
31, SE-115 89 Stockholm

Switzerland
Embassy: (☎ 0900555154, Jubiläumsstrasse 95,
3005 Bern

UK
Embassy: (☎ 020-7499-9000, Ⓦ www.usembassy
.org.uk) 24 Grosvenor Square, London W1A 1AE
Consulate: (☎ 131-556-8315, fax 557-6023) 3
Regent Terrace, Edinburgh EH7 5BW
Consulate: (☎ 1232-328239, Queens House, 14
Queen St, Belfast BT1 6EQ

Embassies & Consulates in the USA

Embassies are in Washington, DC. Some
countries maintain consulates, honorary
consuls or consular agents in Boston. To get
the telephone number of an embassy or
consulate not listed below, call the directory
assistance (information) number for the city
in which you hope to find a diplomatic
office (Boston: ☎ 617-555-1212; Washington:
☎ 202-555-1212).

Australia
Embassy: (☎ 202-797-3000, fax 797-3168,
Ⓦ www.austemb.org) 1601 Massachusetts Ave
NW, Washington, DC 20036

Canada
Embassy: (☎ 202-682-1740, Ⓦ www.cdn
embwashdc .org) 501 Pennsylvania Ave NW,
Washington, DC 20001
Consulate: (☎ 617-262-3760) 3 Copley Place,
Suite 400, Boston, MA 02116

France
Embassy: (☎ 202-944-6000) 4101 Reservoir Rd
NW, Washington, DC 20007-2171

Consulate: (☎ 617-542-7374) 31 St James Ave, Suite 750, Boston, MA 02116

Germany
Embassy: (☎ 202-298-4000, fax 298-4249, [w] www.germany-info.org) 4645 Reservoir Rd NW, Washington, DC 20007-1998
Consulate: (☎ 617-536-4414, fax 536-8573) 3 Copley Place, Suite 500, Boston, MA 02116

Ireland
Embassy: (☎ 202-462-3939, [w] www.irelandemb .org) 2234 Massachusetts Ave NW, Washington, DC 20008
Consulate: (☎ 617-267-9330) Chase Bldg, 535 Boylston St, Boston, MA 02116

Israel
Embassy: (☎ 202-364-5500, fax 364-5423, [w] www.israelemb.org) 3514 International Drive NW, Washington, DC 20008

Italy
Embassy: (☎ 202-612-4400, fax 462-3605, [w] www.italyemb.nw.dc.us/italy) 3000 Whitehaven St NW, Washington, DC 20008
Consulate: (☎ 617-542-0483) 100 Boylston St, Suite 900, Boston, MA 02116

Japan
Embassy: (☎ 202-238-6700, fax 238-2187, [w] www.embjapan.org) 2520 Massachusetts Ave NW, DC 20008

Mexico
Embassy: (☎ 202-736-1002, [w] www.embassy ofmexico.org) 2827 16th St NW, Washington, DC 20006

Netherlands
Embassy: (☎ 202-244-5300, fax 362-3430, [w] www.netherlands-embassy.org) 4200 Linnean Ave NW, Washington, DC 20008
Consulate: (☎ 617-542-8452) 20 Park Plaza, Boston, MA 02116

New Zealand
Embassy: (☎ 202-328-4800, fax 667-5227, [w] www.emb.com/nzemb) 37 Observatory Circle NW, Washington, DC 20008

UK
Embassy: (☎ 202-588-6500, fax 588-7850, [w] britain-info.org)
3100 Massachusetts Ave NW, Washington, DC 20008
Consulate: (☎ 617-248-9555, fax 248-9578) Federal Reserve Plaza, 25th floor, 600 Atlantic Ave, Boston, MA 02210

Your Own Embassy

As a tourist, it's important to realize what your own embassy – the embassy of the country of which you are a citizen – can and can't do.

Generally speaking, it won't be much help in emergencies if the trouble you're in is remotely your own fault. Remember that you are bound by the laws of the country you are in. Your embassy will not be sympathetic if you end up in jail after committing a crime locally, even if your actions are legal in your own country.

In genuine emergencies you might get some assistance, but only if other channels have been exhausted. For example, if you need to get home urgently, a free ticket home is exceedingly unlikely – your embassy will expect you to have insurance. If you have all your money and documents stolen, it might assist in getting a new passport, but a loan for onward travel is out of the question.

Embassies used to keep letters for travelers, and had small reading rooms with home newspapers, but these days the mail-holding service has been stopped and even the newspapers tend to be out of date.

CUSTOMS

The US Customs Service allows each person 21 years of age or older to bring 1 liter of liquor and 200 cigarettes duty-free into the USA. US citizens are allowed to import $400 worth of duty-free gifts from abroad, while non-US citizens are allowed to bring in $100 worth.

Should you be carrying more than $10,000 in US and foreign cash, traveler's checks, money orders and the like, you need to declare the excess amount. There is no legal restriction on the amount that may be imported, but undeclared sums may be subject to confiscation.

MONEY
Currency

The US currency is the dollar ($), divided into 100 cents (¢). Coins are in denominations of 1¢ (penny), 5¢ (nickel), 10¢ (dime), 25¢ (quarter), 50¢ (half dollar – rare) and $1 (three distinct coins, all fairly rare). Common notes ('bills') are in denominations of $1, $2 (rare), $5, $10, $20, $50 and $100.

Exchange Rates

At press time, exchange rates were as follows:

country	unit		US dollars
Australia	A$1	=	US$0.52
Canada	C$1	=	US$0.62
EU	€1	=	US$0.89
Hong Kong	HK$10	=	US$1.28
Japan	¥100	=	US$0.75
New Zealand	NZ$1	=	US$0.43
UK	UK£1	=	US$1.43

Exchanging Money

Cash & Traveler's Checks Only a few banks, mostly in Boston, are prepared to exchange foreign cash. If you are coming to the US from abroad, you should plan on using your bank cash card (ATM card, cashpoint card, etc) to obtain cash easily at the most advantageous rate of exchange. Also plan to use your major credit card (Visa, MasterCard, EuroCard, Access, Diners Club, American Express) often. If you don't have credit cards or a cash card, plan to buy US-dollar traveler's checks before leaving home or upon arrival in the US.

Some banks in small vacation towns frequented by Canadian tourists will buy and sell Canadian currency; some businesses near the border will offer to accept Canadian dollars 'at par,' meaning that they will accept Canadian dollars as though they were US dollars, in effect giving you a substantial discount on your purchase.

There are three Travelex America (☎ 617-567-9881) foreign currency exchange booths at Boston's Logan Airport in Terminals B, C and D – open long hours for foreign arrivals and departures. Fleet Boston bank (☎ 800-841-4000) has exchange locations in Boston and Cambridge (see the Information section in the Boston chapter).

ATMs Cash (cashpoint, debit) cards from many banks may be used to pay at hotels, restaurants, shops, gas stations, etc, and to obtain cash from automated teller machines (ATMs). Look for ATMs in or near banks, shopping malls, large supermarkets, airports and train stations, and on busy streets. In urban settings, use caution at ATMs after dark. In order for your card to be useful in New England, your home bank must be a member of one of the large interbank card systems such as Cirrus, Interlink, Plus Systems or Star Systems.

You can use major credit and charge cards at car rental agencies and at most hotels, restaurants, gas stations, shops and larger grocery stores. The most commonly accepted cards are Visa, MasterCard (Euro-Card, Access) and American Express. However, Discover and Diners Club cards are also accepted by a fair number of businesses. You'll find it hard to perform certain transactions without a credit card. Ticket-buying services, for instance, won't reserve tickets over the phone unless you offer a credit card number, and it's difficult to rent a car without a credit card (you might have to put down a cash deposit of several hundred dollars).

Some inns, B&Bs and restaurants in the most popular resorts (Nantucket, Martha's Vineyard, etc) and in rural areas do not accept credit cards.

Carry copies of your credit card numbers separately from the cards. If you lose your credit cards or they are stolen, contact the company immediately. The following are toll-free numbers for the main credit card companies:

American Express	☎ 800-528-4800
Diners Club	☎ 800-234-6377
Discover	☎ 800-347-2683
MasterCard	☎ 800-826-2181
Visa	☎ 800-336-8472

Costs

New England is among the more expensive regions in the USA for travel, but you can travel quite cheaply here if you know how. What you spend depends on when and where you travel, how you travel and your age.

Seasonal Costs New England's busiest travel seasons are July and August (high summer) and late September through mid-

October (foliage season). Prices for hotels, transportation and attractions are highest at these times. (See the Planning section, earlier in this chapter, for more details.)

City vs Country In general, accommodations in cities are more expensive during the week, and less expensive on Friday, Saturday and sometimes Sunday nights. Resorts, country inns, rural B&Bs and small-town motels, however, are cheapest during the week and more expensive on weekends. To economize you should plan to visit cities on weekends, and venture out into the country during the week, if possible.

Budget Ranges The most inexpensive way to see New England is to camp with a tent, share a rental car among four people and have picnics for lunch. Traveling this way, your daily budget for food, lodging and transport can be as low as $25 to $35 per person; figure $10 to $15 more per person per day if you plan to spend lots of time in the big cities or resorts. Remember that camping is only practical from May through mid-October.

Traveling frugally, a couple can expect to spend between $70 and $85 per person per day. Such travel entails staying in budget motels, eating breakfast/lunch in fast-food places (or lunchrooms), taking dinner in a moderately priced restaurants and getting around by rental car. If you spend lots of time in resorts and cities, your costs might be $80 to $100 per person. Two people touring in a rental car, staying at luxury hotels or inns, and dining as they please should expect to spend $130 to $180 per person per day.

Discounts
Some state tourism information centers have racks of brochures for hotels, motels, inns, restaurants, tours and attractions. Some of these accommodations offer discounts to travelers who present handbills or coupons given out at the information centers. For some lodgings, you must call and make a reservation from the information center to obtain the discount. Also, call the state tourism office for publicity materials, which will be mailed to you and may contain discount coupons for savings on car rentals, lodgings and meals.

Discounts on rentals and accommodations are often available to members of auto clubs affiliated with the American Automobile Association (AAA). Many motels, and some inns and hotels, offer discounts of 10% to 20% to association members. (See Useful Organizations, later in this chapter, for details.)

Students Many museums and attractions offer lower rates to college students. Though there are many special student deals available in college towns like Boston, often these special rates for cultural attractions are available only through individual colleges and universities. You must buy your tickets through the university, not at the attraction itself.

Families Virtually all hotels and motels allow one or two children to share their parents' room at no extra charge. If a rollaway bed is needed, there might be a charge (often $10 to $20). Usually, children must be younger than 18 years of age. At country inns and B&Bs, however, this policy does not usually apply. In fact, many B&Bs and inns do not allow children under 12 at all.

Most local activities and attractions – museums, theme parks, whale-watching expeditions, etc – offer reduced admission charges for children. Some offer special family rates; always ask if they do.

Seniors Older travelers are eligible for discounts at attractions, museums, parks and many hotels, on car rentals and train and bus fares, and on other items. The age at which such discounts apply varies, and you must have photo identification as proof of your age. See Senior Travelers, later in this chapter, for more information.

Tipping
Taxi drivers, hairdressers and baggage carriers expect tips. Waiters and bartenders rely on tips for their livelihoods. Tip 15% unless

Taxes

state	meal	lodging	sales
Connecticut	8%	8%	8%
Maine	5%	5%	5%
Massachusetts	5%	5.7%	5%
New Hampshire	8%	8%	–
Rhode Island	6%	11%	6%
Vermont	6%	–	6%

the service is terrible (in which case a complaint to the manager is warranted), or about 20% if the service is great. Never tip in fast food, takeout or buffet-style restaurants where you serve yourself. Baggage carriers in airports and hotels get US$1 for the first bag and 75¢ for each additional bag. In hotels with daily housekeeping, leave a few dollars in the room for the staff when you check out – ask at the desk regarding the appropriate amount per day. In budget hotels, tips are not expected, but always appreciated.

Taxes

There is no national sales tax (such as VAT) in the USA. Some states levy sales taxes, and states and cities/towns may levy taxes on hotel rooms and restaurant meals. Room and meal taxes are not normally included in prices quoted to you, even though (or perhaps because) they may increase your final bill by as much as 11% or 12%. Be sure to ask about taxes when you ask for hotel room rates.

Taxes on transport services (bus, rail and air tickets, gasoline, taxi rides) are usually included in the prices quoted to you. See the boxed text 'Taxes' for more details.

POST & COMMUNICATIONS

There's a post office in every town, providing the familiar postal services such as parcel shipping and international express mail. For 24-hour postal information, call ☎ 800-275-8777 or check W www.usps.gov. For hours of operation, see Sending Mail, below. Private shippers such as United Parcel Service (UPS; ☎ 800-742-5877) and Federal Express (FedEx; ☎ 800-463-3339) ship much of the nation's load of parcels and important time-sensitive documents to both domestic and foreign destinations.

Postal Rates

US postal rates are fairly cheap and fairly stable, changing every few years. At press time, rates for 1st-class mail within the USA were set at 34¢ for letters up to 1oz, 23¢ for each additional ounce, and 21¢ for postcards.

The rates for international airmail from the USA (except to Canada and Mexico) start at 80¢ for a 1oz letter. The international postcard rate is 70¢.

Letters to Canada and Mexico are 60¢ for a half-ounce letter and 85¢ for a letter up to 2oz. Postcards are 40¢. Aerograms are 70¢.

Sending Mail

If you have the correct postage, you can drop your mail into any blue mailbox. However, to send a package weighing 16oz or more, you must bring it to a post office. Addresses of towns' main post offices are given in this book. For the address of the nearest, call the main post office listed under 'Postal Service' in the US Government section of the local 'white pages' telephone directory.

Usually, post offices are open from 8am or 8:30am to 5pm weekdays; some major post offices in cities stay open until 5:30pm or 6pm. Weekend hours are normally 8am to noon or 2pm on Saturday, closed Sunday.

Receiving Mail

You can have mail sent to you at the address 'c/o General Delivery' at any post office that has its own zip (postal) code. Mail is usually held for 10 days before it's returned to the sender; you might request that your correspondents write 'hold for arrival' on letters. When you pick up your mail, bring some photo identification. Your passport is best. Alternatively, have mail sent to the local representative of American Express or Thomas Cook, both of which provide mail service for their clients.

Telephone

All phone numbers in the USA consist of a three-digit area code followed by a seven-digit local number. Because of the exponential growth of telephone numbers in New England (for faxes, cellular phones, etc), you now must dial ☎ 1 + area code + the seven-digit number for local as well as long-distance calls in many areas, particularly in eastern Massachusetts. If you're calling from abroad, the international country code for the USA is 1.

For directory assistance dial ☎ 411. For US directory assistance outside the local area, dial ☎ 1 + the three-digit area code of the place you want to call + 555-1212. The 800, 888 and 877 area codes are designated for toll-free numbers within the USA and Canada. These calls are free (unless you are dialing locally, in which case the toll-free number is not available). To obtain directory assistance for a toll-free number, dial ☎ 800-555-1212 or 888-555-1212. If you don't know the area code, dial ☎ 0 for operator assistance (free of charge).

Area codes for places outside the region are listed in telephone directories. Due to demand for phone numbers, New England (and the USA) has been assigned a host of new area codes. These changes are not always reflected in older phone books. When in doubt, ask the operator. See the boxed text 'New England Area Codes.'

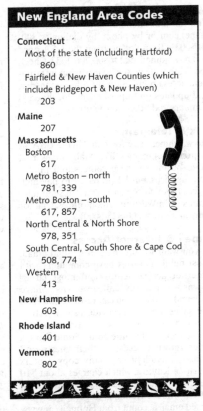

New England Area Codes

Connecticut
  Most of the state (including Hartford)
    860
  Fairfield & New Haven Counties (which include Bridgeport & New Haven)
    203

Maine
    207

Massachusetts
  Boston
    617
  Metro Boston – north
    781, 339
  Metro Boston – south
    617, 857
  North Central & North Shore
    978, 351
  South Central, South Shore & Cape Cod
    508, 774
  Western
    413

New Hampshire
    603

Rhode Island
    401

Vermont
    802

Paying for Calls Local calls at pay phones currently cost 35¢ to 50¢ for three minutes or more, depending upon the town. But these rates may go as high as 75¢ as cell phones become ubiquitous and make pay phones less cost effective for phone companies. For specific rate information, call the operator (☎ 0). Don't ask the operator to put your call through, however, because operator-assisted calls are much more expensive than direct-dial calls. Generally, nights (11pm to 8am), all day Saturday and 8am to 5pm Sunday are the cheapest times to call (60% discount). Evenings (5pm to 11pm Sunday to Friday) are mid-priced (35% discount). Day calls (8am to 5pm weekdays) are full-price calls within the USA.

International Calls To make a direct international call from the USA, dial ☎ 011, then the country code, followed by the area code and the phone number. You may need to wait as long as 45 seconds for the ringing to start. International rates vary depending on the time of day and the destination. Call the operator (☎ 0) for rates. The first minute is always more expensive than extra minutes.

Phone Debit Cards There's a wide range of local and international phone cards. Lonely Planet's eKno Communication Card is aimed specifically at independent travelers and provides budget international calls, a range of messaging services, free email and travel information. (For local calls, you're usually better off with a local card.) You can join online at Ⓦ www.ekno.lonely planet.com or by phone by dialing ☎ 800-707-0031. To use eKno from the USA once you have joined, dial ☎ 800-706-1333. Check the eKno website for membership information, access numbers from other countries, and updates on 'super-budget' local access numbers and other new features.

Fax & Telegram

Fax machines are easy to find in the USA, at shipping companies like Mail Boxes Etc, hotel business-service centers and photocopy services, but be prepared to pay high prices (over $1 a page). You can send telegrams from Western Union offices. Call for information (☎ 800-325-6000).

Email & Internet Access

If you want to surf the Net or send email, most public libraries have computers with Internet access. Cities and most larger towns – especially college towns – have cybercafes where you can retrieve and send messages. For a worldwide lists of cybercafes, browse Ⓦ www.traveltales.com or Ⓦ www.netcafeguide.com. Some hotels offer Internet access to their guests, and access is available at many copy centers (such as Kinko's, which charges about $10 per hour). The cheapest way to have email access while traveling is to get a free Web-based email account from Hotmail (Ⓦ www .hotmail.com), Yahoo (Ⓦ www.yahoo.com) or Netscape (Ⓦ www.netscape.com) that you can access from any online computer with a browser.

INTERNET RESOURCES

The World Wide Web is a rich resource for travelers. You can research your trip, hunt down bargain airfares, book hotels, check on weather conditions, or chat with locals and other travelers about the best places to visit (or avoid!).

There's no better place to start your Web explorations than the Lonely Planet website (Ⓦ www.lonelyplanet.com). Here you'll find succinct summaries on traveling to most places on earth, postcards from other trav-

elers, and the Thorn Tree bulletin board, where you can ask questions before you go or dispense advice when you get back. You also can find travel news and updates to many of our popular guidebooks. The sub-WWWay section links you to the most useful travel resources elsewhere on the Web.

You will find website addresses throughout this book for state and city information services, accommodations and other helpful organizations and businesses.

BOOKS

Books often are published in different editions in different countries, and even by different publishers. Fortunately, local bookstores and libraries can search by title or author, so these are the best places to find out whether the following recommended books are available.

For literature, see that section in the Facts about New England chapter.

Lonely Planet

Lonely Planet's *Boston; New York City; New York City Condensed; New York, New Jersey & Pennsylvania;* and *Washington, DC* are good supplemental guides for travelers exploring the East Coast. Travelers covering even more of the coast might want to read *Virginia & the Capital Region* and *Georgia & the Carolinas.* Lonely Planet's *Canada* is useful for those who intend to continue their journey north. If New England will be your first American experience, you might also enjoy Lonely Planet's *USA,* and those who travel primarily to get outdoors can use *Hiking in the USA.*

Guidebooks

A guide specific to Boston's historic and modern architecture is Susan and Michael Southworth's *The Boston Society of Architects' AIA Guide to Boston.* It details general walking tours as well as specific buildings not only in the city but also in Charlestown and Cambridge.

Excellent, detailed trail guides (with maps) of the Appalachian Trail and the White Mountain National Forest trail system are published by the Appalachian

Mountain Club (AMC; ☎ 617-523-0636, ⓦ www.outdoors.org, 5 Joy St, Boston, MA 02108).

The Green Mountain Club (☎ 802-244-7037, RR1, Box 650, Waterbury Center, VT 05677) publishes some excellent hikers' materials, including the *Guide Book of the Long Trail* ($10), complete with 16 color topographical maps. The Long Trail is a primitive footpath that follows the crest of Vermont's Green Mountains 265 miles from Canada to Massachusetts, with 175 miles of side trails and more than 62 rustic cabins and lean-tos for shelter.

For more on hiking, see the Activities section, later in this chapter.

History

The Flowering of New England, by Van Wyck Brooks, is a Pulitzer Prize–winning work on New England writers, such as Hawthorne and Thoreau, who shaped contemporary ideas.

Literary New England, by William Corbett, is a guidebook to the historic literary sites of New England.

Inside New England, by Judson Hale, is a witty combination of anecdotes, history and highly opinionated satire.

How New England Happened, by Christina Tree, is the definitive traveler's history of the New England region.

Logs of the Dead Pirates Society, by Randall Peffer, is a seafarer's tale of schooner adventures that evokes the history of the Massachusetts coast, from Indian wars and the American Revolution to whaling and rum-running.

FILMS

Little Women (1994), Louisa May Alcott's wonderful book about girls growing up in 19th-century Concord, MA, has been made into a movie starring Susan Sarandon as Marmie.

Jaws (1975), the improbable but still terrifying story of a great white shark attacking swimmers on New England beaches (set on Martha's Vineyard), is available on video.

On Golden Pond (1981), the story of two lovers in their declining years, was filmed at New Hampshire's Squam Lake and features fine performances by Henry Fonda and Katharine Hepburn.

John Huston's classic *Moby Dick* (1956), with Gregory Peck and Orson Welles, is a wonderful introduction to New England maritime life in the 19th century.

School Ties, the story of a working-class scholarship student at an elite New England prep school, was filmed at the Middlesex School in Concord, MA. *The Witches of Eastwick* was filmed in Duxbury, MA.

Housesitter, with Steve Martin and Goldie Hawn, is a light romantic comedy set in a fictional New England town somewhere west of Boston, but it was filmed in Concord and Duxbury, MA.

The Crucible, with Daniel Day-Lewis and Winona Ryder, is a 1996 film adaptation of Arthur Miller's play about the Salem witch trials.

Good Will Hunting, with local-boys-turned-stars Ben Affleck and Matt Damon, is the 1998 hit that tells the story of a blue-collar boy from South Boston who becomes a math/physics savant at the Massachusetts Institute of Technology (MIT).

The Cider House Rules won Michael Caine the Academy Award in 2000 for his role as a doctor in an orphanage in rural Maine.

NEWSPAPERS & MAGAZINES

The region's major newspaper, on sale throughout New England, is the highly regarded *Boston Globe,* followed by the popular tabloid, *Boston Herald.*

Many smaller cities and large towns have their own local newspapers, published daily or weekly.

Boston and Cambridge have newsstands that sell many foreign publications; see the boxed text 'Bookstores,' in the Boston chapter.

For the frequent traveler to New England, *Yankee Traveler* is a helpful newsletter. Its nine issues a year offer destination recommendations and reviews, but it isn't available at newsstands. For a subscription ($36) or single copies ($5), write to PO Box 37021, Boone, IA 50037-0021. It's produced

by the travel editors of *Yankee* Magazine
(Ⓦ www.newengland.com, PO Box 523,
Dublin, NH 03444), which is available at
stores throughout New England.

RADIO & TV

All rental cars have radios, and travelers can
choose from hundreds of radio stations.
Each station follows a format, which may be
to play classical music, country & western,
rock & roll, jazz, easy-listening, or 'golden
oldies.' FM stations mainly carry popular
music. On the AM (middle wave) frequen-
cies, 'talk radio' rules: A more or less intelligent or outrageous radio host receives
telephone calls from listeners, makes comments and expresses opinions.

National Public Radio (NPR) features a
level-headed approach to news, discussion,
music and more. NPR normally broadcasts
on the lower end of the FM dial.

University-run stations like Emerson College's WERS, 88.9 FM in Boston, feature
live folk sessions and reggae, Israeli, French,
Brazilian and Middle Eastern shows.

Most hotel and motel rooms have color
TVs that receive several dozen channels, in-
cluding the major broadcast networks:
Public Broadcasting System (PBS), the
American Broadcasting Company (ABC),
National Broadcasting Company (NBC),
FOX and Columbia Broadcasting System
(CBS), as well as the many cable stations, in-
cluding CNN.

PHOTOGRAPHY & VIDEO

There are virtually no restrictions on pho-
tography in New England, except within
museums and at some musical and artistic
performances.

Every town of any size has at least one
photo shop that stocks a variety of fresh
film, cameras and accessories. All major
brands of film are available at reasonable
prices. In most towns and tourist centers,
some shops can develop your color print
film in one hour, or at least on the same day,
for an extra charge. The charge for processing a 24-exposure roll of 100 ASA 35mm
color print film typically will be about $7 for
regular service.

A note on video equipment for overseas
visitors: Remember that the USA and Canada use the National Television System Committee (NTSC) color TV and video standard,
which is not compatible, unless converted,
with the PAL and SECAM standards used in
Africa, Europe, Asia and Australia.

As always with film and expensive
cameras, a bit of prevention goes a long way.
Film can be damaged by excessive heat, so
don't leave your camera and film in the car
on a hot day, and avoid placing your camera
on the dashboard while you are driving.
Also, it's worth carrying a spare battery for
your camera to avoid disappointment when
your camera dies in the middle of nowhere.
If you're buying a new camera for your trip,
do so several weeks before you leave and
practice using it.

Since the terrorist attacks of September
11, 2001, security is *very* serious business at
US airports. Passengers must pass their
luggage through X-ray machines, which are
said to pose no danger to most films. If
you'd like to bypass the X-ray scanner,
prepare: Unpack your film from boxes and
plastic film cans and have all the film canisters readily visible in a plastic bag. You
really only need to do this for very high-
speed film (1600 ASA and above).

TIME

The USA (excluding Alaska and Hawaii)
spans four time zones.

New England is on US Eastern Time, five
hours earlier than GMT/UTC, and three
hours later than US Pacific Time. When it's
noon in Boston, it's 5pm in London and
9am in San Francisco.

New England observes daylight saving
time, which involves setting clocks ahead
one hour on the first Sunday in April and
back one hour on the last Sunday in October.

ELECTRICITY

Electric current is 110 to 120 volts, 60-cycle.
Appliances built to take 220- to 240-volt, 50-
cycle current (as in Europe and Asia) will
need a converter (transformer) and a US-
style plug adapter with two (flat) pins, or
three (two flat, one round) pins. Plugs with

three pins don't fit into a two-hole socket, but adapters are easy to buy at hardware shops and drugstores.

WEIGHTS & MEASURES

The USA uses the imperial system to measure the volume of gasoline (gallons). Distances are in feet, yards and miles; volume is measured in ounces for most beverages, such as milk or beer. You will find the weight of grocery items such as meat measured in ounces and pounds. See the inside back cover of this book for a conversion chart.

LAUNDRY

Pricier hotels and motels usually provide laundry and dry-cleaning services, but it is often faster, and certainly cheaper, to find the nearest laundromat (self-service coin-operated laundry) or dry cleaners yourself. Ask a local or check the local yellow pages under 'Laundries – Self-Service' and 'Cleaners.'

RECYCLING

It is illegal to litter highways, streets, sidewalks or other public spaces. Fines can be stiff, though enforcement is usually lax.

Virtually all commercial beverage containers sold in the USA are recyclable. In Connecticut, Maine, Massachusetts and Vermont, containers for soft drinks, beer, etc, are subject to a deposit fee of 5¢ or 10¢ each, payable at purchase and refundable when you redeem the container at a recycling center. Supermarkets, liquor stores and other places where beverages are sold in these states will redeem beverage containers, so you can get your nickel or dime back. In New Hampshire and Rhode Island, beverage containers are not subject to deposit, although they are of course recyclable.

Wine bottles are not subject to deposit but are recyclable, as are most sanitary paper drink containers, such as milk and juice boxes.

Many other packaging materials made of plastic, metal, paper or cardboard are recyclable but are collected by towns according to local recycling plans.

It is a serious legal offense in most states to dispose of hazardous materials such as petroleum fuels or lubricants in any way other than through an establishment licensed to accept them, such as an auto repair shop or town recycling center.

TOILETS

Americans have many names for public toilet facilities. The most common names are 'restroom' or 'bathroom.' Other popular names include 'ladies'/men's room,' 'comfort station,' 'facility' and 'sanitary facility.' Of course, you can just ask for 'the toilet.'

You will find public toilets in airports, bars, large stores, museums, state and national parks, restaurants, hotels and tourist information offices, as well as bus, train and highway gas stations. Public toilets in city parks and other public places have mostly been closed due to criminal and sexual misuse.

HEALTH

In an emergency, dial ☎ 911 from any telephone for assistance.

Boston is among the world's most highly regarded centers for medical care and research, with a dozen major hospitals and a half-dozen medical schools. The quality of care is high, as are its costs.

All other cities in New England – even small ones – have hospitals. To find one, look on the highways and roads for the standard hospital symbol, a white 'H' on a blue background. Many cities also have walk-in clinics where you can show up without an appointment, see a nurse, nurse-practitioner or doctor for a minor ailment or preliminary diagnosis, and pay for it in cash or by credit card.

For most foreign visitors, no immunizations are required for entry to the USA, though cholera and yellow fever vaccinations may be required of travelers from areas with a history of those diseases. There are no unexpected health dangers in New England; good medical attention is readily available and the only real health concern is that a collision with the medical system can cause severe injuries to your finances.

Predeparture Preparations

Make sure you're healthy before you start traveling. If you are embarking on a long trip, make sure your teeth are in good shape. If you wear glasses, take a spare pair and your prescription. You can get new spectacles made up quickly and competently for under $100, depending on your prescription and the frame you choose. If you require a particular medication, take an adequate supply and bring a prescription in case you lose your medication.

Health Insurance

A travel insurance policy to cover theft, lost tickets and medical problems is a good idea, especially in the USA, where some hospitals will refuse care without evidence of insurance. (See Travel Insurance, earlier in the chapter.) There are a wide variety of policies; your travel agent will have recommendations. International student travel policies handled by STA Travel and other student travel organizations are usually a good value. Some policies offer the option of lower- or higher-priced medical expense coverage. The higher price is chiefly for countries that, like the US, have extremely high medical costs. Check the fine print.

Some policies specifically exclude 'dangerous activities' such as motorcycling, scuba diving and even trekking. If these activities are on your agenda, avoid this sort of policy. You may prefer a policy that pays doctors or hospitals directly rather than making you pay first and claim later. If you have to claim later, keep *all* documentation. Some policies ask you to call back (reverse charges) to a center in your home country for an immediate assessment of your problem. Check whether the policy covers ambulance fees or an emergency flight home. If you have to stretch out, you will need two seats, and somebody has to pay for it!

Travel Health Guides

Take a look at *Travelers' Health: How to Stay Healthy All Over the World,* by Dr Richard Dawood. The text is comprehensive, easy to read, authoritative and generally highly recommended. Unfortunately, it's rather large to lug around. You might read it before your trip and make copies of the sections you think you might need while you're away.

Food & Water

A crucial health rule is to take care in what you eat and drink. Stomach upsets are the most common travel-related health problem (between 30% and 50% of travelers in a two-week stay experience one), but the majority of these upsets will be relatively minor. In New England, standards of cleanliness in places serving food and drink are generally high.

Bottled drinking water, both carbonated and noncarbonated, is widely available. Tap water is OK to drink throughout the region.

Everyday Health

Normal body temperature is 98.6°F or 37°C; more than 4°F or 2°C higher indicates a 'high' fever. The normal adult pulse rate is 60 to 80 per minute (children 80 to 100, babies 100 to 140). You should know how to take a temperature and a pulse rate.

Respiration (breathing) rate is also an indicator of illness. Count the number of breaths per minute: Between 12 and 20 is normal for adults and older children (up to 30 for younger children, 40 for babies). People with a high fever or serious respiratory illness (such as pneumonia) breathe more quickly than normal. More than 40 shallow breaths a minute usually means pneumonia.

Travel & Climate-Related Problems

Motion Sickness Eating lightly before and during a trip will reduce the chance of motion sickness. If you are prone to motion sickness, try to find a place that minimizes disturbance: near the wing on aircraft, or near the center on buses. Fresh air usually helps. Commercial anti-motion-sickness preparations, which can cause drowsiness, have to be taken before the trip commences; once you feel sick, it's too late. Ginger, a natural preventive, is available in capsule form from health-food stores.

Jet Lag This condition is experienced when a person travels by air across more than three time zones (each time zone usually represents a time difference of one hour). It occurs because many of the functions of the human body are regulated by internal 24-hour cycles called circadian rhythms. When we travel long distances rapidly, our bodies take time to adjust to the 'new time' of our destination, and we may experience fatigue, disorientation, insomnia, anxiety, impaired concentration and/or a loss of appetite. These effects will usually be gone within three days of arrival, but there are ways of minimizing the impact of jet lag:

• Rest for a couple of days prior to departure; try to avoid late nights and last-minute dashes for traveler's checks or your passport.

• Try to select flight schedules that minimize sleep deprivation; arriving in the early evening means you can go to sleep soon after you arrive. For very long flights, try to organize a stopover.

• Avoid excessive eating (which bloats the stomach) and alcohol (which causes dehydration) during the flight. Instead, drink plenty of noncarbonated, nonalcoholic drinks such as fruit juice or water.

• Make yourself comfortable by wearing loose-fitting clothes and perhaps bringing an eye mask and ear plugs to help you sleep.

• Avoid smoking, even if it's legal, as this reduces the amount of oxygen in the airplane cabin even further and causes greater fatigue.

Sunburn Most doctors recommend the use of sunscreen with a high protection factor for easily burned areas such as your shoulders and, if you'll be on nude beaches, areas not normally exposed to sun.

Heat Exhaustion Dehydration or salt deficiency can cause heat exhaustion. Take time to acclimatize to high temperatures, and make sure that you get enough liquids. Salt deficiency is characterized by fatigue, lethargy, headaches, giddiness and muscle cramps. Salt tablets may help. Vomiting or diarrhea can also deplete your liquid and salt levels. Anhydrotic heat exhaustion, caused by the inability to sweat, is quite rare, but unlike the other forms of heat ex-

haustion, it is likely to strike people who have been in a hot climate for some time rather than newcomers. Again, always carry – and use – a water bottle on long trips.

Heat Stroke Long, continuous periods of exposure to high temperatures can leave you vulnerable to this serious, sometimes fatal, condition, which occurs when the body's heat-regulating mechanism breaks down and body temperature rises to dangerous levels. Avoid excessive alcohol intake or strenuous activity when you first arrive in a hot climate to help prevent heat stroke.

Symptoms include feeling unwell, lack of perspiration and a high body temperature of 102°F to 105°F (39°C to 41°C). In extreme cases, hospitalization is essential, but meanwhile get victims out of the sun, remove their clothing, cover them with a wet sheet or towel and fan them continually.

Fungal Infections

These infections, which occur with greater frequency in hot weather, are most likely to occur on the scalp, between the toes or fingers (athlete's foot), in the groin (jock itch or crotch rot), and on the body (ringworm). You get ringworm (which is a fungal infection, not a worm) from infected animals or by walking on damp areas such as shower floors.

To prevent fungal infections, wear loose, comfortable clothes, avoid artificial fibers, wash frequently and dry carefully. If you do get an infection, wash the infected area daily with a disinfectant or medicated soap and water, and rinse and dry well. Apply an antifungal powder and try to expose the infected area to air or sunlight as much as possible. Change underwear and towels frequently and wash them often in hot water.

Infectious Diseases

Diarrhea Any change of water, food or climate can cause 'the runs.' Diarrhea caused by contaminated food or water is more serious. Despite all your precautions, you may still have a mild bout of traveler's diarrhea from exotic food or drink. Dehydration is the main danger with any diarrhea, particularly for children, in whom dehydration can occur quite quickly. Fluid replacement remains the mainstay of management. Weak black tea with a little sugar, soda water, and soft drinks diluted 50% with water are all good. With severe diarrhea, a rehydrating solution is necessary to replace lost minerals and salts. Such solutions, like Pedialyte, are available at pharmacies.

Hepatitis This is a general term for inflammation of the liver. There are many causes of this condition: poor sanitation, contact with infected blood products, drugs, alcohol and contact with an infected person are but a few. The symptoms are fever, chills, headache, fatigue, and feelings of weakness and aches and pains, followed by loss of appetite, nausea, vomiting, abdominal pain, dark urine, light-colored feces and jaundiced skin. The whites of the eyes may also turn yellow. Hepatitis A is the most common strain. You should seek medical advice, but there is not much you can do apart from resting, drinking lots of fluids, eating lightly and avoiding fatty foods. People who have had hepatitis should avoid alcohol for some time after the illness, as the liver needs time to recover. Viral hepatitis is an infection of the liver, which can have several unpleasant symptoms or no symptoms at all, and the infected person may not even know that he or she has the disease.

HIV/AIDS HIV, the human immunodeficiency virus, develops into AIDS, acquired immune deficiency syndrome, which is almost always a fatal disease. Any exposure to blood, blood products or body fluids may put the individual at risk. The disease is often transmitted through sexual contact or dirty needles – vaccinations, acupuncture, tattooing and body piercing can potentially be as dangerous as intravenous drug use.

Fear of infection by HIV should never preclude treatment for serious medical conditions. A good resource for help and information is the US Center for Disease Control AIDS hotline (☎ 800-342-2437, 800-344-7432 in Spanish).

Cuts, Bites & Stings

The stings of bees and wasps and nonpoisonous spider bites are usually painful rather than dangerous. Calamine lotion will give relief, and ice packs will reduce the pain and swelling.

If you get caught in jellyfish tentacles, peel off the tentacles using paper or a towel to protect your fingers. Then wash the area with alcohol (rum works). To alleviate the itchy sting, cover the affected area with meat tenderizer, ammonia or urine.

Ticks & Lyme Disease

Ticks are parasitic arachnids that may be present in brush, forest and grasslands, where hikers often get them on their legs or in their boots. Adult ticks suck blood from hosts by burying their heads in the skin but are often found unattached and can simply be brushed off.

Deer ticks, which can carry and spread a serious bacterial infection called Lyme disease, are found throughout New England. The ticks are usually very small (some as small as a pinhead) and thus are not likely to be noticed casually – you must look carefully for them. A bite from a Lyme disease–infected deer tick may show a red welt and circular 'halo' of redness within a day or two, or there may be no symptoms beyond a minor itch. Also, mild flu-like symptoms – headache, nausea, etc – may follow or may not.

Lyme disease can be treated successfully, but early treatment is essential. If left untreated, Lyme disease causes mental and muscular deterioration.

The best preventive measures are to wear clothing that covers your arms and legs when walking in grassy or wooded areas, apply insect repellent containing DEET on exposed skin and around ankles and trouser leg openings, and always check your body (and especially check your children's and pets' bodies) for ticks after outdoor activities.

If one has attached itself to you, use tweezers to pull it straight out – do not twist it. If a small chunk of skin comes out along with the head, that's good – you've got it all, and no part of the tick will be left to cause infection. Contrary to folk wisdom, do *not* touch the tick with a hot object like a match or a cigarette, because this can cause it to regurgitate noxious gut substances or saliva into the wound. And do not rub oil, alcohol or petroleum jelly on it. If you get sick in the next couple of weeks, consult a doctor.

WOMEN TRAVELERS

Contemporary women in New England can take some comfort in knowing that generations of the region's women have won respect and equality for females in business, arts, science, politics, education, religion and community service. In fact, in some communities like Nantucket, which developed as a matriarchy run by the Quaker 'gray ladies' (while the men were at sea, whaling), women still dominate commercial and community affairs.

Nevertheless, women travelers everywhere, including New England, face challenges peculiar to their gender. In general, you might want to ask for advice at your hotel or telephone the visitor center if you are unsure which areas are considered unsafe, especially when making reservations.

Avoiding vulnerable situations and conducting yourself in a common-sense manner will help you to avoid most problems. You're more vulnerable if you've been drinking or using drugs than if you're sober, and you're more vulnerable alone than if you're with company. If you don't want company, most men will respect a firm but polite 'no thank you.'

At night, avoid getting out of your car to flag down help; turn on your hazard lights and/or display a white cloth outside the driver's-side window or from the radio antenna and wait for official help to arrive. Leaving the hood (bonnet) of your car raised is also a signal that you need assistance.

Some women protect themselves with a whistle, pepper spray or self-defense training. If you decide to purchase a spray, ask local police which sprays are legal. Laws regarding sprays vary from state to state. It is a federal felony to carry defensive sprays on airplanes.

If despite all your precautions you are assaulted, call the police (☎ 911). Many cities have rape crisis centers to aid victims of rape. For the telephone number of the nearest center, call directory information (☎ 411 or 1 + area code + 555-1212).

The headquarters of the National Organization for Women (NOW; ☎ 202-331-0066, e now@now.org, w www.now.org, 1000 16th St NW, Suite 700, Washington, DC 20036) is a good resource for a variety of information and can refer you to state and local chapters. Planned Parenthood (☎ 212-541-7800, e communications@ppfa.org, w www.plannedparenthood.org, 810 Seventh Ave, New York, NY 10019) can refer you to clinics throughout the country and offer advice on medical issues. Check the telephone book's yellow pages under 'Social & Human Services,' 'Clinics' and 'Health Services' for local resources.

GAY & LESBIAN TRAVELERS

Out and active gay communities are visible across New England, especially in cities such as Boston, New Haven and Burlington, which have substantial gay populations, and where it is easier for gay men and women to live their lives with a certain amount of openness. When you travel outside of large cities, it is a bit harder to be open about your sexual preferences. Gay travelers should be careful – holding hands in public might get you bashed.

New England cities often have a gay neighborhood. One example is the South End in Boston. Provincetown, on Cape Cod, and Ogunquit, ME, are gay meccas during the summer. College and university towns have lively gay scenes. Northampton, MA, and Burlington, VT, have well-established lesbian communities. Most cities have a gay or alternative newspaper like Boston's *Bay Windows* that lists current events or at least provides phone numbers of local organizations.

Some good national guidebooks are *The Women's Traveller,* providing listings for lesbians; *Damron's Address Book,* for men; and *Damron Accommodations,* with listings of gay-owned or gay-friendly hotels, B&Bs

and guesthouses nationwide. All three books are published by the Damron Company (☎ 415-255-0404, 800-462-6654, Ⓦ www.damron.com, PO Box 422458, San Francisco, CA 94142-2458).

Ferrari's *Places for Women* and *Places for Men* are useful, as are guides to specific cities. (Check out *Betty & Pansy's Severe Queer Reviews* of various cities, available in some bookstores; it's also available online from Ⓦ www.gaymart.com.)

Another good resource is the *Gay Yellow Pages* (☎ 212-674-0120, Ⓦ gayyellowpages .com, PO Box 533, Village Station, NY 10014-0533), which has a national edition as well as regional editions.

National resource numbers include the National AIDS/HIV Hotline (☎ 800-342-2437), the National Gay/Lesbian Task Force in Washington, DC (☎ 202-332-6483), and the Lambda Legal Defense Fund in New York City (☎ 212-995-8585) and Los Angeles (☎ 213-937-2727).

DISABLED TRAVELERS

Travel within the USA and New England is becoming easier for people with disabilities. Public buildings (including hotels, restaurants, theaters and museums) are now required by law to be wheelchair accessible and to have appropriate restroom facilities. Public transportation services (buses, trains and taxis) must be made accessible to all, including those in wheelchairs, and telephone companies are required to provide relay operators for the hearing impaired. Many banks now provide ATM instructions in Braille. Curb ramps are common, and some of the busier roadway intersections have audible crossing signals.

Larger private and chain hotels have suites for disabled guests. Major car rental agencies offer hand-controlled models at no extra charge. All major airlines, intercity buses and Amtrak trains allow guide dogs to accompany passengers and frequently sell two-for-one packages when seriously disabled passengers require attendants.

Airlines also provide assistance with flight connections, boarding and deplaning – just ask for assistance when making your reservation. (Note: Airlines must accept wheelchairs as checked baggage and have an onboard chair available, though some advance notice may be required on smaller aircraft.) Of course, the more populous the area, the greater the likelihood of facilities for the disabled, so it's important to call ahead to see what is available.

A number of organizations and tour providers specialize in the needs of disabled travelers:

Mobility International USA
(☎ 541-343-1284, fax 541-343-6812, Ⓦ www.miusa .org) PO Box 10767, Eugene, OR 97440. Advises disabled travelers on mobility issues; it primarily runs an educational exchange program

Moss Rehabilitation Hospital's Travel Information Service
(☎ 215-456-9600, TTY 215-456-9602) 1200 W Tabor Rd, Philadelphia, PA 19141-3099

Society for the Advancement of Travel for the Handicapped
(SATH; ☎ 212-447-7284) 347 Fifth Ave, No 610, New York, NY 10016

Twin Peaks Press
(☎ 360-694-2462, 800-637-2256) PO Box 129, Vancouver, WA 98666. A quarterly newsletter; also publishes directories and access guides

SENIOR TRAVELERS

Though the age at which senior discounts apply varies with the attraction, travelers aged 50 years and older can expect to receive cut rates and benefits at many places in the USA. Be sure to inquire about such rates at hotels, museums and restaurants *before* you make your reservation.

Visitors to national parks and campgrounds can cut costs by using the Golden Age Passport, a card that allows US citizens aged 62 or over (and those traveling in the same car) free admission to parks nationwide and a 50% reduction on camping fees. You can apply in person for the Passport at any national park – the only one in New England is Acadia, in Maine – or at regional offices of the US Forest Service (USFS) or National Park Service (NPS). Or call ☎ 800-280-2267.

Some national advocacy groups that can help in planning your travels and finding discounts on travel in New England include the following:

American Association of Retired Persons
(AARP; ☎ 800-424-3410, W www.aarp.org, 601 E St NW, Washington, DC 20049) Advocacy group for Americans 50 years old and older; a good resource for travel bargains. US residents can get one-year/three-year memberships for US$8/20. Citizens of other countries can get the same memberships for US$10/24.

Elderhostel
(☎ 617-426-8056, 75 Federal St, Boston, MA 02110-1941) Nonprofit that offers seniors the opportunity to attend academic college courses throughout the USA and Canada. Programs last one to three weeks, include meals and accommodations, and are open to people at least 55 years old and their companions.

TRAVEL WITH CHILDREN
Some resorts like the Chatham Bars Inn on Cape Cod offer camp-style programs for children three to 15 (see Places to Stay in relevant chapters). For information on enjoying travel with young ones, read *Travel With Children* by Cathy Lanigan, with a foreword by Lonely Planet cofounder Maureen Wheeler.

USEFUL ORGANIZATIONS
American Automobile Association
AAA ('Triple-A'; ☎ 407-444-8000, 800-222-4357, fax 407-444-8030, W www.aaa.com, 1000 AAA Drive, Heathrow, FL 32746) is an umbrella organization uniting myriad local and regional auto clubs that use the AAA name. Members who belong to a certain club may use the facilities of any other AAA club in the USA. Clubs have offices in all major cities and many resort towns, where they provide useful information, free maps, and routine road services such as tire repair and towing (free within a limited radius).

AAA members often receive discounts on attraction admission fees and on lodgings. The annual membership fee depends upon the particular club you join, but may range from $30 to $60; you might also pay a smaller one-time initiation fee. Members of

foreign affiliates, such as the Automobile Association in the UK, are entitled to the same services. (See the Car & Motorcycle section in the Getting Around chapter.)

The New England affiliate is AAA of Southern New England (☎ 800-222-7448, W www.aaasne.com).

Appalachian Mountain Club & Appalachian Trail Conference
The Appalachian Mountain Club (AMC; ☎ 617-523-0636, W www.outdoors.org, 5 Joy St, Boston, MA 02108) sells hiking guides and maps to the White Mountains and other New England backcountry. See the Activities section, later in this chapter, for more details on hiking.

The Appalachian National Scenic Trail is administered by the Appalachian Trail Conference (☎ 304-535-6331, W www.nps.gov/aptr, PO Box 807, Harpers Ferry, WV 25425-0807), in cooperation with the National Park Service (see below). See the Activities section, later in this chapter, for details on the trail.

Hostelling International– American Youth Hostels
HI-AYH (☎ 202-783-6161, fax 202-783-6171, W www.hiayh.org, PO Box 37613, Washington, DC 20013), is the successor to the International Youth Hostel Federation (IYHF). For hostel listings in the USA and Canada, get HI-AYH's official guide, *Hostelling North America,* which is also available online. For a list of New England hostels and organizations by state, see the Accommodations section, later in this chapter.

National Park Service & US Forest Service
The NPS and USFS administer the national parks and forests. National forests are less protected than parks, allowing commercial use of some areas (usually logging or privately owned recreational facilities).

National parks most often surround spectacular natural features and cover hundreds of square miles. A full range of accommodations can be found in and around national parks. In New England, there's only one national park, Acadia National Park in Maine, but the NPS also administers the Freedom Trail in Boston and other frequently visited historic places in the area.

For national park campground information, or for reservations, contact the NPS (☎ 800-365-2267) at National Park Service Public Inquiry, Dept of the Interior, 18th & C Sts NW, Washington, DC 20013.

Current information about national forests can be obtained from ranger stations or at Ⓦ www.recreation.gov. National forest campground and reservation information can be obtained by calling ☎ 800-280-2267 or writing to the NPS address listed above.

DANGERS & ANNOYANCES

The USA has a widespread reputation, partly true but also exaggerated by the media, as a dangerous place because of the availability of firearms. New England's cities – Boston, Burlington, Hartford, New Haven, Portland, Providence, Springfield, Worcester – are among the safer ones, but all suffer to some degree from the crimes of pickpockets, muggers (robbers), carjackers and rapists.

As in cities throughout the world, most crimes take place in the poorest neighborhoods among the local residents. The signs of a bad or dangerous neighborhood are obvious, and pretty much the same as in any other country. Observe the following standard common-sense urban safety rules and you should have no trouble:

• Street people and panhandlers may approach visitors in the larger cities and towns; nearly all of them are harmless. It's an individual judgment call as to whether it's appropriate to offer them money or anything else.

• Carry valuables such as money, traveler's checks, credit cards, passport, etc, in a money belt or pouch underneath your clothing for maximum safety from pickpockets. This is usually only necessary in crowded areas such as airports, subways, city buses, markets or concerts, but it doesn't hurt to do it all the time. Never turn your back on your suitcases, even at the hotel desk.

• Lock valuables in your suitcase in your hotel room or, better yet, put them in the hotel safe when you're not there.

• Don't leave anything visible in your car when you park it – city or country, day or night, crowded or not. Always lock your car when you leave it.

• Avoid walking or driving alone through poorer neighborhoods, especially at night. Don't walk in parks at night. Avoid walking along any empty street at night. Try to use ATMs only in well-trafficked areas. Well-lit streets busy with other walkers are usually all right.

As for rural dangers, avoid forests – or indeed anywhere where game and hunters roam – during the November hunting season, especially at dawn and dusk, when game is most active. 'No Hunting' signs are widely ignored and are not a guarantee of safety.

EMERGENCIES

Most states, cities and towns in New England are connected to the emergency notification system reached by dialing ☎ 911 from any telephone (no money required). Operators who answer 911 calls can fill your need for help from the police, firefighters, emergency medical response teams or other emergency services.

In areas without 911 service (or if dialing ☎ 911 does not work), dial ☎ 0 for the telephone operator, who will connect you to the necessary local emergency service.

The Travelers Aid Society (☎ 617-542-7286, Ⓦ www.travelersaid.org, 17 East St, Boston, MA 02111) is an organization of volunteers who do their best to help travelers solve their problems. Volunteers are on duty at Boston's Logan International Airport Terminal E (☎ 617-567-5385) and at Boston's Amtrak South Station (☎ 617-737-2880). For offices in other large New England cities, look in the local yellow pages or call directory assistance (☎ 411) and ask for the Travelers Aid Society.

LEGAL MATTERS

If you are stopped by the police for any reason, bear in mind that there is no system of paying fines on the spot. For traffic offenses, the police officer will explain your options to you. Attempting to pay the fine to the officer is frowned upon at best and may lead to a charge of bribery to compound your troubles. Should the officer decide that you should pay up front, he or she can take you directly to a magistrate instead of allowing you the usual 30-day period to pay the fine.

If you are arrested for more serious offenses, you are allowed to remain silent, entitled to have an attorney present during any interrogation and presumed innocent until proven guilty. All persons who are arrested have the right to make one phone call. If you don't have a lawyer or family member to help you, call your embassy or consulate. The police will give you the number upon request.

The minimum age for drinking alcoholic beverages is 21. You'll need a government-issued photo ID (such as a passport or US driver's license) to prove your age. Stiff fines, jail time and penalties can be incurred if you are caught driving under the influence of alcohol or providing alcohol to minors. During festive holidays and special events, police agencies sometimes set up roadblocks with breathalyzer tests to deter drunk drivers.

BUSINESS HOURS

Public and private office hours are normally 8am to 5pm weekdays.

For post office business hours, see Post & Communications, earlier in this chapter.

Banks

Traditional 'banker's hours' are 9am to 3pm weekdays, but most banks have extended customer service hours until 5pm weekdays (or even 8pm or 9pm on Thursday or Friday), and added Saturday service from 9am to early afternoon. No banks are open on Sunday except the currency exchange booths at international airports.

Gas Stations

Gas stations on major highways are open 24 hours a day, seven days a week. City gas stations usually open at 6am or 7am and stay open until 8pm or 9pm. In small towns and villages, hours may be only from 7am or 8am until 7pm or 8pm.

Museums

Most museums open at 10am and close at 5pm Tuesday through Sunday (closed on Monday), but there are variations, so call to be sure.

Some smaller museums and exhibits are seasonal and open only in the warmer months.

Many museums and attractions close on Thanksgiving Day (the fourth Thursday in November), Christmas Day and New Year's Day.

Stores & Markets

Most stores are open Monday through Saturday 9:30am or 10am to 5:30pm or 6pm (usually later in big cities). Many stores are also open on Sunday from about 11am or noon until 5pm.

All cities, and many large towns, have at least a few 'convenience stores,' open 24 hours a day, which sell food, beverages, newspapers and some household items. Many highway gas stations, also open 24 hours a day, have small shops selling snacks, beverages, magazines, small automotive products and frequently needed items.

Most city supermarkets stay open from 8am or 9am until 9pm or 10pm, with shorter hours on Sunday, but some in large cities remain open 24 hours a day, closing only from Sunday evening to Monday morning for maintenance.

PUBLIC HOLIDAYS

The US has more than 10 national public holidays. On these days, banks, schools and government offices (including post offices) are closed, and transportation, museums and other services operate on a Sunday schedule. Many stores, however, maintain regular business hours. Holidays falling on weekends are usually observed the following Monday.

New Year's Day January 1
Martin Luther King Jr Day 3rd Monday in January
Presidents' Day 3rd Monday in February
Memorial Day Last Monday in May
Independence Day (the Fourth of July) July 4
Labor Day 1st Monday in September

Columbus Day 2nd Monday in October
Veterans' Day November 11
Thanksgiving 4th Thursday in November
Christmas Day December 25

SPECIAL EVENTS

Special events never cease in New England, including holiday celebrations, harvest celebrations and craft fairs. Here are a few that you may not want to miss, from modern jazz festivals to traditional Thanksgivings. Tourist information offices and websites have complete information on these events as well as others in specific states and towns.

January
Chinese New Year celebrations in late January fill Boston's Chinatown with parades, fireworks, steaming rice, shrimp and chicken.

February
Hanover, NH, has been hosting its winter carnival (held in late February) for more than 90 years, with games, drink and cultural events.

March
On March 17 (or the nearest Monday) Boston's Irish (and tens of thousands of wannabees) attend parades, speeches and pubs 'til the wee hours, in honor of St Patrick's Day.

April
Massachusetts celebrates Patriots Day (April 19), marking the first battles of the American Revolution at Lexington and Concord. There are speeches and reenactments in those towns, but the big event is the massive Boston Marathon.

July
Fourth of July celebrations in Boston include an outdoor performance by the Boston Pops symphony orchestra and fireworks over the harbor.
Maine's Bangor State Fair in late July is a huge assemblage of agricultural exhibits, carnival rides and enough fried dough to feed an army.

August
Newport, RI, hosts the JVC Jazz Festival and the Folk Festival on separate weekends in early August.

September
Country fairs like the Big E in Springfield, MA, come by the dozens to every corner of the region.

October
In early October, Boston's Head of the Charles Regatta, the world's largest single-day rowing event, draws multitudes of the preppie class to picnic on the banks of the Charles River.

November
Living history interpreters at Massachusetts' Old Sturbridge Village and Plimoth Plantation celebrate a traditional Thanksgiving with everyone invited.

December
Many cities in the region (but especially Boston) host First Night celebrations on New Year's Eve. These are alcohol-free festivals, featuring live entertainment in a plethora of venues as well as outdoor events like ice and snow sculpting.

ACTIVITIES

New England's mountains may not be as high as the Rockies, but the region has many virtues as an outdoor paradise. With its hundreds of colleges and universities, and cutting-edge research and technology companies, New England has a large population of young, eager outdoor enthusiasts who support efforts to expand recreational opportunities and preserve natural resources.

New Hampshire's White Mountains, Vermont's Green Mountains and the dense forests of northern Maine offer good hiking, rock climbing, camping, canoeing and white-water rafting. The Appalachian Trail runs through several New England states. The thousands of miles of rugged coastline are good for sailing, canoeing, sea kayaking, windsurfing, whale watching and scuba diving. Swimming, canoeing, boating, fishing and water-skiing are available on many of the region's thousands of lakes and ponds. Though the waters of the Atlantic are usually chilly, swimming and other beach sports are popular in summer, particularly in the warmer waters south of Cape Cod.

Keep in mind that New England is relatively small and manageable. It is entirely possible to begin the day with a climb in New Hampshire's White Mountains and finish it by watching the sunset on a Rhode Island beach.

Hiking & Walking

The Appalachian National Scenic Trail (☎ 304-535-6331, ⓦ www.nps.gov/aptr, PO Box 807, Harpers Ferry, WV 25425-0807), usually just called the Appalachian Trail, runs from its northern terminus at Mt Katahdin (5267 feet) in Maine, heading southward through the Maine woods, New Hampshire's White Mountain National Forest, Vermont's Green Mountains and Massachusetts' Berkshire hills. It then crosses into Connecticut and passes north of New York City before continuing south to Springer Mountain in Georgia, 2158 miles from Mt Katahdin. A full 98% of the trail is on public land (parks, national forests, etc).

Shorter but still challenging, Vermont's Long Trail starts at Jay Peak (3861 feet) in the Northeast Kingdom and follows the Green Mountains south to Bennington. For more on these trails, see the boxed text 'A Month in the Woods,' in the Vermont chapter. See also the Guidebooks and Useful Organizations sections, earlier in this chapter.

If you're seeking a shorter trek, Acadia National Park in Maine has a good system of hiking trails as well as a bikeable system of unpaved 'carriage roads.'

Most of the New England's hundreds of state forests, parks and reservations have walking or hiking trails of varying levels of difficulty. Even many cities and towns have trail systems like Boston's Fenway meandering through woodlands, parks and city reservations.

Mountain Hiking For mountain hiking and rock climbing, by far the most popular area is the White Mountains' Presidential Range in New Hampshire, with Mt Washington (6288 feet) at its apex. Though hardly a challenger to the Rockies or the Alps, Mt Washington has the most severe weather in the region. At least a few hikers perish or are badly injured on its slopes each year.

Maine's Mt Katahdin is for the serious outdoors types who want wilder country, more adventure and fewer people around. It has remained remote backcountry because it is a considerable distance from New England's cities.

In Vermont's Green Mountains, the best hikes are near Stowe and up Mt Mansfield along the Long Trail.

Mt Greylock (3491 feet), the highest peak in the Massachusetts Berkshires, is an excellent goal for a day's walk from Williamstown in the northwest corner of the state.

New Hampshire's accessible Mt Monadnock (3165 feet), near Jaffrey just north of the Massachusetts state line, is a 'beginners' mountain,' a relatively easy climb up a bald granite batholith.

Organized Hikes Should you want to see nature with an organized group, Country Walkers, Inc (☎ 802-244-1387, 800-464-9255, ⓦ www.countrywalkers.com, PO Box 180, Waterbury, VT 05676) organizes four- to five-day walking trips in Vermont and Maine, as well as other parts of the world. Tour participants range from eight to 80 years old and are matched so that they keep about the same pace during each day's 4- to 9-mile trek, covered in three to five hours. Luggage is transported by van and lodgings are usually at country inns in rooms with private baths. Four-day weekend trips cost about $1400, five-day trips about $1500. Lodging and all meals are included.

Another company, New England Hiking Holidays (☎ 603-356-9696, 800-869-0949, ⓦ www.nehikingholidays.com, PO Box 1648, North Conway, NH 03860), runs similar two- to five-day hiking trips throughout New England and other areas, with lodgings and meals at country inns ($650 to $2200).

Camping

Tent camping is popular in New England's national and state forests and parks. Private campgrounds usually have a few places for tents, but they make their money catering to plush recreational vehicles (RVs) that require facilities such as water, sewer and electricity hookups.

For details on camping, see the Accommodations section, later in this chapter, and the Useful Organizations section, earlier in this chapter.

Bicycling

New England's varied and visually interesting terrain makes for great bicycle touring and mountain biking. Thousands of miles of back roads wander through handsome villages and red-brick towns, far enough apart to give cyclists a sense of being in the country but close enough to provide needed services. Bicycle parts and supplies are available in the larger cities and towns, particularly in college towns.

Rubel BikeMaps (☎ 617-776-6567, W www.bikemaps.com, PO Box 1035, Cambridge, MA 02140) publishes good topographic bike maps of the Boston area, Massachusetts' North Shore and Cape Cod.

Bicycle Touring More than 50 miles of bicycle trails start in the Boston area (see Bicycling in the Boston chapter), including the popular circuits along both sides of the Charles River. The Minuteman Commuter Bikeway stretches over 14 miles from Boston and Cambridge through Lexington and Bedford almost to Concord (see West of Boston in the Around Boston chapter).

Cape Cod is among the region's best biking areas, with several remarkable bike paths (Shining Sea Bike Path between Falmouth and Woods Hole; Cape Cod Rail Trail from Dennis to Wellfleet; and the Cape Cod National Seashore bike paths near Provincetown). *Cape Cod Bike Book,* by William E Peace, with maps and information on bike rentals, bike paths, rest stops and other necessities, is sold in bookstores on the Cape, and may also be ordered by mail from Cape Cod Bike Book, PO Box 627, South Dennis, MA 02660, for $4.

Getting your car to the islands of Martha's Vineyard, Nantucket or Block Island is expensive (and often impossible without reservations). But bicycles move easily and cheaply on the ferries (no reservation needed), and each island has a network of bike paths. The flat terrain and fine sea views make these among the best areas for biking. If you don't have a bike, you can rent one there.

Mountain Biking Many of the region's forest and mountain trails are open to mountain bikers. Be sure you know the rules before heading down the trail. If you

plan a mountain-bike tour during the autumn foliage season, probably the best time of the year, reserve your accommodations well in advance.

Many companies operate mountain-bike tours in New England. The Mountain Bike School (☎ 802-464-3333, 800-245-7669, W www.mountsnow.com), at Mt Snow/ Haystack in Vermont, operates on summer weekends, offering mountain-bike tours of varying difficulty.

Craftsbury Outdoor Center (☎ 802-586-7767, PO Box 31, Craftsbury Common, VT 05827) offers mountain-bike programs at a variety of prices. If you bring your own bike, opt for an inn room with shared bath, and provide your own meals you pay less; if you prefer all the comforts, you pay more.

Leaf Peeping
Touring by bicycle, car, bus, train, boat or on foot to enjoy the spectacular colors of the region's fall foliage is one of the glories of New England. Special tours are organized by many commercial and nonprofit organizations. State tourist information offices can give you names and contact information; see the Tourist Offices section earlier in this chapter.

The easiest way to pinpoint where the peak autumn foliage is on any given September or October day is to call the states' Autumn Foliage Hotlines at these numbers:

Connecticut	☎ 800-282-6863
Maine	☎ 800-533-9595
Massachusetts	☎ 800-227-6277
New Hampshire	☎ 800-258-3608
Rhode Island	☎ 800-556-2484
Vermont	☎ 802-828-3239

Swimming & Beaches
The Rhode Island seacoast has excellent beaches. So do Cape Cod and the islands of Martha's Vineyard and Nantucket, all in Massachusetts.

Maine has a scattering of beaches in its coastal towns, including Ogunquit, Old Orchard Beach, Kennebunkport and Bar Harbor. It also has inland lakes, including

Prime Fall Foliage Routes

Leaf-peeping draws hundreds of thousands of tourists to the back roads and harvest festivals of rural New England. From the third week in September (when frosty nights begin changing the colors of the leaves on oaks, maples, birches and elms in northern New England) until the end of October (when the red, orange and yellow leaves fade on the southern coast), residents and tourists alike wonder at the spectacle. Even crusty old Yankees find reasons to take to the highways, and weekends can feature bumper-to-bumper traffic on the most popular routes. If communing with nature is what you have in mind, head for the wilds on a midweek morning and find a trail to hike.

Here are some routes to those trails, taking you over steep hills and along lakes and rivers that afford expansive vistas.

Connecticut
US 7 follows the Housatonic River through the Litchfield Hills from Canaan to New Milford.

CT 154 and its tributaries carry you through the Lower Connecticut River Valley.

Maine
The route between Bethel and Rangeley threads through the state's western lakes and mountains; take US 2 to ME 17 and then take ME 4.

Mt Desert's roads mix steep hills with seascapes and foliage.

Massachusetts
The Mohawk Trail (MA 2) between Fitchburg and North Adams crosses through the northern Berkshire hills.

US 202, between South Hadley and MA 2 at Irving, skirts giant Quabbin Reservoir and runs the eastern ridge of the Pioneer Valley.

New Hampshire
The Kancamagus Highway (NH 112) from Lincoln to Conway winds through White Mountain passes and is probably the most-visited leaf-peeper route in New England. Lots of leaf-peepers continue north from North Conway on NH 302 to Crawford Notch, before circling west to Twin Mountains and Franconia Notch.

For a drive to nowhere, free of tourists, head north from Jackson on NH 16 through Pinkham Notch and the Mt Washington Valley to Dixville Notch. From Gorham to Dixville Notch the road runs through spruce and birch forest along the Androscoggin River. From here you can head east to Bethel, ME, or Rangeley Lakes (see the Maine chapter).

Rhode Island
In northern Rhode Island, RI 101 and RI 116 take you near a reservoir and through apple country.

In the South County, RI 138 runs east/west through woodland from Narragansett Bay to Connecticut, so it's good for folks who are just passing through the state.

Vermont
VT 100 from Killington to Stowe skirts the eastern edge of the Green Mountains National Forest and the Mad River north of Warren.

US 91 runs north from St Johnsbury to the Canadian Border, with long vistas of dairy farms and sugar maples.

Rangeley Lake. Swimming in New England's ponds and lakes (such as Lake Winnipesaukee in New Hampshire) can be warmer and more enjoyable than a dip in the chilly ocean.

Canoeing, Kayaking & Rafting

Canoeing is popular in summer throughout New England, on ponds, lakes, rivers and sheltered parts of the coastline. The heart of riverine canoe activity is undoubtedly North Conway, NH, but there are many canoe outfitters in Maine as well. See North Conway in the New Hampshire chapter and North Woods in the Maine chapter.

Either in rigid or inflatable boats, kayaking is popular wherever there's water, from the quiet ponds of Rhode Island and Connecticut to the Boston waterfront and the wilds of northern Maine. Many outfitters provide rentals and instruction. Perhaps the ultimate New England kayak experience is along the rocky, pine-fringed coasts of Maine.

Adventure Bound (☎ 207-672-4300, 888-606-7238, ☒ www.adv-bound.com, PO Box 88, Caratunk, ME 04925) can take you on white-water rafting and inflatable kayak trips on Maine's Kennebec, Upper Kennebec, Penobscot and Dead Rivers.

Only 20 minutes by ferry from Portland, Maine Island Kayak Co (☎ 207-766-2373, 800-796-2373, ☒ www.maineislandkayak.com, 70 Luther St, Peaks Island, ME 04108) runs half- and full-day kayak tours ($55/95) among the Diamond Islands in Casco Bay. They also have more ambitious weekend and five- to 10-day expeditions covering the best reaches of the Maine coast. Nights are spent at low-impact campgrounds on islands along the way. The guides welcome beginners.

White-water rafting occurs mostly in the northern New England states, particularly on New Hampshire's Saco River and on Maine's Kennebec, Upper Kennebec, Penobscot and Dead Rivers. For adventures closer to Boston, contact Zoar Outdoor (☎ 413-339-8596, 800-532-7483, fax 413-337-8436, PO Box 245, Charlemont, MA 01339).

In addition to the companies mentioned above, you can obtain rental craft (canoes, kayaks, rafts) and equipment, instruction and guide service from these companies:

Magic Falls Rafting Co
(☎ 800-207-7238, ☒ www.magicfalls.com)
PO Box 9, West Forks, ME 04985

Maine Whitewater
(☎ 207-672-4814, 800-345-6246,
☒ www.mainewhitewater.com)
PO Box 633, Bingham, ME 04920

North Country Rivers
(☎ 800-348-8871, ☒ www.ncrivers.com)
PO Box 47, East Vassalboro, ME 04935

Northern Outdoors
(☎ 207-663-4466, 800-765-7238,
☒ www.northernoutdoors.com)
PO Box 100, Route 201, The Forks, ME 04985

Professional River Runners of Maine
(☎ 207-663-2229, 800-325-3911,
☒ www.proriverrunners.com) PO Box 92,
West Forks, ME 04985

Wilderness Expeditions
(☎ 207-534-2242, 800-825-9453, ☒ www.birches
.com) PO Box 41, Rockwood, ME 04478

Windjammer Cruises

The Maine coast in summer is among the world's finest sail-cruising areas. Traditional wooden schooners use Camden, Rockport and Rockland as their home ports.

A cruise of a few days along the gorgeous Maine coast lets you forget your worries and concentrate on nature for a while. For details, see Camden in the Maine chapter.

Windjamming isn't limited to Maine. Day cruises are available in many coastal towns, such as Gloucester and Falmouth, MA. They're also available on the islands: Block Island, RI, and Nantucket and Martha's Vineyard, MA.

Whale-Watching Cruises

Once known for their prowess in seeking out whales for slaughter, New England's sea captains now follow the whales with boatloads of camera-carrying summer tourists.

Whale-watching craft vary from small and old-fashioned fishing vessels to modern, double-hulled speedboats. Cruises depart from South County, RI; Barnstable, Provincetown, Boston, Plymouth, Gloucester and Newburyport, MA; Portsmouth, NH; and Portland, Boothbay Harbor and Bar Harbor, ME, among other coastal towns.

The captains usually have little trouble finding cetacea such as minke whales, humpbacks, fin whales, right whales and dolphins. If for some reason they fail to sight a whale, most boats will give you a pass for another cruise.

For a detailed description of whale watching, see the boxed text 'The New Whalers,' in the Around Boston chapter.

Skiing & Snowboarding

Virtually all ski resorts in New England have substantial snowmaking capacity, and the many gladed trails provide a memorable experience. Smaller, local hills are often cheaper to ski, less crowded and ideal for beginners. Before making reservations at a big resort, check for motels around the smaller hills, which might save you a significant sum.

Snowboarding is very popular on New England slopes; most of the larger ski resorts offer rental equipment, lessons, and special 'snow parks' with half-pipes and jumps for riders.

New England's best skiing is in Vermont at Killington, Mt Snow, Stratton and Stowe; and in New Hampshire's White Mountains at Waterville Valley, the Franconia Notch area (Loon Mountain) and the Mt Washington Valley (Wild Cat). In Maine, Sugarloaf and Sunday River are excellent. Connecticut and Massachusetts' Berkshires have smaller ski areas.

Cross-country (Nordic) skiing is also popular and especially pleasing in the forests or traveling from village to village or inn to inn. Every town seems to have at least a few marked cross-country trails. Resort towns such as North Conway, NH, and Stowe, VT, have elaborate systems of well-groomed cross-country trails.

For more details on particular resorts, see the Activities sections in the appropriate state chapters.

Snowmobiling

You can go snowmobiling in a number of state parks during the winter. Use of the noisy machines is regulated: You must be at least 16 to operate one, and you must stay on approved snowmobile routes and tracks. If you haven't ridden a snowmobile before, you should definitely take a safety training course beforehand, as there are special cautions and dangers associated with them. Maine and New Hampshire are particularly good places to pursue the sport.

WORK

You will find lots of summer jobs at New England seaside and mountain resorts. These are usually low-paying service jobs filled by young people (often college students) who are happy to work part of the day so they can play the rest. If you want such a job, contact the local chambers of commerce or businesses well in advance. You can't depend on finding a job just by arriving in May or June and looking around.

In winter, contact New England's ski resorts, where full- and part-time help is often welcome.

Foreigners entering the USA to work must have a visa that permits it. Apply for a work visa from the US embassy in your home country before you leave. The type of visa varies, depending on how long you're staying and the kind of work you plan to do. Generally, you need either a J-1 visa, which you can obtain by joining a visitor-exchange program (issued mostly to students for work in summer camps), or an H-2B visa, when you are sponsored by a US employer.

The latter can be difficult to procure unless you can show that you already have a job offer from an employer who considers your qualifications to be unique and not readily available in the USA. There are, of course, many foreigners working illegally in the country. Controversial laws prescribe punishments for employers employing 'aliens' (foreigners) who do not have the proper visas. Immigration & Naturalization Service (INS) officers can be persistent and insistent in their enforcement of the laws.

ACCOMMODATIONS

New England provides an array of accommodations from simple campsites, country inns and B&Bs to mid-range and top-end hotels. But truly inexpensive accommodations are rare. The most comfortable accommodations for the lowest price are usually found in that great American invention, the roadside motel.

Camping

If you don't bring your own camping equipment, you can buy gear at many places in New England. Refer to the Shopping section in the Boston chapter and to the Freeport section in the Maine chapter.

You cannot plan to just stop by the road and camp. With few exceptions, you will have to camp in an established campground. New England has lots of them. But most of them are full on weekends in July and August, and many fill up during the week as well. You must reserve in advance or arrive early in the day to give yourself the best chance of getting a site.

Rough camping is permitted in the backcountry of some national forests, but often it must be at established sites; these may have simple shelters and are usually free. Excellent trail guides and maps exist that show and describe these sites; see the Guidebooks section, earlier in this chapter, for details.

An inexpensive option is the primitive forest site with only basic services: pit toilets, cold running water (perhaps from a pump) and fireplaces. These are generally found in national forests and cost about $7.

Standard campsites in state and national parks usually have flush toilets and hot showers (for a fee). Often, they offer a dump station for RVs. Tent sites are usually shaded and are sometimes on wooden platforms or grass, with plenty of space between sites. These sites cost between $6 and $20. Most government-run campgrounds are open only during the summer season, from mid-May to early September or late October. For reservations information, see the Useful Organizations section, earlier in this chapter.

Private campgrounds are usually more expensive ($18 to $40) and less spacious, with sites closer together and less shade. Recreation facilities are usually elaborate, with playgrounds, swimming, game rooms and even miniature golf courses.

Hostels

Hostelling is not nearly as well developed in New England as in Europe. But some prime destinations including Boston, Cape Cod, Bar Harbor, Martha's Vineyard and Nantucket have hostels that allow you to stay in $150-per-night destinations for $12 to $17. Needless to say, advance reservations are essential, but they often can be made by phone if you have a credit card.

US citizens/residents can join Hostelling International–American Youth Hostels (HI-AYH; ☎ 202-783-6161, fax 202-783-6171, ⓦ www.hiayh.org, PO Box 37613, Washington, DC 20013) by calling and requesting a membership form or by downloading a form from the website and mailing or faxing it. Membership can also be purchased at regional council offices and at many (but not all) youth hostels. Non-US residents should buy a HI-AYH membership in their home countries. If not, you can still stay in US hostels by purchasing 'Welcome Stamps' for each night you stay in a hostel. When you have six stamps, your stamp card becomes a valid one-year HI-AYH membership card valid throughout the world.

HI-AYH has its own toll- and surcharge-free reservations service (☎ 800-444-6111), but not all hostels participate in the service, and you need the access codes for the hostels to use it. The HI-AYH card may be used to get discounts at some local merchants and services, including some intercity bus companies.

Two hostelling councils cover New England. HI-AYH Eastern New England Council (☎ 617-779-0900, 1105 Commonwealth Ave, Boston, MA 02215) is the office for hostels in Maine, Massachusetts and New Hampshire. The HI-AYH Yankee Council (☎ 860-683-2847, PO Box 87, Windsor, CT 06095) is the office for hostels in Connecticut and Vermont.

Here's a list of HI-AYH New England hostel locations:

Connecticut
  Hartford
Maine
  Bar Harbor, Portland, Searsport, South Hiram, Augusta
Massachusetts
  Boston, Dudley, Eastham and Truro (Cape Cod), Littleton (near Concord), Martha's Vineyard, Nantucket
New Hampshire
  Conway
Vermont
  Burlington, Middlebury, Montpelier, White River Junction, Woodford (near Bennington)

Boston has more than a half-dozen independent hostels; see Places to Stay in the Boston chapter for details.

Motels

Motels range from 10-room places in need of paint to resorts with manicured gardens, restaurants and resort-style facilities. Prices range from $30 to $100 and up. On the highway or on the outskirts of any but the largest cities, you can get a comfortable motel room for $50 to $75. The cheapest places are invariably the small, privately run ones.

Motels offer standard accommodations: a room entered from the outside, with private bath, color cable TV, heat and air con. Though some smaller, older places may have only twin beds, most motels now have two double beds (or larger beds) or perhaps a queen-size bed and a single bed. In other words, it's easy for a small family (parents and two children) to find one room to accommodate them all. Some motels have small refrigerators, and many provide a simple breakfast of muffins or rolls, fruit and coffee, often at no extra charge. Most also provide toll-free reservations lines.

Efficiencies

An 'efficiency,' in New England parlance, is a hotel, motel or inn room, or one-room cabin, with cooking and dining facilities: stove (cooker), sink, refrigerator, dining table and chairs, cooking utensils and tableware. Efficiencies usually cost slightly more than standard rooms.

B&Bs & Guesthouses

North American B&Bs are often not the casual, inexpensive sort of accommodations found on the continent or in the UK. While they are usually family-run, most B&Bs are like small inns, and they usually require advance reservations. Some are relentlessly charming, with frilly decor and theatrically adorable hosts (and pets). Some have the services and amenities of minor resort hotels, and prices to match. Guesthouses in New England (particularly on Cape Cod, Martha's Vineyard and Nantucket) are more like English country B&Bs with simple rooms and shared baths.

The guesthouses and simpler B&Bs in smaller towns and resorts may charge $60 to $85 for single or double rooms with shared bath, breakfast included. Fancier B&Bs in or near the more popular resorts charge $75 to $150 per night for a room with private bath. At peak times, from mid-July through early September and late September through mid-October, as well as on holiday weekends, prices at the fanciest B&Bs in resort towns may rise to $175 or even above $200. Most have private bathrooms and air con. Some have TVs; most do not.

Breakfasts often include fresh-baked pastries and a selection of brewed stimulants; a full American-style breakfast of bacon or ham and eggs, toast or muffins, fruit, cereal and milk; or any variation of the above.

In the most popular resort towns, B&Bs may have restrictive policies: A minimum stay of two or three days may be required on weekends; bills may have to be paid in advance by check or in cash (not by credit card); and cancellations may be subject to a processing fee, or worse.

Inns

New England has more than 1500 country inns. They vary from small B&Bs (see above) to large, rambling old inns that have been sheltering travelers for several centuries. Quite a few of these inns are historic and authentically furnished, but with modern services. Many of the large mansions and summerhouses built by wealthy families a century ago are now sumptuous inns. Some inns have excellent dining rooms and taverns, and they may also have amenities like swimming pools, gardens, hiking trails or associations with local golf courses or tennis clubs.

Inn rooms are often decorated in antique styles. Most have private baths and air con but may not have TV.

Prices range from $85 to $250 and up, depending upon the inn, the particular room, the town, the season and the day(s) of the week. A room priced at $85 Sunday through Wednesday in Lenox, MA, may cost $150 on Thursday, Friday or Saturday night. As with B&Bs, inns may require minimum stays or payment in advance and may have other restrictions.

Destinnations (☎ 508-790-0577, 800-333-4667, fax 508-790-0565, w www.destinnations.com) is a reservations service for inns and an itinerary-planning service for visitors staying in New England more than a few nights.

Cottages, Cabins & Condos

Renting a cottage or condominium for a week or two is popular in New England, but not particularly easy for those who do not live in the region. You can contact local chambers of commerce and ask for listings of available properties. (Phone numbers and websites for chambers of commerce are listed in the Information sections for the larger towns discussed throughout this book.)

Cottages and cabins, generally found on Cape Cod, Nantucket and Martha's Vineyard and in New England's woods, are two- or three-room vacation bungalows with basic furnishings, bath and kitchen. A condo is a small multiroom apartment with kitchen and dining facilities; it's larger, more elaborate and more expensive than an efficiency. Condos are usually capable of accommodating more people than an efficiency unit – some condos can sleep six, eight or even 10 people. Rates vary greatly, from $70 to $700 per night, depending upon the location, season and size. Mountainside condos are especially popular with skiers, but they're also available – and much cheaper – during the warmer months.

Hotels & Resorts

New England hotels are mostly large and lavish. There are few small, inexpensive 'boutique' hotels. Many city hotels set aside several floors as special 'executive' sections, with more elaborate decoration and a central lounge with an attendant. Resorts feature accommodations of the same ilk. But resorts have spacious, landscaped settings at coastal or mountain vacation spots and usually include a range of guest activities like golf and horseback riding or skiing and water sports.

Prices range from $80 to $200 and up per night, with most between $100 and $150. Weekend discounts and special weekend packages offer significant savings. Be sure to ask about them when you call to inquire about prices and make reservations. Virtually all large hotels have numbers for reservations, but you may find better savings by calling the hotel directly, as some discounts are aimed only at local callers. If you are 55 or older, ask about senior citizen discounts; AAA members (see the Useful Organizations section, earlier in this chapter) may be entitled to discounts as well.

FOOD

A hundred years ago, Boston was famous for baked beans (white/navy beans, molasses, salt pork and onions cooked slowly in a crock) and New England boiled dinner (beef boiled with cabbage, carrots and potatoes). They are not common on menus anymore.

Some traditional cuisine persists, and for good reason. New England's seafood is outstanding. You can buy locally made maple syrup in all the New England states. Vermont dairy products – milk, cream, yogurt and cheese – are only slightly less famous than that state's most famous edible: Ben & Jerry's ice cream.

It is possible to spend anywhere from $2 to $200 per person for a meal. The major cities and the more sophisticated country inns have restaurants serving refined American, continental and international cuisine. Except deep in the forest, you are never far from some place serving food. Some fast-food restaurants (offering hamburgers, pizza, doughnuts and coffee) are open 24 hours a day in cities and on highways.

Restaurants serve breakfast from 6am or 7am to 11am or noon. (Lodgings like B&Bs often start breakfast at 8am.) Some restaurants advertise that they serve breakfast all day. The meal can be a muffin and coffee for less than $2, or a hearty meal of fried eggs or an omelet with bacon, ham or sausage, toast, fruit juice and coffee for $6 or $7.

New Englanders eat lunch from 11:30am to 2pm or 3pm, and in fact many luncheon items are served until the evening closing time. A good simple lunch can cost $3 to $12, a fancy one up to $25. If you like good restaurants but can't afford their dinner prices, go for lunch. Portions are somewhat smaller, but prices may be significantly lower.

Dinner is served in restaurants from 6pm to 10pm. You can get a good dinner in a pleasant, though not fancy, restaurant for $16 to $35 per person, drinks included. In posh big-city restaurants and resorts, it is possible to see a bill of $75 per person. Portions are usually large. Some restaurants continue serving from a lighter, less formal 'bar' or 'tavern' menu until midnight or 1am. Some restaurants close on Monday.

In almost all restaurants, sections are designated as 'smoking' and 'nonsmoking.' Hosts normally ask you which section you want. A growing number of restaurants are completely nonsmoking, meaning that you must step outside for a puff. See the boxed text 'Smoking' for more information.

Fruit

New England produces fruit in abundant variety. Farm or orchard roadside stands are good places to buy fruit, and many farms offer a pick-your-own option.

Strawberries come early, from mid-June through July. Rhubarb is also ripe then, and if you come across a strawberry-rhubarb pie, grab two pieces at least. Late June to mid-July is blueberry season, when pies of fresh blueberries (or huckleberries) appear. September brings peaches, plums and apples, as well as fresh-squeezed apple cider.

Cranberries, a Massachusetts specialty, are harvested in the autumn. The bright-red berries grow in shallow ponds called bogs and are harvested by amphibious machines. The berries are very tart and sour, but when sweetened they make refreshing juice, jelly, sauce, muffins and pies. Tart cranberry sauce is the traditional garnish for a Thanksgiving turkey.

Seafood

Fish Scandinavian fishing boats found bounteous harvests in the fishing grounds of Georges Bank before the arrival of Columbus. In colonial and early American times, the trade in codfish was so important that a stuffed codfish was put in a place of honor in the Massachusetts State House. It's still there.

Intensive fishing, however, has depleted stocks here as in other oceans, raising seafood prices. Still, if you enjoy seafood, you'll enjoy eating in New England.

Fish chowder is whitefish, potatoes, corn and milk. It usually takes second place to the more popular clam chowder (see Oysters, Mussels & Clams, below).

Boston scrod is any bland whitefish. The term 'scrod' is said to have originated at a local hotel restaurant. The chef could never be sure which whitefish (cod, haddock, etc) would be freshest in port that day, so he invented the word 'scrod' and served the catch of the day sautéd in butter or covered with a cheese sauce. Patrons happily ordered the dish and didn't notice any difference. Today, scrod usually refers to young codfish.

Bluefish, a full-flavored fish, can be fried, baked, broiled, grilled, or smoked and made into a pâté appetizer.

Monkfish is a large-flaked whitefish. When sautéd in butter it tastes a bit like lobster.

Halibut, swordfish and tuna steaks are excellent charcoal-grilled and drizzled with lemon juice.

How to Eat a Lobster

Lobster is messy to eat. In early summer, your lobster may come with a bone-hard shell, and you have to use a cracker to break the claws. In mid- to late summer, they have their new shells, which are soft and easily broken with the fingers. Purists believe (perhaps rightly) that spring hard-shell lobsters have the sweetest meat and that soft-shell lobsters are not quite as good.

The best place to eat lobster is in a beachfront shack called a lobster 'pound' or 'pool.' Here you can tear the beasts apart with abandon, using your fingers, which is the only way it can be done. To eat only the tail meat is looked upon by New Englanders as a terrible waste of good body and claw meat.

At lobster pounds or pools, live lobsters are cooked on order. They range in size from 1lb ('chicken lobsters,' or 'chicks') and those weighing 1¼ to 1½lb ('selects') to 'large' lobsters from 2 to 20lb in weight. 'Culls,' those missing a claw, are sold at a discount, as the claw meat is considered choice. 'Shorts,' smaller than chicks, do not meet the legal minimum size for harvesting. Do your part to discourage illegal lobstering and question any lobster that looks very small.

When you order lobster, you'll be brought some special tools: a plastic bib, a supply of napkins, a cracker for breaking the claws, a small fork or pick for excavating claws and other tight places, a bowl in which to throw shells, a container of melted butter, a slice of lemon and an alcohol-soaked towelette to wipe your hands after the mess is over.

The lobster may be very hot, with hot water inside the shell. Start by twisting off the little legs and sucking or chewing out the slender bits of meat inside. Go on to the claws: Twist the claws and knuckles off the body, break the claws and knuckles with the cracker and dip the tender claw meat in butter before eating. Each knuckle also has a large, succulent bit of meat in it. Use the cracker and pick to get it, but beware the sharp spines.

Next, pick up the lobster body in one hand and the tail in the other. Twist the tail back and forth to break it off. Break off each of the flippers at the end of the tail and suck out the meat. Then use your finger or an implement to push through the hole at the end of the tail where the flippers were, and the big chunk of tail meat will come out.

There is delicious meat in the body as well, though it takes work to get it. Tear off the carapace (back shell), then split the body in two lengthwise. Behind the spot where each small leg was attached is a chunk of meat, best gotten with pick and fingers.

Oysters, Mussels & Clams Oysters are available on many restaurant menus. Those harvested in Wellfleet on Cape Cod are the region's choicest. They're best eaten raw on the half shell but may come grilled, fried, baked and stuffed, or in rich, creamy oyster stew.

Attached to the rocks and sea floor, blue mussels grow in abundance along the New England coast. Their flavor is coarser than that of oysters or clams.

New England clams come in two types: soft-shell, with chalky, easily breakable shells; and hard-shell clams called 'quahogs' (pronounced '**ko**-hogs'), with shells that resemble porcelain.

The popular soft-shell clams are 'steamers.' They're cooked in steam, which opens the shells. Extract the clam meat, shuck off the wrinkled membrane from the black 'neck,' wash off any sand by dipping the clam in the thin clam 'broth' provided, dip in melted butter, and eat. After about five clams, you'll be shucking those membranes easily. The clam broth, by the way, is just the water the clams have been steamed in. It's used for dipping, not drinking.

The most common quahogs are littlenecks and cherrystones. They're best eaten raw on the half shell with a few drops of lemon juice, tomato sauce or horseradish, but they may be steamed or stuffed and baked as well.

Surf clams are like giant quahogs, larger than your fist. They're usually cut into strips, deep-fried and served as fried clams in seaside clam shacks or chopped and used to make clam chowder. New England clam chowder is made of sliced or chopped quahogs, potatoes, milk, cream and perhaps a bit of seasoning.

The traditional New England clambake is a feast of steamed clams, boiled or roasted corn on the cob and steamed or boiled lobsters. The closest you can easily get to enjoying a traditional clambake is to order a 'shore dinner' (lobster, steamers and corn) at one of the seaside restaurants mentioned in this guide.

Lobster Though lobster has a reputation as a luxury food, it was not always so. In colonial times, a governor of the Massachusetts Bay Colony was forced to apologize to an important visitor because he had only lobster to serve him, as the cod boats could not go out. Lobsters were then so common that they were harvested in great quantity from shallow waters and used as fodder and fertilizer.

Today lobster is perhaps New England's most famous seafood dish. Purists – which means most New Englanders – demand live lobsters cooked to order, usually steamed for 10 to 20 minutes (depending upon size) in a large pot with a few inches of water. Steaming or boiling in seawater gives a distinctive flavor and salty tang. Lobsters may also be split from head to tail and grilled.

Many restaurants serve baked stuffed lobster: The meat is removed and mixed with other ingredients, and the shell is refilled. Most New Englanders look upon this as a tourist dish for the uninitiated.

Store prices for live lobster range from $4 to $8 or more per pound, depending upon the season; restaurant prices can be as low as $10 for a whole small lobster with salad, corn on the cob, and bread and butter, or $15 to $20 for 'twin lobsters' (two small 'chicken' lobsters). Mid-July to September sees the lowest prices for live lobsters.

For tips on eating one of these creatures, see the boxed text 'How to Eat a Lobster.'

Groceries & Markets

Many bakeries, snack shops, cafes and small restaurants in resort areas prepare food to take away. Most supermarkets have delicatessen counters where you can buy cold meats, cheeses, salads, pâtés, dips, spreads and other picnic and quick-meal items. Some markets even have chefs who prepare Asian stir-fry meals to order.

DRINKS
Nonalcoholic Drinks

Familiar soft drinks are readily available, although they sometimes are called 'tonic' or 'pop' rather than soda or soft drinks. Maine has its specialty soda, Moxie (see the boxed text 'I've Got Moxie,' in the Maine chapter). You can also select from a host of bottled fruit juices, iced tea and spring water. Maine's own Poland Spring water is the local favorite. Most drinks come in cups or glasses filled with ice, so you're paying mostly for frozen water. You might want to order your drinks without ice or with 'just a little' ice.

Tap water is safe to drink virtually everywhere and usually is palatable.

Traditionally, American coffee comes from a light-brown roasted bean and is weaker than that preferred in Europe. In some parts of New England, 'regular' coffee means coffee with sugar and milk or cream, so specify 'black coffee' if that's what you want.

Espresso is readily available, as are American versions of other European favorites such as café au lait, cappuccino and caffe latte. The American versions are often elaborate concoctions with endless variations – vanilla, raspberry or cinnamon flavoring, for instance. Cities and most larger towns have specialty coffee shops where beans are roasted frequently, ground shortly before brewing and brewed by bean variety or origin, to order.

Tea likewise comes in bewildering variety. Tea is often served with lemon, unless milk is specified. Herbal teas of many kinds are readily available; decaffeinated tea is also available. Iced tea with lemon is a popular summer drink.

Alcoholic Drinks

New England has vineyards, wineries and craft breweries producing palatable, even excellent, regional vintages and beers.

Beverage Laws In Maine, New Hampshire and Vermont, you may only buy liquor in state government-operated stores; in Connecticut, Massachusetts and Rhode Island, liquor stores are private, and some food markets are licensed to sell wine and beer. Depending on local ordinances, retail liquor stores might not sell alcohol on Sunday, though most restaurants and bars with liquor licenses can serve liquor by the drink on Sunday. The minimum age for drinking is 21 years, and anyone who looks younger than 21 is 'carded' – that is, asked to produce a photo ID card bearing a birth date. A driver's license or a passport is acceptable proof.

A restaurant may have a 'full liquor license' (for liquor, wine and beer), a 'wine and beer' license or no license. Some small or new restaurants without liquor licenses allow you to 'brown-bag' or 'BYO' (Bring Your Own alcoholic beverages). Such restaurants typically offer 'set-ups' (ice buckets for wine, glasses, corkscrews, mixers for mixed drinks, etc). A few New England towns (Cape Ann's Rockport and Vineyard Haven on Martha's Vineyard, both in Massachusetts, come to mind) are 'dry': No shop, restaurant or hotel can sell you alcohol, but you can buy wine or beer in another town,

bring it into the dry town and drink it legally.

Few fast-food restaurants, such as hamburger, doughnut or sandwich shops, serve alcohol (or permit brown bagging) but quite a few pizza parlors have wine and beer licenses or allow you to BYO. When in doubt, look for beer advertisements, such as a neon sign in the window, or ask inside.

Laws prohibit public drinking outdoors – you may not take alcoholic beverages to the park, beach or forest trail, or drink on a sidewalk – though if you are discreet and keep bottles out of view, you can usually get away with having wine or beer with your picnic.

Do not have any open alcoholic beverage containers in your car. In some states, the driver may be prosecuted for drunk driving (a serious offense) if *any* open alcoholic beverage container is found in a car he or she is operating – even if the alcohol is being drunk exclusively by the passengers.

Wine Grapes grow wild in New England. The Concord grape, a labrusca variety developed in Concord, MA, is used for grape juice, sweet and ceremonial wines, jellies, jams and fillings.

Modern growing methods and careful study of microclimates have allowed vintners in the southern New England states to produce drinkable table wines, white, red and 'blush' (a favorite euphemism for rosé). Some vintage wines from hybrid and even vinifera grapes are of respectable quality and interesting flavor. Eastern Massachusetts, southeastern Rhode Island and northwestern Connecticut have vineyards. Try the wines of Sakonnet Vineyards, RI; Chicama Vineyards on Martha's Vineyard, MA; Haight Vineyards near Litchfield, CT; and Hopkins Vineyard on Lake Waramaug, CT.

Wines made from other fruits – apples, blueberries, pears, peaches, raspberries, etc – are produced at a few wineries. Though lacking the complexity and body of grape wines, they can be tasty. Nashoba Valley Winery, near Concord, MA, makes refreshing fruit wines, and you may find drinkable blueberry wine in Maine.

Beer New England's microbreweries produce interesting and often fine brews. The smallest microbreweries are really brewpubs, serving their beers in only a few of the local establishments. Slightly larger microbreweries may distribute throughout their home states. A few, such as Boston Brewing Company's famous Samuel Adams dark lager and Harpoon Lager are exported in volume to other states and countries.

Liquor stores stock a bewildering variety of 'coolers' – flavored sparkling wines and beers, which might be best described as alcoholic soda pop.

Liquor Strong liquors of all kinds, both domestic and imported, are widely available. Favorite mixed drinks on hot days are gin, rum or vodka and tonic water, and drinks made with liquor and fruit or fruit juice, perhaps beaten or blended with ice.

If you're visiting from abroad and you like whiskey, be sure to try some Kentucky bourbon. (If it's not distilled in Kentucky, it can't be called bourbon.) Representative brands are Old Granddad, Wild Turkey and Maker's Mark. The premium brand is Knob Creek, well aged, smooth as cognac and nearly as expensive. One of the best-known American whiskeys is Jack Daniel's – not a bourbon but a 'sour mash' whiskey distilled in Tennessee.

ENTERTAINMENT

New England offers rich opportunities for entertainment in music, dance and theater. Local newspapers have listings.

Classical Music

The most famous symphony orchestra in the area is the Boston Symphony Orchestra (BSO), but New England's other large cities have their own orchestras as well. The winter season runs from October to April and is followed in the spring by a 'Pops' season of informal concerts held indoors in a music-hall atmosphere. (See Boston's Entertainment section for information on tickets.)

In summer, the orchestras move outdoors: The BSO heads for its season at the Tanglewood estate in Lenox, MA, where it performs along with guest and student artists and ensembles. (See the Lenox section in the Central Massachusetts & the Berkshires chapter.) There are other good chamber music series at Tanglewood as well as in Great Barrington, MA; Stowe and Marlboro, VT; and Blue Hill, ME, among other venues.

There is no major opera house in New England. It is surprising that Boston, with such a rich cultural life and many distinguished musical performance halls, does not have a proper opera house, although satisfying opera performances are staged in several large theaters.

Popular Music

Boston, Burlington, Hartford, New Haven, Newport, Portland, Providence and Worcester are on the circuit for rock, pop and jazz performers year-round. Warm-weather concerts take place outdoors in several cities and resorts, especially in Boston, in Massachusetts' Berkshire hills, on Cape Cod and in Newport, RI. Ticket prices vary widely, from a few dollars for standing room to $50 to $100 for the best seats. During the summer many small towns offer evening band or ensemble concerts for free in a central park.

Theater

Boston is a proving ground for Broadway plays and musicals. (See Boston's Entertainment section for information on tickets.) Many of New England's universities have superb theater departments. In summer, local theater companies in resort areas provide live 'summer stock' drama at moderate prices, often with well-known stars.

If you love theater, it's worth making a special trip to the summer Williamstown Theatre Festival in Williamstown, MA. See the Williamstown section in the Central Massachusetts & the Berkshires chapter for more details.

An evening of Shakespeare at the Mount, the late Edith Wharton's mansion in Lenox, MA, is a delight as well. See the Lenox section in the Central Massachusetts & the Berkshires chapter for information.

Dance

Boston has many award-winning dance companies, including the Boston Ballet Company and a number of modern and experimental dance companies. In summer, the Jacob's Pillow Dance Festival in Lee, MA, in the Berkshires, is the region's premiere dance festival, presenting ballet, jazz and modern dance. See the Lee section in the Central Massachusetts & the Berkshires chapter for more information.

Pubs & Clubs

Boston (with over 225,000 party-hungry college students) has a vast pub and club scene that ranges from grunge, soul, Latin and Caribbean music haunts to jazz caves, martini bars, Euro-discos and belly dancing clubs. New England's university towns and resort areas are almost as lively. And every city and town has at least a few clubs, lounges or bars with live entertainment: pop music, jazz, rock & roll, or stand-up comedy. In the larger cities and summer resorts, the choice and variety are great. Many places require you to pay a cover (admission) charge of a few dollars or spend a minimum amount on food or drinks, if you're there when the entertainment is on.

But night owls beware: Most pubs and clubs in New England close between midnight and 2am, and Boston's T (subway) generally closes about midnight (although the city is experimenting with late-night bus service on weekends; see Entertainment in the Boston chapter for details).

Coffeehouses & Bars

In the cities and college towns, many coffeehouses and bars (which are usually more downscale than clubs) have live entertainment several nights a week. The groups are usually local but are sometimes regional or even national talent. Prices, which may include a cover charge of $3 to $10 or a minimum order of drinks or food, are reasonable. Look in local newspapers and free tourist handouts, in the cafes and bars themselves, or on their websites for programs of events.

Cinemas

Boston, Cambridge and New Haven, being university towns, have the most cinemas with the widest range of offerings, including art houses and film festivals. Most towns of any size have at least one cinema, usually a 'multiplex' housing several small theaters showing different movies. Admission ranges from a few dollars for some of the student shows to $6 to $8 for first-run flicks.

SPECTATOR SPORTS

In the fall, regardless of the temperature or class of play, an American football game makes for an exhilarating experience. The same goes for baseball in the spring, summer and fall. Minor-league and college-team games are sometimes significantly less expensive, yet more fun, than those of professional teams, with their blazing egos and contract disputes.

Boston has major-league teams in baseball (Boston Red Sox), ice hockey (Boston Bruins), soccer (New England Revolution) and basketball (Boston Celtics). For information on the Basketball Hall of Fame, see the Springfield section in the Central Massachusetts & the Berkshires chapter. Also, Boston's colleges and universities support some excellent National Collegiate Athletic Association (NCAA) sports. See Spectator Sports in the Boston chapter for details.

The New England Patriots, Massachusetts' professional football team, plays in Foxboro Stadium, Foxboro, about 50 minutes south of Boston (see the Boston chapter).

In Rhode Island, the Pawtucket 'Paw-Sox' are a big minor-league Triple-A baseball draw.

In Vermont, Burlington has a Triple-A baseball team and the University of Vermont (UVM) has a good hockey team. In Connecticut, Hartford has the University of Connecticut's excellent basketball team and the major-league Hartford Whalers hockey team. Yale in New Haven has an athletic rivalry with Harvard in Cambridge, MA. On Cape Cod, the Cape Cod Baseball League (established 1885) has teams in

Smoking

The USA, which gave the world tobacco, is now mostly a huge no-smoking zone. Government regulations have banished smokers from virtually all public spaces except the out-of-doors, and have also banished most tobacco advertising from the media. Several state governments banded together and sued tobacco companies in order to reclaim the millions of public-health dollars they have had to spend dealing with tobacco-related illnesses. The trial revealed that the tobacco companies had indeed designed their products to be particularly addictive and had suppressed evidence that tobacco use causes various diseases. In short, tobacco products, their manufacturers and their users are now in high disrepute.

Many Americans find smoking unpleasant and know that heavy or habitual smoking is unhealthy and harmful not only to the smoker, but also to those nearby (particularly children and people with asthma or other pulmonary impairments). If you are a smoker from a country that permits smoking in public places, you should be aware of American regulations and social customs.

Smoking is prohibited in most public buildings, such as airports, train and bus stations, offices, hospitals and stores, and on public conveyances (subways, trains, buses, planes, etc). Except for the designated smoking areas in some restaurants, bars and a few other enclosed places, you must step outside to smoke.

Most cities and towns require restaurants to have nonsmoking sections. There is no requirement that there be smoking sections, and indeed more and more restaurants are completely 'smoke-free.' Hotels offer 'nonsmoking' rooms – that is, rooms used only by nonsmoking guests so that the rooms have no stale tobacco smell.

If you are in an enclosed space (a room or car, for example) with other people, it's polite to ask permission of all others before you smoke and to refrain from smoking if anyone protests.

Brewster, Chatham, Falmouth, Harwich, Hyannis, Orleans and Yarmouth-Dennis.

SHOPPING

Regional gifts and souvenirs include maple syrup and maple-sugar candy, silver or pewter items in designs originally made by Paul Revere, and scrimshaw (carved whale ivory – but today it's plastic 'imitation ivory'). The Bull & Finch Pub, inspiration for the popular television series *Cheers*, is Boston's most prolific souvenir factory, selling everything from T-shirts to buttons to beer mugs. The Black Dog Restaurant & Bakery on Martha's Vineyard is a close second.

Shoppers love searching for discounted clothing, shoes, accessories, china, jewelry and all manner of other items at Filene's Basement in Boston and at factory outlet stores in Fall River, New Bedford and Worcester, MA. North Conway, NH, and Freeport and Kittery, ME, also have massive factory outlet malls.

See the Shopping sections in the regional chapters for more details on things to buy.

Getting There & Away

While the two most common ways to reach New England are by air and by car, you can also get here easily by train and by bus. Served by three major airports, two train terminals and a massive bus depot, New York City is the most important transportation hub in the northeastern USA and, like Boston, a popular gateway to New England for many travelers.

AIR

Because of New England's location on the densely populated US Atlantic seaboard between New York and eastern Canada, air travelers have a number of ways to approach the region.

Airports

New England Boston's Logan International Airport (BOS, ☎ 800-235-6426, W www.massport.org) is the major gateway to the region and is easily accessible – usually by nonstop or direct flight – from other major airports in the USA and abroad.

Several other airports in the region receive national and international flights: Bradley International Airport in Windsor Locks, CT (serving Hartford, CT, and Springfield, MA); TF Green State Airport in Warwick, RI; Manchester Airport in Manchester, NH; Burlington, VT; and Bangor and Portland, ME. See the Getting Around chapter for more information on these airports.

New York City Most international flights coming to the northeastern USA land at John F Kennedy International Airport (JFK), just 15 miles from Midtown Manhattan. La Guardia Airport (LGA), 8 miles from Midtown, serves mostly domestic flights, including air shuttles to Boston and Washington, DC. Newark International Airport in New Jersey, 10 miles west of Manhattan, is the hub for Continental Airlines. Many major carriers use its new international arrivals terminal. The Port

Authority of New York & New Jersey operates all three airports and maintains a website with detailed information about each airport at W www.panynj.gov.

Numerous flights go to Boston daily from each of New York's three major airports. Smaller New York airports, such as MacArthur and Islip, offer commuter flights to Boston. US Airways and Delta operate hourly shuttle flights between La Guardia and Boston. No reservation is required, but it's good to have one in order to avoid disappointment. Continental operates similar flights between Newark (EWR) and Boston. One-way fares range between $70 (weekends, with advance purchase) and $200 (weekdays, without advance purchase) for the 40-minute flight.

Scheduled flights also connect New York City with these New England area airports: Albany, New York; Hyannis, Martha's Vineyard, Nantucket and Worcester, MA;

Bridgeport, New Haven, New London and Hartford, CT; Providence, RI; Burlington, VT; Lebanon and Manchester, NH; and Bangor, Portland and Presque Isle, ME.

Serving 35 million passengers a year, **JFK International Airport** is sprawling. Its crowded International Arrivals terminal rivals the chaos of London's Heathrow Airport. Airlines used to build showcase terminals at JFK, and thus the airport grew to its uncoordinated state with no coherent plan. While some of the original airlines (Eastern, Pan Am) have disappeared, the terminals remain, linked by the JFK Expressway and a free shuttle bus. American Airlines, British Airways and Delta have their own terminals; most other airlines use the International Arrivals Building.

To find out if the airport is closed in bad weather, call the information line (☎ 718-244-4444), as individual airlines may be reluctant to give honest information about flight delays over the phone.

If you're arriving or departing in the middle of the day, **La Guardia Airport** (☎ 718-533-3400) is a more convenient choice than JFK. US Airways and the Delta Shuttle to Boston have their own terminals; all other airlines use the Central Terminal Building in front of the parking garage.

La Guardia isn't equipped to accommodate wide-body jets, so cross-country or transatlantic flights can't land there. The airport mainly serves destinations in Canada and the northeastern USA.

Newark International Airport (☎ 973-961-6000, Ⓦ www.newarkairport.com) is the best choice at the moment for foreign visitors, thanks to a new, well-organized international arrivals terminal. This airport's advantages include a large immigration hall that speeds passport checks and a monorail system that links the terminals for quick transfers to domestic flights to New England and elsewhere. Flights to Newark are usually a bit cheaper because of the erroneous perception that the airport is less accessible than JFK.

Most people who fly into the New York area with plans to travel on to New England by ground transport have to travel into

Manhattan to make bus or train connections. If you'd rather not face the potential gridlock of a bus, limo or taxi ride into Manhattan from the Newark International Airport, you can take a short shuttle bus ride to the PATH train, which travels from Newark's Penn Station into New York City. Call ☎ 800-234-7284 for more information.

In 2002–03, the Newark airport plans to link its monorail system with New Jersey Transit trains; this should make for a speedy trip into Manhattan.

Canada Montreal's Dorval airport, 14 miles southwest of the city center, handles Canadian domestic flights and flights to the USA. Mirabel, 34 miles northwest of Montreal, handles intercontinental flights. Delta Air Lines operates routes from Dorval airport to Boston and Hartford. When flying to the USA from Toronto or Montreal, you clear US customs and immigration right in the Canadian airport before departure.

Airlines

These major airlines serve Boston and/or New York City:

Aer Lingus	☎ 800-223-6537
Air Canada	☎ 800-776-3000
Air France	☎ 800-237-2747
Air New Zealand	☎ 800-262-1234
America West Airlines	☎ 800-235-9292
American Airlines*	☎ 800-433-7300
British Airways	☎ 800-247-9297
Canadian Airlines	☎ 800-426-7000
China Airlines	☎ 800-227-5118
Continental Airlines*	☎ 800-523-3273
Delta Air Lines*	☎ 800-221-1212
El Al Israel	☎ 800-223-6700
Icelandic	☎ 800-223-5500
Japan Air Lines	☎ 800-525-3663
KLM Royal Dutch	☎ 800-374-7747
Lufthansa German Airlines	☎ 800-399-5838
MetroJet	☎ 888-638-7653
Midwest Express	☎ 800-452-2022
Northwest Airlines*	☎ 800-447-4747
Northwest Airlines (domestic)	☎ 800-225-2525
Scandinavian Airlines	☎ 800-221-2350

Swissair	☎ 800-221-4750
United Airlines*	☎ 800-241-6522
US Airways*	☎ 800-428-4322
Virgin Atlantic Airways	☎ 800-862-8621

* denotes major domestic carriers

A dozen smaller domestic airlines, such as Air Tran Airways (☎ 800-247-8726), have route systems concentrated in a particular region, plus a few national flights. Several of these are discount airlines that offer lower fares and fewer restrictions on their flights, but usually have fewer flights than major carriers. Southwest Airlines (☎ 800-435-9792) offers discounted fares to and from Rhode Island's TF Green State Airport, south of Providence; the Manchester, NH, airport; and Bradley International Airport near Hartford, CT.

Commuter airlines shuttle passengers from large and intermediate-size local airports, such as Bradley International Airport, TF Green State Airport and Albany, to the airports of smaller cities. Others make short hops across bodies of water, such as from Massachusetts' New Bedford to Nantucket, or Westerly to Block Island, off Rhode Island. See the Getting Around chapter and the Getting There & Away heading under individual destinations for information on these commuter airlines.

Buying Tickets
Airfares in the US range from incredibly low to obscenely high. At the time of this writing, roundtrip fares between Boston and Washington, DC, ranged from $176 to $975.

To get an idea of fares, try these online reservations services:

- Ⓦ www.atevo.com
- Ⓦ www.bestfares.com
- Ⓦ www.counciltravel.com
- Ⓦ www.statravel.com
- Ⓦ www.ticketplanet.com
- Ⓦ www.travelocity.com

In the USA, major newspapers such as *The Boston Globe*, *The New York Times*, the *Los Angeles Times*, *Chicago Tribune*, and *San Francisco Chronicle* have weekly travel sec-tions packed with advertisements for discounted airfares. Council Travel (☎ 800-226-8624, Ⓦ www.counciltravel.com) and STA Travel (☎ 800-777-0112, Ⓦ www.statravel .com), with offices in major cities nationwide, might be offering good fares.

Travel CUTS (Ⓦ www.travelcuts.com), with offices in all major Canadian cities, often has fare bargains. The *Toronto Globe & Mail* and *Vancouver Sun* carry ads for low fares, and the magazine *Great Expeditions* (PO Box 8000-411, Abbotsford, BC V2S 6H1) also is useful.

The travel sections of magazines such as *Time Out* and *TNT* in the UK, or the Saturday editions of the *Sydney Morning Herald* and *The Age* in Australia, carry ads offering cheap fares. STA Travel also has offices worldwide.

The magazine *Travel Unlimited* (PO Box 1058, Allston, MA 02134) publishes details of the cheapest international airfares and courier possibilities.

A return (roundtrip) ticket usually works out cheaper – often *much* cheaper – than buying a one-way ticket each way. But not always, so ask.

Discount Tickets If you call a major airline and book a same-day roundtrip flight to Boston from Washington, DC, the fare can be as high as $600 or even more. If you purchase the ticket at least a week in advance, however, and stay over a Saturday night before returning, the roundtrip fare can be as low as $78.

The rules are complex, but buying as far in advance as possible and staying over a Saturday night usually get you the best fare. Also, flying is cheaper at certain times of the year, particularly mid-January through March and October to mid-December (except Thanksgiving). See When to Go in the Facts for the Visitor chapter.

Also, flights on Tuesday, Wednesday, Thursday, Saturday and Sunday are cheaper than those on Friday and Monday, and flights at certain times (10am to 3pm and after 8pm on weekdays; Saturday afternoon and Sunday before noon) may be cheaper as well.

Air Travel Glossary

Cancellation Penalties If you have to cancel or change a discounted ticket, there are often heavy penalties involved; insurance can sometimes be taken out against these penalties. Some airlines impose penalties on regular tickets as well, particularly against 'no-show' passengers.

Courier Fares Businesses often need to send urgent documents or freight securely and quickly. Courier companies hire people to accompany the package through customs and, in return, offer a discount ticket which is sometimes a phenomenal bargain. However, you may have to surrender all your baggage allowance and take only carry-on luggage.

Full Fares Airlines traditionally offer 1st class (coded F), business class (coded J) and economy class (coded Y) tickets. These days, so many promotional and discounted fares are available that few passengers pay full economy fare.

Lost Tickets If you lose your airline ticket, an airline will usually treat it like a traveler's check and, after inquiries, issue you with another one. Legally, however, an airline is entitled to treat it like cash: if you lose it, it's gone forever. Take good care of your tickets.

Onward Tickets An entry requirement for many countries is a ticket out of the country. If you're unsure of your next move, the easiest solution is to buy the cheapest onward ticket to a neighboring country or a ticket from a reliable airline that can later be refunded if you do not use it.

Open-Jaw Tickets These are return tickets that permit you to fly into one place but return from another. If available, these tickets can save you backtracking to your arrival point.

Overbooking Because almost every flight has some passengers that fail to show up, airlines often book more passengers than they have seats. Usually excess passengers make up for the no-shows, but occasionally somebody gets 'bumped' onto the next available flight. Guess who it is most likely to be? The passengers who check in late.

Promotional Fares These are officially discounted fares, available from travel agencies or direct from the airline.

Reconfirmation If you don't reconfirm your flight at least 72 hours prior to departure, the airline may delete your name from the passenger list. Call to find out if your airline requires reconfirmation.

Restrictions Discounted tickets often have various restrictions – for example, they may need to be paid for in advance, or altering them may incur a penalty. Other restrictions include minimum and maximum periods you must be away.

Round-the-World Tickets RTW tickets give you a limited period (usually a year) in which to circumnavigate the globe. You can go anywhere the carrying airlines go as long as you don't backtrack. The number of stopovers or total number of separate flights is decided before you set off, and these tickets usually cost a bit more than a basic return flight.

Transferred Tickets Airline tickets cannot be transferred from one person to another. Travelers sometimes try to sell the return half of a ticket, but officials can ask you to prove that you are the person named on the ticket. On an international flight, tickets are compared with passports.

Travel Periods Ticket prices vary with the time of year. There is a low (off-peak) season and a high (peak) season, and often a low-shoulder season and a high-shoulder season as well. Usually the fare depends on your outward flight – if you depart in the high season and return in the low season, you pay the high-season fare.

The cheapest tickets are what the airlines call 'nonrefundable,' even though you may be able to get your money (or at least some of it) back under certain circumstances. A good strategy to use when buying a nonrefundable ticket is to schedule your return flight for the latest possible date you're likely to use it. In many cases, an airline will allow you to fly standby at no extra charge if you return earlier than your scheduled flight; but if you want to fly later, you may have to pay a penalty or buy another ticket entirely.

Holiday Periods At holiday times travelers will find it difficult to get the flights and fares they want unless they plan – and purchase their tickets – well in advance. Holiday times include Christmas, New Year's, Easter, Memorial Day, Labor Day and Thanksgiving.

Special Fares for Foreign Visitors Many domestic carriers offer special fares to visitors who are not US citizens. Typically, you must purchase a booklet of coupons in conjunction with a flight into the USA from a foreign country other than Canada or Mexico. Each coupon in the booklet entitles you to a single flight segment on the issuing airline. However, you may have to use all the coupons within a limited period of time, and there may be other restrictions, such as a limit of two transcontinental flights (ie, flights all the way across the USA).

Continental Airlines' Visit USA pass costs $559 for three coupons (minimum purchase) and $1059 for eight coupons (maximum purchase) in high summer. Changes of itinerary incur a $50-75 penalty. Northwest has a similar program.

On American Airlines, you must reserve your flights one day in advance.

Delta has two different programs: 'Visit USA' grants discounts on fully planned itineraries; 'Discover America' allows purchase of coupons good for standby travel anywhere in the continental USA. The minimum purchase is three coupons, and the maximum is 10.

When flying standby, call the airline one or two days before the flight and make a standby reservation. This way you get priority over all the others who just appear and hope to get on the flight the same day.

Round-the-World Tickets Round-the-world (RTW) tickets can be a great deal if you want to visit other regions as well as the USA. Often they work out to be no more expensive – or even cheaper – than a simple roundtrip ticket to the USA, so you get the extra stops for nothing. They're of most value for trips that combine travel to the USA with Europe, Asia and Australia or New Zealand. RTW itineraries that include stops in South America or Africa can be substantially more expensive.

Official airline RTW tickets are usually put together by a combination of two or three airlines, and they permit you to fly to a specified number of stops on their routes as long as you don't backtrack. Other restrictions are that you must usually book the first sector in advance, and cancellation penalties apply. The tickets are valid for a fixed period, usually one year. An alternative type of RTW ticket is one put together by a travel agent using a combination of discounted tickets.

Most airlines do restrict the number of sectors that can be flown within the USA and Canada to three or four, and some airlines even 'black out' a few heavily traveled routes. In most cases, a 14-day advance purchase is required. After the ticket is purchased, dates can usually be changed without penalty, and tickets can be rewritten to add or delete stops for $50 each.

From Australia, a Qantas RTW ticket permits six stops in North America and the Caribbean, four stops in Europe, four stops in Asia, and back to Australia for A$2599. There are other possibilities with Qantas and various partner airlines, ranging from A$1600 to A$3350.

From New Zealand, a RTW ticket via North America, Europe and Asia with Air New Zealand and other airlines costs NZ$3099 and up.

Baggage & Other Restrictions

Baggage regulations are set by each airline but usually allow you to check two bags of average size and weight and to carry one smaller bag (in addition to a purse or computer) onto the plane. If you are carrying many pieces of luggage, or pieces that are particularly big, bulky, fragile or heavy (such as a bicycle or other sports equipment), check with the airline about special procedures and extra charges.

Your ticket folder usually gives details of items that are illegal to carry on airplanes, either in checked baggage or on your person. These include weapons, knives of ANY kind, scissors, aerosols, tear gas and pepper spray, camp stove fuel canisters and full oxygen tanks. You may carry matches and lighters on your person, but do not put them in checked luggage.

Smoking is prohibited on all domestic flights within the USA and on most international flights to and from the USA. Most airports in the USA prohibit smoking except in designated areas.

Travelers with Special Needs

If you have special needs of any sort – a broken leg, dietary restrictions, dependence on a wheelchair, responsibility for a baby, fear of flying – airports and airlines can be surprisingly helpful, but you should let them know as soon as possible so that they can make arrangements accordingly. You should also remind them when you reconfirm your booking (at least 72 hours before departure) and again when you check in at the airport.

Guide dogs for the blind and hearing impaired must often travel in a specially pressurized baggage compartment with other animals, away from their owners, though smaller guide dogs may be admitted to the cabin. Guide dogs are not subject to quarantine as long as they have proof of being vaccinated against rabies.

Deaf travelers can ask that airport and in-flight announcements be written down for them.

Children under two years of age travel for 10% of the standard fare (or free on some airlines), as long as they don't occupy a seat, but they usually don't receive a baggage allowance. 'Skycots' may be provided by the airline if requested in advance; these will hold a child weighing up to 22lb. Children between the ages of two and 12 sometimes can occupy a seat for half to two-thirds of the full fare, while getting a baggage allowance. Strollers usually must be checked at the aircraft door; they are returned at the door upon disembarking.

Departure Tax

A $6 airport departure tax is charged to all passengers bound for a foreign destination from the USA. A $6.50 North American Free Trade Agreement (or NAFTA) tax is charged to passengers entering the USA from a foreign country. There may be other small airport usage and security fees, depending upon the airport. Departure taxes are normally included in the cost of tickets bought in the USA. If you bought your ticket outside the USA, you may have to pay the tax when you check in for your departing flight.

Arriving in the USA

As you approach the USA, your flight's cabin crew will hand out a customs and immigration form for you to fill in.

Arriving from outside North America, you must complete customs and immigration formalities at the airport where you first land, whether or not it is your final destination. Choose the proper immigration line: US citizens or non-US citizens.

After you have cleared immigration procedures, pick up your luggage in the customs area and proceed to an officer, who will ask you questions concerning your destination and length of stay, and perhaps check your luggage. The dog sniffing around the luggage is looking for drugs, explosives and restricted agricultural and food products.

If the airport where you enter the country is not your final destination, you must recheck your luggage.

See also the Customs section in the Facts for the Visitor chapter.

Leaving the USA

You should check in for international flights at least three hours early. During check-in procedures, you might be asked for photo identification, and you will be asked questions about whether you packed your own bags, whether anyone else has had access to them since you packed them and whether you have received any parcels to carry. These questions are for security purposes.

Canada

Boston receives daily direct and nonstop flights from most major Canadian cities, with Toronto, Montreal and Halifax having the most frequent service. Carriers include Air Atlantic, Air Canada, Air Nova, American, Canadian Airlines, Delta, Northwest and United. Canadian fares to Boston are reasonable: As this book was written, round-trips could be found from Halifax at $165, from Montreal at $175, Toronto at $168 and Vancouver at $465. See Canada under Airports near the beginning of this chapter.

Major Canadian newspapers such as the *Toronto Globe & Mail* carry travel agencies' advertisements. The Canadian Federation of Students' Travel CUTS travel agency (W www.travelcuts.com) offers low fares and has offices in major cities throughout Canada.

The UK

Globetrotters Club (W www.globetrotters .co.uk, BCM Roving, London WC1N 3XX) publishes a newsletter called *Globe* that covers obscure destinations and can help you find traveling companions. Check the free magazines widely available in London – start by looking outside the main railway stations.

Travel Agents Most British travel agents are registered with the Association of British Travel Agents (ABTA; W www .abta.com). Some agents are bonded under agreements such as the Air Transport Operators License (ATOL); if you buy a ticket from such an agent and the airline then goes out of business, ATOL guarantees a refund or an alternative.

Besides the many official fares published by the airlines and sold by them and their travel agencies, there are also 'unofficial' bucket shop (consolidator) fares. These seats are sold by the airlines in bulk at a big discount to wholesale brokers, who then sell them to the public and hope to make a profit. If you deal with a reputable shop or agency, these fares can be a good value on the major airlines. Most such fares are non-refundable (see Discount Tickets under Buying Tickets, earlier in this chapter).

London is arguably the world's headquarters for bucket shops, which are well advertised and can usually beat published airline fares. Two reliable agents for cheap tickets in the UK are STA Travel (☎ 020-7581-4132, W www.statravel.co.uk, 86 Old Brompton Rd, London SW7) and Trailfinders (☎ 020-7938-3939, W www.trailfinders.co.uk, 194 Kensington High St, London W8 7RG). Trailfinders produces a lavishly illustrated brochure including airfare details.

The very cheapest flights are often advertised by obscure bucket shops whose names haven't yet reached the telephone directory. Many such firms are honest and solvent, but there are a few rogues who will take your money and disappear, only to reopen elsewhere a month or two later under a new name. If you feel suspicious about a firm, don't give them all the money at once: Leave a deposit of 20% or so and pay the rest when you receive the ticket. If they insist on cash in advance, go elsewhere. And once you have the ticket, phone the airline to confirm that you are booked on the flight.

Fares Virgin Atlantic has a roundtrip in-season fare from London to Boston for £420 (US$676), or to New York for £384 (US$618), allowing a one-month maximum stay and requiring a 21-day advance purchase. Off-season (wintertime) flights from London can be as low as £200 (US$292) to Boston or £190 (US$277) to New York.

British Airways flies nonstop between London and Boston. For flights from London to Montreal, Canadian Airlines International is a good bet, with off-season fares beginning around £210 (US$306).

Aer Lingus offers direct flights from Shannon and Dublin to New York City, but because competition on flights from London is so much fiercer, it's generally cheaper to fly to London first then connect with a flight to the USA.

Continental Europe

Virgin Atlantic flights from Paris to New York are substantially cheaper than alternatives; a ticket with seven-day advance purchase ranges from €356 (US$405) up to €661 (US$752). In Paris, Council Travel (☎ 01 44 41 89 80, ⓦ www.counciltravel.com) is popular.

Lufthansa has nonstop service to Boston from its Frankfurt hub.

Australia & New Zealand

In Australia and New Zealand, STA Travel (ⓦ www.statravel.com) is a major dealer in cheap airfares.

Qantas flies to Los Angeles from Sydney, Melbourne (via Sydney or Auckland) and Cairns. United flies to San Francisco from Sydney and Auckland (via Sydney), and also flies to Los Angeles. Connector flights are available to the East Coast. Fares are generally around A$2450 (US$1249) to A$2800 (US$1463) roundtrip from Melbourne or Sydney to Boston.

Asia

Hong Kong is the discount-ticket capital of the region, but its bucket shops can be unreliable. Ask the advice of other travelers before buying a ticket. STA Travel (ⓦ www .statravel.com) has branches in Hong Kong, Tokyo, Singapore, Bangkok and Kuala Lumpur. Airfares may be available for as low as US$950 roundtrip from Hong Kong to New York or Boston, though normal fares are more like US$1200.

Central & South America

Most flights from Central and South America go to Boston via Miami, Dallas–Fort Worth or Los Angeles, though a few go nonstop to New York. American, Continental, Delta, Northwest and United all have routes to Mexico and Central and South America. Aeroméxico, Mexicana and the airlines of the Central American nations (Aeroquetzal, Aeronica, Aviateca, COPA, LACSA and TACA) have flights to either Miami or New York, with connections to Boston. Fares are somewhat expensive: US$510 roundtrip to Boston from Mexico City, US$714 from Guatemala City.

BUS

Comfortable, air-conditioned buses connect most cities and some towns in the USA. You can get to New England by bus from all parts of the USA, Canada and Mexico, but the trip will be long and may not be much less expensive than a discounted flight.

As with planes and trains, New York City is the region's major hub for buses, and many routes from around the country come through New York on their way to New England.

The Port Authority Bus Terminal (☎ 212-564-8484, ⓦ www.panynj.gov/tbt/pabframe .HTM, Eighth Ave & W 42nd St), in Manhattan, is the city's main bus terminal.

Boston has a modern, indoor, user-friendly bus station (no ☎, 700 Atlantic Ave at Summer St), conveniently adjacent to the South Station train station and above a T stop for the Red Line.

See the Getting Around chapter for details on bus travel within the region.

Fares

Bus companies sometimes offer special travel plans and promotional fares, and these can reduce fares substantially, especially on the longer trips. Ask about them when you call the bus company.

The table below shows sample seven-day advance purchase fares (one-way/roundtrip) to Boston:

from	fare	duration
Chicago, IL	$69/138	20 hours
Montreal, Canada	$50/98	8 hours
New York, NY	$42/79	5 hours
San Francisco, CA	$109/218	67 hours
Toronto, Canada	$73/135	12 hours
Washington, DC	$49/98	9 hours

Bonanza

Bonanza Bus Lines (☎ 212-564-8484, 800-556-3815, ⓦ www.bonanzabus.com) operates routes from New York City to Albany via the Berkshires (Great Barrington, Stockbridge, Lee, Lenox and Pittsfield, MA), and from New York City to Cape Cod (Falmouth, Woods Hole and Hyannis) via Providence. Bonanza also operates buses to Newport and New Bedford.

Green Tortoise

For travel between the West Coast and New England, Green Tortoise (☎ 415-956-7500, 800-867-8647, ⓦ www.greentortoise.com) buses are more relaxing than Greyhound and a lot more entertaining. Foam mattresses and booths with tables replace bus seats, the maximum number of passengers is 38, and food, music and merriment prevail. Tortoise buses leave about every two weeks from San Francisco and spend 12 to 14 days winding across the country via New York to Boston, and vice versa. Along the way you visit state and national parks, monuments, forests and anywhere else your fellow passengers agree to stop; flexibility is key. Fares run from $469 to $499, plus a food fund payment of $121 to $131 per person.

Greyhound

In addition to some 40 New York-Boston trips a day, Greyhound Lines (☎ 212-635-0800, 800-231-2222, ⓦ www.greyhound.com) operates buses from New York City to Hartford, Springfield, Worcester, New Haven, New London and Providence. Service to Cape Cod is provided in conjunction with Bonanza.

Vermont Transit

Vermont Transit Lines (☎ 802-864-6811, 212-594-2000, 800-451-3292 in New England, ⓦ www.vermonttransit.com) serves Montreal, Vermont, Boston, Maine and several points in New Hampshire in conjunction with Greyhound.

TRAIN

Rail passenger service in the USA is operated primarily by Amtrak (☎ 800-872-7245,

ⓦ www.amtrak.com), a quasi-governmental corporation. Service in the 'Northeast Corridor' (connecting Boston with New York and Washington, DC) is some of the most frequent in Amtrak's system. Amtrak operates high-speed 'tilt' trains on a fully electrified line at up to 150mph between Boston, New York and Washington, DC, cutting travel time from New York City center to Boston to three hours. Amtrak calls the high speed train the 'Super Acela'; regular trains are simple 'Acela.'

Several Amtrak routes pass through New York City's Pennsylvania Station (Penn Station), from which about 10 trains depart daily for Boston. In Boston, Amtrak trains stop at the South Station terminal, at Atlantic Ave and Summer St, as well as Back Bay Station, at Dartmouth St. Half the trains that run between Boston and New York are unreserved; the other half are all-reserved trains with somewhat higher fares. Book reservations through Amtrak or a travel agent.

Fares

Amtrak offers excursion fares, seasonal discounts and rail passes good for unlimited travel during a certain period of time. Children receive discounts as well. The fares listed below are unreserved, coach class, peak-season fares, one-way/roundtrip, to Boston. They're subject to change and do not include meals. You can either buy snacks or meals on board or take your own food. If you travel 1st class in a club or sleeping car, meals are included.

from	fare	duration
Chicago, IL	$107/181	22 hours
New York, NY	$58/116	4 hours
San Francisco, CA	$214/395	72 hours
Washington, DC	$78/156	9 hours

One-way weekend special fares aboard the high-speed Super Acela train are $102 from New York and $138 from Washington, DC.

Routes

Boston is the northern terminus of Amtrak's *Northeast Corridor* train service, connecting Hartford, Providence, New Haven, New York City, Philadelphia, Baltimore and Washington, DC.

The main line from New York to Boston, the *Shore Route,* follows the coast for much of the way, stopping in New Rochelle, New York, and Stamford and Bridgeport, CT, before coming to New Haven (Yale University); Old Saybrook, CT (for Old Lyme, Essex and Ivoryton); New London (for the US Coast Guard Academy); Mystic, CT (for the Mystic Seaport Museum); Westerly, RI (for Stonington and Rhode Island beaches); Kingston, RI (for Narragansett, Port Galilee and Block Island); and Providence before reaching Boston.

The *Inland Route* itinerary follows the main line from New York City as far as New Haven, then runs west up the Connecticut River Valley, stopping off at Wallingford, Meriden, Berlin (New Britain), Hartford, Windsor, Windsor Locks (for Bradley International Airport) and Springfield, MA. One or two trains daily continue past Springfield to Worcester and Framingham, MA, then to Boston. This route takes much longer than the *Shore Route* via Providence.

Metro-North trains (☎ 212-532-4900, 800-638-7646, W www.mta.nyc.ny.us) link New York City's Grand Central Station to New Haven (with stops in between) every hour on the hour from 7am until after midnight on weekdays, with extra trains during the peak morning and evening hours. Service on Saturday, Sunday and holidays is less frequent, but there is a train at least every two hours. The trip from Grand Central to New Haven takes 1½ hours.

During July and August, Amtrak operates special weekend trains from New York City to Hyannis on Cape Cod with stops at Bridgeport, New Haven, New London and Mystic, CT; Westerly and Providence, RI; and Buzzards Bay, Sandwich and West Barnstable on Cape Cod.

The *Vermonter* Amtrak route begins in Washington, DC, and runs to Newark; New York City; Stamford, New Haven and Hartford; Springfield and Amherst; and then on to St Albans in Vermont, near the Canadian border.

The *Montrealer* runs between New York City and northern Vermont along the Connecticut River Valley. At the Canadian border, you'll board a bus for Montreal. Stops include Essex Junction (for Burlington), White River Junction and Brattleboro, VT; Amherst; and New Haven.

The Amtrak *Lake Shore Limited* departs Chicago's Union Station each evening for Boston, making stops at Toledo and Cleveland, Ohio; Buffalo, Rochester, Syracuse and Albany-Rensselaer; and at Springfield, Worcester and Boston. You can connect with a New York–bound train at Springfield.

The *Downeaster* between Boston and Portland, ME, has resumed running after decades without train service over this route. For details, see the Train section in the Getting Around chapter.

CAR

Foreign visitors who arrive via their own motor vehicles must carry the vehicle's registration papers, proof of liability insurance, and an international driving permit, in addition to their domestic driver's license.

Though the easiest way to get to New England is by airplane, the best way to get around is by car, so you might want to drive. Interstate highways crisscross New England, and offer forest, farm and mountain scenery once you are clear of urban areas and the I-95 corridor between Boston and New York. These interstate highways connect the region to New York, Washington, DC, Montreal and points south and west.

Drive-Aways

A drive-away is a car that belongs to someone who can't drive it to a specific destination but is willing to allow someone else to drive it. For example, if somebody moves from Denver to Boston, they may elect to fly and leave the car with a drive-away agency. The agency will find a driver and take care of all the necessary insurance and permits. If you happen to want to drive from Denver to Boston and have a valid driver's license and a clean driving record, you can apply to drive the car. Normally, you have to pay a small, refundable deposit and pay for the gas (though sometimes a gas allowance is given). You are given a set number of days within which to deliver the car – usually based on driving eight hours a day – and a limited number of miles, based on the best route and allowing for reasonable side trips. This is an economical way to get around if you like long-distance driving and meet the eligibility requirements.

Drive-away companies often advertise in the classified sections of newspapers under 'Travel.' They are also listed in the yellow pages under 'Automobile Transporters & Drive-Away Companies.' You will need to be flexible about dates and destinations when you call. The most easily available routes are coast-to-coast, although intermediate trips are certainly possible.

Getting Around

The best way to get around New England is by car. The region is relatively small, the highways are good and public transportation is not as frequent or as widespread as in some other countries. Still, there are the alternatives of air, train, bus and boat.

AIR
Domestic Airports
Regional and commuter airlines connect New England's cities and resorts with Boston and New York City. The following airports receive scheduled flights.

The Albany County Airport (☎ 518-869-9611), in Albany, New York, on I-90 across the Massachusetts border from Stockbridge, serves the Berkshires and western Massachusetts as well as Vermont.

Barnstable Municipal Airport (☎ 508-775-2020), in Hyannis, MA, serves Cape Cod. The Martha's Vineyard Airport (☎ 508-693-7022) serves that island, just as the Nantucket Airport (☎ 508-325-5300) serves Nantucket Island.

Worcester Municipal Airport (☎ 508-792-0610), in Worcester, MA, serves central Massachusetts.

Bradley International Airport (☎ 860-292-2000), in Windsor Locks, CT, serves all of Connecticut and greater Springfield, the Pioneer Valley and the Berkshires in Massachusetts, plus Vermont.

Manchester Airport (☎ 603-624-6556), in Manchester, NH, serves south-central New Hampshire and metropolitan Boston.

Groton/New London Airport (☎ 860-445-8549), in Connecticut, serves the southeastern Connecticut coast. Nearby Igor Sikorsky Memorial Airport (☎ 203-576-7498) and Tweed–New Haven Airport (☎ 203-787-8283) also have commuter flights.

TF Green State Airport (☎ 401-737-4000) in Warwick (near Providence) is Rhode Island's largest airport, served by several major and regional carriers.

Burlington Airport (☎ 802-862-9286) is Vermont's major airport, but you can also reach Vermont from airports in Albany, Boston and Hartford, as well as Montreal, Canada.

Regular flights reach Maine's regional airports in Augusta, Bangor, Bar Harbor/Hancock County (which serves Acadia National Park), Portland, Presque Isle and Rockland/Knox County. For more on these airports, see the destination headings in the Maine chapter.

Domestic Airlines
Delta Express Airlines (☎ 800-221-1212, Ⓦ www.delta.com), also operating Business Express, is the largest of New England's regional airlines, flying from Boston to Washington, DC; Philadelphia, Pennsylvania; Albany, Islip, Rochester, Syracuse and White Plains, New York; Burlington, VT; Bangor, Portland and Presque Isle, ME; Halifax, Nova Scotia; Ottawa, Ontario; and Quebec City, Quebec. It also runs flights between Providence and New York City's La Guardia Airport.

US Airways Express (☎ 800-428-4322, Ⓦ www.usairways.com) flies from Boston to Augusta, Bar Harbor and Rockland, ME; Rutland, VT; and Hyannis, Martha's Vineyard and Nantucket in Massachusetts. It also flies between Nantucket and New York's La Guardia Airport.

Cape Air (☎ 508-771-6944, 800-352-0714, Ⓦ www.flycapeair.com) serves the Massachusetts destinations of Hyannis, Martha's Vineyard, Nantucket and Provincetown from Boston and New Bedford, as well as Providence, RI. Nantucket Airlines (☎ 508-790-0300, 800-635-8787, Ⓦ www.nantucketairlines.com), a division of Cape Air, offers hourly shuttle service from Hyannis to Nantucket.

Continental Express (☎ 800-525-0280) flies to Nantucket and Martha's Vineyard, MA, from Newark, NJ.

New England Airlines (☎ 800-243-2460, Ⓦ www.block-island.com/nea/) flies from Westerly, RI, to Block Island, RI.

BUS

Buses go to more places than airplanes or trains, but the routes still leave a lot out, bypassing some prime destinations. Except on the most heavily traveled routes, there might be only one or two buses per day.

The major bus companies, with routes that cover several New England states, are Bonanza, Greyhound, Peter Pan and Vermont Transit.

Bonanza

Bonanza Bus Lines (☎ 212-564-8484, 401-331-7500, 800-556-3815, W www.bonanza bus.com), with its hub in Providence, RI, runs buses from New York City via Danbury and Hartford, CT, to Providence, and via New Milford, Kent and Canaan, CT, to Massachusetts' Berkshire hills and to Bennington, VT. Other routes connect Providence with Newport, RI, and with Boston, Fall River, Falmouth, Hyannis and Woods Hole (Cape Cod), all in Massachusetts.

Greyhound

Greyhound (☎ 212-635-0800, 617-526-1810, 800-231-2222, W www.greyhound.com), working in conjunction with Bonanza, Peter Pan and Vermont Transit, runs buses connecting Boston with New York City and Albany, NY; Hartford and New Haven, CT; Newark, New Jersey; and the Berkshire hills, Springfield and Worcester, MA, with connecting service to many other parts of the country.

Other Greyhound routes, on which service is pooled with carriers such as Vermont Transit, run north via Portsmouth, NH, along the Maine coast, with stops in Portland, Freeport, Brunswick, Bath, Wiscasset, Camden and Bangor. Connecting services can carry you onward to Ellsworth, for Bar Harbor and Acadia National Park, and into New Brunswick and Nova Scotia.

Peter Pan

Peter Pan Bus Lines (☎ 413-781-3320, 800-343-9999, W www.peterpanbus.com), based in Springfield, runs routes connecting Boston with Washington, DC; Baltimore; Philadelphia; Albany (with connections as far as Toronto) and New York City; Amherst, Greenfield, Holyoke, Lee, Northampton, Pittsfield, Springfield, Sturbridge, Williamstown and Worcester, MA; and Bridgeport, Danbury, Hartford, Middletown, New Britain, New Haven, Norwalk and Waterbury, CT.

Peter Pan buses also run from Springfield and the Pioneer Valley to Bradley International Airport, north of Hartford.

Vermont Transit

Vermont Transit Lines (☎ 212-594-2000, 802-864-6811, 800-451-3292 in New England, W www.vermonttransit.com), based in Burlington, has routes connecting major Vermont towns with New York's Albany, Binghamton and New York City; Boston; Manchester and Portsmouth, NH; and Bangor, Bar Harbor, Brunswick and Portland, ME. There are connections via Greyhound to many other points in New England. There are connections at Burlington to Montreal.

Massachusetts Service

Plymouth & Brockton Street Railway Co (☎ 508-778-9767, W www.p-b.com), at Boston's Peter Pan Terminal, goes to Plymouth, Sagamore, Barnstable, Hyannis, Chatham and Provincetown on Cape Cod.

American Eagle (☎ 508-993-5040, 800-453-5040) runs between Boston and the ferry terminal that serves Bourne, Falmouth and Woods Hole on Cape Cod. They also have buses from Boston to New Bedford, Fall River, Providence, Hartford and New York.

New Hampshire Service

Concord Trailways (☎ 603-228-3300, 617-426-8080, 800-639-3317, W www.concord trailways.com), based in Concord, provides most of the bus service in the state, running from Boston up I-91 all the way to Littleton, and also via Laconia and Conway to Gorham and Berlin.

C&J Trailways (☎ 800-258-7111, W www .cjtrailways.com) serves Boston's Logan International Airport and South Station from Newburyport, MA, and Portsmouth, NH.

Maine Service

Concord Trailways (☎ 603-228-3300, 617-426-8080, 800-639-3317, Ⓦ www.concord trailways.com) serves coastal Maine, including Portland, Bangor and Camden. Greyhound and Vermont Transit also run buses within Maine.

TRAIN

Good news: Train service between Boston and Portland, ME, has resumed after a decades-long hiatus. The *Downeaster* makes three trips daily each direction. The ride lasts about 2½ hours; there are brief stops in Dover and Durham (University of New Hampshire), NH. Other Amtrak (☎ 800-872-7245, Ⓦ www.amtrak.com) routes in New England are covered in the Getting There & Away chapter.

Connecticut Commuter Rail Service's Shore Line East (☎ 800-255-7433, Ⓦ www .rideworks.com/rwsl.htm) connects the coastal towns between the New York border and New Haven. Metro-North trains (☎ 212-532-4900, 800-638-7646, Ⓦ www .mta.nyc.ny.us) make the 1½-hour run between New York City's Grand Central Station and New Haven. Other branches of Metro-North's service go north to Danbury, New Canaan and Waterbury.

In Boston, North Station serves the MBTA Commuter Rail trains (☎ 800-392-6100, Ⓦ www.mbta.com) that travel out of the city to the west and north, making stops at Concord, Rockport, Gloucester and Manchester. See Boston's Getting There & Away section for more information.

CAR & MOTORCYCLE

Yes, driving is the best way to see New England. But heads up: New England drivers, particularly around Boston and other cities, are aggressive, speedy and unpredictable. Traffic jams are common in urban areas.

Theft from cars is not uncommon, especially in urban areas. To avert theft, do not leave expensive items, such as purses, CDs, cameras, leather bags or even sunglasses, visibly lying around in your car. Tuck items under a seat or, even better, put them in the

---

Accidents Happen

It's important to know the appropriate protocol when involved in a 'fender-bender.'

- Remain at the scene of the accident until you have exchanged information with the police or the other driver(s) involved, especially if there has been substantial damage or personal injury. It may be necessary to move your car off the road for safety's sake, but leaving the scene of an accident is illegal.

- Call the police (and an ambulance, if needed) immediately, and give the operator as much specific information as possible (your location, any injuries etc). The emergency phone number is ☎ 911.

- Get the other driver's name, address, driver's license number, license plate number and insurance information. Be prepared to provide any documentation you have, such as your passport, international driving license and insurance documents.

- Tell your story to the police carefully. Refrain from answering any questions until you feel comfortable doing so (with a lawyer present, if need be). That's your right under the law. The only insurance information needed is the name of your insurance carrier and your policy number.

- If you've hit a large animal, such as a deer or moose, and it's badly injured, call the police to report it immediately. If your car is damaged in any way, report it to your insurance company or rental agency.

- If a police officer suspects that you are under the influence of alcohol, he or she may request that you submit to a breath-analysis test. If you do not, you may have your driving privileges suspended until a verdict is delivered in your court case.

- If you're driving a rental car, call the rental company promptly.

trunk and don't leave valuables in your car overnight.

Road Rules

Driving laws are different in each of the New England states. Generally, you must be 16 years of age to have a driver's license.

Speed Limits The maximum speed limit on most New England interstate highways is 65mph (but traffic is likely to be moving at more than 70mph). Some interstates have a limit of 55mph. On undivided highways, the speed limit will vary from 30 to 55mph. In cities and towns, it is usually 25 to 35mph, and even lower near schools and medical facilities.

Police enforce speed limits by patrolling in police cruisers and in unmarked cars. 'Radar traps' often are placed so that you won't see them until it's too late. The fine for a first speeding offense is $350 in Connecticut, and it's similarly expensive in other states.

Safety Regulations Most New England states require the use of safety belts, fining both the driver and the beltless passenger for riding unsecured.

In every state, laws require children under four years of age to be placed in child safety seats secured by a seat belt. Older children must wear safety belts. Child safety seats are available from car rental firms, sometimes at a small extra charge. In any car equipped with a front-passenger-seat air bag, no child should sit in the front passenger seat. Air bags, which inflate at 200mph, are designed to protect a full-size, full-weight adult and can seriously injure or kill a small or light person. Seat children in the back and buckle their seat belts for added safety.

Most US states have laws requiring motorcycle riders to wear helmets whenever they ride. In any case, use of a helmet is highly recommended.

Rental

You must be at least 21 years of age (and in some cases 25) and have a valid driver's license to rent an automobile. A major credit card is a practical necessity as well. Without one, you may have to put down a cash deposit of up to $2000.

Well-known national car rental companies such as Avis, Budget, Dollar, Hertz, National and Thrifty tend to have higher rates but more efficient service. Local companies are the cheapest. Quality, service and car condition are most variable among the local firms, which often specialize in rentals to people whose own cars are under repair.

National Companies Here are numbers, local to Boston and national, for some major rental companies:

Alamo	☎ 617-561-4100
	☎ 800-327-9633
Avis	☎ 617-534-1400
	☎ 800-331-1212
Budget	☎ 617-497-1800
	☎ 800-527-0700
Dollar	☎ 800-800-4000
Enterprise	☎ 617-262-8222
	☎ 800-736-8222
Hertz	☎ 617-338-1500
	☎ 800-654-3131
National	☎ 617-661-8747
	☎ 800-227-7368
Payless Car Rental	☎ 800-729-5377
Rent-A-Wreck	☎ 617-576-3700
	☎ 800-535-1391
Thrifty	☎ 617-569-6500
	☎ 800-367-2277

Local Companies Some local rental companies and automobile dealerships rent cars as well, often providing good service at cheaper rates than national companies. Most offer free delivery and pickup at the airport or a hotel, unlimited mileage and quality cars.

Before you rent from a local agency, you might want to check their Reliability Report at the Better Business Bureau (☎ 508-652-4800, Ⓦ www.bosbbb.org, 235 W Central St, Suite 1, Natick, MA 01760-3767) serving eastern Massachusetts, Maine and Vermont. All of the reports are available on the bureau's website. The following are a few choices:

Americar Auto Rental
(☎ 617-776-4640, 800-540-4642)
90 Highland Ave, Somerville, MA 02143

Cartemps
(☎ 617-924-7147)
40 Joy St, Somerville, MA 02143

Peter Fuller Rent-a-Car
(☎ 617-926-7511)
43 N Beacon St, Watertown, MA 02172

Insurance If you are planning to rent a vehicle, be sure to consider the added price of 'liability' insurance, which covers you in case you hit another person or damage someone's property, and 'collision' coverage, which pays for damage to the rental vehicle itself. Various insurance packages can add $10–16 a day to the cost of the overall rental.

You do not necessarily have to buy these inflated insurance packages. You are free to refuse them, but it would be risky to rent without insuring the vehicle in some way.

If you own a car registered in the USA, your own auto insurance may cover damage to a rental car. Check with your insurance agent to be sure. Some major credit card companies provide coverage for any vehicle rented with their cards. Check your credit card agreement to see what coverage is provided for rentals.

Note that in case of damage, a rental company might require that you not only pay for repairs, but also that you pay normal rental fees for all the time that the rental car is off the road for repairs. Your policy should cover this loss as well.

Saving Money The cheapest rates are for the smallest cars, from noon Thursday through noon Monday (or for an entire week or more), returning the vehicle to the place of rental (or at least to the city of rental).

Because of airport taxes, a rental is often more expensive if you pick it up at the airport. A taxi ride to the off-airport office of a local firm may result in a lower price.

You may be offered a choice of 'fuel plans': You can pick up and return the car with a full tank of fuel, or you can pay for the gas that's in the car and return it empty. The full tank is always the better choice. As it's virtually impossible to return a car empty of gas, you will end up turning over several gallons of fuel to the rental company, which will then try to sell it to the next renter.

RV Rental Most private campgrounds accommodate recreational vehicles, from camper vans to the largest motor homes. Rentals can cost anywhere from $75 to $125 per day, and as they are large vehicles, they use lots of fuel. In addition, parking them and sleeping in them overnight outside of campgrounds is not allowed in many areas (although the Wal-Mart chain often permits campers to stay in their lots).

Before you decide on an RV rental, read about camping under Accommodations in the Facts for the Visitor chapter. For further information, contact the Recreation Vehicle Rental Association (☎ 703-591-7130, 800-336-0355, fax 703-591-0734, ☒ www.rvra.org, 3930 University Drive, Fairfax, VA 22030). Companies that rent RVs can be found in the yellow pages of the phone book under 'Recreational Vehicles – Renting & Leasing,' 'Trailers – Camping & Travel' and 'Motor Homes – Renting & Leasing.'

Fuel

Gas stations are ubiquitous and many are open 24 hours a day. Small-town stations may be open only from 7am to 8pm or 9pm.

At some stations, you must pay before you pump; at others, you may pump before you pay. The more modern pumps have credit/debit card terminals built into them, so you can pay with plastic right at the pump. At more expensive, 'full service' stations, an attendant will pump your gas for you; no tip is expected.

Plan on spending $1.40 to $1.80 per US gallon, more around bigger cities and for higher-octane fuels. Leaded gasoline is not sold in the USA.

New England Road Distances

Boston bears the nickname 'The Hub' for a good reason: It is the center of New England and the axis from which most major roads branch off to the corners of the region. For drivers, it is convenient to see the driving distance to Boston from points around New England.

New York City	227
Montreal	332
Connecticut	
Hartford	108
Mystic	108
New Haven	114
Litchfield	136
Maine	
Ogunquit	70
Portland	108
Boothbay Harbor	167
Camden	195
Bar Harbor	269
Aroostook County	311
Massachusetts	
Gloucester	33
Worcester	40
Sturbridge	65
Hyannis	79
Springfield	87
Falmouth/Woods Hole	89
Provincetown	120
Lenox	138
New Hampshire	
Portsmouth	57
Concord	72
Laconia	95
North Conway	144
Rhode Island	
Providence	45
Newport	75
Vermont	
Woodstock	155
Montpelier	182
Stowe	205
Middlebury	210
Burlington	230

Road Maps

State tourism offices (see Tourist Offices in the Facts for the Visitor chapter) distribute detailed road maps, usually for free. You can buy maps (see Maps in Facts for the Visitor) in gas stations, newsstands, bookstores, convenience shops and drugstores for $2 to $4.

Parking

Municipalities control parking by signs on the street stating explicitly what may or may not be done. A yellow line or yellow-painted curb means that no parking is allowed there.

Breakdowns & Assistance

If your car breaks down and you need help, a few highways in New England have Motorist Aid Call Boxes with emergency telephones posted every few miles along the roadside. On other highways, raise the hood (bonnet) of your vehicle and/or tie a white cloth (such as a handkerchief) to the radio aerial to signal that you need help, and await a police patrol, which often comes within an hour.

The American Automobile Association (AAA; ☎ 800-222-4357, W www.aaa.com) provides battery charging, short-range towing, gasoline delivery and minor repairs at no charge to its members and to those of affiliated auto clubs. However, members are still liable for long-distance towing and for major repairs.

BICYCLE

Bicycling is a popular New England sport and means of transport on both city streets and country roads. Several of the larger cities have systems of bike paths that make bike travel much easier and more pleasant. Disused railroad rights-of-way have also been turned into bike trails. The Shining Sea Bicycle Path between Falmouth and Woods Hole is a prominent example.

Bicycle rentals are available in most New England cities, towns and resorts at reasonable prices (often $15 to $20 per day). Many rental shops are mentioned in this guide. For others, look in the yellow pages under 'Bicycles.'

For more on bicycling, see Activities in the Facts for the Visitor chapter.

HITCHHIKING

Don't! Hitchhiking is never entirely safe in any country in the world, and we don't recommend it. Travelers who decide to hitchhike should understand that they are taking a small but potentially serious risk – creeps and criminals might see a hitchhiker as easy prey. People who do choose to hitchhike will be safer if they travel in pairs and let someone know where they are planning to go.

WALKING

Walking and jogging are very popular in New England. Most cities and resort towns have sightseeing trails marked by signs and shown on brochure maps, and jogging/bike trails along rivers, lakes or the seashore. In the countryside, several trail systems offer interstate hikes. The Appalachian Trail, which stretches from Maine to Georgia, is the most famous, but Vermont's Long Trail is also impressive. See Activities in the Facts for the Visitor chapter for more on walking.

BOAT

Boat service is mostly local, and tends to be more for pleasure excursions than transportation. Ferries offer a few exceptions.

In Massachusetts, you can take a ferry between Boston and Provincetown (on Cape Cod). Ferries leave for Martha's Vineyard from Falmouth, Woods Hole, New Bedford and Hyannis. You can reach Nantucket from Woods Hole and Hyannis.

In Connecticut, ferries travel between Bridgeport and Port Jefferson (Long Island, New York); New London and Block Island; New London and Orient Point (Long Island) and New London and Fisher's Island (New York).

In Vermont, there's a ferry running from Burlington to New York state, traversing Lake Champlain.

In Maine, you can travel by ferry between Bar Harbor and Portland and Yarmouth, Nova Scotia; local ferries also service island communities like Monhegan, North Haven and Vinalhaven.

LOCAL TRANSPORTATION
Bus & Subway

City buses, and the T (the subway/underground system) in Boston, provide useful transportation within the larger cities and to some suburbs. Resort areas also tend to have regional bus lines. See relevant regional sections.

Taxi

Taxis are common in the largest cities. In smaller cities and towns, you will probably have to telephone a cab to pick you up. Taxi drivers are usually willing to take you just about anywhere if you can afford the fare. For longer trips, this may be about $2.50 or $3 per mile.

City taxis have fare meters, which usually begin at $2 and then add a certain price per mile. Extra charges may be added for extra passengers or an extra 50¢ charge may apply for driving after sundown. Town taxis may not have meters but will quote you the fare when you call. On top of cab fare, you should add a tip of about 15%.

For longer journeys that you plan in advance (such as trips to the airport), you may want to hire a limo instead (see below). The cost is about the same, the comfort and service better.

Limousine

A limousine (limo for short) is either an 'executive sedan' (a luxury car such as a Lincoln Town Car) or a 'stretch limo' (an executive sedan that has been lengthened to provide more interior room). A limo takes you anywhere you like at either a predetermined or an hourly fare. Executive sedans are often not much more expensive than regular taxis, though they cannot be hailed on the street and must be booked in advance.

Some shuttle van services (see below) use the term 'limo' or 'limousine' for their comfortable – but hardly luxurious – shuttle vans. Ask what you're getting when you reserve.

Shuttle Services

You can reserve a seat in a comfortable van or minibus that shuttles passengers between the airport and the city center or suburbs. Shuttles hold from eight to 25 passengers and may serve cities as much as an hour or two away from the airport. Shuttle fares are often less expensive than taxi fares. The shuttle may pick you up at your hotel (or other point), or you may have to meet it at a predetermined stop or station. For the telephone numbers of airport shuttle companies, look in the yellow pages under 'Airport Transportation Service.'

ORGANIZED TOURS
Local Tours

City tours by bus or 'trolley' (actually a bus disguised as a light-rail trolley) are popular in the major cities, tourist towns and resort areas. Most are useful for getting a look at the major sights, though the commentary is often bland.

There are some adventurous exceptions, such as the 'duck' tours in Boston, a 'duck' being a huge military amphibious vehicle that cruises the city streets, then glides into the river or bay for a nautical cruise.

Regional Tours

Regional tours are the way to go if you don't have time to make many different reservations or don't have a car. By far the most popular are the autumn foliage tours – they can be a good way to get out of the city. They are often fully booked early on and may be more expensive than normal tours.

In the mountain towns of Maine, New Hampshire and Vermont, tours by bicycle, canoe, raft and kayak are popular. See the Activities section of the Facts for the Visitor chapter for more information.

The company Destinnations (☎ 508-790-0577, 800-333-4667, fax 508-790-0565, Ⓦ www.destinnations.com, PO Box 1173, Osterville, MA 02655) tailors individual tours according to budget and interests. You could do a 'Cape and Island Hop,' a B&B & Inns tour, a factory outlet mall tour and more. A five-day seasonal value package could run as low as $500, giving you lodging at B&Bs around New England.

Boston

Most visitors to Boston come to the same opinion: This city is lively, attractive, interesting and educational, and, perhaps most importantly, it's manageable.

The city's liveliness comes in large part from the huge population of college-age residents. Having 60-odd colleges and universities in greater Boston means that there are always lots of sporting activities, cultural pursuits (cinema, theater, galleries, literary cafes, bars and musical performances for all tastes), shopping and nightlife.

Boston's attractiveness comes in part from its being a wealthy port and commercial city since colonial times. During the 19th century, Boston prided itself on being the 'Athens of America' because of its many beautiful buildings, its large population of literati, artists and educators, and its varied cultural institutions of the highest standard.

The Atlantic Ocean, Boston Harbor and the Charles and Mystic Rivers vary the cityscape and provide light and a sense of openness. Urban planning, including a long 'emerald necklace' of parks, gardens and verdant thoroughfares designed by the great American landscape architect Frederick Law Olmsted, brings a bit of the country right into the city.

Boston suffers a bit by being within a four-hour drive of New York City, the great American metropolis. When Boston's top professionals and artists reach the pinnacle of success, many of them take that final step up the career ladder to New York City. But Boston is cleaner, safer, friendlier and easier to negotiate. It is a city of vibrant neighborhoods, from working-class Charlestown to staid, old Beacon Hill to the Italian North End. And just 30 minutes outside of town, you'll find yourself among cornfields, gardens, beautiful colonial towns, scenic rivers and country roads ideal for cycling.

HISTORY

Called 'Trimountain' (for its three hills) in its earliest days, Boston took its permanent

Highlights

- Deciding for yourself who makes the best New England clam chowder
- Walking across the Longfellow Bridge from Kendall Square at dusk
- Finding the oldest tombstone in the Old Granary Burying Ground
- Hiking on the Boston Harbor Islands
- Taking an NPS guided tour of the Black History Trail
- Eating cannoli in the North End
- Checking out the street musicians in Harvard Square
- Catching some rays and the Boston Pops on the Esplanade
- Walking Beacon Hill's cobblestone streets after the gas street lanterns have come on

name from the English town of that name. The vanguard of English settlers, led by the Reverend William Blaxton, arrived in 1624 – less than four years after the Pilgrims arrived in nearby Plymouth.

The colony of Massachusetts Bay was established in 1630 when the elder John Winthrop, official representative of the Massachusetts Bay Company, took up residence. From the beginning, this was the center of Puritan culture and life in the New World.

Puritanism was intellectual and theocratic, and so the leading men and women of early Boston society were those who understood and followed Biblical law – and could explain in powerful rhetoric why they did. Thus it comes as no surprise that the Boston Public Latin School was established in 1635 (and continues as an elite public high school today). A year later, Harvard College (now Harvard University) was founded in neighboring Cambridge. By 1653, Boston had a public library, and by 1704 the 13 original colonies had their first newspaper, the *News-Letter*.

Though the New England coast had many excellent natural ports such as Essex, Plymouth, Providence and Salem, Boston was blessed by geography with the best of all. By the early 1700s it was well on its way to being what it remains today: New England's largest and most important city.

As the chief city in the region, it drew London's attention. When King George III and Parliament chose to burden the colonies with taxation without representation, the taxes were first levied in Boston. When resistance surfaced, it was in Boston. The Boston Massacre and the Boston Tea Party were significant turning points in the development of revolutionary sentiments, and the Battle of Bunker Hill solidified colonial resolve to declare independence from the British crown.

Following the Revolutionary War, Boston suffered economically as the British government cut off American ships' access to other ports in the British Empire. But as new trading relationships developed, Boston entered a commercial and industrial boom that lasted from the late 1700s until the mid-1800s. Fortunes were made in shipbuilding, maritime trade and manufacturing textiles and shoes. Chartered as a city in 1822, Boston's Beacon Hill soon was crowned with fine mansions built by the leading families, and Back Bay was filled in to make room for more.

These same prominent families also patronized arts and culture heavily. Though typically conservative and traditionalist in their general outlook, Bostonians were firm believers in American ideals of freedom. They were also supporters of the Underground Railroad and were for the abolition of slavery.

As the 19th century drew to a close, Boston's prominence was challenged by the growth of other port cities and the westward expansion of the national borders. New England's economic boom turned into a bust when the textile and shoe factories moved to cheaper labor markets in the South.

The Irish potato famine drove thousands of immigrants to the New World, especially Boston, changing the city's ethnic and economic profiles. The new arrivals were soon to be joined by immigrants from Italy, the Ottoman Empire and Portugal.

In the 20th century, however, Boston managed to remain an important port, becoming a prominent center for medical education, treatment and research, and the premiere university center in the USA. Many graduates have chosen to stay in the Boston area, which has helped to fuel booming local commerce in computer research, development and manufacturing.

At the beginning of the 21st century, Boston is poised to continue its preeminent contributions in the technology and financial services sectors.

ORIENTATION

For a city of its stature, Boston is quite small. The sights and activities of principal interest to travelers are contained within an area that's only about a mile wide by 3 miles long. It's bounded on the eastern edge by Boston Harbor and the Atlantic Ocean, on

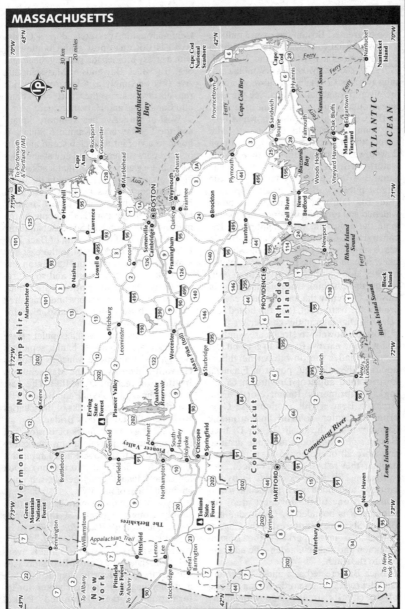

the north by the Charles River and Cambridge. Boston proper has almost 600,000 people; 'greater' Boston has over 3 million.

Most of what you'll want to see in Boston is easily accessible by MBTA (the 'T'; ☎ 617-222-3200, 800-392-6100, W www.mbta.com) subway trains. Convenient T subway stations are given throughout the text. See the Getting Around section for more information.

The Central Artery (also known as I-93, the John F Fitzgerald Expressway and simply 'the expressway') cuts right through downtown, separating the North End and waterfront from the rest of the city. The Central Artery, currently undergoing the largest public works construction project (the 'Big Dig') in US history, is being widened and rerouted underground to alleviate the persistent traffic nightmares. The construction, of course, is creating its own set of surface-artery issues, which will most likely remain until the project is completed in 2005. Don't let this deter you from visiting; do, though, think twice about driving in Boston. Currently the hardest-hit areas are around the waterfront. (See the boxed text 'The Big Dig,' later in this chapter.)

Boston's downtown streets are winding, one-way and narrow. Expect to get a bit lost as you wander the downtown neighborhoods of the small but powerful Financial District (and adjacent Downtown Crossing), the primarily Italian North End, Brahmin Beacon Hill, no-nonsense Government Center, colorful and aromatic Chinatown and the small Theater District. Boston's neighborhoods are quite distinct, and since all of the above areas abut one another, they're best explored on foot.

Beacon Hill, its brick streets lit by gas lanterns and lined with patrician townhouses, is one of the loveliest areas for strolling. It is bounded by Cambridge and Beacon Sts and extends west to the Charles River. Two large parks – the Boston Common and Public Garden – lie adjacent to it to the south.

Back Bay, created as a mid-19th-century landfill project, is more orderly than the rest of the city. Its streets, lined with lovely brownstones and flowering trees, are laid out east to west in alphabetical order: Arlington, Berkeley, Clarendon and so on to Hereford. Commonwealth Ave (referred to as 'Comm Ave') is Boston's most grand boulevard, with a grassy promenade running the length of it. The Back Bay ends at Massachusetts Ave (known simply as 'Mass Ave'), which runs northwest across the Charles River and into Cambridge and Harvard Square.

West of Mass Ave lies Kenmore Square and the Fenway area. Kenmore Square is home to a vibrant nightclub scene and lots of university students. The Fenway includes a 4-mile-long grassy byway that leads in one direction to an arboretum, and in the other to two important museums, the Museum of Fine Arts and the Isabella Stewart Gardner Museum. Fenway Park is the home of the much-loved Boston Red Sox baseball team.

The South End is just south of Back Bay. It lies between Berkeley St to the east and Mass Ave to the west, with Huntington and Shawmut Aves to the north and south, respectively. This newly gentrified area, thick with restaurants, artsy shops and renovated Victorian brownstones, is also nice for walking.

The Charles River, with a popular grassy esplanade along both its banks, separates Boston and Cambridge, which is home to Harvard University and the Massachusetts Institute of Technology (MIT). The best views of the Boston skyline and Beacon Hill are from the northern banks of the Charles River near the Longfellow Bridge.

You can get good maps of Boston and New England at just about any bookstore (see the boxed text 'Bookstores,' later in this chapter, for additional information). Look for Lonely Planet's manageable, full color laminated map of the city.

If you plan on doing more bicycling than simply along the banks of the Charles River, get *Boston's Bike Map* produced by Rubel BikeMaps (☎ 617-776-6567, W www.bikemaps.com). It costs $4.25 and is available from the Globe Corner Bookstore (see 'Bookstores') or directly from Rubel. See also Bicycling, later in this chapter, for information on their laminated 'Pocket Rides.'

The Cape Cod Rail Trail, a 26-mile bicycling path from Dennis to Wellfleet, MA

A small boat awaits its owner in an estuary near Plymouth, MA.

Colonists vs the British: an annual dawn reenactment of the Battle of Lexington Green

Cranberry harvest brightens the Cape Cod bogs.

Massachusetts Bay
Transportation Authority

LEGEND

Transit lines & stop

Commuter rail & station

Terminal station

Free interchange with other lines

Accessible Station

Parking

*Chinatown: Accessible only in Oak Grove direction

*Haymarket: Accessible for Orange line only.

*North Station: Accessible for Green line only.

*State: Not accessible for Blue line inbound.

Boston Harbor Ferry Services

① Lovejoy Wharf to Charlestown Navy Yard

② Lovejoy Wharf to U.S. Courthouse to World Trade Center

③ Long Wharf to Charlestown Navy Yard

④ Hingham Ship Yard to Rowes Wharf, Boston

⑤ Pemberton Point, Hull to Long Wharf, Boston

For schedule & fare information, call (617) 222-3200 or visit our website at www.mbta.com

© MBTA 2002

KIM GRANT

INFORMATION
Tourist Offices

Write or call the Greater Boston Convention and Visitors Bureau (GBCVB; ☎ 617-536-4100, 800-888-5515, ⓦ www.bostonusa.com, 2 Copley Place, Suite 105, Boston, MA 02116) in advance of your visit. They'll send an information packet.

Once in Boston, drop in at the GBCVB's year-round Visitor Information Center (Map 2; ☎ 617-426-3115, Tremont & West Sts) on Boston Common. You can pick up a subway and bus route map, as well as other maps and information. The center (which has public restrooms) is open 8:30am to 5pm daily (Sunday from 9am). ⓣ Red or Green Line to Park St.

In Back Bay, the GBCVB has an information booth in the center court of the Prudential Center mall, 800 Boylston St. It's open 9am to 6pm daily. ⓣ Green Line to Hynes/ICA or Green Line 'E' branch to Prudential.

The National Park Service Visitor Center (NPS; Map 2; ☎ 617-242-5642, 15 State St), across from the Old State House, has plenty of historical literature, a short slide show and free walking tours of the Freedom Trail (see the boxed text 'Walking Tours,' later in this chapter). The center is open 9am to 5pm daily. ⓣ Orange or Blue Line to State.

For city and statewide information, write to or stop in at the Massachusetts Office of Travel & Tourism (Map 2; ☎ 617-973-8500, 800-227-6277, ⓦ www.massvacation.com, State Transportation Building, 10 Park Plaza, Suite 4510, Boston, MA 02116). The office is open 9am to 5pm weekdays. ⓣ Green Line to Boylston.

In Cambridge, the Visitor Information Booth (Map 5; ☎ 617-441-2884, 800-862-5678, ⓦ www.cambridge-usa.org, Harvard Square) has plenty of detailed information on current Cambridge happenings and self-guided walking tours. The visitor information kiosk is staffed 9am to 5pm Monday through Saturday, 1pm to 5pm Sunday. ⓣ Red Line to Harvard.

The Appalachian Mountain Club Headquarters (the AMC; Map 2; ☎ 617-523-0636, ⓦ www.outdoors.org, 5 Joy St) is *the* resource for outdoor activities in Boston and throughout New England. AMC Headquarters, complete with bookstore, is open 8:30am to 5pm weekdays. ⓣ Red or Green Line to Park St.

Discount Tickets

The Boston Citypass, a discount attraction ticket program, provides a great value if you plan on going to most of the following sites: the Museum of Fine Arts, Museum of Science, New England Aquarium, Isabella Stewart Gardner Museum, John F Kennedy Library & Museum and Harvard's Museum of Natural History. The pass costs $28.25 for adults, $21.75 for seniors and $18 for children. (Purchased separately, the tickets would cost double that.) Once the pass is purchased, there's no more waiting in line. Passes may be purchased either prior to your arrival by calling Boston's Official Visitors Information Line (☎ 888-733-2678), or at the visitor information centers on Boston Common or within the Prudential Center or at any of the participating attractions.

Bostix (see 'Discount Tickets,' later in this chapter) offers a booklet for discounted admission to museums and attractions. It's well worth it.

Money

There are Cirrus and Plus ATM machines all around the city. To exchange foreign currency, head to any Fleet Boston bank (☎ 800-841-4000). Fleet branches include: 100 Federal St in Downtown; 6 Tremont St at Government Center; 557 Boylston St at Copley Square; 540 Comm Ave at Kenmore Square and the International Personal Banking office in Harvard Square (☎ 877-353-3939) at 1414 Mass Ave, Cambridge.

At the airport, you can exchange currency at the Travelex America (☎ 617-567-9881) kiosks in terminals B, C and E, which keep long hours timed with international arrivals and departures.

Post

The General Mail Facility (Map 2; ☎ 617-654-5326, 25 Dorchester Ave, Boston, MA 02205),

[continued on page 107]

MAP 1 METROPOLITAN BOSTON

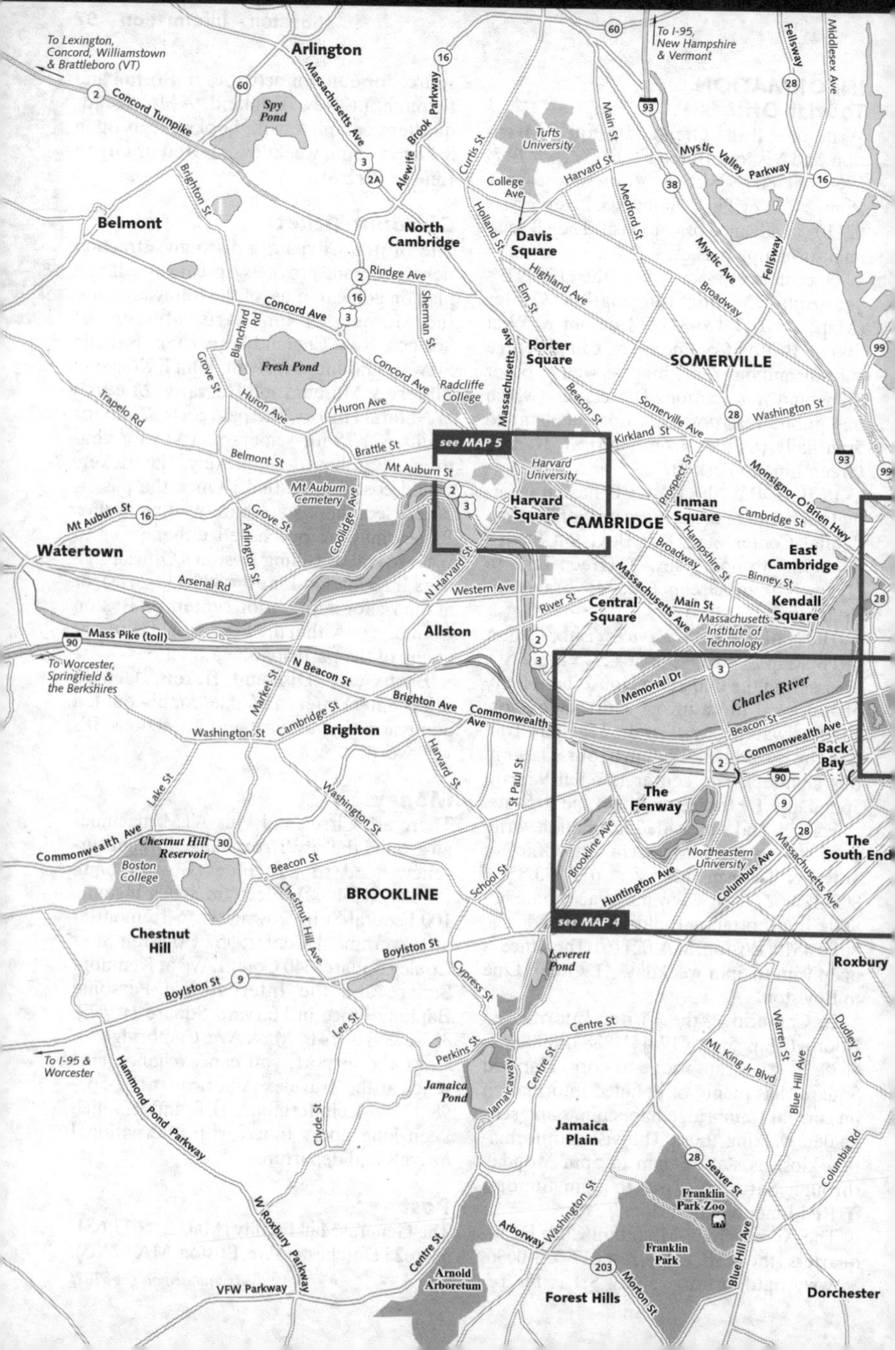

Everett

Revere

To I-95, Salem,
New Hampshire & Maine

To Marblehead & Salem

North Shore Rd

Revere Beach

60

1

107

16

99

Broadway

Revere Beach Parkway

Everett Ave

Chelsea

Broadway

Central Ave

Marginal St

Pearl St

Eastern Ave

Lee Burbank Hwy

Revere Beach Parkway

1A

Massachusetts
Bay

145

Saratoga St

Bennington St

145

William F McClellan Hwy

Meridian St

Winthrop

Pleasant St

Mystic River

Main St

Charlestown

1

1A

East Boston

Maverick St
Sumner St

Logan
International
Airport

Boston
Inner
Harbor

see MAP 2

The
North End

Beacon
Hill

3

Downtown

New Northern Ave

Ted
Williams
Tunnel
(toll)

Deer
Island

A St

D St

Summer St

Broadway

South
Boston

Ferry to Provincetown (seasonal)

Ferry to Gloucester & Salem (seasonal)

E First St

E Broadway

L St

Day Blvd

Pleasure
Bay

Boston Harbor

Dorchester Ave

Old Colony Ave

Boston St

Old Harbor

Spectacle
Island

Long
Island

Columbia
Point

Dorchester
Bay

Morrissey Blvd

UMass

Thompson
Island

Boston Harbor
Islands State Park

Rainsford
Island

Dorchester Ave

3

1

93

Southeast Expressway

To I-95, Plymouth,
Cape Cod &
Providence (RI)

Moon
Island

Squantum

0   1   2 km
0   .5   1 mile

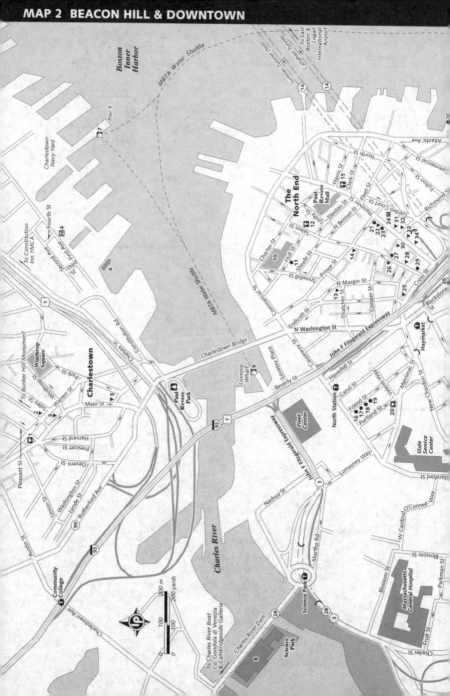

MAP 2 BEACON HILL & DOWNTOWN

Boston Inner Harbor

MBTA Water Shuttle

To East Boston & Logan International Airport

Callahan Tunnel (toll)

Sumner Tunnel (toll)

1A

1A

Atlantic Ave

Pier 4

Charlestown Navy Yard

27

The North End

Paul Revere Mall

North St

Harris St

Clark St

15

Commercial St

Fulton St

Richmond St

Hanover St

Snelling Court

N Bennet St

12

Charter St

St Stephen St

10

Hull St

11

Snowhill St

Prince St

Fleet St

14

N Margin St

Thatcher St

13

Cooper St

Endicott St

Commercial St

35

Blackstone

Cross St

25

26

27

28

29

30

31

32

33

34

21

22

23

24

Salem St

Charlestown Navy Yard

Fourth St

Third Ave

Second Ave

First Ave

4

6

To Constitution Inn YMCA

1

Charlestown

Winthrop Square

Bunker Hill/Monument

Soley St

Park St

Warren St

Main St

5

2

3

Harvard St

Prescott St

Pleasant St

Union St

Washington St

Lynde St

Rutherford Ave

99

Devens St

Austin St

93

Community College

Charlestown Ave

Constitution Rd

Chelsea St

Charlestown Bridge

Paul Revere Park

N Washington St

John F Fitzgerald Expressway

Haymarket

Beverly St

Lovejoy Place

Lovejoy Wharf

39

Canal St

North Station

Friend St

16

17

18

19

20

Portland St

Valenti Way

Merrimac St

New Chardon St

State Service Center

Staniford St

Fleet Center

Lomasney Way

Nashua St

3

Martha Rd

Science Park

93

1

Charles River

Charles River Dam

28

28

3

Science Park

8

W Cardinal O'Connell Way

Blossom St

Parkman St

Massachusetts General Hospital

Fruit St

Charles St

Blossom St

To Charles River Boat Co, Gondola di Venezia & Cambridgeside Galleria

0

100

200 m

100

200 yards

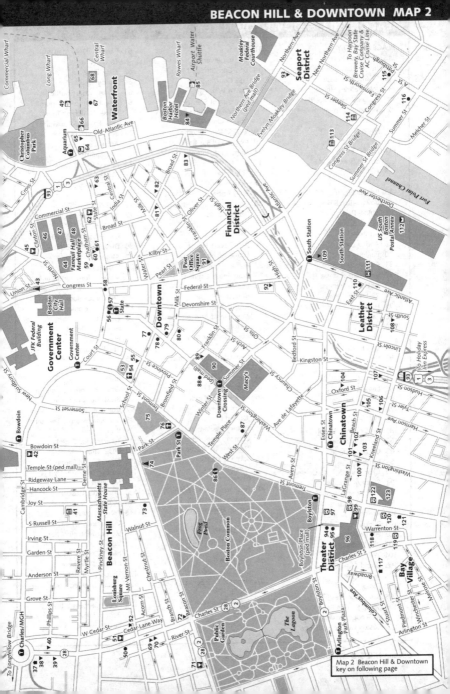

Commercial Wharf

Long Wharf

Central Wharf

68

Waterfront

67

Moakley Federal Courthouse

Northern Ave

Seaport District

New Northern Ave

93

To Harpoon Brewery, Bay State Cruise Company & AC Cruise Line

Airport Water Shuttle

85

Rowes Wharf

Boston Harbor Hotel

84

Northern Ave Bridge (ped mall)

Evelyn Moakley Bridge

Farnsworth St

Congress St

115

116

Summer St

114

Sleeper St

113

Congress St Bridge

Summer St Bridge

Melcher St

Fort Point Channel

Dorchester Ave

US South Boston Postal Annex

112

Christopher Columbus Park

Aquarium

65

64

Old Atlantic Ave

Cross St

93

1

3

63

State St

India St

Central St

82

81

Oliver St

High St

Broad St

83

Financial District

Atlantic Ave

South Station

109

South Station

111

Commercial St

46

47

48

Clinton St

Faneuil Hall Marketplace

44

45

59

60 61

Chatham St

58

Water St

Kilby St

Pearl St

Post Office Square

91

Congress St

North St

Union St

43

Boston City Hall

57

56

State

Downtown

Milk St

Federal St

Devonshire St

Milk St

Otis St

92

110

East St

Leather District

South St

Lincoln St

JFK Federal Building

Government Center

Government Center

77

78

80

79

Franklin St

89

90

Arch St

Summer St

Bedford St

Kingston St

108

107

93

1

3

Hudson St

To Holiday Inn Express

Court St

53

54

55

Province St

School St

Bromfield St

88

Winter St

Downtown Crossing

87

Macy's

Chauncy St

Washington St

Oxford St

104

105

106

Chinatown

Tyler St

New Sudbury St

Somerset St

75

76

Park St

Tremont St

Temple Place

West St

Avery St

Ave de Lafayette

Chinatown

101

102

103

Beach St

Kneeland St

Harrison Ave

122

123

Bowdoin

Bowdoin St

42

Temple St (ped mall)

Ridgeway Lane

Hancock St

Joy St

41

S Russell St

Irving St

Garden St

Anderson St

Grove St

Cambridge St

Derne St

74

Park St

86

Boston Common

73

Massachusetts State House

Beacon Hill

Walnut St

Pinckney St

Mt Vernon St

Chestnut St

Branch St

Frog Pond

Boylston St

Tremont St

LaGrange St

94

95

96

Theater District

97

98

99

100

118

119

120

121

Warrenton St

Boylston

Charles St

117

Bay Village

Broadway

Melrose St

Winchester St

Piedmont St

Stuart St

Charles/MGH

To Longfellow Bridge

Phillips St

W Cedar St

37

38

39

40

28

Cedar Lane Way

51

52

50

69

70

71

72

Charles St

28

2

River St

Acorn St

Louisburg Square

Revere St

Myrtle St

Beacon St

Arlington

28

Public Garden

The Lagoon

Arlington St

Columbus Ave

Park Plaza

Boylston St

2

Map 2 Beacon Hill & Downtown key on following page

BEACON HILL & DOWNTOWN KEY

PLACES TO STAY
16 Shawmut Inn
18 Irish Embassy Hostel
19 Beantown Hostel
37 John Jeffries House
117 Radisson Hotel Boston
121 Wyndham Tremont;
    The Roxy;
    Matrix

PLACES TO EAT
2 Sorelle Bakery Café
3 Figs
5 Olives
13 Regina Pizzeria
14 Bova Italian Bakery
22 Mike's Pastry
25 J Pace & Son
26 Terramia
28 Antico Forno
30 Pagliuca's
31 Galleria Umberto
32 Salumeria Italiana
33 La Piccola Venezia
34 Restaurant Bricco
35 Haymarket Farmer's Market
38 Savenor's
39 Panificio
40 King & I
52 Lala Rokh
55 Ben's Café
60 Bertucci's
63 Tsatsukichi
65 Legal Sea Foods
69 The Paramount
70 Figs
72 DeLuca's Market
81 Mr Dooley's Boston Tavern
82 Sultan's Kitchen
83 Country Life
84 Intrigue
89 Chacarero Chilean Cuisine
91 Post Office Cafe
92 Cosi Sandwich Shop
93 Barking Crab
100 Penang
101 Buddha's Delight
102 Hu Tieu Nam Vang
103 Pho Pasteur
104 Wai Wai
105 Grand Chau Chow
106 Apollo Grill
107 Ginza
108 Les Zygomates
109 South Station Food Court;
    JB Scoops; Rosie's Bakery;
    Boston Coffee Exchange

OTHER
1 Warren Tavern
4 USS Constitution Museum
6 USS Constitution
7 MBTA Water Shuttle
8 Museum of Science;
    Hayden Planetarium;
    Mugar Omni Theater
9 MBTA Water Shuttle
10 Copp's Hill Burying Ground
11 Narrowest House
12 Old North Church
15 St Stephen's Church
17 Hilton's Tent City;
    Polly Esther's
20 Commonwealth Fish &
    Beer Company
21 Caffe dello Sport
23 Caffè Vittoria
24 Paul Revere House;
    Pierce-Hichborn House
27 Polcari's Coffee
29 Dairy Fresh Candies
36 Bed & Breakfast Agency
    of Boston
41 African Meeting House;
    Museum of Afro-American
    History;
    Abiel Smith School
42 Red Hat
43 New England Holocaust
    Memorial
44 Faneuil Hall;
    Out of Left Field
45 Rack Billiard Club
46 North Market;
    Durgin Park
47 Quincy Market;
    Comedy Connection;
    Todd English Rustic Kitchen
48 South Market;
    KingFish Hall;
    Cheers
49 Ferry to Boston Harbor
    Islands State Park;
    Boston Harbor Cruises
50 Eugene Galleries
51 The Sevens
53 King's Chapel Burying
    Ground
54 King's Chapel
56 Old State House
57 National Park Service Visitor
    Center
58 Boston Massacre Site
59 Bostix

61 Rand McNally Map &
    Travel Store
62 Black Rose
64 Trolley Tours
66 MBTA Water Shuttle
67 New England Aquarium
    Whale-Watching Tours
68 New England Aquarium
71 Bull & Finch Pub
73 Appalachian Mountain Club
    Headquarters
74 Robert Gould Shaw
    Memorial
75 Old Granary Burying
    Ground
76 Park St Church
77 Boston Globe Store
78 Borders
79 Old South Meeting House
80 Dreams of Freedom
85 Airport Water Shuttle
86 Boston Park Rangers;
    Visitor Information Center;
    Trolley Tours
87 The Brattle Book Shop
88 Barnes & Noble
90 Filene's;
    Vacation Outlet;
    Filene's Basement
94 The Big Easy
95 La Boom
96 State Transportation
    Building; Massachusetts
    Office of Travel & Tourism;
    Brush Hill/Gray Line
97 Colonial Theater
98 Emerson Majestic Theater
99 Brew Moon
110 Travelers Aid Society
111 Bus Station
112 General Mail Facility
113 Boston Tea Party Ship &
    Museum
114 Children's Museum
115 Mobius
116 Fort Point Arts
    Community Gallery
118 Vapor Nightclub/Chaps;
    Venu;
    Nick's Comedy Stop
119 Charles Playhouse
120 Shubert Theater
122 Wilbur Theater;
    Aria
123 Wang Center for the
    Performing Arts;
    Boston Ballet

Beacon Hill & Downtown map on previous page

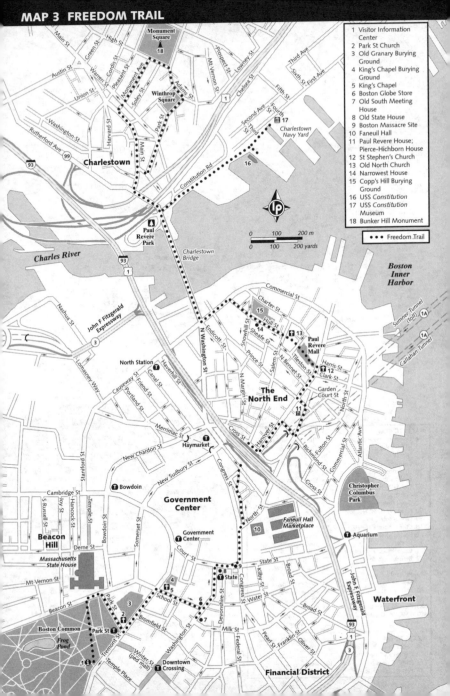

MAP 3 FREEDOM TRAIL

1 Visitor Information Center
2 Park St Church
3 Old Granary Burying Ground
4 King's Chapel Burying Ground
5 King's Chapel
6 Boston Globe Store
7 Old South Meeting House
8 Old State House
9 Boston Massacre Site
10 Faneuil Hall
11 Paul Revere House; Pierce-Hichborn House
12 St Stephen's Church
13 Old North Church
14 Narrowest House
15 Copp's Hill Burying Ground
16 USS Constitution
17 USS Constitution Museum
18 Bunker Hill Monument

••• Freedom Trail

MAP 4 BACK BAY, THE FENWAY & THE SOUTH END

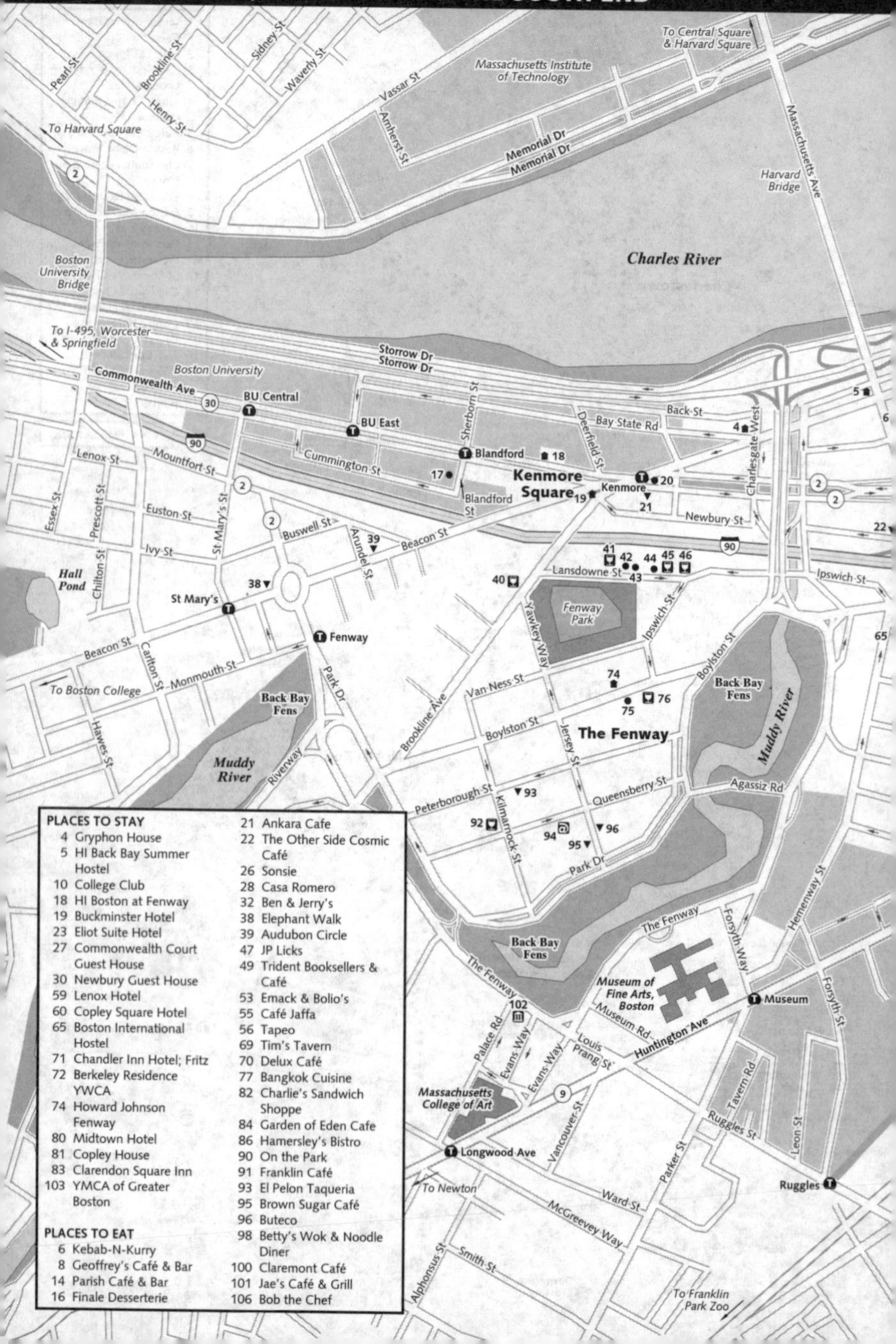

To Central Square & Harvard Square

Massachusetts Institute of Technology

Pearl St
Brookline St
Sidney St
Waverly St
Henry St
Vassar St
Amherst St
Memorial Dr
Memorial Dr
Harvard Bridge
Massachusetts Ave

To Harvard Square

Boston University Bridge

Charles River

To I-495, Worcester & Springfield

Storrow Dr
Storrow Dr

Commonwealth Ave

Boston University

BU Central

Back St

Charlesgate West

5
6

Lenox St
Prescott St
Essex St
Mountfort St
Cummington St
Sherborn St
Deerfield St
Bay State Rd
4

Blandford
18

17
Kenmore Square
19 Kenmore
20
21

Euston St
St Mary's St
Buswell St
Blandford
Newbury St
22

Ivy St
Chilton St
Arundel St
39
Beacon St

Hall Pond

38

St Mary's

Ipswich St

41 42 44 45 46
43
40
Lansdowne St
Fenway Park

65

Fenway

Park Dr

Back Bay Fens

Carlton St
Beacon St
Monmouth St
Haviland St

To Boston College

Van Ness St
74
75 76

Back Bay Fens

Muddy River

Back Bay Fens

Riverway

Muddy River

Boylston Ave
Boylston St

The Fenway

Jersey St

Agassiz Rd

Peterborough St
93

92
Kilmarnock St
94
95 96

Queensberry St

Park Dr

PLACES TO STAY
4 Gryphon House
5 HI Back Bay Summer Hostel
10 College Club
18 HI Boston at Fenway
19 Buckminster Hotel
23 Eliot Suite Hotel
27 Commonwealth Court Guest House
30 Newbury Guest House
59 Lenox Hotel
65 Copley Square Hotel
65 Boston International Hostel
71 Chandler Inn Hotel; Fritz
72 Berkeley Residence YWCA
74 Howard Johnson Fenway
80 Midtown Hotel
83 Clarendon Square Inn
103 YMCA of Greater Boston

PLACES TO EAT
6 Kebab-N-Kurry
8 Geoffrey's Café & Bar
14 Parish Café & Bar
16 Finale Desserterie

21 Ankara Cafe
22 The Other Side Cosmic Café
26 Sonsie
28 Casa Romero
32 Ben & Jerry's
38 Elephant Walk
39 Audubon Circle
47 JP Licks
49 Trident Booksellers & Café
53 Emack & Bolio's
55 Café Jaffa
56 Tapeo
69 Tim's Tavern
70 Delux Café
77 Bangkok Cuisine
82 Charlie's Sandwich Shoppe
84 Garden of Eden Cafe
86 Hamersley's Bistro
90 On the Park
91 Franklin Café
95 El Pelon Taqueria
95 Brown Sugar Café
96 Buteco
98 Betty's Wok & Noodle Diner
100 Claremont Café
101 Jae's Café & Grill
106 Bob the Chef

The Fenway
Forsyth Way
Hemenway St
Forsyth St

Museum of Fine Arts, Boston

102
Palace Rd
Evans Way
Louis Prang St
Museum Rd
Huntington Ave
Museum

Massachusetts College of Art

Tavern Rd

Longwood Ave

9

Vancouver St
Parker St
Ruggles St
Leon St

To Newton

Ward St

McGreevey Way

Ruggles

Alphonsus St
Smith St

To Franklin Park Zoo

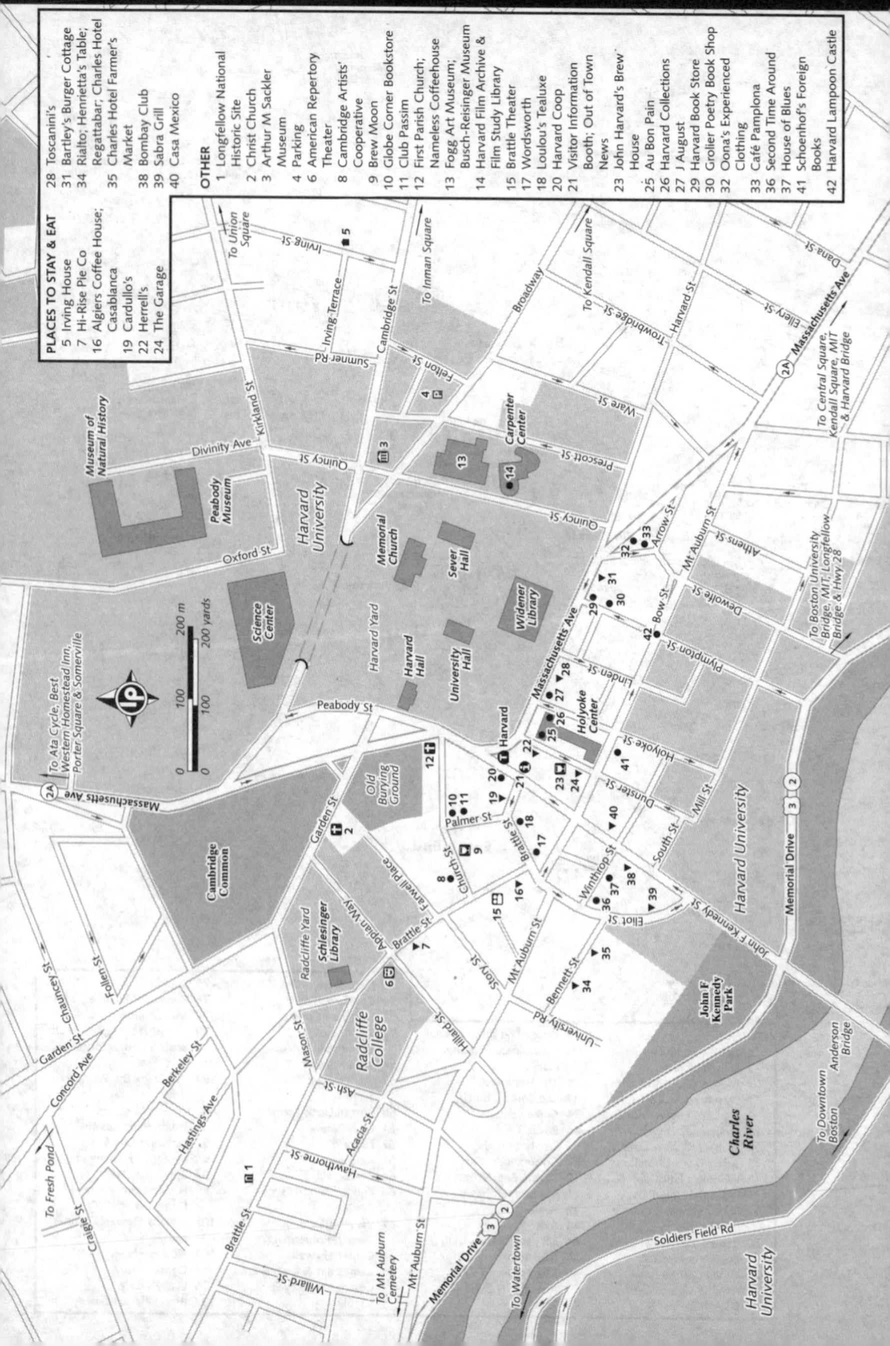
PLACES TO STAY & EAT
5 Irving House
7 Hi-Rise Pie Co
16 Algiers Coffee House; Casablanca
19 Cardullo's
22 Herrell's
24 The Garage
28 Toscanini's
31 Bartley's Burger Cottage
34 Rialto; Henrietta's Table; Regattabar; Charles Hotel
35 Charles Hotel Farmer's Market
38 Bombay Club
39 Sabra Grill
40 Casa Mexico
OTHER
1 Longfellow National Historic Site
2 Christ Church
3 Arthur M Sackler Museum
4 Parking
6 American Repertory Theater
8 Cambridge Artists' Cooperative
9 Brew Moon
10 Globe Corner Bookstore
11 Club Passim
12 First Parish Church; Nameless Coffeehouse
13 Fogg Art Museum; Busch-Reisinger Museum
14 Harvard Film Archive & Film Study Library
15 Brattle Theater
17 Wordsworth
18 Loulou's Tealuxe
20 Harvard Coop
21 Visitor Information Booth; Out of Town News
23 John Harvard's Brew House
25 Au Bon Pain
26 Harvard Collections
27 J August
29 Harvard Book Store
30 Grolier Poetry Book Shop
32 Oona's Experienced Clothing
33 Café Pamplona
36 Second Time Around
37 House of Blues
41 Schoenhof's Foreign Books
42 Harvard Lampoon Castle
0 100 200 m
0 100 200 yards
To Ata Cycle, Best Western Homestead Inn, Porter Square & Somerville
Museum of Natural History
Peabody Museum
Science Center
Harvard University
Harvard Yard
Memorial Church
Sever Hall
Harvard Hall
University Hall
Widener Library
Carpenter Center
Holyoke Center
Cambridge Common
Old Burying Ground
Radcliffe Yard
Schlesinger Library
Radcliffe College
John F Kennedy Park
Charles River
To Union Square
To Inman Square
To Kendall Square
To Central Square, Kendall Square, MIT & Harvard Bridge
To Boston University Bridge, MIT, Longfellow Bridge & Hwy 28
To Downtown Boston
Anderson Bridge
To Watertown
To Mt Auburn Cemetery
To Fresh Pond
Massachusetts Ave
Memorial Drive
Soldiers Field Rd
John F Kennedy St
Brattle St
Mt Auburn St
Garden St
Concord Ave
Harvard

[continued from page 97]
Boston's 24-hour main post office, is just one block southeast of South Station at Fort Point. The friendly folks on the graveyard shift might give you cookies. Ⓣ Red Line to South Station.

Branch post offices include the following:

Back Bay
(☎ 617-267-8162, 800 Boylston St), in the Prudential Center

Beacon Hill
(☎ 617-723-1951, 136 Charles St)

Cambridge
(☎ 617-876-0620, 770 Mass Ave, Central Square)

Faneuil Hall Marketplace
(☎ 617-723-1791, in the original Faneuil Hall), no packages

Financial District
(☎ 617-720-5314, 90 Devonshire St, Post Office Square)

North End
(☎ 617-723-5134, 217 Hanover St)

Most are open 7:30am or 8am to 5pm or 6pm weekdays and on Saturday morning.

All general delivery (poste restante) mail must be sent to the main post office; branch offices cannot accept it.

Email & Internet Access

You can access the Internet (free, for 15 minutes) at the Boston Public Library (Map 4; ☎ 617-536-5400, 666 Boylston St), at Exeter St. Or get a visitor courtesy card at the circulation desk and sign up for one hour of free terminal time. Arrive at 9am when the library opens; otherwise you'll be waiting for a long time to get online. Copy shops like Kinko's have Internet access; look for them in the yellow pages. Or head to Designs for Living (Map 4; ☎ 617-536-6150, 52 Queensberry St), a little cafe where you can surf for $2 for 15 minutes, $8 per hour; Ⓣ Green Line 'D' branch to Fenway or 'E' branch to Museum.

Internet Resources

Websites are listed in this book for places to stay, information bureaus and in newspapers, which are particularly useful in checking up-to-the-minute entertainment offerings.

Travel Agencies

Budget travel specialists include the Council on International Educational Exchange's Council Travel (CIEE; Map 4; ☎ 617-266-1926, 800-226-8624, Ⓦ www.ciee.org, 273 Newbury St). They can satisfy just about every travel-related need that arises. The Council's offices are open 10am to 6pm Monday to Saturday, until 8pm Thursday. Ⓣ Green Line to Hynes/ICA.

Other CIEE offices include one in Harvard Square (12 Eliot St, 2nd floor), which is open 10am to 6pm Monday to Saturday; and on the MIT campus at Stratton Student Center (84 Mass Ave), open 9:30am to 5pm Monday to Friday.

The Vacation Outlet agency at Filene's Basement (Map 2; ☎ 617-267-8100, 800-527-8646, Ⓦ www.vacationoutlet.com, 426 Washington St at Downtown Crossing) offers lots of last-minute deals that tour consolidators could not sell. The idea is that they'd rather sell the package at the last minute for a pretty nominal fee than take a complete loss on it. Their loss could be your gain. Ⓣ Red or Orange Line to Downtown Crossing.

Libraries

The venerable Boston Public Library (Map 4; ☎ 617-536-5400, Ⓦ www.bpl.org, 666 Boylston St) is the country's oldest free city library; it dates back to 1852. Although more than two million people visit annually, most unfortunately bypass the walled-in tranquil garden courtyard, which has a reflecting pool and trees, where you can read when the library is open. Don't make the same mistake as most people. Hours are 9am to 9pm Monday to Thursday, 9am to 5pm Friday and Saturday, 1pm to 5pm Sunday. Ⓣ Green Line to Copley.

Also see the John F Kennedy Library & Museum, which has an Ernest Hemingway archive, later in this chapter.

Newspapers & Magazines

The major daily newspapers include *The Boston Globe* (Ⓦ www.boston.com), which publishes an extensive and useful Calendar section every Thursday, and the competing *Boston Herald* (Ⓦ www.bostonherald.com),

Bookstores

Boston and Cambridge are a book lover's paradise. In fact, the Harvard Square Visitor Information Booth has a free brochure of Harvard Square's abundant bookstores, and the yellow pages lists more than 100. Here are some worth searching out.

Boston

The **Avenue Victor Hugo Bookshop** (Map 4; ☎ 617-266-7746, 339 Newbury St) is one of Boston's best used bookstores. You could browse an entire day away here. Ⓣ Green Line to Hynes/ICA.

Barnes & Noble at Boston University (Map 4; ☎ 617-267-8484, 660 Beacon St) is one of New England's biggest, with three floors of books. Ⓣ Green Line to Kenmore.

Barnes & Noble Downtown (Map 2; ☎ 617-426-5502, 395 Washington St) offers discounts on hardcover books and *New York Times* bestsellers. Ⓣ Orange or Red Line to Downtown Crossing.

Borders (Map 2; ☎ 617-557-7188, 10–24 School St) is well-stocked; the espresso bar helps maintain a browsing buzz . Ⓣ Red or Green Line to Park St.

The **Brattle Book Shop** (Map 2; ☎ 617-542-0210, 9 West St) is a treasure, crammed with out-of-print, rare and first-edition books. Ⓣ Red or Green Line to Park St.

Brookline Booksmith (☎ 617-566-6660, 279 Harvard St) is an excellent general bookstore with informed service. Ⓣ Green Line 'C' branch to Coolidge Corner.

In business since the 1930s, the outdoor **Copley Square News** (Map 4; no ☎, cnr Boylston St & Dartmouth Sts) sells magazines and foreign-language periodicals. Ⓣ Green Line to Copley.

An excellent choice for travel guides and maps is the **Rand McNally Map & Travel Store** (Map 2; ☎ 617-720-1125, 84 State St), near Faneuil Hall Marketplace. Ⓣ Orange or Blue Line to State.

Trident Booksellers & Café (Map 4; ☎ 617-267-8688, 338 Newbury St) specializes in New Age titles. Ⓣ Green Line to Hynes/ICA.

We Think the World of You (Map 4; ☎ 617-574-5000, 540 Tremont St) specializes in gay titles. Ⓣ Orange Line to Back Bay.

---

which has its own Scene section published every Friday.

The *Boston Phoenix* (Ⓦ www.boston phoenix.com), the 'alternative' paper that focuses on arts and entertainment, is published weekly. The sassy, biweekly *Improper Bostonian* and *Stuff @ Night* (Ⓦ www .stuffatnight.com) are free from sidewalk dispenser boxes. *Boston Magazine* (Ⓦ www .bostonmagazine.com) is the city's monthly. *Bay Windows* serves the gay and lesbian community.

Universities

The greater Boston area has many, many college campuses – too many to mention here. Cultural and sporting events are often open to the public, and this brief listing should help you get further information (see also Spectator Sports, later in this

chapter). For the Berklee College of Music, see the Entertainment section.

Harvard University (Map 5; ☎ 617-495-1000), founded in 1636, stretches for a few blocks east and west along Mass Ave from the Harvard T stop in Cambridge. You'll find the main gates leading to Harvard Yard across the street from the Red Line T stop in Cambridge. Free hour-long historical tours of the Yard run during the school year at 10am and 2pm Monday to Friday and at 2pm Saturday from the information office (☎ 617-495-1573, Holyoke Center, 1350 Mass Ave). There are additional tours June through August. Ⓣ Red Line to Harvard.

The Massachusetts Institute of Technology (MIT; ☎ 617-253-4795), a world-renowned scientific mecca founded in 1861, is also spread out along Mass Ave in Cambridge, about 1½ miles east of Harvard Square.

Bookstores

Cambridge

Unless otherwise noted, all stores are reached via ⓣ Red Line to Harvard.

Known simply as 'the Coop,' the **Harvard Cooperative Society** (Map 5; ☎ 617-499-2000, 1400 Mass Ave) has three floors of books, music and every other 'essential' thing a student could need. Anyone can buy just about anything emblazoned with the Harvard logo.

Specializing in travel, the outstanding **Globe Corner Bookstore** (Map 5; ☎ 617-497-6277, ⓦ www.globecorner.com, 49 Palmer St) also carries hundreds of specialty maps, including topographical maps of New England. (For more topos, check out the AMC Headquarters, listed under Information.)

The **Grolier Poetry Bookshop** (Map 5; ☎ 617-547-4648, 6 Plympton St) is simply one of the most famous poetry bookstores in the USA.

The **Harvard Book Store** (Map 5; ☎ 617-661-1515, 1256 Mass Ave), not related to the Coop, is considered the premiere intellectual bookstore on the Square.

New Words Women's Bookstore (☎ 617-876-5310, 186 Hampshire St), in Inman Square, is devoted to books by, for and about women. ⓣ Red Line to Central and then a 10-minute walk.

Out of Town News (Map 5; ☎ 617-354-7777, Harvard Square) is no ordinary newsstand; in fact, it's a National Historic Landmark, selling papers from virtually every major US city, as well as from dozens of cities around the world.

Schoenhof's Foreign Books (Map 5; ☎ 617-547-8855, 76A Mt Auburn St) is a national center for foreign-language materials, books and dictionaries.

Wordsworth, a large general bookstore, has three locations in Harvard Square within a block of one another on Brattle St: the original Wordsworth (Map 5; ☎ 617-354-5201, 30 Brattle St); Wordsworth Abridged (☎ 617-354-5277, 5 Brattle St); and Curious George Goes to Wordsworth (☎ 617-498-0062, 1 John F Kennedy St).

Free tours of the campus are given at 10am and 2pm Monday to Friday from 77 Mass Ave, Building 7 lobby. The number of excellent museums and sheer amount of public art on the campus are impressive. ⓣ Red Line to Kendall.

Northeastern University (Map 4; ☎ 617-373-2000, 360 Huntington Ave) boasts one of the country's largest work-study cooperative programs. ⓣ Green Line 'E' branch to Northeastern.

Boston University (BU; Map 4; ☎ 617-353-2000, 617-353-2169, 881 Comm Ave), west of Kenmore Square, enrolls about 30,000 graduate and undergraduate students, and has a huge campus and popular sports teams. ⓣ Green Line 'B' branch to BU East, BU Central or BU West.

The University of Massachusetts, Boston (UMass; ☎ 617-287-5000, 100 Morrissey Blvd), at Columbia Point on Dorchester Bay, is a commuter campus adjacent to the John F Kennedy Library & Museum. ⓣ Red Line to JFK/UMass, then take a quick shuttle bus.

Other well-established colleges and universities on the city's fringe include the following.

Boston College (BC; ☎ 617-552-8000, 140 Comm Ave/MA 30, Chestnut Hill) boasts a large green campus, Gothic towers, stained glass, a good art museum and excellent Irish and Catholic ephemera collections in the library. Its basketball and football teams are usually high in national rankings. This is also the nation's largest Jesuit community. ⓣ Green Line 'B' branch to the last stop.

Wellesley College (☎ 781-283-1000, 106 Central St, Wellesley), a Seven Sisters women's college, also sports a hilly, wooded campus and the excellent Davis Museum & Cultural Center. To get to Wellesley, take the MBTA commuter rail plus a 10-minute walk, or drive MA 16 to MA 135.

Tufts University (☎ 617-628-5000, College Ave, Medford) has about 8500 students and a good basketball team. Ⓣ Red Line to Davis Square, then a free Tufts shuttle across from the station takes you directly to the campus.

Brandeis University (☎ 781-736-2000, South St, Waltham), a short train ride out of Boston, is a small campus that includes the Rose Art Museum, specializing in New England art. Take the MBTA commuter rail from North Station to the Brandeis/Roberts stop.

Massachusetts College of Art (Map 4; ☎ 617-232-1555, Huntington Ave) hosts regular exhibitions at its galleries. The main gallery (621 Huntington Ave) is open 10am to 6pm Monday to Friday, 10am to 5pm Saturday. Ⓣ Green Line 'E' branch to Longwood Ave.

Cultural Centers
The French Library (Map 4; ☎ 617-266-4351, 53 Marlborough St), founded in 1946, sponsors regular lectures on travel, cooking and all things French; receptions often follow. The library sponsors an annual Bastille Day celebration (July 14) during which Marlborough St is closed off. Hours are 10am to 8pm Tuesday to Thursday, 10am to 5pm Friday and Saturday. Ⓣ Green Line to Arlington.

The Goethe Institute (Map 4; ☎ 617-262-6050, 170 Beacon St) sponsors a cultural program of German events; its reference library is also well stocked with books, tapes and periodicals. They also offer evening classes. Hours are 10am to 5:30pm Monday to Friday. Ⓣ Green Line to Arlington.

Medical Services
Massachusetts General Hospital (MGH; Map 2; ☎ 617-726-2000) is arguably the city's biggest and best. They can often refer you to smaller clinics and crisis hotlines. MGH's traveler's clinic (☎ 617-724-1934) offers immunization services. Ⓣ Red Line to Charles/MGH.

CVS (☎ 617-876-5519), in the Porter Square shopping mall on Mass Ave, Cambridge, is the area's only 24-hour pharmacy. Ⓣ Red Line to Porter.

Emergency
The police, ambulances and fire department can be reached by dialing ☎ 911.

Travelers Aid Society (Map 2; ☎ 617-542-7286, 17 East St), just off Atlantic Ave, across from South Station, is a nonprofit agency that helps stranded travelers. From stolen wallets to practical information to transportation assistance to 'bedless in Boston,' Travelers Aid is there to assist (8:30am to 5pm weekdays). They also have a booth at the information desk in South Station (☎ 617-737-2880), open 9am to 5pm weekends. The Logan Airport 'Terminal E' Travelers Aid (☎ 617-567-5385) is open noon to 9pm daily and is staffed by volunteers.

Dangers & Annoyances
As with most big US cities, there are rundown sections of Boston in which crime is a problem. We have not listed any things to see or do in these sections. Avoid parks (such as Boston Common) after dark if there are not many other people around. The same goes for unfamiliar, unpeopled streets and subway stations at night. The Back Bay Fens, a gay cruising area, can be dangerous for gays at night. Lastly, you might find a few vestiges of 'skankiness' near the Chinatown subway station, along Washington and Essex Sts, where one or two X-rated shops are hanging on by the thread of a G-string.

BEACON HILL & DOWNTOWN (MAP 2)
Established in 1634, the 50-acre **Boston Common**, bordered by Beacon, Tremont and Charles Sts, is the country's oldest public park. During the Revolutionary War, British troops camped here, and until 1830 the Common was used for cattle-grazing. Although there is still a grazing ordinance on the books, today the Common serves picnickers, sunbathers and people-watchers. Colorful characters are often heard spouting off from atop a soapbox near the corner

of Tremont and Park Sts. Ⓣ Red or Green Line to Park St.

The **Public Garden**, a 24-acre botanical oasis of cultivated flower beds, clipped grass, ancient trees and a tranquil lagoon, is adjacent to the Boston Common. You can't picnic on the lawn like you can on the Common, but there are plenty of benches. Pick one in front of the Swan Boats, pedal-powered boats that ferry children and adults around the pond while ducks swim alongside squawking for bread crumbs. A bit tame for modern families accustomed to fast-paced video games, rides nonetheless cost $2 for adults and $1 for children. Ⓣ Green Line to Arlington.

Beacon Hill is Boston's most handsome and affluent residential neighborhood. Adjacent to Boston Common and the Public Garden, Beacon Hill extends northward to Cambridge St and west to the Charles River. Charles St, which divides the flat and hilly parts of the neighborhood, is lined with shops and eateries. Distinguished 19th-century brick townhouses, lavender windowpanes, gas lanterns, little courtyards, rooftop gardens and picturesque narrow alleyways – this is the stuff of Beacon Hill. Ⓣ Red Line to Charles/MGH, Blue Line to Bowdoin, Red or Green Line to Park St.

Seek out the cobblestone **Acorn St** (the city's often-photographed and narrowest street), **Mt Vernon** and **Pinckney Sts** (two of Beacon Hill's prettiest) and **Louisburg Square** (pronounced Lewis-burg), an elegant cluster of multimillion-dollar homes that face a private park owned by the square's residents. Beacon Hill was never the exclusive domain of blue-blood Brahmins, though. Waves of immigrants, and especially African Americans, free from slavery, settled here in the 19th century.

The **Museum of Afro-American History** (☎ 617-725-0022, 46 Joy St; adult/child $3/1; open 11am-5pm Tues-Sat & 1pm-5pm Sun) has two adjacent buildings. Abolitionists Frederick Douglass and William Lloyd Garrison delivered some passionate speeches from the **African Meeting House**, the country's oldest African American meeting house. The house may be closed for restora-

tion when you visit (the reopening date was uncertain at press time). Next door, the **Abiel Smith School** housed the country's first primary school for blacks. The best place to learn about Beacon Hill's African American roots, its permanent exhibits include an extensive library and interactive computer kiosks.

High atop Beacon Hill, the idiosyncrasies of Massachusetts government and politics are played out like a sporting match within the golden-domed **Massachusetts State House** (☎ 617-727-3676, Beacon & Bowdoin

Sts; admission free; open 9am-5pm daily). The commanding state capitol building was designed by Boston's beloved Charles Bulfinch and completed in 1798. A free 40-minute tour (10am to 3:30pm Monday to Saturday) includes a discussion of the history, art works, architecture and political personalities as well as a visit to the legislative chambers when it's in session. Reservations are recommended. Ⓣ Red or Green Line to Park St.

Across the street, the **Robert Gould Shaw Memorial**, an extraordinary bas-relief at Beacon and Park Sts, honors the nation's first all-black Civil War regiment, which was depicted in the 1989 film *Glory*. The soldiers, led by Shaw (the son of a notable white family in Boston), refused their $10 monthly stipend for two years until Congress upped it to $13, the amount white regiments were paid.

One block south on Park St, the **Park St Church** (☎ 617-523-3383, cnr Tremont St; open 8:30am-3:30pm Tues-Sat July & Aug) is noted for its graceful and narrow 200-foot steeple. Duck inside to see what musical program is being offered; the schedule is irregular but full. In 1829, William Lloyd Garrison railed against slavery from the church's pulpit. And on Independence Day in 1895, Katherine Lee Bates' hymn *America the Beautiful* was first sung.

The adjacent **Old Granary Burying Ground** *(Tremont St)* dates to 1660 and is crammed with expressive headstone carvings. Revolutionary heroes including Paul Revere, Samuel Adams and John Hancock are buried here, as are Crispus Attucks (the freed slave who died in the Boston Massacre when British soldiers fired into a group of angry Bostonians in 1770), Benjamin Franklin's parents (he's buried in Philadelphia) and Peter Faneuil (of Faneuil Hall fame).

Continue north to the **King's Chapel & King's Chapel Burying Ground** (☎ 617-523-1749, 58 Tremont St; church open 10am-4pm Mon & Thur-Sat, 1pm-4pm Tues & Wed mid-June–early Sept; 10am-4pm Sat rest of year). Bostonians were not pleased at all when the original Anglican church was

erected in 1688. (Remember, it was the Anglicans – the Church of England – whom the Puritans were fleeing.) The granite church standing today was built in 1754 around the original wooden structure. Then the wooden church was taken apart and tossed out the windows. If the church seems to be missing something, it is: Building funds ran out before a spire could be added. The church houses the largest bell ever made by Paul Revere as well as a lovely sounding organ. An eclectic line-up of recitals is given at 12:15pm Tuesday year-round. The adjacent burying ground contains the grave of John Winthrop, the first governor of the fledgling Massachusetts Bay Colony. Ⓣ Red or Green Line to Park St.

Head south on School St to ponder the **Boston Globe Store** (☎ 617-367-4000, 1 School St). Now a monument pantheon to retailing, this circa-1718 building once housed Boston's most illustrious publishing company. As the Old Corner Bookstore, run by Ticknor & Fields (a set of names later used as a publisher's imprint), it produced books by Thoreau, Emerson, Hawthorne, Whittier, Longfellow and Harriet Beecher Stowe. The 19th-century authors often held lively discussions and meetings here. Today you can purchase front-page reprints of historical events covered in the *Boston Globe*. Ⓣ Blue or Orange Line to State, or Red or Orange Line to Downtown Crossing.

Diagonally across the street, **Old South Meeting House** (☎ 617-482-6439, 310 Washington St; adult/senior & student/child $3/2.50/1; open 9:30am-5pm daily Apr-Oct, 10am-4pm daily Nov-Mar) is graceful and traditional. After one typically feisty town meeting in this brick-and-wood meeting-house, colonists decided to protest the British tea taxation (see the Waterfront section, later).

Dreams of Freedom (☎ 617-338-6022, 1 Milk St; adult/senior/child $7.50/6.50/3.50; open 10am-6pm daily Apr-Dec, 10am-5pm Tues-Sun Jan-Mar) This new museum chronicles the history of immigrants from the Puritans in 1620 to the waves of Irish and Italians and more recent Vietnamese and Portuguese. The intimate gallery space personalizes the emotional stories with interactive and high-tech exhibits.

Downtown Crossing, the pedestrian-only shopping district near the intersection of Washington, Summer and Winter Sts, bustles with pushcart vendors and street musicians. Thanks to a high volume of nearby office workers, plenty of places offer inexpensive, quick lunches. Ⓣ Orange or Red Line to Downtown Crossing.

The rest of downtown and the **Financial District** lie east of Tremont St and stretch all the way to the waterfront (a 10-minute walk). Bounded by State St to the north and Essex St to the south, this area was once the domain of cows. Their well-trodden 17th- and 18th-century paths eventually gave rise to the maze of streets occupied by today's high rises, a distinctive blend of modern and historic architecture. To get a feel for Boston's weekday pace head to **Post Office Square** (Congress, Pearl and Franklin Sts). This postage stamp–size oasis, built atop an underground parking garage, boasts a small cafe (see Places to Eat, later), a fountain and live summertime lunch music.

From Post Office Square, head north on Congress St to State St for the **Old State House** (☎ 617-720-3290, 206 Washington St; adult/senior & student/child $3/2/1; open 9am-5pm daily). Dating to 1713 but dwarfed by encroaching modern structures today, this building is perhaps best known for its balcony, where the Declaration of Independence was first read to Bostonians in 1776. Operated by the Bostonian Society, the museum is definitely worth a visit since it houses Revolutionary memorabilia pertinent to Boston's (and thus the nation's) history. The NPS Visitor Center (see Information, earlier in this chapter) is across the street on State St. Ⓣ Orange or Blue Line to State.

Encircled by cobblestones, the **Boston Massacre site**, directly in front of the Old State House balcony, marks the spot where, on March 5, 1770, British soldiers fired upon an angry mob of protesting colonists, killing five of them. This incident inflamed anti-British sentiment, which led to the outbreak of the Revolutionary War.

Heading north on Congress St brings you smack up against a coldly impersonal mass of concrete buildings dating to the 1960s. **Government Center** is home to the fortress-like Boston City Hall. Although there are perennial plans for creating a more inviting City Hall Plaza, city and state politics crawl at a snail's pace even when dealing with the most benign ideas for change. What few vestiges remain of the Old West End, as the neighborhood was once called, are found in the little byways between Merrimac and Causeway Sts. Ⓣ Green or Blue Line to Government Center.

On your way to Faneuil Hall Marketplace (see below), pose with the two lifelike bronzes of Boston's former Mayor Curley, a cherished but controversial Irish American politician. You'll find them on North St between Union and Congress Sts.

Oddly juxtaposed, the six glass columns of the adjacent, sobering **New England Holocaust Memorial** (between Union & Congress Sts) were erected in 1995. Inside each tower is a pit, representing the major Nazi death camps, with smoldering coals sending plumes of steam up through the glass corridors. It's particularly dramatic at night.

Faneuil Hall Marketplace (☎ 617-338-2323, Congress & North Sts), due east of Boston City Hall, is the granddaddy of East Coast waterfront revitalizations. Pronounced 'fan'l' or 'fan-yool,' the actual hall was constructed as a market and public meeting place in 1740. Look for the brick building with the beloved grasshopper weathervane on top. The austere 2nd floor is still used for public meetings. Behind Faneuil Hall, three long granite buildings make up the rest of the marketplace, the center of the city's produce and meat industry for almost 150 years. In the 1970s, **Quincy Market** was redeveloped into today's touristy, festive shopping and eating mecca. For Faneuil Hall restaurants or shops, see the Places to Eat and Shopping sections later in this chapter. Ⓣ Blue or Orange Line to State.

To escape Faneuil Hall Marketplace crowds, head to the waterfront **Christopher**

Columbus Park, barely northeast of the marketplace. (You'll have to brave the Big Dig construction, though, to reach it.) The park, complete with benches, grassy knolls, moored sailboats and a trellised archway, is a nice place for picnicking.

THE NORTH END & CHARLESTOWN (MAP 2)

Until the I-93 expressway is demolished after the Big Dig, the North End will remain physically separated from the city. Psychologically, the enclave is more like a continent and a century away. Old-world Italians have held court in this warren of narrow, winding streets and alleys since the 1920s. Walk around and you'll soon hear passionate discussions in Italian by old-timers dressed in black. You'll see bocce being played in parks and children running through the streets. Ritual Saturday morning shopping is done at specialty stores selling flowers, handmade pasta, cannoli or biscotti, fresh cuts of meat, a little of this or that – all within a quarter-mile radius of Boston's oldest colonial buildings. When you get tired or hungry, there are a dozen cafes and more *ristoranti* per block than anywhere else in Boston. ⊤ Green or Orange Line to Haymarket (for all North End and Charlestown sites).

From Faneuil Hall walk north on Union St, past the Union Oyster House (the oldest restaurant in the city, established in 1826) and cross under the expressway at Cross St. (These simple directions remain subject to ever-changing Big Dig street closures and diversions. Follow your nose.)

Then follow the red-brick (or painted red line) Freedom Trail (see Map 3 and the boxed text 'Walking Tours' for more information) north on Hanover St, the principal commercial thoroughfare, to reach the Paul Revere House (☎ 617-523-1676, 19 North Square; adult/senior & student/child $2.50/2/1; open 9:30am-5:15pm daily mid-Apr–Oct, 9:30am-4:15pm Tues-Sun Nov–mid-Apr). This small clapboard house, originally built in 1680, is worth a visit – and not just because it's the oldest house in Boston. The hour-long tour also provides a great history lesson. The blacksmith Revere was one of three horse-

back messengers who carried advance warning on the night of April 18, 1775, of the British march into Concord and Lexington (see those towns in the Around Boston chapter). Revere lived here for 10 years during the Revolutionary period.

Tour the adjacent Pierce-Hichborn House (☎ 617-523-1676, 19 North Square) with a combination ticket purchased (for nominally more) at the Revere House. Built in 1710 and owned by Revere's cousin, this is a fine example of an English Renaissance brick house. It's open for tours only at 12:30pm and 2:30pm on the days that the Paul Revere House is open. Call the morning you want to visit.

Head back to Hanover St and walk northeast for a few blocks to reach the 1804 St Stephen's Church, at Harris St. St Stephen's is Boston's only remaining church designed by renowned architect Charles Bulfinch.

Across the street, the shady Paul Revere Mall (called 'the prado' by locals) perfectly frames the Old North Church. In addition to being a lively meeting place for locals of all generations, it's also one of the few places in the cramped quarter where you can rest as long as you want.

The 1723 Old North Church (☎ 617-523-6676, 193 Salem St; open 9am-6pm Mon-Fri, 9am-5pm Sat & Sun) is Boston's oldest church, best known as the place where two lanterns were hung from the steeple on the night of April 18, 1775, as a signal that the British were coming by sea. Tall white box-pews, many with brass nameplates of early parishioners, occupy the graceful interior. Look for the little terraces and gardens behind the church. Sunday Episcopal services are held at 9am, 11am and 5pm. A little museum and gift shop are next door.

Head up Hull St to the particularly moving Copp's Hill Burying Ground, the city's second-oldest cemetery (1660), with headstones chipped and pocked by Revolutionary War musket fire.

Across the street, 44 Hull St is Boston's narrowest house, measuring a whopping 9½ feet wide. The circa-1800 house was reportedly built out of spite to block light from the neighbor's house and to obliterate the view of the house behind it.

From the often decrepit vantage point at Copp's Hill Terrace, which is to the north on Charter St, Charlestown and the last two Freedom Trail sites – Charlestown Bridge and the USS *Constitution* – are barely visible through the trees. If you decide to skip them, retrace your steps to **Salem St**, the neighborhood's most colorful street, chockablock with specialty markets and restaurants. Stop at the Bova Italian Bakery (134 Salem St), open 24/7; the aromatic Polcari's Coffee (105 Salem St); and Dairy Fresh Candies (57 Salem St), for an unsurpassed selection of nuts, chocolates, candies and dried fruit. Around the corner to the north is J Pace & Son (☎ 617-227-9673, 42 Cross St), a neighborhood Italian grocer with fresh cheese, olives, bread and prosciutto.

To reach the last two Freedom Trail sites, walk a mile or so across the **Charlestown Bridge** from Commercial St and follow the shoreline to the **USS** *Constitution* (☎ 617-242-5670, *Charlestown Navy Yard; admission free; tours noon-4pm Thur-Sun*). Despite its wooden hull, the oldest commissioned US Navy ship (1797) was nicknamed Old Ironsides for never having gone down in a battle. Navy personnel give guided tours of the top deck, gun deck and cramped quarters. In order to maintain the ship's commissioned status, she is taken out onto Boston Harbor every Fourth of July, turned around and brought back to the dock.

You might as well stop at the **USS** *Constitution* **Museum** (☎ 617-426-1812; admission free; open 9am-6pm daily May-Oct, 10am-5pm daily Nov-Apr), across from the ship, which shows informative displays and films about ship life and the ship's battles.

The Charlestown Navy Yard was a thriving ship-building center from 1800 until the early 1900s. Although it was closed in 1974, it's been making a comeback ever since. Walk around the impressive granite buildings, which have been transformed into shops and residential and office space. There's a panoramic view of Boston from the Navy Yard. You can also get here by boat; see Cruises, later in this chapter.

Make a short detour through the heart of Charlestown's winding, narrow streets lined with colonial houses and gas lanterns to reach the **Bunker Hill Monument** (☎ 617-242-5641, *Monument Square; admission free; open 9am-4:30pm daily, with slightly longer afternoon hours late June-early Sept).* The 220-foot granite hilltop obelisk rewards physically fit visitors with fine Boston views – after you've climbed its 295 steps. The adjacent small lodge contains interesting historical dioramas, and NPS park rangers give summer talks.

On June 17, 1775, in **Monument Square** (Charlestown's most impressive spot), Colonel Prescott told his revolutionary soldiers, 'Don't fire until you see the whites of their eyes.' A reenactment of this event takes place every June.

The narrow streets immediately surrounding Monument Square are lined with restored mid-19th-century Federal and colonial houses. But venture four or five blocks beyond it in any direction and you'll see another side of Charlestown. Many homes around the square are owned by working-class families who've lived here all their lives. Indeed, there is a bit of tension between the 'townies' and the yuppies.

Charlestown, the monument and the *Constitution* are worth at least a couple of hours. The circa-1780 Warren Tavern (see Entertainment, later), at Pleasant and Main Sts, is an atmospheric and boisterous place for a late afternoon drink, or a burger at lunch or dinnertime.

CHARLES RIVER ESPLANADE (MAP 4)

Boston and Cambridge are graced with grassy banks and paved byways along both sides of the curvaceous Charles River. These paths are perfect for bicycling, jogging or walking. On the Boston side, it's about 2 miles from the Museum of Science at the Esplanade's eastern end to the Anderson Bridge (which turns into JFK St and leads into Harvard Square).

For a great view of Boston, walk – or take the T Red Line, between Charles/MGH and Kendall – across the **Longfellow Bridge**, nicknamed the 'Salt and Pepper' bridge because of its towers' resemblance to the condiment shakers.

From Beacon St near Arlington St, cross Storrow Dr (a noisy but necessary auto way) via the Arthur Fiedler Footbridge to reach the Esplanade. This is its most popular and picturesque portion, which includes the **Hatch Memorial Shell**, the scene of free outdoor concerts and movies (see Entertainment, later in this chapter). On warm days, Bostonians migrate here to sunbathe, sail and feed waterfowl gliding along the tranquil riverbank.

The **Museum of Science** (☎ 617-723-2500, *Science Park, Charles River Dam; adult/senior & child $11/8; open 9am-5pm Sat-Thur & 9am-9pm Fri Sept-June, 9am-7pm daily July & Aug)* is an educational ball of fun, especially for children. With more than 600 interactive exhibits, the favorites include the world's largest lightning bolt generator, a full-scale space capsule, a World Population Meter (a baby is born every second or so) and a 20-foot-tall Tyrannosaurus rex dinosaur model. The Skyline Room Cafeteria offers good food and skyline views. ⓣ Green Line to Science Park.

The museum also houses the **Hayden Planetarium** and **Mugar Omni Theater**; combination tickets (to the museum and one show) save you a few bucks. Generally there are shows on the hour, but call for exact times, especially since you can't count on waltzing in and finding tickets available for the next show. The planetarium boasts a state-of-the-art projection system that puts on a heavenly star show and programs about black holes and other astronomical mysteries. The Omni, a four-story, wraparound theater, makes you feel as if you're experiencing whatever is projected around you: the Grand Canyon, Antarctica or even the human body.

BACK BAY (MAP 4)

During the 1850s, when Boston was experiencing a population and building boom, Back Bay was an uninhabitable tidal flat. To solve the problem, urban planners em-

barked on an ambitious and wildly successful 40-year project: Fill in the marsh, lay out an orderly grid of streets, erect magnificent Victorian brownstones and design high-minded civic plazas.

Back Bay is one of Boston's most cherished treasures. You could easily spend a half-day here, strolling down shady Comm Ave, window-shopping and sipping a latte on chic Newbury St, taking in the remarkable Victorian architecture or popping into grand churches. Although the neighborhood is home to young professionals and blue-blood Bostonians, Back Bay also has a large student population that keeps it from growing too stodgy.

The area is bounded by the Public Garden and Arlington St to the northeast, Mass Ave to the southwest, the Charles River to the northwest and Stuart St and Huntington Ave to the southeast. Cross streets are laid out alphabetically from Arlington St to Hereford St.

Back Bay is at its most enchanting during May, when magnolia, tulip and dogwood trees are in bloom. Marlborough St, one block north and parallel to Comm Ave, is the most tranquil of Back Bay's shady, patrician streets.

The jam-packed **Gibson House Museum** (☎ 617-267-6338, *137 Beacon St; admission $5; 1pm-3pm Wed-Sun),* near Arlington St, will give you an idea of what these opulent 19th-century mansions were like. Tours are given at this splendid six-story Victorian brownstone at 1pm, 2pm and 3pm. ⓣ Green Line to Arlington.

High-minded **Copley Square**, set between Dartmouth, Clarendon and Boylston Sts, is surrounded by historic buildings. **Trinity Church** (☎ 617-536-0944, *206 Clarendon St; open 8am-6pm daily)* is one of the nation's truly great buildings. Designed by Henry Hobson Richardson from 1872 to 1877, the grand French and Romanesque building still holds Sunday services. There are organ recitals at 12:15pm Friday. Across the street, the 62-story **John Hancock Tower** (*200 Clarendon St),* constructed with more than 10,000 panels of mirrored glass, stands in stark contrast to Trinity Church. Designed in 1976 by IM Pei, the tower suffered serious initial problems: Inferior glass panes were installed and when the wind whipped up, the panes popped out, falling hundreds of feet to the ground. The area was quickly cordoned off and all the panes were replaced. (No one was ever hurt.) Ⓣ Green Line to Copley.

The esteemed **Boston Public Library** (☎ 617-536-5400, 666 Boylston St), between Exeter and Dartmouth Sts, lends credence to Boston's reputation as the 'Athens of America.' The reading room is splendid and the garden courtyard tranquil. For details, see Information, earlier in this chapter.

Adjacent to Copley Square, the enormous and modern **Copley Place** is the largest privately funded development in Boston's history. Another large shopping development, the **Prudential Center**, lies a few blocks southwest of Copley Place.

For a bird's-eye view of Boston, head to the 50th-floor **Prudential Center Skywalk** (☎ 617-859-0648, 800 Boylston St; adult/senior & child $6/4; open 10am-10pm daily), which offers a spectacular 360° view of metro Boston and Cambridge. There is no outdoor observation deck, so you'll be photographing the skyline through glass. Last tickets are sold 30 minutes prior to closing. Ⓣ Green Line to Hynes/ICA or Green Line 'E' branch to Prudential.

When it comes to shopping, **Newbury St** is to Boston what Fifth Ave is to New York City. International boutiques and galleries get tonier and tonier the closer you get to the Public Garden. Approaching Mass Ave in the other direction, you'll see more and more nose rings, platform shoes and dyed hair. Newbury St is also fun to wander at night when shops are closed but the well-lit windows are dressed to the nines, and when the darkness cloaks your less-than-Armani attire. Newbury St is epitomized by its cafe culture and a worldly, haute-couture crowd. Ⓣ Green Line to Arlington, Copley or Hynes/ICA, depending on which part of the street you want to tackle first.

The Episcopal **Emmanuel Church** (☎ 617-536-3355, 617-536-3356 concert information, 15 Newbury St; open for services 10am Sun & 6pm Thur Sept-May), near Arlington St, is highly regarded for its musical and cultural offerings. Call for a complete music schedule.

The **Old South Church** (☎ 617-536-1970, 645 Boylston St; open 9am-7pm Mon-Thur, 9am-5pm Fri, 10am-4pm Sat, 9am-4pm Sun), a distinctive Italian Gothic structure complete with a campanile and multicolored granite, is often referred to as the 'new' Old South Church because up until 1875 the congregation worshipped in their original home, what is now called the Old South Meeting House. It's open on Saturday only when other events are scheduled. Sunday services are held at 11am.

The **Arlington St Church** (☎ 617-536-7050, 351 Boylston St; open noon-6pm Wed-Sun May-Oct, during services Sun year-round) was the first public building to be erected in Back Bay. The church features 16 commissioned Tiffany windows, a bell tower and steeple modeled after London's well-known church St Martin-in-the-Fields. By the way, the church's Unitarian Universalist ministry is purely progressive.

Beyond the Pru on the southwestern edge of Back Bay, the **Institute of Contemporary Art** (☎ 617-266-5152, 955 Boylston St; adult/senior & student $6/4, child under 12 yrs free, free to all 5pm-9pm Thur; open noon-5pm Wed & Fri, noon-9pm Thur, 11am-5pm Sat & Sun) livens up Boston's often conservative art scene by showing avant-garde art created by well-known national and unknown regional artists. The ICA's galleries are currently housed within a renovated 19th-century firehouse, but the ICA has plans to build on the waterfront. Ⓣ Green Line to Hynes/ICA.

At Mass Ave, the **Christian Science Church** (☎ 617-450-3790, 175 Huntington Ave; open 10am-4pm Mon-Sat; open only for tours 11:30am, 1pm, 2pm Sun), built in 1894, is the home base for the Church of Christ, Scientist, or Christian Science, founded by Mary Baker Eddy in 1866. Tour the grand basilica, which can seat 3000 worshippers, listen to the 14,000-pipe organ or linger on the expansive plaza with its 670-foot-long reflecting pool. Tours (not required) are given on the hour Monday to Saturday. ⓉGreen Line 'E' branch to Symphony.

Next door are the offices of the internationally regarded daily newspaper, the *Christian Science Monitor* (ⓌWwww.csmonitor.com), an elegant reading room and the **Mapparium**, one of Boston's hidden treasures. The Mapparium is a room-size, stained-glass globe that you can walk through on a glass bridge. Geopolitical boundaries are drawn as the world appeared in 1935. Interestingly, it gets about the same number of visitors today as it did in 1935. The acoustics, which surprised even the designer, are a wonder: No matter how softly you whisper into the ear of your companion, everyone in the room will hear it perfectly! The Mapparium is scheduled to reopen after extensive renovations in late 2002.

Diagonally across the street, **Symphony Hall** (☎ 617-266-1492, 301 Mass Ave) is the world's first concert hall designed in accordance with acoustic principles. Free tours are offered only at 4:30pm Wednesday and the first Saturday of each month from October to May. The preeminent Boston Symphony Orchestra plays here; see the Entertainment section, later in this chapter. ⓉGreen Line 'E' branch to Symphony.

KENMORE SQUARE (MAP 4)

West of Back Bay, Beacon St and Comm Ave converge at Kenmore Square, the epicenter of student life in Boston. In addition to the behemoth Boston University (see Information, earlier in this chapter), which stretches along Comm Ave, there are more than a half-dozen colleges in the area. Kenmore Square has more than its share of clubs (see Entertainment, later in this chapter), inexpensive but nondescript eateries and dormitories disguised as innocuous brownstones. You'll know you're in Kenmore Square when you spot the 60-sq-foot Citgo sign. This mammoth neon sign has marked the spot since 1965. ⓉGreen Line to Kenmore.

Head one block west of Kenmore Square for the **Photographic Resource Center** (☎ 617-353-0700, 602 Comm Ave; adult/senior & student $3/2; open noon-5pm Tues,

Wed & Fri-Sun, noon-8pm Thur Sept-July). One of the few centers in the country devoted exclusively to this art form, the PRC's ever-changing exhibits lean toward the modern and experimental. The library is very well stocked.

THE FENWAY (MAP 4)

South of Kenmore Square is the Fenway, an area wherein the names can be confusing, even to Bostonians. In addition to referring to the area, the Fenway is also the name of a highway, and Fenway Park is where the Boston Red Sox play baseball. But when people refer to 'Fenway,' they're generally talking about the **Back Bay Fens**, a tranquil and interconnected park system that extends south from the Charles River Esplanade (at Park Dr or Charlesgate East), along a winding brook to the lush Arnold Arboretum and Franklin Park Zoo. It's part of the **Emerald Necklace**, a series of parks throughout the city, linked in the 1880s and 1890s by landscape architect Frederick Law Olmsted. Two renowned museums, the Museum of Fine Arts and the Isabella Stewart Gardner Museum (see below), reside in the Fenway. It's not advisable, however, to linger in the Fenway after dark, especially near the tall reeds. In recent years there have been a number of gay-bashing incidents here.

The 265-acre **Arnold Arboretum** (☎ 617-524-1717, 125 the Arborway, Jamaica Plain; admission free; open dawn-dusk daily) is a gem. Under a public/private partnership with the city and Harvard University, it's planted with over 13,000 exotic trees, flowering shrubs and other specimens. It's particularly beautiful in the spring. Dog walking, Frisbee throwing, bicycling and general contemplation are encouraged (but picnicking is not allowed). A visitor center is located at the main gate, just south of the rotary at Rte 1 and Rte 203. ⓉOrange Line to Forest Hills and walk a quarter-mile northwest to the Forest Hills gate.

While the 70-acre **Franklin Park Zoo** (☎ 617-541-5466, Peabody Circle at Blue Hill Ave & Columbia Rd; adult/senior/child $7/6/4; open 10am-5pm Mon-Fri, 10am-6pm

Sat & Sun Apr-Sept; 10am-4pm daily Oct-Mar) is surrounded by one of the city's less safe neighborhoods, the zoo itself is safe. It boasts a well-designed Tropical Forest pavilion, complete with lush vegetation, waterfalls, lowland gorillas, a panther, warthogs and over 30 species of free flight birds. While the mixed-species Bongo Congo features zebras, wildebeests, ostrich and ibex, the Australian Outback Trail highlights wallabies, kookaburras, emus and kangaroos. Ⓣ Orange Line to Forest Hills, then ride the

No 16 bus, which departs every 15 minutes and takes about four minutes to reach the Franklin Park Zoo.

The collections at the **Museum of Fine Arts, Boston** *(MFA; ☎ 617-267-9300, 465 Huntington Ave; adult/senior & student $14/12, child under 17 yrs free, admission by donation after 4pm Wed, admission reduced by $2 Thur & Fri evening, admission valid for two days within a 30-day period; open 10am-4:45pm Mon & Tues, 10am-9:45pm Wed-Fri, 10am-5:45pm Sat & Sun; only the*

Fenway Park

Boston's most cherished landmark? Site of Boston's greatest dramas and worst defeats? To many Bostonians it's not Bunker Hill or the Freedom Trail, not Harvard or MIT, but tiny Fenway Park, home of baseball's Red Sox, where names like Babe Ruth, Ted Williams, Carl Yastrzemski, Jim Rice and Roger Clemens are uttered and remembered as reverently as any heroes from Boston's colonial history. Stars in today's constellations, known to true fans simply by their first names, include Pedro, Nomar and Manny.

Fenway Park has earned the reputation of baseball's mecca, the class of the major leagues. Only Wrigley Field in Chicago can rival Fenway's age and uniqueness.

Nestled between the Back Bay Fens and the Mass Pike, Fenway Park is truly an integral part of downtown Boston. The park is little more than 100 yards from Kenmore Square and adjoins Lansdowne St (also known as Ted Williams Way), which sports many of Boston's most popular nightclubs. Even closer to the park are the hearts of the Red Sox fans, who have remained loyal (the Red Sox are a top draw in the major leagues) despite the team's failure to win a World Series in close to 80 years.

Much of the team's ill fate is attributed to the 'Curse of the Great Bambino,' the sale of their best young pitcher, Babe Ruth, to the hated rival New York Yankees in 1918. The Red Sox have not won a World Series since that season, while Babe Ruth and the Yankees went on to achieve legendary success and fame. Many believe the sale of Ruth to be among the worst transactions in professional sports history.

Baseball played in Fenway is made special by the unique geometry of the park. Thanks to its downtown location, an economy of space gives the fans an intimate proximity to the playing field. The Fenway Faithful claim to feel more a part of the ball game than might be possible in larger, more modern parks. Fenway also has the one and only 'Green Monster,' a towering wall in left field that compensates for the relatively short distance from home plate. The Green Monster consistently alters the regular course of play – what appears to be a lazy fly ball could actually drop over the Monster for a home run, and what appears to be a sharp double into the gap may be played off the wall to hold the runner to a single.

So fabled and important a site as Fenway Park certainly should have protection against urban development. However, that's not the case. There are plans afoot to move the park to a nearby site or to unceremoniously move it to South Boston so that it can abut the 'historic' World Trade Center and Expressway areas. The debate continues, as Boston is slow to decide anything.

For more information on attending a game at Fenway, see Spectator Sports.

West Wing is open Thur & Fri evening) are second in this country only to those of New York's Metropolitan Museum of Art. Particularly noteworthy are its holdings of American art, which include major works by John Singleton Copley, Winslow Homer, Edward Hopper and the Hudson River School; American decorative arts are also well represented. The museum also has more Asian treasures, including a full-scale Japanese Buddhist temple, than any other collection in the world. Furthermore, European paintings from the 11th to the 20th centuries, including a huge collection of French impressionists, are outdone by only a handful of museums around the globe.

When it's time to rest your feet, there is a very good indoor cafe, a ground-floor cafeteria, the indoor/outdoor Frasier Court cafe and a tranquil Japanese garden (also known as *Tenshin-en,* which means 'Garden of the Heart of Heaven'). Ⓣ Green Line 'E' branch to Museum.

The **Isabella Stewart Gardner Museum** (☎ 617-566-1401, 280 the Fenway; adult/ senior/student $11/7/5, child under 17 yrs free; open 11am-5pm Tues-Sun), a magnificent Venetian-style palazzo built to house 'Mrs Jack' Gardner's collection, was also her home until her death in 1924. A monument to one woman's exquisite taste for acquiring unequaled art, the Gardner is filled with almost 2000 priceless objects, primarily European, including outstanding tapestries and Italian Renaissance and 17th-century Dutch paintings.

Since Mrs Jack's will stipulated that her collection remain exactly as it was at the time of her death, nothing in the museum will ever change. That helps explain the few empty spaces on the walls: In 1990, the museum was robbed of nearly $200 million worth of paintings, including a rare and beloved Vermeer. The walls on which they were mounted will remain barren until the paintings are recovered (highly unlikely). The palazzo itself, with a four-story greenhouse courtyard, is a masterpiece, a tranquil oasis alone worth the price of admission. The Gardner's fine cafe serves lunch. Ⓣ Green Line 'E' branch to Museum.

THE SOUTH END (MAP 4)

Not to be confused with South Boston ('Southie'), which is still remembered for its residents' violent opposition to integrating the Boston public schools in the 1970s, the South End is a study in ethnic, racial, sexual and economic diversity. The South End doesn't have any sights per se, but it's worth exploring to get a sense of Boston's vibrancy. Huge portions have been claimed by artists, gay men, architects and young professionals, but other parts are less gentrified. Housing projects and halfway houses rub elbows with converted condos. Ⓣ Orange Line to Back Bay.

South of Back Bay and west of the Theater District, this neighborhood is bounded by Huntington, Mass and Shawmut Aves and the Mass Turnpike to the north. Columbus Ave and Tremont St are the principal commercial streets, lined with trendy restaurants.

Almost 5 miles long, the **Southwest Corridor** is a one-way, paved and landscaped walkway, running between and parallel to Columbus and Huntington Aves. Walk north from Mass Ave for rewarding views of the Back Bay skyline.

South End side streets, which boast the country's largest concentration of Victorian row houses, have a more British temperament than other parts of Boston. The tiny, elliptical **Union Park Square** between Tremont St and Shawmut Ave feels particularly tranquil. Also visit the lovely Rutland Square, just north of Tremont St.

THEATER DISTRICT (MAP 2)

Although tiny by New York standards, Boston's theater district has long served as an important pre-Broadway staging area for shows. Thanks to the 1980s building boom, many landmark theaters received long-needed face-lifts. Little more than a square block, the Theater district is bounded by Boylston St, Stuart St, Tremont St and Charles St South. Don't overlook the area's smaller venues (see Entertainment, later in this chapter) where better value is often found. Ⓣ Orange Line to NE Medical Center or Chinatown.

Off Boylston St, **Boylston Place** is a pedestrian-only alleyway lined with nightclubs. As suburban patrons spill out of theaters, America's youth are just beginning to descend on these clubs.

Much of the daytime action takes place within the drearily named **State Transportation Building** (10 Park Plaza), an atrium-like space with eateries, free lunchtime concerts and art exhibits.

Wedged inside Stuart, Arlington, Marginal and Charles St South, **Bay Village** is an often overlooked but charming neighborhood that's certainly worth a stroll. The tiny, early-19th-century brick houses were built and occupied by those who built the Beacon Hill mansions. Today, the tight-knit neighborhood is more gay and bohemian than most. T Green Line to Arlington.

CHINATOWN (MAP 2)

Adjacent to the eastern edge of the Theater District, the most colorful part of Chinatown is bounded by Tremont, Essex, Kneeland and Kingston Sts. This tiny area is overflowing with authentic restaurants (many open until 4am), bakeries, markets selling live animals, import and textile shops, and phone booths topped with little pagodas. Don't miss the enormous gate that guards Beach and Kingston Sts. In addition to the Chinese, who began arriving in the late 1870s, the community of 8000 also includes Cambodians, Vietnamese and Laotians. T Orange Line to Chinatown.

WATERFRONT (MAP 2)

The **New England Aquarium** (☎ 617-973-5200, Central Wharf, off Atlantic Ave; adult/senior/child $13/11/7; open 9am-5pm Mon-Fri, 9am-6pm Sat & Sun Sept-June; 9am-6pm Mon, Tues & Fri, 9am-8pm Wed & Thur, 9am-7pm Sat & Sun July & Aug) teems with sea creatures of all sizes, shapes and colors. Outdoor harbor seals and sea otters introduce the main indoor attraction: a three-story, cylindrical saltwater tank swirling with over 600 creatures – including turtles, sharks and eels. Leave a little time to be mesmerized by the Echo of the Waves sculpture, not to mention the 'Coastal Rhythms' exhibit, which explores the lives and habitats of coastal animals, and the new 3-D IMAX films featuring aquatic themes. You can also have a quick meal here and catch whale-watching cruises; see Cruises, later in this chapter. Sea lion presentations take place every half-hour beginning at 11am. T Blue Line to Aquarium.

South of the aquarium and across Fort Point Channel (a waterway separating Boston proper from South Boston), the newly designated **Seaport District** is comprised of old brick warehouses, design studios, and a diminishing number of artists' lofts and waterfront businesses like seafood markets and shipping docks. District development, the likes of which haven't been seen since Back Bay was filled in, is driven by a forthcoming convention center. There are dramatic skyline views from the stunning Moakley Federal Courthouse on Northern Ave. T Red Line to South Station plus a 10-minute walk.

The delightful **Children's Museum** (☎ 617-426-8855, 300 Congress St; adult/senior & child 2-15 yrs/child 1 yr $7/6/2, admission $1 5pm-9pm Fri; open 10am-5pm Sat-Thur, 10am-9pm Fri) can entertain preschoolers to teenagers for an entire day with interactive educational exhibits. There are bubble exhibits, Arthur's World, a two-story climbing maze, a rock-climbing wall, a Latino-themed supermarket and a beautiful play space for kids three and under.

The **Boston Tea Party Ship & Museum** (☎ 617-269-7150, Congress St Bridge; adult/student/child $8/7/4; open 9am-5pm daily Mar-late May & early Sept-early Dec; 9am-6pm daily late May-early Sept) stands as testimony to the spirited colonists who refused to pay the levy imposed on their beloved beverage. In 1773, they left a town meeting at the Old South Meeting House and donned Native American garb as a disguise before boarding the Beaver (the Beaver II, which you board today, is an approximate replica) and dumping all the tea overboard in rebellion. Costumed guides tell the complicated story brilliantly, while the adjacent museum offers multilingual information and a free cup of tax-free Salada tea.

BOSTON HARBOR ISLANDS (MAP 1)

Until recently, Boston Harbor had the unenviable distinction of being the country's dirtiest harbor. Following a massive, multimillion-dollar clean-up in the mid-1990s, the harbor is well on its way to regaining a healthier reputation. Good thing, too, since it has more than 30 large and small islands that offer plenty of history, picnic spots, nature walks and fishing. Visiting the islands is refreshing, even on a short visit to Boston.

George's Island, the jumping-off spot for all the other islands, features a 19th-century fort, Fort Warren. **Lovell's Island** is the largest, its 62 acres good for walking along dunes, marshes and meadows. Look for wild raspberries on **Bumpkin Island** and for a variety of birds on **Grape Island**. **Great Brewster Island** has great city views, a visitor center and walking trails and is home to a bird sanctuary.

To get to the islands, **Boston Harbor Cruises** (*☎ 617-227-4320, 1 Long Wharf, off Atlantic Ave; roundtrip adult/senior/child $8/7/6; service 10am-4pm late Apr–early Oct*) offers regular seasonal ferry service. Boats operate hourly late June to early September, every other hour in the shoulder seasons. Purchase a roundtrip ticket to George's Island, where you then catch a free water taxi (another five to 10 minutes) to the smaller islands.

For information on camping on the islands, see Places to Stay, later.

JOHN F KENNEDY LIBRARY & MUSEUM

The library and museum (*☎ 617-929-4500, Columbia Point, Dorchester; adult/senior & student/child $8/6/4; open 9am-5pm daily*) are set dramatically on the harbor adjacent to the UMass, Boston, campus. Designed by architect IM Pei (who is also responsible for the mirror-like John Hancock Tower in Back Bay), the stark white structure successfully blends cylindrical elements with strong pyramid-like lines. Together, they take up most of the peninsula, which is nice for strolling.

The JFK museum is the repository for memorabilia related to the 35th US president: papers, videotape, speeches and photographs. Check out the good introductory film about JFK.

Interestingly, the library has an archive of writer Ernest Hemingway's manuscripts and papers. About 95% of his works can be accessed if you're interested in research, but there is no exhibit space. What's the connection? Kennedy was key in helping Mary Hemingway, Ernest's fourth wife and widow, get the manuscripts and papers out of Cuba during the first and most intense days of the embargo. When she died, she willed them here, because the library offers the public better access than most archival libraries.

The **Commonwealth Museum** (*☎ 617-727-9268, Columbia Point; admission free; open 9am-5pm Mon-Fri, 9am-3pm Sat*) exhibits documents dating back to the first days of colonization. Exhibits are drawn from the Massachusetts Archives (*☎ 617-727-2816*), a research facility and depository for Massachusetts' history.

Ⓣ Red Line to JFK/UMass, and catch a free shuttle bus (departures every 20 minutes) to Columbia Point.

CAMBRIDGE

Cambridge is known around the globe as the home of the intellectual heavyweights Harvard University and MIT; see Information, earlier in this chapter, for details. With thousands of students, Cambridge is a diverse and youthful place, to say the least.

Founded in 1638, Cambridge was home to the country's first college (Harvard) and first printing press, virtually putting an early lock on its reputation as a hotbed for ideas and intellectualism.

Cambridge has always been known for its progressive politics, much of it centering around Harvard Square. Cantabrigians, as residents are called, vehemently opposed the Vietnam War before others did; they embraced the environmental movement before recycling became profitable; and they were one of the first communities to ban smoking in public buildings. And when Irish gays and lesbians were excluded from marching in South Boston's traditional St Patrick's Day parade in the mid-1990s, Cambridge immediately pledged to hold its own inclusive parade.

Harvard Square (Map 5)

You'll find Harvard Square overflowing with cafes, bookstores, restaurants and a lot of street musicians. Although many Cantabrigians rightly complain that the 'Square' has lost its edge – once independently owned shops are continually gobbled up by national chains – Harvard Square is still worth an afternoon.

The Square isn't a square at all, but rather a triangle of brick pavement above the Harvard T station. When people refer to the Square, they are referring to the four- or five-block area that radiates from the Mass Ave and JFK St intersection. Look for the newspaper and periodicals shop Out of Town News (see the boxed text 'Bookstores') and an information kiosk here (for kiosk hours, see Information, earlier in this chapter). Ⓣ Red Line to Harvard.

Most of **Harvard University** lies east of JFK St and east of Mass Ave after it jogs north out of the Square. The gates to famed **Harvard Yard**, a quadrangle of ivy-covered brick buildings, are just across Mass Ave from the T station. Informative campus tours depart from the Holyoke Center (1350 Mass Ave), although the guides probably won't tell you tidbits like the fact that the university's multibillion-dollar endowment is the world's second-largest private endowment. (Only the Catholic Church's is bigger.)

Harvard operates four distinct museums (archaeology, botany, minerals and zoology) that seem to be more devoted to teaching than they are geared to visitors. Under the aegis of the **Museum of Natural History** (☎ 617-495-3045, 26 Oxford St; adult/senior/child $6.50/5/4, free 9am-noon Sun & 3pm-5pm Wed Sept-May; open 9am-5pm daily), you'll find the Museum of Comparative Zoology, with impressive fossil collections. The multicultural Peabody Museum of Archaeology and Ethnology boasts a strong collection of North American Indian arti-

facts. The Botanical Museum, perhaps the most well-known of these museums, houses over 800 lifelike pieces of handblown-glass flowers and plants. Tickets are good for all four museums.

The **Fogg Art Museum** (☎ 617-495-9400, 32 Quincy St; adult/senior/student $5/4/3, youth under 18 yrs free, free 10am-noon Sat & all day Wed; open 10am-5pm Mon-Sat, 1pm-5pm Sun) concerns itself with no less than the history of Western art from the Middle Ages to the present. There is also a good selection of decorative arts. Free tours are given at 11am Monday to Friday (except during summer, when they are given only on Wednesday). Tickets include admission to the Busch-Reisinger and Arthur M Sackler Museums (see below).

Entered through the Fogg, the **Busch-Reisinger Museum** (admission & hours as per Fogg) specializes in Central and Northern European art. Free tours are given at 1pm Monday to Friday (only on Wednesday June to August).

Across the street, the **Arthur M Sackler Museum** (☎ 617-495-9400, 485 Broadway; admission & hours as per Fogg) is devoted to Asian and Islamic art. It boasts the world's most impressive collection of Chinese jade as well as fine Japanese woodblock prints. Free tours are given at 2pm Monday to Friday (only on Wednesday June to August).

One of Cambridge's most distinctive and humorous buildings is the **Harvard Lampoon Castle** (Mt Auburn St at Plympton St). The namesake student humor magazine, which has had its offices here for years (at press time its lease was uncertain), was said to have inspired the creation of the National Lampoon magazine.

Two blocks north of Harvard Square is **Christ Church** (Garden St near Mass Ave), designed by Peter Harrison, who designed Boston's King's Chapel.

Next door is tranquil and verdant **Radcliffe Yard**, wedged between Brattle and Garden Sts, and Appian Way and Mason St. Radcliffe College, founded in 1879 as the sister school to the then-all-male Harvard, merged with its behemoth brother in 1975.

Across the street to the east, George Washington pitched camp from 1775 to 1776 on **Cambridge Common**. The adjacent **Old Burying Ground** is a tranquil Revolutionary-era cemetery, where Harvard's first eight presidents are buried. Around the corner, you'll find the **First Parish Church**.

Brattle St, one of the area's most prestigious residential addresses, is lined with magnificent 18th- and 19th-century homes. In the early 1770s, Brattle St, dubbed Tory Row, was generally home to British loyalists. But in 1775, Washington got his revenge by appropriating most of these houses for his patriots.

The stately home now known as the **Longfellow National Historic Site** (☎ 617-876-4491, 105 Brattle St) was no exception to the appropriation. Washington liked it so much that he moved his headquarters here during the siege of Boston. Henry Wadsworth Longfellow lived and wrote here for 45 years, from 1837 to 1882. Now under the auspices of the NPS, the Georgian mansion contains many of Longfellow's belongings and lush period gardens. After a long period of restoration, the site is expected to open in spring 2002; call for hours.

Elsewhere in Cambridge

On a sunny day, the **Mt Auburn Cemetery** (☎ 617-547-7105, 580 Mt Auburn St; open 8am-7pm daily daylight saving time, 8am-5pm daily rest of year) is worth the 30-minute walk west from Harvard Square. Developed in 1831, its 170 acres were the first 'garden cemetery' in the US. Until then, the colonial notion of moving a body and grave marker around a cemetery was commonplace. Pick up a self-guided map of the rare botanical specimens and of the notable burial plots, including those for Mary Baker Eddy (founder of the Christian Science Church), Isabella Stewart Gardner (of the Gardner Museum), Winslow Homer (19th-century American painter extraordinaire) and Oliver Wendell Holmes (US Supreme Court justice).

Central Square, just east of Harvard Square, used to be grittier and funkier than

it is today, but vestiges of its former incarnation are still apparent. This is where you'll find Boston's largest contingent of body-pierced youth, a good concentration of pubs and clubs and Cambridge's punk scene.

Mass Ave to Porter Square, just north out of Harvard Square, is what Harvard Square used to be in its heyday. Lined with independent, quirky shops, it's a nice stroll up to Porter Square.

Davis Square, on the Red Line officially in Somerville, is more hip than any square in Cambridge. You'll find plenty of trendy bars, clubs, an old movie house and a few cafes. Just hanging in this square is a pastime for many.

In East Cambridge, **Kendall Square** at Main St has come alive in recent years, thanks to the high-tech industry and the takeover of the neglected brick warehouses. The One Kendall Square complex, at Hampshire and Broadway Sts, is its nucleus; see also Places to Eat, later. Ⓣ Red Line to Kendall.

The **MIT** campus extends south and west of Kendall Square. Join an excellent guided campus tour to best appreciate MIT's contributions to the sciences. Wander around the East Campus (on the east side of Mass Ave), bejeweled with public art. The nearby **List Visual Arts Center** (☎ 617-253-4680, Weisner Building, 20 Ames St, Cambridge; suggested donation $5; open noon-6pm Tues-Thur, Sat & Sun, noon-8pm Fri) mounts rewarding and sophisticated shows.

From the East Campus, head one block south to the Charles River for great Boston views.

BICYCLING

More than 50 miles of bicycle trails originate in the Boston area. One of the most popular circuits runs along both sides of the Charles River, but you can also ride for miles out to the Arnold Arboretum or out to nearby Watertown and back. For a trip to the historic countryside, follow the Minuteman Bikeway from Boston and Cambridge through Lexington and Bedford almost to Concord.

Although you have to be something of a kamikaze to take to the inner-city streets, people do it. You can take your bike on any of the MBTA subway lines except the Green Line, but you must avoid rush hours (6am to 9am and 4pm to 7pm weekdays). Be sure to get on the last train car.

Rubel BikeMaps (☎ 617-776-6567) produces little laminated 'Pocket Rides,' 50 different loop rides ($8.95 for five) in greater Boston or from area commuter rail stations. For the metro Boston area, look for the 'BU Bridge Bike Pack,' in which all tours start from the BU Bridge. The rides are incredibly detailed and worth every penny. See also Orientation, near the beginning of the chapter.

Community Bicycle Supply (*Map 4;* ☎ *617-542-8623, 496 Tremont St*), at Berkeley St, is open year-round for sales, and April through September for rentals (prices $10/20 per two/24 hours). **Back Bay Bicycles** (*Map 4;* ☎ *617-247-2336, 336 Newbury St*), at Mass Ave, has year-round rentals (same price). In Cambridge, the same rates are offered at **Ata Cycle** (☎ *617-354-0907, 1773 Mass Ave*), between Harvard and Porter Squares.

JOGGING

The safest and most popular place to run is along either side of the Charles River, between the Longfellow Bridge (near the Hatch Memorial Shell) and the Larz Anderson Bridge, which runs to Harvard Square. That complete circuit, winding along both sides of the river, covers about 6 miles.

IN-LINE & ICE SKATING

Beacon Hill Skate (*Map 4;* ☎ *617-482-7400, 135 Charles St South; $8/20 per hour/day*), in Bay Village, rents in-line skates. Glide over to the Esplanade or, better yet, to Memorial Dr on the Cambridge side of the Charles River, which is closed to auto traffic from 11am to 7pm on Sunday in warm weather.

Ice skating on the human-made Frog Pond on Boston Common is a very popular winter activity. Skate rentals, lockers and restrooms are available at the kiosk next to the pond.

BOATING & KAYAKING

Charles River Canoe and Kayak Center (☎ *617-965-5110, 2401 Comm Ave, Newton; rates per hour: canoes $11, rowboats $12, double kayaks $14, kids' kayaks $5*), near the intersection of MA 30 and I-95, rents boats April to October. Rowing shells are available for $25 per session. The center is across from a tranquil stretch of the Charles River. Ⓣ Green Line 'D' branch to Riverside and then a 20-minute walk. It's best to call for directions for the Newton location or the Soldiers Field Rd location (☎ *617-462-2513*), which is open May to mid-October.

Community Boating (☎ *617-523-1038, Charles River Esplanade; watercraft $50 per two days; open Apr-Oct*), near the Charles St footbridge, offers experienced sailors unlimited use of sailboats, kayaks and windsurfers. You'll have to take a little test to demonstrate your ability. Ⓣ Red Line to Charles/MGH.

ORGANIZED TOURS

See the Cruises section, below, for information on Boston Harbor cruises. For organized walking tours, see the boxed text 'Walking Tours.'

If you're only going to be in town a couple of days, **trolley tours** offer great ease and flexibility because you can hop on and off as you like, catching the next trolley that comes along. The narration is a strange mix of the arcane, endless lists of Boston firsts, bad jokes, substantive information, drivel, more entertainment than scholarly erudition and lots of tidbits that elicit a quizzically uplifting 'huh?' Except for the color of the trolleys (red, ☎ 617-720-6342; orange-and-green, ☎ 617-269-7150; and white, ☎ 617-742-1440), all operators offer essentially the same services for the same price (adult/senior & student/child $23/21/7). It really depends on who's behind the wheel, jabbering into the mic. It's convenient to board trolleys across from the New England Aquarium, at Atlantic Ave and State St, and from the trolley booths on Tremont St next to the visitor information center. You must purchase a ticket before boarding. Tours are

Walking Tours

Boston is a walker's paradise, best explored by foot. Several special-interest maps are available from the Boston Common Visitor Information Center.

The 2½-mile **Freedom Trail** (Map 3; ☎ 617-242-5642) is the granddaddy of walks. Sixteen historically important sites, including colonial and Revolutionary-era buildings, are linked by a double row of red sidewalk bricks (or a painted red line) that begins near the MBTA Park St station, winds through downtown Boston and the North End and ends in Charlestown at the USS *Constitution*. In addition to each site being marked by a bronze medallion in the sidewalk, directional signposts and kiosks have been installed along the route.

The NPS (☎ 617-242-5642, Ⓦ www.nps.gov/bost, 15 State St) offers excellent and free ranger-led walking tours (frequency is highly dependent on federal funding) along the Freedom Trail from mid-April to mid-November. Ⓣ Orange or Blue Line to State.

The Boston Park Rangers (☎ 617-635-7383, Tremont St), on Boston Common, offer free naturalist-led walks and historical talks around the Emerald Necklace, Boston Common and the Boston Public Garden. The extensive schedule varies so it's best to call ahead. Ⓣ Red or Green Line to Park St.

The **Black Heritage Trail**, about 1.6 miles long, encompasses more than a dozen 19th-century Beacon Hill sites. Pick up a self-guiding map at the visitor information center on Boston Common or the Museum of Afro-American History (☎ 617-725-0022, 46 Joy St). Better yet, take a guided walk of the trail (☎ 617-720-0753) daily at 10am, noon and 2pm from late May to early September; the two-hour tour departs from the Shaw Memorial, facing the State House.

Maps for the **Women's Heritage Trail** are available from the NPS. There are four walks (downtown, in the North End, Chinatown and on Beacon Hill) detailed in an inexpensive booklet sold at the NPS.

year-round and take 1¾ hours if you don't get off.

Brush Hill/Gray Line (Map 2; ☎ 617-720-6342, 800-343-1328, adult/child $26/13) has a 3½-hour motor coach tour of Cambridge, Lexington and Concord from late April to mid-November. Buses depart at 9:30am from the State Transportation Building (16 Charles St South), at Stuart St, near the Public Garden.

CRUISES

Boston Harbor Cruises (☎ 617-227-4320, 1 Long Wharf), off Atlantic Ave near the Aquarium, operates a number of harbor cruises from about mid-April to mid-October, depending on the weather. There are 90-minute narrated sightseeing trips around the outer harbor (adult/senior & student/child $17/15/14); 90-minute sunset cruises (same price); and boats to the USS *Constitution* in Charlestown (adult/senior &

student/child $10/9/3). For details on BHC service to George's Island in Boston Harbor, see Boston Harbor Islands, earlier in this chapter. For details on BHC whale-watching tours, see Whale-Watching Cruises, below. Ⓣ Blue Line to Aquarium.

Boston Duck Tours (Map 4; ☎ 617-723-3825, Prudential Center, 800 Boylston St; adult/senior & student/child $22/19/12; daily Apr-Nov) offers unusual land and water tours using modified amphibious vehicles from WWII. Rain or shine, the narrated tour splashes around the Charles River for about 25 minutes, and then competes with cars on Boston city streets for another 55 minutes. The ticket booth within the Prudential Center opens at 9am but people are in line before then. Tickets sell out by noon on weekends. Boats depart (on the Boylston St side of the Pru) every 30 minutes from 9am to 30 minutes prior to sunset. (You can also purchase tickets at the Aquarium, but remember that boats depart from the Pru.) Ⓣ Green Line 'E' branch to Prudential for tickets, Green Line to Copley for tours.

Charles River Boat Co (☎ 617-621-3001, Cambridgeside Galleria; adult/senior/child $8/7/6; trips 10:30am-5pm Sat & Sun May & Sept, 10:30am-5pm daily late May-early Sept) runs an hour-long narrated trip of the Charles River Basin. The boat cruises upstream to Harvard and downstream to the Boston Harbor locks. Meet at the ticket counter outside the mall food court near the fountain.

Gondola di Venezia (☎ 617-876-2800, Canal Park, Cambridgeside Galleria; $15 per person for 15 minutes, $65 per couple for 45 minutes; tours 2pm-10pm daily mid-May–mid-Oct) provides a distinctly different way to get a sense of the river. Make no mistake about it – the Charles River is not the Grand Canal. But the gondolier's technique and the craftsmanship of the gondola certainly give the experience a run for the money. It's a fine way to see the city shores.

Bay State Cruise Company (☎ 617-748-1428, Commonwealth Pier, 200 Seaport Blvd; tickets $16-20; trips 8:30pm-11:30pm Fri & Sat June-Sept), next to the World Trade Center, offers a three-hour evening harbor cruise with music or other entertainment.

The **AC Cruise Line** (☎ 617-261-6633, 800-422-8419, 290 Northern Ave, South Boston; adult/senior & student $20/16; trips late May-early Sept) offers a family-style trip to Salem. The boat departs at 9:30am and arrives at Salem Willows Park by 11:30am, where you'll have four hours to picnic on the beach before taking the boat back to Boston. Ⓣ Red Line to South Station and then a 15-minute walk.

The same **AC Cruise Line** (see above; adult/senior & student $23/18; trips late May-early Sept) ship continues from Salem north to Gloucester with a 2½-hour layover for you to walk around town. Up to four children are permitted free when accompanied by two adults.

Whale-Watching Cruises

Whale sightings are practically guaranteed at Stellwagen Bank, a fertile feeding ground 25 miles out to sea. The big humpback whales are most impressive, breaching and frolicking, but in the spring and fall, huge pods of dolphins making their way to and from summers in the Arctic are also impressive. Trips take about 4½ to 5 hours, with onboard commentary provided by naturalists. Dress warmly even on summer days.

AC Cruise Line (see above; adult/senior & student $25/19; trips 10am Fri-Sun June-Sept) rewards young families with its rates, since up to four children (under age 12) are free when accompanied by two paying adults. Ⓣ Red Line to South Station and then a 15-minute walk.

Boston Harbor Cruises (☎ 617-227-4320, 1 Long Wharf; adult/senior/child $29/25/23; trips mid-May–mid-Oct) also has daily whale-watching tours.

New England Aquarium Whale-Watching Tours (Map 2; ☎ 617-973-5277, Central Wharf; adult/senior & student/child $27/21.50/17-19; May-Oct), off Atlantic Ave, has more frequent boats than the other companies. Even though the Aquarium's faster catamaran may be more tempting than its 'slow' boat because it cuts an hour off the travel time, whales actually prefer the engine sounds of the slow boat. No children under three are permitted on the trip. Ⓣ Blue Line to Aquarium.

SPECIAL EVENTS

Once in town, Thursday's Boston Globe Calendar section has up-to-the-minute details on all events. Prior to your arrival, check with the GBCVB (see Information, earlier in this chapter). Remember that accommodations are much, much harder to secure during big events.

January/February

Chinese New Year climaxes with a colorful parade in Chinatown in late January or early February.

March

The large and vocal South Boston Irish community hosts the St Patrick's Day Parade on W Broadway St in mid-March. Since the mid-1990s, the St Patrick's Day Parade has been marred by the council's decision to exclude gay and lesbian Irish groups from marching.

April

On the third Monday in April, Patriot's Day is celebrated with a reenactment of Paul Revere's historic ride from the North End to Lexington. On the same day, thousands of runners compete in the Boston Marathon, a 26.2-mile run that has been an annual event for more than a century. Starting in Hopkinton west of the city, the race finishes on Boylston St in front of the Boston Public Library. Swan Boats return to the lagoon in the Public Garden in April.

May

Magnolia trees bloom all along Newbury St and Comm Ave. The third Sunday in May, Lilac Sunday at Arnold Arboretum celebrates the arrival of spring when more than 400 varieties of fragrant lilacs are in bloom. It is the only day of the year that visitors can picnic on the grass at the venerable arboretum.

June

Bunker Hill Day (June 17) includes a parade and battle reenactment at Charlestown's Bunker Hill Monument. The Gay Pride Parade in Boston (mid-month) draws tens of thousands of participants and spectators; the parade culminates in a big party on Boston Common.

July

The Fourth of July weekend extends to a week-long Harborfest. This is very big in Boston. The Boston Pops gives a free concert on the Esplanade, attended by hundreds of thousands of people. Fireworks cap off the evening. During Chowderfest, you can sample dozens of fish and clam chowders prepared by Boston's best restaurants.

July/August

In the North End, Italian festivals honoring patron saints are celebrated with food and music on the weekends.

August

The August Moon festival takes place in Chinatown while the Caribbean-American Carnival takes place around Boston.

September

The Cambridge River Festival takes place along the banks of the Charles River. The Boston Film Festival screens a variety of movies at dozens of venues all over the city.

October

The mid-month Head of the Charles Regatta draws more than 3000 collegiate rowers, while preppy fans line the banks of the river, lounging on blankets and drinking beer (technically illegal). It's the world's largest rowing event.

December

The Boston Ballet's Nutcracker at the Wang Center plays from late November to early January. The huge Prudential Center Christmas tree and trees that ring Boston Common are lit in early December and remain lit throughout the month. The mid-month Boston Tea Party reenactment involves costumed actors who march from downtown to the waterfront and dump bales of tea into the harbor. First Night celebrations begin early on the 31st and continue past midnight, culminating in fireworks over the harbor. Buy a special button that permits entrance into many events.

PLACES TO STAY

It's convenient to stay in the city's central neighborhoods. But if you're willing to spend a little time getting into the city from suburbs like Brookline or Braintree, you'll have more moderately priced options. A few require a car; most don't. Remember that city hotels are usually less expensive on weekends, when packages are offered.

Boston hotels enjoy high occupancy rates. That means you may have trouble finding a bed. Reserve months in advance, especially for less expensive places. To help visitors, the GBCVB has an affiliation with Hotel Hot Line (☎ 800-777-6001, ⓦ www .hoteldiscounts.com). Other reservation bureaus can also secure lower rates than you can by calling yourself. Try Central Reservation Services of New England (☎ 617-569-3800, 800-332-3026, fax 617-561-4840, ⓦ www.bostonhotels.net) and Citywide Reservation Services (☎ 617-267-7424, 800-248-9121, fax 617-267-9408, ⓦ www .cityres.com). For those in the UK, look for special deals before you depart.

Hotel prices are generally lowest from mid-November to mid-March with the exception of major holidays. Many hotels refer to prices during this time as their 'winter' or 'off-season' rates ('summer' constituting the rest of the year!). Regardless of what they call it, if occupancy is tight, off-season rates may not exist.

Price ranges for budget, mid-range and top-end accommodations are generally as follows: budget, less than $100; mid-range, $100 to $200; top end, $200 and up, up, up.

LOU JONES

The Charles River sees nearly nonstop action.

KIM GRANT

Cross-country skis are just one way to get around Boston's winter wonderland.

KIM GRANT

New Hampshire's Mt Washington Cog Railway chugs along the world's second-steepest rail track.

NEIL SETCHFIELD

Cafe terraces line lively Newbury St, Boston's premier shopping area.

RICHARD CUMMINS

ANGUS OBORN

LEE FOSTER

Boston, the place where everybody knows your name

KIM GRANT

Harvard University's Weld Boathouse perches on the Cambridge side of the Charles River.

PLACES TO STAY – BUDGET
Camping

Boston Harbor Islands Permits required. Both the Dept of Environmental Management *(DEM; ☎ 877-422-6762, ⓦ www.state.ma.us/dem/forparks.htm)* and the Metropolitan District Commission *(MDC; ☎ 617-727-5293, 98 Taylor St, Dorchester, MA 02122)* manage campsites on this 30-island park. There are about 50 campsites total on four islands: Peddock's, Lovell's, Grape and Bumpkin. The islands are jointly administered by the National Park Service (☎ 617-223-8666; ⓦ www.bostonislands.com).

Contact the DEM for Grape and Bumpkin permits ($10 to $12 nightly). Bumpkin is more remote and less populated, but both are open for camping May to September.

Call and then write the MDC for free permits to Peddock's and Lovell's, which are open for camping late June to mid-October (Saturday only from early September to mid-October). Lovell's has a lifeguard-attended swimming beach and 14 sites, but Peddock's is bigger with open field camping. No matter where you stay, bring water and supplies; facilities are limited to primitive sites and composting toilets.

Regular ferry service is provided by Boston Harbor Cruises (for details, see the Boston Harbor Islands section, earlier).

Wompatuck State Park *(☎ 781-749-7160, 877-422-6762 reservations, Union St, Hingham)* Sites without/with electric $12/15. Open late May–mid-Oct. Wompatuck offers 400 undeveloped campsites on almost 4000 acres; it's about 30 minutes south of Boston by car. The park boasts a network of paved paths and mountain-bike trails. Take I-93 south out of Boston to MA 3 south to MA 228 (exit 14). Go 7 miles north on Free St to Union St.

Canoe River Family Campground *(☎ 508-339-6462, 137 Mill St, Mansfield)* Sites without/with hookups $19/21. Open year-round (although only weekends mid-Oct–mid-Apr). A popular developed campground with over 200 sites, this facility rents kayaks and rowboats. It's about 50 minutes from Boston by car; take I-93 south to I-95 south to MA 140 east (exit 7A) to MA 106 and follow signs.

Normandy Farms Family Campground *(☎ 508-543-7600, 72 West St, Foxboro)* Sites $29-48, with hookups $48-53. Open year-round. This fully developed campground caters more to RVs than tenters. It has a big recreation room and four pools (one indoor), and 450 open and wooded sites on more than 100 acres. It, too, is about 50 minutes from Boston by car; take I-93 south to I-95 south to MA 1 south for 7 miles; go east on Thurston St to West St.

For other campgrounds on the fringes, see the Around Boston chapter.

Hostels

Irish Embassy Hostel *(Map 2; ☎ 617-973-4841, ⓔ embassyh@aol.com, 232 Friend St)* Dorm beds $22. Near the North End and Faneuil Hall, this hostel rents 54 beds (with four to 10 people per room) above its lively eponymous pub. You'll get a tidy place; free sheets; free admission to hear live bands at McGann's Pub around the corner *(197 Portland St);* free barbecue on Tuesday, Friday and Sunday; inexpensive pub lunches; and $1.50 beers. For the price, you can't complain, but don't get too comfortable; there's a six-night maximum stay. There's no lockout. The hostel is full by 9am in summer, so it's best to make reservations as far in advance as possible. Ⓣ Green or Orange Line to North Station.

Beantown Hostel *(Map 2; ☎ 617-723-0800, 222 Friend St)* Dorm beds $22. Since these 56 beds are operated by the adjacent Irish Embassy Hostel, prices and information are the same as at the Irish Embassy.

Strathmore Manor *(☎ 617-730-4118, 1876 Beacon St, Brookline)* Dorm beds $25-30. Open May–early Sept. The Irish Embassy has branched out to leafy suburbia with another acquisition, about 20 minutes from Kenmore Square by public transportation. These 32 beds are in largish four- and two-bedded rooms in a quiet neighborhood. Ⓣ Green Line 'C' branch to Englewood.

Boston International Hostel *(Map 4; ☎ 617-536-9455, 800-909-4776, fax 617-424-6558, ⓦ www.bostonhostel.org, 12 Hemenway*

St) Dorm beds $29/32 members/nonmembers. Conveniently located close to the Museum of Fine Arts and Kenmore Square, this hostel's dorm-style bunk rooms hold four to six people each (same sex), plus there are some rooms for coed couples. In addition to selling discount tickets to museums and whale-watching cruises, the hostel also offers some walking tours and other group events. Don't expect this to be one of the best-run hostels you'll ever encounter. Kitchen implements are often lacking, too. Try to reserve a month ahead of time in summer; make reservations with a credit card either by phone, fax or email. There is a 14-night maximum stay. If the hostel is full, they'll guide you elsewhere. Ⓣ Green Line to Hynes/ICA.

HI Back Bay Summer Hostel (Map 4; ☎ 617-353-3294 summer only, 536-9455 off-season, Ⓦ www.bostonhostel.org, 512 Beacon St) Dorm beds $29/32 members/nonmembers. Open June-late Aug. This 250-bed hostel, which supplements HI's Hemenway location, has relatively spacious rooms with two to four beds in each. Ⓣ Green Line to Hynes/ICA.

HI Boston at Fenway (Map 4; ☎ 617-267-8599, fax 617-424-6558, Ⓦ www.bostonhostel.org, 575 Comm Ave) Dorm beds $35/38 members/nonmembers; private rooms $99 for 1-3 people. Open June-late Aug. This former bi-level hotel, purchased by Boston University for student dormitories, also serves as a summertime hostel with 465 beds. It's a bit unusual, with air-conditioned rooms, in-suite bathrooms, no more than three beds per room, a TV and reading lounge, an information center in the lobby, 24-hour reception, housekeeping and on-call bell-staff. It's scheduled to open June 2002.

YMCA of Greater Boston (Map 4; ☎ 617-536-7800, fax 617-267-4653, Ⓦ www.bostonYMCA.org, 316 Huntington Ave) Singles/doubles/triples without bath $45/65/81, with breakfast. Near the Fenway and the Museum of Fine Arts, this Y rents 39 rooms to both sexes, though only men are allowed from September through May. There are also a limited number of rooms

for four people. Use of the excellent gym and pool is included. Reserve by mail two weeks prior to your visit or walk in after 11am; otherwise the rooms will be taken. Ⓣ Green Line 'E' branch to Northeastern.

Berkeley Residence YWCA (Map 4; ☎ 617-375-2524, fax 617-375-2525, Ⓦ www.YWCAboston.org, 40 Berkeley St) Singles/doubles/triples $65/100/125 with breakfast. Straddling the South End and Back Bay, this Y rents over 200 small rooms (some overlooking the garden) to women on a nightly and long-term basis. Guests can use the library, TV room, laundry room and garden. Ⓣ Orange Line to Back Bay.

Constitution Inn YMCA (☎ 617-241-8400, 800-495-9622, fax 617-241-2856, 150 Second Ave, Charlestown Navy Yard, Charlestown) Rooms $99. A short, scenic boat ride from downtown Boston's Long Wharf, this excellent choice accommodates active and retired military personnel as well as civilian guests. You won't see proportionally more crew cuts here than on the streets, nor will strident anti-war types be put off sleeping here. What you'll find is a good fitness center, pool and about 140 tidy twin- and queen-bedded rooms (all with refrigerator, private bath and cable TV). Ⓣ Green or Orange Line to North Station.

Motels

Motel 6 Boston/Braintree (☎ 781-848-7890, 800-466-8356, fax 781-843-1929, Ⓦ www.motel6.com, 125 Union St, Braintree) Singles $80-86, doubles $86-92. Although 15 miles south of Boston, you can travel into Boston in 30 minutes via public transportation, which stops one block away from here. Ⓣ Red Line to Braintree.

PLACES TO STAY – MID-RANGE
Motels & Hotels

Buckminster Hotel (Map 4; ☎ 617-236-7050, 800-727-2825, fax 617-262-0068, 645 Beacon St) Rooms $69-89, suites $129-149 off-season; rooms $109-149, suites $169-289 May-Nov. With small singles to suites that can accommodate families, this is as close as Boston comes to pensions. Each floor has its own laundry and kitchen facilities, fine if you're traveling with your own pots and pans. Rooms have air con, TV, microwave, fridge and phone. Ⓣ Green Line to Kenmore.

John Jeffries House (Map 2; ☎ 617-367-1866, fax 617-742-0313, 14 David Mugar Way) Rooms $85-110, suites $130-165 off-season; rooms $95-120, suites $140-175 Apr-Oct. This four-story hotel, at the base of Beacon Hill and near the Charles River, has 46 rooms and suites in an early-20th-century building owned by the Mass Eye and Ear Infirmary. (You don't have to know someone having an operation to stay here.) Rooms are nicely decorated, and some still have original molding and hardwood floors; most have a kitchenette. Ⓣ Red Line to Charles/MGH.

Chandler Inn Hotel (Map 4; ☎ 617-482-3450, 800-842-3450, fax 617-542-3428, Ⓦ www.chandlerinn.com, 26 Chandler St) Rooms $89-109 off-season, $139-124 Apr-mid-Nov. Popular with Europeans and gays, this central hotel has 56 clean, albeit nondescript, rooms. Single rooms are about $10 less than doubles. Ⓣ Orange Line to Back Bay.

Shawmut Inn (Map 2; ☎ 617-720-5544, 800-350-7784, fax 617-723-7784, Ⓦ www.shawmutinn.com, 280 Friend St) Singles/doubles $99/109 off-season, singles/doubles $129/139 Apr-mid-Nov, all with continental breakfast. Popular with Europeans, this friendly five-story hotel has 66 darkish rooms with kitchenettes. Suites with a fold-out couch are available for reduced weekly rentals. Rooms facing the elevated subway line are noisy, but the staff tries to accommodate noise level preferences. Children under 12 stay free. Ⓣ Green or Orange Line to North Station.

Holiday Inn Express (☎ 617-288-3030, 800-465-4329, fax 617-265-6543, Ⓦ www.basshotels.com, 69 Boston St, Dorchester) Rooms $109-129 off-season, $159-169 June-Sept. About 3 miles south of Boston (take exit 16 off I-93), this 118-room chain hotel is six blocks from public transportation and right on the expressway. Pluses include free parking and an adjacent 24-hour grocery store. Ⓣ Red Line to Andrew.

Best Western Terrace Inn (☎ 617-566-6260, 800-528-1234, fax 617-731-3543, Ⓦ www.bestwestern.com, 1650 Comm Ave, Brighton) Rooms $119-159 off-season, $139-179 mid-June-Nov. About 2 miles west of Kenmore Square, and about 20 minutes from Boston Common via public transportation, this place has 72 rooms, some with kitchenettes. All include TV, refrigerator and air con, plus parking. Ⓣ Green Line 'B' branch to Mt Hood.

Howard Johnson Fenway (Map 4; ☎ 617-267-8300, 800-654-2000, Ⓦ www.hojo.com, fax 617-267-2763, 1271 Boylston St) Rooms $125-155 off-season, $155-175 May-Oct. With 92 standard rooms, this place is within a 15-minute walk of the Museum of Fine Arts and about 15 minutes from downtown on the subway. Rates include parking. Ⓣ Green Line to Kenmore.

Best Western Homestead Inn (☎ 617-491-8000, 800-491-4914, fax 617-491-4932, Ⓦ www.bestwestern.com, 220 Alewife Brook Parkway, Cambridge) Rooms $169 off-season, $199 Sept-Nov with continental breakfast. An easy 10-minute walk to public transportation, this three-story motel has 69 rooms, friendly management and a small indoor pool. A health-food supermarket and movie theater are right next door. Ⓣ Red Line to Alewife.

B&Bs

The Bed & Breakfast Agency of Boston (Map 2; ☎ 617-720-3540, 800-248-9262, 0800-895128 from the UK, fax 617-523-5761, Ⓦ www.boston-bnbagency.com, 47 Commercial Wharf) lists about 150 B&Bs and apartments, most of which are located downtown. Some are in historic Victorian-furnished brownstones, some are waterfront lofts; one is even in a docked wooden sailboat. The agency details what's available at any given time. Expect to pay from $90 to $110 nightly for a double with shared bath, $100 to $180 with private bath. From mid-November to mid-February, stay two nights and get the third night free, based on availability, of course.

Commonwealth Court Guest House (Map 4; ☎ 617-424-1230, 888-424-1230, *fax 617-424-1510,* W *www.commonwealth court.com, 284 Comm Ave)* Rooms $75-105 off-season, $99-130 April–mid-Nov. These 20 rooms with kitchenettes, cable TV and free local calls aren't spiffy, but the price is right for the great location. Inquire about weekly in-season deals; all rates fluctuate. T Green Line to Hynes/ICA.

College Club (Map 4; ☎ 617-536-9510, fax 617-247-8537, W *www.thecollegeclubof boston.com, 44 Comm Ave)* Singles without bath $90, doubles with bath $150, all with continental breakfast. Originally a private club for women college graduates in the 1940s, this place has just 11 rooms, open to both sexes. Some furnishings are a bit shabby, but most rooms are enormous. The location couldn't be better: one block from the Public Garden and Newbury St, just three from the grassy Charles River Esplanade. T Green Line to Arlington.

Irving House (Map 5; ☎ 617-547-4600, 877-547-4600, fax 617-576-2814, W *www .irvinghouse.com, 24 Irving St, Cambridge)* Singles without bath $89, with bath $129-199, doubles without bath $109, with bath $129-219, all with breakfast. Staffed 24 hours a day and with a whopping 44 rooms, this is a good value made better by its prime location. With luck and timing, you might get one of the limited free parking spaces and a museum pass, too. If full, they'll direct you to their nearby Harding House. T Red Line to Harvard.

Copley House (Map 4; ☎ 617-236-8300, 800-331-1318, fax 617-424-1815, W *www .copleyhouse.com, 239 W Newton St)* Rooms $95-145 daily , $575-875 weekly. (Rates drop about 10-15% Nov-Mar.) There are accommodations in seven area buildings but everyone checks in at W Newton St. The studio and one-bedroom apartments are worn but serviceable with fully equipped mini kitchens, cable TV and free local calls. The units are popular with folks looking for an apartment; theater and business people; and tourists. T Green Line 'E' branch to Prudential.

Newbury Guest House (Map 4; ☎ 617-437-7666, 800-437-7668, fax 617-670-6100, W *www.newburyguesthouse.com, 261 New-* bury St) Rooms $125-190 with continental breakfast. This 32-room, four-story, circa 1882 renovated brownstone has an unbeatable Back Bay location, unless you get a room facing the back when the trash truck comes. There is even limited parking for $15! T Green Line to Hynes/ICA.

Clarendon Square Inn (Map 4; ☎ 617-536-2229, W *www.clarendonsquare.com, 198 W Brookline St)* Rooms $129-195 off-season, $169-259 Mar-Nov with breakfast. This stylish brick townhouse, complete with an airy living room and hot tub on the rooftop deck, has only three rooms. But if you're lucky enough to get one, you'll understand why chichi South End living is all the rage. T Orange Line to Back Bay.

PLACES TO STAY – TOP END

Midtown Hotel (Map 4; ☎ 617-262-1000, 800-343-1177, fax 617-262-8739, 220 Huntington Ave) Rooms $119-149 off-season, $149-279 mid-May–mid-Nov. This two-story hotel, on the edge of the South End, is a mere two blocks from the 4½-mile-long Southwest Corridor Park (great for walking). With free parking and an outdoor pool, the 159-room hotel fills up with families, business people and tour groups. T Green Line 'E' branch to Symphony.

Radisson Hotel Boston (Map 2; ☎ 617-482-1800, 800-333-3333, fax 617-482-0242, W *www.radisson.com, 200 Stuart St)* Rooms $129-179 off-season, $299-319 mid-Mar–Nov. Although the Radisson is popular with business travelers, tourists also appreciate its proximity to Boston Common. This 24-story hotel has 356 rooms, private balconies, free movie channels, a fitness center and an indoor swimming pool. T Green Line to Boylston.

Gryphon House (Map 4; ☎ 617-375-9003, fax 617-425-0716, W *www.innboston.com, 9 Bay State Rd)* Rooms $149-208 off-season, $185-245 May-Oct, with continental breakfast. On a quiet side street, this elegant five-story brownstone B&B features eight suites with in-room gas fireplaces, air con, TV and VCR, CD player, on-site parking (free!), two phone lines and DSL. Rooms have retained late-19th-century period details.

Each room has a different theme. It's easily one of the nicest places to stay in the city. Ⓣ Green Line to Kenmore.

Wyndham Tremont (Map 2; ☎ 617-426-1400, 800-331-9998, fax 617-423-0374, Ⓦ www.wyndham.com, 275 Tremont St) Rooms $149-289 off-season, $249-394 May-Oct. In the Theater District near Chinatown and a favorite among actors and stagehands, this hotel has 322 smallish guest rooms nicely decorated with early American reproduction furniture and prints from the Museum of Fine Arts. The 1925 hotel retains an ornate and elegant lobby, complete with chandeliers and a marble stairway and columns. Ⓣ Green Line to Boylston or Orange Line to NE Medical Center.

Lenox Hotel (Map 4; ☎ 617-536-5300, 800-225-7676, fax 617-236-0351, Ⓦ www .lenoxhotel.com, 710 Boylston St) Rooms $189-244 off-season, $308-348 June-Oct. This early-20th-century hotel has also undergone recent extensive renovations. A fancy Old-Worldish lobby (complete with crackling fireplace) gives way to 213 soundproofed guest rooms with classical furnishings, high ceilings, big closets and sitting areas. Ⓣ Green Line to Copley.

Copley Square Hotel (Map 4; ☎ 617-536-9000, 800-225-7062, fax 617-267-3547, Ⓦ www .copleysquarehotel.com, 47 Huntington Ave) Rooms $195-405. Constructed in 1891, this modest seven-story Back Bay hotel attracts a low-key European crowd who appreciate its eco-friendly attitude. The 143 refurbished rooms vary considerably in size and boast windows that open. What a novelty! Ask about special packages. The hotel's Original Sports Saloon features all-you-can-eat ribs for $15 on Wednesday. Inquire about the hotel's special packages. Ⓣ Green Line 'E' branch to Prudential.

Eliot Suite Hotel (Map 4; ☎ 617-267-1607, 800-443-5468, fax 617-536-9114, Ⓦ www.eliothotel.com, 370 Comm Ave) Rooms $255-365 off-season, $315-415 mid-Apr–mid-Nov. This European-style, nine-story hotel has 85 suites and 10 regular rooms on the edge of Back Bay near Kenmore Square. Although the hotel dates to 1925, rooms were elegantly remodeled

with marble tubs, antiques and French doors separating the living room and bedrooms. Ⓣ Green Line to Hynes/ICA.

PLACES TO EAT

The Boston restaurant scene is exploding with variety and imagination. You'll find most restaurants concentrated in the North End, the South End, Back Bay, Chinatown and Harvard Square in Cambridge. The places that seem a bit more difficult to reach are also worth seeking out. In Boston, eating cheaply doesn't have to mean eating badly. Conversely, if you want to splurge, there are memorable places to enjoy an evening.

See the Entertainment section for breweries, pubs and music venues that offer dining as well. (Also see the North End & Charlestown section, earlier, for specialty markets.)

Beacon Hill (Map 2)

All these eateries are reached via Ⓣ Red Line to Charles/MGH.

Try these gourmet shops, at either end of Charles St, for gathering picnic supplies to take to the Common or the Esplanade. (Remember when assembling a picnic that drinking alcoholic beverages in public is illegal.) *Savenor's* (☎ 617-723-6328, 160 Charles St) and *DeLuca's Market* (☎ 617-523-4343, 11 Charles St) are not cheap, but both offer fine selections of cheeses, deli items, baked goods and fresh produce. Both are open daily.

The Paramount (☎ 617-720-1152, 44 Charles St) Lunch $5-8, dinner $7-15. Open for all 3 meals daily. Not what you'd expect on tony Charles St, this neighborhood hangout is the choice of locals who don't want to cook but don't feel like dressing up. Breakfast and lunch are cafeteria-style with basic diner fare: pancakes, steak and eggs, meatloaf, lasagna. The place goes upscale at dinner without losing its down-home charm. It has arguably the tastiest chicken piccata in town.

Panificio (☎ 617-227-4340, 144 Charles St) Lunches average $6, dinner $9-18. Open for all 3 meals Mon-Fri, brunch Sat & Sun.

Arrive early for frittatas and French toast if you intend to linger over coffee and a newspaper. This cozy cafe and bistro is particularly known for weekday breakfast and weekend brunch. Pastas are de rigueur for dinner; lunches focus on soups and fancy sandwiches.

King & I (☎ *617-227-3320, 145 Charles St)* Mains $6-10, lunch specials $6.50. Open for lunch Mon-Sat, dinner daily. This is a good choice for Thai, with good service and ample portions. Seafood dishes and pad thai ($6.95) are good bets. Vegetables and tofu can be substituted for meat in any of the dishes.

Figs (☎ *617-742-3447, 42 Charles St)* Mains $11-20. Open for lunch Sat & Sun, dinner daily. Figs excels in fancy pasta dishes, salads and creative pizzas (with whisper-thin crusts) topped with goat cheese, prosciutto, portabello mushrooms and the like. Although it's pricier than most, it will also feel more like a night out than most pizza joints.

Lala Rokh (☎ *617-720-5511, 97 Mt Vernon St)* Mains $14-20. Open for dinner daily. Ask the helpful waitstaff if you want Lala Rokh's Persian menu translated; many ingredients will sound familiar to Middle Eastern cuisine fans. The differences, though subtle – an aromatic spice here or savory herb there – set the cooking here apart. Try *morgh,* saffron-seared chicken in a light tomato broth accompanied by basmati rice with cumin, cinnamon, rose petals and barberries ($15). The delectable baklava, fragrant with rose water, is heavenly. You can order a multicourse feast for the price of one entrée at other high-end restaurants.

Downtown (Map 2)

Touch the produce at the outdoor ***Haymarket Farmer's Market*** *(off Blackstone St)* and you risk the wrath of pushcart vendors. No one else in the city matches their prices on ripe-and-ready fruits and vegetables. The spectacle takes place every Friday and Saturday, with the best bargains on Saturday afternoon. ⓣ Green or Orange Line to Haymarket.

Downtown Crossing *(Summer St)* Between Washington and Chauncy Sts, these lunch cart vendors offer tasty, inexpensive fast food like burritos (look for Herrera's), sandwiches, sausages, hot dogs and veggie wraps. Check out the almost-daily produce market. ⓣ Red or Orange Line to Downtown Crossing.

Faneuil Hall Marketplace (☎ *617-338-2323)* Open 10am-9pm Mon-Sat, noon-6pm Sun. Northeast of Congress and State Sts, this food hall offers the greatest number and variety of places under one roof: There are about 20 restaurants and 40 food stalls. You'll find chowder, bagels, Indian, Greek, baked goods and ice cream. The center rotunda has tables. ⓣ Green or Blue Line to Government Center.

Chacarero Chilean Cuisine (☎ *617-542-0392, 426 Franklin St)* Sandwiches $4-6. Open 11am-6pm Mon-Fri. Arrive for an early or late lunch or be prepared to queue up with masses of humanity. They come for hefty takeout grilled chicken, beef or savory vegetarian sandwiches with guacamole and green beans, in fresh crusty rolls and wrapped in foil. Head to a nearby sidewalk bench or to Boston Common with your takeout. ⓣ Red or Orange Line to Downtown Crossing.

Cosi Sandwich Shop (☎ *617-292-2674, 133 Federal St)* Dishes from $6.25. Open 7am-5pm Mon-Fri. The latest import from Paris by way of New York, Cosi has taken the Boston lunch crowd by storm. Line up behind the suits and select from 20 fillings to be sandwiched between pieces of crusty, fresh, hearth-baked flat bread. Possibilities include cranberry roasted turkey, tandoori grilled chicken and roasted red pepper with eggplant feta spread. 'Cosi One' (one filling) goes for $6.25, 'Cosi Two' for $7.25 and so on. One sandwich may be big enough to share. ⓣ Red Line to South Station.

Country Life (☎ *617-951-2534, 200 High St)* Lunch buffet $7, dinner mains $7. Open for lunch Mon-Fri, dinner Sun & Tues-Thur, brunch Sun. Worth seeking out for its all-you-can-eat lunch buffet, you'll also find tasty lasagna, pot pies and lots of different soups, but no meat, dairy or refined grains.

The décor is pleasant enough and the self-service keeps the prices reasonable. ⓣ Red Line to South Station.

Post Office Cafe *(☎ 617-350-7275, Post Office Square)* Sandwiches $7.50. Open 7am-6pm Mon-Fri. This is a favorite of the Financial District suit crowd, but don't let that deter you from large servings of above-average lunch fare like pastas, salads, soups, sandwiches and pastries. The park location is pleasant in summer, when cafe tables are set out and diners spill onto the greenery. ⓣ Red or Orange Line to Downtown Crossing.

Mr Dooley's Boston Tavern *(☎ 617-338-5656, 77 Broad St)* Lunches average $8, dinner $11. Open for all 3 meals Mon-Sat, breakfast & dinner Sun. One of the few area joints open on weekends, this pub offers 'real' Irish breakfasts on Saturday and Sunday. Look for imported sausage, bacon, black-and-white pudding, eggs, home fries, homemade brown soda bread, fish and chips and other similar grub. Live Irish music rounds out the weekend scene. ⓣ Red or Orange Line to Downtown Crossing.

Sultan's Kitchen *(☎ 617-338-7819, 72 Broad St)* Mains average $9. Open 11am-8pm Mon-Fri, 11am-3pm Sat. Line up with the crowds at this self-service find and you'll be rewarded with sizable portions of complex and delicately flavored Turkish dishes. Head upstairs to dine. Standbys include baba ghanoush, stuffed grape leaves, falafel, shish kebobs, salads and baklava. If you can't decide, get the sampler ($8.25). Save room for arguably the world's best rice pudding ($2.75). ⓣ Red or Orange Line to Downtown Crossing.

Bertucci's *(☎ 617-227-7889, 22 Merchants Row)* Dishes $10-17. Open for lunch & dinner daily. Next to Faneuil Hall Market-place, Bertucci's is one of the most popular places for sit-down, brick-oven pizza ($10.50 for a large cheese, $15 to $17 for a large 'specialty'). Try not to fill up on the tasty, piping-hot rolls, because they also have salads, pasta dishes and calzones. ⓣ Green or Blue Line to Government Center.

Cheers *(☎ 617-227-0150, South Market, Faneuil Hall Marketplace)* Dishes average $9. Open 11am-2am daily. Responding to hordes of tourists who are disappointed that the 'real' Bull & Finch pub on Beacon Street doesn't resemble the erstwhile television show, this Cheers was born. With high-quality reproduction props – from the bartender's Red Sox jacket to soundstage artifices to bar stools – you should have no trouble recognizing the place. This, dear readers, is life imitating art, if you can call the sitcom *Cheers* 'art.' Oh yeah, the food is average pub grub. ⓣ Green or Blue Line to Government Center.

Durgin Park *(☎ 617-227-2038, North Market, Faneuil Hall Marketplace)* Dishes $7-20. Open 11:30am-10pm Mon-Sat, 11:30am-9pm Sun. Known for no-nonsense service, sawdust underfoot on the old floor-boards and family-style dining at large tables, Durgin Park fare hasn't changed much since the restaurant was built in 1827: huge slabs of prime rib, fish chowder, chicken pot pie, Boston baked beans, and strawberry short-cake and Indian pudding for dessert. Be prepared to make friends with the other parties seated at your table. ⓣ Green or Blue Line to Government Center.

Les Zygomates *(☎ 617-542-5108, 129 South St)* Lunch $8-15, dinner $15-30 (multicourse prix-fixe options available at both meals). Open 11:30am-1am Mon-Fri, 6pm-1am Sat. In the Leather District near South Station, this trendy and sophisticated late-night place serves great live jazz music along with its oh-so-creative bistro menu highlighting, perhaps, poached lobster with roasted pepper blini or smoked pork with plantain chutney. ⓣ Red Line to South Station.

Ben's Café *(☎ 617-227-3370, 45 School St)* Lunch $12-25. Open for lunch Mon-Fri, dinner daily. Within Old City Hall and arguably the city's finest traditional French restaurant, Maison Robert, Ben's boasts two prix-fixe lunch menus ($18 and $25) featuring smaller portions of the famed French fare. Whether on the terrace or in the cozy, romantic dining room, you won't remember that you are in the 'bargain base-ment' of one of Boston's best. ⓣ Red or Green Line to Park St.

Tsatsukichi (☎ *617-720-2468, 189 State St*) Mains $12-15. Open for dinner daily. Tsatsukichi serves fine traditional Japanese cuisine, especially sushi, in understated elegant surroundings. It's a nice place to take a break from the bustle of Faneuil Hall Marketplace. ⓣ Green or Blue Line to Government Center.

KingFish Hall (☎ *617-523-8862, South Market, Faneuil Hall Marketplace*) Lunch $13-16, dinners average $22. Open noon-10pm or 11pm daily. Chef-entrepreneur Todd English, of Olives and Figs fame, has struck again. Seek out the exceptional original chowder, the fancy lobster and corn version, seafood gumbo and Thai-spiced grilled squid. Seafood reigns, obviously. As for the décor, it's cool kitsch, again with a seafood motif. Look for a second Faneuil Hall location in Quincy Market, ***Todd English Rustic Kitchen*** (☎ *617-523-6334*), featuring casual flat breads, panini, appetizers and polenta dishes (lunch mains $8 to $14, dinner mains $16 to $25). ⓣ Green or Blue Line to Government Center.

The North End (Map 2)

All these eateries are reached via ⓣ Green or Orange Line to Haymarket.

Salumeria Italiana (☎ *617-523-8743, 151 Richmond St*) Open 8am-7pm Mon-Sat, 10am-4pm Sun. Assemble an Italian-style picnic complete with prosciutto, salami, cheese, bread and olives.

Mike's Pastry (☎ *617-742-3050, 300 Hanover St*) Open 8am-9:30pm daily. Before heading off to the waterfront to enjoy your sandwich from Salumeria Italiana, stop at the neighborhood's favorite bakery. Muscle your way through the crowds and grab the attention of one of the staff as they scurry to and fro. Order a ricotta cannoli ($2.25), which they will make fresh in the back room, rather than opting for an already-filled pastry shell.

Regina Pizzeria (☎ *617-227-0765, 11½ Thatcher St*) Large pies $11-17. Open 11am-11pm daily. The North End wouldn't be the same without this legendary, bustling place with seemingly brusque but actually endearing waitstaff. The crispy, thin-crust pizza –

$15 for a large with two toppings – is best consumed with a pitcher of beer (about $9) There's also a branch in Faneuil Hall Marketplace (☎ *617-227-8180*), but it's not as good as the original.

Galleria Umberto (☎ *617-227-5709, 289 Hanover St*) Slices 85¢. Open 11am-2pm or 2:30pm Mon-Sat. This place certainly rivals its counterpart, above, in quality, but its crust is as thick and chewy as Regina's is thin and crispy. Furthermore, the slices are usually gone by mid-afternoon, at which time the joint closes.

La Piccola Venezia (☎ *617-523-3888, 263 Hanover St*) Dishes $8-16. Open 11:30am-10pm daily. This cafe provides consistently great values with huge portions of old-fashioned dishes: eggplant parmagiana ($12 at dinner, less at lunch), spaghetti and meatballs drenched with red sauce ($11) and more unusual but authentic dishes like tripe and gnocchi.

Pagliuca's (☎ *617-367-1504, 14 Parmenter St*) Lunch $6-12, dinner $8-19. Open 11am-10pm daily. A favorite amongst the old-fashioned North End establishments, there's nothing fancy at Pagliuca's, just dependable, hearty home-style Italian fare like eggplant parmesan, chicken cacciatore and veal marsala.

Antico Forno (☎ *617-723-6733, 93 Salem St*) Pizza $10-15, mains $15-20. Open 11:30am-10pm daily. Named for its beehive, wood-burning brick oven, the source of all that's warm and wonderful in this Neapolitan place, Antico Forno specializes in pizza. Try the *vesuvio* (spicy sausage, cherry tomatoes, roasted peppers, mozzarella and ricotta). Southern Italian home cooking and roasted meats aren't slighted either.

Terramia (☎ *617-523-3112, 98 Salem St*) Dishes $11-30. Open for lunch Sun, dinner daily. Antico Forno's sibling is the creation of impresario Mario Nocera, who hand-selects every mushroom that enters the kitchen. The creative menu changes seasonally and showcases the essential beauty of vintage balsamic vinegars and rare Italian cheeses from the country. Dishes could be pasta- and rice-based ($11 to $18) or centered around seafood and meat ($17 to $30).

You'll have to go elsewhere for dessert and coffee – not a problem in the cafe-filled North End.

Restaurant Bricco (☎ 617-248-6800, 241 Hanover St) Mains $18-32. Open for dinner daily. Brilliantly fused flavors from northern Italy, California, southern France and northern Africa reign in a handsomely Euro-chic dining room. In good weather, casement windows open onto the street. Order traditionally or order lots of antipasti (tastings are $7 to $8 each), but save room for diverse breads and sweet finales.

Charlestown (Map 2)

All these eateries are reached via ⓣ Green or Orange Line to North Station or Orange Line to Community College.

Sorelle Bakery Café (☎ 617-242-2125, 1 Monument Ave) Dishes average $5. Open 6:30am-5pm Mon-Fri, 8am-3pm Sat & Sun. This tiny place serves coffees, pastries, salads, sandwiches and cold pasta dishes.

Figs (☎ 617-242-2229, 67 Main St) Dishes $11-20. Open from 5:30pm daily. This is another branch of Figs (see Beacon Hill, earlier), perfect after a late afternoon spent climbing the Bunker Hill Monument.

Olives (☎ 617-242-1999, 10 City Square) Mains average $22-25. Open 5:30pm-10pm Mon-Sat. Olives draws some rave reviews for its creative Mediterranean–New American menu, all of which is prepared in the exposed kitchen. You can easily blow $100 for two people here, feasting on the house specialties of spit-roasted meats and savory fish. Expect a high noise level and a wait, unless you arrive very early (at 4:45pm) or very late.

Back Bay (Map 4)

Boston is ground zero for ice cream wars. Decide for yourself which is best; take the Green Line to Copley and fan out onto Newbury St. ***Emack & Bolio's*** (☎ 617-247-8772, 290 Newbury St) takes pride in its status as an old-timer on the Boston gourmet ice cream scene. Many consider its Oreo cookie ice cream definitive; nonfat yogurt creations like latte espresso chip are also good. ***Ben & Jerry's*** (☎ 617-536-5456, 174 Newbury St) has ever-changing choices, including triple caramel chunk. At ***JP Licks*** (☎ 617-236-1666, 352 Newbury St), it's a toss-up between white coffee and chocolate macadamia. For more best–ice cream contenders, see the Chinatown and Harvard Square sections.

Finale Desserterie (☎ 617-423-3184, 1 Columbus Ave) Dishes average $8. Open 11:30am-10pm daily. Choose from a long list of tempting treats, from crème brulee to chocolate souffle, and enjoy them with coffee, wine or port. The elegant yet comfortable dining room is set up so that, through mirrors over the pastry chefs' workstation, you can watch their magic. There are also light soups, salads and sandwiches at lunchtime and appetizer-size dinner dishes so you don't eat sweets on an empty stomach. ⓣ Green Line to Arlington.

Bangkok Cuisine (☎ 617-262-5377, 177A Mass Ave) Lunch $5-6, dinner $8-13.50. Open 11:30am-3pm & 5pm-10:30pm daily. Near the Boston International Hostel, this was Boston's first Thai restaurant, and it's still one of the best. Conventional choices of satay (grilled $4.75) and pad thai ($5 at lunch, $6.75 at dinner) are very good. When the menu says hot, it means it. ⓣ Green Line to Hynes/ICA.

The Other Side Cosmic Café (☎ 617-536-9477, 407 Newbury St) Dishes $7 & under. Open 11am-1am daily. The 'other side' refers to the other side of Mass Ave, which few strollers crossed before this place opened. The 'cosmic' alludes to its funky, Seattle-inspired style. The 1st floor is done in cast iron, while the 2nd floor is softened by velvet drapes, mismatched couches and low ceilings. Vegetarian chili, sandwiches, fruit and veggie drinks and strong coffee are the order of the day. Some of the twenty-something clientele hang out here all day and night. ⓣ Green Line to Hynes/ICA.

Kebab-N-Kurry (☎ 617-536-9835, 30 Mass Ave) Lunch $6-7, dinners average $13. Open noon-3pm Mon-Fri, 5pm-11pm daily. Always crowded, this small basement eatery boasts consistently good dishes at consistently good prices. ⓣ Green Line to Hynes/ICA.

Geoffrey's Café & Bar (☎ *617-266-1122, 160 Comm Ave*) Dishes $7-15. Open 9am-11pm daily. Geoffrey's serves up eclectic home cooking with a healthy dose of camp on the side. Try a delicious pasta dish, hearty sandwiches and creative meat and potatoes variations. ⓣ Green Line to Copley.

Café Jaffa (☎ *617-536-0230, 48 Gloucester St*) Dishes $8-11. Open for lunch & dinner daily. This storefront eatery is a surprising bargain in the middle of this blue-blood neighborhood. When was the last time you had authentic Turkish coffee, shwarma or falafel in a place with polished wooden floors and exposed brick? The servings are large and the prices more than reasonable. You can take out or eat in. ⓣ Green Line to Hynes/ICA.

Betty's Wok & Noodle Diner (☎ *617-424-1950, 250 Huntington Ave*) Dishes $8-16. Open noon-10pm or 11pm Tues-Sun. Although it's adjacent to Symphony Hall, the Huntington Theater and Northeastern University, this funky and intentionally retro eatery still feels a bit on the edge. But it's worth seeking out for innovative noodle dishes and spicy and saucy Asian and Latin flavors. Pick a main dish, then customize it with your choice of noodles and sauces. Wait until after 8pm on weekends to avoid theater crowds. ⓣ Green Line 'E' branch to Symphony.

Parish Café & Bar (☎ *617-247-4777, 361 Boylston St*) Sandwiches $10-12. Open noon-2am daily. Next to the Public Garden, this cafe is known for creative and hearty sandwiches, each designed by a local celebrity chef. Try the one by Rialto chef Jody Adams: prosciutto and buffalo mozzarella with pesto and a touch of basil oil on grilled white bread – not your average sandwich. Some are accompanied by a salad. Other draws include an outdoor patio, a stylish interior, 76 different brands of beer and 20 wines by the glass. ⓣ Green Line to Arlington.

Trident Booksellers & Café (☎ *617-267-8688, 338 Newbury St*) Dishes $10-15. Open 9am-midnight daily. If you think 'Boston, books and breakfast' go together, head here. The shelves are primarily filled with New Age titles, while the tables are crowded with decidedly down-to-earth salads, soups, sandwiches, pasta entrées and desserts; breakfast is served all day. Vegetarians rejoice with the vegan cashew chili. ⓣ Green Line to Hynes/ICA.

Tapeo (☎ *617-267-4799, 266 Newbury St*) Tapas $4-7.50, mains $18-24. Open for lunch Sat & Sun, dinner daily. This festive Spanish tapas restaurant has bodega-style dining rooms and, in fine weather, a patio fronting Newbury St (a nonstop parade). It's also perfect for sangria-guzzling and sherry-sipping. ⓣ Green Line to Copley.

Casa Romero (☎ *617-536-4341, 30 Gloucester St*) Mains $12-24. Open from 5pm daily. Delicious, authentic Mexico City–style cuisine in a lovely courtyard or intimate Talavera-tiled dining room – what more could you want? The enchiladas, verdes or poblanas, are excellent, as is the *puerco adobado,* roasted pork marinated in sweet oranges and smoked chipotle chile. ⓣ Green Line to Hynes/ICA.

Sonsie (☎ *617-351-2500, 327 Newbury St*) Dinner $16-27. Open 7am-1am daily. This is perhaps the hippest place to sip a cappuccino. Europeans descend on the place wearing basic black and dark sunglasses. In warm weather, a wall of French doors is flung open, making the indoor tables almost al fresco. During busy mealtimes, cafe tables are reserved for diners. Pizza, pasta and other light dishes are available. Although full-fledged dining here is pricey (make reservations), the French and Asian fusion menu is worth it. ⓣ Green Line to Hynes/ICA.

Kenmore Square (Map 4)

Appealing to students on a budget is the sandwich joint *Ankara Cafe* (☎ *617-437-0404, 472 Comm Ave*) Dishes $4-6.50. Open 8am-midnight daily. It has triple deckers named for local schools as well as pizzas and custom blended frozen yogurt. Seating is quite limited. ⓣ Green Line to Kenmore.

Elephant Walk (☎ *617-247-1500, 900 Beacon St, Brookline*) Lunch $8-10, dinner $11-17 (Cambodian), $8.50-23 (French). Open 11:30am-2:30pm Mon-Fri, 5pm-10pm daily. Just west of Kenmore Square, the Elephant Walk is highly regarded for its dual menus of classic French and traditional Cambodian cuisine served in a large dining room. Make reservations. ⓣ Green Line 'C' branch to St Mary's.

The Fenway (Map 4)

All these eateries are reached via ⓣ Green Line to Kenmore.

El Pelon Taqueria (☎ *617-262-9090, 92 Peterborough St*) Dishes under $6. Open 11:30am-10:30pm daily. Come here for authentic Mexican, including burritos, chile rellenos, tamales and huge *tortas* (grilled meat on a toasted roll and heaped with black beans, the chef's special limed onions, lettuce and avocado). How do they serve such generous servings of high-quality food? Paper plates and plastic cutlery help.

Audubon Circle (☎ *617-421-1910, 838 Beacon St*) Dishes $6-13. Open 11:30am-1am Mon-Fri, 4:30pm-1am Sat & Sun. This lively pub and restaurant exudes a good vibe for hanging out or eating. It serves one of the best burgers (and good noshing appetizers) in town.

Buteco (☎ *617-247-9508, 130 Jersey St*) Mains average $8. Open noon-10pm Mon-Fri, 3pm-10pm Sat-Sun. Serving bountiful, hearty Brazilian home cooking in a relaxed atmosphere, this place is justly known for meat dishes. But there are a few chicken, fish and vegetarian dishes, too. The weekend dinner special is usually *feijoada*, a rich stew of black beans, pork, sausage and dried beef.

Brown Sugar Café (☎ *617-266-2928, 129 Jersey St*) Lunches average $6.50, dinners average $12. Open for lunch & dinner daily. You'll have trouble leaving this small cafe. The delectable Thai food is beautifully presented – try the mango curry, with tender chicken simmered in a yellow curry with chunks of ripe mango, tomato, red and green pepper, onion and summer squash. Portions seem even larger when you take out.

The South End (Map 4)

Lawyers in suits and laborers in work boots frequent the classic *Charlie's Sandwich*

Shoppe (☎ *617-536-7669, 429 Columbus Ave*) Dishes $4-8. Open 6am-2:30pm Mon-Fri, 7:30am-1pm Sat. This coffee shop has been serving creative omelets, cranberry French toast and other breakfast platters since 1927. For lunch, favorites include turkey hash with two eggs, hot pastrami and homemade pies at a few shared tables or the counter. ⓣ Orange Line to Back Bay.

Tim's Tavern (☎ *617-437-6898, 329 Columbus Ave*) Dishes $1.25-13. Open 11am-midnight Mon-Sat. Another great neighborhood joint serving fabulous food but cloaked as a divey bar, Tim's has some of the best (and biggest and cheapest) burgers. Splurge on fries or onion rings for another buck. Baby back ribs also get raves. ⓣ Orange Line to Back Bay.

Delux Café (☎ *617-338-5258, 100 Chandler St*) Dishes $3-10. Open for dinner Mon-Sat. Appearances can be both revealing and deceiving. This place looks like a small, dark bar, and it is; but it is also serves decidedly upscale, globally inspired food in a friendly, funky-kitschy atmosphere. A secret no longer, the place is packed (with more than a few smokers, too). ⓣ Orange Line to Back Bay.

Garden of Eden Cafe (☎ *617-247-8377, 571 Tremont St*) Lunch $7-9, dinner $6.50-14. Open 7:30am-10pm (at least) daily. This neighborhood storefront eatery, with two big communal tables for solo diners, is just as apropos for coffee and dessert as it is for a full-blown meal. There are lots of hearty specials (chicken dijonnaise anyone?), creative sandwiches, salads and lush artisanal cheese platters. Breakfast dishes, such as perhaps a vegetarian egg souffle, are available until 2pm. ⓣ Orange Line to Back Bay.

Jae's Café & Grill (☎ *617-421-9405, 520 Columbus Ave*) Lunch specials $9-10, dinner $15-19. Open for lunch & dinner daily. This place specializes in Korean food but offers a full pan-Asian menu, so you can order sushi, satay, pad thai or vegetarian noodle dishes. The spot is cozy, so expect to wait for dinner unless you arrive by 6pm. ⓣ Orange Line to Mass Ave.

Bob the Chef (☎ *617-536-6204, 604 Columbus Ave*) Dishes average $10-13.

Open 11:30am-10pm Tues & Wed, 11:30am-midnight Fri & Sat, 10am-9pm Sun. This is Boston's best down-home soul food: We're talking barbecue ribs with a hunk of cornbread or fried chicken with collard greens or black-eyed peas. Sit at the long counter or in a booth. The Sunday jazz brunch ($18), served 11am to 3:30pm, is a local favorite. Ⓣ Orange Line to Mass Ave.

Franklin Café (☎ 617-350-0010, 278 Shawmut Ave) Mains $12-16. Open 5:30pm-1:30am daily. Perhaps the neighborhood's most beloved restaurant (and that's saying something in this restaurant-rich neighborhood), the Franklin has been discovered by suburbanites (gasp!). No fear; watching hard bodies at the bar while you wait for a table can still be fun. As for the food, think New American comfort food prepared by a gourmet chef: steamed mussels with Pernod, leeks, garlic and white wine or roasted turkey meatloaf with spiced fig gravy and chive mashed potatoes. Ⓣ Orange Line to Back Bay.

Claremont Cafe (☎ 617-247-9001, 535 Columbus Ave) Dishes $12-25. Open for all 3 meals Tues-Sat, brunch 9am-3pm Sun. This tiny, romantic place offers large portions of its South American- and Mediterranean-inspired cuisine; you'll do well with rice dishes, paella and roast chicken. The cafe draws an artsy group of neighborhood residents, especially in the morning for terrific scones. Reservations suggested. Ⓣ Orange Line to Mass Ave.

On the Park (☎ 617-426-0862, 1 Union Park) Dinner $15-20, brunch $4-9. Open 5:30pm-10:30pm Tues-Sat, brunch 9am-2:30pm Sat & Sun. This friendly little neighborhood place feels a bit like it belongs in New York's Greenwich Village. It's bright and funky, with lots of local art on the walls. The food tends toward creative American: marinated pork chops, gingered lamb stew or whole wheat pasta. The weekend brunch with mimosas is particularly popular. No reservations are taken, but call to put your name on a waiting list. Ⓣ Orange Line to Back Bay.

Hamersley's Bistro (☎ 617-423-2700, 553 Tremont St) Mains $23-33. Open for dinner daily. Consistently at the top of every 'best restaurants' list, Hamersley's serves French/country American cuisine. The seasonal menu might include grilled filet of beef or hot-and-spicy grilled tuna. Roasted chicken with garlic, parsley and lemon ($23) is a house specialty. The ambiance is urban and cool, but not too cool; you could spend $150 for two with nice wine, but you only *have* to spend $75 for two. Reservations are highly recommended. Ⓣ Orange Line to Back Bay.

Chinatown (Map 2)

All these eateries are reached via Ⓣ Orange Line to Chinatown.

Wai Wai (☎ 617-338-9833, 26 Oxford St) Wai Wai is Boston's most offbeat entry in the ice cream wars. Although the tiny basement eatery exudes an aroma of roasting chickens, don't be scared. In addition to quick meals, Wai Wai offers five or six homemade tropical ice cream flavors including ginger, coconut and banana. (If you're feeling down and out after a long day, medicate yourself with the Wong Lo Kat 'medical' tea for $1).

Pho Pasteur (☎ 617-482-7467, 682 Washington St) Dishes $5-8. Open 9am-11pm daily. Pho Pasteur serves hearty, hot and cheap meals in a bowl. Although there are other Vietnamese dishes from which to choose, most people come for *pho*, the sometimes exotic, always fragrant and flavorful noodle soup ($5).

Hu Tieu Nam Vang (☎ 617-422-0501, 7 Beach St) Dishes $5-10. Open 8:30am-10pm daily. Delicious and authentic Vietnamese specialties, from pho to vermicelli, are a great value. Try a hot pot – a crock of rice, vegetables and any combination of meat, seafood or tofu, cooked together in a spicy aromatic sauce. It's enough for two people. There are over 40 kinds of cold drinks and fresh fruit shakes.

Grand Chau Chow (☎ 617-426-6266, 45 Beach St) Lunch $5, dinner $8-10. Open 10:30am-4am daily. Highlighting food from various regions in China, this restaurant has excellent daily seafood specials, ample portions and renowned ginger and black bean sauces. Try the garlicky sautéd pea pod stems and the crispy, chewy fried squid.

Apollo Grill (☎ 617-423-3888, 84-86 Harrison Ave) Dishes $5-15. Open 11:30am-2:30pm Mon-Fri, 5pm-4am daily. This Japanese-Korean late-night hot spot features tables with built-in hibachi grills. Tasty appetizers and sushi are a draw, too.

Buddha's Delight (☎ 617-451-2395, 3 Beach St) Lunch specials $7, dinner $7-10. Open 11am-9:30pm or 10:30pm daily. Vegetarians will be thrilled with noodle soups, tasty tofu dishes and imitation meat dishes like soybean 'roast pork.' Try a fruit and milk drink for dessert.

Ginza (☎ 617-338-2261, 16 Hudson St) Lunches average $10. Open 11:30am-2:30pm Mon-Fri, 5pm-2am Mon-Thur & Sun, 5pm-4am Fri & Sat. This hip Japanese restaurant serves some of the best sushi and maki in Boston. For those who prefer their fish hot, there's always tempura. All this excellence doesn't come cheap, though; expect to spend $20 to $25 per person for dinner.

Penang (☎ 617-451-6373, 685 Washington St) Mains average $12. Open 11:30am-11:30pm daily. Penang serves creative Malaysian fare in a festive atmosphere. Although you can test your fortitude with fish heads, intestines and pig's feet, it's not required. There are several vegetarian options for the less than intrepid. Some items come with the admonition 'Ask your server for advice before you order!!!'

Waterfront (Map 2)
South Station Food Court (Atlantic Ave at Summer St) Within the grandly renovated train terminal, the food court offers a range of fast food for about $6, but hidden among the usual suspects are some gems. *Rosie's Bakery* (☎ 617-439-4684) satisfies the most demanding sweet tooth and challenges the most determined dieter; try a pecan sticky bun. *JB Scoops* (☎ 617-443-0500) dishes out homemade ice cream in old-fashioned flavors like maple walnut and pumpkin pie ($2.15 for one scoop). *Boston Coffee Exchange* brews flavorful espresso and cappuccino. Ⓣ Red Line to South Station.

Barking Crab (☎ 617-426-2722, 88 Sleeper St) Dishes $8.50-23. Open 11:30am-9:30pm daily. Everything an indoor clam shack should be, the Barking Crab offers big servings of delicious fried seafood on paper plates at communal picnic tables on the water. The platters, with fries and cole slaw, are worth every penny. It doesn't get more authentic than this. One wonders, though, how long it can last. Ⓣ Red Line to South Station.

Intrigue (☎ 617-856-7744, 70 Rowes Wharf) Lunch $9.50-14.50, dinner $10.50-16.50. Open 7am-10pm daily. Within the Boston Harbor Hotel, this is a refined but unpretentious place for a sumptuous breakfast, light meal or dessert and wine. The casually elegant room, complete with harbor view, also serves afternoon tea. Ⓣ Red Line to South Station.

Legal Sea Foods (☎ 617-227-3115, 255 State St, Long Wharf) Lunch $8-15, dinners average $20. Open 11am-10pm Mon-Fri, 11am-11pm Sat & Sun. With a reputation and local empire built on the motto 'If it's not fresh, it's not Legal,' Legal has few rivals. The menu is simple: every kind of seafood, it seems, broiled, steamed, sautéd, grilled or fried. Freshness comes at a price, though. The servings are generous, so depending on your appetite, the fried calamari appetizer ($8) could be a main dish. The clam chowder ($4.50) is justifiably considered New England's best. Does anyone else see the irony of a big seafood restaurant across from the Aquarium? Ⓣ Blue Line to Aquarium.

There are also branches at the Prudential Center (☎ 617-266-6800, 800 Boylston St), at Park Square (☎ 617-426-4444), at the Copley Place shopping mall (☎ 617-266-7775) and in Kendall Square (☎ 617-864-3400, 5 Cambridge Center, Cambridge). All branches are open about the same hours.

Harvard Square (Map 5)
All these eateries are reached via Ⓣ Red Line to Harvard.

Cambridge is ripe for a farmer's market, but the plaza at the ritzy Charles Hotel hardly seems the obvious site. Nonetheless, the *Charles Hotel Farmer's Market* (☎ *617-864-2100, 5 Bennett St*) is a great market. It's open 10am to 3pm Saturday mid-June to mid-November.

Ice cream wars continue unabated at *Toscanini's* (☎ *617-354-9350, 1310 Mass Ave*), where gingersnap molasses and Vienna finger cookie are excellent, and *Herrell's* (☎ *617-497-2179, 15 Dunster St*), where favorites include malted vanilla and chocolate pudding.

Cardullo's (☎ *617-491-8888, 6 Brattle St*) Open 8am-8pm Mon-Sat, 11am-7pm Sun. This deli carries an impressive assortment of international goods, but more importantly, they make sandwiches to go.

The Garage (*36 John F Kennedy St, Harvard Square*) With about a dozen places to eat under one roof, you're bound to find something fast, filling and cheap here.

Hi-Rise Pie Co (☎ *617-492-3003, 56 Brattle St*) Dishes $5-7. Open 8:30am-5pm Mon-Fri, 9am-5pm Sat, 10am-4pm Sun. Well known for wonderful scones, cookies and crusty loaves, Hi-Rise also serves light meals (sandwiches and soups) in the cafe. Outdoor tables are popular in warm weather; indoors is cozy.

Sabra Grill (☎ *617-868-5777, 20 Eliot St*) Mains $4.50-8. Open 10am-10pm daily. Sabra served fresh and delicious Middle Eastern takeout long before it was trendy. Try the chicken shwarma and shish kebab; vegetarians and their contrarians alike will be happy with spinach pie and Greek salad.

Algiers Coffee House (☎ *617-492-1557, 40 Brattle St*) Dishes $4-12. Open 8am-midnight daily. Although service can be glacial, the palatial Middle Eastern décor makes this a comfortable rest spot. Head to the airy 2nd floor and order a falafel sandwich, a bowl of lentil soup, *merguesa* (lamb sandwich) or a lamb kebab. The one good thing about the 'relaxed' service is that you won't be rushed to finish your pot of Arabic coffee or mint tea.

Bartley's Burger Cottage (☎ *617-354-6559, 1246 Mass Ave*) Dishes under $10. Open 11am-10pm Mon-Sat. Packed with small tables and hungry college students, Bartley's is *the* primo burger joint, offering at least 40

different burgers. But if none of those suits your fancy, create your own 7oz juicy masterpiece topped with guacamole or sprouts. They do make a veggie burger (for vegetarians who don't mind being surrounded by all that red meat). French fries and onion rings complete the classic American meal.

Bombay Club (☎ *617-661-8100, 57 John F Kennedy St*) Lunch buffet $8, dinner mains $12-15. Open 11:30am-11pm daily, lunch buffet 11:30am-3pm daily. This a good choice for lunch because of the bargain buffet, but dinner features cooked-to-order northern Indian dishes like chicken *tikka masala* ($11).

Casa Mexico (☎ *617-491-4552, 75 Winthrop St*) Lunch $6, dinners average $12. Open noon-2:30pm Mon-Sat, 6pm-11pm daily. The best place for inexpensive and authentic Mexican on either side of the Charles River, the basement dining room is usually crowded with patrons who come for rich chocolatey *mole* sauce (as in chicken *mole poblano*), tostadas and enchiladas. It's been around since the 1970s, so it must be doing something right.

Casablanca (☎ *617-876-0999, 40 Brattle St*) Lunch $8-13, dinner $17-23. Open for lunch & dinner daily, bar until 1:30pm. Combining a romantic atmosphere inspired by the eponymous film with modern Mediterranean cuisine catapults this classic restaurant to the top of the tried-and-true list. The menu changes but look for something along the lines of grilled sea scallops with basmati, lentil and pistachio pilaf.

Henrietta's Table (☎ *617-864-1200, 1 Bennett St*) Lunch $10-14, dinner $14-22, Sat brunch $21, Sun brunch $42. Open for all 3 meals daily, brunch noon-3pm Sat & Sun. Within the Charles Hotel, this eatery features a New England regional menu highlighting locally grown produce. The creative and 'fresh and honest' preparations, country inn décor and friendly service make it *the* choice for better-than-home cooking. You'll need an appetite to get your money's worth out of the abundant and deservedly popular brunch (reservations suggested). While Sunday is an all-you-can-eat buffet, Saturday's is a three-course a la carte affair.

Rialto (☎ *617-661-5050, 1 Bennett St*)
Mains $25-30. Open 5:30pm-9:45pm daily.
Also within the Charles Hotel, you'll pay
handsomely ($150 for two, all inclusive) for
dining in this understated, Euro-chic elegance, but it will be romantic and memorable. Mediterranean-inspired dishes include
creamy mussel and saffron stew with leeks or
seared beef tenderloin with cognac sauce
and shellfish paella. The vegetarian main
course is always equally creative. Reservations are advised.

Elsewhere in Cambridge

Emma's (☎ *617-864-8534, 40 Hampshire St*)
Dishes average $10. Open for lunch &
dinner daily. This thin-crust pizza instills a
maniacal devotion in its customers. Before
or after a flick at the Kendall Square
Cinema, make a point of stopping here.
Ever tried dried cranberries or sweet potatoes on a pizza? You might. Slices and salads
are sold from the front window. Ⓣ Red Line
to Kendall.

Summer Shack (☎ *617-520-9500, 149
Alewife Brook Parkway*) Dishes from $11
(prices fluctuate with the market). Open
11:30am-10pm Mon-Thur, 11:30am-11pm
Fri, 5pm-11pm Sat, 3pm-9pm Sun. Longtime
Boston chef Jasper White knows fish and
every other type of seafood. He's written
cook books on them and has perfected the
art of preparing chowder and lobster dishes
better than anyone else in Boston. His
restaurant is as big and noisy as the lobster
is delectable. Traditional lobster rolls, with
only a whisper of filler stuffed into hot dog
buns, are as divine as steamed clams. Portions are large and preparations are
straightforward. Solo diners aren't shafted
here. Ⓣ Red Line to Alewife.

The following eateries, around Central
Square, are reached via Ⓣ Red Line to
Central:

Check out the community bulletin board
and organic offerings at ***Harvest Co-Op
Market*** (☎ *617-661-1580, 581 Mass Ave*).
Nearby, two blocks north of Mass Ave, the
whole-food supermarket ***Bread & Circus***
(☎ *617-492-0070, 115 Prospect St*) boasts an
excellent if pricey selection.

Mary Chung (☎ *617-864-1991, 464 Mass
Ave*) Dishes $5-10. Open for lunch & dinner
Wed-Mon. This neighborhood institution is
perhaps the most beloved Mandarin-Szechuan in Cambridge. Its wide-ranging
menu features about 150 dishes.

India Pavillion (☎ *617-547-7463, 17
Central Square*) Lunch $4.50-6, lunch buffet
$6, dinner $9-12. Open lunch & dinner daily.
You can't go wrong here. The décor is
simple and the dining area tiny, but the excellent and authentic dishes more than
make up for it. There is a lunch buffet
Thursday to Sunday.

Miracle of Science Bar & Grill (☎ *617-
868-2866, 321 Mass Ave*) Dishes under $10.
Open 11:30am-1am daily. Hang with the
cool MIT types downing creative burgers,
sandwiches, salads and grilled entrées.

Green St Grill (☎ *617-876-1655, 280
Green St*) Dishes $11-20. Open 3pm-1am
(for food 6pm-10pm). Central Square's
recent face-lift is reflected in this joint
changing from a 'scrungy' joint to a cleaned-up version of its former self. It's still deservedly popular, serving seriously spicy
Caribbean fare. Tuesday through Saturday
is especially lively with live music.

ENTERTAINMENT

The breadth and depth of cultural offerings
in Boston and Cambridge is impressive.
There's no doubt that much of it is fueled by
the vital university scene. For up-to-the-minute listings of cultural events, entertainment and nightlife, check out the cool
weekly *Boston Phoenix,* the irreverent *Improper Bostonian* and *Stuff @ Night,* and
the mainstream *Boston Globe* (Thursday)
and *Boston Herald* (Friday).

Note: The drinking age for alcoholic beverages in New England is 21, and in most
cases you must be 21 to enter a drinking establishment. Some clubs offer '19-plus'
nights; check the papers for details. Bars
usually close at 1am, clubs at 2am. The last
Red Line trains pass through Park St at
about 12:30am (depending on the direction),
but all T stations and lines are different. To
reliably count on catching the last train,
head over to the nearest T station at about

midnight. At press time, MBTA was testing a pilot plan (at least through summer 2002) to operate late-night bus service that mirrors the subway lines. Service has been extended until 2:30am on weekends. Although the program was enjoying incredible popularity at press time, call the MBTA (☎ 617-222-3200, 800-392-6100) and ask about the 'Night Owl Service.'

Cafes

Boston Of the dozens of North End cafes, two really stand out. (Both reached via ⓣ Green or Orange Line to Haymarket.) *Caffè Vittoria (Map 2; ☎ 617-227-7606, 296 Hanover St)*, an atmospheric, Old-World cafe, has been here since the 1930s, and, undoubtedly, so have some Italian-speaking patrons. To get the full effect, wait for a table in the original dining room. *Caffe dello Sport (Map 2; ☎ 617-523-5063, 308 Hanover St)* is the primo place for watching any sporting event, especially soccer.

Francesca's (Map 4; ☎ 617-482-9026, 564 Tremont St) Open 8am-11pm daily. While espresso and cannoli reign in the North End, the South End is rich with lattes and scones. The area's most dependable place, this lively storefront coffee bar has tables and counter service. ⓣ Orange Line to Back Bay.

Cambridge Preferred by lovers of steeped leaves rather than brewed beans is the tiny storefront dispensary *Loulou's Tealuxe (Map 5; ☎ 617-441-0077, Zero Brattle St)* Open 8am-11pm daily. This place has only a few tables, but if you're lucky, you can take in the ever-engaging *passeggiata* (passers-by) while you sip. ⓣ Red Line to Harvard Square.

Café Pamplona (Map 5; no ☎, 12 Bow St) Open 11am-1am Mon-Sat, 2pm-1am Sun. Located in a cozy cellar on a backstreet, this decidedly no-frills, European cafe is *the* choice among old-time Cantabrigians. In addition to espresso, Pamplona has light snacks like gazpacho, sandwiches and biscotti. The tiny outdoor terrace is a delight in summer. ⓣ Red Line to Harvard Square.

Au Bon Pain (Map 5; ☎ 617-497-9797, 1316 Mass Ave) Open 6am-12:30am daily. The square's only true sidewalk cafe, this spot transcends its popular image as a Frenchified fast-food takeout counter. Students, tourists and locals gather here to read, people-watch and chat just like Matt Damon and Minnie Driver in *Good Will Hunting*. An informal, never-ending tournament takes place at the outdoor chess tables. ⓣ Red Line to Harvard Square.

1369 Central (☎ 617-576-4600, 757 Mass Ave) Open 7am-11pm Mon-Fri, 8am-11pm Sat, 8am-10pm Sun. Featuring a bohemian atmosphere and attitude, this place has good music, serious coffee, a laudable tea selection, a limited snack list and a friendly waitstaff. ⓣ Red Line to Central.

Someday Café (☎ 617-623-3323, 51 Davis Square) Open 7am or 8am-11pm or midnight daily. Furnished with well-worn thrift-store couches, this slacker joint has boisterous music and board games, espresso and pastries. ⓣ Red Line to Davis.

Bars & Pubs

Boston Near Government Center and thus a favorite of Boston politicos is *Red Hat (Map 2; ☎ 617-523-2175, 9 Bowdoin St)* Open 11:30am-2am Mon-Sat, 11:30am-midnight Sun. Red Hat feels more like *Cheers* than its below-mentioned brethren. ⓣ Blue Line to Bowdoin.

The Sevens (Map 2; ☎ 617-523-9074, 77 Charles St) Open 11:30am-1am daily. This popular and friendly Beacon Hill pub is always crowded and usually smoky. Pull up a bar stool or hop in a booth and order a sandwich and beer ($9). ⓣ Red Line to Charles/MGH.

Bull & Finch Pub (Map 2; ☎ 617-227-9605, 84 Beacon St) Open 11am-1:45am daily. This is an authentic English pub (it was dismantled in England, shipped to Boston and reassembled in this townhouse, the Hampshire House), but that's not why hundreds of tourists descend on the place daily. The pub inspired the TV sitcom *Cheers*. However, if there was ever a reason to go here, it's gone. ⓣ Green Line to Arlington.

Rack Billiard Club *(Map 2; ☎ 617-725-1051, 20 Clinton St)* Open 11:30am-2am daily. On the edge of Faneuil Hall Marketplace and always hopping, this upscale pool hall, bar and outdoor cafe serves up above-average pub grub and live music. The young professionals who frequent the place are generally still attired in their business duds. For everyone else, the dress code is strictly enforced. The 22 pool tables cost $14 for a full hour after 5 pm, half-price prior to that. Ⓣ Green or Blue Line to Government Center.

Black Rose *(Map 2; ☎ 617-742-2286, 160 State St)* Open 11:30am-2am daily. Also on the edge of Faneuil Hall Marketplace, this boisterous Irish-American pub has live Irish music and well-poured pints. Ⓣ Green or Blue Line to Government Center.

Warren Tavern *(Map 2; ☎ 617-241-8142, 2 Pleasant St)* Open 11:15am-1am daily. This circa-1780 Charlestown pub, at Main St, is one of the most atmospheric places for a drink in Boston. Ⓣ Orange or Green Line to North Station, or Orange Line to Community College.

Cottonwood Café *(Map 4; ☎ 617-247-2225, 222 Berkeley St)* Open 11am-11pm daily. This upscale place serves Boston's best margaritas. Ⓣ Green Line to Arlington.

Clery's Bar & Restaurant *(Map 4; ☎ 617-262-9874, 113 Dartmouth St)* Open 11am-2am daily. At Columbus Ave in the South End, this neighborhood place gets pretty boisterous on weekends. Simple pub grub complements the drafts ($3.50) and Guinness ($4.25). Ⓣ Orange Line to Back Bay.

Behind Fenway Park near Kenmore Square, clubs are lined up like ducks in a row on Ipswich and Lansdowne Sts; the following are reached via Ⓣ Green Line to Kenmore:

Jillian's Billiard Club *(Map 4; ☎ 617-437-0300, 145 Ipswich St)* Open 11am or noon-2am daily. Although this three-story club has more than 50 billiards tables, people also come here to play darts, snooker, table tennis and over 250 virtual reality games. There are six bars and a full-service menu in this cavernous 70,000-sq-foot place.

Atlas Bar & Grille *(Map 4; ☎ 617-437-0300, 145 Ipswich St)* Open 5:30pm-2am daily. With a funky industrial atmosphere once aptly described as 'the Jetsons meet the Copacabana,' Atlas is a fun place to congregate for a beer – before or after serious club-hopping. A DJ spins recent top 40 tunes 10:30pm to 2am Friday and Saturday.

Jake Ivory's *(Map 4; ☎ 617-247-1222, 1 Lansdowne St)* Open 7:30pm-2am Thur-Sun. This joint features dueling rock 'n' roll pianos and, believe it or not, sing-alongs.

Modern *(Map 4; ☎ 617-536-2100, 36 Lansdowne St)* Open 10pm-2am Tues & Thur-Sat. With its sleek silver bar and upholstered seats, this is a sophisticated addition to the Lansdowne St scene. Order a martini and take your place among the diverse but glamorous crowd.

Linwood Grill & Bar *(Map 4; ☎ 617-247-8099, 81 Kilmarnock St)* Open 11:30am-2am daily. At the other end of the spectrum, this Fenway mainstay is a true neighborhood place to have a beer (make that a Bud!), chow on some barbecue, and talk sports. At the adjacent bar you can also play darts, pool and pinball and listen to live music a few nights a week.

Cambridge Between Central and Harvard Squares you'll find the friendly Irish bar ***Plough & Stars*** *(☎ 617-441-3455, 912 Mass Ave)* Open 11:30am-1am daily. This place has the requisite Guinness and Bass on tap, as well as televised English football matches on weekends September through May. Rock bands play most nights ($3 cover on weekends). Ⓣ Red Line to Central.

The Phoenix Landing *(☎ 617-576-6260, 512 Mass Ave)* Open 11am-1am daily. This social Irish pub has space for talkers in front and dancers in back (where a DJ spins tunes). Ⓣ Red Line to Central.

The Field *(☎ 617-354-7345, 20 Prospect St)* Open noon-1am daily. The funky pulse of Central Square is still discernible at this unpretentious neighborhood bar. Ⓣ Red Line to Central.

Temple Bar *(☎ 617-547-5055, 1688 Mass Ave)* Open 11am-10pm daily. Between

Harvard and Porter Squares, this bar (with windows that open onto the street) is reminiscent of the Temple Bar area in Dublin's SoHo. Ⓣ Red Line to Porter.

Under Bones (☎ 617-628-2200, 55 Chester St) Open 5pm-1am daily. Specializing in rare brews from Belgium to Boston, this amiable bar is in the basement of Redbones barbecue joint. Ⓣ Red Line to Davis.

The Burren (☎ 617-776-6896, 247 Elm St) Open noon-1am daily. Cover $3. A very popular and amiable place oozing Irish atmosphere, the Burren features traditional Irish music nightly in the front room and various bands (and an 'open mike' night) in the back. Try to catch the Tarbox Ramblers, a local country & blues band, on Saturday night. Ⓣ Red Line to Davis.

Brewpubs & Brewery Tours

Bostonians take beer seriously. In the past decade, a number of 'microbreweries' have sprung up in Boston. While all those listed below are recommended for beer and snacks, some serve noteworthy, moderately priced meals.

Boston Beer Co (☎ 617-368-5000, 30 Germania St, Jamaica Plain) Tours & tastings 2pm Thur & Fri, noon-2pm Sat. Also known as the Samuel Adams brewery and Boston Beer Museum, Boston Beer Co produces the only local brew that's achieved international fame. In July and August, there's an additional tour at 2pm Wednesday. Ⓣ Orange Line to Stony Brook, then follow signs for two blocks.

Boston Beer Works (Map 4; ☎ 617-536-2337, 61 Brookline Ave) Open 10:30am-1am daily. Near Fenway Park and Kenmore Square, this place has seasonal concoctions brewed in exposed tanks and pipes. About 16 different kinds of beer, including Boston Red, IPA and Buckeye Oatmeal Stout, are usually available. The appetizers and munchies are pretty good, too. If you don't like sporting crowds, avoid this place after a Sox game. Ⓣ Green Line to Kenmore.

Brew Moon (Map 2; ☎ 617-523-6467, 115 Stuart St & Map 5; ☎ 617-499-2739, 50 Church St, Cambridge) Open 11am-11:30pm or midnight. Lunch $8-13, dinner $11-17. Deservedly popular with a sophisticated dining room and sleek bar, Brew Moon offers seven seasonal brews, pizzas, and a creative menu. Head brewer Darrah Bryans is one of the country's only female master brewers; she's generally at the Harvard Square location. Ⓣ Green Line to Boylston; Red Line to Harvard.

Commonwealth Fish & Beer Company (Map 2; ☎ 617-523-8383, 138 Portland St) Open 11:30am-1am daily. Within gleaming copper kettles, the casual Commonwealth produces over 10 kinds of English-style suds served at various temperatures. The menu is heavy on seafood (crispy calamari, grilled fish, chowder), but you can get a BBQ chicken sandwich, too. The basement tap room is comfortably 'clubby.' The place is packed when bands play on game nights. (The Bruins and Celtics play at the nearby Fleet Center.) The kitchen closes at 9pm or 10pm. Ⓣ Green or Orange Line to North Station.

Harpoon Brewery (☎ 617-574-9551, 306 Northern Ave) Tours & tastings 11am, 1pm, 3pm Tues-Sat. Although this place is not a brewpub, the Harpoon Brewery is the largest facility in the state. Ⓣ Red Line to South Station, and then a 20-minute walk over the Northern Ave Bridge to the Marine Industrial Park.

John Harvard's Brew House (Map 5; ☎ 617-868-3585, 33 Dunster St, Cambridge) Open 11:30am-12:30am Sun-Thur, 11:30am-1:30am Fri & Sat. Lunch $6-10, dinner $10-17. This subterranean pub smells and feels more like an English pub than the others and has perhaps the best beer among the crowded microbrewery field. You'll find ales and stouts here (plus a sampler rack). Above-average pub grub is available at lunch and dinner and for Sunday brunch. Ⓣ Red Line to Harvard.

Joshua Tree (☎ 617-623-9910, 256 Elm St) Open 11:30am-1am daily. This trendy bar-cum-restaurant has a giant-screen TV for sports action, 26 beers on tap and a DJ or live music Thursday to Saturday night. Ⓣ Red Line to Davis.

The Druid (☎ 617-497-0965, 1357 Cambridge St) Open 3pm-1am Mon & Tues, 1:30am-1am Wed-Sun. Welcoming and well adorned with original Celtic artwork, this Inman Square pub pours a proper pint of Murphy's and boasts no TV. The traditional Sunday Irish jams ('seisiuns') draw a loyal crowd at 5:30 pm. Ⓣ Red Line to Central and then a 15-minute walk.

Flat Top Johnny's (☎ 617-494-9565, One Kendall Square) Open 3pm-1am daily. Situated within Kendall Square, Flat Top Johnny's place is clean and attracts MIT students and young computer professionals for relaxed billiards games and beers. Ⓣ Red Line to Kendall.

Live Music

Rock Plenty of nationally known alternative and rock bands got their start in Boston clubs; there are more than 5000 bands registered here.

The Middle East (☎ 617-354-8238, 472 Mass Ave, Cambridge) Cover $8-15. Open nightly. This excellent venue usually has three different gigs going simultaneously. There's always a free jazz show in the 'corner.' The Middle East also serves pretty good (well-priced) food until midnight. Ⓣ Red Line to Central.

Johnny D's Uptown (☎ 617-776-2004, 17 Holland St, Somerville) Cover $8-12. Open 11:30am-1am daily. One of the area's best and most eclectic venues, with a different style of music every night, Johnny D's has everything from blues and Cajun to swing and rock 'n' roll. Sunday night blues jams are popular while weekend jazz brunches are mellow. Ⓣ Red Line to Davis.

TT the Bear's (☎ 617-492-0082, 10 Brookline St, Cambridge) Cover $3-15. Open 6pm or 7pm-midnight or 1am nightly. This intimate diehard rock joint has been going strong in Central Square for more than 25 years. Ⓣ Red Line to Central.

Lizard Lounge (☎ 617-547-0759, 1667 Mass Ave, Cambridge) Cover varies. Open nightly. Between Harvard and Porter Squares and beneath the Cambridge Common Restaurant, this intimate, basement-level club features live original music nightly. Casual dress is cool. Ⓣ Red Line to Harvard.

Toad (☎ 617-497-4950, 1920 Mass Ave, Cambridge) Admission free. Open nightly. Local bands perform funk, R&B, rock and soul nightly at this tiny, ultra-casual place. Ⓣ Red Line to Porter.

The Paradise (☎ 617-562-8800, 967 Comm Ave) Cover $10-30. Open when bands are booked; call for schedule. This small club books groups from all walks of the musical spectrum and has shows throughout the week. Ⓣ Green Line 'B' branch to Pleasant St, the sixth stop after Kenmore.

Blues & Jazz The music rests squarely on up-tempo traditional jazz and fusion at *Wally's Café* (Map 4; ☎ 617-424-1408, 427 Mass Ave) Admission free. Open 9pm-2am Mon-Sat, noon-2am Sun. Gritty, smoky and storied, this club is the last survivor of the jazz clubs that once enlivened this neighborhood. Monday is blues; Tuesday and Wednesday are jazz-Latin fusion; Thursday is progressive Latin jazz; Friday and Saturday are progressive jazz; and Sunday sees afternoon jam sessions and evening urban funk. There's a one-drink minimum. Ⓣ Orange Line to Mass Ave.

Berklee Performance Center (Map 4; ☎ 617-266-7455 professional shows, ☎ 747-8820 faculty & student shows, ☎ 747-2261 box office, 136 Mass Ave) This venue hosts jazz concerts given by the Berklee College of Music's renowned faculty members and exceptional students for a mere $4 during the school year. The center also hosts big-name professional performers at big-buck prices. Ⓣ Green Line to Hynes/ICA.

House of Blues (Map 5; ☎ 617-491-2583, 96 Winthrop St, Cambridge) Cover $7-40. Open (for food) 11am-11pm daily. This original House of Blues was opened by 'Blues Brother' Dan Aykroyd in 1992 and has since become a major force on the national blues scene. The music begins at 9pm or 10pm. It's free during lunch on Friday and Saturday from 1pm to 3pm. The all-you-can-eat-and-listen-to Sunday gospel brunch ($26, or $15 for just the food) is a downright religious experience for some. Reservations are required. ⓣ Red Line to Harvard.

The Cantab Lounge (☎ 617-354-2685, 738 Mass Ave, Cambridge) Cover $3-8. Open nightly. Grungy, dark and laid-back, in keeping with the longtime tradition of pre-rehab Central Square, the Cantab Lounge is a well-established bluegrass, blues and oldies venue where students hang with locals. ⓣ Red Line to Central.

Ryles (☎ 617-876-9330, 212 Hampshire St, Cambridge) Cover $7-12. Open 7pm-1am Tues-Thur, 7pm-2am Fri-Sat, 10am-3pm Sun. This great Inman Square jazz venue boasts two intimate floors of local and national recording acts. The music is free during the Sunday jazz brunches. ⓣ Red Line to Central.

Regattabar (Map 5; ☎ 617-661-5000, 876-7777 tickets, 1 Bennett St, Cambridge) Tickets $10-26. Open Tues-Sat. Within the Charles Hotel in Harvard Square, this upscale yacht-club-sort-of-place books international-ally known groups. A limited number of general seating tickets go on sale one hour before show time. Ticket prices vary depending on the fame quotient. ⓣ Red Line to Harvard.

Folk Although other clubs occasionally book folk acts, these two places are devoted to giving struggling folk singers a venue. Both are reached via ⓣ Red Line to Harvard.

Club Passim (Map 5; ☎ 617-492-7679, 47 Palmer St, Cambridge) Cover $5-15. Open nightly. This venerable nonprofit club is nationally known for supporting the early careers of singer-songwriters Jackson Browne, Tracy Chapman, Nanci Griffith and Patty Larkin. The small club has only 125 seats. Call ahead for the nightly programs and show times. Tuesday is 'open mike' night. Passim also serves lunch and dinner daily in an alcohol- and smoke-free environment.

Nameless Coffeehouse (Map 5; ☎ 617-864-1630, 3 Church St, Cambridge) Admission by donation. Open Sept-May. Within the First Parish Church (Unitarian Universalist), this low-key place, run by volunteers, sponsors acoustic singer-songwriters on the first Saturday of each month.

Dance Clubs

The thriving club scene is fueled by the constant infusion of thousands of American and international students. Clubs are fairly stable, although the nightly line-up often changes. Check the *Boston Phoenix* or *Improper Bostonian* or *Stuff @ Night* for up-to-the-minute information. The clubs along Lansdowne St near Kenmore Square cater to a university crowd, while those in the Theater District are favored by young professionals; Man Ray, in Cambridge, defies categorization. Cover charges vary widely, from free (if you arrive early) to $15, but the average is more like $10 on weekends. Most clubs are open 10pm to 2am.

Downtown (Map 2) If you're yearning for tunes from the bubble gum '80s and slick '90s, head to **Polly Esther's** (☎ 617-720-1966, 262 Friend St) Open Thur-Sat. This four-story emporium attracts an international and young professional set. ⓣ Orange or Green Line to North Station.

Theater District (Map 2) The following places are all reached via ⓣ Green Line to Boylston.

La Boom (☎ 617-357-6800, 25 Boylston Place) Open Thur-Sat. If your ears can take a booming subwoofer system (with DJs) that'll make your body piercings shudder, this place is for you.

The Big Easy (☎ 617-351-7000, 1 Boylston Place) Open Thur-Sat. The atmosphere here tries to replicate a New Orleans Mardi Gras–style playground. In addition to eclectic cover bands, a DJ spins Latin, international, hip-hop and everything else imaginable. You can just watch from the 2nd-floor balcony if you prefer. 'Proper dress' is required; the crowd is a bit older here. And the drinks are cheaper.

The Roxy (☎ 617-338-7699, 279 Tremont St) Open Thur-Sat. Within the Wyndham Tremont hotel's stylish, 3rd-floor ballroom, the Roxy plays Latin and salsa, and international and house classics, depending on the night. No jeans, T-shirts or sneakers.

Venu (☎ 617-338-8061, 100 Warrenton St) Open 11:30pm-2am Tues-Sun. To signal your insider status at this super-chic club that appeals to the authentic Versace/Prada set, pull out your best Armani knockoff and arrive fashionably late for DJ-spun tunes. Jackets are required for men on Friday.

Matrix (☎ 617-542-4077, 275 Tremont St) Open Thur-Sun. Downstairs from the Wyndham Tremont hotel, the oh-so-hip Matrix plays high-energy techno, house, top 40 and disco in two rooms. Check out the laser light show and one of a dozen bars.

Aria (☎ 617-338-7080, 246 Tremont St) Open Tues-Sun. From hip-hop to R&B to Latin and house, this exclusive red velvet club below the Wilbur Theater is for a highly stylized, glam set. If you don't fit the bill, save yourself the embarrassment.

Kenmore Square (Map 4) The following places are all reached via Ⓣ Green Line to Kenmore.

Avalon (☎ 617-262-2424, 15 Lansdowne St) Open Thur-Sun. Boston's premier, huge dance club features international house music, progressive national bands and some '19-plus' nights. The weekend light shows burst with energy.

Axis (☎ 617-262-2437, 13 Lansdowne St) Open Thur-Sun. Called 'Avalon's little sister,' the crowd here is a bit younger and the feel more subterranean. The clientele is still monied, though. Cover includes access to Avalon on Friday and Saturday.

Karma Club (☎ 617-421-9595, 9 Lansdowne St) Open Thur-Sun. More formal and with a strict dress code (dress to the nines or you'll be left standing in the cold), Karma caters to sophisticates. What would Krishna think of the hip-hop, house and reggae?

Embassy (☎ 617-536-2100, 30 Lansdowne St) Open Thur-Sat. You might as well be in Europe for all the myriad faces, fashion and world music you'll encounter.

Bill's Bar (☎ 617-421-9678, 5½ Lansdowne St) Open nightly. The self-mocking 'bastard child of Lansdowne Street,' this smaller club, with live music and DJs, is packed with BU students who live by alternative music. The popular hip-hop night 'Fat Tuesday' is renowned.

Sophia's (☎ 617-351-7001, 1270 Boylston St) Open Tues-Sun. Popular with the Euro glamour set, this Latin salsa and merengue club has hardwood floors, exposed brick and a rooftop terrace. In the winter, a tent keeps the rooftop hot (as if the music didn't).

Cambridge Creative attire is encouraged at Central Square's most 'underground' club, *Man Ray* (☎ 617-864-0400, 21 Brookline St) Open 10pm-2am Wed-Sat. As they say, dress to impress, express or distress. (When in doubt wear black; fetishwear is suggested on Friday.) The line-up varies from industrial rock and high-energy dance tunes to campy, classic disco trash and '80s new wave. Ⓣ Red Line to Central.

Gay & Lesbian Venues

Many straight clubs feature gay and lesbian nights. Since schedules and venues change often, check *Bay Windows* or talk to the folks at We Think the World of You bookstore (see the boxed text 'Bookstores').

Vapor Nightclub/Chaps (Map 2; ☎ 617-695-9500, 100 Warrenton St) One of Boston's most popular gay bars and dance clubs, the line-up at this Theater District club is diverse. Monday it's an 'open mike' and quiet piano bar (complimentary pizza is served); Tuesday there's retro disco with a DJ; Wednesday features Latin house music; Thursday starts out quiet as a piano bar and then picks up with a rap, hip-hop and new wave mix; Friday is soulful house; Saturday (19-plus) begins quiet and ends with serious dance music; and Sunday tea dances start at 7pm. Ⓣ Green Line to Boylston.

Jacques (Map 4; ☎ 617-426-8902, 79 Broadway St) Cover $5-6. Shows nightly. Behind the Radisson Hotel on Stuart St in the Theater District, drag queen cabaret attracts the crowds at Jacques. Ⓣ Green Line to Arlington.

Club Café *(Map 4; ☎ 617-536-0966, 209 Columbus Ave)* A mixed crowd gathers at this South End bar and restaurant. Thursday is girls' night, in the front anyway. Sunday brunch is always packed. Ⓣ Orange Line to Back Bay.

Avalon *(Map 4; ☎ 617-262-2424, 15 Lansdowne St)* The most popular Sunday night venue, Avalon dominates with blistering house music. Ⓣ Green Line to Kenmore.

Axis *(Map 4; ☎ 617-262-2437, 13 Lansdowne St)* Just about anything goes on 'Statik' Monday, when the transgender community, gays and drag queens converge. Ⓣ Green Line to Kenmore.

Man Ray *(☎ 617-864-0400, 21 Brookline St, Cambridge)* Thursday is reserved for the boys here. Ⓣ Red Line to Central.

Europa/Buzz *(☎ 617-482-3939, 51 Stuart St)* Women converge on Friday 'Circuit Girl' nights, while Saturday features hard gay bodies. You can always shoot a bit of pool, sip a quiet martini or hang at the mahogany bar. Ⓣ Green Line to Boylston.

Luxor *(Map 4; ☎ 617-423-6969, 69 Church St)* This is a more casual men's bar behind Park Plaza, but women are always welcome. Ⓣ Green Line to Arlington.

Ramrod *(Map 4; ☎ 617-266-2986, 1254 Boylston St)* This is a traditional men's leather bar. Ⓣ Green Line to Kenmore.

Machine *(Map 4; ☎ 617-536-1950, 1254 Boylston St)* Below Ramrod, you'll find a hot, high-tech dance club. Ⓣ Green Line to Kenmore.

Fritz *(Map 4; ☎ 617-482-4428, 26 Chandler St)* Within the Chandler Inn, this casual watering hole has a nice low-key atmosphere; it's mostly men, but women certainly aren't turned away. Ⓣ Orange Line to Back Bay.

Cinemas

Brattle Theater *(Map 5; ☎ 617-876-6837, 40 Brattle St, Cambridge)* The Brattle is a film lover's 'cinema paradiso.' Film noir, independent films and series that celebrate directors or periods are shown regularly in this renovated 1890 repertory theater. You can often catch a classic double feature. Ⓣ Red Line to Harvard.

Coolidge Corner Theater *(☎ 617-734-2500, 290 Harvard St, Brookline)* The area's only not-for-profit movie house shows documentaries, foreign films and first-run movies on two enormous screens in a grand art deco theater. Ⓣ Green Line 'C' branch to Coolidge Corner.

Somerville Theater *(☎ 617-625-5700, Davis Square, Somerville)* Another classic theater that survived the megaplex movie house invasion, this theater alternates second-run films with live musical performances. Ⓣ Red Line to Davis.

Kendall Square Cinema *(☎ 617-494-9800, One Kendall Square, Cambridge)* Kendall has nine screens as well as espresso machines that can churn out a cup of java in 10 seconds. Ⓣ Red Line to Kendall, then a 10-minute walk.

Harvard Film Archive & Film Study Library *(Map 5; ☎ 617-495-4700, 24 Quincy St, Cambridge)* At least two films per day are screened at the Carpenter Center for the Visual Arts at Harvard University. Directors and actors are frequently on hand to talk about their work. Ⓣ Red Line to Harvard.

Boston Public Library *(Map 4; ☎ 617-536-5400, 666 Boylston St)* Free, film festival–quality flicks are screened at 6pm Monday night in the Rabb Lecture Hall on the lower level. Ⓣ Green Line to Copley.

Museum of Fine Arts, Boston *(Map 4; ☎ 617-369-3770, 465 Huntington Ave)* At the West Wing entrance of the museum, in the Remis Auditorium, a wide variety of films – silent, avant-garde and local – are screened. Ⓣ Green Line 'E' branch to Museum.

French Library *(Map 4; ☎ 617-266-4351, 53 Marlborough St)* This Back Bay library shows classic and contemporary French films at 8pm Friday and at 3pm Sunday. Ⓣ Green Line to Arlington.

Hatch Memorial Shell *(Map 4; ☎ 617-787-7174, Charles River Esplanade)* 'Free Friday Flicks' under the stars are shown at dusk Friday late June to August. You'll be sitting on the lawn, so bring a blanket and picnic. Many movies are family-oriented. Ⓣ Green Line to Arlington.

Comedy Clubs

Comedy Connection *(Map 2; ☎ 617-248-9700, Quincy Market, Faneuil Hall Marketplace)* Tickets $10-12 Sun-Thur, $14-40 Fri & Sat. Shows daily. This 2nd-floor club, above the food court, is one of the city's oldest and biggest comedy venues. Ⓣ Green or Blue Line to Government Center.

Nick's Comedy Stop *(Map 2; ☎ 617-482-0930, 100 Warrenton St)* Tickets $10-15. Shows Thur-Sat. This Theater District venue features both local and nationally known jokesters. Ⓣ Green Line to Boylston.

Improv Boston *(☎ 617-576-1253, 1253 Cambridge St, Cambridge)* Tickets $12. Shows Thur-Sun. This witty, long-running ensemble performs at the Back Alley Theater in Inman Square and makes things up as they go along; oftentimes, audience members throw out ideas and the cast is off and running. The show redefines itself with every fast-paced performance. Sunday shows (7pm) are family-oriented. Ⓣ Red Line to Central, then walk 5 minutes up Prospect St.

Performing Arts

Theater There isn't a bad seat in Harvard University's **American Repertory Theater** *(Map 5; ☎ 617-547-8300, 64 Brattle St, Cambridge)* Tickets $25-45. The prestigious 'A-R-T' stages new plays and experimental interpretations of classics. There's a cheap way to get in: Every Monday morning the theater sets aside 50 tickets for the following Saturday matinee. You literally 'pay what you can.' Student 'rush' tickets are sold for $12 30 minutes prior to the curtain call. Ⓣ Red Line to Harvard.

Huntington Theater Company *(Map 4; ☎ 617-266-0800, 264 Huntington Ave)* Tickets $12-62. Boston University's highly regarded theater company performs both modern and classical plays annually in its Greek revival theater. Rear balcony seats are usually available and the least expensive ($12). Student 'rush' tickets for $15 are dispensed two hours prior to curtain call. Ⓣ Green Line 'E' branch to Symphony.

Charles Playhouse *(Map 2; 74 Warrenton St)* Shows Tues-Sun. This two-stage Theater

Discount Tickets

Half-price tickets to same-day performances are available beginning at 11am at Bostix (Map 2; ☎ 617-723-5181), on the south side of Faneuil Hall Marketplace. (You can always buy full-price tickets here, too. Either way, it's cash only.) Another kiosk is located in Back Bay's Copley Square (Map 4; ☎ 617-723-5181), at Dartmouth and Boylston Sts. Both kiosks are open 10am to 6pm Tuesday to Saturday, 11am to 4pm Sunday; the Copley Square kiosk is also open 10am to 6pm Monday.

District venue has presented *Shear Madness* (☎ 617-426-5225), a comical murder mystery with audience participation, since 1980. It holds the record for the world's 'longest-running nonmusical play.' Tickets cost $34. *Blue Man Group* (☎ 617-426-6912, 617-931-2787 tickets), a mixed-media performance art piece staged since 1996, pokes fun at the arts community with music and percussion and by plucking members from the audience. Tickets are $43 to $53. One hour before show time on Tuesday and Wednesday, remaining tickets are released for $25 to students , but don't get your hopes up. Ⓣ Green Line to Boylston or Orange Line to NE Medical Center.

Boston Center for the Arts *(Map 4; ☎ 617-426-7700, 539 Tremont St)* Three distinctive performance spaces (as well as the Mills Gallery, a contemporary art space) are well suited to unusual productions. Indeed, there's rarely a dull moment at the BCA. Ⓣ Orange Line to Back Bay or Green Line to Copley.

Mobius *(Map 2; ☎ 617-542-7416, 354 Congress St, 5th floor)* The avant-garde performance artists who belong to this ensemble present experimental dance, music and other art-in-progress almost every weekend. Tickets are sometimes free, but usually about $10 to $12. Ⓣ Red Line to South Station.

Other Performing Arts Venues The following venues host big production and pre-Broadway musicals and plays, as well as excellent nonprofit performances. All are reached via Ⓣ Green Line to Boylston.

The **Colonial Theater** (Map 2; 106 Boylston St) and **Wilbur Theater** (Map 2; ☎ 617-426-9366, 931-2787 tickets, 246 Tremont St) both get pre- and post-Broadway touring companies. Although the lavish Colonial is now enveloped by an office building, it is still resplendent with all the gilded ornamentation, mirrors and frescoes it had in 1900.

Emerson Majestic Theater (Map 2; ☎ 617-824-8000, 219 Tremont St) In a beaux-arts-style building owned by Emerson College, a private performing arts school, this theater has been recently restored to its former majesty and luster.

Wang Center for the Performing Arts (Map 2; ☎ 617-482-9393, 800-447-7400 tickets, 270 Tremont St) This opulent and enormous hall, built in 1925, has one of the largest stages in the country. The Boston Ballet performs here, but the Wang also hosts extravagant music and modern dance productions, as well as occasional giant-screen movies. (The center was originally built as a movie palace.) As cavernous as the Wang is, its illustrious sister venue, the **Shubert Theater** (Map 2; ☎ 617-482-9393, 800-447-7400 tickets, 265 Tremont St) is intimate.

Classical Music Professional and student chamber and orchestral concerts are hosted in an acoustically superlative hall at the **New England Conservatory** (Map 4; ☎ 617-585-1122 concert line, ☎ 536-2412 box office, Jordan Hall, 30 Gainsborough St). Most student and faculty concerts are free; call for a schedule. Ⓣ Green Line 'E' branch to Symphony or Orange Line to Mass Ave.

Hatch Memorial Shell (Map 4; ☎ 617-727-9547, Charles River Esplanade) This venue has lots of free summertime concerts. Check the newspapers for its evening shows (midweek) and midday shows (on weekends). There are public restrooms and an inexpensive snack bar here. Ⓣ Green Line to Arlington.

Symphony Hall (Map 4; ☎ 617-266-1492, 266-1200 tickets, 301 Mass Ave) Tickets $25-87. Near-perfect acoustics match the ambitious programs of the world-renowned Boston Symphony Orchestra (BSO), which performs from October to April. The Boston Pops plays popular classical music and show tunes from May to mid-July and offers a popular holiday show in December. A cafe (open 5:30pm to 7:30pm) offers buffet-style dining before evening concerts.

For same-day discounted 'rush' tickets ($8; one per person, you don't have to be a student), line up at the box office on Tuesday and Thursday at 4pm for the 8pm show, Friday at 9am for the 2pm show. (No rush tickets are sold for the Saturday show.) The only other way to beat the high cost of the BSO is to get lucky by catching one of its sporadic (once-monthly) open rehearsals at 7:30pm Wednesday or at 10:30am Thursday. These $15 tickets can be purchased in advance and they usually are; you'll be fortunate to get one. Ⓣ Green Line to Symphony.

Dance Both modern and classical works are staged by the **Boston Ballet** (☎ 617-695-6950) Tickets $25-78. The troupe performs at the Wang Center. Student 'rush' tickets for $12.50 are available one hour before the performance. Ⓣ Green Line to Boylston or Orange Line to NE Medical Center.

SPECTATOR SPORTS

Boston is a big sports town, and emotions run high during the various sporting seasons. Be prepared that the simple question, 'Hey, what do you think of the Sox this season?' could kick off an impassioned conversation with a local. For sports talk radio all the time, tune into 850 AM.

Boston Red Sox (Map 4; ☎ 617-267-1700 tickets, 4 Yawkey Way) Tickets $18-20 bleachers, $25-55 regular seats. Season early Apr-late Sept. The Sox play in Fenway Park, the nation's oldest ballpark, built in 1912, and certainly one of the most storied (see the boxed text 'Fenway Park'). Sit with the 'common fan' in outfield bleacher seats or splurge behind the plate. During sold-out games, there are often first-come, first-served standing-room-only tickets sold at 9am for same-day games; head to the ticket windows on Yawkey Way. Game times are at 1:05pm, 5:05pm and 7:05pm. Ⓣ Green Line to Kenmore.

Boston Celtics (Map 2; ☎ 617-523-3030 information, ☎ 931-2000 tickets, Fleet Center, 150 Causeway St) Tickets $10-85. Season late Oct-Apr. The Celtics, who've won more basketball championships than any other NBA team, play across from North Station. Tickets start at $10, but it's a rare bird who can find one for that price, and you won't be able to see anything from there anyway. Ⓣ Orange or Green Line to North Station.

Boston Bruins (Map 2; ☎ 617-624-1900 information, ☎ 931-2000 tickets, Fleet Center, 150 Causeway St) Tickets $20-77. Season mid-Oct–mid-Apr. The Bruins, under the former star power of Bobby Orr, Phil Esposito and Ray Bourque, play ice hockey. You can buy tickets at the box office, at the western end of the Fleet Center. Ⓣ Orange or Green Line to North Station.

New England Patriots (☎ 508-543-8200, 800-543-1776, Foxboro Stadium, Route 1, Foxboro) Tickets $47. Season late Aug-late Dec. The Super Bowl XXXVI champs play football about 50 minutes south of Boston, but it's hard to get a ticket (most seats are sold to season ticket holders). Their new, state-of-the-art stadium should be ready for the 2002-03 season. There are direct trains ($8 roundtrip) from South Station; contact the MBTA (☎ 617-222-3200) for exact times.

New England Revolution (☎ 877-438-7387, Foxboro Stadium, Route 1, Foxboro) Tickets $16-32. Season mid-Apr–early Oct. The local soccer team also plays in Foxboro. For transportation information, see New England Patriots, above.

Many colleges also have teams worth watching, and spirited, loyal fans. In April, look for the annual Bean Pot Tournament, college hockey's premier event.

Boston University (☎ 617-353-3838, Case Athletic Center, Babcock St) Tickets $14. BU's hockey team plays just off Comm Ave. Ⓣ Green Line 'B' branch to Babcock St.

Boston College (☎ 617-552-3000, Conte Forum, 140 Comm Ave) Football tickets $40; hockey tickets $13/8 adult/child. BC has a tough hockey team and its football fans are devoted, so tickets are nearly impossible to get. Basketball is also good here. Ⓣ Green Line 'B' branch to the end.

Harvard University (Map 5; ☎ 617-495-2211, N Harvard St & Soldiers Field Rd) Tickets $12. Football matches are played across the Anderson Bridge south of Harvard Square. When Harvard plays other Ivy League rivals, tickets get snatched up quickly. Ⓣ Red Line to Harvard.

SHOPPING
Stores are generally open 9am or 10am until 6pm or 7pm Monday to Saturday, unless otherwise noted. Most are also open noon to 5pm Sunday.

Shopping Districts & Malls
Faneuil Hall Marketplace (Map 2; ☎ 617-338-2323) Open 10am-9pm Mon-Sat, noon-6pm Sun. Northeast of Congress and State Sts, these five buildings are filled with 100 or so one-of-a-kind shops (catering mainly to tourists), pushcart vendors and national chain stores. It's expensive and crowded (almost every visitor stops here at some point or another), especially on the weekends, but it's rather festive, too. There are lots of fast-food outlets (see Places to Eat, earlier), street performers and outdoor benches to rest your weary feet. Ⓣ Green or Blue Line to Government Center.

Downtown Crossing (Map 2; Winter, Summer & Washington Sts) This outdoor pedestrian mall has practical shops geared to everyday Bostonians. There are lots of small retail outlets for clothing, jewelry, shoes, books and electronic equipment, as well as two department stores, *Filene's (☎ 617-357-2100, 426 Washington St)* and *Macy's (☎ 617-357-3000, 450 Washington St)*. This area is enlivened by street musicians, food and souvenir pushcart vendors, a few outdoor cafes and benches for people-watching. Ⓣ Red or Orange Line to Downtown Crossing.

Newbury St (Map 4), between Arlington St and Mass Ave, is filled with chic boutiques, cafes and galleries. These eight high-rent blocks are great for strolling and window-shopping even if you can't afford to buy. You'll find everything from used CDs and books to Armani and Louis, Boston, clothing. Don't get too discouraged about the high prices; as you walk west you'll find that prices begin to drop back into this stratosphere as shops get more youth oriented. Ⓣ Green Line to Arlington (for the eastern end of the street) or Hynes/ICA (for the western end).

Loulou's Lost & Found (☎ 617-859-8593, 121 Newbury St) Check out this eclectic inventory of retro objects for the home, some from the early 20th century.

The Hempfest (☎ 617-421-9944, 207 Newbury St) This store sells all manner of products made from hemp, the botanical cousin of marijuana: items to wear, to furnish one's home and even to eat.

John Fluevog (☎ 617-266-1079, 302 Newbury St) The shoes here are more fun to look at than comfortable to walk in.

Condom World (☎ 617-267-7233, 332 Newbury St) One size will not fit all.

Newbury Comics (☎ 617-236-4930, 332 Newbury St) In addition to namesake comics, they sell new and used alternative rock CDs and records.

Patagonia (☎ 617-424-1776, 346 Newbury St) Patagonia carries the finest outdoor fleecewear.

Urban Outfitters (☎ 617-236-0088, 361 Newbury St) This shop has the latest in trendy clothing and housewares.

The Shops at the Pru (Map 4; ☎ 617-267-1002, 800 Boylston St) An upscale indoor mall boasting 70 stores and eateries within an atrium-like space, the mall also has one of the few inner-city grocery stores, *Star Market*, on the ground level. Ⓣ Green Line 'E' branch to Prudential.

Copley Place (Map 4; ☎ 617-369-5000, 100 Huntington Ave) You'll find American consumerism alive and well at this enormous indoor shopping mall that encompasses hotels, a first-run cineplex, glass walkways, restaurants and dozens of pricey shops. Ⓣ Green Line to Copley or Orange Line to Back Bay.

Harvard Square Although there used to be dozens of independent stores in Cambridge's Harvard Square, most have been replaced by national chains. However, there's still a spirited street life with plenty of musicians and performance artists. Look for a cluster of shops within *The Garage* (Map 5; 36 John F Kennedy St). Head northwest out of the square on Mass Ave to find a diverse array of one-of-a-kind shops all the way to Porter Square (about a 30-minute walk). Ⓣ Red Line to Harvard.

Cambridgeside Galleria (☎ 617-621-8666, 100 Cambridgeside Place, Cambridge) Just beyond the Museum of Science, this three-story mall has 100 shops, including the big and moderately priced department store *Sears* (☎ 617-252-3500). Ⓣ Green Line to Lechmere.

Clothing

Filene's Basement (Map 2; ☎ 617-542-2011, 426 Washington St) The granddaddy of bargain stores, Filene's carries overstocked and irregular items at everyday low prices in Downtown Crossing. But the deal gets better: Items are automatically marked down the longer they remain in the store. With a little bit of luck and lots of determination you could find a $300 designer jacket for $30; but be forewarned, the chances of finding something perfect (ie, that is well made, undamaged, your size and in a color other than neon purple or fire-engine red) are pretty slim. Patience is a prerequisite since customers rip through piles of merchandise, turning the place upside down as if a tornado hit it. Even so, it's a sight to see, an experience unique to Boston; don't miss it. Ⓣ Red or Orange Line to Downtown Crossing.

The Levi's Store (Map 4; ☎ 617-375-9010, 800 Boylston St) Located within the Prudential Center, this store sells nothing but the real thing. Ⓣ Green Line 'E' branch to Prudential.

The Garment District (☎ 617-876-5230, 200 Broadway, Cambridge) If your memories of the fashion-conscious '60s and '70s have faded like an old pair of jeans, entering this store will bring it all back with a vengeance. Ⓣ Red Line to Kendall.

Dollar-a-Pound Plus *(☎ 617-876-5230, 200 Broadway, Cambridge)* Below the Garment District, this venue has different merchandise and pricing methods. Like a flea market gone berserk, piles of clothing are dumped on the warehouse floor and folks wade through it looking for their needle in the haystack. Upon checkout, your pile is weighed and you pay 'by the pound.' The price per pound is usually $1.50, but on Friday it's lowered in order to move the merchandise faster. There are also books, records and cassettes, and kitchen supplies, all priced to move. Hours are irregular; call ahead. Ⓣ Red Line to Kendall.

Second Time Around *(Map 5; ☎ 617-491-7185, 8 Eliot St, Cambridge)* and ***Oona's Experienced Clothing*** *(Map 5; ☎ 617-491-2654, 1210 Mass Ave, Cambridge)* Both these Harvard Square shops deal in used threads. Ⓣ Red Line to Harvard.

Boston Souvenirs

Out of Left Field *(Map 2; ☎ 617-722-9401, Faneuil Hall)* These folks specialize in Boston sports mementos. Ⓣ Green or Blue Line to Government Center.

J August *(Map 5; ☎ 617-864-6650, 1320 Mass Ave, Cambridge)* and ***Harvard Coop*** *(Map 5; ☎ 617-499-2000, 1400 Mass Ave, Cambridge)* Both shops have a good selection of Harvard University–related items. But please, don't wear them until you get home. Ⓣ Red Line to Harvard.

Eugene Galleries *(Map 2; ☎ 617-227-3062, 76 Charles St)* Browse this remarkable selection of antique Boston prints and maps. Ⓣ Red Line to Charles/MGH.

Boston Globe Store *(Map 2; ☎ 617-367-4000, 3 School St)* Buy selected pages from the city's principal newspaper for the day you were born, but don't be disappointed if your arrival on earth didn't make the front page. Ⓣ Orange or Blue Line to State.

Newspapers & Magazines

The outdoor ***Copley Square News*** *(Map 4; Boylston St at Dartmouth St)* has sold hundreds of magazines and many foreign-language periodicals on this corner since the 1930s. Ⓣ Green Line to Copley.

Out of Town News *(Map 5; ☎ 617-354-7777, Harvard Square, Cambridge)* Open 5am-10pm. This is no ordinary newsstand; in fact, it's a National Historic Landmark. Despite the fact that you can read news on the Internet, this place still sells papers from virtually every major US city, as well as from cities around the world. Ⓣ Red Line to Harvard.

Art Galleries

While Newbury St has the most expensive and dense concentration of galleries, there are also a number of avant-garde galleries in the Leather District, an area near South Station bounded by South, Lincoln, Essex and Kneeland Sts. There are also a few galleries throughout the city that allow you to support local and national artists and artisans without losing your shirt.

Fort Point Arts Community Gallery *(Map 2; ☎ 617-423-4299, 300 Summer St)* The focal point for Boston's cutting edge arts community, there's always something interesting on display here. Ⓣ Red Line to South Station.

Bromfield Art Gallery *(Map 4; ☎ 617-451-3605, 560 Harrison Ave)* This South End gallery is one of the more accessible, affordable and reputable galleries on the Boston art scene. It also happens to be the city's oldest cooperative. Ⓣ Orange Line to Back Bay, then a 15-minute walk.

Barbara Krakow Gallery *(Map 4; ☎ 617-262-4490, 10 Newbury St)* This gallery provides an elegant venue for contemporary artists. It's worth a look even if you can't afford to buy anything. Ⓣ Green Line to Arlington.

Arts & Crafts

Harvard Collections *(Map 5; ☎ 617-496-3532, 1350 Mass Ave, Cambridge)* If you prefer unique Harvard-related gifts without the Harvard name and seal emblazoned all over them, stop by this place. They have fine reproductions and original works inspired by the immense holdings of the various University museums, from African masks and carvings to jewelry crafted from ancient coins. Ⓣ Red Line to Harvard.

Society of Arts & Crafts (Map 4; ☎ 617-266-1810, 175 Newbury St) This prestigious, nonprofit gallery was founded in 1897. Within the exhibition and retail space you'll find high-quality weaving, leather, ceramics, furniture and other handcrafted items. Ⓣ Green Line to Copley.

Women's Education & Industrial Union (Map 4; ☎ 617-536-5651, 356 Boylston St) Handcrafted gifts from quilts to toys, books and stationery take center stage at this historic shop. Ⓣ Green Line to Arlington.

Cambridge Artists' Cooperative (Map 5; ☎ 617-868-4434, 59A Church St, Cambridge) Craftspeople double as sales staff at this Harvard Square co-op that displays over 200 handcrafted objects ranging from $3 to $1000. Ⓣ Red Line to Harvard.

Antiques

In Boston antiques are pricey, but if you want to do some window-shopping, head to Charles and River Sts on Beacon Hill. Ⓣ Red Line to Charles/MGH.

Cambridge Antique Market (☎ 617-868-9655, 201 Monsignor O'Brien Hwy, Cambridge) With five floors of furniture, glass, clothing, pottery and jewelry, you'll probably find a little something to take home. Ⓣ Green Line to Lechmere.

Justin Tyme (☎ 617-491-1088, 91 River St, Cambridge) For a more intimate shopping experience, try this shop, specializing in antiques, collectibles, costume jewelry and vintage clothing. Ⓣ Red Line to Central, and then head west on Western Ave for one block until River St forks to the left.

Camping Supplies

Hilton's Tent City (Map 2; ☎ 617-227-9242, 272 Friend St) Although it's dusty and musty, Hilton's boasts four floors of tents (set up to test out) and all the camping and backpacking accessories, equipment and clothing you'll ever need – all at the lowest prices around. Ⓣ Orange or Green Line to North Station.

Eastern Mountain Sports (EMS; ☎ 617-254-4250, 1041 Comm Ave, Brighton) This is another good source for hiking and camping gear, books and maps. If you can't find it at

Hilton's, you'll find it here. Ⓣ Green Line 'B' branch to Babcock.

GETTING THERE & AWAY

Air

Logan International Airport (Map 1; ☎ 800-235-6426, MA 1A, East Boston) is served by most major national and international carriers. Its five separate terminals are connected by a frequent shuttle bus (No 11). The nonprofit Travelers Aid Society (☎ 617-567-5385), an agency that assists travelers in need, maintains a booth at Terminal 'E,' where all international flights arrive and depart; the booth is staffed by volunteers noon to 9pm daily. Also, look for volunteers roaming around being helpful in Terminal 'E.' Logan has been undergoing an expansion for years and the congestion and confusion that it brings comes as a shock to travelers. You'll fare better if you assume the worst: Don't expect much logic or ease in navigation.

Bus

Boston has a modern, indoor, user-friendly bus station (Map 2; no ☎, 700 Atlantic Ave), at Summer St, conveniently adjacent to the South Station train station and above a T stop for the Red Line.

Greyhound (☎ 617-526-1800, 800-231-2222, Ⓦ www.greyhound.com) buses depart for New York City throughout the day. Express buses take only 4½ hours, but others take up to two hours longer. Adult fares are $42 one-way (children ages two to 11 are half-price). Other sample destinations and adult one-way fares from Boston include the following:

destination	fare	duration
Albany, NY	$30	3½ to 4¾ hours
Hartford, CT	$21	2 to 2½ hours
New Haven, CT	$29	3½ hours
Newark, NJ	$42	5¾ to 6½ hours
Providence, RI	$7.50	1 hour
Springfield, MA	$20	2 to 2½ hours

Inquire about special offers like buying one roundtrip ticket with a three-day advance purchase and getting a companion ticket free. A seven-day advance purchase on one-way tickets often beats all other quoted fares; inquire.

Bonanza Bus Lines (☎ 617-720-4110, 800-556-3815, w www.bonanzabus.com) serves Falmouth and Woods Hole on Cape Cod, as well as Providence and New York City.

Plymouth & Brockton (☎ 508-778-9767, w www.p-b.com) provides frequent service to most towns on Cape Cod, including Hyannis and Provincetown.

Peter Pan Bus Lines (☎ 800-343-9999, w www.peterpanbus.com) serves Northampton and Lenox in western Massachusetts, Hartford, New Haven and New York City.

Concord Trailways (☎ 617-426-8080, 800-639-3317, w www.concordtrailways.com) plies routes from Boston to New Hampshire, and Boston to Portland and Bangor in Maine.

C&J Trailways (☎ 800-258-7111, w www .cjtrailways.com) provides daily service to Newburyport, MA, and Portsmouth, NH.

Vermont Transit (☎ 800-451-3292, w www .vermonttransit.com) operates its buses to White River Junction and Keene, NH; Portland (year-round) and Bar Harbor (seasonal), ME. In Vermont, buses go to Burlington, Brattleboro, Bennington and lots of small towns in between.

Train
Amtrak (Map 2; ☎ 800-872-7245, w www .amtrak.com) trains stop at the South Station terminal, at Atlantic Ave and Summer St (Ⓣ Red Line to South Station), as well as Back Bay Station (Map 4), at Dartmouth St (Ⓣ Orange Line to Back Bay). Service to New York City's Penn Station costs $58 to $63 one-way, depending on the day and time, and takes 4 to 4½ hours. Service to Manhattan on the high-speed Acela train (3½ hours) is a lot more expensive ($99 to $116 one-way); reservations are required. Amtrak's online 'Rail Sale' program offers substantial discounts on many reserved tickets.

When it was built in 1900, South Station was the world's largest railroad station. Decades of heavy use took their toll, but a renovation in the late 1980s brought the

magnificent gateway back up to par. Today, the curved, five-story building is alive with pushcart vendors, fast-food eateries, cafe tables, a newsstand and live concerts on many summer afternoons.

North Station (Map 2; ☎ 617-222-3200, 150 Causeway St) serves MBTA commuter rail trains (☎ 800-392-6100, w www.mbta.com) to the west and north of the city, including Concord. Catch the 'beach trains' to Salem, Gloucester and Rockport here. North Station is on the T Green and Orange Lines.

Car
From western Massachusetts, the Massachusetts Turnpike ('Mass Pike' or I-90; a toll road) takes you right into downtown. After paying a toll in Newton, drive east 10 more minutes on the pike and pay another 50¢; then the fun begins.

There are three exits for the Boston area: Cambridge, Copley Square (Prudential Center) and Kneeland St (Chinatown). Then, the turnpike ends abruptly. At that point you can head north or south of the city on the I-93 Expressway (the Central Artery; see the Orientation section at the beginning of this chapter) or right past South Station, into downtown.

From New York and other southerly points, take I-95 north to MA 128 to I-93 north, which cuts through the heart of the city. From northerly points, take I-93 south across the Tobin Bridge, which merges into the Central Artery.

As for a few sample distances from Boston to various points around New England, it takes 4½ hours to travel 220 miles to Burlington, VT; 4½ hours to travel 227 miles to New York City; just over an hour to drive 57 miles to Portsmouth, NH; an hour to drive 45 miles to Providence, RI; and 2¼ hours to travel 108 miles to Portland, ME.

Boat
Boston Harbor Cruises (Map 2; ☎ 617-227-4320) operates boats to George's Island from Long Wharf; see the Boston Harbor Islands section for details.

Bay State Cruise Company (☎ 617-748-1428) operates boats from Commonwealth

The Big Dig

The combined construction of the Ted Williams Tunnel and the depression of the Central Artery is scheduled for completion in 2005 (with a little luck). Approaching the city, you'll feel the Big Dig's greatest impact from the south. Once in the city, there are serious traffic problems along the entire waterfront area, South Station and the North End. Although the project managers have done a commendable job rerouting auto and pedestrian traffic, snarls can be monumental. Admittedly, it's fascinating to watch the around-the-clock phalanx of workers, the enormous cranes and the convoys of trucks hauling away mega-tons of earth.

Pier in South Boston to Provincetown at the tip of Cape Cod; see the Getting There & Away section for Provincetown in the Cape Cod chapter for details. For information on its summertime evening cruises, see Cruises, earlier in this chapter.

The AC Cruise Line (☎ 617-261-6633, 290 Northern Ave) operates boats to Gloucester and Salem on the North Shore; see Cruises, earlier in this chapter.

GETTING AROUND
To/From the Airport

Downtown Boston is just a few miles from Logan International Airport and is accessible by subway (the 'T'), water shuttle, van shuttle, limo, taxi and rental car.

The T, or the MBTA subway (☎ 617-222-3200, 800-392-6100, ⓦ www.mbta.com), is the fastest and cheapest way to reach the city from the airport. From any terminal, take a free, well-marked shuttle bus (No 22 or No 33) to ⓣ Blue Line to Airport, purchase a $1 token and you'll be downtown within 30 minutes, including waiting. The subway operates daily from about 5:30am to about 12:30am.

Taxis are plentiful but pricey; traffic snarls can translate into a $20 fare to downtown.

If you are driving to downtown from the airport, take the Sumner Tunnel ($2 toll) downtown to Government Center and the North End, where there are immediate on-ramps for the I-93 Expressway (Central Artery) north and south. When you're going *from* Boston *to* the airport, take the Callahan Tunnel (no toll). The Third Harbor Tunnel (Ted Williams Tunnel; $2 toll), a mile south of the city off I-93, is open to buses, taxis and limos every day, but to noncommercial vehicles (that's you) only on weekends. There's a hefty fine for going through it when you're not supposed to. When it's open, it saves travelers approaching from the south a great deal of time.

The Airport Water Shuttle (☎ 617-951-0255, 800-235-6426), also accessible via free shuttle buses from each terminal, whisks passengers to downtown Rowes Wharf (at Atlantic Ave; Map 2) in seven minutes. Once downtown, though, you'll probably still have to take the subway. (The closest T station to Rowes Wharf is ⓣ Blue Line to Aquarium, a five-minute walk.) However, the water shuttle across Boston Harbor provides a great view of Boston's skyline. Purchase tickets onboard; one-way tickets cost $10/5 adult/senior, free for children under

12. The shuttle runs every 15 minutes from 6am to 8pm weekdays, every 30 minutes from 10am to 8pm Saturday and Sunday.

'Logan Dart' has traditionally provided a direct bus connection (☎ 800-235-6426) from Logan airport to the South Station Transportation Center. At press time this service had been canceled and was under review for future operation.

The T

The MBTA (☎ 617-222-3200, 800-392-6100) operates the USA's oldest subway, built in 1897, known locally as 'the T.' There are four lines – Red, Blue, Green and Orange – that radiate from the principal downtown stations. These are Park St (which has an information booth), Downtown Crossing, Government Center and State. When traveling away from any of these stations, you are heading outbound.

Tourist passes with unlimited travel are available for periods of one week ($22), three days ($11) and one day ($6). Kids ages five to 11 pay half-fare. Passes may be purchased at the visitor information center on Tremont St and at the following T stations: Park St, Government Center, Back Bay, Alewife, Copley, Quincy Adams, Harvard, North Station, South Station, Hynes and Airport. For even longer stays, monthly unlimited-travel passes are available from around the first of the month to the 15th; subway-only passes are $35, subway-plus-bus passes are $57.

Otherwise, buy tokens at all stations ($1 adult, 50¢ children) except those west of Symphony ('E' branch) and Kenmore ('B', 'C' and 'D' branches) on the Green Line, which are above ground. You need exact change to board. No fare is collected when heading outbound from an above-ground Green Line station. Some fares heading inbound, though, are higher than $1.

The T operates from about 5:30am to 12:30am. See MBTA map that precedes page 97.

Bus

The MBTA also operates bus routes within the city, but these can be difficult to figure out for short-term visitors. The subway goes to 95% of the places you'll want to go.

Car

With any luck you won't have to drive in or around Boston. Not only are the streets a maze of confusion, choked with construction (see the 'Big Dig' boxed text) and legendary traffic jams, but Boston drivers use their own set of rules. Driving is often considered a sport – in a town that takes its sports very seriously.

Two highways skirt the Charles River: Storrow Dr runs along the Boston side and Memorial Dr (more scenic) parallels it on the Cambridge side. There are exits off of Storrow Dr for Kenmore Square, Back Bay and Government Center. Both Storrow Dr and Memorial Dr are accessible from the Mass Pike and the I-93 Expressway.

All major rental car agencies are represented at the airport; free shuttle vans will take you to their nearby pick-up counters. (See also the Car & Motorcycle section in the Getting Around chapter.) When returning rental cars, you'll find gas stations on US 1 north of the airport. Rental car companies with offices downtown include:

Avis
(☎ 617-534-1400, 800-331-1212)
3 Center Plaza at Government Center

Budget
(☎ 617-497-1800, 800-527-0700)
24 Park Plaza

Enterprise
(☎ 617-262-8222, 800-736-8222)
Prudential Center, 800 Boylston St

Hertz
(☎ 617-338-1500, 800-654-3131)
30 Park Plaza near the Public Garden

National
(☎ 617-661-8747, 800-227-7368)
1663 Mass Ave, between Harvard Square and Porter Square

Rent a Wreck
(☎ 617-576-3700, 800-535-1391)
Monsignor O'Brien Hwy, near Lechmere, Cambridge

Thrifty
(☎ 617-330-5011, 800-367-2277)
125 Summer, near South Station

Hertz has installed its 'Never Lost' navigational system in its Boston cars. With road configurations in Boston that literally change overnight, the system will surely be put to a test. Regardless, these cars cost an additional $6 daily.

Taxi

Cabs are plentiful (although you'll have to walk to a major hotel to find one with any degree of assurance), but expensive. Expect to pay about $10 to $15 between most tourist points within the city limits, without much traffic. You'll have lots of trouble hailing a cab during bad weather and between 3:30pm and 6:30pm weekdays. Again, head to major hotels or Faneuil Hall.

Recommended taxi companies include Independent (☎ 617-426-8700) and Metro Cab (☎ 617-242-8000).

Bicycle

Daredevil Bostonians cycle around town, but there are no bike lanes, so use caution if you take to the Boston city streets on two wheels. For information on biking and renting bicycles in Boston, see the Bicycling section earlier in this chapter. Be sure to get a hold of *Boston's Bike Map*; see Orientation, at the beginning of this chapter.

Boat

City Water Taxi (☎ 617-422-0392) makes on-demand taxi stops from April to October at about 10 waterfront points, including the airport, the Children's Museum, Long Wharf, Burroughs Wharf in the North End, the USS *Constitution* and the Charlestown Navy Yard. The fare is usually $10 per person between any two points, with the exception of the airport.

MBTA Water Shuttle (☎ 617-222-3200) plies the waters year-round between Lovejoy Wharf near North Station, Charlestown Navy Yard and Long Wharf. Tickets cost $1.25 one-way.

For information on the airport water shuttle, see the beginning of the Getting Around section. For information on cruises, see Cruises, earlier in this chapter.

Around Boston

Famous village greens, national parks and historic harbors, rich in the evocation of New England's past, lie within an hour's excursion (by car or train) from Boston. But history and museums are far from the only draws here. Hiking, whale watching, canoeing, biking, beaching and picnicking tempt the wild at heart.

West of Boston

To trace the events leading to the outbreak of the American Revolution in 1775, travelers can follow patriot Paul Revere's famous ride to Lexington's Battle Green, about 18 miles northwest of Boston, then continue along the Battle Road (a national park) another 6 miles through rolling fields and forests to Concord.

From Boston, you can reach Lexington by bus and Concord by train, but consider making the trip by bike. The **Minuteman Commuter Bikeway** follows an old railroad right-of-way from near the Alewife Red Line subway terminus in Cambridge, through Arlington to Lexington and Bedford, a total distance of about 14 miles. From Bedford, ride along MA 4 northwest, then MA 62 southwest, to reach Concord, another 6 miles along. For bicycle rental information, see the Boston chapter.

LEXINGTON

This upscale suburb, about 18 miles from Boston's center, has a bustling village of white churches, eateries, boutiques, historic taverns and tour buses surrounding the Battle Green. Here, the skirmish between patriots and British troops announced the start of the War for American Independence. And if you come to Lexington on an early weekend morning when the mist hangs on the Battle Green, you may still sense the peace shattered by cries of 'The British are coming!'

History

On April 18, 1775, Paul Revere, William Dawes and Samuel Prescott set out on their midnight ride from Boston to Lexington

Highlights

- Strolling through the gracious, historic villages of Lexington and Concord
- Visiting the picturesque coastal town of Salem
- Touring Gloucester, the region's most famous fishing port
- Spending the day wandering in Rockport or sailing on the bay

NH

Cape Ann
(Gloucester & Rockport)
page 185

Salem
page 176
Marblehead
page 182

Concord
page 167

Plymouth
page 199

Cape Cod Bay

Around Boston
pages 162-163

RI

ATLANTIC
OCEAN

AROUND BOSTON

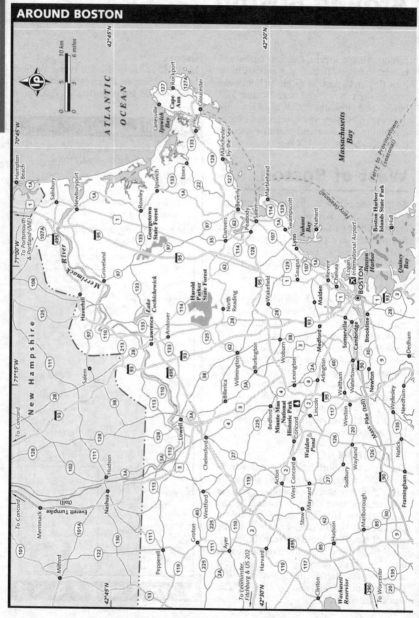

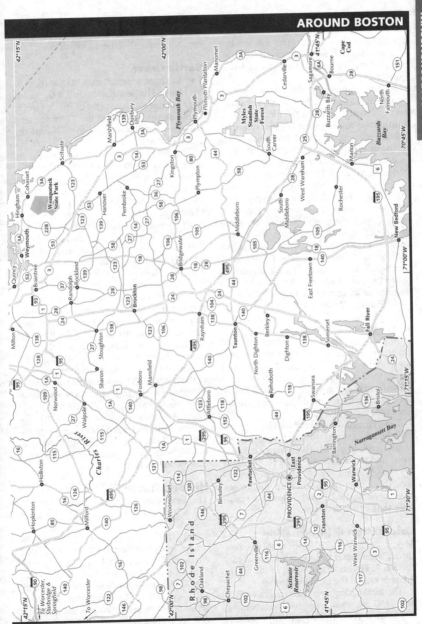

and Concord. They rode to warn these communities and others that General Gage, the British commander in Boston, was sending an expeditionary force to search for arms and matériel rumored to be stockpiled at Concord.

Revere, Dawes and Prescott were part of a colonial intelligence and communications network so efficient that the local troops of militia, the minutemen, turned out long before the tramp of British boots was heard on the dirt road approaching Lexington.

When the advance body of 700 redcoats, under Major John Pitcairn, marched up to Lexington Green just after daybreak, they found Capt John Parker's company of 77 minutemen lined up in formation to meet them. Capt Parker and his men were there to defend their homes from what they deemed an unreasonable search; the British were there to do their duty. Clearly outnumbered, and perhaps fearing capture of his force, Capt Parker ordered his men to disperse peaceably, which they slowly began to do. But the British took this as capitulation and began trying to arrest the 'rebels' who had raised arms against them.

A shot rang out – from which side has never been clear – and then others, and soon eight minutemen lay dead on the green, with 10 others wounded. Pitcairn regained control of his troops with difficulty and marched them out of Lexington toward Concord.

The skirmish on Lexington Green (now called Battle Green) was the first organized, armed resistance to British rule in a colonial town, and the beginning of the Revolutionary War. Without the bloodshed at Lexington, the Concord minutemen might not have been steeled to offer spirited resistance to the British troops.

Orientation & Information
MA 4 and MA 225 follow Mass Ave through the center of Lexington, passing by the Battle Green. The green is at the northwestern end of the business district.

The local Chamber of Commerce (☎ 781-862-1450, ⓦ www.lexingtonchamber.org, 1875 Mass Ave, Lexington, MA, 02421)

maintains a visitor center opposite Battle Green, next to Buckman Tavern. It's open 9am to 5pm daily (10am to 4pm in winter).

Battle Green
The Lexington minuteman statue (crafted by Henry Hudson Kitson in 1900) stands guard at the southeast end of Battle Green, honoring the bravery of the 77 minutemen who met the British here in 1775 and the eight who died.

The green is tranquil today, shaded by tall trees. A boulder marks the spot where the minutemen faced a force almost 10 times their strength. Just off the green, by the church, is **Ye Olde Burying Ground**, with tombstones dating back as far as 1690.

Every year on April 19, minuteman companies in colonial dress, bearing colonial matchlock firearms, reenact the battle on Lexington Green. The British heavies – somewhat fewer than their original force of 700 – come dressed authentically as well, and the air is again filled with the tramp of hobnailed boots, barked commands, explosions of musket fire and clouds of gun smoke. Authenticity is pursued with some vigor, so the reenactment starts at the same time as the original event: just after dawn.

For a look at the most famous depiction of the battle of Lexington, walk southeast of the green to **Isaac Harris Cary Memorial Hall** (*the town hall; ☎ 781-862-0500, 1625 Mass Ave; admission free; open 8:30am-4:30pm Mon-Fri*). Sandham's famous painting *The Dawn of Liberty* hangs flanked by marble statues of patriots John Hancock and Samuel Adams.

Historic Houses
The **Lexington Historical Society** (*☎ 781-862-1703, 1332 Mass Ave*) maintains three historic houses.

Facing the green next to the visitor center, **Buckman Tavern** (*☎ 781-862-5598, 1 Bedford Rd; adult/child $5/3; open 10am-5pm Mon-Sat, 1pm-5pm Sun mid-Apr–Oct; extended hours until 8pm June-Aug*), built 1709, was where the minutemen spent the tense hours between the original midnight call to arms and the dawn arrival of the redcoats. It also served as a field hospital where the wounded were treated after the fight. Today, it is a museum of colonial life, with instructive tours given by 'interpreters' in period costume.

Now serving as the Lexington Historical Society's headquarters, **Munroe Tavern** (☎ 781-674-9238, 1332 Mass Ave; adult/child $5/3; open 10am-5pm Sat, 1pm-5pm Sun mid-Apr–Oct; extended hours until 8pm June-Aug), built in 1695, is about seven long blocks southeast of the green and was used by the British as a command post and field infirmary. It's now furnished with antiques, mementos of the battle and artifacts from President George Washington's visit in 1789.

The **Hancock-Clarke House** (☎ 781-861-0928, 36 Hancock St; adult/child $5/3; open 10am-5pm Sat, 1pm-5pm Sun mid-Apr–Oct; extended hours until 8pm June-Aug), built in 1698, is about a block north of Battle Green. It was the parsonage of the Reverend Jonas Clarke in 1775, and the goal of Paul Revere as he rode out to warn the colonials of the British troops' advance. John Hancock and Samuel Adams, 'rabble-rousers' wanted by the British crown, hid here on the fateful day.

Museum of Our National Heritage
The museum (☎ 781-861-6559, 33 Marrett Rd/MA 2A; admission free; open 10am-5pm Mon-Sat, noon-5pm Sun), just off Mass Ave (MA 4 and MA 225), stands more than a mile southeast of Battle Green. Founded by the Scottish Rite Masons in 1975, it has four large galleries with several exhibits depicting events of April 1775 in Lexington and Concord.

Places to Stay
The chamber of commerce visitor center has a list of B&Bs; see the Orientation & Information section, earlier in this chapter.

Battle Green Inn (☎ 781-862-6100, 800-343-0235, W www.battlegreeninn.com, 1720 Mass Ave) Doubles/twins $99/104. This is a motel-style lodging right in the center of Lexington's business district. A light self-service breakfast is included in the rates.

Sheraton Tara Lexington Inn (☎ 781-862-8700, fax 863-0404, W www.sheraton .com, 727 Marrett Rd) Rooms $109 and up. This establishment has 119 rooms, in a full-service facility favored by business travelers. Ask about weekend discounts. It's just west of I-95 exit 30B; follow the signs for Hanscom Field.

Places to Eat & Drink
More than a dozen eateries lie within a five-minute walk of the Battle Green. Most are open for lunch and dinner daily.

Vila Lago Gourmet Foods (☎ 781-861-6174, 1845 Mass Ave) Prices $4-10. Here's a cafe with high ceilings, intimate tables, the scent of fresh-roasted coffee and a great deli case. You'll often see cyclists in here kicking back with the daily paper, a cup of exotic java or tea (around $1) and a sandwich of roasted turkey, Swiss and sprouts.

Bertucci's (☎ 781-860-9000, 1777 Mass Ave) Dishes $5-14. In the very center of town, Bertucci's serves pizzas baked in a wood-fired brick oven, pastas, salads and other light meals. This is a good place to catch a draft beer ($3) after cycling.

Mario's Italian Restaurant (☎ 781-861-1182, 1733 Mass Ave) Mains $4-9. The consummate Umbrian bistro, with just 15 tables and red-and-white checkered tablecloths, Mario's offers great value on pizza ($7 and up) and carbo loading for cyclists. Try the spaghetti lunch special ($5).

Dabin (☎ 781-860-0171, 10 Muzzey St) Dishes $10-15. Travelers can pause here for sushi ($9 to $12) or other Japanese and Korean dishes. It's a half-block south of Mass Ave.

Lemon Grass Thai Cuisine (☎ 781-862-3530, 1710 Mass Ave) Mains $10-15. A little place with cane chairs and the scent of ginger, the Lemon Grass has huge meals like 'boat trip noodles,' and curries with shrimp, chicken, onions and red pepper.

Yangtze River (☎ 781-861-6030, 21 Depot Square) Lunch buffet Mon-Fri $6, Sat-Sun $7.50; dinner buffet Mon-Fri $11, Sat-Sun $12. This restaurant, off Mass Ave just south of the Battle Green, features Szechuan and Mandarin cuisine, like sesame beef.

Peking Garden (☎ 781-862-1051, 27–31 *Waltham St*) Mains $8-14. Peking Garden has a large dining room with lots of gold paint and birds of paradise. We think the moo shu vegetables ($7) are a good value.

Vinny Testa's (☎ 781-860-5200, 20 *Waltham St*) Mains $13-25. For more elaborate Italian fare, head across the street from the Peking Garden to Vinny's for huge pasta plates ($6 to $19) like penne gratinate. Dark paneling, Roman murals and Italian torch songs set the tone. The bar is a popular stop for urban professionals during the evening.

Getting There & Away

Take MA 2 west from Boston or Cambridge to exit 54 (Waltham St) or exit 53 (Spring St). From I-95 (MA 128), take exit 30 or 31.

MBTA buses (☎ 800-392-6100) No 62 (Bedford VA Hospital) and No 76 (Hanscom Field) run from the Red Line Alewife subway terminus through Lexington center at least every hour weekdays, less frequently on Saturday; no buses on Sunday.

If you have a bike, or rent one (see the Boston chapter), a good day's biking excursion is the 8-mile ride along the Minuteman Bikeway from Cambridge to Lexington. From here you can follow the bikeway west to Bedford and Concord.

CONCORD

Tall white church steeples rise above ancient oaks, elms and maples in colonial Concord, giving the town a stateliness that belies the Revolutionary War drama that occurred here. In warm weather, tourists flock to the Minute Man National Historic Park, Thoreau's Walden Pond and the homes of literary figures like Emerson, Hawthorne, and Alcott. The placid Concord River offers canoeing possibilities, and the country roads are excellent for cycling.

History

Revolutionary History At about 7am the morning of April 19, 1775, after the skirmish on Lexington Green, General Gage's expeditionary force of 700 British soldiers marched to nearby Concord and commandeered the Wright Tavern at the corner of Main St and Lexington Rd as their headquarters. Their commander sent seven companies off to the north to seize arms reported by spies to be stored at Colonel James Barrett's farm, leaving only three of these companies to secure the North Bridge.

The Yankee minutemen, outnumbered, mustered on Punkatasset Hill, northeast of the town center, and awaited reinforcements, which came steadily from surrounding towns. When several hundred had assembled, the minutemen saw smoke rising from the town. The British searchers had found nothing but a few gun carriages, which they burned, but the minutemen assumed the worst.

'Will you let them burn the town down?' shouted their commander. Enraged that the regulars would burn down their homes, the minutemen fired on the now-outnumbered British troops, wounding half of their officers and forcing them back across the North Bridge. Soon the British were on their way out of Concord.

The battle at North Bridge, called 'the shot heard 'round the world' by Emerson, was the first successful armed resistance to British rule. But it did not end there.

The British suffered 11 wounded and two dead at North Bridge, but it was only the beginning of the calamity. Minutemen pursued the British troops on their march back to Boston, firing at the redcoats from behind trees, walls and buildings. Most of this fire did little harm, but occasionally a bullet would find its mark, and in places where the minutemen had defensible positions, British troops fell. They were tired, dispirited and angry when they reached Lexington and encountered 1000 reinforcements.

These guerrilla tactics were unusual for the time and were looked upon as cowardly and unfair by the British troops. Enraged by the locals' resistance, and by their own ever-mounting casualties, the British rioted and murdered innocent colonials whom they encountered along their line of march. At Menotomy (modern Arlington), 5000 men battled one another. By the time the British regained the safety of Boston, they

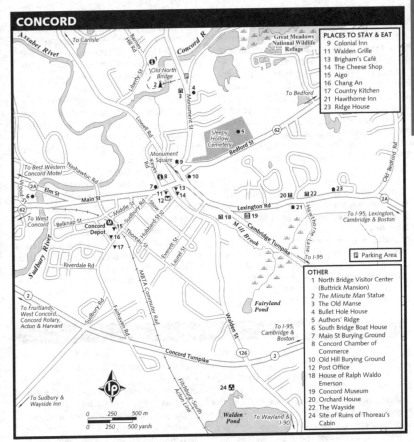

CONCORD

PLACES TO STAY & EAT
9 Colonial Inn
11 Walden Grille
13 Brigham's Café
14 The Cheese Shop
15 Aigo
16 Chang An
17 Country Kitchen
21 Hawthorne Inn
23 Ridge House

P Parking Area

OTHER
1 North Bridge Visitor Center
   (Buttrick Mansion)
2 The Minute Man Statue
3 The Old Manse
4 Bullet Hole House
5 Authors' Ridge
6 South Bridge Boat House
7 Main St Burying Ground
8 Concord Chamber of
   Commerce
10 Old Hill Burying Ground
12 Post Office
18 House of Ralph Waldo
   Emerson
19 Concord Museum
20 Orchard House
22 The Wayside
24 Site of Ruins of Thoreau's
   Cabin

had suffered 73 dead, 174 wounded and 26 missing. The American losses amounted to 49 dead, 40 wounded and five missing.

The die had been cast. The American colonies stood in armed rebellion against the forces of the British crown.

19th-Century Literary History Concord in the 19th century was a very different place. Though still a town of prosperous farmers, it was home to prominent literary figures of the age, including essayist, preacher and poet Ralph Waldo Emerson (1803–82); essayist and naturalist Henry David Thoreau (1817–62); short-story writer and novelist Nathaniel Hawthorne (1804–64); and novelist and children's book author Louisa May Alcott (1832–88).

Emerson was the paterfamilias of literary Concord, one of the great literary figures of his age and the founding thinker of the Transcendentalist movement. While traveling in Great Britain, he befriended Thomas Carlyle, Samuel Taylor Coleridge and William Wordsworth. His Concord house is now a museum.

Thoreau took the naturalist beliefs of Transcendentalism out of the realm of theory and into practice when he left the comforts of the town and built himself a rustic cabin on the shores of Walden Pond, several miles from the town center. His famous memoir of his time spent there, *Walden, or Life in the Woods* (1854), was full of praise for nature and disapproval of the stresses of civilized life – sentiments that have found an eager audience ever since. Many of his readers visit the site of his cabin at Walden Pond (see Walden Pond, later in this section).

Hawthorne, author of *The Scarlet Letter, Twice-Told Tales* and *The House of the Seven Gables,* was born and raised in Salem, MA, but lived in Concord at the Old Manse next to the North Bridge for three years just after his marriage. His residence in Concord gave him material for several later stories.

Alcott was a junior member of this august literary crowd, but her work proved more durable than that of the others. *Little Women* (1868–69), her mostly autobiographical novel about women coming of age in Concord, is among the most popular young-adult books ever written. Its several sequels continued her portrayal of family life in Victorian America with keen perception and affection. Her childhood home, Orchard House, is among Concord's most-visited sites (see Historic Houses, later in this chapter).

Daniel Chester French (1850–1931) was a young sculptor living in Concord when the town asked him to create a bronze statue of a minuteman to commemorate the 100th anniversary in 1875 of the battle at Old North Bridge. French went on also to create the marble statue of Emerson now in Concord's public library; the equestrian statue of General George Washington that now stands in Paris; the great marble statue in the Lincoln Memorial (1922) in Washington, DC; and many other works.

Resident Ephraim Bull had a different kind of success altogether. Around 1850, his hybrid Concord grape gave birth to commercial table-grape agriculture in the USA. For many years, the Welch's company had its headquarters on Main St.

Transcendentalism

Transcendentalism was a 19th-century American social and philosophical movement that flourished from 1836 to 1860 in Boston and Concord. Though small in numbers, the Transcendentalists had a significant effect on American literature and society.

The core of Transcendentalist belief was that each person and element of nature had within them a part of the divine essence, that God 'transcended' all things. The search for divinity was thus not so much in scripture and prayer, nor in perception and reason, but in individual intuition or 'instinct.' By intuition we can know what is right and wrong according to divine law. By intuition we can know the meaning of life. Living in harmony with the natural world was very important to Transcendentalists.

Bronson Alcott (1799–1888), educational and social reformer and father of Louisa May Alcott, joined Emerson, Thoreau, Margaret Fuller and other Concordians in turning away from their traditional Unitarianism to Transcendentalism.

The Transcendentalists founded a periodical, the *Dial*, to disseminate their views, and established the community of Brook Farm (1841–47) based on Transcendentalist doctrines of community life and work, social reform and opposition to slavery. Hawthorne was a resident for a time, and both he and novelist Herman Melville were influenced by Transcendentalist beliefs.

Bronson Alcott was also a founder of Fruitlands, an experimental vegetarian community in Harvard, MA, established in 1843. He lived here with his family (including 10-year-old daughter Louisa) and others for a year before abandoning the project. Fruitlands is now a museum open to the public (see the Fruitlands section, later in this chapter).

Orientation

Concord (population 18,000) lies about 22 miles northwest of Boston along MA 2. The center of this sprawling, mostly rural town is Monument Square, marked by its war memorial obelisk. The Colonial Inn stands on the square's north side.

Main St runs westward from Monument Square through the business district to MA 2. Walden and Thoreau Sts run southeast from Main St and out to Walden Pond some 3 miles away.

The MBTA commuter rail train station, the Concord Station ('the Depot'), is on Thoreau St at Sudbury Rd, a mile west of Monument Square.

Information

Concord's Chamber of Commerce (☎ 978-369-3120, W www.concordmachamber.org, Keyes Rd, Concord, MA 01742) has a new visitor center (complete with public rest rooms) behind the Middlesex Savings Bank, across from the Main St Burying Ground at the center of town. The chamber is open 9:30am to 4:30pm daily mid-April to October, 9am to 2pm Monday to Friday off-season.

Minuteman National Historic Park's Minute Man Visitor Center (☎ 978-862-7753) is on MA 2A between Lexington and Concord, in the heart of the Battle Road section of the park. Concord's North Bridge Visitor Center (☎ 978-369-6993) is on Liberty St just north of the North Bridge. Both centers are open 9am to 5pm daily in summer, until 4pm in winter; closed Christmas and New Year's Day.

There are lots of links to Concord information at W www.concordma.com, or stop by Concord Bookshop (☎ 978-369-2405, 65 Main St) for the local scoop and a new novel.

Walking Tours

If you'd like a guided walking tour, contact the Concord Chamber of Commerce (☎ 978-369-3120, $15/10/5 adult/senior & student/child under 12). It offers 1½-hour walking tours of the town's revolutionary and literary sites.

The grassy center of Monument Square is a favorite resting and picnicking spot for cyclists touring Concord's scenic roads. It's the best place to start your walk around historic Concord. At the southeastern end of the square is Wright Tavern, one of the first places the British troops searched in their hunt for arms on April 19, 1775. It became their headquarters for the operation. At the opposite end of the square is the Colonial Inn (see Places to Stay, later in this section), the oldest part of which dates from 1716.

Walk northeast out of Monument Square (keep the Colonial Inn on your left), along Monument St. It's a 15-minute walk past some of the town's most beautiful colonial houses to Old North Bridge, site of the first battle of the Revolutionary War. Along the way, watch for the yellow Bullet Hole House on the right-hand (east) side. British troops fired at the owner of the house as they retreated from the engagement at North Bridge, and a hole made by one of their bullets can still be seen in the wall of the shed attached to the house.

The wooden span of Old North Bridge, now part of Minuteman National Historic Park, has been rebuilt many times but still gives a good impression of what it must have looked like at the time of the battle. Across the bridge is Daniel Chester French's first statue, *The Minute Man,* which is on the way up the hill to the Buttrick Mansion, the park's visitor center.

Walking south and east from Monument Square for five minutes brings you to the Concord Museum (☎ *978-369-9609, 200 Lexington Rd; family/adult/senior & child $16/7/3; open 9am-5pm Mon-Sat).* Among the museum's exhibits is one of the lanterns hung in the steeple of Boston's Old North Church as a signal to Revere, Dawes and Prescott; furnishings from Ralph Waldo Emerson's study; and the world's largest collection of Thoreau artifacts.

Historic Houses

Across from the Concord Museum is the House of Ralph Waldo Emerson (☎ *978-369-2236, 28 Cambridge Turnpike; adult/child*

$5/3, child under 7 yrs free; open 10am-4:30pm Thur-Sat, 2pm-4:30pm Sun mid-Apr–Oct). The house, where Emerson lived from 1835 until his death in 1882, often hosted his renowned circle of friends and still contains many original furnishings.

About a mile east of Monument Square is Louisa May Alcott's home, **Orchard House** (☎ *978-369-4118, 399 Lexington Rd; adult/senior/child/family $7/6/4/16; open 10am-4:30pm Mon-Sat, 1pm-4:30pm Sun Apr-Oct; 11am-3pm Mon-Fri, 10am-4:30pm Sat, 1pm-4:30pm Sun Nov-Mar),* on the left-hand (north) side as you come from the center of Concord. Her father, Bronson Alcott, bought the property in 1857 and lived here with his family until his death in 1888. Louisa wrote *Little Women* here in 1868 and died here 20 years later (two days after her father). The house, furnishings and Bronson's Concord School of Philosophy, on the hillside behind the house, are open to visitors, but you must take a guided tour to enter. Call ☎ 978-369-5617 on the day you wish to visit, ask tour times, then get to the house in plenty of time to get your tickets. The tours fill up, particularly in summer.

A short stroll to the east is **The Wayside** (☎ *978-369-6975, 455 Lexington Rd; admission $4; open 10am-6pm daily mid-Apr–Oct),* another house in which Louisa May Alcott lived and which she described in *Little Women.* At another time, it was Nathaniel Hawthorne's home, but most of the remaining furnishings are those of Margaret Sidney, author of *Five Little Peppers.*

Right next to Old North Bridge, **The Old Manse** (☎ *978-369-3909, 269 Monument St; adult/senior & student/child 6-16 yrs $6.50/5.50/4.50; open 10am-5pm Mon-Sat, noon-5pm Sun mid-Apr–Oct)* was built in 1769 by the Reverend William Emerson and was owned by the Emerson family for the following 169 years, until it was deeded to the NPS. Today it's a museum filled with mementos of the Emerson family, and also of Nathaniel and Sophia Hawthorne, who lived here from 1842 to 1845 following their marriage. Admission price includes a guided tour; last tour at 4:30pm.

Historic Graveyards

Old Hill Burying Ground, with graves dating from colonial times, is on the hillside at the southeastern end of Monument Square. **Main St Burying Ground**, at the intersection of Keyes Rd in the commercial center, has the town's oldest tombstones, dating from Concord's founding in the 17th century. Legend says the town has two burying grounds because in earlier times it was considered bad luck to carry a corpse across a stream (the Mill Brook runs beneath Main St just off Monument Square).

It is in spacious **Sleepy Hollow Cemetery** (☎ *978-371-6299, Bedford St),* however, that the most famous deceased Concordians rest. Though the cemetery is only a block east of Monument Square, along MA 62, the most interesting part, Authors' Ridge, is a 15-minute hike (or a shorter drive) farther. Enter the gate from MA 62 and follow signs to Authors' Ridge.

Henry David Thoreau and his family are buried here, as are the Alcotts and Nathaniel Hawthorne and his wife. Ralph Waldo Emerson's tombstone is a large uncarved rock of New England marble, an appropriate Transcendentalist symbol. Down the hill a bit is the tombstone of Ephraim Bull, developer of the famous Concord grape.

Nearby is the Melvin Memorial, a much-photographed monument to the memory of three Concord brothers who died in the Civil War. It is the work of Daniel Chester French, who is buried in Sleepy Hollow as well.

Walden Pond

The glacial pond (☎ *978-369-3254, Walden St; admission free, parking $2; open sunrise to sunset daily),* near which Henry David Thoreau spent the years 1845–47, is now a state park. It lies about 3 miles south of Monument Square, along Walden St (MA 126) south of MA 2. There's a swimming beach and facilities on the southern side and a footpath that circles the large pond (about a half-hour stroll). The site of Thoreau's cabin is on the northeast side, marked by a cairn and signs.

Fruitlands

Thirty miles west of Boston, but just a half-hour drive west of Concord on MA 2, lies the town of Harvard and **Fruitlands Museums** (☎ 978-456-3924, 102 Prospect Hill Rd; admission $5; open 10am-5pm mid-May–mid-Oct). The original hillside farmhouse, set on spacious grounds with panoramic views of rural hills, dates from the 18th century and was used by Bronson Alcott and his utopian 'Con-Sociate' (communal) family in 1843. Other museums have been moved to the 200-acre estate, including the 1794 Shaker House, an American Indian museum and a picture gallery featuring paintings by 19th-century itinerant artists and Hudson River School landscape painters.

The tearoom at Fruitlands offers lunch ($5 to $10) and beverages 10am to 4pm (Sunday brunch is 10am to 3pm), with outdoor dining so you enjoy the excellent views.

Canoeing

The South Bridge Boat House (☎ 978-369-9438, 496–502 Main St/MA 62; $10 per hour/$43 per day on weekends, discounts weekdays and for students), a mile west of Monument Square, rents canoes for cruising the Concord and Assabet Rivers from April until the first snowfall. The favorite route is downstream to Old North Bridge and back past the many fine riverside houses and the campus of prestigious Concord Academy – a paddle of about two hours.

Places to Stay

While there is a paucity of hotels and motels in Concord, travelers will find more than a dozen B&Bs in the Concord area. Most rooms have private baths, and furnishings from the Federal or Victorian periods. Rates generally start at about $125. You can get a complete list of accommodations at W www.concordmachamber.org.

Best Western Concord Motel (☎ 978-369-6100, 800-528-1234, W www.bestwestern.com, 740 Elm St) Rooms $99-124 with breakfast. Rooms are the freshly appointed, well-scrubbed units typical of this chain. The motel is at MA 2 near the Concord rotary. Several restaurants are next door.

Ridge House (☎ 978-369-9796, 533 Lexington Rd) Rooms $85-105. Set in the historic district, this small but welcoming 1850s house has one double and one twin room with shared bath. You can walk to Orchard House and the Wayside. It's a mile to the village center.

Colonial Inn (☎ 978-369-9200, fax 978-371-1533, W www.concordscolonialinn.com, 48 Monument Square) Rooms $135-225. The original building of this inn dates from 1716 and houses 12 of the more expensive guest rooms, a lobby, dining rooms and tavern (featuring afternoon tea). The other 48 guestrooms are less expensive and are in a modern brick annex. The inn's dining room, tavern and front porch are a center of town social life. Ask about the ghost in room 24.

Hawthorne Inn (☎ 978-369-5610, W www.concordma.com, 462 Lexington Rd) Rooms $175-285 with breakfast. Artists Greg Burch and Marilyn Mudry have made this inn their life's work. The Hawthorne has seven rooms, with oriental carpets and antique Japanese ukiyo-e prints and sculpture, air con and private baths. You'll find the inn about a mile southeast of Monument Square, across the street from Orchard House (see Historic Houses, earlier).

Wayside Inn (☎ 978-443-8846, fax 978-443-8041, 76 Wayside Rd, Sudbury) Rooms $99-112 with breakfast. This inn is 13 miles south of Concord on US 20, in the town of Sudbury. The inn, dating from 1700, was made famous by Longfellow's poems Tales from a Wayside Inn, and it now boasts that it is the oldest operating inn in the USA. It was restored by Henry Ford in the 1920s and still operates as a restaurant and hostelry, with 10 period rooms.

Places to Eat

Country Kitchen (☎ 978-371-0181, 181 Sudbury Rd) Prices $3-8. Open 5am-4pm. The 'Little Yellow House by the Tracks' is the queen of cheap takeout in Concord. You can get a medium cup of franks and beans

($3) and eat on the picnic table out front. A veggie pocket runs $3.50.

The Cheese Shop (☎ 978-369-5778, 29 Walden St) Prices $4-8. Closed Mon. Stop here for a huge luncheon sandwich like the mixed grilled veggie pocket ($6) or for picnic supplies. Wine tasting starts at noon on Saturday.

Brigham's Café (☎ 978-369-9885, 17 Main St) Mains $5-9. Open 7am-9pm. This popular breakfast and lunch spot hums with the sound of silver and plates hitting the Formica table tops. Two eggs, bacon, toast and coffee go for less than $4. The fried clam roll runs $5.

Walden Grille (☎ 978-371-2233, 24 Walden St) Mains $6-18. Across from the Cheese Shop, this place, formerly called Walden Station, is a tavern-restaurant with soft lighting, exposed brick walls and lyrical landscape paintings. The menu features international favorites. You can get the salmon niçoise salad for $10 at lunch or the chicken andouille fettucine (about $15) for dinner with black pepper pasta, sausage, and adobo sauce.

Chang An (☎ 978-369-5288, 10 Concord Crossing) Mains $8-20. Chang An is an elegant (linen tablecloths) oasis with the most popular Chinese cuisine in town. You can go light with the broccoli in garlic sauce ($8) or feast on the tai chi shrimp (about $15), which come with both a hot sauce and a white wine sauce.

Aigo (☎ 978-371-1333, 84 Thoreau St) Mains $8-25. This Pronveçal bistro is upstairs in the Concord Depot. The French Mediterranean cuisine is refined and inventive, with offerings like mushroom-crusted chicken breast ($24).

Getting There & Away

Driving west on MA 2 from Boston or Cambridge, it's 20-some miles to Concord. Coming from Lexington, follow signs from Lexington Green to Concord and Battle Rd, the route taken by the British troops on April 19, 1775.

MBTA commuter rail trains (☎ 617-722-3200, 800-392-6100) run between Boston's North Station and Concord and West Concord Stations 16 times each weekday on the Fitchburg/South Acton line. The 40-minute ride costs about $4, half-price for children five to 11 (under five free). In Concord, buy your tickets at Coggins Bakery (☎ 978-371-3040, 68 Thoreau St), just northwest of the depot building.

LOWELL

Located at the confluence of the Concord and Merrimack Rivers, 25 miles northwest of Boston, Lowell (population 105,000) was the crucible of the Industrial Revolution in America and remains a textile mill town. The national park in the heart of the city is a gem, with a working textile mill, canal boat tours, and trolley rides that evoke the birth of America as an industrial giant. The town is also the center of a 40,000-person community of Southeast Asian immigrants, who bring their native cuisines to local restaurants. Painter James McNeill Whistler and Beat writer Jack Kerouac were both Lowell natives.

History

A farming community since its founding in 1653, Lowell took on its modern aspect after 1822 when it was chosen by Boston merchant Francis Cabot Lowell as the site of a new kind of industrial project. Lowell, who had toured England's factories, paid for the development of a new and better power loom. Breaking with the traditional model of a factory that's funded and founded by one investor or family, Lowell assembled a group of investors called the Boston Associates, who pooled all of their capital to fund a huge and complex industrial installation.

Driven by the abundant waterpower of the town's Pawtucket Falls, Lowell's new factories were soon turning out cloth by the mile. A network of canals and, after 1835, the Boston & Lowell Railroad shipped raw materials in and finished cloth out. In 1834, Anna Mathilda (McNeill) Whistler, wife of the local agent for the Locks and Canals Corporation, gave birth to James Abbott McNeill Whistler (1834–1903). The coming of the railroad made locks and canals less important, and the Whistlers moved away from Lowell in 1837. Young James went on to the US Military Academy at West Point and, with that superb training as a soldier under his belt, became one of America's greatest 19th-century painters.

The Industrial Revolution in America echoed the one in England: Huge amounts of wealth grew from investments leveraging the efforts of low-paid, unorganized laborers working long hours under dangerous conditions. Heroic efforts at labor organization and reform efforts, such as those by Sarah Bagley for the 'mill girls' of Lowell, were often frustrated by influxes of unskilled immigrants willing to work for any wage under any conditions. But ultimately, workers' rights were acknowledged in the body of American labor law.

In the 1920s, a century after the birth of modern Lowell and just as workers' rights were being recognized in law, Lowell's textile business began to decline as capital moved to southern states with cheaper labor. By mid-century, the city was a wasteland of abandoned mills and high unemployment. Beat generation author Jack Kerouac (1922–1969) was born into this milieu, and used it as the setting for his five novels, most famous of which is *On the Road*. Poet, painter and author, Kerouac is remembered annually during the **Lowell Celebrates Kerouac! festival**, held in early October.

During the 1980s, re-industrialization efforts brought in high-tech and other industries to provide a strong economic base. Restoration of the city's 19th-century buildings and the declaration of the city center as a National Historic Park have now made Lowell an attraction for many travelers.

Orientation

From I-495, follow the Lowell Connector to its end at exit 5-C to reach the city center. Signage is excellent, allowing you to find all the attractions easily.

Trains from Boston terminate at the Gallagher Transportation Terminal on Thorndike St, a 15-minute walk southwest of the city center, or you can take the downtown

shuttle bus (30¢, every 30 minutes) to the Downtown Transit Center, in the heart of the city.

Once in the city center, you can walk to most of the sights. Merrimack St is the main commercial thoroughfare, holding the Downtown Transit Center, the chamber of commerce office and several restaurants.

Information

The National Park Service Visitor Center (☎ 978-970-5000, 246 Market St) is the place to start your exploration of historic Lowell. It's open 9am to 5pm daily. The Greater Merrimack Valley Convention & Visitors Bureau (☎ 978-459-6150, 800-443-3332, Ⓦ www.merrimackvalley.org, 9 Central St, Lowell, MA 01852), two blocks east of the visitor center, also has information and is open 8:30am to 5pm Monday to Friday. The bureau has an information center at I-495, exit 32 (☎ 978-250-9504). Hours vary.

Lowell National Historical Park

A network of buildings in the city center, connected by the trolley and canal boats, make up Lowell National Historical Park. The park has a visitor center (☎ 978-970-5000, 246 Market St, Market Mills; admission free; open 9am-5pm Mon-Sat, 10am-5pm Sun).

The **Boott Cotton Mills Museum** (☎ 978-970-5000, foot of John St; adult/child $4/2; open 9am-5pm Mon-Sat, 11am-5pm Sun) includes a working power loom and exhibits that chronicle the rise and fall of the Industrial Revolution in Lowell.

To see how the 'mill girls' lived and worked in Lowell, visit the **Working People Exhibit** in the Patrick J Mogan Cultural Center (☎ 978-970-5000, 40 French St; admission free; open 1pm-5pm daily).

Whistler House Museum of Art

James McNeill Whistler's birthplace (☎ 978-452-7641, 243 Worthen St; adult/child $4/3; open 11am-4pm Tues-Sat), built in 1823, is now the home of the Lowell Art Association. It contains a permanent collection of the artist's works and hosts exhibits of works by him, his contemporaries and modern

New England artists. Whistler's most famous painting, *Arrangement in Grey and Black* (popularly known as *Whistler's Mother*), is not here, unfortunately, but in the Musée d'Orsay in Paris.

The Whistler House is on the west side of the Merrimack Canal, less than two blocks west of the National Park Service Visitor Center.

Other Museums

Lowell is also home to the **American Textile History Museum** (☎ *978-441-0400, 491 Dutton St; adult/senior & student $5/3; open Tues-Fri 9am-4pm, weekends 10am-4pm*), a block south of the Whistler House; and the **New England Quilt Museum** (☎ *978-452-4207, 18 Shattuck St; adult/senior $4/3; open 10am-4pm Tues-Sat*), a half-block from the NPS Visitor Center.

Places to Eat & Drink

Athenian Corner (☎ *978-458-7052, 207 Market St*) Dishes $3-10. Across the street from the NPS Visitor Center, this restaurant is a hallmark of Lowell's immigrant Greek community. Athenian Corner offers soups, salads, and main courses like mousaka ($10).

Quick Pickin's Deli (☎ *978-452-8161, 96 Merrimack St*) Sandwiches $3-6. Here's one of the favorite lunch stops for park rangers. Walk north on Shattuck St for one long block to Merrimack St and turn right to find this place, opposite John St, which sells huge sandwiches like hot pastrami for $4. Greek salads cost $5.

Southeast Asian Restaurant (☎ *978-452-3182, 343 Market St*) Mains $5-14. Aficionados of Lao, Thai, and Vietnamese cuisines come here from all over New England to feast on the legendary 'bowl of fire' (Lao spicy beef) and the all-you-can-eat lunch buffet ($6). The restaurant and associated market are a beacon of culture for Lowell's Southeast Asian immigrants. Southeast Asian vet Joe Antonaccio and his Thai/Lao wife Chan Khip have put together one of the most varied, authentic collection of delicious recipes from the 'Golden Triangle' west of Chang Mai.

Dubliner (☎ *978-458-2120, 197 Market St*) Mains $5-15. Here's a classic Irish pub to suck you in for a corned beef sandwich ($6) with a jar of Harp or Guinness ($4). The pub scene rocks here with an under-30 crowd after 9pm.

La Boniche (☎ *978-458-9473, 143 Merrimack St*) Entrees $8-28. Closed Mon. The two dining rooms in this restored storefront nook fill with scents of French nouvelle cuisine and attract an upscale crowd for lunch and dinner. The grilled lamb salad ($12) rivals the daily quiche (about $8) for luncheon popularity. Don't miss the braised salmon ($22) for dinner.

Getting There & Around

Lowell is at the end of the Lowell Connector, a spur road that goes north from MA 3 and I-495.

MBTA (☎ 617-722-3200, 800-392-6100) trains depart Boston's North Station for Lowell (45 minutes, fare about $4) 21 times on weekdays, eight times a day on the weekends.

The Lowell Regional Transit Authority (☎ 978-452-6161) operates the bus system, including the downtown shuttle buses that link the Gallagher Transportation Terminal and the Downtown Transit Center.

North Shore

The entire coast of Massachusetts claims a rich history, but no part offers more recreational, cultural and dining diversions than does the shore north of Boston. Salem was one of America's wealthiest ports in the 19th century; Marblehead is among the premier yachting ports in the USA, and Gloucester is the nation's most famous fishing port. Trade and fishing have brought wealth, sumptuous houses and great collections of art and artifacts to the area.

MBTA commuter rail trains (☎ 617-722-3200, 800-392-6100) run from Boston's North Station to Salem (30 minutes, $3), Gloucester (one hour, $4.50) and Rockport (70 minutes, $5) on the Rockport line. Trains run every 30 minutes during the morning and evening rush hours, hourly during the rest of day, with trains every two or three hours in the evening and on weekends. Buy your ticket before you board; there's a $2 surcharge to buy a ticket on the train during the time when tickets are being sold at the station.

If you're driving, note that street signage north of Boston is often confusing, making it easy to get lost here. Be prepared to ask the way.

SALEM

This town's very name brings thoughts of witches and witchcraft. The famous Salem witch trials of 1692 burn in the national memory, and Halloween (October 31) is the city's biggest holiday, with all lodgings booked a year in advance and 'witch shops' selling all manner of real and ersatz wiccan accessories. These phenomena obscure Salem's true claim to fame: its glorious days as a center for clipper-ship trade with China.

Today, Salem is a commuter suburb of Boston with light industry, though not quite enough to make it wealthy. Visit Salem to take in its world-class Peabody Essex Museum, the National Historic Site, 19th-century ship captains' and merchants' homes, the House of the Seven Gables (made famous in Hawthorne's novel of that name) and – particularly for children – some of the kitschy witch museums and shops.

History

Roger Conant and a band of 20 hearty settlers established Salem in 1626. Within a century, the town was a port of note, and by 1762 it counted among its residents Elias Hasket Derby, America's first millionaire. Derby and his father, Capt Richard Derby, built the half-mile-long Derby Wharf, which is now the center of the Salem Maritime National Historic Site.

During the Revolutionary War, Salem's merchants fitted 158 vessels as privateers – private vessels that preyed on enemy shipping – and held the distinction of sinking or capturing more British ships than all the ships of all the other American ports combined.

After the war, the privateers went into trade. Since their traditional British Empire ports abroad had been closed to them, they were forced to sail farther afield. Elias Derby's ship *Grand Turk* sailed around the Cape of Good Hope, the first Salem vessel to do so, reaching Canton in 1786. Many Salem vessels followed, and soon the owners founded the East India Marine Society to provide warehousing services for their ships' logs and charts. The new company's charter required the establishment of 'a museum in which to house the natural and artificial curiosities' to be brought back by members' ships. The collection, grown to a half-million artifacts, was the basis for what is now the Peabody Essex Museum (see below).

Salem's golden age lasted until the mid-19th century, when New England clipper ships emerged onto the scene. These swift new ships that raced around the world – even carrying New England ice to tropical ports – needed harbors that were deeper than Salem's. As the tall masts gradually disappeared from Salem's harbor, the harbor silted up, ending a chapter in colonial and early US maritime history.

Orientation

The main areas of interest in Salem are the Essex St Mall, a pedestrian way through the heart of historic Salem; Salem Common, adjoining the mall; and the Derby Wharf, a block away (see Salem Maritime National Historic Site, below). All are walkable. The train station is a five-minute walk from Essex St Mall.

The Heritage Trail is a 1.7-mile route connecting Salem's major historic sites. Follow the red line painted on the sidewalk.

Information

Travelers can stop at the NPS Central Wharf Visitor Center (☎ 978-744-4323, 2 Liberty St) to get oriented. There are very helpful rangers at the information desk and racks of maps, brochures and accommodations information. It's open 9am to 5pm daily.

The place to call or visit online for information is the Salem Office of Tourism &

MASSACHUSETTS

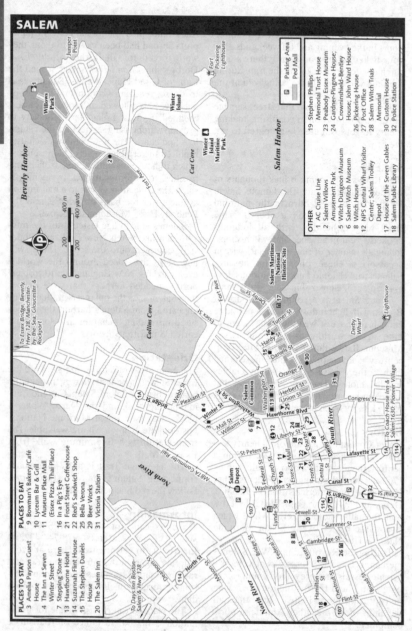

SALEM

PLACES TO STAY
3   Amelia Payson Guest
     House
4   The Inn at Seven
     Winter Street
7   Stepping Stone Inn
13   Hawthorne Hotel
14   Suzannah Flint House
15   The Stephen Daniels
     House
20   The Salem Inn

PLACES TO EAT
9   Bowman's Bakery/Café
10   Lyceum Bar & Grill
11   Museum Place Mall
     (Essex Pizza, Thai Place)
16   In a Pig's Eye
21   Front Street Coffeehouse
22   Red's Sandwich Shop
25   Bella Verona
29   Beer Works
31   Victoria Station

OTHER
1   AC Cruise Line
2   Salem Willows
     Amusement Park
5   Witch Dungeon Museum
6   Salem Witch Museum
8   Witch House
12   NPS Central Wharf Visitor
     Center; Salem Trolley
     Depot
17   House of the Seven Gables
18   Salem Public Library
19   Stephen Phillips
     Memorial Trust House
23   Peabody Essex Museum
24   Gardner-Pingree House;
     Crowninshield-Bentley
     House; John Ward House
26   Pickering House
27   Post Office
28   Salem Witch Trials
     Memorial
30   Custom House
32   Police Station

Parking Area
Ped Mall

Beverly Harbor

Salem Harbor

Cultural Affairs, Destination Salem (☎ 877-SALEM-MA, Ⓦ www.salem.org).

Peabody Essex Museum

You will find the art, artifacts and curiosities brought back from the Far East by ships out of Salem at the Peabody Essex Museum (☎ 978-745-1876, ☎ 745-9500 taped information, ☎ 800-745-4054, Essex St Mall, New Liberty St; adult/senior & student $10/8, child 16 yrs and under free; open 10am-5pm Mon-Sat, noon-5pm Sun June-Oct; 10am-5pm Tues-Sat, noon-5pm Sun Nov-May).

This is America's oldest private museum in continuous operation. It has expanded many times since 1824 and is now in the midst of a $100 million expansion, which will add five new galleries by summer 2003.

The museum includes exhibits from New England's history, including clocks, ceramics, costumes, dolls and toys, military uniforms and weapons, lamps, lanterns and glassware. The town's maritime history is particularly well documented with ship captains' portraits, scale models, paintings of ships, 18th-century navigation instruments, scrimshaw (carved whalebone) and carved ships' figureheads. There's even a reproduction of the main cabin of Cleopatra's Barge, the first oceangoing yacht in the USA, built in 1816 for a member of the East India Marine Society.

The Asian collections cover arts and crafts of peoples native to America, the Pacific Islands and East Asia, including porcelain, paintings, silver, furniture and other arts from China, Japan, Polynesia, Micronesia and Melanesia. The collection from pre-industrial Japan is rated the best in the world.

There are also exhibits on the natural history of Essex County. The Museum Café (☎ 978-740-4551) serves lunch and afternoon tea.

Historic Houses

Salem's most famous house is the House of the Seven Gables (☎ 978-744-0991, 54 Turner St; adult/child 6-17 yrs $8/5; open 10am-5pm Mon-Sat, noon-5pm Sun), made famous in Nathaniel Hawthorne's 1851 novel of that name. The novel brings to life the gloomy Puritan atmosphere of early New England and its effects on the people's psyches; the house does the same. The admission fee allows entrance to the site's four historic buildings, the Gables Garden Café and luxuriant gardens on the waterfront.

Furnished in antiques, Pickering House (☎ 978-744-1647, 18 Broad St; admission $4; open 10am-3pm Mon, other times by appointment) is said to be the oldest house in the USA continuously occupied by the same family.

House lovers should also seek out Chestnut St, which with its beautiful homes is among the most architecturally lovely streets in the country. It's a block south of western Essex St.

The Stephen Phillips Memorial Trust House (☎ 978-744-0440, 34 Chestnut St; adult/senior, student & child $3/2, child under 6 yrs free; open 10am-4:30pm Mon-Sat late May–mid-Oct) displays the family furnishings of Salem sea captains and includes a collection of antique carriages and cars. Last tours leave at 4pm.

The following three historic houses are operated by the Peabody Essex Museum (see earlier in the Salem section for details) and tickets for the houses need to be bought at the museum. Guided House Tours (☎ 800-745-4054; adult/senior & student/child $10/8/free; open 10:30am-3pm Mon-Fri, 10:30am-4pm Sat & Sun) include Gardner-Pingree House, built in 1804, the Crowninshield-Bentley House, built in 1727, and the John Ward House, built in 1684.

Salem Maritime National Historic Site

The Custom House on Derby Wharf is the centerpiece of this national historic site, and the Central Wharf Visitor Center (☎ 978-740-1660, 193 Derby St; admission free; open 9am-5pm daily) is the first place for visitors to go.

Nathaniel Hawthorne, a Salem native, was surveyor of the port from 1846 to 1849. Other buildings at the site include the Government Bonded Warehouse, containing

Salem Witch Trials

In the late 17th century, it was widely believed that one could make a pact with the devil in order to gain evil powers to be used against one's enemies. Thousands had been found guilty of witchcraft in Europe in previous centuries. The judges of the Massachusetts Bay Colony had tried 44 persons for witchcraft (hanging three of them) before 1692.

The Reverend Cotton Mather, one of the colony's most fiery preachers, had added his own book on witchcraft to the already considerable literature on the subject. In March 1692, a girl named Betty Parris, who lived in what is now Danvers, and her cousin Abigail began acting strangely. Other children copied their bizarre antics, and their parents came to believe that 'the Devil' had come to their village. (More likely, the girls got hold of a copy of Reverend Mather's book, read how the 'possessed' were thought to behave and acted it out.)

Partly as a prank, the girls accused a slave named Tituba of being a witch. The accused, a half-black, half-Indian woman, 'confessed' under torture and accused two other women of being accomplices, in order to save her own life. Soon, the accusations flew thick and fast, as the accused confessed to riding broomsticks, having sex with the devil and participating in witches' sabbaths. They implicated others in attempts to save themselves. The girls, afraid of being discovered as fakes, kept the accusations coming.

Governor Phips appointed a special court to deal with the accusations, but its justices saw fit to accept 'spectral evidence' (evidence of 'spirits' seen only by the witness). With imaginations, superstitions and religious passions enflamed, the situation soon careened out of control.

By September 1692, 156 people stood accused, 55 people had pleaded guilty and implicated others to save their own lives, and 14 women and five men who would not 'confess' to witchcraft had been hanged. Giles Corey, who refused to plead either guilty or not guilty, was pressed to death, and at least four people died in jail of disease.

The frenzy died down when the accusers began pointing at prominent merchants, clergy and even the governor's wife. With the powers-that-be in jeopardy, the trials were called off, the jails were opened and the remaining accused were released. Judges and witnesses confessed to having been misled or having used bad judgment, and the families of many victims were compensated for the injustice.

This cautionary tale of justice gone awry and innocents sacrificed to popular hysteria came powerfully to mind in the 1950s during Senator Joseph R McCarthy's destructive career of ill-considered condemnation and character destruction.

Salem probably never had any witches. The Salem Witch Trials Memorial, a modest monument off Charter St, honors the innocents who died. If their spirits linger here, however, the pervasive 'witch' commercialism and the circus atmosphere of Halloween that today capitalize on the tragedy of 1692 are hardly a fitting epitaph.

cargoes typical of the trade in 1819; the Scale House; West India Goods Store, a working store with many items similar to those sold two centuries ago; Derby House, home of the famous shipping family; Hawkes House, used as a privateer-prize warehouse during the Revolutionary War; Narbonne-Hale House, a more modest house owned by artisans and their families; and the lighthouse on Derby Wharf.

Witchcraft Sights

The tragic events of 1692 have proved a boon to modern operators of witch-related attractions.

Most authentic of more than a score of witchy sites is the **Witch House** (☎ 978-744-0180, 310½ Essex St; adult/senior/child $5/4/2; open 10am-4:30pm daily mid-Mar–June & Sept-Nov; 10am-6pm daily July & Aug; closed Dec–mid-Mar), operated by the Salem parks and recreation department. This was the home of Magistrate Jonathan Corwin, where some preliminary examinations of persons accused of witchcraft were held.

The **Salem Witch Museum** (☎ 978-744-1692, 19½ Washington Square North; adult/senior/child 6-14 yrs $6/5.50/4; open 10am-5pm daily Sept-June; 10am-7pm daily July & Aug) is on Brown St at Hawthorne Blvd. This churchlike building holds dioramas, exhibits, audiovisual shows and costumed staff who help you to understand the witchcraft scare.

The **Witch Dungeon Museum** (☎ 978-741-3570, 16 Lynde St; adult/senior/child $6/5/4; open 10am-5pm daily Apr-Nov) stages re-creations of a witch trial based on historical transcripts.

Parks

Salem Common is the broad green space at the town center, next to the Hawthorne Hotel. On the west side of the common is Washington Square, marked by the dramatic, brooding statue of Roger Conant (1592–1679), Salem's first Anglo settler. If you look closely at 'the Puritan,' as it's usually known, you'll see a number of bullet holes in its bronze skirts.

Less than 2 miles northeast of Salem center is **Salem Willows Amusement Park** (☎ 978-745-0251, 171 Fort Ave; pay per attraction; open 10am-11pm Mon-Sat, 11am-11pm Sun Apr-Oct), with beaches, children's rides and games and harbor cruises. Just south of it is **Winter Island Maritime Park**, the site of Fort Pickering and its lighthouse, now a public park and campground (see below).

Forest River Park, less than 2 miles south of the town center, has beaches, picnic areas and a saltwater swimming pool. **Salem 1630: Pioneer Village** (☎ 978-744-0991, West St; admission adult/child 6-17 yrs $7/5; open 10am-5pm Mon-Sat, noon-5pm Sun April-Nov) is a replicated Puritan village of the 1600s with costumed interpreters, period buildings, gardens, crafts and animals.

Places to Stay

Camping Less than 2 miles east of the center of town is *Winter Island Maritime Park* (☎ 978-745-9430, 50 Winter Island Rd) Tent/RV sites with electricity $15/30. Open May-Oct. There is space for 25 tents and 30 RVs.

Motels & Hotels Salem's centerpiece, at the corner of Hawthorne Blvd and Essex St, is the *Hawthorne Hotel* (☎ 978-744-4080, 800-729-7829, fax 978-745-9842, ⓦ www.hawthornehotel.com, 18 Washington Square West) Rooms $135-182. This historic (1920s) full-service hotel has 89 double rooms, and offers discounts of 8% to 10% off-season.

Days Inn Boston-Salem (☎ 978-777-1030, 800-325-2525, www.daysinn.com, 152 Endicott St, Danvers) Singles/doubles $99/109 with breakfast. Four miles from the center of Salem on MA 114 on the northwest side of MA 128 (take exit 24), this 130-room complex features queen-size beds.

Inns & B&Bs Salem has more than 10 B&Bs. All are nonsmoking and include breakfast. Virtually all rooms have direct-dial phones and cable TVs. For a complete list and links, consult ⓦ www.salem.org.

Suzannah Flint House (☎ 978-744-5281, 888-752-5281, 98 Essex St) Doubles with bath $80-130. Here's an 1808 Federal house just off Salem Common. All three rooms have queen beds.

Stepping Stone Inn (☎ 978-741-8900, 800-338-3022, 19 Washington Square North) Rooms with bath $80-130. Just off Salem Common, facing the statue of Roger Conant, stands this restored house built for naval officer Benjamin True in 1846. It has eight rooms.

Amelia Payson Guest House (☎ 978-744-8304, 16 Winter St) Doubles with bath $85-125. This place is within walking distance of Salem's sights and has all the comforts.

Coach House Inn (☎ 978-744-4092, 800-688-8689, fax 978-745-8031, 284 Lafayette St) Doubles $95-155. Built in 1870, the Coach House Inn is about a mile south of the center on MA 1A/MA 114. Nine of the 11 rooms have bath; all rooms have air con.

The Inn at Seven Winter Street (☎ 978-745-9520, 800-932-5547, 7 Winter St) Doubles $105-175. Here's an 1870 Second Empire Victorian mansion about four blocks from the center. The seven rooms all have private baths. A few have kitchens.

The Stephen Daniels House (☎ 978-744-5709, 1 Daniels St) Rooms $115. Two blocks north of the waterfront, at Essex St, this must be Salem's oldest lodging, with parts dating from 1667 – before the witch trials – and many period antiques. Several of the four bedrooms adjoin, making them perfect for families, two couples or small groups. Be sure to call Mrs Katherine Gill, the proprietor, for reservations.

The Salem Inn (☎ 978-741-0680, 800-446-2995, 7 Summer St) Doubles $119-285 with breakfast. This place offers a variety of accommodations, in 40 rooms with all the conveniences, in three historic houses, including the Captain West House, a large brick sea captain's home built in 1834; the Curwen House (1854); and the Peabody House (1874). There are more expensive Jacuzzi-equipped rooms and suites as well.

Places to Eat & Drink

The town's historic district and waterfront sport a lot of eateries, most open for lunch and dinner.

Red's Sandwich Shop (☎ 978-745-3527, 15 Central St) Dishes $2-9. Situated in the old London Coffee House building (1698), this shop has breakfast plates like cheese and tomato omelet for under $4, chicken marsala for $6.

Bowman's Bakery/Café (☎ 978-744-5200, 266 Essex St). Prices $2-5. Here's an old-school bakery with fantastic cheap eats, where a cup of chili or chowder runs $2 and chicken wings are $3.75.

Front Street Coffeehouse (☎ 978-740-6697, 20 Front St) Prices $2-8. This is currently the cool place for a hot latte ($2.75). It also serves sandwiches.

Museum Place Mall (2 East India Square). Just west of the Peabody Essex Museum along Essex St, this mall has several breakfast and lunch places, including ***Essex Pizza***, where you pay about $6 for a small pie.

Thai Place (☎ 978-741-8008, Museum Place Mall) Prices $5-27. We like the big plate of vegetarian pad thai for $7.

Lyceum Bar & Grill (☎ 978-745-7665, 43 Church St) Lunch $6-9, dinner $15-25. This historic place is Salem's all-purpose eatery. A varied lunch menu consists of sandwiches, salads and entrees; at dinner you get hearty traditional main-course favorites like rack of lamb ($25) with New American accents.

Beer Works (☎ 978-745-2337, 278 Derby St) Brunch $7-9. The postmodern decor in this brewpub draws in folks for lunch and dinner, but we favor the brunch choices here like veggie quesadilla ($7) and the salmon tarragon ($9). A pint of the house brew runs under $4.

In a Pig's Eye (☎ 978-741-4436, 148 Derby St) Mains $14 and under. A dark pub, the Pig's Eye boasts an eclectic menu of Greek salads, vegetarian dishes, pastas and many steak, chicken and seafood main courses. Monday and Tuesday are Mexican nights, and there's live entertainment most evenings. The musicians include some of the region's best acoustic performers. The crowd ranges from 20-somethings to 50-somethings, and they're all hip and in love with their pints of Guinness ($3.50).

Bella Verona (☎ *978-825-9911, 107 Essex*) Mains $8-15. Open for dinner. This little Italian bistro with 10 tables, low lights, and walls decorated with the pots and pans of a Northern Italian kitchen can't be beat for romance or cuisine. Try the *trota* (trout) *alla mugnaia con capperi* ($13).

Victoria Station (☎ *978-745-3400, Pickering Wharf*) Mains $14-24. Here's a broad deck for waterfront dinning overlooking Salem Harbor. You can strap on the feed bag for the all-you-can-eat BBQ beef ($15) or go light with the salad bar ($8).

Getting There & Around
Salem lies 20 miles northeast of Boston, a 35-minute drive (mostly on MA 1A) if it's not rush hour.

See the beginning of this North Shore section for train information.

The MBTA buses (Nos 450 or 455) from Boston's Haymarket Square (near North Station) take longer than the train and cost no less.

The Salem Trolley (☎ 978-744-5469, 8 Central St; all-day ticket adult/senior/child five to 12 yrs/family $10/9/5/12) runs a figure-eight route, with a running commentary, past most of the town's places of interest, departing on the hour 10am to 4pm (last departure) daily. July to October, departures are on the hour and half-hour.

MARBLEHEAD
First settled in 1629, Marblehead's Old Town is a maritime village with winding streets, brightly painted colonial and Federal houses, and 1000 sailing yachts bobbing at moorings in the harbor. As indicated by the number of boats, this is the Boston area's premier yachting port, and one of New England's most prestigious addresses.

It has been so for a long time. Incorporated in 1649, citizens of Marblehead boast that their town was the 'birthplace of the navy' because the Marblehead schooner *Hannah* (1775) was the first ship to be commissioned by General George Washington in the Revolutionary War.

Marblehead makes a good diversion from Boston. Travelers can lose themselves in its narrow streets, admire its historic houses, go to the beach, picnic in a seaside park, and rub shoulders with the preppie crowd in lively restaurants and pubs.

Orientation
You pass through the modern districts of Marblehead along Pleasant St (MA 114) on the way to the Marblehead Historic District, called Old Town, with its network of narrow, winding streets, many of them one-way. Old Town is difficult to negotiate by car. Parking is a problem in summer, particularly on weekends, so it's best to find a parking place inland and explore the town on foot.

Washington St, State St and Mugford St intersect by the Old Town House, once the town hall. Heading southeast from the Old Town House along Washington and State Sts brings you to the State Street Landing, the town's main dock, with views across the harbor to the yacht clubs and mansions on Marblehead Neck.

Information
The local Chamber of Commerce (☎ 781-631-2868, ⓦ www.marbleheadchamber.org) operates an information booth during warm weather on MA 114 (Pleasant St), near the corner of Essex and Spring Sts. Look for it on the right-hand side as you approach Old Town and pick up a copy of their walking tour brochure and map. The chamber's business office (which serves as its information office during the winter) is at 65 Pleasant St, Marblehead, MA 01945. It's open 9am to 5pm Monday to Friday.

Things to See & Do
Every American is familiar with *The Spirit of '76*, the patriotic painting (c. 1876) by Archibald M Willard. It depicts three Revolutionary War figures – a drummer, a fife-player and a flag bearer. The painting hangs in the selectmen's meeting room in the red-brick **Abbott Hall** (☎ *781-631-0000, Washington Square at Washington St; admission free; open 8am-5pm Mon, Tues, Thur, 7:30am-7:30pm Wed, 8am-1pm Fri, 9am-6pm Sat, 11am-6pm Sun)*, home of the

MASSACHUSETTS

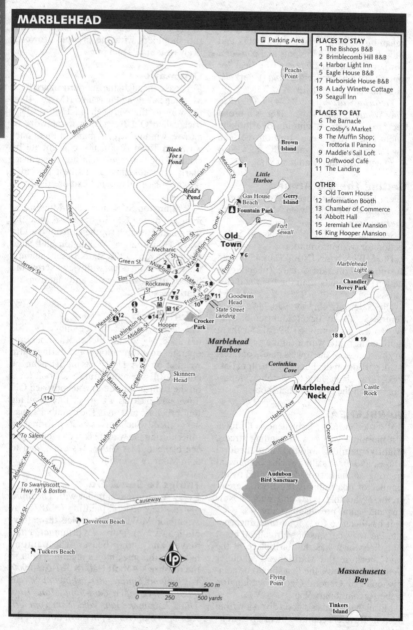

MARBLEHEAD

☐ Parking Area

PLACES TO STAY
1 The Bishops B&B
2 Brimblecomb Hill B&B
4 Harbor Light Inn
5 Eagle House B&B
17 Harborside House B&B
18 A Lady Winette Cottage
19 Seagull Inn

PLACES TO EAT
6 The Barnacle
7 Crosby's Market
8 The Muffin Shop;
    Trottoria Il Panino
9 Maddie's Sail Loft
10 Driftwood Café
11 The Landing

OTHER
3 Old Town House
12 Information Booth
13 Chamber of Commerce
14 Abbott Hall
15 Jeremiah Lee Mansion
16 King Hooper Mansion

Marblehead Historical Commission. The building (look for the lofty clock tower) is the seat of Marblehead's town government, and houses artifacts of Marblehead's history, including the original title deed to Marblehead from the Nanapashemet Indians, dated 1684.

The Georgian **Jeremiah Lee Mansion** (☎ 781-631-1069, near cnr Hooper & Washington Sts; adult/senior & student/child under 10 yrs $5/4.50/free; open 10am-4pm Tue-Sat, 1pm-4pm Sun June-Oct) was built in 1768 on the order of a prominent merchant. It is now a museum with period furnishings and collections of toys and children's furniture, folk art and nautical and military artifacts.

The **King Hooper Mansion** (☎ 781-631-2608, 8 Hooper St; admission free, donations accepted; open 10am-4pm Mon-Sat, 1pm-5pm Sun), more or less across the street from the Jeremiah Lee Mansion, is the home of the Marblehead Arts Association. The historic 1728 house holds four floors of exhibit space, with shows changing monthly.

Old Town is perfect for strolling, cafe-sitting, window-shopping, photo-snapping and picnicking.

A block west of State Street Landing, hilltop **Crocker Park** has views of the harbor, a swimming float and excellent scenic picnic possibilities.

At the eastern end of Front St, the earthworks of **Fort Sewall** also provide a prime venue for picnics, on a rocky rise at the mouth of the harbor. The fort, built in the 17th century, expanded during the Revolutionary War and is now a park.

Access to Marblehead's **Audubon Bird Sanctuary** (Ocean Ave; admission free; open sunrise to sunset) is on the southwest side of Ocean Ave on Marblehead Neck.

At the eastern end of Marblehead Neck, **Chandler Hovey Park**, by Marblehead Light, offers views of Cape Ann and the islands of Salem Bay.

On the southeastern side of Marblehead Neck, a short walk takes you to **Castle Rock**, with views of the Boston Ship Channel and Boston's Harbor Islands, plus cool breezes on hot days.

Places to Stay

Marblehead has about two dozen B&Bs, charging from $60 with shared bath to $125 and up with private bath for a double room; highest prices are for weekend stays. None have more than a few rooms, so reservations are essential. You will find a complete list of B&Bs at [W] www.marbleheadchamber.org.

Brimblecomb Hill B&B (☎ 781-631-6366 daytime, ☎ 631-3172 evenings, 33 Mechanic St) Room with/without bath $95/75. There is a private entrance for guests.

A Lady Winette Cottage (☎ 781-631-8579, 3 Corinthian Lane) Rooms with shared bath $85-95. This Victorian cottage has two rooms.

The Bishops B&B (☎ 781-631-4954, fax 631-2102, 10 Harding Lane) Rooms $85-145. This place is right on the water. It has three rooms and a two-night minimum stay on weekends.

Eagle House B&B (☎ 781-631-1532, 800-572-7335, 96R Front St & 6½ Merritt St) Rooms $85-125. Here you get two suites with sitting room, kitchenette and separate entrance.

Harbor Light Inn (☎ 781-631-2186, 58 Washington St) Rooms with bath $105-275. This is Marblehead's 'big' hostelry, with 20 rooms, some with fireplaces and Jacuzzis. There's a heated pool as well.

Harborside House B&B (☎ 781-631-1032, 23 Gregory St) Rooms $70-90. There are two clean, simple rooms here with a shared bath.

Seagull Inn (☎ 781-631-1893, fax 631-3535, [e] host@seagullinn.com, 106 Harbor Ave) Suites $100-250. This inn is on Marblehead Neck. It has luxury suites with kitchenettes, air-conditioning and ocean views.

Places to Eat & Drink

Crosby's Market (☎ 781-631-1741, 118 Washington St) Deli $2-7. Visit this place in Old Town for all of your picnic needs, including wine and beer. This large, upscale market with an extensive deli is rife with the scent of freshly baked pumpernickel, dill pickles and roasted veggie salad.

The Muffin Shop (☎ 781-631-8223, 126 Washington St) Deli $2-7. Open 6am-6pm.

Strollers love this spot for its fresh bagels ($1), latte ($2.50), café tables and newspapers.

The ***Driftwood Cafe*** (☎ 781-631-1145, 63 Front St) Dishes $3-7. Open 5:30am-5pm. Right near State Street Landing, this inexpensive cafe in a frame shack is a Marblehead fixture, serving hearty mariners' breakfasts like French toast ($4) to early risers.

Maddie's Sail Loft (☎ 781-631-9824, 15 State St) Dishes $5-16. Here's the rallying place for the sailing crowd, airline flight crews (many live in town) and a lot of other party animals of all ages. Maddie's is a block inland from State Street Landing. Moderately priced foods (burgers $5, fish and chips $10) top the menu. But the main attractions in this tiny pub are cheap beer (Pabst under $2), stiff drinks (killer Mud Slides) and the chance to pack a small, smoky room with a lot of hot bodies ages 21-60.

The Barnacle (☎ 781-631-4236, 141 Front St) Lunch $5-9, dinner $10-14. Perched on a rocky outcropping at harbor's edge, the tiny Barnacle has both porch and indoor seating. The smallness of the restaurant and its popularity make for a crowd. Consider the open steak sandwich ($9) or lobster caesar (about $12) for Sunday brunch.

Trottoria Il Panino (☎ 781-631-3900, 126 Washington St) Mains $9-21. Hidden in the basement of the Muffin Shop, this trottoria has the feel of Napoli, with outdoor café tables, and nooks tucked throughout the open-beam cellar. Try the *zuppa di pesce* with lobster, clams, mussels, calamari and shrimp in cherry tomato sauce.

The Landing (☎ 781-631-1878, 81 Front St) Lunch $9-18, dinner $20-40. Across the parking lot from the Driftwood, this restaurant is aptly named. It is a both a full-service restaurant and a pub with a long menu (plenty of seafood) and a variety of dining spaces inside and on the porch with a harbor view. We like the mussels provençal ($9).

Getting There & Away

From Salem, follow MA 114 southeast 4 miles to Marblehead, where it becomes Pleasant St.

MBTA buses Nos 441/442 and 448/449 run between Boston's Haymarket Square (near North Station) and Marblehead.

See the beginning of the North Shore section for information on MBTA trains to neighboring Salem. From Salem's train station, you can take a taxi ($8) to Marblehead.

GLOUCESTER

Founded in 1623 by English fisherfolk, just three years after the colony at Plymouth, Gloucester is among New England's oldest towns. The port, on Cape Ann (see the Cape Ann map), has made its living at fishing for most of 400 years and inspired books and films like Kipling's *Captains Courageous* and Junger's *The Perfect Storm*.

But overfishing on Georges Bank and the Grand Banks offshore has imperiled New England's fish stock. Strict government limits on catches started in 1994 and have dealt Gloucester an economic blow, putting thousands of anglers out of work. Since the summer of 2000, fish stocks have begun to rebound, but Gloucester's industrious workers are reinventing the town's economy. Local fish-processing operations are converting to plants that process seafood brought in from other regions, and there's an active search for new industries like tourism and whale watching. Recently, more than a half-dozen hip new eateries have come to town. Four large whale-watching operations run from here, along with a cruise on a traditional fishing schooner.

The town still smells of fish. You'll see fishing boats (many now run by Italian or Portuguese immigrants), festooned with nets, dredges and winches, tied to the wharves or motoring into Gloucester Harbor with clouds of hungry seagulls hovering above. The Crow's Nest bar, made famous in *The Perfect Storm,* still attracts fishing crews on the threshold of a fishing trip, just as it did the crew of the *Andrea Gail,* the swordfish boat in the book and film.

Orientation

Washington St runs from Grant Circle (a rotary out on MA 128) into the center of

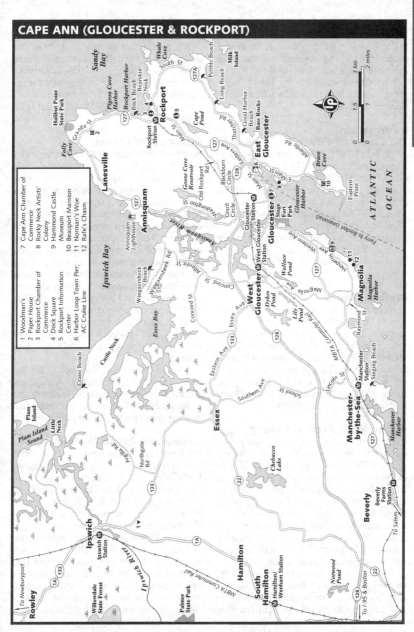

CAPE ANN (GLOUCESTER & ROCKPORT)

1   Woodman's
2   Paper House
3   Rockport Chamber of
     Commerce
4   Dock Square
5   Rockport Information
     Center
6   Harbor Loop Town Pier;
     AC Cruise Line

7   Cape Ann Chamber of
     Commerce
8   Rocky Neck Artists'
     Colony
9   Hammond Castle
     Museum
10 Beauport Mansion
11 Norman's Woe
12 Rafe's Chasm

Gloucester at St Peter's Square, an irregular brick plaza overlooking the sea. Rogers St, the waterfront road, goes east from the plaza; Main St, the business and shopping thoroughfare, is one block inland.

East Gloucester, with the Rocky Neck artists' colony, is on the southeastern side of Gloucester Harbor.

Information

The Cape Ann Chamber of Commerce (☎ 978-283-1601, 800-321-0133, W www .capeannvacations.com, 33 Commercial St, Gloucester, MA 01930) provides information and maps. Look for it south of St Peter's Square. It's open 8am to 5:30pm Monday to Friday, 10am to 6pm Saturday, 10am to 4pm Sunday.

In summer, a visitor information office is open in Stage Fort Park, on the west side of the Annisquam River up the hill (follow the signs).

Walking Tours

You can follow the town's Maritime Trail by using a brochure from the chamber of commerce or by following signs posted around town. Highlights are the Harbor Cove, Inner Harbor, Fish Pier and Leonarde Craske's famous statue, *The Gloucester Fisherman,* often called 'The Man at the Wheel.' The statue is dedicated to 'They That Go Down to the Sea in Ships, 1623–1923.'

Rocky Neck Artists' Colony

Cape Ann's rocky coast and fishing fleet have attracted artists for more than a century. The narrow peninsula of Rocky Neck, jutting into Gloucester Harbor from East Gloucester, offers some of the best views around. Between the world wars, artists began renting little seaside shacks from local fisherfolk, which they used as studios. Today many of these same shanties, considerably gentrified, are galleries displaying the work of local artists.

Follow Main St east and south around the northeastern end of Gloucester Harbor to East Gloucester. Turn onto Rocky Neck Ave and park in the lot on the right (parking farther on in the village proper is nearly impossible in high summer).

It's only a five-minute walk from the parking lot to the galleries and restaurants. Stroll along enjoying the view, poke your head into a gallery or two, then stop for refreshments at one of the restaurants overlooking Smith Cove (see Places to Eat, later in this section).

Beauport Mansion

Beauport (☎ *978-283-0800, 75 Eastern Point Blvd, Eastern Point, East Gloucester; adult/ senior/child 6-12 yrs $6/5.50/3; open 10am-4pm Mon-Fri mid-May–mid-Sept, 10-4pm daily mid-Sept–mid-Oct),* the Sleeper-McCann mansion, is a lavish 'summer cottage' constructed between 1907 and 1934 by Henry Davis Sleeper. Its builder, a prominent interior designer and collector of antiques, worked to make his fantasy palace a showplace of American decor. He toured New England in search of houses about to be demolished and bought up selected elements from each: wood paneling, architectural elements and furniture. In place of unity, Sleeper created a wildly eclectic but artistically surprising – and satisfying – place to live.

Now in the care of the Society for the Preservation of New England Antiquities, Beauport is open to visitors. Beauport also holds afternoon teas, evening concerts and other special events. Call for schedules.

Hammond Castle Museum

Dr John Hays Hammond, Jr (1888–1965) was an electrical engineer whose inventions were important to the development of radar, sonar and radio remote-control systems, including torpedo guidance. Despite his genius with electrical things, it was not Dr John, but rather Laurens Hammond (unrelated), who invented the electric organ.

Defense contracts filled his bank account, and with this wealth Hammond pursued his passion for collecting European art and architecture. His eccentric home is a castle with four sections, each epitomizing a period in European history: Romanesque, medieval, Gothic and Renaissance. Furnishings, including an 8200-pipe organ in the Romanesque Great Hall, are eclectic, quirky, and, at times, beautiful.

The museum (☎ 978-283-7673, Hesperus Ave, Magnolia; adult/senior & student/child 4-12 yrs $6.50/5.50/4.50; open 10am-5pm daily) offers a 45-minute guided tour as part of the entrance fee. For a schedule of concerts and special programs, call ☎ 978-283-2080.

Hammond Castle overlooks several natural features famous in literature. Rafe's Chasm is a cleft in the rocky shoreline that is characterized by turgid and thrashing water. Near it is **Norman's Woe**, the reef on which the ship broke up in Longfellow's poem 'The Wreck of the Hesperus.'

Beaches

Gloucester has several excellent beaches that draw thousands of Boston-area sun-and-sea worshippers on any hot day in July or August. (See also Ipswich, later in this chapter.)

Perhaps biggest and best of all is **Wingaersheek Beach**, a wide swath of sand on Ipswich Bay by the Annisquam River. At low tide, a long sandbar stretches for more than a half-mile out into the bay. At its tip, you have a clear view of the Annisquam lighthouse.

On weekends and very hot days in July and August, plan to arrive by mid-morning at the latest. The parking lot fills up by then, and latecomers are turned away. To get there, take the Concord St exit from MA 128 (the exit just before the Grant Circle rotary). Follow Concord St north for several miles, turning at the sign.

Admission costs $15 per car on weekends, $10 on weekdays. There are showers, toilets and refreshments available. If you come too late and the parking lot is full, retrace your route. Several homeowners on the way to the beach rent parking space on their front lawns on busy weekends. The beach is closed at sunset.

Another large beach is **Good Harbor Beach**, east of East Gloucester off MA 127A

on the way to Rockport. Fees, facilities and parking policies are similar to those at Wingaersheek Beach. On hot days and weekends, make sure you come early to avoid disappointment.

A short distance farther east and north along MA 127A are two smaller beaches, **Long Beach** and **Pebble Beach**, in the neighboring town of Rockport.

There is a small, but usually uncrowded, beach down the hill in **Stage Fort Park Beach**, off Western Ave on the west side of Gloucester. Parking costs $10, but you can park for free on Western Ave; it's a 10-minute walk over the hill to the beach.

Whale Watching & Windjamming

Gloucester has a good selection of vessels to take you to sea to observe whales on nearby Stellwagen Bank or to sail like a traditional Gloucester schooner hand; see the 'New Whalers' boxed text.

Cruises out of Gloucester cost about $26 for adults, $21 seniors, $16 for children under 16. You can sometimes find discount coupons at the chamber of commerce or in local publications. Here are some recommended companies:

Cape Ann Whale Watch (☎ 978-283-5110, 800-877-5110, Rose's Wharf, 415 Main St) Cruises depart from Rose's Wharf, east of Gloucester center (on the way to East Gloucester).

Capt Bill & Sons Whale Watch (☎ 978-283-6995, 800-339-4253, 33 Harbor Loop) The boat leaves from behind Captain Carlo's Seafood Market & Restaurant.

Seven Seas Whale Watch (☎ 978-283-1776, 800-238-1776, Rogers St) Seven Seas vessels depart from Rogers St in the center of Gloucester, between St Peter's Square and the Gloucester House Restaurant.

Yankee Whale Watch (☎ 978-283-0313, 800-942-5464, 75 W Essex Ave/MA 133) The Yankee fleet ties up at the dock next door to the Gull Restaurant on MA 133 (MA 128 exit 14).

Schooner Thomas E Lannon (☎ 978-281-6634, Rogers St) This 65-foot schooner is the spit and image of the Gloucester fishing schooners. It leaves on two-hour sails from the Seven Seas wharf (see Seven Seas Whale Watch, above).

Special Events

Gloucester's **St Peter's Festival**, held on a weekend in late June, brings a carnival to St Peter's Square, with rides, snacks, musical performances and special events such as a greased pole-climbing competition and boat races. The main event is the procession through the streets of a statue of St Peter, patron saint of fisherfolk. Customarily, the cardinal of the Catholic Archdiocese of Boston attends to bless the fishing fleet.

Gloucester's **Fourth of July** parade takes place on the evening of July 3 and is called the Fishtown Horribles Parade. By tradition, children dress up in fanciful costumes (from horrible to humorous) and march, hoping to win a prize for the best. Politicians and local businesses enter floats, and various bands perform.

Places to Stay

Camping If you want to pitch your pup on 50 wooded, hilltop acres, consider *Cape Ann Campsite* (☎ 978-283-8683, Ⓦ *www .capeanncampsite.com, 80 Atlantic St*) Tent sites/full hook-ups $18/21. Open May-Oct. This place has 250 sites.

Motels & Hotels Follow Eastern Point Ave until it becomes Atlantic Rd to find the

---

The New Whalers

A century and a half ago, many New England mariners made their livings – if not their fortunes – hunting the great mammals of the sea. With the discovery of petroleum and natural gas, the importance of whale oil faded away, and with it New England's whaling business.

Whaling is still a business, of course. Japan and Norway both have active whaling programs even though whale-hunting is condemned by most other nations. A kilo of whale meat can be worth up to $400 at retail in Tokyo. For more information, see Ⓦ www.physics.helsinki.fi/whale.

The great whales still produce income for New England mariners, too, but they don't give their lives to do it. Whale-watching cruises are very popular.

Vessels

The typical whale-watch vessel is a steel-hulled, diesel-powered boat of 80 to 100 feet in length. Boats are equipped with snack bars, toilets, indoor and outdoor seating areas and full safety equipment. Sonar helps track the schools of fish that often indicate where the whales will be feeding that day. A naturalist accompanies the cruise to provide full information on the species of whales, their habits, and even, in some cases, their 'names,' as many of the whales are regulars, known to the crews.

Schedules

The typical cruise is a four- or five-hour voyage departing at breakfast-time, mid-morning or just after lunch. Cruises run from late April to late October. From late June to early September, many boats make two cruises daily.

Preparations

To prepare for your cruise, call ahead and confirm departure times and ticket prices. Ask about maritime conditions: If it's been stormy in the past few days, the seas may still be rough, which means most landlubbers will suffer from seasickness.

Take a warm sweater and/or jacket (a lined windbreaker is perfect), as it will be considerably cooler out on the windy ocean – particularly on morning cruises – even on warm days. Wear rubber-soled shoes.

Sunglasses, sunscreen or sunblock and a hat are also necessary, as you will be exposed to direct sunlight as well as the harsh light reflected off the water.

following sea-view motels. They're open only in warm weather.

Ocean View Resort & Inn *(☎ 978-283-6200, 800-315-7557, fax 978-282-7723, 171 Atlantic Rd)* Rooms $80-160. What do you get when you combine an inn and a resort? This great place, with two pools, pub, dining room, billiards and rooms in Tudor mansions.

Atlantis Motor Inn *(☎ 978-283-0014, 800-732-6313, 125 Atlantic Rd)* Rooms $90-150. This inn features a heated pool, coffee shop and motel-style rooms with air con and cable.

Bass Rocks Ocean Inn *(☎ 978-283-7600, 800-528-1234, 103 Atlantic Rd)* Rooms $125-190. Bass Rocks Ocean Inn has 48 renovated ocean-view rooms and a pool. Children are welcome.

B&Bs The B&B phenomenon is just taking hold in Gloucester, bringing a new level of character and value to accommodations. You can search out this emerging market at ⓦ www.capeannvacations.com. Here are a couple of the tried and true.

Gray Manor *(☎ 978-283-5409, 14 Atlantic Rd, East Gloucester)* Rooms $60-75. Just a three-minute walk from popular Good Harbor Beach, this spot has three rooms and six efficiencies. All rooms in this classic

The New Whalers

Take your camera and perhaps binoculars. Though not all whale sightings are photogenic, you may be in luck and should be prepared.

Nonalcoholic beverages, snacks and sometimes even light meals are available onboard. Only a few boats sell alcoholic beverages or allow them to be served. If the sea is not dead calm, and if you are not an experienced mariner, forget the booze.

Seasickness Prevention

If possible, carry capsules of powdered ginger (from a health-food store) and take one or two before departure. Ginger helps to settle the stomach on rocky voyages. There are also anti-seasickness drugs such as Dramamine (ask your doctor or pharmacist). Bring paper napkins and a plastic bag in case these don't work.

If you feel queasy, sit outside, breathe the sea air deeply and look at land or the horizon until the feeling passes. Don't read for long periods on a rocking boat, as that is the short, fast route to nausea.

Sightings

Your boat motors out to sea for about an hour to where the whales customarily hunt for food, perhaps at the National Marine Sanctuary of Stellwagen Bank. It will then cruise slowly for about two hours looking for whales. Most boats have enviable records, sighting whales over 99% of the time, not to mention seabirds, dolphins and seals. If your cruise fails to sight a whale, the company usually gives you a pass good for another cruise.

The **humpback** whales are baleen (filter-feeding) whales of up to 50 feet in length and weighing 30 tons, with flippers up to 15 feet long. They're the ones most sought because they're big and playful, sometimes 'breaching' (leaping out of the water).

The **finbacks**, or fin whales, are more slender and longer (up to 70 feet) and heavier (up to 50 tons). They're second only to the great blue whales in size. They don't breach, but lunge and spout in the water.

The **minke** (min-kee) whales are smaller (23 to 28 feet in length) and lighter and do not breach, but lunge on the surface.

You might also see **Atlantic white-sided dolphins**, 8 or 9 feet in length, which have teeth rather than baleen and feed on fish and squid. The dolphins love to leap in the air and sport in boat wakes.

summer mansion have fridge, air con, TV & private bath.

Jullietta House (☎ *978-281-2300, 84 Prospect St*) Rooms $75-118. You'll find five rooms in this Victorian Inn, complete with period furnishings and decorations. It's walking distance from downtown.

Places to Eat

Gloucester has become the new 'in' place to window shop for eateries as the town blooms with new restaurants. Most places are open for lunch and dinner unless noted.

Downtown Gloucester For a snack, grab a slab of pizza ($1.50) or a canoli ($1) at *Virgilio's Italian Bakery* (☎ *978-283-5295, 29 Main St*) Prices $1-6.

Café Sicilia (☎ *978-283-7345, 40 Main St*) Prices $2-7. This cafe is at Short St, and has Italian pastries and also good, strong espresso (under $2).

Valentino's (☎ *978-283-6186, 38 Main St*) Dishes $5-15. Across the street from Virgilio's at Short St, Valentino's serves whole pizzas ($9 to $15) and pasta plates.

Halibut Point Restaurant & Pub (☎ *978-281-1900, 289 Main St*) Dishes $5-13. Open 11:30am-11:30pm daily. Here's a narrow little Gloucester pub with good food and drink at reasonable prices. Patronized mostly by locals, it serves chowder, sandwiches and burgers in cozy, congenial surroundings. You'll love the Italian fish stew (under $5). There's a lively bar scene from noon 'til closing.

Blackburn Tavern (☎ *978-282-1919, 2 Main St*) Dishes $5-13. This tavern is at the corner of Washington St. It's an upscale saloon with a varied bar menu of sandwiches like the rueben ($7), main courses and, of course, drinks.

The Gull (☎ *978-281-6060, 75 Essex Ave/ MA 133*) Dishes $10-24. This is a bit out of the way, in West Gloucester, but it's worth the trip. The Gull's a bright, upbeat place with large windows overlooking a busy marina. Seafood is the strong point, from excellent lobster rolls to grilled tuna and swordfish steaks and clambakes. There's a bar popular with locals.

Jalapeño's (☎ *978-283-8228, 86 Main St*) Lunch $11-17. Check out this place for authentic Mexican cuisine at decent prices. Try the *pollo con mole* (chicken in a spicy chocolate sauce, $13) or a cactus salad ($4).

White Rainbow (☎ *978-281-0017, 65 Main St*) Dinner $35-50. For elegant dining, this restaurant serves dinner in a cozy brick-lined basement dining room. The menu lists classic main courses – steak, roast duckling, rack of lamb, grilled shrimp. Gloucester gentry come here to see and be seen. Call for reservations.

Rocky Neck & East Gloucester Parking is tight on E Main St and Rocky Neck Ave, so allow a bit of time to find a place.

The Studio (☎ *978-283-4123, 51 Rocky Neck Ave*) Mains $17-21. This is great spot for lunch, a light dinner, or a drink on the deck overlooking Smith's Cove. We recommend the sugar cane skewered BBQ shrimp (about $10).

The Rudder (☎ *978-283-7967, 73 Rocky Neck Ave*) Mains $17-24. Just down the street from the Studio, the Rudder looks like a neat little lobsterman's shack. Here's a great date restaurant, with dining in the intimate basement or on a small waterfront deck with candlelight and jazz. Chef Robert Hartley fires up fusion like Yucatan spice-rubbed halibut ($20).

L'Amante (☎ *978-282-4426, 197 E Main St*) Mains $17-25. Kevin and Kathleen Cleary run this chic storefront bistro in East Gloucester. The menu changes monthly and always features imaginative mains like fettuccini with lobster ($24).

Entertainment

Gloucester Stage Company (☎ *978-281-4099, 267 E Main St*) Tickets $15-30. During the summer, this company stages excellent small-theater productions of classics and modern works, and new plays by acclaimed playwright Israel Horovitz.

Gloucester gets its party on, particularly on summer weekends. Check out the following.

The Crow's Nest (☎ *978-281-2965, 334 Main St*) Yep, here's the very down-and-dirty fisherfolk bar made famous in *The*

Perfect Storm. But this is the real McCoy, not the set the movie folks threw up for a few weeks during filming. If you want to drink with the fish crews, and listen to 'No Woman No Cry' on the jukebox, get here around 7am for a breakfast Bud. By noon (in summer), the tourists have moved in.

Rhumb Line (☎ 978-283-9732, 40 Railroad Ave) This place is across from the train station. The upstairs is the liveliest disco in town on the weekend, with an under-30 crowd pulsing to mainstream and alternative rock. Downstairs brings in acoustic and blues acts. On Wednesday, you get open-mike night.

Madfish Grille (☎ 978-281-4554, 77 Rocky Neck Ave, East Gloucester) On a wharf at Rocky Neck, the Madfish has been rock & roll heaven for decades under a series of names. And it's still going strong during the summer, when the tan, hardbody posses pack the open-air deck bar. You get mainstream rock cover bands on Friday and Saturday. Sunday stirs it up with reggae. Note the excellent pickup action.

Blackburn Tavern (see Places to Eat). There's live blues and rock here Thursday to Saturday. The crowd is older and tamer than at the Madfish, but this is the place to come in cool weather.

Getting There & Away

See the beginning of the North Shore section, earlier in this chapter, for train information.

You can reach Gloucester quickly from Boston or North Shore towns via four-lane Rte 128, but the scenic route on MA 127 follows the coastline through the prim villages of Prides Crossing, Manchester-by-the-Sea and Magnolia.

AC Cruise Line (☎ 617-261-6633) sails from Boston to Gloucester daily in summer. Departure from Boston (290 Northern Ave, in the Seaport district) is at 9:30am, arriving at Harbor Loop Town Pier at 12:30pm. The return trip leaves at 3pm, arriving back in Boston at 5pm. Roundtrip tickets cost $20 for adults, $16 for seniors; children 12 and under ride with their parents for free. Call for advance reservations.

ROCKPORT

What a metamorphosis. In the 19th century, Rockport was a sheltered harbor town from which granite blocks were shipped to construction sites up and down the Atlantic seaboard and even to Europe. Cut at a half-dozen quarries just west of the Rockport Granite Quarry Wharf, the stone became the favored local building material. Monuments, curbstones, building foundations, pavements and piers on Cape Ann (see the Cape Ann map) all remain as a testament to Rockport's past. The town's several granite buildings are particularly handsome.

A century ago, Winslow Homer, Childe Hassam, Fitz Hugh Lane and other acclaimed artists came to Rockport's rugged shores. They painted pictures of the hearty fisherfolk who wrested a hard, but satisfying, living from the sea. The artists told their friends about this retreat. Those friends told other friends, and today Rockport makes its living from tourists who come to look at the artists. The artists have long since given up looking for hearty fishermen because the descendants of the fishers are all running boutiques and B&Bs.

Still, Rockport is just about as visually appealing as it was a century ago, although in summer it can be mobbed with daytrippers and travelers who stay in the more than 30 local inns and B&Bs. Beaches, boutiques, restaurants, seaside walks and drives are the main attractions. You might even see some artists…but most of the serious ones have studios hidden in the woods.

The **Rockport Chamber Music Festival** (☎ 978-546-7391, 2 Main St) sponsors internationally acclaimed performers, who give concerts in the Rockport Art Association gallery from mid-June to early July.

Orientation

The center of town is Dock Square, at the beginning of Bearskin Neck. Most everything is within a 10-minute walk of it. The railroad station is less than a 15-minute walk west of Dock Square.

Parking is very difficult on summer weekends. Unless you get here in time for breakfast, you'd do well to park at one of the lots

MASSACHUSETTS

on MA 127 from Gloucester and take the shuttle bus ($1) to the center. The few lots in town charge $8 per day, but fill early. Meters (25¢ an hour) are policed vigorously; if you overstay your meter it'll cost you $10. Scrupulously observe the parking regulation signs everywhere.

Information
The Rockport Chamber of Commerce (☎ 978-546-6575, 888-726-3922, W www.rockportusa.com, PO Box 67, 3 Main St at Pier Ave, Rockport, MA 01966) is in the town center just off Main St, uphill from Dock Square. It's open 9am to 5pm Monday to Saturday (10am to 4pm weekdays in winter). The Rockport Information Center, on MA 127 as you enter Rockport from Gloucester, is open in summer. The staff will help you find a room if you need one.

Toad Hall Bookstore (☎ 978-546-7323, 51 Main St) is not only a good place to buy books, but the shop donates some of its income to environmental projects.

Walking Tours
Rockport is a town for wandering. Start at Dock Square and flow with the crowds along Bearskin Neck, window-shopping, stopping for coffee, ice cream or a snack and finally emerging at the Breakwater, which overlooks Rockport Harbor to the south and Sandy Bay to the west.

For a guided tour, contact **Footprints** (☎ 978-546-7730, 3 North St) on Bearskin Neck, which sponsors walking tours at 11am, 1pm, and 3pm daily. There are also lantern tours. Expect to pay $8/5, adult/child.

The red fishing shack decorated with colorful buoys is *Motif No 1*. So many artists of great and minimal talent have been painting and photographing it for so long that it well deserves its tongue-in-cheek name. Actually, it should be called Motif No 1-B, as the original shack vanished during a great storm in 1978 and a brand-new replica was erected in its place.

Follow Main St west and north from Dock Square to reach **Back Beach** on Sandy

Bay, which is the nearest beach to the town center.

About a mile north of Dock Square on the water, Wharf Rd heads west from the **Rockport Granite Company Wharf**, the granite pier from which there are panoramic views of the town and Sandy Bay.

Pigeon Cove, the neighborhood about 2 miles north of Dock Square, remains a working fishing and lobster-boat harbor (except for a block of luxury condos).

For excellent views of the town and the sea, walk southeast from Dock Square along Mt Pleasant St, then east along Atlantic Ave or Heywood Ave to the public footpath marked as the 'Way to the Headlands.' The walk from Dock Square takes only 10 or 15 minutes, and you'll be rewarded with a view of the town that takes you back 100 years.

Halibut Point State Park
Only a few miles north of Dock Square along MA 127, just northeast of the Old Farm Inn, is Halibut Point State Park (☎ 978-546-2997, admission per person $2, per car $5; open sunrise to sunset daily). A 10-minute walk through the forest brings you to yawning, abandoned granite quarries, huge hills of broken granite rubble and a granite foreshore of tumbled, smoothed rock perfect for picnicking, sunbathing, reading or painting. The surf can be strong here, making swimming unwise, but natural pools can be good for wading or cooling your feet.

Park rangers lead nature walks, explaining the marine life in tidal pools, the working of granite quarries, the local bird life and the area's edible plants. Call to learn about current programs.

Paper House
Inland from Pigeon Cove is the Paper House (☎ 978-546-2629, 52 Pigeon Hill St; admission by donation; open 10am-5pm daily Apr-Oct), a curiosity begun in 1922 when Mr Elis F Stenman decided something useful should be done with all those daily newspapers lying about. He and his

family set to work folding, rolling and pasting the papers into suitable shape as building materials.

Twenty years and 100,000 newspapers later, the house was done. The walls are 215 layers thick, the furnishings – table, chairs, lamps, sofa, even a grandfather clock and a piano – are all made of newspapers. Some pieces even specialize: One desk is made from *Christian Science Monitor* reports of Charles Lindbergh's flight, and the fireplace mantel is made from rotogravures drawn from the *Boston Sunday Herald* and the *New York Herald Tribune*. On all of the papers in the house, the text is still readable.

Activities

You can go on the 1½-hour **Rockport lobstering trip** (☎ 978-546-3642, at T Wharf; adult/child $10/6, islands $8/5) with Capt Fred aboard the 38-foot *Dove* each morning at 9:30am or 11:30am from the T-wharf at the center of town. Hour-long island cruises depart at 1:30pm and 3pm.

North Shore Kayak Outdoor Center (☎ 978-546-5050, 9 Tuna Wharf; kayaks $25-40, bikes $16) rents out kayaks and offers tours. You can also rent bikes.

Essex River Adventures (☎ 978-768-3722, 66R Main St, Essex; tours $20-70), in neighboring Essex, offers kayak tours of the islands and bays of the extensive Essex River estuary.

Rockport Whale Watch (☎ 978-546-3377, 9 Tuna Wharf; adult/senior/child under 13 yrs $26/21/17), off Bear Neck, will take you on a half-day whale-watching cruise.

Places to Stay

Rockport has dozens of inns and B&Bs, as well as a few motels. The competition keeps the rates quite a bit lower than what you might find in some other historic towns. Most hostelries lie within an easy walk of Dock Square. Many require two-night minimum stays on weekends (three nights on holiday weekends); some do not accept children. Virtually all are nonsmoking and include at least a light breakfast in the room price. Most all of these places are seasonal operations and do not maintain fax lines. For a complete list, see W www.rockportusa.com.

Motels If you want the convenience of a modern motel, try the *Sandy Bay Motor Inn* (☎ 978-546-7155, 800-437-7155, 173 Main St) Rooms $98-130. This place, less than 2 miles inland along Main St (MA 127), has a restaurant and enclosed swimming pool. The summer rates given here don't include breakfast.

Captain's Bounty Motor Inn (☎ 978-546-9557, 1 Beach St) Rooms $100-130. Its prime location, right on the beach and only a few minutes' stroll from Dock Square, allows this 24-room inn to set these high summer rates, without breakfast.

Inns & B&Bs Come on, girls! Take a break at *Rockport Lodge* (☎ 978-546-2090, 61 South St) Singles/doubles/triples $50/45/40 with two meals. This is a special lodging for women only. Founded in 1906 by the National League of Working Women, it was meant to be a place where women of low or moderate income could find a restful vacation from the drudgery of factory labor at affordable prices. It continues to fulfill that mission, offering beds and two meals. If you just stay the night and have no meals, the charge is $30 per person. Weekly rates are equally reasonable. Guests get linens, but you bring your own towels and soap and tidy up your own room.

The Inn on Cove Hill (☎ 978-546-2701, 37 Mt Pleasant St) Doubles with shared bath $55, with private bath $70-135. This is an early-American house (1791), built, so they say, with pirates' gold discovered nearby. The double rooms are furnished in Federal style with canopy beds. The location, a block from the harbor in the center of town, is hard to beat.

Lantana House (☎ 978-546-3535, 800-291-3535, 22 Broadway) Doubles/twins $78-95. Conveniently located, Lantana House has some of the least expensive rooms in Rockport. Some have kitchenettes and air con.

Carlson's B&B (☎ 978-546-2770, 43 Broadway) Doubles with bath $78-94 with full breakfast. This is the Victorian home of prominent local artist Carol Carlson. Guests use a private entrance and have garage parking.

Tuck Inn (☎ *978-546-7260, 800-789-7260, 17 High St*) Rooms $80-130. This inn is a recently renovated 1790s colonial home, offering nine rooms and a four-person suite. Elegant public rooms feature period decor, and most rooms have private entrances. There is a large pool.

Sally Webster Inn (☎ *978-546-9251, 877-546-9251*, W *www.sallywebster.com, 34 Mt Pleasant St*) Rooms with bath $82-96. This is a handsome brick colonial, built in 1832, offering eight rooms with early-American decor.

Linden Tree Inn (☎ *978-546-2494, 800-865-2122, 26 King St*) Rooms $86-130. This Victorian-style place has a variety of 18 double rooms plus one small single. Check out the view from the cupola.

Addison Choate Inn (☎ *978-546-7543, 800-245-7543, 49 Broadway*) Rooms $115-145 with breakfast. Lisa and Scott Reiter's Greek revival residence stands out among Rockport's historic inns, with a swimming pool and six rooms/suites complete with four-poster beds and oriental carpets. Rates include afternoon tea.

Places to Eat

Rockport is 'dry,' meaning there's no alcohol for sale, either in stores or restaurants (there are no bars). You can buy bottles in Gloucester or Lanesville, and most restaurants (but not fast-food places) will open and serve them for a corkage fee of about $1.50 per person. Lanesville Package Store, on MA 127 in Lanesville (4 miles from central Rockport), is open 8am to 10pm (10:30pm on Friday and Saturday, closed Sunday). There are numerous liquor stores in Gloucester as well. In high summer, make reservations for dinner in the better restaurants.

Dock Square, at the beginning of Bearskin Neck, has several cafes. And Bearskin Neck is crowded with ice cream shops, cafes and cozy restaurants. As you walk out the neck, you'll pass several small wharf buildings where you can catch a bowl of chowder, fish and chips, and relatively cheap lobster. Quite a few of the seaside restaurants close during the winter. Eateries listed here are open for lunch and dinner unless noted.

Hula Moon Café (☎ *978-456-5185, 27 Mt Pleasant St*) Dishes $1-12. This little place has some of the best bargains and imaginative cooking in the village. The emphasis is on Hawaiian-style cuisine. Mini veggie sandwiches run as low as $1.25. Feast on the Kalua pig and cabbage ($8).

Helmut's Strudel (☎ *978-546-2824, 49 Bearskin Neck*) Prices $2-5. For coffee or tea and dessert, try this bakery, almost near the outer end, serving various strudels, filled croissants, pastries, cider and coffee. Four shaded tables overlook the yacht-filled harbor.

Ellen's Harborside (☎ *978-546-2512, 1 Wharf Rd*) Breakfast $2-5, mains $6-15. Open 6am-9pm daily. By the T-wharf in the center of town, Ellen's has grown famous serving a simple menu of American breakfasts, chicken, ribs and lobster, since 1954. You get decent portions, fresh food and low prices. Bring your own bottle, and go wild on the baked stuffed lobster tails (around $14). Consider the Cubano sandwich, oven-baked with ham, Swiss, pickles and French bread ($6).

Roy Moore Lobster Company (☎ *978-546-6696, 29 Bearskin Neck*) Dishes $3-16. This takeout kitchen has the cheapest lobster-in-the-rough (around $11) on the Neck. Your beast comes on a tray with melted butter, a fork and a wet wipe for cleanup. Claws and shell are pre-cracked for convenience.

Roy Moore's Fish Shack Restaurant (☎ *978-546-6667, 29 Bearskin Neck*) Mains $4-18. If you'd like a bit more refinement, go upstairs right next door to Roy Moore's Lobster Company. The prices are still fairly low given its water-view dining room. Bring your own wine or beer and dive into a bowl of chowder (about $4).

The Greenery (☎ *978-546-9593, 15 Dock Square*) Lunch $6-12, dinner $11-15. Here's a classic storefront cafe that opens at the rear to a view of Motif No 1. Consider the salad bar (under $7) or try the turkey and avocado sandwich for the same price.

Brackett's (☎ *978-546-2797, 25 Main St)* Mains $11-15. Locals swear by this cozy little dining nook with a pub atmosphere. The scrod, shrimp, crab and scallop casseroles (about $14), rich in sherry and cream, are to die for. Better make reservations.

My Place by the Sea (☎ *978-546-9667, 68 Bearskin Neck)* Lunch $8-12, dinner $20-30. Barbara Stavropolos and Kathy Milbury run Brackett's rival. This spot is right out at the end of the Neck. The location offers panoramic views of the bay, indoor and outdoor seating, excellent service and imaginative nouvelle cuisine. Lunch is a good value, with a roasted red pepper on a baguette (under $8). For dinner, consider pan-seared Szechuan lobster ($22); you'll need dinner reservations.

Getting There & Away
Rockport is the terminus for MBTA commuter rail trains (see the beginning of the North Shore section for details).

MA 127/127A loops around Cape Ann. You can join this loop at several points in Gloucester and meet Rockport halfway around the loop. Driving the entire loop is worth it for the bold seaside scenery in East Gloucester, Laneville, and Annisquam.

The Cape Ann Transportation Authority (CATA; ☎ 978-283-7916) operates bus routes among the towns of Cape Ann. Most fares are less than $1.

IPSWICH
Famous for its clams, Ipswich is one of those New England towns that is pretty today because it was poor in the past. With no harbor, and no source of waterpower for factories, commercial and industrial development went elsewhere in the 18th and 19th centuries. As a result, Ipswich's 17th-century houses were not torn down to build grander residences. Today, antique shops abound.

It's also famous as the home of novelist John Updike and is the setting for some of his novels and short stories like 'A&P,' which is based on the local market.

Beachgoers must try **Crane Beach** (admission $5 per car), at the end of Argilla Rd. It's 4 miles of fine-sand barrier beach on Ipswich Bay. Above the beach, on Castle Hill, you'll find the 1920s estate of Chicago plumbing-fixture magnate Richard T Crane. The 59-room Stuart-style **Great House** (☎ *978-356-4351, 290 Argilla Rd)* was the setting for the film *The Crucible* with Daniel Day-Lewis and is the site of summer concerts and special events.

Woodman's (☎ *978-768-6057, 121 Main St/MA 133)* Mains $7-25. This roadhouse is the most famous spot in New England to come for clams (raw, stewed, fried), and is in neighboring Essex, on the way to Ipswich from Rockport on MA 128 exit 14.

MBTA trains (☎ 617-222-3200, 800-392-6100) on the Newburyport line leave Boston's North Station for Ipswich (50 minutes, about $4) 12 times each weekday, five times on Saturday, no trains Sunday.

NEWBURYPORT
Architecturally, Newburyport is lost in time. Among the five largest towns in America at the outset of the Revolution in 1775, Newburyport (at the mouth of the Merrimack River, 35 miles north of Boston) prospered as a shipping port and center for silversmiths until the river's dangerous sandbars and the Industrial Revolution took trade and industry to more modern ports. This left Newburyport limping along with few changes until the early 1970s, when people began noticing that the town had the largest stock of Federal-period brick buildings and churches in all of Massachusetts.

Today, the center of this town of 17,000 is a model of historic preservation and gentrification. For the traveler this means creative restaurants, pubs, museums and entertainment. If you need more of a temptation, consider that Newburyport is the gateway to Plum Island, an 8½-mile barrier strand that is largely a national wildlife refuge with some of the best bird watching in New England.

Orientation & Information
All major roads (MA 113, US 1, and US 1A) lead to the center of the town's commercial

and historic district, around the junction of Water St and State St.

The Greater Newburyport Chamber of Commerce (☎ 978-462-6680, ⓦ www.new buryportchamber.org, 29 State St, New buryport, MA 01950) greets visitors 9am to 5pm weekdays, 10am to 4pm Saturday, noon to 4pm Sunday. There is a seasonal information booth in Market Square open June to October.

Custom House Maritime Museum

The museum (☎ 978-462-8681, 25 Water St; admission adult/senior & child $3/2; open 10am-4pm Tues-Sat, 1pm-4pm Sun) sits in the 1835 granite Custom House. The museum exhibits artifacts from Newburyport's maritime history as a major shipbuilding center and seaport, when it sent ships to the Far East and around the world. Your ticket also give you access to Lowell's Boat Shop in neighboring Amesbury, the oldest boat shop in America.

Cushing House Museum

This 21-room Federal home (☎ 978-462-2681, 98 High St; admission adult/child $4/1.50; open 10am-4pm Tues-Fri, 11am-2pm Sat May-Oct) houses the Historical Society of Old Newbury. Visitors see the treasures of the area's past, encompassing every aspect of life from the countryside to the city. There are guided tours, exhibits, special events and lectures. Last tour begins one hour before closing.

Parker River National Wildlife Refuge

The 4662-acre sanctuary (☎ 978-465-5753, Plum Island; admission car & bike/pedestrian $5/$2; open sunrise-sunset daily) is 4 miles east of Newburyport and home to more than 800 species of birds, plants and animals. The refuge has beaches, sand dunes, salt pans, salt marshes, freshwater impoundments and maritime forests.

The salt pans are excellent spots to see shorebirds during fall migration (July to September) and egrets and herons from mid-April to October. The Hellcat Wildlife

Swamp Interpretive Area has freshwater impoundments, as well as an extensive swamp and forest. Here you'll see waterfowl and shorebirds, including herons. During the spring and fall, you can observe migrating songbirds, including magnificent wood-warblers in the woods. In winter, the refuge is a good place to see waterfowl, the rough-legged hawk and snowy owl.

The Joppa Flats Education Center of the Massachusetts Audubon Society (☎ 978-462-9998) offers interpretive natural history programs for families and adults.

Beaches

Plum Island has 9 miles of sandy beaches. Sandy Point on the southern tip of Plum Island is a state park and a popular spot to swim, sun and go tidepooling. Parking is available at the refuge, Sandy Point or in private parking lots. Note: Beaches in the refuge are generally closed April to June because of nesting piping plover, but you can go to the public beaches at the north end of the island, where there is a community of vacation homes.

Whale Watching

Newburyport Whale Watch (☎ 800-848-1111, the Boardwalk at 54 Merrimac St; adult/senior/child under 13 yrs $26/21/17) runs daily trips during the summer.

Places to Stay

Like many historic North Shore towns, Newburyport has become a mecca for B&Bs. For a complete list of places to stay and website links check out ⓦ www.new buryportchamber.org.

Essex Street Inn (☎ 978-465-3148, 7 Essex St) Rooms $90-175. Here's a cross between an inn and a boutique hotel with 17 rooms. Many of the rooms have a fireplace and spa, some have decks. All have air con and 19th-century decor. You might miss the lack of public space.

The Garrison Inn (☎ 978-499-8500, 11 Brown Square) Doubles $100-140. Joy McFarland runs this boutique hotel with 24 rooms. Once a private mansion, the building has been a hostelry for 100 years. All rooms have private baths, air con, and cable TV. An elevator makes the inn wheelchair accessible. *David's* (☎ 978-462-8077) restaurant, downstairs, features Asian and American haute cuisine for $16 and up.

The Windsor House (☎ 978-462-3778, 38 Federal St) Rates $100-145 with full English breakfast. Guests in this five-room B&B rave about English ambiance and the personal attention they get from innkeeper Judith Harris and her husband John, a Cornish raconteur. Tea's served at 4pm in the common room. Three of the rooms have private baths.

The Clark Currier Inn (☎ 978-465-8363, 45 Green St) Rates $100-150. Travelers in search of a genteel experience can luxuriate in this 1803 Federal mansion with its period sitting room, library, fish pond and gazebo. Mary and Bob Nolan have eight rooms for guests, all with private bath. One has a Franklin stove; many have canopy beds.

Places to Eat & Drink

Couples love exploring Newburyport on warm evenings when the scents from restaurants fill the streets. Unless noted, eateries listed here are open for lunch and dinner.

Angie's Food (☎ 978-462-7959, 7 Pleasant St) Breakfast & lunch $3-7. Open 6am-4pm. You gotta love the blue Formica tabletops as well as the three-egg omelet ($4) and sizzling joe in this classic coffee shop, where locals gather for breakfast and gossip.

Szechuan Taste (☎ 978-463-0686, 19 Pleasant St) Mains $5-12. One of the attractions of this popular takeout spot is that you can catch some shrimp lo mein ($8) until midnight or later on weekends.

The Rockfish (☎ 978-465-6601, 35 State St) Dishes $5-18. Here's a great place to people-watch. In warm weather you can take a table downstairs in the pub by the large, street-side open windows. Snarf some spicy rockfish cakes ($7), suck on a cold brewski, network with the locals, and watch the evening strollers sashay up and down State St. Upstairs you get tablecloths and candlelight. Chef/owner Chris Leary fires up some inventive fusion dishes: Check out

the 'rippin' red-hot roll-up' (chicken breast in Thai chili sauce with roasted pepper and blue cheese dressing, $8). The pub scene is intense on weekend nights with an under-35 crowd.

Mr India Restaurant (☎ 978-465-8600, 114 Merrimack St) Mains $7-12. This eatery is perched on the edge of the historic district. The building is Depression-era New England, but the scents and tastes are pure Bombay. We like the curried chicken ($10).

The Grog (☎ 978-465-8008, 13 Middle St) Mains $7-16. Mexican cuisine rules in a pub atmosphere on the 1st floor. Try the quesadillas ($9). You'll find the under-25 crowd filing in for rock & roll cover bands after about 9pm.

Ciro's Restaurant (☎ 978-463-3335, 1 Market Square) Lunch $7-12. This streetside cafe at Water St is the spot to be and be seen on warm weekend afternoons. Pizza (about $10) and chilled chardonnay spritzers with lime ($5) set the tone. Big salads!

Scandia Restaurant (☎ 978-462-6271, 25 State St) Dinner $15-24. This spot is one of the great date restaurants on the North Shore. Couples love cuddling into the pillow-filled window seats in this small, storefront restaurant. The ambiance is soft jazz and candles. You'll relish every bite of the seared yellowfin tuna ($19).

Entertainment

The Firehouse Center for the Performing Arts (☎ 978-462-7336, 1 Market Square) Tickets $12-22. There are two art galleries, a 190-seat theater, and Ciro's Restaurant (see above) in this restored 1823 firehouse at Water St. The theater offers year-round concerts, plays and children's theater with top performers from around New England.

Getting There & Away

The MBTA (☎ 800-392-6100) runs a line from North Station to Newburyport. There are more than 10 trains daily on weekdays, six on weekends. The fare is $5.

There is a C&J Trailways (☎ 800-258-7111) terminal on Storey Ave just off I-95; about 12 buses run daily from Logan Airport and Boston's South Station. The fare is $9.

From Boston follow I-95 north. Take exit 57 and follow signs to downtown Newburyport. There are free parking lots on Green and Merrimack Sts.

South Shore

PLYMOUTH

Historic Plymouth, 'America's Home Town,' is synonymous with Plymouth Rock. Thousands of visitors come here each year to look at this weathered granite ball and to consider what it was like for the Pilgrims, who stepped ashore in this strange land in the autumn of 1620, seeking a place where they could practice their religion as they wished without interference from government, and for the Native Americans who were soon wiped out. You can see Plymouth Rock in a mere minute, but the rock is just a symbol of the Pilgrims' struggle, sacrifice and triumph, which are elucidated in many museums and exhibits nearby. If your time is short, put Plimoth Plantation and *Mayflower II* atop your list. Then add Pilgrim Hall if you don't have kids, and Plymouth National Wax Museum if you do. The historic houses are for die-hard enthusiasts.

Orientation & Information

'The rock,' on the waterfront, is on Water St at the center of Plymouth, within walking distance of most museums and restaurants. Main St, the main commercial street, is a block inland. Some lodgings are within walking distance, but others require a car.

The 'Destination Plymouth' visitor information center (☎ 508-747-7525, 508-747-7533 in winter, Ⓦ www.visit-plymouth.com, 130 Water St, Plymouth, MA 02360) is a half-mile north of Plymouth Rock. It's open 9am to 5pm April to November, until 8pm late May to early September. Its staff can help with B&B reservations.

The Massachusetts Tourist Information Center (☎ 508-746-1150, MA 3 exit 5) has information on many regional destinations in addition to Plymouth. It's open year-round 6am to 5pm Monday to Thursday, 6am to 8pm Friday and 8am to 8pm Saturday and Sunday.

Yankee Books (☎ 508-747-2691, 10 North St) has a selection of books on Pilgrim history.

Plymouth Rock

Though the Pilgrims came from England, Plymouth Rock came from Pangaea, the gigantic continent that split in two to form Europe and Africa on the eastern side and North and South America on the western side, leaving the Atlantic Ocean in between. The boulder is of Dedham granite, a rock some 680 million years old. Most of the Dedham granite went to Africa when Pangaea split; bits were left in the Atlantica terrain, the geologic area around Boston. About 20,000 years ago, a glacier picked up Plymouth Rock, carried it and dropped it here.

We don't really know that the Pilgrims landed on Plymouth Rock; it's not mentioned in any early written accounts. But the colonial news media picked up the story and soon the rock was in jeopardy from its adoring fans. In 1774, 20 yoke of oxen were harnessed to the rock to move it – and they split it in the process. Half of the cloven boulder went on display in Pilgrim Hall from 1834 to 1867. The sea and wind lashed at the other half, and innumerable small pieces were chipped off and carried away by souvenir hunters over the centuries.

By the 20th century, the rock was an endangered artifact, and steps were taken to protect it. In 1921, the reunited halves were sheltered in the present granite enclosure, designed by McKim, Mead & White. In 1989, the rock was repaired and strengthened to withstand weathering.

Plymouth Rock – relatively small, broken and mended, with the date '1620' cut into it – is a symbol of the quest for religious freedom. It's open for viewing all the time, for free.

Mayflower II

If Plymouth Rock tells us little about the Pilgrims, *Mayflower II* (☎ 508-746-1622, State Pier; adult/child $8/6; combined ticket to Plimoth Plantation adult/senior & student/child $22/20/14; open 9am-5pm daily Apr-Nov), a replica of the small ship in which they made the fateful voyage, speaks volumes. As you enter, you'll think it impossible that 102 people with all the household effects, tools, provisions, animals and seed to establish a colony could have lived together on this tiny vessel for 66 days, subsisting on hard, moldy biscuits, rancid butter and brackish water as the ship passed through the stormy north Atlantic waters. But they did, landing on this wild, forested shore in the frigid December of 1620 – eloquent tes-

timony to their courage, spirit and the strength of their religious beliefs.

Mayflower II, moored at State Pier only a minute's walk north of Plymouth Rock, was built in England in 1955 and sailed the Atlantic to Plymouth in 1957.

Plimoth Plantation

During the winter of 1620–21, half of the Pilgrims died of disease, privation and exposure to the elements. But the survivors were joined by new arrivals in 1621, and by 1627, just before an additional influx of Pilgrims founded the colony of Massachusetts

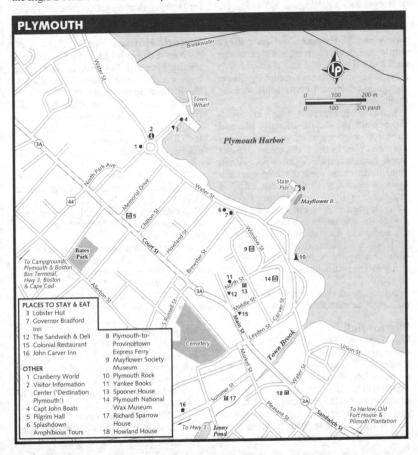

PLYMOUTH

PLACES TO STAY & EAT
3 Lobster Hut
7 Governor Bradford Inn
12 The Sandwich & Deli
15 Colonial Restaurant
16 John Carver Inn

OTHER
1 Cranberry World
2 Visitor Information Center ('Destination Plymouth')
4 Capt John Boats
5 Pilgrim Hall
6 Splashdown Amphibious Tours

8 Plymouth-to-Provincetown Express Ferry
9 Mayflower Society Museum
10 Plymouth Rock
11 Yankee Books
13 Spooner House
14 Plymouth National Wax Museum
17 Richard Sparrow House
18 Howland House

Bay, Plymouth colony was sturdily built and on the road to prosperity.

The Plimoth Plantation (☎ *508-746-1622, MA 3A; adult/child $20/12; see combination tickets prices under* Mayflower II; *open 9am-5pm daily Apr-Nov*), a mile or so south of Plymouth Rock, authentically re-creates the Pilgrim's 1627 settlement. Everything in the village – costumes, implements, vocabulary, artistry, recipes and crops – has been painstakingly researched and remade. Even the animals have been bred to be very similar to those which the Pilgrims had. You can see them in Nye Barn.

Hobbamock's (Wampanoag) Homesite replicates the life of a Native American community in the same area at the same time. While the Homesite huts are made of wattle and daub (a framework of woven rods and twigs covered and plastered with clay), the inhabitants occupying them engage in traditional crafts while wearing traditional garb.

Costumed interpreters, acting in character, explain the details of daily life and answer your questions as you watch them work and play. In the crafts center, artisans weave baskets and cloth, throw pottery and build fine furniture using the techniques and tools of the early 17th century. Exhibits explain how these manufactured goods were shipped across the Atlantic in exchange for colonial necessities. An interactive audio and video exhibit, 'Irreconcilable Difference,' illuminates the contrasts between a 'typical' Native American woman and a Pilgrim woman living between 1627 and 1690.

A picnic area, bakery and several restaurants provide modern sustenance.

Pilgrim Hall

This 1824 museum (☎ *508-746-1620, 75 Court St; adult/senior/child $5/4.50/3; open 9:30am-4:30pm daily Feb-Dec*) boasts that it is the oldest continually operating public museum in the USA. Its exhibits are not re-productions, but the real things the Pilgrims and their Wampanoag neighbors used in their daily lives, right down to Miles Standish's sword. Monumental paintings in the museum's collection depict scenes of everyday Pilgrim life.

Plymouth National Wax Museum

This museum (☎ *508-746-6468, 16 Carver St; adult/child 5-12 $6/75¢; open 9am-5pm daily Mar & Apr; 9am-7pm daily May & June, Sept & Oct; 9am-9pm daily July & Aug*), across the street and up the hill from Plymouth Rock, is a good place to give children a sense of Pilgrim history. The life-size wax figures – 180 in 26 scenes – show the progress of the Pilgrims as they left England for Holland, then set sail for, and arrived in, America.

Historic Houses

As New England's oldest European community, Plymouth has its share of fine old houses, some very old indeed. The oldest is the **Richard Sparrow House** (☎ *508-747-1240, 42 Summer St; adult/child $2/1; open 10am-5pm Thur-Tues Apr-late Dec*), built by one of the original Pilgrim settlers in 1640. There aren't many houses like this remaining in the US and it'd be a shame to miss it.

The 1667 **Howland House** (☎ *508-746-9590, 33 Sandwich St; adult/senior & student/child $4/3/2; open 10am-4:30pm daily late May-mid-Oct*) was originally the residence for an immigrant family that came over on the *Mayflower*.

The **Mayflower Society Museum** (☎ *508-746-2590, 4 Winslow St; adult/child $4/1; open 10am-4pm daily July-early Sept; 10am-4pm Sat-Sun late May-June & early Sept-mid-Oct*) dates from 1754 and shows how wealthy the town of Plymouth became in a little more than a century. Note especially the house's flying staircase.

The 1677 **Harlow Old Fort House** (☎ *508-746-0012; 119 Sandwich St; adult/child $4/2; open 10am-3pm Mon-Fri July-Aug*) is staffed with costumed interpreters who'll describe how the second generation of Plymouth colonists lived.

The 1747 **Spooner House** (☎ *508-746-0012; 27 North St; adult/child $4/2; open 10am-4pm Thur-Sat June-early Oct*) was occupied by the same family for more than two centuries, which accounts in part for its very rich collection of period furnishings.

Cranberry World

Soon after the Pilgrims arrived, they discovered the tart red berries that filled the sandy bogs near Plymouth and south to Cape Cod. Cranberries made it onto that first Thanksgiving menu and have been there ever since. You can learn all about the sour, yet appealing and healthful, fruit at Cranberry World (☎ 508-747-2350, 158 Water St; adult/child $2/free; open 9:30am-5pm daily May-Nov), near the rotary and town wharf. Sample cranberry refreshments are free.

Organized Tours

Whale-watching cruises on **Capt John Boats** (☎ 508-746-2643, 800-242-2469, Town Wharf; adult/senior/child $27/22/17; tours Apr-Oct) leave the harbor at least once daily during the summer for a four-hour whale-watching cruise. During the educational and fun trip, an onboard marine biologist explains the differences between the humpback, finback, minke, right and pilot whales you may encounter. The outfit has a 99% sighting record.

Splashdown Amphibious Tours (☎ 508-747-7658, 800-225-4000, Harbor Place; adult/child 3-12 yrs/child under 3 yrs $17/10/3; tours daily mid-May-Sept, Sat & Sun mid-Apr-mid-May & Oct) utilize authentic WWII beach-assault vehicles to transport modern-day out-of-towners. You can't miss the behemoths rolling through the town's historic district and plunging into the harbor for a continuation of the hour-long tour. Exact departure times are tide-dependent, so you'll have to call.

Places to Stay

The Plymouth area offers a broad range of accommodations, but you'll want to reserve early for a summer stopover.

Camping There are plenty of scenic and commercial camping options in the surrounding area.

Myles Standish State Forest (☎ 508-866-2526, 877-422-6762 reservations mid-May-early Sept, Cranberry Rd) Sites $12. Open for camping mid-Apr-mid-Oct; park open year-round. This closest state facility is about 6 miles south of Plymouth. Take MA 3 exit 5 or MA 58 to South Carver and look for Standish signs. Within the 16,000-acre park are 15 miles of biking and hiking trails, nine ponds (two with beaches and one with a bathhouse) and 400 campsites. Campsites right on water's edge are a little more expensive.

Wompatuck State Park (☎ 781-749-7160, 877-422-6762 reservations late May-early Sept, Free St) Sites without/with electricity $12/15. Open for camping mid-Apr-mid-Oct; park open year-round. From Boston, take MA 3 to exit 14 in Hingham and head 5 miles north on MA 228 to the park. It's about 30 miles north of Plymouth. The 2900-acre park has 262 campsites, 12 miles of paved biking trails and even more mountain-biking and hiking trails.

Pinewood Lodge Campground (☎ 508-746-3548, 190 Pinewood Rd) Sites without/with hookups $20/30. Open May-Oct. Off US 44 in Plymouth, this campground has 160 sites and is among the closest to the town center.

Sandy Pond Campground (☎ 508-759-9336, 834 Bourne Rd) Sites without/with hookups $22/26. Open mid-Apr-Sept. This establishment has 80 sites with water and electricity, 25 for tents, two sandy beaches and hiking trails. From Boston take MA 3 south to exit 3, bear right, then turn left onto Long Pond Rd and follow signs.

Plymouth Rock KOA Kampground (☎ 508-947-6435, Plymouth St, Middleboro) Sites without/with hookups $26/31.50. Open Mar-Nov. This developed campground is farther away than Sandy Pond or Pinewood and has upwards of 400 sites. From Boston take I-93 south to MA 24 south to I-495 south to exit 6 (US 44 west) and follow signs.

Motels Across the street from the entrance to Plimoth Plantation is *Pilgrim Sands Motel* (☎ 508-747-0900, 800-729-7263, fax 508-746-8066, Ⓦ www.pilgrimsands.com, 150 Warren Ave) Doubles $70-130 off-season, $118-160 mid-June-mid-Oct. Open year-round. This typically appointed, basic motel has 64 rooms. It's the only motel with a private beach, which is sandy at low tide.

Governor Bradford Inn (☎ 508-746-6200, 800-332-1620, fax 508-747-3032, ⓦ *www .governorbradford.com, 98 Water St)* Doubles $79-149 off-season, $109-179 late June-late Aug. Open year-round. Smack in the middle of town, these 94 rooms are convenient. Rooms with sea views are at the high end of the rate range.

John Carver Inn (☎ 508-746-7100, 800-274-1620, fax 508-746-8299, ⓦ *www.john carverinn.com, 25 Summer St)* Doubles $99-169 off-season, $139-209 early June-late Oct. Open year-round. This 85-room establishment has four categories of rooms, and both smoking and nonsmoking. Suites are more expensive than the rooms quoted above.

B&Bs Around the corner from Plimoth Plantation and about a mile from town is *Foxglove Cottage* (☎ 508-747-6576, 800-479-4746, fax 508-747-7622, ⓦ *www.foxglove cottage.com, 101 Sandwich Rd)* Doubles $115 ($95 for multinight stays) with full breakfast. Open year-round, this renovated early-19th-century B&B has three rooms, each with a working fireplace and each decorated with the utmost care. The back deck and living room provide ample common space. To find the B&B, head out of town along Sandwich St, which inexplicably turns into Sandwich Rd.

Places to Eat

Fast-food shops line Water St opposite the *Mayflower II*. For better food at lower prices, walk a block inland to Main St, the attractive thoroughfare of Plymouth's business district, where restaurants are open year-round.

The Sandwich & Deli (☎ 508-746-7773, *65 Main St)* Dishes $4-6. Open for breakfast and lunch. This deli, at North St, has clam chowder and BLTs for $3.75. Huge reuben and pastrami sandwiches are $5.75, and many other quick-lunch plates are priced in between.

Colonial Restaurant (☎ 508-746-0838, *39 Main St)* Dishes $4-11. There's no atmos-

phere to speak of, but the portions are healthy and the seafood fresh. Locals swear by it. Try the fish cakes ($6.75).

Lobster Hut (☎ 508-746-2270, *Town Wharf)* Mains $6-18. Right on the town wharf, five short blocks north of *Mayflower II*, the seaside Lobster Hut has big plates of fried clams (market price) and fish and chips ($7). Most lunch sandwiches and platters are in the $4 to $10 range. Seating is both indoors and out.

Getting There & Away

Bus Plymouth & Brockton buses (☎ 508-746-0378, 778-9767) connect Boston with Plymouth (one hour; $9 one-way) and Hyannis (45 minutes; $6 one-way); service is quite frequent. The P&B terminal is at the visitor center, exit 5 off MA 3. From there catch a Greater Attleboro Taunton Regional Transit Authority (GATRA) bus (75¢) to the center of town, about 2 miles away.

You can reach Plymouth from Boston by MBTA commuter trains (☎ 617-222-3200, 800-392-6100). From the station at Cordage Park, GATRA buses connect to Plymouth Center. One-way tickets are $5.

Car Plymouth is 41 miles south of Boston via MA 3; it takes an hour with some traffic. From Providence, it's the same distance and time, but you'll want to head west on US 44.

Boat The Plymouth-to-Provincetown Express Ferry (☎ 508-747-2400, 800-242-2469, State Pier) operated by the ubiquitous Capt John Boats, deposits you on the tip of the Cape faster than if you drove. The 90-minute journey departs Plymouth at 10am and leaves Provincetown at 4:30pm. During the summer (mid-June to early September), service is daily. Late May to mid-June and for most of September, the ferry also runs on the weekend, with additional service on Tuesday and Wednesday in September. Roundtrip ferry tickets cost adult/senior/child $25/22/18; bikes cost an additional $3.

NEW BEDFORD

During its heyday as a whaling port (1765–1860), New Bedford commanded as many as 400 whaling ships. This vast fleet brought home hundreds of thousands of barrels of whale oil for lighting America's lamps. So famous was the town's whaling industry that Herman Melville set his great American novel, *Moby-Dick; or, The Whale*, in New Bedford. (At the time, he lived in Pittsfield, MA.) If you're interested in whaling history, this is the place to find it.

When petroleum and electricity supplanted whale oil, New Bedford turned to fishing, scalloping and textile production for its wealth. In the early 20th century, the textile industry headed south, then offshore, in search of cheaper labor, and in recent years New England's Atlantic fishing grounds have been exploited to near extinction, so New Bedford is again in search of a source of wealth.

The city, with a population of 94,000, gets its share of bad press like any city its size. But the city center, complete with cobblestone streets and gas lanterns and designated a National Historical Park in late 1996, is really worth a look.

Orientation & Information

The heart of the old city center is the restored historic district around Melville Mall. The area is about a mile south of I-195 via MA 18 (take the downtown exit 18S). At the first set of lights, take a right and park in the municipal garage on the right. Parking is cheap. The National Historical Park visitor center is one block away.

The New Bedford Whaling National Historical Park Visitor Center (☎ 508-996-4095, 33 William St, New Bedford, MA 02740) is open 9am to 5pm daily. Highly recommended walking tours are offered twice daily in July and August.

The waterfront New Bedford Office of Tourism (☎ 508-979-1745, 800-508-5353, W www.ci.new-bedford.ma.us, Wharfinger Building, Pier 3, New Bedford, MA 02740) provides general and lodging information; it's open 9am to 5pm weekdays and 10am to 4pm weekends. Staff can also tell you about the Whaling City Festival in mid-July. Pick up a self-guided brochure for the 'dock walk,' which orients you to the working harbor.

Whaling Museum

The New Bedford Whaling Museum (☎ 508-997-0046, 18 Johnny Cake Hill; adult/senior/child 6-14 yrs $6/5/4; open 9am-5pm daily), which recently underwent a $10 million renovation project, encompasses seven buildings situated between William and Union Sts. To learn what whaling was all about, you need only tramp the decks of the *Lagoda*, a fully rigged, half-size replica of an actual whaling bark. The onboard tryworks (a brick furnace where try-pots are placed) converted huge chunks of whale blubber into valuable oil. Old photographs and a 22-minute video of an actual whale chase bring this historic period to life. Don't ignore a new 66-foot blue-whale skeleton and the 100-foot-long mural depicting sperm whales or the exhibits of delicate scrimshaw, the carving of whalebone into jewelry, notions and beautiful household items.

Seamen's Bethel

This small chapel (☎ 508-992-3295, 15 Johnny Cake Hill; admission free, donations accepted; open 10am-5pm Mon-Fri late May–mid-Oct), across from the Whaling Museum, was a refuge for sailors from the rigors and stresses of the maritime life. Melville, who suffered from terrible conditions aboard a whaling ship, immortalized it in *Moby-Dick*.

New Bedford Fire Museum

Antique fire trucks and fire-fighting equipment fill this century-old building (☎ 508-992-2162, 51 Bedford St; adult/child $3/2; open 9am-4pm Mon-Sat July-early Sept). Recently expanded into an adjacent, former fire station at 6th St, the museum appeals to children, who love the old trucks, uniforms, pumps and fire poles.

Rotch-Jones-Duff House & Garden Museum

New Bedford's most grand historic house (☎ 508-997-1401, 396 County St; adult/senior/child 4-12 yrs $4/3/2; open 10am-4pm daily Apr-Dec; 10am-4pm Tues-Sun Jan-Mar) was designed in Greek revival style in 1834 by Richard Upjohn (1802–1878), first president of the American Institute of Architects. The English-born architect later rebuilt New York's Trinity Church (1839). You can wander or tour the grand house.

Places to Stay & Eat

Historic New Bedford offers plenty of eateries, but it is not thick with lodging possibilities. New Bedford Office of Tourism (☎ 508-979-1745, 800-508-5353, ⓦ www.ci .new-bedford.ma.us) can direct you to places to stay in the surrounding area.

The Melville House (☎ 508-990-1566, ⓦ www.melvillehouse.net, 100 Madison St) Doubles $135 with organic continental breakfast. Herman Melville often visited his sister at this 1855 Victorian manse. The current owner rents two bedrooms and conducts an alternative healing practice from here.

Antonio's (☎ 508-990-3636, 267 Coggeshall St) Mains $6-15. Don't miss this hopping taverna, just a block off I-195 in New Bedford's North End, if you want authentic Portuguese cuisine. Paella ($26 for two) will transport you to Lagos and Sintra.

Freestone's City Grille (☎ 508-993-7477, 41 Williams St) Lunch $7-10, dinner $14-19. Standing almost right next to the national park visitor center, Freestone's offers 'gay '90s' ambiance in a reclaimed bank building complete with a stained glass mirror and a brass monkey. You get an upscale pub menu with items like herbed roast beef wrapper ($7.50) and grilled sea scallops ($16).

The Candleworks Restaurant (☎ 508-997-1294, 72 N Water St) Lunch $8-11. Here's a chic spot in a restored brick candle factory. You can eat in the cool cellar or under the umbrellas on the patio. The lunch menu offers dinner-size portions at half the price. We like the shrimp candleworks ($9), sautéed in garlic, pepper and a Mozambique sauce.

Getting There & Away

American Eagle (☎ 508-993-5040) operates between New Bedford (cnr Elm and Pleasant Sts) and Boston's South Station ($10 one-way, $18 return), with frequent weekday

service and buses about every four hours on weekends.

New Bedford is 15 miles from Fall River via I-195. It's another 25 miles via I-195 to Cape Cod's Bourne Bridge.

The Steamship Authority (☎ 508-997-1688, ⓦ www.islandferry.com, Billy Wood's Wharf, 1494 E Rodney French Blvd) operates a passenger ferry between New Bedford and Oak Bluffs on Martha's Vineyard. The service runs mid-May to September. In the summer, there are three daily voyages in each direction (1½ hours; adult/child/bike $20/10/10 roundtrip). From I-195, take exit 15 to MA 18 south. Continue on MA 18 to the fourth set of lights, turn left and follow signs 0.8 mile to Billy Wood's Wharf and the ferry. Parking is $10. At time of writing, political wrangling between the Steamship Authority board and city cast New Bedford passenger service into question for the 2002 season. With a little luck, the repairing of egos and the healing of turf wars, there will be both regular and high-speed ferry service.

FALL RIVER

Fall River has a good harbor, rivers for water power and a humid climate that's well suited to working woolen thread, so it was natural that it became one of New England's most important textile production centers during the 19th century. Thousands of tons of the local granite were hewn to build the huge textile mills that are still the most prominent feature of Fall River's cityscape. But Fall River was the victim of its own success. Industrial wealth led to inflation and higher costs. After the turn of the 20th century, the textile trade moved to cheaper labor markets in the southern states and then moved overseas, leaving Fall River's great textile mills empty.

Today, the great granite buildings are busy again. Fall River has become an off-price shopping mecca, the 'largest factory-outlet shopping center in New England,' as the signs say. Most of the spacious mills are again filled with textiles – goods not made here, but imported from Asia and Latin America.

Factory Outlet Stores

The concept of the factory outlet store began a century ago when flawed, but still usable, products would be sold to locals at very low prices. Today, prices often are much the same as in city department stores and specialty shops. But in Fall River, cheap rents in the old mills allow manufacturers to pass on savings to consumers. Over 100 merchants have set up shop in the mills, selling everything from cut-price jeans to designer dresses that are a little out of fashion. You'll find accessories, baskets, books, candy and nuts, carpets, children's clothing, cosmetics, crystal and glass, curtains, furniture, gift wrap and greeting cards, kitchenware, leather goods, linens, lingerie, luggage, toys, raincoats and overcoats, shoes, sweaters, ties, towels and even wallpaper. You can easily reach the outlets via I-195 (they are visible from the road).

Battleship Cove

Take I-195 exit 5 at the Braga Bridge, then follow the signs to Battleship Cove (☎ *508-678-1100, 800-533-3194, 1 Water St; adult/senior/child $10/8/5; open 9am-5pm daily)*, a quiet corner of Mt Hope Bay that holds well-preserved WWII-era vessels that you can visit. The 46,000-ton battleship USS *Massachusetts*, longer than two football fields and taller than a nine-story building, carried a crew of 2300 and was the first and last battleship to fire her 16-inch guns in WWII. The USS *Joseph P Kennedy, Jr*, named for President John F Kennedy's older brother, did battle in the Korean and Vietnam Wars and is now a museum. The USS *Lionfish* is a WWII submarine still in full working condition. There are also two PT boats, a landing craft, a Japanese attack boat and other craft. Food is available at the site. You can even dine in the *Massachusetts'* wardroom if you like.

Just past the battleship, the **Marine Museum** at Fall River (☎ *508-674-3533, 70 Water St; adult/senior/child $5/4/4; open 9am-5pm Mon-Sat, 9am-4pm Sun)* is especially strong in intricate ship models, including a scale model of the Titanic that was used in the 1950s movie on the subject.

Cape Cod

'The Cape,' as it is universally called by locals, is among New England's favorite summer vacation destinations and it thrives on tourism. Vacationers come in search of fresh seafood (commercial fishing still contributes to the economy) and to enjoy the beaches that cover much of the Cape's 400 miles of shore. There is real New England beauty in the Cape's dune-studded landscapes cloaked in scrub oak and pine, in its fine stands of tall sea grass, and in the grace and dignity of its colonial towns.

History

Mariner Bartholomew Gosnold (1572–1607) sailed the New England coast in 1602, naming natural features as he went. He gave the name Cape Cod to the sandy, 65-mile-long peninsula that juts eastward from mainland Massachusetts into the Atlantic.

When the Pilgrims first set foot in the New World in November 1620, it was at the site of Provincetown, at the tip of Cape Cod. They rested only long enough to draw up rules of governance (the Mayflower Compact) before setting sail westward in search of a more congenial place for their settlement, which they found at Plymouth. Later settlers stayed on the Cape, founding fishing villages along the coasts. The fishing industry drew boat builders and salt makers. Soon there were farmers working the cranberry bogs as well, and whaling ships bringing home rich cargoes of oil and whalebone.

In the mid-19th century, Henry David Thoreau made a walking tour of Cape Cod, reporting on the peninsula just before it became a popular summer vacation destination for wealthy families from Boston and Providence. In 1879, Cape Cod was connected to Europe by an undersea telephone cable, which ran from Orleans to Brest, France, a distance of 4000 miles. Early in the next century, Guglielmo Marconi (1874–1937) set up a wireless telegraph station on the beach in South Wellfleet to communicate with Great Britain.

Highlights

- Watching the sunrise over Nobska Lighthouse in Woods Hole
- Biking the Cape Cod Rail Trail
- Clambering across the dunes at Cape Cod National Seashore
- Taking an airplane ride above the Outer Cape
- Eating oysters and other delicacies in Wellfleet
- People-watching and gallery-hopping in Provincetown
- Exploring Chatham's Monomoy Island, accessible only by boat

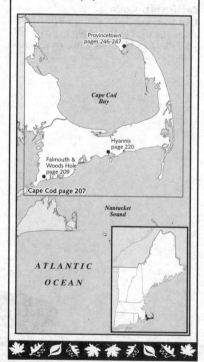

At the beginning of the 20th century, the US government financed construction of the Cape Cod Canal (1909–14), which joined Buzzards Bay and Cape Cod Bay, cutting long hours off voyages between Boston and Providence or New York. It also cut off Cape Cod from the mainland, making Cape Cod an island.

Information

You can get Cape-wide information at the Massachusetts Tourist Information Center (☎ 508-746-1150) in Plymouth at exit 5 off MA 3 (for those heading from Boston to

Cape Cod). The well-stocked and staffed building is open at least 8:30am to 4:30pm daily year-round. For those coming from the south or west, the Cape Cod Chamber of Commerce's satellite office (☎ 508-759-3814), 3 miles east of the Bourne Bridge on MA 25, is open 9am to 5pm daily year-round, with varied longer hours mid-May to mid-October.

Once on Cape Cod, stop in at the main Cape Cod Chamber of Commerce information office (☎ 508-862-0700, 800-332-2732, W www.capecodchamber.com) just off US 6 at exit 6 in Hyannis. In addition, all towns have their own information bureaus.

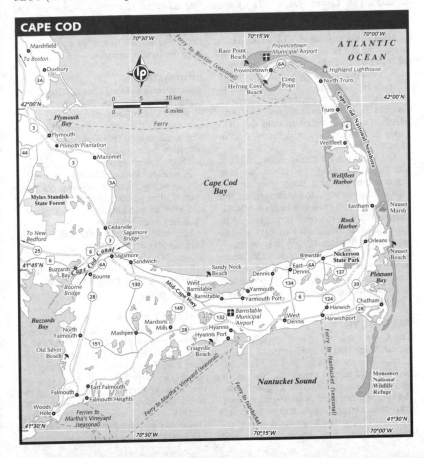

CAPE COD

Getting There & Around

The Sagamore (northeast) and Bourne (southwest) Bridges span the Cape Cod Canal, linking mainland Massachusetts to the Cape. Take the Bourne Bridge if your destination is Falmouth and Woods Hole (or Martha's Vineyard). Use the Sagamore Bridge for the rest of the Cape. The bridges are only 4 miles apart via US 6.

Locals use a somewhat confusing nomenclature for the various Cape Cod districts. The 'Upper Cape' is nearest the canal and the mainland. 'Mid-Cape' extends from Barnstable and Hyannis eastward to Orleans. The 'Lower' (or 'Outer') Cape extends north and east from Orleans to Provincetown.

Main roads include MA 28, which heads south from the Bourne Bridge to Falmouth, where it takes a sharp turn east and runs along the southern edge of the Cape through Hyannis and into Chatham, where it takes a northern jog before it ends in Orleans. Between Falmouth and Chatham, MA 28 is overbuilt with strip malls, fast-food joints and motels; it's quite congested in summer.

The Cape's main transit route is US 6, also called the Mid-Cape Hwy, a four-lane divided highway that stays more or less inland from the canal to Orleans, where the Cape begins to narrow as it heads north. Although US 6 is the only through-road to Provincetown, traffic on this part of it is usually free-flowing, if heavy in summer.

MA 6A, the highly recommended alternative to the Mid-Cape Hwy, is a rural and scenic two-lane road between Sandwich and Orleans, offering occasional views of Cape Cod Bay.

FALMOUTH

The Cape's second-largest town, a year-round town that is quite spread out, is known for its village green, Main St, beaches and nature preserves. Nothing is more quintessentially 'New England' than the village green here: A white picket fence surrounds a large triangle of grass bordered by fine 19th-century houses and a Congregational church with a white steeple. The church's bell was cast in 1796 by patriot Paul Revere. Main St has some nice shops, and the green is a nice place for a picnic. Get off the main drag, too, and explore the back roads near Quissett Harbor and Sippewissett, west of MA 28.

Orientation

MA 28 leads to Main St and the town green, the center of activity for inns, dining and shopping. Farther east on MA 28, college students flock to the Falmouth Heights area on Grand Ave and Falmouth Heights Rd, known for sweeping ocean views and beachside activities. The town's best beach, Old Silver Beach, is 5 miles north of town, off leafy and tranquil MA 28A. Party boats and passenger ferries to the Vineyard depart from the Inner Harbor.

Information

The main office of the Falmouth Chamber of Commerce (☎ 508-548-8500, 800-526-8532, Ⓦ www.falmouth-capecod.com, 20 Academy Lane), off Main St, is open 8:30am to 5pm weekdays year-round. It's also open Saturday from mid-May to mid-October and on Sunday from June to early September.

A smaller office at 320 Palmer Ave (on MA 28 barely north of the town center) is open 8:30am to 5pm Monday to Saturday mid-May to mid-October and on Sunday from July to early September.

Falmouth Hospital (☎ 508-548-5300, 100 Terheun Dr), off MA 28 just north of town, is open 24 hours a day.

The independent Booksmith (☎ 508-540-6064), in Falmouth Plaza off MA 28, has all the right titles.

Historic Houses

The Falmouth Historical Society's **Museums on the Green** (☎ 508-548-4857, 55-65 Palmer Ave; adult & child over 12 yrs $4; open 10am-4pm Tues-Sun mid-June–Aug, 10am-1pm Sat & Sun early Sept-early Nov) operates two historic buildings just off the town green. In addition to scrimshaw and 18th-century sailors' valentines, the Conant House has a room dedicated to Katherine Lee Bates, the town resident who wrote the

FALMOUTH & WOODS HOLE

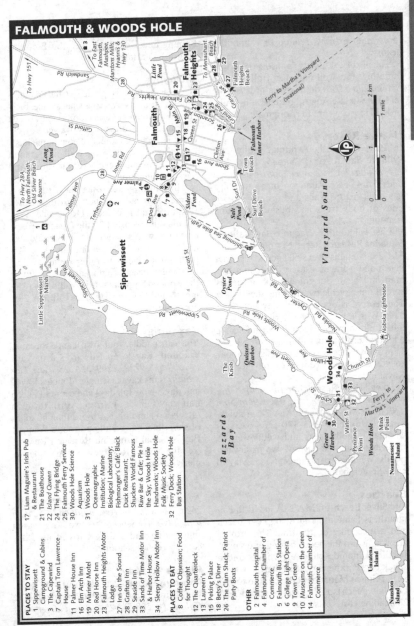

PLACES TO STAY
1 Sippewissett
  Campground & Cabins
7 The Capewind
7 Captain Tom Lawrence
  House
11 Palmer House Inn
16 Elm Arch Inn
19 Mariner Motel
20 Red Horse Inn
23 Falmouth Heights Motor
  Lodge
27 Inn on the Sound
28 Grafton Inn
29 Seaside Inn
33 Sands of Time Motor Inn
  & Harbor House
34 Sleepy Hollow Motor Inn

PLACES TO EAT
8 Coffee Obsession; Food
  for Thought
12 The Quarterdeck
13 Laureen's
15 Peking Palace
18 Betsy's Diner
26 The Clam Shack; Patriot
  Party Boats

17 Liam Maguire's Irish Pub
  & Restaurant
21 The Boathouse
22 Island Queen
24 The Flying Bridge
25 Falmouth Ferry Service
30 Woods Hole Science
  Aquarium
31 Woods Hole
  Oceanographic
  Institution; Marine
  Biological Laboratory;
  Fishmonger's Café; Black
  Duck Restaurant;
  Shuckers World Famous
  Raw Bar & Cafe; Pie in
  the Sky; Woods Hole
  Handworks; Woods Hole
  Folk Music Society
32 Ferry Dock; Woods Hole
  Bus Station

OTHER
2 Falmouth Hospital
4 Falmouth Chamber of
  Commerce
5 Falmouth Bus Station
6 College Light Opera
9 Town Green
10 Museums on the Green
14 Falmouth Chamber of
  Commerce

popular patriotic hymn 'America the Beautiful.' Next door, the Julia Wood House features quiet exhibits related to Falmouth's history.

The historical society sponsors richly illuminating and well-narrated **trolley tours** (adult/child $12/8) on many Saturdays from mid-June to late August. Inquire at the Julia Wood House, where they originate.

Nature Reserves

In East Falmouth, **Ashumet Holly and Wildlife Sanctuary** (☎ 508-362-1426, MA 151; adult/child $3/2; open sunrise to sunset daily), a 45-acre Audubon bird sanctuary, has eight nature trails and dozens of varieties of holly trees and bushes. It's quite tranquil.

East Falmouth's **Waquoit Bay National Estuarine Research Reserve** (☎ 508-457-0495, MA 28) contains over 2500 acres of barrier beach and a fragile estuary. Pick up a trail map and head out for a walk or simply spread out a picnic overlooking the estuary. The reserve is open during daylight hours daily. With a bit of advance planning (permits are required), you might wish to camp on Washburn Island, within the reserve. The 11 primitive sites are only accessible by boat, so you'd have to rent a canoe (see the Kayaking section).

Lowell Holly Reservation (no ☎, off Sandwich Rd; admission free; open 9am-5pm daily), off MA 130 from MA 28 in neighboring Mashpee, is a 130-acre oasis of woodlands, holly trees and wildflowers. A trail runs along the edge of two freshwater ponds. Weekend parking is $6 late May to early September.

Beaches

Old Silver Beach, off MA 28A in North Falmouth, is Falmouth's most popular beach and a nice bike destination. The crowds are young and the beach is long and sandy. Facilities include changing rooms and a snack bar. Parking costs $10 daily.

Parking at **Menauhant Beach** (the town's best bay beach), off Central Ave from MA 28 heading east, costs $10.

Surf Drive Beach, off Main St, is popular with kayakers and accessible from the Shining Sea Bike Path (see the Bicycling section). Parking costs $10.

Bicycling

Because the town is spread out and summertime car traffic slows to a snail's pace, bicycling here makes sense. Additionally, beach 'entrance' fees are usually waived for cyclists. The local chamber of commerce has a bicycling route map as well as detailed information on bicycle rental shops and parking regulations.

The **Shining Sea Bike Path** follows a former railroad bed between downtown Falmouth and Woods Hole. The very popular and pleasant 7-mile (roundtrip) excursion rewards peddlers with some ocean and lighthouse views along the way. This path also connects to other routes leading to smaller beaches and harbors, including the wooded Sippewissett area and West Falmouth and Quissett Harbors (off MA 28A north of town).

Kayaking

You can paddle your own canoe, because **Waquoit Kayak** at Edward's Boatyard (☎ 508-548-9722, 1209 MA 28, East Falmouth) rents kayaks (singles/doubles $30/40 half day, $45/55 full day) and canoes ($40/55 half day/full day) from April through October. Falmouth has more than 60 miles of shoreline, but paddling around Waquoit Bay National Estuarine Research Reserve (see the Nature Reserves section) is particularly rewarding.

Cruises

Avast, there. **Patriot Party Boats** (☎ 508-548-2626, 227 Clinton Ave; adult/child $25/20; trips July-early Sept) offers two-hour coastal sightseeing and sailing trips in an 18th-century replica schooner.

Places to Stay

Camping About 2 miles north of town, you'll find *Sippewissett Campground & Cabins* (☎ 508-548-2542, 836 Palmer Ave)

Sites without/with hookups $30/32; cabins $220-425 weekly off-season, $325-575 July-Aug. Open mid-May–mid-Oct. Off MA 28, this 13-acre place has 125 wooded campsites and 11 camping cabins. Although the campground caters to RVs, tenters are also happy campers. Bonuses include a free beach and Vineyard ferry shuttle.

Motels A five-minute walk from the center of town is the *Mariner Motel* (☎ 508-548-1331, 800-233-2939, W www.marinermotel .com, 555 Main St) Doubles $49-119 off-season, $89-139 July-Aug. Open year-round. This motel has an outdoor pool and 30 motel-style rooms with refrigerators.

Falmouth Heights Motor Lodge (☎ 508-548-3623, 800-468-3623, fax 508-548-3623, W www.falmouthheightsmotel.com, 146 Falmouth Heights Rd) Doubles $55-104 off-season, $105-150 late June-early Sept. Open May-Oct. A mile from the center of town and within walking distance of the beach and Vineyard ferry, this 24-room motor lodge also has a few studios with kitchenettes.

Seaside Inn (☎ 508-540-4120, fax 508-548-5653, W www.seasideinnfalmouth.com, 263 Grand Ave S) Doubles $49-109 off-season, $105-225 June-early Sept. Open year-round. These 23 newly renovated rooms and efficiencies are within a stone's throw of the beach. Prices are determined by your answers to the following questions: Do you want a balcony, a limited or full ocean view, a view of the parking lot, a kitchenette, a weekend or a weekday stay?

The Capewind (☎ 508-548-3400, 800-267-3401, fax 508-495-0316, W www.capewind .com, 34 Maravista Extension) Doubles $70-110 off-season, $115-150 July-Aug. Open Apr-Oct. Off MA 28 about 2 miles east of Falmouth village green, these 32 rooms and efficiencies have a more secluded location than most and overlook a salt pond.

Red Horse Inn (☎ 508-548-0053, 800-628-3811, fax 508-540-6563, W www.redhorse inn.com, 28 Falmouth Heights Rd) Doubles $110-135 off-season, $152-184 July-Aug. Open May-Oct. A mere five-minute walk to the island ferries, this motel entices cus-

tomers with free parking during your Vineyard stay. The 22 standard-issue rooms have requisite refrigerators.

B&Bs Dating to the early 19th century is the rambling *Elm Arch Inn* (☎ 508-548-0133, 26 Elm Arch Way) Doubles $80-90 off-season, $100-125 mid-June–mid-Sept. Open Apr-Oct. It has 20 colonial-style guest rooms (many with shared bath and all with an in-room sink), lots of common rooms and a pool. There's a modern annex, too. Pricier rooms have TVs. Credit cards are not accepted.

Captain Tom Lawrence House (☎ 508-540-1445, 800-266-8139, fax 508-457-1790, W www.captaintomlawrence.com, 75 Locust St) Doubles $90-130 off-season, $135-170 May-Oct, with full breakfast. Open year-round. This unpretentious B&B, with six guest rooms, is thankfully set back from the road to Woods Hole. A separate apartment, well suited to families, rents for $260 for four people.

Palmer House Inn (☎ 508-548-1230, 800-472-2632, fax 508-540-1878, W www.palmer houseinn.com, 81 Palmer Ave) Doubles $90-199 off-season, $140-225 mid-June–mid-Oct, with full breakfast. Open year-round. This early-19th-century Victorian house has 17 luxurious rooms decorated with heavy period antiques. Service includes amenities like nightly turn-down and triple sheeting.

Inn on the Sound (☎ 508-457-9666, 800-564-9668, fax 508-457-9631, W www.innon thesound.com, 313 Grand Ave S) Doubles $125-250 off-season, $150-295 May-Oct, with expanded continental breakfast buffet. Open year-round. Across from the beach, Falmouth's nicest place exudes a simple, breezy beach elegance. The 10 rooms, many with private decks, are contemporary and stylish.

Grafton Inn (☎ 508-540-8688, 800-642-4069, fax 508-540-1861, W www.graftoninn .com, 261 Grand Ave S) Doubles $110-169 off-season, $169-250 mid-May–Oct, with full buffet breakfast. Open Mar-early Dec. Also across from the beach, Grafton Inn has 10 lacy rooms with TV.

MASSACHUSETTS

Places to Eat

The java is strong at **Coffee Obsession** (☎ 508-540-2233, 110 Palmer Ave) Open 6am-7:30pm daily. 'Coffee O,' an alternative place with communal newspapers, is great for hanging out and sipping coffee drinks.

Laureen's (☎ 508-540-9104, 170 Main St) Dishes $6-10. Open 8:30am-5pm Mon-Sat year-round. This upscale deli has fancy sandwiches, cold pasta salads, veggie burritos, rich desserts and good coffee.

Food for Thought (☎ 508-548-4498, 37 N Main St) Dishes $3-10. Open for breakfast & lunch year-round; call ahead for hours. The eclectic menu highlights real French omelets, blintzes, smoked salmon plates and such. Lunch ranges from burgers, soups and Mexican dishes to an excellent vegetarian eggplant parmesan.

Betsy's Diner (☎ 508-540-0060, 457 Main St) Breakfast and lunch $2-8, dinner mains average $6-7. Open for all meals daily. Betsy's is always crowded with locals who appreciate large portions of no-frills, inexpensive old-fashioned American fare.

Peking Palace (☎ 508-540-8204, 452 Main St) Dishes $6-10. If you're tired of eating fish, this restaurant serves remarkably good Cantonese, Szechuan and Mandarin dishes.

The Clam Shack (☎ 508-540-7758, 227 Clinton Ave) Prices fluctuate with the market. This is a classic of the genre: tiny, with picnic tables on the back deck and lots of fried clams and such.

The Quarterdeck (☎ 508-548-9900, 164 Main St) Lunch $7.50-12, dinner $12-22. A year-round tavern with barnboard walls, the Quarterdeck has a deservedly popular local following. Try the fish-and-chips, the daily seafood special or the traditional baked seafood platter.

Chapoquoit Grill (☎ 508-540-7794, 410 MA 28A) Dinner mains $7-18. A few miles north of town, this place has excellent pizzas loaded with garlic and even better nightly seafood and swordfish specials. You'll wait in line in summer, but it's worth it.

Entertainment

Sing along at **Liam Maguire's Irish Pub & Restaurant** (☎ 508-548-0285, 273 Main St)

Weekend cover $2. As authentic as it gets this side of the Atlantic: Between Guinness on draft, Irish waiters and boisterous songfests, you'll weave out the door in search of the Blarney Stone.

The Boathouse (☎ 508-548-7800, 88 Scranton Ave) With live music nightly in summer and DJs in the spring and fall, this place packs in boisterous twentysomethings.

College Light Opera (☎ 508-548-0668, Depot Ave) Tickets $22. This is a well-regarded summer theater of singers and musicians.

Getting There & Around

Bonanza buses (☎ 800-556-3815, Ⓦ www.bonanzabus.com) serve Falmouth from Boston, Providence and New York City. At least 10 buses go from Boston to Falmouth daily ($13.50 one-way, 1½ hours). The bus stops on Depot Ave, near the center of town.

By car, from the Bourne Bridge, take MA 28 South into town. In the center of Falmouth, MA 28 makes a left turn and heads east toward Hyannis and Chatham. The directional names for MA 28 can be confusing: Even though you are heading due east toward Hyannis, West Dennis and Chatham, the road signs say MA 28 South. It takes 1½ hours (75 miles) to reach Falmouth directly from Boston via MA 3 and MA 28.

By boat, from Falmouth you can catch a passenger ferry (no cars) to Martha's Vineyard. (Car ferries to the Vineyard depart from nearby Woods Hole.) See the Martha's Vineyard & Nantucket Island chapter for information on getting to the Vineyard from Falmouth.

The Whoosh Trolley (adult/senior & child $1/50¢) operates from 9:30am to 7pm daily late May to mid-October. It loops around main attractions in Falmouth before heading to the ferry in Woods Hole. The chamber of commerce has schedules; otherwise, just flag down the bus anywhere along Main St.

WOODS HOLE

Woods Hole, a postage-stamp-size village and seaport, is a world-famous center for marine research and exploration. Besides

Nobska Light and Eel Pond, the only places to visit are a few small maritime exhibits and popular waterside restaurants built on old wharves.

Most travelers passing through town are headed for the Steamship Authority's big car ferries to Martha's Vineyard. From MA 28 in Falmouth, Locust St (which becomes Woods Hole Rd) leads directly to the ferry terminal. Water St, the main road, branches off Woods Hole Rd and leads to restaurants and the research institutions. The chamber of commerce in Falmouth has information on Woods Hole; see Information under Falmouth.

If you're lucky, your visit will coincide with performances of the *Woods Hole Folk Music Society* (☎ 508-540-0320, *Community Hall, Water St*). There are performances on the first and third Sunday of each month between October and May. Tickets are about $8.

For souvenirs, *Woods Hole Handworks* (☎ 508-540-5291, *68 Water St*), next to the drawbridge, carries creative items crafted by cooperative members.

Things to See & Do

Dramatically situated on a point overlooking Vineyard Sound, **Nobska Lighthouse** on Church St off Woods Hole Rd is a great place for a picnic or for watching the sun slowly set or quickly rise.

Walk around **Eel Pond**, west of Water St, stopping at St Joseph's Bell Tower and the quiet St Mary's Garden, opposite the drawbridge, for a respite from the crowds.

The **Shining Sea Bike Path** runs between Falmouth and Woods Hole. See the Bicycling section under Falmouth.

The **Woods Hole Science Aquarium** (☎ 508-495-2001, *cnr Water & Albatross Sts; admission free; open 10am-4pm daily mid-June–mid-Sept, 10am-4pm Mon-Fri Sept–mid-June*), part of the National Marine Fisheries, was founded here in 1871 to study and promote the well-being of the USA's fisheries. The aquarium, where seals are fed twice daily in front, is the country's first.

The Marine Fisheries was followed in 1888 by the **Marine Biological Laboratory** (☎ 508-289-7623 *for tour reservations, 127 Water St; admission free; tours daily late June–late Aug*), set up to do basic biology research based on marine life forms. The one-hour tours are popular, so you'll need to make reservations two weeks in advance. Otherwise, you could pop into their tiny visitor center across the street (*open 10am-4pm Mon-Fri late June–late Aug*).

In 1930, the **Woods Hole Oceanographic Institution** (☎ 508-289-2100, *15 School St; suggested donation $2; open 10am-4:30pm Tues-Sat, noon-4:30pm Sun late May-Dec, plus 10am-4:30pm Mon late May-early Sept*) was created to pursue deep-sea research using funding from the Rockefeller Foundation. The exhibit center, a block off Water St, is informative, especially for children.

Places to Stay

Just out of town is the *Sleepy Hollow Motor Inn* (☎ 508-548-1986, fax 508-548-5932, *527 Woods Hole Rd*) Doubles $65-115 off-season, $95-125 mid-June–mid-Sept. Open May-Oct. It offers 24 basic rooms.

Sands of Time Motor Inn & Harbor House (☎ 508-548-6300, 800-841-0114, fax 508-457-0160, W *www.sandsoftime.com, 549 Woods Hole Rd*) Doubles $100-150/145-172 off-season/June-Sept. Open Apr–mid-Nov. A 10-minute walk from town and overlooking the harbor, this modern 20-room motel also has 15 inn-style guest rooms (some with fireplaces) in the adjacent Victorian house.

Places to Eat

Fortunately, all of Woods Hole's eateries overlook the water.

Pie in the Sky (☎ 508-540-5475, *10 Water St*) Prices $2-5. Open 7am-5pm Mon-Fri, 7am-3:30pm Sat year-round & 8am-noon Sun July-Aug. While waiting for the ferry, run over here to pick up coffee, pastries and sandwiches.

Fishmonger's Café (☎ 508-548-9148, *56 Water St*) Lunch $6-16, dinner $9-23. Open for all three meals daily mid-Apr–Nov. The first place you see as you enter the village is also the very best. And it's just what you'd expect: rustic, atmospheric, with lots of good food, including lots of veggie options.

Black Duck Restaurant (☎ 508-548-9165, 73 Water St) Lunch $6-11, dinner $13-22. Open for all three meals Mar-Jan. Across from the 'Monger, the Black Duck has a good seafood menu, but there's less emphasis on creativity.

Shuckers World Famous Raw Bar & Cafe (☎ 508-540-3850, 91A Water St) Lunch under $10, dinner under $20. Open May–mid-Oct. Behind the WHOI's News and Information Offices, Shuckers really does have fresh-shucked clams and oysters. You can also get light meals and full dinners but it'd be a shame to miss these oysters.

Getting There & Around

Bonanza buses (☎ 800-556-3815, [W] www.bonanzabus.com) discharge passengers at the Woods Hole ferry terminal from Boston ($15.50, 1½ hours), Providence ($19.75, two hours) and New York City ($49, six hours). In theory, bus schedules are designed to coincide with ferry departures and arrivals, but in practice, neither waits if the other is late. Don't rely on the last connection of the day.

For travel by boat, see the Martha's Vineyard & Nantucket Island chapter for details on getting to the island from Woods Hole.

For a nominal fee, the Whoosh Trolley (see the Getting There & Around section under Falmouth) connects the ferry terminal to points of interest in Falmouth.

MASHPEE

When the Pilgrims landed in Plymouth in 1620, over 30,000 Wampanoag people lived in southeastern Massachusetts. Today there are barely 500 Wampanoag members in Mashpee. (Aquinnah, on Martha's Vineyard, has the only other sizeable community.) These days, Mashpee is best known for a huge development of condos and golf courses at New Seabury and an upscale mall on MA 28, Mashpee Commons. But Mashpee, on the road from Falmouth to Hyannis, also has two small Wampanoag museums and a long beach.

The desirable **South Cape Beach State Park** (☎ 508-457-0495), off Great Neck Rd from MA 28, has a 2-mile-long sandy beach

overlooking the Vineyard and nature trails. Parking costs $7.

The **Old Indian Meetinghouse** (☎ 508-477-0208, Meetinghouse Way; admission free; open 10am-2pm Wed & Fri July-Aug), off MA 28, is the Cape's oldest meetinghouse, built in 1684. It's inspiringly simple.

The rudimentary **Wampanoag Indian Museum** (☎ 508-477-0208, MA 130; admission by donation; open 10am-2pm Mon-Fri) houses exhibits of baskets, traditional clothing, a reconstructed wigwam and a model of a pre-European tribal village.

At the **Mashpee Powwow** (☎ 508-477-0208, Barnstable County Fairgrounds on MA 151, East Falmouth; adult/child $8/4), Native Americans from tribes all over the country (and the whole of the Americas) gather in traditional dress, exchanging stories and demonstrating crafts, music and dancing. There are also contemporary food stalls of the carnival variety. The powwow takes place on Fourth of July weekend.

SANDWICH

The Cape's oldest town (founded in 1637) is also the first one of note you'll encounter across the Sagamore Bridge. The village center couldn't be more sylvan, complete with duck pond and grist mill, fine historic houses, a famous glass museum, a renowned horticultural park with Americana collections and an adequate town beach. After exploring the village, head east out of town on MA 6A, the Cape's most scenic byway.

As for getting to Sandwich, Plymouth & Brockton buses (☎ 508-778-9767) do not serve Sandwich but they stop near the Sagamore Bridge. If you must, call for specifics about the inconvenient location.

In a car, it takes just over one hour to get from Boston to Sandwich (64 miles) via MA 3 to US 6.

Orientation & Information

Cross the Sagamore Bridge to US 6 East to MA 130 North (also called Water St) into the center. Water, Main and Grove Sts converge in the small village center. Tupper Rd, off MA 6A, leads to the marina and town beach.

The Cape Cod Canal Region Chamber of Commerce (☎ 508-759-6000, 🆆 www .capecodcanalchamber.org, 70 Main St) occupies a former railroad station in the village of Buzzards Bay, on the mainland side of the Bourne Bridge. The office (open 9am to 5pm weekdays year-round) dispenses information on Sandwich, Bourne and Cape Cod Canal activities.

If you're visiting during summer, head to the Chamber's seasonal booth (no ☎, MA 130 North). It's open at least from 10am to 3pm mid-April to late October.

The Chamber's Sagamore Bridge rotary booth (MA 3 at US 6) in a little building just before the bridge, has the same seasonal hours.

Titcomb's Book Shop (☎ 508-888-2331, 432 MA 6A) is most worthy of a stop.

Things to See & Do

About a mile from the center of town, **Heritage Plantation of Sandwich** (☎ 508-888-3300, Grove St; adult/senior/child $9/8/4.50; open 10am-5pm daily mid-May–mid-Oct) has a number of fine collections (vintage automobiles, crafts and folk art, firearms and miniatures) spanning various American periods. The lovely grounds include 76 acres of naturalized plantings and an outdoor cafe.

The **Sandwich Glass Museum** (☎ 508-888-0251, 129 Main St; adult/child $3.50/1; open 9:30am-5pm daily Apr-Dec, shorter hours Feb-Mar) celebrates Sandwich's famous glassmaking heyday from 1825 to 1888. There are fine examples of molded, blown and etched glass, dioramas showing how the glass was formed and a video recounting the industry's dramatic rise and fall.

Dexter Mill (no ☎, Water St; adult/child $1.50/75¢; open at least 1pm-4:45pm daily mid-June–mid-Sept), on the edge of Shawme mill pond, was originally built in 1654, but the present one was rebuilt in 1961. In addition to touring the small mill, you can purchase bags of freshly ground cornmeal.

The restored circa-1675 **Hoxie House** (☎ 508-888-1173, 18 Water St; adult/child $1.50/75¢; open 10am-5pm Mon-Sat, 1pm-5pm Sun mid-June–mid-Oct), Sandwich's finest historic house, is filled with period antiques.

The **Thornton W Burgess Museum** (☎ 508-888-4668, 4 Water St; admission by donation; open 10am-4pm Mon-Sat, 1pm-4pm Sun mid-Apr–Oct) is dedicated to the Sandwich native, naturalist and children's book author (he wrote all the Peter Rabbit books). Children enjoy the 'see-and-touch' room, story hours and Peter Rabbit puzzles and games.

Barely off MA 6A a few miles east of town, the **Green Briar Nature Center** (☎ 508-888-6870, 6 Discovery Hill Rd; kitchen open 10am-4pm Mon-Sat, 1pm-4pm Sun mid-Apr–Dec, trails open year-round) offers 57 acres of conservation land with walking trails and wildflower and herb gardens. But for many, the old-fashioned kitchen making and selling jams is the real draw.

The **Cape Cod Scenic Railroad** (☎ 508-771-3788, Jarves St; adult/senior/child $13/11/9; trips late May-Oct), off MA 6A, makes a two-hour return journey to Hyannis, passing cranberry bogs, salt marshes and small villages along the way. There are two daily departures (except on Mondays). You could conceivably hop off in Hyannis, wander around and take the last train back.

Off Tupper Rd from MA 6A, **Town Neck Beach** is long and pebbly, best visited at high tide if you want to swim. There are restrooms; parking costs $5.

Cape Cod Canal

The canal, which effectively separates the Cape from mainland Massachusetts, took five years to dig and was opened in 1914, just a couple of weeks before the Panama Canal. Every year it saves thousands of ships from having to sail an extra 135 miles around the tip of the Cape at Provincetown, a treacherous route studded with constantly changing sandbars.

You can take a two- to three-hour boat ride through the seven-mile-long canal with Hy-Line's **Cape Cod Canal Tours** (☎ 508-295-3883, Onset Bay Town Pier; adult $10-14, child $5-8; trips daily late May-late Sept, Sat & Sun early May & early Oct), off US 6 and MA 28, a few miles west of the Bourne

Bridge. If you're so inclined, hop aboard their sunset cocktail or jazz trips.

The canal is flanked by a well-maintained bike trail. In Buzzards Bay across from the old railroad station near the canal, head to **P&M Cycles** (☎ *508-759-2830, 29 MA 6A; $10/15 2 hr/half day*) for bike rentals.

Places to Stay

Camping Off MA 6A about 2 miles from the center of town is *Shawme Crowell State Forest* (☎ *508-888-0351, 877-422-6762 for reservations, off MA 130*) Sites $12. Open year-round. Shawme has 285 wooded sites (none with hookups) distributed over 3,000 acres.

Scussett Beach State Reservation (☎ *508-888-0859, 877-422-6762 for reservations, off MA 3*) Sites without/with hookups $15/20. Open year-round. Off MA 3 on the mainland side of the canal just before the Sagamore Bridge, Scussett Beach State Reservation has 103 camp sites adjacent to the canal.

Peter's Pond Park (☎ *508-477-1775, 185 Cotuit Rd*) Sites without/with hookups $25/37. Open mid-Apr–mid-Oct. Off MA 130 South, Peter's rents tents, teepees ($250 weekly in-season, $45 daily off-season) and is more developed than the others. There are 480 sites (mostly shaded, some along the pond) on 100 acres with walking trails and a pond for swimming.

Motels About 5 miles east of town is the *Spring Garden Motel* (☎ *508-888-0710, 800-303-1751, fax 508-833-2849,* Ⓦ *www.spring garden.com, 578 MA 6A*) Doubles $69-99 off-season, $89-125 July-Aug. Open Apr-Nov. This proudly maintained motel has eight rooms and three efficiencies overlooking a tranquil salt marsh and tidal creek. There's also a pool.

Sandy Neck Motel (☎ *508-362-3992, 800-564-3992, fax 508-362-5170,* Ⓦ *www.sandy neck.com, 669 MA 6A*) Doubles $65-89 off-season, $89-99 mid-June–early Sept. Open Apr-Nov. At the entrance to Sandy Neck Beach (see the Things to See & Do section under Barnstable), this motel has 12 standard rooms.

Shadynook Inn & Motel (☎ *508-888-0409, 800-338-5208, fax 508-888-4039,* Ⓦ *www.shadynookinn.com, 14 MA 6A*) Doubles $55-95 off-season, $95-125 mid-June–early Sept. Open year-round. This nicely landscaped and well-shaded place has 30 clean, simple and large rooms, some of which are efficiencies. A two-room suite is a bargain at $140 in-season.

B&Bs In the center of town is *Summer House* (☎/fax *508-888-4991, 800-241-3609,* Ⓦ *www.summerhousesandwich.com, 158 Main St*) Doubles $70-95 off-season, $85-110 late May–mid-Oct, with full breakfast. Open year-round. These five simple but nice guest rooms share whimsical common space in a mid-19th-century Greek Revival house. Tea is served on the back porch or in the garden.

Dillingham House (☎ *508-833-0065,* Ⓦ *www.dillinghamhouse.com, 71 Main St*) Rooms $100-130 with full breakfast. Open Apr-Oct. A mile or so out of town, this circa-1650 house is one of the Cape's most unusual B&Bs. Yes, there are traditional wide-pine floors, low ceilings and pancakes with fruit compote for breakfast, but the living rooms are also painted black and gold. In addition to four comfortable rooms, there is a detached cottage.

Captain Ezra Nye House (☎ *508-888-6142, 800-388-2278, fax 508-833-2897,* Ⓦ *www.captainezranyehouse.com, 152 Main St*) Doubles $90-105 off-season, $110-125 mid-May–Oct, with full breakfast. Open year-round. This B&B has friendly, well-traveled hosts and six carpeted guest rooms, one with a working fireplace. One of the eclectic living rooms has a TV and VCR.

Places to Eat

Take a booth or carry food out at *Marsh-land Restaurant* (☎ *508-888-9824, 109 MA 6A*) Dishes $3-10. Open for breakfast daily, lunch Mon-Sat, dinner Tues-Sat. This small and simple roadside place serves lunch specials (for about $6) like down-home meatloaf or fancier scallop sauté.

Horizons on Cape Cod Bay (☎ *508-888-6166, Town Neck Beach*) Right on the beach, this is a fine place for a sunset drink but save your appetite for elsewhere.

Captain Scott's (☎ *508-888-1675, 71 Tupper Rd)* Dishes $4-15. Basic Italian dishes, fried seafood and simply prepared fish in casual surroundings draw the locals.

Dunbar Tea Room (☎ *508-833-2485, 1 Water St)* Dishes average $9. Ever crowded, the Tea Room specializes in ploughman's lunch (choice of three cheeses, baguette, side salad and pickled beets and onions), quiche, Scottish shortbread and authentic English tea ($10, plus tea) in a slightly countrified setting.

Sagamore Inn (☎ *508-888-9707, 1131 MA 6A)* Dishes $7-12. This friendly restaurant, owned and staffed by locals, is classic 'old Cape Cod' with tin ceilings, wooden floors, wooden booths and country curtains. In addition to a beloved Yankee pot roast, the kitchen serves hearty Italian and seafood dishes.

Bee-Hive Tavern (☎ *508-833-1184, 406 MA 6A)* Lunch around $8, dinner $8-17. This dark tavern is popular with locals who come for value-conscious servings of pasta, fried seafood, burgers and sandwiches. You can also get more complete meals like chicken teriyaki.

Dan'l Webster Inn (☎ *508-888-3622, 149 Main St)* Breakfast $3-7, lunch $11-16, dinner $15-25. Open for breakfast, lunch & dinner daily mid-Apr–mid-Nov. Sandwich's most conservative place is teeming with gray-headed grannies lunching in a sunny solarium filled with potted plants. You could retreat to the tavern for lighter evening meals and drinks. Or join 'em and dress neatly for continental cuisine in the main dining room.

Belfry Inne Bistro (☎ *508-888-8550, 8 Jarves St)* Dinner mains $19-27. Carved from a former church, with dramatic flying buttresses and stained glass still intact, this elegant restaurant serves grilled salmon, a seafood medley and the like. It's not at all sacrilegious.

Shopping

Open daily year-round, *Pairpoint Crystal* (☎ *508-888-2344, 800-899-0953, 851 MA 6A)*

has been renowned since 1837 for its glass-blowing techniques and original designs. You can watch artisans working 9am to 4pm weekdays May through December.

BARNSTABLE

The stretch of MA 6A that passes through Barnstable lives up to its scenic reputation, affording glimpses of the ocean and salt marshes. The winding road is also dotted with antique stores, art galleries, craft shops and pricey B&Bs. Take practically any northern turn off of MA 6A and you'll reach Cape Cod Bay. Perhaps the best thing about Barnstable is Sandy Neck Beach, a 6-mile-long stretch of barrier beach and dunes.

The town of Barnstable includes seven distinct villages and stretches the width of the Cape, from Cape Cod Bay on the north shore to Nantucket Sound on the south. Historic MA 6A is simultaneously referred to as Main St and Old King's Hwy.

Contact the Hyannis Area Chamber of Commerce (☎ 508-362-5230, 800-449-6647, W www.hyannis.com, 1481 MA 132, Hyannis) for information on all seven of Barnstable's villages. The office is open 9am to 5pm Monday to Saturday year-round, and on Sunday in high season.

The convenient Cape Cod Chamber of Commerce (☎ 508-862-0700, 888-332-2732, W www.capecodchamber.com), at exit 6 from US 6, promotes the entire Cape. It's open 8:30am to 5pm daily June to mid-October, and 10am-4pm weekdays mid-October to April.

MA 6A runs from Sandwich through Barnstable, Yarmouth, Dennis and Brewster. If you're in a hurry, take US 6 to exit 5 for West Barnstable, exit 6 for Barnstable. The Plymouth & Brockton bus (☎ 508-778-9767) from Boston stops at the commuter lot on US 6 in Barnstable ($14, 1½ hours), a few miles from anything of interest in town.

Since MA 6A is winding and narrow, it's not well-suited to bicycles.

Things to See & Do

Members of the 1717 **West Parish Meeting-house** (☎ *508-362-8624, MA 149; admission* *free; open 10am-4pm daily late May–mid-Oct),* between US 6 and MA 6A, belong to the country's oldest Congregational parish. They can trace their origins back to London's First Congregational Church.

The **Donald Trayser Memorial Museum Complex** *(☎ 508-362-2092, 3353 MA 6A; admission by donation; open 1:30pm-4:30pm Tues-Sun mid-June–mid-Oct)* served as the Old Customs House from the mid- to late 19th century. At that time, Barnstable Harbor was the busiest port on the Cape. (It silted up in the early 20th century.) The museum contains a random assortment of items: the custom keeper's office, imported ivory, a collection of Sandwich glass, a bicycle dating to 1900 and a late-17th-century jail cell. History buffs will find it charming.

Sandy Neck Beach *(☎ 508-362-8300),* Cape Cod Bay's best beach, is 6 miles long and backed by a rather extensive network of high dunes. Facilities include a changing room, restrooms and a snack bar; parking is $10. To reach it take Sandy Neck Rd off MA 6A on the Sandwich-Barnstable town line. A 10-mile (roundtrip) salt marsh trail begins at the gatehouse parking lot and heads into the dunes. Along the way, there are four cross trails that connect the main trail to the beach. It's well worth the four-hour walk.

Hyannis Whale Watcher Cruises *(☎ 508-362-6088, 888-942-5392, Barnstable Harbor, off MA 6A; adult/child $26/16; cruises mid-Apr–mid-Oct)* offers trips with an onboard naturalist. If you're not going to Provincetown, Gloucester or Boston, take a trip out of Barnstable Harbor.

Places to Stay
MA 6A is lined with former sea captains' houses that have been converted into romantic B&Bs. If you have a bit of money to spare, you'll find a few places to spend it here.

Lamb and Lion Inn (☎ 508-362-6823, 800-909-6923, fax 508-362-0227, ⓦ www.lamband lion.com, 2504 MA 6A) Doubles $125-160 off-season, $145-220 mid-May–Oct, with continental breakfast. Open year-round. In addition to a cottage and barn well suited to families (inquire about the rates), this inn has 10 rooms surrounding a pool. It's all very pleasant and cheery, thanks to cloud and sky murals brightening the long hallways.

Honeysuckle Hill (☎ 508-362-8418, 866-444-5522, fax 508-362-8386, ⓦ www.honey

---

Field of Dreams

The crack of a wooden bat making contact with a well-seen curve ball. The night lights and fireflies. The rudimentary aluminum seats within spitting distance of the third baseman. The free admission. The hopes and dreams of making it big time.

If you've never been to a baseball game, or you think the major leagues have been sullied by salaries and egos, the Cape Cod Baseball League will give you faith. The nation's oldest amateur league (founded in 1885), the CCBL is also the country's most competitive summertime college proving ground. The beloved league's slogan, 'Where tomorrow's stars shine tonight,' isn't far from the truth. Former CCBL players who went to the major leagues include Hall-of-Famer Red Sox catcher Carlton Fisk and the late Thurman Munson. Current Boston Red Sox shortstop Nomar Garciaparra and catcher Jason Varitek are among more than a hundred major leaguers playing today who went through the Cape League's ranks.

So, take me out to the ball game, but don't forget to bring your own peanuts, Cracker Jack and hot dogs. The season runs from mid-June to mid-August. There are 10 team franchises located in Bourne, Brewster, Chatham, Cotuit (Barnstable), Falmouth, Harwich, Hyannis, Orleans, Wareham (barely off-Cape) and Yarmouth. Stop into the local chambers of commerce for schedules and game locations.

sucklehill.com, 591 MA 6A) Doubles $100-130 off-season, $130-160 May-Oct, with full breakfast. Open year-round. One of the friendliest B&Bs along MA 6A, the completely renovated Honeysuckle Hill has four modestly elegant rooms featuring feather beds and white wicker. A two-bedroom suite can comfortably accommodate a family.

Places to Eat

Named after the four bodies of water surrounding the Cape, *Four Seas* (☎ *508-775-1394, 360 S Main St, Centerville)* dispenses what is arguably the Cape's best homemade ice cream. The shop scoops its ultra-fresh riches to crowds who pack the parking lot as densely as the shop packs pints of beach plum ice cream. Don't think about the fat content, especially if you can visit only once.

Mill Way Fish and Lobster Market (☎ *508-362-2760, Barnstable Harbor)* Dishes $6-15. This harborside joint makes great fish sandwiches, fried seafood and fish chowder to take to the harbor.

Barnstable Tavern (☎ *508-362-2355, 3176 MA 6A)* With an appealing central location, the front patio is pleasant for a warm-weather drink. But, really, stick to liquids rather than solids here.

Dolphin (☎ *508-362-6610, 3250 MA 6A)* Lunch $6-11, dinner $17-22. This low-key restaurant and bar, a popular local hangout, has a *really* extensive seafood menu, but the Greek salad with balsamic vinaigrette is also recommended.

Entertainment

Barnstable Comedy Club (☎ *508-362-6333, 3171 MA 6A)* Tickets $12-14. Performances year-round. Despite its name, the country's oldest nonprofessional theater group performs musicals and plays. They aren't exactly on the cutting edge; their motto is, 'To produce good plays and remain amateurs.' We suppose that Kurt Vonnegut, an alumnus, didn't get the message. Call for a schedule.

HYANNIS

The Cape's commercial and transportation hub has a rejuvenated waterfront and Main St area, which make it a pleasant place to wait for a ferry or a bus. Hyannis draws crowds of summer college workers for their one night off per week, and also attracts Kennedy fans: Hyannisport is the summer home to this US political family.

From US 6, take MA 132 South (exit 6) to the airport rotary to Barnstable Rd to Main St. From Falmouth or Chatham, take MA 28 directly to Main St (one-way), the principal shopping and dining thoroughfare. Both ferry terminals (the Ocean St Dock and the South St Dock) are about a 10-minute walk from the bus station, which is just one block north of Main St.

The Hyannis Area Chamber of Commerce (☎ 508-362-5230, 800-449-6647, Ⓦ www.hyannis.com, 1481 MA 132), about a mile south of US 6, is generally open 9am to 5pm Monday to Saturday year-round. In high season it's also open from 10am to 2pm Sunday. The Cape-wide Cape Cod Chamber of Commerce has a booth (☎ 508-771-7156) across from Macy's in the Cape Cod Mall, MA 132, that keeps long mall hours daily year-round.

Borders (☎ 508-862-6363) and Barnes & Noble (☎ 508-771-1400), both on MA 132, are the big players in town.

Cape Cod Hospital (☎ 508-771-1800, 27 Park St), a few blocks from the center of town, is open 24 hours a day.

John F Kennedy Hyannis Museum

This museum (☎ *508-790-3077, 397 Main St; adult/child under 16 yrs $3/free; open 10am-4pm Mon-Sat & 1pm-4pm Sun mid-Apr–mid-Oct, 10am-4pm Wed-Sat mid-Oct–Dec & mid-Feb–mid-Apr)* celebrates John F Kennedy's life in Hyannis through more than 100 heartwarming photographs. The 35th President of the US summered in Hyannisport (an exclusive section of Hyannis) with his family from the early 1930s until he was assassinated in 1963. Many Kennedy family members still have family homes here. The 'Kennedy Compound,' as it is called, is just a group of private houses (albeit lovely ones), surrounded in most cases by tall fences and shrubs.

HYANNIS

PLACES TO STAY
10 Hyannis Travel Inn
17 Seacoast on the Towne
18 Anchor Inn
31 Memories by the Sea
33 Inn on Sea Street
33 Captain Gosnold Village
34 Sea Breeze Inn

PLACES TO EAT
5 Starbuck's
7 Ying's
12 Fazio's Trattoria
14 Prodigal Son
15 La Petite France
19 Spiritus
21 Baxter's Boathouse
22 RooBar City Bistro
23 The Egg & I
27 Hyannisport Brewing Company
28 Sweetwaters Grille & Bar
29 Roadhouse Cafe

OTHER
1 Hyannis Area Chamber of Commerce
2 Borders
3 Barnes & Noble
4 Cape Cod Mall
6 Cape Flight
8 Trek (Car Rental)
9 Bus Station
11 Spectrum Gallery
13 Cape Cod Hospital
16 John F Kennedy Hyannis Museum
20 Cape Cod Mobile Duck Tours
24 Ocean St Dock; Cat Boat; Hy-Line Cruises; Hyannisport Harbor Cruises
25 South St Dock; Steamship Authority
26 Cape Cod Melody Tent
30 Plush & Plunder

To Eastern Mountain Sports, US 6, Hwy 6A, Barnstable & Sandwich

To Yarmouthport, US 6, Hwy 6A & Yarmouth

Barnstable Municipal Airport

Iyanough Rd

Falmouth Rd

To Marstons Mills, Falmouth & Bourne Bridge

Hinckley Rd

Bearses Way

Bassett Lane

Winter St

Spring St

Central St

Ridgewood Ave

Cape Cod Central Railroad

Barnstable Rd

Camp St

Yarmouth Rd

To West Dennis, Harwichport, Chatham & Orleans

Iyanough Rd

Main St

Train Station

Elm St

High School Rd

North St

Stevens St

Main St

Sea St

Stevens St

Pleasant St

School St

Lewis Bay Rd

Park St

South St

Aunt Betty's Pond

To Craigville Beach

Village Green

Pine St

Old Colony Rd

Hyannis Inner Harbor

West End Rotary

Sea St

Oak Neck Rd

S Harvard

Snows Creek

Ferry to Nantucket

Ferry to Nantucket & Martha's Vineyard (seasonal)

Greenwood Ave

Marston Ave

Ocean Ave

Norris St

Crocker St
Studley Rd

Angell Rd

Gosnold St

Estey Ave

Ocean St

Town Park

Veteran's Beach

Lewis Bay

Scudder Ave

To Hyannisport

Sea Street Beach

Hawes Ave

Kalmus Park Beach

Dunbar Point

Hyannis Harbor

A simple JFK memorial was erected off Ocean St overlooking the harbor where he often sailed.

Beaches
The **Sea Street Beach**, off Sea St from the western end of Main St, is a narrow but decent beach with restrooms and a bathhouse; parking is $10.

Kalmus Park Beach, off Ocean St, has a restroom, bathhouse and good windsurfing conditions; parking is $10.

Veteran's Beach, off Ocean St at the town park, is equal parts park and beach. Families picnic and barbecue (there's a snack bar, too), play paddle ball and swim in shallow waters. Parking is $10.

West Hyannisport (technically Centerville) boasts popular **Craigville Beach**, the Cape's largest beach. It has restrooms and changing rooms; parking is $10.

Activities
For adventure-sports lovers, **Eastern Mountain Sports** (*EMS;* ☎ *508-362-8690, 1513 MA 132*) rents kayaks ($40-50 daily) and gives instructional clinics throughout the year on everything related to outdoor activities, from using a compass to where to bicycle.

Cape Flight (☎ *508-775-8171, Barnstable Municipal Airport, East Ramp, MA 132 rotary*) offers hour-long sightseeing trips in twin-engine propeller planes high above this fragile strip of land. Fly to Provincetown, along the beautiful east-side beaches, over the Chatham lighthouse and Monomoy and then out to the Vineyard and Nantucket. It's a great way to fully appreciate the Cape's unique geology and topography. The grand loop tour ($320 up to five people) is great, but you many be able to arrange a shorter flight for less money.

The **Cape Cod Central Railroad** (☎ *508-771-3800, 888-797-7245, cnr Center & Main Sts; adult/senior/child $13/11/9; trips late May-Oct*) makes a two-hour scenic run between Hyannis and Sandwich. There are three trips daily except Monday. You could take either early train, get off in Sandwich, mosey into the village (about a 10-minute walk) and catch the last train back.

Cruises
Laid-back sailors will enjoy the **Cat Boat** (☎ *508-775-0222, Ocean St Dock; adult/senior/child under 90lb $25/20/5; trips mid-Apr–late Nov*), which offers a variety of voyages designed to maximize wind power and minimize motor noise. It sails far into Nantucket Sound, around the bay at twilight and along the coast in front of the Kennedy compound.

Hyannisport Harbor Cruises (☎ *508-778-2600, Ocean St Dock; adult/child 5-12 yrs $10/5; trips late Apr–late Oct*) offers hour-long sightseeing trips of the harbor and bay. It's a fine way to get onto the water inexpensively. They also have special blues and jazz cruises, lobster luncheons and ice cream sailings.

Cape Cod Duck Mobile Tours (☎ *508-362-1117, 437 Main St; adult/senior/child under 5 yrs $14/11/5; trips late May–mid-Oct*) utilizes amphibious vehicles on a narrated 45-minute tour of Hyannis' harbor and side streets. If you take it, you'll understand what it means to feel like a 'duck out of water.'

Places to Stay
Motels 'Towne' is the key to *Seacoast on the Towne* (☎ *508-775-3828, 800-466-4100, fax 508-771-2179,* W *www.seacoastcapecod .com, 33 Ocean St*) Doubles $48-78 off-season, $78-118 late June-early Sept. Open May-Oct. Right in the middle of the action, this place offers 26 cheery rooms, some with refrigerators.

Hyannis Travel Inn (☎/*fax 508-775-8200, 800-352-7190,* W *www.hyannistravelinn.com, 18 North St*) Doubles $49-79 off-season, $95-125 July-Aug. Open Feb-Nov. This 83-room establishment has both indoor and outdoor swimming pools.

Anchor Inn (☎ *508-775-0357, fax 508-775-1313,* W *www.anchorinn.com, 1 South St*) Doubles $69-125 off-season, $105-179 mid-June–early Sept. Open year-round. These 43 simple rooms are basically next door to the ferry and enjoy a heated pool and balconies overlooking the harbor.

Cottages You'll find plenty of wooded space between the units at *Captain Gosnold*

Village (☎ 508-775-9111, ⓦ *www.captain gosnold.com, 230 Gosnold St*) Doubles $55/90, studios $65/105, 1-bedroom cottages $100/170 off-season/mid-June–early Sept. Open Apr-Oct. A block from Sea Street Beach, this compound offers motel rooms, fully equipped cottages and efficiency apartments that can sleep up to eight people. This is a good place for longer stays and for families since there's a playground and a pool. Cottage prices increase with their size; inquire about two- and three-bedroom units.

B&Bs Open year-round is *Sea Breeze Inn* (☎ 508-771-7213, fax 508-862-0663, ⓦ *www .seabreezeinn.com, 270 Ocean Ave*) Doubles $60-110 off-season, $80-140 mid-June–mid-Sept, with expanded continental breakfast. Sea Breeze Inn has 14 clean and pleasant motel-style rooms within a sandal-shuffle of the beach. A few rooms have ocean views.

Inn on Sea Street (☎ 508-775-8030, fax 508-771-0878, ⓦ *www.innonseastreet.com, 358 Sea St*) Rooms without bath $85-95, with bath $110-130, cottage $150, with full breakfast. Open Apr-Oct. Within an easy walk of the beach, this is a very nice place. Most of the nine rooms have private bath; all are decorated with tasteful Victorian or English country antiques. If you want to splurge, rent the simple, all-white cottage with a complete kitchen.

Memories by the Sea (☎ 508-775-9300, 877-737-9300, ⓦ *www.memoriesbythesea .com, 162 Sea St*) Doubles $90/120 off-season/May-Sept with continental breakfast. Just a 10-minute walk from the beach, this guesthouse has three rooms with cable TV, a sitting area and fireplace. It's one of the few B&Bs well suited to families.

Places to Eat

Unless otherwise noted, the establishments listed here are open for lunch and dinner, many year-round.

Spiritus (☎ 508-775-2955, 500 Main St) Sandwiches under $5. Spiritus serves good strong coffee, pizza by the slice and filling sandwiches. The funky storefront cafe is a popular hangout, especially since it's open until 2am on summer weekends.

The Egg & I (☎ 508-771-1596, 521 Main St) Dishes under $6. Open 6am-1pm Apr-Nov. It's hard to beat the value here. Despite cheap egg dishes galore, pancakes and good old-fashioned corned beef hash, you could always splurge on the seafood omelet.

La Petite France (☎ 508-771-4445, 349 Main St) Dishes $5-7. Presided over by a hands-on Frenchman, this cafe serves excellent onion soup, cold Mediterranean salads and clam chowder. Their sandwiches are made with baguettes and home-roasted meats.

Prodigal Son (☎ 508-771-1337, 10 Ocean St) Sandwiches $6. This laid-back, borderline-grunge coffeehouse is perhaps more apropos of the West Coast than the Cape. A good selection of microbrews and wine outshines its limited but sufficient selection of sandwiches. The coffee is strong. The comfortable touches are perfect for listening to live folk, blues and jazz music. Stop in to check out the listings of upcoming events. Maybe it'll be an open-mike night.

Hyannisport Brewing Company (☎ 508-775-8289, 720 Main St) Dishes $6-15. The onion rings, burgers and chili at this popular microbrewery are all made with the same beer you'll be drinking. But the beer is better than the beer batter.

Baxter's Boathouse (☎ 508-775-4490, 177 Pleasant St) Dishes $7-20. Baxter's serves the requisite fish-and-chips, but it also boasts a raw bar and lively bar scene. For many, though, the harborfront location with picnic tables on a floating dock is the real draw.

Ying's (☎ 508-790-2432, 59 Center St) Lunch $8, dinner $10-18. Possibly the best Thai food on Cape Cod, Ying's also has Japanese and Korean dishes and dozens of noodle dishes.

Starbuck's (☎ 508-778-6767, MA 132) Dishes $5-15. Open for lunch & dinner daily year-round. Starbuck's (which has nothing to do with the major coffee chain) serves dependable standbys: burgers, pasta, Tex-Mex, shrimp and chicken sandwiches. It's also known for frozen cocktails and other 20oz libations, but keep in mind that this pleasant, lively place serves as many families as it does drinks.

Fazio's Trattoria (☎ 508-775-9400, 294 *Main St)* Dinner mains $11.50-17.50. Open daily year-round. This storefront bistro offers authentic and contemporary Italian dishes including thin-crust pizzas, homemade pasta and veal specialties.

Sweetwaters Grille & Bar (☎ 508-775-3323, 644 *Main St)* Lunch $6-9, dinner $11-17. Open daily year-round. It's hard to go wrong ordering any of the Southwestern dishes here: black bean soup, burritos and chicken fajitas.

Roadhouse Cafe (☎ 508-775-2386, 488 *South St)* Open year-round. The bistro section of this restaurant features a piano bar nightly in summer and jazz on Monday year-round. But in order to listen, which is free, you'll have to buy dinner; stick to the thin-crust pizzas. There are more than 40 kinds of beer.

RooBar City Bistro (☎ 508-778-6515, 586 *Main St)* Dinner mains $15-25. Open daily year-round. Known for its lively bar scene (which rocks from 4pm to 1am), this hip place features an exposed kitchen, high ceilings and New American 'fusion' cuisine. If grilled swordfish served with sunflower seed and jalapeño pesto makes your mouth water, this is your place. You can always get a pizza for about $12.

Entertainment

The *Cape Cod Melody Tent* (☎ 508-775-9100, W *Main St)* is just that: a giant tent. Big-name musicians and comedians, such as Tony Bennett, Lyle Lovett and Joan Rivers, perform here.

Several restaurants also have lively bar scenes; see the Places to Eat section.

Shopping

In addition to used bookstores, Main St offers a mishmash of shops, from funky ones geared to tattooed high schoolers to a few upscale galleries. Mostly, it's everything in between. Try *Spectrum Gallery* (☎ 508-771-4554, 342 *Main St)*, featuring handmade contemporary American crafts, and *Plush & Plunder* (☎ 508-775-4467, 605 *Main St)*, a

funky store with retro accessories. The sprawling *Cape Cod Mall* (☎ 508-771-0200, *cnr MA 28 & MA 132)* is geared to one-stop shopping.

Getting There & Around

Air The Barnstable Municipal Airport (☎ 508-775-2020), at the rotary intersection of MA 28 and MA 132, is served by a few regional carriers. You can reach Hyannis from Boston on Cape Air (☎ 508-790-0300, 800-635-8787, W www.flycapeair.com), as well as from New York's La Guardia Airport on Colgan Air (☎ 888-265-4267), a division of US Airways.

See also the Getting There & Away sections in the Martha's Vineyard & Nantucket Island chapter.

Bus The Plymouth & Brockton bus (☎ 508-778-9767, cnr Center & Elm Sts) connects Boston to Hyannis and Provincetown. There are about 30 daily buses from Boston to Hyannis ($12 one-way) and four daily buses from Hyannis to Provincetown ($9 one-way).

Bonanza buses (☎ 800-556-3815, W www.bonanzabus.com) carry passengers to Hyannis from New York City and Providence. From New York there are about six buses daily ($45 one-way, six hours), from Providence about five buses daily ($19.75 one-way, two hours)

Car Hyannis is one of the few Cape Cod locations where you can pick up a rental car. Hertz (☎ 800-654-3131), National (☎ 800-227-7368) and Avis (☎ 800-331-1212) are all at the airport. Trek (☎ 508-771-2459) is just a few blocks away.

Although traffic volume along MA 28 fluctuates from winter to summer like the tides from high to low, count on it taking at least 45 minutes to get to Chatham, 20 miles away. It's a tad further to Falmouth in the other direction.

Boat See the Martha's Vineyard & Nantucket Island chapter for information on getting to the islands via ferry service departing from Hyannis.

Trolley An intricate network of trolleys (☎ 508-385-8326) runs along Main St, the waterfront area, to some beaches and onto other towns. For the casual visitor, it's more trouble than it's worth. Nonetheless, look for schedules at the Steamship Authority, Chamber of Commerce and other high tourist traffic areas; the trolleys (adult/child $1/50¢) run daily from late May to early September.

YARMOUTH

The north side of Yarmouth along MA 6A is quiet and dignified, lined with shady trees, antique shops and former sea captains' homes. Along MA 28 on the south side, Yarmouth is thick with low-slung motels built right on the narrow beaches.

By car, it takes 30 minutes from the Bourne Bridge (20 miles) via US 6 without stopping (which would be silly). Take US 6 exit 7 (Willow St) into Yarmouthport, or exit 8 for Yarmouth and South Yarmouth. Better yet, keep wending your way along MA 6A. The villages of Yarmouthport and Yarmouth are on MA 6A; South Yarmouth and West Yarmouth are on MA 28. Everything you'll need is on or just off these two roads. On rainy or overcast days families might cruise MA 28, chockablock with over-the-top mini golf courses, trampoline cages and indoor amusement centers.

For information, the Yarmouth Chamber of Commerce (☎ 508-778-1008, 800-732-1008, Ⓦ www.yarmouthcapecod.com, 657 MA 28, West Yarmouth) is open 9am to 5pm daily (with slightly shorter hours on Sunday) early May to mid-October and 9am to 5pm on weekdays the rest of the year.

The Parnassus Book Service (☎ 508-362-6420, 220 MA 6A) is delightfully cluttered with antiquarian and used books.

Things to See & Do

The **Winslow Crocker House** (☎ 508-362-4385, 250 MA 6A; adult/child $4/2; tours hourly 11am-4pm Sat & Sun June–mid-Oct), a lovely Georgian house overseen by the Society for the Preservation of New England Antiquities, is filled with notable antiques from the 17th, 18th and 19th cen-turies. This is one historic house that's worth the admission price.

The **Captain Bangs Hallet House** (☎ 508-362-3021, 11 Strawberry Lane; donation requested adult/child $3/50¢; tours 1pm, 2pm, 3pm Thur-Sun June–mid-Oct), behind the post office off MA 6A, was once home to a prosperous sea captain who made his fortune sailing to China and India. After touring the house, take a walk on the short nature trails behind it.

The historic store **Hallet's** (☎ 508-362-3362, 139 MA 6A; open Apr-Dec) occupies a revered place in Yarmouth's history. It began as an apothecary in 1889 and has also served as a post office and town meeting hall. It still boasts its original soda fountain, complete with swivel stools. Stop in for coffee, ice cream or a sandwich. Upstairs there is a wonderfully nostalgic little museum chock-full of items collected over the last 100 years.

Grey's Beach (also known as Bass Hole Beach), off Centre St from MA 6A, isn't known for great swimming but it does have a long boardwalk that stretches out into the tidal marsh and across a creek. Parking is free.

Seagull Beach, off S Sea Ave from MA 28, is Yarmouth's best south-side beach. The approach is actually prettier, alongside a tidal river. Parking is $10; there is a bathhouse.

Places to Stay

Motels You'll find a relatively quiet locale at the **Beach 'n Towne Motel** (☎ 508-398-2311, 800-987-8556, 1261 MA 28, South Yarmouth) Doubles $38-54 off-season, $70 late June-early Sept. Open Feb-Nov. This single-story motel has 21 standard rooms.

Tidewater (☎ 508-775-6322, 800-338-6322, fax 508-778-5105, Ⓦ www.tidewater ml.com, 135 MA 28, West Yarmouth) Doubles $43-119 off-season, $109-169 late June-early Sept. Open year-round. Tidewater offers 101 rooms located as close to the Nantucket ferry as you can get without being in Hyannis traffic.

All Seasons Motor Inn (☎ 508-394-7600, 800-527-0359, fax 508-398-7160, Ⓦ www .allseasons.com, 1199 MA 28, South Yarmouth) Doubles $45-99 off-season, $115-145

July-Aug. Open year-round. This attractive two-story complex has 114 modern motel rooms (with refrigerators), two pools (one indoor heated), saunas, a whirlpool, game room and lots of other facilities.

B&Bs Old-fashioned properties here include the *Village Inn* (☎ 508-362-3182, W www.thevillageinncapecod.com, 92 MA 6A, Yarmouthport) Doubles $75-89 off-season, $75-109 mid-May–mid-Oct, with full breakfast. Open year-round. This family-run hostelry has lots of common room and 10 modest guest rooms of varying sizes. Two share a bath.

Lane's End Cottage (☎ 508-362-5298, 268 MA 6A, Yarmouthport) Doubles $120-135 with full breakfast. Open year-round. This small, circa-1710 English-style B&B is surrounded by flowers and tucked back in the woods, with three simple rooms, one with a terrace. The brick patio, where breakfast is served by a delightful host, is ringed with potted plants. No credit cards are accepted.

Wedgewood Inn (☎ 508-362-5157, fax 508-362-5851, W www.wedgewood-inn.com, 83 MA 6A, Yarmouthport) Doubles $115-165 off-season, $135-205 June-Oct, with full breakfast. Open year-round. Easily the loveliest B&B along MA 6A, this inn has nine rooms (some with private porches and fireplaces) in the main house and restored adjacent carriage house. Nary an undesirable room at the inn, they're spacious and filled with antiques, Oriental carpets and fireplaces.

Places to Eat

Don't look for frills at *Jack's Outback* (☎ 508-362-6690, 161 MA 6A, Yarmouthport) Dishes $3-7. Open for breakfast & lunch daily year-round. This no-frills, pine-paneled place serves good, cheap American food. Pour your own coffee, write your own order and pick up your plate when it's ready. Jack's has been insulting patrons and doing things this way for years, and patrons love it. You'll be well fed and out the door for under $7.

Lobster Boat (☎ 508-775-0486, 681 MA 28, West Yarmouth) Dishes average $15.

Open 4pm-10:30pm daily early Apr-late Oct. You can't miss this touristy, overgrown and hybridized pirate-ship-cum-lobster-boat. Come for twin lobsters and early-bird specials for $10 to $15.

Clancy's (☎ 508-775-3332, 175 MA 28, West Yarmouth) Lunch $5-16, dinner $10-20. With a pleasant country-tavern atmosphere, Clancy's has a more-than-adequate menu of burgers, sandwiches, peel-and-eat shrimp and chicken fingers.

Inaho (☎ 508-362-5522, 157 MA 6A, Yarmouthport) Dinner mains $12-23. This authentic Japanese restaurant has excellent sushi, traditional bento boxes, tempura and more exotic dishes. If green tea ice cream doesn't strike your fancy, try the distinctly American flourless chocolate cake made by the Japanese owner.

Abbicci (☎ 508-362-3501, 43 MA 6A, Yarmouthport) Lunch $7.50-13, dinner $18-28, early dinner specials $12.50-17.50. For a creative meal served in sophisticated but unpretentious surroundings, head to Abbicci. Contemporary Italian dishes like ravioli stuffed with game or duck breast with mustard sauce are served in a 1775 house modernized with track lighting, contemporary art and an upscale bar. The early-bird dinner specials are a bargain and Sunday brunch is a treat.

Spectator Sports

Cape Cod Crusaders (☎ 508-790-4782, Dennis-Yarmouth High School) Adult/child $8/5. The Crusaders, a farm team for the professional New England Revolution, play soccer from early May to mid-August here. Take exit 8 off US 6 and call for exact times and dates.

DENNIS

Similar to Yarmouth's sprawl, Dennis stretches from Cape Cod Bay to Nantucket Sound. Along MA 6A you'll find cranberry bogs, salt marshes and lots of antique stores and artisans' shops. Dennis also has a very good museum dedicated to area artists, a highly regarded summer theater, an art cinema and a fine lookout point. If you don't like moving around nightly, it serves as a good mid-Cape location for exploring in either direction.

To get there, continue heading along MA 6A or take exit 9 from US 6 (north to MA 6A or south to MA 28). East Dennis and Dennis are on MA 6A; West Dennis and Dennisport are along MA 28. MA 134 runs north-south (through South Dennis), linking MA 6A to MA 28. The section of MA 6A that passes through Dennis is only 3 miles long, and MA 28 is about the same, so there isn't much problem with navigation. From MA 6A, it's a mile east to Scargo Tower and 2 miles west to Chapin Memorial Beach.

The Dennis Chamber of Commerce (☎ 508-398-3568, 800-243-9920, Ⓦ www .dennischamber.com, MA 28 at MA 134, West Dennis) is open 9am to 5pm weekdays late June to early September; 10am to 4pm weekends early May to mid-Oct; 9am to 5pm weekdays mid-Oct to early May.

Depending on where you are, stop in at the exceptional Arm Chair Bookstore (☎ 508-385-0900, 619 MA 6A); the very good independent Booksmith (☎ 508-398-8380, Patriot Square, MA 134), near US 6; and Paperback Cottage (☎ 508-760-2101, 927 MA 28), at MA 134. Since many summer visitors are voracious readers, Paperback Cottage also *rents* books, by the week.

Things to See & Do

The Cape Museum of Fine Arts (☎ 508-385-4477, MA 6A; adult/child under 17 yrs $7/ free; open 10am-5pm Tues-Sat, 1pm-5pm Sun year-round & 10am-5pm Mon late May–mid-Oct) represents Cape artists, both living and dead, famous as well as up-and-coming, working in a variety of media. Part of the modern and airy museum is housed in a wonderfully restored old barn. Admission is by donation 10am to 1pm Saturday.

From Scargo Tower (take MA 6A to Old Bass River Rd to Scargo Hill Rd) you can see all the way to Provincetown on a clear day. The high vantage point gives you a good idea of just how delicate the ecology of this little peninsula really is. Directly below is Scargo Lake, one of the Cape's 365 freshwater lakes.

Cape Cod Waterways (☎ 508-398-0080, MA 28, Dennisport; open May–mid-Oct), near MA 134, allows you to explore the small but interesting Swan River from the vantage point of a canoe, kayak or paddleboat – a nice alternative to go-carts and batting cages, both of which are also on MA 28. Ninety-minute kayak rentals are $15/25 single/double.

Beaches

Wade on in at Chapin Memorial Beach, off MA 6A – a long, dune-backed beach with a gently sloping grade. As with all bay-side beaches during low tide, you can walk for a mile out onto the tidal flats. Parking is $10.

West Dennis Beach, off MA 28 in West Dennis, is a narrow, mile-long beach on Nantucket Sound. It's quite popular (the parking lot holds 1000 cars); facilities include a snack bar and restrooms. Parking is $10.

Cruises

The schooner Freya (☎ 508-385-4399, Town Marina; adult $16-18, child $10; trips July-Aug) takes peaceful and leisurely two-hour sails into Cape Cod Bay and hour-long sunset trips. Save $4 by going on the morning sail.

Water Safari's Starfish (☎ 508-362-5555, Bass River Bridge, 38 MA 28, West Dennis; adult/child $12.50/7; open late May–mid-Oct) offers 90-minute narrated trips on flat-bottom boats up the largest tidal river on the East Coast. Trips depart at 11am and 1pm, but in the heart of the summer, there's also a boat at 4pm.

Cape Cod Rail Trail

The 26-mile paved Cape Cod Rail Trail follows the flat Old Colony Railroad bed from Dennis to Wellfleet. Along the way you'll pass ponds, forests, a country store or two, a few ocean vistas, beaches and salt marshes. It's one of the Cape's most pleasant excursions, but there are stretches that many find a tad dull.

Park at the trailhead on MA 134 in South Dennis, just south of US 6. You can rent bikes ($10/20 two hours/full day) and in-line skates ($15 daily) at **Barbara's Bike and Sports Equipment** (☎ 508-760-4723, 430 MA 134). The shop is open from April to mid-November, weather permitting.

Places to Stay

Motels Chill at the *Holiday Hill Motor Inn* (☎ 508-394-5577, 352 MA 28, Dennisport) Doubles $35-79 off-season, $59-99 late June-late Aug. Open May–mid-Oct. This two-story motor inn has 56 large rooms with refrigerators.

Huntsman Motor Lodge (☎ 508-394-5415, 800-628-0498, fax 508-398-7852, 🅦 www.thehuntsman.com, 829 MA 28, West Dennis) Doubles $49-59 off-season, $79-89 late June-early Sept. Open year-round. This establishment has 17 simple rooms and nine efficiencies.

B&Bs Among good local properties is the *Isaiah Hall B&B Inn* (☎ 508-385-9928, 800-736-0160, fax 508-385-5879, 🅦 www.isaiah hallinn.com, 152 Whig St, Dennis) Doubles $96-131 Apr-late Oct with continental breakfast. This practically perfect B&B offers 11 unpretentious rooms with TV (one with a fireplace) in a 19th-century farmhouse and an attached, renovated barn. In addition to lovely gardens, an enthusiastic host and plenty of common space both inside and out, the inn is a 10-minute walk from the beach. There is even a DSL line for guests! Whig St is off MA 6A.

By The Sea (☎ 508-398-8685, 800-447-9202, fax 508-398-0334, 🅦 www.bytheseaguests .com, 57 Chase Ave, Dennisport) Doubles $80-120 off-season, $100-175 July-early Sept, with continental breakfast. Open May-Nov. This hostelry, at Inman Rd, smack on Inman Beach, has 12 spacious rooms with well-maintained but old-fashioned beach-house furnishings, TV and updated bathrooms. Five spiffy one- and two-bedroom suites are quite desirable.

Places to Eat

Captain Frosty's (☎ 508-385-8548, 219 MA 6A, Dennis) Dishes $3-14. Of the Cape's ubiquitous clam shacks, this excellent one offers more than fried clams and burgers. You might also order a daily special such as grilled shrimp with a salad. Look for casual indoor seating on rainy days or an outdoor patio.

Bob Briggs' 'Wee Packet' (☎ 508-398-2181, 79 Depot St, Dennisport) Dishes $3-14. Open for lunch & dinner daily May-Sept, breakfast daily July-Aug. This simple, diner-style place is packed with locals and visitors who appreciate moderately priced, piping hot meals. The menu extends from broiled seafood, sandwiches and quiche to homemade desserts. A 'Wee Packet,' by the way, is a small ship and this homey place is no bigger than one. Check out their homemade doughnuts next door.

Kream 'n Kone (☎ 508-394-0808, 527 MA 28, Dennisport) Meals average $15. If you appreciate a side serving of family-style kitsch with your fried seafood, this place dishes it out like nobody else on the Cape.

Contrast Bistro and Espresso Bar (☎ 508-385-9100, 605 MA 6A, Dennis) Lunch $5-12, dinner $9-26. This mod bistro is lively with bold colors and large canvases. The food is less bold than the decor, but you'll find large portions of such disparate dishes as a frittata, grilled chicken sandwich with sun-dried tomato pesto and moussaka. The desserts are luscious and the coffee strong.

Scargo Café (☎ 508-385-8200, 799 MA 6A, Dennis) Lunch $5-12, dinner $10-20. Awash in polished wood and natural light, sedate Scargo appeals to a pre-matinee and theater crowd, who munch on specials such as grilled lamb, shrimp and pasta and chicken with ginger sauce.

Gina's By The Sea (☎ 508-385-3213, 143 Taunton St, Dennis) Dinner mains $9-22. Off MA 6A, Gina's is deservedly popular, popular, popular. Arrive early (no reservations are taken), put your name on the waiting list and go to the beach, just steps away. The northern Italian menu features traditional, wickedly garlicky dishes. The interior is pleasant, with knotty-pine paneling, exposed ceiling beams and a small bar. Maybe you'll get lucky and land an outdoor table.

Entertainment

It's a different production each week at the **Cape Playhouse** (☎ 508-385-3838, 820 MA 6A, Dennis) Tickets $20-38, children's shows $6. Generally regarded as the Cape's best summer theater, the playhouse features well-known actors and rising stars.

Cape Cinema (☎ 508-385-2503, 820 MA 6A, Dennis) On the grounds of the Cape Playhouse, this cinema shows foreign, art and independent films. The exterior looks like a Congregational church, but it was built as a cinema in 1930. The art deco ceiling, not to be missed, was painted with a huge mural depicting heaven.

Christine's (☎ 508-394-7333, 581 MA 28, West Dennis) Open year-round, but entertainment only from 'March-ish through September-ish.' The liveliest place outside of Hyannis on the Cape's south side, Christine's hosts dance bands, cabaret, jazz and comedy.

Shopping

Pricey **Scargo Pottery** (☎ 508-385-3894, 30 Dr Lords Rd S) offers a change from the omnipresent antique shops. Barely east of Scargo Lake beach, off MA 6A, this pottery shop features playful interpretations of architectural icons that double as birdhouses.

BREWSTER

Brewster, another tranquil little town on MA 6A, is home to an excellent natural history museum, an equally exceptional state park with camping, and many fine restaurants worth a splurge.

From US 6 take exit 10 (MA 124 North) into town or continue along MA 6A; everything of interest is on or just off of MA 6A. From Brewster, it's only 5 miles (10 minutes) to Orleans and 9 miles (about 15 minutes) to Chatham.

The Brewster Chamber of Commerce (☎ 508-896-3500, W www.brewstercapecod.org, 2198 MA 6A), a half-mile east of MA 124 and behind the town offices, is open most days from 9am to 2pm or 3pm from late April to mid-October.

The Brewster Book Store (☎ 508-896-6543, 2648 MA 6A) is well-stocked with local titles as well as children's books.

Things to See & Do

The mission of the **Cape Cod Museum of Natural History** (☎ 508-896-3867, 869 MA 6A; adult/senior/child $5/4.50/2; open 9:30am-4:30pm Mon-Sat, 11am-4:30pm Sun year-round) is to 'educate, enlighten, and entertain' people about the Cape's unique natural history. And they certainly do a good job at it. To that end, you'll find a series of marine tanks teeming with all sorts of swimming life forms, whale displays and three short but highly recommended nature trails that cross cranberry bogs, salt marshes and beech groves.

The museum sponsors a variety of excellent naturalist-led canoe and kayak trips and seal-watching trips. Since the lineup of programs fluctuates from season to season, it's best to call for an exact schedule and prices.

With 2000 acres, **Nickerson State Park** was a local businessman's hunting and fishing estate in the early 1900s. It boasts eight ponds, a network of trails for bicycling and walking, picnic sites and sandy beaches. And it's all free. The **Cape Cod Rail Trail** (see the Cape Cod Rail Trail section under Dennis) runs through here; there are bike rentals on site. **Rail Trail Bike & Blades** (☎ 508-896-8200, 302 Underpass Rd; open year-round), off MA 6A, also rents in-line skates as well as bikes. **Jack's Boat Rentals** (☎ 508-896-8556), on Flax Pond within Nickerson State Park, rents canoes, kayaks and other flotation devices.

The **tidal flats** off MA 6A are a great place to explore at low tide, when you can walk almost a mile into Cape Cod Bay. You can usually park for free at town beaches when the surge of sunbathers has dissipated (late afternoon and anytime between early September and mid-June).

The **Stony Brook Grist Mill** (☎ 508-896-6745; 830 Stony Brook Rd; admission by donation; open 2pm-5pm Thur-Sat Apr-June; 2pm-5pm Fri July & Aug) and **Herring Run** (no ☎; admission free), adjacent to each other off MA 6A, are one of the Cape's most tranquil and lush spots. Try to visit the open-air Herring Run from mid-April to mid-May, when thousands of herring migrate from the ocean to fresh water in order to spawn. As for the mill, the water wheel still turns the machinery that grinds cornmeal.

The **New England Fire & History Museum** (☎ *508-896-5711, 1439 MA 6A; adult/child $5/2.50; open 10am-4pm Mon-Fri, noon-4pm Sat & Sun late May–mid-Sept; noon-4pm Sat & Sun mid-Sept–mid-Oct)*, arranged to resemble a 19th-century village, includes a blacksmith's shop, apothecary's shop and 30 working fire engines. Kids will enjoy it, but unfortunately, there are no Dalmatians.

Places to Stay

Camping The best campsites on the Cape are at **Nickerson State Park** (☎ *508-896-3491, 877-422-6762 for reservations, 3488 MA 6A)* Sites $15. Open mid-Mar–Dec. It's tough to get a spot here; reserve up to six months in advance if you can. There are 418 wooded sites, some waterfront. About 80 additional sites are rented on a first-come, first-served basis, but you may have to wait a few days to get one. In the summer, don't get your hopes up. From mid-October through December and mid-March to mid-April, the sites are only rented Thursday through Sunday nights. There are also six rustically furnished, canvas yurts that rent for $25 to $35 nightly for 4 to 6 people.

Sweetwater Forest (☎ *508-896-3773, 676 MA 124)* Sites $22-29. Open year-round, but only self-contained RVs permitted in winter. Sweetwater has 150 sites on 60 acres, a playground, small swimming beach for children and a rec room for rainy days.

Shady Knoll Campground (☎ *508-896-3002, cnr MA 6A & MA 137)* Sites $28. Open mid-May–mid-Oct. If Nickerson is full, try this place with 100 mostly shady sites in natural surroundings.

Inns Brewster's inns are good examples of how almost anything can be turned into charming accommodations.

Old Sea Pines Inn (☎ *508-896-6114, fax 508-896-7387, W www.oldseapinesinn.com, 2553 MA 6A)* Doubles $65-110 off-season, $75-150 July-Aug, with full buffet breakfast. Open mid-Mar–mid-Dec. A former girls' school, this establishment has 24 rooms and suites that range from small to moderately roomy. Some have antique iron and brass beds; some have shared bath or a fireplace; others in the rear annex are more motel-like but quite pleasant. The living room is spacious and the front porch set with rockers. The family suites can accommodate three to four people.

The Blue Cedar B&B (☎ *508-896-4353, fax 508-896-1235, W www.thebluecedar.com, 699 MA 6A)* Doubles $95-110 off-season, $110-135 late May–mid-Sept, with continental breakfast. Open May-Oct. This renovated mid-19th-century farmhouse has three tasteful rooms that are delightfully free of clutter. There's even nightly 'turndown.'

Isaiah Clark House (☎ *508-896-2223, 800-822-4001, fax 508-896-2138, W www.isaiahclarkhouse.com, 1187 MA 6A)* Doubles $115-120 off-season, $140-150 mid-May–Oct, with full breakfast. Open Mar-Dec. This late-18th-century house has seven unpretentious and homey guest rooms, some with a fireplace. Breakfast is served in the historic keeping room or on the back deck.

Captain Freeman Inn (☎ *508-896-7481, 800-843-4664, fax 508-896-5618, W www.captainfreemaninn.com, 15 Breakwater Rd)* Doubles $115-190 off-season, $140-250 June-Oct, with full breakfast. Open year-round. The lovely Captain Freeman Inn, just off MA 6A, is the most upscale area inn and offers some rooms with TV, VCR, fireplace, refrigerator and whirlpool tub. A couple of the more 'simple' rooms have floor-to-ceiling windows and parquet floors. The innkeeper makes such exceptional low-fat breakfasts that you might bet your guidebook they're laden with carbs and calories. (You'd lose the bet.) Breakfast is served overlooking the pool.

Places to Eat

Most of these restaurants are open only during the summer and shoulder seasons.

Cobie's (☎ *508-896-7021, 3260 MA 6A)* Dishes $3-12. Just off the Cape Cod Rail Trail, Cobie's dishes out requisite fried seafood platters; crunch and munch it at outdoor picnic tables.

JT's (☎ *508-896-3355, 2689 MA 6A*) Prices average $10-12. With a longer season, this informal eatery offers way-above-average fried seafood and sea food rolls. The evening's specials are always worthy.

Brewster Fish House (☎ *508-896-7867, 2208 MA 6A*) Lunch $8-13, dinner $15-26. Highly regarded for its simple, creatively prepared seafood at moderate (for Cape Cod) prices, the Fish House is a very pleasant albeit small place to savor a spicy lobster bisque or perhaps scallops with sun-dried tomatoes. Expect a serious wait if you arrive after 6:30pm for dinner.

Bramble Inn (☎ *508-896-7644, 2019 MA 6A*) 4-course dinner $44-66 by reservation only. The Bramble's exceptional world-influenced cuisine consistently shines above the vast majority of other Cape Cod fine dining establishments. Elegantly casual and romantic, the chef-owned restaurant serves dishes like parchment-roasted chicken with grilled lobster and seafood curries.

Chillingsworth (☎ *508-896-3640, 2449 MA 6A*) Lunch mains $9-13, bistro mains $15-23, fixed-price dinner $55-63. Chillingsworth is the Cape's best French restaurant. Their seven-course, fixed-price dinner will set you back, but there are ways to experience this place without losing your shirt. Come for an à la carte lunch and feast on grilled duck salad – or select from the bistro dinner menu in the less formal but still upscale Garden Room.

Entertainment

Much of the entertainment in Brewster is homegrown, but that doesn't mean it's not fun.

Woodshed (☎ *508-896-7771, 1993 MA 6A*) Cover $5. Just east of the town common within the Brewster Inn, locals hang out at this rustic bar and restaurant, which hosts local bands nightly in summer.

Cape Repertory Theatre (☎ *508-896-1888, 3397 MA 6A*) Adult $14-18, child $6. On the north side of MA 6A in East Brewster, this group stages creative outdoor productions in a natural amphitheater surrounded by trees (or indoors in cool and inclement weather). The company also stages a Sunday evening musical revue dinner theater at the Old Sea Pines Inn ($42.50 including a four-course dinner mid-June to mid-September).

Shopping

Brewster has the most dense concentration of antique shops on MA 6A, but the following are also worth visiting.

Brewster Store (☎ *508-896-3744, cnr MA 6A & MA 124*) This old-fashioned country store has managed to stay in operation since 1866. After picking up a few modern conveniences, pop upstairs to see some of the town memorabilia dating from the mid-19th to the mid-20th century.

The Sydenstriker Galleries (☎ *508-385-3272, 490 MA 6A*) Open year-round. The craftspeople here employ a glass-fusing technique developed by a Brewster local. You can watch 'em work mid-days except Sunday.

For fine pottery, stop at *Clayworks (3820 MA 6A)*, *Kemp Pottery (258 MA 6A)* and *Heart Pottery (1145 MA 6A)*.

HARWICH

There's not much to recommend in Harwich, but if you're passing through from Hyannis to Chatham, you'll find a couple of decent restaurants, some modest B&Bs, many motels, and an alternative Nantucket ferry. Tranquil Wychmere Harbor, with a convenient grassy picnic spot overlooking it, sits right on MA 28. Like other townships that sprawl along MA 28, Harwich's stretch is jammed with go-carts, bumper boats, pitching cages and trinket shops selling huge inflated beach toys.

The Harwich Chamber of Commerce (☎ 508-432-1600, 800-441-3199, Ⓦ www.harwichcc.com, MA 28) is open 9am to 5pm daily late May to mid-October. The business office is a couple of doors away, within the Cape Cod Five Cents Savings Bank, and that office is open 9am to 3pm weekdays year-round.

Wychmere Book & Coffee (☎ 508-432-7868, 587 MA 28) has the market nicely covered.

Cape Water Sports (☎ *508-432-5996, 337 MA 28*) rents canoes ($50 daily) and kayaks

($50/65 single/double daily) for paddling on the Herring River. At the corner of MA 28 and MA 124, they're open year-round. You'll need your own roof rack if the boat won't fit inside your car.

Wychmere Village Lodging (☎ 508-432-1434, 800-432-1434, fax 508-432-8904, W www.wychmere.com, 767 MA 28) Doubles $55-85 off-season, $104-140 mid-June–mid-Sept. Open Apr-late Oct. Right on MA 28, this tidy complex has 24 simple motel rooms outfitted with cable TV, air con and kitchenette. They can all accommodate families. Try to get a room facing the pool and playground.

Augustus Snow House (☎ 508-430-0528, 800-320-0528, fax 508-432-6638, W www .augustussnow.com, 528 MA 28) Doubles $125-160 off-season, $170-190 mid-May–mid-Oct, with full breakfast. This circa-1901 Victorian inn, fanciful with its turrets and gabled dormers, rents five spacious guest rooms which have some of the most unusual bathroom fixtures in New England. All rooms have a gas fireplace and TV. For a real splurge, ask about the two-room suite.

Bonatt's Restaurant & Bakery (☎ 508-432-7199, 537 MA 28) Dishes $4-10. In the center of town, this short-order kitchen serves consistent, inexpensive fish-and-chips, steak sandwiches and the like. The atmosphere is pleasant and friendly.

Mason Jar (☎ 508-430-7600, 544 MA 28) Sandwiches $5.50. Mason Jar offers fancy sandwiches, cheeses and pâtés.

Lambert's (☎ 508-432-5415, 710 MA 28) More an upscale grocery store than anything else, Lambert's has a great deli section and some indoor tables.

Seafood Sam's (☎ 508-432-1422, 302 MA 28) Dishes $5-12. This family-style, fast-food seafood joint has reliable fryolator standbys.

Harwich Junior Theatre (☎ 508-432-2002, cnr Division & Willow Sts, West Harwich) Adult/senior/child $14/12/10. The country's oldest children's theater stages four shows in summer, when all tickets cost $10.

See Nantucket's Getting There & Away section (in the Martha's Vineyard & Nantucket Island chapter) for Nantucket ferry information.

CHATHAM

The patriarch of Cape Cod towns, Chatham has a genteel, refined reserve that is evident along its shady Main St; the shops are upscale and expensive, the lodging-places tony. Though the bulk of the town's summer residents are regulars, there is certainly an ardent transient tourist trade.

Orientation

From US 6, take MA 137 South (exit 11) to Old Queen Anne Rd to MA 28 and Main St. From Hyannis and points west, continue on MA 28 North (you're actually heading due east) into the center of town. From Orleans and points north, take MA 28 South into town to Shore Rd, which runs along the shore, past the Fish Pier, the lighthouse and onto Morris Island. Main St is about a mile long from the MA 28 rotary to Shore Rd.

Surrounded on three sides by bays, coves and inlets, Chatham is blessed with over 60 miles of shorelines. You'll be rewarded with ocean views when you veer off Main St near the center of town and east of MA 28 as it jogs north towards Orleans.

Information

A tiny shed suffices as the centrally located Chatham Information Booth (☎ 508-945-5199, 800-715-5567, W www.chathamcapecod.org, 533 Main St). It's staffed with knowledgeable locals and crammed with information. The booth is open 10am to 5pm daily mid-May to mid-October. If you're coming from Hyannis, a more seasonal booth is located at the intersection of MA 28 and MA 137.

Two independent bookstores grace Main St: the excellent Cabbages and Kings (☎ 508-945-1603) and Yellow Umbrella Books (☎ 508-945-0144).

Things to See & Do

For expansive and dramatic vistas of sand and sea, head to the **Chatham Light** viewing area on Shore Rd. A ferocious 1987 winter storm split the long spit of sand called Nauset Beach into two sections; residents still talk about the environmental consequences. The present light, by the way, dates to 1878 and is visible 15 miles out to sea. There is free parking and a fine beach below (see the Activities section).

Head to the **Fish Pier** on Shore Rd in the mid- to late afternoon to watch the fishing fleet come in with its daily catch. Chatham's boats haul in some of the freshest fish around because they're too small to stay out overnight. On Chatham menus, the term 'daily catch' really has meaning! Shellfish farming is also increasingly popular as an industry; look for bay scallops on local menus.

The little family-friendly **Railroad Museum** (*no ☎, 153 Depot Rd; admission by donation; open 10am-4pm Tues-Sat mid-June–mid-Sept*) is fashioned from an 1887 depot and features a 1910 wooden caboose. From Main St, take Old Harbor Rd north to Depot Rd.

The Historical Society's **Old Atwood House** (*☎ 508-945-2493, 347 Stage Harbor Rd; adult & child 12 yrs & over $3; open 1pm-4pm Tues-Fri mid-June–Sept*), off the western end of Main St from the rotary, contains a historical collection of over 2000 items pertaining to Chatham's past. It's a fine rainy-day activity.

Activities

Directly below the lighthouse on Shore Rd, **Chatham Light Beach** is a long, wide sandy beach. It's best to walk or bicycle to get here, because parking at the lighthouse is limited to 30 minutes.

Desolate and long **North and South Beaches** are accessible only by shuttle boat. They're worth the added expense of getting there. See the Getting There & Around section.

Monomoy Island, a 2700-acre wildlife refuge, is a haven for offshore birds and seals; it's only accessible by boat. You'll be well rewarded for making the additional effort to reach it. Try to make time for a naturalist-led tour with the **Wellfleet Bay Wildlife Sanctuary** (*☎ 508-349-2615*) or the **Cape Cod Museum of Natural History** (*☎ 508-896-3867*); call for reservations. Prices and departure times and days vary

greatly. See also the Getting There & Around section.

The Beachcomber (*☎ 508-945-5265, 680-5064*) has boats docked at the fish pier, Ryder's Cove and Stage Harbor for various trips. They take passengers to desolate stretches of beach or to Monomoy for seal-watching excursions.

Outermost Harbor Marine (*☎ 508-945-2030*), off Morris Island Rd, also offers transportation to South Beach (adult/child from $10/5 return) and Monomoy ($15) from late May to mid-October. Like a taxi service, call them when you're ready to depart and don't forget to schedule a pick-up time.

Chatham's side streets and shady lanes are well suited to bicycling. Rent bikes at **Bert & Carol's** (*☎ 508-945-0137, 347 MA 28, North Chatham*) from April to December. They have on-site parking and a good Chatham bike map ($3).

The waters off Chatham are decent for windsurfing and surfing (it's not the Banzai Pipeline), and the friendly folks at **Monomoy Sail & Cycle** (*☎ 508-945-0811, 275 MA 28, North Chatham*) rent sailboards ($45 for 24 hours).

The **Cape Cod Flying Circus** (*☎ 508-945-9000, Chatham Municipal Airport, 240 George Ryder Rd, West Chatham; flights 25/55 min $80/150; open year-round*), off MA 28, offers excellent sightseeing flights over the immediate coastline, bays and inlets. Both trips circle Monomoy Point before heading north; the short trip stops above Wellfleet harbor while the longer one skirts the tip of Provincetown.

Places to Stay

Motels Within walking distance of town is the *Chatham Highlander* (*☎ 508-945-9038, fax 508-945-5731, W www.realmass.com/highlander, 946 MA 28*) Doubles $65-110 off-season, $115-155 mid-June–early Sept. Open Apr-Nov. Just beyond the rotary, the motel's 28 rooms are extremely well maintained, each with TV and refrigerator. The friendly proprietors take deserved pride in their work.

Chatham Motel (☎ *508-945-2630, 800-770-5545,* W *www.chathammotel.com, 1487 MA 28)* Doubles $85-125 off-season, $115-165 mid-June–early Sept. Open mid-May–late Oct. Two miles west of town, this is also a good choice. The 33 nice rooms are set back from the highway in a pine grove.

Hawthorne Motel (☎ *508-945-0372,* W *www.thehawthorne.com, 196 Shore Rd)* Doubles $110-130 off-season, $150-170 late June–mid-Sept. Open mid-May–mid-Oct. It's all about location. The 27 rooms and efficiencies are standard, but they overlook the ocean and have access to a stunning private beach. The motel has no trouble with its four-night minimum stay policy in summer.

Hotels The Cape's grande dame of resort hotels is the *Chatham Bars Inn* (☎ *508-945-0096, 800-527-4884, fax 508-945-5491,* W *www.chathambarsinn.com, Shore Rd)* Rooms $190-290 off-season, $310-440 mid-June–mid-Sept, with breakfast off-season. Open year-round. The hotel comprises 205 pricey rooms and cottages on or near the beach. Facilities include an oceanside heated pool, tennis courts, a private beach and exercise facilities. It's an impressive place, especially from the vantage point of a rocking chair on the expansive veranda. You can always come just for a drink.

B&Bs All rooms are equally choice but some are more equal than others at our two listings.

Bow Roof House (☎ *508-945-1346, 59 Queen Anne Rd)* Doubles $75-85 with continental breakfast. Open year-round. Just off the rotary and within walking distance of the town and town beach, this six-room, late-18th-century house is delightfully old-fashioned in price and offerings. It's hard to find places like this anymore.

The Moorings (☎ *508-945-0848, 800-320-0848, fax 508-945-1577,* W *www.moorings capecod.com, 326 Main St)* Rooms $80-165 off-season, $142-230 mid-June–mid-Sept, with full breakfast. Open mid-Feb–Dec. In the middle of town, this first-rate complex features a great array of upgraded accommodations surrounded by immaculately landscaped private grounds. All 16 of the rooms are comfortably elegant, but some have private decks and gas fireplaces.

Places to Eat
Tired of sandwiches? See below.

Marion's Pie Shop (☎ *508-432-9439, 2022 MA 28)* Open 7am-6pm mid-Mar–Jan. Stop here for a chicken pot pie ($7.25 for a small) or some tempting breakfast baked goods.

Carmine's (☎ *508-945-5300, 595 Main St)* Slices $2-2.50, pies $10-13. For a quick pick-me-up, Carmine's dishes pizza and scoops of gelato in a faux old-fashioned ice cream parlor setting.

Beach House Grill (☎ *508-945-0096, 297 Shore Rd)* Dishes $7-16. Open for breakfast & lunch daily mid-June–mid-Sept. Across from the Chatham Bars Inn, you might expect to pay through the nose for such a privileged beachside perch. But even though this is one of a handful of Cape Cod eateries right on the beach, you don't. The ever-so-slightly upscale menu doesn't stray far from burgers, salads and fried seafood.

Chatham Squire (☎ *508-945-0945, 487 Main St)* Lunch $6-13, dinner $15-19. The town's most popular all-purpose tavern dishes out a long and varied lunch menu. At dinner, try the shrimp and chicken stir-fry or seafood stew ($19). The bar, to the left as you walk in, offers the same food, served at a higher noise level.

Christian's (☎ *508-945-3362, 443 Main St)* Dinner mains $10-21. Although the central location is enticing, there are better places to drop some bucks. If you must, opt for meatloaf with gravy and chicken with biscuits. Cajun french fries are a highlight.

Sosumi Asian Bistro & Sushi Bar (☎ *508-945-0300, 14 Chatham Bars Ave)* Dinner mains $15-21. Sosumi's exotic flavors light up any palate bored with sautéed seafood. Dishes at the hip bistro range from scallops tempura to a tuna burger with wasabi mayo to homemade parsnip chips. You can always eat tapas-style, by choosing lots of little dishes.

Chatham Wayside Inn (☎ 508-945-5550, 512 Main St) Breakfast $5-8, lunch $6-11, dinner $16-24. This touristy place, dominating the center of town, has middle-of-the-road service and offerings. It's not bad; it's just not as good as it should be. The menu ranges from eggs Benedict to lunchtime chicken Caesar salads to evening attempts at creativity pairing duck with pineapple.

Impudent Oyster (☎ 508-945-3545, 15 Chatham Bars Ave) Lunch $7-14, dinner $18-24. Barely off Main St, this place attracts conservative palates with its seafood menu and fresh-shucked oysters. Follow the locals, ordering from the daily specials menu. Lunch is far more reasonable than dinner.

Entertainment

There's something here for everyone.

Outdoor Band Concerts (no ☎, Kate Gould Park) Performances 8pm Fri early July-early Sept. Most Cape towns have summertime outdoor concerts, but Chatham boasts the granddaddy. Thousands of folks have gathered since the mid-1930s to listen and dance to big-band music from the gazebo off Main St. Bring a picnic blanket and follow the crowds.

Monomoy Theatre (☎ 508-945-1589, 776 MA 28) Shows late June-late Aug. On the way toward Harwich, this well-known Equity playhouse with Ohio University students stages a new production weekly.

Chatham Squire (see Places to Eat) Hundreds of college kids who work the area resorts gather here with local fishermen and summer folk to rock and roll every night of the summer. You may not find the love of your life here, but you will probably find somebody to love.

Shopping

Main St is bursting with shops that could drain your pockets fast. Three galleries, in particular, are more like museums:

Chatham Glass Company (☎ 508-945-5547, 758 Main St) Just west of the rotary, this shop displays brilliant glass pieces blown on the premises.

Munson Gallery (☎ 508-945-2888, 880 Main St) You won't find tacky 'tourist' art' within this renovated horse barn.

Odell's Studio and Gallery (☎ 508-945-3239, 423 Main St) In the middle of town, Odell's features work by two exceptional artists, a metalsmith and a painter.

Getting There & Around

It takes 15 minutes (9 miles) to head up MA 28 to the Orleans rotary, and another 45 minutes to buzz up to Provincetown on US 6 from the rotary.

Chatham is best explored on foot; it's about a 30-minute walk from the western end of Main St to the lighthouse on Shore Rd and another 15 minutes from the lighthouse to the fish pier.

For South Beach shuttles and birdwatching and seal trips to Monomoy, use the Monomoy Island Ferry (☎ 508-945-5450) from Wikis Way off Morris Island Rd. Make reservations the night before you want to go; prices vary widely with the services rendered.

ORLEANS

To some, Orleans is simply the place where MA 28 and US 6 converge and US 6 heads north to Provincetown. Others know that Nauset Beach is exceptional, that Nauset Marsh has a rich ecosystem worth exploring and that there are lots of good restaurants here. But fewer know that Orleans has a military history: The British fired upon Orleans during the War of 1812 and a German submarine fired a few torpedoes at it during WWI. Rock Harbor, off the rotary, consists of little more than a colorful clam shack, charter fishing fleet and a small beach, but it is quiet and worth a detour.

Orientation & Information

US 6, MA 6A and MA 28 all converge at the rotary on the northern edge of town.

Main St, which intersects with MA 6A and 28, runs northwest to picturesque Rock Harbor and east to East Orleans center and Nauset Beach (where it turns into Beach Rd). The stretch of MA 28 that heads south through Orleans, along Pleasant Bay, is particularly scenic.

The Orleans Chamber of Commerce (☎ 508-240-2484, W www.capecodorleans .com, Eldredge Park Way), off MA 6A just north of US 6, maintains a seasonal information booth, open 10am to 6pm Monday to Saturday and 11am to 3pm Sunday late May to mid-October. The administrative office (44 Main St) is open 10am to 2pm weekdays year-round.

Activities

One of the Cape's best beaches for walking, sunning or bodysurfing is **Nauset Beach**, at the end of Beach Rd from Main St in East Orleans. The 9-mile-long barrier beach on the Atlantic Ocean has good facilities, including restrooms, changing rooms and a snack bar. Parking costs $10, though it's usually free off-season.

You can explore the quiet back roads and coves on bicycles rented at **Orleans Cycle** (☎ 508-255-9115, 26 Main St); they're open April through December.

The excellent **Goose Hummock Outdoor Center** (☎ 508-255-2620, off MA 6A, Town Cove) rents canoes and kayaks (singles $25-35, doubles $35 for four hours) for use on the protected and calm waters of Pleasant Bay and Nauset Marsh. They also have half-day tours ($60) of Nauset Marsh and introductory paddling courses (2½-hour lessons $50) daily May through October.

Clamming with Casey Jones (☎ 508-896-4048; $35 per person) is an adventure you won't soon forget. There's more to digging clams than having a rake and bucket and going to the beach. It's an art that takes a lifetime to perfect, and Casey dispenses her wisdom with grace and humor. She'll take you out for a 2½- to four-hour adventure and show you the ropes. You get to keep the clams!

Rock Harbor Charter Fleet (☎ 508-255-9757, 800-287-1771; $100-120 for a 4- to 8-hr trip), the Cape's largest charter fishing fleet, is docked here at Rock Harbor on Cape Cod Bay. The best way to find a captain is to cruise the slips and talk to them. At various

KIM GRANT

Roll up your sleeves and step into your special pants: clam digging in Pleasant Bay, Cape Cod

Trans-Atlantic Communication

The multibillion dollar telecommunications industry owes a debt of gratitude to Cape Cod's Atlantic Shore. Long before cell phones and beepers and satellites, there were underwater cables, which came ashore in Orleans. Forget the information superhighway. We're talking the information slow lane here.

Between 1890 and 1941 the **French Cable Station** transmitted communications via a 4000-mile-long cable between Orleans and Brest, France. Among the messages relayed: Lindbergh's arrival in Paris and Germany's invasion of France. With the aid of the Smithsonian Institution, the little museum in Orleans (☎ 508-240-1735, Cove Rd at MA 28; admission free; open 1pm-4pm Mon-Sat July & Aug, 1pm-4pm Fri-Sun June & Sept) contains all the original equipment used to send messages. The displays look every bit as complicated as today's circuit boards, but not-so-nerdy staff members help decipher things.

Up the road off US 6 in South Wellfleet, the **Marconi Wireless Station** was the first place in the US to transmit messages across the Atlantic Ocean without the aid of wires and cables. With the technology of the day, however, it took 25,000 volts of electricity to place a long-distance call. In 1903 President Roosevelt used Guglielmo Marconi's invention to send 'most cordial greetings and good wishes' to King Edward VII in England. Because of wartime security, the station was shuttered in 1917. Little remains today except for interpretive plaques, an expansive vista, a walking trail and a fine beach.

times of the season, the waters teem with bluefish, striped bass and mackerel. To reach Rock Harbor from MA 6A, turn northwest on Main St and keep going until you reach the water.

Places to Stay

Efficiencies A half-hour's walk from Nauset Beach is *Kadee's Gray Elephant* (☎ 508-255-7608, fax 508-240-2976, 216 Main

St, East Orleans) Apartments $95/140 off-season/July-Aug. Open mid-May–mid-Oct. These 10 fancifully painted, artsy efficiency apartments were carved out of a 200-year-old sea captain's house.

Motels Prices don't fluctuate at the *Ship's Knees Inn* (☎ 508-255-1312, fax 508-240-1351, 186 Beach Rd, East Orleans) Doubles $65-140 year-round. Of the 18 rooms here, a few are nice inn-style rooms but more are plain motel-style rooms. Some share a bath.

Olde Tavern Motel (☎ 508-255-1565, 800-544-7705, 151 MA 6A) Doubles $54-81 off-season, $82-120 mid-June–early Sept. Open Apr-Nov. This one-story brick motel is about a half-mile east of the rotary and has 28 of the least expensive (standard) motel rooms in town.

The Cove (☎ 508-255-1203, 800-343-2233, fax 508-255-7736, ⓦ www.thecoveorleans.com, 13 MA 28) Rooms $59-138 off-season, $109-199 late June-early Sept. Open year-round. In the middle of town but apart from the bustle, the Cove has 47 very nice motel rooms and suites with refrigerators, free movies and coffeemakers. Some are situated right on Town Cove, and all have access to private shoreline, barbecue grills and a heated pool. Deluxe rooms can handle four people.

B&Bs Easily one of the best area lodgings is the *Nauset House Inn* (☎ 508-255-2195, ⓦ www.nausethouseinn.com, Beach Rd) Single $65, doubles $75-140, with full breakfast. Open Apr-Oct. This property has friendly innkeepers, comfortable rooms, plentiful common areas (including a greenhouse conservatory) and an excellent beach location – it's about a 10-minute walk to Nauset Beach. What more could you ask for? OK, afternoon snacks and drinks.

Parsonage Inn (☎ 508-255-8217, 888-422-8217, fax 508-255-8216, ⓦ www.parsonageinn.com, 202 Main St, East Orleans) Doubles $95-105 off-season, $120-145 May-Oct, with full breakfast. Open Feb-Dec. This rambling 18th-century residence has eight nice guest rooms with wide pine floors and canopy beds. Breakfast is a treat. For longer stays, opt for the roomy studio apartment or the renovated barn.

Places to Eat

Orleans has a remarkably diverse selection of high-quality eateries, and many are open year-round. If you're staying nearby, chances are you'll be eating in Orleans.

Hot Chocolate Sparrow (☎ *508-240-2230, Old Colony Way*) Behind the CVS on MA 6A and adjacent to the Cape Cod Rail Trail, the Sparrow has the strongest and most consistent espresso around, bar none. They also hand-dip chocolate.

New York Bagels (☎ *508-255-0255, 125 MA 6A*) This bona fide place deals in bagels, smoked whitefish, kosher pastrami and everything else you'd expect to find at a Jewish deli in Brooklyn.

Land Ho! (☎ *508-255-5165, 38 MA 6A*) Dishes $9-15. Locals and tourists alike flock here for inexpensive sandwiches, fried seafood platters, barbecue ribs, clam pie and burgers. An informal atmosphere is created with wooden floors, old business signs on the walls and newspapers hanging on a wire that separates the tables from the bar.

Cap't Cass Rock Harbor Seafood (no ☎, *117 Rock Harbor Rd*) Lunch $6-12, dinner $10-30. This little harborside seafood shack is more quaint than most and offers generous lobster rolls, clam chowder and daily blackboard specials.

Lobster Claw (☎ *508-255-1800, 42 MA 6A*) Lunch about $7, dinner mains $9-16. Near the rotary and filled with nautical paraphernalia, this informal family-friendly place has been owned by the same folks since 1970. Lobsters, mixed-seafood plates and all kinds of fish – they're all on the menu. Generous portions don't generally allow room for dessert.

Joe's Beach Road Bar & Grille (☎ *508-255-0212, 5 Beach Rd, East Orleans*) Dinner mains $8-17. Open year-round. This rustic and rockin' hangout for locals and tourists serves creative and hearty seafood, steak, pizza, burgers, sandwiches and pasta. Keep your eyes peeled for lobster specials.

Binnacle Tavern (☎ *508-255-7901, 20 MA 28*) Dinner mains $11-18. This cozy tavern is known for gourmet pizza, but it also offers Italian specialties like eggplant parmigiana and homemade pasta.

Kadee's Lobster & Clam Bar (☎ *508-255-6184, 212 Main St, East Orleans*) Lunch $6-14, dinner $10-18. Prices are a bit high, but the seafood is fresh and outdoor tables draw 'em in after a day at Nauset Beach, just down the road. You know the choices by now: oysters, seafood stew, lobster, scallops.

Nauset Beach Club (☎ *508-255-8547, 222 Main St, East Orleans*) Pastas $10-24, 'proteins' $19-30. Authentic and creative northern Italian and fish specials appeal to a more fashionable crowd. The restaurant, a former duck-hunting cottage, is small but the portions are enormous (no sharing is permitted).

Christian's Academy Ocean Grill (☎ *508-240-1585, 2 Academy Place at MA 28*) Dinner mains $19-24. This outstanding seafood restaurant never disappoints. Look for such creative dishes as swordfish with a basil glaze, sole Française and roasted duck (it's not all seafood). All mains are dressed with a trio of different veggies. The house vinaigrette is good to the last drop.

Entertainment

Next to the windmill is the *Orleans Inn* (☎ *508-255-2222, Town Cove, cnr MA 28 & US 6*). The inn's outdoor sundeck is a fine place for an après-beach or sunset drink. Focus on the drinks rather than the food.

Academy of Performing Arts Playhouse (☎ *508-255-1963, 120 Main St*) Tickets $12-16. Performances year-round. The Playhouse stages a variety of dramas, musicals and comedies in the 1873 former town hall.

Shopping

A diverse arts and crafts gallery, the *Left Bank Gallery* (☎ *508-247-9172, 8 Cove Rd*) is a treat for the visual senses.

The Bird Watcher's General Store (☎ *508-255-6974, 36 MA 6A*) Near the rotary, this place is more devoted to our feathered friends than many people are to

Cape Cod National Seashore

With the backing of President Kennedy, who appreciated the Cape's uniqueness and considered it his home, Congress established the Cape Cod National Seashore (CCNS) in 1961. The CCNS includes the whole eastern shoreline of the Outer Cape, from South Beach in Chatham to Race Point Beach in Provincetown. It covers more than 42 sq miles, including at least half (and often more) of the land mass in Eastham, Wellfleet, Truro and Provincetown. The seashore is known for pristine and virtually endless beaches, crashing waves, dunes, nature trails, ponds, salt marshes and forests.

Everything of interest is on or just off of US 6, the only highway that runs from Orleans to Provincetown.

The **Salt Pond Visitor Center** (☎ 508-255-3421, www.nps.gov/caco), off US 6 in Eastham, anchors the southern portion of the CCNS. There are excellent exhibits and films about the Cape's geology, history and ever-changing landscape. Check out the daily list of ranger- and naturalist-led walks and talks, which are usually free. There are two short walking trails that lead from the visitor center. The center is open 9am to 4:30pm daily March to December (until 5pm in summer) and on weekends in January and February.

The **Province Lands Visitor Center** (☎ 508-487-1256, Race Point Rd), in Provincetown, has similar services and exhibits; you can also pick up local trail and bike maps here. It's open 9am to 5pm daily May to October.

Parking permits at CCNS beaches are transferable at all beaches, which means that you can spend the morning at one, the afternoon at the other and not have to pay the parking fee again.

their mothers. The staffers are quite knowledgeable about where and when to spot the various species of birds that flock to the Cape.

Getting There & Around

The Plymouth & Brockton bus (☎ 508-778-9767) stops at the CVS drugstore on MA 6A on its way from Provincetown ($6) to Hyannis ($4) and Boston ($14).

It's about 3 miles from the center of Orleans to Nauset Beach, and about half that distance in the opposite direction to Rock Harbor. If you shoot directly north on US 6 to Provincetown, it takes about 45 minutes (29 miles).

EASTHAM

Home to the Cape's oldest windmill, Eastham is one of the Cape's quietest, most compact towns, just 3 miles wide from bay to ocean, and 6 miles long. It's perhaps best known for what happened in 1620: The Pilgrims first 'encountered' Native Americans

on a stretch of land now aptly called First Encounter Beach. The meeting was less than amicable, though there were no fatalities, and the white guys didn't return to the area for another 24 years.

Just north of the Fort Hill area, the chamber of commerce (☎ 508-255-3444, 240-7211, Ⓦ www.easthamchamber.com, US 6) is open 10am to 5pm daily late May through September, with slightly longer hours in July and August.

For more tourist information, go to the Cape Cod National Seashore Salt Pond Visitor Center (☎ 508-255-3421, off US 6); see also the boxed text 'Cape Cod National Seashore.'

The Plymouth & Brockton bus (☎ 508-778-9767) stops across from the Eastham Town Hall (MA 6) on its way from Boston ($18) and Hyannis ($4) to Provincetown ($5).

Heading north on US 6, it's 15 minutes (11 miles) to Wellfleet and 35 minutes (25 miles) to Provincetown.

Things to See & Do

Definitely stop at **Fort Hill**, east of US 6, which commands a high position above the extensive and fragile Nauset Marsh, and boasts a short but lovely 1½ mile (round-trip) walking trail that skirts the marsh and heads inland through a red maple swamp.

Atop Fort Hill, the **Edward Penniman House** (☎ 508-255-3421; admission free; tours 10am Sat & Mon), a mid-19th-century sea captain's house, is slowly being restored to its former grandeur by the National Park Service (NPS). Although visiting hours are erratic, you can always peek in the windows. The Salt Pond Visitor Center has current opening times.

The **Old Schoolhouse Museum** (☎ 508-255-0788, Nauset Rd; admission free; open 1pm-4pm Mon-Fri July & Aug), marked by a huge set of whale jawbones across from the Salt Pond Visitor Center, features a small exhibit on Henry Beston's year spent in a cottage on Coast Guard Beach. (Beston lived alone on the beach in 1928 and recorded the natural environment around him in The Outermost House.)

The **bike trail** from the visitor center to Coast Guard Beach traverses a dramatic salt marsh and winds through a pretty forest. From April through November, rent bikes across from the Salt Pond Visitor Center at **Little Capistrano Bike Shop** (☎ 508-255-6515, Salt Pond Rd; adult $10/16, child $8/12 for 2 hr/8 hr). Look for it behind the colorful Lobster Shanty restaurant.

Beaches

The long **Coast Guard Beach**, east of the visitor center on the Atlantic Ocean, is backed by tall, undulating dune grasses. Facilities include restrooms, showers and changing rooms. Parking costs $7/20 daily/seasonally. In summer, a bus shuttles folks from a parking lot near the visitor center to the beach.

Nauset Light Beach, north of Coast Guard Beach, is also the stuff of dreams. Its features and facilities are similar to Coast Guard Beach, but you can park right at the beach for $7/20 daily/seasonally. **Nauset Lighthouse**, a picturesque red-and-white striped tower, guards the shoreline. (Threatened by an ever-encroaching shoreline, the lighthouse was moved about 250 feet from the current cliff in 1996, so that these days it looks, in fact, rather far from the coastline.) Even more incongruously placed, the **Three Sisters Lighthouses** are set even farther back in the woods.

Places to Stay

Hostels It's all dorm style at **Hostelling International, Mid-Cape** (☎ 508-255-2785, 800-909-4776 for reservations in-season, fax 508-240-5598, W www.hiayh.org, 75 Goody Hallet Dr, Eastham) Beds for members/nonmembers $15/19. Open mid-May–mid-Sept. With only 50 beds in eight cabins, reservations (by mail or by phone with credit card) are essential for July and August. Off-season, write to Hostelling International Boston, 12 Hemenway St, Boston, MA 02215 or call ☎ 617-531-0459. To get there, from US 6 and the Orleans rotary, follow Harbor Rd to Bridge Rd to Goody Hallet Dr.

Motels Some units can accommodate a whole family at the **Midway Motel** (☎ 508-255-3117, 800-755-3117, fax 508-255-4235, W www.midwaymotel.com, 5460 US 6) Doubles $58-90 off-season, $94-97 late June-Aug. Open Apr-Oct. These 11 excellent units are set back from the highway and shaded by pine trees.

Captain's Quarters (☎ 508-255-5686, 800-327-7769, fax 508-240-0280, W www.captains-quarters.com, US 6) Doubles $69-79 off-season, $135 mid-June–early Sept. Open Apr-Nov. About a half-mile north of Brackett Rd, this motel offers 75 large rooms (many well suited to four people), a heated pool and tennis courts. Bicycle use is complimentary.

Hotels One can stay year-round at the **Four Points Hotel – Eastham Cape Cod** (☎ 508-255-5000, 800-533-3986, fax 508-240-1870, W www.fourpoints-eastham.com, 2700 US 6) Doubles $79-169 off-season, $249 July-Aug.

Less than a mile north of Salt Pond Visitor Center, this Sheraton is expensive in summer for what you get. But during the rest of the year, the rates drop as the occupancy does. Half the 107 rooms overlook the indoor pool; the others are larger and have refrigerators.

B&Bs Queue up for a cue at the *Overlook Inn* (☎ 508-255-1886, fax 508-240-0345, Ⓦ www.overlookinn.com, 3085 US 6) Doubles $95-160 off-season, $140-190 June–mid-Oct, with full breakfast. Open year-round. Across from the Salt Pond Visitor Center, the inn is set back from the road and offers 14 antique-filled guest rooms. The common rooms are somewhat eccentric but charming and include a billiard room. The Cape Cod Rail Trail is out the back door.

Whalewalk Inn (☎ 508-255-0617, 800-440-1281, fax 508-240-0017, Ⓦ www.whale walkinn.com, 220 Bridge Rd) Doubles $145-250 off-season, $175-300 mid-May–mid-Oct, with full breakfast. Open year-round. This establishment, off the Orleans-Eastham rotary, is the Outer Cape's best B&B. If you want to splurge, there are five private suite/cottages here (most with kitchen), five elegant guest rooms in the main inn and six luxurious carriage-house rooms. The living room exudes a sophisticated country elegance and breakfast is served on a private flagstone patio.

Places to Eat
These two eateries focus on seafood.

Arnold's Lobster & Clam Bar (☎ 508-255-2575, 3580 US 6) Dishes $7-16. Open for lunch & dinner mid-May–mid-Sept. With the exception of a raw bar, great onion rings and weekday lunch specials as low as $3, you know the menu: baskets and buckets of fried seafood.

Eastham Lobster Pool (☎ 508-255-9706, 4360 US 6) Mains average $20. Open 11:30am-9pm daily Apr-Oct. The Pool offers informal indoor and outdoor dining on lobsters (surprise!), tasty clam chowder ($3/4 cup/bowl) and fish cooked practically any way you'd like it.

Entertainment
Off US 6 from the windmill, look for *First Encounter Coffee House* (☎ 508-255-5438, Samoset Rd) Tickets $10-15. This little yellow chapel hosts acoustic and folk performances on the second and fourth Saturday of each month, except in December and May. Off-season, it's a real insider's place.

WELLFLEET
Like most Outer Cape towns, Wellfleet is relatively untouched by development and rampant commercialism. Although Wellfleet is full of professional people who have taken up summer residence for the season, day-trippers are lured by art galleries, fine beaches, quiet scenic roads and the famous Wellfleet oysters. The town is extremely quiet from early September to late June.

Orientation & Information
Main and Commercial Sts run parallel to each other in the center of town. Continue west along either road to scenic Chequessett Neck Rd. West of US 6, Pilgrim Spring Rd is also pretty; there is a nice harbor view from its terminus. East of US 6, LeCount Hollow Rd leads to Ocean View Drive and Atlantic Ocean beaches.

The Wellfleet Chamber of Commerce (☎ 508-349-2510, Ⓦ www.wellfleetchamber .com, off US 6, South Wellfleet) is open 9am to 6pm daily late May to early September and 10am to 4pm Friday through Sunday in spring (from mid-May) and fall (until mid-October).

Things to See & Do
The Massachusetts Audubon Society's 1000-acre **Wellfleet Bay Wildlife Sanctuary** (☎ 508-349-2615, US 6; adult/child $3/2; visitor center open 8:30am-5pm daily May-Oct, 8:30am-5pm Tues-Sun Nov-Apr; trails open sunrise-sunset year-round) boasts walking trails that cross tidal creeks, salt marshes and a Cape Cod Bay beach.

Marconi Beach, off US 6, is a narrow Atlantic beach backed by high sand dunes. Parking is $7/20 daily/seasonally; facilities include changing rooms, restrooms and showers.

Both **Cahoon Hollow Beach** and **White Crest Beach**, on the Atlantic Ocean, are excellent but parking is $10 daily. White Crest is popular with hang gliders.

The 8-mile **Great Island Trail**, off Chequessett Neck Rd, requires four hours, lots of sunscreen, water and a bit of stamina since you'll be walking on soft sand out to a spit of sand that curves around into Wellfleet Bay. The lack of human presence more than compensates for the extra effort. The road to the Great Island Trail is narrow, hilly and winding.

The **Cape Cod Rail Trail**, which begins in Dennis 26 miles southwest, ends at LeCount Hollow Rd, a couple miles from two good beaches. You can rent bikes at the small **Idle Times** (☎ 508-349-9161, US 6) mid-May to early September.

Jack's Boat Rentals (☎ 508-349-9808, US 6), near Wellfleet Center, rents kayaks, canoes and sailboards. Inquire about their guided trips on local rivers and glacial ponds. They also have a Gull Pond location if you want the ease of paddling where you pick up.

Places to Stay

Camping Large commercial campgrounds are the rule here.

Paine's Campground (☎ 508-349-3007, 800-479-3017, Old Colony Rd) Sites $18-24. Open late-May-Sept. Paine's, off US 6, offers 150 sites, most of which are large, wooded and reserved for tenters. It's a 20-minute walk to the beach.

Maurice's Campground (☎ 508-349-2029, US 6) Sites $20, cabins $70, cottages $450 weekly. Open late May–mid-Oct. Just north of the Eastham town line and on the Cape Cod Rail Trail, this campground reserves about a quarter of its 180 shaded sites for tents. They also have some cabins and cottages rented weekly and accommodating three or four people.

Motels & Cottages You can choose a room or a cottage at **Even' Tide Motel** (☎ 508-349-3410, 800-368-0007, fax 508-349-7804, Ⓦ www.eventidemotel.com, 650 US 6) Rooms $59-79 off-season, $92-112 mid-

June–early Sept. Open Apr-Oct. This nice 31-room motel, about 4 miles north of the Salt Pond Visitor Center and set back in a grove of trees, also has nine cottages. If you're lucky enough to get one, it can accommodate up to eight people. Other pluses include an indoor heated pool, a nearby 1-mile hiking trail to Marconi Beach, and the Cape Cod Rail Trail, which runs right behind the motel.

Wellfleet Motel & Lodge (☎ 508-349-3535, 800-852-2900, fax 508-349-1192, Ⓦ www.wellfleetmotel.com, 146 US 6) Doubles $65-130 off-season, $135-250 July-Aug. Open year-round. Across from the wildlife sanctuary, this place has two pools and 65 above-average suites and rooms, each with refrigerator, coffeemaker and free movies.

B&Bs They keep it simple at the **Holden Inn** (☎ 508-349-3450, 140 Commercial St) Singles $53, doubles $70-80. Open May–mid-Oct. This decidedly old-fashioned hostelry hasn't changed much since the mid-1920s. The 26 sparsely furnished guest rooms, many with shared bath, are housed in three buildings. You can't beat the price for the location and front-porch rocking chairs, but you get what you pay for (namely, a roof over your head if it's raining).

Inn at Duck Creek (☎ 508-349-9333, fax 508-349-0234, Ⓦ www.innatduckcreeke.com, 70 Main St) Doubles $65-90 off-season, $75-100 late June-early Sept, with continental breakfast. Open early May-late Oct. The nicest rooms at this 25-room complex, near US 6, are in the cottage and carriage house. Otherwise the old-fashioned rooms at Inn Duck Creek are adequate, with rates depending on the bath situation (whether it is shared or private).

Blue Gateways (☎ 508-349-7530, Ⓦ www .bluegateways.com, 252 Main St) Doubles $90-110 off-season, $100-120 late May-early Sept, with light breakfast. Open Apr-Jan. This homey and completely renovated small B&B has three tidy guest rooms within walking distance of many galleries. Fireplaces make the B&B appealing off-season.

Places to Eat

Many of Wellfleet's restaurants close for the winter.

Box Lunch (☎ 508-349-2178, 50 Briar Lane) Dishes $2-7. Open for breakfast & lunch year-round. Box Lunch serves deli meats and salads rolled up in pita bread.

Lighthouse (☎ 508-349-3681, 317 Main St) Breakfast $3-7, lunch $4-8.50, dinner $9-15. It's nothing fancy, just decent food at good prices: omelets ($5), grilled codfish and other sandwiches at lunch, burgers and steaks at dinner and Guinness on tap. Try to get a table in the glassed-in dining room; it's quieter.

Moby Dick's (☎ 508-349-9795, US 6) Dishes $8-20. This excellent self-service place, where patrons dine on indoor picnic tables, features large portions of very fresh seafood. The clam chowder, onion rings and steamers (clams) are particularly good. Bring your own beer or wine.

Captain Higgins Seafood Restaurant (☎ 508-349-6027, Town Pier) Lunch $7-17, dinner $12-22. The outdoor deck is key at this informal seafood place. Try the lobster rolls, native bluefish and especially the Wellfleet oysters.

Painter's Restaurant (☎ 508-349-3003, 50 Main St) Dinner mains $10-23. The 'in' crowd hangs out here, downing fresh oysters, Portuguese stew, and New American seafood (pan-seared mustard-sesame tuna) for dinner. The restaurant also serves breakfast, weekend pizzas and coffee.

Upstairs Bar at Aesop's Tables (☎ 508-349-6450, 316 Main St) Dishes $5-15. This place has an old-world feel with velveteen chairs, comfortable couch groupings and low lighting. It's a nice place to go for a lighter meal (steak sandwiches or barbecue ribs, for instance), dessert or an after-dinner drink and a quiet conversation. You can hear live music occasionally.

Entertainment

For a cool beachside hangout, try the **Beachcomber** (☎ 508-349-6055, Cahoon Hollow Beach) Cover varies. Off Ocean View Dr, this indoor-outdoor, all-in-one restaurant, bar and nightclub has live music

nightly. Sunday afternoon concerts and happy hours – with drinks poured to a reggae beat – are quite popular. If you've had too much to drink, watch that first step over the cliff; it's a doozy.

Tavern Room (☎ 508-349-7369, 70 Main St) While listening to live jazz and folk music (Thursday to Sunday), you can munch on good burgers, seafood and upscale but light bistro treats (roasted eggplant on focaccia, for instance). It's a cozy place, with beamed ceilings.

Wellfleet Drive-In (☎ 508-349-7176, US 6) Adult/child $6.50/4. One of the few remaining drive-in theaters in New England shows first-run double features at dusk.

Wellfleet Harbor Actors Theater (WHAT; ☎ 508-349-6835, 1 Kendrick Ave) Tickets $18. This venue, on the harbor off Commercial St, stages contemporary, experimental plays. The productions are always lively, occasionally bawdy and usually the subject of animated conversation long after the curtain falls. The box office is on Main St, next to the pharmacy. Half-price student 'rush tickets' are available just before curtain time.

Shopping

Wellfleet has over 20 galleries representing both fine art and tourist art. Most galleries host receptions (with free food and drink) on Saturday nights in July and August. It's best to just wander Main and Commercial Sts and look for the galleries that are open. Having said that, don't miss the **Nicholas Harrison Gallery** (275 Main St) or **Jules Besch Stationers** (15 Bank St).

Wellfleet Flea Market (☎ 508-349-2520, US 6) Open Sat & Sun mid-Apr–mid-Oct, Wed & Thur July & Aug. On the grounds of the drive-in theater, the Cape's biggest venue has both treasure and junk.

Getting There & Around

The Plymouth & Brockton bus (☎ 508-778-9767) stops at the town hall in Wellfleet center (off US 6) on its way from Boston ($21) and Hyannis ($7) up to Provincetown ($4).

The center of Wellfleet is best explored by foot or bike since there is very little parking in town. From Wellfleet, it's 7 miles north to Truro center and 15 miles to Provincetown.

TRURO

An odd collection of elements coexist peacefully in Truro: strip motels and cookie-cutter cottage complexes, huge homes built in the hills and dales west of US 6 and undeveloped forests and beaches to the east. There's very little to do in this sleepy little town, but you'll find good camping and beaches.

Truro is about 10 miles long and only a few miles wide, with no town center per se. Everything you'll need is on or just off US 6. In North Truro, MA 6A veers off US 6 and is filled with motels as it heads into Provincetown. Take any winding road east or west of US 6, get lost a bit and soak in the distinct scenery.

The chamber of commerce (☎ 508-487-1288, US 6, North Truro) is open 10am to 5pm daily late June to early September, with additional weekend hours a month before and after that.

Things to See & Do

The Highland Light, also known as **Cape Cod Light**, east of US 6 in North Truro, replaced the Cape's first lighthouse, built on this spot in 1798. Daily lighthouse **tours** (☎ 508-487-1121; tours $3; open early May-late Oct) include a short video and a little exhibit in the Keeper's House. Children must be at least 51 inches tall; the lighthouse has a measuring tape, if you don't. The Cape's oldest public golf course, a windswept links-style course, is adjacent to the lighthouse.

Once a summer hotel, the adjacent **Highland House Museum** (☎ 508-487-3397, Highland Light Rd; adults $3; open 10am-4:30pm daily June-Sept) is an interesting local museum dedicated to Truro's farming and maritime past.

The **Pilgrim Heights Area**, east of US 6, has two short trails with splendidly expansive views. One trail leads to the spot where the Pilgrims purportedly tasted their first spring water in the New World.

A 4-mile **bike path** runs along the ocean from Head of the Meadow Beach (see below), past the Pilgrim Heights Area, to the end of Highhead Rd.

Head of the Meadow Beach, east off US 6, is a wide, dune-backed beach with lots of parking for $7/20 daily/seasonally. There are restrooms and changing rooms.

Corn Hill Beach, off US 6 on Cape Cod Bay, is nice for walking at low tide and windsurfing at high tide. Head up the street above it for a great view of the rolling dunes. Parking is $5.

Places to Stay

It's a short walk to the beach from **North of Highland Camping Area** (☎ 508-487-1191, 52 Head of the Meadow Rd, North Truro) Sites $20. Open late May–mid-Sept. This great camping area has 237 sites on 60 forested acres shared by tents and pop-up trailers.

North Truro Camping Area (☎ 508-487-1847, 46 Highland Rd) Sites without/with hookups $16/21. Open year-round. This worthy campground reserves about 100 of its 350 mostly wooded sites for tents.

Hostelling International, Truro (☎ 508-349-3889, 800-909-4776 for reservations in-season, W www.hiayh.org, N Pamet Rd, North Truro) Dorm beds members/nonmembers $15/19. Open late June-early Sept. At the end of N Pamet Rd, abutting Ballston Beach, this former Coast Guard station (now with 42 beds) has a dramatic location amid dunes and marshes, just a five-minute walk from the beach. Reserve by mail or by phone with credit card; off-season, write to Hostelling International Boston, 12 Hemenway St, Boston, MA 02215 or call ☎ 617-531-0459.

The Seaside Village (☎ 508-487-1215, fax 508-487-0819, W www.seasidevillage.com, 482 MA 6A, North Truro) Doubles $75-95 off-season, $115-145 July-Aug; apartments $850-1000 weekly. Open May-Nov. This place has 32 above-average motel rooms with refrigerators and 18 efficiencies rented weekly in July and August.

East Harbour (☎ 508-487-0505, fax 508-487-6693, W www.eastharbour.com, 618 MA

6A) Rooms $55-80, cottages $525-625 weekly off-season; rooms $105-120, cottages $825-925 weekly late June-early Sept. Open Apr-Oct. This beachfront complex of seven cottages and nine motel units is one of the better colonies that line MA 6A in North Truro like ducks in a row. Considering the communal grills and in-room microwaves and refrigerators, it suits longer stays. Cottage rates are for two people; add $200 weekly for each additional adult, $100 weekly for each additional child.

Places to Eat
All of the places listed here close for the colder months.

Jams, Inc (☎ 508-349-1616, *off US 6*) In 'downtown' Truro (blink and you'll miss it), this place has fancy picnic foods like rotisserie chicken, salmon pâté and imported cheese. The espresso is rich and strong.

Village Cafe (☎ 508-487-5800, *4 Highland Rd*) Dishes $4-6. Open for breakfast & lunch May–mid-Oct & dinner July-Aug. In the center of Truro, this pleasant little place has outdoor seating, bagels, sandwiches and soups.

Adrian's (☎ 508-487-4360, *US 6, North Truro*) Breakfast $3-8, dinner $8-23. Adrian's has big picture windows that take advantage of a commanding view atop a bluff overlooking the dunes and ocean. Try the *huevos rancheros* or frittatas at breakfast. An Italian menu with brick-oven pizzas and pasta dishes reigns at dinner. You can't go wrong here.

Terra Luna (☎ 508-487-1019, *MA 6A, North Truro*) Dinner mains $14-20. Nondescript from the outside, this bistro-style place is gussied up with local art on barnboard walls. Creative dishes lean toward New American and Italian with some vegetarian overtones.

Getting There & Away
The Plymouth & Brockton bus (☎ 508-778-9767) stops at Jams in Truro center and at Dutra's Market in North Truro on its way from Boston ($21 to $22) and Hyannis ($7) to Provincetown ($4). Both of these stops are just off US 6.

Truro is 8 hilly miles south of Provincetown via US 6.

PROVINCETOWN
Cape Cod's most lively resort town is also New England's gay mecca. Painters and writers, Portuguese American fishermen and solitude seekers and their families make up this tolerant year-round community of 3400. Walking down Commercial St on any given day, you may see cross-dressers, children eating saltwater taffy, leather-clad motorcyclists, barely clad inline skaters, women strolling hand in hand and unwitting tourists wondering what they've stumbled into on their way to a whale-watching ferry.

This outpost also has long stretches of pristine beach, dramatic sand dunes, contemporary art and one-of-a-kind shops and boutiques. Beyond the main thoroughfare, there are 4000 acres within the protected CCNS through which to bicycle, walk or gallop.

'P-town,' as it's known to outsiders but never to locals, is jam-packed from June through September as its seasonal population swells to 45,000. Even though there are hundreds of rooms to rent, it's essential to arrive with lodging reservations during summer. Because of special events, it also remains crowded on weekends through October. From January through March Provincetown becomes a desolate but hauntingly beautiful place to visit. Just enough restaurants and guesthouses remain open to service visitors.

Orientation
Three exits off US 6 go into town: Snail Rd heads to the quieter East End, Conwell St leads to the center and MacMillan Wharf, Shank Painter Rd leads to the West End. To reach the CCNS beaches and dunes, take Race Point Rd north off US 6 or follow US 6 to its end and head north on Province Lands Rd.

Commercial St is the town's main drag, lined with shops, restaurants, places to stay, entertainment venues and a few museums and historic houses. About 3 miles long, the one-way street runs parallel to the shoreline and functions as the town's boardwalk. Bradford St runs parallel to Commercial St and receives less foot but more auto traffic. Quiet guesthouses line the narrow streets linking Bradford and Commercial Sts. On-street parking is difficult and driving slow, but there are plenty of public parking lots. Commercial St is eminently strollable, as long as you are willing to share it with kamikaze in-line skaters and convertibles cruising the strip at 5mph.

Information

The chamber of commerce (☎ 508-487-3424, fax 508-487-8966, W www.ptown chamber.com, 305 Commercial St, MacMillan Wharf) is open 9am to 5pm daily June to September and 10am to 4pm Monday to Saturday October to May (except it's closed in January and February).

The Province Lands Visitor Center (☎ 508-487-1256, Race Point Rd) sponsors dozens of nature-oriented programs. By all means, stop in. (See the boxed text 'Cape Cod National Seashore,' earlier.)

The Provincetown Business Guild (☎ 508-487-2313, 800-637-8696, W www.ptown.org, Freeman St) promotes gay- and lesbian-owned businesses.

Public toilets are located behind the chamber of commerce information office and on the 2nd floor of the town hall.

Outer Cape Health Services (☎ 508-487-9395, Harry Kemp Way), off Conwell St from US 6, is open in summer for walk-ins, and year-round by appointment.

Art Museums & Galleries

Provincetown began attracting artists in the early 1900s shortly after the Cape Cod School of Art was founded in 1899 by Charles Hawthorne. By the 1920s artists drawn to the clear light had created a fashionable art colony, much like those in Taos, New Mexico; East Hampton, New York; and Carmel, California. Provincetown remains a vital center on the American arts scene with more than 20 galleries representing artists of various persuasions, from avant-garde to representational.

Organized in 1914, the **Provincetown Art Association & Museum** (☎ *508-487-1750, 460 Commercial St; suggested admission adult/child $5/free; open daily late May-Sept, Sat & Sun Oct-late May, call for hours*) is one of the country's foremost small museums. Paintings from the permanent collection, including works by Marsden Hartley and Milton Avery, rotate throughout the year; changing exhibits often highlight emerging local artists.

Pick up the *Provincetown Gallery Guide* for the latest offerings. Drop into these well-established galleries: **Berta Walker Galleries** (☎ *508-487-6411, 208 Bradford St*), **Packard Gallery** (☎ *508-487-4690, 418 Commercial St*) and **Rice/Polak Gallery** (☎ *508-487-1052, 430 Commercial St*).

Pilgrim Sights

In search of a place to settle where they could freely practice their religion, the Pilgrims first set foot on American soil in 1620 at Provincetown. A **plaque** marks the spot at the western end of Commercial St near the Provincetown Inn. The Pilgrims anchored here for five weeks in search of fresh water and fertile ground; when they failed to find adequate supplies of either, they forged on to Plymouth.

Despite their short stay, the Pilgrims made history here. The **Pilgrim Bas Relief**, on Bradford St behind the Provincetown Town Hall, commemorates the Mayflower Compact, which the Pilgrims drew up while anchored in the harbor. The compact, a predecessor to the US Constitution, was designed to quell brewing insurrection by the indentured servants on board by granting them full rights in the new land.

The **Pilgrim Monument & Provincetown Museum** (☎ *508-487-1310, High Pole Rd; adult/child 4-12 yrs $6/3; open 9am-7pm daily July & Aug, 9am-5pm daily Apr-June & Sept-Nov*), off Winslow St from Bradford St, is modeled after the Torre del Mangia in Siena, Italy. Climb the 116 stairs and 60 ramps for a great view of town, the beaches, the spine of the Outer Cape and even Boston on a clear day (it's 30 miles away as the crow flies). The museum portrays the

PROVINCETOWN

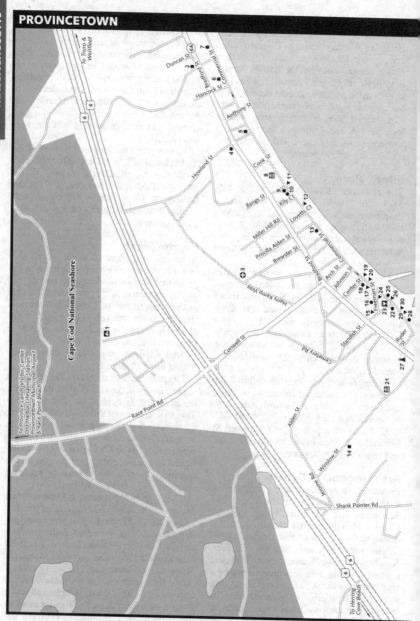

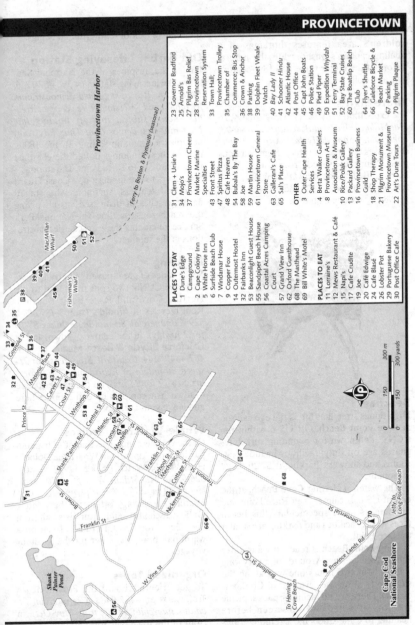

PLACES TO STAY

1 Dune's Edge Campground
2 Cape Colony Inn
5 White Horse Inn
6 Surfside Beach Club
7 Windamar House
9 Copper Fox
14 Outermost Hostel
32 Fairbanks Inn
53 Beaconlight Guest House
55 Sandpiper Beach House
56 Coastal Acres Camping Court
57 Grand View Inn
62 Oxford Guesthouse
68 The Masthead
69 Bill White's Motel

PLACES TO EAT

11 Lorraine's
12 Mews Restaurant & Café
15 Napi's
17 Cafe Crudite
19 Joe
20 Café Edwige
24 Cafe Blasé
26 Lobster Pot
29 Portuguese Bakery
30 Post Office Cafe

31 Clem + Ursie's
34 Mojo's
37 Provincetown Cheese Market; Marine Specialties
43 Front Street
47 Spiritus Pizza
48 Cafe Heaven
54 Bubala's By The Bay
58 Joe
59 Martin House
61 Provincetown General Store
63 Gallerani's Cafe
65 Sal's Place

OTHER

3 Outer Cape Health Services
4 Berta Walker Galleries
8 Provincetown Art Association & Museum
10 Rice/Polak Gallery
13 Packard Gallery
16 Provincetown Business Guild
18 Shop Therapy
21 Pilgrim Monument & Provincetown Museum
22 Art's Dune Tours

23 Governor Bradford
25 Arnold's
27 Pilgrim Bas Relief
28 Provincetown Reservation System
33 Town Hall; Provincetown Trolley
35 Chamber of Commerce; Bus Stop
36 Crown & Anchor
38 Parking
39 Dolphin Fleet Whale Watch
40 Bay Lady II
41 Schooner Hindu
42 Atlantic House
44 Post Office
45 Capt John Boats
46 Police Station
49 Pied Piper
50 Expedition Whydah
51 Ferry Terminal
52 Bay State Cruises
60 The Boatslip Beach Club
64 Flyer's Shuttle
66 Galeforce Bicycle & Beach Market
67 Parking
70 Pilgrim Plaque

Pilgrims' struggle to survive and the lives of whaling captains who later settled here. A children's area features dioramas of a whaling captain's onshore life, the natural history of the Outer Cape and 18th-century toys and dolls.

Pirate Sights

The **Expedition *Whydah*** (*☎ 508-487-8899, 16 MacMillan Wharf; adult/senior/child $6/4/3; open 10am-5pm daily late Apr–mid-Oct*) showcases booty and artifacts from a famous pirate ship recovered from waters near Marconi Beach. The *Whydah* sank only 1500 feet off Wellfleet in 1717 and was recovered in 1984 by a Cape Cod team.

Beaches

High dunes stretch as far as the eye can see at **Race Point Beach**. Off US 6 within the CCNS, it's known for pounding surf. Lifeguards are on duty; facilities include restrooms and showers. Parking is $7/20 daily/seasonally.

The water at **Herring Cove Beach**, at the end of US 6, is calmer than Race Point and the sunsets more spectacular (this beach faces west). Facilities and parking are similar to Race Point.

Long Point Beach is reached via a water shuttle (see Getting Around) or a very long walk (about two hours one-way along the stone jetty at the western end of Commercial St). There are no facilities; pack a picnic and lots of water and sunscreen before heading to Cape Cod's most remote grains

of sand. It's well worth the effort because of the relative lack of fellow human beings.

Old Harbor Lifesaving Station

Under the auspices of the National Seashore, the lifesaving station (*☎ 508-487-1256, Race Point Beach; suggested demonstration fee adult/child $3/1; station free & open irregular hours subject to staff funding late May–mid-Oct; demos 6pm Thur July-Aug*) occupies a dramatic setting. In the 1800s, nine of these buildings dotted the coastline from Chatham to Race Point. The stations – precursors to the modern-day Coast Guard – housed fearless 'surfmen' who staged daring rescues of distressed vessels plying the treacherous coastline. The National Park Service re-creates these rescue demonstrations in the summer.

Bicycling

Seven miles of great paved bike trails crisscross the CCNS; two spur trails lead to the Herring Cove and Race Point Beaches. Rent bicycles at **Arnold's** (*☎ 508-487-0844, 329 Commercial St; mountain bikes $7/16 for 2 hr/day*), in the center of town, and at **Galeforce Bicycle & Beach Market** (*☎ 508-487-4849, 144 Bradford St Extension; 21-speed mountain or hybrid bikes $6-8 for 2 hrs, $16-19 for 24 hrs*), on the western edge of town. You can pick up deli supplies here and leave your car, too.

Whale-Watching Cruises

Of the various companies that offer trips departing from MacMillan Wharf, the **Dolphin Fleet Whale Watch** (*☎ 508-349-1900, 800-826-9300, MacMillan Wharf; adult/senior/child 7-12 yrs $19/17/16; trips mid-Apr–Oct, weather permitting*) offers the best tours. Onboard scientists and naturalists hail from the Center for Coastal Studies. Even on a warm day, bring a sweater for the 3½-hour voyage.

Organized Tours

To get oriented, board the **Provincetown Trolley** (*☎ 508-487-9483, Commercial St; adult/senior/child $8/7/5; trips May-Oct*), in front of the town hall, for a 40-minute narrated sightseeing tour. Tours depart on the half-hour 10am to 4pm and on the hour 5pm to 8pm mid-June to August. (In the 'shoulder season' the schedule is slightly more limited.) Hop on and off at various points including the Provincetown Art Association and the Province Lands Visitor Center.

Art's Dune Tours *(☎ 508-487-1950, cnr Commercial & Standish Sts; adult $12, senior $11, child $8-10; trips mid-Apr–mid-Nov)* offers great hour-long, narrated, 4WD dune tours within the CCNS. Reservations are recommended for the sunset trip. Inquire about summertime sunrise breakfasts and afternoon clambakes, too. If you only do one or two things in Provincetown, the basic trip should be one.

The **Schooner** *Hindu (☎ 508-487-3000)* and *Bay Lady II (☎ 508-487-9308)*, both traditional schooners, depart from MacMillan Wharf mid-May to mid-October for two-hour bay sails. On the *Hindu* adults pay $20, children under 12 cost $10. The *Bay Lady II* is cheaper: $12 to $16 for adults (depending on the time of day), $7 for children.

Places to Stay
Camping RVs and tenters can be accommodated at two commercial campgrounds.

Dune's Edge Campground (☎ 508-487-9815, US 6) Sites without hookups $25-28, with hookups $31-34. Open May-late Sept. True to its name, this campground is on the edge of the dunes just off US 6. There are 120 pine-shaded RV and tent sites. It's a bit of a walk from here into town, so you'd better have a bicycle or car if you're staying here.

Coastal Acres Camping Court (☎ 508-487-1700, W Vine St Extension) Sites without/with hookups $22/32. Open Apr-Oct. This campground is off Bradford St, on the western edge of town.

Hostels Backpackers can look for the *Outermost Hostel (☎ 508-487-4378, 26-28 Winslow St)* Dorm beds $18.50. Open May-Oct. This privately run hostel, one step below camping, has five cabins housing six bunks. Barbecues and picnic tables come in handy since you'll want to avoid the cabins as long as possible.

Efficiencies About a mile west of the town center, you'll find *The Masthead (☎ 508-487-0523, 800-395-5095, fax 508-487-9251, W www.themasthead.com, 31-41 Commercial St)* Rooms $63-168 nightly off-season, rooms & efficiencies $81-197 nightly July & Aug, cottages & apartments $992-1905 weekly July & Aug. Open year-round, this funky establishment sits right on the bay. A variety of room configurations are available (have them fax you a listing): multiroom apartments, cottages, efficiencies and simple motel rooms.

Motels On the edge of town and across from dunes and marshes is *Bill White's Motel (☎ 508-487-1042, fax 508-487-2346, W www.billwhitesmotel.com, 29 Bradford St Extension)* Doubles $65/80 off-season/July-early Sept. Open early May-late Oct. This 12-unit motel is well maintained by a proud family.

Cape Colony Inn (☎ 508-487-1755, 800-841-6716, W www.capecolonyinn.com, 280 Bradford St) Doubles $67-70 off-season, $107-110 July-Aug. Open May-Oct. These 54 units, eight with two bedrooms, are nicely maintained and fairly large. The motel also has a heated pool, playground and barbecue grills. The two-bedded suites are a bargain at $148 for four people in the summertime ($95 off-season).

Surfside Beach Club (☎ 508-487-1726, 800-421-1726, fax 508-487-6556, W www.surfsideinn.cc, 543 Commercial St) Doubles $85-150 off-season, $129-249 June-early Sept. Open mid-May–Oct. Although it's arguably the least-attractive building in town, the Surfside does have 84 rooms, which means that it'll have rooms when others don't. Half the rooms have balconies overlooking the bay; others overlook the pool and a parking lot. Rates are dependent on views.

Guesthouses & B&Bs Provincetown has a hundred small inns and guesthouses that provide the most interesting accommodations. Most guesthouses are gay-owned and operated with a mix of rooms with private or shared bath. In summer, most will also be booked in advance. If you can't make an advance reservation, arrive early in the day and ask the chamber of commerce for help. Better yet, try to visit before June or after early September.

White Horse Inn (☎ *508-487-1790, 500 Commercial St*) Singles $40-50, doubles $50-60 off-season; singles $50-80, doubles $75-80 mid-June–early Sept. Open year-round. Twelve basic rooms, most with shared bath, are decorated with original local art. The six bungalow-style apartments are far more interesting and bohemian. They rent for $125-140 in summer, with a three-night minimum. No credit cards are accepted.

Windamar House (☎ *508-487-0599, fax 508-487-7505, 568 Commercial St*) Doubles $50-125, apartments $115-125 off-season; doubles $65-140 late May–mid-Sept, apartments $125-140 late May-early Sept, with continental breakfast. Open Apr-Dec. This former sea captain's house has six lovely rooms (shared and private bath) and two even-better apartments. The house's manicured backyard is one of the most tranquil in town. No credit cards are accepted, but there is free, on-site parking (a rarity).

Grand View Inn (☎ *508-487-9193, 888-268-9169, fax 508-487-2894, 4 Conant St*) Doubles $40-90 off-season, $70-145 mid-June–mid-Sept. Open year-round. This well-kept place, on a quiet street convenient to the center, has 12 rooms with shared or private bath.

Fairbanks Inn (☎ *508-487-0386, 800-324-7265, fax 508-487-3540,* Ⓦ *www.fairbanksinn.com, 90 Bradford St*) Doubles $50-175 off-season, $99-155 mid-June–mid-Sept, with continental breakfast. Open year-round. A gracious and historic 18th-century hostelry that's retained its integrity, the Fairbanks Inn boasts restored wide-pine floors and fireplaces. One of the nicest places to stay in town, it's also been upgraded with fine amenities and down comforters. A couple of the 15 rooms have shared bath.

Beaconlight Guesthouse (☎/*fax 508-487-9603, 800-696-9603,* Ⓦ *www.beaconlightguesthouse.com, 12 Winthrop St*) Doubles $65-155 off-season, $115-245 mid-June–early Sept, with expanded continental breakfast. Open

year-round. Among Provincetown's other welcoming and elegant guesthouses, this B&B has 10 harmoniously decorated rooms and comfortable suites.

Copper Fox (☎ *508-487-8583, fax 508-487-3238, 448 Commercial St*) Doubles $85-100 off-season, $140-195 mid-June–mid-Sept, with full breakfast. Open year-round. Set back from the street by a lovely front yard, this renovated B&B has three rooms, two suites and two apartments with private entrances, perfect for longer stays. There's plenty of common space, including a relaxing front porch.

Oxford Guesthouse (☎ *508-487-9103, 888-456-9103,* Ⓦ *www.oxfordguesthouse.com, 8 Cottage St*) Doubles $75-185 off-season, $135-265 mid-June–early Sept, with expanded continental breakfast. Open year-round. The innkeepers of Beaconlight Guesthouse also run this nearby place, with seven equally refined but perhaps more sophisticated rooms.

Sandpiper Beach House (☎ *508-487-1928, 800-354-8628, fax 508-487-8828,* Ⓦ *www.sandpiper.com, 165 Commercial St*) Doubles $85-145 off-season, $215-245 late May-early Sept, with continental breakfast. Open year-round. This 12-room place is nicely kept and conveniently located; the front porch is good for people-watching.

Places to Eat

While there are plenty of moderately priced eateries and takeout joints hawking sandwiches, pizza, pasta and seafood, Provincetown also has a surprising number of fine but pricey restaurants. Dining options range from down-home Portuguese to fried seafood to Italian to exceptional New American. A few are open year-round. The spots listed here are open for lunch and dinner unless otherwise noted.

No matter where you are on Commercial St, you'll never be far from the ***Provincetown Cheese Market*** (☎ *508-487-3032, 225 Commercial St*) or the ***Provincetown General Store*** (☎ *508-487-0300, 147 Commercial St*), both of which are open year-round.

Joe (☎ *508-487-6656, 148A Commercial St*) Open daily year-round. Joe offers consistently excellent cappuccino. You can also get a fix at Joe's East End location (☎ 508-487-6868, 353A Commercial St), open May through October.

Spiritus Pizza (☎ 508-487-2808, 190 Commercial St) Without a doubt this is *the* place to go for a late-night slice. Strong coffee and a pastry will jump-start you after a long night.

Portuguese Bakery (☎ 508-487-1803, 299 Commercial St) Provincetown's favorite old-fashioned snack is a big wad of hot, sugar-dusted fried dough ($1.50) from this place. This simple bakery-lunchroom, which has been here for a century, also sells the town's cheapest breakfasts and sandwiches.

Mojo's (☎ 508-487-3140, MacMillan Wharf, Ryder St) Prices $2-15. Every town has a classic clam shack and Provincetown is no exception. You can get everything from a hot dog ($1.80) to a pint of clams ($15). There are also some good veggie options.

Cafe Blasé (☎ 508-487-9465, 328 Commercial St) Dishes $10-20. The principal activity for many at this, the town's premier outdoor cafe for people-watching, is dishing people as they saunter by. But the cafe has some good dishes to eat, too: crabmeat salad, Caesar salad with grilled tuna, smoked turkey sandwiches and garden burgers.

Cafe Heaven (☎ 508-487-9639, 199 Commercial St) Dinner mains $16-23. Light and airy but small and crowded, this is an excellent breakfast and lunch place. From fluffy omelets ($6) to cold salads and sandwiches ($6 to $7), there is more value here than at most eateries. At press time, the dinner concession had been sublet to another tenant, so we can't vouch for their duck breast, salmon and free-range chicken dishes.

Gallerani's Cafe (☎ 508-487-4433, 133 Commercial St) Dinner mains $11-24. Beloved by locals, especially off-season, this bistro-style eatery is fun and friendly. Hundreds of multipaned windows expose flickering candles, beckoning patrons. Look for chicken stuffed with chutney, red peppers and mozzarella or a variety of pasta dishes or almost anything grilled.

Napi's (☎ 508-487-1145, 7 Freeman St) Lunch $6-13, dinner $18-26. An institution

since 1973, this unusual and art-filled restaurant has an eclectic menu ranging from organic salads to stir-fry to Portuguese linguiça. There's plenty of reason for vegetarians do cartwheels in the aisles. It's always lively, funky and welcoming.

Post Office Cafe (☎ 508-487-3892, 303 Commercial St) Breakfast $4-12, lunch $4-18, dinner $6-25. This casual eatery attracts drag queens and gets points for always being open. The menu is laden with sandwiches, fried things, platters and salads.

Front Street (☎ 508-487-9715, 230 Commercial St) Dinner mains $13-23. This cozy basement restaurant has two menus: fine Italian cuisine and more creative 'Mediterranean-American fusion' creations. Both are consistently well prepared. Look for dishes like tea-smoked duck and softshell crabs. Desserts are outstanding, as is the service.

Clem + Ursie's (☎ 508-487-2333, 85 Shank Painter Rd) Most dishes $8-18. After the beach, this casual open-air hangout is great for steamed lobsters, anything from the raw bar and barbecue. Watch your wallet or you'll end up dropping a wad.

Bubala's By The Bay (☎ 508-487-0773, 183 Commercial St) Breakfast $4-9, lunch $7-15, dinner $7-26. If the food was as good as the people-watching, you'd never get a table. It's difficult as it is. Keep it simple with omelets and burgers and check out the streetside parade.

Cafe Crudite (☎ 508-487-6237, 336 Commercial St) Dishes under $10. This cafe, on a 2nd-floor deck overlooking the street, boasts a world-influenced vegan and vegetarian menu, a traditional Japanese macrobiotic menu and a veggie burger with upwards of 28 ingredients.

Café Edwige (☎ 508-487-2008 breakfast, 487-4020 dinner, 333 Commercial St) Breakfast $4.50-8.50, dinner $17-25. P-town's most popular breakfast place features frittatas, tofu casserole, broiled flounder and fruit pancakes. Expect to wait unless you arrive by 8:30am. At dinnertime the cafe is transformed into a romantic bistro offering an eclectic menu with the likes of Thai stir-fry, crab cakes and Asian-style paella. The solicitous service and creative cuisine make it a top place to dine.

Sal's Place (☎ 508-487-1279, 99 Commercial St) Dinner mains $12-25. Sal's serves simple but good southern Italian dishes at outdoor tables on the bay or indoors in a classic trattoria.

Lobster Pot (☎ 508-487-0842, 321 Commercial St) Dishes $6-22. There's a reason why lines form outside this old-fashioned touristy place: Inside you'll find fresh seafood and fish, chowder, a bakery, filling serves, tables overlooking the harbor and fast service.

Lorraine's (☎ 508-487-6074, 463 Commercial St) Dinner mains $15-26. This cozy waterfront place features Mexican cuisine with a touch of a New England accent. Local littleneck clams are served in a cilantro lime broth with roasted garlic, shallots and scallions; fresh sea scallops are served with tomatillos in a green chile sauce, flambéed with tequila.

Martin House (☎ 508-487-1327, 157 Commercial St) Dinner mains $15-33. Open year-round. This rustic 18th-century house with fireplaces is particularly well suited to winter dining. It's difficult to categorize the innovative menu except to say that some dishes are internationally inspired, some lean towards continental, others celebrate vegetarians. One thing is certain: Leave room for desserts like the caramelized banana and lime tart.

Mews Restaurant and Cafe (☎ 508-487-1500, 429 Commercial St) Cafe menu upstairs $8-15, downstairs mains $18-28. Open for Sunday brunch & dinner year-round. This waterfront place is the best place to splurge and offers less-expensive food upstairs than at the fancier downstairs dining room, but it's still from the same exceptional kitchen that thinks of food as an art form. Go all out with a mixed-seafood grill or bouillabaisse or hold back with a fancy pasta dish. But it could be the best $22 you spend on grilled tuna.

Entertainment

Besides people-watching and drinking in restaurant bars, there's plenty to do here, including several live (and lively) entertainment venues. The best approach is to check in with the Provincetown Reservation System (☎ 508-487-2400, 800-648-0364, 293 Commercial St), since they sell tickets to practically every show and special event in town. Check to see who's performing at the **Post Office Cabaret**, **Antro** and **Vixen**.

Having said that, we must admit that much of the action is in the bars and clubs, both gay and straight. (It is, frankly, hardly worthwhile to distinguish gay clubs from straight ones in Provincetown, since nearly all are gay and all are open to everyone.) Here are some of the popular scenes.

Governor Bradford (☎ 508-487-9618, 312 Commercial St) Open year-round. This local dive, with big picture windows overlooking Commercial, has pool tables, chess boards and lots of smoke. It attracts many of P-town's straight night owls with live reggae and rock. This is a vestige of old Provincetown, along with the **Old Colony**, the no-frills mariners' haunt across the street, where filmmakers shot scenes for Norman Mailer's cult classic flick Tough Guys Don't Dance.

The Boatslip Beach Club (☎ 508-487-1669, 161 Commercial St) This place is known for its wildly popular afternoon tea dances (from 4pm to 7pm). They rent pool chairs for $3 a day, although you must depart by 4pm so they can set up for the tea dances. The Boatslip attracts a highly eclectic crowd, and in the summer, more often than not, the place is packed with gorgeous guys.

Pied Piper (☎ 508-487-1527, 193A Commercial St) Open May-Oct. This waterfront place is the women's bar in town. They host 'after-tea' tea parties at 6:30pm.

Atlantic House (☎ 508-487-3821, 4 Masonic Place) Open year-round. Referred to simply as the 'A-House,' this club features three distinct men's bars: leather, disco and an intimate bar with an off-season fireplace. The gay scene pretty much started here 50 years ago, and the disco is still a raging shirts-off club-kids scene!

Crown & Anchor (☎ 508-487-1430, 247 Commercial St) Open year-round. Crown & Anchor draws a gay and mixed crowd to its 'leather and Levi's' bar (dubbed 'the vault'), video bar, disco, drag and cabaret shows. Crown & Anchor was rebuilt better than ever since a fire in early 1998 burned it to the ground.

Shopping

Commercial St is lined with the most creative specialty shops on the Cape. You'll find almost anything that could suit your fancy, from leather implements of torture to rubber stamps, from cutting-edge women's clothing to artsy T-shirts, from sculpture to handcrafted jewelry. It's best to wander. There are two shops you shouldn't miss:

Marine Specialties (☎ 508-487-1730, 235 *Commercial St*) A cavernous store filled with random, surplus Army and Navy stuff and other odd items, all priced to sell.

Shop Therapy (☎ 508-487-9387, 346 *Commercial St*) Open year-round. With its psychedelic exterior, this shop carries retro and cutting-edge goods that tip the scales away from 'normal.'

Getting There & Away

Provincetown is a magnet for traffic by land, sea and air.

From Boston, Cape Air (☎ 508-487-0241, 800-352-0714, W www.flycapeair.com) provides daily year-round service to Provincetown's Municipal Airport, about 4 miles from town and served by taxi. One-way fares hover around $115, roundtrips range from $99 to $199. The flight takes 25 minutes gate to gate.

The Plymouth & Brockton bus (☎ 508-778-9767) stops at the chamber of commerce. Four daily buses ($21 one-way, 3½ hours) travel between Provincetown and Boston, with stops in Truro, Wellfleet, Eastham, Orleans, Hyannis and West Barnstable.

In a car, from the Cape Cod Canal via US 6, it takes almost 1½ hours to reach Provincetown (65 miles), depending on traffic.

You can reach Provincetown by passenger ferry from Boston and Plymouth.

Bay State Cruises (☎ 508-487-9284 in summer, ☎ 617-748-1428 for year-round information) links Provincetown's MacMillan Wharf and Boston's Commonwealth Pier on Northern Ave. The three-hour voyage costs $30/21/5 adult/child/bicycle one way. Boats depart Provincetown at 3:30pm and Boston at 9:30am Friday to Sunday from late May to early September. Bay State's high-speed ferry takes 1½ hours. It departs Boston and Provincetown three times daily from late May to mid-October and costs $28 one-way, $49 roundtrip.

Capt John Boats (☎ 508-747-2400, 800-242-2469), on State Pier next to the *Mayflower* in Plymouth, departs Plymouth at 10am and returns from Provincetown at 4:30pm on weekends late May to September and daily mid-June to early September. Return tickets are $27/22/18/3 adult/senior/child under 12/bicycle. The voyage takes 90 minutes.

Getting Around

From late May to mid-October, the Summer Shuttle (☎ 508-385-8311) travels up and down Bradford St, to MacMillan Wharf, to Herring Cove Beach and south to the campgrounds in North Truro between 8am and midnight. Flag the bus down anywhere along the route. The fare is $1 per ride, $3 for a one-day pass. Pick up a route map at the chamber of commerce.

The Flyer's Shuttle (☎ 508-487-0898, 131A Commercial St) ferries sunbathers across the bay to remote Long Point mid-June to mid-September. The fare is $7 one-way, $10 roundtrip.

Martha's Vineyard & Nantucket Island

In the 18th century, these islands off New England's coast grew into bustling havens for whaling vessels and merchant fleets. With the coming of the Age of Steam in the 19th century, they became vacation resorts, charming places where city dwellers could escape the summer's heat and find a cool, constant sea breeze. For most of the 20th century, Martha's Vineyard and Nantucket have been pleasure destinations for New Englanders of all social classes. But recently these two islands have gone noticeably upscale: President and Mrs Clinton chose Martha's Vineyard for most of their annual vacations in the mid- to late 1990s, as did an increasing number of the rich and famous. Still, generally, Martha's Vineyard attracts a more ethnically and economically diverse holiday crowd than Nantucket.

Nantucket, meanwhile, continues to overbuild with more and more multimillion-dollar 'trophy' homes. No wonder the island's small airport experiences more takeoffs and landings of private jets in summer than most other places in the country. Almost everything is very expensive on Martha's Vineyard and Nantucket Island, even more expensive than on Cape Cod. But these two special places are beguiling, historic and beautiful, and there are ways to visit the islands without hemorrhaging money.

Martha's Vineyard

In 1602, mariner Bartholomew Gosnold cruised the New England coast, charting it for later exploration. It is thought that he found wild grapes when he stopped at this island and named it Martha's Vineyard in honor of his daughter. Today, the island has an actual working vineyard that you can visit. There are also lots of beaches, bike paths, charming towns, open spaces, restaurants and inns. To the residents of eastern Massachusetts, it's simply 'the Vineyard.'

Highlights

- Touring the gingerbread Victorian houses of Oak Bluffs
- Walking deserted off-season beaches on Chappaquiddick Island
- Wandering up-island on Martha's Vineyard to buy farm-fresh produce
- Canoeing or kayaking on a quiet inlet
- Taking Nantucket's Great Point natural history tour
- Bicycling Nantucket's Polpis Rd
- Snapping pictures of the rose-covered cottages of 'Sconset

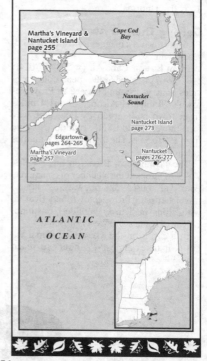

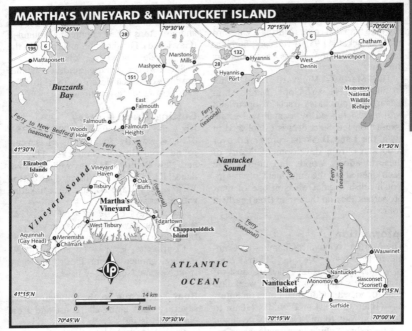

MARTHA'S VINEYARD & NANTUCKET ISLAND

History

Prior to 1640, 3000 Wampanoag Indians populated the island. Over the next century, English settlers colonized the Vineyard and converted the Wampanoags to Christianity. Many Wampanoags died from diseases the English imported, and by the mid-18th century there were only 300 native islanders left. Today, many of their descendants live in Aquinnah (known as Gay Head until the late 1990s).

Vineyarders are a proud, fiercely independent lot, relishing their separation from the mainland. Nevertheless, they've opened their island to a thriving tourist trade: The year-round population of 11,000 swells to 100,000 in July and August.

Orientation

The main entry ports are Vineyard Haven, the island's year-round commercial center, and Oak Bluffs, a seasonal, somewhat honky-tonk town with ornate Victorian houses and

a history of racial integration. It's 3 miles from Vineyard Haven to Oak Bluffs east along Beach Rd. Edgartown, the Vineyard's pricey grande dame, is the island's other principal town. Its patrician back lanes are filled with lovely houses built by whaling captains and separated by white picket fences. It's 5 miles south along the shoreline from Oak Bluffs to Edgartown.

You can reach Chappaquiddick, a spit of land within a stone's throw of Edgartown, via a five-minute ferry from Edgartown center. The small island, relatively free of tourists, has pristine beaches. The other towns on Martha's Vineyard – West Tisbury, Chilmark, Menemsha and Aquinnah – are relatively undeveloped and collectively referred to as 'up-island.' An up-island visit will probably be the highlight of your trip. The western tip of the island belongs to the colorful cliffs of Aquinnah, a hilly 21 miles from Edgartown or Vineyard Haven.

Maps Rubel BikeMaps (☎ 617-776-6567, Ⓦ www.bikemaps.com) produces an excellent bike map that covers Martha's Vineyard and Nantucket ($1.95). If you can't find it at your local bookstore, contact the company directly.

The Martha's Vineyard Land Bank (☎ 508-627-7141, 167 Upper Main St), in Edgartown, purchases tracts of open land with a trust funded by a small real estate transaction fee. Since it was established in 1986, the Land Bank has preserved over 1500 acres from development. Many of these meadows, woods and moors have been opened for the enjoyment of visitors. You'll relish a quiet walk on one of their properties. Pick up their map (free) early in your visit.

Information

The Martha's Vineyard Chamber of Commerce (☎ 508-693-0085, fax 508-693-7589, Ⓦ www.mvy.com) is on Beach Rd just off Main St. It's open 9am to 5pm weekdays year-round, with additional hours on Saturday (10am to 4pm) and Sunday (10am to 2pm) mid-May to mid-October. The chamber publishes a guide to attractions and accommodations, distributes maps and offers other practical advice. There is also a visitor center in the ferry terminal, which is open 8am to 8pm daily in July and August and 8:30am to 5:30pm Friday to Sunday from late May through June and September to mid-October.

Pick up the weekly *Martha's Vineyard Times* or *Vineyard Gazette* (Ⓦ www.mv gazette.com) for a current calendar of events. For general, independent information, check out Ⓦ www.mvweb.com.

The Martha's Vineyard Hospital (☎ 508-693-0410) is off the Vineyard Haven-Oak Bluffs Rd.

Organized Tours

All operated by the same company, **Gay Head Sightseeing, MV Sightseeing** and **Island Transport** *(☎ 508-693-1555; adult/child $15/5)* buses depart from the ferry terminals in Vineyard Haven and Oak Bluffs from late April to early November. Buses are timed

with ferry arrivals, more or less. The 2½-hour island-wide tour takes in all the major towns and also stops for 30 minutes at Aquinnah (Gay Head). For those on a short visit, the tour provides a good overview.

See also the 'Chappaquiddick Island' boxed text, which describes tours by The Trustees of the Reservations.

Getting There & Away

Air Cape Air (☎ 508-790-0300, 800-352-0714, Ⓦ www.flycapeair.com) flies year-round from Boston, Nantucket, Hyannis and New Bedford, MA, as well as Providence, RI, to Martha's Vineyard Airport in West Tisbury. Cape Air has joint ticketing with major airlines.

US Airways Express (☎ 800-428-4322, Ⓦ www.usairways.com) serves the Vineyard from Boston in the summer.

Continental Express (☎ 800-525-0280, Ⓦ www.continental.com) flies to the island from Newark, New Jersey, in season.

Boat Ferries run to the Vineyard from several points along the coast and from Nantucket Island.

From **Woods Hole**, car and passenger ferries of the Steamship Authority (☎ 508-477-8600 for auto reservations, ☎ 508-548-3788 for day-of-sail information, Ⓦ www .islandferry.com) sail daily in summer to Vineyard Haven (14 trips) and Oak Bluffs (four trips). In other seasons, all 14 daily trips dock in Vineyard Haven. In the summer, make automobile ferry reservations months in advance, especially if you are traveling on Friday or a weekend.

On Tuesday, Wednesday and Thursday in summer, the Authority has a 'guaranteed standby policy,' which means that if your car is in line by 2pm, you are guaranteed to get on or off the island that day (although you may not leave until midnight).

Roundtrip fares from mid-May to mid-October are $104 for cars; $11/5.50 for adult/child passengers. Roundtrip bicycle fare is $6. Off-season, the fare for cars drops to $62 roundtrip; for people it stays the same. The trip takes about 45 minutes. Parking in Woods Hole costs $8 to $10 daily.

MARTHA'S VINEYARD

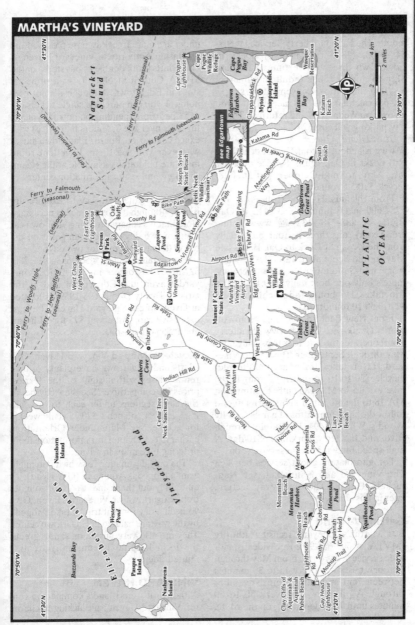

Nantucket Sound

41°30'N

70°30'W

Ferry to Nantucket (seasonal)

Ferry to Hyannis (seasonal)

Ferry to Falmouth (seasonal)

Cape Pogue Lighthouse

Cape Pogue Bay

Cape Pogue Wildlife Refuge

41°20'N

Wasque Reservation

Edgartown Harbor

Mytoi

Chappaquiddick Island

Chappaquiddick Rd

Katama Bay

Katama Beach

see Edgartown map

Katama Rd

Edgartown

South Beach

Ferry to Falmouth (seasonal)

Joseph Sylvia State Beach

Bike Path

Felix Neck Wildlife Sanctuary

Bike Path

Parking

Meetinghouse Way

Herring Creek Rd

Edgartown Great Pond

ATLANTIC OCEAN

Ferry to Woods Hole (seasonal)

East Chop Lighthouse

Oak Bluffs

Beach Rd

County Rd

Owens Park

Vineyard Haven

Main St

West Chop Lighthouse

Lagoon Pond

Sengekontacket Pond

Vineyard Haven Rd

Bike Path

Airport Rd

Edgartown–West Tisbury Rd

Lake Tashmoo

Chicama Vineyard

Edgartown

Manuel F Correllus State Forest

Martha's Vineyard Airport

Long Point Wildlife Refuge

Ferry to New Bedford (seasonal)

70°40'W

Cove Rd

State Rd

Lambert's Cove

Tisbury

West Tisbury

Tisbury Great Pond

Lambert's Cove Rd

Indian Hill Rd

Cedar Tree Neck Sanctuary

Old County Rd

State Rd

Polly Hill Arboretum

North Rd

Middle Rd

Tabor House Rd

South Rd

Lucy Vincent Beach

Vineyard Sound

Nashorn Island

Westend Pond

Elizabeth Islands

Buzzards Bay

Paqua Island

Menemsha

Menemsha Cross Rd

Chilmark

Menemsha Beach

Menemsha Harbor

Lobsterville Beach

Menemsha Pond

Lobsterville Rd

Squibnocket Pond

Nashawena Island

70°50'W

Lighthouse Rd

South Rd

Aquinnah (Gay Head)

Moshup Trail

Clay Cliffs of Aquinnah & Aquinnah Public Beach

Gay Head Lighthouse

41°20'N

4 km

2 miles

0   1   2

70°30'W

If you're not bringing a car, two passenger-only ferries operate out of **Falmouth.** The Falmouth Ferry Service (☎ 508-548-9400, 278 Scranton Ave) docks in Edgartown three to five times daily late May to mid-October (adult/child/bicycle $24/18/6 roundtrip). Convenient parking is $12 per calendar day. That means that if you go over on Wednesday and return on Thursday, parking will cost $24.

The *Island Queen* (☎ 508-548-4800, Ⓦ www.islandqueen.com, Falmouth Heights Rd) docks in Oak Bluffs. Service operates late May to mid-October (adult/child/bicycle $10/5/6 roundtrip).

From **Hyannis,** Hy-Line Cruises (☎ 508-778-2600 in Hyannis, ☎ 693-0112 in Oak Bluffs, ☎ 888-778-1132, Ⓦ www.hy-line cruise.com) runs three or four boats daily from the Ocean St Dock to Oak Bluffs late May to mid-September. In early May and from mid-September to late October, there's only one boat daily, at 9:15am. The trip takes 1½ hours (adult/child/bicycle $27/13.50/10 roundtrip).

From **New Bedford,** the Steamship Authority (☎ 508-997-1688, Ⓦ www.islandferry .com) operates three to four trips daily mid-May through September. The trip to Vineyard Haven takes 1½ hours (adult/child/bicycle $20/10/10 roundtrip). From I-195, take exit 15 to MA 18 south. Continue on MA 18 to the 4th set of lights, turn left and follow the signs four-fifths of a mile to Billy Wood's Wharf, 1494 E Rodney French Blvd, and the ferry. Parking is $10/day. A high-speed ferry may be in service soon.

For information about service between The Vineyard and Nantucket, see Nantucket's Getting There & Away section, later in this chapter.

Getting Around

Bus Martha's Vineyard Transit Authority (MVTA; ☎ 508-627-9663) provides island-wide service year-round. From May through October, buses run every 15 to 30 minutes between 7am and 1am. From November through April, they run every 30 to 60 minutes until 7pm, depending on the route.

Passes are an old-fashioned bargain: $5/10/15 one day/three days/one week. Children under age 6 are free. Purchase passes at the Steamship Authority in Vineyard Haven or Oak Bluffs (both double as bus stops) or the MVTA Church St office (also a principal stop) in Edgartown. Although it's not economical, you can purchase single tickets ($1 to $3 per trip, depending on how far you go, for folks over age 7; seniors half-price) with exact change on board. Flag down buses wherever you see them. Excellent route maps are ubiquitous, available at the steamship, inns and visitor information centers.

Car A car is the best way to explore up-island, although it is by no means necessary. Note that it's cheaper to bring your own car over for two days (if you can get it on the ferry) than to rent one for two days.

For rentals, Budget (☎ 508-693-1911, 800-527-0700) has offices in Oak Bluffs, Vineyard Haven and Edgartown and at the airport. Thrifty (☎ 508-693-1959) is located at Five Corners, Vineyard Haven. The least expensive cars cost about $75 for 24 hours, about $55 off-season.

Bicycle & Moped Vineyard Haven, Oak Bluffs and Edgartown have plenty of bike rental shops within sight of the ferries; prices are competitive. (See the Activities or Bicycling sections under each town heading.) Expect to spend $20/75 daily/weekly for a bike. See Maps under Orientation, earlier in this chapter, for information about ordering bike maps in advance.

The only destination for which you might want a moped is Aquinnah (Gay Head); it's quite hilly out there and it is 20 or so miles from Edgartown or Vineyard Haven. Give yourself a day for that trip by bike. Mopeds, by the way, are banned in Edgartown center. They are also very unsafe on sandy streets; the local hospital is constantly treating injured riders.

VINEYARD HAVEN

Although it's the island's commercial center, Vineyard Haven isn't lacking in charm.

Its harbor is filled with more traditional wooden schooners and sloops than any harbor of its size in New England, and its back streets, especially William St, are lined with sturdy sea captains' homes. It's the most mellow of the three principal towns – the most 'real,' if you will. It's also a year-round community, so if you're coming off-season, this is the place to stay.

Orientation & Information

The principal section of Vineyard Haven is just four or five blocks wide by about half a mile long. Steamship Authority ferries dock at the end of Union St, a block from Main St. From the terminal, Water St leads to Beach Rd and the infamous 'Five Corners' intersection: Five roads come together and no one really has the right of way. Good luck. From Five Corners, Beach Rd heads to Oak Bluffs along the ocean. For a picnic place, head west on Main St to Owen Park, a nice patch of lawn that slopes down to the harbor.

Bunch of Grapes Bookstore (☎ 508-693-2291, 44 Main St) has a fine reputation and constant 'author events.' Among the art galleries in town, **Shaw Cramer Gallery** (☎ 508-696-7323, 2nd floor, 76 Main St) is an excellent one, specializing in a wide array of contemporary crafts.

Things to See & Do

Making wine is not easy in New England, but **Chicama Vineyard** (☎ 508-693-0309, State Rd; admission free; open 11am-5pm Mon-Sat mid-May–mid-Oct; 1pm-4pm Jan–mid-Apr; shoulder season hours vary), about 3½ miles south of town off State Rd, does a fairly credible job. You'll have no illusions about being in the Loire Valley. Nonetheless, it only seems right that there be a working vineyard on the Vineyard. Stop by for a free tour and tasting from mid-May to mid-October.

West Chop Lighthouse, at the northern end of Main St, was built in 1817 with wood and replaced with brick in 1838.

If you're looking for beaches, head up-island or to Edgartown.

Activities

Strictly Bikes (☎ 508-693-0782, 24 Union St; daily rentals $20/15 adult/child), near the ferry, rents bikes. Before heading out to Oak Bluffs (a flat route along the ocean), bicycle 2 miles northwest on Main St to see West Chop Lighthouse.

Wind's Up (☎ 508-693-4252, 199 Beach Rd; double canoes & kayaks $20/50/65 per hour/4 hours/24 hours), at the drawbridge, rents boats and offers paddling lessons. The adjacent lagoon is perfect for 'intro to wind-surfing,' so Wind's Up gives lessons and rents equipment for windsurfing, too. The 'Beginner Package' costs $100 and includes two lessons and three hours of practice. (Experienced windsurfers who want to harness stronger winds around the island will appreciate the staff's wisdom.)

MV Parasail (☎ 508-693-2838, Pier 44, Marina, Beach Rd; June–mid-Sept) offers an assortment of lessons and rentals for water-skiing, wakeboarding, kneeboarding, para-sailing and inner-tubing for ages four and up. Mark, the owner, has never met anyone he couldn't teach. Is that a challenge? If you're into jet skiing, you might take Mark's guided, 2-hour water tour for $125/150 single/double. It's a different way to see the island, that's for sure.

Sports Haven (☎ 508-696-0456, 5 Beach St), near the ferry, rents in-line skates ($15/30 half/two days). In Vineyard Haven, skating is not permitted on Main St or at the Steamship Authority. You'll also have to remove the skates in downtown Edgartown and on Circuit Ave in Oak Bluffs. Where can you skate? Try the excellent paths in the state forest. Sports Haven also rents tennis racquets.

Places to Stay

Island-wide, most places require a minimum multi-day summertime stay. Make reservations as far in advance as possible for summer and for fall weekends. Better yet, go mid-week in May, June or October, when the rates are often lower. You'll find a comprehensive list of accommodations and links at Ⓦ www.mvy.com.

Camping The island's only campground is *Martha's Vineyard Family Campground* (☎ 508-693-3772, 569 Edgartown Rd) No hookups/hookups $36/40, cabins $100-120. Open mid-May–mid-Oct. This property offers 130 wooded sites for tenters and 50 for RVs. The dozen or so rustic cabins sleep four to six people.

Motels They're open year-round at *Vineyard Harbor Motel* (☎ 508-693-3334, fax 508-693-0320, 60 Beach Rd) Doubles $65-105 off-season, $130-185 mid-June–mid-Sept. These 40 uniformly plain rooms have TV and a refrigerator. Some rooms have small kitchens, and since the motel's on the edge of the harbor (and town), some rooms also have water views. Two apartments rent for $155 in-season.

B&Bs Off the beaten path, you'll find *The House at New Lane* (☎ 508-696-7331, New Lane) Singles $65, doubles $85 year-round with full breakfast. Can't spare $300 a night for a mattress and pillow? Luckily this place is as comfortable as the rates are reasonable. Delightfully out of the way, these three rooms with shared bath are homey and comfy. Bonuses include beach passes and friendly innkeepers. One room has a private deck.

Kinsman Guest House (☎ 508-693-2311, 278 Main St) Doubles $100 off-season, $125 June–mid-Oct. Open year-round. A pleasant 10-minute walk from the center of town, these three guest rooms (two of which share a bath) have been decorated with care and pride by the hands-on owner.

Crocker House Inn (☎ 508-693-1151, 800-772-0206, fax 508-693-1123, Ⓦ www.crocker houseinn.com, 12 Crocker Ave) Doubles $95-265 off-season, $205-385 June–mid-Oct with expanded continental breakfast. Open year-round. If you have a good arm, these eight guest rooms are a stone's throw from the harbor. The nicely renovated rooms exude a cheery, summery feel and the front porch rockers are a quiet place for a second cup of coffee.

Captain Dexter House (☎ 508-693-6564, 866-624-8424, fax 508-693-8448, Ⓦ www

.captaindexter.com, 92 Main St) Doubles $95-175 off-season, $150-250 late May–mid-Oct with continental breakfast. Open year-round. This centrally located 1843 residence has eight large rooms furnished with Victorian, colonial and New England antiques. A couple of rooms have a fireplace; some have four-poster canopy beds.

Places to Eat

Vineyard Haven has a surprising range of eateries, many of which are open year-round. It's a 'dry' town, so no alcohol is served in restaurants or sold in stores, but you can 'bring your own bottle' (BYOB) and waiters will uncork it for you for a nominal charge. Unless otherwise noted, these places are open for lunch and dinner.

Black Dog Bakery (☎ 508-693-4786, Water St) Open at least 5:30am-5pm daily year-round. Only 100 yards east of the Steamship Authority terminal, this bakery is often the first place people head for good coffee and sweet treats as they disembark from the ferry.

90 Main St Market & Deli (☎ 508-693-0041, 90 Main St) Dishes $4-7. This shop serves up salads and sandwiches at decent prices.

Sandwich Haven (☎ 508-696-8383, 32 Beach Rd) Dishes $6-15. With the exception of specialties like falafel, this joint is dedicated to pizzas, calzones and subs.

Vineyard Gourmet (☎ 508-693-5181, Main St) Dishes by the pound. For an upscale alternative, you might try pâté, smoked salmon and spiced asparagus spears.

Zephrus (☎ 508-693-3416, 9 Main St) Lunch mains $8-14, dinner mains $19-31. In seasonal locales, the rare combination of above average atmosphere, cuisine and service make this place a consistent winner. The wide-ranging menu bounces from steamed mussels to strip steak to nightly veggie and pasta dishes.

Black Dog Tavern (☎ 508-693-9223, 21 Beach St Extension) Breakfast dishes $6-9, lunch mains $6-14, dinner mains $10-25. In the summer, when sales of Black Dog T-shirts and baseball caps outpace that of swordfish, this harborfront tavern is too popular for its own good. The food is good but pricey, ranging from beef stew ($10) to lobster ($25). Mostly, the American menu leans toward seafood and locally grown vegetables. Reservations are not accepted, and the lines are usually quite long, so try to arrive before 5:30pm for dinner in the summer.

Le Grenier (☎ 508-693-4906, 96 Main St) Mains $20-31. Open for dinner only. Lovely in a low-key, Vineyard sort of way, this well-established and highly regarded bistro serves traditional and exceptional French cuisine.

Entertainment
Sit in the dark year-round at *Capawock Movie House* (☎ 508-627-6689, Main St) Built in 1912, this cinema is a particularly good place to pick up off-season island gossip.

Vineyard Playhouse (☎ 508-693-6450 information, ☎ 508-696-6300 tickets, 24 Church St) Tickets outdoor $5-15, main stage $20-30. Open year-round. The Playhouse presents fine and challenging plays, musicals and other performances (daily except Monday in summer) in a former Methodist meeting-house. Every now and then, there are performances by famous 'washashores.' If you're even luckier, there may be unsold 'rush' tickets available 10 minutes before the curtain goes up ($20).

OAK BLUFFS
Nicknamed 'Sin City,' Oak Bluffs is the island's summer fun center: informal, downscale, pierced, interracial, even gaudy. Brightly colored Victorian 'gingerbread houses' line many back streets, and there's an old-fashioned carousel that some say is the oldest in the country.

Orientation & Information
The *Island Queen* ferry from Falmouth docks at the end of Circuit Ave Extension, which is lined with inexpensive outdoor eateries. The Steamship Authority's ships dock at Sea View and Oak Bluffs Aves (seasonal).

Oak Bluffs Ave (lined with bike and car-rental shops) turns into Lake Ave, which runs parallel to the harbor. Keep going west to reach Vineyard Haven. Sea View Ave, also called the Oak Bluffs-Edgartown Rd, heads south out of town, along the shore, to Edgartown.

Circuit Ave is the main drag. To the left and right of it, on the side streets, are the gingerbread houses for which the town is famous.

The information booth (☎ 508-693-4266), behind the Flying Horses Carousel on Circuit Ave at Lake Ave, is open 9am to 5pm daily May to mid-October.

Gingerbread Houses
Wesleyan Grove is bounded by Lake, Sea View and Dukes County Aves and sliced in the middle by Circuit Ave. The grove contains the renowned Victorian gingerbread cottages that look like they're dripping with icing. Bold colors and whimsical ornamental woodwork characterize what architects call a 'Carpenter Gothic' style.

In 1835, when the Methodist Campmeeting Association began holding summer revival meetings here, the congregation camped in tents. As the meetings grew, participants who returned year after year began putting up bigger tents. Then they pitched their tents on wooden platforms, which evolved into small cottages. Every year, they adorned their cottages with more and more fanciful wooden trim. *Voilà!* A Carpenter Gothic village.

This neighborhood is no museum: Members of the religious congregation still live here, so note the posted rules, especially no 'rude or loud behavior.' Services are still held in the 1879 wrought-iron Trinity Park Tabernacle.

The **Cottage Museum** (☎ 508-693-0525, 1 Trinity Park; admission by nominal donation; open 10am-4pm Mon-Sat mid-June–mid-Oct) is typical of the 300 or so tiny 19th-century cottages in Oak Bluffs. It's filled with furniture, artifacts and memorabilia from the cottages' heydays.

The **Flying Horses Carousel** (no ☎, Circuit Ave; rides $1; open 11am-4:30pm

Sat-Sun late Apr–mid-Oct & 10am-10pm daily late May–early Sept), at Lake Ave, claims to be the country's oldest operating merry-go-round (1876). More adults ride the merry-go-round than you might think, hoping to catch the brass ring.

The narrow, 2-mile long **Joseph Sylvia State Beach** on Beach Rd (aka Oak Bluffs-Edgartown Rd) is backed by low dunes. It's also referred to as the Bend-in-the-Road Beach. Parking is free along the road.

Bicycling

Since lots of ferries pull into town, discharging hordes of passengers, there are lots of places renting lots of bicycles. Try **Anderson Bike Rentals** (*☎ 508-693-9346, Circuit Ave Extension*) and **Vineyard Bike & Moped** (*☎ 508-693-4498, Oak Bluffs Ave*) across from the Flying Horses Carousel. Bikes are competitively priced at about $20 daily.

The Oak Bluffs-Edgartown Rd straddles the ocean, a good beach and a saltwater pond for much of the route. The 5-mile ride is scenic, but you'll be riding parallel to the heavily traveled road on the bike path.

Also, head up to **East Chop Lighthouse**: Take Lake Ave toward Vineyard Haven, turn right on Commercial St along the water and continue on Highland Ave. The bluff commands a nice ocean view and is a good place for a picnic.

Special Events

The actual date of the mid-August **Illumination Night** is kept mum until a week before

The African American Connection

As early as the late 1600s, African slaves tended Vineyard farms. And by 1779, freed slave Rebecca Amos was willed property by her Wampanoag husband upon his death and the death of her master. Shortly after the abolition of slavery in 1783, a freeman from Virginia sailed to the island preaching Methodist sermons. By 1834 the Methodist Campmeeting Association was born, which in turn spurred Vineyard tourism. At the same time in the mid-19th century, African Americans, like their white counterparts, shipped out on whaling boats in the hope of quick prosperity. Not surprisingly,

the island's first black whaling captain, William Martin, traced his roots back to Rebecca Amos.

These days, Oak Bluffs is a prime vacation land for East Coast African American movers and shakers. Famed Harlem Renaissance writer Dorothy West, author of *The Wedding* (which Oprah Winfrey turned into a miniseries starring Halle Berry), was an early convert to the island's charms. She died on the island in 1998 and is buried here. Filmmaker Spike Lee owns a house in 'OB' and Harvard academician Henry Louis 'Skip' Gates Jr frequents the island. Former president Bill Clinton vacationed here with Hillary and Chelsea during most of his White House years and played golf with über lawyer-lobbyist and FOB (Friend of Bill) Vernon Jordan.

For more thorough coverage of African American island folklore, history and contemporary connections, look for African American Heritage Trail pamphlets in local bookstores or take a tour (*☎ 508-693-4361*) from late May to early September.

Vineyard resident Spike Lee

it becomes obvious: Residents gather for a heartwarming community sing, then the town of Oak Bluffs shuts off all electrical lights, and the eldest resident lights a Japanese lantern. When the rest of the Methodist Campmeeting Association follows suit, an eerie glow illuminates the neighborhood.

Places to Stay

Motels & Hotels Centrally located is the *Surfside Motel* (☎ 508-693-2500, 800-537-3007, fax 508-693-7343, ⓦ www.mvsurfside .com, 7 Oak Bluffs Ave) Doubles $60-170 off-season, $150-295 mid-June–mid-Sept. Open year-round. Since the motel is right in the middle of the action, it's not the right choice for light sleepers. Of the 38 rooms, the more expensive ones have refrigerators and water views.

Wesley Hotel (☎ 508-693-6611, 800-638-9027, fax 508-693-5389, ⓦ www.wesleyhotel .com, 70 Lake View Ave) Doubles $110-135 off-season, $185-230 mid-June–mid-Oct. Open May–mid-Oct. There are two worthy features of this three-story, turn-of-the-19th-century hotel: the sheer number of rooms (95) and its long verandah dotted with rocking chairs facing the marina. Half the basic furnished rooms have water views, while many annex rooms are darkish.

B&Bs There was a stem-to-stern renovation in 2000 at the *Nashua House* (☎ 508-693-0043, ⓦ www.nashuahouse.com, 30 Kennebec Ave) Doubles $59-89 off-season, $99-109 late May-early Sept. Open Apr-Nov. The 15 shared-bath rooms are simple, and this place is a welcome relief from the higher-priced hostelries.

Attleboro House (☎ 508-693-4346, 42 Lake Ave) Doubles $75-115, family rooms $95-175. Open mid-May–Sept. This decidedly old-fashioned gingerbread-style house has 11 basic rooms, all with shared bath. A few rooms have sinks, and some can handle an extra person or two. An attic room sleeps six. The house enjoys unobstructed views of the protected marina from the rocking chairs on the front porch.

Narragansett House/Iroquois Cottage (☎ 508-693-3627, 888-693-3627, fax 508-693-4573, ⓦ www.narragansetthouse.com, 46 Narragansett Ave) Doubles $85-225 off-season, $100-275 late May–mid-Sept. Open May–mid-Oct. This Victorian-style house, smack in the middle of the gingerbread-cottage community, has 13 simple and decidedly old-fashioned rooms, two apartments that can accommodate larger groups and six spiffy, renovated rooms in the adjacent Iroquois Cottage. Many of these latter rooms, at the higher end of the price range above, are small but boast cathedral ceilings or little balconies. Call for apartment rates.

Four Gables (☎ 508-696-8384, ⓦ www .fourgablesmv.com, 41 New York Ave) Doubles $75-105 off-season, $100-145 June-Sept with continental breakfast. Open year-round. Barely on the outskirts of town, these four rooms are a fine choice for independent travelers who relish a bit of quirkiness. It's all very comfortable, very low-key. The expansive 3rd-floor suite, when it's available, costs $145 off-season, $190 in season.

Admiral Benbow Inn (☎ 508-693-6825, fax 508-693-7820, ⓦ www.admiral-benbow inn.com, 81 New York Ave) Doubles $85-110 off-season, $130-180 late June-late Sept with continental breakfast. Open year-round. On the edge of a well-traveled road into town, the inn's seven rooms are decorated with Victorian furnishings.

Oak House (☎ 508-693-4187, 800-245-5979, fax 508-696-7293, Seaview Ave) Doubles $120-210 off-season, $180-275 mid-June–early Sept with continental breakfast and extensive afternoon tea. Open mid-May–mid-Oct. The Oak House is aptly named; guest rooms have oak furniture, oak walls and oak ceilings! It's all quite Victorian: cozy, nicely put together and expensive. Most of the 10 rooms have water views, and some have private balconies.

Oak Bluffs Inn (☎ 508-693-7171, 800-955-6235, fax 508-693-8787, ⓦ www.oakbluffs inn.com, 64 Circuit Ave) Doubles $100-185 off-season, $190-250 mid-June–mid-Sept with continental breakfast. Open May-Oct. The inn, on the edge of Wesleyan Grove with great views of the camp meetinghouses, has nine guest rooms and suites decorated with bright and fanciful cottage-style furniture.

Places to Eat

In addition to inexpensive eateries offering burgers, sandwiches, shrimp and lobster, Oak Bluffs has some fine choices if you're ready to splurge. Unless otherwise noted, these restaurants are open for lunch and dinner; some are seasonal.

Mocha Mott's (☎ 508-696-1922, 10 Circuit Ave) Open 6am-6pm (at least) daily year-round. Java junkies follow their noses to this basement hangout which also has newspapers and sweets.

Linda Jean's (☎ 508-693-4093, 25 Circuit Ave) Dishes $3-18. Open 6am-8pm daily year-round. The town's best all-around inexpensive eatery has three-egg omelets filled with vegetables ($6), chowder ($3), burgers ($3.50), and platters of fried seafood ($18). It's a beloved institution, packed with locals.

The Strip The waterfront strip, or boardwalk, where the Hy-Line and *Island Queen* ferries dock, is lined with fast food eateries of varying quality. You've seen the menus elsewhere: fried clams, burgers, raw bar, frozen drinks and the like.

Offshore Ale Co (☎ 508-693-2626, 30 Kennebec Ave) Lunch mains $6-12, dinner mains $10-25. Open noon-3pm daily May-Sept & 5pm-midnight daily year-round. Within the shell of an old barn, this place brews its own beer and serves it alongside great burgers, greater brick-oven pizzas and modest seafood dishes. Entertainment (nightly in summer, less often in winter) often accompanies the free-flowing supply of peanuts on each table.

Lola's Southern Seafood (☎ 508-693-5007, 15 Beach Rd) Pub menu $7-15, dining room mains $20-35, brunch $12-15. Open for dinner and Sunday brunch year-round. A bit out of town, this hopping joint has excellent, authentic barbecue ribs, seafood jambalaya and other New Orleans-style dishes. The all-you-can-eat brunch is a steal, but if you just want a lively place to hang out a while, you can easily make do with the lighter pub menu. Portions are huge. There's a varied lineup of entertainment throughout the year, including jazz and gospel during brunch.

Giordano's (☎ 508-693-0184, 107 Circuit Ave) Mains $8-16. At the corner of Lake Ave, Giordano's has been in business since 1930, serving large portions of moderately priced home-style Italian-American food. Known for its salad bar and hefty cocktails, they also sell excellent fried clams from the take-out window.

Zapotec Cafe (☎ 508-693-6800, 14 Kennebec Ave) Mains $11-18. Mexican and Southwestern dishes like chicken suiza and chimichangas vie for attention with Vineyard variations like swordfish fajitas. Still, the sangria and chili pepper lights remind you of the restaurant's essential debts to El Paso and points south.

Jimmy Sea's Pan Pasta (☎ 508-696-8550, 32 Kennebec Ave) Dinner mains $15-23. Open for dinner year-round. This small, casual place offers large portions; you'd better come with an appetite or have a place to reheat leftovers. Their fancy pasta dishes are cooked to order, served in the skillet and infused with fresh herbs from the

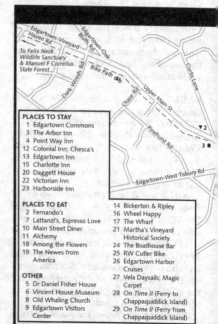

PLACES TO STAY
1 Edgartown Commons
3 The Arbor Inn
4 Point Way Inn
12 Colonial Inn; Chesca's
13 Edgartown Inn
15 Charlotte Inn
20 Daggett House
22 Victorian Inn
23 Harborside Inn

PLACES TO EAT
2 Fernando's
7 Lattanzi's; Espresso Love
10 Main Street Diner
11 Alchemy
18 Among the Flowers
19 The Newes from America

OTHER
5 Dr Daniel Fisher House
6 Vincent House Museum
8 Old Whaling Church
9 Edgartown Visitors Center

14 Bickerton & Ripley
16 Wheel Happy
17 The Wharf
21 Martha's Vineyard Historical Society
24 The Boathouse Bar
25 RW Cutler Bike
26 Edgartown Harbor Cruises
27 Vela Daysails; Magic Carpet
28 *On Time II* (Ferry to Chappaquiddick Island)
29 *On Time II* (Ferry from Chappaquiddick Island)

front garden. President Clinton and family have feasted here.

Sweet Life Cafe (☎ 508-696-0200, 63 Circuit Ave) Mains $24-38. Open May-Nov. This chef-owned bistro easily serves the best cuisine in town, and features an ever-changing New American menu. You can count on something along the lines of oven-roasted halibut with garlic mashed potatoes. Note to foodies: Run, don't walk, to Sweet Life Cafe.

Entertainment

Oak Bluffs is the island's liveliest town during the summer, but many pubs close October to late May.

Atlantic Connection (☎ 508-693-7129, 19 Circuit Ave) Cover $4-8. There's usually something rowdy going on here all summer. Live reggae bands share the stage with hip-hop DJs and comedians who appeal to twenty-somethings.

Ritz Cafe (☎ 508-693-9851, 1 Circuit Ave) Open year-round. This blues dive, with an emphasis on 'dive,' has live music weekends off-season, nightly except Sunday in summer. You see a lot of not-so-young island long-hairs, fisherfolk and sailors here.

Lampost/Rare Duck (☎ 508-693-9847, Circuit Ave) The 2nd-floor Lampost features dancing and pool for an under-30 crowd, while the 1st-floor Rare Duck entertains older patrons more simply with frozen drinks. In summer, you can usually catch some live entertainment here, too.

EDGARTOWN

Patrician Edgartown is the island's architectural showpiece. Its 18th- and 19th-century whaling captains' houses are perfectly maintained, with clipped lawns, blooming gardens and white picket fences. Though it's crowded in summer, Edgartown is downright quiet between October and April.

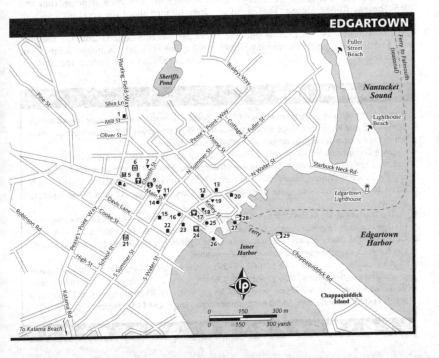

Orientation & Information

You'll probably come into town via Main St, which extends down to the harbor. Water St is parallel to the harbor. N Water St, lined with fine sea captains' houses, leads out to the Edgartown Lighthouse.

The Edgartown Visitors Center (no ☎), around the corner from the Old Whaling Church on Church St, is open 9am to 5pm daily, June to early September, with additional summer evening hours. You'll find public restrooms and a post office here.

Bickerton and Ripley (☎ 508-627-8463, 100 Main St) is a great bookstore; it is open April through December.

Martha's Vineyard Historical Society

The historical society (☎ 508-627-4441, 59 School St; adult/child $7/4; open 10am-5pm Tues-Sat mid-June–mid-Oct; 1pm-4pm Wed-Fri & 10am-4pm Sat mid-Oct–mid-June) occupies several buildings, including the 1765 Thomas Cooke House. The island's most interesting museum contains whaling and maritime relics, scrimshaw and the huge Fresnel lens taken from the Gay Head Lighthouse.

Historic Buildings

You'll find the **Vincent House Museum** (☎ 508-627-8619 for tours, ☎ 627-8017 for information, 99 Main St; over age 12 $4; open noon-3pm daily late May–mid-Oct) behind the stunningly simple **Old Whaling Church.** Since the house, built in 1672, was in the same family until 1977, its architectural integrity has been well-guarded. Three rooms appear as they would have in the 17th, 18th and 19th centuries.

The Old Whaling Church, by the way, was constructed in 1843 using the same techniques as those employed in building whaling ships. Next door, the **Dr Daniel Fisher House** is a magnificently preserved 1840s Federal-style house once owned by the founder of the Martha's Vineyard National Bank. It's yours for the touring at 11am, noon, 1pm and 2pm daily.

An $8 combination ticket gets you into all three quietly impressive buildings, where there are tours of each at noon, 1pm and 2pm. Inquire about the good walking tour **Ghosts, Gossip & Downright Scandals** ($10 per person) that departs from the museum daily; the schedule is unpredictable but there are always tours daily in the summer.

Chappaquiddick Island

A stone's throw from Edgartown Harbor, Chappaquiddick is perhaps most widely known for US Senator Edward Kennedy's tragic accident there in 1969. A passenger in Kennedy's car drowned when the car he was driving plunged off a small wooden bridge.

Since Chappaquiddick has very few houses and no shops or eateries, the prime attractions are natural. Check out the 500-acre **Cape Pogue Wildlife Refuge** (complete with a remote lighthouse) and the 200-acre **Wasque Reservation**, both unspoiled and unfrequented stretches of sand. In addition to its beautiful open space, the island contains the meditative 14-acre **Mytoi** Japanese garden.

The Trustees of the Reservations (☎ 508-627-3599) offer three-hour naturalist-led expeditions of Cape Pogue and Wasque Reservation twice daily in summer (adult/child $30/15; late May–mid-Oct), as well as shorter trips that include a tour of the Cape Pogue Lighthouse (adult/child $15/6). Call for exact departure times and to make reservations.

A six-car ferry, *On Time II* (☎ 508-627-9427), at the corner of Daggett and Dock Sts, takes people and cars to the island daily year-round. 'Chappy' is only 200 yards or so away, and the ferry leaves whenever there are people who want to go; that way, it's always 'on time.' Roundtrip tickets cost $6 car and driver, $1.50 each additional passenger and $4 for bicycles.

Sanctuaries & Beaches

The 350-acre **Felix Neck Wildlife Sanctuary** (☎ 508-627-4850, off Edgartown-Vineyard Haven Rd; trail access adult/senior & child $3/2; visitor center open 8am-4pm daily June-Sept; 8am-4pm Tues-Sat Oct-May) is crisscrossed with 5 miles of trails that traverse woods, meadows, marshes and the beach.

The dense 4400-acre **Manuel F Correllus State Forest** (☎ 508-693-2540, off the Edgartown-Vineyard Haven Rd; open dawn-dusk) occupies a huge chunk of the island's midsection. It has walking and biking trails. Park near the Barnes Rd exit.

South of Edgartown, **Katama Beach** (extending west as South Beach), off Katama Rd, is 3 miles long, with moderate surf. The big parking lot is a good indicator of the beach's popularity.

Lighthouse Beach is easily accessible from the end of N Water St. The lighthouse is particularly striking at sunset, but it's fun to watch boats put into Edgartown Harbor from here any time.

College students and summer workers hang out on **Fuller St Beach**, at the end of Fuller St near Lighthouse Beach.

Bicycling

You can rent bikes at both **RW Cutler Bike** (☎ 508-627-4052, 1 Main St) and **Wheel Happy** (☎ 508-627-5928, 8 S Water St). Prices are about $20/75 daily/weekly.

Cruises

For an old-fashioned and intimate sail (only six people at a time), climb aboard a 50-foot wooden sloop at **Vela Daysails** (☎ 508-627-1963, Memorial Wharf; adult/child $55/25; open mid-June–mid-Sept) next to the Chappy Ferry. Reservations are recommended. It's particularly nice for families. If the *Vela* is full, try the *Magic Carpet* (☎ 508-627-2889, Memorial Wharf), which also has a nice captain and can accommodate 18 people.

Edgartown Harbor Cruises (☎ 508-939-9282, Lower Main St; adult/child $18/8; daily late May-early Sept), near the Edgartown Yacht Club, offers short narrated tours on the hour 11am to 6pm.

Special Events

Even with all the Vineyard's various seasonal events, the 'Possible Dreams Auction,' usually held in Edgartown at the Harborside Inn, is unique. Early in August, nationally known celebrities with second homes on the island throw a creative auction to benefit island community services. Highest bidders might win a tour of the *60 Minutes* studios in New York by anchor Mike Wallace or a personal performance by singer Carly Simon.

Places to Stay

Efficiencies If you're planning a longer stay, try the ***Edgartown Commons*** (☎ 508-627-4671, 800-439-4671, fax 508-627-4271, 🔲 www.edgartowncommons.com, 20 Pease's Point Way) Studios & one-bedrooms $90-110, two-bedrooms $140-160 off-season; studios & one-bedrooms $160-185, two-bedrooms $235-260 mid-June–early Sept. Open May-Oct. Just a couple of blocks from the town center, the Commons is actually a complex of seven buildings with 35 well-kept studios and multi-bed apartments. Guests (most of whom are families) also have access to outdoor barbecues and a pool. Apartments can accommodate two to six people.

Hotels In the middle of the action is the ***Colonial Inn*** (☎ 508-627-4711, 800-627-4701, fax 508-627-5904, 🔲 www.colonialinnmvy.com, 38 N Water St) Doubles $135-270 off-season, $195-370 late May-Sept. Open mid-Apr–Nov. This rambling three-story place has 43 comfortable rooms, each with a TV and air-con. Rates vary with size and view; ask about mid-week specials.

Harborside Inn (☎ 508-627-4321, 800-627-4009, fax 508-627-7566, 🔲 www.theharborsideinn.com, 3 S Water St) Doubles $100-225 off-season, $215-295 June-early Sept. Open mid-Apr–mid-Nov. One of the island's few waterfront properties, this time-share hotel has 90 fairly standard-issue rooms in seven buildings. Rates depend on harbor proximity and whether you have a private balcony. A couple of very small rooms are available for $130/150 off-season/in-season.

Inns & B&Bs The best bargain in town is the *Edgartown Inn* (☎ 508-627-4794, 🖳 *www .edgartowninn.com, 56 N Water St)* Doubles with shared bath $60-75, with private bath $100 off-season, doubles with shared bath $100-165, with private bath $130-220 June–mid-Sept. Open mid-Apr–Oct. Fortunately, the inn is also friendly and tidy. The main inn has 20 simple rooms, but the two airy rooms in the adjacent Garden Cottage are the nicest. No credit cards are accepted.

The Arbor Inn (☎ 508-627-8137, 888-748-4383, fax 508-627-9104, 🖳 *www.mvy.com/ arborinn, 222 Upper Main St)* Doubles $110-155 off-season, $140-190 mid-June–mid-Sept with continental breakfast. Open mid-Apr–mid-Nov. A 10-minute walk from the harbor, the Arbor's location keeps prices fairly reasonable. Most of the nine guest rooms, furnished with a combination of antiques and modern pieces, have private baths.

Daggett House (☎ 508-627-4600, 800-946-3400, fax 508-627-4611, 🖳 *www.thedaggett house.com, 59 N Water St)* Doubles $100-220 off-season, $150-295 mid-May–mid-Sept. Open year-round. Daggett House has 31 rooms and suites in four buildings. One cottage is right on the harbor; more modern rooms are across the street. (The lawn stretches down to the harbor, so wherever you stay you can sit on the water.) The main house served as the island's first tavern in the 17th century; breakfast is served in this atmospheric, museum-style room.

Victorian Inn (☎ 508-627-4784, 🖳 *www .thevic.com, 24 S Water St)* Doubles $100-195 off-season, $185-385 June-Sept with full breakfast and tea. Open mid-Feb–Dec. This 14-room inn has a talkative innkeeper, four-poster beds, upscale furnishings and a private patio.

Point Way Inn (☎ 508-627-8633, 888-711-6633, fax 508-627-3338, 🖳 *www.pointway .com, 104 Main St)* Doubles $100-200 off-season, $225-375 June–mid-Oct with full breakfast and tea. Open year-round. This former whaling captain's house has been transformed into a stylish enclave with 13 rooms and suites, many with four-poster canopy beds and fireplaces. A tranquil courtyard protects you from the hordes of tourists. As a further bonus, the owners have an extra car that they loan to guests (on a first-come, first-served basis) for free. Will wonders never cease!

Charlotte Inn (☎ 508-627-4751, fax 508-627-4652, 27 S Summer St)* Doubles $250-695 off-season, $295-895 June-Oct with continental breakfast. Catering to a well-heeled crowd, the inn really does deserve its reputation as one of the finest inns in New England. The Charlotte Inn's 23 rooms and two suites, connected by English gardens and brick walkways, are furnished with practically priceless antiques. If you're going to go all the way, it has an outstanding (and equally expensive) French restaurant, too: *L'étoile.*

Places to Eat

With the exception of the following suggestions, the quality of food in Edgartown is generally lower than prices warrant. These eateries are open for lunch and dinner unless noted; some are seasonal.

Espresso Love (☎ 508-627-9211, 17 Church St)* Lunch mains $6-10, dinner mains $8-26. Open for all three meals. This cafe boasts the richest cup o' joe in town and good breakfast muffins. Dine on the outside patio or the enclosed deck just off Main St. Lunch revolves around sandwiches and soups, while dinner ranges from black angus burgers to penne pasta to grilled salmon.

Among the Flowers (☎ 508-627-3233, 17 Mayhew Lane)* Lunch mains $4-10, dinner mains $8-20. Open breakfast & lunch May-Oct, dinner July & Aug. It's hard to find a more down-to-earth eatery on the island. There are only a few tables outdoors, but don't let that deter you from getting an omelet, soup, salad or a quiche. Dinner offerings are a bit more upscale.

Main Street Diner (☎ 508-627-9337, 65 Main St)* Breakfast & lunch mains $5-8, dinner mains $10-14. Open 7am-8 or 9pm daily. Can't find a place to feed your starving family without selling the farm? This kitschy, faux 1950s-style diner helps with reasonably priced grilled cheese sandwiches, PB&J and a smattering of Italian dishes.

The Newes from America (☎ *508-627-4397, 23 Kelley St*) Mains $7-13. The Newes has very good traditional pub grub, as well as excellent burritos and burgers. (Don't order anything too fancy, though.) It's a dark and cozy place with a low-beamed ceiling. You'll find a lot of preppy summer folk here. They're a fun-loving and boisterous crowd.

Lattanzi's (☎ *508-627-8854, Old Post Office Square*) Pizzas $10-20, dinner mains $22-40. Open 5:30pm-closing. Lattanzi's is fashionable for brick-oven pizzas. There aren't a lot of bells and whistles here, just really good Italian food. If you're in the mood, look for their more formal, fine dining section next door, which serves extraordinary cuisine, and their new traditional gelateria and bakery.

Alchemy (☎ *508-627-9999, 71 Main St*) Lunch mains $10-15, dinner mains $26-30. This open, two-story bistro and bar has a good buzz. Venture out on a limb (it'll hold you here) for a pressed Cuban sandwich or stick with a highly evolved seared salmon. Save room for chocolate truffle cake, and keep your ears peeled for live music over the din.

Fernando's (☎ *508-627-8344, 227 Upper Main St*) Mains $13-23. Open 5pm-10pm daily. A favorite with locals who come for traditional pasta and steaks, Fernando's also has a children's menu.

Chesca's (☎ *508-627-1234, 38 N Water St*) Dishes $17-30. Open for dinner Apr-Oct. Quite pleasant and very popular, the backbone of Chesca's menu is Italian, featuring mix-and-match pastas with sauces or vegetarian risotto. But the rest of the menu reflects an Italian who travels a bit: try the frilled salmon with a spicy Thai glaze or a seafood paella.

Entertainment

The house specialty at *The Newes from America* (see Places to Eat) is a 'rack of beer,' a sampler with five unusual brews. The entire microbrew menu, in fact, is worth a sample.

The Wharf (☎ *508-627-9966, Main St*) Open year-round. This pub is popular and lively with the under-25 preppy set and quite a pick-up scene.

The Boathouse Bar (☎ *508-627-4320, 2 Main St*) Open May–mid-Oct. Similar to the Wharf, and situated within the waterfront Navigator restaurant, the Boathouse Bar has live entertainment on Friday and Saturday in the summer. The place is popular with couples over 30.

UP-ISLAND

This pastoral landscape is a patchwork of rolling fields, lined with stone walls and private dirt roads and dotted with barns and grazing sheep. There's very little to do up-island, except soak up the scenery, take a little hike, pop into a gallery, stop at a farm stand and head to the beach. But that's why you'll treasure the time spent.

Orientation

From West Tisbury, all roads – South, Middle and North – lead to Menemsha. But take South Rd (it's the prettiest) to 'Beetlebung Corner,' which is the center (just a crossroads, really) of Menemsha. To reach the harbor, follow Menemsha Cross Rd and look for signs to Dutcher's Dock. Only South Rd leads to Aquinnah (Gay Head) from Menemsha. At one particularly high point, you can see Menemsha Harbor to the north.

There are public restrooms near the parking area at the Clay Cliffs of Aquinnah (Gay Head) and at Dutcher's Dock, Menemsha Harbor.

Things to See & Do

A favorite local gathering place is **Alley's General Store** (☎ *508-693-0088, State Rd in West Tisbury*), which has served up-island residents since 1858. It was in danger of succumbing to the pressures of modern retailing in the mid-1990s, but fortunately a group of locals created a foundation to save and overhaul it. In 1998, the Wampanoag Indians stepped up to the plate to operate it.

Menemsha, a truly quaint little fishing village, was used as one of the sets for the movie *Jaws* (Edgartown and Chappy also figured large). There's a quiet beach and a good restaurant, Home Port, here. The sunsets are pretty spectacular, too.

The multicolored **Clay Cliffs of Aquinnah** were formed by glaciers more than 100 million years ago. Rising 150 feet from the ocean, they're dramatic any time of day. The cliffs are a National Historic Landmark owned by the Wampanoag Indians, and it's illegal to bathe in the mud pools that form at the bottom of the cliffs, or to remove clay from the premises. The 1844 brick **lighthouse**, standing precariously at the edge of the bluff, is open to visitors from late June to mid-September, Friday through Sunday evenings ($3); it's open 90 minutes prior to sunset and closes 30 minutes after sunset.

The **Cedar Tree Neck Sanctuary** *(☎ 508-693-5207, off Indian Hill Rd off State Rd, West Tisbury)* has a few trails crossing the 300 acres of bogs, fields and forests.

The 600-acre **Long Point Wildlife Refuge** *(☎ 508-693-7662, off Edgartown-West Tisbury Rd)* also has a few short trails, but a particularly good one leads to a deserted stretch of South Beach. Parking costs $7, and each adult pays $3.

The 20-acre **Polly Hill Arboretum** *(☎ 508-693-9426, 809 State Rd, West Tisbury; adult/child over 12 $5/3; open sunrise to sunset Thur-Tues mid-Oct–late May & 7am-7pm Thur-Tues late May–mid-Oct)* celebrates local woodlands and protects endangered species. This summer oasis shouldn't be overlooked in spring and fall. A little visitor center keeps slightly shorter hours.

It's a long and hilly **bicycle ride** from Edgartown to Aquinnah (21 miles one-way), but you'll be rewarded with expansive vistas and the quiet, intimate details of island life. With the exception of the path that borders the state park, you'll be riding on narrow winding roads with all the other traffic. Watch out for sandy patches.

The catamaran *Arabella* *(☎ 508-645-3511, Menemsha Harbor; sailing mid-June to late September)* makes a daily run to nearby Cuttyhunk Island (10am to 4pm; $60) and an evening sunset trip ($40) around the cliffs. Captain Hugh Taylor is singer James Taylor's brother, but he doesn't like to make a big deal about it.

Beaches

Also known as Gay Head Beach, **Aquinnah Public Beach** is a whopping 5 miles long. Head north for the cliffs; the farther you go in this direction, the less clothing you'll see. To the south, the beach is wider, but it's technically restricted to residents only. Stick to the water's edge, and you'll have no problem. Parking costs $15 daily or $5 for one hour.

Menemsha Beach, northeast of Dutcher's Dock and the harbor, is pebbly, but the water is calm. Across the 'cut' of water, to the southwest, **Lobsterville Beach** is popular with families because of the gentle surf and shallow water. From mid-June to late September, there's a little ferry (☎ 508-645-3511) that takes people and their bikes ($7 roundtrip, $4 one-way) across the cut. Parking at Lobsterville is restricted to residents, so you'll have to bike here to use the beach.

Lucy Vincent Beach, off South Rd about a half mile before the junction with Middle Rd, is open to Chilmark residents only. That's unfortunate because it's the loveliest stretch of sand (complete with dune-backed cliffs) on the island. You shouldn't have trouble using the unmarked beach off-season.

Places to Stay

Unless you stay at the hostel, it's impractical to stay up-island without a car.

Hostels For cheap digs, you can't beat the *Manter Memorial AYH Hostel* *(☎ 508-693-2665, 800-909-4776 in-season, ☎ 617-779-0900 off-season, fax 508-693-2699, Edgartown-West Tisbury Rd, West Tisbury)* Dorm beds members/non-members $15/19. Open Apr–mid-Nov. The 78-bed building was designed to be a hostel, so it's got a great kitchen. In summer, when reservations are essential, the hostel sponsors weekly programs on such topics as stargazing, the environment, budget travel and the Wampanoags. The hostel is accessible via bike (it's 8 miles from Vineyard Haven), thumb and MVTA bus (see Getting Around, earlier in this chapter). To make reservations before the hostel opens for the season, write to Hostelling International Boston (Attn: Reservations), 12 Hemenway St, Boston, MA 02215, or fax them at 617-424-6558.

Inns, B&Bs & Cottages For authentic up-island flavor, try *The Old Parsonage* (☎ 508-696-7745, 866-765-9777, fax 508-696-6712, ⓦ *www.swiftsite.com/oldparsonage, 1005 State Rd, West Tisbury*) Rooms/suite $90-145/165 late May-Nov with continental breakfast. Owned and operated by fifth-generation islanders and dating to 1668, this atmospheric hostelry has three rooms (two of which share a bath) and one large suite. The tranquil setting couldn't be more …dare we say…picturesque.

Captain Flanders' House (☎ 508-645-3123, ⓦ *www.captainflanders.com, North Rd*) Singles $65, doubles $115-150, cottage $175 off-season, singles $80, doubles $175-195 cottage $275 late-May–early Oct, all with continental breakfast. Open mid-Apr–Oct. This 17th-century house, located between Menemsha Cross and Tabor House Rds in Chilmark, enjoys a tranquil setting on 60 acres of rolling farmland overlooking a pond. Accommodations include four very modest guest rooms (two with private bath) in the main house and two snug, romantic cottages. Rates include a coveted pass to Lucy Vincent Beach.

Menemsha Inn and Cottages (☎ 508-645-2521, fax 508-645-9500, ⓦ *www.menemsha inn.com, North Rd, Menemsha*) Rooms $105-155 off-season, rooms $175-275 mid-June–mid-Sept with continental breakfast; cottages $170 nightly off-season & $1800 weekly mid-June–mid-Sept. Open May-Oct. Between Menemsha Cross Rd and Menemsha Harbor, this secluded place offers 12 charmingly simple and tidy one-bedroom cottages, each with a kitchen, fireplace and distant harbor views. There are also 15 motel-style rooms and suites. Guests get passes to Lucy Vincent Beach, but you can also walk through the woods to Menemsha Beach from here. No credit cards.

The Duck Inn (☎ 508-645-9018, fax 508-645-2790, off State Rd, Aquinnah) Doubles $85-175 off-season, $110-210 July-Aug with full organic breakfast. On a bluff practically overlooking Philbin Beach (adjacent to Aquinnah Beach), the rooms here are individually decorated, to say the least, with perhaps a feather duvet or marble wash basin or French door for the toilette. The 1st floor, draped in kilims (Middle Eastern rugs) and Native American carpets, is devoted to bohemian-style common space. Plenty of picture windows offer scenic views.

Places to Eat
Most up-island eateries are open from late May to early October.

West Tisbury Farmer's Market (no ☎, State Rd) Head to the Grange Hall (in the center of West Tisbury – you can't miss it) on Saturday from 9am to noon. The homey, all-island affair is also open 2:30pm to 5:30pm on Wednesday in July and August.

Inexpensive take-out shacks litter the route to the Clay Cliffs of Aquinnah.

Chilmark Store (☎ 508-645-3739, State Rd, Chilmark) This borderline bourgeois store will satisfy your need for a quick energy fix and a thirst quencher if you're bicycling to Aquinnah (Gay Head). Picnic fixings will cost a bit more than if you'd done it in Edgartown.

The Galley (☎ 508-645-9819, Menemsha Harbor) Dishes $4-10. This little shack with picnic tables sells meaty lobster rolls and arguably the island's best chowder.

Home Port (☎ 508-645-2679, Menemsha Harbor) Dinner mains $24-40. Open for dinner only. This place is very good, but basic; make reservations or be prepared to wait. Better yet, go to the back door and order the same food that everyone else is getting – fresh seafood and surf-and-turf combos – and take it to the dock and watch the sunset. Ordering à la carte from the back door costs less than eating inside.

Shopping
Looking for a tchotchke? Try the *Flea Market in the Meadow* (no ☎, Middle Rd, Chilmark) Open 8:30am-2pm Wed & Sat late June-early Sept.

Craven Gallery (☎ 508-693-3535, State Rd, Middletown Exchange, West Tisbury)

This modest-appearing gallery is a delight. Big-name artists like Milton Avery and Edward Hopper hang alongside, or are stacked behind, lesser-known artists who will probably be known in due time, if the eagle-eye owner is any judge. And she is.

Field Gallery and Sculpture Garden (☎ 508-693-5595, State Rd, West Tisbury) If you're remotely conscious, you can't miss this field of large white sculptures, playfully posing while tourists dance around them. There's an indoor gallery, too.

Chilmark Pottery (☎ 508-693-6476, off State Rd, West Tisbury) The island's rutted dirt roads lead to many potters, but this is one of the better known.

Martha's Vineyard Glass Works (☎ 508-693-6026, State Rd, West Tisbury) Master craftspeople turn sand into fragile and colorful creations here and, if you can stand the heat, you can watch it.

Nantucket Island

Thirty miles south of the Cape Cod coast, Nantucket is an island of grassy moors, salt bogs, warm-water beaches and historic villages – with prices to match the tony New Yorkers and Bostonians who summer here.

History

Within 40 years of the Pilgrims landing at Plymouth in 1620, there were white settlers living on Nantucket, going out in boats and hunting whales. By 1686, one of these whalers, a certain Jethro Coffin, had made a fortune large enough to afford a grand house built of brick. The house still stands. Throughout the 18th century, Nantucket grew ever richer from the whaling trade. The wealthy island's contribution to the Revolutionary War effort was exemplary: Around 2000 Nantucketers lost their lives and more than 100 whaling vessels were lost in battle. Though ultimately victorious in the war, Nantucketers were economically defeated by the peace. Before the island could recover from these huge losses, the War of 1812 began and robbed them of yet more men and ships. By the mid-19th century, the

great age of the sailing ship was over, supplanted by steam. With the advent of coal and petroleum as fuels, the trade in whale oil suffered a fatal decline.

The same steamships that robbed Nantucket of its whaling wealth brought a new means of prosperity: tourism. Nantucket's mariners abandoned whaling and took up cruising, shuttling visitors between the coast and the island. In the late 19th century, huge, rambling, wood-frame hotels were built to house vacationers, and the island settled into a comfortable, seasonal trade. In the early 1960s, islander and developer Walter Beinecke, Jr, began to revitalize the waterfront. He convinced merchants, restaurateurs and innkeepers that since the island had finite resources, it was far better to attract a moneyed crowd than folks with just a few dollars to spend. The theory continues to drive the island: You'll see far more jewelry stores than T-shirt shops.

Organized Tours

There's no better way to orient yourself and get a quick overview of Nantucket Island's main attractions than to take a 90-minute tour.

Ara's Tours (☎ 508-228-1951) Tours adult/child $12/6; late Apr-Oct. Ara's micro-bus has huge windows and a raised ceiling that makes it appealing for touring. Call for a reservation; Ara picks up at guest houses and ferries. You might want to inquire about special photographic charter expeditions.

Gail's Tours (☎ 508-257-6557) Tours $12. Tours 10am, 1pm & 3pm daily year-round. Gail's offers the perspective of a seventh-generation islander. Although she is full of interesting island trivia, there's a lot of commentary about which famous islanders owns which enormous houses. Don't be afraid to ask questions to change the direction of the patter. Tours depart from the Visitor Services & Information Bureau (25 Federal St). Call ahead off-season.

Barrett's Tours (☎ 508-228-0174, 20 Federal St) and **Nantucket Island Tours** (☎ 508-228-0334, Straight Wharf). Five or six daily tours ($14 per person) May-Oct. Buses generally depart after ferries arrive.

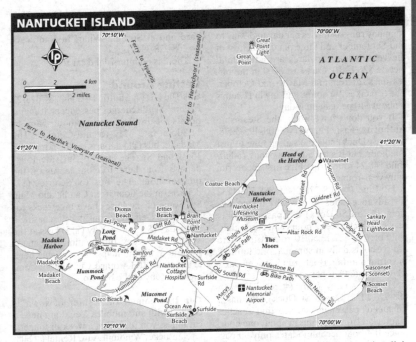

NANTUCKET ISLAND

For information on guided walking tours, see the Organized Tours section for Nantucket town. See also Lighthouses, under Around the Island, later in this chapter.

Getting There & Away

Air For the Fortune 500 executives among us who don't have private corporate planes, Nantucket's Memorial Airport is primarily served by small commuter planes. With the exception of the evening rush hour, just show up at the airport in Hyannis, New Bedford, Providence (RI) or Martha's Vineyard, buy a ticket for the next flight and you'll be on the island in less than 45 minutes. The taxi ride into Nantucket town costs $8.

Cape Air and Nantucket Airlines (☎ 508-790-0300, 800-352-0714, Ⓦ www.flycapeair .com) offer daily shuttle flights to and from Boston ($160 to $240 roundtrip in summer), Hyannis ($76), New Bedford ($111 to $141) and Martha's Vineyard ($75 to $90). Nantucket Airlines (☎ 508-790-0300, 800-635-

8787, Ⓦ www.nantucketairlines.com), a division of Cape Air, offers hourly shuttle service from Hyannis to Nantucket.

Island Air (☎ 508-228-7575, 800-248-7779) also operates from Hyannis at similar prices; flying time is 20 minutes.

US Airways Express (☎ 800-428-4322, Ⓦ www.usairways.com) services the island from New York's La Guardia Airport year-round and from Boston during the summer.

Continental Express (☎ 800-525-0280, Ⓦ www.continental.com) flies to Nantucket from Newark, New Jersey, in the summer.

Boat Nantucket is reached by ferries from Cape Cod and Martha's Vineyard.

From **Hyannis**, ferries of the Steamship Authority (☎ 508-477-8600 for car reservations, ☎ 508-771-4000 for day-of-sailing information, Ⓦ www.steamshipauthority.com, South St Dock) carry people and autos to Nantucket year-round. Make car reservations as early as possible (months in advance for summer, if you can). Reservations are not necessary for passengers or bicycles. The company runs six ferries per day mid-May to mid-September and three per day the rest of the year. Roundtrip fares are adult/child/bicycle $26/13/10. Cars cost $200 in the off-season, $320 from mid-May to mid-October. The trip takes 2¼ hours. Parking in Hyannis is about $10 per calendar day.

If you don't have a car, the Steamship Authority Fast Ferry (☎ 508-495-3278, South St Dock) cuts the sailing time to just one hour, but it's for a pretty penny (adult/child $48/24 roundtrip). Five to six boats run daily year-round.

Hy-Line (☎ 508-778-2600, 888-778-1132 for advance sales, W www.hy-linecruises.com, Ocean St Dock) has passenger-only service, which takes 2 hours and costs adult/child/bicycle $27/13.50/10 roundtrip. There are six boats daily in summer, one to three in spring and fall. Boats run between early May and late October.

Hy-Line's *Grey Lady* (☎ 508-778-0404, 888-778-1132, Ocean St Dock) also has a 'hi-speed' passenger service that reaches Nantucket from Hyannis in about one hour. Since the boat accommodates only 90 passengers, advance reservations are recommended. The boat makes six trips a day in summer, five the rest of the year. A roundtrip ticket costs adult/child/bicycle $58/41/10.

You can avoid Hyannis traffic if you come to Nantucket from **Harwichport**. Freedom Cruise Line (☎ 508-432-8999, W www.nantucketislandferry.com, Route 28 at Saquatucket Harbor) offers one daily morning ferry from late May to mid-October. As a daytripper, you'd have 6½ hours on the island. From mid-June to early September there are additional noontime and early evening ferries. The voyage takes 1½ hours and costs adult/child/bicycle $43/36/10. Advance reservations are highly recommended for the first two boats. Parking is free for the first day, then it jumps to $12 per day.

From **Martha's Vineyard**, Hy-Line Cruises (☎ 508-693-0112) operates three daily inter-island passenger ferries, early June to mid-September. The trip takes 2¼ hours; one-way

tickets cost adult/child/bicycle $13.50/6.75/5. The ferry docks in Oak Bluffs on the Vineyard and at Straight Wharf in Nantucket (☎ 508-228-3949).

There is no inter-island car ferry.

Getting Around

Bus The NRTA Shuttle (☎ 508-228-7025, 22 Federal St) discharges passengers at major points of interest from about 7am to 11:30pm, late May to mid-October. The Madaket bus ($1) departs on the hour from 15 Broad St. The bus to Surfside (50¢) departs from here, too, but leaves on the quarter hour. The bus to 'Sconset ($1) departs on the hour from Candle and Main Sts. Some of the buses have bike racks for two bikes. Definitely consider purchasing a three-day ($10) or weekly ($15) pass at the Visitor Services & Information Bureau, 25 Federal St. Route maps are available here, at the main NRTA office, Chamber of Commerce or any of the bus stops.

Car In summer, the center of town is choked with automobiles. You don't need a car unless you're staying a week or longer.

Nantucket Windmill Auto Rental (☎ 508-228-1227, 800-228-1227) is based at the airport but offers free pick-up and delivery. In town, head to Young's (☎ 508-228-1151, 6 Broad St) or Affordable Rental (☎ 508-228-3501, S Beach St). Expect to shell out $75 to $89 daily for a car in summer, $59 to $69 off-season. A 4WD vehicle, if you can get one in the summer, costs $200/995 per day/week.

Taxi Taxis are plentiful, especially on Lower Main St and at Steamboat Wharf, and rates are fixed. Rides from town cost $16 to 'Sconset, $10 to Cisco Beach and $8 to the airport. A nominal charge is added for each additional person in the taxi, and another charge is added after dark. Most taxi drivers can give you a personal tour of the island; you'll have to negotiate a price.

Bicycle & Moped Virtually every able-bodied person takes a bicycle or moped ride while on the island. Bicycling is the best way to get away from summertime crowds (don't try it on the cobblestones of Main St if you plan to have children), savor the island's natural beauty and reach much of the protected conservation land. Besides, the generally flat island has honest-to-goodness bike paths.

For the location of bicycle rental shops, see Bicycling under Nantucket town, later in this chapter. Rent mopeds at the **Nantucket Bike Shop** (*☎ 508-228-1999, 4 Broad St; $50/70 single/double in-season, about $10 less off-season*).

NANTUCKET
The only town of any size on this island, Nantucket town boasts movie-set-perfect cobblestone streets shaded by towering elms and lined with gracious 19th-century homes. The whole town is a National Historic Landmark, boasting the country's largest concentration of houses built prior to 1850. In summer, Nantucket's Main St is always jammed with shoppers, strolling daytrippers and cyclists walking their wheels.

Orientation
There are two ferry terminals, Steamboat Wharf and Straight Wharf, both a block or two off Main St in the center of town. Both terminals are within walking distance of most of the town's lodgings. The majority of tourist/visitor facilities – restaurants, inns, bicycle rental shops and stores – are within a 10-minute radius of Main St and the wharves. These principal areas are bounded by Main, Centre, Broad and S Water Sts. If you walk 30 minutes in any direction from the wharves, you will be on the outskirts of town.

If you need a map, Rubel BikeMaps (☎ 617-776-6567, W www.bikemaps.com) produces an excellent bike map covering routes on Martha's Vineyard and Nantucket ($1.95). If you can't find it at your local bookstore, contact the company directly.

Information
The tourism industry here is a well-oiled machine. Nantucket's chamber of commerce (☎ 508-228-1700, W www.nantucket chamber.org, 48 Main St) is stocked with

tons of information on seasonal activities and special events. The office is open 9am to 5pm weekdays year-round. Call for the free *Official Guide*.

Nantucket's Visitor Services & Information Bureau (☎ 508-228-0925, 25 Federal St) is the place to go for up-to-the-minute information on room availability and bus schedules. The bureau is open 9am to 5:30pm daily year-round (closed Sunday December through April). The bureau also maintains seasonal kiosks (late May to early September) at both of the island's ferry terminals (see Getting There & Away, earlier).

At Nantucket.net (☎ 508-228-6777, W www.nantucket.net, 2 Union St) you can access the Web for $5 per 30 minutes. The public access room is on the second floor, behind Nantucket Looms.

Nantucket Bookworks (☎ 508-228-4000, 25 Broad St) and Mitchell's Book Corner (☎ 508-228-1080, 54 Main St) have very good selections. The Hub (no ☎, cnr Main & Federal Sts) has magazines and newspapers.

There are public restrooms at the information bureau, the Steamship Authority ferry terminal and the end of Straight Wharf.

Nantucket Cottage Hospital (☎ 508-228-1200, S Prospect St at Vesper Lane) is on the edge of town. It's open 24 hours.

Nantucket Historical Association
The NHA (*☎ 508-228-1894, 15 Broad St; passes adult/child $12/8*) oversees nine of the island's most important historic buildings. Together, these buildings and their contents represent island life from its farming beginnings to its prosperous whaling days. Passes allow unlimited seasonal visits to the following buildings. Most buildings are open 10am to 5pm Monday through Saturday and noon to 5pm Sunday late May to mid-October; off-season hours are quite changeable.

Of the association's properties open to the public, don't miss the island's **oldest house**, built in 1686 on Sunset Hill Rd as a wedding present for Jethro Coffin and Mary Gardner Coffin. On the corner of S Mill and S Prospect Sts, a working **windmill** was built in 1746. The **Old Gaol** (*15R Vestal St*), was the island prison from 1805 to 1933. The first prisoner to escape was also the last. You can also tour the **Hadwen House** (*96 Main St*), a rarefied example of privileged life in the 19th century.

The historical association's most famous property is the **Nantucket Whaling Museum** (☎ *508-228-1736, 13 Broad St; also open spring and fall weekends 11am-4pm & for a tour and talk at 1pm Sat Jan-Mar*), which memorializes the island's principal industry, the original source of its prosperity. This is the only NHA property for which you can buy a single ticket (*adult/child $8/6*). But for an extra $4, it really makes sense to get the pass. The pass also entitles you to a complimentary walking tour which depart in front of the Whaling Museum at 10:30am and 2:30pm daily from late May to mid-October. The tours aren't nearly as good as Dirk Roggeveen's (see Organized Tours), but they are free.

Other Museums & Buildings

Climb the **First Congregational Church steeple** (☎ *508-228-0950, 62 Centre St; donation suggested adult/child $2/50¢; open 10am-4pm Mon-Sat mid-June–mid-Oct*), for an eagle-eye view of town. If your only goal is photography, you'll be a tad disappointed.

The Greek Revival **Atheneum** (☎ *508-228-1110, Lower India St; admission free; open 9:30am-5pm Tues-Sat year-round, 9:30am-5pm Mon late May–early Sept & 5pm-8pm Tues & Thur late May–early Sept*) is one of the town's greatest cultural resources. It's filled with whaling-ship records, island genealogy, scrimshaw and other historical articles dating back to 1816. One feels a great sense of history just reading the morning newspaper here. Often there are special events in the Great Hall on the 2nd floor, where notables such as Frederick Douglass and Ralph Waldo Emerson once spoke.

The small **Lightship Basket Museum** (☎ *508-228-1177, 49 Union St; nominal admission; open 10am-5pm Wed-Sun late May–mid-Oct*), with a re-created workshop, illuminates the simple but incredibly time

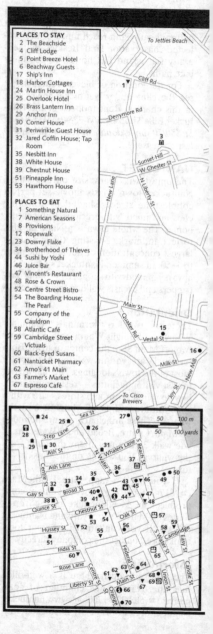

PLACES TO STAY
2 The Beachside
4 Cliff Lodge
5 Point Breeze Hotel
6 Beachway Guests
17 Ship's Inn
18 Harbor Cottages
24 Martin House Inn
25 Overlook Hotel
26 Brass Lantern Inn
29 Anchor Inn
30 Corner House
31 Periwinkle Guest House
32 Jared Coffin House; Tap Room
35 Nesbitt Inn
38 White House
39 Chestnut House
51 Pineapple Inn
53 Hawthorn House

PLACES TO EAT
1 Something Natural
7 American Seasons
8 Provisions
12 Ropewalk
23 Downy Flake
34 Brotherhood of Thieves
44 Sushi by Yoshi
46 Juice Bar
47 Vincent's Restaurant
48 Rose & Crown
52 Centre Street Bistro
54 The Boarding House; The Pearl
55 Company of the Cauldron
58 Atlantic Café
59 Cambridge Street Victuals
60 Black-Eyed Susans
61 Nantucket Pharmacy
62 Arno's 41 Main
63 Farmer's Market
67 Espresso Café

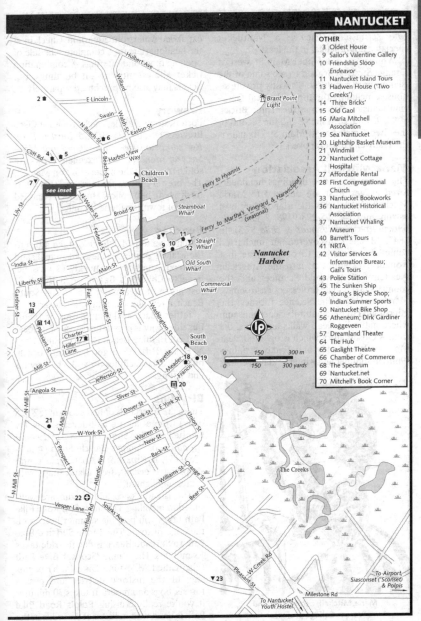

NANTUCKET

OTHER
3 Oldest House
9 Sailor's Valentine Gallery
10 Friendship Sloop
   Endeavor
11 Nantucket Island Tours
13 Hadwen House ('Two
   Greeks')
14 'Three Bricks'
15 Old Gaol
16 Maria Mitchell
   Association
19 Sea Nantucket
20 Lightship Basket Museum
21 Windmill
22 Nantucket Cottage
   Hospital
27 Affordable Rental
28 First Congregational
   Church
33 Nantucket Bookworks
36 Nantucket Historical
   Association
37 Nantucket Whaling
   Museum
40 Barrett's Tours
41 NRTA
42 Visitor Services &
   Information Bureau;
   Gail's Tours
43 Police Station
45 The Sunken Ship
49 Young's Bicycle Shop;
   Indian Summer Sports
50 Nantucket Bike Shop
56 Atheneum; Dirk Gardiner
   Roggeveen
57 Dreamland Theater
64 The Hub
65 Gaslight Theatre
66 Chamber of Commerce
68 The Spectrum
69 Nantucket.net
70 Mitchell's Book Corner

consuming process of making these expensive and artistic baskets, topped with intricate scrimshaw. They're a Nantucket specialty, not practical in the least.

While you're on Upper Main St, west of Orange St, stroll around to see some of the island's most beautiful — mostly private — houses, including the three identical Georgian mansions known as the **'Three Bricks'** at 93, 95 and 97 Main St; and the second of the **'Two Greeks'** at 94 Main St. (Its pair is the Hadwen House, above.)

Maria Mitchell Association

The association's five buildings headquartered at Vestal St are devoted to Maria Mitchell (1818–1889), the island's foremost astronomer (☎ *508-228-9198, 2 Vestal St; museum pass adult/senior & child $7/5)*. In 1847, Mitchell discovered an uncharted comet and went on to become the first woman ever admitted into the American Academy of Arts and Sciences and the country's first female professor of astronomy.

You can visit the Science Library; the Hinchman House, a natural science museum where naturalists lead walks and talks; the Loines Observatory which is open on clear Monday, Wednesday and Friday evenings (9pm) in summer and winter Friday evenings

Maria Mitchell, astronomer and
Vassar College professor

(8pm); Mitchell's birthplace, which has lovely wildflower and herb gardens; and an expanded waterfront aquarium. Check in at the headquarters for a complete schedule of opening times and offerings. A combination ticket allows entry to all buildings, but tickets may also be purchased separately.

Brewery

Porters, stouts and ales can be found at **Cisco Brewers** (☎ *508-325-5929, 5 Bartlett Farm Rd; admission free; open 10am-6pm Mon-Sat year-round)*. Cisco's excellent brews are sold here and at the liquor store on Main St. The brewery offers tastings, too. (It's all as fresh as can be.) Follow Hummock Pond Rd south of town for about 2½ miles.

Beaches

You'll have to pedal, hitch or take a bus to the island's prime beaches, but to feel sand between your toes as quickly as possible, head to **Children's Beach**, off S Beach St just north of Steamboat Wharf, and **South Beach**, a few blocks south of the wharf.

Jetties Beach, a 20-minute walk or a short bus ride away, is popular because of its location, off Bathing Beach Rd (accessible from N Beach Rd). It's a good walking beach, but it also has facilities for volleyball, tennis and sailing.

Bicycling

There are thousands of bikes to rent ($20-25 daily) from at least a half-dozen shops. Try **Nantucket Bike Shop** (☎ *508-228-1999, 4 Broad St)* or **Young's Bicycle Shop** (☎ *508-228-1151, 6 Broad St)*. All bicycle rental shops have decent, free island maps with routes highlighted.

The island's pace and terrain are well-suited to bicycling. The short **Cliff Road Bike Path** takes you past big summer houses on the edge of town. The 3-mile **Surfside Bike Path** to Surfside Beach is flat; the ride takes 15 minutes. The 7-mile **'Sconset Bike Path** (also called Milestone Bike Path) begins east of the historic district and passes forests, bogs and moors. It takes 30 minutes if you're really cruising. **Polpis Road Bike Path** is lined with millions of daffodils in the springtime. The circular loop from town to 'Sconset and back via Polpis is about 17 miles. To reach the western end of the island, take the **Madaket Bike Path**, a hilly and winding 6-mile path that passes beautiful terrain.

Boating
Paddle your own canoe at **Sea Nantucket** (☎ 508-228-7499, Washington St Extension, Francis St Beach). Half- and full-day tours (prices vary considerably) of the scallop-shaped harbor, on non-rollable sea kayaks. Don't want a tour? Half-day kayak rentals cost $30/50 single/double May through September. On choppy days, boats can be delivered to quieter inland ponds.

Indian Summer Sports (☎ 508-228-3632, 6 Broad St; $30 daily) rents body boards and sailboards in summer.

The Sunken Ship (☎ 508-228-9226, 12 Broad St) offers full-service, year-round dive shop paraphernalia.

Friendship Sloop Endeavor (☎ 508-228-5585, Slip 1015, Straight Wharf; tickets $15-35) runs three daily harbor sails and a sunset cruise. Prices vary with the length of the sail.

Striped bass and bluefish 'run' off Nantucket's shores. A half-dozen or so charter boats dock at Straight Wharf. It's best to walk around and talk to the captains and see who you like.

Organized Tours
Since practically every building in Nantucket town is a historical showpiece with a story to tell, take an organized walking tour to get the most out of a visit. **Dirk Gardiner Roggeveen** (☎ 508-221-0075), a 12th-generation islander, offers delightfully informative tours around the core of town for $10 per person. It's well worth it. You'll meet in front of the Atheneum, but call first to secure a spot on his seasonal tour.

Maria Mitchell Association (☎ 508-228-9198, 2 Vestal St) Adult/senior & child $10/6. Tours mid-June–mid-Oct. This association offers nature and birding walks. On Sunday mornings (8am) in winter, the walks are free for those hearty souls willing to brave the elements.

Places to Stay
Staying overnight in Nantucket is generally not cheap. To get around this, it's best to visit in spring or fall (or even winter if you don't mind gray, windy days). It's difficult to find a room in July and August without advance reservations. In addition, many places require a two-night minimum and do not accept credit cards. Camping or sleeping under the stars, or even in your car, is not permitted on the island. This policy is strictly enforced. You'll find a very complete list of island accommodations and web links on the Chamber of Commerce website (W www.nantucketchamber.org).

Hostels About 3 miles from the center of town on Surfside Beach is the *Nantucket Youth Hostel* (☎ 508-228-0433, 617-531-0459 for off-season information, fax 508-228-5672, W www.usahostels.org, 31 Western Ave) Dorm beds members/non-members $19/22. Open late Apr–mid-Oct. This beach-front hostel (yes, that's right!) occupies the island's first lifesaving station, an architectural gem. Its bunk rooms accommodate a total of 50 people. Advance reservations are absolutely essential in summer, but there is usually plenty of room in spring and fall. Nonetheless, make reservations on shoulder-season weekends. To make reservations before the hostel opens, contact Hostelling International Boston (Attn: Reservations), 12 Hemenway St, Boston, MA 02215, or send a fax to 617-424-6558.

Hotels One of the cheapest places in town is *Overlook Hotel* (☎ 508-228-0695, 3 Step Lane) Singles $100-110, doubles without bath $110-115, doubles with bath $125 off-season, doubles without bath $130-155, doubles with bath $170 late May–early Sept. Open late May-Oct. This three-story summer hotel has wraparound porches and 25 serviceable rooms.

Point Breeze Hotel (☎ 508-228-0313, 800-365-4371, fax 508-325-6044, W www.point breeze.com, 71 Easton St) Doubles $99-235, cottages $275-525 off-season, doubles $180-300, cottages $325-690 mid-June–mid-Sept. Open late May–mid-Oct. This rambling 1893 hotel, a 10-minute walk from Main St, has 30 simple but clean rooms, suites and cottages that are well-suited to families (who can afford them). There are six two-bedroom cottages can sleep up to six.

The Beachside (☎ 508-228-2241, 800-322-4433, fax 508-228-8901, ⓦ www.thebeachside.com, 30 N Beach St) Doubles $130-190 off-season, $240-285 mid-June–mid-Sept with continental breakfast. Open Apr-Oct. This upscale, two-story motel offers an excellent island-style family value, since the many of the 92 rooms contain two double beds. Surrounding an attractive pool, all the rooms are decorated with cheery furnishings and many have private grassy patios.

Inns & B&Bs For a real find, check out the **Nesbitt Inn** (☎ 508-228-0156, fax 508-228-2446, 21 Broad St) Singles $55-75, doubles $65-95, quads $95-125 with continental breakfast. This centrally located inn has 12 rooms with shared bath and two apartments. A real bargain and a favorite among Europeans, the 1872 house has many original Victorian furnishings.

Martin House Inn (☎ 508-228-0678, 61 Centre St) Singles $60-70, doubles $90-145 off-season, singles $70-85, doubles $110-225 mid-June–mid-Sept, all with continental breakfast. Open Mar-Dec. Elegantly but simply furnished with canopy beds and antiques, many of this inn's 13 rooms have a fireplace. Four rooms have shared bath.

Beachway Guests (☎ 508-228-1324, 3 N Beach St) Doubles $100/125-150. These seven rooms, all with mini-fridge and microwave, are just a few blocks from the center.

White House (☎ 508-228-4425, 888-577-4425, fax 508-228-8114, ⓦ www.nantucketwhitehouse.com, 48 Centre St) Doubles $75-150 off-season, $150-195 mid-June–mid-Oct with voucher for full breakfast at nearby restaurant. Open mid-Apr–Oct. This simple and inexpensive guesthouse, in the center of the historic district, has three rooms and a suite.

For historical value, you can't beat the **Jared Coffin House** (☎ 508-228-2405, 800-248-2405, fax 508-228-8549, ⓦ www.jared coffinhouse.com, 29 Broad St) Singles $75-100, doubles $225-275 off-season, singles $125, doubles $265-320 June-Sept. Open year-round. The island's most well-known and historic lodging place has 60 rooms housed in an 1845 Federal-style brick mansion and four adjacent buildings. Colonial-style reproduction furniture is the norm; all rooms have a TV. History aside, for the price, there are more elegant beds in town.

Brass Lantern Inn (☎ 508-228-4064, 800-377-6609, fax 508-325-0928, ⓦ www.brasslanternnantucket.com, 11 N Water St) Doubles $85-150 off-season, $150-250 July-Aug with continental breakfast. Open year-round. A few blocks from the waterfront, this inn has 17 traditionally furnished and modern rooms. The inn's one four-person suite costs $295 in-season, $200 off-season.

Corner House (☎ 508-228-1530, ⓦ www.cornerhousenantucket.com, 49 Centre St) Doubles $75-165 off-season, $155-225 mid-June–Sept with continental breakfast and afternoon tea. Open year-round. This antique-filled house has 17 lovely historic rooms and suites and very professional service. It's a top choice. Even the least expensive, smaller, third-floor rooms are quite nice. Afternoon tea is served on the brick patio or sun porch. Ask about off-season packages.

Cliff Lodge (☎ 508-228-9480, fax 508-228-6308, 9 Cliff Rd) Singles $95-110, doubles $105-165 off-season, singles $125, doubles $165-225 June-early Sept with continental breakfast. Open year-round. In a converted 1771 sea captain's house 10 minutes from Straight Wharf, Cliff Lodge has 11 fresh, light and airy rooms and an apartment ($205/325 off-season/June-early Sept) decorated in an English-country style.

Hawthorn House (☎/fax 508-228-1468, ⓦ www.hawthorn-house.com, 2 Chestnut St) Doubles $70-105 off-season, $160-190 June-Sept. These nine modest rooms, most with private bath, are comfortable, homey and old-fashioned. Rates include breakfast at one of two bona-fide nearby restaurants.

Chestnut House (☎ 508-228-0049, fax 508-228-9521, ⓦ www.chestnuthouse.com, 3 Chestnut St) Doubles $95-105 off-season,

$170-210 mid-June–mid-Oct. Open year-round. This friendly establishment, full of family-made arts and crafts, has four suites and one room, each with TV and refrigerator. Most rooms can sleep four people for an additional $25 per person. A four-person cottage with a complete kitchen rents for $200/300 off-season/mid-June–mid-Oct. A full breakfast is included at two recommended restaurants nearby.

Anchor Inn (☎ *508-228-0072,* W *www .anchor-inn.net, 66 Centre St)* Doubles $65-135 off-season, $175-215 mid-June–mid-Sept, with continental breakfast. Open Mar-Dec. This sea captain's house, built in 1806, has friendly innkeepers and 11 nicely appointed rooms with queen-size canopy beds, tiled bath, cable TV, phones and seasonal air-con. This is easily another top choice.

Periwinkle Guest House (☎ *508-228-9267, 800-588-0087, fax 508-325-4046,* W *www.robertshouseinn.com, 7–9 N Water St)* Doubles without bath $75, with bath $175-225 off-season, doubles without bath $125, with bath $195-250 late May-early Sept with continental breakfast. Open year-round. Periwinkle has 16 rooms just a few minutes from Steamboat Wharf. Rooms come in a variety of sizes and shapes, with and without bath. A couple of singles with shared bath start at $35 off-season; call to see what's available

Ship's Inn (☎ *508-228-0040, 888-872-4052, fax 508-228-6524, 13 Fair St)* Singles without bath $75, doubles with bath $175 off-season, singles without bath $100, doubles with bath $210 May–mid-Oct with continental breakfast and afternoon tea. Open May-Oct. This 1831 whaling captain's house has 10 large, nice, airy and comfortable rooms that are a 10-minute walk from Straight Wharf on a quiet residential street. Also see Places to Eat, later.

Pineapple Inn (☎ *508-228-9992, fax 508-325-6051,* W *www.pineappleinn.com, 10 Hussey St)* Doubles $110-250 off-season, $185-325 mid-June–Sept with full breakfast. Open late Apr-late Oct. Easily one of the best places to stay, the 12 guest rooms at this 1838 whaling captain's house have been

completely renovated with an understated elegance. With marble baths, canopy beds and strong cappuccino at breakfast, you'll feel pampered.

Cottages Up to six people can stay in the larger *Harbor Cottages* (☎ *508-228-4485, fax 508-228-2451,* W *www.nisda.org, 71 Washington St)* Units $120-185/night, $750-925/week, June-Sept. Call for off-season rates, when this area becomes more of an artist colony. Open year-round. Rustic by island standards, these 10 simple studios and one-bedroom cottages have painted floorboards, exposed rafters and whitewashed walls. The complex, across from a kayaking beach, is about a 10-minute walk from 'downtown.'

Places to Eat

Nantucket town has inexpensive sandwich shops and bistros, all generally creative and inventive. But it's also renowned for its concentration of exceptional restaurants. If you've been waiting to splurge, this may be the place to do it, but you'll have to be careful not to burn a hole through your pocket. Reservations are essential for the moderate and expensive restaurants in summer. Many places close during the off-season.

Farmer's Market Locally grown produce is sold on Main St from the backs of trucks during the growing season (daily except Sunday, May through October).

Cafes As you might expect, the coffee is strong at *Espresso Cafe* (☎ *508-228-6930, 40 Main St)* Dishes under $11. Open 7:30am-10pm late May-early Sept & 7:30am-4:30pm early Sept-late May. This cafe serves breakfast pastries, vegetarian dishes, hearty soups and cold salads. If it wasn't so popular, it would be more of a find. There's a quiet rear patio.

Juice Bar (☎ *508-228-5799, 12 Broad St)* Purveyor of fruit and veggie drinks, the Juice Bar also serves delicious ice cream and nonfat yogurt concoctions.

Nantucket Pharmacy (☎ *508-228-0180, 45 Main St)* This classic drugstore has a soda fountain with swivel stools and dispenses cheap coffee, peanut butter and jelly sandwiches and the like for a few bucks.

Something Natural (☎ 508-228-0504, 50 Cliff Rd) Dishes $4-7. On the way to Madaket Beach, this shop prepares sandwiches and natural snacks.

Downy Flake (☎ 508-228-4533, 18 Sparks Ave) Dishes $4-8. Open 5:30am-2pm Mon-Sat & 6am-noon. Known for doughnuts and blueberry pancakes, this tiny place been a local institution since the 1960s.

Provisions (☎ 508-228-3258, Straight Wharf) Sandwiches $6.75. Provisions makes huge sandwiches, such as a smoked turkey sandwich with cranberries, that are large enough for most people to share.

Restaurants The locals eat year-round at *Hutch's* (☎ 508-228-5550, Nantucket Memorial Airport) Breakfast and lunch dishes $4-9, dinner mains $12-13. Starving after a day at the beach? Hutch's will get you in and out (within minutes) with seafood omelets, chicken fingers and fish and chips. Since Jamaicans work the short-order line, you can safely assume the Wednesday-night homeland specials are great.

Black-Eyed Susan's (☎ 508-325-0308, 10 India St) Breakfast $5-8, dinner mains $14-27. Open 7am-1pm daily & 6pm-10pm Mon-Sat. This small storefront eatery is beloved for its combination of downscale atmosphere and upscale preparations. The creative kitchen puts out everything from Dutch pancakes to North African spiced chicken (at different times of the day, of course).

Centre Street Bistro (☎ 508-228-8470, 29 Centre St) Breakfast and lunch $5-10, dinner mains $15-22. Open for breakfast Sat-Sun, lunch Mon-Fri & dinner year-round. Dine at a few indoor tables, a quiet back patio or the front patio, which is great for people-watching. Try the poached eggs with pan-fried grits (a trademark) for breakfast. The changing dinner menu is hard to pin down, but if we mention warm goat cheese tarts or seared salmon with crispy wontons, do you get the idea? For the money and quality, this is one of Nantucket's better places.

Vincent's Restaurant (☎ 508-228-0189, 21 S Water St) Lunch mains $7-12, dinner mains $10-22. The family-friendly restaurant offers plain and fancy pasta dishes, pizzas and seafood for lunch and dinner.

Sushi by Yoshi (☎ 508-228-1801, 2 E Chestnut St) Platters $7-20. The name says it all: A transplanted Japanese chef prepares fresh sashimi, sushi and more exotic creations from a tiny shop.

Atlantic Café (☎ 508-228-0570, 15 S Water St) Dishes $7-23. Open year-round. This casual and fun place gets louder and louder as the night wears on. The 'AC' serves generous portions of noshing food like nachos, buffalo wings, chowder and burgers.

Rose & Crown (☎ 508-228-2595, 23 S Water St) Dishes $7-23. A former livery stable, this large eatery has a pub-style menu similar to the AC. Kids love it.

Brotherhood of Thieves (no ☎, 23 Broad St) Dishes $9-15. Open year-round. This dark tavern is a friendly and boisterous place frequented by locals chowing on chowder, burgers and sandwiches. Since there's always a long line, you'll be seated at tables with fellow patrons.

Arno's 41 Main (☎ 508-228-7001, 41 Main St) Breakfast and lunch dishes $10, dinner mains $15-26. Arno's serves decent portions of well-priced food in a pleasant storefront eatery with high ceilings. Sandwiches, Thai peanut noodles, fish and chips and a few vegetarian dishes are offered, as are banana pancakes and eggs Benedict at breakfast.

Cambridge Street Victuals (☎ 508-228-7109, 12 Cambridge St) Dinner mains $14-24. Dim and boisterous, this place specializes in over-the-top portions of barbecue, but you can also get good *schwarma* (roasted lamb on a spit), thin-crust pizza and tandoori-style chicken. Microbrews reign.

Tap Room (☎ 508-228-2400, 29 Broad St) Lunch mains $8-14, dinner mains $16-23. Open daily year-round. In the basement of the Jared Coffin House, this cozy 19th-century tavern serves hearty and traditional American dishes like cod cakes with molasses baked beans year-round. In nice weather, head for the shaded terrace.

Ropewalk (☎ 508-228-8886, *Straight Wharf*) Lunch mains $9-14, dinner mains $23-26. Although it might look too pricey, this harborfront restaurant offers relative bargains at lunch. Focaccia pizza, oysters, raw bar shellfish and frozen drinks rope the patrons in every time.

Ship's Inn (☎ 508-228-0040, *13 Fair St*) Mains $22-38. Open for dinner. This fine chef-owned restaurant is well known for healthy and creative California-French cuisine.

The Boarding House (☎ 508-228-9622, *12 Federal St*) Mains $22-38. Open for dinner. The Boarding House consistently rises to the top of 'must eat' places, and offers innovative American cuisine. Entrées like grilled lobster tail and pan-roasted salmon are served in a cozy basement setting or outdoors on a brick patio, great for people-watching.

American Seasons (☎ 508-228-7111, *80 Centre St*) Mains $23-30. Open for dinner. Celebrating the four corners of the country with an eclectic menu, American Seasons highlights jazzed-up dishes inspired by the Wild West, the Pacific Coast, the South and New England. The dining room features lots of folk art and artfully presented entrées. It may be pricey, but you won't have to eat again for 24 hours.

The Pearl (☎ 508-228-9701, *12 Federal St*) Open for dinner. Mains $30-45. The Boarding House's adjacent sister restaurant is even more fashionable and trendy. Try their signature 'oyster shooters,' in which the shucked shellfish are served in shot glasses with condiments.

Company of the Cauldron (☎ 508-228-4016, *5 India St*) Fixed-price dinner $48-52 per person. Open for dinner. A creative New American menu is served at two seatings in romantic surroundings (tables are placed too close together, though, to whisper serious sweet nothings). Although the menu changes nightly, it might go something like this: roasted red-and-yellow-pepper soup, Nantucket greens, baked jumbo shrimp stuffed with crab and a chocolate tart to finish up.

Entertainment

Nantucket Map & Legend and *Yesterday's Island*, two free weeklies, have up-to-the-minute listings of island concerts, theater productions and festivals.

Many restaurants mentioned above provide entertainment as well as food. You'll find bands, DJs and dancing to classic rock at the boisterous *Rose & Crown* (☎ 508-228-2595, *23 S Water St*) and perhaps folk music at the *Brotherhood of Thieves* (no ☎, *23 Broad St*). *Atlantic Café* (☎ 508-228-0570, *15 S Water St*) is a popular place to hang out later in the evening. The crowd in all of these places is a mix of locals and up-scale summer folk under 35 (or pretending).

Gaslight Theatre (☎ 508-228-4435, *1 N Union St*) This theater screens art films and in the winter, you can BYOB. That should warm you up.

Dreamland Theater (☎ 508-228-5356, *19 S Water St*) Open year-round. This cinema shows first-run movies.

Shopping

There are dozens of pricey antique shops, clothing boutiques, jewelry stores, art galleries and specialty shops that carry the island's trademark woven 'lightship baskets,' which can cost between $300 and $3000.

Sailor's Valentine Gallery (☎ 508-228-2011, *Lower Main St*) This gallery has one of the island's most eclectic contemporary art collections.

The Spectrum (☎ 508-228-4606, *26 Main St*) Open Apr-Dec. This shop features high-quality contemporary American crafts.

AROUND THE ISLAND

The island, measuring 14 miles by 3 miles, has a ring of sandy beaches, almost all of which are open to the public. The narrow strips of beach at Great Point and Coatue Point are only accessible by 4WD vehicle. Because over one-third of the island is protected conservation land, the island's interior has plenty of places to walk and enjoy nature.

The only town of note besides Nantucket town is Siasconset, always referred to locally as 'Sconset. The few other towns on the map are really just residential communities with ongoing home construction. To get to 'Sconset, head out of Nantucket town on Milestone Rd, which will take you directly to the village.

You'll definitely want to balance the history that seeps from the town's cobblestones with the natural open spaces around the island. In fact, it would be a travesty not to get out of town and explore the island. Head west for the largest tracts of conservation land; head east to Polpis Rd for the Lifesaving Museum, The Moors, Wauwinet and Sankaty Head Lighthouse.

'Sconset

The residential village of 'Sconset, awash with blooming roses in the summertime, is definitely worth a detour. In the 17th century, fishermen and whalers lived in the tiny weathered cottages, adding 'warts' (equally tiny rooms) when their families came out to stay with them. By the late 1800s, 'Sconset was fashionable with New York City actors who summered here. 'Sconset is 7 miles from Nantucket town; the best way to reach it is by bicycle, although you can take a bus (see Getting Around under Nantucket Island).

'Sconset Beach is long and narrow (it's suffered much erosion in recent years), with a good deal of surf and undertow. It's just south of 'Sconset on the island's eastern shore.

There are a few options for both serious or quick dining. Next to the post office in the tiny center of town, **'Sconset Market** (☎ 508-257-9915) and **Claudette's** (☎ 508-257-6622) have picnic supplies and sandwich fixings for cyclists and beachgoers.

'Sconset Cafe (☎ 508-257-4008, Post Office Square) Lunch mains $8-14, dinner mains $20-28. Open for all three meals. This cafe serves an eclectic lunch menu with creative soups and salads. If you pedal out for breakfast, you'll be rewarded with cranberry and blueberry pancakes. The cafe also serves fancier New American dinners in the same airy setting, surrounded by local artwork. BYOB.

The Chanticleer (☎ 508-257-6231, 9 New St) Lunch mains $20-25, dinner mains $25-35, fixed-price dinner $70 per person. One of the island's two best restaurants, The Chanticleer serves exquisite and memorable French cuisine in an elegant and romantic setting, in the courtyard of a rose-covered cottage or in small dining rooms overlooking the courtyard.

Nantucket Lifesaving Museum

The museum (☎ 508-228-1885, 158 Polpis Rd; adult/child $5/2; open 9:30am-4pm daily mid-June–mid-Oct), about 5 miles east of Nantucket town, displays lifesaving boats, photographs and accounts of dramatic sea rescues. On the edge of a pond, it's an inviting place for a picnic.

The Moors

Off Polpis Rd, Altar Rock, the island's highest point, offers expansive views of the moors, heather and cranberry bogs. The Moors, crisscrossed with walking trails and rutted dirt roads, are spectacular in autumn and are lovely at dawn or dusk throughout the year.

Conservation Land

Much of the island's wetlands, moors and grasslands is protected from development and is a naturalist's delight. If you plan to be here for any length of time, stop by the Nantucket Conservation Foundation (☎ 508-228-2884, 118 Cliff Rd) in Nantucket town, for an up-to-date map ($3) of the foundation's ever-expanding holdings.

Quiet walking and biking trails within Sanford Farm, Ram Pasture and the Woods crisscross a former 900-acre farm you get to off Madaket Rd.

Lighthouses

Not surprisingly, the island has a cache of working lighthouses. **Brant Point Light** guards the entrance to the harbor. 'Sconset's **Sankaty Head Lighthouse**, visible 30 miles out to sea, stands on the edge of a rapidly eroding 90-foot bluff.

Stately and lonesome **Great Point Light**, accessible only by 4WD vehicle, is remote but well worth the expense it takes to get there. The Trustees of the Reservations (☎ 508-228-6799; adult/child $40/15; open late-May–mid-Oct) offer an excellent three-hour natural history tour of Great Point that culminates at the top of the lighthouse. Tours run at 10am and 2pm daily in July and August.

Wauwinet

A neighborhood of 20 or so exclusive summer houses on a private (guard house), windswept spit of land near the northeast corner of the island, Wauwinet tempts travelers in search of a chic getaway.

The Wauwinet (☎ 508-228-0145, 800-426-8718, fax 508-325-0657, Ⓦ www.wauwinet .com, 120 Wauwinet Rd) Doubles $230-800 off-season, $590-900 late June-early Sept with full breakfast. Open May-Oct. This is the ultimate island splurge when price is no object. Set on a dramatic and narrow strip of land between the harbor and Atlantic Ocean, 8 miles from Nantucket town, The Wauwinet has 35 luxuriously appointed rooms. A free jitney service shuttles guests to and from town. Service is absolutely exceptional here, and lots of amenities are included.

Topper's (☎ 508-228-8768, 120 Wauwinet Rd) Brunch $38, lunch $22-31 for tasting menu, dinner mains $36-44. Within the inn, Topper's vies for the title of 'best island dining.' Again, when price is no object, you are sure to depart with memories that will last for years. Skillful New American cuisine, utterly gracious service and a wine list to knock your socks off could set you back as little as $150 for two people (if you're really, really careful). For lunch, inside or beachside, the set-up is more unusual: select three to five dishes from the tasting menu. Lunch is a bargain when you consider that it includes complimentary passage aboard the *Wauwinet Lady*, departing from Straight Wharf, and gains you access to the rarified Wauwinet world, if only for a couple of hours.

Beaches

The island's only beach with dunes is **Dionis Beach**, about 3 miles from Nantucket town off Eel Point Rd (accessible from the Madaket Bike Path). It's good for swimming (the water is relatively calm) and shelling.

Surfside Beach, 3 miles from Nantucket town and accessible by frequent shuttle bus, is popular with the college and twenty-something crowd. It's a wide beach with moderate-to-heavy surf.

Madaket Beach, at the end of the namesake bike path, is the most popular place to watch sunsets. Strong currents and heavy surf make for less-than-ideal swimming conditions.

Cisco Beach, 4 miles from Nantucket town off Hummock Pond Rd (accessible from Milk St), is popular with surfers.

Central Massachusetts & the Berkshires

To unschooled travelers, Massachusetts' major attractions west of Boston are in the Berkshire Hills, near the New York state border. But on the way to the Berkshires, largely rural Central Massachusetts begs for exploration.

Early settlers used the Connecticut River and the Blackstone River as highways into the interior and as the routes out for crops and local products. Pioneer Valley, as the Connecticut River basin is called in Massachusetts, and the Blackstone Valley have a mix of colonial, early American and 19th-century industrial villages and towns that evoke simpler times. Numerous colleges and universities bring a youthful, cosmopolitan spirit to the region.

Getting There & Around

Air US Airways Express (☎ 800-428-4322) flies out of Worcester Regional Airport (☎ 888-359-9672). Bradley International Airport (see Getting There & Around in the Connecticut chapter), across the state line in Windsor Locks, CT, also serves Springfield and the Pioneer Valley towns.

Bus Peter Pan Bus Lines (☎ 617-426-7838, 800-343-9999), a Trailways affiliate, has its hub in Springfield, and runs buses daily throughout New England and eastern New York.

Bonanza Bus Lines (☎ 212-947-1766, 800-556-3815) runs buses daily between New York City and Bennington, VT, via Great Barrington, Stockbridge, Lee, Lenox, Pittsfield and Williamstown.

Train Amtrak's (☎ 800-872-7245) *Lakeshore Limited* departs from Boston's South Station (☎ 617-482-3660) in the afternoon, stopping at Framingham, Worcester, Springfield and Pittsfield before reaching Albany, New York, and heading west to Chicago. There are also trains to Springfield from New York City and Vermont.

Highlights

- Scouring the stalls for treasures at the Brimfield Antique Show

- Immersing yourself in early American life at Historic Deerfield Village

- Taking in a performance at the Jacob's Pillow Dance Festival near Lee, or at Tanglewood Music Festival in Lenox

- Hiking the trails of Mt Greylock

- Exploring the enormous Massachusetts Museum of Contemporary Art in North Adams

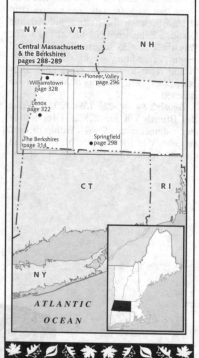

Car The Massachusetts Turnpike (or Mass Pike, I-90) and MA 2 are the major east-west roads connecting Boston with central and western Massachusetts. It takes about three hours to drive across Massachusetts from Boston to Lenox on the Mass Pike, which between Boston and Springfield is a toll road.

MA 2, running between Boston and Williamstown, is mostly four lanes between Cambridge and I-91 at Greenfield. West of Greenfield to Williamstown it's a scenic two-lane road known as the Mohawk Trail.

Central Massachusetts

If you have a few days to spend, Central Massachusetts will reward you with drives, bike rides and hikes through a rolling terrain of dairy farms and forests. Along the way you will find engaging museums, hip and historic towns, B&Bs, and an array of both imaginative and 'down-home' restaurants.

WORCESTER
Blessed with fine museums, one of America's best concert hall/arenas, well-preserved 19th-century buildings and re-spected institutions of higher learning, Worcester (pronounced 'woosta' by locals), population 172,000, is starting to emerge as an urban attraction after a half-century of neglect. In spite of urban renewal, the city has the gritty feel of a place that remains home to a legion of working families, not the gentry.

History
Once the home of the Nipmuck Indians, Worcester boomed as one of New England's centers for industry and invention during the 19th century. All sorts of new devices, implements and conveniences were thought up in these cities' small workshops and passed on to the water-powered mills nearby for large-scale manufacture. Worcester produced machines that were the first to weave carpets, fold envelopes and turn irregular shapes on a lathe.

During its heyday, Worcester hosted the first national convention on women's suffrage (1850) and saw the founding of several colleges and universities, including Clark, Holy Cross and Worcester Polytechnic Institute, as well as several significant museums. One of its native sons, Dr Robert Goddard (1882–1945), for whom the Goddard Space Flight Center in Greenbelt, Maryland, is named, launched the first liquid-fuel rocket from Pakachoag Hill in 1926, inaugurating the age of American rocketry.

But the spirit of invention moved on to other parts of the country, and manufacturing largely moved to the Far East after WWII, leaving Worcester to reminisce about its lost prosperity.

During the 1990s major efforts at urban renewal brought a huge outlet shopping mall to the center of town, with large-scale restoration of downtown buildings. Restaurants, bars, and clubs have taken root in the historic buildings around the Centrum arena, Worcester Common Outlets, City Hall and the University of Massachusetts Medical Center.

Orientation & Information
Commercial St, three blocks west of I-290 and one block south of Main St, is the city's center of commerce. The clock tower on City Hall marks the center of town.

The Worcester County Convention and Visitors Bureau (☎ 508-753-2920, Ⓦ www .worcester.org, 30 Worcester Center Blvd, Worcester, MA 01608), across the street from the Centrum, can help with travelers' questions or problems. The CVB also administers the Central Massachusetts Tourist Council (☎ 800-231-7557). The council operates a visitor center in the Worcester Common Outlets (☎ 508-754-0305, 110 Front St). These sites are generally open 8:30am to 5pm Monday to Friday.

Worcester Art Museum
During Worcester's golden age, its captains of industry bestowed largesse upon the town and its citizens. The Worcester Art Museum (☎ 508-799-4406, 55 Salisbury St; adult/senior & student & child 13-18 yrs/

child under 7 yrs $8/6/free, free Sat mornings; open 11am-5pm Wed-Sun, Sat 10am-5pm) off Park and Main Sts (follow the signs) is a generous and impressive bequest.

This small museum has a comprehensive collection, ranging from ancient Chinese, Egyptian and Sumerian artifacts to European masterworks, and from the work of Japanese *ukiyo-e* (17th- to 19th-century woodcut) painters to great North American paintings and primitives. Edward Hick's *Peaceable Kingdom* is perhaps the most easily recognizable piece in the collection, but you can also see Mary Cassatt's *Woman Bathing,* Paul Gauguin's *Brooding Woman* and Rembrandt's *St Bartholomew.*

The museum's collection of more than 2000 photographs spans the history of the medium, from Matthew Brady to Gary Winogrand.

The Museum Café makes a convenient place to eat before moving on; see Places to Eat later in this chapter.

Salisbury Mansion

Very near the art museum, the Salisbury Mansion (☎ 508-753-8278, 40 Highland St; admission $3; open 1pm-4pm Thur-Sun), built in 1772, was the Salisbury family home until 1851. It was moved to its present site in 1929 and is now preserved as a museum, decorated in the style of the early 19th century.

Worcester Historical Museum

The Worcester Historical Society (☎ 508-753-8278, 30 Elm St; admission $2; open 10am-4pm Tues-Sat, 1pm-4pm Sun), just around the corner from the art museum, preserves the record of Worcester's history, particularly its 19th-century golden age.

American Antiquarian Society

If you're interested in doing research in the largest single collection of printed source materials relating to the first 250 years of US history, the American Antiquarian Society (☎ 508-755-5221, 185 Salisbury St; admission free; open 9am-5pm Mon-Fri), a few blocks from the art museum, is a must-see. The society was founded in 1812, and

the documents in its library cover all aspects of colonial and early American culture, history and literature. Free tours run each Wednesday at 2pm.

Higgins Armory Museum

John Woodman Higgins, president of the Worcester Pressed Steel Company at the beginning of the 20th century, loved good steel. Medieval armorers made good steel, so he collected it: more than 100 full suits of armor for men, women, children and even dogs. His collection got so big that in 1929 he built a special armory to house it – this art deco building with interior neogothic accents is the Higgins Armory Museum (☎ 508-853-6015, 100 Barber Ave; adult/senior/child 6-16 yrs $5.75/5/4.75; open 10am-4pm Tues-Sat, noon-4pm Sun), off W Boylston St (MA 12). Children will like the Quest Gallery, where they can try on 'castle clothing' and replica suits of armor.

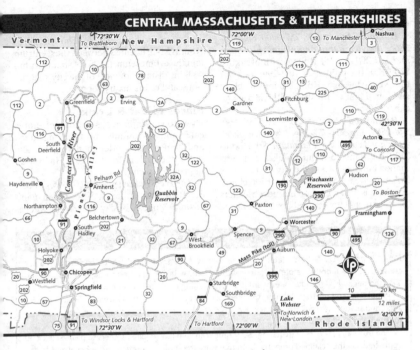

Mechanics Hall

Mechanics Hall (☎ 508-752-5608, 321 Main St) took shape in 1857 on the orders of the Worcester County Mechanics Association, a group of artisans and small business owners who typified Worcester's inventive and industrial strength in the mid–19th century. The hall boasts superb acoustics and is regarded as the finest standing pre–Civil War concert hall in the USA. Henry David Thoreau and Ralph Waldo Emerson spoke here, as did Charles Dickens, Mark Twain and Theodore Roosevelt. Restored in 1977, the hall is still used for concerts, lectures and recording sessions. Call for information on visiting hours, or call the box office (☎ 508-752-0888) for tickets to a lecture or performance.

Blackstone River Bikeway

When it is finished in the next three to five years, the Blackstone River Bikeway (☎ 401-789-4625, Union Station, 45 Shrewsbury St) will offer a mostly off-road bike trail from Worcester to Providence, RI, which is 45 miles to the south. The trail laces through historic mill villages and follows remnants of the Blackstone River Canal as well as a railroad right-of-way. Until the bikeway is complete, you can follow the trail on marked roads.

Places to Stay

Worcester's hotels serve Centrum arena concertgoers and high-tech firms on the outskirts of the city. This demand has jacked up the rates on most of Worcester's hosteleries. You will find more economical tourist lodgings about 20 miles southwest, in and around Sturbridge.

Best Western Inn & Suites (☎ 508-852-2800, 800-932-3297, fax 508-852-4605, [W] www.bestwestern.com, 50 Oriol Drive/I-290 exit 20) Rooms $79. This establishment has 114 comfortable rooms, amid landscaped grounds in a quiet setting.

Hampton Inn (☎ 508-757-0400, 800-426-7866, W *www.hamptoninn.com, 110 Summer St/I-290 exit 16*) Rooms with breakfast $109-120. It's right next to I-290; look for the Aku-Aku sign. Rooms here are clean and functionally furnished, with air con and cable TV.

Beechwood Hotel (☎ 508-754-5789, 800-344-2589, fax 508-752-2060, W *www.beechwoodhotel.com, 363 Plantation St*) Rooms $139-169. This 73-room hotel, a cylinder-shaped building east of the city center along MA 9 near the Massachusetts Biotechnology Park, is well known to business travelers for its personal service and luxury rooms.

Crowne Plaza-Worcester (☎ 508-791-1600, 800-465-4329, fax 508-791-1796, W *www.crowneplaza.com, 10 Lincoln Square*) Rooms $145. Located between the Centrum and the art museum, the hotel stands within walking distance of most of the city's attractions, and offers luxury rooms.

Places to Eat & Drink

Downtown Worcester is a trove of ethnic cafes and restaurants, most serving lunch and dinner. Many offer food you can take out to the park in front of City Hall for an impromptu picnic.

The Ivy Kitchen (☎ 508-831-7696, 6 Waldo St) Breakfast & lunch $2-6. Open 6am-2:30pm Monday-Friday only. John Keene-

---

Johnny Appleseed

John Chapman (1774–1845), later known as Johnny Appleseed, was born in Leominster, Massachusetts, a few months before his father was to fight with the minutemen at Concord. Around 1797 he began his legendary westward journey, planting apple seeds as he went.

Popular legend portrays Johnny Appleseed as a happy, barefoot hobo wearing a saucepan for a hat and scattering seeds from a sack over his shoulder, providing free apple trees – and apples – for the good of one and all.

The true story is no less fascinating. Early American land law required settlers to plant at least 50 apple trees on their claimed property, both to ensure the settler's nutrition and survival and to discourage claims made without intention of settlement.

Chapman was a pioneer, setting out ahead of the waves of westbound settlers. He bought apple seeds in bulk from cider mills in Pennsylvania and traveled west as far as Indiana, staking many claims, gaining title to the land, and cultivating the land as nurseries for the apple trees that would be required by the settlers.

For 50 years he sold seedlings to the settlers, donated others, and preached the tidings of the Swedenborgian Church of the New Jerusalem to one and all. In March 1845, Chapman arrived in Fort Wayne, Indiana, to find someone damaging one of his nurseries. In the altercation that followed, Chapman died, putting an end to the planting, but giving a beginning to the legend.

In the early 1990s, the owners of Harvey Farm in Nova, Ohio, identified a huge, ancient apple tree on the farm's property as one planted by Chapman. Soon after arborists took cuttings from it, the tree was destroyed in a storm. The cuttings survived, however, and have been propagated to produce 30,000 new trees, which will carry on the legend of Johnny Appleseed.

way and Sue McFarland do a doubles act in this little short-order place, which is hard to match for friendliness, wit and down-home cooking. An old-school coffee shop, complete with green Formica counters and swiveling stools, the Ivy Kitchen lies just two blocks north of the Centrum and Worcester Common Outlets. A three-egg cheese omelette runs just $3. Try the shepherd's pie ($4.25) for lunch.

Moynagh's Tavern (☎ *508-753-9686, 25 Exchange St)* Beer under $2. Right next door to the Ivy Kitchen (which supplies the pub with food), you will find the oldest bar in Worcester, an authentic Irish-American pub of the first order. Babe Ruth once bowled here when the place was a bowling alley. In more recent times, Red Sox catcher Carlton Fisk stopped in for a beer and ended up tending bar for the whole night. The crowd here is still working folk.

The Irish Times (☎ *508-797-9599, 244 Main St)* Prices $4-16. Set in a 19th-century three-story building, this place really feels like a Dublin pub, with dark paneling, high ceilings, the scent of Caffrey's brew, and bartenders with Irish brogues. Downstairs you get acoustic and Irish folk music. On Friday and Saturday, the upstairs is a disco where the DJ spins out techno and dance tunes for an under-30 crowd. The dinner patrons are largely urban professionals who come for the onion soup ($4) or Irish lamb stew ($8).

Woosta Pizza (☎ *508-791-3333, 8 Franklin St)* Mains $5-15. This amusingly named pizza joint has imaginative pizza toppings, such as asparagus. A slice and a soda can cost as little as $3.

The Atrium (☎ *508-363-1392, 1 Exchange Place)* Lunch $5-11. You get courtyard cafe dining here, just a block from the Centrum. Duke's roast beef sandwich ($6) is a popular item. The complex also has a martini bar, sports bar and a DJ spinning classic rock like Aerosmith on weekend Friday and Saturday nights for the 24-35 age group.

Seol Leecci (☎ *508-363-0891, 385 Main St)* Lunch $6-8, dinner $8-15. A Korean-Japanese restaurant and sushi bar less than a block from the landmark City Hall, this place offers exceptional luncheon values

like *bi bim bab* ($6), veggies, fried egg, rice and hot sauce.

Museum Café (☎ *508-799-4406, 55 Salisbury St)* Dishes $6-18. This cafe, in the Worcester Art Museum, is a good choice for light meals and moderate prices at a location you'll probably visit. It serves soups, salads and sandwiches. Locals favor the chicken Caesar ($7).

Tiano's (☎ *508-756-7262, 108 Grove St)* Mains $15-24. In the Northworks Marketplace, a restored mill complex, Tiano's serves up imaginative Tuscan fare like pan-caramelized beef tips ($21) and seared fillet of salmon ($21). This is a popular date spot; you will need reservations on Friday and Saturday nights.

Entertainment
Worcester has made a name for itself by attracting big-name musical performers to its two high-quality venues.

Mechanics Hall (☎ *508-752-0888, 321 Main St)* Tickets $15-30. The hall is used for classical and jazz performances.

Centrum (☎ *508-798-8888, 617-931-2000 for tickets, 50 Foster St)* Tickets $18-150. This huge venue attracts nationally known rock groups and other big-crowd acts.

Shopping
Built as part of a plan to draw people to a revitalized city center, the huge ***Worcester Common Outlets*** (☎ *508-798-2581, 110 Front St)* shopping complex is right in the city center, with acres of parking, and shops such as Saks Fifth Avenue, Polo, Ann Taylor, London Fog, Media Play and Sports Authority.

Getting There & Away
Worcester Regional Airport (☎ 508-799-1741, 888-359-9672), several miles due west of the city center along MA 122 (Chandler St), is served by US Airways Express (☎ 800-428-4322).

Peter Pan Bus Lines (☎ 508-753-1515, 754-4600, 800-343-9999, 75 Madison St) has direct services between Worcester and Albany, Amherst, Bennington, Boston (and Logan Airport), Deerfield, Hartford,

Holyoke, Hyannis, New York City, Northampton, Pittsfield, Plymouth, South Hadley, Springfield, Sturbridge, Toronto, and Williamstown.

Amtrak trains (☎ 508-755-0356, 800-872-7245, 45 Shrewsbury St) stop here enroute between Boston and Chicago. MBTA Commuter Rail (☎ 617-722-3200, 800-392-6099) operates five trains each way from Boston to Worcester Monday to Friday, three on Saturday and Sunday.

Worcester stands at the junction of four interstate highways. About an hour's drive will bring you here from the Boston, Providence, Springfield, and Hartford, CT, areas.

STURBRIDGE

Mercy! The bittersweet taste Sturbridge leaves in the traveler's mouth! Here is one of the most visited attractions in New England and one of the rudest examples of how far US culture has traveled in less than 200 years in search of the Yankee dollar.

This small, central Massachusetts town kept much of its colonial character until after WWII. When the Mass Pike (I-90) and I-84 arrived and joined just south of the town, commerce and change came all at once. To take advantage of the handy highway transport, the town became host to one of the country's first 'living museums.' Curators moved old buildings here from throughout the region. Others were replicated, as needed, to recreate a typical 1830s New England village. Rather than labeling the exhibits, this museum has 'interpreters' – people who dress in costume, ply the trades and occupations of their ancestors and explain to visitors what they are doing and why.

The concept of the living museum was new when Old Sturbridge Village started. It has now spread throughout the world. Sadly, in the community's effort to preserve a working example of a traditional Yankee community within the borders of OSV, it generated a mammoth attraction on whose borders motor inns, fast-food chains, gas stations and more than 50 roadside shops have sprouted to sell the visitor everything from ersatz Indian moccasins to collectible Beanie Babies.

Sturbridge is very busy with visitors in summer and the autumn foliage season. Traffic increases exponentially during the three times per year (early May, early July and early September) when the Antiques and Flea Market is held in Brimfield, 5 miles east of town along US 20.

Orientation & Information

There are actually three Sturbridges. The first one you see is the relentless commercial strip along US 20 (Main St), just south of I-90 exit 9, which has most of the town's motels and restaurants. The second is Sturbridge as it used to be, best seen at the town common, backed by the historic Publick House Inn, on MA 131 half a mile southeast of US 20. The third is Old Sturbridge Village, entered from US 20.

The Sturbridge Area Tourist Association information office (SATA; ☎ 508-347-7594, 800-628-8379, 380 Main St/US 20) is opposite the entrance to Old Sturbridge Village. It's open 9am to 5pm daily. The Peter Pan/Trailways bus stop is here as well. The SATA is a division of the Tri-Community Area Chamber of Commerce, whose name you will see on the sign.

Old Sturbridge Village

During the first half of the 20th century, two brothers, Albert Wells and J Cheney Wells, lived in Southbridge and carried on a very successful optics business. They were enthusiastic collectors of antiques – so enthusiastic, in fact, that by the end of WWII their collections left no free space in their homes.

They bought 200 acres of forest and meadow in Sturbridge and began to move old buildings to this land. Opened in 1946, Old Sturbridge Village (OSV; ☎ 508-347-3362, US 20; adult/senior/child 6-15 yrs/child under 6 yrs $20/18/10/free; open 9am-5pm daily April-early Nov, 10am-4pm Sat and Sun Jan–mid-Feb) is a recreated New England town of the 1830s, with 40 restored structures filled with the Wells' antiques.

Although some historians find the layout of the village less than accurate, attention to detail is high here. The country store displays products brought from throughout the world by New England sailing ships. Crafters and artisans ply their trades with authentic tools and materials. The livestock has even been back-bred to approximate the animals – smaller, shaggier, thinner – that lived on New England farms a century and a half ago. The OSV library has more than 20,000 manuscripts and books describing various aspects of early-19th-century life in the region.

Admission is good for two consecutive days. Food services in the village include the Bullard Tavern, with buffet and à la carte service for full meals, light meals and snacks. There is also a picnic grove with grills and a play area.

St Anne Shrine

Monsignor Pie Neveu, a Roman Catholic Assumptionist bishop, ministered to a diocese in Russia from 1906 to 1936. While at his post, Bishop Neveu collected valuable Russian icons, a hobby no doubt made easier by the fall of the old order and the advent of secularist communism. Bishop Neveu's collection was further augmented by acquisitions brought to the USA by the Assumptionist fathers who served as chaplains at the US embassy in Moscow between 1934 and 1941. The collection was installed at the St Anne Shrine in 1971.

Since WWII, it has been illegal to export icons from Russia, so the collection of 60 rare works preserved at the icon museum at the St Anne Shrine (*☎ 508-347-7338, 16 Church St; admission free; donations accepted; open 9am-6pm daily*) is a treasure. The icon museum is one building in the shrine complex, just off US 20 at the western end of Sturbridge in the neighborhood sometimes called Fiskdale. Watch for the sign just east of the intersection of US 20 and MA 148.

Mellea Winery

Ten miles southeast of town, along MA 131 in West Dudley, just north of the Connecticut state line, is **Mellea Winery** (*☎ 508-943-5166, 108 Old Southbridge Rd; admission free; open noon-5pm Wed-Sun late May-Dec*).

Joe Compagnone, a chemist-industrialist, has planted his French-American hybrid vines and vinifera on a gravelly, south-facing hillside and produces a variety of wines, from table-grade to premium, using his own grapes and others imported from southeastern Massachusetts, Long Island and Oregon. Visit for a free tour and tasting.

Hyland Orchard & Brewery

If beer is your beverage, visit the **Hyland Orchard & Brewery** (*☎ 508-347-7500, 199 Arnold Rd; admission free; guided tours 1pm & 3pm Sat, call for current hours*), a 150-acre farm with its own craft brewery that produces Sturbridge Amber Ale. To find Hyland, go west on Main St/US 20 to Arnold Rd, turn right and go 2 miles north on Arnold Rd to the farm.

Brimfield Antique Shows

Six miles west of Sturbridge along US 20 is Brimfield, a mecca for collectors of antique furniture, toys, tools and collectibles. Up to 5000 sellers and 35,000 buyers come from a dozen states and beyond to do business in 23 farmers' fields here, the largest outdoor antiques fair in the USA. The town has numerous shops open year-round, but the major antiques and collectibles shows are held in early to mid-May, early July and early September, usually on the second weekends in those three months. Actually, there are 20 separate fairs set up in fields surrounding the town.

Contact the Brimfield Antique Show Promoters' Association (*☎ 203-763-3760; US 20 in Brimfield; admission to grounds Mon-Fri $3, Sat-Sun $5; open 6am-sunset*) or the SATA (*☎ 508-347-7594, 800-628-8379*) for dates and details. Be sure to have advance hotel reservations.

Places to Stay

Even though Sturbridge is packed with places to stay, many lodgings fill on Friday and Saturday nights in summer and, especially, in autumn. When the Brimfield Antiques and Flea Market is in progress (see above), local lodging prices rise substantially and advance reservations are necessary. If you come in the off season (April or November), the competition keeps the prices low.

Camping North of I-90 you'll find *Wells State Park* (☎ 508-347-9257, *Mountain Rd/ MA 49, Sturbridge*) Sites $9-12. This campground offers 59 wooded sites on its 1470 acres. The higher prices are for the lakefront sites. You can reserve your site in advance with a two-night deposit.

Yogi Bear's Sturbridge Jellystone Park (☎ 508-347-9570, *River Rd/I-84 exit 2*) Sites $40-42, cabins $60-78. This park has 400 sites, as well as amusements that include two pools, a hot tub, waterslide and other entertainment. Rates vary depending upon hookups. The rustic cabins sleep up to five people.

Motels Lying along a one-mile stretch of US 20, just off Exit 9 of I-20, are *Red Roof, Best Western, Days Inn, Econo Lodge, Super 8, Comfort Inn, Holiday Inn* and *Hampton Inn*. If you don't have a reservation when you arrive in Sturbridge, go to the SATA information office (see the Information section for Sturbridge, above) and look through the motel brochures. Some include coupons that are good for special rates or discounts. Expect to pay around $75 for a room in the winter or shoulder seasons and $95 June to October. The cheapest lodgings are several family-run motels.

Sturbridge Heritage Motel (☎ 508-347-3943, *99-501 Main St*) Rooms $50-55. This motel is a mile west of OSV, across from the Whistling Swan restaurant, and has eight relatively quiet rooms.

Village Motel (☎ 508-347-3049, *Main St*) Rooms $55. Here's a family-run motel more or less across the road from Sturbridge Heritage and down an unpaved lane. It too is quiet and inexpensive.

Inns & B&Bs Staying in an inn or B&B remote from US 20 and the wheels of commerce is how many travelers preserve that 'jaunt in the country' feeling they get when visiting Sturbridge/Brimfield. In fact, if it's fresh air and tranquility that you're seeking, the best option may be to get out of town completely and stay at a farm B&B. The

SATA (☎ 508-347-7594, 800-628-8379) can direct you to its member B&Bs, and it can help you make same-day reservations if you stop in at the information office.

Publick House Inn (☎ 508-347-3313, 800-782-5425, fax 508-347-1246, *MA 131 on the Common*) Rooms $99-160. Sturbridge's most famous historic inn (1771), the Publick House faces the village common (half a mile away from the mania of US 20) and is now a mini-industry, with frequent weekend theme programs, several dining rooms and three separate lodgings. The Publick House itself has 17 guestrooms decorated in Early American and Federal period furnishings like canopy beds.

Sturbridge Country Inn (☎ 508-347-5503, fax 347-5319, *530 Main St*) Rooms $85-165. The inn is a stately Greek Revival mansion about a mile west of OSV on US 20 in the commercial district. Its nine sybaritic rooms all have fireplaces, whirlpool baths, TV and air-con. There's a bit of traffic noise in front.

Pine Hill Farm (☎ 508-791-1762, *Pond St, Paxton*) Rooms $120 & up. About 15 miles north of Sturbridge in rural Paxton, this 30-acre farmstead has stood by the 'Old Mill Stream' for 250 years. Arnold and Sally Fay have three rooms full of country antiques and quilts. You get a full farm breakfast with homemade baked goods.

Zukas Homestead Farm (☎ 508-885-5320, fax 508-885-5546, Ⓦ www.zukas.com, *89 Smithville Rd, Spencer*) Suite $130. Set on a hilltop 2 miles from the town of Spencer and a 20-minute drive north from Sturbridge, this B&B was a working dairy farm until 1995 when Peter and Lynn Zukas scaled back on the dairy herd and opened the B&B. The sole suite includes a private bath, Jacuzzi tub, TV/ VCR, working fireplace, fridge, microwave and popcorn popper. Children are welcome and will enjoy the Zukas children and the array of cows, miniature horses, kittens, chickens and Labrador Retriever.

Places to Eat
US 20 is awash in fast-food outlets, breakfast joints and independent restaurants that offer lunch and dinner.

Annie's Country Kitchen (☎ 508-347-2320, 140 Main St/MA 131) Breakfasts $3-6. This is the place for an early breakfast, such as the lumberjack special of ham and three eggs, toast, homefries, juice and coffee for under $5.

Heritage Family Restaurant & Pizza (☎ 508-347-7673, Charlton Rd) Dishes around $7. For low prices and good food, escape the tourist crowds by following US 20 to the east side of I-84, where you'll find this place. You can fill up with a pizza, grinders, calzone, salad or fish and chips.

Rom's (☎ 508-347-3349, MA 131) Prices $2-9. A Sturbridge roadside institution, Rom's serves up big portions of its traditional Italian-American fare (and drinks) for moderate prices. You can get a shrimp plate for under $7.

The Casual Cafe (☎ 508-347-2281, 538 Main St) Mains $8-12. Open for dinner Tues-Sat. This cafe serves Italian dishes, such as linguine in white clam sauce and tortellini *con carciofi* (with artichokes), at very moderate prices.

Publick House (see Places to Stay, above) Mains $20-30. This classic country inn features a formal dining room, with traditional New England dishes like hearthbaked chicken breast ($20); try the rainbow trout flambée ($21). Full three-course dinners with drinks run $32 to $50; less for lunch.

Cedar Street Restaurant (☎ 508-347-5800, 12 Cedar St) Mains $15-21. Just west of the Sturbridge Coach Motor Lodge, this restaurant off US 20 offers innovative New American preparations of filet mignon, rack of lamb and seared yellowfin tuna. The menu includes a good number of vegetarian dishes as well. Prices are moderate for the quality: $25 to $40 for a full dinner.

Salem Cross Inn (☎ 508-867-2345, Ware Rd, West Brookfield) Mains $18-25. If you're up for taking a drive, follow US 20 (2 miles west of OSV) to MA 148 North; 7 miles along, turn left (west) onto MA 9 and go 5 miles to this tranquil inn. The Salem Cross, built in 1705 and set on 600 acres of farmland, provides a respite from the commercial fury of Sturbridge. You can get traditional New England meals like a baked scrod dinner or rack of lamb for $35 to $55 per person, with drinks, tax and tip included.

Getting There & Away

Peter Pan Bus Lines (☎ 508-347-7594, 800-343-9999) runs one-day excursion buses right to OSV from Boston (☎ 617-426-7838), via Worcester, and from New York City (☎ 212-564-8484) via Hartford and Springfield. For other bus routes you must connect at Boston or Springfield. The Peter Pan bus stop is opposite the entrance to OSV, at the SATA information office.

Pioneer Valley

In Massachusetts, folks call the Connecticut River basin the Pioneer Valley because of its early settlement. Within a few years after the Pilgrims landed at Plymouth in 1620, fur traders and settlers were making their way up the great river, deep into the center of New England. Springfield and other valley towns later became pioneers of technical advancement.

For information on the Connecticut River valley in Massachusetts, check out Ⓦ www.valleyvisitor.com.

SPRINGFIELD

Springfield, the largest city in western Massachusetts, with a population of about 152,000, is at the region's transportation nexus. Here the traditional east-west route from Boston to Albany crosses the Connecticut River valley. Its 19th-century industrial might (America's largest handgun manufacturer, Smith & Wesson, is here) and a major Civil War armory brought its residents the wealth to build several excellent museums (closed Monday and Tuesday), a library and a grand symphony hall. Basketball players all over the world pay tribute to Springfield with every shot. The game originated here, and now the city has a much-enlarged Basketball Hall of Fame. Springfield is also the home of 'The Cat in the Hat,' of children's literature fame. The cat's creator, Theodor Geisel, was

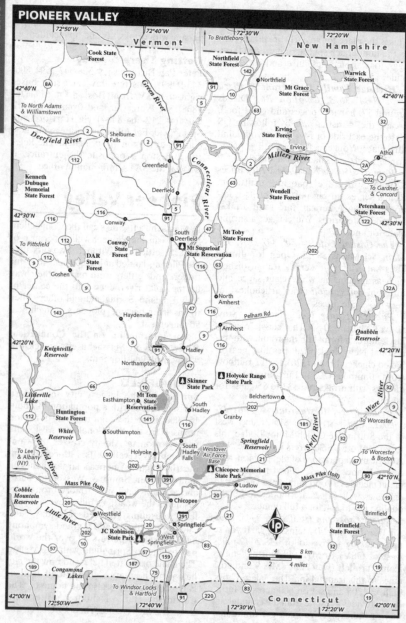

a Springfield native who used the pen name Dr Seuss. He died in 1991.

Today Springfield is a city of commuters in suits, and a large immigrant population mostly from Puerto Rico who, surprisingly, have brought little of their art, music and cuisine to the downtown area. The Romanesque buildings around Court Square and the nearby modern office blocks disgorge an army of workers (there's a huge insurance industry here) who flee the city at the end of the workday. Nevertheless, you will find an active night scene downtown that only the young and the restless seem to know about. Most travelers make Springfield a daylong stop while staying in Northampton, Amherst or the Berkshires.

History

By 1636, pioneers and settlers had come up the Connecticut River to Springfield to trade for furs with the Omiskandoagwiak ('Wolf People,' the Connecticut River Valley Indians) and to farm the valley's fertile alluvial soil. Later, industry sprang up here because the river provided cheap waterpower and transport to the markets of Hartford, New York and Philadelphia.

Springfield's prosperity was assured in 1777, when General George Washington and his chief of artillery, Colonel Henry Knox, decided upon this spot for the first arsenal in the USA. Though centrally located and easy to access, it was safely distant from the major theaters of the Revolutionary War. Muskets, cannons and other arms were stored here, and paper cartridges were manufactured for them. After the revolution, Springfield continued to be the new nation's major arsenal.

In 1786, the American Revolution was successful, but the new nation found itself suffering a severe economic depression. The paper money issued to fund the war was still in circulation, but rarely accepted at face value.

Boston merchants and traders, for whom 'sound money' was essential, led a movement to adopt a gold standard. Public officials with fat salaries and Boston lawyers acting on behalf of the rich went along. But

farmers in western Massachusetts, who could not pay in kind, were opposed to a gold standard. Country people were burdened with heavy land and poll taxes, the foreclosure of mortgages on their farms and debtors' prison; those without property could not vote at all.

The discontent broke out in rebellion on August 29, 1786, when Daniel Shays (1747–1825), formerly a captain in the Revolutionary army, led armed men to prevent the sitting of the courts in Northampton that were handing down judgments against debtors. Shays and his followers planned their moves in an Amherst tavern. Their action forced even the state supreme court to adjourn its session in Springfield.

Early in 1787, Governor Bowdoin sent General Benjamin Lincoln and 4400 men to put down the rebellion. As the troops marched to Springfield, Daniel Shays and his 1200 men attacked the federal armory on January 25, but were repulsed by the Massachusetts state militia and suffered several casualties before being captured or dispersed.

Shays' Rebellion alerted Boston to the dire conditions in the western part of the state. Governor John Hancock later pardoned Daniel Shays and other rebellion leaders. Similar rebellions in other states influenced public opinion in the direction of a strong federal government capable of preserving public order.

Orientation

Take I-91 exit 6 northbound or exit 7 southbound, follow it to State St (east) then Main St (north), and you'll be at Court Square in the heart of Springfield, a good place to start your explorations. Museum Quadrangle is a few blocks northeast, and the Tower Square complex, which includes the Springfield Marriott Hotel, is two blocks northwest. The Springfield Armory is a 10-minute walk northeast and the Basketball Hall of Fame is a 10-minute walk south.

Information

The Greater Springfield Convention & Visitors Bureau (☎ 413-787-1548, 800-723-1548, ⓦ www.valleyvisitor.com, 1441 Main St,

MASSACHUSETTS

Springfield, MA 01103) is a block and a half north of Court Square. It's open 9am to 5pm Monday to Friday.

The post office is on Main St at the corner of Liberty St, eight blocks north of Court Square.

Court Square

Fine buildings surround this shady square. You'll see **Symphony Hall** and **City Hall** on its west side. To the south stand the **First Congregational Church** (1819) and the granite **Hall of Justice** (Hampden County Superior Courthouse) by Henry Hudson Richardson, inspired by the Palazzo Vecchio in Venice. William Pynchon, who led the group of Puritans that settled here in 1636, and incorporated the town five years later, is honored with a statue.

Museum Quadrangle

The **Springfield Library & Museums** (☎ 413-263-6800, 220 State St; adult/senior/child 6-16yrs/child under 6yrs $6/3/2/free; open noon-5pm Wed-Sat, 1pm-4pm Sun) surround Museum Quadrangle, two blocks northeast of Court Square. Look for Merrick Park, at the entrance to the quadrangle, and Augustus Saint-Gaudens' statue The Puritan. All four of these museums have the same hours, and one ticket grants entrance to them all.

The **George Walter Vincent Smith Art Museum** (☎ 413-263-6800, 220 State St; admission & hours as per Springfield Library & Museums, above) is the gift of a man who amassed a fortune manufacturing carriages and then spent his money on works of art and artifacts. There are fine 19th-century American and European paintings, textiles, ceramics, and works in several other media. The Japanese armor collection is among the finest outside of Asia.

The **Museum of Fine Arts** (☎ 413-263-6800, 220 State St; admission & hours as per Springfield Library & Museums, above) has

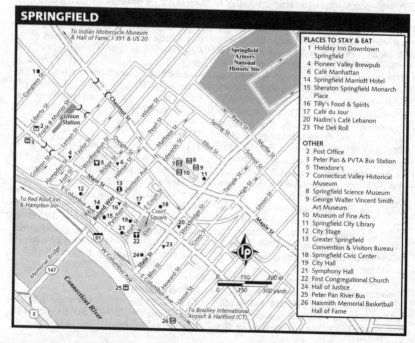

SPRINGFIELD

To Indian Motorcycle Museum & Hall of Fame, I-391 & US 20

Springfield Armory National Historic Site

PLACES TO STAY & EAT
1 Holiday Inn Downtown Springfield
4 Pioneer Valley Brewpub
6 Café Manhattan
14 Springfield Marriott Hotel
15 Sheraton Springfield Monarch Place
16 Tilly's Food & Spirits
17 Café du Jour
20 Nadim's Café Lebanon
23 The Deli Roll

OTHER
2 Post Office
3 Peter Pan & PVTA Bus Station
5 Theodore's
7 Connecticut Valley Historical Museum
8 Springfield Science Museum
9 George Walter Vincent Smith Art Museum
10 Museum of Fine Arts
11 Springfield City Library
12 City Stage
13 Greater Springfield Convention & Visitors Bureau
18 Springfield Civic Center
19 City Hall
21 Symphony Hall
22 First Congregational Church
24 Hall of Justice
25 Peter Pan River Bus
26 Naismith Memorial Basketball Hall of Fame

To Red Roof Inn & Hampton Inn

To Bradley International Airport & Hartford (CT)

0   150   300 m
0   350   300 yards

more than 20 galleries filled with lesser paintings of the great European masters and the better works of lesser masters. Among the masterworks here is Erastus Salisbury Field's *The Rise of the American Republic,* hung above the main stairway. In the impressionist and expressionist galleries, look for Monet's *Haystacks* and artworks by Edgar Degas, Raoul Dufy, Gauguin, Camille Pissarro, Pierre-Auguste Renoir, Georges Rouault and Maurice de Vlaminck. In the contemporary gallery there are works by George Bellows, Lyonel Feininger, Georgia O'Keeffe and Picasso. Modern sculptors featured include Leonard Baskin and Richard Stankiewicz.

The **Springfield Science Museum** (☎ 413-263-6800, 220 State St; admission & hours as per Springfield Library & Museums, above) is a good place for children. The Dinosaur Hall has a full-size replica of a Tyrannosaurus rex. The African Hall has many exhibits about peoples, animals and ecology. The historic Seymour Planetarium has eight weekly shows (which cost $1 extra).

At the **Connecticut Valley Historical Museum** (☎ 413-263-6800, 220 State St; admission & hours as per Springfield Library & Museums, above) you'll discover exhibits on the decorative and domestic arts of the Connecticut River valley from 1636 to the present. There are collections of furniture, pewter and glass, as well as four rooms decorated authentically in period styles: a 17th-century kitchen, a Federal-period dining room and two rooms from an early-19th-century tavern.

The **Springfield City Library** (413-263-6800, cnr State & Chestnut Sts; admission free; 10am-8pm Tues-Sun) has more than a million books, records and videos in its system.

Springfield Armory
The **Springfield Armory National Historic Site** (☎ 413-734-8551, 1 Armory Square, Federal St; admission free; open 10am-4:30pm Wed-Sun) preserves what remains of the USA's greatest federal armory. During its heyday in the Civil War, 3400 people worked in the armory, turning out

Pioneers of Invention

In 1794, President George Washington selected Springfield as a location for one of two federal armories that would manufacture muskets for the US Army. The first musket produced here in 1795 was a copy of the French 'Charleville,' popular with US soldiers during the Revolutionary War.

During the 19th century, Yankee ingenuity went to work at Springfield. In 1819, Thomas Blanchard invented a wood-turning lathe to produce identical gun stocks quickly and cheaply. Percussion ignition replaced the flintlock, and breech-loaders replaced muzzle-loaders. The Model 1903 Springfield rifle was what American doughboys carried into battle in WWI, and the M-1 Garand, built in Springfield, armed the troops in WWII.

After WWII, the armory evolved into a design and testing laboratory for small arms, machine-guns, grenade launchers and similar armaments, but these were built elsewhere by private contractors. Finally, in 1968, the Department of Defense decided to close down the armory. It had served the military needs of the nation for almost two centuries.

Arms were not Springfield's only contribution to American life and world culture. It was here, in 1891, that Dr James Naismith conceived the game of basketball, now played and loved around the world. Appropriately, Springfield is home to the Naismith Memorial Basketball Hall of Fame.

Springfield's impressive list of inventions goes on: the monkey wrench, steel-bladed ice skates, the first planetarium in the USA and the gasoline-powered motorcycle (1901). Another invention was the first practical internal-combustion engine automobile, built in 1894 on the top floor of the building at 41 Taylor St by the Duryea brothers, Charles and Frank. For a short time in the 1930s the world's most elegant auto, the Rolls-Royce, was also assembled in this city.

1000 muskets a day. Springfield Technical Community College now occupies many of the former firearm factories and officers'

quarters, but exhibits in several of the old buildings recall the armory's golden age quite effectively.

The Armory is a 10-minute walk northeastward from Court Square along State St past Museum Quadrangle. If you are driving, take I-291 exit 3 to Armory St and follow it to Federal St.

On the site, the Small Arms Museum holds one of the world's largest collections of firearms, including lots of Remingtons, Colts, Lugers and even weapons from the 1600s. For a truly weird weapon, don't miss the Organ of Rifles.

Basketball Hall of Fame

The founder would have approved (see boxed text Having a Ball): The **Naismith Memorial Basketball Hall of Fame** (☎ *413-781-6500, 1150 W Columbus Ave; adult/senior & child 7-14 yrs/child under 7yrs $10/7/free; open 10am-5pm daily)* is a mile south of I-91 exit 7, on the west side of I-91. It's pretty cool, hoopsters. The hall of fame completed a new building in 2002 that doubles its size. The new facility is an active place where you can shoot baskets, feel the center-court excitement in a wraparound cinema and learn about the sport's history and great players. Plan at least an hour's stop, though you could easily stay all morning.

Indian Motorcycle Museum & Hall of Fame

Springfield claims the birth of the gasoline-powered motorcycle, invented here in 1901. Up to 1953, the Indian Motorcycle Company produced its cycles here in a sprawling factory complex. The company also made cars, aircraft engines, air conditioners and, in 1947, the 'snowboat,' a precursor of the snowmobile.

The last of the company's buildings, once the engineering division, is now the Indian Motorcycle Museum & Hall of Fame (☎ *413-737-2624, Hendee St; adult/child 6-12 yrs $3/1; open 10am-4pm daily)*, with the largest, finest collection of Indian motorcycles and memorabilia in the world. There are other makes as well, and lots of funky period mementos. All of the machines are in working order (note the oil-drip pans underneath), and are taken out and run every three months. If you like bikes, don't miss this place. It's fascinating.

To find the museum, take I-291 exit 4 (St James Ave), then follow the signs north on Page Blvd to Hendee St. You'll find the museum in a low brick building in an industrial area.

Forest Park

Forest Park (☎ *413-787-6440, off Sumner Ave; admission cars/walkers & bikers $3/free; open 8am-sunset)*. Two miles south of the Springfield shopping center off of Sumner Ave (MA 83) is an 800-acre swath of lawns, woods, gardens, ponds, fountains, walking and horse trails, swimming pools and tennis courts. The **Zoo** at Forest Park (☎ *413-733-2251, admission adult/senior/child under 12 $3.50/2.50/1; open 10am-5pm daily)* has more than 200 animals, a miniature train and educational field trips.

Cruises

Springfield's Peter Pan Bus Lines operates the **Peter Pan River Bus** (☎ *413-746-6679, River Front Park; adult/child 3-9 yrs $11/7; open May-Oct)*. The Connecticut River cruises last 1½ hours and depart Springfield's River Front Park off W Columbus Avenue at the foot of State St. Families enjoy special discounts.

Special Events

In mid-September, sleepy West Springfield, on the west bank of the river, explodes into activity with the annual **The Big E**, the Eastern States Exposition (☎ *413-737-2443, 800-334-2443 ticket orders only, fax 413-787-0271, 1305 Memorial Ave/MA 147)*. The fair goes on for two weeks, with farm exhibits, horse shows, carnival rides, regional and ethnic food, parades, Wild West and high-diver shows, a circus, a petting zoo and country and pop music performances. In addition, each of the six New England states hosts a large pavilion with its own exhibits.

There's an admission charge (weekdays/weekends $8/12, child under six free). Once you're in the fairgrounds, all the shows are free; carnival rides cost extra. Hotels fill up when the Big E is in session, particularly on Friday and Saturday nights.

Places to Stay

With the help of *Berkshire Bed & Breakfast* (☎ 413-268-7244, fax 413-268-7243) you can make a reservation at small B&Bs in historic neighborhoods of Springfield, such as Maple Hill or Forest Park. Rooms cost $70 to $120 double, breakfast included.

Most of Springfield's inexpensive motels, including the *Red Roof Inn* (☎ 413-731-1010) and the *Hampton Inn* (☎ 413-732-1300) are actually in West Springfield on or near Riverdale St off I-91 exit 13, near the intersection with US 5 and I-391. The hotels in downtown Springfield tend to be luxurious business accommodations.

Holiday Inn Downtown Springfield (☎ 413-781-0900, 800-465-4329, fax 413-785-1410, Ⓦ www.sixcontinentshotels.com, 117 Dwight St) Rooms $125. This hotel is at Congress St, just over half a mile north of Court Square, and has 245 rooms.

The city's top two hotels are right in the city center facing one another across Boland Way, at I-91 exit 6 northbound or exit 7 southbound, a block north of Court Square.

One is the *Springfield Marriott Hotel* (☎ 413-781-7111, 800-228-9290, fax 413-731-8932, Ⓦ www.marriott.com, Boland Way at Columbus St Ave) Rooms $124-174. The Springfield Marriott has a sauna, an indoor pool and 265 sparkling business-class rooms with data ports.

The other is the *Sheraton Springfield Monarch Place* (☎ 413-781-1010, 800-426-9004, fax 413-734-3249, Ⓦ www.sheraton .com, Boland Way at Columbus St) Rooms $130-140. The Sheraton has 304 luxury rooms, an athletic club and swimming pool.

Places to Eat & Drink

Downtown Springfield has no chic restaurant district. There are, however, lunch places, pubs and bistros in the vicinity of Court Square and the railroad station that serve up tasty fare. Unless noted, the eateries listed here serve lunch and dinner.

Café du Jour (☎ 413-732-3900, 1369 Main St) Prices $2-5. This cafe is just northwest of Court St, serving good coffee and light meals to the office workers from the towers nearby. Danish, pound cake and chocolate chip cookies are $1. A large cappuccino runs under $3.

The Deli Roll (☎ 413-827-7007, 91 State St) Dishes $4-8. A sandwich shop a block southeast of Court Square, the Deli Roll has a plethora of meals on bread like the 'tuna-cado' (under $5), which is hot tuna plus avocado on a Portuguese roll. Most folks come for takeout, but there are several tables inside, and more on the sidewalk in front during nice weather.

Tilly's Food & Spirits (☎ 413-732-3613, 1390 Main St) Prices $6-12. Tilly's is an Irish pub serving soups, pasta and steaks at moderate prices: You can get a filling lunch for under $10.

Nadim's Café Lebanon (☎ 413-781-0800, 141 State Street) Lunch specials $6. Here's a cheery Middle Eastern eatery where you can get a choice of chicken, lamb, beef or swordfish kabob with a soup or salad for lunch.

Pioneer Valley Brewpub (☎ 413-732-2739, 51-59 Taylor St) Lunch $6-12, dinner $10-20. This is Springfield's art deco brewpub and bistro, at Main St four blocks northwest of Court Square. It serves its own beer ($3.50 a pint) and offers full lunch and dinner menus inside the dining room and at the courtyard tables. Try the hot corned beef on rye ($6).

Café Manhattan (☎ 413-737-7913, 301 Bridge St) Lunch $8-11, dinner $16-21. A bright spot in the food picture is this cafe at Barnes St. It is an upscale storefront bistro 2½ blocks northwest of Court Square serving traditional American and continental cuisine for lunch and dinner. Consider the cashew-crusted chicken breast ($18).

Entertainment

Pick up a copy of the *Valley Advocate* (W www.valleyadvocate.com), a free weekly newspaper, for entertainment listings.

Symphony Hall (☎ 413-788-7033, off *Court Square*) Tickets $18-35. Recitals and concerts by the members of the **Springfield Symphony Orchestra** (☎ 413-733-2291) occur year-round in this grand hall.

City Stage (☎ 413-788-7033, *Bridge St*) Tickets $20-30. For theater try this venue, off Main St in Columbus Center.

Springfield Civic Center (☎ 413-787-6600, *1277 Main St*) This modern building northeast of Court Square is the venue for exhibits, rock concerts and athletic events.

You don't need to be bored or lonely if you make camp in Springfield overnight. The area around Union Station and nearby Worthington St has been an entertainment district for 100 years, and it is alive with pubs and clubs that draw a large, well-educated crowd of 20- and 30-somethings.

Theodore's (☎ 413-736-6000, *201 Worthington St*) Check out this authentic Roaring '20s saloon and pool hall for some of the hottest BBQ and coolest jazz (almost nightly) in the Pioneer Valley. Owner Keith Weppler brings in national blues acts like Sleepy Labeef, who started doing his 'blues thang' in the 1940s down in Arkansas. The cover is usually $3 on weekends. There are 18 pool tables in the upstairs hall, where both the place and some of the tables date back to 1910. The bar is a hot cruising scene on Friday and Saturday nights when the music comes from below the belt. The kitchen will serve you some spicy ribs (under $10) until midnight on Friday and Saturday.

Getting There & Around

Springfield is served by the Bradley International Airport (☎ 860-292-2000) in Windsor Locks, CT, 18 miles to the south. See Getting There & Away in the Hartford section in the Connecticut chapter.

Springfield is the home of Peter Pan Bus Lines (☎ 413-781-2900, 800-343-9999), which serves New England, New York City, Philadelphia, Baltimore and Washington, DC. The bus station is at 1776 Main St at Liberty St, a 10-minute walk northwest of Court Square. Daily buses from Springfield go to Albany, New York; Amherst, MA; Bennington, VT; Boston and Deerfield, MA; Hartford, CT; Holyoke, Lee and Lenox, MA; New Haven, CT; New York City; and North Adams, Pittsfield, South Hadley, Williamstown and Worcester, MA.

Peter Pan's service connecting the college towns of the Pioneer Valley (Amherst, Holyoke, Northampton and South Hadley) with Springfield and Boston is frequent, with 15 buses daily. Buses run from each of these towns to Springfield almost hourly from 5am to 6pm, with two additional late-evening buses. From Springfield, frequent connecting buses go on to Boston. There is also direct service via Boston between the Pioneer Valley towns of Springfield and Hyannis.

The Pioneer Valley Transportation Authority (PVTA; ☎ 413-781-7882, 1776 Main St, in the Peter Pan terminal) runs 43 routes to 23 communities in the region.

Bonanza Bus Lines (☎ 800-556-3815) routes connect the cities of Providence, Springfield, Lee, Lenox, Pittsfield, Williamstown and Bennington.

Amtrak's (☎ 800-872-7245) *Lakeshore Limited*, the train running between Boston and Chicago, stops at Springfield's Union Station (☎ 413-785-4230, 66 Lyman St), a 10-minute walk northwest of Court Square. See the beginning of this chapter for details on trains.

If you're driving, you'll find Springfield stands at the junction of I-90 and I-91 about 90 miles from Boston and 140 miles from New York City.

For airport transport, contact Valley Transporter (☎ 413-733-9700, 413-253-1350) or Peter Pan Bus Lines (☎ 413-781-2900).

SOUTH HADLEY

North of Springfield lies Hampshire County. This is the central region of the Pioneer Valley, sometimes known as the Five College

Area because it is home to Amherst College, Hampshire College, Mount Holyoke College, Smith College and the University of Massachusetts at Amherst.

The village of South Hadley (population about 2000), 15 miles north of Springfield on MA 116, is the most southerly of the Five College towns, with the USA's oldest college for women, Mount Holyoke College, at its center.

With views of hills, fields and tobacco barns, MA 116 between South Hadley and Amherst, and MA 47 between South Hadley and Hadley, are among the prettiest drives in the Pioneer Valley. For bicycling information, see Activities in the Amherst section, later in this chapter.

Information

For information on the town, visit the South Hadley Chamber of Commerce (☎/fax 413-532-6451, 362 N Main St, South Hadley, MA 01075). Have a look at the Odyssey Book Shop (☎ 413-534-7307, 9 College St) for a sophisticated selection of fiction and nonfiction.

Mount Holyoke College

Founded in 1837 by teacher Mary Lyon, Mount Holyoke College (☎ 413-538-2222, W *www.mtholyoke.edu, on MA 116 in the center of South Hadley)* is the country's oldest women's college, with a current enrollment of about 2000 students. You can arrange campus tours any day by phoning the number provided.

The great American landscape architect Frederick Law Olmsted laid out the center of Mount Holyoke's parklike 800-acre campus in the latter part of the 1800s. Among the college's other 19th-century legacies is a hand-crafted organ in the chapel, one of the last built by New England's master organ maker, Charles B Fisk.

In the 20th century, the college added a multimillion-dollar sports complex, an

---

Having a Ball

The Pioneer Valley seems to be the cradle of big-ball games: Both basketball and volleyball were invented here.

Born in Canada, James Naismith (1861–1939) graduated from McGill University in Montreal, then came to Springfield to work as a physical education instructor at the International YMCA Training School (later Springfield College). He wanted to develop a good, fast team sport that could be played indoors during the long New England winters. Sometime around December 1, 1891, he took two empty wooden half-bushel peach baskets and nailed them to opposite walls in the college gymnasium. He wrote down 13 rules for the game (12 of which are still used), and thus basketball was born.

Students at the college took to the new game enthusiastically. News of the game's invention spread fast and far, as students carried their enthusiasm with them when they went home for Christmas vacation that year.

Naismith went on to become basketball coach at the University of Kansas. His successor in that post, Forrest Allen (1885–1974), worked to have basketball included in the Olympic Games, and was successful in 1936.

Volleyball was invented in nearby Holyoke by William G Morgan, who worked for the Holyoke YMCA. It was intended to be an indoor game for businessmen who found basketball too strenuous. Morgan named his new game 'mintonette,' but a professor at Springfield College thought 'volleyball' more appropriate, because of the back-and-forth movement of the ball.

The rules of the game took shape in 1897, and the United States Volleyball Association was founded in 1922.

MASSACHUSETTS

equestrian center and a Japanese garden and teahouse.

Besides a walk around the pastoral campus, you can enjoy the **College Art Museum** (☎ 413-538-2245; admission free; open 11am-5pm Tues-Friday, 1-5pm Sat-Sun).

Skinner State Park

This mountaintop park (☎ 413-586-0350, north of South Hadley off MA 47 in Hadley; admission free; open sunrise-sunset daily) is at the summit of Mt Holyoke. The summit house affords panoramic views of the Connecticut River, its oxbow curve and its fertile valley. There are hiking trails and a picnic area as well.

Holyoke Range State Park

This park (☎ 413-253-2883, a few miles north of South Hadley on MA 116; admission free; open sunrise-sunset daily) has trail hikes ranging from three-quarters of a mile to 5.4 miles on the Metacomet-Monadnock Trail (see the boxed text) and side trails.

Places to Stay & Eat

Lodgings are in Amherst, Northampton and Springfield.

Woodbridge's Restaurant (☎ 413-536-7341, cnr MA 47 & MA 116) Dinner $13-19, Sunday brunch $13. For a satisfying meal, try this place in the center of South Hadley. Sunday brunch is served 10:30am to 2pm. The front terrace tables are the best in good weather. We like a bowl of chili ($4) or a Monte Cristo sandwich ($6) after hiking.

Entertainment

The stage is under the stars at *Mount Holyoke Summer Theater* (☎ 413-538-3222, in the Brook Theater at Mt Holyoke College) Tickets $15-30. This group stages outdoor evening performances Tuesday through Saturday on the common.

Getting There & Away

Springfield is the long-distance transportation center for the region. PVTA buses (see Getting There & Around in the Springfield section, earlier in this chapter) can bring you to South Hadley.

NORTHAMPTON

Described by the 'Swedish Nightingale,' Jenny Lind, as the 'Paradise of America' during her visit in 1850, and currently promoted as the 'number one small arts town in America,' Northampton (population 30,000), dates from 1654. The Hampshire County seat and the home of highly regarded Smith College is a cultural oasis, where New York's Greenwich Village meets rural New England. Northampton is also the dining and entertainment center of the region, with a large selection of moderately priced ethnic restaurants and world-class entertainment.

The presence of college students and their professors gives the town a liberal political atmosphere. There is an outspoken and active lesbian community, such that the college-town lineup of shops, banks, bookstores, cafes, copy shops and pizza parlors reflects a strong feminist sensibility.

For information on bicycling, see Activities in the Amherst section, later in this chapter.

Orientation & Information

The center of town is at the intersection of Main St (MA 9) and Pleasant St (MA 5). Restaurants, banks, shops and other services are within a few blocks, although most lodgings are on the outskirts.

Check in at the Greater Northampton Chamber of Commerce (☎ 413-584-1900, W www.northamptoncommon.com, 99 Pleasant St, Northampton, MA 01060). It's open 9am to 5pm Monday to Friday, 10am to 2pm Saturday and Sunday May to October.

Smith College

Smith College (☎ 413-584-2700, W www.smith.edu, Elm St, Northampton), at the western end of the downtown area, was founded 'for the education of the intelligent gentlewoman' in 1875 by Sophia Smith. The student body, numbering about 2700, continues to consist largely of women, with a sprinkling of men. The wooded 125-acre campus along Elm St holds an eclectic architectural mix of nearly 100 buildings, as well as Paradise Pond.

Visitors are welcome at the **Lyman Plant House** (☎ 413-585-2740), a collection of Victorian greenhouses that are the venue for the Bulb Show and Chrysanthemum Show (see Special Events, below). You should also take a look at the **Smith College Museum of Art** (☎ 413-585-2770, Elm St at Bedford Terrace; admission free; open 9:30am-4pm Tues, Wed, Fri & Sat, 9:30am-8pm Thur, noon-4pm Sun) when it reopens after renovation in 2003. There is a strong collection of 17th-century Dutch and 19th- and 20th-century European and North American paintings, including fine works by Degas, Winslow Homer, Pablo Picasso and James Abbott McNeill Whistler.

Guided campus tours can be arranged through the Office of Admissions (☎ 413-585-2500), or you can guide yourself using the good campus folder available for free at the college switchboard in College Hall, or from the Office of Admissions.

Special Events

Flower-lovers should check out the renowned annual **Bulb Show** in mid-March and the **Chrysanthemum Show** in November, both held at the Lyman Plant House at Smith College (☎ 413-585-2740).

Springfield has the Big E, but Northampton has the **Tri-County Fair** (☎ 413-584-2237), starting on the Friday of Labor Day weekend. The fair, first held in 1818, features agricultural and livestock exhibits, horse races, food and rides. The Tri-County Fairgrounds, on MA 9 just west of I-91 exit 19 North and US 20 South, is also the site of the **New England Morgan Horse Show** (☎ 413-527-8994), held annually in July.

Places to Stay

It's usually easy to find a room during the summer. At other times of year, room price and availability depend on the college's schedule of ceremonies and cultural events.

Motels One of the cheapest places to stay is the *Econo Lodge* (☎ 413-584-9816, fax 586-7512, ☒ www.econolodge.com, 237 Russell St (MA 9), Hadley) Rooms $68. It is 4 miles northeast of central Northampton. Some

rooms have kitchenettes, and there's a swimming pool.

Autumn Inn (☎ 413-584-7660, fax 413-586-4808, 259 Elm St/MA 9) Singles/doubles $86/112. Despite its motel-like layout, this 34-room place has an innlike ambiance and a swimming pool.

Hotel Northampton (☎ 413-584-3100, fax 584-9455, 36 King St) Rooms $135 and up. This 72-room hotel behind the county courthouse has been receiving Northampton's important guests since 1916. You can walk to everywhere in town from here. Rooms have all the amenities.

B&Bs While the B&B phenomenon is strong in the Pioneer Valley accommodations scene, few are actually in Northampton, although there are many in and around nearby Amherst (see Places to Stay in the Amherst section, later in this chapter).

Lupine House (☎ 413-586-9766, 185 North Main St) Rooms $65-75. Three miles from downtown Northampton, Evelyn and Gil Billings offer three rooms in their home, each with a private bath and air con. The attractions here are the big family-style breakfast and the inn's proximity to Look Park (just up the street) with its hiking/biking trails and tennis courts.

The Salt Box (☎ 413-584-1790, 173 Elm St) Rooms $85-130, $575-850 a week. The draw here is the elegance of this colonial home, in the Smith College neighborhood with an easy walk to all of the attractions of downtown Northampton. The caveat is that the innkeepers prefer to rent their three rooms for a week or longer. All rooms have a fridge, air con, coffeemaker, private bath, private entrance. Many visiting scholars stay here.

Places to Eat

Compared to the high prices of Boston and Cape Cod, a Northampton restaurant tab is a joy. And so are the number and variety of eateries. A survey of the restaurants, on and off Main St, reveals American, Chinese, French, Greek, Indian, Italian, Japanese, Mediterranean, Mexican, Moroccan, Persian, Thai and Turkish cuisine, not to mention a handful of cafes. In addition, most Northampton restaurants offer lunches and dinners with vegetarian fare and alcoholic drinks.

Jake's (☎ *413-584-9613, 17 King St*) Breakfasts and lunches $2-5. A full service cafe with plenty of tables, Jake's is the most popular and most economical breakfast joint in town. You can get a three-stack of pancakes and a smile for $3. We go for the Syrian sub ($4) at lunch.

Java Net Café (☎ *413-587-3400, 241 Main St*) Prices $3-8. Northampton's cybercafe serves up coffee, tea, baked goods and the Internet; it's like a library with large easy chairs for lounging. You'll pay about $2 to log on for 20 minutes. Curiously, we found the staff here rather indifferent to customers on our last visit, an anomaly in such a generally welcoming town.

Bart's (☎ *413-584-0721, 235 Main St*) Prices $3-8. Bart's specializes in custom-made ice cream (you pick the 'add-ins'), but also serves coffee, pastries and light lunches. You've got to try the ice cream called 'Three Geeks and a Redhead' (coconut, strawberry and maybe sex hormones).

Bakery Normand (☎ *413-584-0717, 192 Main St*) Prices $3-7. Head into this tiny bakery for picnic supplies like fresh baguettes ($2.50) or Danish, cakes, tarts and coffee to go.

Sylvester's (☎ *413-586-5343, 111 Pleasant St*) Prices $5-7. We caught the whole crew from the chamber of commerce lined up here at lunch for noho veggie quesadillas (about $7) and the pesto cheddar veggie burger (under $6).

Nini's La Pizzaria (☎ *413-584-1711, 71 Pleasant St*) Pies $7-17. Check out this little takeout shop selling the cheapest slice of pizza ($1) in Northampton. We've fed three happy road guerrillas on the *aglio olio* (garlic, oil, eggplant, mushrooms, broccoli) pie ($17).

Paul and Elizabeth's (☎ *413-584-4832, 150 Main St*) Lunches $6-10. Known locally as P&E's, this airy cafe sits in back of Thornes Marketplace (an urban minimall in a reclaimed department store). P&E's is the town's premier natural foods restaurant,

serving vegetarian cuisine and seafood, as well. A three-course dinner with wine can cost $22 to $26, but you can tank up for a lot less at lunch on the smoked salmon wrap or tabouli salad (both about $7).

La Veracruzana (☎ *413-586-7181, 31 Main St*) Dishes $3-8. This eatery has down-home Mexican food such as tamales, enchiladas, tostadas and taco plates.

La Taqueria Cha Cha Cha! (☎ *413-586-7311, 134 Main St*) Prices $6-12. Northampton's other centrally located Mexican eatery, La Taqueria has a young, hip and informal mood. A meal of burritos or quesadillas with a glass of wine costs about $10.

Northampton Brewery (☎ *413-584-9903, 11 Brewster Court*) Prices $7-12. Enjoy this modern brewpub, which features excellent beer, light meals and nouvelle cuisine entrees. A pint and a sandwich cost under $12. Dine in the verdant beer garden in good weather. The main entrance is actually on Hampton Rd, one long block south of Main St.

Mulino's Trattoria (☎ *413-586-8900, 21 Center St*) Dishes $5-16. At this storefront bistro you'll find a long list of homestyle Italian dishes, including pizza from a wood-fired oven, panini (Italian sandwiches) and pasta, meat and fish. There's a piano bar downstairs.

La Cazuela (☎ *413-586-0400, 7 Old South St*) Dinners $16-30. For fancy Mexican fare, head for this Southwest/Mexican restaurant and cantina off Main St. Eat in the terrace dining area during good weather. Look out for two types of salsa on every table – hot and very hot. Dinner prices include killer margaritas.

Eastside Grill (☎ *413-586-3347, 19 Strong Ave*) Dishes under $18. Eastside Grill, a half block south of Main St, has a vast and eclectic menu listing everything from Louisiana fried oysters and chicken étouffée to steaks and pecan pie. The tenderloin costs $18; everything else is several dollars less, and there's an extensive and reasonably priced wine list. You'll find the clientele is well dressed.

Spoleto (☎ *413-586-6313, 50 Main St*) Dinner $25-40. Open for dinner 4pm-10pm.

Many people rate Spoleto as Northampton's best restaurant. The classic dishes such as veal scaloppini and chicken saltimbocca have California accents. Vegetarians should try the eggplant rollatini.

Entertainment
Northampton is the center of nightlife for residents, students and faculty in the Five College Area. For listings of what's happening throughout the Pioneer Valley, pick up a copy of *The Valley Advocate* (W www.valley advocate.com), a local free weekly newspaper with lots of listings.

Theater At Smith College is the *New Century Theatre* (☎ 413-585-3220) Tickets $16-22. Local talent stage modern works in July and August.

Music The town's prime folk and jazz venue is the *Iron Horse Music Hall* (☎ 413-584-0610, 20 Center St) Tickets $10-20. Call for the current program, then look for the small storefront half a block off Main St with the line of people waiting to get in. Note: They serve booze, too.

Calvin Theater (☎ 413-584-1444, 19 King St) Tickets $20-100. World-class acts like Ray Charles and Graham Nash regularly perform here, in the intimate setting of a restored movie house.

Pearl St (☎ 413-584-7771, 10 Pearl St). This place, at the corner of Strong Ave, is the hottest dance club in town, drawing local, regional and national performers and enough loyal patrons to produce a line Friday and Saturday nights. Wednesday is gay night, Thursday is 18-plus, Friday is retro and Saturday is for modern rock.

Fire & Water Vegetarian Café & Performance Space (☎ 413-586-8336, 5 Old South St). This basement cafe features folk, jazz, blues and new talent nightly. You can get local microbrews here as well as caffeine. Sarah Pepper Ryan and her pal Carlos from Trinidad will make you feel at home.

Pubs You usually get live rock or acoustic on Friday and Saturday nights at the *Northampton Brewery* (☎ 413-584-9903, 11 Brewster Court). This pub packs in a mixed gang (both in age and sexual preference) every evening.

Packard's (☎ 413-584-5957, 14 Masonic St). Hit this pub, off Main St, for the billiard tables on the 3rd floor or the dartboards. This is the most popular place to be and be seen for the under-30 crowd. At $3, beer ain't cheap.

FitzWilly's (☎ 413-584-8666, 23 Main, at Strong Ave) Dishes $5-8. This is a centrally located fern bar and restaurant. A longtime favorite, with an extensive menu of burgers, salads and pizzas, FitzWilly's is currently popular with middle-age couples out for a date.

Gay & Lesbian Venues
The entire town of Northampton is gay-friendly, and couples are obviously 'out' in public. The lesbian community is much more prominent in the town's social dynamic than gay males. Most clubs and pubs are a congenial mix of straights and gays.

The Grotto (☎ 413-586-6900, 25 West St). Seven nights a week this hopping club floods with femme lesbians from the college, plus local cruisers and couples, some gay men, drag queens, and their straight friends, who all boogie to house and techno.

Getting There & Away
See the Springfield section, earlier in this chapter, for information on air, bus and train service.

If you're driving, you'll find Northampton lies 18 miles north of Springfield on I-91 and 108 miles from Boston.

AMHERST
Best known as the home of prestigious Amherst College, Amherst also is home to the main campus of the University of Massachusetts and smaller artsy Hampshire College. The town has produced its share of famous people, among whom poet Emily Dickinson, 'the belle of Amherst,' is perhaps the best known. With the influence of almost 30,000 college students, this former farm town (population 17,000 without the college kids) rocks!

Orientation & Information

At the center of Amherst is the town common, a broad New England green framed by churches and inns.

The Amherst Area Chamber of Commerce (☎ 413-253-0700, W www.amherst common.com, 409 Main St at Railroad St, Amherst, MA 01002) is less than half a mile east of Pleasant St. It's open 9am to 5pm Monday to Friday. The chamber maintains a summer information booth on the common facing S Pleasant St, directly across from the Peter Pan bus station (which is at 79 S Pleasant St). The post office (☎ 413-549-0418) is on N Pleasant St at Kellogg Ave. There's a Council Travel agency (☎ 413-256-1261) at 44 Main St. For full-service bookstores, check out the Jeffrey Amherst Bookshop (☎ 413-253-3381) at 55 Pleasant St and Atticus bookshop (☎ 413-256-1747), 8 Main St.

Dickinson Homestead

Emily Dickinson (1830–86) was raised in the strict Puritan household of her father, a prominent lawyer. When he was elected to the US Congress, she traveled with him to Washington and Philadelphia, then returned to Amherst and this house to live out the rest of her days in near seclusion. Some say she was in love with the Reverend Charles Wadsworth, a local married clergyman. Unable to show her love, she withdrew from the world into a private realm of pain, passion and poignancy.

Dickinson wrote finely crafted poems on scraps of paper and old envelopes and stuffed them in her desk. She published only seven poems during her lifetime, and no one recognized her then as a major talent. After her death, more than 1000 of her exquisite poems were discovered and published. Dickinson's verses on love, death, nature and immortality have made her one of the most important poets in the United States.

Emily Dickinson's former home (☎ 413-542-8161, 280 Main St; admission adult/senior/child over 12 $5/4/3; open 1pm-4pm Wed-Sun) has several rooms open for touring. Call for reservations.

Hampshire College

The region's newest and perhaps most innovative center of learning, Hampshire College (W www.hampshire.edu), is 3 miles south of Amherst center on MA 116. It has a verdant campus. Contact the admissions office (☎ 413-582-5471) to schedule a tour.

Amherst College

Founded in 1821, Amherst (W www.amherst .edu) has retained its character and quality partly by maintaining its small size (1575 students); thus its prestige has grown. The main part of the campus lies just south of the town common. The information booth has a map and brochure for self-guided walking tours, or you can ask questions at Converse Hall (☎ 413-542-2000).

University of Massachusetts at Amherst

The University of Massachusetts at Amherst (☎ 413-545-0111, W www.umass.edu), founded in 1863 as the Massachusetts Agricultural College, is now the keystone of the public university system in Massachusetts. About 24,000 students study at the sprawling UMass campus, which is to the northwest of the common. A free PVTA bus line serves the campus, making for easy local transport.

Atkins Farms Country Market

This recently expanded farm-produce center (☎ 413-253-9528, MA 116 & Bay Rd; admission free), about 3 miles south of Amherst, offers maple sugar products in spring, garden produce in summer and apple-picking in autumn. Other activities, such as a scarecrow-making workshop in October, take place throughout the year. A deli/bakery sells picnic supplies; Atkins Farms will also ship gift baskets.

Activities

See the South Hadley section, earlier in this chapter, for information on hiking in the Holyoke Range, south of Amherst.

The **Norwottuck Rail Trail** (nor-**wah**-tuk) is a foot and bike path that follows the former Boston & Maine Railroad right-of-way from Amherst to Hadley to Northampton, a total distance of 8.5 miles. For much of its length, the trail parallels MA 9. Parking and access to the trail can be found on Station Rd in Amherst, at the Mountain Farms Mall on MA 9 in Hadley and at Elwell State Park on Damon Rd in Northampton.

Biking the trail is particularly enjoyable. You can rent bikes for the day from **Valley Bicycles** (☎ 413-256-0880, 319 Main St less than half a mile east of Pleasant St; $20 per day).

Places to Stay

There aren't many campgrounds in this region. One is **White Birch Campground** (☎ 413-665-4941, 122 North St, Whately) Sites $22-24. Open May-Nov. Follow MA 116 North through North Amherst and Sunderland to South Deerfield, then go southwest to Whately, where you'll find this wooded campground with 40 sites.

Motels & Hotels Just over the town line in Hadley, you'll find the **Amherst Motel** (☎ 413-256-8122, 408 Northampton Rd/MA 9) Rooms $54-68, with breakfast. This motel is on the south side of MA 9, a mile west of the Amherst town common. Rooms are simply furnished but clean.

University Lodge (☎ 413-256-8111, 345 North Pleasant St/MA 116) Rooms $72-99. The attraction here is the location: only a few blocks north of the town common in the heart of Amherst's restaurant district.

Campus Center Hotel (☎ 413-549-6000, fax 545-1210, the Murray D Lincoln Campus Center at UMass off N Pleasant St) Rooms $79-95. This hotel is inside the high-rise tower on campus. Rooms compare to those you will find in an attractive motel, and the staff features cheery college students.

Inns & B&Bs The Amherst Area Chamber of Commerce (see Orientation & Information, above) has a list, which includes phone numbers and prices, of more than two dozen member B&Bs.

Allen House (☎ 413-253-5000, W www .allenhouse.com, 599 Main St) Rooms $45-

135, with breakfast. This is a prim, Queen-Anne-style Victorian cottage, and the bath-equipped rooms are air-conditioned. It is over half a mile east of Pleasant St, and Main St has some traffic noise during the day.

Lord Jeffrey Inn (☎ 413-253-2576, 800-742-0358, fax 413-256-6152, 30 Boltwood Ave) Rooms $79-139. A 49-room residence facing the town common, this is the classic college-town inn: colonial, collegiate, cozy and comfortable. Right on the common, the location couldn't be better.

Places to Eat

Being a college town, Amherst has lots of places serving pizza, sandwiches, Mexican *antojitos* (appetizers), Chinese takeout and fresh-brewed coffee. The fast-food and restaurant zone is on N Pleasant St, north of Main St to Kellogg Ave.

Antonio's Pizza by the Slice (☎ 413-253-0808, 31 N Pleasant St) Slices $1.50-3. This is Amherst's most popular pizza place, which is saying a lot. No cheap cheese-on-cardboard here: The variety of toppings, flavorings and spices are vast, and prices are low.

Rao's Coffee Roasting Company (☎ 413-253-9441, 17 Kellogg Ave) Prices $2-6. Rao's is a half-block east of Pleasant St along Boltwood Walk. It serves specialty coffees ($1 to $3) and appropriate nibbles at its indoor and outdoor cafe tables.

Nancy Jane's (☎ 413-253-3343, 36 Main St) Breakfast $2-6. Opens 6:30am. Wander into this storefront cafe for a transfusion of home-style eggs and bacon after a long night in the pubs. We crave the Rueben omelette ($6).

La Veracruzana (☎ 413-253-6900, 63 S Pleasant St) Dishes $2.50-7. This eatery is convenient to the common and the bus station. It serves burritos, quesadillas and tacos; we love the seafood enchiladas with crab, cilantro, onion and tomato (under $6).

Panda East (☎ 413-256-8923, 103 N Pleasant St) Prices $5-12, lunch specials $5-6. Panda East is on Boltwood Walk at Kellogg Ave. Here you'll find Chinese and Japanese cuisine at very reasonable prices in attractive surroundings, and you can choose from the long list of luncheon specials like kung pao shrimp, which comes with soup and steamed rice.

Amherst Chinese Food (☎ *413-253-7835, 62 Main St*) Lunch $5-8, dinner $6-12. This one is a long block east of Pleasant St. It has been serving Chinese dishes for decades. We go for the veggie lo mein ($5).

Atlantis (☎ *413-253-0025, 41 Boltwood Walk*) Prices $6-22. To find some of the most imaginative cooking in the Pioneer Valley, you have to head down a narrow alley off N Pleasant St, next to Antonio's Pizza. In a building tucked behind the storefronts, you'll find a little bistro to make your taste buds jump up and rumba. Come for the Sunday brunch with mains like Moroccan chicken ($8), with couscous and curried veggies.

Top of the Campus Restaurant (☎ *413-545-0636, Murray D Lincoln Campus Center at UMass*) Dinner $12-18. For a meal and a view, try this restaurant. The food is traditional Yankee fare like baked scrod (about $15); prices are moderate and the view of the campus and the countryside is impressive at sunset.

Judie's (☎ *413-253-3491, 51 N Pleasant St*) Lunch $11-15, dinner $16-35. This restaurant, in a converted house, has an eclectic menu of original – some would say 'odd' – dishes, such as a chicken 'sandwich' with apple butter, bananas, peanuts, coconut, raisins, cranberry sauce and a curry glaze, served in a popover. There's usually a luncheon special priced around $5.50.

The Windowed Hearth (☎ *413-253-2576, 30 Boltwood Ave*) Dinners $35 to $60 with wine. This restaurant is in the Lord Jeffrey Inn, facing the common, and is where folks go when they crave a fancy meal. Pecan-crusted duck breast and venison *osso buco* typify the offerings in the formal colonial dining room.

Entertainment
Although a lot of the college crowd head to nearby Northampton to get their party on, you can find plenty of action in Amherst.

Fine Arts Center (☎ *413-545-2511, UMass campus*) Tickets $12-35. The university's en-

tertainment auditorium has a full program of concerts, shows, folk, jazz and rock.

Amherst Brewing Company (☎ *413-253-4400, 24-36 N Pleasant St*). Here you'll find a full calendar of jazz, blues, rock and reggae groups performing, usually with no cover charge. Pints of summer brew run $3.50. This is a good place to go scouting on Thursday night for your weekend date.

Black Sheep (☎ *413-253-3442, 79 Main St*). Welcome to the town's most popular folk club.

The Pub (☎ *413-549-1200, 15 E Pleasant St*). A place of local legend, the Pub attracts brewski-pounding frat men and the young women who love them.

Getting There & Away
Amtrak (☎ 800-872-7245) runs its daily *Vermonter* between New York and Montreal, with a stop at Amherst depot just off Main St, half a mile east of the common.

Peter Pan's Amherst Center Bus Terminal (☎ 413-256-0431, 79 S Pleasant St) is just south of Main St, offering direct or connecting rides throughout New England.

Amherst is 80 miles from Boston, 24 miles from Springfield and 7 miles from Northampton via MA 9.

Getting Around
UMass Transit Service (☎ 413-586-5806) runs free buses along MA 116/Pleasant St between the town center and the UMass campus.

DEERFIELD
History lovers thrill to this rural village, where zoning and preservation keep the community looking like a ghost of the 18th century. During the mid-17th century, pioneers settled at Deerfield in the fertile Connecticut River valley 16 miles northwest of what is now Amherst. But the valley was the borderland of colonial settlement and it was open to attack by the area's Native Americans.

Massasoit (1580–1661), great *sachem* of the Wampanoags, signed a treaty of peace with the Pilgrims at Plymouth in 1621, and he scrupulously observed it until his death.

In the four decades after the founding of Plymouth, English settlers poured into the region. The Wampanoags and other native peoples became dependent on English goods and found themselves yielding their lands in exchange for English cloth, kitchen utensils and firearms.

Upon Massasoit's death, his son Metacomet (called 'King Philip' by the English) became sachem, and, though he preserved peace for several years, he and his people became increasingly agitated by the colonists' steady encroachment.

In 1671 the English government, suspicious of Metacomet's motives, brought him in for questioning, levied a fine and demanded that the Wampanoags give up their arms. They did.

Still, friction increased, and in 1675, when three Wampanoags were tried and executed for the murder of a Christian Indian who had been an informer for the English, war broke out.

King Philip's War, as it was called by the English, brought devastation to frontier settlements such as Deerfield. In the autumn of 1675, an Indian force a thousand strong massacred 64 residents here.

The survivors rebuilt the town, only to have the Indians attack again in 1704. Nearly 50 residents were killed and the rest marched off to Canada; many others died along the way. But the survivors returned and rebuilt the town once again.

Later in the 18th century, when peace had returned to the region, more settlers arrived to farm the rich bottomlands.

Orientation & Information

The modern commercial center is in South Deerfield. The original settlement of Deerfield, 6 miles to the north, has been preserved and restored to something like its appearance in earlier, more dangerous times.

To get information before you arrive, contact Historic Deerfield (☎ 413-774-5581, Ⓦ www.historic-deerfield.org, PO Box 321, Deerfield, MA 01342) or the Franklin County Chamber of Commerce (☎ 413-773-5463, Ⓦ www.co.franklin.ma.us, 395 Main

Metacomet-Monadnock Trail

The Metacomet-Monadnock Trail is part of a 200-mile greenway and footpath that extends from Connecticut along the Connecticut River valley to New Hampshire's Mt Monadnock and beyond.

In Connecticut, the trail takes its name from Metacomet (the Indian leader who waged war on the colonists in 1675). It enters Massachusetts near the Agawam/Southwick town line to become Massachusetts' Metacomet-Monadnock Trail, 177 miles long. From the state line, the trail proceeds north up the river valley through public and private lands, ascends Mt Tom, then heads east along the Holyoke Range, through Skinner State Park and Holyoke Range State Park, before bearing north again.

After entering New Hampshire, the trail ascends Mt Monadnock, where it joins the Monadnock-Sunapee Greenway.

The easiest access to the trail for day hikes is in the state parks, where leaflets and simple local trail maps are available. For longer hikes, it's good to have the Metacomet-Monadnock Trail Guide (9th edition, 1999), published by the Berkshire Chapter Trails Committee of the AMC (PO Box 9369, North Amherst, MA 01059). It's also available through the AMC's main office (☎ 800-262-4455, 5 Joy St, Boston, MA 02108) and at bookshops and outdoors stores.

St, Greenfield, MA 01302). When you arrive in town, inquire at the information desk in the museum across from the Deerfield Inn. It has maps, brochures and an audiovisual presentation that gives you an overview of Historic Deerfield Village.

Historic Deerfield Village

The main street of Historic Deerfield Village (☎ 413-774-5581, The Street; adult/child 6-21 yrs $12/5; single house admission $6/3; open 9:30-4:30 daily) escaped the ravages of time and now presents a noble prospect: a dozen houses dating from the 1700s and 1800s, well preserved and open to the public. It costs nothing to stroll along the Street, or you can take a half-hour tour of the buildings and the guides in the houses provide commentary.

The **Wright House** (1824) has collections of American period paintings, Chippendale and Federal furniture and Chinese export porcelain. The **Flynt Textile Museum** (1872) has textiles, costumes and needlework from Europe and the US. There's also the **Henry N Flynt Silver and Metalwork Collection** (1814). Furnishings in **Allen House** (1720) were made in the Pioneer Valley and Boston.

The **Stebbins House** (1799–1810) was the home of a rich land-owning family, and is furnished with typical luxury items of the time. In the **Barnard Tavern**, many of the exhibits are touchable, which makes this a favorite with children. The rooms of the **Wells-Thorn House** (1717–51) are furnished according to period, from colonial times to the Federal period.

The **Dwight House**, built in Springfield in 1725, was moved to Deerfield in 1950. It now holds locally made furniture and an 18th-century doctor's office. **Sheldon-Hawks House** (1743) was the 18th-century home of the Sheldons, wealthy Deerfield farmers. Contrast its furnishings with those in the Stebbins House, built and furnished a half century later.

The local parsonage was the **Ashley House** (1730). The **Ebenezer Hinsdale Williams House**, which took 22 years to build, has recently been restored to its original appearance (it was built between 1816 and 1838).

Memorial Hall Museum

Here's the original building (☎ 413-774-7476, cnr Memorial St, US 5 & 10; adult/child under 12 $6/3; open 9:30am-4:30pm daily May-Oct) of Deerfield Academy (1798), the prestigious preparatory school in town. It's now a museum of Pocumtuck Valley life and history. Puritan and Indian artifacts include carved and painted chests, embroidery, musical instruments and glassplate photographs (1880–1920).

When visiting the museum, don't miss the Indian House Door, a dramatic relic from the French and Indian Wars. In February 1704, Indians attacked the house of the Sheldon family. The attackers chopped and bashed at the door, but it wouldn't yield. Finally, they hacked a hole through its center and did in the inhabitants with musket fire.

Cruises

For a junket on the Connecticut River, try the **Northfield Mountain Recreation and Environmental Center** (☎ 413-659-3714, on MA 63 north of MA 2; boat cruises adult/senior/child 14yrs and under $9/8/5; cruises 11am, 1pm and 3pm Wed-Sun). Take I-91 north to exit 27, then MA 2 east, then MA 63 north. The Quinnetukut II glides on 12-mile, 1½-hour trips in summer. A lecturer fills you in on the history, geology and ecology of the river and the region. Call for reservations.

Places to Stay

Among possible campgrounds is **Erving State Forest** (☎ 413-544-3939, 877-422-6262, MA 2A, Erving) Bare sites $7. This vast forest, on the north side of MA 2A, has 32 campsites and is about 16 miles east of Greenfield.

Barton Cove Campground (☎ 413-659-3714, fax 413-659-4460, off MA 2 in Gill) Bare site $15. Barton Cove has 27 family tent sites on a mile-long wooded peninsula on the Connecticut River. The nature trail takes you to dinosaur footprints and nesting bald eagles. Take I-91 exit 27, then MA 2 East for 4 miles and look for the sign on the right.

The Franklin County Chamber of Commerce (☎ 413-773-5463) can recommend dozens of B&Bs in the region.

The Deerfield Inn (☎ 413-774-5587, 800-926-3865, fax 413-773-8712, W www.deerfield inn.com, The Street, Deerfield) Doubles $150-235 with breakfast and afternoon tea. This establishment has 23 modernized, comfortable rooms right at the head of Historic Deerfield's main street. The inn, built in 1884, was destroyed by fire and rebuilt in 1981.

Getting There & Away

Air, rail and bus service connect to Springfield (see that section, earlier in this chapter), and Peter Pan bus service goes to Greenfield.

By car, Deerfield lies just off I-91 on MA 5, about 39 miles north of Springfield.

The Berkshires

Few places in America combine culture with rural countryside as well as the Berkshire hills in western Massachusetts. Extending from the highest point in the state – Mt Greylock (3491 feet), near North Adams – southward to the Connecticut state line, the Berkshires have been a summer refuge for more than a century since the rich and famous, such as industrialist Andrew Carnegie, author Edith Wharton and the like, arrived to build more than 75 'summer cottages' of grand proportions. Many of these relics survive today as inns or venues for theater, musical concerts or dance recitals. On summer weekends when the sidewalks are scorching in Boston, New York and Hartford, crowds of city dwellers jump in their cars and head for the cool shade and breezes of the Berkshires to hike, bike, canoe and swim.

In the evenings, culture beckons. The Boston Symphony Orchestra's summer concert series at Tanglewood, near Lenox, draws the biggest crowds. The Williamstown Theatre Festival attracts many well-known New York and Hollywood actors, who also want to escape the city. Nearby, the Clark Art Institute's collection of impressionist works rivals any big-city museum.

Most visitors congregate in the southern half of the Berkshires, from Great Barrington to Lenox, where you will find considerable traffic and commercial development along the main road, US 7. Williamstown, to the north, is far less crowded, resembling the pastoral setting of Vermont to the north and Connecticut's Litchfield Hills to the south. To experience the natural beauty of the Berkshires, stay off US 7 and take to the back roads like MA 43 and 41. Better yet, hike the Appalachian Trail, which traverses the hills north to south.

GREAT BARRINGTON

Great Barrington's Main St used to consist of Woolworth's, several hardware stores, thrift shops and a run-down diner. They have given way to artsy boutiques, antique shops, coffeehouses and restaurants. The industrial-looking Union Bar & Grill could easily fit into Manhattan's SoHo district. Indeed, locals are beginning to call their town 'Little SoHo,' perhaps to appeal to the many city travelers that are now stopping to shop and eat at the best selection of restaurants in the region. But beware: The town's popularity makes for traffic jams on summer weekends.

Barringtonians are down-to-earth and highly independent – traits that stem from their past. In 1774 local citizens, chafing under the abuses of the king's governors in Boston, prevented the royal judges from meeting in the local courthouse.

Great Barrington also saw the birth of the great African American teacher and civil rights leader William Edward Burghardt DuBois (1868–1963). After receiving a PhD from Harvard, WEB DuBois became a pioneer for civil rights and a cofounder of the NAACP.

Great Barrington is 146 miles west of Boston off I-90. New York City is 150 miles to the south.

Orientation & Information

The Housatonic River flows through the center of town just east of Main St/US 7, the central thoroughfare. Most lodgings and restaurants are on Main St or on heavily congested US 7 North, or MA 23/41 southwest of the town. However, the finest accommodations (most of which are B&Bs) are on small roads outside of town in the farmlands.

The Southern Berkshire Chamber of Commerce (☎ 413-528-1510, Ⓦ www.great barrington.org, 362 Main St, Great Barrington, MA 01230) has maps, brochures, restaurant menus and accommodations lists. It's open 9am to 5pm Tuesday to Saturday.

THE BERKSHIRES

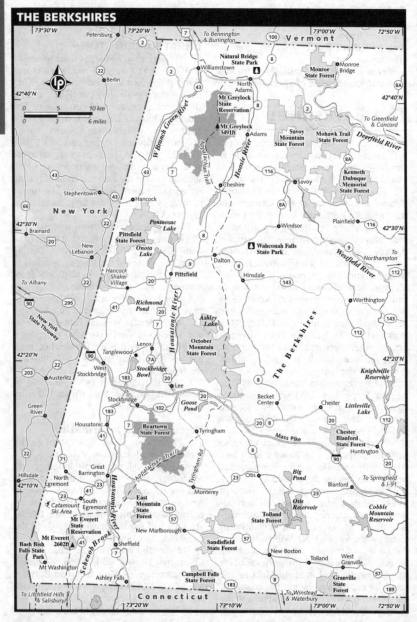

Searles Castle

Edward Searles and his wife, Mary Searles, were Great Barrington's most wealthy and prominent citizens in the late 19th century. Mary, the widow of railroad tycoon Mark Hopkins, built an imposing mansion here in 1886. Now called Searles Castle, it stands behind high walls on Main St at the southern end of the town center. Today the great house is the home of John Dewey Academy, a private school.

Monterey & Tyringham

Take MA 23 East out of Great Barrington 8 miles to the village of Monterey. Its general store is much like it was when it opened a half-century ago. If you buy lunch at the deli here, try the local goat cheese.

The village of Tyringham, several miles north of Monterey via the back road, is the perfect destination for an excursion deep into the heart of the countryside. Once the home of a Shaker community (1792–1870s), the village is now famous for its **Gingerbread House**, an architectural fantasy designed at the beginning of the 20th century by sculptor Henry Hudson Kitson. Kitson's best-known work graces the Lexington Green – a statue of Captain Parker as the minuteman. The thatched cottage, once Kitson's studio, now houses the **Santerella Museum & Gardens** (☎ 413-243-3260, 75 Main Rd; adult/child under four $4/free, open 10am-5pm daily). For places to stay in Tyringham, see Inns & B&Bs under Places to Stay, later in this section.

Hiking

To residents of southwestern Massachusetts, a 'cobble' is a high, rocky knoll of limestone, marble or quartzite. These knobby hills, which were formed about 500 million years ago, are now a curiosity. **Bartholomew's Cobble**, 10 miles south of Great Barrington along US 7 and MA 7A toward Ashley Falls, is a 277-acre reservation open to the public, cloaked in trees, ferns, flowers and moss. Six miles of hiking trails provide routes for enjoying the cobble and the woods, which are set beneath a flyway used by over 200 species of birds. Try the Ledges Trail that weaves along the Housatonic River. This property belongs to the Trustees of Reservations (☎ 413-229-8600; adult/child $3/1; open 9am-5pm daily mid-April–mid-Oct), a private, statewide conservation and preservation organization.

Twelve miles south of South Egremont, right on the New York state line, is **Bash Bish Falls**, a scenic waterfall that plunges down a 1000-foot gorge. You can take two paths to reach it. Follow MA 41 south out of Great Barrington and turn right onto Mt Washington Rd, following signs for the Catamount Ski Area. Then follow signs to the falls, taking East St, then West St and finally Bash Bish Falls Rd, deep in the Mt Washington State Forest.

On US 7, less than 5 miles north of Great Barrington center, **Monument Mountain** has two trails to the summit. Writer Nathaniel Hawthorne wrote that Monument's summit resembled 'a headless sphinx wrapped in a Persian shawl.' On August 5, 1850, Hawthorne climbed up Monument Mountain with Oliver Wendell Holmes and Herman Melville. It was the first time Hawthorne and the young Melville met, but they quickly became good friends and kept in touch throughout their lives.

Special Events

The **Aston Magna Festival** (☎ 413-528-3595; tickets about $20) celebrates classical music (especially baroque) every July and August. If you like Bach, Brahms and Buxtehude, buy your tickets well in advance. Concerts are held in the St James Church, on Main St (US 7) at Taconic Ave, near the Town Hall.

The **Berkshire Opera Company** (☎ 413-644-9988; tickets $20-60) stages full-dress productions of classic and modern operas in the restored Mahaiwe theater in Great Barrington and at other venues in the southern Berkshires.

Places to Stay

A good half-hour drive from Lenox and Tanglewood, Great Barrington is nonetheless a popular place for people to stay in the summer. Unless otherwise stated, rates quoted are for Friday and Saturday nights in the high-peak months of July and August (when Tanglewood is in session). Prices for rooms midweek and off-season are substantially lower.

Camping Mostly backpackers rent sites at *Beartown State Forest* (☎ 413-528-0904, *Blue Hill Rd, Monterey*) Sites $7. This campground, 8 miles east of Great Barrington via MA 23, has 12 simple sites that overlook Benedict Pond. RVs have trouble getting up the winding road.

Mt Washington State Forest (☎ 413-528-0330, *East St, Mt Washington*) Tent sites $7. There are 15 wilderness sites for hikers at the village of Mt Washington, which is to the southwest of South Egremont.

Tolland State Forest (☎ 413-269-6002, *MA 8, Otis*) Tent sites $7. Otis is 16 miles east of Great Barrington along MA 23. This campground in deep woods has 90 sites.

Prospect Lake Park (☎ 413-528-4158, *Prospect Lake Rd, North Egremont*) Sites $25. Open May–mid-Oct. There are 140 sites and a snack bar on a lake.

Most of the other campgrounds are in or near Otis, which is near the junction of MA 8 and MA 23.

Laurel Ridge Camping Area (☎ 413-269-4804, *Old Blanford Rd, East Otis*) Sites $22. Laurel Ridge has 140 sites. Here you get large, flat wooded sites, a pool and a rec hall.

Motels Just north of the center of town is the *Lantern House Motel* (☎ 413-528-2350, *254 Stockbridge Rd, US 7*) Rooms Sun-Wed/Thur-Sat $64-72/$87. This motel is the best value. There's a large swimming pool.

Briarcliff Inn (☎ 413-528-3000, *506 Stockbridge Rd*) Rooms $65-125. Positioned on a far more scenic stretch of Route 7 than the motels in town, this one stands directly across from Monument Mountain. Rooms have been renovated and offer air con, TV and king beds.

Days Inn (☎ 413-528-3150, fax 413-528-3150, ⓦ *www.daysinn,com, 372 Main St*) Rooms Mon-Fri/Sat & Sun $89/130. On the southern side of the town center, this conveniently located motel is right behind the chamber of commerce.

Inns & B&Bs There are well over 50 inns and B&Bs within 10 miles of Great Barrington. For links and a full list, log on to ⓦ www.greatbarrington.org.

Littlejohn Manor (☎ 413-528-2882, *1 Newsboy Monument Lane*) Rooms $80-95, with breakfast and afternoon tea. This is a big Victorian house perched above a pond and cornfields. The four guestrooms have shared bath but rates include a full English breakfast.

Manor Lane B&B (☎ 413-528-8222, *145 Hurlburt Rd*) Rooms $125-145. Manor Lane nestles between horse farms, and is a five-minute drive from the center of town. The large house has three spacious rooms, a cozy sitting room with piano and Turkish carpets, and a glassed-in breakfast area. Outside are a pool, tennis courts and trails into the woods.

The Wainwright Inn (☎ 413-528-2062, *518 S Main St*) Rooms with bath $110-150. The Wainwright bills itself as 'a country bed and breakfast,' although it's a short walk from the center of town. The historic 1776 house has eight guestrooms. Rates vary depending on the day of the week.

The Pink House (☎ 413-528-6680, *42 East St*) Rooms $90 with breakfast. This is an apt name for the rosy-colored building with three rooms, located in a quiet residential neighborhood. Owner Barbara Beach has created a charming garden, where guests are served home-cooked breakfast and fresh fruit.

Baldwin Hill Farm B&B (☎ 413-528-4092, *121 Baldwin Hill Rd*) Rooms $89-110 with breakfast. Baldwin Hill Farm is off MA 71 in South Egremont, and has four rooms, a pool and over 400 acres of hilltop land with glorious views of the surrounding mountains.

Race Brook Lodge (☎ 413-229-2916, fax 413-229-6629, ⓦ *www.rblodge.com, 864 S Undermountain Rd/MA 41 Sheffield*) Rooms from $75. This lodge sits at the base of Mt Race. Take the strenuous trail behind the lodge to Race's summit, where the Appalachian Trail leads you on a ridge walk. The 21 guest rooms are in a 200-year-old converted barn.

Sunset Farm B&B (☎ *413-243-3229, fax 413-243-0730,* W *www.sunsetfarminn.com, 74 Tyringham Rd)* Rooms $90-110. If you fall in love with Tyringham, you can spend the night here. Situated on a hillside overlooking one of the first Shaker settlements in the Berkshires, Sunset Farm Inn commands a view of the Tyringham Valley. There are four bedrooms, plus a guest apartment, all complete with hand-sewn quilts and early American Shaker furniture.

The Old Inn on the Green *(413-229-3131, 800-286-3139,* W *www.oldinn.com, MA 57, New Marlborough)* Rooms $175-245. Once a relay stop on the post road from Westfield to Albany, the Old Inn, c. 1760, is exactly what most people picture when they think of a New England country inn. The old inn offers 5 guestrooms upstairs and a restaurant downstairs. The dining rooms are lit entirely by candlelight, and there are fireplaces in each room. Windsor chairs and mahogany tavern tables furnish the dining rooms. In the summer, dinner is served outside on the garden terrace. Rooms have 18th-century furnishings and décor, with private baths.

Places to Eat & Drink

Fare in the restaurants in the town center ranges from Middle Eastern food to sushi to old-time diner eats.

Berkshire Coffee Roasting Company *(☎ 413-528-5505, 286 Main St)* Prices $2-7. Open 8am-5pm. Here's a good place to meet locals in the morning over a cup of joe ($1.25).

The Neighborhood Diner *(☎ 413-528-8226, 282 Main St)* Prices $4-10. This diner is an inexpensive place for breakfast (tasty blueberry pancakes) or sandwiches for lunch.

La Chosa *(☎ 413-528-6390, 284 Main St)* Burritos $4-6. If it's filling Mexican takeout that fits your needs, don't miss this spot, in the same arcade as Helsinki Tea Company. We get fired up for the portobello mushroom asada ($6).

Cheesecake Charlie's *(☎ 413-528-7790, 271 Main St)* Lunch $4-11. As the name suggests, here you'll find 50 varieties of cheesecake as well as an espresso bar. It also offers extremely affordable pastas and sandwiches, starting at $5. Charlie's has an evening cabaret that includes dinner, and shows with themes like 'Broadway' or 'Texas.' The cover runs $5 and up; you can get a show and a meal for $45.

Baba Louie's *(☎ 413-528-8100, 284 Main St)* Prices $4-16. Baba's is known for its wood-fired pizza with organic sourdough crust. A large vegetable pizza costs $11.50.

Helsinki Tea Company *(☎ 413-528-3394, 284 Main St)* Mains $7-20. In the back of the small arcade, this is a good place to plop down on an overstuffed sofa and order a pot of green tea. The eclectic menu features such fare as the Moroccan-style lamb and the Sibelius barbecue, a honey-orange-roasted half-chicken named for Finland's most famous composer. In 2001 Helsinki started a coffee house/bar in the back room, which features nationally known musical acts like Pete Seeger and the John Scofield Project. There's entertainment Thursday to Saturday. The crowd is hip, ranging from carpenters and waitresses to Mia Farrow and James Taylor. Cover runs $5 to $35.

Bizen *(☎ 413-528-4343, 17 Railroad St)* Sushi $8-16. Bizen is a Japanese restaurant featuring a small sushi bar, sashimi and tempura. All meals are served on pottery created by owner Michael Marcus when he spent four years in Japan.

Union Bar & Grill *(☎ 413-528-6228, 293 Main St)* Prices $12-20. This is considered one of the hottest restaurants in the Berkshires, but don't come here expecting an intimate candlelight dinner. Intriguing entrees like portobello lasagna and duck quesadillas are served on aluminum tables against a backdrop of metallic walls. The trendy, yet moderately priced, restaurant is one of the few places open late, so you can venture here after going to Tanglewood.

The Old Mill *(☎ 413-528-1421, 53 Main St, South Egremont)* Mains $15-25. This is a 1797 grist mill and blacksmith's shop, turned into a highly praised restaurant serving American and continental cuisine, such as diver scallops ($22) and smoked salmon ($20).

Castle St Café *(☎ 413-528-5244, 10 Castle St)* Mains average $17. Just off Main St, this cafe features a piano bar. The piano in the back once belonged to Nat King Cole, who owned a summer home in Tyringham. Chef/owner Michael Ballon uses lots of fresh local ingredients, like Hillsdale chèvre cheese and Pittsfield fettuccine, to create his innovative menu.

STOCKBRIDGE

Stockbridge is a picture-perfect New England village, almost too perfect – the way Norman Rockwell might have seen it.

In fact, Rockwell *did* see it: He lived and worked here during the last 25 years of his life. Whether it has always been this beautiful, or whether it has remade itself in Rockwell's image, we will never know. Both the town and the artist attract the summer crowds. They come to stroll its streets, inspect its shops and sit in the rockers on the porch of the grand old Red Lion Inn. And they come (by the busload) to visit the Norman Rockwell Museum on the town's outskirts.

Also of interest in this pretty town are Chesterwood, the country home and studio of sculptor Daniel Chester French; Naumkeag, a lavish early-20th-century 'Berkshire cottage' and the Berkshire Theatre Festival.

Orientation & Information

Stockbridge is 7-mile drive from Great Barrington to the south and Lenox to the north.

Main St in Stockbridge is MA 102. The central district is only a few blocks long.

Volunteers sometimes staff an information kiosk on Main St in the summertime months. For accommodations information, you can get in touch with the Stockbridge Lodging Association (☎ 413-298-5200, Ⓦ www.stockbridgechamber.org, PO Box 224, Stockbridge, MA 01262). It's open 9am to 5pm Monday, Wednesday and Friday.

Norman Rockwell Museum

Norman Rockwell (1894–1978) was born in New York City, and he sold his first magazine cover illustration to the *Saturday Evening Post* in 1916. In the following half

century he did another 321 covers for the *Post,* as well as illustrations for books, posters and many other magazines. His clever, masterful, insightful art made him the best-known and most popular illustrator in US history. His wonderful sense of humor can be seen in his painting *Triple Self Portrait* (1960), where an older Rockwell looks in a mirror, only to paint a much younger version of himself.

The museum *(☎ 413-298-4100, MA 183; adult/child under 10yrs $10/free; open 10am-5pm daily)* has the largest collection of his original art, and contains his studio (moved here from behind his Stockbridge home). Picnic tables are set in a grove near the museum.

To find the museum follow MA 102 west from Stockbridge, turn left (south) on MA 183, and look for the museum on the left side.

Chesterwood

Daniel Chester French (1850–1931) is best known for his statue *The Minute Man* (1875) at the Old North Bridge in Concord, and his great seated statue of Abraham Lincoln in the Lincoln Monument in Washington, DC (1922).

French's work was mostly monumental sculpture. He created more than 100 great public works and became a wealthy man as a result. His home was in New York City, but he spent most summers after 1897 at Chesterwood *(☎ 413-298-3579, 4 Williamsville Rd; family/adult/youth 13-18 yrs/child 6-12 yrs $18/8.50/5/3; open 10am-5pm daily May-Oct),* his gracious Berkshire estate. He continued work on his sculptures here while enjoying the society of the other 'cottage' owners.

The sculptor's house and studio are substantially as they were when he lived and worked here, with nearly 500 pieces of sculpture, finished and unfinished, in the barnlike studio.

The museum is near the village of Glendale, off MA 183, south of the Norman Rockwell Museum. Follow MA 102 west from Stockbridge and turn left onto Glendale Middle Rd, proceed through Glendale to Williamsville Rd and turn left; the museum is on the right.

Naumkeag

This grand Berkshire 'cottage' on Prospect Hill is well worth a visit. It was designed in 1885 by Stanford White for attorney and diplomat Joseph Hodges Choate. Choate was a noted collector of art, so his summer house is filled with Oriental carpets, Chinese porcelain and other luxury goods. The gardens are the result of 30 years of devoted work on the part of prominent landscape architect Fletcher Steele and the Choate family.

You can take a guided tour of the house and gardens (☎ 413-298-3239, 5 Prospect St; adult/child 6-12 yrs $8/2.50, gardens only adult/child $5/free; open 10am-5pm daily, June–mid-Oct). Follow Pine St from the Red Lion Inn to Prospect St.

Mission House

This historic residence (☎ 413-298-3239, 19 Main St; adult/child 6-12 yrs $5/2.50; open 10am-5pm daily late May-early Sept) was the home of the Reverend John Sergeant, the first missionary to the native peoples in this area. He built the original part of the house in 1739. It's furnished with 17th- and 18th-century effects and houses a small museum of Native American artifacts.

Merwin House

This late-Federal-style brick residence (☎ 413-298-4703, 14 Main St; admission $5; open 11am-5pm. Sat & Sun June–mid-Oct) is furnished with an eclectic mix of European and American pieces. There are tours on the hour.

Berkshire Botanical Garden

Two miles from the center of Stockbridge, the 15-acre Berkshire Botanical Garden (☎ 413-298-3926, 5 W Stockbridge Rd/MA 102; adult/senior/child 12yrs and under $5/4/free; open 10am-5pm daily) is within walking distance of the Norman Rockwell Museum. Wildflowers, herbs, perennials, water plants, an alpine forest and rock gardens are yours to enjoy daily.

West Stockbridge

Though not nearly as picturesque as Stockbridge, West Stockbridge still retains its historic charm. Old country stores and the 19th-century train station stand next to new galleries and art studios. This is a great place to stay during Tanglewood season, because Lenox is less than a 15-minute drive away on rarely used backcountry roads.

Places to Stay

There are numerous inns and B&Bs in and around Stockbridge. The following are among the least expensive.

Red Lion Inn (☎ 413-298-5545, fax 298-5130, W www.redlioninn.com, 30 Main St) Rooms with shared bath $77-80, private bath $167-235. This huge 108-room white frame hotel dominates the town center both by its size and activity and is the very heart of Stockbridge. Founded in 1773, it was completely rebuilt after a fire in 1897.

Williamson Guest House (☎ 413-298-4931, 32 Church St) Rooms with shared bath $85-100. This large yellow house on a country road is a mile from the Stockbridge town center; it has four rooms.

Card Lake Inn (☎ 413-232-0272, fax 413-232-0294, W www.cardlakeinn.com, 29 Main St, West Stockbridge) Rooms $110-165 with breakfast. Owned by a young family with twins, this stage coach stop dating from 1805 is a good place for families to stay. There are eleven rooms, and breakfast is hearty.

The Williamsville Inn (☎ 413-274-6118, fax 413-274-3539, W www.williamsvilleinn .com, MA 41, West Stockbridge) Rooms $130-150. This is a 1797 farmhouse 5 miles from the center of West Stockbridge. It is worth the splurge to stay in one of the 16 rooms that reek and creak with history. Thick wood floors, exposed beams, and red brick fireplaces are de rigueur.

Places to Eat

The secret might be the cows that provide **Berkshire Ice Cream** (☎ 413-232-4111, 4 Albany Rd, West Stockbridge) Prices $2-6. This establishment won against big boys Haagen-Dazs and Ben & Jerry's in a taste test sponsored by the Boston Globe. The increasingly popular ice cream, now featured at Tanglewood, is made with pure Golden Guernsey milk from the owner's farm. Try a scoop of the black raspberry.

Elm St Market (☎ 413-298-3654, 4 Elm St) Prices $2.25-5. This little market off Main St also has a deli counter and a few tables. It's a great place to eat in or take out on the cheap. Consider the juicy Rueben sandwich ($5), dripping with Swiss cheese.

Daily Bread Bakery (☎ 413-298-0272, 31 Main St) Prices $4-8. 'On the sunny side of Main St,' this bakery sells cakes, cookies, bread and rolls that are good for snacks or picnics.

Caffe Pomodoro (☎ 413-232-4616, 6 Depot St, West Stockbridge) Prices $4-10. This cafe in the 1838 railroad station right next to the post office is where local artisans lunch on large sandwiches and freshly made soups. Don't miss the tomato and fennel soup (under $4).

Main Street Café (☎ 413-298-3060, 40 Main St) Dishes $5-8. This is a fine place for sandwiches and salads; try the soup and half a roast beef sandwich ($6).

Once Upon a Table (☎ 413-298-3870, 36 Main St) Dinner mains $12-18. In the Mews shopping arcade, this place serves upscale fare such as pan-seared sea bass or sweet potato-filled ravioli, on its glass-enclosed porch.

The Williamsville Inn (☎ 413-274-6118, 286 Great Barrington Rd) Mains $17-23. The inn, on MA 41 in West Stockbridge, is the ideal choice for an intimate candlelit dinner. Book a table in the private Library Room, and while away the hours dining on butterfly pasta served with roasted red peppers, garden peas, garlic and pine nuts.

Red Lion Inn (☎ 413-298-5545, see Places to Stay, earlier in this section) The Red Lion is Stockbridge's premier place for dining. Besides the elegant formal dining room (mains $21-30), there's the **Widow Bingham Tavern**, a rustic colonial pub (mains $9-19). The **Lion's Den**, downstairs, is the cocktail lounge, and has a sandwich and salad menu (prices $3-8). On Friday and Saturday nights they have cool jazz and folk music. In fair weather you can dine in the courtyard out

back. We go for the Nantucket fish stew ($15) in the tavern.

Entertainment
Theater comes in stages at **Berkshire Theatre Festival** (☎ 413-298-5576, PO Box 797, Stockbridge, MA 01262-0797). During this festival, running from late June through early September, new and innovative plays are staged at the Mainstage and smaller Unicorn Theatre. Tickets $18-31. There's a Children's Theatre ($5) as well. Call or write for current offerings.

LEE
Lee, incorporated in 1777, is a historic town, like many of its neighbors. Though there is nothing wrong with Lee, most people go barreling through it, forgetting that they're no longer on the turnpike.

Lee is 134 miles from Boston, just off Exit 2 of I-90. Great Barrington and Lenox are less than a 10-minute drive away except on busy summer weekends, when the traffic on US 7 can be maddening.

Orientation & Information
The town of Lee, at I-90 exit 2, is the gateway to Lenox, Stockbridge and Great Barrington. US 20 is Lee's main street, and leads to Lenox.

The Lee Chamber of Commerce (☎ 413-243-0852, W www.leelodging.org, PO Box 345, Lee, MA 01238-0345) maintains an information booth on the town green in front of the town hall in summer. The chamber of commerce is open 10am to 4pm Tuesday to Saturday.

Jacob's Pillow Dance Festival
Founded by Ted Shawn in an old barn in 1932, Jacob's Pillow (☎ 413-243-0745, fax 243-4744, PO Box 287, Lee, MA 01238-0287; $18 to $55; performances mid-June–early Sept) has developed into one of premier summer dance festivals in the USA. Through the years, Alvin Ailey, Merce Cunningham, the Martha Graham Dance Company, the Bill T Jones/Arnie Zane Dance Company and other leading interpreters of the dance have taken part.

The festival theaters are in the village of Becket, 7 miles east of Lee along US 20 and MA 8.

October Mountain State Forest

Most out-of-towners who venture to the Berkshires head to the Mt Greylock State Reservation (see the Williamstown section, later in this chapter) to see the state's highest peak, and thus leave October Mountain State Forest, a 16,500-acre state park (☎ 413-243-1778) and the largest tract of green space in Massachusetts, to the locals. Canoe Buckley Dunton Reservoir, a small body of water stocked with bass and pickerel and hidden amid the hardwoods. For hikers, a 9-mile stretch of the Appalachian Trail pierces the heart of the forest through copses of hemlocks, spruces, birches and oaks. To get there from Lee, follow Route 20 West for 3 miles and look for signs.

Places to Stay

For a comprehensive list of area accommodations visit Ⓦ www.leelodging.org online.

October Mountain State Forest (☎ 877-422-6762, Center St) Sites $7. This state forest campground, near the shores of the Housatonic River, is for campers only and has 45 sites, with hot showers. To find the campground, turn east off US 20 onto Center St and follow the signs.

Appalachian Mountain Club (☎ 413-499-4262, on the Appalachian Trail 2 miles south of MA 20) Bunk bed $3. This is a primitive cabin on the shores of scenic Upper Goose Pond run by the Berkshire chapter of the Appalachian Mountain Club. To get there, follow MA 20 West from Lee for 2 miles until you see signs for the Appalachian Trail. Park the car and continue on foot 2 miles south along the AT. This cabin in the woods has bunks for eight campers; first come, first served.

Motels in Lee are clustered around I-90 exit 2, on heavily trafficked Route 7. They include the following, for which prices range from $65 to $145: *Super 8 Motel (☎ 413-243-0143)*, *Sunset Motel (☎ 413-243-0302)* and *Pilgrim Motel (☎ 413-243-1328)*.

Places to Eat

Lee offers a clear choice of lifestyles at breakfast.

Juice and Java (☎ 413-243-3131, 60 Main St) Prices $1-6. Head to this place to stock up on sandwiches, such as grilled eggplant ($4), and beverages before heading out to hike in October Mountain State Forest.

Joe's Diner (☎ 413-243-9756, 63 Center St) Prices $3-10. Open 24 hours. There's no better slice of Americana in the Berkshires than Joe's Diner. Norman Rockwell's famous painting of a policeman sitting at a counter talking to a young boy, *The Runaway* (1958), was inspired by this diner. Every politician who's ever run for office in Massachusetts, including US Senator Ted Kennedy, has stopped at Joe's to get his or her picture taken and put on the wall. Pancakes or an omelette runs $3.50.

LENOX

Originally named Yokuntown after a local Native American leader, Lenox took its current name in honor of Charles Lenox, Duke of Richmond, who had been sympathetic to the American Revolution.

This gracious, wealthy town is an historical anomaly: Its charm was not destroyed by the Industrial Revolution, and then, prized for its bucolic peace, the town became a summer retreat for wealthy families (like Andrew Carnegie's) who had made their fortunes by building factories in other towns.

Today, Lenox is home to the Tanglewood Music Festival, an incredibly popular summer event since its inception in 1934.

Orientation & Information

It's easy to get around Lenox on foot, though some of its many inns are a mile or two from the center. Tanglewood is 1½ miles west of Lenox's center along West St/ MA 183.

The Lenox Chamber of Commerce (☎ 413-637-3646, Ⓦ www.lenox.org, in the landmark Curtis building on Main St at Walker St, PO Box 646, Lenox, MA 01240) is the local source of information, open Tuesday to Saturday 10am to 6pm, Sunday 10am to 2pm.

MASSACHUSETTS

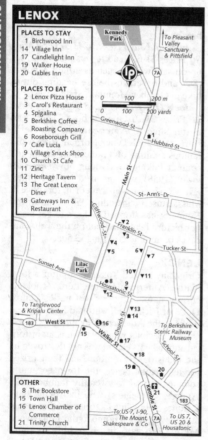

LENOX

PLACES TO STAY
1 Birchwood Inn
14 Village Inn
17 Candlelight Inn
19 Walker House
20 Gables Inn

PLACES TO EAT
2 Lenox Pizza House
3 Carol's Restaurant
4 Spigalina
5 Berkshire Coffee
  Roasting Company
6 Roseborough Grill
7 Cafe Lucia
9 Village Snack Shop
10 Church St Cafe
11 Zinc
12 Heritage Tavern
13 The Great Lenox
  Diner
18 Gateways Inn &
  Restaurant

OTHER
8 The Bookstore
15 Town Hall
16 Lenox Chamber of
  Commerce
21 Trinity Church

Simply called the Bookstore (☎ 413-637-3390, 9 Housatonic St), this shop is the place to stop for that map, atlas or summer novel you need.

Berkshire Scenic Railway Museum

This museum (☎ 413-637-2210, Willow Creek Rd; admission free; 10am-4pm Sat-Sun May-Oct), 1½ miles east of Lenox center, is a nonprofit museum of railroad lore set up in Lenox's 1902-vintage railroad station.

The museum's two elaborate model railroad displays are favorites with children, as is the short train ride in a full-size train on the museum grounds (adult/child $3/2).

The Mount

Almost 50 years after Nathaniel Hawthorne left his home in Lenox (now part of the Tanglewood estate), another writer found inspiration in the Berkshires. Edith Wharton (1862–1937) came to Lenox in 1899 and proceeded to build her palatial estate, the Mount. Wharton summered at the Mount for a decade before moving permanently to France. When not writing, she would entertain friends such as Henry James.

The dramatic conclusion of *Ethan Frome* (1911) was based on an actual sleigh ride accident on Courthouse Hill in Lenox.

You can tour the Mount (☎ 413-637-1899, 2 Plunkett St; adult/senior/child 13-18 yrs $7.50/6/5; open 9am-4pm daily), which is on the outskirts of Lenox at US 7.

Pleasant Valley Sanctuary

This 1112-acre wildlife sanctuary (☎ 413-637-0320, 472 W Mountain Rd; admission free; open sunrise-sunset) has several pleasant walking trails through forests of maples, oaks, beeches and birches. It's not uncommon to see beavers here if you come at dawn or dusk. To reach the sanctuary, go north on US 7 or MA 7A. Three-quarters of a mile north of the intersection of US 7 and MA 7A, turn left onto W Dugway Rd and go 1½ miles to the sanctuary.

Tanglewood Music Festival

In 1934, Boston Symphony Orchestra conductor Serge Koussevitzky's dream of a center for serious musical study came true with the acquisition of the 400-acre Tanglewood Estate (☎ 413-637-1600, 297 West St) in Lenox. Young musicians – including Leonard Bernstein and Seiji Ozawa – came to Tanglewood to study at the side of the great masters. Along with the lessons came musical performances: concerts by masters and students together.

Today, the Tanglewood Music Festival is among the most esteemed music events in the world. Symphony, pops, chamber music, recitals, jazz and blues are performed from late June through early September. Performance spaces include the coyly named 'Shed,' a simple 6000-seat concert shelter with several sides open to the surrounding lawns. The newest space is the Seiji Ozawa Concert Hall. Electronic amplification systems boost the volume for those seated on the lawn, making the music easier to hear, but less worth hearing.

The Boston Symphony Orchestra concerts on Friday, Saturday and Sunday in July and August are the most popular events at Tanglewood. Most casual (as opposed to devoted) attendees – up to 8000 of them on a typical summer weekend evening – arrive three or four hours before concert time. They stake out good listening spots on the lawn outside the Shed or the Concert Hall, then relax and enjoy elaborate picnic suppers until the music starts. The event is for everyone, including young families, many of whom come with their babies in tow.

Contemporary star performers include Midori, Itzhak Perlman, Anne-Sophie Mutter, Yo-Yo Ma and Andre Watts. Popular performers such as Frank Sinatra, James Taylor, Wynton Marsalis (in jazz mode), the Manhattan Transfer, Joshua Redman Quartet and Ray Charles have given Tanglewood concerts.

Tickets Tickets range from $14 per person for picnic space on the lawn to $88 for the best seats at the most popular concerts. If you pay for general admission to the lawn and it rains during the concert, you get wet. (Sorry, no refunds or exchanges.)

For information, call ☎ 617-266-1492 in Boston; ☎ 413-637-1600 in Lenox. Tickets may be purchased at the box office at Tanglewood's main entrance, online (W www.bso .org) or through Ticketmaster, which can be reached at ☎ 617-931-2000 in Boston; ☎ 413-733-2500 in the Berkshires; ☎ 212-307-7171 in New York City; and ☎ 800-347-0808 from other areas.

If you arrive two or three hours before concert time, you can often get lawn space; Shed and Concert Hall seats should be bought in advance.

Parking Ample concert parking is available. Keep in mind that parking – and, more importantly, *unparking* – 6000 cars can take time. It's all organized very well and runs smoothly, but you will still have to wait a while in your car during the exodus.

Organized Tours You can take a walking tour of the Tanglewood grounds on Wednesday at 10:30am or Saturday at 1:15pm, starting from the visitor center.

Several tour companies operate special Tanglewood concert buses that take you directly to the concert, then back home. In Boston, call **K&L Tours** (☎ 617-267-1905); in New York City, call **Biss Tours** (☎ 718-426-4000) for information.

Shakespeare & Company

Among the most enjoyable cultural events of a Lenox summer are the performances of the Bard's great plays by Shakespeare & Co (☎ 413-637-1199, fax 637-4274; tickets $12.50-35; plays Tues-Sun). The company is currently building a replica of the Elizabethan Rose Theater for their productions.

Activities

Kennedy Park in downtown Lenox is popular with mountain bikers in the summer and cross-country skiers in the winter. The **Arcadian** (☎ 413-637-3010, 91 Pittsfield Rd/ US 7) rents mountain, road, and children's bikes ($25), and cross-country skies and snowshoes ($11). They also rent tents ($15) and sleeping bags ($15).

Places to Stay

Lenox has no hotels and only a few motels. The *Super 8* (☎ 413-637-3560) and *Quality Inn* (☎ 413-637-4244) stand on US 7 outside the village to the east. Expect to pay $85 and up.

However, there are lots of inns. Because of Tanglewood's weekend concerts, many inns require a two- or three-night minimum stay on Friday and Saturday nights in summer. That means a Lenox weekend can cost $280 to $500 just for lodging. Faced with such prices, thrifty travelers opt to sleep in lower-priced communities such as

Great Barrington. But if you can afford them, Lenox's inns provide charming digs and memorable stays. Log on to W www .lenox.org for a list and links.

Most inn rooms have a private bath, and include a full breakfast and perhaps afternoon tea. Prices are always quoted per double room. Very few Lenox inns accept children under 10 or 12, or pets.

Candlelight Inn (☎ 413-637-1555, 35 Walker St) Doubles $69-189. This inn is well known for its candlelit restaurant. The guestrooms are simple but comfy and convenient to the village.

The Birchwood Inn (☎ 413-637-2600, 800-524-1646, fax 413-637-4604, 7 Hubbard St) Doubles $75-175. The mansard-roofed house, dating from 1767, is now a quite gracious, 12-room inn, enjoying fine views of the town.

Walker House (☎ 413-637-1271, fax 413-637-2387, 74 Walker St) Rooms $90-200. This inn, which looks relatively modest from the front, is convenient to everything in the town center. Behind the classic façade are the friendliest innkeepers in town and three acres of gardens. The eight rooms have private bath.

The Gables Inn (☎ 413-637-3416, 103 Walker St) Doubles $90-250. The Gables was originally known as Pine Acre. Built in 1885, the Queen Anne–style 'cottage' was the summer home of Mrs William C Wharton, whose son Teddy married Edith Newbold Jones (see the Mount, above). The house has been nicely restored, and now rents its 17 rooms.

The Village Inn (☎ 413-637-0020, fax 413-637-9756, 16 Church St) Doubles with bath $135-500. The Federal-style Village Inn was built in 1771 and has 32 rooms, a dining room serving breakfast, afternoon tea and dinner, and a tavern featuring English ales, draft beer and light meals.

Blantyre (☎ 413-637-3556, fax 413-637-4282, Blantyre Rd) Rooms $315-850. If money is no object, then this is the place for you. It is 3 miles west of I-90 exit 2 along US 20. An imitation Scottish Tudor mansion built in 1902, Blantyre sits on 85 acres of grounds equipped with four tennis courts,

croquet lawns, a swimming pool, hot tub and sauna. Accommodations are available in 23 rooms, suites and cottages; continental breakfast is included.

Kripalu Center (☎ 413-448-3400, fax 413-448-3384, W www.kripalu.org, MA 183) Dorm beds from $86-113, including meals and workshops. Shadowbrook, the former summer home of Andrew Carnegie, is now one of America's finest yoga centers. The center's spectacular 300-acre grounds, within walking distance of Tanglewood, overlook Stockbridge Bowl (a small lake). Kripalu accommodates some 300 students, who come to study yoga and meditation in peaceful surroundings. Check out the popular program, 'Retreat & Renewal,' online.

Places to Eat & Drink

This little village is rife with eateries, serving lunch and dinner (unless noted).

Village Snack Shop (☎ 413-637-2564, 35 Housatonic St) Prices $3-7. Open for breakfast & lunch. At this classic diner at Church St, you can sit with the locals at the counter, inhale some coffee and keep your travel budget intact. Omelettes start at $4.

The Berkshire Coffee Roasting Company (☎ 413-637-1606, 52 Main St) Prices $3-8. This is where locals linger over steaming bowls of café au lait.

Carol's Restaurant (☎ 413-637-8948, 8 Franklin St) Breakfast & lunch $4-8. Open at 8am. You've gotta love the cinderblock walls, florescent lights and Carol's effusive personality (get her started on 'healing stones'). Actress Julia Roberts does; she's a breakfast (served all day) patron here when she's in town. We like to create our own omelettes ($4.50 plus 75¢ for each add-in).

Heritage Tavern (☎ 413-638-0884, Housatonic St) Pub food $4-8. If you're looking for the saloon in town, this is it. Unlike most of trim Lenox, the Heritage has a natural shagginess about both the interior and exterior of its 1860s-era building. The last remodeling (adding ersatz wood paneling and beer signs) probably occurred in the 1970s. But, dude, a bottle of domestic beer costs just $1.25, and there's Guinness on tap. Chicken wings and jalapeño poppers run under $5.

Many of the area youth, including counselors from the surrounding camps who are imports from Australia, New Zealand and Germany, make the Heritage their clubhouse on summer evenings. Come for the scene, pool table, cheap, strong drinks and the Thursday night DJ, who plays rock and dance tunes. Actor Woody Harrelson has been known to show up for the Guinness.

Lenox Pizza House(☎ *413-637-2590, 7 Franklin St)* Large pie $6-17. This pizzeria serves pan pizza (whole pie or by the slice), grinders, Greek salads and pasta.

The Great Lenox Diner (☎ *413-637-3204, 30 Church St)* Dishes $7-10. This is your best bet for a cheap dinner in town. The diner serves typical diner fare such as meat loaf, Yankee pot roast and rotisserie chicken.

Church Street Cafe (☎ *413-637-2745, 69 Church St)* Lunch under $10, dinner $18-26. This cafe has made customers happy for years with its reasonably priced lunches and inventive dinners, served in a large festive dining room and on the deck. Consider the Maine crab cakes ($23).

Spigalina (☎ *413-637-4455, 80 Main St)* Prices $15-23. This is one restaurant in town that local inn owners rave about. Tantalizing pasta, fish and meat dishes are served in a room where dim lighting and yellow walls create a Mediterranean ambiance. Don't miss the *zuppa di pesce* ($19), with five different kinds of crustacean and calamari.

Zinc (☎ *413-637-8800, 56 Church St)* Mains $17-21. Very, very hip. The postmodern décor here is all metal surfaces, light woods and gleaming curves, with doors made of French wine crates. The tin ceiling, parquet floors and Aretha Franklin singing 'Forever' add to the LA feel of this place. The cuisine features tempting New American offerings like pan-seared halibut with olive tapenade ($20).

Roseborough Grill (☎ *413-637-2700, 83 Church St)* Mains $18-24. Just down from the Church Street Cafe, this is a converted house with tables set out on the front porch. The emphasis here is on fresh local produce, home-baked goods and grilled meats, poultry, fish and vegetables. We like the blackened, sesame seed–encrusted salmon ($19).

Cafe Lucia (☎ *413-637-2640, 90 Church St)* Prices $18-24. This cafe serves classic, though somewhat pricey, Italian dinners. The linguini with littleneck clams runs $22.

A number of inns in Lenox serve elegant dinners. Here are two tried and true:

The *Candlelight Inn* has four dining rooms, with meals running $17 to $25, decorated in early-20th-century style (see Places to Stay, above, for location). Come for dinner (you can sit outside in good weather) or to get after-performance drinks and desserts. Consider the pecan and tarragon chicken breast ($18).

Gateways Inn & Restaurant (☎ *413-637-2532, 51 Walker St)* Mains $17-27. This was the mansion of Harley T Procter (of Procter & Gamble). He supposedly wanted the house to look like a bar of Ivory Soap (not even close). Its elegant dining room is known as the place to go in town for an anniversary or birthday dinner. The fettuccine with lobster meat is the chef's signature dish.

Getting There & Away

The nearest airports are in Windsor Locks and in Albany. Peter Pan Bus Lines (☎ 800-343-9999) operates between Lenox and Boston. See the Tanglewood Music Festival, earlier in this section, for organized tours information.

Trains stop in nearby Pittsfield (see Pittsfield, later in this chapter, for details).

If you're driving, Lenox is 15 miles north of Lee and I-90 on US 7.

PITTSFIELD

Pittsfield is the service city of the Berkshires and the least attractive part of the region. This is where the trains stop and where one finds the biggest stores. For travelers, there are two or three first-rate historical attractions worth a stop.

The tourist information booth in Park Square is open daily in summer. The Berkshire Visitors Bureau (☎ 413-443-9186, 800-237-5747, Ⓦ www.berkshires.org), inside the Berkshire Common building by the Crowne Plaza Hotel, is open 8:30am to 5pm Monday to Friday.

Park Square, at the intersection of North, South, East and West Sts, is the center of Pittsfield. North and South Sts are also US 7.

Hancock Shaker Village

The Shakers were among the earliest of the numerous millennial Christian sects that flourished in the fertile climate of religious freedom in the New World. Hancock Shaker Village, 5 miles west of Pittsfield on US 20, gives you a studied look at the peaceful, prayerful Shaker way of life.

Twenty of the original buildings at Hancock Shaker Village are carefully restored and are open to view. Most famous is the Round Stone Barn (1826), but other structures, including the Brick Dwelling (1830), the laundry and the machine shop (1790), the trustees' office (1830–1895), the meetinghouse (1793) and the sisters' and brethren's shops (1795) are of equal interest.

The Hancock Shaker Village (☎ 413-443-0188, US 20; family/adult/child 6-17 yrs $33/13.50/5.50; open 9:30am-5pm daily May-Oct) lies southwest of Pittsfield center near the intersection with MA 41 (not in the village of Hancock). The village was known as the City of Peace and occupied by Shakers until 1960. At its peak, in 1830, the community numbered some 300 souls. Preserved as a historic monument, the village still gives you a good look at what the work-focused principles of Shakerism could accomplish.

Interpreters in the historic buildings demonstrate the quiet, kindly, hard-working Shaker way of life; there are guided tours at 10am and 3pm in April and November. On Saturday evening, you can feast on a bountiful Shaker candlelit dinner while being entertained by Shaker music. Call for details and reservations.

Shakes of Ecstasy

The United Society of Believers in Christ's Second Appearing, or the Millennial Church, popularly known as the Shakers, an offshoot of Quakerism, began in 1747 in England. Followers of the sect believed in, and strictly observed the principles of, communal possessions, pacifism, open confession of sins and equality – but celibacy – between the sexes.

Shakers believed that God had both a male and a female nature. Ann Lee, an ardent follower of the sect, proclaimed that she had been blessed with the 'mother element' of the spirit of Jesus. Calling herself Mother Ann, she pressed her claim so zealously that she was imprisoned.

On her release, she set sail with a handful of followers for New York. The group founded the first Shaker community in the New World, near Albany, in 1774.

Mother Ann died in 1784, but her followers went on to found Shaker communities in northern New England. In addition to Hancock, there are surviving Shaker communities at Canterbury, NH (near Concord), and Sabbathday Lake, ME (north of Portland).

With celibacy as a tenet, Shakerism depended upon conversion for its growth and sustenance. Converts to the church turned over all their worldly possessions to the movement and worked selflessly on its behalf, although members were free to leave at any time. Shaker worship services were characterized by a communal dancelike movement, during which some congregants would be overcome with religious zeal and suffer tremors ('shakes') of ecstasy.

Each community was organized into 'families' of 30 to 90 members, who lived and worked together. Though there was equality of the sexes, there was also a good deal of segregation. Communities were largely self-sufficient, trading produce and handicrafts with the rest of the world for the things they could not produce themselves. Work, among Shakers, was considered a consecrated act, an attitude reflected in the high quality of workmanship and design of Shaker furniture and crafts. In effect, every product was a prayer.

Berkshire Museum

Pittsfield's major repository of art, history and natural science is the Berkshire Museum (☎ 413-443-7171, 39 South St/US 7 just south of Park Square; adult/senior, student/child 12-18 yrs/child under 12 yrs $6/5/4/free; open 10am-5pm Mon-Sat, noon-5pm Sun). The museum's painting collection holds the works of 19th-century masters such as Bierstadt, Church, Copley, Inness and Peale. The history collections are strong in regional artifacts, tools, firearms, dolls and costumes. The natural science section highlights the ecology, flora and fauna of the Berkshires and has a rock and mineral collection numbering over 3000 pieces.

Melville's Arrowhead

Novelist Herman Melville (1819–1891) lived in Pittsfield from 1850 to 1863. Melville moved to Pittsfield to work on a farm so he could support himself while he wrote. It was here, in the house he called Arrowhead (☎ 413-442-1793, 780 Holmes Rd; adult/senior/child 6-16 yrs $6/4/2; open 9:30am-5pm daily), that he wrote his masterwork, Moby Dick.

Inspired by the view of Mt Greylock in winter, which supposedly reminded him of a whale, Melville completed the 600-plus pages of Moby Dick in less than a year. The house is now a museum maintained by the Berkshire County Historical Society and is open for visits and guided tours (last tour begins at 4pm).

Places to Stay & Eat

Pittsfield has the usual selection of business-oriented hotels and motels for a city of its size. Most visitors prefer to stay in one of the more hip or historical communities such as Lenox, Great Barrington or Williamstown.

If you plan to stop, there are plenty of places to pick up a quick meal on North and South Sts/US 7 as you pass through or around Park Square.

Elizabeth's (☎ 413-448-8244, 1264 East St) Dishes $9-15. Don't be put off by the locale of this nondescript pink building across the street from a vacant General

Electric plant. Chefs travel from New York and Boston to sample Tom and Elizabeth Ellis' innovative pasta dishes.

Start with the insalata mista, a house salad overflowing with crisp greens, veggies, fruits and cheeses. Then choose the pasta of the day, often something as imaginative as linguine with clam sauce infused with Thai spices (lemongrass and ginger).

Getting There & Away

The nearest airports are in Windsor Locks and in Albany. For airport transportation, contact Peter Pan Bus Lines.

The Pittsfield Bus Terminal (☎ 413-442-4451) is at 57 S Church St. Peter Pan Bus Lines (☎ 800-343-9999) operates routes connecting Pittsfield with Albany, Bennington, Boston, Hartford, Lee, Lenox, North Adams, Springfield, Toronto, Williamstown and Worcester. Its many other destinations include Amherst, Hyannis, New Haven and New York City.

Bonanza Bus Lines (☎ 800-556-3815) runs daily buses between New York City and Bennington through Great Barrington, Stockbridge, Lee, Lenox, Pittsfield (with connecting service to Albany) and Williamstown. The ride between New York City and Pittsfield takes about four hours.

For Amtrak information, see the Train section in the Getting There & Around section at the beginning of this chapter.

Pittsfield is 7 miles north of Lenox on US 7.

WILLIAMSTOWN

After all the domestic architectural extravagances of the southern and central Berkshires, Williamstown comes as something of a surprise. The big buildings here are not palatial mansions, but marble-faced college halls. The northwestern corner of Massachusetts, though far from university-strewn Boston or the college-crowded Pioneer Valley, has its own prestigious institution of higher learning, Williams College. Bennington College is only 30 minutes north, in Vermont, making this area of the Berkshires an academic enclave with quite possibly the best summer theater in America.

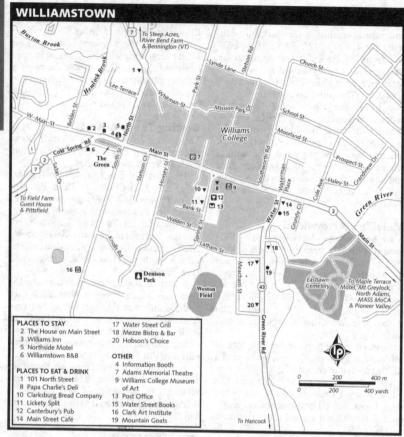

WILLIAMSTOWN

PLACES TO STAY
2 The House on Main Street
3 Williams Inn
5 Northside Motel
6 Williamstown B&B

PLACES TO EAT & DRINK
1 101 North Street
8 Papa Charlie's Deli
10 Clarksburg Bread Company
11 Lickety Split
12 Canterbury's Pub
14 Main Street Café

17 Water Street Grill
18 Mezze Bistro & Bar
20 Hobson's Choice

OTHER
4 Information Booth
7 Adams Memorial Theatre
9 Williams College Museum
    of Art
13 Post Office
15 Water Street Books
16 Clark Art Institute
19 Mountain Goats

History

Ephraim Williams Jr, born in 1714, was a soldier in the British colonial army. He worked at surveying this area until he was given command of the line of British frontier forts facing the French North American territories. Fort Massachusetts, in North Adams, was one of these forts. Six miles to the west was the town of West Hoosuck.

In 1755, Williams led a column of Massachusetts troops toward Lake George and the French positions there. He died in the fighting. His will provided a substantial amount of money for the founding of a college in West Hoosuck if the town would rename itself after him. Luckily for future Hoosuckers, it did. Williams College, in Williamstown, enrolled its first students in 1793. The college is the lifeblood of the town.

Orientation & Information

US 7 and MA 2/Main St intersect on the western side of town. The small central commercial district is off Main St on Spring St. Other businesses, including motels, are on US 7 and MA 2 on the outskirts of town. The marble-and-brick buildings of Williams College fill the town center.

In the summer, the Williamstown Board of Trade (☎ 413-458-9077, PO Box 357, Williamstown, MA 01267) operates a self-service information booth at the intersection of MA 2 and US 7, a short distance from the Williams Inn.

For information about Williams College, contact the Office of Public Information (☎ 413-597-3131, Williams College, PO Box 676, Williamstown, MA 01267).

The Northern Berkshire Chamber of Commerce (☎ 413-663-3735, W www.nberk shirechamber.com, in the Windsor Mill, Union St/MA 2, North Adams, MA 01247) is another information source. It's open 9am to 5pm Monday to Friday.

Water Street Books (☎ 413-458-0249, 26 Water St) is the Williams college bookstore, with a friendly staff that knows both books and the area.

Clark Art Institute

The Sterling and Francine Clark Art Institute (☎ 413-458-9545, 225 South St; admission permanent collection/summer exhibit $5/10, permanent collection free Tues; open 10am-5pm Tues-Sun) is a gem among US art museums.

Robert Sterling Clark (1877–1956), a Yale engineer whose family had made money in the sewing machine industry, began collecting art in Paris in 1912. He and his French wife, Francine, eventually housed their wonderful collection in Williamstown, in a white marble temple built expressly for the purpose. The Clarks' collections are particularly strong in the impressionists, their academic contemporaries in France and the mid-century Barbizon artists, including Jean-François Millet, Constant Troyon and Camille Corot. Mary Cassatt, Winslow Homer, Frederic Remington and John Singer Sargent represent contemporary American painting. From earlier centuries, there are excellent works by Piero della Francesca, Hans Memling, Jan Gossaert, Jacob van Ruisdael, Jean-Honoré Fragonard, Thomas Gainsborough, Joseph Mallord William Turner and Francisco de Goya. There are some sculptures, including Degas' famous Little Dancer of Fourteen

Years, as well as prints, drawings and noteworthy collections of silver and porcelain.

Even if you are not an avid art lover, you should not miss this museum. It is less than a mile south of the information booth at the intersection of US 7 and MA 2.

Williams College Museum of Art

The Clark Art Institute's sister museum in Williamstown is the Williams College Museum of Art (☎ 413-597-2429, Main St between Water St & Spring St; admission free; open 10am-5pm Mon-Sat, 1pm-5pm Sun). This is in Lawrence Hall, the Greek Revival building backed by a big modern addition. The museum hosts traveling exhibits and stages its own with works from community and regional artists. Call for current offerings.

Massachusetts Museum of Contemporary Art

The MASS MoCA (☎ 413-662-2111; 87 Marshall St, North Adams; admission adult/child $8/3; open 10am-6pm daily) is no ordinary gallery. It's housed in the former Sprague Electric Company factory; more than $31 million was spent to modernize 'the largest gallery in the United States.' The museum includes 220,000 sq feet of space in five buildings, with 19 galleries, art construction areas and performance centers. The spaces are huge, large enough to exhibit Robert Rauschenberg's immense The 1/4 Mile or 2 Furlong Piece, which was exhibited at the museum's opening in 1999. The museum has become a venue for a regular series of concerts and entertainment and has attracted Williamstown's popular restaurant Mezze (see Places to Eat, below) to open a bistro here.

Mt Greylock State Reservation

Mt Greylock (3491 feet) is Massachusetts' highest peak. It sits in an 18-sq-mile forest reservation of fir, beech, birch, maple, oak and spruce that also includes Mt Prospect, Mt Fitch, Mt Williams and Saddle Ball Mountain.

Wildlife in the reservation includes bears, bobcats, deer, porcupines, raccoons and birds such as hawks, grouse, thrushes, ravens and wild turkeys.

The **Hopper** is a stunning V-shaped wedge of trees that fills a valley between Mts Greylock, Williams and Prospect and Stoney Ledge. Its forests have some old-growth trees (more than 150 years old).

There's an access road to the summit that begins in North Adams, 6 miles east of Williamstown along MA 2. Several miles up the road, as you reach the summit, you'll see the 92-foot-high **War Veterans Memorial Tower** (1932).

Bascom Lodge (☎ *413-743-1591, fax 413-743-0622, 1 Summit Rd*) Bunks $36, private room $98. This is a mountain hostelry built as a federal work project in the 1930s at the summit of Mt Greylock. Bascom Lodge is administered by Nature's Classroom; it can provide beds for 32 people from mid-May to mid-October. Reservations are essential.

The Mt Greylock State Reservation (☎ 413-499-4262) has some 45 miles of hiking trails, including a portion of the Appalachian Trail. Several state parks have campsites (see Camping in the Places to Stay section, below).

Bicycling & Hiking

Williamstown and environs, with its rolling farmland and quiet country roads, are excellent for biking. Route 43, along the Green River, is one of the prettier roads. **Mountain Goats** (☎ *413-458-8445, 130 Water St; bikes $20*) has cycles as well as hiking, camping and fly fishing gear. They also sponsor free weekly hikes.

Special Events

From the third week in June to the third week in August, the *Williamstown Theatre Festival* (☎ *413-597-3399, tickets 597-3400, PO Box 517, Williamstown, MA 01267*) mounts the region's major theatrical offerings, and tickets are usually inexpensive. This is one of the most renowned stages in the country for summer-stock theater. Kevin Kline, Richard Dreyfuss and Gwyneth Paltrow are but a few of the well-known thespians who have performed here. The main works are presented in the 500-seat

Adams Memorial Theatre on Main St. Plays in the 96-seat Other Stage are new and experimental. There are also cabaret performances in area restaurants. On Sundays, the Clark Art Institute is the scene for special dramatic events.

Places to Stay

Camping It's possible to camp in a number of places at *Mt Greylock State Reservation* (☎ *413-499-4262, 877-422-6762*) Sites $6. The 35 campsites near scenic Stoney Ledge should be your first choice.

If you follow MA 8 north from North Adams, you'll pass *Natural Bridge State Park* (☎ *413-663-6392*), a day-use area for picnicking; a bit farther along is *Clarksburg State Park* (☎ *413-664-8345, 877-422-6762, Middle Rd*) Sites $12. There are 47 campsites here and pit toilets, but no showers. This place is a bit farther along MA 8 after Natural Bridge State Park.

Savoy Mountain State Forest (☎ *413-663-8469, Central Shaft Rd*) Sites $12. This wooded campground has 45 sites, some of which may be reserved in advance. There are showers and flush toilets. This is one of the top state parks for mountain biking.

Motels & Hotels You'll find a score of hotels and motels on the outskirts of town on MA 2 East US 7 North. Here are a few that distinguish themselves with location and/or service.

Northside Motel (☎ *413-458-8107, 45 North St*) Rooms $70-90. This motel is very near the information booth, the museums and the center of town. It has 33 rooms and a small pool.

Maple Terrace Motel (☎ *413-458-9677, W www.mapleterrace.com, 555 Main St*) Rooms $73-98 with light breakfast. A small, 15-room place on the outskirts to the east of town, the Maple Terrace is a big old house with motel units behind it. There's a secluded heated pool. All guest rooms are nonsmoking.

Williams Inn (☎ *413-458-9371, fax 413-458-9371, W www.williamsinn.com, 1090 Main St*) Rooms $120-200. On the green, the inn is Williamstown's major hotel, with a restaurant and indoor pool. Its 100 rooms have luxury-hotel comforts.

Inns & B&Bs Most of these have a two-night minimum on Friday and Saturday nights and some require a three-night stay on holidays and during special college events. Breakfast is included in the rates.

Steep Acres (☎ 413-458-3774, Ⓦ www.steepacres.com, 520 White Oaks Rd) Rooms $55-150. The gregarious Gangemi family welcome travelers to their 30-acre hilltop farm just two miles north of Williamstown. From here you get spectacular views of both the Berkshires and the Green Mountains of Vermont. Furnishings and décor feature a 'country' motif (simple elegance), and all rooms have a private bath. We love the trout and swimming pond (complete with beach toys) for picnics and kicking back.

River Bend Farm (☎ 413-458-3121, 643 Simmons Rd) Rooms $90. Four doubles share two baths here. This one, just off US 7 on the north side of the little bridge over the Hoosic River, is a favorite among European travelers. A Georgian tavern since revolutionary times, River Bend owes its carefully and authentic restoration to hosts Judy and Dave Looms.

The House on Main Street (☎ 413-458-3031, fax 413-458-2254, Ⓦ www.houseonmainstreet.com, 1120 Main St) Rooms $90-110. Timothy and Donna Hamilton run this Victorian near the center of town that was once owned by the daughter of President Woodrow Wilson. There are six rooms (three with private baths).

Williamstown B&B (☎ 413-458-9202, fax 413-458-9331, Ⓦ www.williamstownbandb.com, 30 Cold Spring Rd) Rooms with bath $85-110. Friendly Kim Rozell runs this Victorian B&B with three rooms in the center of town, just off the green.

Field Farm Guest House (☎ 413-458-3135, Ⓦ www.thetrustees.org, 554 Sloan Rd) Rooms with bath $145-165. This was the country estate of Lawrence and Eleanore Bloedel, collectors of 20th-century art. Built in 1948, in spare, clean-lined post-WWII style on 296 wooded acres, the estate was willed to the Trustees of Reservations, which now operates it. There are five modern rooms available. You will also find a pond, 4 miles of walking trails, a tennis court, and a swimming pool. Follow US 7 South to MA 43 West, and, just past the intersection, turn on Sloan Rd. Field Farm is just over a mile down Sloan Rd.

The Harbour House Inn (☎ 413-743-8959, Ⓦ www.harbourhouseinn.com, 725 N State Rd/US 8, Cheshire) Rooms $150. This inn, with five rooms, is about 15 miles from Williamstown and 17 miles from Lenox, but it's worth mentioning because of its spectacular location, on the back side of Mt Greylock. Part of a 200-year-old farm, the Harbor House is now an elegant manor house run by a family whose two young daughters are the ideal hosts.

Places to Eat & Drink

For pizza, a sandwich or a light meal, wander along Spring St, the main shopping street. Other areas of town have restaurants serving full lunches and dinners.

Papa Charlie's Deli (☎ 413-458-5969, 28 Spring St) Dishes $4-5. Here's a welcoming breakfast spot with sunny tables, and omelettes for $3.50. The sandwiches are named after stars who've performed in Williamstown. We like the Richard Chamberlain with turkey, Swiss and cranberry.

Clarksburg Bread Company (☎ 413-458-2251, 37 Spring St) Prices $3-8. This bakery has fresh-baked biscuits, breads, coffee cakes, cookies, muffins, pies, rolls, scones and squares, as well as coffee, tea and juices. Consider it as a breakfast stop or a place to provision for a picnic or hike. Baguettes run $2.

Lickety Split (☎ 413-458-1818, 68 Spring St) Prices $4-6. Check out this spot for homemade ice cream, soups and sandwiches. We like to sit at a table in the bay window, nibble a slice of quiche ($3) and watch the world stroll by.

Water Street Grill (☎ 413-458-2175, 123 Water St) Prices $4-18. Here's a large restaurant that features moderately priced steaks, seafood and salads. It's open late, so it's a good choice in summer after a play. You'll find live acoustic, folk and blues playing to a mixed crowd here many nights during the summer (no cover). The best deal from the kitchen is a huge plate of nachos for $6.

Canterbury's Pub (☎ *413-458-2808, 46 Spring St)* Prices $5-10. This pub features Olde English decor, Guinness on tap, a salad bar, soups and sandwiches. You get a lively gang here after eight to play pool and suck down $4 pitchers of Busch. Some nights have a local rock band or DJ who spins hip-hop. The crowd is a mix of locals and college folk.

Hobson's Choice (☎ *413-458-9101, 159 Water St)* Mains $12-18. Just down the street from the Water Street Grill, Hobson's has a country-home feel that's popular with Williams students and faculty. Soups and sandwiches for lunch are served in cozy booths. Dinner mains include grilled chicken and seafood pasta.

101 North Street (☎ *413-458-4000, 101 North St)* Prices $15-21 Down the hill from the information booth, this eatery serves contemporary American cuisine, like coriander-crusted grilled halibut ($19).

Main Street Café (☎ *413-458-3210, 16 Water St)* Mains $15-22. Another choice for fine dining is this place. Walk though the small garden to a vibrant yellow room, which features continental cuisine. Consider the charcoal grilled scallops ($22) or make a request for a favorite recipe: The chef loves a challenge.

Mezze Bistro & Bar (☎ *413-458-0123, 84 Water St)* Mains $17-22. This is the place where actors from the Williamstown Theatre tend to go for a drink after performances. You can listen to subtle African pop on the sound system while sitting on the patio outside overlooking a waterfall on the Green River. International offerings like shiitaki mushroom ravioli with celeriac, fennel broth and truffle oil ($17) tempt the hungry.

Entertainment
During the academic year, call Concertline (☎ 413-597-3146) of the Williams College Department of Music for information on concerts, recitals and performances.

Williamstown Chamber Concerts (☎ *413-458-8273)* Tickets $15-22. In the summer this group stages concerts at the Clark Art Institute.

Getting There & Away
North Adams has a small airport and the Mohawk Soaring Club, but no scheduled air service.

Williamstown's bus station is in the lobby of the Williams Inn (☎ 413-458-2665), on Main St close to the intersection of US 7 and MA 2.

Peter Pan Bus Lines (☎ 800-343-9999) runs daily buses between Bennington and Boston via Williamstown, Pittsfield, Lee and Springfield.

Bonanza Bus Lines (☎ 800-556-3815) runs its daily buses between New York City and Bennington via Great Barrington, Stockbridge, Lee, Lenox, Pittsfield and Williamstown.

Boston lies 145 miles to the east; Lenox is 29 miles south on US 7.

Rhode Island

Geographically the smallest state in the US, Rhode Island and its population of about a million manage to fit two ass-kickin' cities and dozens of top-notch beaches within its tiny borders.

Providence, arguably the second-largest city in New England, serves as the state's capital. After surviving a massive 15-year-long face-lift, aimed at preserving the city's historic buildings, Providence recently emerged looking swell.

Newport, the famed 19th-century summer playground of the colossally wealthy, is now the region's yachting capital and summer home to the merely inordinately wealthy.

Perfect for day trips or overnights, Block Island, 13 miles off the south coast, keeps bird watchers happy. The hundreds of miles of seacoast ringing the convoluted shoreline of Narragansett Bay provide ever-changing scenery and long, sandy beaches.

Information

Visit the Rhode Island Tourism Division (☎ 401-222-2601, 800-556-2484, fax 401-222-2102, W www.visitrhodeisland.com, 1 W Exchange St, Providence, RI 02903). The Travelers Aid Society of Rhode Island, also based in Providence, provides a helpline (☎ 401-351-6500, 800-367-2700, W www.travelersaidri.org, 177 Union St, Providence, RI 02903) that can provide information and assist you with accomodations and directions, and in emergencies.

Bed & Breakfast of Rhode Island (☎ 401-849-1298, 800-828-0000, W www.visitnewport.com/bedandbreakfast, PO Box 3291, Newport, RI 02840) can make reservations for you at more than 200 B&Bs and inns in the state for a $5 postage and handling fee.

There's a Rhode Island Welcome Center as you head north on I-95, between exits 2 and 3; it's open 8am to 5pm daily year-round, and until 6:30pm from Memorial Day to Columbus Day.

Highlights

- Strolling through the college campuses and museums of Providence
- Touring the mansions of Newport's Gilded Age
- Chilling on a South County beach
- Biking the narrow roads and trails of Block Island

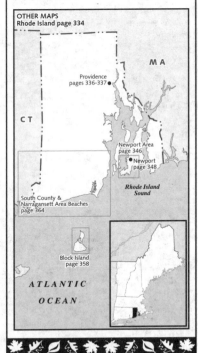

OTHER MAPS
Rhode Island page 334

M A

Providence
pages 336-337

C T

Newport Area
page 346

Newport
page 348

Rhode Island
Sound

South County &
Narragansett Area Beaches
page 364

Block Island
page 358

ATLANTIC

OCEAN

Getting There & Around

See the following Providence section for transportation information. Rhode Island state law requires automobile passengers to wear seat belts; violators are subject to a fine of $30.

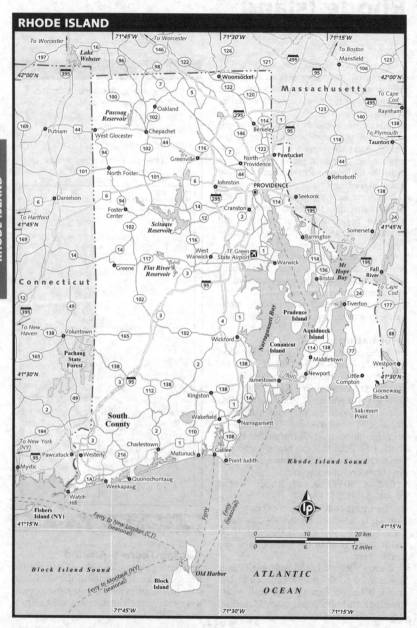

RHODE ISLAND

PROVIDENCE

Yep, this is the place where they make the popular TV series of the same name. And since the show about Dr Sydney Hansen and her family started in the late 1990s, Providence has gained a certain amount of national chic from its prime-time exposure. And why not? The town has its lures.

Providence is a compact, walkable city of some 173,000 people, offering the discriminating visitor a sense of history and a wealth of fine architecture. Home to Johnson & Wales University, one of the nation's best culinary arts programs, excellent restaurants in all price ranges fill the city.

Providence's high-profile universities and colleges (Brown; the Rhode Island School of Design, or RISD; Johnson & Wales) keep the city's social and arts scenes lively by providing a student population of nearly 20,000. The bands-per-capita ratio is high, so you shouldn't find yourself in too much trouble if you need to see a rock show.

For such a historic city, Providence looks shiny and new these days. A billion-dollar downtown renovation project under the guidance of architect Bill Warner, begun in 1983, is completed after more than 15 years of construction. Taking a cue from San Antonio, Texas, Providence has been busily reclaiming its long-neglected waterfront. The Waterplace Park project and its Riverwalk extensions moved the city's two central rivers – the Moshassuck and the Woonasquatucket Rivers, which merge into the Providence River – back to their historic positions after more than a century of filling and dredging had reduced them to near-invisibility. You can even rent kayaks and canoes to go paddling on the reconstructed rivers.

The city's skyline is punctuated by the art deco lines of the Fleet Bank Building (often referred to as 'the Superman building' because of its resemblance to the structure in the old TV show, which the Caped One was able to 'leap over in a single bound'). The skyline now sports a towering Westin Hotel, part of the Rhode Island Convention Center complex in the heart of the new downtown.

History

Ever since Roger Williams (1603–83), a religious outcast from Boston, founded Providence in 1636, it has been a city with an independent frame of mind. The gilded statue atop the Rhode Island State House is called, appropriately, *The Independent Man*.

Williams' guiding principle, the one that got him ostracized from the Puritan Massachusetts Bay Colony, was that all people should have freedom of conscience. He was an early advocate of separation between civil and religious authorities. With his new settlement of Providence, he put these core beliefs into practice, remaining on friendly terms with the local Narragansett Indians after purchasing from them the land for his bold experiment in tolerance and peaceful coexistence.

It should perhaps not be surprising that Rhode Island became the first colony to declare independence from England, in May 1776. From that time until 1900, the state's two big cities – Providence and Newport – alternated as state capital, with Providence, which became the state's premier port city following the devastation wrought on Newport during the Revolutionary War, destined to win.

The most significant name in Providence history (after that of Roger Williams) is Brown. John Brown, whose magnificent mansion on the East Side is now a museum, was a slave trader who also opened trade with China to establish the family's wealth. John's brother Joseph was an architect whose excellent buildings, including John Brown's mansion, the First Baptist Meeting House and Market House, are among the most distinguished in the city. And Moses Brown, who unlike his slave-trader brother was an abolitionist and a pacifist, founded the Quaker school in Providence that is named for him. The last of the Brown brothers, Nicholas, founded Brown University in 1764 in the town of Warren; it was then a Baptist institution named Rhode Island College.

Like many small East Coast cities, Providence went into a precipitous decline in the 1940s and '50s as its manufacturing industries

PROVIDENCE

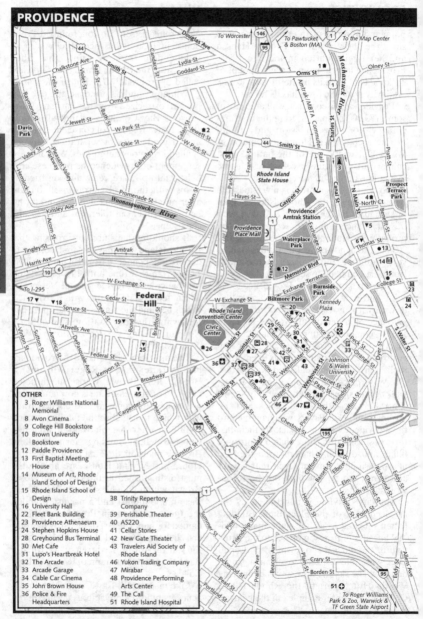

OTHER
3 Roger Williams National Memorial
8 Avon Cinema
9 College Hill Bookstore
10 Brown University Bookstore
12 Paddle Providence
13 First Baptist Meeting House
14 Museum of Art, Rhode Island School of Design
15 Rhode Island School of Design
16 University Hall
22 Fleet Bank Building
23 Providence Athenaeum
24 Stephen Hopkins House
28 Greyhound Bus Terminal
30 Met Cafe
31 Lupo's Heartbreak Hotel
32 The Arcade
33 Arcade Garage
34 Cable Car Cinema
35 John Brown House
36 Police & Fire Headquarters
38 Trinity Repertory Company
39 Perishable Theater
40 AS220
41 Cellar Stories
42 New Gate Theater
43 Travelers Aid Society of Rhode Island
46 Yukon Trading Company
47 Mirabar
48 Providence Performing Arts Center
49 The Call
51 Rhode Island Hospital

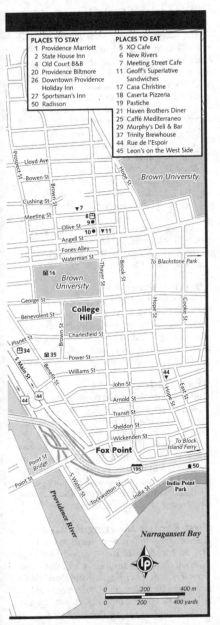

PLACES TO STAY	PLACES TO EAT
1 Providence Marriott	5 XO Cafe
2 State House Inn	6 New Rivers
4 Old Court B&B	7 Meeting Street Cafe
20 Providence Biltmore	11 Geoff's Superlative
26 Downtown Providence	Sandwiches
Holiday Inn	17 Casa Christine
27 Sportsman's Inn	18 Caserta Pizzeria
50 Radisson	19 Pastiche
	21 Haven Brothers Diner
	25 Caffé Mediterraneo
	29 Murphy's Deli & Bar
	37 Trinity Brewhouse
	44 Rue de l'Espoir
	45 Leon's on the West Side

RHODE ISLAND

(textiles and costume jewelry) faltered. In the 1960s, preservation efforts led by Antoinette Downing salvaged the historic architectural framework of the city, and following a few stalls and starts in the decades since, a new and much finer Providence has arisen.

Orientation

Providence is situated at the head of Narragansett Bay astride two rivers, the Moshassuck and the Woonasquatucket, which merge at Waterplace Park to form the Providence River. Surrounding Providence are the populous bedroom suburbs of Warwick, Cranston, Johnston, Pawtucket and East Providence.

I-95 is the primary north-south artery through Providence, with I-195 splitting from it eastward toward Cape Cod. Take exit 22 (Downtown) from I-95 or the Wickenden St exit from I-195 to reach Kennedy Plaza and the Amtrak train station. For the Italian neighborhood and restaurant district of Federal Hill, take exit 21 (Atwells Ave/Broadway).

Kennedy Plaza, with the Providence Biltmore hotel and City Hall on its southwestern side, is the center of the city. To the west of the Biltmore are the Westin Hotel and the Rhode Island Convention Center. The old Union Station building is on the northwestern side of Kennedy Plaza, and beyond it, across the river, are the new Providence (Amtrak) Station (☎ 800-872-7245) and the Rhode Island state capitol, called the State House, on its hilltop perch. The huge new Providence Place Mall is to the west between Kennedy Plaza and the State House. The Greyhound bus terminal is on Fountain St, five blocks southwest of Kennedy Plaza.

East of the Providence River is the East Side, marked by College Hill and its wealth of 18th- and 19th-century buildings, plus RISD and Brown University. Federal Hill, the Italian neighborhood to the west, has dozens of good restaurants, pastry shops and taverns along its main axis, Atwells Ave.

The heart of the city is a surprisingly compact area, and you'll get more of the flavor of Providence on foot than you will in a car. Remember to look up! Many of downtown's most architecturally interesting building facades are several stories above street level.

Information

The Rhode Island Tourism Division (☎ 401-222-2601, 800-556-2484, W www.visitrhode island.com, 1 W Exchange St, Providence, RI 02903) will send you booklets and maps on the whole state and update you on special events. It's open 8:30am to 4:30pm weekdays. Also see the Information section at the beginning of this chapter.

The Providence-Warwick Convention & Visitors Bureau (☎ 401-274-1636, 800-233-1636, W www.providencecvb.com, 1 W Exchange St, Providence, RI 02903) also provides information.

Brown University Bookstore (☎ 401-863-3168, 244 Thayer St) and College Hill Bookstore (☎ 401-751-6404, 252 Thayer St), near each other on College Hill, are the city's most comprehensive bookstores.

For maps and a small selection of guidebooks, try The Map Center (☎ 401-421-2184, 671 N Main St).

For a quality selection of used books, try Cellar Stories (☎ 401-521-2665, 111 Mathewson St) downtown.

The daily newspaper for Providence and indeed all of Rhode Island is the *Providence Journal.* 'Lifebeat,' a daily arts and entertainment section, includes listings of performances and events; the Thursday edition carries an expanded weekend listings section called 'Live.' Visitors should also have a look at its website, W www.projo.com.

The Providence *Phoenix,* which appears Thursday, is the city's free alternative weekly, with nightclub listings and reviews. Find it in record stores and bookstores on Thayer Street.

Boston-based *Fun* (☎ 617-266-6670), which provides listings for gays and lesbians, gets printed every month or so. You can find it, and other pink newspapers, in most gay and lesbian venues.

If you need medical attention, go to Rhode Island Hospital (☎ 401-444-4000, 593 Eddy St), south of the center near I-95 exit 19.

Rhode Island State House

The Rhode Island State House (☎ 401-222-2357; admission free; open 8:30am-4:30pm Mon-Fri) rises above the Providence skyline, easily visible from the highways that pass through the city. Modeled in part on St Peter's Basilica in Vatican City, this very white building not only has the world's fourth-largest self-supporting marble dome, it also houses Gilbert Stuart's portrait of George Washington, which you might want to compare to a dollar bill from your wallet. Inside the public halls are the battle flags of Rhode Island military units and a curious Civil War cannon, which sat here for a century loaded and ready to shoot until someone thought to check whether it was disarmed.

Visitors are welcome for free guided tours at the Smith St (US 44) entrance. Call a week in advance to arrange one, or drop in for a self-guided version.

Walking Tours

The Rhode Island Historical Society (☎ 401-331-8575, 110 Benevolent St; tours $10 from June 15-Oct 15) offers daily walking tours of Benefit St and downtown Providence during summer and early fall. The tours don't run very often, so call ahead for times.

The Arcade

This 1828 Greek Revival building, America's first mall (☎ 401-598-1199, 65 Weybosset St; open 10am-5pm Mon-Fri, 11am-4pm Sat), bustles at lunchtime with the downtown business crowd. The 1st floor of the Arcade has several inexpensive lunch spots, such as Jensen's, Villa Pizza and the Providence Cookie Co, and the 2nd and 3rd floors have gift and clothing boutiques. Park across Weybosset St in the Arcade garage.

First Baptist Meeting House

The congregation now resident in the First Baptist Meeting House (☎ 401-454-3418, 75 N Main St; admission free; open 10am-4pm Mon-Fri May-Oct) began with Roger Williams and his followers in 1638. Free guided tours show you the building, or you can use a free pamphlet for a self-guided tour.

Providence Athenaeum

Anyone who has a visceral attraction to books will enjoy a visit to the Athenaeum (☎ 401-421-6970, 251 Benefit St; admission free; open daily, call for hours), a private subscription library. It's one of the oldest libraries in the country (1831). In these stacks poet Edgar Allan Poe carried on his courtship of Providence's Sarah Helen Whitman, who was the inspiration for his poem 'Annabel Lee.'

This is a library of the old school: They store the card catalog in old-fashioned wooden drawers rather than in a computer, and plaster busts and oil paintings on the walls fill in spaces not occupied by books.

Brown University

Dominating the crest of the College Hill neighborhood on the East Side, the campus of Brown University (☎ 401-863-2378, Ⓦ www.brown.edu) has Ivy League charm. University Hall, a 1770 brick edifice used as a barracks during the Revolutionary War, sits at its center. To explore the campus, start at the wrought-iron gates opening from the top of College St and make your way across the green toward Thayer St.

Free tours of the campus leave five times daily on weekdays, and on Saturday morning from mid-September to mid-November, beginning from the college admission office (Corliss Brackett House, 45 Prospect St).

John Brown House

Called the 'most magnificent and elegant mansion that I have ever seen on this continent' by John Quincy Adams, this brick residence was built in 1786 for Providence merchant John Brown by his brother Joseph. The Rhode Island Historical Society now operates it as a museum house (☎ 401-331-8575, 52 Power St; adult/senior & student/child $6/5/3; open 10am-5pm Tues-Sat, noon-4pm Sun). The 45-minute tours run between 11am and 3:30pm.

Museum of Art, Rhode Island School of Design

Exhibits in the small but select Museum of Art, Rhode Island School of Design (☎ 401-454-6500, 224 Benefit St; adult/senior/student/child 5-18 yrs $5/4/2/1; open 10am-5pm Wed, Thur, Sat & Sun, 10am-8pm Fri) include 19th-century French paintings; classical Greek, Roman and Etruscan art; medieval and Renaissance works; European and Asian decorative arts; and examples of 19th- and 20th-century American painting, furniture and decorative arts. The museum stays open until 9pm on the third Thursday of the month; on those days, admission is free after 5pm.

Providence Architecture

Even though much of Providence is new, the city's main appeal is its historic buildings. You can see the city's colonial history reflected in the multihued 18th-century houses that line Benefit St on the East Side. These are, for the most part, private homes, but many are open for tours one weekend in mid-June during the annual Festival of Historic Homes, organized by the Providence Preservation Society (☎ 401-831-7440, 21 Meeting St).

Benefit St is a fitting symbol of the Providence renaissance, rescued by local preservationists in the 1960s from misguided urban-renewal efforts that would have destroyed it. Its treasures range from the 1708 **Stephen Hopkins House** (15 Hopkins St at Benefit St; donations accepted; open Wed & Sat Apr-Oct) to the clean Greek revival lines of the 1838 Providence Athenaeum, a privately operated subscription library and rare books collection that is a must-see for bibliophiles. The Rhode Island Historical Preservation & Heritage Commission (☎ 401-222-2678) is at 150 Benefit St.

Downtown, the beaux arts style of the city hall makes an imposing centerpiece to Kennedy Plaza, and the stately white dome of the Rhode Island State House (designed by McKim, Mead & White in 1904) is visible from many corners of the city. The USA's first indoor shopping mall – the 1828 Greek revival Arcade – is an airy, tile-floored space with shops and cafes on three floors.

RHODE ISLAND

Neighborhoods

Federal Hill Among the most colorful of Providence's neighborhoods is fervently Italian Federal Hill. (There's a 1990s feature film of the same name about the neighborhood.) It's a great place to wander, taking in the aromas of sausages, peppers and garlic from neighborhood groceries such as Tony's Colonial Market, Providence Cheese and Roma Gourmet. Scialo Bakery on Atwells is a typical Italian pastry shop, with sweet confections poised atop paper doilies in its glass cases. Many of Providence's best restaurants are on Atwells Ave.

College Hill Headquarters of Brown University and the Rhode Island School of Design, College Hill contains a dense population of wood-framed houses, largely from the 18th century. Among the (relatively) quiet tree-lined streets of this residential neighborhood, you'll find the two campuses and a lot of folks walking around with blue hair. The cafes, cheap eateries and used record stores that nourish all the college-types are located on Thayer St, College Hill's main commercial drag.

Fox Point The city's substantial Portuguese population resides in this waterfront section of the city, though gentrification has taken place with influxes of Brown University professors and students and artists from RISD. Even so, you can still find an Old World–style grocery like the Friends Market on Brook St tucked in among the trendy coffeehouses, salons and galleries. Most of the action in Fox Point centers around Wickenden St.

Parks

Waterplace Park & Riverwalk Cobblestone paths lead along the Woonasquatucket River to this central pool and fountain, overlooked by a stepped amphitheater where outdoor performance artists liven up the scene in warm weather. Virtually all of what you see is new, the result of decades of urban renewal. Take a look at the historical maps and photos mounted on the walls of the walkway beneath Memorial Blvd.

Waterplace Park also serves as a nucleus for *WaterFire*, an exceedingly popular public art installation. Scores of flaming braziers anchored into the city's rivers illuminate the water, often accompanied by live (and canned) music, dancing, gads of concession stands and ostentatious gondolas. *WaterFire* occurs during the evening about 25 times a year, mostly in summer months. For information, call ☎ 401-272-3111.

Prospect Terrace Park A great spot from which to get an overview of the city, Prospect Terrace is a small pocket of green space off Congdon St on the East Side. In warm weather, you'll find students throwing Frisbees, office workers picnicking and kick-ass sunsets. The monumental statue facing the city is that of Providence founder Roger Williams, whose remains were moved to this site in 1939.

Roger Williams Park & Zoo In 1871, Ms Betsey Williams, great-great-great-granddaughter of the founder of Providence, donated her farm to the city as a public park. Today this 430-acre expanse of greenery, only a short drive south of Providence at 1000 Elmwood Ave, includes lakes and ponds, forest copses and broad lawns, picnic grounds, the Planetarium and the Museum of Natural History, a boathouse, greenhouses and Ms Williams' cottage.

Perhaps the park's most significant attraction is the Roger Williams Park Zoo (*☎ 401-785-3510, adult/senior & child over 3 yrs $6/3.50*). The zoo, home to more than 600 animals, is open from 9am to 5pm daily (until 4pm in winter; until 6pm on summer weekends). To reach the park, go south from Providence on I-95 to exit 17 (Elmwood Ave). If you are heading north from Connecticut or from the Rhode Island beaches, take exit 16.

Bicycling

Starting at India Point Park on the Narragansett Bay waterfront in Providence, the scenic **East Bay Bicycle Path** winds its way for 14½ miles south along a former railroad track. The mostly flat, paved path follows the shoreline to the pretty seaport of Bristol. State parks along the route make good spots for picnics.

Boating

You can rent kayaks and canoes from **Paddle Providence** *(☎ 401-453-1633; kayaks/canoes $10/12 per hr)* at Waterplace Park. This joint offers an urban boating experience, with paddlers heading into the heart of the city along the landscaped riverways.

Places to Stay

Camping Camping areas are outside the city, but since Rhode Island is small, they aren't all that far away.

George Washington Management Area (☎ 401-568-2013, US 44) Sites $8/12 residents/out-of-staters. This area, 2 miles east of the Connecticut state line in West Glocester, has 45 simple tent and RV sites. There are also two shelters ($20 per night) in a wooded area overlooking the Bowdish Reservoir.

Bowdish Lake Camping Area (☎ 401-568-8890, US 44) Sites $16-45. If the state-operated campground is full, try this neighboring private campground. The 450 sites range in price, depending upon the location and facilities.

Motels As usual, inexpensive motels lurk on the outskirts near interstate exits, about 3 to 5 miles from the city center. Head south to Warwick for the *Motel 6 (☎ 401-467-9800, 20 Jefferson Blvd)*, offering doubles for $65 to $90, as well as the *Fairfield Inn (☎ 401-941-6600, 800-524-2538, 36 Jefferson Blvd)*, with rooms for $100 to $119. Both are generic, clean and situated at I-95 exit 15.

Hotels The rates at Providence's hotels vary widely, depending on season and availability. The big universities' parents' weekends and graduations fill up rooms more quickly than do major holidays.

Downtown Providence Holiday Inn (☎ 401-831-3900, 800-465-4329, fax 401-751-0007, ⓦ www.sixcontinentshotels.com, 21 Atwells Ave) Rooms $99-209. This 274-room hotel, at I-95 exit 21, is right next to the Civic Center between downtown and Federal Hill. It runs free shuttles to TF Green State Airport in Warwick.

Radisson (☎ 401-272-5577, fax 401-272-0251, ⓦ www.radisson.com, 220 India St) Rooms $109-209. The Radisson is just north of India Point Park off I-195 near Wickenden St. You can see the harbor from many of its 136 rooms.

Providence Marriott (☎ 401-272-2400, fax 401-273-2686, ⓦ www.marriott.com, 1 Orms St) Rooms $129-275. This hotel features 345 deluxe rooms and suites, an indoor/outdoor pool, whirlpool, sauna and fitness center.

Providence Biltmore (☎ 401-421-0700, 800-294-7709, fax 401-455-3040, ⓦ www.providencebiltmore.com, Kennedy Plaza) Rooms $159-275. With 289 rooms, this granddaddy of the 1920s, newly refurbished, easily beats out the other hotels as the prettiest.

Inns & B&Bs Bed & Breakfast of Rhode Island (☎ 401-849-1298, 800-828-0000, fax 401-849-1306, ⓦ www.visitnewport.com/bedandbreakfast, PO Box 3291, Newport, RI 02840) provides listings for the entire state, including Providence.

Sportsman's Inn (☎ 401-751-1133, 122 Fountain St) Singles/doubles $55/65. In a city with no hostels, this combination inn and 'gentleman's club' boasts the cheapest lodging in the Providence area and a central downtown location. Expect clean(ish) rooms, seedy patrons, an impatient front desk clerk and naked women.

State House Inn (☎ 401-351-6111, fax 401-351-4261, ⓦ www.providence-inn.com, 43 Jewett St) Rooms $109-159. State House Inn is a restored 1880s house close to the Rhode Island State House. The 10 simple rooms, decorated with tasteful colonial and Shaker-style furnishings, have private bath, TV and phone.

Old Court B&B (☎ 401-751-2002, fax 401-272-4830, ⓦ www.oldcourt.com, 144 Benefit St) Rooms $125-165. Well positioned among the historic buildings of College Hill, this 1863 Italianate building offers discounts in the winter.

Places to Eat

Both the Rhode Island School of Design (RISD) and Johnson & Wales University have culinary programs that annually turn out creative new chefs who liven up the city's restaurant scene. The large student population assures that plenty of good, inexpensive places exist. Unless otherwise noted, eateries listed here are open for lunch and dinner.

Kennedy Plaza Area For a quick, light meal, don't forget *The Arcade*, described in the section by that name, earlier.

Haven Brothers Diner Grub $3-5. Open 5pm-3am daily. Parked next to City Hall on Washington St, this diner sits on the back of a truck that has rolled into the same spot every evening for decades. Climb up a rickety ladder to get hamburgers, hot dogs, fries, cabinets, lobster salad and little else. Everyone who has lived in Providence for a year or more is likely to have eaten here at least once.

Murphy's Deli & Bar (☎ 401-621-8467, 55 Union St) Sandwiches $4-7. For a sandwich and a beer right in the city center, head straight for Murphy's, in the back of the

---

Coffee Milk & Cabinets

In 1993, two popular beverages battled each other for the honor of becoming Rhode Island's official state drink: coffee milk and Del's Frozen Lemonade.

Though Del's tastes great, no one really doubted that coffee milk would come out on top. A mixture of coffee syrup and milk, RI kids have guzzled it since before the Great Depression. To try it, head to a grocery store, pick up a bottle and go to town.

While we've got your attention, please note this crucially important distinction: In Rhode Island, a milkshake is traditionally syrup and milk blended together *without* ice cream. Rhode Islanders call the version *with* ice cream a 'cabinet' or 'frappe.' (The term 'cabinet' is pretty much specific to Rhode Island, while 'frappe' gets thrown around by folks as far away as Boston.)

Del's, a lemonade stand gone global

Biltmore parking garage. Besides serving up standard deli sandwiches such as hot pastrami and Swiss cheese ($5.25) since 1929, Murphy's offers a broad selection of instant lottery tickets.

Trinity Brewhouse (☎ *401-453-2337, 186 Fountain St*) Dishes $5-9. Open 11:30am-2am daily. A favorite college hangout in the evenings, this brew house serves only its own hop-heavy Irish/British-style beer. There's entertainment most nights, and the kitchen, serving sandwiches (some vegetarian), burgers and pizzas, closes at midnight.

College Hill There's a massive selection of sandwiches at ***Geoff's Superlative Sandwiches*** (☎ *401-751-9214, 283 Thayer St*) Sandwiches $3-6. Open daily. A favorite with college-types and drummers, Geoff's menu includes lots of veggie options. Some kosher meats are available. While you wait, use the big-ass barrel of free pickles to keep your blood sugar up.

Meeting Street Cafe (☎ *401-273-1066, 220 Meeting St*) Prices $7-12. For larger and more expensive sandwiches, as well as lox-oriented breakfasts, head to this delicatessen. Its enormous oatmeal cookies ($3), voted best in Rhode Island by several polls, measure about 10 inches in diameter.

Rue de l'Espoir (☎ *401-751-8890, 99 Hope St*) Mains $17-28. The city's long-running favorite is not as French as it sounds. The menu is eclectic and ever changing, with several vegetarian options.

New Rivers (☎ *401-751-0350, 7 Steeple St*) Mains $18-25. Open dinner only from 5:30pm. New Rivers specializes in 'contemporary American cooking,' which is to be interpreted as innovative and fancy, using organic and locally grown produce when possible. 'Small meals' include pastas and polentas, while grilled and baked main courses cost a little more.

XO Cafe (☎ *401-273-9090, 125 N Main St*) Mains $18-30. Open dinner only from 5pm. The menu of this artsy, trendy little bistro changes with the seasons. Besides the New American cuisine, there's always wood oven–baked pizza ($14) as well as weirdo cocktails and a cigar menu.

Federal Hill The Italian district is just west across the bridge from the Holiday Inn. Look for the huge concrete arch with a big pineapple marking Atwells Ave, which has dozens of eateries. All of the following suggestions close Monday.

Pastiche (☎ *401-861-5190, 92 Spruce St*) Desserts $4-5. For sweets and coffee, Pastiche, awash in soothing colors and warmed by a fire in winter, offers a seasonal dessert.

Caserta Pizzeria (☎ *401-621-3618, 121 Spruce St*) Pizza $4.25-12. This Federal Hill icon serves possibly the best pizza in New England (no exaggeration). The cavernous interior houses a black and white floor and cheap Formica tables. It's so popular with local Italian Americans that you need to order several days in advance if you want a pie on Christmas Eve.

Leon's on the West Side (☎ *401-273-1055, 166 Broadway*) Mains $12-20. Good food at the best prices is the specialty at Leon's, two blocks south of Atwells Ave. Inventively prepared Italian classics, salads, pizzas and pastas are served for dinner. There's no lunch on weekdays, but great brunches are offered weekends.

Casa Christine (☎ *401-453-6255, 145 Spruce St*) Mains $13-20. Open lunch & dinner Tues-Fri, dinner only Sat. You'd never stumble across it, but locals in the know find their way to this family-run dining room on a drab back street near Caserta to fill up on heaps of home-cooked veal, chicken and fish.

Caffé Mediterraneo (☎ *401-331-7760, 134 Atwells Ave*) Mains $15-30. This traditional Italian American trattoria serves filling dinners and tries to be a touch more upscale than its neighbors. It's a favorite with ladies at lunchtime.

Entertainment

Providence Civic Center (☎ *401-331-6700, 1 LaSalle Square*) This is the place to see sporting events (see Spectator Sports, later), occasional big-name rock groups and boat shows.

Theater Classic and contemporary plays are performed by the ***Trinity Repertory***

Company (☎ 401-351-4242, 201 Washington St) Tickets $35. Trinity performs in the historic Lederer Theater downtown. Trinity is a favorite try-out space for Broadway productions, and it's not unusual for well-known stars to turn up in a performance. Over several decades, Trinity Rep has earned a reputation for adventurous productions, but mainstream audiences usually come away satisfied.

Several smaller theater companies stage contemporary and avant-garde productions. Check local listings in the newspaper or call the following theater companies for upcoming performances: **Perishable Theater** (☎ 401-331-2695, 95 Empire St) and **New Gate Theater** (☎ 401-421-9680, 134 Mathewson St).

AS220 (☎ 401-831-9327, 115 Empire St) This nonprofit venue supports area creative-types and hosts a bunch of artists' works. A variety of action goes down here; you can catch bands, performance artists and theater troupes. If you need a cup of coffee or a vegan cookie, it's also got a cafe.

Leeds Theatre at Brown University (☎ 401-863-2838, off Waterman St) This company stages traditional and contemporary productions featuring student actors.

Providence Performing Arts Center (☎ 401-421-2787, 220 Weybosset St) Tickets $30-60. This popular venue for touring Broadway shows is in a former Loew's Theater building, dating from 1928. It has a lavish art deco interior, recently restored to its original splendor.

Cinemas Offbeat and foreign films are featured at **Cable Car Cinema** (☎ 401-272-3970, 204 S Main St) Patrons can sit on couches and enjoy all-you-can-eat popcorn while watching the show. Local talents often perform to warm up the audience before the movie. The Cable Car's sidewalk cafe brews excellent coffee; Danny DeVito drank it recently.

Avon Cinema (☎ 401-421-3315, 260 Thayer St) On College Hill, Avon also features foreign films, cult classics and experimental movies.

Nightclubs With its large population of students, Providence has a lively nightclub scene. Refer to the 'Lifebeat' section in the daily *Providence Journal* or the *Phoenix* for listings of performers, venues and schedules.

Lupo's Heartbreak Hotel (☎ 401-272-5876, 239 Westminster St) Cover $10-20. Lupo's is legendary in the city. It hosts national acts (progressive rock, R&B and blues) in an intimate space that usually accommodates some dancing.

Met Cafe (☎ 401-861-2142, 130 Union St) Adjacent to Lupo's, this hole-in-the-wall provides an outlet for Rock-with-a-capital-R, featuring local bands and lesser-known national talents. In the back, find the classic video game Centipede; the well-used machine is in excellent condition. At the time this book went to print, a skilled local with the initials C-U-M was impressively topping the high-scores list.

The Call (☎ 401-751-2255, 15 Elbow St) The Call, a blues and rock venue, sits in the basement of a turn-of-the-century warehouse. Its well-designed two-tiered floor provides clear views of the stage, which has lately hosted a range of musicians from notable Frank Black to cheesy Grateful Dead cover bands to quality locals. There's a pool table and, best of all, amazingly clean bathrooms.

Gay & Lesbian Venues The venerable establishment **Mirabar** (☎ 401-331-6761, 35 Richmond St) attracts devoted regulars; most know the bartenders' names. It's got two floors. The second, a sort of promenade, overlooks the action of the main level's dance floor, where you can observe a bunch of muscle in small white T-shirts.

Yukon Trading Company (☎ 401-274-6620, 124 Snow St) If you want a club full of leather, liquor, some more leather and a few stuffed game heads, find your way over to this remote bar.

Deville's (☎ 401-751-7166, 🅦 www.devilles providence.com) Forced to move away from Allens Ave because of plans to expand the highway, Deville's, Rhode Island's favorite lesbian club, will soon have a new home.

Check its website or drop in at Mirabar to find out details.

Spectator Sports

Pawtucket Red Sox (☎ *401-724-7300*) This Triple-A (minor league) farm team for the Boston Red Sox plays all spring and summer at McCoy Stadium in Pawtucket, just north of Providence. A night here, complete with hot dogs and peanuts, is a favorite way for baseball addicts to get a fix without the hassle and cost of driving to and parking at Fenway Park in Boston. Call for directions.

Providence Bruins (☎ *401-331-6700, 1 LaSalle Square*) Another farm team for Boston, this hockey squad plays a regular schedule at the Civic Center in the fall and winter.

Getting There & Around

Air TF Green State Airport (☎ 401-737-8222) is in Warwick, about 20 minutes south of Providence. Green is served by most major airlines. There is no airport bus available, though some luxury hotels have shuttle buses. Taxi services include Airport Taxi (☎ 401-737-2868) and Checker Cab (☎ 401-273-2222).

Bus Rhode Island Public Transit Authority (RIPTA; ☎ 401-781-9400, 800-221-3797, W www.ripta.com) links Providence's Kennedy Plaza with the rest of the state for fares ranging from $1.25 to $4.

RIPTA bus No 11 (Broad St) takes you from Kennedy Plaza to Broad and Montgomery Sts, from where you can walk to Roger Williams Park & Zoo. Bus No 60 (Providence-Newport) makes 38 trips from Kennedy Plaza to Newport on weekdays, 21 trips on Saturday and 17 trips on Sunday and holidays.

Bonanza Bus Lines (☎ 401-751-8800, 888-751-8800) connects Providence and TF Green State Airport with Boston and Boston's Logan Airport with 12 express buses daily. Pick it up at Kennedy Plaza or Bonanza's terminal 2 miles north at I-95 exit 25 (Route 126/Smithfield Ave). The Providence-Boston fare is $18 one-way.

From the Greyhound bus terminal (☎ 401-454-0790, 100 Fountain St at Mathewson), buses depart for Boston (11 daily, 1¼ hours, $8); New York City (11 weekdays, 15 weekends, four to 5½ hours, $23); New London ($15), New Haven ($19), and Foxwoods Resort Casino ($16 roundtrip), CT, among other destinations.

Train Twelve daily Amtrak trains connect Providence with Boston (one hour) and New York (four hours). High-speed Super Acela trains now operate as well; they shorten your trip but cost more. Call ☎ 800-872-7245 for details.

For information on Amtrak's *Shore Route* between New York and Boston, see the Getting There & Away chapter at the front of this book.

Boston's MBTA commuter rail trains (☎ 617-222-3200, 800-392-6100) also run between Providence and Boston's South Station, for $4.75 each way.

Car With hills, two interstates and two rivers defining its downtown topography, finding your way around in Providence can be confusing. Parking can be difficult in the city center as well. Be patient and allow time.

All of the major car rental companies have offices at TF Green State Airport in Warwick. Avis (☎ 401-521-7900) has an office downtown as well.

Boat Interstate Navigation Co runs summer ferries to Block Island from its terminal at the southern end of Water St, at the India St Dock west of India Point Park. See the Block Island section, later in this chapter, for additional details.

NEWPORT

Perfectly situated for access by sea, Newport was an important commercial port, a conquered war prize and a wealthy summer resort before becoming one of New England's busiest and most entertaining tourist destinations. The town is packed all summer by young day-trippers, older bus tourists, foreign visitors and families whose

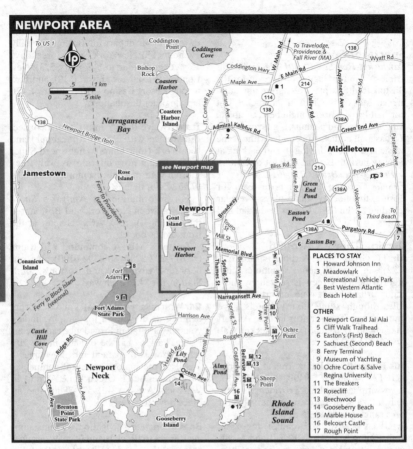

NEWPORT AREA

To US 1

Coddington Point

Coddington Cove

Bishop Rock

Coasters Harbor

Coddington Hwy

Maple Ave

To Travelodge, Providence & Fall River (MA)

Wyatt Rd

W Main Rd

E Main Rd

214

138

0   .5   1 km
0   .25   .5 mile

Coasters Harbor Island

Girard Ave

114

138

Turner Rd

Aquidneck Ave

Paradise Ave

Narragansett Bay

JT Connell Rd

Admiral Kalbfus Rd

138

2

Valley Rd

Green End Ave

138A

Rose Island

Newport Bridge (toll)

Bliss Rd

Bliss Mine Rd

214

Prospect Ave

Middletown

Wolcott Ave

138A

3

Jamestown

Ferry to Providence (seasonal)

see Newport map

Newport

Broadway

Touro St

Green End Pond

Easton's Pond

To Third Beach

Goat Island

Mill St

Memorial Blvd

138A

4

Purgatory Rd

6   Easton Bay

7

Newport Harbor

Spring St

Thames St

Bellevue Ave

Cliff Walk

5

PLACES TO STAY
1 Howard Johnson Inn
3 Meadowlark Recreational Vehicle Park
4 Best Western Atlantic Beach Hotel

Conanicut Island

Fort Adams

8

9

Narragansett Ave

Ochre Point Ave

10

Ochre Point

11

OTHER
2 Newport Grand Jai Alai
5 Cliff Walk Trailhead
6 Easton's (First) Beach
7 Sachuest (Second) Beach
8 Ferry Terminal
9 Museum of Yachting
10 Ochre Court & Salve Regina University
11 The Breakers
12 Rosecliff
13 Beechwood
14 Gooseberry Beach
15 Marble House
16 Belcourt Castle
17 Rough Point

Fort Adams State Park

Harrison Ave

Spring St

Ruggles Ave

Castle Hill Cove

Ridge Rd

Hazard Rd

Carroll Ave

Lily Pond

Coggeshall Ave

12

13

Sheep Point

Newport Neck

Ocean Ave

Almy Pond

14

15

16

17

Rhode Island Sound

Harrison Ave

Brenton Point State Park

Ocean Ave

Gooseberry Island

cars pack the narrow colonial streets, bringing traffic to a standstill.

Once the home of the America's Cup race, Newport is still one of the East Coast's premier yachting ports, with an enthusiasm, which borders on mania, for the sport. The plethora of yachts and tippling aristocrats led one wag to comment that 'Newport is a drinking town with a yachting problem.'

Much of Newport is beautiful, with restored colonial buildings, cobbled streets and surprising attractive sea views. A good deal, however, is humdrum: a collection of crowded residential areas, cheerless condominium developments and decaying maritime industry facilities.

Most people visit Newport to look at the sumptuous mansions – disingenuously called 'summer cottages' by their fabulously wealthy owners – ranged along Bellevue Ave, with peerless views of the sea. Others come by yacht to visit friends, who may still live in some of the more secluded mansions. Still other tourists come to the music festivals – classical, folk, jazz – which are among the most important in the USA. Newport also boasts several of New England's most beautiful and oldest religious buildings.

July and August are the busiest months. If you come in late April, May, late October or early November, you'll enjoy lower prices, smaller crowds and easier parking. Whenever you come, you'll enjoy Newport more if you carefully plan where to park your car and your body.

Orientation

Newport occupies the southwestern end of Aquidneck Island. Adjoining it to the north is Middletown, which holds many of the services, less-expensive residential areas and unsightly commercial strips not allowed in Newport. Most cheap motels and guesthouses are in Middletown, several miles north of the center, while the more expensive inns, B&Bs and hotels are in Newport proper.

Downtown Newport's main north-south commercial streets are America's Cup Ave and Thames (that's 'thaymz,' not 'temz') St, just in from the harbor. There are public toilets at the entrance to the parking lot at Bowen's Wharf.

Your initial destination in Newport should be the Newport Gateway Transportation & Visitors Center (see Information, below), which holds the bus station, tourist office and public toilets. Walking or biking around town is probably the best way to go; see Bicycling, later in this section, for bike rentals.

Parking is particularly difficult and expensive. The cheapest is at the Newport Gateway Transportation & Visitors Center, which gives you the first half-hour for free, the next for $1 and each additional half-hour for 75¢, to a maximum of $12.25 per day. If you park at a meter (25¢ for 15 minutes, up to two hours), scrupulously observe its time limit or you'll end up with a ticket.

Information

The Newport County Convention & Visitors Bureau (☎ 401-849-8048, fax 401-849-0291, 🌐 www.gonewport.com, 23 America's Cup Ave) operates the information office inside the Newport Gateway Transportation & Visitors Center, open 9am to 5pm daily. Information personnel won't make room

reservations, but they post a list of B&Bs, inns and hotels with vacancies, and you can call those for free from a bank of special phones.

For books on Newport and Rhode Island and especially the New England coast, look for the Armchair Sailor Bookstore (☎ 401-847-4252, 543 Thames St), which stocks an extensive nautical collection.

There are many ATM machines on Thames Street, such as Citizens Bank, just north of the post office.

Internet access is available for a fee at Ship to Shore (☎ 401-846-4537, 337 Thames St), which does most of its business providing support to sailors. It's located inside of the Perry Mill Market Place.

Walking Tours

The Newport Historical Society *(☎ 401-846-0813; tours $7)* will take you on a walking tour of Historic Hill, the Cliff Walk and Bellevue Ave on Thursday, Friday or Saturday from mid-May through mid-October. Tours begin at the Museum of Newport History, on Thames St.

If you'd rather go on your own, the Historical Society has erected a system of 26 self-guided walking-tour signs on the sidewalks of Historic Hill describing many of the prominent and historic buildings found there.

Newport Mansions

During the 19th century, the wealthiest New York bankers and business families chose Newport as their summer resort. This was pre–income tax America, their fortunes were fabulous and their 'summer cottages' – actually mansions and palaces – were fabulous as well. Most mansions are on Bellevue Ave. You must visit at least a few of them, because they are incredible. They frequently turn up as settings for films like *The Great Gatsby*.

Many of the mansions are under the management of the **Preservation Society of Newport County** *(☎ 401-847-1000, 🌐 www.newportmansions.org, 424 Bellevue Ave)*, which offers combination tickets that save you money if you intend to visit several of

NEWPORT

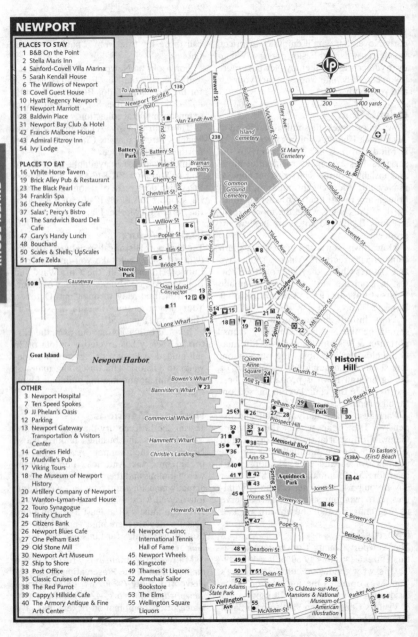

PLACES TO STAY
1 B&B On the Point
2 Stella Maris Inn
4 Sanford-Covell Villa Marina
5 Sarah Kendall House
6 The Willows of Newport
8 Covell Guest House
10 Hyatt Regency Newport
11 Newport Marriott
30 Baldwin Place
31 Newport Bay Club & Hotel
42 Francis Malbone House
43 Admiral Fitzroy Inn
54 Ivy Lodge

PLACES TO EAT
16 White Horse Tavern
19 Brick Alley Pub & Restaurant
23 The Black Pearl
34 Franklin Spa
36 Cheeky Monkey Cafe
37 Salas'; Percy's Bistro
41 The Sandwich Board Deli
    Cafe
47 Gary's Handy Lunch
48 Bouchard
50 Scales & Shells; UpScales
51 Cafe Zelda

OTHER
3 Newport Hospital
7 Ten Speed Spokes
9 JJ Phelan's Oasis
12 Parking
13 Newport Gateway
    Transportation & Visitors
    Center
14 Cardines Field
15 Mudville's Pub
17 Viking Tours
18 The Museum of Newport
    History
20 Artillery Company of Newport
21 Wanton-Lyman-Hazard House
22 Touro Synagogue
24 Trinity Church
25 Citizens Bank
26 Newport Blues Cafe
27 One Pelham East
28 Old Stone Mill
30 Newport Art Museum
32 Ship to Shore
33 Post Office
35 Classic Cruises of Newport
38 The Red Parrot
39 Cappy's Hillside Cafe
40 The Armory Antique & Fine
    Arts Center
44 Newport Casino;
    International Tennis
    Hall of Fame
45 Newport Wheels
46 Kingscote
49 Thames St Liquors
52 Armchair Sailor
    Bookstore
53 The Elms
55 Wellington Square
    Liquors

RHODE ISLAND

its mansions. Visiting just one will cost adults $10 and kids $4. Most of the Preservation Society's mansions are open 10am to 5pm daily, though some close for the winter season.

Other interests operate several mansions. A few mansions are still in private hands and aren't open to visitors.

The best way to see the mansions is by bicycle. Cruising along Bellevue Ave at bike speed allows you to enjoy the view of the grounds, explore side streets and paths and ride right up to the mansion entrances without having to worry about parking or holding up traffic. If you can't bring your own bike, you can rent one (see Bicycling, later in this section).

The following are the mansions you pass going from north to south along Bellevue Ave. The only mansions described here not managed by the Preservation Society are Ochre Court, Beechwood, Belcourt Castle and Rough Point.

Kingscote This Elizabethan fantasy, complete with Tiffany glass, was Newport's first 'cottage' strictly for summer use, designed by Richard Upjohn in 1841 for George Noble Jones of Savannah, Georgia. It was later bought by China-trade merchant William H King, who gave the house its name.

The Elms Edward J Berwind, a graduate of the US Naval Academy and a Navy officer, made his fortune by selling coal to the US Navy after his retirement. He had this supremely graceful summerhouse designed by Horace Trumbauer and built in 1901.

Threatened with imminent destruction – incredibly – the mansion was to be replaced with a housing project. However, thanks to the efforts of the Preservation Society, good sense prevailed. The Elms, nearly identical to the Château d'Asnieres built near Paris in 1750, offers a 'behind-the-scenes' tour that snakes through the complex basement, servants' quarters and up onto the roof.

Château-sur-Mer Originally designed by Seth Bradford and built of granite for retired banker William S Wetmore in 1852, this Victorian neo-Gothic house was remodeled by Richard Morris Hunt during the 1870s and '80s for the original owner's son. Compared to the others, it has a more 'lived-in' feel.

Ochre Court Designed by Richard Morris Hunt and built in 1892, Ochre Court (*☎ 401-847-6650; admission free; open 9am-4pm Mon-Fri*) is now the administration building of Salve Regina University. You can visit much of the main floor anytime during opening hours. In summer, there are guided tours.

The Breakers Most magnificent of all the Newport mansions is the Breakers, a 70-room Italian Renaissance palace designed by Richard Morris Hunt for Cornelius Vanderbilt II and completed in 1895 at Ochre Point, a prime oceanside site next to Ochre Court. Sumptuous is the only way to describe it. The furnishings, most made expressly for the Breakers, are all original. Don't miss the Children's Cottage on the grounds.

The Breakers' grand **Stable & Carriage House**, also designed by Hunt, is inland several blocks, on the west side of Bellevue Ave. It is now a museum of Vanderbilt family memorabilia, much of which provides a detailed look at the lifestyle of one of the USA's wealthiest families at the turn of the century.

The Vanderbilt's summer 'cottage,' the Breakers

Rosecliff Stanford White designed Rosecliff to look like the Grand Trianon at Versailles – but in some respects it is even more grand. Its Marie Antoinette was Mrs Hermann Oelrichs (née Theresa Fair), an heiress of the Comstock Lode silver treasure. Mrs Oelrichs liked to entertain, so she saw to it that her house had Newport's largest ballroom. Rosecliff played opposite Robert Redford and Mia Farrow in *The Great Gatsby*.

Beechwood William B Astor built this home in 1856 (☎ *401-846-3772, 580 Bellevue Ave; adult/senior & child 12 yrs & under $10/8; open 10am-5pm daily mid-May–Nov, 10am-4pm daily Feb–mid-May, call for times Nov-Dec*). Today, it is occupied by Beechwood Theater Company actors, who bring the house to life by portraying a 'typical' summer's houseful of family, staff and guests.

Marble House Designed by Richard Morris Hunt and built in 1892 for William K Vanderbilt, the younger brother of Cornelius II, Marble House was inspired by the palace of Versailles, complete with original Louis XIV–style furnishings, which were custom-made for the mansion. The aptly named Gold Room was created for the Vanderbilts' grand balls. Don't miss the Chinese Teahouse.

Belcourt Castle Oliver Hazard Perry Belmont, heir to the American Rothschild fortune, had Hunt design him a 60-room castle according to the 17th-century tastes of France's King Louis XIII. He stocked it with period art, tapestries, furniture, glassware and suits of armor from 32 countries. Staffed by 30 servants, it even had a private menagerie. He and his wife, Alva, the former Mrs William K Vanderbilt, lived here in regal splendor. Tours of Belcourt Castle (☎ *401-846-0669, 657 Bellevue Ave; adult/senior/student 13-17 yrs/child 6-12 yrs $10/8/7/5; open 9am-5pm daily late May– mid-Oct*) are offered daily; call for times.

Rough Point In 1889, Frederick W Vanderbilt built this Gothic-style mansion on a rocky piece of land jutting out into the ocean. Later purchased by the tobacco baron, James B Duke, the mansion and the rest of his wealth fell into the hands of Duke's only daughter, Doris (aged 13 years). She left the estate to the Newport Restoration Society upon her death.

Rough Point is just recently opened to tourists. You can purchase tickets (*adult/ senior $25/22*) to Rough Point at Newport's Gateway Center. There are no advance tickets, and you must travel to the estate using a courtesy shuttle. For information, call ☎ 401-849-7300.

Museums
Newport has more than its share of museums, from the ponderous to the sublime.

The Griswold Mansion (1864), a vast Victorian frame summer cottage, houses the **Newport Art Museum** (☎ *401-848-8200, 76 Bellevue Ave; adult/senior & student 13-18 yrs $6/4, free for child 12 yrs & under; open 10am-5pm Mon-Sat, noon-5pm Sun*). It has changing exhibits of paintings, sculpture, metalwork, ceramics, photography, etc. Call for current shows. The admission fee depends upon the exhibit, but is usually close to the listed prices.

In Newport's historic Brick Market building, the **Museum of Newport History** (☎ *401-846-0813; adult/senior/child 5 yrs & older $5/4/3; open 10am-5pm Mon & Wed-Sat, 1pm-5pm Sun*) is run by the Newport Historical Society (☎ *401-846-0813*) and traces the town's eventful history.

Constructed in 1675, the **Wanton-Lyman-Hazard House** (☎ *401-846-0813, 17 Broadway; admission $4, free for children under 12*) is the oldest restored house in the city. Used as a residence by colonial governors and well-to-do residents, it's now a museum of colonial Newport history operated by the Newport Historical Society. Call the society for hours of operation.

The **Old Stone Mill**, off Bellevue Ave in Touro Park, is a curious stone tower of uncertain provenance. Some people believe it was built by Norse mariners before the voyages of Columbus, making it the oldest existing structure in the United States; others say it's a windmill's base, built by an early governor of the colony.

The **International Tennis Hall of Fame** (☎ 401-849-3990, 194 Bellevue Ave; adult/senior/child 16 yrs & under/family $8/6/4/20; open 10am-5pm daily), just south of Memorial Blvd, is in the historic Newport Casino building (1880), once the wealthy Newporters' summer club. The forerunners of today's US Open Tennis Tournament were held here in 1881. Playing on one of its 13 grass courts costs $25 per person per hour, though the grass courts close for winter.

For decades, Newport was the homeport for America's Cup races, which is why it has a **Museum of Yachting** (☎ 401-847-1018, Fort Adams State Park; adult/senior & child under 12 $4/3; open 10am-5pm daily mid-May–Oct).

The **Artillery Company of Newport** (☎ 401-846-8488, 23 Clarke St; adult/child $3/2; call for hours) has an extensive collection of military uniforms, paraphernalia and other memorabilia on view.

The newly opened **National Museum of American Illustration** (☎ 401-851-8949, 492 Bellevue Ave; tickets $25; open Fri & Sat, call for hours) houses pieces by the likes of Norman Rockwell and NC Wyeth, inside of Vernon Court, a mansion dating from 1898. Exceedingly popular, admission to the museum sells out months in advance; you must make advance arrangements. The museum won't admit children under 12.

Touro Synagogue

This house of worship (☎ 401-847-4794, 85 Touro St; tours 10am-5pm Sun-Fri July-Sept; 11am-3pm Sun, 1pm-3pm Mon-Sat Sept-Oct & May-June; 11am-3pm Sun, 1pm Mon-Fri Nov-Apr), designed by Peter Harrison (who did King's Chapel in Boston) and built by the nascent Sephardic Orthodox Congregation Yeshuat Israel in 1763, has the distinction of being North America's oldest Jewish synagogue. Inside, a letter to the congregation from President George Washington, written in 1790, hangs in a prominent spot. There's a historic cemetery just up the street.

The synagogue opens for worship only on Saturday. To visit outside of the listed winter hours, call to make an appointment.

Trinity Church

This Episcopal church (☎ 401-846-0660, cnr Spring & Church Sts; open 10am-4pm daily mid-June–early Sept, 1pm-4pm daily May & mid-Sept–mid-Oct, 10am-1pm daily rest of year), on Queen Anne Square, follows the design canon of Sir Christopher Wren's Palladian churches in London. Built in 1725 and 1726, it has a fine wineglass-shaped pulpit, tall windows to let in light and traditional box pews to keep out drafty air.

Cliff Walk

This footpath runs along the eastern edge of the peninsula, with vast views of the sea to one side and the mansions along Bellevue Ave to the other. It starts at the inn called Cliff Walk Manor, just west of Easton's Beach, and goes south and then west almost to Bailey's Beach. Strolling its entire length takes about an hour.

Beaches

Newport's public beaches are on the eastern side of the peninsula along Memorial Blvd. All are open 9am to 6pm in summer and charge a parking fee of $10 per car ($15 on weekends).

Easton's Beach (☎ 401-848-6491), also called **First Beach**, is the largest, with a pseudo-Victorian pavilion containing bathhouses and showers, a snack bar and a small aquarium where children can see and touch a variety of tidepool creatures and fish. It's within walking distance of Newport's center.

East of Easton's Beach along Purgatory Rd lies **Sachuest (Second) Beach** (☎ 401-846-6273), named for the nearby wildlife sanctuary. It's prettier and cleaner than Easton's Beach and has showers, a snack bar and a lovely setting, overlooked by the neo-Gothic tower of St George's prep school.

Third Beach (☎ 401-847-1993) is a short distance east of Second Beach. Popular with families because it is protected from the open ocean, Third Beach also appeals to windsurfers because the water is calm and the winds steady.

RHODE ISLAND

Other 'pocket' beaches exist along Ocean Ave, but most of these, such as **Bailey's Beach**, are private. An exception is **Gooseberry Beach**, open to the public for a fee of $10 per car, $3 for pedestrians and cyclists.

State Parks

Fort Adams, built between 1824 and 1857, crowns a rise at the end of the peninsula, which juts northward into Newport Harbor. Like many American coastal fortresses, it had a short, practical life as a deterrent and a long life as a tourist attraction. It's the centerpiece of **Fort Adams State Park** (☎ 401-847-2400; admission free; open 6am–11pm daily), the venue for the Newport Jazz and Folk Festivals and special events. A beach, picnic and fishing areas and a boat ramp are open daily. You can take a guided tour of the park from mid-May to September (adults/seniors and children under 12 $5/4). The Museum of Yachting (see Museums, above) and the ferry to Block Island are here as well.

At the opposite end of the peninsula, **Brenton Point State Park**, due south of Fort Adams on Ocean Ave, is a prime place for gazing at the ocean and for flying kites.

Bicycling

Newport is a fine town for bicycling, with only a few gentle slopes. Observe traffic laws just as you would in a car: Ride in the direction of traffic and do not ride on the sidewalk.

Perhaps the most beautiful and satisfying ride is the 10-mile loop around Ocean Ave, which includes Bellevue Ave and its many beautiful mansions.

Rent your wheels at **Newport Wheels** (☎ 401-849-4400, 411 Thames St; $5/20 per hr/day, $10 each additional day). You can get one with a baby seat for $7.50 per hour. Motor scooters cost $35/45/65/100 for one/two/four/eight hours, or $130 for 24 hours (which is about three times what a four-person rental car would cost). You can also rent bikes at **Ten Speed Spokes** (☎ 401-847-5609, 18 Elm St), really on America's Cup Ave next to the Newport Gateway Transportation & Visitors Center.

Cruises

Viking Tours (☎ 401-847-6921, 23 America's Cup Ave; adult/child $10/5; trips mid-May–mid-Oct) offers narrated harbor tours aboard the Viking Queen departing several times daily; among other sights, you'll see Hammersmith Farm, Jacqueline Kennedy's summer home.

Classic Cruises of Newport (☎ 401-849-3033, Christie's Landing; adult/child $17/12; trips mid-May–mid-Oct) runs excursions on the Rum Runner II, a Prohibition-era bootlegging vessel. The narrated tour will take you past mansions and former speakeasies.

Special Events

Newport has a crowded calendar of community celebrations. During your visit, you may find special events involving polo, yachts, flowers and horticulture, yachts, Irish music, clam chowder, yachts, traditional crafts, soapbox racers, tennis, beer and yachts. There's even a winter festival (☎ 401-847-7666, 800-976-5122) in mid-February. For the full schedule, see ⓦ www.gonewport.com.

If you plan to attend any of the major events described below, make sure you reserve accommodations and tickets in advance (tickets usually go on sale in mid-May).

Newport Music Festival – In mid-July, this includes classical music concerts in many of the great mansions for $28 to $50 per ticket. For a schedule, write to the Newport Music Festival, PO Box 3300, Newport, RI 02840, or call ☎ 401-846-1133.

International Tennis Hall of Fame Championships – In July, this event hosts top professionals. Contact the Hall of Fame (☎ 401-849-3990, 194 Bellevue Ave, Newport, RI 02840).

Ben & Jerry's Folk Festival/Newport – In early August, big-name stars and up-and-coming groups perform at Fort Adams State Park and other venues around town. Call ☎ 401-847-3700 for information; tickets cost $25 to $40.

JVC Jazz Festival/Newport – This event (☎ 401-847-3700) usually takes place on a mid-August weekend, with concerts at the Newport Casino (International Tennis Hall of Fame) and Fort Adams State Park.

Newport International Boat Show – The boat show (☎ 401-846-1115), held in late September, is the biggest and best known of Newport's many boat and yacht shows.

Places to Stay

Newport's lodgings are expensive. The cozy inns and harborside hotels in the center of town generally charge $125 to $200 and up for a double room with breakfast in summer. Rhode Island sales tax of 7% and Newport lodging tax of 5% will be added to your bill.

On Friday and Saturday, prices are high; during the music festivals, they're higher still. Sunday through Thursday, rates fall as much as 30%. Many lodgings require a two-night minimum on summer weekends, and a three-night minimum on holidays.

As rooms can be scarce in summer, you might want to use a reservation service. Anna's Victorian Connection (☎ 401-849-2489, fax 401-847-7309, 5 Fowler Ave, Newport, RI 02840) will make a reservation at any one of 250 hostelries in Rhode Island and southeastern Massachusetts at no cost to you.

Bed and Breakfast of Newport Ltd (☎ 401-846-5408, 800-800-8765, fax 401-846-1828, W www.bbnewport.com, 33 Russell Ave, Newport, RI 02840) represents 350 establishments in the Newport area. Taylor-Made Reservations (☎ 800-848-8848, fax 401-848-0301, W www.Enjoy-Newport.com) represents a full range of lodgings as well.

If you arrive without a reservation, go to the visitor center and ask to see its list of vacancies. Except in summer, you may find handbills in the brochure racks that entitle you to special reduced rates.

Camping Off RI 138A in Middletown is *Meadowlark Recreational Vehicle Park* (☎ 401-846-9455, 132 Prospect Ave) RV sites $24. Open mid-Apr–Oct. Meadowlark has 40 RV sites.

Melville Ponds Campground (☎ 401-849-8212, 181 Bradford Ave) Tent sites $15, RV sites $21-24. Open Apr-Oct. This is a municipal campground in Portsmouth, off RI 114, about 10 miles north of Newport's center. It has 57 tent sites and 66 RV sites. To find it, take RI 114 to Stringham Rd, go to Sullivan Rd, then head north to the campground.

Fort Getty State Park (☎ 401-423-7264) Tent sites $20, RV sites $25. This park is across the Newport Bridge on Conanicut Island in Jamestown, with 25 tent sites and 100 RV sites. From RI 138, go south on North Rd, cross Narragansett Ave and continue on Southwest Ave, then merge into Beaver Tail Rd and turn right onto Fort Getty Rd.

Motels Compared to Newport's many wonderful inns, its motels lack character, but they make up for it with modern amenities and lower prices. Most are in Middletown on RI 114 (W Main Rd) and RI 138 (E Main Rd). RIPTA bus No 63/Purple Line will take you to downtown Newport, saving you the expense and bother of parking.

Travelodge (☎ 401-849-4700, 800-862-2006, fax 401-848-7704, 1185 W Main Rd/RI 114, Middletown) Rooms $79/120 Sun-Thur/Fri & Sat. This place hired a friendly staff that knows how to clean.

Howard Johnson Inn (☎ 401-849-2000, 800-654-2000, fax 401-849-6047, W www.hojo.com, 351 W Main Rd/RI 114, Middletown) Rooms $89/149 Sun-Thur/Fri & Sat. If you love strip malls, stay here.

Best Western Atlantic Beach Hotel (☎ 401-847-5330, fax 401-847-8041, W www.bestwestern.com, 34 Wave Ave) Rooms $89-169. Nicely situated across the street from Easton's Beach, this place offers a well-used volleyball court.

Hotels Newport's downtown hotels are convenient and pricey.

Newport Bay Club & Hotel (☎ 401-849-8600, fax 401-846-6857, W www.newportbayclub.com, 337 Thames St) Suites $89-199 winter, $139-349 summer. On the waterfront at the foot of Memorial Blvd, this hotel sits in an old stone wharf building. Its one-bedroom suites range hugely in price. Call about the several off-season packages, one of which involves in-room massages.

Newport Marriott (☎ 401-849-1000, fax 401-849-3422, W www.marriott.com, 25 America's Cup Ave) Rooms $229-249 Sun-Thur, $249-399 Fri & Sat. Come to this 317-room establishment if you want on-site pools, racquetball courts, saunas and weight machines.

Hyatt Regency Newport (☎ 401-851-1234, fax 401-851-3201, ⓦ www.hyatt.com, 1 Goat Island) Rooms $129-169 winter, $250-385 summer. The 264 rooms of this hotel, sandwiched between Goat Island's harbor and a small lighthouse, feature views of the Newport Bridge and downtown. It's got a ton of amenities.

Inns & B&Bs Unless otherwise mentioned, all inn and B&B rooms have private baths and rates include breakfast.

North of the Newport Gateway Transportation & Visitors Center is the quiet residential district called the Point, with a good collection of small inns and B&Bs. Prices here are generally a bit lower than at lodgings south of the visitor center.

B&B on the Point (☎ 401-846-8377, ⓦ www.bandbonthepoint.com, 102 3rd St) Rooms $90/115 Sun-Thur/Fri & Sat. Between Sycamore and Van Zandt, this is a comfy, plain place (rooms have color TV) and a bit farther than most from Newport's center, so you can except a more reasonable rate.

Sarah Kendall House (☎ 401-846-7976, 800-758-9578, ⓦ www.sarahkendallhouse .com, 47 Washington St) Rooms $125-195 off-season, $150-275 in-season. The rooms boast working fireplaces, air-conditioning and cable TV. If you stay here, climb the B&B's tower to a rooftop cupola for a view of everywhere. The perfect manicured garden might even be too nice.

Stella Maris Inn (☎ 401-849-2862, 91 Washington St) Rooms $120-130 Sun-Thur, $150-180 Fri & Sat. This big, quiet stone-and-frame inn has numerous fireplaces and heaps of black-walnut furnishings. Rooms with garden views rent for less than those overlooking the water.

Sanford-Covell Villa Marina (☎ 401-847-0206, ⓦ www.sanford-covell.com, 72 Washington St) Rooms $125-255. This Victorian 'Stick-style' place was perhaps Newport's most lavish house when a cousin of Ralph W Emerson built it in 1869. Restored by a team of historians from RISD and beyond in the 1980s, every detail enjoys period accuracy. Outside, kick back on the

waterfront wraparound veranda or take a dip in a saltwater swimming pool. Rooms vary in size, and some have shared baths. The most expensive provide water views. One of them contains the oldest bathtub in the States.

Admiral Fitzroy Inn (☎ 401-848-8000, 866-848-8780, fax 401-848-8006, ⓦ www .admiralfitzroy.com, 398 Thames St) Rooms $85-165 off-season, $125-225 May-Oct. Set a bit back from the street, the location of this inn provides guests some (but not complete) protection from the noise of Newport's nightlife. Each of the 17 large rooms has some period furnishings, a mini-fridge and color TV. Enjoy the ample parking behind the inn (a valuable asset in Newport).

Covell Guest House (☎ 401-847-8872, 43 Farewell St) Rooms $100-155 Sun-Thur, $125-170 Fri & Sat. This five-room guesthouse is several blocks to the east of the Point. It was built in 1805 and renovated in 1982.

South of the visitor center, on Historic Hill and off lower Thames St, are many more inns and B&Bs at slightly higher prices. Here are a few of the better-value, quieter ones.

Baldwin Place (☎ 401-847-3801, 888-880-3764, 41 Pelham St) Rooms $100-200 off-season, $150-300 May-Oct. This is a lovely, centrally located Second Empire–style house, built around 1865 and recently restored to its original splendor. Each of its four rooms is individually decorated; an English garden and hot tub are ideal places to relax, and several cats are effective lap-warmers on chilly days. Stuart, one of the proprietors, can recommend all kinds of places to visit.

Ivy Lodge (☎ 401-849-6865, 800-834-6865, 12 Clay St) Rooms $135-185 with buffet breakfast. Though not quite as grand as other Bellevue mansions nearby, the three-story entrance hall of this impressive place packs a wallop, with elaborate oak paneling, a series of interior balconies and a Moorish fireplace. The rooms ain't too shabby either.

The Willows of Newport (☎ 401-846-5486, ⓦ www.thewillowsofnewport.com,

8 Willow St) Rooms $128-158 off-season, $188-278 in-season. The four rooms of the Willows feature poetry, mints and canopy beds, breakfast in bed included; check out the 'French Victorian secret garden,' full of frog statuary, wooden cartoon bunnies and massive pink bird feeders.

Francis Malbone House (☎ *401-846-0392, 800-846-0392, fax 401-848-5956,* W *www .malbone.com, 392 Thames St*) Doubles $155-225 off-season, $175-285 May-Oct. This grand brick mansion was designed by the Touro Synagogue's architect and built in 1760 for a shipping merchant. Now beautifully decorated and immaculately kept, with a lush garden in back, it is one of Newport's finest inns. Some guest rooms have working fireplaces, as do the public rooms. Breakfast and afternoon tea are included.

Places to Eat

From June through September, reserve your table for dinner in advance, then show up on time or lose your spot. Some restaurants do not take reservations, in which case you must get in line early. Many Newport restaurants don't accept credit cards; ask about payment when you reserve. Unless otherwise noted, eateries listed here are open for lunch and dinner.

The richest selection of restaurants in all price ranges is undoubtedly along lower Thames St, south of America's Cup Ave. Some allow you to 'BYO' (bring your own wine or beer), which you can buy at ***Thames St Liquors*** (☎ *401-847-0017, 517 Thames St*) or at ***Wellington Square Liquors*** (☎ *401-846-9463, 580 Thames St*).

Gary's Handy Lunch (☎ *401-847-9480, 462 Thames-St*) Breakfast & lunch $1.50-5.50. Open 5am-3pm Sun-Fri, 5am-8pm Sat. Locals crowd the booths of this cheap and popular old-school diner for eggs and ground beef.

Franklin Spa (☎ *401-847-3540, 229 Spring St*) Breakfast $2-7. Open 6am-2pm Mon-Sat, 7am-1:30pm Sun. This joint slings hash, eggs and grease for cheap. Watch from the bar as the fellas at the grill struggle to keep up with heavy weekend demand while you ease down your OJ.

The Sandwich Board Deli Cafe (☎ *401-849-5358, 397 Thames St*) Dishes $2-6. Breakfast bagels, luncheon salads and cheap sandwiches can be consumed at sidewalk tables.

Salas' (☎ *401-846-7088, 345 Thames St*) Mains $8-15. Above Percy's Bistro but with a separate entrance, this Newport institution for the hearty, hungry and thrifty serves simple and tasty Italian, American, 'Oriental' and seafood dishes, plus a children's menu. The meatball sandwich costs $4, and the huge plates of pasta in red clam sauce are sold by weight.

Brick Alley Pub & Restaurant (☎ *401-849-6334, 140 Thames St*) Mains $8-18. This centrally located, ever-popular place has a huge menu of snacks, sandwiches, bar food, Mexican specialties and full meals, as well as Newport's most elaborate drinks list. Try the all-you-can-eat soup, salad and bread bar for $9. There is also an outdoor eating area.

The Black Pearl (☎ *401-846-5264, Bannister's Wharf*) This is Newport's 'old reliable,' offering three types of dining. ***The Tavern***'s sandwich board and seafood menu ($8 to $20) are long and varied, the atmosphere suitably nautical; have a big bowl of clam chowder and a beer for less than $10. For traditional swordfish, steaks and rack of lamb ($20 to $38) in fancier surroundings, there's the ***Commodore's Room***. The ***Hot Dog Annex*** supplies cheap snacks.

Cafe Zelda (☎ *401-849-4002, 528 Thames St*) Mains $11-20. This dimly lit bistro, whose menu changes seasonally, offers dishes such as seared striper over a potato and gorgonzola pancake with spinach-tomato broth. The very popular bar is in a separate space next door.

Scales & Shells (☎ *401-846-3474, 527 Thames St*) Mains $11-41. This is a moderately priced, plainly decorated retro seafood place, with an open kitchen and a blackboard menu. Have your squid or lobster grilled for a change, with a glass of chardonnay from Greenvale, a local Rhode Island vineyard.

UpScales (☎ *401-847-2000, 527 Thames St*) Scales & Shells' more genteel 2nd-floor dining room has slightly higher prices. Come early or make a reservation; there's often a two-hour wait in summer.

Percy's Bistro (☎ *401-849-7895, 341 Thames St*) Mains $13-20. Just off Memorial Blvd, this is a good, storefront place for a quiet, romantic dinner. Low lights, moderately priced main courses and cheap daily specials are the attractions.

Cheeky Monkey Cafe (☎ *401-845-9494, 14 Perry Mill Wharf*) Dining room mains $22-28. Open Tues-Sat. Popular with the BMW and SUV sets, this chic place offers dishes such as lobster fritters with key lime and white truffle aioli. Cheeky Monkey's lunch and bistro menus will cost you far less than the main dining room's.

White Horse Tavern (☎ *401-849-3600, 26 Marlborough St*) Lunch $13-20, dinner $28-36. For traditional American and continental fare made with local ingredients when possible, try this historic tavern (the oldest in the US), which opened in 1687. Dinner (at which men must wear a jacket) costs big bucks; lunch is somewhat less.

Bouchard (☎ *401-846-0123, 505 Thames St*) Bouchard is great for a splurge. American chef Albert Bouchard prepares nouvelle-French cuisine that's not prissy. A three-course dinner costs about $60 per person, wine, tax and tip included.

Entertainment

This is a resort town, and in July and August it rocks at night (see Special Events, earlier). But really, any day is a good one for finding a congenial cafe, pub or music club. For what's going on, check out the *Providence Journal*'s daily 'Lifebeat' section.

Cappy's Hillside Cafe (☎ *401-847-9419, 8 Memorial Blvd W*) Populated by locals and fishermen, this bar opened on the day the hurricane of '38 devastated New England. Fortunately Cappy's, now one of the oldest bars in Newport, survived. If you feel like surprising the bartender, order a Ballentine ale, stocked for the single regular who drinks it.

Mudville's Pub (☎ *401-849-1408, 8 W Marlborough St*) With a back porch sitting about 10 feet from the foul line of Cardines

Field's outfield (see Spectator Sports, below), this bar fills many local sports fans with pub food and beer. It even sponsors a team (the Mudville Nine) that plays in one of Cardines' leagues.

The Red Parrot (☎ *401-847-3140, 348 Thames St*) This huge three-story restaurant books jazz for Friday night entertainment. The menu lists burgers starting at $6 and other bar dishes up to $18. The warm goat cheese mesclun salad defines 'fresh' and 'good.'

One Pelham East (☎ *401-847-9460, 1 Pelham St*) Opposite Bannister's Wharf, this is the place to come for an Irish theme and live music (not all Irish) on many nights. Pelham St, by the way, was the first street in the USA illuminated by gas (1805) and remains lit that way today.

Newport Blues Cafe (☎ *401-841-5510, 286 Thames St*) This popular rhythm and blues bar draws quality acts. A program gets posted on the door a month in advance, and the cover is often steep.

JJ Phelan's Oasis (☎ *401-848-5555, 162 Broadway*) Surrounded by tattoo parlors, the Oasis, a rock bar specializing in streetcred, provides a space for down-and-out/up-and-coming bands in a small setting. Get your ska, punk and power chords on here, or just play some pool.

Spectator Sports

Cardines Field (*cnr America's Cup Ave & Marlborough St*) Tickets $1-4. Likely the third oldest standing baseball field in the US (after Wrigley Field and Fenway Park), this relic, home to the ancient Newport Sunset league, allows you to see some surprisingly skilled ball for cheap. Because of the seating's close proximity to the field and because the games are sparsely attended, you can easily hear the players trash-talk each other. According to local legend, Babe Ruth once played a game here.

Newport Grand Jai Alai (☎ *401-849-5000, 150 Admiral Kalbfus Rd*) At this supremely tacky gambling facility you can watch jai alai, an obscure Spanish game, that involves guys wearing helmets and white pants, with little sashes around their waists, hurling a ball back and forth with baskets strapped on their hands. You actually can bet on this game. There are slot machines, too. You need to be over 18 to get in.

Shopping

The Armory Antique & Fine Arts Center (☎ 401-848-2398, 365 Thames St) This shop has more than 125 antique dealers in one building – an ivy-covered, castle-like former armory now stuffed with pottery, porcelain, paintings, estate jewelry and furniture.

Getting There & Away

Bonanza Bus Lines (☎ 401-846-1820, 888-751-8800), at the Newport Gateway Transportation & Visitors Center, operates a half-dozen buses daily between Newport and Boston (1¾ hours, including Logan Airport) via Fall River, MA.

The Rhode Island Public Transit Authority (RIPTA; ☎ 401-781-9400, 800-244-0444) runs its buses on RI 60 between Newport (Gateway Center) and Providence (Kennedy Plaza, Francis St Terminus) at least every hour for $4, from around 5am to midnight weekdays, 7am to 11pm weekends and holidays. There's also a shuttle service to TF Green State Airport (☎ 401-737-8222).

From late May through mid-October, RIPTA operates buses connecting Newport with the Amtrak railroad station in Kingston for $3. Express buses make the trip in 35 minutes.

A summer ferry (☎ 401-783-4613) from Providence ($4 one-way) stops at Fort Adams Dock, taking passengers to Block Island (a two-hour trip); see the Block Island section, later, for details.

Getting Around

RIPTA runs several bus routes from the Newport Gateway Transportation & Visitors Center every 30 minutes: Bus No 61/Orange Line runs to First and Second Beaches; bus No 62/Red Line runs along Thames St to Fort Adams; bus No 63/Purple Line runs to Middletown and the motels described in Places to Stay, earlier; and bus No 67/Yellow Line runs along Bellevue Ave to the mansions.

See Bicycling, earlier in this section, for bike-rental information.

GALILEE & POINT JUDITH

Rhode Island's port for car ferries to Block Island is at Galilee State Pier, at the southern end of RI 108 in the village of Galilee, near Point Judith. Galilee – sometimes called Point Judith in ferry schedules – is a real workaday fishing town with docks for fishing craft, a dock for the ferries, Roger W Wheeler Memorial Beach, and Fishermen's Memorial State Park (see Rhode Island Beaches, later in this chapter, for camping information).

All-day parking in Galilee costs about $10 in any of several lots.

The *Portside Restaurant & Chowder House*, the *Top of the Dock Restaurant* and other eateries are good for a drink or snack while you're waiting for the boat. (See the following Block Island section for ferry details.)

Champlin's Seafood (☎ 401-783-3152, 256 Great Rd) Dishes $3-15. This eatery in Galilee's port is casual, with an outdoor deck that overlooks the activity of the port.

George's of Galilee (☎ 401-783-2306, cnr Sand Hill Cove & Great Rds) Prices $3-10. Also at the port, George's has a takeout window where hordes of sandy people line up on summer afternoons for clamcakes that are crisp on the outside, doughy on the inside and studded with bits of clam.

BLOCK ISLAND

This 11-sq-mile island, shaped something like a pork chop, exists as an isolated community for most of the year, until it explodes into a tourist haven during the heat of summer. It gets particularly busy during Block Island Race Week, usually held in June, when yachters come from all over the East Coast to compete in a series of races around the island.

During off-season, the island landscape has the spare, haunted feeling of an Andrew Wyeth painting, with stone walls demarcating centuries-old property lines and few trees to interrupt the ocean views. At this time, the island's population dwindles to a

RHODE ISLAND

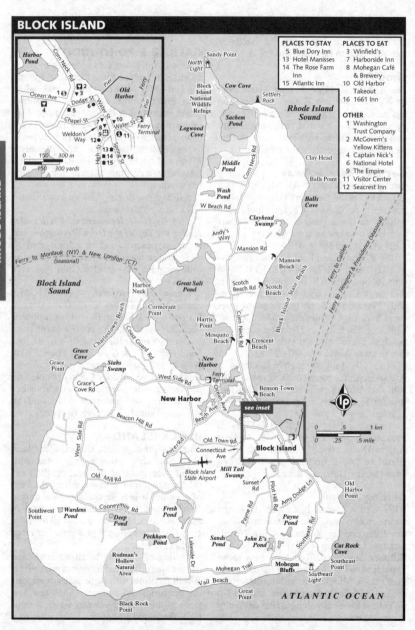

BLOCK ISLAND

PLACES TO STAY
5 Blue Dory Inn
13 Hotel Manisses
14 The Rose Farm Inn
15 Atlantic Inn

PLACES TO EAT
3 Winfield's
7 Harborside Inn
8 Mohegan Café & Brewery
10 Old Harbor Takeout
16 1661 Inn

OTHER
1 Washington Trust Company
2 McGovern's Yellow Kittens
4 Captain Nick's
6 National Hotel
9 The Empire
11 Visitor Center
12 Seacrest Inn

Harbor Pond

Corn Neck Rd

Pier

Old Harbor

Ferry

Ocean Ave

Dodge St

Water St

Chapel St

Weldon's Way

Water St

High St

Spring St

Ferry Terminal

0   150   300 m
0   150   300 yards

North Light

Sandy Point

Cow Cove

Settlers Rock

Block Island National Wildlife Refuge

Sachem Pond

Logwood Cove

Rhode Island Sound

Clay Head

Balls Point

Middle Pond

Corn Neck Rd

Wash Pond

W Beach Rd

Balls Cove

Clayhead Swamp

Andy's Way

Mansion Rd

Mansion Beach

Ferry to Montauk (NY) & New London (CT) (seasonal)

Ferry to Galilee

Ferry to Newport & Providence (seasonal)

Block Island Sound

Harbor Neck

Great Salt Pond

Scotch Beach Rd

Scotch Beach

Block Island State Beach

Charlestown Beach

Coast Guard Rd

Cormorant Point

Harris Point

Mosquito Beach

Corn Neck Rd

Crescent Beach

Grace Cove

Grace Point

Slahs Swamp

Grace's Cove Rd

West Side Rd

New Harbor

Ferry Terminal

Benson Town Beach

New Harbor

Beacon Hill Rd

Beach Ave

Ocean Ave

see inset

Block Island

West Side Rd

Center Rd

Old Town Rd

Connecticut Ave

Block Island State Airport

Mill Tail Swamp

0   .5   1 km
0   .25   .5 mile

Old Mill Rd

Cooneymus Rd

Sunset Rd

Payne Rd

Amy Dodge Ln

Pilot Hill Rd

Old Harbor Point

Southwest Point

Wardens Pond

Deep Pond

Fresh Pond

Peckham Pond

Lakeside Dr

Sands Pond

John E's Pond

Payne Pond

Southeast Rd

Cat Rock Cove

Rodman's Hollow Natural Area

Mohegan Trail

Mohegan Bluffs

Southeast Light

Southeast Point

Vail Beach

Great Point

Black Rock Point

ATLANTIC OCEAN

few hundred. During the summer months, throngs of beachgoers, lemonade stands and cyclists pack it full for a completely different experience.

History

In 1614, before the Pilgrims founded their settlement at Plymouth, MA, a mariner named Adriaen Block stopped at this island and gave it his name.

When colonists attempted to settle a decade later, the local Pequot tribe strongly resisted. In fact, the 1637 murder of an English trader by the Block Island Pequot was one of the principal causes of New England's Pequot War. But by 1672, the thriving fishing town of New Shoreham received a royal charter.

Fishing and farming were mainstays of the island's economy for almost two centuries (bootlegging was a big deal, too). In the mid-19th century, the development of fast, dependable steam-powered vessels and the wealth of the New England economy made it possible for mainlanders to take affordable summer vacations on the island. Steamboats made regular trips from New York and Boston, and the hotels were full of long-skirted ladies and men in straw boaters.

Besides the increasingly large number of seasonal tourists that arrive, not much changes on Block Island from one year to the next. The row of gingerbread Victorian inns along the Old Harbor landing shows the same face to visitors that it did 50 or even 100 years ago, and the island's simple attractions remain much the same as well. In a nutshell, these are the 'four Bs': beaches, boating, bicycling and birds.

Orientation & Information

It's confusing: All of Block Island is incorporated as the town of New Shoreham, but the main settlement is known as Old Harbor, or just 'the town.'

Most of the boating activity is in New Harbor, the island's other main settlement, on the shore of Great Salt Pond.

For tourist information, contact the Block Island Chamber of Commerce (☎ 401-466-2982, 800-383-2474, [W] www.blockisland .com, PO Drawer D, Water St, Block Island, RI 02807). It's open from 9am to 5pm daily during the summer with shorter hours other seasons.

Southeast Light

You'll likely recognize this red-brick lighthouse building from postcards of the island. Set dramatically atop 200-foot red-clay cliffs called **Mohegan Bluffs**, the lighthouse had to be moved back from the eroding cliff edge in 1993. With waves crashing below and sails moving across the Atlantic offshore, it's probably the best place on the island to watch the sunset.

North Light

At **Sandy Point**, the northernmost tip of the island, scenic North Light stands at the end of a long sandy path lined with beach roses. The 1867 lighthouse contains a small maritime museum with information about famous island wrecks. As you travel there along Corn Neck Rd, watch for a cluster of competing lemonade stands. On a hot day, you'll pray that one is open. Emily's sells a cup for 50¢.

Beaches

The island's east coast, north of Old Harbor, is lined with 2 miles of glorious beach, the **Block Island State Beach**. The southern part, **Benson Town Beach**, sits closest to town; it's got a pavilion for changing and showering. Heading north, you'll next hit **Crescent Beach**, then **Scotch Beach** and finally **Mansion Beach**, named for a mansion of which nothing is left but the foundation. The farther up you go, the smaller the crowd gets.

Bicycling

The island is a convenient size for biking, and bicycles as well as mopeds are available for rental at many places in Old Harbor. In fact, many people save money by leaving their cars parked at the ferry dock in Galilee on the mainland and bring only their bikes for a day trip.

Rentals are available from the **Old Harbor Bike Shop** (☎ *401-466-2029, 50 yards* *from ferry dock),* **Seacrest Inn** (☎ 401-466-2882, *High St)* and many other places. Expect to pay about $20 per day for bikes, $70 per day for mopeds. Most islanders resent the noise and hazards caused by tourists on mopeds, so you'll get friendlier greetings (and exercise) if you opt for a bicycle.

Boating
Fishing charters, kayaks, canoes and other types of boats may be booked through **Oceans & Ponds – The Orvis Store** (☎ 401-466-5131, *Ocean Ave).*

Hiking & Bird Watching
The island provides some great places to hike: **Rodman's Hollow** (entrance off Cherry Hill Rd) is a 100-acre wildlife refuge laced with trails that end at the beach – perfect for a picnic. The **Clay Head Nature Trail** (off Corn Neck Rd) follows high clay bluffs along the beachfront, then veers inland through a mazelike series of paths cut into low vegetation that attracts dozens of species of bird.

Bird-watching opportunities abound, especially in spring and fall when migratory species make their way north or south along the Atlantic Flyway. The island's verdant landscape and many freshwater ponds provide ample habitat. **The Nature Conservancy** (☎ 401-466-21290) leads visitors on guided nature walks in some refuges. Call for details.

Places to Stay
Camping is not allowed on the island, but there are some 35 cozy B&Bs and small guesthouse-style inns. You should know, however, that many places have a two- or three-day minimum stay in summer (especially on weekends and holidays) and that advance reservations are essential. Many places close between November and April.

The visitor center near the ferry dock keeps track of vacancies, and its staff will try to help you should you make the mistake of arriving without a reservation.

The Rose Farm Inn (☎ 401-466-2034, ⓔ rosefarm@blockisland.com, *Box E, Block Island, RI 02807)* Rooms $109-235. Rose

Farm is convenient both to Old Harbor and the beach. The older part of the inn has fine views of the ocean; a newer addition called the Captain Rose House offers nine rooms with more modern accoutrements.

Atlantic Inn (☎ 401-466-5883, 800-224-7422, Ⓦ www.atlanticinn.com, *High St)* Doubles $130-260. This 1879 establishment in Old Harbor overlooks the activities at the ferry landing from its hilltop perch. The gracefully proportioned Victorian inn features a wide porch, 21 rooms and a well-stocked bar. Bill Clinton ate here in 1997.

Blue Dory Inn (☎ 401-466-5891, 800-992-7290, *Box 488, Dodge St)* Doubles $135-225. With 14 small rooms, this cozy place sits at the edge of Old Harbor near the beach. Decorated in Victorian style, the inn oozes with 'romantic' flourishes. Some love it, others might find it a touch saccharine.

Hotel Manisses (☎ 401-466-2421, 800-626-4773, fax 401-466-3162, *Spring St)* Rooms $50-315 – see below. The fanciest hotel on the island is this place in Old Harbor. With its high Victorian 'widow's walk' turret and small but lushly furnished guest rooms, the Manisses combines sophistication with Block Island's relaxed brand of country charm. It's part of a family accommodations business that includes the 1661 Inn, 1661 Guest House, Dewey Cottage, Dodge Cottage, Nicholas Ball Cottage and Sheffield House, so one call gets you information on dozens of rooms ranging in price from $50 to $315 depending upon the room, the building and the season. Buffet breakfast, wine and cheese hour, an island tour and service (but not tax) are included.

Places to Eat
Block Island specializes in fish, shellfish and more fish. Generally, cheap food = fried fish; expensive food = not-fried fish. Most places are open for lunch and dinner during the summer; many close off season.

Old Harbor Takeout (☎ 401-466-2935, *Water St)* Prices $3-6. This shack provides burgers, cheap sandwiches and frozen lemonade.

Mohegan Café & Brewery (☎ 401-466-5911) Mains $8-20. Besides brewing its own beer, this place serves items such as Jamaican jerked mako and some vegetarian options.

1661 Inn (☎ 401-466-2421, Spring St) Prices $15-25. This place serves an excellent – if somewhat pricey – outdoor buffet brunch on a grassy hillside overlooking the Atlantic.

Harborside Inn (☎ 401-466-5504, Water St) Lunch $10-20. This is a good choice for lunch. You can't miss the red umbrellas on its outdoor patio as you step off the ferry at Old Harbor. Expect to spend $20 and up at dinnertime.

Winfield's (☎ 401-466-5856, Corn Neck Rd) Mains $15-30. For a classier dining experience, try Winfield's. It has exposed wooden ceiling beams, white tablecloths and a menu that features such classics as rack of lamb and filet mignon at prices similar to those at the Hotel Manisses, below.

Hotel Manisses (☎ 401-466-2421, Spring St) Mains $16-35. One of the best dining rooms on the island is at this hotel. Vegetables come from the hotel's garden, and the style of cooking is creative, often featuring fresh local seafood. Full dinners cost around $40 to $50 per person.

Entertainment
Though Block Island quiets down after the last ferry leaves, you can still find some stuff to do at night.

McGovern's Yellow Kittens (☎ 401-466-5855, Corn Neck Rd) Just north of Old Harbor, McGovern's attracts New England–area bands and keeps patrons happy with pool, table tennis and darts. It's been called Yellow Kittens since 1876.

Captain Nick's (☎ 401-466-5670, Ocean Ave) With a patch over one eye, this youngster offers drinks, live music, good times and vivid treasure.

National Hotel (☎ 401-466-2901, Water St) The elevated porch of this hotel, across from the ferry landing, has a relaxed 'Margaritaville' atmosphere, with live music on most summer evenings.

There are two places to catch first-run movies on Block Island: *Oceanwest Theater*

(☎ 401-466-2971, New Harbor) and *The Empire (☎ 401-466-2555, cnr High & Water Sts)*, which is in a former roller-skating rink in Old Harbor.

Shopping
Opportunities for shopping are limited. Most shops are small, seasonal boutiques along Water and Dodge Sts in Old Harbor. Take a look at the *Ragged Sailor* (crafts, paintings and folk art), the *Scarlet Begonia* (jewelry and craft items for the home) and the *Star Department Store*, a wood-floored classic that calls itself 'Block Island's general store.' Come here for saltwater taffy and corny island souvenirs.

Getting There & Away
Air New England Airlines (☎ 401-596-2460, 800-243-2460) provides air service between Westerly State Airport, on Airport Rd off RI 78, and Block Island State Airport (25 minutes) for $70 per person roundtrip.

Boat Interstate Navigation Co and Nelseco Navigation Co (☎ 401-783-4613 reservations, 203-442-7891 or 442-9553 offices, ⓦ www.blockislandferry.com), based in New London, CT, operate the ferry services to Block Island.

Interstate operates the car-and-passenger ferries from Galilee State Pier, Galilee, to Old Harbor, Block Island, a voyage of just over an hour. Adults pay $13.50 for a same-day roundtrip ticket, children half-price. Cars are carried for $26.30 each way; reserve your car space in advance.

A daily Interstate passenger boat runs in summer (late June to mid-September) from Providence's India St Dock (four hours, $13.70) via Newport's Fort Adams Dock (two hours, $7.65) to Old Harbor, Block Island; children pay half of these same-day roundtrip adult fares. This boat takes bikes but not cars; finding safe, inexpensive parking in Providence and Newport can be difficult.

Nelseco runs a daily car-and-passenger ferry from early June to early September. It leaves New London at breakfast time and it returns from Old Harbor, Block Island, in the late afternoon. The two-hour voyage (same-day roundtrip) costs $17.50 for adults, $11 for children, $50 for a car (make your reservations in advance).

Viking Star (☎ 631-688-5700) runs passenger ferries between Montauk, Long Island, and Old Harbor (1¾ hours) from mid-May through mid-October.

Getting Around
Block Island Car Rental (☎ 401-466-2297) rents cars, or you can hire a taxi. There are usually several taxis available at the ferry dock in Old Harbor and in New Harbor. See Bicycling, above, for moped and bicycle rentals.

WATCH HILL
One of the toniest summer colonies in the Ocean State, Watch Hill occupies a spit of land at the southwesternmost point of Rhode Island, just south of Westerly. Drive into the village along winding RI 1A, and the place grabs you: Huge shingled and Queen Anne summerhouses command the rolling landscape from their perches high on rocky knolls. These houses show the wealth of their owners with subtle good taste; though they were built around the turn of the century, contemporaneously with Newport's mansions, they aren't flashy palaces. Perhaps partly because of that, Watch Hill's houses are still in private hands, while Newport's became white elephants, rescued only as tourist attractions.

Visitors not lucky enough to own a summerhouse here spend their time at the beach and browsing in the shops along Bay St, the main street. If you haven't yet hit puberty or if you've brought children, an ice cream cone from St Clair's Annex and a twirl on the Flying Horses Carousel provide immediate gratification and fodder for fond memories.

Watch Hill is at the end of Watch Hill Rd, 6 miles south of Westerly and 12 roundabout miles east of Stonington, CT, by car.

Flying Horses Carousel
The antique merry-go-round at the end of Bay St dates from 1883. Besides being among the few historic carousels still in operation in the country, it boasts a unique design: Its horses are suspended on chains so that they really do 'fly' outward as the carousel spins around. Rides cost $1 apiece. Yes, riders can grab for rings (a brass one equals a free ride), and no, *you* can't, it's for kids only.

Beaches
For a leisurely beach walk, the half-mile stroll to **Napatree Point**, at the westernmost tip of Watch Hill, is unbeatable. With the Atlantic on one side and the yacht-studded Little Narragansett Bay on the other, Napatree is a protected conservation area, so walkers are asked to stay on the trails and off the dunes.

The nearest state beach to Watch Hill is **Misquamicut State Beach** (see that listing, later), 3 miles to the east along RI 1A, but there is a fine beach, **Ocean House Beach**, right in Watch Hill, in front of the Ocean House Hotel. Access to the beach is by a right-of-way off Bluff Ave, but there is no parking nearby, and neighboring property owners are vigilant about restricting beachgoers to the public area below the high-tide line. There's also small **Watch Hill Beach**, open to the public for a fee, behind the Flying Horses Carousel.

Places to Stay
Watch Hill Inn (☎ 401-348-6301, fax 401-348-6301, W www.watchhillinn.com, 38 Bay St) Rooms $85-120 off-season, $165-220 in-season. These wood-floored, air-conditioned rooms overlook the action of Watch Hill's cluster of shops.

Ocean House Hotel (☎ 401-348-8161, 2 Bluff Ave) Doubles $205-260 with breakfast & dinner. Open late June-early Sept. This is the grand old lady of hotels in Watch Hill, the lone survivor of a series of fires and hurricanes that destroyed its Victorian sisters by about 1950. While it's true that the yellow-clapboard Ocean House looks a bit less spiffy inside these days (the last renovation seems to have occurred when indoor plumbing became popular), the hotel's art deco chandeliers and fancy-town ballroom will still kick your butt. The massive ocean-front porch is a great spot to sit with a drink after a day at the beach. It's rumored that Ocean House may get a four-star makeover and new owners at some time in the near future.

Places to Eat

Bay Street Deli *(☎ 401-596-6606, 110 Bay St)* Sandwiches $5.50-8. Locals come here for specialty sandwiches, including good takeout for picnics.

St Clair's Annex *(☎ 401-348-8407, 41 Bay St)* Cones $2 & up. This ice cream shop, across the street from the deli, has been run by the same family for more than a century, and features more than 30 flavors of home-made ice cream.

Olympia Tea Room *(☎ 401-348-8211, 74 Bay St)* Lunch $10-12, dinner $20-28. The most atmospheric restaurant in town, the Olympia is an authentic 1918 soda fountain turned bistro. Varnished wooden booths, black-and-white checkered tiles on the floor and the antique marble-topped soda fountain help to ease baked scrod and ginger-bread down your throat.

Beach Activities

South County's salt ponds and tidal rivers are ideal for **kayaking** and **canoeing**. It's even possible to venture out into the surf in a sea kayak. Outfitters in the area include Quaker Lane Bait & Tackle (☎ 401-294-9642, 4019 Quaker Lane, North Kingstown).

Narragansett Town Beach is considered to be among the top spots on the East Coast for **surfing**. You can rent surfboards, sailboards and any other water-sports gear you might need at The Watershed (☎ 401-789-3399, 396 Main St, Wakefield). The owner offers surfing lessons as well.

For the adventurous, **deep-sea fishing** trips – for a whole or a half day – can be arranged with the Frances Fleet (☎ 401-783-4988, 800-662-2824, 2 State St, Galilee). The Frances fleet also runs whale-watching cruises in summer. If you want to charter a boat for a longer trip, contact Snug Harbor Marina (☎ 401-783-7766, 410 Gooseberry Rd, Galilee).

Rhode Island Beaches

It's not by accident that Rhode Island's nickname is 'the Ocean State.' Though it will take you less than an hour to drive from one end of the state to the other, Rhode Island somehow manages to cram 400 miles of coastline into its borders.

Rhode Island's topography divides its beaches into two general styles: those that sit on the ocean and those that sit on the Narragansett Bay (which is better for boaters than for beachgoers). The best-known beaches in the state lie in what is known as South County, the colloquial name for the southwestern coastline towns from Narragansett to Watch Hill.

Most public beaches in Rhode Island charge parking fees ranging from $5 to $15 per day from mid-June to Labor Day. The best deals are the state beaches, where state residents pay $5 to $7, and out-of-staters $10 to $12, to park. Reasonably priced season passes (which may be used at any state beach) are a good option if you're going to spend more than a few days at the beach during your stay.

Below is a selective look at some of the best beaches the Ocean State has to offer.

SOUTH COUNTY BEACHES

These beaches, which trace the coast like a necklace looped with tidal salt ponds, are similar in nature and, geologically speaking, are all the same beach: a wide apron of pristine sand separating huge salt ponds such as Quonochontaug and Ninigret from the surfy, generally seaweed-free open ocean.

The salt ponds are home to multitudes of waterfowl and shellfish, and some (such as Trustom Pond in South Kingstown) have been designated as national wildlife refuges. If you're the type of person who gets bored

SOUTH COUNTY & NARRAGANSETT AREA BEACHES

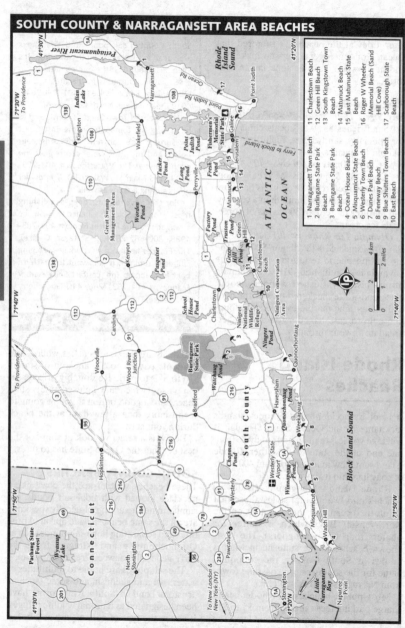

1 Narragansett Town Beach
2 Burlingame State Park Beach
3 Burlingame State Park Beach
4 Ocean House Beach
5 Misquamicut State Beach
6 Westerly Town Beach
7 Dunes Park Beach
8 Feneway Beach
9 Blue Shutters Town Beach
10 East Beach
11 Charlestown Beach
12 Green Hill Beach
13 South Kingstown Town Beach
14 Matunuck Beach
15 East Matunuck State Beach
16 Roger W Wheeler Memorial Beach (Sand Hill Cove)
17 Scarborough State Beach

just lying in the sun, take a bird-watching walk around the salt ponds instead. You're likely to see herons, egrets and sandpipers hunting for lunch, and, at low tide, clams squirting from beneath the muddy sand.

For information on the South County beaches and attractions, contact the South County Tourism Council (☎ 401-789-4422, 800-548-4662, Ⓦ www.southcounty.com, 4808 Tower Hill Rd, Wakefield).

Roger W Wheeler Memorial Beach

Colloquially known as **Sand Hill Cove**, families with small children come here. Not only does it have a playground and other facilities, it also has an extremely gradual drop-off and little surf because of protection afforded by the rocky arms of a breakwater called the Point Judith Harbor of Refuge. Roger W Wheeler Memorial Beach is just south of Galilee.

South Kingstown Town Beach

A sandy beach that epitomizes the South County model, the Town Beach provides a small pavilion with restrooms and convenient parking in nearby Wakefield.

Blue Shutters Town Beach

A Charlestown-managed beach, this is also a good choice for families. There are no amusements other than nature's, but there are convenient facilities, a watchful staff of lifeguards, generally mild surf and smaller crowds.

Misquamicut State Beach

With good surf and close proximity to the Connecticut state line, Misquamicut draws huge crowds. It offers families low prices and convenient facilities for changing, showering and eating. Another plus is that it's near an old-fashioned amusement area, Atlantic Beach Park, which ranges between charming and derelict. Here you'll find plenty to enjoy or avoid – water slides, miniature golf, T-shirt hawkers, kiddie rides, arcade games and, for a lucky few, tetanus shots. Misquamicut is situated just south of Westerly.

Places to Stay

Camping The state-managed campgrounds (Ⓦ www.riparks.com) in South County are among the prettiest spots in the state. The fee to camp at these campgrounds is $12, $16 for hookups.

Legrand G Reynolds Horsemen's Camping Area (☎ 401-539-2356, 277-1157, *Escoheag Hill Rd, Exeter*) Sites $3. You must be on horseback to camp in one of the 20 sites. To get there, take I-95 exit 5S, then follow RI 102, then take RI 3 to RI 165 west, and go north on Escoheag Hill Rd.

Burlingame State Park Campsites (☎ 401-322-7994, 322-7337, *off US 1, Charlestown*) Sites $12. This campground has more than 750 wooded sites near crystal-clear Watchaug Pond. First-come, first-served is the rule, but you can call ahead to check on availability.

Charlestown Beachway (☎ 401-364-7000, 322-8910, *off Charlestown Beach Rd, Charlestown*) RV sites $12. Open mid-Apr–Oct. This state-run place has 75 RV sites with running water only, and spots to fish and swim.

Ninigret Conservation Area (☎ 401-322-0450, *off E Beach Rd, Charlestown*) Sites $12. This area has 30 RV sites, but you need a special summerlong permit ($50).

Private campgrounds include the following properties:

Worden's Pond Family Campground (☎ 401-789-9113, 416A Worden's Pond Rd, South Kingstown*) Tent/RV sites $17/20. This pleasantly wooded campground, with 75 tent sites and 125 RV sites, provides access to a calm pond where you can fish and swim. From US Hwy 1, follow RI Hwy 110, and turn at the second left (Worden's Pond Rd); from there, it's less than a mile to the campground.

Wakamo Park Resort (☎ 401-783-6688, *Succotash Rd, South Kingstown*) RV sites $45. Open mid-Apr–mid-Oct. This resort has 30 RV sites. To get there from I-95 south, take RI 2 to RI 78 to US 1, then follow signs for East Matunuck.

Hotels & B&Bs For extra listings, contact Bed & Breakfast Referrals of South Coast

Rhode Island (☎ 800-853-7479), which takes calls between 9:30am and 9:30pm for 20 quality places.

Grandview Bed & Breakfast (☎ 401-596-6384, 800-447-6384, Ⓦ *www.grandviewbandb .com, 212 Shore Rd/RI 1A)* Rooms $75-95 off-season, $85-110 mid-May–mid-Oct. Within the town limits of Westerly, yet close to the beach town of Weekapaug, this is a comfortable, modestly furnished guesthouse. Its proprietor, Pat Grande, provides good tips on what to do in South County.

Admiral Dewey Inn (☎ 401-783-2090, *668 Matunuck Beach Rd, South Kingstown)* Rooms $90-140. Near the beachy town of Matunuck, this 1898 National Historic Register building with 10 rooms offers reasonable rates in the middle of cutesville. The inn is complete with a porch (also, of course, cute).

Weekapaug Inn (☎ 401-322-0301, Ⓦ *www .weekapauginn.com, 25 Spray Rock Rd, Weekapaug)* Singles $275, doubles $390-425, with all meals. A classic with its wraparound porch and lawn sloping down to Quonochontaug Pond (a saltwater tidal pool), this vast shingled inn caters to a rather sedate crowd, many of whom have been regulars for decades. Expect croquet, shuffleboard, tennis and no phones. The inn's setting, with its own private ocean beach, is one of the loveliest in New England. Men must wear jackets to dinner.

Places to Eat

Not surprisingly, seafood is the order of the day in South County. Most spots are casual and beachy; shorts and T-shirts are far more common than suits and ties. See the Galilee & Point Judith section for listings.

Entertainment

Quiet, seaside South County is not noted for its nightlife, but there are a couple of places in the area where folks can stay up past 9pm.

Theatre-by-the-Sea (☎ 401-782-8587, *Cards Pond Rd, South Kingstown)* Tickets $30. Located in a scenic area close to the beaches of Matunuck, this venue offers a summer schedule of likable musicals and plays in one of the oldest barn theaters in the US.

Ocean Mist (☎ 401-782-3740, *145 Matunuck Beach Rd, South Kingstown)* For live rock music geared to a younger crowd, try this place, set so close to the beach that if it weren't for the crashing bass, you might hear the crashing surf.

Shopping

The Fantastic Umbrella Factory (☎ 401-364-6616, *RI 1A, Charlestown)* A sprawling collection of 19th-century farm buildings and elaborate, unkempt gardens, this former commune got its start as one of Rhode Island's strangest stores in 1968. You can find almost anything in the series of sheds filled with a wide variety of gift items: everything from flower bulbs and perennials to greeting cards, toys and handmade jewelry. The organic cafe (a rarity in Rhode Island) serves quality stuff, and exotic birds and farm animals walk all over the place.

Getting There & Away

Though the *Shore Route* Amtrak trains between Boston and New York stop in Westerly, you really need a car to get to the beaches.

Distances are not great (this is Rhode Island); from Westerly to Wakefield is only about 21 miles. Traffic to and from the South County beaches can be horrendous on hot summer weekends. Come early, stay late.

NARRAGANSETT AREA BEACHES

Though South County's beaches are more famous, don't overlook the smaller ones along the shores of Narragansett Bay. Many are in coves surrounded dramatically by huge boulders. These are particularly lovely early and late in the day when the sun slants on the granite, stage-lighting the scene.

For local information, contact the Narragansett Chamber of Commerce (☎ 401-783-7121, Ⓦ www.narragansettri.com/chamber, The Towers, RI 1A, PO Box 742, Narragansett, RI 02882).

Car is the transportation of choice around Narragansett Bay. Ferries connect

Block Island (see that section) to the mainland at Galilee, Newport and Providence.

Scarborough State Beach
Scarborough (sometimes written as 'Scarboro') is the prototypical Rhode Island beach, considered by many the best in the state. A massive, castle-like pavilion, generous boardwalks, a wide and long beachfront, and great, predictable surf make Scarborough special. It tends to attract a lot of teenagers, but it's large enough that other people can take them or leave them. On a hot summer day, expect extra hordes of beachgoers.

Narragansett Town Beach
Narragansett tends to be crowded because it's an easy walk from the beachy town of Narragansett Pier. It's the only beach in Rhode Island that charges a per-person admission fee ($4) on top of a parking fee ($5). Still, people – surfers in particular – adore it.

Places to Stay & Eat
Fishermen's Memorial State Park (☎ 401-789-8374, off RI 108) Tent sites without hookups $8/12, with hookups $14/16 for residents/out-of-staters. In the fishing port of Galilee, this place is so popular that many families return year after year to the same site. There are only 180 campsites at Fishermen's, so it's wise to reserve early by requesting the necessary form from the park management (1011 Point Judith Rd, Narragansett, RI 02882) or the Division of Parks and Recreation (☎ 401-222-2632, 2321 Hartford Ave, Johnston, RI 02919).

The Richards (☎ 401-789-7746, 144 Gibson Ave) Rooms $95-200. Built of locally quarried granite, the Gothic English-manor look sets it apart from other B&Bs in Narragansett. Elisabeth Shue slept here, likely dreaming of her favorite movie, *Cocktail*.

Every beach has its collection of clam shacks and snack shops good for a quick lunch. For a more elaborate meal, you might just head to Newport or Providence.

For a filling dinner, try *The Coast Guard House (☎ 401-789-0700, 40 Ocean Rd, Narragansett)*, with entrées for $14 to $22. For a fancy night out, this eatery has traditional American favorites such as steak, veal and seafood. It also occupies a dramatic seaside site – one that has made it vulnerable to hurricanes in recent years.

LITTLE COMPTON AREA
Lovely, remote, ocean-facing **Goosewing Beach** is the only good public beach in Little Compton, a town on the east shore of Narragansett Bay. Access can be tricky. Due to an ongoing wrangle between the town and the Nature Conservancy over control of the beach, parking and lifeguard coverage are perennially in question. Still, since the dispute began it has been possible to get onto Goosewing by the unusual means of parking at the town beach called South Shore ($10) and walking across a small tidal inlet to the more appealing Goosewing. What makes it so appealing is immediately apparent: The long sand beach with its wide-open ocean view is backed by rolling farmland that's almost a throwback to another era. With no facilities to speak of, Goosewing can't be called convenient, but you won't forget a summer's day spent here.

To find the beach, head south on RI 77, then make a left onto Swamp Rd. Make a second left onto South Shore Rd, at the end of which you'll find South Shore Beach and Goosewing.

Connecticut

Connecticut is about paradox. To travelers along I-95, Connecticut may seem like one large industrial zone or a bedroom community for New York City. But while the coastal region does indeed manufacture everything from helicopters to submarines, and the towns bordering the commuter rail lines house an army that migrates to work in 'the City' five days a week, the harbors of these industrial and commuter towns are also home to working watermen who fish lobsters and oysters from Long Island Sound. And although Connecticut is among the most densely populated states in the US, fully three-quarters of the state is rural. Hartford, the capital, is a thicket of skyscrapers amid tobacco fields.

The state takes its name from the Connecticut River, which bisects it. Called by the area's original inhabitants the 'Quinnehtukqut,' or 'long tidal river,' the Connecticut is navigable 50 miles inland to Hartford. And the great river was one of the reasons the colony, and then the state, prospered in the days before highways.

Today, most of Connecticut's visitors come to see Mystic Seaport, the re-creation of a 19th-century working coastal town; to gamble at casinos; or to visit the campus and museums of Yale University at New Haven. This chapter will help you discover another Connecticut as well: a castle guarding the banks of author Mark Twain's beloved Connecticut River, the forests and lakes of the Litchfield Hills, the sophisticated restaurants and pubs of the capital, vineyards and dinosaur footprints.

The Connecticut Office of Tourism (☎ 800-282-6863, W www.ctbound.org, 505 Hudson St, Hartford, CT 06106-7106) will send you a free, comprehensive *Connecticut Vacation Guide*, or you can pick one up at a Welcome Center.

You will find Connecticut Welcome Centers at Bradley International Airport (Terminals A and B) and on major highways entering the state.

Highlights

- Stepping into the 19th century at the Mystic Seaport Museum

- Submerging in the restaurant, museum, theater and club scene of New Haven

- Wine-tasting at a vineyard in the Litchfield Hills

- Admiring the Victorian splendor of Mark Twain's mansion in Hartford

- Discovering towns lost in the history of the Lower Connecticut River

- Trying your luck at the Native American gambling casinos north of Mystic

OTHER MAPS
Connecticut page 369

Litchfield Hills
page 402

M A

Hartford
● page 371

Mystic
page 394

New Haven
page 384

N Y

New London
& Groton Area
page 390

Lower Connecticut
River Valley
page 379

N Y

ATLANTIC
OCEAN

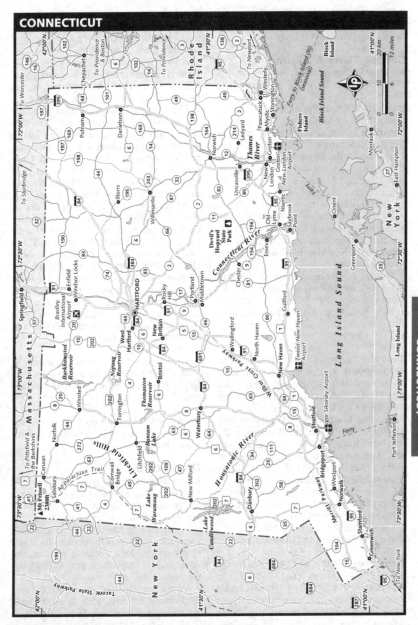

CONNECTICUT

There's a 12% hotel tax levied on all accommodations charges. Figure it in when calculating your lodging costs.

Getting There & Around

Air Bradley International Airport (☎ 860-292-2000), 12 miles north of Hartford in Windsor Locks (I-91 exit 40), serves the Hartford, CT, and Springfield, MA, area. Direct flights by Air Ontario, America West, American, Continental, Delta, Midway, Northwest, Southwest, United and US Airways connect Bradley with about 60 other US airports. Bus and shuttle services transport passengers between the airport and major towns and cities in central Connecticut and Massachusetts.

Tweed–New Haven Airport (☎ 203-787-8283), in New Haven, serves the southeastern part of the state with flights by US Airways. See New Haven's Getting There & Around section.

Groton–New London Airport (☎ 860-445-8549), in Groton, and Igor Sikorsky Memorial Airport (☎ 203-576-7498), closer to New York City in Bridgeport-Stratford, also serve the coast with commuter flights and US Airways.

Bus Peter Pan Bus Lines (☎ 413-781-3320, 800-343-9999), with its hub in Springfield, operates routes connecting Bridgeport, New Haven, Middletown and Hartford with New York City, Springfield and Boston.

Bonanza Bus Lines (☎ 401-331-7500, 800-556-3815), with its hub in Providence, RI, runs buses from New York City via Danbury and Hartford to Providence; and via New Milford, Kent and Canaan, CT, to Massachusetts' Berkshire hills and Bennington, VT. Connect at Providence with buses to Newport, RI, to Boston and to Cape Cod's Falmouth, Hyannis and Woods Hole.

Greyhound Bus Lines (☎ 800-231-2222) also serves Hartford and coastal cities.

Train Metro-North trains (☎ 212-532-4900, 800-638-7646) make the 1½-hour run between New York City's Grand Central Station and New Haven almost every hour from 7am to midnight on weekdays, with more frequent trains during the morning and evening rush hours. On weekends, trains run about every two hours.

Other branches of Metro-North service also have frequent stops and go north to Danbury (connect at South Norwalk), New Canaan (connect at Stamford) and Waterbury (connect at Bridgeport).

Connecticut Commuter Rail Service's *Shore Line East* service (☎ 800-255-7433) travels along the shore of Long Island Sound, connecting New London, Old Saybrook, Westbrook, Clinton, Madison, Guilford, Branford and New Haven. At New Haven, the *Shore Line East* trains connect with Metro-North and Amtrak routes.

Amtrak (☎ 800-872-7245) trains depart New York City's Pennsylvania Station for Connecticut on three lines: New Haven, Hartford, Springfield; New Haven, Hartford, Windsor Locks, Boston; and New Haven, New London, Mystic, Providence, Boston. Most tickets and trains allow stopovers along the way at no extra charge, so a ticket on the shore route between New York City and Boston may allow you to see New Haven, New London, Mystic and Providence for the same fare.

Car Connecticut fuel prices are usually at least 10% higher than in neighboring New England states and increase as you approach New York City.

Boat For information on ferry travel, see the New Haven and New London & Groton sections.

HARTFORD

It's a rare person who goes to Hartford on vacation – it's a workaday city rather than a tourist destination – but once you're here, you'll be surprised at how much Connecticut's capital city has to offer visitors, with particular strengths in history and art. If you plan your visit for a weekend, you can take advantage of surprisingly reasonable lodging prices.

With a population of about 124,000, Hartford's main business, aside from the state government, is insurance. In fact, the city is

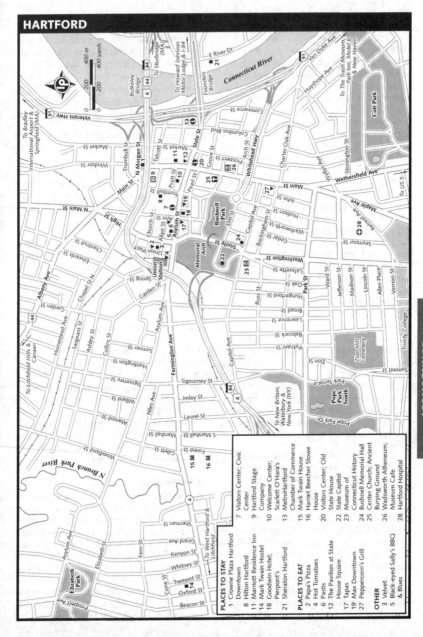

HARTFORD

PLACES TO STAY
1 Crowne Plaza Hartford
   Downtown
8 Hilton Hartford
11 Marriott Residence Inn
14 Mark Twain Hostel
18 Goodwin Hotel;
   Pierpont's
21 Sheraton Hartford

PLACES TO EAT
2 Papa's Pizza
4 Hot Tomatoes
6 Pastis
12 The Pavilion at State
   House Square
17 Tapas
19 Max Downtown
27 Peppercorn's Grill

OTHER
3 Velvet
5 Black-eyed Sally's BBQ
   & Blues

7 Visitors Center; Civic
   Center
9 Hartford Stage
   Company
10 Welcome Center;
   Scarlett O'Hara's
13 MetroHartford
   Chamber of Commerce
15 Mark Twain House
16 Harriet Beecher Stowe
   House
20 Visitors Center; Old
   State House
23 State Capitol
23 Museum of
   Connecticut History
24 Bushnell Memorial Hall
25 Center Church; Ancient
   Burying Ground
26 Wadsworth Atheneum;
   Museum Cafe
28 Hartford Hospital

CONNECTICUT

the insurance capital of the nation, home to more than 30 major insurance companies.

History

Before European colonists arrived, the Saukiog Indians called Hartford their home. In 1633, the Dutch, venturing north from New York, established a trading post called the House of Good Hope on the shore of the Connecticut River. At the same time, a second group of Europeans came west to the Hartford area from the Massachusetts Bay Colony under the leadership of the Reverend Thomas Hooker.

The Hartford Colony, named for a town in England, became the Colony of Connecticut under the charter granted by King Charles II in 1662. A watershed event in the city's history took place 25 years later when the English governor, Sir Edmund Andorra, threatened the charter's provisions. In defiant response, the citizenry hid the charter in the trunk of a large oak tree in Hartford, and never afterward surrendered it. A plaque at Charter Oak Place now marks the spot where the tree stood until 1856.

The insurance industry got its start in Hartford as early as the late 18th century: The establishment of the Hartford Fire Insurance Co was a means of guaranteeing the profitability of the shipping trade. By the late 19th century, Hartford was a thriving city, and its location between New York and Boston made it appealing to writers and artists. Samuel Clemens (Mark Twain) first visited the city in 1869, calling it:

> ...the best-built and handsomest town I have ever seen. They have the broadest, straightest streets, and the dwelling houses are the amplest in size, and the shapeliest, and have the most capacious ornamental grounds about them.

Twain eventually made Hartford his home, building his dream house in the pastoral area of the city then called Nook Farm and living in it from 1874 to 1891, years he later called the happiest of his life. Among the famous author's neighbors were writers Harriet Beecher Stowe and William Dean Howells. Poet Wallace Stevens spent much of the first half of the 20th century as an insurance executive in Hartford while contemplating 'Complacencies of the peignoir.'

Hartford entered a decline in the first half of the 20th century from which it has only partly recovered. In the 1960s, an urban planning project gave the city Constitution Plaza, a complex of office buildings in the heart of downtown, and in the '70s, the city opened its Civic Center, a venue for concerts and sporting events with associated shops and a hotel. But Hartford today suffers from an excess of commuters: people who drive in to work in the insurance towers, but who live – and pay taxes – in smaller towns. Urban renewal will not bring back the prosperous city of Twain's day until the people who work here live here.

Orientation

On its hilltop perch, the pseudo-Gothic Connecticut State Capitol is visible from most of the interstate highways entering the city. The tallest building, with a brilliant laser beacon shining atop it at night, is the Travelers Tower. The Hartford Civic Center is the huge building complex at the city's heart, with plenty of parking.

The easiest way to take in most of the Hartford attractions – the Wadsworth Atheneum, Old State House and Center Church – is on foot. The houses of literary figures Mark Twain and Harriet Beecher Stowe are a mile or so west of the town center off Farmington Ave.

Continue west on Farmington Ave as it becomes the main street of gentrified West Hartford, a 10-minute drive from downtown. It's lined with shops and cafes.

Information

You will find the bulk of tourist services at the centrally located Welcome Center (☎ 860-244-0253, 45 Pratt St). For literature or online information, contact the Greater Hartford Convention & Visitors Bureau (☎ 860-728-6789, 800-446-7810, W www.grhartfordcvb.com, One Civic Center Plaza, Hartford 06123). It's open 8:30am to 5pm Monday to Friday. Other visitor centers are in the Old State House (☎ 860-522-6766) and the Civic Center (☎ 860-275-6456).

The MetroHartford Chamber of Commerce (☎ 860-525-4451, W www.metrohartford.com, 250 Constitution Plaza) has information as well.

Hartford Guides (☎ 860-522-0855) offers guided walking tours. The Hartford Friends and Enemies Web Site (W www.wesleyan.edu/wstevens/stevens.html) sponsors literary events and walking tours illustrating poet Wallace Stevens' life in the city.

You'll find well-stocked shelves at the Gallows Hill Bookstore (☎ 860-297-5231, 300 Summit St). Bookworm (☎ 860-233-2653, 968 Farmington Ave) is on the shady main street of West Hartford.

The city's major medical facility is Hartford Hospital (☎ 860-524-2525, 80 Seymour St), south of downtown.

State Capitol

The Connecticut State Capitol (☎ 860-240-0222, cnr Capitol Ave & Trinity St; admission free; open 8am-5pm Mon-Fri), on Capitol Hill, is an imposing white marble building with Gothic details and a gold-leaf dome. Because of the variety of architectural styles it reflects, it has been unkindly dubbed 'the most beautiful ugly building in the world.' Designed by Richard Upjohn in 1879, it's open for free visits. One-hour guided tours, also free, depart hourly from the Legislative Office Building, on Capitol Ave near Broad St, from 9:15am to 1:15pm on weekdays (also 2:15pm in July and August). On Saturday from April to October, they depart hourly from the southwest (Capitol Ave) entrance to the capitol from 10:15am to 2:15pm.

Museum of Connecticut History

While you're up on Capitol Hill, have a look at this museum (☎ 860-566-3056, 231 Capitol Ave; admission free; open 9am-4pm Mon-Fri, 10am-4pm Sat, noon-4pm Sun) housed in the State

Library and Supreme Court Building just across from the State Capitol. Nationally known for its genealogy library, it also holds Connecticut's royal charter of 1662, a prime collection of Colt firearms (which were manufactured in Hartford), clocks and the table at which Abraham Lincoln signed the Emancipation Proclamation.

Bushnell Park

Hartford's 37-acre Bushnell Park (☎ 860-522-3668, center city; admission free; open sunrise-sunset daily), spreading down the hill from the capitol, was designed by Jacob Weidenmann in the 1850s. The Tudor-style **Pump House Gallery** (1947) in the park features art exhibits and a summer concert series.

Children will enjoy the **Bushnell Park Carousel** (☎ 860-585-5411; rides 50¢; open 11am-5pm Tues-Sun mid-May–Aug, 11am-5pm Sat & Sun mid-Apr–mid-May & Sept), a 1914 merry-go-round designed by Stein and Goldstein, with 48 horses and a Wurlitzer band organ.

The **Gothic Soldiers & Sailors Memorial Arch** (☎ 860-522-3668), which frames the Trinity St entrance, was designed by George Keller and dedicated in 1886. It commemorates Civil War veterans and offers fine views from its turrets – after you've climbed the 97 steps to the top.

CONNECTICUT

RICHARD CUMMINS

Bushnell Memorial Hall in downtown Hartford

Wadsworth Atheneum

The nation's oldest continuously operating art museum, the Wadsworth Atheneum (☎ 860-278-2670, 600 Main St; adult/senior & student/child 6-17 yrs $7/5/3; open 11am-5pm Tues-Sun) houses more than 40,000 pieces of art in a castlelike Gothic Revival building. Included are paintings by members of the Hudson River School, including some by Hartford resident Frederic Church; 19th-century impressionist works; 18th-century furniture; and the mobile and stabile sculptures of the Connecticut artist Alexander Calder. The Amistad Foundation Gallery has an outstanding collection of African American art and historical objects; the Matrix Gallery features works by contemporary artists.

You can have lunch here, too; see Places to Eat. If you visit on weekends, there's free parking in Travelers Lot No 7 on Prospect St.

Old State House

Connecticut's Old State House (☎ 860-522-6766, 800 Main St; admission free; open 10am-4pm Mon-Fri, 11am-4pm Sat Sept–mid-Aug) boasts that it is the oldest state capitol in the country. Designed by Charles Bulfinch – who also did the Massachusetts State House in Boston – it was the site of the trial of the Amistad prisoners (see the boxed text 'Amistad'); reenactments of the trial are held periodically. Gilbert Stuart's famous portrait of George Washington hangs in the senate chamber. Children will like the blasts from antique cannons at 10am and 4pm daily. There's a tourist information office as well and free tours of the building.

Center Church

This church (☎ 860-249-5631, 675 Main St; admission free; open 11am-2pm Wed & Fri) was established by the Reverend Thomas Hooker when he came to Hartford from the Massachusetts Bay Colony in 1636. The present building dates from 1807 and was modeled on St Martin's-in-the-Fields in London. In the **Ancient Burying Ground** behind the church lie the remains of Hooker and Revolutionary War patriots Joseph and Jeremiah Wadsworth. Some headstones date from the 17th century.

Mark Twain House

One of the premier attractions in Hartford is this eccentric home (☎ 860-247-0998, 351 Farmington Ave; adult/senior/child 6-12 yrs $9/8/5; open 9:30am-5pm Mon-Sat, noon-5pm Sun, closed Tues Nov-May), in an area once called Nook Farm. For 17 years, Samuel Langhorne Clemens (1835–1910) lived in this striking orange-and-black brick Victorian house that architect Edward Tuckerman Potter lavishly embellished with turrets, gables and verandas. Some of the interiors were done by Louis Comfort Tiffany. Here, the author penned some of his most famous works, including The Adventures of Tom Sawyer, The Adventures of Huckleberry Finn, The Prince and the Pauper and A Connecticut Yankee in King Arthur's Court. A guided tour is part of the admission fee. The last tour leaves at 4pm.

Harriet Beecher Stowe House

Next door to the Twain house is this author's home (☎ 860-525-9317, 73 Forest St; adult/senior/child 6-12 yrs $6.50/6/2.75; open 9:30am-4pm Mon-Sat, noon-4:30pm Sun). Stowe was the woman who Abraham Lincoln said started the Civil War with her book Uncle Tom's Cabin. Built in 1871, the Stowe house reflects the author's strong ideas about decorating and domestic efficiency as she expressed in her best seller American Woman's Home, which was nearly as popular as the phenomenal Uncle Tom's Cabin. The house is light-filled, with big windows draped in plants.

Tickets include admission to the adjoining Katharine S Day House, named for Stowe's grandniece, who sought to preserve the memory of her great-aunt's community spirit and works. The house has 1880s decor as well as changing exhibits.

Elizabeth Park Rose Gardens

Known for its fine collection of roses, Elizabeth Park (☎ 860-722-6514, *Prospect Ave; admission free; open sunrise-sunset daily, greenhouses open 8am-3pm Mon-Fri),* at Asylum Ave, is a 100-acre preserve on the Hartford–West Hartford town line. More than 14,000 rose plants – 900 varieties such as climbers, American Beauties, ramblers and heavily perfumed damasks – cover the grounds. June and July are the months to see the roses in full flower, but they bloom, if less profusely, well into fall. Elizabeth Park also has greenhouses, landscaped walking paths and a pretty gazebo.

Places to Stay

Hartford's city center luxury hotels charge high rates on weekdays and surprisingly low rates (less than half the weekday rates) on weekends. The suburban motels' rates go up on weekends.

Mark Twain Hostel (☎ *860-523-7255, 800-909-4776, fax 860-233-1767,* W *www.hiayh .org, 131 Tremont St)* Dorm beds $18. This 42-bed place has clean beds, and guests can use the fully equipped kitchen and laundry facilities. It's in the city's West End off Farmington Ave (I-84 exit 46), a 25-minute walk from downtown and Union Station. Call for pick-up service.

Just outside the center of Hartford are many of the usual chain motels, usually offering the best-value accommodations.

Motel 6 (☎ *860-563-5900, 800-466-8356, fax 860-563-1213,* W *www.motel6.com, 1341 Silas Deane Hwy)* Rooms $49-54. The 146 rooms here are comfortable and clean. There's a coin-operated laundry in the building and a restaurant next door. It is 10 miles south of the city center in Wethersfield at I-91 exit 24 (Silas Deane Hwy).

Howard Johnson Motor Lodge (☎ *860-875-0781, fax 860-872-8449,* W *www.hojo.com, 451 Hartford Turnpike)* Rooms $52 with light breakfast. This 64-room lodge, at I-84 exit 65, is northeast of the city in Vernon, on the way to Boston. There's a swimming pool as well.

Park Inn (☎ *860-525-9306, 800-670-7275, fax 860-525-2990, 185 Brainerd Rd)* Rooms/

suites $79/89 with continental breakfast. At I-91 exit 27, this establishment has 130 units, 60 of them suites. There's a fitness room and outdoor swimming pool as well.

Sheraton Hartford (☎ *860-528-9703, fax 860-289-4728,* W *www.sheraton.com, 100 E River Dr)* Rooms weekday/weekend $149/ 89. Across the river in East Hartford (I-84 West exit 54, I-84 East exit 53, I-91 North exit 29, I-91 South exit 30, CT 2 exit 4), you find a pool, fitness center, restaurant and lounge. The spacious rooms were redecorated in 2001 with lush ribbed carpets, high-speed data ports and ergonomically designed workstations.

Crowne Plaza Hartford Downtown (☎ *860-549-2400, fax 860-527-2746,* W *www .crowneplaza.com, 50 N Morgan St)* Rooms Sun-Thur/Fri & Sat $160/80. Close to the Civic Center (I-91 exit 32B, I-84 exit 50) and with 350 guest rooms, this is a chain hotel with luxury rooms and many guest services, including shuttle service to Bradley Airport, an outdoor pool, an on-site restaurant and baby-sitting services.

Hilton Hartford (☎ *860-728-5151, 800-325-3535, fax 860-240-7394,* W *www.hilton .com, 315 Trumbull St)* Rooms Sun-Thur/ Fri & Sat $165/85. For convenient location, this high-rise is hard to beat. The 22-story, 388-room hotel is connected to the Hartford Civic Center with a skyway and within easy walking distance of everything downtown.

Marriott Residence Inn (☎ *860-524-5550, fax 860-534-0624,* W *www.marriott.com, 942 Main St)* Rooms Sun-Thur/Fri & Sat $169/89. This all-suite hotel with 100 units came on line with the millennium. Each room has a full kitchen, data ports, voice-mail and cable TV. There's an exercise facility here, too.

Goodwin Hotel (☎ *860-246-7500, 800-922-5006, fax 860-247-4576,* W *www.goodwin hotel.com, 1 Haynes St)* Rooms Sun-Thur/ Fri & Sat $229/299. Here's the fanciest hotel in Hartford, and it faces the Civic Center. The five-story, 124-room, 1881 redbrick building looks historic on the outside, but inside it has been entirely remodeled to appeal to modern preferences for large, light-filled rooms. Decor is traditional, with antique reproduction furniture. Staff serves afternoon tea in the lobby.

There are currently no B&Bs in the city, but there are a number in the surrounding countryside. Call Nutmeg Bed & Breakfast Reservation Agency (☎ 860-236-6698, 800-727-7592, ⓦ www.BnB-Link.com) for a list and profile of Hartford area B&Bs or log onto their website.

Places to Eat
Recent years have seen an influx of eateries to the downtown area between Main St and Union Station in all price ranges, most serving lunch and dinner (unless noted).

The Pavilion at State House Square *(cnr Main & State Sts)* Dishes $4-12. Across from the Old State House on Main St, the food court here opened in 2001 and has a dozen vendors selling ethnic and vegetarian takeout food to eat at counters and tables in the airy interior courtyard of a high-rise office palace. We like ***Bangkok*** where the pad thai costs $4.

Papa's Pizza *(☎ 860-727-9930, 54 Union Place)* Pies $6-14. You find this no-frills cafe across from Union Station. We actually favor this place for a cheap breakfast as well as 'za. Pancakes or French toast runs about $3.

Tapas *(☎ 860-525-5988, 126 Ann St)* Lunch $6-10. The crowd packs this storefront bistro at lunch and happy hour for good reason. You can sit at high tables or stand at wall counters and rub shoulders with three neighbors while eating blackened chicken tapas ($6.50) or souvlaki (under $6) and listening to '70s rock.

Museum Cafe *(☎ 860-728-5989, 600 Main St)* Mains about $11. Open 11:30am-3pm Tues-Sun. This cafe in the Wadsworth Atheneum is casual and menu offerings tend to be light and sophisticated. Consider the seasonal soups like pumpkin ($4).

Peppercorn's Grill *(☎ 860-547-1714, 357 Main St)* Mains $12-20. Modern American interpretations of traditional Italian dishes are the specialty of the house at this restaurant, between Capitol and Buckingham. In this family-run place, you might find anything from veal saltimbocca ($18) to a zesty dish of ravioli with scallops and lobster ($19).

Max Downtown *(☎ 860-522-2530, 185 Asylum St)* Mains $14-22. A favorite spot of the downtown 'in' crowd is this urbane place at Haynes St, serving a wide selection of international bistro dishes like Chinese BBQ spareribs (about $12 at lunch).

Pastis *(☎ 860-278-8852, 201 Ann St)* Mains $17-25. A great date restaurant, this French brasserie wins your heart with intimate tables, candlelight and French acoustic music. Consider the seared scallops with saffron rice ($20).

Pierpont's *(☎ 860-522-4935, 1 Haynes St)* Mains $18-25. This restaurant in the Goodwin Hotel is a top choice for a romantic dinner on the town. Named for financier J Pierpont Morgan, a sometime Hartford resident, Pierpont's offers expert preparation, serving traditional continental dinners like roast duck (about $20).

Hot Tomatoes *(☎ 860-241-9100, One Union Place)* Lunch $7-14, dinner $23-35. A lot of locals love this place with its cafe deck overlooking Bushnell Park and the State Capitol. The interior is postmodern chrome with a squad of waitstaff dressed in matching polo shirts. It's a place to be and be seen. And it will cost you; the Oriental chicken salad runs $10, and you can drop $35 on a tenderloin with sweet onion–potato lasagna.

Entertainment
Hartford Civic Center Coliseum *(☎ 860-727-8010, 1 Civic Center Plaza)* Tickets $25-125. Big shows and ice hockey rule.

Bushnell Memorial Hall *(☎ 860-987-5900, 166 Capitol Ave)* Tickets $20-45. This historic building is where you go for most ballet, symphony and chamber music performances. For current performances, contact the Hartford Downtown Council (☎ 860-522-6400) or the Greater Hartford Arts Council (☎ 860-525-8629). For events in Bushnell Park, call ☎ 860-722-6500.

Hartford Symphony *(☎ 860-244-2999)* and ***Dance Connecticut*** *(☎ 860-987-5999)* Tickets $20-30. Both have full winter performance seasons.

Hartford Stage Company *(☎ 860-527-5151, 50 Church St)* Tickets $20-35. Contemporary as well as classic dramas play from

A Trashy Museum

For all but the most recent fraction of recorded history, humankind didn't think about trash at all. It barely existed. Since the end of WWII, however, trash has become one of the planet's most vexing and expensive problems.

The **Trash Museum** (☎ 860-247-4280, 211 Murphy Rd; admission free; open 10am-4pm Wed-Fri year-round, 10am-4pm Tues & Sat July & Aug), at I-91 exit 27, at the Connecticut Resources Recovery Authority Visitors Center, examines the advent of trash, follows its creation and disposal and educates the public on what can be done to reuse and recycle it. Don't miss the Temple of Trash – recycling at its best.

September to June. The theater building is striking, designed by Venturi & Rauch of red brick with darker red zigzag details.

Real Art Ways (☎ 860-232-1006, 56 Arbor St) Admission free. Open 10am-5pm Mon-Fri, noon-5pm Sat & Sun. This gallery combines contemporary works on paper and canvas with works on video, poetry and musical events, and it's consistently offbeat and adventurous. Performances usually cost $5 to $10.

Cinestudio (☎ 860-297-2463 for show times, ☎ 297-2544 for office, 300 Summit St) If you want to catch a movie, this gorgeous, velvet-seated cinema at Trinity College shows first-run and art films at lower-than-average prices.

Scarlett O'Hara's (☎ 860-728-8290, 59 Pratt St) We're talkin' the dead moose (and other hunting trophies) motif here. Stop in during the vigorous happy hour to mingle with lots of young professionals from the insurance offices. A sign on the wall proclaiming 'Milk sucks, got beer?' gives you a sense of the ethos. There are two free pool tables. A DJ spins rock and blues on weekends. Some folks dance. Domestic pints run $2.50 and you can score pub food like fried shrimp ($6).

Black-eyed Sally's BBQ & Blues (☎ 860-278-7427, 350 Asylum St) Cover $4-8, mains $11-16. Wow. Just Wow! This blues palace is the real thing, dragging in national acts like Walter Trout. It's a big old joint with high walls and lots of booths and tables. The walls are covered with graffiti, some penned by visiting bands. There's live blues Thursday to Saturday. Try the jambalaya ($16).

Velvet (☎ 860-278-6333, 50 Union Place) Cover about $5. Here's a dance club for the young and wild. The music is body-numbing house and techno in a smoky, strobe-lit bunker.

Getting There & Around

See this chapter's introductory Getting There & Around section for information on air travel (via Bradley International Airport in Windsor Locks) and intercity bus service. Airport Connection (☎ 860-627-3400, 800-627-3400) runs shuttles between Bradley International Airport and downtown hotels. Rates run about $20.

By train, Amtrak (☎ 800-872-7245) connects Hartford to New York and Boston.

By car, interstates connect Hartford to Boston (102 miles), New Haven (36 miles), New York (117 miles) and Providence (71 miles).

In Hartford, Union Station (☎ 860-247-5329, One Union Place), at Spruce St, is the city's transportation center and the place to catch trains, airport shuttles, intercity buses and taxis.

Connecticut Transit (☎ 860-525-9181), the city bus service, has an information booth at State House Square and Market St.

Check the taxi stand outside Union Station, or call Yellow Cab Co (☎ 860-666-6666).

AROUND HARTFORD

The environs of Hartford hold many things to see and do. Here are several of the best.

CONNECTICUT

Old Wethersfield

Historic Wethersfield, 5 miles south of Hartford off I-91 exit 26, boasts that George Washington stayed here while planning the final victorious campaign of the Revolutionary War. 'Old Wethersfield' (the historic district) has a cache of Revolutionary-era and colonial houses. Three 18th-century houses comprise the **Webb-Deane-Stevens Museum** (☎ *860-529-0612, 211 Main St; adult/senior/student & child 5 yrs & older $8/7/4; open 10am-4pm Wed-Mon May-Oct, 10am-4pm Sat & Sun Nov-Apr*). Exhibits in all the houses bring to life the America of more than two centuries ago. In the Webb House, grand murals commissioned in 1916 depict the strategy conference between Generals Washington and Rochambeau, held right here to plan what became of the victorious American campaign against the British-held Yorktown.

Dinosaur State Park

Two hundred million years ago, dinosaurs traipsed across mudflats near Rocky Hill, 10 miles due south of Hartford along I-91. Their tracks hardened in the mud and remained safely buried until the 20th century, when road-building crews serendipitously uncovered them. Connecticut's answer to Jurassic Park is Dinosaur State Park (☎ *860-529-8423, 400 West St; admission free to park, admission to exhibit center adult/child 6-17 yrs $2/1; open 9am-4:30pm Tues-Sun*), where you can view the hundreds of footprints preserved beneath a geodesic dome, tour an 80-foot-long diorama that shows how – and by what – the tracks were made, and view other dinosaur-related exhibits. The park also has a picnic area and 2 miles of nature trails. Take I-91 exit 23, then go a mile east.

Lake Compounce Theme Park

Here's a 100-acre lakeshore amusement park in the town of Bristol, 18 miles southwest of Hartford. Lake Compounce Theme Park (☎ *860-583-3300, 822 Lake Ave; adult/child $26/18; open 11am-8pm daily mid-June–late Sept*), at the junction of CT 61 and CT 132, includes two roller coasters, a whitewater raft ride, a historic steam train, an interactive haunted house and many other amusements. Splash Harbor Water Park, with its pools, jets and waterslides, is perfect for a hot summer's day, and the 180-foot free-fall 'swing' will thrill even the most jaded of extreme sports enthusiasts – not to mention the rest of us. Every member of the family will find something fun to do here.

Admission includes unlimited access to most rides and amusements; the child price applies only to children under 52 inches tall. You can also visit just the park for $8 (no rides) and there's a $5 parking charge as well.

Lower Connecticut River Valley

The Connecticut River has escaped the bustle of industry and commerce that so often mar the major rivers of the Northeast. The Connecticut is the longest river in New England (with its headwaters near New Hampshire's Canadian border), but it is surprisingly shallow near its mouth at Long Island Sound. This lack of depth led burgeoning industry to look for better harbors elsewhere, and thus the lower end of the Connecticut has preserved much of its 18th-century appearance.

Historic Connecticut towns grace the river's banks, including Old Lyme, Old Saybrook, Essex, Ivoryton, Chester, Hadlyme and East Haddam. Each offers its own charms, and together they present visitors with fine dining, theater, river excursions, art museums, a castle and a steam train. The sections on places to stay and places to eat, later, include information on all these towns as a group.

Note: Lodging prices are substantially higher on weekends (Friday and Saturday nights), and campgrounds fill up early on those days.

Information

Contact the Connecticut River Valley and Shoreline Visitors Council (☎ 860-347-0028,

800-486-3346, W www.cttourism.org, 393
Main St, Middletown, CT 06457) or Lyme
and Old Lyme Chamber of Commerce
(☎ 860-434-1665, 70 Lyme St, PO Box 268,
Old Lyme, CT 06371).

OLD LYME

Near the mouth of the Connecticut River,
on the east bank, Old Lyme (I-95 exit 70)
was home to some 60 sea captains in the
19th century. Since the early 20th century,
however, Old Lyme has been known as a
center for the American impressionist art
movement. Numerous artists, including
Charles Ebert, Childe Hassam, Willard Met-
calfe, Henry Ward Ranger and Guy and
Carleton Wiggins came here to paint,
staying in the mansion of local art patron
Florence Griswold.

The house (which her artist friends often
decorated with murals in lieu of paying
rent) is now a museum containing a good
selection of both impressionist and Barbizon paintings, the **Florence Griswold
Museum** (☎ 860-434-5542, 96 Lyme St;
adult/senior & student $5/4; open 10am-5pm
Tues-Sat, 1pm-5pm Sun).

The neighboring **Lyme Academy of Fine
Arts** (☎ 860-434-5232, 84 Lyme St; admission free; open 10am-4pm Tues-Sat, 1pm-
4pm Sun), and the **Lyme Art Association
Gallery** (☎ 860-434-7802, 90 Lyme St; admission free; open noon-4pm Tues-Sun) feature
recent works by local artists.

OLD SAYBROOK

Colonists founded Old Saybrook on the
west bank of the mouth of the Connecticut
River in 1635. Exhibits at **Fort Saybrook
Monument Park** (☎ 860-395-3123, Saybrook
Point; admission free; open sunrise-sunset
daily) tell the story. The park also offers
panoramic views of the mouth of the mighty
Connecticut River. Take CT 154 or CT 9
exit 2.

For even better views of the river valley,
go to the park wharf and hop aboard one of
the boats of the **Deep River Navigation
Company** (☎ 860-526-4954; 2-hr/1-hr cruises
$12/8; departures noon, 1:30pm & 3pm daily
mid-June–early Sept).

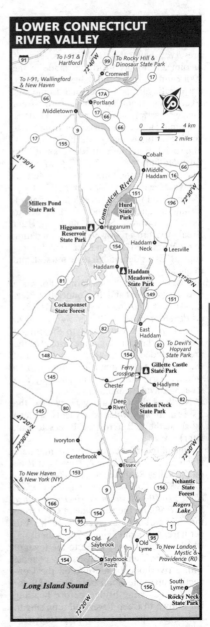

LOWER CONNECTICUT
RIVER VALLEY

CONNECTICUT

ESSEX

Established in 1635, Essex stands as the chief town of the region and features well-preserved Federal-period houses, legacies of rum and tobacco fortunes made in the 19th century. Essex today has the genteel, aristocratic air of historical handsomeness. Everything from landscaping to street signage is scripted to look good, and it does.

Coming into the town center from CT 9, you'll eventually find yourself on Main St. The social centerpiece of Essex is the 1776 **Griswold Inn** (☎ 860-767-1776, 36 Main St), a hostelry since the time of the Revolutionary War (see Places to Stay, later). 'The Gris,' as locals call it, is today both an inn and a restaurant, and its taproom is the place to meet the townfolk. Sunday morning 'Hunt Breakfasts' are a renowned tradition dating to the War of 1812, when British soldiers occupying Essex demanded to be fed well and in quantity.

Past the Gris at the eastern end of Main St is the riverfront and the **Connecticut River Museum** (☎ 860-767-8269, foot of Main St; adult/senior/child 6-12 yrs $4/3/2; open 10am-5pm Tues-Sun), next to Steamboat Dock. Its exhibits recount the history of the area. Included among them is a replica of the world's first submarine, the *Turtle*, a wooden barrel-like vessel built here by Yale student David Bushnell in 1776.

North of the Gris along Ferry St is the Essex marina, crowded with yachts. You can lunch at the deli here (see Places to Eat, later).

One of the most enjoyable activities here is the Essex Steam Train & Riverboat Ride on the **Valley Railroad** (☎ 860-767-0103, 800-377-3987, 1 Railroad Ave; train only adult/child $10.50/5.50, train & riverboat cruise $16.50/8.50), on the west side of CT 9 from the main part of Essex. Take CT 9 exit 3A to get here. A steam engine powers the train, which rumbles slowly north to the town of Deep River. There passengers may connect with a riverboat for a cruise on the Connecticut up to the Goodspeed Opera House and CT 82 swing bridge before heading back down to Deep River and returning to Essex via train. The roundtrip train ride takes about an hour, covering about 12 miles; with the riverboat ride, the complete excursion takes 2½ hours. Trains leave the Railroad Ave station five times on weekdays in summer, six times on weekends. Fall foliage runs are usually scheduled as well.

IVORYTON

A mile west of Essex, on the west side of CT 9, is the sleepy town of Ivoryton. Named for the African elephant tusks imported during the 19th century by the Comstock-Cheney piano manufacturers for use in making piano keys, it is also the home of witch hazel, a traditional folk medicine. Today, the ivory industry is long gone, and most people visit Ivoryton to dine at the Copper Beech Inn (see Places to Stay).

CHESTER

Cupped in the valley of Pattaconk Brook, Chester is another sedate river town. A general store, post office, library and a few shops pretty much account for all the activity in the village. Most visitors come either for fine dining (see Places to Eat) or to browse in the antique shops and boutiques on the town's charming main street.

HADLYME

From Chester, a small car ferry (☎ 860-566-7635) crosses the Connecticut River to Hadlyme. The trip takes just five minutes; the ferry – which carries just eight cars – is the second oldest in continuous operation in the state, operating daily April to mid-December. Crossing eastbound, the ferry drops you at the foot of Gillette Castle in East Haddam.

EAST HADDAM

Two first-rate attractions mark this small town on the east bank of the Connecticut. Looming on one of the Seven Sisters hills above the ferry dock is **Gillette Castle** (☎ 860-526-2336, 67 River Rd; adult/child 6-11 yrs $5/3; open 10am-5pm Fri-Sun late May-early Sept), a turreted, 24-room riverstone mansion that is one of Connecticut's curiosities. Built between 1914 and 1919 by eccentric actor William Gillette, it was

What Is a 'Connecticut Yankee'?

A Connecticut Yankee made it all the way to King Arthur's court in Twain's famous novel. Connecticut Yankees were also peddlers that traveled up and down the Atlantic seaboard selling soap, tin, etc. The expression also implies a certain character of ingenuity and marketing, especially in the peddlers' case, for useful household items like combs, pins and clocks. (Waterbury was the clockmaking capital of the US in the mid-1800s, and Timex was born from it; see W www.timexpo.com.) Such ingenuity rubbed off on Eli Whitney, inventor of the cotton gin, and Hartford entrepreneur Samuel Colt, who gained fame through the repeating pistol, better known as the Colt .45 revolver.

modeled on the medieval castles of Germany's Rhineland. Gillette made his name and his considerable fortune on stage in the role of Sherlock Holmes. He created the part himself, based on the famous mystery series by Sir Arthur Conan Doyle. In a sense, he made his castle/home part of the Holmes role as well: An upstairs room replicates Conan Doyle's description of the sitting room at 221B Baker St, London.

Following Gillette's death in 1937, his dream house and its surrounding 117 acres were designated a Connecticut state park.

North of Gillette Castle stands the **Goodspeed Opera House** *(☎ 860-873-8668, CT 82 at the bridge; performances Wed-Sun Apr-Dec)*, a Victorian music hall renowned as the only theater in the country dedicated to both the preservation of old and the development of new American musicals.

The shows *Man of La Mancha* and *Annie* premiered at the Goodspeed before going on to national fame. The six-story, Victorian-style theater, built in 1876, enjoyed a huge reputation before the Great Depression. It was saved from demolition in 1959 by a group of concerned citizens, then refurbished and reopened in 1963.

Also in East Haddam is the **Nathan Hale Schoolhouse** *(☎ 860-873-9547, Main St; admission free; open by appointment)*, behind St Stephen's Church in the center of town. Hale taught in this one-room building from 1773 to 1774 when it was called the Union School. He was a peripatetic pedagogue, and numerous other one-room Connecticut schoolhouses bear his name, and corresponding museum status. Hale (1755–1776) is famous for his patriotic statement, 'I only regret that I have but one life to lose for my country,' as he was about to be hanged for treason by the British without trial. Today it is a museum of Hale family memorabilia and local history.

STATE PARKS & FORESTS

The Lower Connecticut River Valley has a half-dozen state parks and forests good for outdoor activities. For information on any park, contact the Bureau of Outdoor Recreation (☎ 860-424-3200, 79 Elm St, Hartford, CT 06106-5127).

Cockaponset State Forest, in Haddam, has fishing, hiking and swimming.

Devil's Hopyard State Park, just off CT 82 in East Haddam, has 860 acres of parkland for camping and hiking, including the 60-foot Chapman Falls.

Haddam Meadows State Park, in Haddam, is good for boating and fishing.

Hurd State Park, in East Hampton, offers camping, fishing, hiking and picnicking.

Selden Neck State Park, in Lyme, features camping places for those making canoe trips on the river, as well as hiking trails.

PLACES TO STAY
Camping

Devil's Hopyard State Park (☎ 860-424-3200, 877-668-2267, off CT 82 in East Haddam) Sites $9. The 860-acre park is the site of Chapman Falls and the potholes at the base that give the park its name. There are 20 basic tent sites here with water and toilets.

CONNECTICUT

Wolf's Den Campground (☎ 860-873-9681, 256 Town St/CT 82, East Haddam) Sites $27. Wolf's has 205 sites, bath houses and a store.

Markham Meadows (☎ 860-267-9738, 7 Markham Rd, East Hampton) Sites about $28. Markham Meadows has 75 sites.

Nelson's Family Campground (☎ 860-267-5300, 71 Mott Hill Rd, East Hampton) Sites $30. Nelson's is a large, busy campground with 300 sites and all the amenities.

Motels

Moderately priced motels stand along the Boston Post Rd (US 1) in Old Saybrook, reached via I-95 exit 66.

Saybrook Motor Inn (☎ 860-399-5926, 1575 Boston Post Rd) Rooms Sun-Thur/Fri & Sat $55/85. Saybrook offers 24 well-used rooms with refrigerators, TVs and beach passes.

Super 8 Motel (☎ 860-399-6273, 800-800-8000, fax 860-399-2525, ⓦ www.super8.com, 37 Spencer Plain Rd) Rooms Sun-Thur/Fri & Sat $70/110 with continental breakfast. The 44 rooms have air con and cable TV.

Days Inn (☎ 860-388-3453, 800-329-7466, fax 860-395-0209, ⓦ www.daysinn.com, 1430 Boston Post Rd) Rooms Sun-Thur/Fri & Sat $88/134 with continental breakfast. There are 52 standard motel rooms here with a two-night minimum stay on weekends in the summer. You get an outdoor pool here and microwaves in the rooms.

There's another cluster of motels near I-95 exits 67 North and 68 South.

Inns & B&Bs

Griswold Inn (☎ 860-767-1776, fax 860-767-0481, ⓦ www.griswoldinn.com, 36 Main St, Essex) Rooms $95-120, suites $150 with light breakfast. This is the town's landmark lodging and dining place. Despite the Gris' antiquity (it has been serving travelers since the Revolutionary War), its 25 guest rooms have modern conveniences. Hint: Room No 24 costs only $80. The inn's famous all-you-can-eat Hunt Breakfasts (served 11am to 2:30pm Sunday) cost $13. Otherwise, lunch in the dining room costs $10 to $20, full dinners $30 to $50.

Inn at Chester (☎ 860-526-9541, 800-949-7829, fax 860-526-4387, 318 W Main St/CT 148, Chester) Rooms $115. The original inn at Chester was a farmhouse built in 1776. Several buildings were added during the 20th century to produce a colonial-style inn with modern conveniences in its 42 air-conditioned rooms. To reach the inn from the center of Chester, follow CT 148 west for 4.4 miles and go past CT 9 exit 6 and Killingworth Reservoir to the inn, which is right on the Chester-Killingworth town line. The inn's spacious dining room serves traditional game dishes (venison, duck) with nouvelle-cuisine touches. The entrées cost about $24.

Bee & Thistle Inn (☎ 860-434-1667, ⓦ www.beeandthistle.com, 100 Lyme St, Old Lyme) Rooms $85-160. This is a 1756 Dutch Colonial farmhouse with 11 rooms, some of which share baths. The dining room features innovative cuisine and romantic ambience, so it's a very good idea to reserve your table in advance. Expect to spend over $25 for an entrée like filet mignon.

Copper Beech Inn (☎ 860-767-0330, 888-809-2056, ⓦ www.copperbeechinn.com, 46 Main St, Ivoryton) Rooms $110-180. Built in the 1890s as the residence of ivory importer AW Comstock, the inn has four guestrooms in the main house and nine more luxurious rooms in the Carriage House. To find the inn, take CT 9 exit 3 and follow the signs on to Ivoryton, going west 1.6 miles through Centerbrook to the inn, on the left-hand side of the road. The **dining room**'s updated French classic dishes, like stuffed breast of roasted pheasant served, are both superb and in high demand. Reserve well in advance and expect to pay $45 to $65 per person for dinner with wine.

PLACES TO EAT

In the Connecticut River Valley, you'll find some of the best restaurants in country inns, such as the **Copper Beech** in Ivoryton, the **Griswold** in Essex, the **Bee & Thistle** in Old Lyme and the **Inn at Chester**. For details, see Places to Stay.

Olive Oyl's Carry-Out Cuisine (☎ 860-767-4909, 77 Main St, Essex) Dishes $5-8.

For inexpensive but good sandwiches and picnic fare in pricey Essex, you need go no farther than this place behind the Strong Real Estate office. You can sample good breads, cheese, pâtés, pastries and sandwiches like smoked salmon salad with capers and sundried tomatoes on a roll ($5.50).

Crow's Nest Gourmet Deli (☎ 860-767-3288, Pratt St, Essex) Dishes $5-9. Open for breakfast & lunch daily. This aptly named place overlooks the boatyard and marina from its perch at Brewer's Shipyard. The yachting crowd roosts here after a day on the water. Locals favor the chicken fajita for about $7. Follow Ferry St from the Gris to reach the Crow's Nest.

Chester has several good places to dine, including the following.

Fiddler's (☎ 860-526-3210, 4 Water St) Lunch $9-17, dinner $20-35. The specialty here is seafood, such as bouillabaisse ($28) and inventive lobster dishes.

Restaurant du Village (☎ 860-526-5301, 59 Main St) Mains $21-27. Here's a little piece of Provençe in Connecticut's countryside. With its flower-filled windowboxes set beneath multipaned windows, the restaurant features country French variations on chicken and lamb dishes.

SHOPPING

The Connecticut River Artisans Cooperative (☎ 860-526-5575, 4 Water St, Chester) Open 10am-5pm Wed-Sun mid-Mar–Dec, 10am-5pm Fri-Sun Jan–mid-Mar. This co-op features one-of-a-kind art and craft pieces including clothing, folk art, furniture, jewelry, paintings, photographs and pottery.

Connecticut Coast

Connecticut's coastline on Long Island Sound is long and varied. Industrial and commercial cities and bedroom communities dominate the western coast. The central coast, from New Haven to the mouth of the Connecticut River, is less urban, with historic towns and villages. The eastern coast includes New London and Groton, both important in naval history, and Mystic, where the Mystic Seaport Museum brings maritime history to life.

NEW HAVEN

Bravo, New Haven! Much maligned for decades as a stagnant urban seaport, this city of 123,000 souls has risen from its own ashes to become an arts mecca. As you roll into town along I-91 or I-95, New Haven appears bustling and muscular – it's still an important port, as it has been since the 1630s. Shipping, manufacturing, health care and telecommunications power New Haven's economy. But at the city's center is a tranquil core: New Haven Green, decorated with graceful colonial churches and venerable Yale University. Scores of ethnic restaurants, theaters, museums, pubs and clubs dot the neighborhood and make the Yale University area almost as lively as Cambridge's Harvard Square.

History

The Puritan founders of New Haven established their colony in 1637–38 at a spot where the Quinnipiac and other small rivers enter Long Island Sound. The new town was to be no haven of religious freedom: This was a theocracy, so only believers could be citizens, and the Bible was the law. The strictness of religious law was softened somewhat in 1665 when New Haven reluctantly joined the larger province of Connecticut. It served as joint provincial (and then state) capital, along with Hartford, from 1701 to 1875.

Prominence first came from the town's port, but by the late 18th and early 19th centuries, Yankee ingenuity had made New Haven an important manufacturing city as well.

In 1702, James Pierpont founded a collegiate school in nearby Clinton. The school soon moved to Old Saybrook, and in 1717 went to New Haven in response to a generous grant of funds by Elihu Yale. In 1718, the name changed to Yale in honor of the benefactor.

Re-chartered in 1745, Yale grew extensively during the following century, adding

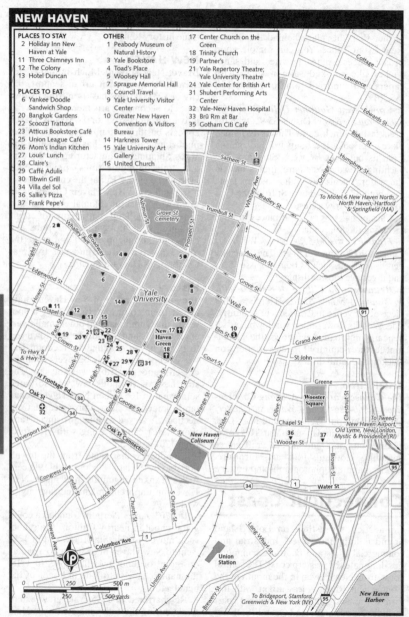

NEW HAVEN

PLACES TO STAY
2　Holiday Inn New Haven at Yale
11　Three Chimneys Inn
12　The Colony
13　Hotel Duncan

PLACES TO EAT
6　Yankee Doodle Sandwich Shop
20　Bangkok Gardens
22　Scoozzi Trattoria
23　Atticus Bookstore Café
25　Union League Café
26　Mom's Indian Kitchen
27　Louis' Lunch
28　Claire's
29　Caffé Adulis
30　Tibwin Grill
34　Villa del Sol
36　Sallie's Pizza
37　Frank Pepe's

OTHER
1　Peabody Museum of Natural History
3　Yale Bookstore
4　Toad's Place
5　Woolsey Hall
7　Sprague Memorial Hall
8　Council Travel
9　Yale University Visitor Center
10　Greater New Haven Convention & Visitors Bureau
14　Harkness Tower
15　Yale University Art Gallery
16　United Church
17　Center Church on the Green
18　Trinity Church
19　Partner's
21　Yale Repertory Theatre; Yale University Theatre
24　Yale Center for British Art
31　Shubert Performing Arts Center
32　Yale-New Haven Hospital
33　Brü Rm at Bar
35　Gotham Citi Café

schools of medicine, divinity, law, art and architecture, music, forestry, engineering and drama, and a graduate school. By 1887 it was time to rename it Yale University. The third-oldest university in the nation, Yale can boast many distinguished alumni and alumnae, including Presidents George W Bush, Bill Clinton, George HW Bush, Gerald Ford and William Howard Taft, as well as Hillary Rodham Clinton, Samuel FB Morse Noah Webster and Eli Whitney.

Orientation

Entering New Haven along I-95 or I-91 (which joins I-95 right in the city), take I-95 exit 47 for CT 34, the Oak St Connector, to reach New Haven Green, the city center, with Yale to its west. From the Wilbur Cross Parkway, take exit 57, 59 or 60 and follow the signs to the center.

Most hotels and sights are within a few blocks of the green. The bus and train stations are near I-95 in the southeast part of the city.

Information

The Greater New Haven Convention & Visitors Bureau (☎ 203-777-8550, 800-332-7829, W www.newhavencvb.org, 59 Elm St, New Haven, CT 06510) is open 8:30am to 5pm Monday to Friday.

Yale University has a visitor center (☎ 203-432-2300, 149 Elm St), at Temple St, on the north side of the green, where you can get free campus maps and a self-guided walking-tour pamphlet. For information on guided tours, see the Yale University section, below.

New Haven has a Council Travel office (☎ 203-562-5335, 84 Wall St).

The Yale Bookstore (☎ 203-772-0670, 77 Broadway) not only has a rich collection of books but also Yale sweatshirts and souvenirs. Atticus Bookstore Café is another favorite; see Places to Eat.

As for dangers and annoyances, New Haven has urban pleasures and problems, including street crime. You should avoid run-down neighborhoods and empty streets after dark, and don't leave *anything* visible in your parked car to tempt thieves.

New Haven Green

New Haven's spacious town green, the spiritual center of the city, claims three historic churches. The **Trinity Church** (Episcopal), on Chapel St, resembles England's Gothic York Minster. The Georgian-style **Center Church on the Green** (UCC), a good example of New England's interpretation of Palladian architecture, harbors many colonial tombstones in its crypt. At the northeastern corner of the green is **United Church** (UCC), another Georgian-Palladian work.

Grove St Cemetery *(227 Grove St),* three blocks north of the green, holds the graves of several famous New Havenites behind its grand Egyptian Revival gate (1845), including rubber magnate Charles Goodyear, the telegraph inventor Samuel Morse, lexicographer Noah Webster and cotton gin inventor Eli Whitney.

Yale University

Crowded with University Gothic buildings, Yale's old campus dominates the northern and western portions of downtown New Haven. Tallest of its Gothic spires is Harkness Tower, from which a carillon peals at appropriate moments throughout the day. On the south side of the Oak St Connector is an extensive modern campus holding the Yale–New Haven Hospital and medical science buildings. For more information about Yale and its history, see the History section, earlier.

Stop at the visitor center at Elm St and Temple St (see Information) and pick up a free campus map and a walking-tour brochure. For a free one-hour student-guided walking tour, arrive slightly before 10:30am or 2pm weekdays or at 1:30pm weekends.

Yale's museums have outstanding collections, and the art museums are free.

Peabody Museum of Natural History

The museum (*☎ 203-432-5050, 170 Whitney Ave; adult/senior & child 3-15 yrs $6/3; open 10am-5pm Mon-Sat, noon-5pm Sun),* five blocks northeast of the green along Temple St, has a vast collection of animal, vegetable and mineral specimens, including dinosaur fossils, wildlife dioramas, meteorites and minerals.

Yale Center for British Art This museum (☎ 203-432-2800, 1080 Chapel St; admission free; open 10am-5pm Tues-Sat, noon-5pm Sun), at the corner of High St, a block west of the green, holds the most comprehensive collection of British art outside the UK. The collections cover the period from Queen Elizabeth I to the present, with special emphasis on the period from Hogarth (born 1697) through Turner (died 1851).

Yale University Art Gallery Masterworks by Frans Hals, Peter Paul Rubens, Manet, Picasso and van Gogh fill the Yale Gallery (☎ 203-432-0600, 1111 Chapel St; admission free; open 10am-5pm Tues-Sat, 1pm-6pm Sun), between High and York Sts, opposite the Yale Center for British Art. Besides the masterworks, there are important collections of American silver from the 18th century and art from Africa, Asia, the pre- and post-Columbian Americas and Europe: 75,000 objects in all.

Places to Stay
Camping There are no campgrounds near New Haven. The closest are 21 miles east along I-95 near Clinton.

Hammonasset Beach State Park (☎ 860-566-2304, 877-668-2267, I-95 exit 62) Sites $12. This campground is on the coast between Madison and Clinton, and despite its 558 sites, it is often full in high summer. Reserve early.

Riverdale Farm Campsites (☎ 860-669-5388, River Rd, Clinton) Sites $28. Open mid-Apr–Sept. Riverdale Farm has 250 sites, showers, toilets and a camp store. Tent sites have water and electricity; some have full hookups.

Motels A few miles north of the city is *Motel 6 New Haven North* (☎ 203-469-0343, 800-466-8356, fax 203-468-0787, W www .motel6.com, 270 Foxon Blvd) Rooms $56-64. To get to this 58-room motel, take I-91 exit 8. All rooms are well-used, standard motel issue with bath, air con and TV.

Quality Inn (☎ 203-387-6651, 800-228-5151, fax 203-387-6651, W www.qualityinn .com, 100 Pond Lily Ave) Rooms $109-119 with light breakfast. This inn is just off the Wilbur Cross Parkway (exit 59), several miles to the northeast of town, and has 125 rooms. You get an indoor pool, fitness center and spa along with a well-furnished motel unit.

Hotels & Inns New Haven's classic hostelry is *Hotel Duncan* (☎ 203-787-1273, fax 203-787-0160, 1151 Chapel St) Singles/ doubles/suites $44/60/70. This is a gem for travelers who love European three-star hotels. At this period piece, more than a century old, the décor and facilities of fin-de-siècle New Haven have been preserved (the least expensive rooms have fans rather than air con). The elevator (with an old-school lever) holds only about five people and actually has an operator. Today there are 65 rooms let on a long-term basis and 35 for daily rental. Rooms have all the basic amenities and are extremely clean. You will find the staff as cheery as the rooms are clean. Check out the wall in the manager's office filled with autographed pictures of celebrity guests like Jodie Foster, Christopher Walken, Kevin Bacon and Colleen Dewhurst.

The Colony (☎ 203-776-1234, 800-458-8810, fax 203-772-3929, 1157 Chapel St) Singles/doubles $99/109. Only a few steps from the Duncan, this is a modernish hotel with 86 luxury rooms (including four-poster beds) within walking distance of everything. Ask about special discounted rates.

Holiday Inn New Haven at Yale (☎ 203-777-6221, fax 203-772-1089, W www.sixconti-nentshotels.com, 30 Whalley Ave) Rooms from $115. This hotel is only a few minutes' walk from the green. It has 160 rooms (the higher rooms have good views) and room rates vary depending upon the exact date and room. Make sure you ask for their discount rates.

Three Chimneys Inn (☎ 203-777-1201, 800-443-1554, fax 203-776-7363, 1201 Chapel St) Rooms $180 with full breakfast. Here's an 1870 Victorian townhouse that's been well restored. The 10 rooms are decorated in period style, mostly Victorian.

Places to Eat

Not so long ago the area west of Chapel St was a neighborhood in decay. Today Chapel St, adjacent Crown St and a half-dozen connecting streets constitute a restaurant and entertainment zone with cuisines from every part of the globe. Most of the restaurants here serve lunch and dinner.

Yankee Doodle Sandwich Shop (☎ 203-865-1074, 258 Elm St) Dishes $1-6. This is a classic hole-in-the-wall American lunch counter – Formica countertop, chrome and plastic stools – with prices to match: hamburgers for under $2, ham and cheese sandwiches for $3. You can get a couple of fried eggs for under $2.

Louis' Lunch (☎ 203-562-5507, 261-263 Crown St) Dishes around $4.50. Open 11am-4pm Mon-Thur, 11am-1am Fri & Sat. This joint, between College and High Sts, claims to be the place where the hamburger was invented – well, almost. Around 1900, when the vertically grilled ground beef sandwich was first introduced at Louis', the restaurant was in a different location. It still uses the historic vertical grills, and serves other sandwiches as well.

Atticus Bookstore Café (☎ 203-776-4040, 1082 Chapel St) Dishes $3-8. Open 8am-midnight daily. Between High and York Sts, this cafe has been serving coffee, soups, sandwiches and pastries amid the stacks for almost two decades. Mocking McDonald's, it proclaims 'Millions of scones served since 1981.' Prices are not low, and a slice of choice pastry or cheesecake might cost as much as $5. We like the Portuguese kale soup ($4). The bookstore adjoins, and both are open true college-town hours.

Claire's (☎ 203-562-3888, 1000 Chapel St) Dishes $5-7. At College St, this is the local favorite for vegetarian cuisine and breakfast (chocolate scones for $2), eat-in or take-out. Bright and airy, it's always busy with students picking up light Mexican meals or gooey desserts. In good weather you can catch rays at a streetside table, but clear it when you're done.

Bangkok Gardens (☎ 203-789-8684, 172 York St) Lunch $5-6, dinner $9-11. Just off Chapel St, this is the center's most popular Thai eatery. At lunch, big plates of pork, beef and chicken with vegetables are inexpensive, and the special three-course lunch is only $7.

Wooster Square, six blocks east of the green, is a mostly residential neighborhood, but it's famous for its pizza parlors.

Frank Pepe's (☎ 203-865-5762, 157 Wooster St) Dishes $5-20. Pepe's serves good pizza, just as it has for decades, in Spartan surroundings. Prices vary depending on size and toppings; the large mozzarella pie runs $12.

Sallie's Pizza (☎ 203-624-5271, 237 Wooster St) Pies $7-15. A nearby challenger to Pepe's, Sallie's is younger but even more highly regarded by many New Havenites.

Mom's Indian Kitchen (☎ 203-624-8771, 283 Crown St) Mains $7-10. If you like hole-in-the wall ethnic dining and air that drips with curry, you've got to stop at Mom's. There are only nine tables (with calming green table clothes) in this storefront operation. Consider the chicken *tikka masala* (spiced and cooked in a yogurt sauce) for $9.

Villa del Sol (☎ 203-785-9898, 236 Crown St) Lunch $6-13, dinner $13-18. The décor here is an upscale rendition of a Oaxacan cantina, with mariachi music (recorded) to match. The guacamole burritos ($7) are a good lunch value.

Caffé Adulis (☎ 203-777-5081, 228 College St) Mains $9-21. Want to try something different? New Haven is one of the few cities in New England with an Ethiopian-Eritrean restaurant. Eritrean cooking is distinguished by the use of sun-dried hot peppers called *berbere*, which are simmered in some dishes. Check out the *birzen*, or lentil stew ($9).

Scoozzi Trattoria (☎ 203-776-8268, 1104 Chapel St) Mains $16-23. At York St next to the Yale Repertory Theatre, Scoozzi serves trendy Italian fare with strong New American cuisine accents. Their little pizzettes and other appetizers are favorites with the before- and after-theater crowd, who combine them with wine by the glass to make a light supper. More substantial fare includes pasta combinations like ravioli di funghi ($20) and new variations on traditional Italian meat courses.

Tibwin Grill (☎ *203-624-1883, 220 College St)* Mains $17-21. At the corner of Crown St, this is an upscale New American bistro just a short stroll from the green. Grilled beef, lamb, pork and fowl turn on the spits as diners nibble exotic appetizers and quaff select wines and beers. Despite the red-meat emphasis, it does have a few vegetarian dishes (this *is* a college town).

Union League Café (☎ *203-562-4299, 1032 Chapel St)* Mains $17-23. Here's an upscale European bistro in the historic Union League building. Expect a menu featuring continental classics like *cassoulet de canard* (duck sausage with spring root veggies) along with those of nouvelle cuisine. The Sunday dinner is a fixed-price ($28) repast.

Entertainment

As a college town and a city of some size, New Haven has amassed an unusual number of theater, dance and musical companies – almost 20 at last count!

Theater & Ballet From September to May, a full and varied program of performances is offered by the *Yale Repertory Theatre* and *Yale University Theatre* (☎ *203-432-1234, 222 York St)* Tickets $10-36. Performing in a converted church at the corner of Chapel St, these Tony-winning companies perform classics and new works, featuring graduate students of the Yale School of Drama (Meryl Streep is an alum) as well as professionals.

Long Wharf Theatre (☎ *203-787-4282, 222 Sargent Dr)* Tickets $15-45. This famous theater, at I-95 exit 46, is on the waterfront near the Howard Johnson, with a theater season extending from October through June.

Shubert Performing Arts Center (☎ *203-562-5666, 800-228-6622, 247 College St)* Tickets $15-50. Dubbed 'Birthplace of the Nation's Greatest Hits,' the Shubert Center has been hosting ballet and Broadway musicals on their trial runs before heading off to the Big Apple since 1914. Shows run September to May.

Live Music Yale's Woolsey Hall is home to performances by the *New Haven Symphony Orchestra* (☎ *203-776-1444, 800-292-6476)* Tickets $10-48. The orchestra holds concerts at 8pm each Tuesday evening October to June.

Chamber Music Society of Yale (☎ *203-432-4158, 470 College St)* Tickets $8-25. This Yale society sponsors concerts at 8pm Tuesday evening from September through April in the Morse Recital Hall of Sprague Memorial Hall (470 College St).

Other concerts are hosted by the *Yale School of Music* (☎ *203-432-4157)* and by the *Yale Collection of Musical Instruments* (☎ *203-432-0822)*.

Greater New Haven Acoustic Music Society (☎ *203-468-1000)* Tickets $6-18. This society hosts folk concerts and performances in the summer in the Eli Whitney 1816 Barn, and in the winter in Dodds Hall (300 Orange Ave), on the University of New Haven (not Yale) campus.

New Haven Coliseum (☎ *203-772-4200, 275 S Orange St)* Tickets $15-55. The Coliseum is the place to come for rock concerts by world-class acts.

Clubs Get your swerve on at the hot, well-known nightclub *Toad's Place* (☎ *203-624-8623 recording,* ☎ *562-5589 office, 300 York St)* Cover free-$25, depending on the act. Performers such as Iggy Pop, Damien Marley and Michael Bolton work the stage.

Brü Rm at Bar (☎ *203-495-1111, 254 Crown St)* Cover $4-8. Check out this club, facing Louis' Lunch. The Brew Room (as its name translates) serves up brewpub beer, brick-oven pizza and dancing most nights. Friday nights see a long line at the door waiting to shuck and jive to underground house rhythms.

Gay Venues You get great cruising on three floors at *Partner's* (☎ *203-776-1014, 365 Crown St)* Cover free-$5. There are pool tables, quiet alcoves for conversation, busy bars and a DJ who cranks out dance rhythms. A lot of college boys hang here.

Gotham Citi Café (☎ 203-498-2484, 130 Crown St) Cover $5. Want a New York–style dance scene where the club kids pull off their shirts and pump it up? Head down to the Gotham. The music is dance and house; the guys are young studs.

Getting There & Around

Air Connecticut Transit (☎ 203-785-8930) can shuttle you to Tweed–New Haven Airport (☎ 203-787-8283, I-95 exit 50), from where several commuter airlines can take you to Boston or New York.

Bus Peter Pan Bus Lines (☎ 800-343-9999) connects New Haven with New York City, Hartford, Springfield and Boston, as does Greyhound Bus Lines (☎ 203-772-2470, 800-221-2222), inside New Haven's Union Station (☎ 203-773-6177, 50 Union Ave).

New Connecticut Limousine (☎ 800-472-5466) runs buses between New Haven and New York City's airports (La Guardia and JFK, plus Newark).

Train Metro-North trains (☎ 212-532-4900, 800-223-6052, 800-638-7646) make the 1½-hour run between New York City's Grand Central Station and New Haven's Union Station (☎ 203-773-6177, 50 Union Ave), at I-95 exit 47, almost every hour from 7am to midnight on weekdays, with more frequent trains during the morning and evening rush hours. On weekends, trains run about every two hours. Commuter Connection buses (☎ 203-624-0151) run at peak morning hours and during the afternoon/evening commuter times to shuttle passengers from Union Station to New Haven Green.

Several daily Amtrak trains (☎ 800-872-7245) run from New York's Pennsylvania Station, but at a higher fare.

See the beginning of this chapter for information on *Shore Line East* trains from New Haven east to New London.

Car Avis, Budget and Hertz rent cars at Tweed–New Haven Airport. New Haven is 141 miles southwest of Boston, 36 miles south of Hartford, 75 miles from New York and 101 miles from Providence via interstate highways.

Boat The Bridgeport & Port Jefferson Steamboat Company (☎ 888-443-3779 in CT, ☎ 631-473-0286 on Long Island, 102 W Broadway, Port Jefferson, NY 11777) operates its daily car ferries year-round between Bridgeport, 10 miles southwest of New Haven, and Port Jefferson on Long Island about every 1½ hours. The 1½-hour voyage one-way costs $13/10/6 adult/senior/child six to 12. The fee for a car and driver runs $30 to $40 depending on the number of passengers. Call to reserve space for your car.

NEW LONDON & GROTON

Stretching 6 miles along the west bank of the Thames (pronounced Thaymz) River, New London is an industrial, commercial and military city with a small tourist trade. During its golden age in the mid-19th century, New London was home port to some 200 whaling vessels, more than twice as many as were based at all other Connecticut ports combined. Its whaling commerce even rivaled that of Massachusetts' great whaling ports of Nantucket and New Bedford. Unlike Nantucket, however, New London is short on charm and long on industrial bustle.

On the east bank of the Thames in Groton, you'll find the General Dynamics Corporation, a major naval defense contractor, and the US Naval Submarine Base, the first (1881) and now the largest in the country. It's a fitting place for these establishments, because the first submarine was launched in 1776 just down the coast in Old Saybrook.

Orientation & Information

New London and Groton are 101 miles from Boston and 52 miles from Hartford via interstates.

For information on the area, contact the Chamber of Commerce of Southeastern Connecticut (☎ 860-443-8332, 105 Huntington St, New London, CT 06320) or the Southeastern Connecticut Tourism District

CONNECTICUT

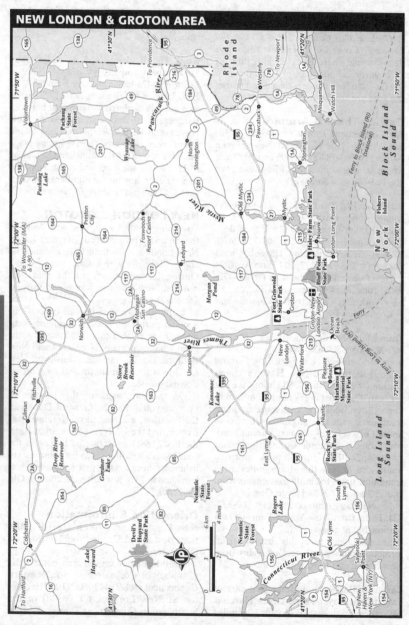

(☎ 860-444-2206, 800-863-6569, Ⓦ www
.mysticmore.com, 470 Bank St, PO Box 89,
New London, CT 06320). Both are open
8:30am to 5pm Monday to Friday.

Things to See & Do
New London This town has a well-laid-out
walking tour that starts along the restored
pedestrian mall called the **Captain's Walk**
(State St). Among the major sites are the
city's 19th-century railroad station and the
nearby **Nathan Hale Schoolhouse** (☎ 860-
443-7949, Union Plaza; admission free; open
noon-4pm Thurs-Sat mid-May–mid-Oct), a
tiny two-story building where Hale taught
before enlisting in the Connecticut militia.
There is also the 1833 **Custom House**, the
front door of which was made from the
wood of the USS Constitution.

Between Federal St and Governor
Winthrop Blvd, **Whale Oil Row** features
four identical white mansions with imposing
Doric facades built for whaling merchants
in 1830. They're not open to the public, but
the exterior view is impressive.

Of the two **Hempstead Houses** (☎ 860-
443-7949, 11 Hempstead St; adult/child $4/2;
open noon-4pm Thurs-Sun mid-May–mid-
Oct), the older one (1678) is one of the best-
documented 17th-century houses in the
country. Maintained by the descendants of
the original owners until 1937, it is one of the
few 17th-century houses remaining in the
area, having survived the burning of New
London by Benedict Arnold and the British
in 1781. The house is insulated with seaweed,
of all things.

You'll find more historic houses on Starr
St; shops and cafes line Bank St southwest
of the Amtrak train station near the waterfront.

Monte Cristo Cottage (☎ 860-443-0051,
325 Pequot Ave; admission $5; open 10am-
5pm Tues-Sat, 1pm-5pm Sun mid-June–early
Sept) was the boyhood home of playwright
Eugene O'Neill. Near Ocean Beach Park in
the southern districts of the city (follow the
signs), the Victorian-style house is now a research library for dramatists. Many of
O'Neill's belongings are on display, including his desk. You might recognize the living

room: It was the setting for two of O'Neill's
most famous plays, Long Day's Journey into
Night and Ah, Wilderness! (Theater buffs
should be sure to visit the Eugene O'Neill
Theater Center in nearby Waterford, which
hosts an annual summer series of readings
by young playwrights.)

The **Lyman Allyn Art Museum** (☎ 860-
443-2545, 625 Williams St; adult/senior &
student $4/3; open 10am-5pm Tues-Sat, 1pm-
5pm Sun) is a neoclassical building with exhibits that include early American silver
and Asian, Greco-Roman, European and
ethnic art of many cultures. There is also a
collection of dolls and dollhouses. Included
on the grounds of the museum is the
Deshon-Allyn House, a whaling captain's
Federal-style house, furnished with period
antiques and American regional fine art.

At the southern end of Ocean Ave is
Ocean Beach Park (☎ 860-510-SAND, 1225
Ocean Ave), a popular beach and amusement area with waterslides, a picnic area,
miniature golf, an arcade, a swimming pool
and an old-fashioned boardwalk.

Visitors can tour the grounds of the **US
Coast Guard Academy** (☎ 860-444-8270, 15
Mohegan Ave; admission free; open 9am-
5pm daily), one of the four US military
academies, any day. From May through
October, the visitors pavilion boasts a multi-
media show on cadet life; the academy's
museum is open year-round. You can climb
aboard the tall ship Eagle, used for cadet
training and boat parades, when it's in port
(usually on Sunday).

Groton At the **Historic Ship Nautilus &
Submarine Force Museum** (☎ 860-694-3174,
800-343-0079, 1 Crystal Lake Rd; admission
free; open 9am-5pm Wed-Mon, 1pm-5pm
Tues mid-May–Oct; 9am-4pm Wed-Mon
Nov–mid-May), on the Naval Submarine
Base, visitors can board the world's first
nuclear-powered submarine, the Nautilus,
launched on January 21, 1954. Other exhibits
chronicle the history of the US submarine
force and feature working periscopes and
mini-subs.

Fort Griswold State Park (☎ 860-445-1729,
cnr Monument St & Park Ave; admission

free; open 10am-5pm daily late May-early Sept; 10am-5pm Sat & Sun early Sept–mid-Oct) has a 130-foot obelisk that marks the place where colonial troops were defeated and massacred by Benedict Arnold and the British in 1781, in a battle that saw the death of colonial Colonel William Ledyard and the British burning of Groton and New London. Monument House features the Daughters of the American Revolution's collection of Revolutionary and Civil War memorabilia.

Places to Stay

In summer, rates are highest on Friday and Saturday nights and lower from Sunday to Thursday. The lowest rates quoted are for November to March. For a complete list and links to accommodations in eastern Connecticut, consult 🆆 www.mysticmore.com.

For camping not far from New London and Groton, see the Mystic section.

Motels & Hotels The coming of the Foxwoods and Mohegan Sun casinos (see the boxed text 'Foxwoods') has spurred motel development around every exit of I-95 in eastern Connecticut. The result is over 60 different motor inns and competitive pricing. All of the major chains are here. These motels see a *lot* of clients so don't expect pristine furnishings or meticulous housekeeping.

Thames Inn & Marina (☎ 860-445-8111, 193 Thames St, Groton) Rooms $40-100. This inn has 26 rooms (with fully equipped kitchens) and a coin-operated laundry on the premises.

Motel 6 (☎ 860-739-6991, 800-466-8356, fax 860-691-1828, 🆆 www.motel6.com, 74 Flanders Rd, Niantic) Rooms $45-66. A bit farther west, Motel 6 stands off I-95 at exit 74. There are 93 modern units here, an outdoor pool and a free shuttle to Foxwoods Resort Casino.

Holiday Inn (☎ 860-442-0631, 800-465-4329, fax 860-442-0130, 🆆 www.sixcontinents hotels.com, I-95 & Frontage Rd, New London) Rooms $60-160. The motor inn has 136 rooms, plus an outdoor pool, bar, restaurant and fitness center.

Groton Inn & Suites (☎ 860-445-9784, 800-452-2191, fax 860-445-2664, 99 Gold Star Hwy/CT 184, Groton) Rooms $72-198. Groton Inn, at I-95, has 115 rooms with kitchenettes. You also get a restaurant, bar and fitness center.

Radisson Hotel New London/Mystic (☎ 860-443-7000, 800-333-3333, fax 860-443-1239, 🆆 www.radisson.com, 35 Governor Winthrop Blvd, New London) Rooms $70-150. An indoor pool, restaurant, bar and a free shuttle to area casinos are part of the package at the Radisson.

Inns Afternoon tea is included in the rates at the *Queen Anne Inne* (☎ 860-447-2600, 800-347-8818, fax 860-443-0857, 265 Williams St, New London) Rooms $89-185 with full breakfast. This is a Victorian 1903 mansion with an art gallery as well as 10 guest rooms. A 20th-century hot tub is also available.

Lighthouse Inn (☎ 860-443-8411, 888-443-8411, fax 860-437-7027, 🆆 www.light houseinn-ct.com, 6 Guthrie Place, New London) Rooms $90-150, suites $180-250. The hotel, just inland from Guthrie Beach at the southern end of Montauk Ave, offers 51 deluxe rooms in a huge, finely restored 1902 mansion. The Carriage House rooms are cheaper, and you can get a discount rate by booking online.

Places to Eat

New London and Groton are short on fancy restaurants, but you'll find a number of cafes and bars along Bank St in New London.

Recovery Room (☎ 860-443-2619, 443 Ocean Ave, New London) Dishes $6-15. For great, inexpensive pizza (said to rival New Haven's famous Pepe's), try this family-run place near the beach.

Bangkok City (☎ 860-442-6970, 123 Captain's Walk, New London) Mains $8-16. Nobody's holding back on the *prik phao* (crushed red peppers) here. This sit-down restaurant near the ferry docks has memorable *tom yam kong* (spicy shrimp soup) for under $6.

G Williker's (☎ 860-445-8043, 156 King's Hwy/US 1, Groton) Dishes $6-14. This theme restaurant features a lot of Tex-Mex offerings. Consider a stop here on Wednesday for 'half-price Mexican' when you can get tacos or a margarita for $3.

Getting There & Away

New London's transportation center is the Amtrak train station on Water St at State St; the bus station is in the same building and the ferry terminal (for boats to Long Island, Block Island and Fishers Island) is next door.

Air The Groton–New London Airport (☎ 860-445-8549) hosts US Air Express (☎ 800-428-4322) and commuter airlines that connect with the major airlines in Boston and New York City.

Train Amtrak (☎ 800-872-7245) trains between New York and Boston on the shore route stop at New London. See Getting There & Around at the beginning of this chapter for details on Amtrak.

Car For New London, take I-95 exit 84, then go north on CT 32 (Mohegan Ave) for the US Coast Guard Academy, or take I-95 exits 82, 83 or 84 and go south for the city center. The center of the commercial district is just southwest of the Amtrak station along Bank St. Follow Ocean Ave (CT 213) to reach Ocean Beach Park and Harkness Memorial State Park.

For Groton, take I-95 exits 85, 86 or 87.

Boat Cross Sound Ferry (☎ 860-443-5281, 516-323-2525, 2 Ferry St, PO Box 33, New London, CT 06320) operates car ferries and high-speed passenger ferries year-round between Orient Point, Long Island (New York) and New London, a 1½-hour run on the car ferry, 40 minutes on the high-speed ferry. From late June through Labor Day, ferries depart each port every hour on the hour from 7am to 9pm daily (last boats at 9:45pm). Off-season, boats tend to run every two hours. For high-speed ferries, the one-way rates are $15.50/8 adult/child. The rates for car ferries are $10/5 adult/child. Cars cost $36, bicycles $2. Call for car reservations.

The Fishers Island Ferry (☎ 860-442-0165) runs from New London to the wealthy summer colony at Fishers Island, New York.

In summer, there are daily boats between New London and Block Island, RI, as well. See the Rhode Island chapter for details.

MYSTIC

Southeastern Connecticut is the most-visited region of the state because it is here that you find the famous Mystic Seaport Museum and the Foxwoods and Mohegan Sun casinos (see the boxed text 'Foxwoods').

Mystic was a classic seaport town centuries before the Seaport Museum became such a popular tourist attraction, and the town remains a memorable place to stroll, shop and dine.

Orientation & Information

Take I-95 exit 90 for the Mystic Seaport Museum and Mystic town center. Motels are both north and south of I-95; Mystic Seaport Museum is a mile south of the highway on CT 27 (Greenmanville Ave); the center of the town is less than a mile south. Old Mystic is a separate town to the north of I-95. The Foxwoods Resort Casino is north of I-95 off CT 2 and CT 214. The Mohegan Sun casino is off I-395 at exit 79A.

The Mystic River Bascule Bridge (1922), known locally as 'the drawbridge,' carries US 1 across the Mystic River at the center of the town of Mystic. It's a familiar ritual in Mystic to wait while the drawbridge is raised for river traffic. There are shops and restaurants situated on both sides of the bridge; most of the ice cream shops are on the west side.

For information, contact the Mystic Chamber of Commerce (☎ 860-572-9578, Ⓦ www.mysticchamber.org, 16 Cottrell St, PO Box 143, Mystic, CT 06355), south of the drawbridge on the east bank of the river. The visitor center is in the train station on Roosevelt St, open 9am to 5pm Monday to Friday.

Mystic Seaport Museum

From simple beginnings in the 17th century, the village of Mystic grew to become one of

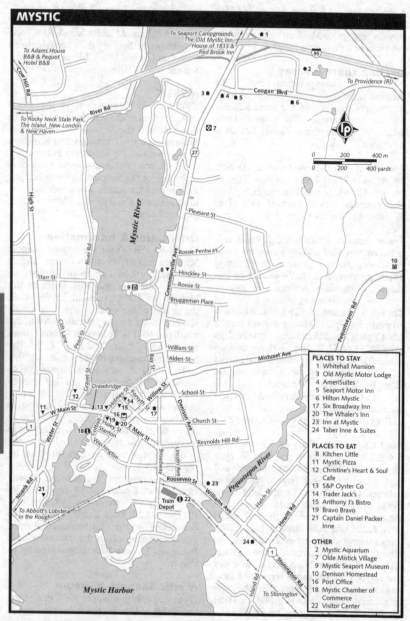

MYSTIC

To Seaport Campgrounds,
The Old Mystic Inn,
House of 1833 &
Red Brook Inn

To Adams House
B&B & Pequot
Hotel B&B

Cow Hill Rd

To Providence (RI)

Coogan Blvd

River Rd

To Rocky Neck State Park,
The Island, New London
& New Haven

High St

River Rd

Mystic River

Starr St

Pleasant St

Rossie Pentway

Greenmanville Ave

Hinckley St

Rossie St

Bruggeman Place

Cliff Lane

Pearl St

Gravel St

William St

Alden St

Mistuxet Ave

Bay St

Drawbridge

Holmes St

Forsyth St

Willow St

School St

Denison Ave

W Main St

Water St

Cottrell

Haley St

Stanton

E Main St

Church St

Washington

Broadway

Lincoln Ave

Reynolds Hill Rd

Noank Rd

To Abbott's Lobster
in the Rough

Roosevelt St

Train
Depot

Williams Ave

Pequotsepos River

Hatch St

Hewitt Rd

To Stonington

Stonington Rd

Island Rd

Mystic Harbor

0   200   400 m
0   200   400 yards

PLACES TO STAY
1 Whitehall Mansion
3 Old Mystic Motor Lodge
4 AmeriSuites
5 Seaport Motor Inn
6 Hilton Mystic
17 Six Broadway Inn
20 The Whaler's Inn
23 Inn at Mystic
24 Taber Inne & Suites

PLACES TO EAT
8 Kitchen Little
11 Mystic Pizza
12 Christine's Heart & Soul
   Cafe
13 S&P Oyster Co
14 Trader Jack's
15 Anthony J's Bistro
19 Bravo Bravo
21 Captain Daniel Packer
   Inne

OTHER
2 Mystic Aquarium
7 Olde Mistick Village
9 Mystic Seaport Museum
10 Denison Homestead
16 Post Office
18 Mystic Chamber of
   Commerce
22 Visitor Center

CONNECTICUT

the great shipbuilding ports of the East Coast. In the mid-19th century, Mystic's shipyards launched clipper ships, many from the George Greenman and Co Shipyard, which is now the site of Mystic Seaport Museum, inaugurated in 1929.

Today, the Mystic Seaport Museum (☎ 860-572-0711, 75 Greenmanville Ave/CT 27; adult/child 6-15 yrs $17/9; open 9am-5pm daily) covers 17 acres and includes more than 60 historic buildings, four ships and many smaller vessels. Some buildings in the Seaport are original to the site, but as at Old Sturbridge Village in Massachusetts, many were transported to Mystic from other parts of New England and arranged to re-create the look of the past.

Costumed interpreters staff the buildings and talk about their crafts and trades with visitors.

Visitors can board the *Charles W Morgan* (1841), the last surviving wooden whaling ship in America; the *LA Dunton*, a three-masted fishing schooner; or the *Joseph Conrad*, a square-rigged training ship. 'Fishermen' interpreters on the *Dunton* show how cod was salted and demonstrate some other skills essential to life at sea in the 19th century. The museum's exhibits include a replica of the 77-foot schooner *Amistad*, the slave ship on which 55 kidnapped Africans cast off their chains and sailed to freedom. In the Steven Spielberg movie *Amistad*, Mystic Seaport Museum was used to stage many of the scenes that actually took place in colonial New London. See the boxed text 'Amistad.'

At the Henry B duPont Preservation Shipyard, visitors can watch large wooden boats being restored. The Seaport also includes a small boat shop, general store, chapel, school, sail loft, shipsmith and the ship chandlery – all the sorts of places that you'd expect to find in a real shipbuilding town of 150 years ago. The Wendell Building has a display of ships' figureheads and carvings.

The *Sabino* (☎ 860-572-5315; adult/child $5/4), a 1908-era steamboat, takes visitors on excursion trips up the Mystic River from May to October.

Mystic Aquarium

Mystic Aquarium (☎ 860-572-5955, 55 Coogan Blvd; adult/senior/child 3-12 yrs $16/15/11; open 9am-5pm daily) has more than 6000 species of sea creatures (including sand tiger sharks), an outdoor viewing area for seals and sea lions, a penguin exhibit and a 1400-seat Marine Theater for dolphin shows. Use I-95 exit 90 to get there.

Denison Homestead

The displays in this 1717 home (☎ 860-536-9248, Pequotsepos Rd; adult/senior & student/child under 16 yrs $4/3/1; open 11am-4pm Thurs-Mon), to the east of Mystic Seaport Museum, illustrate life in New England from the colonial period through the 1940s. The house contains memorabilia from 11 generations of the Denison family arranged in a series of rooms: a colonial kitchen, a Revolutionary-era bedroom, a Federal parlor, a Civil War bedroom and an early-20th-century living room.

Places to Stay

Mystic offers a multitude of motels and inns, many of which post photographs and links at W www.mysticmore.com or the website of Bed & Breakfasts of Mystic (W www.bnbofthemysticcoast.com). In July and August, most lodgings fill up every day. Consider alternatives in nearby communities such as New London, Stonington and Groton.

Camping Though there are several state parks nearer, the closest with camping is *Rocky Neck State Park* (☎ 860-739-5471, 877-688-2267, 244 West Main St, Niantic) Sites $12. South of I-95, this is a well-developed state park with swimming, hiking, horseback riding and a concession stand.

The Island (☎ 860-739-8316, 20 Islanda Court, East Lyme) Tent sites $20, full hookups $25. Off US 1, the Island has 35 sites and full hookups on a pond, 3 miles from t eaches.

Seaport Campgrounds (☎ 860-536-4044, W www.seaportcampground.com, CT 184, Old Mystic) Tent sites $28, RV sites without/

CONNECTICUT

Amistad

On July 2, 1839, the slave ship *Amistad* was sailing along the coast of Cuba with its 'cargo' of 55 Africans who had been abducted and forced into slavery. One of the captives, known to history as Joseph Cinque, managed to remove his shackles surreptitiously and lead a rebellion of other captives against the European crew. The captain and cook were killed, but the mutineers spared the Spanish navigator so that he could guide the ship back to Sierra Leone for them.

The navigator had other plans, however. Though he headed the ship eastward during the day when the sun's position made its course evident to the mutineers, at night he used the stars to head west, hoping to bring the ship to a port where he could get help.

For two months the *Amistad* sailed back and forth, exhausting its supplies of food and water. Finally, a US Coast Guard ship sighted and seized it off Long Island and towed it to New London. The Africans were accused of rebellion, transported to New Haven and imprisoned awaiting trial.

The plight of the *Amistad* abductees became a cause célèbre among abolitionist forces in the state and the nation. A committee of concerned Christian abolitionists was formed to aid in their legal defense. The *Amistad* abductees' case went all the way to the US Supreme Court, and former President John Quincy Adams emerged from retirement to plead their case. The court found that they had been abducted illegally and therefore could not be held liable for mutiny when they sought their own freedom. The decision was a powerful moral and legal victory for the antislavery forces.

The *Amistad* abductees were repatriated to Africa, and the committee formed to help them was incorporated in 1846 as the American Missionary Association. The AMA went on to found more than 500 schools for those emancipated by the Civil War and, later, many noted institutions of higher learning, including Howard University.

with hookups $34/36. Open Mar-Nov. Seaport has 130 RV sites, a separate tenting area, and services from free hot showers to miniature golf.

Motels & Hotels Most of Mystic's motels cluster near I-95 exit 90, most on CT 27 (Greenmanville Ave/Whitehall Ave) north and south of the interstate.

Seaport Motor Inn (☎ 860-536-2621, 800-447-0764, fax 860-536-4493, Coogan Blvd) Rooms $49-149. Just south of I-95, you can't miss this inn. It has 117 clean, simple rooms with motel conveniences and an outdoor pool.

Old Mystic Motor Lodge (☎ 860-536-9666, fax 860-536-2044, 251 Greenmanville Ave/CT 27) Rooms $49-169. Across CT 27, this motor lodge has a large pool and 56 rooms on two floors, all equipped with refrigerators and microwaves.

AmeriSuites (☎ 860-536-9997, 800-833-1516, fax 860-536-9686, 224 Greenmanville

Ave) Suites $79-249. This is the newest lodging in this cluster, with up-to-date suites, many of which sleep four or six people.

Hilton Mystic (☎ 860-572-0731, 800-445-8667, fax 860-572-0328, ⓦ www.hilton.com, 20 Coogan Blvd) Rooms $85-205. The Hilton has predictably comfortable accommodations in a convenient location across from Mystic Aquarium. Special packages may give you more for less; call and ask about them.

Several other good choices lie east of the center of Mystic along US 1.

Inn at Mystic (☎ 860-536-9604, 800-237-2415, fax 860-572-1635, cnr US 1 & CT 27) Rooms $65-275. Quarters range from simple, clean motel-style units to luxury chambers in the hilltop Georgian mansion decorated with colonial-style furniture and antiques. Humphrey Bogart and Lauren Bacall spent their honeymoon here. From the inn's hilltop setting, lawns sweep down to a boat dock, tennis court and swimming pool. The *Flood Tide* restaurant is very well regarded.

Taber Inne & Suites (☎ 860-536-4904, fax 860-572-9140, 66 Williams Ave) Rooms $97-375. This place is a minute's drive east of Mystic center along US 1 and is popular with families. There's quite a range of comfortable accommodations here, from 28 motel-type rooms to luxurious one- and two-bedroom townhouses.

Inns & B&Bs Only 1½ miles from the center of Mystic is the *Adams House B&B* (☎ 860-572-9551, fax 860-572-9552, 382 Cow Hill Rd) Rooms $85-175 with breakfast. The Adams House offers cozy rooms with queen beds and private baths; afternoon tea is included.

Whitehall Mansion (☎ 860-572-7280, 800-572-3993, fax 860-572-4724, 40 Whitehall Ave/CT 27) Rooms $89-250 with breakfast. Perhaps the finest of Mystic's inns, this grand colonial house dates from 1771; it became a luxury B&B in 1996. Each of the five rooms has a fireplace, whirlpool bath and individual climate control. Evening wine and cheese come with the tariff. You'll find the mansion just to the north of I-95 at the Mystic exit.

The Whaler's Inn (☎ 860-536-1506, 800-243-2588, fax 860-572-1250, ⓦ www.whalersinnmystic.com, 20 E Main St) Rooms are $95-139. Right in the center of Mystic by the drawbridge, this establishment consists of an 1865 Victorian house, a contemporaneous inn and a more modern motel structure known as Stonington House. Room rates at Whaler's Inn vary depending upon the number and size of beds and the building they're in.

Pequot Hotel B&B (☎ 860-572-0390, fax 860-536-3380, 711 Cow Hill Rd) Rooms $95-175. This place was once a stagecoach stop. The Greek Revival house, built in 1840, now has three luxury guest rooms with bath (two with fireplaces).

Red Brook Inn (☎ 860-572-0349, fax 860-572-0146, cnr CT 184 & Wells Rd) Rooms $95-189. The Red Brook Inn offers guests a choice of two buildings: the Haley Tavern (1740), with seven guest rooms, and the

Crary Homestead (1770), with three guest rooms.

Six Broadway Inn (☎/fax 860-536-6010, 6 Broadway) Rooms Sun-Thur/Fri & Sat $95/225. This fine old Victorian house is a short distance from the center of Mystic; you'll pass the inn as you drive south from Mystic Seaport Museum to the center. European-style luxury is the aim for guests in its five rooms. There's a two-night minimum on weekends.

House of 1833 (☎ 860-536-6325, 800-367-1833, 72 N Stonington Rd/CT 201) Rooms $99-249. This Greek Revival mansion has five luxury guest rooms furnished in antiques, a swimming pool, a Har-Tru tennis court and bikes for touring.

The Old Mystic Inn (☎ 860-572-9422, fax 860-572-9954, 52 Main St, Old Mystic) Rooms $115-175. Situated in Old Mystic north of I-95, the inn has eight guest rooms (six with working fireplaces, two with whirlpool tubs) named for New England authors.

Places to Eat & Drink

There are several places to grab a snack or sit down to a full meal within Mystic Seaport Museum, but most of Mystic's restaurants are in or near the town center, close to the drawbridge. Most serve lunch and dinner.

Kitchen Little (☎ 860-536-2122, 135 Greenmanville Ave) Dishes $4-10. Check out this spot for breakfast or lunch in a rock garden with a view of the river. In a recent issue of *Gourmet Magazine*, food writers touted the clear-broth clam chowder ($5) as 'a potent elixir that radiates marine fragrance like a summer breeze across a white sand beach.' Some folks actually brown-bag a split of champagne to wash down their omelets.

Mystic Pizza (☎ 860-536-3737, 56 W Main St) Dishes $6-16. This pizzeria calls its pizzas 'little slices of heaven' and also serves salads, hearty grinders and beer. If the name sounds familiar, it may be because it was the title of a low-budget comedy film starring Julia Roberts (one of her first movies). The pizza parlor might have inspired the movie, but the location used as the movie set is actually in Stonington.

Several popular restaurants stand right in the center of town, east of the drawbridge.

S&P Oyster Co (☎ 860-536-2674, 1 Holmes St) Dishes $6-18. Set on the riverbank, this place boasts 'the best view in Mystic.' The large serving of fish and chips ($9) is the number one entrée at lunch and dinner. There's a children's menu, too.

Anthony J's Bistro (☎ 860-536-0448, 6 Holmes St) Mains $9-20. This is a classy trattoria serving pizzas for $8 to $11 and a full menu of Italian specialties, pastas and grills.

Christine's Heart & Soul Cafe (☎ 860-536-1244, 4 Pearl St) Mains $10-20. Open for dinner from 4pm daily, lunch from 11am Sat. Tucked in a colonial building on the west side of the drawbridge, Christine's features an American-continental menu with appetizers like seafood-stuffed portabellos ($7) and entrées such as grilled marinated chicken ($10). The cafe has eclectic décor and a seating capacity of 30. From Wednesday to Sunday, the gang shows up after 9pm for live blues, jazz and acoustic, mostly original compositions. The draw is the music, a selection of 50 beers and an upscale crowd, ages 35 to 55, geared to party. The cover runs $2 to $12.

Trader Jack's (☎ 860-572-8550, 14 Holmes St) Mains $12-20. A block farther north than Anthony's, this tavern at the corner of Church St often has the very best deals at lunch. Consider the Mexican options like the enchiladas ($9).

Bravo Bravo (☎ 860-536-3228, 20 E Main St) Dishes $15-19. This eatery, at Holmes St, serves nouvelle Italian food – flavorful and inventive pastas, seafood and beef – in a bright, sophisticated setting. We like the seafood *zuppa* ($17).

Abbott's Lobster in the Rough (☎ 860-536-7719, 117 Pearl St) Mains $15-22. Open 11:30am-9:30pm daily May-Oct. Lobster lovers should check out Abbott's, on the waterfront in neighboring Noank, just west of Mystic. You order your lobster (or other seafood) at the window, get a number, pick out a picnic table by the water and, when your number is called, pay and eat. New

England doesn't get much better than this on a warm summer night.

Captain Daniel Packer Inne (☎ 860-536-3555, 32 Water St) Mains $22-30. On the west side of the drawbridge, then south on Water St (CT 215; a five-minute walk), this place occupies a historic house dating from 1754. Diners rave about the imaginative American cuisine. A favorite is 'steak blackjack,' a 16oz slab of beef in a sauce laced with whiskey ($28).

Shopping

Olde Mistick Village (☎ 860-536-4941, CT 27) Open 10am-6pm Mon-Sat, noon-5pm Sun. Just south of I-95, this pseudocolonial village green is centered on a Congregational church and surrounded by over 60 shops selling sportswear, gifts, crafts, jewelry and Lladró porcelain.

The town's most interesting shops lie along Main St west of the drawbridge.

Getting There & Around

Amtrak (☎ 800-872-7245) trains between New York and Boston on the shore route stop at Mystic's train depot on Roosevelt St, less than a mile south of Mystic Seaport Museum.

Mystic is 9 miles east of New London and Groton. The best route by car is I-95.

The Mystic Trolley circulates through the town and among the major points of interest, charging $2 per ride or $5 for unlimited rides all day.

STONINGTON

Five miles east of Mystic on US 1, Stonington stands out as one of the most appealing towns on the Connecticut coast. Many of the town's 18th- and 19th-century houses were once sea captains' homes. One of the finest of these belonged to Capt Nathaniel Palmer, who earned fame at the very tender age of 21 by being the first American to see the continent of Antarctica.

It's best to explore this historic town – actually a 'borough,' Connecticut's oldest – on foot. Compactly laid out on a peninsula that juts into Long Island Sound, Stonington is rife with streetscapes of period architecture.

Foxwoods

Rising above the forest canopy of Great Cedar Swamp 7 miles north of Mystic, the gleaming towers of the mammoth *Foxwoods Resort Casino* (☎ 800-752-9244) seem to have been dropped from outer space into the Connecticut countryside.

Under treaties dating back centuries, native peoples have territorial and legal rights separate from those enjoyed by other citizens of the US. In recent times, these aboriginal nations have used the courts and the Congress to elaborate these treaty rights into a potent vehicle for addressing longstanding discrimination against them and its resulting poverty.

One such group, the 700-member Mashantucket Pequot Tribal Nation, known as 'the fox people,' kept a tenuous hold on a parcel of ancestral land in southeastern Connecticut. The tribe had dwindled to insignificant numbers through assimilation and dispersion, but a few souls refused to abandon the reservation. Living in decrepit trailers dragged onto the land, they fought a dispiriting legal battle against attempts to declare the reservation abandoned.

Their tenacity paid off in 1986 when they reached an agreement with the Connecticut state government that allowed the Pequots to open a high-stakes bingo hall. In 1992, again under an agreement with the state, the tribe borrowed $60 million from a Malaysian casino developer and began to build Foxwoods.

The resort features the world's largest gambling casino, nightclubs with free entertainment, cinemas, rides and video-game and pinball parlors for children. There are about 1400 luxury guest rooms (☎ 800-369-9663 for reservations) in three hotels (the *Grand Pequot Tower, Great Cedar Hotel* and *Two Trees Inn*).

The **Mashantucket Pequot Museum & Research Center** (☎ 860-396-6838, Ⓦ *www.mashan tucket.com; adult/senior/child 6-15 yrs $10/8/6; open 10am-7pm daily*) is an ultramodern museum for an ancient people. The last admission is at 6pm.

Take I-95 to exit 92 (the North Stonington exit, east of Mystic), then follow CT 2 West; or take I-395 to exit 79A, 80, 81 or 85 and follow the signs for the 'Mashantucket Pequot Reservation.'

Mohegan Sun Casino (☎ 888-226-7711), at I-395 exit 79A, is a smaller version of Foxwoods operated by the Mohegan tribe on its reservation.

The short main thoroughfare, Water St, features shops selling high-end antiques, colorful French Quimper porcelain and upscale gifts. There are also a couple of waterfront restaurants and delis. At the southern end of Water St is the 'point' or tip of the peninsula, with a park and tiny beach.

History

Settled in 1752 and chartered in 1801, Stonington was a whaling village until the advent of steam power fated it to become a major transfer point on the rail-and-steamship route between New York and Boston. At one time in the mid-19th century, some 17 rail lines converged on the town from Boston and other New England points, bringing passengers and cargo to continue on to New York by steamboat.

When the era of the steamships ended in the 1880s and the Northeast Corridor trip could be made entirely by rail, the once-vital connection at Stonington was no longer needed. Then, a new railroad viaduct across the main north-south road into Stonington had the effect of cutting off the village from the commercial highway corridor of US 1. Many longtime Stonington residents credit (or blame) the railroad viaduct for consigning the mile-long peninsula and its little village to a time warp in which it has remained ever since. Some of Stonington's earliest buildings were destroyed in the Battle of Stonington during the War of

CONNECTICUT

1812, but many more remain, including the sweet little Greek Revival arcade.

The battle was a moment of high drama for the village: On August 9, 1814, four British ships used 158 Royal Navy guns to batter the town, which was suspected of harboring torpedoes. Forty buildings were destroyed, but the Yanks repelled the British. You will see the Yankee cannons that served Stonington on perpetual display in Cannon Square. Cannonballs, recovered from all over the village after the battle, stand atop granite gateposts and hitching posts around town.

Things to See & Do

Stonington has had its share of famous residents over the years. Drive or walk down Water St (one-way southbound) to its southern end for a good look at the town, and then drive north on Main St, the other major north-south street, one block east of Water St.

The **Colonel Amos Palmer House** (1780), on Water St at Wall St, was the home of artist James McNeill Whistler and later of poet Stephen Vincent Benét. (The house is not open to the public.)

At the southern end of Water St, close to the point, the houses become plainer and simpler, many dating from the 18th century. These were the residences of ships' carpenters and fishermen.

At the end of the point, near the small DuBois Beach, is the **Old Lighthouse Museum** (☎ 860-535-1440, 7 Water St; adult/child 6-12 yrs $4/2; open 10am-5pm Tues-Sun May-Oct). The octagonal-towered granite lighthouse, built in 1823 as the first government lighthouse in Connecticut, moved to its present location in 1840 and deactivated 50 years later. Now it's a museum with exhibits on whaling, Native American artifacts, curios from the China trade, wooden boats, weaponry, 19th-century oil portraits, toys and decoys.

Heading back north, the **Portuguese Holy Ghost Society** building on Main St is a reminder of the contributions made to Stonington by the Azoreans who signed onto Stonington-bound whalers during the

19th century and eventually settled in the village. Today, their descendants still form a significant part of Stonington's population, though the small village's ever-increasing appeal to wealthy New Yorkers seeking summer homes is driving the locals out of the real-estate market. Nearby, the old **Custom House** stands as testimony to the days when Stonington was a major port.

Places to Stay

Stonington is the area's quaintest place to stay; see the Mystic or New London & Groton sections for cheaper or chain motels.

There are 260 sites at *Highland Orchards Resort Park* (☎ 860-599-5101, 800-624-0829, CT 49, North Stonington) Sites $29-39. Open year-round. This campground has swimming, fishing and a camp store.

Budget motels – some of the cheapest accommodations in the area – lie northeast of the center of Stonington along US 1 on the way to Pawcatuck.

Stonington Motel (☎/fax 860-599-2330, 901 Stonington Rd/US 1, Stonington) Rooms $53-89. This motel has 12 well-used rooms. Inquire about the 10% discount on weekdays.

Cove Ledge Inn & Marina (☎ 860-599-4130, fax 860-599-1563, Whewell Circle/US 1, Pawcatuck) Rooms $75-250. You get a pool at Cove Ledge and a choice of rooms or cottages. Some accommodations have cooking facilities.

Within walking distance of everything in town is *Lasbury's* (☎ 860-535-2681, 41 Orchard St) Doubles $100-125. Calling itself 'a quiet guest house' – the only one in the heart of Stonington – this unpretentious inn is off Church St (turn left off of Water St at Noah's restaurant).

Randall's Ordinary (☎ 860-599-4540, Ⓦ www.randallsordinary.com, 41 Norwich/Westerly Rd, North Stonington) Rooms $125-300. This is a centuries-old farmhouse (1685) that is now an inn and restaurant (see Places to Eat, below). As you enter the farm, it's easy to believe you've gone back in time: Authenticity of the exterior appearance is a strong point here, even though on the inside the inn has modern conveniences.

In the main house are three guest rooms; nine more are in the barn. All rooms have private baths. The inn is 8.4 miles northeast of the center of Stonington along CT 2, three-tenths of a mile north of I-95 exit 92.

Places to Eat
You will see Stonington's few restaurants as you proceed south on Water St.

Water St Market & Deli (☎ *860-535-0797, 143 Water St)* Dishes $4-8. Across the street from the Water St Cafe, this is perfect for picnic supplies – have your picnic in the park at the southern end of Water St. Try the crab cake roll ($4).

Water St Cafe (☎ *860-535-2122, 142 Water St)* Dishes $5-25. North of Grand St, this cafe boasts a menu that is creative and moderately priced – a rare combination. Recent dishes included escargot pot pie, tuna tartare and a pork empanada. Lunch can cost as little as $10; dinner is more like $25. They serve Sunday brunch as well.

Noah's (☎ *860-535-3925, 115 Water St)* Mains $10-16. Open 7am-9pm Tues-Sun. Noah's is a pretty, informal place at Church St, with two small rooms topped with original stamped-tin ceilings. It has local art on the walls and an authentic old-fashioned atmosphere. We like the roast duck and fennel soup ($3) and asparagus quiche ($7) for lunch.

Randall's Ordinary (see Places to Stay) Mains $18-25. Hearth cooking in the authentic colonial manner is the specialty here. Breakfast and lunch are à la carte, but there is just one dinner seating, at 7pm, for a fixed-price menu of slow-simmered soups, beef, fish, chicken or venison, hearth-baked cornbread and colonial-style desserts. Drinks, tax and tip are additional to the fixed dinner price. Advance reservations are essential.

Skipper's Dock (☎ *860-535-0111, 66 Water St)* Lunch $8-15, dinner $25-35. Here's a casual seafood restaurant with a waterside deck. This is the place to order steamers, lobster or what is locally known as a clam boil – the works, including clams, corn, lobster, fish and sausage. A lunch entrée will fill you for the day.

Shopping
Quimper Faïence (☎ *860-535-1712, 800-470-7339, 141 Water St)* Open 10am-5pm Mon-Sat, noon-5pm Sun. Stonington is one of only two towns in the USA (the other is Alexandria, Virginia) with an official shop for Quimper Faïence. Pronounced 'kamm-**pehr**,' this is the colorfully painted dinnerware handmade in France since the 17th century. Folk-art plates, cups, mugs, platters, figurines and utensils are popular collector's items. Prices are not low, but then, each Quimper piece is one of a kind by definition.

Litchfield Hills

The rolling hills in the northwestern corner of Connecticut take their name from the historic town of Litchfield at their heart. Sprinkled with lakes and dotted with state parks and forests, this region offers an abundance of tranquillity. Only a handful of inns and campgrounds provide for travelers, an intentional curb on development that guarantees the preservation of the area's rural character. In many ways the Litchfield hills are antidotes to the tourist development that lies just to the north in Massachusetts' Berkshire Hills. Quite a few entertainment industry celebrities keep a low profile on their farms and country estates on the back roads here.

One of the most delightful drives in southern New England makes a circle south from Great Barrington, MA, to Litchfield via US 7 and CT 63, turns west on US 202 to Lake Waramaug and heads north on CT 45 and US 7 to Cornwall Bridge, Lime Rock, Lakeville and Salisbury before following CT/MA 41 back to the Berkshires.

LITCHFIELD
The centerpiece of the region is Litchfield, Connecticut's best-preserved late-18th-century town.

Founded in 1719, Litchfield prospered from 1780 to 1840 on the commerce brought through the town by stagecoaches en route between Hartford and Albany. In the mid-19th century, railroads did away

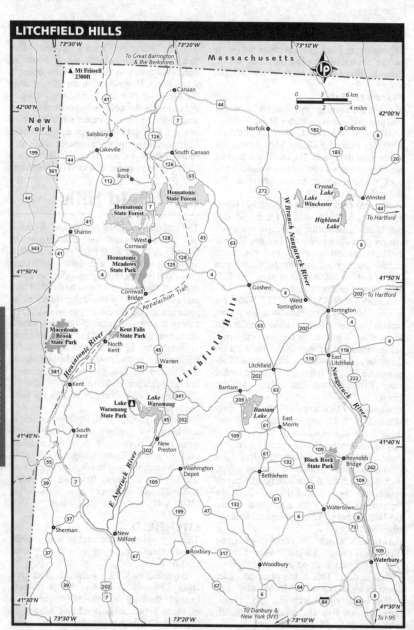

LITCHFIELD HILLS

Massachusetts

To Great Barrington
& the Berkshires

▲ Mt Frissell
2380ft

New
York

Canaan

Salisbury

Lakeville

Lime
Rock

Norfolk

Colbrook

Winsted

To Hartford

South Canaan

Housatonic
State Forest

Crystal
Lake

Lake
Winchester

Highland
Lake

Housatonic
State Forest

West
Cornwall

Sharon

Housatonic
Meadows
State Park

Goshen

West
Torrington

To Hartford

Cornwall
Bridge

Appalachian Trail

Torrington

Macedonia
Brook
State Park

Kent Falls
State Park

North
Kent

Warren

East
Litchfield

Litchfield

Kent

Bantam

Lake
Waramaug
State Park

Lake
Waramaug

Bantam
Lake

East
Morris

Reynolds
Bridge

South
Kent

New
Preston

Black Rock
State Park

Washington
Depot

Bethlehem

Watertown

Sherman

New
Milford

Roxbury

Woodbury

Waterbury

To Danbury &
New York (NY)

To I-95

CONNECTICUT

with the coach routes, and industrial water-powered machinery drove Litchfield's artisans out of the markets, leaving the town to retreat into a torpor of faded gentility. This event proved to be Litchfield's salvation. Its grand 18th-century houses were not torn down to build factories, Victorian mansions or malls.

Orientation & Information
The town green is at the intersection of US 202 and CT 63. An 18th-century milestone stands on the green as it has since stagecoach days, when it informed passengers that they had another 33 miles to ride to Hartford, or 102 to New York City. Several restaurants face the green.

From June through mid-September, locals staff a visitor information booth on the town green; it's open weekends from mid-September through October.

Litchfield Hills Travel Council (☎ 860-567-4506, W www.litchfieldhills.com, PO Box 968, Litchfield, CT 06759) can send you a booklet with precise route details on touring the Litchfield Hills region by car, boat, bike or foot. They also have a listing of over 40 hard-to-find inns and B&Bs in the area.

Barnidge & McEnroe, described in Places to Eat, is the place to find books.

Things to See & Do
A walk around town starts at the information kiosk on the town green. Just north across West St is the town's **historic jail**. Stroll along North St to see the fine houses.

More of Litchfield's well-preserved 18th-century houses are along South St. Set well back from the roadway across broad lawns and behind tall trees, the houses take you back visually to Litchfield's golden age.

The **Litchfield Historical Society** (☎ 860-567-4501, 7 South St; adult/senior $5/3, child under 16 yrs free; open 11am-5pm Tues-Sat, 1pm-5pm Sun mid-Apr–mid-Nov) has set up a museum in its headquarters. Your ticket allows admission both to the museum and to the Tapping Reeve House.

The **Tapping Reeve House** (☎ 860-567-4501, 82 South St; open 11am-5pm Tues-Sat, 1pm-5pm Sun mid-May–mid-Nov), at the corner of Wolcott, dates from 1773. Beside it is a tiny shed (1784) that once housed America's first school of law, established by Tapping Reeve in 1775. Lest it look too modest to have had any effect, you should know that John C Calhoun and 130 members of Congress studied here. The school's most notorious graduate was Aaron Burr, who, while serving as vice president of the US under Jefferson, shot Alexander Hamilton in an upstate New York duel in 1804.

At the southern end of South St is a house that may have been the birthplace of Ethan Allen, leader of Vermont's famous 'Green Mountain Boys' during the Revolutionary War.

One mile southeast of the town center off CT 118, **Haight Vineyards** (☎ 860-567-4045, 800-325-5567, 29 Chestnut Hill Rd; admission free; open 10:30am-5pm Mon-Sat, 11am-5pm Sun) makes wines from vinifera and French-American hybrid grapes grown on the property. Grape varieties include Chardonnay, Maréchal Foch, Seyval Blanc, Vidal Blanc and Vignoles. They even make a sparkling wine by the méthode champenoise. Winery tours and free tastings are available.

At the **White Memorial Conservation Center** (☎ 860-567-0857, US 202; admission free; open sunrise-sunset), 2½ miles west of town along US 202, are 35 miles of hiking and nature trails on 6¼ sq miles. There is a free natural history museum (open 9am-5pm Mon-Sat, noon-4pm Sun).

Topsmead State Forest (☎ 860-567-5694, CT 118, admission free; open 8am-sunset daily), 2 miles east of Litchfield, was once the estate of Ms Edith Morton Chase. You can visit Ms Chase's grand Tudor-style summer home (open for guided tours alternate weekends during summer months, hours vary) complete with its original furnishings, spread a blanket on the lawn and have a picnic while enjoying the view from this perch at 1230 feet. There are hiking trails as well.

You can hike and swim at **Mt Tom State Park** (☎ 860-868-2592, US 202, $5/8 per car Mon-Fri/Sat & Sun, free Sept-May; open 8am-sunset), 3 miles west of Bantam.

Places to Stay

Five miles west of the Litchfield green is *Looking Glass Hill Campground* (☎ 860-567-2050, US 202, Bantam) Sites $27-32. Open Apr–mid-Oct. This simple, appealing place has 30 partially wooded sites.

Hemlock Hill Camp Resort (☎ 860-567-2267, Hemlock Hill Rd) Sites $28. Open May-late Oct. Here's a full-service campground with 125 pine-shaded sites, pools, spa and snack bar. From Litchfield, go west along US 202 for a mile, then right on Milton Rd.

Opposite the lower end of the green, at Spencer, is *Abel Darling* (☎ 860-567-0384, fax 860-567-0384, 102 West St) Rooms $105-125 with continental breakfast. This is an early-American house (1782) with two rooms to rent.

Litchfield Inn (☎ 860-567-4503, 800-499-3444, fax 860-567-5358, US 202) Rooms $125-200 with continental breakfast. Two miles west of Litchfield, set in extensive grounds, this establishment looks like an upscale motel. It has 30 luxury rooms and also has 'theme' rooms with special décor and working fireplaces. The more expensive rooms can sleep three or four people.

Places to Eat

Most of the town's restaurants line up on West St facing the green.

Barnidge & McEnroe (☎ 860-567-4670, 7 West St) Dishes $2-8. Facing the green, this cafe serves up rich coffee ($1 to $3), sweet buns and intellectual satisfaction: It's a bookstore cafe.

Difranco's Restaurant & Pizzeria (☎ 860-567-8872, 19 West St) Dishes $4-12. This is a traditional and inexpensive place with large, private booths. You can get veal marsala for $12, pasta and sandwiches for much less. Wine and beer are available.

The Litchfield Grocer (☎ 860-567-4884, 33 West St) Sandwiches $5-8. Here's a grocery store\deli good for picnic supplies. There are a half-dozen wooden tables with chairs in here where the local gentry gather for coffee clutches on weekday mornings. We favor the hot pastrami sandwich (under $6) for lunch.

Aspen Garden (☎ 860-567-9477, 51 West St) Dishes $5-8. Aspen Garden serves a good selection of light meals with Greek accents: salads, sandwiches and baklava. There's beer as well. Sit at an umbrella-shaded terrace table in good weather.

The County Seat Cafe & Bakery (☎ 860-567-8069, 3 West St) Lunch $8-12, dinner $15-21. Plenty of folks stop in for coffee and a bran muffin, but the County Seat's real claims to fame are the lunches and dinners, with an eclectic menu that includes warm smashed potato salad with artichokes and gorgonzola ($10) and teriyaki-marinated pork tenderloin ($19).

West Street Grill (☎ 860-567-3885, 41 West St) Mains $14-21. This is a sophisticated city grill and tavern serving creative New American cuisine, with full dinners going for about $30 per person, hamburger platters for $9. There's also a pub scene after 9pm.

Village Restaurant (☎ 860-567-8307, 25 West St) Dishes $6-12. This small restaurant with a tin ceiling features gourmet sandwiches and similar lighter fare as well as beer and wine. Try the salmon crab cake ($8).

Getting There & Away

If you are traveling by bus, Bonanza Bus Lines (☎ 800-556-3815) runs four buses between New York City and Bennington, VT, via Danbury, Kent and Cornwall Bridge, CT. No buses stop in Litchfield; these come the closest.

If you're traveling by car, Litchfield lies 34 miles west of Hartford and 36 miles south of Great Barrington, MA, in the southern Berkshires.

LAKE WARAMAUG

Of the dozens of lakes and ponds in the Litchfield Hills, Lake Waramaug, north of New Preston, stands out. Gracious inns dot its shoreline, parts of which are a state park.

As you make your way around the northern shore of the lake on North Shore Rd, you'll come to the **Hopkins Vineyard** (☎ 860-868-7954, 25 Hopkins Rd, Warren; weekend tours $1; open 10am-5pm daily). The wines, made mostly from French-

Outdoor Connecticut

New England's three northern states – Vermont, New Hampshire and Maine – are justly noted for their outdoor activities, but that doesn't mean that Connecticut can't compete.

Northwest Connecticut's Housatonic River is particularly good for canoeing, kayaking, rafting and tubing. With the spring floods, the white water can reach Class III; in summer, it's Class I and II. Expect to pay about $85 for guided white-water rafting during the spring run-off in April and May, and about $25 for unguided rafting the rest of the year.

Clarke Outdoors (☎ 860-672-6365, 163 US 7, West Cornwall, CT 06796) can equip you with a canoe kayak or raft for a run down the Housatonic River. They have guided white-water rafting during spring's high water.

Farmington River Tubing (☎ 860-693-6465), a mobile division of North American Canoe Tours, Inc (☎ 860-739-0791) in Niantic, will take you tubing down the Farmington River at Satans Kingdom State Recreation Area, which is only a dozen miles west of Hartford on US 44.

Huck Finn Adventures (☎ 860-693-0385, PO Box 137, Collinsville, CT 06022) has a similar service on the Farmington River. They also offer a guided tour through the Lost Park River, miles of spacious tunnels buried under Hartford.

American hybrid grapes, are eminently drinkable. Consider a bottle of the semi-sweet Westwind ($9).

Hopkins Inn (☎ 860-868-7295, 22 Hopkins Rd) Rooms $82-100. Right next door to the winery, this inn has a fine restaurant with a traditional continental and American menu that features entrées like chicken cordon bleu (about $20). In good weather, you can catch the cooling west wind and vistas overlooking the lake and hills from the dining terrace.

Lake Waramaug State Park (☎ 860-868-0220, 877-688-2267, 30 Lake Waramaug Rd) Sites $10. Around the bend in the lake is this park with 88 lakeside campsites in a thin forest. The sites usually get booked well in advance. There's a popular snack bar in the park.

The Boulders (☎ 860-868-0541, fax 860-868-1925, ⓦ www.bouldersinn.com, E Shore Rd/CT 45, New Preston) Rooms $260-320 with breakfast. This was once a grand summer house and now makes a genteel inn with a highly regarded restaurant. Rooms

are cheaper during the week. For $35 more per room per night, you can have a full dinner as well.

NORTH TO SALISBURY

Almost every town in the northwest corner of Connecticut has a historic inn or two, a main street with antique and handicraft shops and an art gallery.

From Lake Waramaug, go north on CT 45 via Warren to **Cornwall Bridge**, stopping for a look at its famous namesake covered bridge. Hikers can join the Appalachian trail, which crosses the river here.

North of Cornwall Bridge, **Housatonic Meadows State Park** (☎ 860-927-3238, US 7) is famous for its 2-mile-long stretch of Carse Brook set aside exclusively for fly fishing.

Housatonic Meadows State Park Campground (☎ 860-672-6772, 877-688-2267) Sites $10. Open mid-Apr–mid-Oct. You get 97 sites on the banks of the Housatonic River.

The town of **Lime Rock**, west of US 7 along CT 112, is famous for its automobile racetrack, the Lime Rock Park Raceway (☎ 860-435-0896).

Inn at Iron Masters (☎ 860-435-9844, fax 860-435-2254, 229 Main St, Lakeville) Rooms Sun-Thurs/Fri & Sat $95/155 with breakfast. This one-story inn in nearby Lakeville looks suspiciously like a motel, but the rooms are more elegant and feature an Edwardian theme with butler's tables and regal armchairs.

Interlaken Inn (☎ 860-435-9878, 800-222-2909, fax 860-435-2980, 74 Interlaken Rd, Lakeville) Rooms $99-270. The sprawling resort has six different buildings that feature everything from modern motel units and townhouse suites to rooms in a 19th-century B&B. There is an outdoor pool, two restaurants, tennis, bikes, boats, fitness center and game room.

SALISBURY

This pristine village is Connecticut's answer to the genteel towns of Massachusetts' Berkshire hills to the north. Salisbury prides itself on its inns and restaurants.

White Hart Inn (☎ 860-435-0030, fax 860-435-0030, ⓦ www.whitehartinn.com, cnr CT 41 & US 44) Rooms $119-249. This 23-room inn, on the village green right where these major roads meet, has the perfect front porch for watching the minimal activity in the town, and frilly chintz-filled rooms. The dining room, ***Julie's New American Sea Grill***, serves all three meals. We like the fresh brook trout over wild rice ($19).

Under Mountain Inn (☎ 860-435-0242, 482 Under Mountain Rd) Doubles for two nights $355-410 with breakfast & dinner. Here's an 18th-century farmhouse that's perfect for a country getaway. Rates for the seven rooms are for two nights but are all-inclusive.

Chaiwalla (☎ 860-435-9758, 1 Main St/ US 44) Prices $3-10. Tea-lovers will want to check out Mary O'Brien's shop, which serves a variety of tea, especially unblended Darjeelings (unblended teas are a tea-drinker's equivalent to estate-bottled wines). Traditional accompaniments such as open-faced sandwiches, scones and short-bread are also served 10am to 6pm Wednesday to Sunday. Consider Mary's famous tomato pie (about $8). Meryl Streep is an occasional customer.

Vermont

Vermont is one of the most rural states in the union. We're talking rolling farmlands as green as billiard felt and littered with cows; backcountry roads where the only traffic is the local farmer's tractor; and the backbone of the Green Mountains standing tall. (In fact, the name Vermont is drawn from the French *vert mont,* which means 'green mountain.')

Vermont is small, with a population of only about half a million people. It has only one city worthy of the name – Burlington – with a population of a mere 39,000. It's a land of towns and villages, self-sufficient in the way of the old-fashioned USA before jet planes and interstate highways.

Some of its towns bear the scars of the Industrial Revolution: Once-proud 19th-century brick factories sit by the riverside now somewhat forlorn and dispirited, recycled for storage or retail space. But many Vermont towns and villages are proud inheritors of the New England traditions of hard, honest work, good taste and staunch patriotism. Some could be virtual museums of pristine New England architecture and town planning.

Vermont is busiest with visitors in winter, when its many ski slopes draw enthusiasts from Albany, New York; New York City; Boston; Hartford, CT; and Montreal, Canada. But if you want to see lush green pastures, summer is the more splendid time, and fall foliage is positively glorious.

To enjoy Vermont properly, you must get out of your car and hike into the forests or canoe down a rushing stream. Don't rush it. Enjoy the land and the friendly people.

Information

For pre-trip planning, information is available from the Vermont Dept of Tourism and Marketing (☎ 802-828-3236, 800-837-6668, �W www.1-800-vermont.com, 6 Baldwin St, Montpelier, VT 05633-1301). They'll send a free detailed road and attractions map and camping guide. Or call during fall foliage

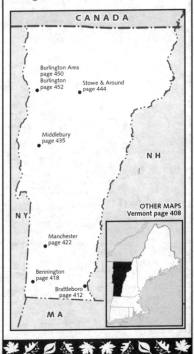

Highlights

- Driving VT 100 from Killington to Stowe
- Strolling through the historic villages of Newfane and Grafton
- Biking a rural route through fall foliage
- Taking a day hike on the Long Trail
- Crossing Lake Champlain by ferry from Burlington
- Touring Shelburne Farms
- Watching cheese being made at the Grafton Village Cheese Company
- Dining at a romantic country inn
- Getting lost on dirt roads in the Northeast Kingdom

CANADA

Burlington Area
page 450
Burlington
page 452

Stowe & Around
page 444

Middlebury
page 435

NH

OTHER MAPS
Vermont page 408

NY

Manchester
page 422

Bennington
page 418

Brattleboro
page 412

MA

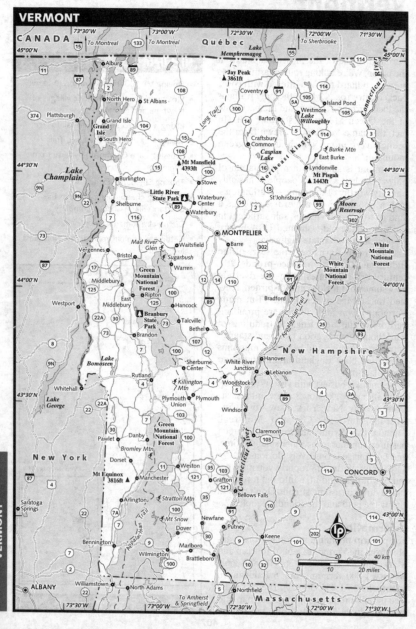

VERMONT

season to find the best viewing spots for colorful foliage. This organization maintains a fabulous Vermont Welcome Center on I-91 near the Massachusetts state line, and others on VT 4A near the New York state line and on I-89 near the Canadian border.

The Vermont Chamber of Commerce (☎ 802-223-3443, W www.vtchamber.com, PO Box 37, Montpelier, VT 05601) offers additional information on hotels, restaurants and other tourist services.

The Vermont Ski Areas Association (☎ 802-223-2439, W www.skivermont.com, 26 State St, Montpelier, VT 05601) provides helpful information on planning area ski trips. For daily ski condition reports (in winter only), call ☎ 802-229-0531.

Contact the Vermont State Parks (☎ 802-241-3655, W www.vtstateparks.com) for full information on camping and play places.

Getting There & Around

Air Vermont's major airport is in Burlington (☎ 802-863-2874), but there is also a commercial airport in Rutland. Delta, Continental, Northwest, United and US Airways service these airports.

Bus Based in Burlington, Vermont Transit (☎ 802-864-6811, 800-552-8737, W www .vermonttransit.com) connects major Vermont towns and makes forays to Manchester and Keene, NH; Boston; and Albany.

Greyhound (☎ 800-231-2222, W www .greyhound.com) operates five buses daily between Burlington and Montreal (three hours, $19.50 one-way).

Train Taking Amtrak's (☎ 800-872-7245, W www.amtrak.com) *Ethan Allen* or *Vermonter* is the relaxing way to travel around the state, albeit inconvenient at times. The *Ethan Allen* (train No 294) departs New York City and stops in Fair Haven and Rutland. From NYC to Rutland costs $54 one-way and takes 5½ hours. The *Vermonter* (train No 56) originates in Washington, DC, heads to NYC and makes two stops in Connecticut (New Haven and Hartford) before venturing into Vermont (stopping at Brattleboro, Bellows Falls, Windsor, White River

Junction, Randolph, Montpelier, Waterbury, Burlington–Essex Junction and St Albans).

If you're a biker, you can buy one ticket on the *Vermonter* and get on and off as many times as you like, as long as you reserve a space for you and your bike ahead of time.

Car Vermont is not particularly large, but it is mountainous. Although I-89 and I-91 provide speedy access to certain areas, the rest of the time you must plan to take it slow and enjoy the winding roads and mountain scenery. Having said that, I-91 north of St Johnsbury offers expansive vistas, as does I-89 from White River Junction to Burlington.

VT 100 is the state's scenic highway, snaking north from the Massachusetts border right through the center of Vermont, almost to Quebec. Along the way it passes through, or near, many of the things you'll want to see. If time allows, take VT 100, not one of the interstate highways.

In western Vermont, consider taking VT 7A north from Arlington to Manchester, and continuing on VT 30 north to VT 22A to Middlebury, through the Champlain River Valley, rather than US 7. Any of the so-called Gap Roads, crossing up and over the Green Mountains north of Rutland, also offer dramatic mountain scenery. Try VT 125 between Hancock (on VT 100) and Middlebury (on US 7); VT 73 between Talcville (on VT 100) and Brandon (on US 7); and the partial dirt road connecting Warren (on VT 100) to Bristol (on VT 116).

Boat Lake Champlain ferries carry passengers, bikes and cars between New York state and Vermont. Service is seasonal, so call for the latest schedules.

Ferries operated by the Lake Champlain Transportation Company (☎ 802-864-9804) run between Plattsburgh, New York, and Grand Isle; Port Kent, New York, and Burlington; and Essex, New York, and Charlotte. It also operates cruises and charters.

The Fort Ti Ferry (☎ 802-897-7999) runs from Larrabees Point (reached via VT 74) in Shoreham to Ticonderoga Landing (also known as Ferry Rd), three-quarters of a

VERMONT

A Taste of Vermont

Vermont is famous for its dairy farms, especially for Vermont cheddar cheese. Ben Cohen and Jerry Greenfield, founders of the Ben & Jerry's premium ice cream company, established themselves in Vermont because of its good dairy industry. You can visit their factory in Waterbury Center near Stowe.

The large number of dairy cattle has also given rise to another Vermont institution: the cow shop. A cow shop may be an elaborate store or a simple pushcart that sells jokey gear based on the black-and-white mottle of the Holstein. The first time you see a cow shop it's funny, the second time boring, the third time depressing.

Vermont maple syrup and maple sugar candy are also big exports, even though maple trees can be tapped well into Canada and as far south as Pennsylvania and west to Wisconsin.

For a complete and handy rundown of statewide farm tours, farmers' markets, overnight farm stays, maple sugaring locations, pick-your-own orchards and cheese-making/dairy operations, contact the Vermont Department of Agriculture, Food and Markets (☎ 802-828-2416, Ⓦ www.state.vt.us/agric).

Perhaps the best of Vermont products are its crafts: textiles, carvings of wood and stone, wrought ironwork and pottery. The Vermont State Craft Center organizes exhibits and sales at outlets, the foremost of which is at Frog Hollow in Middlebury.

–Tom Brosnahan

mile from the center of Fort Ticonderoga, New York. The trip takes only seven minutes, and the ferry runs 8am to 5:45pm daily, except in July and August, when it runs 8am to 9pm. People ride for 50¢; bicycles and motorcycles are $3; cars are $6 one-way and $10 roundtrip. RVs cost $7 to $30 one-way. Service operates late May through October.

Southern Vermont

Tidy white churches and inns surround village greens throughout historic southern Vermont, home to several towns that predate the Revolutionary War. In summer, the roads between the three 'cities' of Brattleboro, Bennington and Manchester roll over green hills; in winter, they wind their way toward the ski slopes of Mt Snow, southern Vermont's cold-weather play-ground. For those on foot, the Appalachian Trail passes through the Green Mountain National Forest here, offering a colorful hiking experience during the fall foliage season.

BRATTLEBORO

The site of Vermont's first colonial settlement (1724), Brattleboro is the first town you're likely to encounter if you drive straight to Vermont from Boston or New York.

Brattleboro is one of Vermont's larger towns (population 12,000), a pleasant and workaday sort of place with an interesting ambience: This is where the USA's 1960s 'alternative' lifestyle settled down to live. You'll see lots of bookstores, a few tattoo parlors and an abundance of male facial hair. Don't be put off by the red brick exterior of Brattleboro's buildings. This might not be quintessential Vermont, but those buildings house some fine restaurants, as well as outdoor gear shops, art galleries and artisans. All in all, Brattleboro is one of Vermont's most welcoming communities.

History

Fort Dummer, a wooden stockade, was built on Whetstone Brook in 1724 to defend the local settlers against Native American raids. The town received its royal charter a year later and took its name from Colonel William Brattle Jr of the King's Militia, who never got the chance to visit his namesake.

Despite its country-town ambience, Brattleboro has seen its share of history. The first postage stamp used in the USA was made here in 1846. Jubilee Jim Fisk, the partner of railroad robber baron Jay Gould, was born here and was buried here after he died in a quarrel over a woman. Dr Robert Wesselhoeft developed the Wesselhoeft Water Cure using the waters of Whetstone Brook and treated such luminaries as Harriet Beecher Stowe and Henry Wadsworth Longfellow from 1846 to 1871.

The Mormon leader Brigham Young was born in nearby Windham County in 1801. Rudyard Kipling married a Brattleboro woman in 1892 and lived for a time in a big Brattleboro house he named Naulaukha. While living there, he wrote *The Jungle Book*.

Orientation & Information

Brattleboro proper is east of I-91; West Brattleboro is west of the highway. Downtown Brattleboro's commercial district is surprisingly compact, with most of the good restaurants clustered around the landmark Latchis Hotel.

A Vermont Information Booth (☎ 802-257-1112) sits on VT 9 on the western outskirts of West Brattleboro, near the town's covered bridge. It's open in the summer only. The Brattleboro Chamber of Commerce (☎ 802-254-4565, W www.brattleboro.com, 180 Main St, Brattleboro, VT 05301) is open 8:30am to 5pm weekdays and 10am to 2pm Saturday. Its good town map details all the cool shops.

Beneath the 2nd-floor restaurant Common Ground (see Places to Eat, below), Everyone's Books (☎ 802-254-8160) sells political literature and T-shirts emblazoned with 'Discover Columbus's legacy – 500 years of racist oppression and stolen land.'

Things to See & Do

The town's commercial district centers around the pure art deco **Latchis Building**, which houses the Latchis Theatre, Latchis Hotel and Lucca Brasserie & Bistro. Built in the 1930s by Demetrius Latchis, a Greek immigrant successful in the fruit business, the nicely restored building still serves its original purposes. You can stay and dine here and watch first-run movies.

The **Brattleboro Museum & Art Center** (☎ *802-257-0124, 10 Vernon St; adult/senior $3/2, child under 12 yrs free; open 10am-6pm Tues-Sun mid-May–Oct*) is in the Union Railroad Station, in the center of town. In addition to a permanent collection of Estey reed organs made in Brattleboro during the late 19th century, the museum displays good changing art and history exhibitions.

Brattleboro Bicycle Shop (☎ *802-254-8644, 178 Main St*) rents hybrid bicycles ($20 daily) and dispenses plenty of advice about where to use them. But it's not really an outfitter, so it doesn't carry racks or kids' bikes.

Vermont Artisan Designs (☎ *802-257-7044, 106 Main St*) This contemporary crafts gallery sells outstanding creations by Vermont artists.

Windham County has 30 **covered bridges** and the Brattleboro Chamber of Commerce (see Orientation & Information, above) distributes a free packet of information about them.

Vermont Canoe Touring (☎ *802-257-5008, Veterans Memorial Bridge, 451 Putney Rd*) offers guided canoe jaunts down the Connecticut or West Rivers. To find this outfitter, head north on US 5 (Putney Rd) to the bridge where the West River meets the Connecticut River.

Robb Family Farm (☎ *802-254-7664, 827 Ames Hill Rd*) welcomes visitors to watch maple sugaring from late February to early

BRATTLEBORO

PLACES TO STAY & EAT
1 Forty Putney Road B&B
5 Collected Works
7 Istanbul Kitchen
10 India Palace
10 Coffee Country Cafe
11 Common Ground;
 Everyone's Books
13 Amy's Bakery Arts Cafe
14 Artist's Loft B&B
16 Mocha Joe's
17 TJ Buckley's
19 Brattleboro Food Co-op

OTHER
2 Police Station; Municipal
 Center
3 Post Office
4 Brattleboro Chamber of
 Commerce
6 Brattleboro Bicycle Shop
8 Moles Eye Cafe
12 Vermont Artisan Designs
15 McNeill's Brewery
18 Latchis Building (Latchis
 Hotel, Lucca Brasserie &
 Bistro, Latchis Theatre,
 Windham Brewery)
20 Brattleboro Museum & Art
 Center

April at this 400-plus-acre family farm. In autumn, they also offer hayrides, and in winter sleigh rides (call ahead for reservations). To reach the farm, head north on I-91, west on VT 9, left on Green Leaf Rd, through the stop sign and up the dirt Ames Hill Rd to the farm.

Places to Stay
Camping Pitch a tent at *Fort Dummer State Park* (☎ 802-254-2610, Old Guilford Rd) Sites $14. Open mid-May–early Sept. This 217-acre park has 61 sites (10 of them lean-to shelters), hot showers and nature

trails. From I-91 exit 1, go north a few hundred yards on US 5, then a half-mile east on Fairground Rd, then a mile south on Main St to Old Guilford Rd.

Hidden Acres Campground (☎ 802-254-2098, 792 US 5) Sites without/with hookups $18/24. Open May–mid-Oct. With only 40 open and wooded sites (many just for tents), Hidden Acres has a surprising amount of facilities. It's on US 5 about 2½ miles north of I-91 exit 3.

Brattleboro North KOA (☎ 802-254-5908, 1238 US 5) Sites without/with hookups $24/28. Open mid-Apr–Oct. A few miles north of Hidden Acres, this 42-site spot is even more elaborate.

Motels & Hotels Motels line Putney Rd (US 5) north of Brattleboro and VT 9 west of town.

Molly Stark Motel (☎ 802-254-2440, *VT 9*) Doubles $50-80. Three miles west of I-91, this motel has 14 nice units.

Colonial Motel & Spa (☎/fax 802-257-7733, Ⓦ www.colonialmotelspa.com, 889 US 5) Doubles $68-85, suites $100. Some of these 73 units are suites; a few have a kitchen. As for the spa aspect, there are two pools, whirlpools, saunas, steam rooms and an exercise room.

Latchis Hotel (☎ 802-254-6300, fax 802-254-6304, 50 Main St) Doubles $65-105, 4-person suites $105-145; foliage rates $10-30 higher. With 30 comfortably renovated rooms, this is one of the better and more interesting places to stay, as it was in the 1930s.

Inns You'll be comfortable at *Crosby House* (☎ 802-257-4914, 800-528-4914, 45 Western Ave) Doubles $105-135 with full breakfast. This perfectly restored mid-19th-century mansion has three guest rooms decorated with great care and comfort.

Artist's Loft B&B (☎/fax 802-257-5181, Ⓦ www.theartistsloft.com, 103 Main St) Room $118-138 with self-catered breakfast. In the heart of Brattleboro, one of Vermont's most unique places is situated in a 125-year-old building. Gracious innkeepers and renowned artists Patricia Long and William Hays have only one room, but what a room! This spacious 3rd-floor suite, the size of a large one-bedroom apartment, overlooks the Connecticut River and the mountains in the background.

Forty Putney Road B&B (☎ 802-254-6268, 800-941-2413, fax 802-258-2673, Ⓦ www.putney.net/40putneyrd, 40 Putney Rd) Doubles $125-235 with full breakfast. This 70-year-old estate with four bedrooms and a cute separate self-contained cottage sits on scenic Putney Rd, bordering the West River. Canoe, kayak and bicycle rentals on the river are a five-minute walk away. There is also a little pub on the premises.

Places to Eat

Mocha Joe's (☎ 802-257-7794, 82 Main St) Open 8am-7pm Sun-Wed, 8am-8pm Thur, 8am-11pm Fri-Sat. Your nose will locate the exceptionally rich brews before your eyes spy the subterranean space.

Coffee Country Cafe (☎ 802-257-0032, 12 Harmony Place) Open 7am-6pm Mon-Fri, 8am-6pm Sat, 9am-4pm Sun. This informal place attracts everyone from tongue-studded teenagers to 65-year-old farmers. Drop in for some good java and hot baked goods.

Brattleboro Food Co-op (☎ 802-257-0236, Canal St) Open 8am-9pm daily. This fragrant co-op has whole food groceries, organic produce and an incredible cheese department offering more than 500 distinct varieties.

Istanbul Kitchen (☎ 802-380-1641, 157 Main St) Dishes $3. Open 11am-6pm Sun-Thur, 11am-8pm Fri-Sat. In the Gibson River Garden complex, Mediterranean vegetarian specialties include hearty casseroles, eggplant pie and feta-spinach pie.

Collected Works (☎ 802-258-4900, 29 High St) Open 8am-6pm Mon-Thur, 8am-9pm Fri, 10am-6pm Sat-Sun. After browsing through Zen titles, women's literature, art books and travel, head through the stacks and beyond the comfy sofas to grab a quick bite at the cafe.

Amy's Bakery Arts Cafe (☎ 802-251-1071, 113 Main St) Lunch $3-5. Open 8am-6pm daily. Enjoy your breakfast breads, pastries and coffee with views of the river and local art. At lunchtime, the offerings revolve around salads, soups and sandwiches.

Common Ground (☎ 802-257-0855, 25 Elliot St) Mains $5-12. Open 11am-9pm Thur-Tues. Common Ground is an institution, perhaps New England's purest expression of 1960s alternative dining. Its 2nd-floor location continues to thrive, and for good reason: It offers excellent, healthy food (vegan and vegetarian) at low prices. Dinner is free on Tuesday night. (Yes, that's right: free.) Soup and homemade breads suffice for light lunches.

India Palace (☎ 802-254-6143, 69 Elliot St) Lunch $5.25-10.25, dinner $9-16. Open daily. If you're in the mood for northern Indian cuisine, especially tandoori, check out this place. Lunchtime curries are extra cheap.

Lucca Brasserie & Bistro *(☎ 802-254-4747, 6 Flat St)* Lunch $7-12, dinner $9-22. Open Wed-Sun. Beneath the Latchis Hotel, this stylishly renovated restaurant serves top-notch New American cuisine.

Marina Restaurant *(☎ 802-257-7563, 28 Spring Tree Lane)* Dishes $8-15. Open for lunch & dinner daily. Off Putney Rd, the Marina's glass-enclosed patio overlooks the West River. Food is reasonably priced, with fish-and-chips ($10), pastas ($8 to $10) and chicken dishes ($11).

TJ Buckley's *(☎ 802-257-4922, 132 Elliot St)* Mains $25-30. Open for dinner Thur-Sun. This upscale but classic and authentic 1927 diner seats just 18 but those lucky 18 are in for an exceptional dinner. The menu of four entrées changes nightly, and locals rave that TJ Buckley's food is Brattleboro's best.

Entertainment

Moles Eye Cafe *(☎ 802-257-0771, cnr Main & High Sts)* Open 4pm-midnight Mon-Thur, 11:30am-1am Fri-Sat. Food is served until 9pm. Cover $4. This popular hangout in an oak-paneled cafe has live entertainment Thursday through Saturday and good meals at moderate prices. Thursday open mike is usually a blast.

Common Ground *(☎ 802-257-0855, 25 Elliot St)* This alternative restaurant has free bluegrass jams on Tuesday and a free house funk band on Thursday. The Friday night DJ and Saturday night bands have a $5 or $10 cover.

Windham Brewery *(☎ 802-254-4747, 6 Flat St)* Open daily. Downstairs at the Latchis Hotel, try a pint of Olde Guilford Porter, a dark, medium-bodied ale ($4).

McNeill's Brewery *(☎ 802-254-2553, 90 Elliot St)* Open from 4pm daily. This is the kind of place where the smell of too many beers spilled on wooden floors never disappears. The classic pub draws a lively, friendly crowd and brews award-winning suds.

Latchis Theatre *(☎ 802-254-5800, 50 Main St)* The 1930s deco palace projects mainstream and indies on three screens nightly.

Getting There & Away

Vermont Transit *(☎ 802-864-6811, 800-552-8737)* runs two daily buses between Brattleboro and Middlebury (three hours, $21) via Rutland, where there are connecting buses northward. The bus stops behind the Citgo station *(☎ 802-254-6066)* at the intersection of US 5, VT 9 and I-91.

Amtrak's *Vermonter* *(☎ 800-872-7245)* stops in Brattleboro. New York City to Brattleboro costs $50 to $55 one-way. See Getting There & Around at the beginning of this chapter for more details on the *Vermonter's* route.

By car, it takes 1¼ hours (40 miles) to traverse scenic VT 9 from Brattleboro to Bennington. From Northampton, MA, it takes less than an hour (40 miles) straight up I-91 to reach Brattleboro.

NEARBY VILLAGES

The Lower Connecticut and West River valleys of southern Vermont are home to a warren of pristine villages worth exploring.

Marlboro

Upon first sight, this village appears pretty but unremarkable: a white church, a white inn, a white village office building and a few white houses, all a short distance off the Molly Stark Trail (VT 9), 8 miles west of Brattleboro.

However, to chamber-music lovers, Marlboro looms very large as the home of the ***Marlboro Music Fest*** *(☎ 215-569-4690, 802-254-2394 after June 15,* Ⓦ *www.marlboromusic.org, 135 S 18th St, Philadelphia, PA 19103)*. The festival was founded and directed for many years by the late Rudolf Serkin and attended by Pablo Casals. On weekends from early July to mid-August, the small Marlboro College is alive with enthusiastic music students and concert-goers, who consistently pack the small, 700-seat auditorium. Many concerts sell out almost immediately, so it's essential to reserve seats, by phone or mail, in advance. Tickets cost $5 to $20.

Heading west from Marlboro on VT 9 brings you to the top of Hogback Mountain (2410 feet). At the high point, there's a lookout and the family-owned *Skyline Restaurant* (☎ 802-464-3536), with dishes for $7 to $10. This place is open for breakfast and lunch, with dinner possibly on weekends. Dine on homemade soups, a 'Vermonter' sandwich and traditional New England comfort foods, all with the backdrop of a marvelous '100-mile' view and knotty pine décor.

Newfane

Vermont has dozens of pretty villages, but Newfane is near the top of everyone's list. All the postcard-perfect sights you'd expect in a Vermont town are here: tall old trees, white high-steepled churches, excellent inns and gracious old houses. In spring, Newfane is busy making maple sugar; in summer, yard sales are in full bloom; fall heralds 'leaf peepers'; and winter brings couples seeking cozy rooms in warm hideaways.

Newfane is on VT 30, just 12 miles northwest of Brattleboro, and 19 miles northeast of Wilmington.

A short stroll exposes Newfane's core – you'll see the stately Congregational church (1839), the Windham County Courthouse (1825), built in Greek Revival style, and a few antique shops.

Townshend State Park (☎ 802-365-7500, VT 30) Sites $14. Open mid-May–mid-Oct. Tucked deep into the forest about 3 miles north of Newfane, this is one of the state's better places to camp, with 34 tent sites. Hiking trails include the sometimes steep, challenging path to the summit of Bald Mountain (1680 feet), a rocky climb that rises 1100 feet in less than a mile. Other trails within Townshend State Park are easier. There's swimming and boating at the nearby Army Corps of Engineers' Recreation Area at Townshend Dam. The West River is good for canoe trips.

West River Lodge (☎ 802-365-7745, fax 802-365-4450, W www.westriverlodge.com, 117 Hill Rd) Doubles $85-125 with full country breakfast. Just outside of town, this lodge features English riding workshops (it

has its own stables) and eight farmhouse accommodations.

Four Columns Inn (☎ 802-365-7713, 800-787-6633, fax 802-365-0022, W www.four columnsinn.com, 21 West St) Doubles $115-340 with full breakfast. Most people with money stop in Newfane just long enough for a meal or a night here. The 1830s Greek Revival inn on the common has 16 guest rooms and an excellent dining room serving New American cuisine.

Grafton

Grafton is right next to Newfane on that short list of must-see villages. At the junction of VT 121 and VT 35, it's about 15 miles north of Newfane.

Graceful Grafton is not that way by accident. In the 1960s, the private Windham Foundation established a restoration and preservation program for the entire village, and it has been eminently successful. It is virtually an open-air museum. The real museum, however, is the **Grafton Historical Society** (☎ 802-843-2584, Main St; suggested donation adult/child $3/free; open 10am–noon & 2pm-4pm Sat-Sun late May–mid-Sept, 10am-noon & 2pm-4pm daily late Sept–mid-Oct), near the post office and south of the Old Tavern.

The **Grafton Village Cheese Company** (☎ 802-843-2221, 533 Townshend Rd; admission free; open 8am-4pm Mon-Fri, 10am-4pm Sat-Sun) is a half-mile south of the village. It makes award-winning Covered Bridge Cheddar, which you can sample while watching it be made. Try the four-year-old stuff; it has a distinctive bite.

The Inn at Woodchuck Hill Farm (☎ 802-843-2398, W www.woodchuckhill .com, off Middletown Rd) Rooms without/ with bath $89/135, suites $155 with full breakfast. This 1790s farmhouse is set up high on 200 acres just outside of Grafton, with its own private hiking and cross-country ski trails. These 10 guest rooms and suites are filled with lovely antiques; the studio suite with a private deck is particularly coveted.

The Old Tavern at Grafton (☎ 802-843-2231, 800-843-1801, fax 802-843-2245,

W *www.old-tavern.com, cnr VT 35 & Town-shend Rd)* Doubles $115-245, suites $150-450 with full breakfast. The inn's double porch is Grafton's landmark. While the original brick inn is quite formal, many of the 47 guest rooms and suites are less so, scattered around houses within the village. The dining room is New England formal and the cuisine is New England classic, but the cafe is less so (the fare is also lighter).

Putney

This village answers the question: Where do old hippies go when they grow up? One look at the general store bulletin board tells you all you need to know about the crafts-people who populate Putney and their grassroots involvement in local affairs. Pick up a quick bite at the general store in the center of town or at the Putney Food Co-op, just south of the village on US 5. Putney is on US 5, just 10 miles north of Brattleboro via I-91.

Curtis' Barbeque (☎ *802-387-5437, US 5)* Dishes $4-8. Open 10am-dusk Wed-Sun June–mid-Oct. This retrofitted school bus dispenses the best ribs and barbecue chicken north of the Mason-Dixon line. The secret's in the sauce, of course, which has hints of Vermont maple syrup.

WILMINGTON

Wilmington is the gateway to Mt Snow/ Haystack, one of New England's best ski resorts and an excellent summertime mountain-biking and golfing spot. Many restaurants and stores cater to families, the resort's predominant clientele.

To reach Mt Snow/Haystack from Wilmington, travel 10 miles north on VT 100. The free bus service, Moover (☎ 802-464-8487), transports skiers from Wilmington to the slopes of Mt Snow at least every hour between 7am and 6pm.

Orientation & Information

The state's central north-south highway, VT 100, goes north from Wilmington past Haystack and Mt Snow. VT 9, the main route across southern Vermont, is Wilmington's main street. Wilmington is 21 miles west of Brattleboro (45 minutes on the winding road) and 20 miles east of Bennington (40 minutes).

The Mt Snow Valley Region Chamber of Commerce (☎ 802-464-8092, W www.visitvermont.com) maintains a village office on West Main St that's open 10am to 5pm daily.

Mt Snow

The terrain at Mt Snow (☎ 802-464-3333, 800-245-7669, W www.mountsnow.com) is diverse, making it popular with the whole family. The resort features 132 trails (20% beginner, 60% intermediate, 20% expert) and 23 lifts, plus a vertical drop of 1700 feet and the snowmaking ability to blanket 85% of the trails. Area cross-country routes cover more than 60 miles. As if that weren't enough, Mt Snow offers snowmobile tours and winter mountain tubing, too. Come summer, Mt Snow has lots of hiking possibilities and hosts one of the best mountain-biking schools in the country. All this activity surely warrants a stop at its full-service Grand Summit Spa (☎ 802-464-1100, ext 6005).

Places to Stay

Molly Stark State Park (☎ *802-464-5460, VT 9)* Sites $14-20. Open late May–mid-Oct. This 160-acre state park, about 3 miles east of Wilmington, has 34 sites (10 lean-tos), hot showers, and hiking trails with panoramic views.

Vintage Motel (☎ *802-464-8824, 800-899-9660,* W *www.vintagemotel.com, VT 9)* Doubles $60-95 with light weekend breakfast. A mile west of the town center, the Vintage has 18 tidy units and a heated pool.

Nutmeg Inn (☎ *802-464-3351, 800-277-5402, fax 802-464-7331,* W *www.nutmeginn .com, VT 9)* Doubles $99-299 with full breakfast. West of Wilmington, this 18th-century renovated farmhouse has 14 rooms and suites furnished with antiques and re-production pieces. Some rooms even have a whirlpool and fireplace.

Snow Goose (☎ *802-464-3984, 888-604-7964, fax 802-464-5322,* W *www.snowgoose inn.com, VT 100, West Dover)* Doubles $105-350 with full breakfast. Only a mile from the ski slopes, this elegant inn has 13 large rooms and suites with large Jacuzzis, fireplaces and private decks overlooking the forest.

Trail's End (☎ 802-464-2727, 800-859-2585, fax 802-464-5532, Ⓦ www.trailsendvt .com, 5 Trail's End Lane) Doubles $110-190 with full breakfast. About 4 miles north of Wilmington, Trail's End has a country-home feel, 15 cozy rooms and suites (many with fireplace) and a game room with billiard table. Outside you'll find a heated swimming pool and a stocked trout and catfish pond. Take VT 100 north to E Dover Rd, which leads to Smith Rd and then Trail's End Lane.

Red Shutter Inn (☎ 802-464-3768, 800-845-7548, fax 802-464-5123, Ⓦ www.red shutterinn.com, VT 9) Doubles $120-240 with full breakfast. Dating from 1894, this grand old house has seven rooms and two suites, each with a unique décor.

White House of Wilmington (☎ 802-464-2135, 800-541-2135, fax 802-464-5222, Ⓦ www.whitehouseinn.com, VT 9) Doubles $118-262 with full breakfast. This white Federal mansion crowns a hill on the eastern outskirts of the town and boasts an indoor pool, a large outdoor pool, great cross-country trails and 25 luxury rooms.

Places to Eat
Cup N' Saucer (☎ 802-464-5813, VT 100, Wilmington) Dishes $2-6. Open 6am-2:30pm daily. Judging from the muddy pickup trucks in the parking lot, locals flock here for burgers or a hot open-faced turkey sandwich. The circular counter is decidedly old-fashioned. Breakfast is served all day; the pancakes are great.

Dot's (☎ 802-464-7284, Main St; ☎ 802-464-6476, VT 100, Mt Snow) Dishes $3-8.25. With locations in the village and near the slopes, Dot's is popular with skiers in search of cheap sustenance like steak and eggs for breakfast. Dot's is also known for quick service and excellent chili.

The Silo (☎ 802-464-2553, VT 100, West Dover) Lunch $4-10, dinner $6-23. Open daily. A bit more upscale, this serious steak house is good for large parties who all want

something different – from stuffed shrimp to chicken pot pie to caesar salad to pastas, pizzas and sandwiches. In the winter, the Silo offers entertainment, DJs, dancing and 10¢ wings (4pm to 6pm daily).

Alonzo's (☎ 802-464-2355, W Main St, Wilmington) Mains $8-15. Open 4pm-10pm daily. Within the Crafts Inn, Alonzo's specializes in Italian food, homemade pastas and grilled dishes.

Poncho's Wreck (☎ 802-464-9320, 10 S Main St, Wilmington) Lunch $5.50-12, dinner $9-26. Open for lunch Sat-Sun & dinner nightly. A casual favorite with the après-ski crowd since 1972, Poncho's menu is extensive, but don't stray too far from nightly seafood specials. There's live entertainment on winter and holiday weekends.

BENNINGTON
Bennington, a felicitous mix of picture-perfect Vermont village (Old Bennington) and workaday town (Bennington proper), is also home to Bennington College and the famous Bennington Museum. It's also a historic place, famed for its tall monument commemorating the crucial Battle of Bennington during the Revolutionary War. Robert Frost, one of the most famous American poets of the 20th century, is buried in Bennington.

Vermont Transit (☎ 802-864-6811, 800-552-8737) runs three daily buses from Bennington to Manchester (30 minutes, $7); the same buses continue on to Middlebury and Burlington. The bus stops at 126 Washington Ave (☎ 802-442-4808).

Bennington is 40 miles west of Brattleboro via VT 9 and 19 miles south of Manchester via US 7.

History
In August 1777, during the Revolutionary War, British General John ('Gentleman Johnny') Burgoyne, his supplies depleted during the battle at Fort Ticonderoga, sent two units toward Bennington to seize military supplies held by the colonials. He misjudged the size of the American defenses and was unaware that General John Stark, a veteran of Bunker Hill and a commander

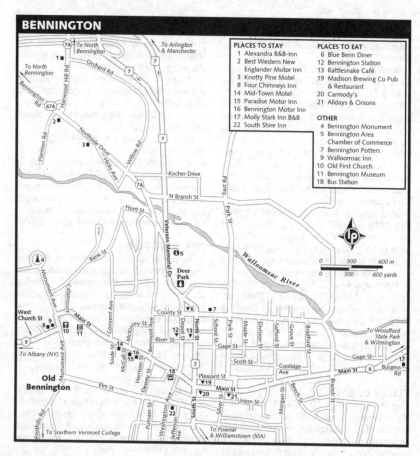

BENNINGTON

PLACES TO STAY
1 Alexandra B&B-Inn
2 Best Western New
   Englander Motor Inn
3 Knotty Pine Motel
8 Four Chimneys Inn
14 Mid-Town Motel
15 Paradise Motor Inn
16 Bennington Motor Inn
17 Molly Stark Inn B&B
22 South Shire Inn

PLACES TO EAT
6 Blue Benn Diner
12 Bennington Station
13 Rattlesnake Café
19 Madison Brewing Co Pub
   & Restaurant
20 Carmody's
21 Alldays & Onions

OTHER
4 Bennington Monument
5 Bennington Area
   Chamber of Commerce
7 Bennington Potters
9 Walloomsac Inn
10 Old First Church
11 Bennington Museum
18 Bus Station

under Washington at the battles of Trenton and Princeton, was leading the defense.

Stark headed off the British advance in Walloomsac, New York, 6 miles west of Bennington. 'There are the redcoats!' he exclaimed. 'They will be ours tonight or Molly Stark sleeps a widow!'

The two sides clashed on August 16, 1777. The ferocious battle lasted two hours, with the Americans victorious, but British reinforcements still posed a threat to Stark's troops. The American victory was assured by Colonel Seth Warner and his Green Mountain Boys, who arrived in time to

counter the British resurgence. The Americans captured more than 800 British regulars, about one-sixth of Burgoyne's total force. (Every year people in Arlington, VT, reenact the exploits of the Green Mountain boys with Ethan Allen Days – 'Fun with the Green Mountain Boys,' held in mid-June. See the boxed text 'Ethan Allen & Vermont,' in the Facts about New England chapter.)

Unable to procure supplies in Bennington and suffering badly from the loss of soldiers, Burgoyne's forces were greatly weakened when they went into the Battle of

Saratoga later that fall. After a disastrous defeat there, General Burgoyne surrendered his entire command to the Americans, ending his drive down the Hudson Valley, which, if successful, would have cut the colonies in two.

Orientation & Information

Bennington is an important crossroads since US 7, VT 7A and VT 9 converge here. Most businesses, lodgings and restaurants are in downtown Bennington, but the Bennington Monument, Bennington Museum and prettiest houses are in Old Bennington, a mile from the center of town, at the western end of Main St on the way to New York state. The actual site of the Battle of Bennington is in Walloomsac, New York, 6 miles west of the monument.

The Bennington Area Chamber of Commerce (☎ 802-447-3311, 🆆 www.bennington .com, 100 Veterans Memorial Dr/US 7) maintains an information office that's open 8:30am to 4:30pm weekdays, 9am to 3pm weekends mid-May to mid-October. Pick up its self-guided walking tour of historic Old Bennington.

The Bennington Bookshop (☎ 802-442-5059, 467 Main St) has all manner of Vermont related books.

Bennington Museum

Head a mile west from downtown Bennington via W Main St (VT 9) for the Bennington Museum (☎ 802-447-1571, W Main St; adult/senior & child 12-17 yrs $6/5, child under 12 yrs free; open 9am-5pm daily Nov-May, 9am-6pm daily June-Oct). The museum's outstanding collection of early Americana includes furniture, glassware and pottery (made in Bennington), sculpture, paintings, dolls, toys and military memorabilia. The museum is especially noted for its rich collection of paintings by Anna Mary Moses (1860–1961), a New York farm wife. At the age of 70, when she could no longer keep up with the heavy physical demands of farm labor, 'Grandma Moses' began to paint. Her lively, natural depictions of farm life were eagerly sought out, and she painted until she was 100 years old.

Old Bennington

A few hundred yards west of the museum, the charming hilltop site of colonial Old Bennington is studded with 80 substantial Georgian and Federal houses (dating from 1761 – the year Bennington was founded – to 1830) arranged along a broad mall.

The **Old First Church**, towering over the village, was built in 1806 in Palladian style. Its churchyard holds the remains of five Vermont governors, numerous Revolutionary War soldiers and poet **Robert Frost** (1874–1963). Frost was born in California of New England stock and lived and wrote in England for a time, but he is famous for his poems of the New England experience, inspired by his life on several New England farms. Although never successful at farming, Frost became the best-known, and perhaps best-loved, American poet of the 20th century. Near Franconia, NH, is one of his farms, the Frost Place (see the Franconia section in the New Hampshire chapter). Another farm is in Ripton, VT, near Middlebury College's Bread Loaf School of English (see Ripton, later in this chapter).

Across from the church, the ramshackle **Walloomsac Inn** (1764) was a working hostelry up until the 1980s, complete with Victorian-era plumbing and spartan appointments. It's now closed.

Up the hill to the north, the **Bennington Monument** (☎ 802-447-0550, Monument Ave; adult/child $1.50/75¢; open 9am-5pm daily Apr-Oct) is Vermont's loftiest structure. The view is quite nice from the impressive obelisk, built between 1887 and 1891. The original staircase has been replaced by an elevator, so you can ride the 306 feet to the top. Purchase tickets at the nearby gift shop.

To reach the actual battle site 6 miles away, follow the 'Bennington Battlefield' signs from the monument, along back roads, through a historic covered bridge (there are two others nearby) to North Bennington, then go west on VT 67 to the **Bennington Battlefield Historic Site**. Admission is free, and picnic tables are provided under welcome shade.

Just off VT 67A in North Bennington, look for the **Park-McCullough House Museum**

(☎ 802-442-5441, *cnr West & Park Sts; adult/ senior/child $6/5/4; open 10am-4pm daily mid-May–mid-Oct).* The 35-room mansion was built in 1865 for Trenor and Laura Hall Park of New York City as their summer 'cottage.' Today, it holds period furnishings and a fine collection of antique dolls, toys and carriages. The house is open for tours (the last tour departs at 3pm). In addition to special spooky Halloween events (call for details), the house is also open for Victorian Christmas celebrations from late November to early December (from 1pm to 4pm Saturday and Sunday).

Activities
Batten Kill Canoe (☎ 802-362-2800, 800-421-5268, 6328 VT 7A; *tandem canoes & kayaks $45-55 daily, solos $25-30),* 20 minutes away in Arlington, can outfit you for a day trip on the Batten Kill River. This lovely stream winds through a Vermont forest down to the Hudson River. The staff also arranges longer trips, from one to 10 days, combined with overnights at inns.

The **Prospect Mountain Cross-Country Ski Touring Center** (☎ 802-442-2575, *VT 9, Woodford),* about 10 minutes east of Bennington, always seems to be covered in snow. More than 40km of groomed trails wind through the area. The center offers ski rentals and lessons as well as snowshoe rentals.

Bennington Potters (☎ 802-447-7531, *324 County St)* sells trademark Bennington pottery.

Places to Stay
Camping & Hostels Ten miles east of Bennington is ***Woodford State Park*** (☎ 802-447-7169, *VT 9)* Sites $14-20. Open mid-May–early Sept. This park has 102 sites (20 lean-tos), a beach, boat and canoe rentals and hiking trails.

Lake Shaftsbury State Park (☎ 802-375-9978, *VT 7A)* Lean-tos $20. Open late May–early Sept. Two miles south of Arlington, this campground has 15 lean-tos. Tent camping is reserved for groups only. There's a beach, boat and canoe rentals and a nature trail.

Howell's Camping Area (☎ 802-375-6469, *212 No Name Rd, Arlington)* Sites $16. Open mid-Apr–mid-Oct. Howell's is a mile off VT 7A/313 and has 72 sites.

Camping on the Batten Kill (☎ 802-375-6663, *VT 7A, Arlington)* Sites $18.50-26.50. Open mid-Apr–mid-Oct. This campground has more than 100 sites.

Greenwood Lodge & Campsites (☎/fax 802-442-2547, W *www.campvermont.com/ greenwood, VT 9, Prospect Mountain)* Sites without/with hookups $17/22, dorm beds $18.35, private room $44. Open mid-May–late Oct. Nestled in the Green Mountains in Woodford, 8 miles east of Bennington, this is one of Vermont's best-sited hostels. Accommodations include 20 budget beds and 40 campsites dispersed over 120 acres. Reserve in advance by phone; no credit cards are accepted.

Motels Two miles north of Bennington is the ***Harwood Hill Motel*** (☎/fax 802-442-6278, *898 VT 7A)* Doubles $57-80. Open Dec-Oct. This place has 16 rooms (larger rooms have more amenities) and three cottages with fine views of the Bennington Monument and the town.

Best Western New Englander Motor Inn (☎/fax 802-442-6311, W *www.bestwestern .com, 220 Northside Dr)* Doubles $57-110. Near the Knotty Pine Motel, this place has 58 rooms in a variety of styles.

Knotty Pine Motel (☎ 802-442-5487, *130 Northside Dr)* Doubles $59-89. On VT 7A in a commercial strip just off US 7, this friendly, family-run motel has a fairly convenient location and 19 country-style rooms paneled in knotty pine (surprise!).

Mid-Town Motel (☎/fax 802-447-0189, *107 W Main St)* Doubles $62-95. This 17-room establishment has economy units as well as deluxe efficiencies. Facilities include a pool and hot tub.

Paradise Motor Inn (☎ 802-442-8351, *fax 802-447-3889,* W *www.theparadisemotor inn.com, 141 W Main St)* Doubles $75-105. Paradise is the big, fancy place in town, with 76 rooms and suites and all the amenities.

Bennington Motor Inn (☎ 802-442-5479, *800-359-9900, 143 W Main St)* Doubles

$76-102. These 16 rooms are within walking distance of most sights.

Inns A big 1890 Victorian holds the **Molly Stark Inn B&B** (☎ 802-442-9631, 800-356-3076, fax 802-442-5224, W www.mollystarkinn.com, 1067 Main St) Doubles $70-105, suites $135, cottage $150, all with excellent breakfast. This inn has six comfy guest rooms. Molly Stark's luxury accommodations include a private honeymoon cottage and two sugar-house suites with vaulted ceilings, hardwood floors and a double-sided fireplace.

Alexandra B&B-Inn (☎ 802-442-5619, fax 802-442-5592, W www.alexandrainn.com, VT 7A) Doubles $85-150 with full breakfast. At Orchard Rd about 2 miles north of Bennington, this tidy house has 12 guest rooms.

Four Chimneys Inn (☎ 802-447-3500, fax 802-447-3692, W www.fourchimneys.com, 21 West Rd) Doubles $105-185 with continental breakfast. The only B&B in Old Bennington, this grand white mansion is set amid verdant manicured lawns, with 11 more conservative rooms.

South Shire Inn (☎ 802-447-3839, fax 802-442-3547, W www.southshire.com, 124 Elm St) Doubles $110-185 with full breakfast. This antique-filled Victorian inn has nine rooms, some with fireplaces.

Many more cozy inns and B&Bs lie north of Bennington in nearby Arlington; call the chamber of commerce (see Orientation & Information, above) for further information on places to stay.

Places to Eat & Drink

Alldays & Onions (☎ 802-447-0043, 519 Main St) Lunch $5, dinner $14-19. Open 7:30am-4pm Mon-Sat, 6pm-8:30pm Fri-Sat. This excellent storefront eatery has creative sandwiches, salads, soups and other light fare during the day. For dinner try the special 'chicken Alldays,' roasted breast meat with blue cheese. The eclectic wine list is quite complementary. Note that, despite its name, Alldays is not open all days.

Blue Benn Diner (☎ 802-442-5140, 314 North St) Dishes $5-11. Open 6am-5pm Mon-Tues, 6am-8pm Wed-Fri, 6am-4pm Sat, 7am-4pm Sun. For a longer menu with several international variations, try this genuine diner. Standard fare is supplemented with Mexican dishes, some Asian fare, omelets and lots of vegetarian plates. Breakfast is served all day.

Madison Brewing Co Pub & Restaurant (☎ 802-442-7397, 428 Main St) Lunch $5-9, dinner $5-18. Open 11:30am-9:30pm daily. This pleasant but pseudo-rustic pub features standard fare ranging from sandwiches and burgers to steak and pasta, plus a good beer selection.

Rattlesnake Café (☎ 802-447-7018, 230 North St) Dishes $6-16. Open 4:30pm-9pm Tues-Sun. At the local Mexican joint, a hefty bean-and-cheese burrito will set you back $8. If you're not driving, try one of the strong margaritas.

Carmody's (☎ 802-447-5748, 421 Main St) Dishes $6-15. This old-fashioned restaurant serves basic American fare: burgers, fries, pasta and seafood.

Bennington Station (☎ 802-447-1080, 150 Depot St) Lunch $6-9, dinner $12-18. Set in an authentic 100-year-old train station, this restaurant features an extensive menu of prime rib, fish, pasta, salad and children's dishes.

MANCHESTER

Manchester has been a fashionable resort for almost two centuries. Formerly, the crowds came for mountain scenery, equable summer climate and the Batten Kill River, one of Vermont's best trout streams. These days, the draw is mostly winter skiing and upscale outlet shopping (there are more than 100 shops), but Manchester is still busy in summer with hikers and golfers. From mid-September to mid-November, one of Vermont's biggest fall festivals, the Stratton Arts Festival, takes place at nearby Stratton Mountain.

Two families put Manchester on the map. The first was that of native son Franklin Orvis (1824–1900), who became a New York businessman but then returned to Manchester to establish the Equinox House Hotel (1849). Orvis did much to beautify

VERMONT

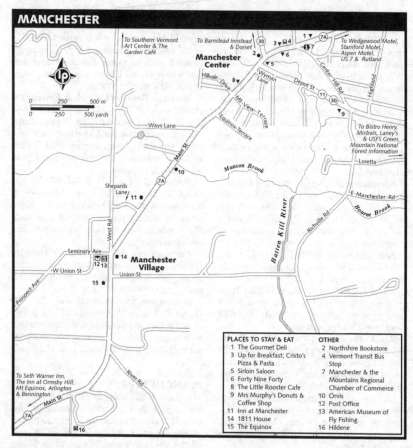

MANCHESTER

To Southern Vermont Art Center & The Garden Café

To Barnstead Innstead & Dorset

To Wedgewood Motel, Stamford Motel, Aspen Motel, US 7 & Rutland

Manchester Center

Hillvale Drive

Wyman Lane

Depot St

Center Hill Rd

Highland

Mt-View-Terrace

Equinox Terrace

Ways Lane

Main St

Munson Brook

To Bistro Henry, Mistrals, Laney's & USFS Green Mountain National Forest Information

Loretta

Shepards Lane

Batten Kill River

E-Manchester-Rd

Richville Rd

Bourne Brook

West Rd

Seminary Ave

W-Union St

Union St

Manchester Village

Prospect Ave

To Seth Warner Inn, The Inn at Ormsby Hill, Mt Equinox, Arlington & Bennington

River Rd

Main St

PLACES TO STAY & EAT	OTHER
1 The Gourmet Deli	2 Northshire Bookstore
3 Up for Breakfast; Cristo's Pizza & Pasta	4 Vermont Transit Bus Stop
5 Sirloin Saloon	7 Manchester & the Mountains Regional Chamber of Commerce
6 Forty Nine Forty	
8 The Little Rooster Cafe	10 Orvis
9 Mrs Murphy's Donuts & Coffee Shop	12 Post Office
11 Inn at Manchester	13 American Museum of Fly Fishing
14 1811 House	
15 The Equinox	16 Hildene

VERMONT

Manchester – by laying marble sidewalks, constructing public buildings and opening forest roads for excursions. Franklin's brother, Charles, founded the Orvis Company, makers of fly-fishing equipment, in 1856. The Manchester-based company now has a worldwide following.

The second family was that of Abraham Lincoln (1809–1865), 16th president of the USA. His wife, Mary Todd Lincoln (1818–1882), and their son Robert Todd Lincoln (1843–1926) came here during the Civil War, and Robert returned to build a mansion, Hildene, a number of years later.

Orientation

US 7 bypasses the town to the east; VT 7A goes right through the town's center.

Manchester has a split personality. When the locals say 'Manchester' or 'Manchester Village,' they're referring to the southern part of the town, a beautiful, dignified, historic Vermont village centered on the huge, venerable, posh Equinox hotel.

'Manchester Center,' a few miles north along VT 7A, used to be called Factory Point, but this name did not fit well with Manchester's resort image, and so it was changed. Manchester Center has several moderately priced inns and inexpensive-to-moderate restaurants, but the area is devoted mostly to upscale outlet stores – Mark Cross, Giorgio Armani, Polo, etc.

Information
The Manchester and the Mountains Regional Chamber of Commerce (☎ 802-362-2100, W www.manchestervermont.net) maintains an information office on the village green in Manchester Center (open 9am to 5pm Monday to Saturday year-round, 10am to 2pm Sunday late May to October). The chamber helps visitors find rooms and distributes printouts for hikes of varying difficulty within the Green Mountain National Forest.

The Northshire Bookstore (☎ 802-362-2200, Main St) is one of New England's best.

Hildene
The wife and children of Abraham Lincoln, one of the USA's greatest presidents, had tragic lives. His wife went mad, and only one of his four sons lived to adulthood. That son was Robert Todd Lincoln, who served on General Grant's staff during the Civil War. He later became a corporate lawyer in Chicago, president of the Pullman Palace Car Company, Secretary of War and minister (ambassador) to Great Britain.

Robert Todd Lincoln built a 24-room Georgian Revival mansion, which he named Hildene (☎ 802-362-1788, VT 7A; adult/child $8/4; open 9:30am-4pm daily mid-May–Oct), a short distance south of Manchester. He enjoyed the house until his death, and his great-granddaughter lived in the house until her death in 1975. Soon after, it was converted to a museum by the Friends of Hildene. Many of the Lincoln family's personal effects and furnishings are still in the house, which has been authentically restored. Tours are given every 30 minutes; grounds close at 5:30pm.

American Museum of Fly Fishing
This museum (☎ 802-362-3300, VT 7A; adult/child $3/free; open 10am-4pm Mon-Sat), just north of the little village center, has perhaps the world's best display of fly-fishing equipment, including historic rods used by novelists Ernest Hemingway and Zane Grey and several US presidents.

To examine or purchase the new stuff, head north about a half-mile to *Orvis* (☎ 802-362-3750, west side of VT 7A), open 9am to 6pm daily. Try out a rod in the trout ponds on the grounds, or inquire about its two-day fly-fishing schools.

Mt Equinox
It's just 5 miles from Manchester to the summit of Mt Equinox (3816 feet). Follow VT 7A south out of Manchester and look for Sky Line Dr (☎ 802-362-1114), a private toll road open 9am to dusk daily May to October. Tickets costs $6 for a car and driver, $2 each additional passenger over age 12.

Activities
About 10 minutes from town, **Bromley Mountain** (☎ 802-824-5522, 800-865-4786 lodging reservations, VT 11, Peru; rides $5-6.50 each, $50 for a book of 10, $50 per day per person) is a small family resort featuring 43 downhill ski runs, 10 chairlifts, and 84% snowmaking capacity. In summer, the mountain has just as many attractions. There's an Alpine Slide (the longest in North America), climbing wall, trampolines, 'zip line,' a kiddie adventure park, and much more. Additionally, chairlifts take hikers and sightseers up to trails beyond the Alpine Slide. Vermont's Long Trail goes right through Bromley.

Stratton Mountain (☎ 802-297-2200, 800-843-6867, VT 30), about 16 miles east of Manchester, is larger and more well known. It has 90 trails, 13 lifts (including a summit gondola) and a vertical drop of more than 2000 feet on a 3875-foot mountain. The longest downhill skiing trail is 3 miles, and there are 20 miles of cross-country trails. In summer, there's lots of golf, tennis, hiking and mountain biking.

As for hiking, the **Appalachian Trail** passes just east of Manchester, and in this area it's called Vermont's **Long Trail**. Shelters pop up about every 10 miles; some are staffed. Good day hikes include one to the

VERMONT

A Month in the Woods

America's first long-distance hiking trail, Vermont's Long Trail is a 264-mile mountainous corridor that runs the length of the state from Massachusetts to Canada.

Backpackers have been hiking the south-to-north ridge of the Green Mountains since 1930, when the Green Mountain Club finished clearing the length of the trail. Today, the Green Mountain Club has approximately 6200 members who maintain the trail system, 440 miles altogether when you include the 175 miles of side-trails.

And what an impressive network of trails it is. Often only 3 feet wide, the Long Trail crosses over streams, skirts every hidden pond from Massachusetts to Canada, weaves up and down mountains on open ridges to bare summits offering exceptional vistas of the entire state. Wave after wave of hillside gently rolls back to a sea of green dotted with the occasional pasture or meadow. A little less than half of the trail is located inside the Green Mountain National Forest.

The trail is best taken from south to north so you don't have to read the *Guide Book of the Long Trail* backwards. Also recommended is *The Long Trail End-to-Ender's Guide*, packed with nitty-gritty details on equipment sales and repairs, mail drops and B&Bs that provide trailhead shuttle services. Both guides are published by the Green Mountain Club.

For shelter, the Green Mountain Club maintains more than 60 lodges, camps and lean-tos along the trail. Hikers can easily walk from one shelter to the next in a day because the rest stops were built at 5- to 7-mile intervals. However, it is imperative that you bring a tent in case a shelter is full. Although the trail is wonderful for a trip of several days, many hikers use it for day hikes.

For more information, contact the Green Mountain Club (☎ 802-244-7037, VT 100, PO Box 650, Waterbury Center, VT 05677).

– Steve Jermanok

summit of Bromley Mountain and another to Stratton Pond. For details and maps, contact the USFS Green Mountain National Forest (☎ 802-362-2307) at the corner of VT 11 and VT 30 about 3 miles east of Manchester Center. The chamber of commerce also has detailed printouts.

The **Batten Kill Sports Bicycle Shop** (☎ 802-362-2734, 800-340-2734, cnr US 7 & VT 11/30) rents road, mountain and hybrid bikes for as little as $20 daily, including helmet, lock, trail recommendations and map. About a mile from Manchester Center, the shop does repairs and is open daily in summer (most days in spring and fall).

Places to Stay

Camping Camping on the Batten Kill River, described earlier in the Bennington section, is just south of Manchester on VT 7A.

Motels Rest easy at *Wedgewood Motel* (☎ 802-362-2145, 5927 VT 7A) Cottages $50-

118 with light breakfast. North of Manchester, this motel has 12 cozy little units trimmed with Wedgewood blue.

Stamford Motel (☎ 802-362-2342, fax 802-362-1935, 6458 VT 7A) Units $60-85. These 14 tidy units have standard comforts.

Eyrie Motel (☎ 802-362-1208, fax 802-362-2948, off US 7, East Dorset) Doubles $60-115. If the above motels are full, try this one, 7 miles north of Manchester Center, with 12 rooms.

Aspen Motel (☎ 802-362-2450, 5669 VT 7A) Doubles $65-105. This sprawling place has 24 rooms and one efficiency.

Chalet Motel (☎ 802-362-1622, 800-343-9900, fax 802-362-1753, ⓦ www.thechaletmotel.com, VT 11/30) Doubles $70-150. Two miles east of the town center, this 43-room motel is similar but more expensive.

Inns There are plenty of inns in the area.

Barnstead Innstead (☎ 802-362-1619, fax 802-362-0688, ⓦ www.barnsteadinn.com,

349 Bonnet St) Doubles $75-220. Barely a half-mile from Manchester Center, this hostelry has some charm, a good location and decent prices. The 14 rooms in a renovated 1830s hay barn, complete with exposed beams and homey braided rugs, have all the usual comforts.

Seth Warner Inn (☎ 802-362-3830, fax 802-362-1268, ☒ www.sethwarnerinn1.prodigy biz.com, 2353 VT 7A) Doubles $100-110 with full breakfast. About 2 miles southwest of town, this five-room inn, dating back to 1800, features country décor, antiques, stenciling, quilts and period restoration.

1811 House (☎ 802-362-1811, fax 802-362-2443, ☒ www.1811house.com, VT 7A) Doubles $120-230 with full breakfast. This refined Federal house, surrounded by 7 acres of lawns and gardens, was built in the 1770s and has been an inn since 1811. In addition to 14 antique-filled rooms and quiet, elegant common space, its cozy little *pub* (open to the public from 5:30pm to 8pm) offers an impressive selection of single-malt scotches.

The Inn at Ormsby Hill (☎ 802-362-1163, 800-670-2841, ☒ www.ormsbyhill.com, 1842 VT 7A) Doubles $125-300 with full breakfast. Just southwest of Manchester, Ormsby Hill is arguably one of the most welcoming inns in all of New England. Waverly fabrics, fireplaces, two-person Jacuzzis, antiques, gracious innkeepers and 2½ acres of lawn draw repeat guests to its 10 rooms. Absolutely bountiful breakfast offerings, perhaps bacon and egg risotto followed by rhubarb crumble and vanilla ice cream (yes, this is breakfast), are unlike anywhere else.

Inn at Manchester (☎ 802-362-1793, 800-273-1793, fax 802-362-3218, ☒ www.innat manchester.com, 3967 VT 7A) Rooms $129-209, suites $179-209 with full breakfast; rates about $40 more mid-Sept–Oct. This restored house and carriage house is set back from the road and offers 18 rooms and four suites to a loyal clientele. There's lots of wicker on the big front porch, an expansive backyard with a pool and frilly common rooms. Tea and Saturday wine and cheese are included in the rates.

Resorts One of Vermont's best resorts is **The Equinox** (☎ 802-362-4700, 800-362-4747, fax 802-362-7782, ☒ www.equinox resort.com, VT 7A) Doubles $199-359. This grand property boasts 183 elegant rooms, an 18-hole golf course, small indoor and outdoor fitness pools and three tennis courts. Other activities include falconry, off-road driving and snowmobiling. Room rates vary with the view and season. The original building here, the Marsh Tavern, dates from 1769. Even if you can't afford to stay, sit on a front-porch rocker, read a newspaper in the morning sun and pretend you belong.

Places to Eat

Mrs Murphy's Donuts & Coffee Shop (☎ 802-362-1874, VT 11/30) Dishes $5. Open 5am-6pm daily. Manchester's down-home favorite (look for the pickup trucks) serves fresh doughnuts and more substantial bacon-and-egg 'tuck-ins' (think Egg McMuffin) throughout the day. You're certainly not paying a premium for atmosphere here.

The Little Rooster Cafe (☎ 802-362-3496, VT 7A) Dishes $5-9. Open for breakfast & lunch Thur-Tues. This place serves dishes like Asian vegetables with noodles and chicken or grilled portobello focaccia.

The Gourmet Deli (☎ 802-362-1254, 4961 Main St) Dishes $6. Open 7am-3:30pm daily. Behind the Green Mountain Village Shopping Plaza, this casual place has inexpensive sandwiches, soups, salads, chili and the like.

Up for Breakfast (☎ 802-362-4204, 4935 Main St) Dishes $4-8. Open 7am-noon daily. Above Christo's, breakfast dishes range from huevos rancheros to wild turkey hash.

Christo's Pizza & Pasta (☎ 802-362-2408, 4931 Main St) Dishes $8-10. Open for lunch & dinner. This no-nonsense, nondescript alternative is fine for a quick slice or bowl of pasta.

The Garden Cafe (☎ 802-366-8297, West Rd) Dishes $5-10. Open for lunch Tues-Sun. At the Southern Vermont Art Center, the indoor and outdoor cafe pairs very good dishes with the tranquil setting of the sculpture garden.

Sirloin Saloon (☎ 802-362-2600, VT 11/30) Mains $9-22. Open daily. The Sirloin Saloon claims to be Vermont's oldest steak house, and that's still the specialty, although there's decent seafood, too. The salad bar is the cheapest thing in the house.

Forty Nine Forty (☎ 802-362-9839, 4940 Main St) All-day menu $7, dinner $10-22. Open daily. In addition to good noshing appetizers, this pleasant, bright bistro serves veggie burgers, Black Angus burgers and grilled Tuscan cheese sandwiches all day. Create your own sandwich at lunchtime. The evening meal is simple, with grilled chicken, stir-fry or pasta alfredo.

Laney's (☎ 802-362-4456, VT 11/30) Pizza $7-10, mains $11-21. Open from 4:30pm daily. About a mile from Manchester Center, this large family-friendly eatery has wood-fired pizzas and lots of pasta dishes.

Bistro Henry (☎ 802-362-4982, VT 11/30) Mains $16-28. Open for dinner. Within the Chalet Motel, this casual chef-owned bistro serves creative modern cuisine highlighting fresh seafood, aged meats and fresh vegetables accompanied by fine wine. You can't go wrong here.

Mistral's (☎ 802-362-1779, 10 Toll Gate Rd) Mains $25. Open for dinner. Nestled deep in the woods and overlooking a stream (off VT 30 and VT 11 toward Bromley), you'll enjoy the scenery before dark and then dine on Norwegian salmon or roast duck in an incredibly intimate setting.

Entertainment

Southern Vermont Art Center (☎ 802-362-1405, West Rd) Open 10am-5pm Tues-Sat year-round & noon-5pm Sun mid-May–Oct. In addition to an excellent outdoor sculpture garden and changing exhibits, this center has a full program of concerts from June through August. Other summer concerts are organized by Hildene (☎ 802-362-1788), the Manchester Music Festival (☎ 802-362-1956) and Barrows House (☎ 802-867-4455), in nearby Dorset.

Getting There & Away

Trains and stagecoaches brought early vacationers to Manchester. Now it's buses and cars. Vermont Transit (☎ 802-864-6811, 800-552-8737) runs three daily buses from Manchester to Middlebury (1½ hours, $12.50) and onward to Burlington and Montreal. The bus stop is at Village Valet (☎ 802-362-1226, 4940 Main St).

From Manchester Village, take the lovely back road, West Rd, north to VT 30 to Dorset. But before reaching Dorset, veer off onto Dorset West Rd to Church St into the Dorset village.

Manchester is 32 miles (one hour with traffic) south of Rutland via US 7, but it's far more scenic to head north on VT 30 through Dorset and onward to Middlebury.

NEARBY VILLAGES

It's hard to get enough of these quintessentially Vermont towns, whether they be town-and-country perfect like Dorset or more blue-collar like Pawlet.

Dorset

Six miles north of Manchester along VT 30, Dorset is a perfect Vermont village like many others, with its village green, stately inn and lofty church. The difference, however, is that in Dorset the sidewalks, the church and lots of other things are made of creamy marble.

Settled in 1768, Dorset became a farming community with a healthy trade in marble. The **quarry**, about a mile south of the village center, supplied much of the marble for the grand New York Public Library building and numerous other public edifices, but it's now filled with water. It's a nice place to picnic.

Much like Manchester, Dorset became a summer playground for well-to-do city folks more than a century ago. Today, in addition to the village's pristine beauty, the **Dorset Playhouse** (☎ 802-867-5777, Cheney Rd) draws visitors. In summer, the actors are professionals; at other times, community players.

Emerald Lake State Park (☎ 802-362-1655, US 7) Sites $14-20. Open late May-mid–Oct. Just north of East Dorset, this 430-acre park has 105 sites, including 32 lean-tos. You can swim and canoe on the

80-foot-deep lake and hike through the mountains; some trails connect with the Long Trail.

Dorset's lodging and dining places are upscale.

Peltier's (☎ 802-867-4400, VT 30) Open daily. An institution since 1816, Peltier's sells all manner of edible Vermont items, especially high-end gourmet goodies and picnic fixings.

Dorset Inn (☎ 802-867-5500, fax 802-867-5542, W www.dorsetinn.com, cnr Church & Main Sts) Singles $80-95, doubles $110-150 with full breakfast. Just off VT 30, facing the village green, this traditional but updated inn has 31 renovated guest rooms. The front-porch rockers provide a nice setting for watching the comings and goings of the sleepy Vermont town. Opt for rates that include dinner since the chef-owned restaurant is highly regarded. It's also open for casual luncheons.

Dovetail Inn (☎ 802-867-5747, 888-867-5747, fax 802-867-0246, W www.dovetail inn.com, VT 30) Doubles $85-175, suite $235 with continental breakfast. Also facing the village green, this inn offers 11 tidy, well-kept rooms.

Cornucopia B&B (☎ 802-867-5751, 800-566-5751, fax 802-867-5753, W www.cornu copiaofdorset.com, VT 30) Doubles $150-270 with full breakfast. This refined and elegant B&B has five perfectly kept guest rooms with canopy and four-poster beds. Among all the special attentions paid to guests, you'll be greeted with champagne on arrival and awakened with morning coffee at your door.

Weston
On the eastern side of the Green Mountains from Manchester, Weston is another of Vermont's pristine towns. Its town common is graced with towering maples and a bandstand, and surrounded by a famous country store and fine summer theater.

Vermont Country Store (☎ 802-824-3184, VT 100) Open 9am-5pm Mon-Sat. Purveyors of all that's unnecessary but makes life's little chores easier, the Vermont Country Store is an experience in nostalgia,

humor and Yankee ingenuity. You will undoubtedly leave with a handful of charmingly eccentric items that you'll use fondly for years. And when you run out of them, you'll send for a down-home black-and-white catalog that will entertain you during long winter nights.

Weston Playhouse (☎ 802-824-5288) Tickets $22-26. Performances late June-early Sept. Vermont's oldest professional theater occupies an old church on the green and backs onto the West River. It enjoys a fine reputation, and if you're in the area, try to obtain tickets. Arrive early for a show or to dine on light fare 'Downstairs at the Playhouse.'

Pawlet
The alternative route from Manchester to Middlebury is VT 30 north. Along the way you'll pass through the blink-of-an-eye village of Pawlet. Stop at *Machs' Market* (☎ 802-325-3405, VT 30), a fine old-fashioned general store that generates its electricity from an adjacent stream passing through a little gorge. You can see all this from inside the store, thanks to a glass counter. The village consists of a few little shops and the *Station Restaurant* (☎ 802-325-3041), a former railroad station converted into a classic diner with swivel stools.

Continuing north, take a quick detour into East Poultney, on VT 140 from VT 30. The classic town green, lined with a fine church and 18th- and 19th-century houses, has a fine old general store.

Central Vermont

Vermont's heart features some of New England's most bucolic countryside. Just north of Rutland, Vermont's second-largest city, cows begin to outnumber people. Outdoors lovers make frequent pilgrimages to central Vermont, especially to the resort area of Killington, which attracts countless skiers and summer hikers. For those interested in indoor pleasures, antique shops and art galleries dot the back roads between picturesque covered bridges.

VERMONT

WOODSTOCK

Woodstock, VT, is the antithesis of that symbol of 1960s hippie living, Woodstock, New York. Vermont's Woodstock, chartered in 1761, has been the highly dignified seat of Windsor County since 1766. It prospered in this role. The townspeople built many grand houses surrounding the town common, and Woodstock's churches boast no fewer than four bells cast by Paul Revere. Senator Jacob Collamer, a friend of President Abraham Lincoln's, once said, 'The good people of Woodstock have less incentive than others to yearn for heaven.' In the 19th century, other New England towns built smoky factories, but the only pollution from Woodstock's main industry, county government, was hot air, and it quickly rose out of sight.

Today, Woodstock is still very beautiful and very wealthy. Spend some time walking around the village green, surrounded by Federal and Greek Revival homes and public buildings. Both the Rockefellers and the Rothschilds own estates in the surrounding countryside, and the well-to-do come to stay at the grand Woodstock Inn & Resort. Despite its high-tone reputation, the town also offers some reasonably priced lodgings and meal possibilities.

Orientation & Information

Woodstock, off US 4, is part of the Upper Connecticut River Valley community that includes Hanover and Lebanon, in New Hampshire, and Norwich and White River Junction, in Vermont. People think nothing of driving from one of these towns to another to find accomodations, a meal or an amusement.

The Woodstock Area Chamber of Commerce (☎ 802-457-3555, Ⓦ www.woodstock vt.com, 18 Central St, Woodstock, VT 05091) operates a small information booth on the village green, open May to October. Parking places are at a premium in Woodstock, and enforcement is strict, so obey the regulations.

For local guidebooks, maps and books in general, stop at the Yankee Bookshop (☎ 802-457-2411, 12 Central St).

Billings Farm & Museum

After your walk around town, pay a visit to this farm museum (☎ 802-457-2355, VT 12; adult $8, senior $7, child $4-6; open 10am-5pm daily May-Oct, 10am-4pm Sat-Sun Dec), less than a mile north of the village green, at River Rd. The railroad magnate Frederick Billings founded the farm in the late 19th century and ran it on sound 'modern' principles of conservation and animal husbandry. In 1871, he imported cattle directly from the Isle of Jersey in Britain, and the purebred descendants of these early bovine immigrants still give milk on the farm today. Life on the working farm is a mix of 19th- and 20th-century methods, all of which delight curious children. Call for details about the daily demonstrations, audiovisual shows and special programs.

Marsh-Billings-Rockefeller National Historical Park

This mansion and park (☎ 802-457-3368, Elm St; tours adult/senior & child $6/3; open 10am-4pm daily late May-Oct; tours every 30 min), off VT 12, focuses on the relationship between land stewardship and environmental conservation. While there is an admission fee to the mansion, the 20 miles of trails and carriage roads are free for exploring. In the winter, they're groomed for cross-country skiing and snowshoeing. Some trails start on the far side of the Ottauquechee River from the village green, along the east edge of the cemetery. When the mansion is closed, the Woodstock Inn & Resort (see Places to Stay, below) has a walking-trail pamphlet.

Quechee Gorge

Eight miles east of Woodstock along US 4, the highway passes over Quechee (pronounced 'kwee-chee') Gorge, a craggy chasm cut by the Ottauquechee River. Though it's less than 170 feet deep, the gorge provides dreamy views, and Quechee Gorge State Park, on the east side of the gorge, has camping, hiking trails and picnic facilities (see Places to Stay, below). The walk through the gorge down to the river takes only 15 minutes.

Long Trail Brewing Company

Halfway between Killington and Woodstock, the **Long Trail Brewing Company** (*☎ 802-672-5011; cnr US 4 & VT 100A; admission free; open 10am-6pm daily*) brews 'Vermont's No 1 Selling Amber.' Sit down at the visitor center, order a sandwich or burger and wash it down with a cold hearty stout or a fruity blackberry wheat ale. Tours are free.

Vermont Raptor Center

Learn all about raptors and other birds of prey at the Vermont Institute of Natural Science (*☎ 802-457-2779, Church Hill Rd; adult $7, senior $6.30, child (varies with age) $1-4; open 10am-4pm Mon-Sat*), 1½ miles southwest of Woodstock's village green. The two dozen species of raptors living here range from the tiny, 3oz saw-whet owl to the mighty bald eagle. The birds have sustained permanent injuries that do not allow them to return to life in the wild. Three self-guided nature trails are delightful for hikes in summer or for snowshoeing in winter.

Activities

Be sure to look out for Woodstock's three covered bridges over the Ottauquechee River.

Nearby state parks offer hiking trails and lakes good for swimming, boating and canoeing. See Camping under Places to Stay for locations.

Bike Vermont (*☎ 800-257-2226*) operates two- to six-night bike tours, including inn-to-inn tours. The price for a three-day/two-night trip, for instance, is $295 to $360 per person; the price varies with the season. Local bicycle shops, including **Woodstock Sports** (*☎ 802-457-1568, 30 Central St*) and **Cyclery Plus** (*☎ 802-457-3377, 490 Woodstock Rd/US 4*) rent bicycles and provide maps of good local routes. Expect to pay $20 for full-day rentals.

In 1934, Woodstockers installed the first mechanical ski-tow in the USA, and skiing is still important here. **Suicide Six** (*☎ 802-457-6661, 800-448-7900, VT 12, Pomfret*), 3 miles north of Woodstock, is known for

challenging downhill runs. The lower slopes are fine for beginners, though. There are 23 trails and three lifts (30% beginner, 40% intermediate, 30% expert).

The full-service **Woodstock Ski Touring Center** (*☎ 802-457-6674, VT 106*), just south of town, rents equipment and has 50 miles of groomed touring trails.

Places to Stay

Camping The following state parks cost $14 to $20 and are open mid-May to mid-October.

Quechee Gorge State Park (*☎ 802-295-2990, 886-2434, 190 Dewey Mills Rd, White River Junction*) Eight miles east of Woodstock and 3 miles west of I-89 along US 4, this 600-acre spot has 54 pine-shaded sites (six lean-tos) a short stroll from Quechee Gorge.

Silver Lake State Park (*☎ 802-234-9451, 886-2434, off VT 12, Barnard*) This 34-acre park is 10 miles north of Woodstock and has 47 sites (seven lean-tos), a beach, boat and canoe rentals and fishing.

Mt Ascutney State Park (*☎ 802-674-2060, Black Mountain Rd, Windsor*) About 22 miles southeast of Woodstock off I-91, these 49 sites (10 lean-tos) are at an elevation of 3144 feet, and they offer great panoramic views. The 2000-acre park also features a playground, hiking trails and cliffs for hang gliding.

Wilgus State Park (*☎ 802-674-5422, 886-2434, US 5, Windsor*) Wilgus is 2 miles south of I-91 exit 8. The 29 sites (nine lean-tos), next to the Connecticut River, offer good possibilities for fishing, canoeing and hiking within the park's 100 acres.

Thetford Hill State Park (*☎ 802-785-2266, Academy Rd, Thetford*) You'll find 16 sites (two lean-tos), plus hiking trails and a playground here. From I-91 exit 14, go a mile west on VT 113 to Thetford Hill, then a mile south on Academy Rd.

Motels East of town is *Braeside Motel* (*☎ 802-457-1366, Ⓦ www.braesidemotel.com, US 4*) Doubles $68-108. This motel has a nice location, a seasonal swimming pool and 12 good rooms.

Shire Motel (☎ 802-457-2211, fax 802-457-5836, ⓦ www.shiremotel.com, 46 Pleasant St) Doubles $68-175. Within walking distance of the town center on US 4 on the east side of town, this place has 33 comfy rooms.

B&Bs Get cozy at **Barr House** (☎ 802-457-3334, 55 South St) Singles $65-70, doubles $70-75 with large country breakfast. Open Mar-Dec. This handsome B&B has only two rooms (shared bath) on VT 106, a five-minute walk south of the green.

Rosewood Inn (☎ 802-457-4485, 674 Bartlett Brook Rd, South Pomfret) Doubles $70-125 with full breakfast. Of the five guest rooms at this small B&B 2 miles north of Woodstock, try to get the large one with private bath.

1830 Shire Town Inn (☎ 802-457-1830, ⓦ www.1830shiretowninn.com, 31 South St) Doubles $75-125 with hearty breakfast. This cozy B&B has three rooms with the requisite period wide floorboards, thick beams and fireplaces.

Applebutter Inn (☎/fax 802-457-4158, 800-486-1374, 7511 Happy Valley Rd, Taftsville) Doubles $75-175 with immense breakfast. Just 3 miles east of Woodstock and set on 12 extraordinary acres with one of Vermont's most picturesque barns, the Applebutter is a Federal-style house (circa 1850) with six guest rooms and a wonderful old kitchen. No credit cards are accepted.

Woodstocker B&B (☎ 802-457-3896, fax 802-457-3897, 61 River St) Doubles $85-135 with full breakfast. This 1830s hostelry offers nine spacious, nicely decorated rooms. For longer stays, ask about the desirable suites.

Canterbury House (☎ 802-457-3077, 800-390-3077, ⓦ www.thecanterburyhouse.com, 43 Pleasant St) Doubles $100-175 with full breakfast. These eight charming guest rooms, filled with antiques, are housed in a restored 1880s Victorian B&B.

Inns & Resorts The **Village Inn of Woodstock** (☎ 802-457-1255, 800-722-4571, fax 802-457-3109, ⓦ www.villageinnofwoodstock.com, 41 Pleasant St) Doubles $85-235

with full breakfast. This lovely Victorian mansion has eight guest rooms, most with feather beds and down comforters, and period details like oak wainscoting and tin ceilings.

Parker House Inn (☎ 802-295-6077, ⓦ www.theparkerhouseinn.com, 1792 Quechee Main St, Quechee) Doubles $115-150 with full breakfast. A Victorian-style place built in 1857 for a former Vermont senator, this antique-laden inn features seven large guest rooms. It's just 100 yards from the Ottauquechee River's covered bridge and waterfall.

Woodstock Inn & Resort (☎ 802-457-1100, 800-448-7900, fax 802-457-6699, ⓦ www.woodstockinn.com, 14 The Green) Rooms $179-365, suites $454-559. One of Vermont's most luxurious hotels, the resort has extensive grounds, a formal dining room, indoor sports center and 144 guest rooms and suites.

Places to Eat & Drink

Pane e Salute (☎ 802-457-4882, 61 Central St) Daytime dishes $3-7, mains $16-18, prix fixe $38. Open for breakfast & lunch Thur-Sun & dinner Fri-Sat. Specialties include authentic Italian pastries and the best cup of espresso this side of the Connecticut River. Expect buttery *panettone*, rolls filled with ricotta, pear and chocolate, and Florentine coffee cake. Get a sandwich to go, or relax with table service. In the evening, you'll be rewarded with classic Italian dishes, from rustic mountainous ones to aristocratic, citified creations. The chefs aren't particularly interested in innovating with new flavors, but rather reacquainting you with nostalgic ones.

If you have a picnic lunch, take it to the George Perkins Marsh Man and Nature Park, a tiny hideaway right next to the river on Central St, across the street from Pane e Salute.

Mountain Creamery (☎ 802-457-1715, 33 Central St) Dishes $4-6. Open 7am-3pm daily. A few steps west of Pane e Salute, you can get a sandwich or other yummy picnic fare here. It also serves Woodstock's most scrumptious apple pie.

Skunk Hollow Tavern (☎ 802-436-2139, *off VT 12, Hartland Four Corners*) Mains $8-24. Open Wed-Sun. Eight miles south of Woodstock, this tiny 200-year-old tavern has worn wooden floors that ooze history. You can have burgers or fish-and-chips ($8) at the bar or head upstairs, where it's more intimate, to enjoy rack of lamb ($24). The same menu is available upstairs and downstairs. It's a treat when there's live music (Wednesday and Friday) and the band takes up half the room.

Village Inn of Woodstock (☎ 802-457-1255, *41 Pleasant St*) Mains $15-20. Open Wed-Sat. This dark green tavern features a limited seasonal menu highlighting Vermont ingredients.

The Prince & the Pauper (☎ 802-457-1818, *24 Elm St*) Bistro menu $13-19, mains $21-24, prix fixe $38. Open nightly. Woodstock's elegant New American bistro serves a sublime three-course prix-fixe menu. You might order applewood-smoked ruby trout with grilled corn cake and *crème fraîche* from the à la carte menu. Lighter bistro fare is always an option.

Parker House Inn (☎ 802-295-6077, *16 Main St, Quechee*) Dishes $16.50-24. Open nightly July–mid-Oct, Fri-Sat mid-Oct–June. Locals concur: The food here is just as tasty as at Simon Pearce next door (see below), but the Parker House prices are better. However, you don't get waterfall views or the chance to use Simon Pearce stemware.

Simon Pearce Restaurant (☎ 802-295-1470, *The Mill, Main St, Quechee*) Lunch $6-15, dinner $19-35. Open 11:30am-2:45pm & 6pm-9pm daily. A 10-minute drive from Woodstock, this creative restaurant enjoys a dramatic setting in an old brick mill overlooking a waterfall and a covered bridge. Influenced by New American cuisine, the menu nevertheless maintains a refreshing simplicity: Try sweet-potato soup, hickory-smoked coho salmon or grilled leg of lamb with garlic, rosemary and balsamic vinaigrette. The restaurant's beautiful stemware is blown by hand in the Simon Pearce Glass workshops, also located in the mill; watch them work while you wait.

Jackson House Inn (☎ 802-457-2065, *114-3 Senior Lane/US 4*) Prix fixe $55. Open for dinner Wed-Sun (nightly July-Oct). Expect tranquillity, exquisite views of Mt Tom and premier cuisine. The prix-fixe menu might feature oysters, scallops or duck in phyllo, followed by a main dish of pepper-crusted tuna or a juicy little squab lightly caramelized with maple syrup. End with the cheese sampler or *tarte Tatin*. For a special occasion, this place is worth the splurge.

Getting There & Away

Many Vermont Transit (☎ 802-864-6811, 800-552-8737) buses stop at nearby White River Junction (☎ 802-295-3011, Sykes Ave). If you take the bus to White River Junction on your way to Woodstock, you might find it easiest to take a taxi (drivers wait at the bus station) from there to Woodstock, a distance of 16 miles. One late-morning bus route travels between White River Junction, Quechee, Woodstock, Sherburne (Killington) and Rutland. Woodstock to Killington costs $5.50 one-way and takes 30 minutes. The Woodstock bus stop is located at the Windmill Copy Center (10 Central St).

Amtrak's daily *Vermonter* (☎ 800-872-7245) stops at nearby White River Junction. (See above for information on continuing on to Woodstock.) For more details on the *Vermonter*'s route, see the Getting There & Around section at the beginning of this chapter.

It's a straight shot (89 miles or 2 hours) via US 4 east to I-89 north to Burlington from Woodstock. It'll take a mere half-hour (20 miles) to reach Killington via US 4 west.

PLYMOUTH

This small farming village, 14 miles southwest of Woodstock, is known only for the Coolidge Homestead and the Plymouth Cheese Company.

History

'If you don't say anything, you won't be called on to repeat it,' said Calvin Coolidge (1872–1933), 30th president of the USA, who was born in Plymouth. He attended nearby Amherst College in Massachusetts, opened a law practice in Northampton, MA, ran for local office, and then served as state senator, lieutenant governor and governor of Massachusetts. Elected as vice president of the USA on the Warren Harding ticket in 1920, he assumed the presidency upon Harding's sudden death in 1923. Vice President Coolidge was visiting his boyhood home in Plymouth when word came of Harding's death, and his father, Colonel John Coolidge, the local justice of the peace, administered the presidential oath of office by kerosene lamp at 2:47am on August 3, 1923.

Known for his simple, forthright New England style and his personal honesty, Coolidge had the good fortune to preside over a time of great prosperity – the Roaring Twenties. His laissez-faire business policies were well accepted but contributed to the stock market crash of 1929. With wonderful *après-moi-le-déluge* luck, he declined to run for another term as president in 1928, although he probably would have won. Instead, he retired to Northampton to write articles for newspapers and magazines.

Thus, the burden of blame for the Great Depression fell hard on the shoulders of the 31st president, Herbert Hoover, who had engineered many of the Coolidge Administration's successes as its Secretary of Commerce. Hoover had only been in office a matter of months when the stock market crashed. In 1931, with many banks failed and a quarter of the nation's workers unemployed, former president Coolidge understatedly reflected, 'The country is not in good shape.'

Coolidge Homestead
The tranquil and perfectly manicured homestead (☎ 802-672-3773, VT 100A; adult/family $6.50/20, child under 14 yrs free; open 9:30am-5pm daily late May–mid-Oct) is open for tours. You can check out the birthplace, homestead and Wilder Barn, a farmers' museum. Wilder House, once the home of Coolidge's mother, has now become a lunchroom. Calvin Coolidge is buried in the local cemetery.

Plymouth Cheese Company
A good Vermont cheese can melt in your mouth like butter or it can have the sharpness of a dry chardonnay. On the grounds of the Coolidge Homestead at the Plymouth Cheese Company (☎ 802-672-3650, VT 100A; admission free) you can see how some of the state's finest cheeses are made and taste the results. Try the granular-curd cheddar that's made from creamy Vermont milk.

Places to Stay
Coolidge State Park (☎ 802-672-3612, 886-2434, PO Box 105, VT 100A) Sites $14-20. Open late May-early Oct. This 165-acre park is 3 miles northeast of Plymouth Union, and even closer to Plymouth itself. The 60 sites (35 lean-tos) sit at an elevation of 2100 feet in a 25-sq-mile state forest with good hiking and fishing. There's a backcountry camping area, as well.

HI-AYH – Trojan Horse Hostel (☎ 802-228-5244, 800-547-7475, Ⓦ www.hiayh.org, 44 Andover St) Dorm beds $15-18 summer, $23 winter. Office open 8am-10am & 5pm-9pm daily May-Mar. On VT 100 just south of Ludlow village, 11 miles south of Plymouth, this hostel is a bit more expensive in winter when it's crowded with skiers from the nearby Okemo Mountain ski area. Reserve in advance by phone December through March.

Golden Stage Inn (☎ 802-226-7744, 800-253-8226, Ⓦ www.goldenstageinn.com, Depot St, Proctorsville) Doubles $79-250 with full breakfast. One of the coziest overnight stays in the Okemo area, this former 18th-century stagecoach stop off VT 103 is now an 11-room inn with views of the mountain.

KILLINGTON MOUNTAIN
The largest ski resort in the East is all about outdoor activities and it's all centrally located on the mountain. Officially, the mountain town is Sherburne, but there's really no there, there.

Vermont Transit (☎ 802-864-6811, 800-552-8737) buses stop at the Deli (☎ 802-775-1599) on US 4 in Killington. The ride from

CHARLES COOK

The Hammond Covered Bridge, in Pittsford, safely floated 1½ miles in a 1927 flood.

Sherburne to Rutland costs $5.50 one-way (30 minutes). Once you're in Rutland, you can catch buses to Burlington, Brattleboro or Bennington.

Information

The Killington Chamber of Commerce (☎ 802-773-4181, W www.killingtonchamber .com), on US 4, is open 9am to 5pm weekdays year-round, and 10am to 2pm Saturday when traffic warrants it during the summer, fall foliage and ski season.

The Killington Lodging Bureau and Travel Service (☎ 800-372-2007, W www .killington.com), the central reservations for the resort, is the best source for area services. They will send you information prior to your visit, but their real raison d'etre is in helping with accommodations. Since there are well over a hundred area places to stay, package deals with sports activities and lodgings can be attractively priced.

Activities

Winter Vermont's prime ski resort, **Killington** (☎ 802-422-3261, 800-621-6867) offers 200 runs on seven mountains, a vertical drop of more than 3000 feet, and 32 lifts, including the Skyeship and K-1 gondola that lifts

up to 3000 skiers per hour in heated cars with closed-circuit radio along a 2½-mile cable. The experts attempt to ski Outer Limits, the steepest mogul run in the East. The area boasts top-notch facilities for every conceivable winter activity, from ice skating to snowboarding. Ski season typically runs from early November through late May.

Summer Killington facilities are used for other outdoor activities, including excellent hiking and biking.

The **Mountain Bike & Repair Shop** (☎ 802-422-6232, Killington Rd) rents mountain bikes ($50 daily; helmet and trail map included). Serious riders will want to take the 1¼-mile K-1 gondola ride to the 4241-foot summit of Killington Mountain and find their way down among the 45 miles of trails. Mountain-bike trail access costs $8 daily or $30 for trail and gondola access.

As for hiking, the Mountain Bike Shop has an excellent (free) map of 14 self-guided nature hikes. Hikers can ride the gondola to the top and hike down (adult/senior & child/family $13/8/31). If you simply want to ride up and down, the gondola costs $9/5/20 adult/senior & child/family.

VERMONT

Places to Stay

Gifford Woods State Park (☎ 802-775-5354, 886-2434, Gifford Woods Rd, Killington) Sites $14-20. Open late May-early Oct. A half-mile north of US 4 and VT 100, this park has 48 campsites (21 lean-tos) on 114 acres. There's a playground, hiking trails and fishing in Kent Pond.

For condo and house rentals and hotels, the Killington Lodging Bureau and Travel Service (see Information, above) really finds the best deals.

Places to Eat & Drink

The mountain has more than 100 restaurants; you won't go hungry or broke. Families should head to *Casey's Caboose* (☎ 802-422-3795, Killington Rd); grazers should head to *Choices Restaurant* (☎ 802-422-4030, Glazebrook Center, Killington Rd).

Mother Shapiro's (☎ 802-422-9933, Killington Rd) Dishes $3-10. Open for all 3 meals. The area's most popular place for breakfast, Mother's also serves juicy burgers and killer-size sandwiches. The service is as friendly as the portions are hefty.

Panache (☎ 802-422-8622, Woods Resort, Killington Rd) Dishes $15-20. Open for dinner. This place has made its mark with exuberant preparations of exotic wild game (kangaroo, rattlesnake) from Australia, Africa and the US. While we're not sure why they'd want to dine here, vegetarians aren't slighted either, strangely enough.

The Vermont Inn (☎ 802-775-0708, US 4) Mains $18-22. Open daily. One of the mountain's best dining values, the inn offers rack of lamb, local veal and variations on the steak theme. Do skiers have appetites or what?

With 25 clubs and lively bars in many restaurants, Killington is a place where the après-ski scene rages. Many of these nightspots lie along the 4-mile-long Access Rd, which is Killington's version of a town. Check out these: *Wobbly Barn* (☎ 802-422-3392), with dancing, blues and rock & roll, and the *Pickle Barrel* (☎ 802-422-3035), with great rock & roll bands. *McGrath's Irish Pub* (☎ 802-775-7181, US 4), at the Inn at Long Trail, has live Irish music on winter weekends.

RUTLAND

Rutland is Vermont's second-largest city (Burlington is larger and more charming). US 7 bypasses the center of Rutland, and you should probably do the same. If you need to find a big hardware store, automobile dealership, airport or hospital, Rutland will do. Otherwise, move on.

In the 19th century, Rutland was important as a railroad town. The trains shipped Vermont marble out and the manufactured goods of the world in. But the city's main railroad station was torn down in the 1960s and replaced by a nondescript shopping mall, leaving Rutland without even a visual memory of its heyday.

The **Vermont State Fair** takes place here in early September. The Rutland Region Chamber of Commerce (☎ 802-773-2747, 256 N Main St/US 7, Rutland, VT 05701) has more information. It's open 8am to 5pm weekdays.

MIDDLEBURY

Prosperity lives at the crossroads, and Middlebury obviously has its share. Aptly named, Middlebury stands at the nexus of eight highways, and as a result the center of town is always busy with traffic. Despite Middlebury's history of marble quarrying, most buildings in the town's center are built of brick, wood and schist (a stone). Middlebury College, however, contains many buildings made with white marble and gray limestone.

History

Middlebury was permanently settled at the end of the 18th century. In 1800, Middlebury College was founded, and it has been synonymous with the town ever since. But the establishment of this renowned liberal arts college was not Middlebury's only educational milestone. In 1814, education pioneer Emma Willard (1787–1870) founded the Middlebury Female Seminary, a college-preparatory boarding school designed to prepare women for college admission – a radical idea in early-19th-century America. The school later moved to nearby New York state.

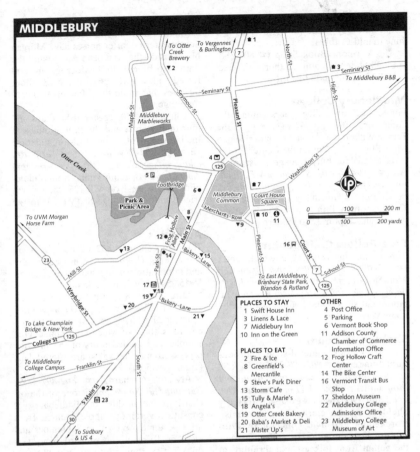

MIDDLEBURY

PLACES TO STAY
1 Swift House Inn
3 Linens & Lace
7 Middlebury Inn
10 Inn on the Green

PLACES TO EAT
2 Fire & Ice
8 Greenfield's Mercantile
9 Steve's Park Diner
13 Storm Cafe
15 Tully & Marie's
18 Angela's
19 Otter Creek Bakery
20 Baba's Market & Deli
21 Mister Up's

OTHER
4 Post Office
5 Parking
6 Vermont Book Shop
11 Addison County Chamber of Commerce Information Office
12 Frog Hollow Craft Center
14 The Bike Center
16 Vermont Transit Bus Stop
17 Sheldon Museum
22 Middlebury College Admissions Office
23 Middlebury College Museum of Art

John Deere was an apprentice blacksmith in Middlebury during the 1820s. He soon moved to Illinois, where he discovered that conventional plows had a hard time with the black prairie soils of the Midwest. He fashioned a plow with a one-piece steel plowshare and moldboard, which proved to be a major advance in plow technology.

Robert Frost (1874–1963) owned a farm in nearby Ripton, and he cofounded the renowned Bread Loaf School of English at nearby Middlebury College. (For more information on Robert Frost, see the Franconia section in the New Hampshire chapter.)

Orientation & Information

Middlebury stands on hilly ground straddling Otter Creek. Main St (VT 30) crosses the creek just above the Otter Creek Falls. The town green and Middlebury Inn are on the north side of the creek; Frog Hollow (a shopping complex in an old mill) and Middlebury College are to the south.

The Addison County Chamber of Commerce (☎ 802-388-7951, W www.midvermont. com, 2 Court St, Middlebury, VT 05753) is also on the north side of the creek and maintains an information office in a grand mansion facing the town green. It's open

9am to 5pm daily year-round, with additional Saturday hours (noon to 4pm) late June to mid-October.

The Vermont Book Shop (☎ 802-388-2061, 38 Main St) features a thorough selection of Vermont and Frost titles.

Middlebury College

For Middlebury College tours, contact the admissions office (☎ 802-443-3000), in the Emma Willard House, on the south side of S Main St (VT 30). Within the Center for the Arts, the **Middlebury College Museum of Art** (☎ 802-443-5007, S Main St/VT 30; admission free; open 10am-5pm Mon-Fri, noon-5pm Sat-Sun) has good collections of Cypriot pottery, 19th-century European and American sculpture, and modern prints.

Frog Hollow Craft Center

This outstanding Vermont state craft center (☎ 802-388-3177, 1 Mill St; open 10am-5pm Mon-Sat & 11am-4pm Sun year-round, with barely longer hours May-Dec) has an exhibition and sales gallery showing works by many Vermont artisans.

Sheldon Museum

This 1829 brick Federal-style mansion-turned-museum (☎ 802-388-2117, 1 Park St; adult/senior/child $4/3.50/2; open 10am-5pm Mon-Sat year-round & 11am-4pm Sun Oct; tours May-Oct) owes its existence to Henry Sheldon, a town clerk, church organist, storekeeper and avid collector of 19th-century Vermontiana. His collection runs the gamut from folk art and furniture to paintings and bric-a-brac.

University of Vermont Morgan Horse Farm

In 1789, Justin Morgan and his thoroughbred Arabian colt, Figure, came to Vermont from Springfield, MA. The colt grew to a small bay stallion, and the hardy farmers and loggers of Vermont looked upon him as pretty but not particularly useful. Morgan, however, proved to them the horse's surprising strength, agility, endurance and longevity. Renamed Justin Morgan after his owner, the little horse became the USA's first native breed, useful for heavy work, carriage draft, riding and even war service. Southwestern quarter horses have Morgan blood, as do the American Albino and the Palomino breeds. Pure Morgans are still raised today, with most of the excellent qualities that made them famous two centuries ago.

You can see 70 registered Morgans and tour their stables and the farm grounds at the University of Vermont's Morgan Horse Farm (☎ 802-388-2011, Horse Farm Rd; adult/teenager/child $4/3/1; open 9am-4pm daily May-Oct), about 3 miles from Middlebury. Drive west on VT 125, then north (right) onto Weybridge St (VT 23) to the farm.

Activities

The Bike Center (☎ 802-388-6666, 74 Main St), at Frog Hollow Alley, has equipment and information on regional biking (rentals $5/15/25 hourly/daily/weekend).

Otter Creek Brewing (☎ 802-388-0727, 800-473-0727, 85 Exchange St) makes a rich Stovepipe Porter, Copper Ale and other microbrews, some of which are organic. Free samples and guided tours of the brewing process from grain to glass are offered daily (1pm, 3pm, 5pm).

Atwood Orchards (☎ 802-897-5592, Barnum Hill, Shoreham) is one of the orchards on the outskirts of Middlebury that constitute Vermont's apple country. Trees are ripe for the pickin' in September and October. To reach this orchard, head west on VT 125, then south on VT 22A; it's located 3 miles south of Shoreham village.

There are lots of good day hikes in the region. Contact the **Green Mountain National Forest District Office** (☎ 802-388-4362, US 7) for free, detailed printouts; it's open 8am to 4:30pm weekdays.

Places to Stay

Camping There is little camping in or very close to Middlebury, but several places are within an easy drive.

Branbury State Park (☎ 802-247-5925, VT 53) Sites $14-20. Open May–mid-Oct. About 10 miles south of Middlebury on

Lake Dunmore, this place has 44 sites (five lean-tos) on 96 acres. Hiking trails lead to spectacular views.

DAR State Park (☎ 802-759-2354, VT 17) Sites $14-20. Open mid-May–early Sept. About 17 miles northwest of Middlebury, DAR enjoys a choice shore location on Lake Champlain between West Addison and Chimney Point. The park has 71 campsites (21 lean-tos) as well as boating, fishing and a playground.

Ten Acre Campground (☎ 802-759-2662, VT 125, Addison) Sites without/with hookups $14/20. Open May–mid-Oct. Fifteen miles west of Middlebury and a mile south of the Lake Champlain Bridge to New York, Ten Acre has 90 sites (78 with hookups), a large tenting area, a pool and lots of amusements.

Lake Dunmore Kampersville (☎ 802-352-4501, VT 53, Salisbury) Sites without/with hookups $19/28. Open May-Oct. A 10-minute drive from Middlebury, this campground has 210 sites with hookups and two swimming pools (one heated), as well as many other services.

Motels Two miles north of the town center is *Sugarhouse Motel* (☎ 802-388-2770, fax 802-388-8616, US 7) Doubles $49-99. Some rooms at this motel have kitchenettes.

Greystone Motel (☎ 802-388-4935, fax 802-388-7810, US 7) Doubles $55-95. Just 2 miles south of the town center, this trim motel has 10 rooms.

Blue Spruce Motel (☎ 802-388-4091, fax 802-388-3003, US 7) Doubles $75-85, suites $125-145. Blue Spruce has 24 comfortable rooms and suites 3 miles south of the town center. Suites are more like mini-apartments that can sleep four.

B&Bs You can walk to town from *Middlebury B&B* (☎ 802-388-4851, 174 Washington St Extension) Doubles without bath $75, with bath $90-100 with expanded buffet breakfast. Liz Hunt's B&B has four rooms (one with private bath). No credit cards are accepted.

Middlebury Inn (☎ 802-388-4961, 800-842-4666, fax 802-388-4563, 🌐 www.middlebury inn.com, 14 Court House Square/VT 7) Singles $75-175, doubles $88-185 with continental breakfast. The inn's fine old main building (1827) has formal public rooms but many of the 75 guest rooms are less desirable modern motel units in the back.

Waybury Inn (☎ 802-388-4015, 800-348-1810, fax 802-388-1248, 🌐 www.waybury inn.com, VT 125, East Middlebury) Doubles $95-195 with full breakfast. This former stagecoach stop has a popular pub and 14 guest rooms. The inn's exterior was used as the setting for the 1980s TV show *Newhart*, which popularized innkeeping.

Linens & Lace (☎ 802-388-0832, 29 Seminary St) Doubles without/with bath $99/129 with full breakfast. In a quiet residential neighborhood and within easy walking distance of the college and village, this place has five simple rooms and a large common area.

Swift House Inn (☎ 802-388-9925, fax 802-388-9927, 🌐 www.swifthouseinn.com, cnr Stewart Lane & US 7) Doubles $100-235 with continental breakfast. This grand white Federal house was built in 1814 and has a large gatehouse and carriage house surrounded by fine lawns and gardens. In addition to 21 luxurious rooms, the inn boasts a welcome steam room and a sauna.

Inn on the Green (☎ 802-388-7512, 888-244-7512, fax 802-388-4075, 🌐 www.innon thegreen.com, 19 S Pleasant St) Doubles $160-260 with continental breakfast. This 1803 Federal-style home offers seven spacious rooms in the house and four more modern rooms in an adjoining carriage house.

Places to Eat

Greenfield's Mercantile (☎ 802-388-8221, 46 Main St) Open daily. Get your smoothies and hemp cookies here. And while you're at it, pick up anything else made of hemp.

Otter Creek Bakery (☎ 802-388-3371, 14 College St) Sandwiches $4-5. Open 7am-6pm Mon-Sat, 7am-3pm Sun. This bakery, with some outdoor seating, is popular for takeout pastries, strong coffee and creative sandwiches. Traveling with a pooch? It'll lick your face if you buy it an Otter Creek dog biscuit.

Baba's Market & Deli (☎ 802-388-6408, 54 College St) Dishes $5-15. Open 11am-3pm Sun-Mon, 9am-8pm Tues-Sat. When Middlebury students tire of college 'mystery meat' served on campus, they come here for cheap calzones, Middle Eastern specialties and pizzas. Check out the dishes held in warming trays before deciding.

Steve's Park Diner (☎ 802-388-3297, 66 Merchants Row) Dishes $6-8. Open 7am-2pm daily. Perhaps the cheapest place in town, Steve's has small wooden booths, pancakes and sandwiches ($3 to $3.75). It's popular with returning students and young faculty families.

Storm Cafe (☎ 802-388-1063, 3 Mill St) Lunch $3-8, dinners-to-go $6-13. Open 11:30am-6pm Tues-Sat. In the basement of Frog Hollow Mill, this creekside cafe has soups, salads, sandwiches and the like. The blackboard menu highlights more substantial dishes like vegetarian lasagna to take away for a late-afternoon picnic or early dinner. In good weather, sit on the terrace overlooking Otter Creek.

Mister Up's (☎ 802-388-6724, 25 Bakery Lane) Dishes $6-14. Open 11:30am-midnight daily. Also overlooking the creek, this is basically a steak, burger and seafood sort of place, with a portobello sandwich or two thrown in for good measure.

Angela's (☎ 802-388-0002, 86 Main St) Dishes average $9. Open 11am-2am Mon-Sat. More a place to drink than eat, Angela's nonetheless offers decent Italian fare like pasta ($5 to $7). A limited menu is served 10pm to midnight, after which only drinks are served.

Tully & Marie's (☎ 802-388-4182, 5 Bakery Lane) Lunch $6-7, dinner $9-20. Overlooking the creek, Tully and Marie's features lots of delicious vegetarian and vegan dishes. At lunch, try the Indian curry soup with chickpeas, a black-bean burrito or a sandwich. Dinner ranges from pad thai to steak.

Fire & Ice (☎ 802-388-7166, 26 Seymour St) Lunch $8-14, dinner $15-25. Open for lunch Tues-Sun & dinner daily. Known for its prime rib and steaks, Fire & Ice also has a good salad bar.

Getting There & Away

Vermont Transit (☎ 802-864-6811, 800-552-8737) operates three buses daily on the Burlington-Rutland-Albany route, which stops in Middlebury. It takes an hour to ride from Middlebury to Burlington ($8.50). You can connect at Albany with buses for New York City and at Burlington with buses for Montreal, Canada. The bus stops at the Exxon Station (☎ 802-388-4373, 16 Court St).

By car, it takes about the same amount of time (an hour) to get from Middlebury to either Warren/Waitsfield or Burlington.

RIPTON

Ten miles east of Middlebury on VT 125, Ripton is a beautiful little hamlet set in the Vermont mountains. Two white churches, a few houses, a schoolhouse and a big old country house converted into an inn – that's Ripton. Sit on the lawn in the sun, go down to the river and pitch stones, read, walk, think, talk.

Chipman Inn (☎ 802-388-2390, 800-890-2390, W www.chipmaninn.com, VT 125) Doubles $105-135 with full breakfast. Open Dec-Mar & May-Oct. The eight-room inn, a beautiful Federal house built in 1828, is big on Frostiana and also on the peace and quiet that Robert Frost sought. The warming hearth and woodstove are key in wintertime. Since guests dine at communal tables, there is a palpable sense of camaraderie here.

Frost spent 23 years on a nearby farm, and just east of Ripton you'll find the **Robert Frost Wayside Recreation Area**. A forest trail, less than a mile in length, is marked with signs with quotations from the poet's works. From Ripton, take VT 125 east for 2 miles, and look for the trail on the right side of the road.

For information on the **Bread Loaf School of English and Writers' Conference** in Ripton, contact Middlebury College (☎ 802-443-5418).

WARREN & WAITSFIELD

North of Killington, VT 100 is one of the finest stretches of road in the country – a bucolic mix of rolling hills, covered bridges, ubiquitous white steeples and farmland so fertile you feel like jumping out of the car and digging your hands in the soil. An hour north of Killington, you'll reach Waitsfield and Warren, towns you might have seen in the advertisements for Vermont tourism. They're places where nothing ever changes. This is especially true of Sugarbush and the nearby Mad River ski area, both popular with locals. Mad River still has a chairlift for single skiers, and both mountains feature the New England skiing of yore, a time when trails were cut by hand and weren't much wider than a hiking path.

Orientation

The 'gap roads' that run east to west over the Green Mountains offer some of the most picturesque views of the region. VT 73 crosses the Brandon Gap (2170 feet) from Brandon to Rochester and Talcville. VT 125 crosses the Middlebury Gap from East Middlebury (2149 feet) to Hancock. A narrow local road crosses Lincoln Gap (2424 feet) from Bristol to Warren. (The Lincoln Gap road is closed in wintertime due to heavy snowfall.)

VT 17 crosses the Appalachian Gap (at 2356 feet) from Bristol to Irasville and Waitsfield, and this route offers the best views of all.

Information

The Sugarbush Chamber of Commerce (☎ 802-496-3409, 800-828-4748, W www .madrivervalley.com), on VT 100 in Waitsfield, is open 9am to 5pm weekdays. During the summer, fall and winter tourism seasons, there are additional Saturday hours from 10am to 5pm.

Local telephone calls from public phones are free in Warren and Waitsfield, courtesy of the Waitsfield-Fayston Telephone Company. Imagine that.

Skiing

The nature of New England downhill skiing is flying down serpentine trails around corners, down quick dips and through tight slots, always in the company of trees. On the best trails, the woods surround you as you whiz by a rolling tapestry of maple, oak, birch, spruce, pine and balsam. That's exactly what happens at **Sugarbush** (☎ 802-583-2381). Paradise, Castlerock and the backcountry runs in between braid through the forest like a crazed snake.

Subaru wagons with Vermont license plates often have bumper stickers that offer this dare, 'Mad River Glen, Ski It If You Can.' Bumper stickers don't lie. **Mad River Glen** (☎ 802-496-3551) is the nastiest lift-served ski area in the East, a combination of rocks, ice, trees – and snow, of course. It's truly a place where the ski slope seems little removed from the mountain's gnarled primal state.

Local ski touring centers feature more than 100 miles of groomed cross-country trails. Call the Sugarbush Chamber of Commerce (see above) for information. One of the biggest ski touring centers is **Ole's Cross Country Ski Center** (☎ 802-496-3430, 2355 Airport Rd, Warren).

Other Activities

Canoeing and kayaking are prime on the Mad River (along VT 100) and White River (along VT 100 near Hancock) in April, May and early June, and on the larger Winooski River (along I-89) in the spring, summer and fall.

Clearwater Sports (☎ 802-496-2708, VT 100, Waitsfield) rents canoes ($30-50 daily, depending on whether you need shuttle service), kayaks, river-floating tubes, in-line skates, bicycles ($20 daily), snowshoes, telemark demo gear, and many other types of sports equipment. Clearwater also organizes one-day guided canoe and kayak trips ($55 per person for four hours, including lessons).

Sugarbush Soaring (☎ 802-496-2290, off VT 100; rides May-Oct) offers an unconventional activity. You take off from Warren-Sugarbush Airport in a glider towed by a conventional aircraft. After gaining altitude, you cast off the tow rope and soar quietly through the skies above the mountains and river valleys, kept aloft by updrafts of warm air. A glider can accommodate one or two

VERMONT

passengers, but the two-person craft has a weight restriction of 300lb. Rides last 20 to 30 minutes and cost $97 to $108 for one person, $119 to $152 for two.

Vermont Icelandic Horse Farm *(☎ 802-496-7141, N Basin Rd, Waitsfield)*, 1000 yards south of the town common, takes folks on half-day ($60) or full-day jaunts ($125 with lunch) year-round. Icelandic horses are fairly easy to ride, even for novice riders.

Places to Stay

Because the Sugarbush area is primarily active in the winter ski season, there are no campgrounds nearby. Many area accommodations are condominiums marketed to the ski trade. The largest selection of condos is rented by **Sugarbush Village** *(☎ 800-451-4326, W www.sugarbushvillage.com)*, located right at the ski area. Rentals cost about $90 to $550 per day, depending on condo size, location, date of arrival and length of stay.

Hyde Away *(☎ 802-496-2322, 800-777-4933, fax 802-496-7829, W www.hyde awayinn.com, VT 17, Waitsfield)* Doubles $59-159 with full breakfast. This 1830 farmhouse, sawmill and barn has its own mountain-bike touring center and 12 rooms, suites and bunks.

The Garrison *(☎ 802-496-2352, 800-766-7829, fax 802-496-9586, VT 17, Waitsfield)* Doubles $65-140. Although mainly a condo complex, with one- to four-bedroom units, the motel section rents basic rooms with kitchenettes.

Inn at Mad River Barn *(☎ 802-496-3310, 800-631-0466, fax 802-496-6696, W www .madriverbarn.com, VT 17, Waitsfield)* Doubles $65-135 with full breakfast. One of the last old-time Vermont lodges, this place rents 15 rooms, some of which are in the annex with queen-size beds, steam baths and TVs.

The Inn at Round Barn Farm *(☎/fax 802-496-2276, 800-721-8029, W www.round barninn.com, 1661 E Warren Rd, Waitsfield)* Doubles $130-295 with huge country breakfast. This premier, elegant inn gets its name from the adjacent 1910 round barn, one of

the few round barns remaining in Vermont. The barn's lower level has an indoor 60-foot lap pool; outdoor pursuits revolve around snowshoeing, cross-country skiing and off-road driving. The decidedly upscale inn features 12 guest rooms with mountain views, gas fireplaces, canopy beds and antiques.

Places to Eat & Drink

Skiers' taverns abound in this area. Restaurants are quite busy in ski season, a bit sleepy at other times.

The Warren Store *(☎ 802-496-3864, Main St, Warren)* Dishes $4-6. Open daily. This atmospheric country store serves the area's biggest and best sandwiches. Eat on the deck overlooking the waterfall in the summer (except when there are swarms of bees).

American Flatbread *(☎ 802-496-8856, VT 100, Waitsfield)* Flatbreads $9-18. Open only for dinner Fri-Sat. These excellent pizza pies are cooked in a primitive wood-fired oven. In fact, the Revolution Flatbread is so good that it's distributed to grocery stores throughout New England.

Miguel's Stowe Away *(☎ 802-583-3858, Sugarbush Access Rd, Warren)* Dishes $9-16. Open for dinner. Miguel's serves Americanized Mexican dishes like tacos and *mole poblano*. The white-corn tortilla chips are pretty darn good.

Spotted Cow *(☎ 802-496-5151, Bridge St Marketplace, Waitsfield)* Lunch $9-12, dinner $17-25. Open Tues-Sun. Just off VT 100, locals rave about the Spotted Cow, owned by a Bermudian. You can't go wrong with a bowl of the Bermudian fish chowder ($6), but then again, the smoked chicken salad at lunch and the pan-fried rainbow trout at dinner are excellent, too.

John Egan's Big World Pub and Grill *(☎ 802-496-3033, VT 100, Waitsfield)* Dishes $10-17. Open for dinner. Don't let the exterior décor fool you. Extreme skier John Egan has hired a renowned chef from Montpelier's New England Culinary Institute, and the venison and lamb dishes are arguably the finest in the Green Mountain State.

The Common Man *(☎ 802-583-2800, 3209 German Flats Rd, Warren)* Mains

$13-25. Open Tues-Sun. Despite its proletarian name, the fancy favorite specializes in French, Italian and a smattering of other European cuisines. It's rather like dining around the Continent without leaving Vermont, especially since it's housed in a restored 19th-century barn. The wine cellar is fine.

Getting There & Away
Area bus and train travel are impractical because the nearest Vermont Transit and Amtrak stations are in Waterbury, 14 miles north of Waitsfield. (See Stowe, later, for details.)

From Waitsfield, it's 22 miles (40 minutes) to Stowe via VT 100, about the same if you're taking a detour to Montpelier (via VT 100 north to I-89 south).

Northern Vermont

Home to the state capital, Montpelier, northern Vermont also contains the state's largest city, Burlington. Never fear, though, this area still features all of the rural charms found elsewhere. Even within Burlington, cafe-lined streets coexist with scenic paths along Lake Champlain. Farther north, the pastoral Northeast Kingdom offers a full range of outdoor activities, from skiing to biking, in the heart of the mountains.

MONTPELIER
Montpelier (mont-**peel**-yer), with its population of 8000 souls, would qualify as a large village in some countries. But in sparsely populated Vermont, it is the quaint capital, and perhaps the most charming capital in the country. You might want to visit Montpelier for a good meal or if you are intensely interested in Vermont history and affairs.

Orientation & Information
Montpelier is quite small. Find the golden dome of the State House to find the three major sights.

The information kiosk on State St, opposite the post office, is open in the summer. The Vermont Chamber of Commerce

(☎ 802-223-3443, fax 802-223-4257, **W** www .vtchamber.com) distributes a wealth of information during the planning stages of your trip.

Look for the worthwhile Bear Pond Books (☎ 802-229-0774, 77 Main St).

State House
The front doors of the State House (☎ 802-828-2228, State St; admission free; open 8am-4pm Mon-Sat) are guarded by a massive statue of Revolutionary War hero Ethan Allen. (See the boxed text 'Ethan Allen & Vermont,' in the Facts about New England chapter.) And the gold dome was built of granite quarried in nearby Barre in 1836. You can wander around the building during weekday business hours, or take one of the free tours given on the half-hour, 10am to 3:30pm (11am to 2:30pm Saturday) from July to mid-October.

Vermont Historical Society
Next door to the State House, the Pavilion Building houses this surprisingly excellent museum (☎ 802-828-2291, State St; adult/ senior & student $3/2; open 9am-4:30pm Tues-Fri, 9am-4pm Sat, noon-4pm Sun), devoted to all that's fascinating about Vermont. At press time, the museum was closed through fall 2002 for expansion and renovation.

TW Wood Art Gallery
This gallery (☎ 802-828-8743, 36 College St; adult $2, child under 12 yrs free, admission free on Sun; open noon-4pm Tues-Sun), at E State St on the Vermont College campus, was founded in 1895 by Thomas Waterman Wood (1823–1903), a native of Montpelier who gained a regional reputation for his portraits and genre paintings. The museum has a large collection of Wood's art, as well as Depression-era paintings. Changing exhibits, especially of arts made in Vermont, fill the main gallery.

If you enjoy crafts shows, the Festival of Vermont Crafts takes place in Montpelier the first weekend of October. The show affords an opportunity to enjoy local crafts and good fall foliage simultaneously.

Progressive Politics

Vermont's independent streak is as long and deep as a vein of marble. Senator Jim Jeffords turned the Senate and the country upside down in 2001 when he switched from Republican to Independent because of the rightward swing Republicans were taking after Bush's election in 2000. With that defection, the scales of an evenly divided Senate tipped back to the Democrats by one vote. Vermont's singular Independent representative, Bernie Sanders, is a registered Socialist.

In April 2000, the Vermont legislature passed and Governor Howard Dean signed HB847 into law. This civil union law declares gay couples have most of the same rights and privileges as heterosexuals. It is the only US state to acknowledge these unions. While it does not put civil unions on the same par as marriage, the law does provide gay couples with legal standing on issues ranging from terminal care and child custody to transfer of property and immunity from compelled testimony. The governor and other pro-CU supporters were harshly criticized for their position and you will still see 'Take Back Vermont' signs posted on barns around the state. Exit polls in the November 2000 election suggested that the law is supported by a slim margin, but most Vermonters have chosen to move on.

Places to Stay

Betsy's Bed & Breakfast (☎ 802-229-0466, fax 802-229-5412, W www.betsysbnb.com, 74 E State St) Doubles $60-105 with full breakfast. This restored Victorian house within the historic district has 12 nicely done rooms and suites. Updated amenities include phone and TV; the suites even have kitchens.

The Inn at Montpelier (☎ 802-223-2727, fax 802-223-0722, W www.innatmontpelier .com, 147 Main St) Doubles $104-177 with continental breakfast. Fortunately, the state capital has a first-rate place to sleep, one that's worth a detour. The 19-room inn, made up of two refurbished Federal houses right in the heart of town, boasts deluxe rooms with fireplaces.

Places to Eat

Home to the New England Culinary Institute (NECI; ☎ 802-223-6324), one of the country's finest cooking schools, Montpelier is an excellent place to stop for a meal. NECI runs three restaurants in town. Depending on the student chefs of the day, you can either have one of the best meals in New England at an affordable price or a damn good attempt. Be a guinea pig and support someone's education.

La Brioche (☎ 802-229-0443, 89 Main St) Sandwiches $5. Open 6:30am-7pm Mon-Fri & 7:30am-5pm Sat-Sun. NECI's first restaurant is a casual bakery and cafe offering soups and sandwiches on homemade bread, among other things. They start running out of sandwich fixings at about 2pm, so you'd better time it right if you're hungry.

Main Street Bar & Grill (☎ 802-223-3188, 118 Main St) Lunch averages $7, dinner $14, Sunday brunch $15. Open daily. Run by first-year NECI students, the grill's fare might feature almond-crusted trout and bouillabaisse. Brunch is an all-you-can-eat affair.

Sarducci's (☎ 802-223-0229, 3 Main St) Lunch $6-14, dinner $8-16. Open 11:30am-9:30pm Mon-Sat, dinner Sun. If you don't feel like tossing the dice and risking a meal made by students, head to this standby. In an old railroad station overlooking the Winooski River, Sarducci's features Italian dishes like chicken marsala, pastas, wood-oven pizza and eggplant parmesan. Lunch portions are very generous.

Chef's Table (☎ 802-229-9202, 118 Main St) Mains $14-28. Open Mon-Sat. Since this upstairs restaurant is run by second-year NECI students, the food is far more innovative than at the Grill. Specials change nightly but you'll always find veal chops, lamb dishes and rosemary seared swordfish ($18.50).

Getting There & Away

Vermont Transit (☎ 802-864-6811, 800-552-8737) runs four buses daily between Boston and Burlington, stopping in Montpelier at the main terminal (☎ 802-223-7112, 1 Taylor St). Boston to Montpelier costs $42 (four hours); Montpelier to Burlington costs $9.50 (one hour).

Amtrak's *Vermonter* (☎ 800-872-7245) stops in Montpelier on its way to St Albans. The fare from Brattleboro to Montpelier is $23 to $35, depending on the day of the week. See the Getting There & Around section at the beginning of this chapter for more details on the *Vermonter*'s route.

From Montpelier to Burlington, it's an easy drive on I-89 (38 miles, 45 minutes).

BARRE

Montpelier's smaller neighbor Barre (pronounced 'bar-ee') touts itself as the 'granite capital of the world.'

Rock of Ages Quarries

The Rock of Ages Quarries (☎ 802-476-3119, 773 Quarry Hill Rd), 4 miles southeast of Barre off I-89 exit 6 off VT 14, are the world's largest granite quarries, covering 50 acres and mining a vein that's 6 miles long, 4 miles wide and 10 miles deep. The beautiful, durable, granular stone, formed more than 330 million years ago, is used for tombstones, building facades, monuments, curbstones and tabletops.

Visit the Rock of Ages Visitor Center between 8:30am and 5pm Monday to Saturday; admission is free. A quarry tour costs adult/senior/child $4/3.50/1.50 and includes a short video and historical exhibits. The 35-minute guided caravan tour of an active quarry heads off-site. At the **Rock of Ages Manufacturing Division**, open 8am to 3:30pm daily, you can see granite products being made – some with an accuracy that approaches 25-millionths of an inch. Or follow a self-guided quarry tour.

Hope Cemetery

Where do old granite carvers go when they die? In Barre, they end up in Hope Cemetery, just a mile north of US 302 on VT 14.

To granite carvers, tombstones aren't dreary reminders of mortality but artful celebrations of the carver's life. And what celebrations! A carver and his wife sit up in bed holding hands, smiling for eternity; a granite cube balances precariously on one corner; a carver's favorite armchair is reproduced, larger than life and tellingly empty. If a cemetery can ever be fun, this one is. It's open all the time.

STOWE

In a cozy valley where the West Branch River flows into the Little River, Stowe has a certain commercial, Vermont-style charm. Its small center is pretty without being prim. Its inns and hotels, ranged along Mountain Rd up to the ski slopes of Mt Mansfield (4393 feet), have adopted central European names to go with their architecture. Stowe also has central European weather, with a lavish amount of rain and snowfall. Despite occasional storms, though, the town's far-flung visitors find plenty to do.

History

Founded in 1794, Stowe was a simple, pretty, backwoods farming town until 1859, when the Summit House was built as a summer resort atop Mt Mansfield. Skiing was introduced around 1912, and in the early 1930s Civilian Conservation Corps (CCC) workers cut the first real ski trails in the mountain's slopes.

In the late 1930s, the Mt Mansfield Corporation was established, and after it installed the longest and highest chairlift in the USA, skiing really took off in Stowe.

An Austrian ski champion named Sepp Ruschp was hired as the resort's first ski school director, and he eventually rose to become head of the corporation. At the time of Ruschp's death in 1990, Stowe was among the best-regarded ski resorts in the eastern USA, a reputation it still maintains.

Orientation & Information

Stowe is 10 miles north of I-89 exit 10, on VT 100. Waterbury, just 3 miles north of I-89 on the way to Stowe, is the home of Ben & Jerry's premium ice cream company.

VERMONT

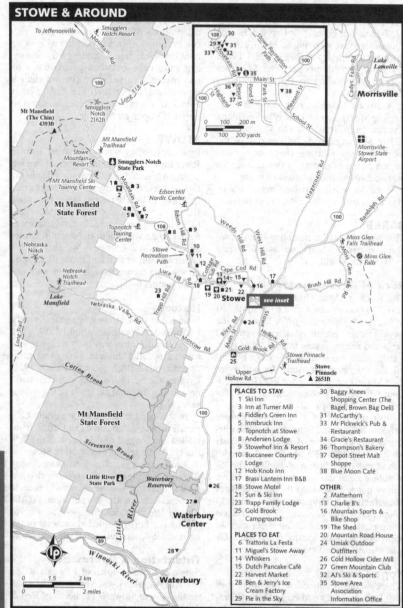

STOWE & AROUND

To Jeffersonville
Smugglers' Mountain Rd
Smugglers Notch Resort
Long Trail
108
Mt Mansfield (The Chin) 4393ft
Smugglers Notch 2162ft
Mt Mansfield Trailhead
Stowe Mountain Resort
Mt Mansfield Ski Touring Center
Smugglers Notch State Park
Mt Mansfield State Forest
Mountain Rd
Edson Hill Nordic Center
Topnotch Touring Center
108
Stowe Recreation Path
Nebraska Notch
Nebraska Notch Trailhead
Lake Mansfield
Nebraska Valley Rd
Edson Hill Rd
Weeds Hill Rd
West Hill Rd
Cape Cod Rd
Cottage Club Rd
Luce Hill Rd
Trapp Hill Rd
Moscow Rd
Long Trail
Cotton Brook
Mt Mansfield State Forest
Stevenson Brook
Little River State Park
Waterbury Reservoir
Waterbury Center
100
89
Little River
Winooski River
Waterbury
Stowe
see inset
Main St
River Rd
Stowe Hollow Rd
Gold Brook Rd
Upper Hollow Rd
Stowe Pinnacle Trailhead
Stowe Pinnacle 2651ft
Brush Hill Rd
Moss Glen Falls Trailhead
Moss Glen Falls
Moss Glen Falls Rd
Stagecoach Rd
Randolph Rd
100
Cadys Falls Rd
Lake Lamoille
Morrisville
Morrisville-Stowe State Airport
108
100
Mountain Rd
Stowe Recreation Path
Main St
Highland St
Depot St
Pond St
Park St
Pleasant St
School St
100
0   100   200 m
0   100   200 yards

PLACES TO STAY
1 Ski Inn
3 Inn at Turner Mill
4 Fiddler's Green Inn
5 Innsbruck Inn
7 Topnotch at Stowe
8 Andersen Lodge
9 Stowehof Inn & Resort
10 Buccaneer Country Lodge
12 Hob Knob Inn
17 Brass Lantern Inn B&B
18 Stowe Motel
21 Sun & Ski Inn
23 Trapp Family Lodge
25 Gold Brook Campground

PLACES TO EAT
6 Trattoria La Festa
11 Miguel's Stowe Away
14 Whiskers
15 Dutch Pancake Café
22 Harvest Market
28 Ben & Jerry's Ice Cream Factory
29 Pie in the Sky

30 Baggy Knees Shopping Center (The Bagel, Brown Bag Deli)
31 McCarthy's
33 Mr Pickwick's Pub & Restaurant
34 Gracie's Restaurant
36 Thompson's Bakery
37 Depot Street Malt Shoppe
38 Blue Moon Café

OTHER
2 Matterhorn
13 Charlie B's
16 Mountain Sports & Bike Shop
19 The Shed
20 Mountain Road House
24 Umiak Outdoor Outfitters
26 Cold Hollow Cider Mill
27 Green Mountain Club
32 AJ's Ski & Sports
35 Stowe Area Association Information Office

0   1.5   3 km
0   1   2 miles

VERMONT

The village of Stowe, at the intersection of VT 100 and VT 108, is small and easily negotiated on foot. However, many of the town's hotels and restaurants are spread out along Mountain Rd (VT 108, officially named the 10th Mountain Division Memorial Hwy), which goes northwest from the town past Mt Mansfield and through the dramatic, rocky gorge known as Smugglers Notch to Jeffersonville (18 miles). Smugglers Notch is closed by snow in the winter months.

The Stowe Area Association (☎ 802-253-7321, 800-247-8693, PO Box 1320, Stowe, VT 05672) is on Main St in the village. It is open daily (9am to 8pm Monday to Saturday and 9am to 5pm Sunday summer, fall and winter; 10am to 6pm Monday to Friday and 9am to 5pm Saturday and Sunday in spring). The association is well organized and can make reservations for your whole package: air travel, rental cars and local accommodations.

Ben & Jerry's Ice Cream Factory
Worked up an appetite and feel you deserve a treat? Head to Waterbury, just south of Stowe, and the prominent Ben & Jerry's Ice Cream Factory (☎ 802-882-1260, VT 100; adult/senior $2/1.75, child under 12 yrs free; open 9am-8pm daily July & Aug, 9am-6pm daily Sept & Oct, 10am-5pm daily Nov-May, 9am-5pm daily June). Take exit 10 off I-89 and go north on VT 100 toward Stowe. The factory is on a hilltop beside the road.

Many years ago, childhood buddies Ben Cohen and Jerry Greenfield sent away $5 for information about how to make ice cream. They opened up shop in a disused gas station in downtown Burlington, and the ice cream shop-cum-luncheonette prospered – partly because of their unorthodox flavor combinations. As the super-premium (full-cream) ice creams became wildly popular, the partners abandoned the gas station location and took to shipping their tasty product nationwide. In 2000 they sold their company to the Dutch and British conglomerate Unilever, but Ben and Jerry are still on the board of directors and operate a foundation funded by the sale of

the ice cream company. You can tour the factory and eat free ice cream. Tours depart every 10 to 30 minutes depending on the season, and they're usually most crowded in the afternoon.

Cold Hollow Cider Mill
Several miles north of Ben & Jerry's on VT 100, you'll want to stop at New England's largest producer of fresh apple cider (☎ 802-244-8771, VT 100; open 8am-7pm daily July–mid-Oct, 8am-6pm daily mid-Oct–June). Sample the goods and stock up on other Vermont goodies such as maple syrup, apple jellies, cheddar cheese and honey mustards.

Skiing
Downhill You're new to the sport, your wife's an expert and the kids love bopping down the intermediate slopes. No worries. Visit **Stowe Mountain Resort** (☎ 802-253-7311). With 48 trails (15% beginner, 60% intermediate, 25% expert), the variety of terrain at Stowe is unparalleled in the East. Beginning skiers can chute through the scenic 3.7-mile Toll Road or venture to Spruce Peak; middle-of-the-roadies can glide down Tyro or Lullaby Lane; the hardcore can tackle the Front Four or Nose Dive.

'The family that skies together, stays together' should be the motto for **Smuggler's Notch Resort** (☎ 800-451-8752, VT 108), just north of Stowe village. The resort's fully equipped condos cater extensively to families, and the lineup of activities for children is longer than a child's wish list for Santa.

The complex, spread out over three mountains, includes indoor pools, outdoor skating rinks, a tube-sliding hill that is lighted at night, 14 miles of cross-country trails and a magic learning trail, where young children ski up to exhibit panels that teach them about various winter animals. Other activities include horse-drawn sleigh rides and nightly family entertainment. Junior won't get bored here, nor will his parents.

Cross-Country With four of the top ski touring centers in the state, including the **Trapp Family Lodge** (☎ *802-253-8511*), made famous by Maria von Trapp, Stowe is easily the Northeast's premier cross-country skiing destination. The other centers, linked by some 200 miles of trails, are the **Mt Mansfield Ski Touring Center** (☎ *802-253-7311*), the **Edson Hill Nordic Center** (☎ *802-253-8954*) and the **Topnotch Touring Center** (☎ *802-253-8585*). The centers connect via some tough backcountry ski runs, like the **Bruce Trail** and **Teardrop Trail**, two of the earliest downhill trails in the country (cut by the Civilian Conservation Corps in the early 1930s).

Within this wide network of trails that traverse mountains and skirt lakes is one 280-mile-long route that runs the length of Vermont. Called the **Catamount Trail**, it starts in southern Vermont at Readsboro and ends at North Troy on the Canadian border. In between lies some of the finest skiing in the East, from backcountry trails that are etched in Mt Mansfield to 11 ski touring centers located in the Green Mountain National Forest, such as Blueberry Hill and Mountain Top. Contact the informative Catamount Trail Association for more information (☎ 802-864-5794).

Hiking

The **Stowe Recreation Path** is the obvious choice for a short walk. It follows the course of the Waterbury River (and Mountain Rd) for 5.3 miles from the village northwest to the Stowe Mountain Resort. The path is for bicycle, roller-skate and foot traffic only.

The **Green Mountain Club** (☎ *802-244-7037, 4711 Waterbury-Stowe Rd, Waterbury*

Center, VT 05677), 5 miles south of Stowe, was founded in 1910 to maintain the Long Trail. The club also publishes some excellent hikers' materials, available from the Green Mountain Club's offices or by mail. For more information on the Long Trail and trail guidebooks, see the boxed text 'A Month in the Woods.'

The Green Mountain Club recommends the following day hikes around Stowe:

Moss Glen Falls
Easy, half-mile, half-hour. Follow VT 100 for 3 miles north of Stowe Center and bear right onto Randolph Rd. Go three-tenths of a mile and turn right for the parking area, then walk along the obvious path to reach a deep cascade and waterfalls.

Stowe Pinnacle
Moderate difficulty, 2.8 miles, two hours. Follow VT 100 south of Stowe and turn east onto Gold Brook Rd, proceeding for three-tenths of a mile; cross a bridge and turn left to continue along Gold Brook Rd. About 1.6 miles later, you come to Upper Hollow Rd; turn right and go to the top of the hill, just past Pinnacle Rd, to find the small parking area on the left. The hike to Stowe Pinnacle, a rocky outcrop offering sweeping mountain views, is short but steep.

Nebraska Notch
Moderate difficulty, 3.2 miles, 2¼ hours. Take VT 100 south of Stowe and turn west onto River Rd, which becomes Moscow Rd. Continue for 5.8 miles to the Lake Mansfield Trout Club. The trail follows an old logging road for a while and then ascends past beaver dams and grand views to join the Long Trail at Taylor Lodge.

Mt Mansfield
Difficult, 7 miles, five hours. Follow VT 108 west from Stowe to the Long Trail parking area, seven-tenths of a mile past Stowe Mountain Resort ski area. Mt Mansfield is thought by some to resemble a man's profile in repose. Follow the Long Trail to the 'chin,' then go south along the summit ridge to Profanity Trail; follow that aptly named route to Taft Lodge, then take the Long Trail back down.

Bicycling

Several bike shops can supply you with wheels for cruising along the Stowe Recreation Path. Rent bikes from the **Mountain Sports & Bike Shop** (☎ *802-253-7919, 580 Mountain Rd; $11/25 per 2 hr/day for* *recreation path bikes, $20/30 per 4 hr/day for mountain bikes; open year-round).* There's also **AJ's Ski & Sports** (☎ *802-253-4593, Mountain Rd),* which rents in-line skates ($7/24 per hour/day) and bikes.

Snowshoeing

Tubbs snowshoes (☎ *802-253-7398)* are manufactured in Stowe and you can purchase or rent them at **Umiak Outdoor Outfitters** (see below). Umiak guides also lead popular three-hour snowshoeing jaunts, lit by headlamp or moonlight, for $38 to $48 per person.

Canoeing & Kayaking

Umiak Outdoor Outfitters (☎ *802-253-2317, 849 S Main St; $30-35 daily)* rents canoes and kayaks and offers two- and four-hour lake and river shuttle trips (paddlers and canoes are shuttled to the river and then picked up at the put-out) for $25 to $35 per person. It also has a seasonal location on Lake Elmore.

Places to Stay

Stowe has a wide variety of lodging, with about 75 inns, motels and B&Bs; many are along Mountain Rd. The Stowe Area Association (☎ 802-253-7321, 800-247-8693, fax 802-253-2159) helps with reservations.

Camping Just north of I-89 is ***Little River State Park*** (☎ *802-244-7103, Little River Rd, Waterbury)* Sites $14-20. Open late May–mid-Oct. This place has 101 campsites (20 lean-tos) next to Waterbury Reservoir, on which you can boat, fish and swim. Head 1½ miles west of Waterbury on US 2, then 3½ miles north on Little River Rd.

Smugglers Notch State Park (☎ *802-253-4014, 7248 Mountain Rd)* Sites $14-20. Open late May–mid-Oct. This 25-acre park, 8 miles northwest of Stowe, has just 35 sites (14 of which are lean-tos).

Gold Brook Campground (☎ *802-253-7683, VT 100)* Sites without/with hookups $18/29. Open year-round. About 7½ miles north of I-89, this campground has 100 campsites (half with hookups), free hot showers and many services. You may need to reserve a site in advance for the busy summer months.

Motels A nicely landscaped inn adjacent to the recreation path is ***Sun & Ski Inn*** (☎ *802-253-7159, 800-448-5223, fax 802-253-7150,* Ⓦ *www.stowesunandski.com, 1613 Mountain Rd)* Doubles $69-101. This 25-room lodge has an outdoor swimming pool (heated to 102°F in winter) and a sauna.

Innsbruck Inn (☎ *802-253-8582, 800-225-8582, fax 802-253-2260, 4361 Mountain Rd)* Doubles $79-120 with full breakfast in winter. A modern interpretation of a traditional Alpine inn, the 24 rooms and efficiencies here are comfy and well equipped. Inquire about the five-bedroom chalet.

Stowe Motel (☎ *802-253-7629, 800-829-7629, fax 802-253-9971,* Ⓦ *www.stowemotel .com, 2043 Mountain Rd)* Doubles $79-89. In addition to 21 efficiencies, suites and houses, this motel's amenities include a swimming pool, tennis court, badminton and lawn games. You can also borrow bicycles for the recreation path.

Hob Knob Inn (☎ *802-253-8549, 800-245-8540, fax 802-253-7621,* Ⓦ *www.hobknobinn .com, 2364 Mountain Rd)* Rooms $85-125. These 21 large rooms (some with fireplace, some with efficiency kitchens) are nicely set back from the road.

Inns Near the Ski Inn, you'll find ***Fiddler's Green Inn*** (☎ *802-253-8124, 800-882-5346,* Ⓦ *www.fiddlersgreeninn.com, 4859 Mountain Rd)* Doubles $60-90. This 1820s farmhouse has rustic pine walls, a fieldstone fireplace and seven guest rooms geared to outdoor enthusiasts. Not surprisingly, guests congregate around the fieldstone hearth; it's all quite homey.

Inn at Turner Mill (☎ *802-253-2062, 800-992-0016,* Ⓦ *www.turnermill.com, 56 Turner Mill Lane)* Units $75-210 (see below). Hidden on 9 acres next to Notch Brook, at Mountain Rd a mile from Stowe's lifts, this inn offers an assortment of efficiencies in a rambling wood building. The inn attracts and encourages folks who appreciate the area's natural resources, and the innkeepers help plan activities. Accommodations range

VERMONT

from simple rooms for two people ($75 in summer with breakfast, $95 in winter without breakfast) to two-bedroom apartments for four people ($158/210 summer/winter).

Buccaneer Country Lodge (☎ 802-253-4772, 800-543-1293, fax 802-253-9486, W www.buccaneerlodge.com, 3214 Mountain Rd) Doubles $75-295 with full breakfast. All 12 rooms here (most with full kitchens) enjoy excellent views of Mt Mansfield, only a 3-mile drive away.

Andersen Lodge (☎ 802-253-7336, 800-336-7336, fax 802-253-4715, 3430 Mountain Rd) Doubles $68-120 with full breakfast. This 17-room Tyrolean-style inn has a good dining room, as well as a swimming pool, tennis courts and sauna.

Brass Lantern Inn B&B (☎ 802-253-2229, 800-729-2980, fax 802-253-7425, W www.brasslanterninn.com, VT 100) Doubles $90-150 with full breakfast. Just north of town on VT 100, this beautifully renovated inn has nine spacious rooms with fireplaces, stenciling, antiques and quilts.

Trapp Family Lodge (☎ 802-253-8511, 800-826-7000, fax 802-253-5740, W www.trappfamily.com, 700 Trapp Hill Rd) Doubles $100-350. Off Luce Hill Rd from Mountain Rd, the hills are alive with the sound of tourism at this Austrian-style chalet, built by Maria von Trapp of *The Sound of Music* fame. There are 116 motel and lodge rooms, as well as time-share units. The 2700-acre spread offers excellent hiking, snowshoeing and cross-country skiing.

Stowehof Inn & Resort (☎ 802-253-9722, 800-932-7136, fax 802-253-7513, W www.stowehofinn.com, 434 Edson Hill Rd) Doubles $103-275 with full breakfast. In addition to a dramatic hillside location, this rustic 44-room inn has a very good dining room and many spa-like amenities including an indoor pool.

Ski Inn (☎ 802-253-4050, fax 802-253-2078, W www.ski-inn.com, 5037 Mountain Rd) Doubles $110 with full breakfast & dinner in winter, $55-65 with continental breakfast in summer. This traditional inn, only a mile from the ski area, opened in

1941 just after the first chairlift was built. Its 10 clean and simple rooms (some with shared bath) exude a family atmosphere.

Topnotch at Stowe (☎ 802-253-8585, 800-451-8686, fax 802-253-9263, W www.topnotch-resort.com, 4000 Mountain Rd) Doubles $230-345. Stowe's most lavish resort has 92 rooms. It really is top-notch. If your wallet can handle it, you may wish to inquire about its townhouses. Amenities include a spa, bar, fine dining, outdoor pool, indoor and outdoor tennis courts, skating rink and touring center.

Places to Eat

Food in Stowe, for the most part, is expensive and mediocre. However, a few places excel.

The Bagel (☎ 802-253-9943, 394 Mountain Rd) Open 6:30am-5:30pm daily. For light breakfast fare, check out The Bagel in the Baggy Knees Shopping Center.

Harvest Market (☎ 802-253-3800, 1031 Mountain Rd) Open 7am-5:30pm daily. This one-stop gourmet purveyor dishes out cold entrees by the pound, wonderful Vermont cheeses, crusty loaves of bread, salads and sandwiches.

Thompson's Bakery (☎ 802-253-9044, Main St) Dishes $2-6. This is a fine place to grab a quick muffin, soup, sandwich or snack. There are tables inside and outside.

McCarthy's (☎ 802-253-8626, 454 Mountain Rd) Dishes $2-7. Behind the Baggy Knees Shopping Center, locals enjoy McCarthy's hearty breakfasts of French toast, apple pancakes with maple syrup and lots of omelets.

Depot Street Malt Shoppe (☎ 802-253-4269, 57 Depot St) Dishes $3-7. Open 11:30am-9pm daily. Burgers and old-fashioned ice cream sodas reign at this 'shoppe.'

Brown Bag Deli (☎ 802-253-4600, Mountain Rd) Sandwiches $4-6. Open 6:30am-4pm daily. In the Baggy Knees Shopping Center, this basic deli makes sandwiches to go.

Dutch Pancake Café (☎ 802-253-8921, 900 Mountain Rd) Dishes $5.50-9.50. Open 8am-11am daily. Within the Grey Fox Inn,

Highland Light, on the site of Cape Cod's first lighthouse (1798)

Keepers of Maine's Nubble Lighthouse (1879) used a pulley to transport supplies from the mainland.

Portland Head Light (1791) is the oldest of Maine's 52 working lighthouses.

RICHARD CUMMINS

A glimpse of Hartford, CT

LEE FOSTER

Portsmouth, NH, is full of well-preserved historic buildings.

ANDRE JENNY

The Elms (1911), a 'summer cottage' in Newport, RI

JON DAVISON

Cape Cod's oldest working windmill, Eastham, MA

KIM GRANT

Boston's State House

the Dutch owner makes more than 75 kinds of *pannekoeken* (Dutch pancakes); some have a southern American twist with sausage and gravy.

Pie in the Sky (☎ *802-253-5100, 492 Mountain Rd*) Dishes $8-12. Open 11:30am-10pm daily. This affordable eatery is a local favorite for pizza and pasta.

Miguel's Stowe Away (☎ *802-253-7574, 3148 Mountain Rd*) Dishes $9-16. Open for dinner. This Mexican farmhouse cantina became so popular that it launched its own line of chips and salsa that's sold around the country. You'll find Tex-Mex, gringo and creative Mexican dishes like salmon with a mango poblano sauce.

Gracie's Restaurant (☎ *802-253-8741, Main St*) Lunch $5-15, dinner $8-23. Open 11:30am-11pm daily. Behind Carlson Real Estate, Gracie's is becoming so popular that supermarkets around the country now carry Gracie's sauces. Specialties include big burgers, hand-cut steaks, Waldorf salad and garlic-laden shrimp scampi.

Trattoria La Festa (☎ *802-253-8480, 4080 Mountain Rd*) Mains $12.50-21.50. Open Mon-Sat. Just north of Topnotch at Stowe, this trattoria has very good Italian fare made by Italian chefs. Try the spaghetti *pescatore*, chock-full of mussels, clams and shrimp ($16.50).

Mr Pickwick's Pub & Restaurant (☎ *802-253-7064, 433 Mountain Rd*) Lunch $5-15, dinner $17-25. Open daily. Situated in Ye Olde England Inne, this place is heavy on the British décor and features 120 beers and ales, including rare Scottish malts. Menu highlights include beef Wellington, bangers and mash, and steak and kidney pie.

Whiskers (☎ *802-253-8996, 1652 Mountain Rd*) Mains $13-32. Open from 4:30pm daily. Although this steakhouse specializes in prime rib, including an 18oz monster portion for $16, you can always get a soup and salad bar for $10. Outdoor dining is nice in summer.

Blue Moon Cafe (☎ *802-253-7006, 35 School St*) Mains $16.50-26. Open for dinner daily. In a converted house with a little sunporch, this intimate bistro is among New England's top restaurants. Entrées change nightly, but they're usually sublime. Look for Maine crabs, salmon dishes, oysters, rabbit and an extensive wine list.

Entertainment

Matterhorn (☎ *802-253-8198, 4969 Mountain Rd*) Cover $5. Open nightly; bands Fri-Sat year-round. At the top of Mountain Rd, this place is always hopping beginning at 5pm (daily), when skiers start to hobble off the slopes.

Charlie B's (☎ *802-253-7355, 1746 Mountain Rd*) Open nightly. If you're searching for an après-ski scene with a bit more class, check out Charlie B's at the Stoweflake Inn and Resort.

Mountain Road House (☎ *802-253-2800, 1677 Mountain Rd*) With a casual setting (peanut shells on the floor), the Road House offers Stowe's best R&B music.

The Shed (☎ *802-253-4364, 1859 Mountain Rd*) Open 11:30am-10pm daily. This cozy microbrewery always has six fresh beers on tap.

Getting There & Around

Vermont Transit (☎ 802-864-6811, 800-552-8737) buses stop at Waterbury, 10 miles south of Stowe. There is one daily bus from Burlington to Waterbury (30 minutes, $8). From Waterbury, you can call Peg's Pick Up (☎ 800-370-9490) for the short drive into Stowe ($20 per person).

Amtrak's daily *Vermonter* (☎ 800-872-7245) stops at Waterbury. Some hotels and inns will arrange to pick up guests at the station. For more details about the *Vermonter*'s route, see the Getting There & Around section at the beginning of this chapter.

By car, it takes 45 minutes (36 miles) to reach Burlington from Stowe; head south on VT 100, then north on I-89.

If you don't have your own vehicle, the Stowe Trolley runs every half-hour daily during ski season from Stowe village, along Mountain Rd, to the ski slopes. Pick up a schedule and list of stops at your inn or the Stowe Area Association's information office (see Orientation & Information, earlier).

BURLINGTON

Vermont's largest city (population 55,000) would be a small city in most other states, but Burlington's small size is one of its charms. With the University of Vermont's (UVM) student population and a vibrant cultural and social life, Burlington has a spirited, youthful character. And when it comes to nightlife, Burlington is Vermont's epicenter.

The city's location adds to its charm. Perched on the shore of Lake Champlain, Burlington is less than an hour's drive from Stowe and other Green Mountain towns. In fact, Burlington can be used as a base for exploring much of northwestern Vermont, where each season brings its own festivals and events (see Special Events, later).

Orientation

Take I-89 exit 14 to reach the city center; or take exit 13 to I-189 west to head for Shelburne and the motel strip that runs along US 7, south of Burlington. Downtown Burlington is easily negotiated on foot. Parking is usually not a big problem. The heart of the city is the Church St Marketplace and the adjacent pedestrian mall. Four

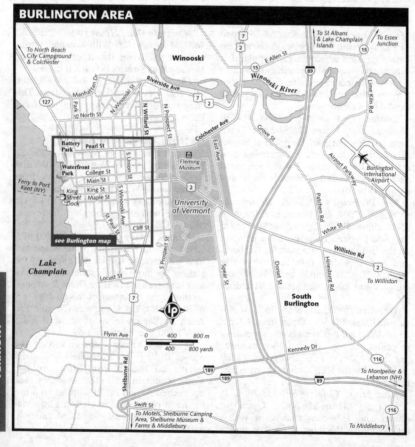

BURLINGTON AREA

blocks west along College St is the city's nice Waterfront Park.

Information

The Lake Champlain Regional Chamber of Commerce (☎ 802-863-3489, 60 Main St, Burlington, VT 05401) provides information. It's open 8:30am to 5pm weekdays (with slightly longer hours in summer and fall).

Check out the Peace and Justice Center (☎ 802-863-8326, 21 Church St) for good leftist reading and support. It's dedicated to community building, inclusion, tolerance and justice. The Adventurous Traveler Bookstore (☎ 802-860-6776, 800-282-3963, 245 S Champlain St) is great.

Shelburne Museum

This extraordinary museum (☎ 802-985-3346, US 7; adult/child 6-14 yrs $17.50/7, child 5 yrs & under free; admission tickets good for 2 consecutive days; open 10am-5pm daily mid-May–late Oct & 1pm-4pm daily mid-Apr–mid-May when only one-third of the buildings are open), 9 miles south of Burlington off US 7, occupies a 45-acre estate once owned by the Havemeyer family. HO and Louisine Havemeyer were patrons of the arts and collectors of European and Old Masters paintings. Their daughter Electra's interests, however, tended toward the more familiar and utilitarian. Electra Havemeyer (1888–1960) amassed a huge, priceless collection of American works of art and craft that she put on display in the numerous buildings of the museum. Indeed, the buildings themselves are exhibits. Many were moved here from other parts of New England to assure their preservation.

The collections, 80,000 objects housed in 39 buildings, include exhibits on folk art, decorative arts, Vermont history, tools and trades, transportation and New England houses. There's also a classic round barn (1901), a railroad station complete with locomotive (1915) and luxury private rail coach (1890), a Circus Building and 1920s carousel, a sawmill (1786), a covered bridge (1845), a lighthouse (1871) and even the

Lake Champlain side-wheeler steamboat called the SS *Ticonderoga* (1906).

A minimal visit takes three hours, but you can easily (and pleasantly) spend all day here. Sustenance is available from the refreshment stand, or from a more elaborate restaurant and eateries in Shelburne village.

A local bus (CCTA) runs from Burlington's Cherry St terminal along US 7 south to the Shelburne Museum frequently on weekdays and four times on Saturday. There is no Sunday service. The fare is $1/50¢ adult/senior & child age six to 18.

Shelburne Farms

In 1886, William Seward Webb and Lila Vanderbilt Webb built a little place for themselves in the Vermont countryside on Lake Champlain. The 1400-acre farm, designed by landscape architect Frederick Law Olmsted (who also designed New York's Central Park and Boston's Emerald Necklace), was both a country house for the Webbs and a working farm. The grand, 24-bedroom English country manor (1899), now an inn, is surrounded by working farm buildings inspired by European romanticism. By all means, visit Shelburne Farms (☎ 802-985-8686, 985-8442, off US 7; adult/senior/child $5/4/3; open 10am-5pm daily winter, 9am-5pm daily summer), buy some of the cheese, maple syrup, mustard and other items produced here, hike the walking trail and visit the animals in the Children's Farmyard.

The farm is 8 miles south of Burlington. Guided 90-minute tours begin at 9:30am, 11am, 12:30pm, 2pm and 3:30pm, mid-May through mid-October. The walking trail and the Children's Farmyard close at 4pm. A ticket for both the walking trail and the Children's Farmyard costs $4/3 adult/child.

University of Vermont

The university (☎ 802-656-3131), occupying a verdant campus east of the town center featuring a number of 18th-century buildings, gives Burlington its youthful vigor. It's said that the students here drink more than the students do at Dartmouth, which might

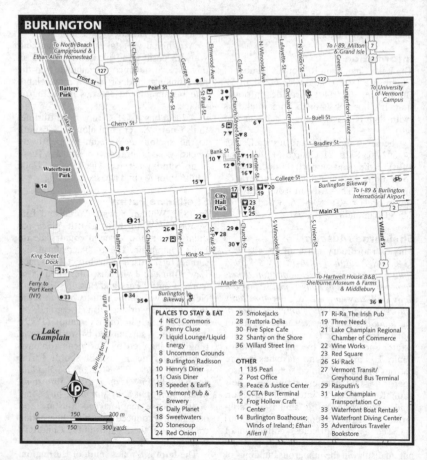

BURLINGTON

PLACES TO STAY & EAT
4 NECI Commons
6 Penny Cluse
7 Liquid Lounge/Liquid Energy
8 Uncommon Grounds
9 Burlington Radisson
10 Henry's Diner
11 Oasis Diner
13 Speeder & Earl's
15 Vermont Pub & Brewery
16 Daily Planet
18 Sweetwaters
20 Stonesoup
24 Red Onion

25 Smokejacks
28 Trattoria Delia
30 Five Spice Cafe
32 Shanty on the Shore
36 Willard Street Inn

OTHER
1 135 Pearl
2 Post Office
3 Peace & Justice Center
5 CCTA Bus Terminal
12 Frog Hollow Craft Center
14 Burlington Boathouse; Winds of Ireland; *Ethan Allen II*

17 Ri-Ra The Irish Pub
19 Three Needs
21 Lake Champlain Regional Chamber of Commerce
22 Wine Works
23 Red Square
26 Ski Rack
27 Vermont Transit/ Greyhound Bus Terminal
29 Rasputin's
31 Lake Champlain Transportation Co
33 Waterfront Boat Rentals
34 Waterfront Diving Center
35 Adventurous Traveler Bookstore

be hard to actually prove, but if true is something of an accomplishment. If you go out at night, you'll no doubt run into them.

From fall to spring, the main event at the Guterson Field House is UVM hockey, which consistently draws sellout crowds; call ahead for information on getting tickets to these thrillers.

Fleming Museum
UVM's art collection (☎ 802-656-2090, 61 Colchester Ave; adult/senior & child $3/2; open noon-4pm Tues-Fri, 1pm-5pm Sat-Sun) consists of more than 17,000 disparate

objects, including African masks, Indian drums, samurai armor, an Egyptian mummy and Vermont paintings.

Ethan Allen Homestead
Ethan Allen, the Revolutionary War hero often referred to as 'Vermont's godfather,' lived in this 18th-century farmhouse (☎ 802-865-4556, off VT 127; adult/senior/child/family $5/4/2.50/14; open 10am-5pm Mon-Sat & 1pm-5pm Sun late May-late Oct, noon-4pm Sat-Sun late Oct-late May). The center features multimedia exhibits documenting the exploits of his Green Mountain

Boys, as well as walking trails behind the house.

Frog Hollow Craft Center
This excellent contemporary and traditional craft center (☎ 802-863-6458, 85 Church St; admission free; open 10am-6pm Mon-Wed, 10am-9pm Thur-Sat & noon-6pm Sun) feels more like a museum than the retail store that it is. A rigorous jury process screens artisans for acceptance.

Walking & Bicycling
The Burlington Recreation Path (☎ 802-864-0123), a popular 7½-mile route for walking, biking and in-line skating, runs along the waterfront through the Waterfront Park and Promenade. You can rent bikes at Ski Rack (☎ 802-658-3313, 85 Main St) for $10 per hour, $16 for four hours or $22 for 24 hours. You can also rent in-line skates, kayaks, snowshoes and skis (of course).

Local Motion (☎ 802-652-2453), a local nonprofit group, is spearheading an effort to link Burlington to Montreal via bike paths. The Island Line Rail Trail is currently 13 miles long; the trail begins just south of the Burlington Boathouse. At the Auer Family Boathouse, about 7½ miles north of Burlington proper, a bike ferry will take you across the breakwater ($1 per person), from where you can continue another 5 miles. It operates noon to sunset June to early Sept and 10am to sunset Saturday and Sunday early September to October.

Boating
Approximately 120 miles long and 12 miles wide, Lake Champlain is the largest freshwater lake in the country after the Great Lakes. Consistently good wind, sheltered bays, hundreds of islands and scenic anchorages combine to make this immense lake one of the top cruising grounds in the Northeast. Winds of Ireland (☎ 802-863-5090, Burlington Boathouse) charters boats (28 to 41 feet) for anywhere from a half-day to a week. Prices start at $200 per half-day, but a captain costs extra.

The Burlington Boathouse (☎ 802-865-3377), at the foot of College St, rents sail-boats. Waterfront Boat Rentals (☎ 802-864-4858), at the foot of Maple St on Perkins Pier, rents canoes and kayaks.

Ethan Allen II (☎ 802-862-8300, Burlington Boathouse) cruises mid-May to mid-October. In addition to lunch and dinner cruises, the vessel plies the lake with 90-minute daily scenic narrated cruises (adult/child $9/4) and a 2½-hour sunset cruise (adult/child $10/5) at 6:30pm Sunday through Thursday.

Diving
Ever since the 18th-century French and Indian War, 120-mile-long Lake Champlain has been a major thoroughfare from the St Lawrence Seaway to the Hudson River. During the Revolutionary War and the War of 1812, numerous historic battles were fought on the lake to control this navigational stronghold. In the latter half of the 19th century, commercial vessels replaced gunboats. Many of these military and merchant ships sank to the lake's deep dark bottom as a result of the cannonball or of temperamental weather.

These vessels' misfortunes are lucky finds for scuba divers. Two hundred wrecks have already been discovered, including the 54-foot Revolutionary War boat Philadelphia, pulled from the waters in 1935 (and now sitting in the Smithsonian Institution in Washington, DC). Unfortunately, many of the earlier wrecks are far too deep for scuba divers, but six of the commercial vessels that lie on the lake's floor have been preserved by the state of Vermont as an underwater historical site.

There are no special permit fees, but all divers must register with the Vermont Division for Historic Preservation (☎ 802-828-3051). In return, you get a nifty little book that details all six wrecks. Register at any state dive shop.

Waterfront Diving Center (☎ 802-865-2771, 214 Battery St) offers rentals, charters and instruction.

Special Events
In early April, nearby St Albans hosts the Vermont Maple Festival. In late May, the

VERMONT

Lake Champlain Islands

For a nice day trip from Burlington, head north on I-89 to US 2 to North and South Hero Islands, connected to the mainland via a causeway road. These unspoiled rural islands, with sweeping water views, are populated year-round by a mere 4000 hearty souls. The flat, relatively untrafficked lanes are perfect for cycling, and the lake, of course, is great for swimming and boating. The Champlain Islands Chamber of Commerce (☎ 802-372-5683, W www.champlainislands.com, PO Box 213, North Hero, VT 05474) maintains an office in the Hero's Welcome General Store (US 2, North Hero) and has detailed information. For overnights, the chamber can direct you to a dozen secluded area B&Bs, each with only a couple of rooms to rent.

Hero's Welcome General Store (☎ 802-372-4161, US 2, North Hero) rents bikes, kayaks and canoes, while the **North Hero Marina** (☎ 802-372-5953) rents power boats, and South Hero's **Apple Tree Bay** (☎ 802-372-3922) rents sailboats.

Alburg Dunes State Park (☎ 802-796-4170, Alburg) has a sandy beach fine for sunning and swimming (day use only). **Knight Point State Park** (☎ 802-372-8389, US 2), on the southern tip of North Hero, offers the best swimming for families.

Allenholm Farm (☎ 802-372-5566, 111 South St, South Hero; open July-Dec) This is orchard country, but area farms offer more than sublime apples. Come here for local cheese, maple syrup, excellent pies, cider and of course crispy, tart and juicy apples.

Places to Stay & Eat

Grand Isle State Park (☎ 802-372-4300, US 2, Grand Isle) Sites $14-20. Open mid-May–mid-Oct. This 226-acre park has 156 tent and RV sites.

Burton Island State Park (☎ 802-524-6353, in Lake Champlain) Sites $14-20. Open mid-May–early Sept. Reached by park boat from the tip of Hathaway Point at Killkare State Park on the eastern shore of the lake (from St Albans, take VT 36 west), this park offers a unique lakeside perspective. The 250-acre island has 42 tent sits, lean-tos, flush toilets and a 100-slip marina. After you debark from the boat, the park service will transport your camping gear to your site.

North Hero House (☎ 802-372-8232, 800-525-3644, W www.northherohouse.com, US 2, North Hero) Doubles $89-249 with full breakfast. This landmark 24-room inn, built in the early 1900s, has lakeside rooms as well as rooms in the main inn across the street from the lake. They've been renovated recently, so grab one if you can. The inn also serves lunch and dinner to the public; dishes run the gamut from steak to pasta to salmon. Friday suppers feature lobsters down on the water.

Hero's Welcome General Store Sandwiches $4-6. Open daily. Do you get the impression that island life revolves around this place? It does; the cafe and bakery has the best area sandwiches, too.

state's proud dairy heritage is celebrated at the Vermont Dairy Festival, held in nearby Enosburg Falls. In late August and early September, the weeklong Champlain Valley Fair dominates nearby Essex. Early October brings the annual Applefest to South Hero.

In Burlington proper, look for the Discover Jazz Festival in June; a patriotic civic celebration on the Fourth of July; the Champlain Shakespeare Festival from July through August; and a very big and festive First Night celebration – a winter festival featuring a parade, an ice- and snow-sculpture exhibition, music and more – on December 31. Contact the chamber of commerce (see Information, earlier) for details.

Places to Stay

Camping Right on Lake Champlain is the **North Beach Campground** (☎ 802-862-0942, 60 Institute Rd) Sites without/with hookups $20/24. Open May–mid-Oct. With 137 sites (mostly for tents) on 45 acres near the city center, North Beach is the first choice for tent campers. To find it, get to Burlington's waterfront, then head north along Battery St and North Ave (VT 127), turning left on Institute Rd.

Shelburne Camping Area (☎ *802-985-2540, Shelburne Rd*) Sites $18-26. Open mid-May–mid-Oct. A mile north of the Shelburne Museum, this campground has 76 sites in a pine grove off the highway.

Hostels Reservations are essential at ***Mrs Farrell's Home Hostel*** (☎ *802-865-3730,* W *www.hiayh.org*) Dorm beds $15-17, doubles $26. Open Apr-Oct. Call at least 24 hours in advance, and between 4pm and 6pm. Arrive by 5pm. Nancy Farrell will give you directions to the hostel (which has six beds) when you call.

Motels & Hotels Burlington's budget and mid-range motels are on the outskirts of town. It's not usually necessary to reserve in advance, but if you call ahead on the day you intend to stay and ask for the 'same-day rate,' you may get a discount. Many of the chain motels lie on Williston Rd east of I-89 exit 14; another cluster is along US 7 north of Burlington in Colchester (take I-89 exit 16). Perhaps the best selection, though, is along Shelburne Rd (US 7) in South Burlington.

Yankee Doodle Motel (☎ *802-985-8004, fax 802-985-9552, 3972 Shelburne Rd*) Doubles $55-129. Only 2 miles north of the Shelburne Museum, this homey motel offers 15 very clean and tidy rooms.

Countryside Motel (☎ *802-985-2839,* W *www.countrysidevt.com, 6475 Shelburne Rd*) Doubles $58-136. This 12-room place is just south of the museum in a decidedly rural setting on spacious grounds.

Howard Johnson Motel & Suites (☎ *802-860-6000, 800-874-1554, fax 802-864-9919, 1720 Shelburne Rd*) Doubles $69-139. A step up in comfort from other Shelburne Rd motels, this 121-room establishment also has a nice swimming pool, whirlpool bath, sauna and a free airport shuttle.

Burlington Radisson (☎ *802-658-6500, 800-333-3333, fax 802-658-4659,* W *www.radisson.com, 60 Battery St*) Rooms $139-269. Downtown Burlington hotels are quite comfortable but much more expensive than the motels above. Of the downtown hostelries, this 256-room hotel has the best location.

Inns In a quiet residential neighborhood just a five-minute drive from the center of town is ***Hartwell House B&B*** (☎ *802-658-9242, fax 802-865-1090,* W *www.vermont bedandbreakfast.com, 170 Ferguson St*) Doubles without bath $55-70 with expanded continental breakfast. Innkeeper Linda Hartwell will pick up folks from the bus and train stations by arrangement. As if that weren't enough, her three clean rooms are a bargain, especially considering the outdoor pool and deck.

Burlington Redstone (☎ *802-862-0508,* W *www.burlingtonredstone.com, 497 S Willard St*) Rooms without/with bath $100/135 with full breakfast. This wonderful old stone house is owned by an avid gardener and you can stroll through her perennial gardens on a lakeside hill. Of the three rooms, one has lake views.

Willard Street Inn (☎ *802-651-8710, 800-577-8712, fax 802-651-8714,* W *www.willard streetinn.com, 349 S Willard St*) Rooms $120-195, suite $225 with full breakfast. Perched on a hill within easy walking distance of UVM and the Church St Marketplace, this Queen Anne–style home was built in the late 1880s. Many of the 14 guest rooms overlook Lake Champlain. The sublime breakfasts might include cranberry-walnut French toast.

Inn at Shelburne Farms (☎ *802-985-8498, fax 802-985-1233,* W *www.shelburnefarms .org, 1611 Harbor Rd*) Doubles without bath $95-180, with bath $200-365 with afternoon tea & continental buffet breakfast. Open mid-May–mid-Oct. The farm is arguably one of the top 10 places to stay in New England. If you've always dreamed of being lord of the manor, you can indulge your fantasies at this sumptuous place, 8 miles south of Burlington off US 7. The inn was once the summer mansion of the wealthy Webb family, and you can play billiards in their game room, read leather-bound books from their library or just relax in front of one of the inn's many fireplaces. The 23 guest rooms vary in size and appointments, which is reflected in the rates. (Less expensive rooms have shared bath.) Outstanding meals are also available.

Places to Eat

Burlington is the only place in Vermont that has a full range of restaurants. Most are in and near the Church St Marketplace.

Uncommon Grounds (☎ 802-865-6227, 42 Church St) Open 7am-10pm most days. Take your newspaper, order a cup of joe and a muffin and blend into the woodwork, or grab a sidewalk table and people watch in good weather.

Speeder & Earl's (☎ 802-860-6630, 104 Church St) Open 8am-6pm daily. This hole-in-the-wall serves a good cup of coffee, but the espresso isn't particularly strong.

Liquid Lounge/Liquid Energy (☎ 802-860-7666, 57 Church St) Drinks $2-5. By day you order wheatgrass concoctions, veggie tonics and other enhanced nutritious drinks, perhaps enjoying them in front of TVs or at DSL Internet stations. By night the groovy place turns more sophisticated, mixing martinis and other cool cocktails.

Penny Cluse (☎ 802-651-8834, 169 Cherry St) Dishes $1-10. Open for breakfast & lunch daily. In the original home of Ben & Jerry's ice cream, Penny Cluse serves one of the best breakfasts in town, including Southwestern selections like the breakfast burrito ($5.75). Indeed, local chefs rave about the innovative morning meals served here.

Stonesoup (☎ 802-862-7616, 211 College St) Dishes $3-6. Open 7am-7pm Mon-Fri, 9am-5pm Sat. Stonesoup is a big lunchtime hit with local vegetarians. Homemade soups (about $3), the salad bar and sandwiches with homemade bread (about $5) are quite popular.

Oasis Diner (☎ 802-864-5308, 189 Bank St) Dishes $4-6. Open 6am-2pm daily. Just off Church St, this old-time stainless steel diner has an equally old-time feel and

serves cheap meals. Try it for Sunday brunch.

Red Onion (☎ 802-865-2563, 140½ Church St) Dishes average $6.50. Open 7:30am-8pm Mon-Fri, 10am-8pm Sat, 11am-6pm Sun. Expect lines at lunch, even in the blustery days of winter, at this popular spot. A few tempting specials include hot open-faced turkey sandwiches or veggie lentil soup.

Henry's Diner (☎ 802-862-9010, 115 Bank St) Dishes under $8. Open 6am-4pm daily. A Burlington fixture since 1925, the diner has daily specials for around $5. The food is simple (you can get breakfast all day), the atmosphere homey and pleasant, the prices unbeatable.

Vermont Pub & Brewery (☎ 802-865-0500, 144 College St) Dishes $5-14. Open 11:30am-2am daily. This pub's specialty and seasonal brews are made on the premises. Try the Burly Irish Ale, Dogbite Bitter and Vermont Smoked Porter. There's plenty of bar food to accompany the pints.

Sweetwaters (☎ 802-864-9800, 120 Church St) Dishes $6.50-18. Open 11:30am-1am Mon-Sat, 10:30am-11pm Sun. Heavily nouveau Victorian in décor, this local watering hole attracts the young and upwardly mobile. In the evening the glass-enclosed patio is loud with chatter and redolent of nachos and chicken wings; the beverage of choice is an exotic beer.

NECI Commons (☎ 802-862-6324, 25 Church St) Lunch $7-10.50, dinner $12.50-19. Open daily. NECI Commons is run by Montpelier's New England Culinary Institute students. Dishes like rotisserie chicken, roasted turkey breast and sea bass are served at a long, welcoming wooden counter, bar, banquettes, booths and quiet tables. Stop by NECI Commons for morning coffee and freshly baked pastries or gourmet lunchtime picnic fare. From 2pm to 4pm on weekdays, a lighter bistro menu is available.

Daily Planet (☎ 802-862-9647, 15 Center St) Dinner $11-20. Open daily. Daily Planet serves creative main courses such as potato-crusted salmon with Moroccan vegetable sauté, or Thai shrimp salad.

Five Spice Cafe (*☎ 802-864-4045, 175 Church St*) Lunch $6.50-9.50, dinner $12-28. Open daily. This cafe is incredibly popular for Sunday dim sum brunches ($1.75 to $2.75 each dish), but it'll be worth the wait. The cafe also serves excellent dishes from China, India, Indonesia, Thailand and Vietnam.

Smokejacks (*☎ 802-658-1119, 156 Church St*) Lunch $5-9, dinner $9-21. Open daily. Smokejacks is known for fresh fish and specialties like smoked Long Island duck breast. The locally famous cheese list features some of America's finest small-farm cheeses.

Shanty on the Shore (*☎ 802-864-0238, 181 Battery St*) Lunch $6-10, dinner $11-23. Open daily. Facing the car ferry dock and with fine lake views, this combined seafood market and eatery serves lobster, fish and shellfish lunches and dinners.

Trattoria Delia (*☎ 802-864-5253, 152 St Paul St*) Mains $10.50-26. Open 5pm-10pm daily. Burlington's top Italian restaurant serves homemade pastas and specialties like *osso bucco*.

Entertainment

The local *Burlington Free Press* carries a special weekend entertainment section in its Thursday issue. This is perhaps the town's best source for up-to-date concert, theater, cinema, lecture and other program information. Otherwise, head to the center of Burlington nightlife, Church St Marketplace, with its many restaurants and sidewalk cafes. See also Liquid Lounge/Liquid Energy, under Places to Eat, above.

Red Square (*☎ 802-859-8909, 136 Church St*) With a stylish Soho-like ambience, Red Square is where knowledgeable Vermonters go to sip martinis or wine, munch on good bar food (including pizzas and sandwiches) and listen to Burlington's best roadhouse music.

Daily Planet (*☎ 802-862-9647, 15 Center St*) This welcoming place is where young, hip and alternative-lifestyle types come for a drink; also see Places to Eat, above.

Wine Works (*☎ 802-951-9463, 133 St Paul St*) Open from 4:30pm Tues-Sat. You've heard of wines by the glass? Well, these folks also offer wines by the ounce, all the better for teaching your palate a lesson. It's a mod place. Small bites of New England delicacies (like scallops wrapped in bacon and mini crab cakes) complement their wines.

Three Needs (*☎ 802-658-0889, 207 College St*) Open 4pm-1am daily. This pleasant microbrewery wins awards year after year for its brews.

Sweetwaters (*☎ 802-864-9800, 120 Church St*) Thirtysomethings who have 'made it' (or hope they have) head here after work, though the action doesn't really pick up until after 9:30pm.

Rasputin's (*☎ 802-864-9324, 163 Church St*) This popular college-age hangout has an Irish band on Friday and a DJ and dancing the rest of the week.

Ri-Ra The Irish Pub (*☎ 802-860-9401, 123 Church St*) Open 11:30am-2am daily. This Irish pub was restored in Ireland, dismantled and shipped to the States, so it really does have an authentic feel, albeit a spanking clean one. Order a pint of Guinness or a dram of Uisce Beatha (whiskey). Check out folk music on Wednesday and Sunday, a DJ on Friday and bands on Saturday night.

135 Pearl (*☎ 802-863-2343, 135 Pearl St*) Open 7:30pm-2am Sun-Thur & 5pm-2am Fri-Sat. This mixed club has been the hub of Vermont's gay, lesbian, bisexual and transgender scene since the mid-1990s. Not segregated in the least, the club has an international feel because of its proximity to Montreal (only 1¼ hours north). Thursday through Saturday features dancing and a DJ; Wednesday is karaoke night. Otherwise, there's a mixed schedule of cabaret, live music, theater, poetry and art shows. Check it out.

Getting There & Away

A number of national carriers serve Burlington International Airport, 3 miles east of the city center. You'll find major car-rental companies at the airport.

Vermont Transit (*☎ 802-864-6811, 800-552-8737*), based in Burlington, provides bus service to major Vermont towns, as well as to Manchester and Keene, NH; Albany, New York; and Boston, MA. The main terminal (☎ 802-864-6811, 345 Pine St) also serves Greyhound (☎ 800-231-2222), which operates four buses daily between Burlington and Montreal (about 2½ hours, $19.50 one-way).

Amtrak's *Vermonter* (☎ 800-872-7245) stops in Essex Junction, 5 miles from Burlington. The fare from Montpelier to Essex Junction is $10 to $13, depending on the day of the week. The station is served by local CCTA buses (☎ 802-864-0211). For additional train details, see the Getting There & Around section at the beginning of this chapter.

By car, it takes 4½ hours (230 miles) to reach Burlington from Boston; take I-93 to I-89. It's another 2¼ hours (102 miles) from Burlington to Montreal.

Lake Champlain Transportation Co (☎ 802-864-9804, King St Dock) runs car ferries connecting Burlington with Port Kent, New York, at least nine times daily from late May to mid-October; there's no service off-season. The one-hour voyage costs $13.25 for a car and driver, $3.50/1.25 additional for each adult/child ages six to 12 (one-way).

The company also operates ferries connecting Charlotte, VT, with Essex, New York (south of Burlington); and Grand Isle, VT (north of Burlington), with Plattsburgh, New York. The latter service runs year-round.

Getting Around

The Chittenden County Transportation Authority (CCTA; ☎ 802-864-0211) operates buses from its Cherry St Terminal to Burlington Airport. Buses depart Cherry St every half-hour or so; there is no Sunday service. Fares to the airport and around town are $1/50¢ adult/senior & child ages six to 18.

A free College St shuttle bus runs a loop route from the Waterfront Park near the Burlington Boathouse, stopping at Battery St, St Paul St, Church St Marketplace, Winooski Ave, Union St, Willard St and ending at the UVM campus. In summer, shuttle buses run every 10 minutes from 11am to 6pm.

NORTHEAST KINGDOM

Speaking to a small group of constituents in Lyndonville, VT, in 1949, Senator George Aiken noted that 'this is such beautiful country up here. It ought to be called the Northeast Kingdom of Vermont.' The locals took the wise senator's advice. The Northeast Kingdom now consists of a large tract of land wedged between the Quebec and New Hampshire borders. In a state known for its rural setting (only Wyoming and Alaska contain fewer people), the Kingdom is Vermont's equivalent to putting on its finest pastoral dress, with a few holes here and there. Wave after wave of unspoiled hillside form a vast sea of green, and small villages and farms spread out in the distance under a few soaring summits. Here, inconspicuous inns and dairy cows have replaced the slick resorts and Morgan horses found in the southern part of the state, and the white steeples are chipped, not freshly painted. Indeed, it is the most authentic area in Vermont, a region that doesn't put on any airs about attracting tourists.

History

It was the 1830s when the Fairbanks family of St Johnsbury, the Kingdom's largest community, began manufacturing weight scales. The Fairbanks clan soon became one of America's wealthiest families and, fortunately for St Johnsbury, began pouring money into the village. They would eventually open one of the finest libraries in America, where leather-bound books would share space with a 19th-century art gallery. They also opened one of the country's first natural history museums. The two sites have remained relatively unaltered and are still open to the public.

Orientation & Information

While St Johnsbury is easily reached by I-91 or I-93 (a three-hour drive from Boston through New Hampshire), the rest of the Northeast Kingdom is incredibly spread out. Use I-91 as your north-south thoroughfare, and then use smaller routes like VT 5A to find dramatically sited Lake Willoughby or VT 14 to find Craftsbury Common, a town of white clapboard houses perfectly set around a village green. Other favorite villages include Greensboro, nestled upon the shores of Caspian Lake, and Barton, near pristine Crystal Lake.

Contact the Northeast Kingdom Chamber of Commerce (☎ 802-748-3678, ⊌ www .vermontnekchamber.org, 357 Western Ave, Suite 2, St Johnsbury, VT 05819) for regional information. It's open 8:30am to 5pm daily. The convenient information booth at Courthouse Park on Main St is open daily from mid-June to mid-October.

St Johnsbury Athenaeum
The athenaeum (☎ 802-748-8291, 1171 Main St; admission free; open 10am-8pm Mon & Wed; 10am-5:30pm Tues, Thur & Fri; 9:30am-4pm Sat), founded in 1871 when Horace Fairbanks gave the town a library, was built around some 8000 finely bound copies of the world's classic literature. Fairbanks then added an art gallery and installed works by such noted Hudson River School painters as Asher B Durand, Worthington Whittredge and Jasper Crospey. His crowning achievement was the purchase of Albert Bierstadt's 10-foot-by-15-foot Domes of the Yosemite. Bierstadt is said to have returned to the gallery every summer until his death to touch up his masterpiece. Today, the Athenaeum's art collection is the oldest art gallery still in its original form in the USA.

Fairbanks Museum & Planetarium
In 1891, when Franklin Fairbanks' collection of stuffed animals and cultural artifacts from across the globe grew too large for his home, he built the Fairbanks Museum of Natural Science (☎ 802-748-2372, 1302 Main St; adult/senior/child/family $5/4/3/12; open 9am-5pm Mon-Sat, 1pm-5pm Sun). This massive stone building with a 30-foot-high barrel-vaulted ceiling still displays more than half of Franklin's original collection.

More than 3000 preserved animals in glass cases can be seen, including a 1200lb moose shot in Nova Scotia in 1898, an American bison from 1902 and a Bengal tiger. There are planetarium shows at 1:30pm daily, and in July and August at 11am ($2 per person).

Activities
Not surprisingly, this sylvan countryside is the perfect playground for New England outdoor activities. Almost any outdoor activity is at its best in this region.

Skiing When it's balmy in Boston in winter, you can still expect a blizzard at Vermont's northernmost ski resort, Jay Peak (☎ 802-988-2611, VT 242), 8 miles north of Montgomery Center. Bordering Quebec, Jay gets more snow than any other ski area in New England (about 350 inches of powder). Being so far north, Jay also accommodates far more Quebecois than New Yorkers. Black-diamond lovers enjoy the steeper tree runs off the tram, while novices find the trails in Bonaventure Basin to their liking. Add the natural off-trail terrain, and you have some of the most challenging backcountry snowboarding and skiing runs in America.

Burke Mountain (☎ 802-626-3305), off US 5 in East Burke, is relatively unknown to anyone outside the Northeast Kingdom. Locals enjoy the challenging trails and empty lift lines. Burke has 33 trails (30% beginner, 40% intermediate, 30% expert) and four lifts, including one quad chair and one lift with a vertical drop of 2000 feet.

Cross-country skiers are bound to end up at the full-service Craftsbury Outdoor Center (☎ 802-586-7767, Lost Nation Rd), 3 miles from Craftsbury Common. The 80 miles of trails, 50 of them groomed, roll over meadows and weave through forests of maples and firs, offering an ideal experience for all levels. Even if you don't plan on skiing, you should take a drive over to Craftsbury Common, where you'll find what may be Vermont's most spectacular village green. White clapboard buildings surround a rectangular lawn that hasn't changed one iota from the mid-19th century.

VERMONT

Nearby, **Highland Lodge** (☎ 802-533-2647, Craftsbury Rd) has 40 miles of trails that slope down to the shores of Caspian Lake.

Mountain Biking On VT 114 off I-91, **East Burke** is a terrific place to start a mountain bike ride. In the summer of 1997, John Worth, co-owner of East Burke Sports, and several other dedicated locals linked together more than 200 miles of single and double tracks and dirt roads to form a network they call the **Kingdom Trails**. Riding on a soft forest floor dusted with pine needles and through century-old farms makes for one of the best mountain-biking experiences in New England. **East Burke Sports** (☎ 802-626-3215, VT 114) rents bikes ($25 to $35 daily) and supplies maps.

Hiking Hiking Lake Willoughby's stunning beauty will leave even a jaded visitor in awe. Sandwiched between Mt Hor and Mt Pisgah, cliffs plummet more than 1000 feet to the glacial waters below and create, in essence, a landlocked fjord. The scenery is best appreciated on the three-hour hike to the summit of **Mt Pisgah**. From West Burke, take VT 5A for 6 miles to a parking area on the left-hand side of the road, just south of Lake Willoughby. The 1.7-mile (one-way) **South Trail** begins across the highway. It's about a 30-minute drive from St Johnsbury to Mt Pisgah.

Places to Stay

The Northeast Kingdom offers some of the most affordable lodging in the state. The best accommodations are at small inns or family-run farms or by the shores of a hidden lake.

Camping The following parks are open mid-May to mid-October and cost $14 to $20.

Brighton State Park (☎ 802-723-4360, off VT 105, Island Pond) About 35 miles north of St Johnsbury, via I-91 north to US 5 north to VT 114 north, this 150-acre park has hiking trails and 84 sites.

Ricker Pond State Park (☎ 802-584-3821, off VT 232, Groton) Between Montpelier

and St Johnsbury, this park has 33 tent sites and 22 lean-tos, many lakeside.

Stillwater State Park (☎ 802-584-3822, off VT 232, Groton) Nearby, Stillwater has 107 sites and a prime swimming spot on the northwestern shores of Lake Groton.

Inns & B&Bs Not far from the shores of Shadow Lake is **Rodgers Country Inn** (☎ 802-525-6677, 800-729-1704, fax 802-525-1103, 582 Rodgers Rd, West Glover) Rates per person $45/250 day/week with breakfast & dinner. Jim and Nancy Rodgers offer five guest rooms in their 1840s farmhouse. Hang out on the front porch and read, or take a stroll on this 350-acre former dairy farm. Smack dab in the middle of farm country, this inn appeals to people who really want to feel what it's like to live in rural Vermont.

Inn on Trout River (☎ 802-326-4391, 800-338-7049, Ⓦ www.troutinn.com, 241 Main St, Montgomery Center) Rates per person $43-66 with full breakfast. One of the better places to stay if you plan on skiing Jay Peak, this inn was built by a lumber baron over a century ago, and features 10 guest rooms, one suite and two restaurants (one fancy and one a pub).

Craftsbury Bed & Breakfast (☎ 802-586-2206, 414 Wiley Hill Rd, Craftsbury Common) Doubles with shared bath $60-75 with full breakfast. Open year-round by reservation. Set in a farmhouse atop Wylie Hill, this six-room B&B offers expansive views of rolling farmland. It's just down the road from the historic village green and close to the Craftsbury Outdoor Center for mountain biking and cross-country skiing.

The Village Inn (☎ 802-626-3161, VT 114, East Burke) Doubles $75 with full breakfast. Conveniently located at the base of Burke Mountain's ski area, the inn has six very clean rooms, an outdoor Jacuzzi, guest kitchen and a living room fireplace. In the wonderful 5-acre garden out back, you can follow a trail that leads to a waterfall. (If only life could be this simple.)

Heermansmith Farm Inn (☎/fax 802-754-8866, 550 Heermanville Rd, Coventry) Doubles $75 with full breakfast. This authentic 1860s farmhouse, off US 5, has six neat, modest rooms lined with rows and rows of books. The inn also has one of the region's best restaurants. See Places to Eat, below.

Willoughvale Inn (☎ 802-525-4123, 800-594-9102, fax 802-525-4514, W www.willough vale.com, VT 5A, Westmore) Rooms $89-155, suites $145-199, cottages $139-245 with continental breakfast. Open Dec-Mar & May-Oct. Overlooking the majestic granite cliffs of Mt Hor and Mt Pisgah, this inn sits on the northern shores of Lake Willoughby. It features eight spacious rooms, two suites, four cottages and elegant common areas. In the summer, cast off from the small beach and kayak (rented for a small fee) on the cool waters of the lake. In the winter, rent snowmobiles and head up into the hills.

The Wildflower Inn (☎ 802-626-8310, 800-627-8310, fax 802-626-3039, W www.wild flowerinn.com, 2059 Darling Hill Rd, Lyndonville) Rooms $95-140, suites $115-280 with full breakfast. Open Dec-Mar & May-Oct. This is a perennial favorite among families. Maybe it's because owners Jim and Mary O'Reilly have eight children and their home is littered with toys. Or perhaps it's the hayrides, mountain-bike trails, petting zoo with sheep and goats, playground, pool, tennis courts, batting cage, basketball courts, cross-country trails, snowshoe trails, skating rink, sledding hill and sleigh rides. Did we forget to mention the exquisite views of the region from atop Darling Hill? There are 10 rooms and 11 suites on the property.

The Highland Lodge (☎ 802-533-2647, fax 802-533-7494, W www.highlandlodge.com, off VT 16, Greensboro) Doubles $102-250 with breakfast and dinner. Open late Dec–mid-Mar & June–mid-Oct. This 11-room lodge (with 11 additional one- to four-bedroom cottages) is perched on a hill over Caspian Lake, down the road from one of Vermont's best country stores, Willey's. A trail leads to a private beach and canoe rental shop. Wintertime guests can enjoy an extensive cross-country skiing network.

The Inn at Mountain View Farm (☎ 802-626-9924, 800-572-4509, fax 802-626-3625,

W www.innmtnview.com, 3383 Darling Hill Rd, East Burke) Doubles $145-220 with full breakfast. Built in 1883 as the quintessential gentleman's farm, this splendid place once housed 100 Jersey cows, pigs and Morgan horses in impressive and very large red barns. Today, the 15-room inn is situated in the former creamery and farmhouse. The farm's 440 acres are ideal for mountain biking, cross-country skiing or simply taking a long stroll on the hillside.

Places to Eat

You might be surprised at the region's fine and inexpensive tabs.

The Bagel Depot (☎ 802-748-1600, 1216 Railroad St, St Johnsbury) Open 6am-3pm daily. This Creamery Building eatery serves the freshest bagels in the Northeast Kingdom.

Miss Lyndonville Diner (☎ 802-626-9890, US 5, Lyndonville) Dishes $2-9. Open for all 3 meals daily. Five miles north of St Johnsbury and popular with locals, this place also enjoys friendly and prompt service. Large breakfasts are cheap, sandwiches a bit more, but the affordable and tasty dinners (like roast turkey with all the fixings) are a real steal.

Anthony's Diner (☎ 802-748-3613, 50 Railroad St, St Johnsbury) Dishes $3-16. Open for all 3 meals. While hanging around the large counter, try the mountain-size Vermont cheddar burger.

Northern Lights Bookshop and Cafe (☎ 802-748-4463, 378 Railroad St, St Johnsbury) Lunch $4-10, dinner $6-15. Open for breakfast & lunch daily & dinner Thur-Fri. The area's best bookstore is also known for its tasty soups, salads, sandwiches and 'extreme veggie burgers.' At night, more substantial dishes like chicken marsala and curried chicken are offered.

Cucina di Gerardo (☎ 802-748-6772, 213 Railroad St, St Johnsbury) Lunch $7-10, dinner $12-22. Open daily. This Creamery Building place serves hearty Italian fare like mussels marinara and fancy pizzas.

The Willoughvale Inn (☎ 802-594-9102, VT 5A, Westmore) Mains $11-17. Open for lunch & dinner. If you don't stay here, at least have a meal in its glass-enclosed dining room overlooking Lake Willoughby. Hearty American fare, including prime rib and turkey, is served. The house specialty is stuffed chicken Willoughvale.

The River Garden Café (☎ *802-626-3514, VT 114, East Burke*) Lunch $8, dinner $18-22. Open Tues-Sun & Sun brunch. This local favorite has salads, pastas, filet mignon and stir-fried dishes. For lunch, try the Green Mountain pizza ($7), topped with Vermont goat cheese, mozzarella, pesto and tomato sauce. The summertime patio is a big draw.

Heermansmith Farm Inn (☎ *802-754-8866, 550 Heermanville Rd, Coventry*) Mains $16-23. Open Wed-Sun year-round. This place might be in the middle of nowhere, but it serves one of the finest dinners in the Kingdom. Try the signature dish, oven-roasted duck à la Heermansmith,

topped with homemade strawberry *chambord* sauce ($18). From I-91, take exit 26 and head north on US 5 for 5 miles. Take a left across from the school and head into Coventry, then make the next left onto Heermanville Rd. The farm and its sign are on the right side of the road.

Getting There & Away

Vermont Transit (☎ 802-864-6811, 800-552-8737) operates buses between St Johnsbury and Burlington (four hours, $29 to $31) and St Johnsbury and Montpelier (three hours, $21), but they're inefficient routes since you have to go south to White River Junction first.

By car, St Johnsbury is 39 miles (45 minutes) from Montpelier via US 2 east, or 76 miles (1½ hours) if you're coming directly from Burlington.

New Hampshire, like neighboring Vermont, is ruggedly mountainous and prime for outdoor pursuits. The dramatic White Mountain Range stars Mt Washington (6288 feet), one of the highest peaks east of the Mississippi River. The state's symbol is the 'Great Stone Face' (also called the Old Man of the Mountain), a natural granite 'profile' of a face at Franconia Notch in the White Mountain National Forest.

New Hampshire is also a lake-lover's paradise. Among its 1300 glacial lakes and ponds, Lake Winnipesaukee is the largest. For saltwater beach fun and honky-tonk partying, New Hampshire even has a short seacoast.

In addition to its natural charms, New Hampshire has several small cities, some good small museums, and Dartmouth College in Hanover, one of the nation's most prestigious institutions of higher education.

New Hampshire's earliest recorded inhabitants were the Abenakis, an eastern woodland people of the Algonquian group. In 1622, the Council for New England awarded the territory between the Merrimack and Kennebec rivers (named 'the Province of Maine') to Captain John Mason and Sir Ferdinando Gorges. A year later, the first English settlers arrived and set up home at Portsmouth.

In 1629, Mason's land grant, which he renamed New Hampshire, was extended from the Merrimack to the Piscataqua River. Later, it was enlarged even further, though these early borders were often in dispute. In 1641, four New Hampshire towns placed themselves under the protection of the royal governor of Massachusetts, but in 1679, New Hampshire received its own royal charter from King Charles II. The border disputes between the two provinces were only settled by royal decree in 1740. The following year, Benning Wentworth of Portsmouth was appointed the colony's first royal governor. By this time, white settlers had long since penetrated the 211-mile-long

Highlights

- Riding the Cog Railway to the top of Mt Washington
- Camping in the White Mountain National Forest
- Sampling Portsmouth restaurants
- Driving Kancamagus Highway
- Hiking in the Presidential Range
- Boating on Lake Winnipesaukee
- Touring Canterbury Shaker Village
- Taking the train through Crawford Notch
- Cross-country skiing in Jackson
- Exploring Monadnock Region villages

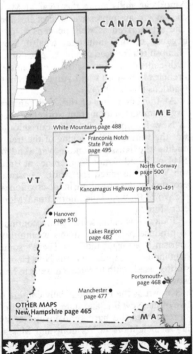

CANADA

ME

White Mountains page 488

Franconia Notch State Park page 495

North Conway page 500

VT

Kancamagus Highway pages 490-491

Hanover page 510

Lakes Region page 482

Portsmouth page 468

Manchester page 477

OTHER MAPS
New Hampshire page 465

MA

Connecticut River Valley and the 100-mile-long Merrimack River.

Four months before the 'shot heard round the world' rang out in Lexington, Massachusetts, on April 19, 1775, the farmer-soldiers of New Hampshire captured Fort William and Mary from the British, signaling the start of the troubles. New Hampshirites provided important supplies, manpower and navy vessels for the Revolutionary War. On June 21, 1788, New Hampshire ratified the US Constitution and provided the ninth and final vote necessary to inaugurate the radically different form of government it described.

By 1790, New Hampshire had a population of almost 142,000. In the mid-19th century, the Industrial Revolution brought considerable wealth to New Hampshire, which was blessed, like much of New England, with abundant water power. The great Amoskeag mills along the river at Manchester are an impressive relic of this era. The arts thrived as well, perhaps in part because of this industrial wealth. New Hampshire produced two of America's best 19th-century sculptors: Daniel Chester French (1850–1931) and Augustus Saint-Gaudens (1848–1907).

At the beginning of the 20th century, large numbers of immigrant workers settled in New Hampshire. In 1905, Portsmouth was the venue for the signing of the treaty ending the Russo-Japanese War. And in 1944, a United Nations conference at Bretton Woods designed the world's postwar economic model, resulting in the creation of the World Bank and the International Monetary Fund.

Today, New Hampshire's farms continue to produce part of the state's wealth, but tourism is a bigger industry. There's some light industry as well, but many New Hampshirites head south to Massachusetts to find work.

Known as the most politically conservative of the New England states, New Hampshire suffers the barbs and insults of its liberal neighbors in Vermont and Massachusetts. New Hampshirites take comfort in the words of native General John Stark,

victor at the crucial Battle of Bennington (1777): 'Live free or die.'

Information

The New Hampshire Division of Travel & Tourism (☎ 603-271-2666, ⓦ www.visitnh .gov, PO Box 1856, Concord, NH 03302), is the statewide information source, but you'll get more complete information from regional tourism offices mentioned elsewhere in the chapter. Prior to your visit, call the number above for the excellent free highway map, a state parks brochure (ⓦ www .nhparks.state.nh.us), information on a statewide bicycle route system and a very complete camping guide.

Another telephone number (☎ 800-258-3608) will serve as your information guide all year. You can call to learn about such things as special events from April through August, fall foliage reports from September to mid-October, and both alpine and cross-country ski conditions from November through April.

Getting There & Around

Air Manchester Airport (☎ 603-624-6539, ⓦ www.flymanchester.com), the state's largest airport, has enjoyed exponential growth in recent years as a 'relief airport' for Boston's overburdened Logan International Airport. Continental, Delta, Northwest, United, US Airways and particularly Southwest Airlines all serve Manchester. Car rentals are available here.

US Airways Express flies into the smaller Lebanon Municipal Airport (☎ 603-298-8878), which serves Hanover.

Bus Concord Trailways (☎ 603-228-3300, 800-639-3317) operates a bus route to and from Boston and Logan International Airport, with stops in Manchester, Concord, Laconia, Meredith, Conway, Jackson, Gorham and Berlin, NH. There's also another route through North Woodstock/Lincoln, Franconia, Littleton and some other points along the way.

In addition, Vermont Transit (☎ 603-436-0163, 800-552-8737) operates a route connecting Boston and Portsmouth, with

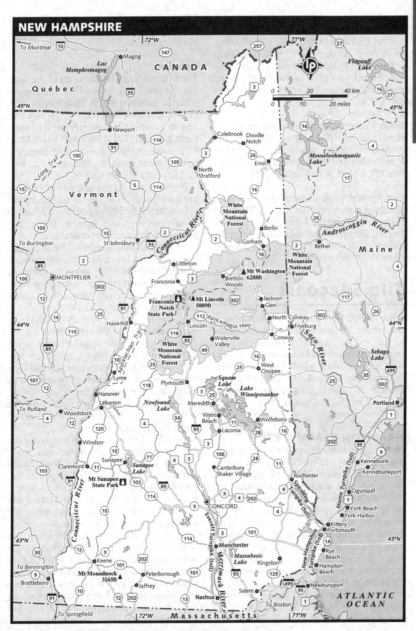

continuing service to Portland, Bangor and Bar Harbor, Maine.

C&J Trailways (☎ 603-430-1100) plies the route from Portsmouth to Boston's South Station ($12.50 one-way) and Logan International Airport ($18 one-way). There are almost 20 buses daily. Same-day return fares cost $17.50.

Train There is no scheduled rail passenger service in New Hampshire, although the Amtrak *Vermonter* runs up the Connecticut River Valley and stops at White River Junction, VT, a town near Hanover, NH.

Car For flexibility, convenience and independence, autos rule for touring. The New Hampshire Turnpike (along the seacoast), Everett Turnpike and Spaulding Turnpike are toll roads (75¢ to $2.50). For road conditions, call ☎ 800-918-9993.

The Seacoast

Even though New Hampshire's coastline is only about 18 miles long, it provides access to the sea and, more importantly, to the beach. Indeed, the coast is mostly beach, with a few rocky headlands and coves. Several state beaches and parks along the coast have orderly, well-regulated access. The rest of the beach has been commercially developed.

HAMPTON BEACH & RYE
New England beachfront honky-tonk at its best (or worst) – that's Hampton Beach. In the summer, clam shacks, cheap motels, hot-dog stands, coin-machine game arcades, free nightly entertainment and weekly fireworks, all spiced with neon and noise, keep the crowds of mostly young sunseekers happy. North of Hampton Beach, the mood changes dramatically. Rye is a town of rolling greenswards and serpentine private drives that lead to oceanfront mansions and 12-bedroom 'summer cottages.'

The Hampton Beach Area Chamber of Commerce (☎ 603-926-8718, ⓦ www.hamp tonbeaches.com or ⓦ www.seacoastnh.com,

1 Park Ave, Suite 3G, Hampton, NH 03842) has a summer office in the town center at 180 Ocean Blvd.

Beaches
The beach actually begins south of the state line, on the north bank of the Merrimack River at **Salisbury Beach State Reservation** in Massachusetts. Take I-95 exit 56 (MA 1A) and head east to Salisbury Beach, then north along NH 1A to **Hampton Beach State Park**, a long stretch of sand with changing rooms, toilet facilities and a snack bar. Parking costs $10 per car.

North of the state park, where NH 1A becomes Ocean Blvd, the town of Hampton is both beach and honky-tonk playground. In summer, the beach is crowded with the young, the tanned, the beautiful and the rest of us. The **Hampton Seashell**, a building with public toilets, a first aid station and a visitor center (☎ 603-926-8717), sits at the center of the long seaside strip. Across the boulevard, the Hampton Beach Casino has video games, fast-food stands and souvenir shops. Beach admission is free, but you'll have to feed quarters to the parking meters.

In the residential neighborhoods north of Hampton Beach, you'll find a few less crowded and less spectacular beaches. Ten minutes north of Hampton Beach, **North Hampton State Beach** is not nearly as wide but it's quieter than its grand southern neighbors. It has bathhouses, lifeguards and a small parking lot.

As NH 1A enters Rye, parking along the road is restricted to vehicles with town parking stickers, but **Jenness State Beach** has a small parking lot that's open to the general public – if you can find a space. Farther north at **Rye Harbor State Park**, however, you're allowed to park along the roadway. Climb over the seawall of rubble and riprap to get to the gravel beach, which is much less crowded than anything to the south. Continuing northward, **Wallis Sands State Beach** has a large parking lot and nice grass lawns for children's games. Last but not least, **Odiorne Point State Park** offers seaside strolls, picnicking and fishing, but there's no beach.

Places to Stay

Whether you're tenting it or dropping big bills in hotels, you'll need reservations around here.

Tidewater Campground (☎ *603-926-5474, US 1 and NH 101*) Sites without/with hookups $25/32. Open mid-May–mid-Oct. This private 40-acre campground, with prime shaded spots near the ocean, has about 100 sites equally divided between tent and RV sites.

Hampton Beach State Park Campground (☎ *603-926-8990, off NH 1A*) Sites $35. Open mid-May–mid-Oct. With only 28 oceanfront RV sites, this place absolutely requires reservations.

Hampton Beach has loads of rental rooms and apartments – booked well in advance. (People start calling in mid-February and March). Contact *Preston Real Estate* (☎ *603-926-2604, 63 Ocean Blvd*) in Hampton Beach for weeklong rentals. Weekly rates range from $725 for a decent but small two-bedroom apartment to as much as $1400 for a three-bedroom place with ocean views. As for hotels, during beach season it's very difficult, if not impossible, to find a room for one night.

Hampton Harbor Motel (☎ *603-926-4432, 210 Ashworth Ave*) Doubles $59-79 off-season, $99-119 late June-Sept. Just a short stroll from the casino and beach, this motel has four efficiency apartments and 18 typical rooms, as well as an outdoor heated rooftop pool.

Ashworth By the Sea (☎ *603-926-6762, 800-345-6736, fax 603-926-2002, 295 Ocean Blvd*) Doubles $89-225. North of Hampton Beach, this conference- and family-friendly hotel has 105 somewhat luxurious rooms. The price depends on the view.

Places to Eat

Neither of these suggested eateries is actually in Hampton Beach.

Galley Hatch (☎ *603-926-6152, US 1*) Mains $6-20. Open for lunch and dinner. This popular restaurant serves everything from the requisite fish and sandwiches to steaks, pastas, pizzas and veggie dishes. It also has a couple of lounges with entertain-ment. If you're hungry, it'll do just fine. It's in Hampton rather than Hampton Beach.

Brown's Seabrook Lobster Pound (☎ *603-474-3331, NH 286*) Mains $8-20. Open for lunch and dinner (Fri-Sun mid-Nov–mid-Apr). Seasonal lobster pounds line the seacoast along US 1 and NH 1A. Make a slight detour to Seabrook, barely south of Hampton Beach, for this year-round pound that overlooks a marsh and serves freshly boiled crustaceans.

PORTSMOUTH

The New England coast is dotted with graceful old cities that grew to importance during the great days of New England's maritime ascendancy, when local merchants made fortunes trading with the world. Portsmouth (population 23,000) is New Hampshire's only such city, but it's one of the region's most attractive and has much of historical interest.

Portsmouth's checkered history has left it with a particularly impressive and eclectic array of historic buildings from all periods. It is neither a prissy, perfectly preserved 'museum town,' nor a modernized city, but more of an architectural museum of real life as lived on the New Hampshire seacoast from 1623 to the present day.

History

In 1623, only three years after the Pilgrims landed at Plymouth Rock, another band of intrepid settlers sailed to the mouth of the Piscataqua River. They landed and scrambled up a bank covered with wild strawberries – a good omen to hungry seafarers. They decided to stay and named the place Strawbery Banke, but the name changed to Portsmouth in 1653.

The purpose of this colony was fishing. The early settlers caught and sold fish and built and sold fishing boats. By the time of the American Revolution, Portsmouth was among the dozen largest cities in the English colonies. Its streets were lined with handsome houses (many of which remain today) built by merchants and ship captains.

The War of 1812 was the beginning of the end for Portsmouth's greatness, as trading

NEW HAMPSHIRE

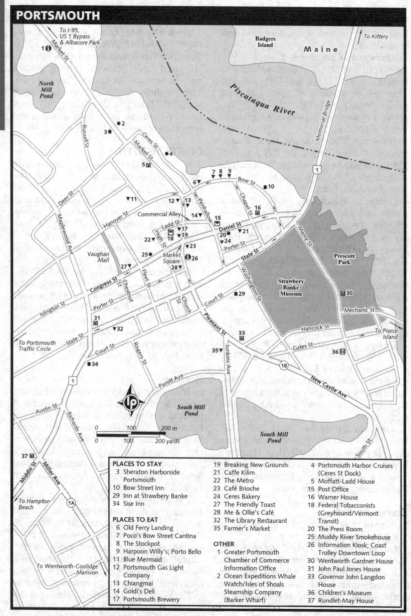

PORTSMOUTH

PLACES TO STAY
3 Sheraton Harborside Portsmouth
10 Bow Street Inn
29 Inn at Strawbery Banke
34 Sise Inn

PLACES TO EAT
6 Old Ferry Landing
7 Poco's Bow Street Cantina
8 The Stockpot
9 Harpoon Willy's; Porto Bello
11 Blue Mermaid
12 Portsmouth Gas Light Company
13 Chiangmai
14 Goldi's Deli
17 Portsmouth Brewery

19 Breaking New Grounds
21 Caffe Kilim
22 The Metro
23 Café Brioche
24 Ceres Bakery
27 The Friendly Toast
28 Me & Ollie's Café
32 The Library Restaurant
35 Farmer's Market

OTHER
1 Greater Portsmouth Chamber of Commerce Information Office
2 Ocean Expeditions Whale Watch/Isles of Shoals Steamship Company (Barker Wharf)

4 Portsmouth Harbor Cruises (Ceres St Dock)
5 Moffatt-Ladd House
15 Post Office
16 Warner House
18 Federal Tobacconists (Greyhound/Vermont Transit)
20 The Press Room
25 Muddy River Smokehouse
26 Information Kiosk; Coast Trolley Downtown Loop
30 Wentworth Gardner House
31 John Paul Jones House
33 Governor John Langdon House
36 Children's Museum
37 Rundlet-May House

and shipping dropped off drastically during the war and other ports grew to take up the slack in the postwar years. But the graceful houses, fine churches and other great buildings from Portsmouth's heyday remain.

Today, the city makes its living from tourism and from manufacturing such things as computers and fiber-optic cable.

Orientation & Information

Historic Portsmouth is surrounded on three sides by water. To the northeast is the Piscataqua River, to the northwest is the North Mill Pond and to the southeast is the South Mill Pond. Market St, reached via I-95 exit 7, is the main commercial street and has shops, restaurants and two information centers. Motels are clustered around I-95 exits 5 and 6.

The Greater Portsmouth Chamber of Commerce (☎ 603-436-1118, Ⓦ www.portsmouth chamber.org, 500 Market St, Portsmouth, NH 03802) answers questions about the region. Stop at its office on Market St just east of I-95 exit 7 or at its information kiosk at Market and Daniel/Congress Sts in the city center at Market Square. The chamber produces a good self-guided Portsmouth Harbour Trail map leading you to most of the city's sights. Inquire about informative walking tours (10:30am Mon & Thur-Sat, 1:30pm Sun mid-June–mid-Oct; adult/child $8/5).

Strawbery Banke Museum

Unlike other New England historic re-creations – Mystic Seaport, Old Sturbridge Village, Plimoth Plantation – Strawbery Banke Museum (☎ 603-433-1100, Marcy St; family/adult/senior/child 7-17 yrs $28/12/ 11/8; open 10am-5pm mid-Apr–Oct) does not limit itself to one historical period. Like Portsmouth itself, the museum is an eclectic mix; its 35 buildings span the town's history. Set on a 10-acre site in the Puddle Dock section, Strawbery Banke includes Pitt Tavern (1766), a hotbed of American revolutionary sentiment, Goodwin Mansion (and other grand 19th-century houses from Portsmouth's most prosperous time) and Abbott's Little Corner Store (1943). The ad-

mission ticket is good for two consecutive days.

Albacore Park

The city's maritime museum, Albacore Park (☎ 603-436-3680, 600 Market St; adult/ senior/child $5/3.50/2; open 9:30am-5pm late May–mid-Oct, 9:30am-4pm Thur-Mon mid-Oct–late May) hosts the USS Albacore, a 205-foot-long submarine. The Albacore was launched from the Portsmouth Naval Shipyard in 1953, and with a crew of 55 men it was piloted around the world for 19 years without firing a shot. When the sub was retired to Portsmouth, it became the centerpiece of the maritime museum. You can tour the 27-foot-wide sub, which is located near I-95 exit 7.

Strawbery Banke Museum, Portsmouth

Children's Museum of Portsmouth

Ensconced in an old meeting house, this exciting museum (☎ 603-436-3853, 280 Marcy St; adult/senior/child $4/3/4; open 10am-5pm Tues-Sat & 1pm-5pm Sun; also open 10am-5pm Mon mid-June–Aug) has changing exhibits, toys and experiments for children one to 10 years old. As you might expect, many displays elucidate the region's maritime history in an engaging way.

Historic Houses

Several of Portsmouth's grand old houses have been beautifully preserved.

John Paul Jones (1747–92) was America's first great naval commander, who coined the phrase, 'I have not yet begun to fight!' The 1758 **John Paul Jones House** (☎ 603-436-8420, 43 Middle St; adult/child $5/2.50; open 10am-4pm Mon-Sat, noon-4pm Sun mid-May–mid-Oct) was a boardinghouse when the naval hero lodged here during the outfitting of the Ranger (1777) and the America (1781). It's now the headquarters of the Portsmouth Historical Society.

The 1760 **Wentworth Gardner House** (☎ 603-436-4406, 50 Mechanic St; adult/ child $5/free; open 1pm-4pm Tues-Sun mid-June–mid-Oct) is simply one of the finest Georgian houses in the USA.

The **Moffatt-Ladd House** (☎ 603-436-8221, 154 Market St; adult/child $5/2.50; open 11am-5pm Mon-Sat & 1pm-5pm Sun mid-June–mid-Oct), originally owned by an influential ship captain, was later the home of General William Whipple, a signer of the Declaration of Independence. The 18th-century chestnut tree and the gardens behind the house are particularly noteworthy. Viewing the old-fashioned gardens by themselves costs $2.

The 1784 **Governor John Langdon House** (☎ 603-436-3205, 143 Pleasant St; adult/ senior/child $6/5/3; open 11am-4pm Wed-Sun June–mid-Oct) was the home of a prosperous merchant who later served as the state's governor.

The Federal-style 1807 **Rundlet-May House** (☎ 603-436-3205, 364 Middle St;

adult/senior/child $6/5/3; open 11am-4pm Sat & Sun June–mid-Oct) was built by a wealthy merchant, and it's furnished with many pieces handcrafted in Portsmouth.

The 1716 **Warner House** (☎ 603-436-5909, Daniel & Chapel Sts; adult/child $5/2.50; open 10am-4pm Mon-Sat & 1pm-4pm Sun June-Oct) is a fine brick residence with rich paneling and lush murals.

The 42-room **Wentworth-Coolidge Mansion** (☎ 603-436-6607, 375 Little Harbor Rd; adult/child $3/free; open 10am-3pm Tues, Thur-Sat & noon-5pm Sun May-Oct), south of the town center, was home to New Hampshire's first royal governor and served as the colony's government center from 1741 to 1767. The lilacs on its grounds are descendants of the first lilacs planted in America, which were brought over from England by Governor Benning Wentworth.

Prescott Park

The city's major waterfront park boasts a large formal garden with fountains and more than 500 varieties of riotous annuals. Musical performances, part of the Prescott Park Arts Festival (☎ 603-436-2848), take place throughout the summer. The haven is open from dawn to dusk, providing shade, flowers and quiet, along with fine views of the river mouth and harbor.

Cruises

Portsmouth Harbor Cruises (☎ 603-436-8084, 800-776-0915, Ceres St Dock; adult $10-17, senior $8.50-16, child $6-9) sponsors (in warm weather) one- to 2½-hour narrated cruises up an inland river, past a couple of lighthouses, through the harbor, along the coast and out to the Isles of Shoals. The summertime evening trips are the shortest, least expensive and perhaps most relaxing offerings.

Isles of Shoals Steamship/Ocean Expeditions Whale Watch (☎ 603-431-5500, 800-441-4620, 315 Market St, Barker Wharf; adult $15-28, child $10-18) runs an excellent narrated harbor and historic Isles of Shoals combo trip aboard a replica 1900s-style ferry mid-June to October. This is a deservedly popular voyage, especially the midday trip, which docks at Star Island for three hours. Look into their all-day whale watches and shorter sunset and dinner cruises.

Places to Stay

Camping Most camping areas are privately run, inland from the seacoast and very busy in the summer. Some campgrounds do not accept tents, only RVs.

Great Bay Camping (☎ 603-778-0226, 56 NH 108, Newfields) Sites without/with hookups $19/23. Open mid-May–Sept. About 13 miles from Portsmouth, this family-oriented camping area has 95 sites best suited to RVs. It's nicely maintained and sited on a tidal river.

Ferndale Acres (☎ 603-659-5082, 132 Wednesday Hill Rd, Lee) Sites $25. Open mid-May–mid-Sept. About 20 miles from Portsmouth, this family-oriented campground is off NH 155 and has 150 shaded sites for both tents and RVs.

Hotels & Motels Many of Portsmouth's motels and hotels cluster at I-95 exits 5 and 6, around the Portsmouth (Interstate) traffic circle. Prices are generally lower during the week (Sunday to Thursday) and rise for Friday and Saturday. The low prices given here are for weekdays June through October, the high prices for summer weekends.

Best Western Wynwood Hotel & Suites (☎ 603-436-7600, 800-528-1234, fax 603-346-7600, W www.portsmouthnh.com/wynwood, 580 US 1 bypass) Motor lodge $79/98, hotel rooms $98/125, suites $125/185-225. This 169-room hotel at the traffic circle also has a generic restaurant (Bickford's) that's open 24 hours.

Anchorage Inn (☎ 603-431-8111, 800-370-8111, fax 603-431-8111, W www.anchorageinn.com, 417 Woodbury Ave) Doubles $100/130. Very close to the traffic circle, this place has 93 rooms, an indoor swimming pool and a sauna.

Sheraton Harborside Portsmouth (☎ 603-431-2300, 800-235-3535, fax 603-431-7805, W www.sheraton.com, 250 Market St) Doubles $190-230. The city's grandest accommodations are these 200 rooms conveniently located across from the Isles of Shoals Steamship docks, only a three-block stroll from Market Square.

Inns & B&Bs At the *Bow Street Inn* (☎ 603-431-7760, fax 603-433-1680, W www.bowstreetinn.com, 121 Bow St), a standard room costs $129 and a river-view room $149-175 with continental breakfast. Just a few blocks from Market Square, this citified inn is housed within a converted redbrick brewery overlooking the river. Most of the 10 rooms have a river view and brass beds.

Inn at Strawbery Banke (☎ 603-436-7242, 800-428-3933, W www.innatstrawberybanke.com, 314 Court St) Doubles $135-150 with breakfast. This adequate seven-room inn, just a five-minute walk from Market Square, is conveniently located among historic houses. Some rooms are in the 19th-century building, others in the more modern addition.

Sise Inn (☎ 603-433-1200, 877-747-3466, fax 603-431-0200, W www.someplacesdifferent.com, 40 Court St) Doubles $165-185, suites $190-260 with continental breakfast. A short walk from the city center, this elegant, Queen Anne–style inn dates from 1881. It has 28 rooms and six suites with hotel-style accoutrements like CD players and telephones.

Places to Eat

Near Market Square Breakfasts, coffee, beer and pizza. Who could ask for more?

Breaking New Grounds (☎ 603-436-9555, 16 Market St) Open 6:30am-10:30pm. Judging by the aroma and the roasting and grinding machines in full view, coffee is the main draw here.

Me & Ollie's Cafe (☎ 603-433-6588, 10 Pleasant St) Open 7am-6:30pm Mon-Sat, 8am-5pm Sun. Mains $3-6. Forgive the grammatical construction of the cafe's name; delectable breads are the focus here. An army of breads is utilized to make little pizzettes (piled with peach and raspberry crumble), grilled panini sandwiches (rife with pesto and veggies) and as bowls for soup (carved French boules are filled with vegetarian delights).

Café Brioche (☎ *603-430-9225, 14 Market Square*) Sandwiches $4-5. Open 6am-6pm Sun-Fri & 6am-11pm Sat. Overlooking Market Square, Brioche is a nice, upscale cafe offering coffee, pastry and light meals. For easy picnicking, try a box lunch for $10.

The Friendly Toast (☎ *603-430-2154, 121 Congress St*) Mains $4.25-7.75. Open 7am-11pm Mon-Thur & 7am Fri to 9pm Sun. Yes that's right; they're open non-stop from Friday morning through Sunday night. This retro, kitschy diner-like eatery dishes out meals ranging from 'plain to strange,' according to one reviewer. The mission burrito is humongous and the falafel tasty.

Portsmouth Brewery (☎ *603-431-1115, 56 Market St*) Mains $10-18. Open 11:30am-11pm. This airy brewpub has a long menu of salads, pastas, sandwiches (about $5), main dishes and even vegetarian fajitas. It's perfectly acceptable to have just a pint and a bite, too. Appetizers like chowder and chili ($5 to $8) hit the spot.

Portsmouth Gas Light Company (☎ *603-430-9122, 64 Market St*) Pizza averages $10, mains $9-17. Open 11:30am-10pm. In a historic building with tin ceilings and exposed ductwork once occupied by its namesake, the specialty here is brick-oven pizza (check out the all-you-can-eat pizza buffet from 11:30am to 2pm for $7), but there are also more elaborate dishes. In fine weather, you can dine on the rear, umbrella-shaded terrace.

The Metro (☎ *603-436-0521, 20 High St*) Lunch $7-10, dinner $13-26. Open 11:30am-2:30pm & 5:30pm-9:30pm Mon-Sat. Among the city's posh places to dine, the New American contemporary menu here is appealing and substantially cheaper for lunch than dinner. Dark paneling, wall sconces and white linen tablecloths lend the place a romantic and conservative feel. Look for live jazz on Friday and Saturday evenings.

Bow & Penhallow Sts A lot of good eating places are packed into a small area.

Caffe Kilim (☎ *603-436-7730, 79 Daniel St*) Open 7am-9pm Mon-Sat & 7am-8pm

Sun. This little Turkish hole-in-the-wall is a funky addition to New Hampshire's espresso scene.

Ceres Bakery (☎ *603-436-6518, 51 Penhallow St*) Open 7am to 4 or 5pm Mon-Sat. This is a good, spartan place to pick up fresh bread or pastry for a snack or picnic. The menu is limited to quiche, soups and a few sandwiches.

Goldi's Deli (☎ *603-431-1178, 106 Penhallow St*) Sandwiches $2-7. Open 8am-3pm. An attractive two-story deli with a long menu of cheap sandwiches with humorous names, Goldi's also has bagels, lox, blintzes and kosher items.

Old Ferry Landing (☎ *603-431-5510, 10 Ceres St*) Lunch $6-10, dinner $13-20. Open 11:30am-8pm mid-Apr–mid-Sept. Next to the tugboats, this inexpensive seafood restaurant in a former ferry terminal has traditional New England seafood like lobster rolls and haddock sandwiches. Note the live lobster tank (always a good sign) just inside the door.

Chiangmai (☎ *603-433-1289, 128 Penhallow St*) Mains $7-15.50. Open for lunch & dinner Tues-Sat & dinner Sun. This pleasant and tasty Thai restaurant features the requisite chicken satay and pad thai.

The Stockpot (☎ *603-431-1851, 53 Bow St*) Lunch dishes under $10, dinner under $18. Open 11am-11:30pm. Advertising 'good food cheap,' The Stockpot delivers. If you want a tugboat view accompanying your clam chowder and sandwich specials, this is the place. You might get lucky with a leg of lamb sandwich or curried chicken and veggie stir fry. After 5pm, more substantial plates are served.

Poco's Bow Street Cantina (☎ *603-431-5967, 37 Bow St*) Mains $9-19. Open 11:30am-10pm. This cantina serves Southwestern dishes with a New England flair to a fun crowd. While tempted by lobster tacos or seafood chimichangas, keep in mind that no-nonsense steak and seafood dishes are more popular. The waterside dining area is pleasant in good weather, but there are nice harbor views inside, too.

Porto Bello (☎ *603-431-2989, 67 Bow St*) Mains $12-22. Open 4:30pm-9:30pm

Wed-Sun. Portsmouth's traditional Italian restaurant, located on the 2nd floor, offers regional dishes from throughout Italy.

Harpoon Willy's (☎ *603-433-4441, 67 Bow St*) Mains $16-22. Open for lunch & dinner spring to fall. Beneath Porto Bello and open in warm weather only (no one can predict when it will open or close for the season), this open-air harbourside eatery specializes in 'lobster in the rough' (simple steamed lobster), large plates of fish-and-chips, fried clams and the like.

Elsewhere Look for fresh produce two blocks from Market Square at the *Farmers Market (Parrot Ave)* Open 8am-1pm Sat May-Oct.

Blue Mermaid (☎ *603-427-2583, The Hill at Hanover and High Sts*) Lunch $8-10, dinner $15-25. Open daily. Portsmouth's hippest restaurant is just a few minute's walk from the center. Wood-grilled seafood, burgers and pizzas are a specialty, particularly enlivened by a margarita or martini. Ethnic dishes from Asian seared pork to Caribbean pan-seared cod, from Bimini chicken to chicken Santa Fe also rule the roost.

The Library Restaurant (☎ *603-431-5202, 401 State St*) Lunch $10-18, dinner $18-28. Open daily. Within a palatial and opulent home built by a prominent judge in 1785, The Library highlights traditional, classic dishes. In addition to the wood-paneled dining room, there's an English pub.

Entertainment
Portsmouth is a local mecca for music as well as dining. Several clubs feature ever-changing schedules of local and national acts playing rock, folk, jazz, R&B, and so on.

The Press Room (☎ *603-431-5186, 77 Daniel St*) This joint has live music nightly and a long menu of bar food priced at less than $8.

Muddy River Smokehouse (☎ *603-430-9582, 21 Congress St*) Barbecue and bands (Wednesday to Sunday) compete at this lively, 2nd-floor Market Square venue. A faux roadhouse look, more appealing with each drink, pervades the back room.

The Metro, mentioned above under Places to Eat, has live jazz on Friday and Saturday evenings.

Getting There & Around
The Coast Trolley Downtown Loop (☎ 603-743-5777) provides free shuttle service from public parking lots. It runs to the major historic sights around town from June to mid-September daily except Sunday. Pick up a schedule and route map at the Market Square information kiosk.

Greyhound/Vermont Transit runs three or four buses daily on a route connecting Boston and Portsmouth with Portland, Bangor and Bar Harbor, Maine. Portsmouth to Boston takes 1¼ hours ($18 one-way). The bus station is located at Federal Tobacconists (☎ 603-436-0163, 10 Ladd St), just off Market Square.

Portsmouth is equidistant from Boston and Portland, Maine. It takes about 1¼ hours to travel the 55 miles via I-95 in either direction. It takes an hour (47 miles) to reach Manchester from Portsmouth.

Monadnock Region

In the southwestern corner of the state, the pristine villages of Peterborough and Jaffrey Center anchor Mount Monadnock (3165 feet), the world's second-most-climbed mountain after Mount Fuji in Japan. Keene (population 23,000), at the junction of commercial NH 12 and NH 10, is the region's largest town, where residents run errands and conduct daily business. US 202 north from Jaffrey to Hancock, from where you can continue on NH 123 north toward Alstead, is a scenic route through a handsome region dotted with lakes.

For more Monadnock information, the Greater Keene Chamber of Commerce (☎ 603-352-1303, 48 Central Square, Keene 03431) is a great source, situated in the center of town. It's open weekdays 9am to 5pm.

PETERBOROUGH
This small village is a convenient regional base for exploration. Pleasant for strolling,

with a growing number of galleries and restaurants, Peterborough served as the inspiration for Thornton Wilder's play, *Our Town*.

Orientation & Information
Peterborough is unavoidably located just north of the intersection of NH 101 and NH 123/US 202. Depot Square is the heart of town. The Greater Peterborough Chamber of Commerce (☎ 603-924-7234, W www. peterboroughchamber.com), at the highway intersection, is a friendly informational source. It's open 9am to 5pm weekdays year-round and 10am to 3pm Saturdays from mid-June through October.

The Toadstool Bookshop (☎ 603-924-3543, 12 Depot St), has good regional and general titles.

Things to See & Do
Sharon Arts Center (☎ 603-924-2787, 20-40 Depot St; admission free), located about 8 miles south of Peterborough on NH 123 in Sharon, also has an annex gallery in Depot Square featuring the same fine arts and crafts. Don't miss it.

The region's back roads were made for cycling and you can rent wheels at **Eclectic Bicycle** (☎ 603-924-9797, 109 Grove St). Mountain bikes cost $15 daily.

The prestigious **Monadnock Music** (☎ 603-924-7610) performs free concerts in meetinghouses and town halls throughout the region's villages from mid-June to mid-September. Look for the schedule at the information center.

Places to Stay
For a complete list of smaller places to stay, surf W www.monadnocklodging.com or W www.nhlodging.com.

Camping Choose from 250 lakeside tent sites at *Greenfield State Park* (☎ 603-547-3497, off NH 136) Sites $16. Open mid-May–mid-Oct. Twelve miles northeast of Peterborough, this 400-acre park has fine swimming and hiking.

B&Bs Traveling with a crowd? *Peterborough Manor B&B* (☎ 603-924-9832, W www

.peterboroughmanor.com, 50 Summer St) Doubles $55 with continental breakfast. This late-19th-century manse still harbors shades of its AYH past. Some of the seven rooms have multiple beds and the kitchen remains communal. This is a find.

Hannah Davis House (☎ 603-585-3344, 186 Depot Rd) Doubles $70-140 with full breakfast. This excellent B&B features six rooms and suites decorated with great attention and flair. One has a fireplace and another has both a fireplace and a separate entrance.

The Amos Parker House (☎ 603-585-6540, NH 119) Doubles $105-125 with full breakfast. In addition to formal breakfasts served by candlelight, this comfortably refined bed and breakfast property has six rooms and suites furnished with antiques. Be sure to visit in warm weather since the friendly innkeeper's acre-sized plot has been transformed into a rare oasis. Gardeners, confident they've died and gone to heaven, might never want to leave.

Places to Eat
Twelve Pine (☎ 603-924-6140, Depot St) Mains $2-6. Open 8am-7pm Mon-Fri, 9am-4pm Sat. A former train station, this sweet-smelling cafe has a good deli selection and specialty foods, as well as a nice coffee and juice bar.

Peterborough Diner (☎ 603-924-6202, Depot St) Mains $2-10. Open 6am-9pm. This 1950s diner has typical fare served at the counter or in booths.

Aesop's Tables (☎ 603-924-1612, 12 Depot St) Mains $3-6. Open 7:30am-4pm Mon-Sat. Within the Toadstool Bookstore, which in turn occupies a cavernous former grocery store, this cafe serves good blackboard specials, sweet treats and coffee. In summer the ice-cream window and patio are popular.

JAFFREY
The town proper is less interesting than Jaffrey Center, picture-perfect and 2 miles due west of Jaffrey. For a bit of local color, try to catch the Temple Band, the oldest town band in the country, which gives free

concerts on the Jaffrey Town Green on many Wednesday evenings in the summer.

The Jaffrey Chamber of Commerce (☎ 603-532-4549, W www.jaffreycoc.org, 28 Main St), behind the Bank of New Hampshire, is a good source of information. It's open 9:30am to 2:30pm Monday through Wednesday, until 5pm on Thursday and Friday and from 9am to noon on Saturday.

Mt Monadnock
This commanding peak (☎ 603-532-8862, *Dublin Rd off NH 124; admission $3 over age 12)*, which you can see from 50 miles away in any direction, is the area's spiritual vertex. Complete with a visitor center where you can get good hiking information, 12 miles of ungroomed cross-country ski trails and over 40 miles of hiking trails (6 miles of which reach the summit), this state park is a nice place to spend an afternoon. Take the White Dot Trail (which turns into the White Cross Trail) from the visitor center to the bare-topped peak. The hike takes about 3½ hours roundtrip. Monadnock, by the way, means 'mountain that stands alone' in Algonquian parlance.

Maple Sugaring
For more than 200 years, **Bacon's Sugar House** (☎ 603-532-8836, *Dublin Rd; admission free; open for sales year-round)* has been a family farm and sugaring operation. Bacon's is conveniently located just south of the Mt Monadnock State Park entrance. Always call ahead; nature is unpredictable in March, and if the sap isn't flowing, maple sugar producers aren't boiling.

Places to Stay
Primitive is the word at popular *Monadnock State Park* (☎ 603-532-8862, 603-271-3628 for reservations, NH 124) Sites $12-16. Open year-round. Four miles west of US 202, this 1000-acre park has 21 sites. From November until mid-May there is no water and since they don't plow the road, you must pack in supplies. (It's less than a mile hike.)

Emerald Acres Campground (☎ 603-532-8838, 39 Ridgecrest Rd) Sites without/with hookups $14/21.50. Open May–mid-Oct. Off NH 124, these 52 forested sites are adjacent to a lake with swimming and boat rentals.

Benjamin Prescott Inn (☎ 603-532-6637, 888-950-6637, fax 603-532-6637, W www .benjaminprescottinn.com, NH 124) Doubles $80-155 with full breakfast. In East Jaffrey, this classic mid-19th-century farmhouse has 10 country-style guest rooms that have been meticulously restored. Expansive views of the surrounding 500-acre dairy farm and fields are icing on the cake.

AREA VILLAGES
The region is a web of narrow, indirect roads connecting vintage towns. And you could easily spend a couple of days bopping from one village to another. There isn't much to do in any of them, but they'll linger in your mind long after departing. If you're tooling around, stop for a short spell in **Fitzwilliam**, with its town green surrounded by lovely old houses and a graceful town hall (with a stunning steeple). Fitzwilliam is on NH 119, 13 miles southwest of Jaffrey.

Harrisville, northwest of Peterborough via NH 101 and Dublin, is a former mill village that looks much as it did in the late 1700s, when woolen mills reigned. But this is no living museum; today, the brick and granite mill buildings have been renovated into functionally aesthetic commercial spaces.

It's hard to get enough of these quintessential towns and **Hancock**, north of Peterborough on NH 123, is one of the best. The town's showpiece is one of the oldest continuously operating inns in New England. *Hancock Inn* (☎ 603-525-3318, 800-525-1789, fax 603-525-9301, W www.hancock inn.com, 33 Main St) Doubles $120-250 with full breakfast. New Hampshire's oldest inn, with 15 rooms, has been completely renovated and features canopy beds, quilts and braided rugs. They serve traditional New England dinners.

Hillsborough Center, 14 miles north of Hancock on NH 123, is another classic, not to be confused with Hillsborough Lower Village and Upper Village. Steeped in the late 18th and early 19th century, the trim little town boasts a number of art studios. Stop into **Caron's Diner** (☎ *603-464-3575, 85 Henniker St*) to get the local lowdown and a piece of meatloaf.

Although Concord Trailways (☎ 603-228-3300, 800-639-3317) buses stop at the Fitzwilliam Inn in Fitzwilliam (☎ 603-585-9000, 526 Main St), the region's wealth is certainly best explored by car. Vermont Transit (☎ 603-436-0163, 800-552-8737) serves Keene from its terminal (☎ 603-352-1331) at 6 Gilbo Ave.

To reach Peterborough and Jaffrey from Manchester, head south then east on NH 101. Expect the 40-mile trip to take about 1½ hours. It also makes sense to visit the region on the way to or from Brattleboro, VT.

Manchester & Concord Area

Although New Hampshire is noted more for mountains than cities, Manchester, a historic mill city, and Concord, the state's tidy capital, are worth a look. In local tourist parlance, the surrounding region is called the Merrimack Valley.

MANCHESTER
Exploiting the abundant water power of the Merrimack River, Manchester (population 106,000) became the state's manufacturing and commercial center in the early 19th century. It's now the banking center as well. Students crowd the campuses of New Hampshire Technical College, Notre Dame College and the University of New Hampshire.

Orientation & Information
Manchester stretches along the east bank of the Merrimack River; West Manchester is on the river's west side. If you enter Manchester from I-93, you miss the view that defines the city's history: the redbrick swath of the great Amoskeag textile mills stretching along the east bank of the river for over a mile. To get the view, follow I-293 along the west bank of the river. After you've

passed the mills, exit via the Amoskeag Bridge or the Queen City Bridge to enter the town.

The heart of Manchester lies along Elm St (US 3), running north-south through the business and commercial district. The Currier Gallery of Art is six blocks east of Elm St along Beech St (follow signs). Many hotels and motels are clustered at the interstate exits.

The Greater Manchester Chamber of Commerce (☎ 603-666-6600, Ⓦ www.manchester-chamber.org, 889 Elm St, Manchester, NH 03101) offers good information.

Currier Gallery of Art
The state's premier fine-arts museum (☎ *603-669-6144, 201 Myrtle Way; adult/senior $5/4, child under 18 yrs free, free for all 10am-1pm Sat; open 11am-5pm Sun, Mon, Wed, Thur, 11am-8pm Fri, 10am-5pm Sat*) has an excellent collection of 19th- and 20th-century European and American glass, English and American silver and pewter and colonial and early American furniture. As for European painters, Degas is the highlight.

Amoskeag Mills
These former textile mills, impressive brick buildings with hundreds and hundreds of tall windows, stretch along Commercial St on the Merrimack riverbank for almost 1½ miles. Other mills face the buildings from across the river in West Manchester. For almost a century, from 1838 to 1920, the Amoskeag Manufacturing Company was the world's largest textile manufacturer. The mills employed up to 17,000 people a year (out of a city population of 70,000). Many mill employees lived in the trim brick tenements stretching up the hillside eastward from the mills. The restored tenements are still used as housing.

As for the mills, the company abandoned them in 1935. Many are now offices, college classrooms, restaurants, warehouses, and broadcasting studios. To appreciate the scale of the buildings, follow the restored riverwalk that runs north and south from the Notre Dame Bridge.

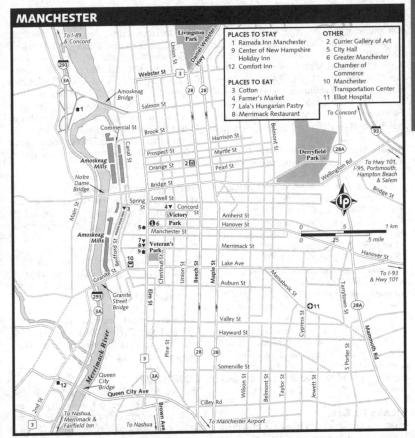

MANCHESTER

PLACES TO STAY
1 Ramada Inn Manchester
9 Center of New Hampshire
   Holiday Inn
12 Comfort Inn

PLACES TO EAT
3 Cotton
4 Farmer's Market
7 Lala's Hungarian Pastry
8 Merrimack Restaurant

OTHER
2 Currier Gallery of Art
5 City Hall
6 Greater Manchester
   Chamber of
   Commerce
10 Manchester
   Transportation Center
11 Elliot Hospital

Anheuser-Busch Brewery

The Anheuser-Busch Company (☎ 603-595-1202, 221 Daniel Webster Hwy; admission free; open 10am-4pm daily), which brews Budweiser and Michelob, has a large brewery in nearby Merrimack, one of a dozen throughout the USA. The world's largest beer brewer makes 86 million barrels annually. Tour the plant, watch the foamy stuff fermenting, then lift a sample glass yourself.

Animal lovers should not miss the **Clydesdale Hamlet**, home of the majestic draft horses that are Anheuser-Busch's trademark. (You may have seen their advertisements with the Clydesdales pulling an old-fashioned brewer's wagon.) To reach the brewery, go south on I-293 to the Everett Turnpike (US 3) and then take exit 10 (Industrial Drive).

Places to Stay

Camping Although there are no camping places in greater Manchester, southern New Hampshire has a number of nice state parks.

Bear Brook State Park (☎ 603-485-9869, 603-271-3628 reservations, NH 28, Allenstown) Sites $15. Open mid-May–mid-Oct. Halfway to Concord, this 10,000-acre park has 98 sites, hiking and lake swimming. Follow US 3 north, turn right onto NH 28 and follow signs.

Pawtuckaway State Park *(☎ 603-895-3031, 603-271-3628 reservations, NH 156, Nottingham)* Sites without/with water view $16/22. Open late May–mid-Oct. If you're willing to drive 40 minutes, you can camp at these 192 sites on 6500 acres. Halfway between Manchester and Portsmouth, take NH 101 east to Raymond and follow signs.

Hotels

Most lodging here is for business travelers, so hotel discounts are often available when business is slow.

Comfort Inn *(☎ 603-668-2600, 800-228-5150, fax 603-668-2600, ⓦ www.comfort inn.com, 298 Queen City Ave)* Doubles $89-99. While it is in a commercial district west of the highway and river, this newer 103-room hotel is still convenient to the Queen City Bridge. Take exit 4 off I-293.

Ramada Inn Manchester *(☎ 603-669-2660, 800-272-6232, fax 603-669-1135, ⓦ www .ramada.com, 21 Front St)* Doubles $89-149. The Ramada has 120 comfortable rooms off I-293 exit 6, on the west side of the river.

Center of New Hampshire Holiday Inn *(☎ 603-625-1000, 800-465-4329, fax 603-625-4595, ⓦ www.sixcontinentshotels.com, 700 Elm St)* Doubles $139-179. This 250-room place is right in the middle of the business district.

Places to Eat

Most restaurants are on Elm St (US 3) in the center of the business district (take I-293 exit 5 and cross the Granite St Bridge). The best one, by far, is in the mill district.

Farmers Market *(Concord Street)* Open 3pm-6:30pm Thur June-Sept.

Lala's Hungarian Pastry *(☎ 603-647-7100, 836 Elm St)* Mains $5-7. Open 7am-5pm Mon-Fri & 9am-2pm Sat. No-nonsense Lala's has wondrous Hungarian pastries to spoil your diet, as well as savory ethnic luncheon specials, including chicken goulash and schnitzel.

Merrimack Restaurant *(☎ 603-669-5222, 786 Elm St)* Lunch $5-6, dinner $8-17. Open for all three meals Mon-Sat, breakfast Sun.

This old-fashioned restaurant with Naugahyde booths and swivel stools has familiar American fare – salads, sandwiches, seafood, chicken and steaks – at low prices.

Cotton *(☎ 603-622-5488, 75 Arms Park Drive)* Lunch $7-10, dinner $13-20. Open for lunch Mon-Fri, dinner daily. For artfully prepared fare in urbane and sophisticated surroundings, this hip cafe near the river and the Amoskeag mills wins hands down. In warm weather, the vine-shaded terrace is romantic and secluded. Expect organic field greens, thin-crust pizzas, ginger-soy glazed mahi-mahi and the like.

Getting There & Away

Manchester Airport *(☎ 603-624-6539)*, off US 3 south of Manchester, is a civilized alternative to Boston's Logan International Airport.

Concord Trailways, at the Manchester Transportation Center *(☎ 603-228-3300, 800-639-3317, 119 Canal St)*, runs frequent daily buses to Boston (one hour; $15). An equal number of buses go north to Concord (30 minutes; $4.50).

Driving from Boston to Manchester via I-93 and the Everett Turnpike takes an hour. It's another 30 minutes from Manchester to Concord via I-93.

CONCORD

The New Hampshire state capital (population 38,000) is a well-rounded town. Its citizens work at government, light manufacturing, crafts, education and retail sales, as you'll see immediately when you approach the gigantic shopping mall beside I-93. They also quarry granite, a suitable occupation in the Granite State. The facades of the State House and many of the buildings surrounding it, as well as that of the Library of Congress in Washington, DC, were fashioned from stone quarried nearby. Despite its modest charms, Concord will not grip you, and after a visit of several hours, you'll be on your way again.

Orientation & Information

I-93 passes just east of the city center, and US 3 is Main St, where you'll find everything worth visiting. Take I-93 exit 14 or 15 for Main St.

The Greater Concord Chamber of Commerce (☎ 603-224-2508, Ⓦ www.concordnh chamber.com, 40 Commercial St, Concord, NH 03301) maintains a small information kiosk in front of the State House on N Main St (open noon to 6pm Friday, 10am to 4pm Saturday and noon to 4pm Sunday from late May to mid-October).

State Capitol

The handsome State House (☎ 603-271-2154, 107 N Main St; admission free; open 8am-4pm Mon-Fri) was built in 1819 and the state legislature still meets in the original chambers. It's the longest such tenure in the USA. A self-guided tour brochure tells you all you'll need to know. The Hall of Flags holds the standards that state military units carried into battle. Portraits and statues of New Hampshire leaders, including the great orator Daniel Webster, line its corridors and stand in its lofty halls. A statue of Franklin Pierce (see Pierce Manse, below) stands in front of the building.

Museum of New Hampshire History

The New Hampshire Historical Society operates this intriguing two-story warehouse (☎ 603-228-6688, 7 Eagle Sq/N Main St; family/senior/adult/child 6-18 yrs $15/5/4/2.50, free 5pm-8:30pm Thur; open 9:30am-5pm Tues-Wed & Fri-Sat; 9:30am-8:30pm Thur; noon-5pm Sun; 9:30am-5pm daily Dec & July–mid-Oct).

The chronological displays illuminate such arcane subjects as the Concord Coach, the stagecoach that provided transport to much of America's western frontier. One of the most compelling exhibits considers the state's famous residents, from Shaker 'eldresses' to Robert Frost to President Franklin Pierce. The museum also has beautiful 19th-century landscape paintings of the White Mountains. The handsome building itself – granite again – is a good place for a stroll. And the small park outside, with a fountain and sidewalk cafe, is a good place to rest.

Pierce Manse

The home of Franklin Pierce (1804–69), 14th president of the US, is now a museum. The manse (☎ 603-225-2068, 224-7668, 14 Penacook St; adult/child $3/50¢; open 11am-3pm Mon-Fri mid-June–mid-Sept) was completed in 1839 and served as his family home from 1842 to 1848. Pierce was the son of a two-term New Hampshire governor, a member and later speaker of the New Hampshire General Court (legislature) and a representative and senator in Congress. He retired from the US Senate to practice law in Concord, maintaining an interest in politics but having little interest in further public service. But during the Democratic party's convention of 1852, there were so many strong candidates for the presidency that none could achieve a majority vote. On the 49th ballot, Pierce, a compromise candidate, became the party's nominee, and he went on to win the presidential election.

Christa McAuliffe Planetarium

This planetarium (☎ 603-271-7827, 2 Institute Dr; adult/senior, child $8/5; open 10am-5pm Thur-Sat, noon-5pm Sun, with expanded hours during the summer), just off exit 15 from I-93, honors the New Hampshire schoolteacher chosen to be America's first teacher-astronaut. McAuliffe and her fellow astronauts died in the tragic explosion of the Challenger spacecraft on January 28, 1986. Call for a schedule of the hour-long shows, many open to the public.

Places to Stay

Several highway hotels and motels attract government business, but most tourists rocket through to the mountains or lakes.

Comfort Inn (☎ 603-226-4100, 800-228-5150, fax 603-228-2106, Ⓦ www.comfortinn .com, 71 Hall St) Doubles $79-109 off-season, $99-189 May-Oct. While this standard 100-room inn is in a residential area, it is still centrally located off I-93 exit 13. It has a heated indoor pool, a spa and a fitness center.

Holiday Inn (☎ 603-224-9534, 800-465-4329, fax 603-224-8266, Ⓦ www.sixcontinents hotels.com, 172 N Main St) Doubles $89-149.

This comfortable 122-room hotel is downtown and has amenities similar to the Comfort Inn's.

Centennial Inn (☎ 603-225-7102, 800-360-4839, fax 603-225-5031, 96 Pleasant St) Rooms $99-199, suites $149-275 with continental breakfast. This turn-of-the-20th-century turreted manse has 32 luxurious rooms and suites outfitted with computer modems and VCRs.

Places to Eat

Most restaurants catch the legislative lunch crowd across from the State House on N Main St at Park St.

Bread and Chocolate (☎ 603-228-3330, 20 S Main St) Open Mon-Sat. This exceptional European-style bakery could hold its own in the French or German countryside. Their sandwiches are very good, too, although the selection is limited.

In a Pinch Cafe (☎ 603-226-2272, 146 Pleasant St) Mains $4-6. Open for breakfast & lunch Mon-Sat. Good sandwiches, soups and salads provide sustenance here. Grab some picnic fare or relax on the sun porch.

Durgin Lane Deli (☎ 603-228-2000, 88 Washington St) Mains $4-6. Open for breakfast & lunch Mon-Sat. The Middle Eastern dishes are a nice alternative to ubiquitous and prosaic sandwiches.

The Common Man (☎ 603-228-3463, 25 Water St) Lunch $4-9, dinner $12-22. Open daily. Oven baked sandwiches constitute the lunch specialties, but dinner is more serious with scrod, baked stuffed shrimp and house specialties including chicken Kiev and prime rib.

Hermanos Cocina Mexicana (☎ 603-224-5669, 11 Hills Ave) Mains $5-18. Open for lunch and dinner. Just off Main St in an unlikely, historic brick building, Hermanos serves authentic and creative Mexican dishes, from pork taquitos to chimichangas. Head to the upstairs bar for excellent margaritas and catch some live jazz (many nights).

Getting There & Away

Concord Trailways, at the Trailways Transportation Center (☎ 603-228-3300, 800-639-3317, 30 Stickney Ave, I-93 exit 14), has frequent daily service between Concord and Boston ($12.50; 1½ hours). From Concord to Lincoln, there is one bus daily ($13.50; 1½ hours).

Driving from Concord to Lincoln via I-93 takes 1¼ hours. It's about 45 minutes from Concord to Weirs Beach via I-93 to US 3 North.

CANTERBURY SHAKER VILLAGE

Members of the United Society of Believers in Christ's Second Appearing were called 'Shakers' because of the religious ecstasies they experienced during worship. (For a history of Shakers, see the Facts about New England chapter or the Pittsfield, Massachusetts, section of this book.)

This particular Shaker community was founded in 1792 and was actively occupied for two centuries. Sister Ethel Hudson, last member of the Shaker colony here, died in 1992 at the age of 96. Canterbury Shaker Village (☎ 603-783-9511, 800-982-9511, 288 Shaker Rd; family/adult/child 6-12 yrs $25/10/5; open 10am-5pm daily May-Oct (last guided tours at 4pm); 10am-5pm Sat & Sun Apr, Nov & Dec) is now preserved as a nonprofit trust to present Shaker history. The lone surviving Shaker community, at Sabbathday Lake, Maine, still accepts new members.

Canterbury Shaker Village has 'interpreters' in period garb who perform the tasks and labors of community daily life: fashioning Shaker furniture and crafts (for sale in the gift shop) and growing herbs and producing herbal medicines. The guided tour takes you to an herb garden, a meetinghouse (1792), apiary (bee house), ministry, 'Sisters' shop (a crafts shop run by Shaker women), laundry, horse barn, infirmary and schoolhouse (1826).

On Friday and Saturday evenings, you can join in an illuminating, traditional four-course candlelight dinner. There's one seating per evening, and it begins at 6:45pm sharp. Dinner is served family style at long tables, and you can choose from a poultry, meat or fish main course. Recipes, ingredi-

Vermont, ablaze with autumn colors, is a leaf-peeper's heaven.

Tranquillity along the Cape Cod National Seashore

One of Vermont's countless classic farms

Sunset on the Mystic Seaport Museum in Mystic, CT

A quiet and glorious end to the day, Newport, RI

Franconia Notch State Park, NH

Red snappers snappin', clam shells clappin', Seal Harbor, ME

ents and cooking methods are all true to Shaker form and philosophy. After a memorable dinner, you'll be guided through the village by candlelight, or if it's off-season and the village is closed, you'll be treated to an evening of folksinging. Dinner costs $40 per person. Alternatively, The Creamery restaurant is open for lunch 11:30am to 2pm when the village is open.

Take I-93 exit 18 and follow the signs, or head 15 miles north of Concord on MA 106.

Lakes Region

Centered on vast Lake Winnipesaukee, the Lakes Region is an odd mix of wondrous natural beauty and commercial tawdriness. Most visitors are New England families who have cottages on or near the lakeshore or who take their annual vacations in one of the roadside motels. The forest-shrouded lakes have beautiful, sinuous coastlines stretching for hundreds of miles. The roads skirting the shores and connecting the lakeside towns, however, are a riotous festival of mindless popular culture, lined with a hodgepodge of shopping malls, gas stations, miniature-golf courses, amusement arcades, auto dealerships, go-cart tracks, motels, private zoos, clam shacks, tourist cottages, junk-food outlets and boat docks.

If you're heading north to the White Mountains or south to Boston, you can spend a day or two pleasantly enough here. Lake Winnipesaukee, New Hampshire's largest, has 183 miles of coastline, more than 300 islands and, despite being landlocked, excellent salmon fishing. Stop for a swim, a lakeside picnic or a cruise. If you have children, don't miss a chance to prowl the video arcades, bowldromes and junk-food cafes of Weirs Beach.

Orientation & Information

Laconia is the population center, with a hospital, an auto parts store and other services. Most visitors stay in the small towns near the lake, such as sedate Glendale, with its small hotels, motels and cottages shaded by pines. Weirs Beach has honky-tonk game arcades and boat rides, while Wolfeboro is aristocratic. Meredith is a more substantial town, with many lodging and dining possibilities.

Larger towns have their own information offices; see the Information section for each destination. You can also try the Lakes Region Association (☎ 603-744-8664, 800-605-2537, Ⓦ www.lakesregion.org, NH 104, New Hampton, NH 03256).

LACONIA AREA

The largest town of the Lakes Region, Laconia occupies itself with light manufacturing of shoes and electrical components. Neighboring Gilford, in the shadow of Belknap Mountain (pronounced 'bell nap'; 2384 feet), is joined at the hip to and indistinguishable from Laconia. In the sedate lakeside town of Glendale, you'll find Ellacoya State Park and its fine beach.

The Greater Laconia-Weirs Beach Chamber of Commerce (☎ 603-524-5531, Ⓦ www.laconia-weirs.org, 11 Veterans Square, Laconia, NH 03246) maintains an information office in the old railroad station in the center of town. It's open 8:30am to 5pm weekdays and noon to 4pm Saturday year-round. The staff can help find same-day accommodations.

Lake Winnipesaukee

The lake (Ⓦ www.winnipesaukee.com) is the region's big attraction. Its euphonious Indian name means 'smile of the Great Spirit'). The stretch between Glendale and Alton Bay is much prettier and less commercial than Laconia itself. To get there, follow NH 11 south from Gilford. Watch for signs for Belknap Point Rd, which is the narrower shoreline drive (NH 11 is well back from the shore). The northeastern side of the lake, on NH 109 between Wolfeboro and Moultonborough is also much more scenic. From Alton Bay, head north on NH 28 to NH 109.

Most lakeshore lodgings have water access, but if your place does not, head for **Ellacoya State Beach Park** (☎ 603-293-7821;

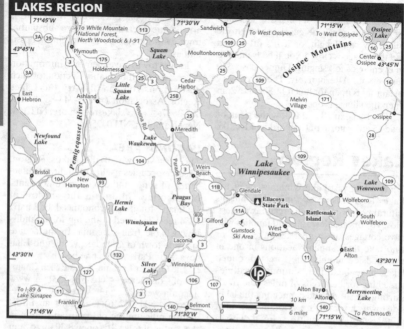

LAKES REGION

admission $3.50/free adults 12-55 yrs/others; open late May–mid-October), which has a 600-foot-wide beach, a picnic area and a campground (see Places to Stay).

Activities

Within the Belknap Mountain State Forest, the Mt Major Trail is a good 2-mile trek up Mt Major (1780 feet). The trail head is a few miles south of West Alton on NH 11; park just off the road.

When the snow covers the ground, Belknap Mountain becomes **Gunstock** (☎ 800-486-7862, NH 11A, Gilford), a ski area with a campground (see Places to Stay). Gunstock sports 45 downhill runs on a vertical drop of 1400 feet. There are seven lifts, as well as a ski school, day care facilities and night skiing. Most mountain trails are intermediate, with more advanced than beginner trails. Over 30 miles of cross-country trails follow the wooded paths around Gilford. Rental skis are available, as are snowboards,

snowskates (boots attached to shortened skis) and telemark skis.

Special Events

The annual Motorcycle Week takes place in early to mid-June and draws two-wheeled crowds to the New Hampshire International Speedway (☎ 603-783-4931) on NH 106 in Loudon, south of Laconia. Races, shows and other events create quite a scene. Bikers are everywhere. Lodgings, particularly campgrounds and motels, are expensive and can be impossible to find, so reserve well ahead.

Places to Stay

Camping It's a long trip for a glass of water at **Gunstock** (☎ 603-293-4341, 800-486-7862, NH 11A, Gilford) Sites without/with hookups $24/31. Open mid-May–mid-Oct & Dec-Feb. Basically a ski area with a campground, these 275 sites offer access to heated bathrooms, but there is no water at the sites.

Ellacoya State Beach Park (☎ 603-293-7821, 603-436-1552 for reservations, off NH 11, Gilford) Sites $35. Open mid-May–mid-Oct. There are 35 unshaded sites with full RV hookups here.

Clearwater Campground (☎ 603-279-7761, NH 104, Meredith) Sites without/with hookups $34/38. Open mid-May–mid-Oct. Lots of family facilities accompany these 151 sites on 35 lakeside acres. You can rent rowboats, canoes and paddleboats; play horseshoes; or use the playground and game room. When Clearwater closes for the winter, its sister campground across the street, *Meredith Woods*, remains open year-round.

Motels Here are a couple of area motels that are reasonable, but not cheap.

Super 8 Motel (☎ 603-286-8882, 800-800-8000, fax 603-286-8788, Ⓦ www.super8 motel.com, 7 Chilton Rd, Tilton) Doubles $55-135 off-season, $70-165 May–mid-Oct. This 63-room place is off I-93 exit 20.

Belknap Point Motel (☎ 603-293-7511, 888-454-2537, fax 603-528-3552, Ⓦ www .bpmotel.com, 107 Belknap Point Rd, Gilford) Doubles $62-92 off-season, $95-115 mid-June–early Sept. Along Belknap Point Rd, just northwest of Ellacoya State Park, these 16 lakeside motel rooms and efficiencies are a good choice because of their nice views of the lake and mountain.

Places to Eat

Look in the old downtown railroad station for *Las Piñatas (☎ 603-528-1405, 9 Veterans Square)* Lunch $7-10, dinner $11-19. Open daily in summer, lunch Thur-Sat & dinner Wed-Mon in winter. This place has mostly traditional Mexican specialties, with a few Tex-Mex dishes thrown in for good measure.

Getting There & Around

Concord Trailways (☎ 603-228-3300, 800-639-3317) discharges passengers in Laconia (but doesn't pick any up) on a route between Concord and Conway. The daily bus stops at the Laconia Chamber of Commerce (see Information section above). There is no service to Weirs Beach or Wolfeboro.

The Greater Laconia Transit Agency (☎ 603-528-2496, 800-294-2496) runs shuttle trolleys through town to Weirs Beach and Meredith (adult/child $2/1 all day) from July to early September.

Driving from Laconia to North Conway takes 1½ hours (50 miles); take US 3 to NH 25 to NH 16.

WEIRS BEACH

Weirs Beach is the honky-tonk heart of Lake Winnipesaukee's childhood amusements, famous for video game arcades and the great variety of junk food available. But there's also a nice lakefront promenade, a small state park with a beach, the dock for the MS *Mount Washington* cruise boat and a train station for the local scenic railroad. Above town on US 3, you'll find a water slide and a drive-in theater.

Surprisingly, the town also has a lot of evocative, Victorian-era, lakeside-vacation-cottage fantasy architecture. It's as though Weirs Beach found its cultural and commercial niche a century ago and has remained there ever since.

Called 'Aquedoctan' by its Native American settlers, Weirs Beach (Ⓦ www.weirs beach.com) takes its English name from the Indian weirs (enclosures for catching fish) that the first white settlers found along the small sand beach that still draws swimmers.

The Greater Laconia – Weirs Beach Chamber of Commerce (☎ 603-524-5531, Ⓦ www.laconia-weirs.org) has a seasonal information booth a mile south of Weirs Beach on US 3. The staff helps with same-day accommodations.

Activities

The touristy **Winnipesaukee Scenic Railroad** *(☎ 603-745-2135, adult/child 4-11 yrs $8.50/6.50; operational 11am-5pm daily mid-June–early Sept; 11am-5pm Sat & Sun late May–mid-June & early Sept–mid-Oct)* departs Weirs Beach for a one-hour lakeside ride aboard '20s and '30s train cars. Rail enthusiasts can ask about their two-hour trip.

The **MS *Mount Washington*** *(☎ 603-366-2628; adult/child 4-12 yrs $18/9; mid-May–mid-Oct)* steams out of Weirs Beach on relaxing 2½-hour scenic lake cruises several times daily. Should this be your first visit to New Hampshire's Lakes Region, put this activity on your short list of things to do. There are evening dinner cruises with entertainment (ask what the night's theme will be).

The same company also operates the MV *Sophie C*, a veritable floating post office. This US Mail boat delivers packages and letters to quaint ports and otherwise inaccessible island residents on 1½ hour morning and afternoon runs (adult/child $14/7). The MV *Doris E* makes one-hour runs (adult/child $10/5) from Weirs Beach hourly on the half-hour (10:30am to 7:30pm) from late June to early September.

Places to Stay
Camping Campgrounds are north of Weirs Beach along US 3 (Daniel Webster Hwy). Reserve well in advance if you can.

Hack-Ma-Tack Campground (☎ 603-366-5977, US 3) Sites without/with hookups $22/28. Open mid-May–mid-Oct. This 17-acre, family-friendly campground is 1½ miles north of Weirs Beach and has 80 open and shaded sites (most with hookups).

Paugus Bay Campground (☎ 603-366-4757, 96 Hilliard Rd) Sites without/with hookups $31/33. Open mid-May–mid-Oct. Off US 3, Paugus has 170 wooded sites overlooking the lake and lots of facilities like a rec room and beach.

Motels Some of the nicer moderately priced area motels lie on US 3 (Weirs Blvd) between Gilford and Weirs Beach.

Baytop Motel (☎ 603-366-2225, 🌐 www.baytop.com, 1025 Weir Blvd) Doubles $55-84 off-season, $79-109 June-early Sept. Just a half-mile south of Weirs Beach, these eight traditional motel rooms and four efficiencies overlook the lake.

Birch Knoll Motel (☎ 603-366-4958, 🌐 www.birchknollmotel.com, 867 Weirs Blvd) Doubles $59-99 off-season, $79-109 June-early Sept. Open May–mid-Oct. A mile south of Weirs Beach and overlooking Paugus Bay, this 24-room motel is among the region's better ones.

Places to Eat
Weirs Beach is all about lobsters and fast food: burgers, hot dogs, fried dough, ice cream, doughnuts and anything sweet and fatty. Cruise Lakeside Dr for the snack shops.

Weirs Beach Lobster Pound (☎ 603-366-2255, US 3) Mains $5-10. Open mid-May–mid-Oct. Across from the Weirs Beach Water Slide, this restaurant's been here forever. It serves local seafood and steaks and has a children's menu.

MEREDITH
More sedate and upscale than Weirs Beach, Meredith is still a real Lakes Region town, with a long lakeside commercial strip of restaurants, shops and places to stay.

US 3, NH 25 and NH 104 converge in Meredith, which is spread along the lakeshore. The Meredith Chamber of Commerce, at Mill St on US 3 (☎ 603-279-6121, 🌐 www.meredithcc.org, 272 Daniel Webster Hwy, Meredith, NH 03253), is open 9am to 5pm weekdays year-round, with additional weekend hours (9am to 5pm Saturday and 9am to 2pm Sunday) from mid-May to mid-October.

Places to Stay
Camping A mile and a half east of the town of Meredith you will find *Harbor Hill Camping Area* (☎ 603-279-6910, NH 25) Sites without/with hookups $24/30. Open late May–mid-Oct. This area has 140 sites, mostly wooded and with hookups, and has a pool and rec hall.

Long Island Bridge Campground (☎ 603-253-6053, Moultonboro Neck Rd) Sites without/with hookups $22/25. Open mid-May–mid-Oct. Thirteen miles northeast of Meredith near Center Harbor, this camping area overlooking the lake has popular tent sites and a private beach. In July and August, there is a three-day minimum. Follow NH 25 east for 1½ miles from Center Harbor, then go south on Moultonboro Neck Rd for 6½ miles.

White Lake State Park (☎ 603-323-7350, off NH 16, West Ossipee) Sites without/with water views $18/24. Open mid-May–mid-Oct. White Lake, 22 miles northeast of

Meredith, has 200 tent sites on over 600 acres, plus swimming and hiking trails.

Inns A five-minute walk from the town center is *Tuckernuck Inn (☎ 603-279-5521, 888-858-5521, ⓦ www.thetuckernuckinn .com, 25 Red Gate Lane)* Doubles $95-135 with full breakfast. Tuckernuck has five cozy, quiet rooms (one has a fireplace) with stenciling and quilts. From Main St, head inland along Water St, then turn right (uphill) onto Red Gate Lane.

Meredith Inn B&B (☎ 603-279-0000, fax 603-279-4017, ⓦ www.meredithinn.com, Main St) Doubles $109-159 with full breakfast. This delightful Victorian inn has eight guest rooms with luxurious bedding and antiques; most large bathrooms have a whirlpool tub. ·

Places to Eat

It's traditional food and plenty of it at *Meredith Bay Bakery & Cafe (☎ 603-279-2279, 7 Main St)* Mains $5-6. Open for breakfast and lunch. Facing the big Mill Falls Marketplace, just inland from the main intersection in town, the bakery draws locals with its huge sandwiches made with fresh-baked bread. The traditional breakfast menu ranges from steak and hash to eggs Benedict to pancakes.

The Boathouse Grille (☎ 603-279-2253, US 3 & NH 25) Lunch $6-11, dinner $13-25. Open daily. Within the Inn at Bay Point, the grille is owned by the statewide 'Common Man' family of restaurants and features a wide-ranging menu of well-prepared American dishes. Once seated, you may never want to leave the breezy lakeside deck.

The Camp (☎ 603-279-3003, US 3) Mains $15-20. Open for dinner. The interior of this restaurant and friendly bar (formerly a rustic summer camp) is atmospheric, with birch logs and a fieldstone fireplace. As for the food, try the stuffed pork, duck dishes and grilled tuna.

Getting There & Away

Concord Trailways (☎ 603-228-3300, 800-639-3317) stops in Meredith (at a Mobil gas station on NH 25; ☎ 603-279-5129) on a route between Concord and Conway. The daily bus from Meredith to Conway costs $8.50 one-way (one hour).

WOLFEBORO

Named for General Wolfe, who died vanquishing Montcalm on the Plains of Abraham in Quebec, Wolfeboro (founded in 1770) claims to be 'the oldest summer resort in America.' Whether that's true or not, it is now the most pleasant lakeside resort town, with an agreeable bustle and plenty of services.

The Wolfeboro Chamber of Commerce information booth (☎ 603-569-2200, ⓦ www .wolfeborochamber.com, 32 Central Ave) is inside the old train station. It's open 10am to 5pm Monday through Saturday and 11am to 3pm Sunday July to mid-October (10am to 3pm weekdays & 9am to noon the rest of the year).

Things to See & Do

Wolfeboro is a pretty town with some good examples of New England's architectural styles, from Georgian through Federal, Greek Revival and Second Empire. The information office has several **walking tour** pamphlets, including the half-mile-long Bridge Falls Path, which runs along the southern shore of Back Bay; the 10-minute walk to Abenaki Tower; and the Wolfeboro-Sanbornville Recreational Trail, which follows an abandoned railroad bed for 12 miles.

At the age of 40, Dr Henry Forrest Libby, a local dentist, began collecting things. And in 1912, he built a home for his collections, the **Libby Museum** *(☎ 603-569-1035, NH 109, Winter Harbor; tickets $3; open 10am-4pm Tues-Sun June-early Sept)*, 3 miles north of Wolfeboro. Starting with butterflies and moths, the amateur naturalist built up a private natural history collection. Other collections followed, including Abenaki relics and early-American farm and home implements.

The **Clark House** *(☎ 603-569-4997, 233 S Main St; adult/child under 12 yrs $4/free; open 11am-3:30pm Mon-Fri, 10am-1:30pm Sat July-early Sept)*, Wolfeboro's eclectic historical museum, has colonial artifacts, fire engines and equipment dating back to 1872, and a one-room schoolhouse from 1868.

The **MV** *Judge Sewall* (☎ *603-569-3016, off N Main St; $10; daily in summer*), a 65-foot, 75-passenger diesel-powered launch, plies the lake with tranquil tours. Board the Wolfeboro Inn's quaint 1946 vessel at the town dock.

The MV *Mount Washington* also has a daily 3½-hour cruise from Wolfeboro. See Weirs Beach, above, for details and fares.

Places to Stay
Camping A mile from Lake Wentworth State Beach is *Willey Brook Campground* (☎ *603-569-9493, NH 28*) Sites without/with hookups $16/19. Open mid-May–mid-Oct. It's 3 miles north of Wolfeboro and has 48 sites.

Wolfeboro Campground (☎ *603-569-9881, 61 Haines Hill Rd*) Sites without/with hookups $18/19. Open mid-May–mid-Oct. Off NH 28, and about 4½ miles north of Wolfeboro, this campground has 50 well-spaced, wooded sites.

Motels Less than a mile north of Wolfeboro's center is *Lakeview Inn* (☎ *603-569-1335,* W *www.lakeviewinn.net, 200 N Main St*) Doubles $55 off-season, $75-95 May-Oct. This inn and motor lodge has 17 nice rooms and efficiencies. Its dining room is a local favorite for continental cuisine such as scampi, veal and venison.

Inns & B&Bs Breakfast is big at *Tuc' Me Inn B&B* (☎ *603-569-5702, 118 N Main St*) Doubles $90-100 off-season, $100-110 mid-Apr–Oct with country breakfast. Barely north of Wolfeboro Inn, the conveniently located, 7-room B&B offers shared or private baths .

Wolfeboro Inn (☎ *603-569-3016, 800-451-2389, fax 603-569-5375,* W *www.wolfeboroinn .com, 44 N Main St*) Doubles $89-169 off-season, $139-279 May-Oct with continental breakfast. The town's best-known spot, on the lake with a private beach, has been the region's first choice since 1812. It has 44

very comfortable, country-style rooms in the main inn and a modern annex that resembles an old barn.

Places to Eat
Things are indeed yummy at the *Yum Yum Shop* (☎ *603-569-1919, 16 N Main St*) Mains $1-4. Open for breakfast and lunch. From bagels to croissants to doughnuts, this cafe serves all sorts of baked goods, as well as light sandwiches and strong coffee.

Bailey's (☎ *603-569-3662, NH 28*) Mains $2-6. Open long hours May–mid-Oct. This old-time fave has scooped ice cream for generations of families. Their casual, family-friendly dining room produces good clam chowder and barbecued chicken.

Strawberry Patch (☎ *603-569-5523, 50 N Main St*) Mains $3-8. Open for breakfast and lunch Mar-early Nov. The extensive menu here includes a litany of entirely homemade items: Belgian waffles, eggs with hollandaise sauce, crab omelets and lots of concoctions with strawberries. Lunch specials include cashew chicken, quiche and roast turkey.

Wolfe's Tavern (☎ *603-569-3016, 44 N Main St*) Mains $5-15. Open for all three meals. The bar menu at the rustically colonial Wolfeboro Inn ranges from burgers to substantial 'tuck-ins,' pasta and grilled meats. Terrace tables are set outside in good weather.

The Cider Press (☎ *603-569-2028, 30 Middleton Rd*) Mains $10-16. Open for dinner. Off NH 28 south of town, this deservedly popular spot is cozy with rustic barn board walls, fireplaces and antiques. As for the cuisine, it roams from baby back ribs to grilled salmon. Don't overlook the creative blackboard specials.

Love's Quay (☎ *603-569-3303, Mill St*) Lunch $7-10, dinner $10-25. Open daily. In addition to everyday pasta dishes, this lakeside eatery has a dozen nightly specials highlighting fish and lamb, and a spicy jambalaya.

1812 Steakhouse (☎ *603-569-3016, 44 N Main St*) Mains $15-22. Open daily late May–mid-Oct & Sat-Sun mid-Oct–late May. The Wolfeboro Inn's main dining area is formal and serves conservative American and continental fare.

Getting There & Around
There is no bus to Wolfeboro. Driving from Wolfeboro to North Conway takes just under 1½ hours (43 miles) via NH 28 to NH 16.

The narrated Molly the Trolley (☎ 603-569-5257) trundles along Main St from 10am to 5pm daily July to early September. An all-day pass costs $3/1 adult/child.

White Mountain Region

The White Mountains are New England's greatest range, and have become one of its prime outdoor playgrounds. Fortunately, most of the range is protected from over-development as part of the White Mountain National Forest. Activities here include hiking, rustic and backwoods camping, canoeing, kayaking and skiing.

Among the region's highlights are Waterville Valley, a planned mountain resort community; the Kancamagus Hwy, a beautiful wilderness road over Kancamagus Pass; North Conway and Jackson, centers for downhill and cross-country skiing, canoeing and kayaking; Mt Washington, with Bretton Woods and its famous Mount Washington Hotel; and the Franconia Notch area, which has several ski areas and many dramatic geological formations (including New Hampshire's symbol, the Old Man of the Mountain).

The nerve center for information on outdoor pursuits is the White Mountain National Forest headquarters (WMNF; ☎ 603-528-8721, W www.fs.fed.us/r9/white/, 719 Main St, Laconia, NH 03247). Their information offices just off I-93 at exits 32, 28 and 23 (☎ 603-744-9165) are particularly convenient.

It costs $3/5/20 daily/weekly/seasonally to park at National Forest trailheads. Purchase parking permits at any of the visitor center ranger stations mentioned above.

WATERVILLE VALLEY
This beautiful mountain valley was developed as a complete mountain resort community. Sports facilities include downhill and cross-country ski trails, hiking trails, tennis courts, a golf course, road- and mountain-bike routes and in-line skating paths.

As early as 1829, there was an incorporated town here in the shadow of Mt Tecumseh, on the banks of the Mad River, but the valley took its present shape during the last decades of the 20th century. Hotels, condominiums, vacation villas, golf courses, ski runs, roads and services were all laid out according to plan by the Waterville Company. The result is a harmonious, although somewhat sterile, resort with lots of organized sports activities.

Driving from Boston to Waterville Valley is a straight 3-hour shot via I-93. Pushing northward 27 miles from the valley to Lincoln takes another 45 minutes via I-93.

Orientation & Information
Take exit 28 (Campton) off I-93 and continue 13 miles northeast into Waterville Valley (☎ 800-468-2553, W www.waterville.com) and its resort. Town Square is the valley's main service facility, with a post office, bank, information office, laundry, restaurants and shops. Scenic Tripoli Rd (unpaved, closed in winter) goes northwest from Waterville Valley to I-93 exit 31 and north to Lincoln.

The Waterville Valley Region Chamber of Commerce (☎ 603-726-3804, 800-237-2307, W www.watervillevalleyregion.com, 12 Vintinner Rd, Campton, NH 03223) has lots of information and is easily visible on NH 49. It's open 9am to 5pm daily year-round.

Places to Stay & Eat
Camping Three USFS campgrounds (sites $16), in Campton on I-93 south of Waterville Valley, are convenient to the valley.

Waterville Campground (☎ 603-536-1310, I-93) Open year-round. Waterville has 27 very basic sites, some of which can be reserved in advance.

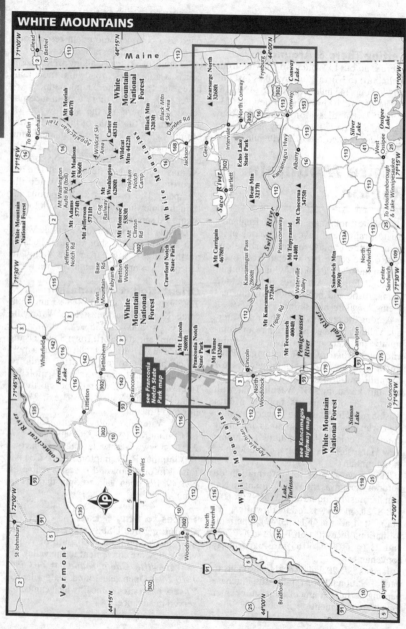

WHITE MOUNTAINS

Geography of New Hampshire

Southern New Hampshire is a region of glacial lakes and low mountains, many of which are batholiths – huge rounded granite domes formed deep underground and brought to the surface by upheavals and erosion. Mt Monadnock (3166 feet), southeast of Keene, is the most famous of New Hampshire's batholiths.

The Merrimack River Valley drains the central and southern portions of the state. The river itself is easily traceable on any road map because it shares its valley with I-93 and I-293. Originating at Newfound Lake, the river flows southeastward through Concord, Manchester, Merrimack and Nashua-Hudson before turning northeastward and entering the Atlantic at Newburyport, Massachusetts.

South-central New Hampshire's major feature is vast Lake Winnipesaukee, with 183 miles of shoreline. Surrounding lakes, which would be large in most other places, look small by comparison.

North-central New Hampshire is dominated by the White Mountain Range and the northern end of the Appalachian Mountains, including the famous Presidential Range, which has peaks named after many US presidents. Mt Washington (6288 feet) is the highest, of course.

Most of the White Mountain Range is included in the vast White Mountain National Forest. Several 'notches' (narrow passes) provide passage between major mountains. The most famous of these is Franconia Notch, a 5-mile-long gap within the serene and unwavering gaze of the rock formation known as the Old Man of the Mountain.

Campton Campground (☎ 603-536-1310, I-93) Open mid-Apr–mid-Oct. Campton, with pay showers and flush toilets, has 58 sites near the Mad River; some can be reserved in advance.

Russell Pond Campground (☎ 888-226-7764, Tripoli Rd) Open mid-May–mid-Oct. Four miles off I-93, this beautifully sited campground has 86 campsites, many pondside, with flush toilets and pay showers.

Hotels There is no cheap lodging in Waterville Valley resort, although there are economical lodgings in Campton, 13 miles southwest. Valley reservations are made through a central service (☎ 800-468-2553, fax 603-236-4174, Ⓦ www.waterville.com). If you call a hotel directly, they may ask if you've ever stayed there before. A 'yes' answer (regardless of your previous lodging history) will probably get you a 'previous-guest' discount of up to 10%. Don't be bashful. For valley condominium rentals, call Waterville Lodging at ☎ 800-556-6522.

The Black Bear Lodge (☎ 603-236-4501, 800-349-2327, Ⓦ www.black-bear-lodge.com, 3 Village Rd) Suites $88-300, plus 15%

resort fee. This lodge, with an indoor pool and children's movie theater, has 107 one- and two-bedroom suites that can sleep up to six people. Kitchens are fully equipped.

Snowy Owl Inn (☎ 603-236-8383, 800-766-9969, Ⓦ www.snowyowlinn.com, 4 Village Rd) Doubles $99-259 with continental breakfast, plus 15% resort fee. This handsome place has 85 accommodations ranging from Superior (actually rather modest) to Deluxe, Premium, Loft/Studio and Fireside. Kids 12 and under stay free. Among the dozens of amenities, you'll find indoor and outdoor heated pools, a fitness center and a three-story hearth in the main lobby where afternoon wine and cheese are served.

The Valley Inn (☎ 603-236-8336, 800-343-0969, fax 603-236-4294, Ⓦ www.valleyinn.com, Tecumseh Rd) Doubles $90-130, condos $160-185, plus 15% resort fee. The Valley Inn consists of a mix of hotel-style rooms and condominiums (sleeping up to six people). All prices include use of the many resort facilities, from tennis courts and health club to mountain-bike trails and golf course.

Most Waterville Valley hotels have decent **dining rooms**, and there are a number of **theme restaurants** in the Town Square complex.

KANCAMAGUS HIGHWAY

The winding Kancamagus Hwy (NH 112) between Lincoln and Conway runs right through the White Mountain National Forest and over Kancamagus Pass (2868 feet). Unspoiled by commercial development, the paved road offers easy access to USFS campgrounds.

History

In about 1684, Kancamagus, 'the fearless one,' assumed the powers of *sagamon* (leader) of the Penacook Confederacy of Native American peoples in this region. He was the third and the final sagamon, succeeding his grandfather, the great Passaconaway, and his uncle Wonalancet. Kancamagus worked to keep the peace between the indigenous peoples and European explorers and settlers, but provocations by the newcomers pushed his patience past the breaking point. He finally resorted to battle to rid the region of Europeans. The tide of history was against him, and by 1691, he and his followers were forced to escape northward.

Hiking

The **White Mountain National Forest** is laced with excellent hiking trails of varying difficulty. For detailed trail-by-trail information, stop at any of the WMNF ranger stations (see the introductory paragraphs of the White Mountain Region Information section earlier in this chapter) or the White Mountains Attractions Association (see the North Woodstock & Lincoln Information section below).

If you like to plan ahead, get the AMC White Mountain Guide from the Appalachian Mountain Club (☎ 617-523-0636, 🆆 www.outdoors.org, 5 Joy St, Boston, MA 02108) or from an outfitter or local bookshop. Here are some hiking suggestions:

Lincoln Woods Trail The trailhead (elevation 1157 feet) for this 2.9-mile route is located on the Kancamagus Hwy, 5 miles east of I-93. Among the easiest and most popular in the forest, the trail ends at the Pemigewasset Wilderness Boundary (elevation 1450 feet).

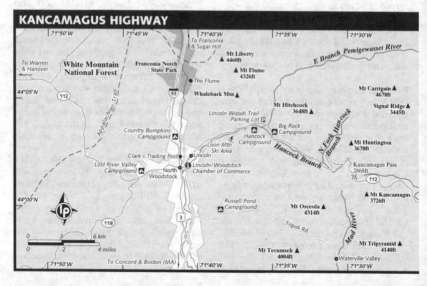

KANCAMAGUS HIGHWAY

Wilderness Trail This easy trail begins where the Lincoln Woods Trail ends, and it continues for 6 miles to Stillwater Junction (elevation 2060 feet). You can follow the Cedar Brook and Hancock Notch Trails to return to the Kancamagus Hwy, which is some miles east of the Lincoln Woods trailhead parking lot.

Places to Stay

The heavily wooded USFS campgrounds east of Lincoln along the Kancamagus Hwy are primitive sites (mostly with pit toilets only). Since they're in heavy demand in the warm months, arrive in the morning to get a site and on Thursday or Friday morning to pin one down for the weekend. Call ☎ 603-536-1310 or 603-447-5448 for more information on camping here. The following campgrounds are listed from west to east (Lincoln to Conway).

Hancock Campground Sites $14. Open year-round. Four miles east of Lincoln, this place has 56 sites near the Pemigewasset River and the Wilderness Trail.

Big Rock Campground Sites $14. Open year-round. Big Rock has 28 sites near the Wilderness Trail and is 6 miles east of Lincoln.

Passaconaway Campground Sites $14. Open mid-May–Oct. This campground is 12 miles west of Conway, and has 33 sites on the Swift River, which is good for fishing.

Jigger Johnson Campground Sites $16. Open mid-May–mid-Oct. Jigger's is 10 miles west of Conway, has 75 sites, flush toilets and pay hot showers. There are nature lectures on summer weekends.

Covered Bridge Campground Sites $14. Open mid-May–mid-Oct. Six miles west of Conway, this place has 49 sites, some of which can be reserved. And yes, you do cross the Albany Covered Bridge to reach the campground.

Blackberry Crossing Campground Sites $14. Open year-round. Six miles west of Conway, this former Civilian Conservation Corps (CCC) camp has 26 sites.

NORTH WOODSTOCK & LINCOLN

These twin towns serve a diverse clientele. Outdoorsy types in heavy boots stop for provisions on their way to camp and hike along the Kancamagus Hwy (NH 112). And retirees in huge road cruisers stop for cocktails after photographing the Old Man of

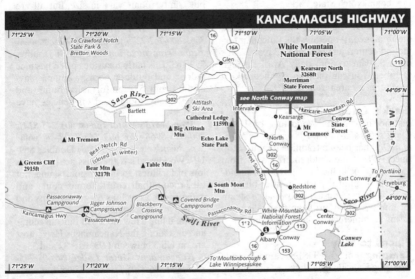

the Mountain in Franconia Notch State Park. If you've come as far as North Woodstock and Lincoln, you must see the 'Old Man' and enjoy the park's other natural wonders. See the Franconia Notch State Park section, later in this chapter, for more details.

Skiers will find that **Loon Mountain** (☎ 603-745-8111), along the Kancamagus Hwy east of Lincoln, is a good option.

Orientation & Information

The shallow, boulder-strewn Pemigewasset River springs forth just south of Franconia Notch, runs south parallel to I-93 and is joined by its eastern branch at North Woodstock. Lincoln, on the east branch, is east of I-93. Both are pretty much one-street towns. The Kancamagus Hwy reaches them from Conway, 18 miles east of Kancamagus Pass (286 feet).

The Lincoln/Woodstock Chamber of Commerce (☎ 603-745-6621, W www.lincoln woodstock.com, on the Kancamagus Hwy, Lincoln, NH 03251), is located above the Laconia Savings Bank. It's open 9am to 5pm weekdays year-round. There's also a small office in the Flume Visitor Center in Franconia Notch State Park.

The White Mountains Attractions Association (☎ 603-745-8720, W www.visitwhite mountains.com) operates the Lincoln information center, just east of I-93 exit 32. It's open 8:30am to 5pm daily April through October. You can pick up detailed hiking brochures for area trails here.

Clark's Trading Post

Just north of North Woodstock on US 3, Clark's (☎ 603-745-8913; open late May–mid-Oct) has been a traditional family stop since 1928. If the children are bored from too much time in the car, Clark's has an old-fashioned photo parlor, water-bumper boats, a magic house, narrow-gauge steam locomotive and a gift shop that sells moccasins. Commercial? You bet, but fun.

Places to Stay

Camping For the USFS campgrounds along the Kancamagus Hwy east of Lincoln,

see Camping in the Kancamagus Highway section, earlier.

Country Bumpkins Campground (☎ 603-745-8837, US 3) Sites without/with hookups $17/19 and up. Open Apr-Oct. Near the Pemigewasset River and Bog Brook, this campground has 46 sites. To reach them, take I-93 exit 33 and head south on US 3.

Lost River Valley Campground (☎ 603-745-8321, NH 112) Sites without/with hookups $22/31.50. Open mid-May–mid-Oct. This excellent, 200-acre campground has 125 sites, many of which are near streams. Inquire about camping cabins ($40 double).

Motels Heading north from Lincoln and North Woodstock along US 3 brings you to many motels.

Franconia Notch Motel (☎ 603-745-2229, 800-323-7829, W www.franconianotch.com, US 3) Doubles $35-80. This tidy place has 18 attractive rooms and cottages facing a stream. In winter, there are only 8 rooms open.

Red Doors Motel (☎ 603-745-2267, 800-527-7596, fax 603-745-3646, W www.red doorsmotel.com, US 3) Doubles $40-80. Yes, this place does have red doors. The 30 plain but comfy rooms vary in size, but all are well maintained.

Drummer Boy Motor Inn (☎ 603-745-3661, 800-762-7275, fax 603-745-9829, W www .drummerboymotorinn.com, US 3) Doubles $59-165. This fairly luxurious place has nice indoor and outdoor pools, a sauna, playground and 53 comfortable rooms and suites. Many rooms and efficiencies have kitchens.

Woodward's Motor Inn (☎ 603-745-8141, 800-635-8968, fax 603-745-3408, W www .woodwardsresort.com, US 3) Doubles $69-119. Woodward's is the class act here with lots of facilities: an indoor pool, sauna, hot tub, racquetball court, tennis court and game room, as well as 85 good rooms and attractive landscaping.

You'll find a few motels in Lincoln center and east along the Kancamagus Hwy; most are on US 3 between I-93 exits 32 and 33.

Kancamagus Motor Lodge (☎ 603-745-3365, 800-346-4205, fax 603-745-6691, W www

.kancmotorlodge.com, NH 112) Doubles $79. This lodge has 34 modern rooms with steam baths, and a heated indoor pool.

B&Bs Just south of the junction is *Wilderness Inn* (☎ 603-745-3890, 800-200-9453, W *www.thewildernessinn.com, junction US3 and NH 112)* Doubles $60-145 with breakfast. this former lumbermill owner's house offers lots of mahogany, congenial hosts and seven guest rooms (ranging from small to suite size). A separate cottage by the river rents for $90-160, depending on the season. The highlight of your stay will probably be the huge breakfast, cooked from scratch and ordered off a menu.

Places to Eat
Lincoln The Kancamagus Hwy (NH 112) through Lincoln bears the usual assortment of fast-food emporia – *Burger King, McDonald's* and the other franchise shops.

Elvio's Pizzeria (☎ 603-745-8817, Lincoln Plaza, NH 112) Mains $4-10. Open for lunch and dinner. When you're in a hurry to hit the highway or trails, Elvio's submarine sandwiches and pizzas will hit the spot.

The Italian Garden (☎ 603-745-2626, NH 112) Mains $7-15. Open year-round. In the Millfront Marketplace, you'll find lighter meals (sandwiches, pastas) and Italian classics like chicken and veal piccata, scampi and eggplant parmesan. The bar is a popular gathering place.

The Olde Timbermill Restaurant & Pub (☎ 603-745-3603, NH 112) Pub menu $8-13, mains $13-19. Open for lunch and dinner. In the Millfront Marketplace, this glass-fronted, family-friendly eatery is lofty (it served as a mill in its former incarnation). The pub menu concentrates on sandwiches, burgers and a few Mexican dishes. Downstairs offers an equally vast array of dishes more seriously prepared. There are lots of chicken, pasta and beef entrées. The lounge gets rambunctious on ski weekends, when there are live bands.

Gordi's Fish & Steak House (☎ 603-745-6635, NH 112) Mains $11-18. Open for lunch late May–mid-Oct, dinner year-round. In the Depot shopping center, this

big place has a hearty menu suiting appetites sharpened by outdoor exercise. Big steaks and fish are featured, but a pub menu has cheaper fare.

The Common Man (☎ 603-745-3463, NH 112) Mains $12-23. Open daily. This successful local chain combines a simple menu of pasta, prime rib and lobster dishes with a massive hearth and warm bar. The mix can't be beaten.

North Woodstock Plenty of variety and some entertainment is available at the relatively few places here.

Peg's Restaurant (☎ 603-745-2740, Main St) Mains $3-6. Open 5:30am-4pm (until 2pm Nov-June). Locals flock to this no-frills eatery for hearty, early breakfasts and late luncheon sandwiches like roast turkey and meat loaf with gravy.

Sunny Day Diner (☎ 603-745-4833, US 3) Mains $3-15. Open 7am-2pm Thurs-Mon, dinner Fri & Sat. North of town, this authentic diner serves classic fare: peanut butter and jelly sandwiches and blue plate specials like pot roast, roast pork and salmon. The basement bakery supplies all the bread, rolls and pies.

Truant's Taverne & Restaurant (☎ 603-745-2239, Main St) Lunch and dinner dishes under $14. Skip the food and come for live winter weekend entertainment.

Woodstock Station & Brewery (☎ 603-745-3951, Main St) Mains $9-17. Open for lunch and dinner. Formerly a railroad station, this eatery tries to be everything to everyone. In the end, it can probably satisfy any food craving successfully. Woodstock Station & Brewery's menu boasts upwards of 150 items, from Mexican dishes and Peking ravioli to seafood, pasta and burgers. The beer-sodden rear tavern here is one of the most happening places in this neck of the woods.

Getting There & Away
Concord Trailways buses (☎ 603-228-3300, 800-639-3317) stop at the Shell Quick Mart (☎ 603-745-3195) on Main St.

From Lincoln it takes just over one hour to reach North Conway (42 miles) on the

Kancamagus Highway. It's about 3¼ hours (140 miles) from Boston via I-93.

FRANCONIA NOTCH STATE PARK

Franconia Notch, a narrow gorge shaped over the eons by a wild stream cutting through craggy granite, is a dramatic mountain pass (notch). The symbol of the Granite State is a natural rock formation here called the Great Stone Face, or Old Man of the Mountain, who gazes across Franconia Notch from his lofty perch high on the west wall of the gorge.

Southeast of the Old Man lies the undulant crest of Mt Liberty, which some people think resembles George Washington lying in state. Use your imagination; this is, after all, the Presidential Range.

Orientation & Information

The most scenic parts of the notch are protected by the narrow Franconia Notch State Park. Reduced to two lanes, I-93 (renamed the Franconia Notch Parkway) squeezes through the gorge. Services are available in Lincoln and North Woodstock, and, to a lesser extent, in Franconia and Littleton, farther to the north.

The visitor center (☎ 603-745-8391) at the Flume (see below) includes a Flume ticket office, cafeteria, gift shop and auditorium.

There's another visitor center at Lafayette Place (☎ 603-823-9513), between the Basin and Profile Lake. (Also see Information in the Franconia section, later in this chapter.)

The Flume

After paying your admission fee *(adult/ child 6-12 $8/5; open 9am-4:30pm daily mid-May–Oct)*, take a 2-mile self-guided nature walk that includes the 800-foot boardwalk through the Flume, a natural cleft (12 to 20 feet wide) in the granite bedrock. The granite walls tower 70 to 90 feet above you, with moss and plants growing from precarious niches and crevices. Signs along the way explain how nature formed this natural phenomenon. A nearby covered bridge is thought to be one of the oldest in the state, perhaps erected as early as the 1820s.

The Basin

This huge glacial pothole 20 feet in diameter was carved deep into the granite 15,000 years ago by the action of falling water and swirling stones. The Basin offers a nice (short) walk and a cool spot to ponder a minor wonder of nature.

Lafayette Place

There's a visitor center here, as well as a *campground (☎ 603-823-9513; sites $16; open late May–mid-Oct)* with 97 tent sites that are in heavy demand in summer. Arrive early in the day to claim a site. Many of the state park's hiking trails start here.

Old Man of the Mountain

After 200 million years in the making, the Old Man of the Mountain was 'discovered' early in the 19th century by white settlers passing through the notch. The striking profile of a man's face (à la Picasso, perhaps) can be seen from the north (follow signs for 'Old Man Viewing'). From the parking lot, a path leads down to Profile Lake, where plaques tell you all about the Old Man.

Marketed as the symbol of the Granite State, the Great Stone Face looms larger in the imagination than in real life. Some viewers find it small. A 40-foot-tall, 25-foot-wide face is indeed big, but when perched 1200 feet above the ground, it is less impressive than its super close-up photographs. Since the Old Man is an important tourist attraction and state symbol, it would not be cool for him to tumble down. He's been stabilized with (invisible) concrete and rebar to protect him from the natural consequences of tremors and erosion.

Cannon Mountain Aerial Tramway

Just north of the Old Man, the tramway *(☎ 603-823-7722; adult/child 6-12 yrs $10/6 roundtrip; open 9am-5pm late May–mid-Oct)* offers a breathtaking view of Franconia Notch and the surrounding mountains. In 1938, the first passenger aerial tramway in North America was installed on this slope. Thankfully, it was replaced in 1980 by

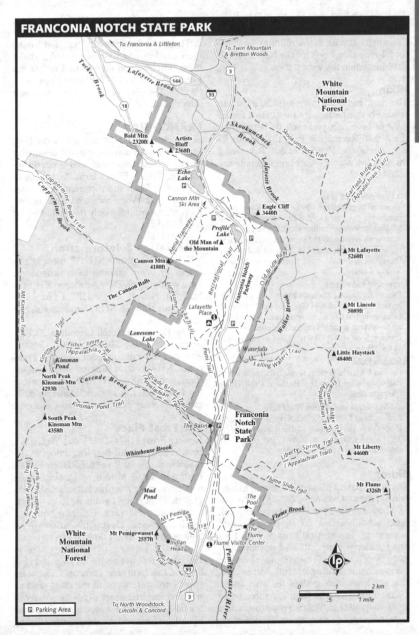

FRANCONIA NOTCH STATE PARK

the current, larger cable car, capable of carrying 80 passengers up to the summit of Cannon Mountain in five minutes – a 2022-foot, 1-mile ride. Look for the New England Ski Museum in the base station.

Hiking

The park has good hiking trails; most are relatively short, some are steep. For a casual walk or bike ride, you can't do better than the 8-mile Recreation Path that wends its way along the Pemigewasset River and through the notch. Other hikes include the following:

Mt Pemigewasset Trail
This trail begins at the Flume Visitor Center and climbs for 1.4 miles to the 2557-foot summit of Mt Pemigewasset (Indian Head), offering excellent views. Return by the same trail or the Indian Head Trail, which joins US 3 after 1 mile. From there, it's a 1-mile walk north to the Flume Visitor Center.

Lonesome Lake Trail
Departing from Lafayette Place and its campground, this trail climbs 1000 feet in 1½ miles to Lonesome Lake. Various spur trails lead farther up to several summits on the Cannon Balls and Cannon Mountain (3700 to 4180 feet) and south to the Basin.

Kinsman Falls
On the Cascade Brook, these falls are a short, half-mile hike from the Basin via the Basin Cascade Trail.

Bald Mountain and Artists Bluff Trail
Just north of Echo Lake, off NH 18, this 1½-mile loop skirts the summit of Bald Mountain (at 2320 feet) and Artists Bluff (2368 feet), with short spur trails to the summits.

Skiing

They even have a nursery at **Cannon Mountain Ski Area** (☎ 603-823-7722, off I-93 at exit 2). They also have three cafeterias, lounges, a ski school, and a ski shop with rental equipment. The vertical drop is 2146 feet, and the slopes are positioned so they naturally receive and retain more than the average amount of white stuff. Just in case, the ski area also makes its own snow. Cannon has an aerial tramway, three triple and two quad chairlifts, two rope tows and a wonder carpet (a moving walkway for beginners) for accessing its 26 miles of trails and slopes.

Thanks to the extensive national forest, there are lots of cross-country trails at the downhill areas and elsewhere. Contact the Lincoln/Woodstock Chamber of Commerce (☎ 603-745-6621) for details on rentals and directions.

FRANCONIA

A few miles north of the notch via I-93, Franconia is a pleasant, tranquil town with splendid mountain views and a poetic attraction: Robert Frost's farm. As a place to stay, it's prettier, more tranquil and a bit cheaper than Woodstock and Lincoln, but most places are open only from late May to mid-October.

Orientation & Information

NH 18, NH 116 and NH 117 meet at the center of town, marked by a prominent, local prep school, Dow Academy. NH 18 is Main St. Nearby Sugar Hill, a few miles west along tranquil NH 117, has several fine country inns.

The Franconia Notch Chamber of Commerce (☎ 603-823-5661, 800-237-9007, W www.franconianotch.org, Main St, Franconia, NH 03580) maintains a seasonal information booth on NH 18 just southeast of the town center. It's open 11am-5pm daily except Monday mid-May to mid-October.

The Frost Place

Robert Frost (1874–1963) was America's most renowned and best-loved poet in the middle of the 20th century. Born in San Francisco, Frost moved to Massachusetts with his mother after his father's death. He attended – but didn't graduate from – Dartmouth, then Harvard. He then bought a small farm near Derry in southern New Hampshire but didn't do well as a farmer.

After a sojourn of several years in England, Frost lived with his wife and children on this farm near Franconia. The years spent here were some of the most productive and inspired years of his life. Many of his best and most famous poems describe life on this farm and the scenery surrounding it, including 'The Road Not Taken' and 'Stopping by Woods on a Snowy Evening.'

The farmhouse has been kept as faithful to the period as possible, with numerous exhibits of Frost memorabilia. In the forest behind the house, there is a half-mile-long nature trail. Frost's poems are mounted on plaques in sites appropriate to the things the poems describe, and in several places the plaques have been erected at the exact spots where Frost composed the poems.

The Frost Place (☎ 603-823-5510; Ridge Rd; adult/senior/child 6-15 yrs $3/2/1.25; open 1pm-5pm Sat-Sun late May-June & 1pm-5pm Wed-Mon July–mid-Oct), marked on some signs as the Frost Museum, is a memorial to the poet's life and work. Admission includes a 20-minute slide show about Frost's early life and work and about the countryside here.

To find Frost's farm, follow NH 116 south from Franconia. After exactly a mile, turn right onto Bickford Hill Rd, then left onto unpaved Ridge Rd. It's a short distance along on the right.

Places to Stay
Camping Outdoor living is available in nearby Lafayette Place in Franconia Notch State Park; see that section, earlier in this chapter.

Fransted Family Campground (☎ 603-823-5675, NH 18) Sites without/with hookups $18/24. Open May-Oct. Two miles northwest of Franconia Notch State Park, this wooded campground caters more to tenters (with 91 sites) than RVers (26 sites). Many sites are along a stream.

Motels Heated pools set the pace at both of these properties.

Stonybrook Motel & Lodge (☎ 603-823-8192, 800-722-3552, NH 18) Doubles $55-100. Open mid-May–mid-Oct & mid-Dec–mid-Mar. A mile south of town, on a river, this mountain motel has heated indoor and outdoor pools and 23 tidy, comfortable rooms that vary greatly in size.

Gale River Motel & Cottages (☎ 603-823-5655, 800-255-7989, fax 603-823-5280, Ⓦ www.galerivermotel.com, 1 Main St)

Frost's Accomplishments

In addition to writing very popular poetry, Robert Frost (1874–1963) also garnered significant critical acclaim. He won Pulitzer Prizes for his collections *New Hampshire* (1923), *Collected Poems* (1930) and *A Further Range* (1936).

In 1958, Frost was appointed the Poetry Consultant to the Library of Congress, and he later received honorary doctorates from Oxford and Cambridge. At John F Kennedy's 1961 inauguration as president of the US, Frost read his poem 'The Gift Outright.' At his death, Frost was considered the unofficial poet laureate of the US. Not bad for a college dropout.

Rooms $65-95, cottages $110-120. Open May-late Oct. This classic roadside motel with mountain vistas has 10 rooms and two cottages, a heated pool, hot tub and spas.

Hotels The rooms are modern at *Franconia Village Hotel* (☎ 603-823-7422, 888-669-6777, fax 603-823-5638, Ⓦ www.franconiavillagehotel.com, 87 Wallace Hill Rd)

Doubles $69-150. Franconia's most prominent lodging place (exit 38 off I-93) has 61 rooms, an indoor pool, spa and health club. Inquire about the lone apartment with kitchen ($115-250).

Inns Among the possible accommodations in Franconia is a rarity: a working farm. *Pinestead Farm Lodge* (☎ 603-823-8121, NH 116) Doubles $36-45. The family rents 11 clean, simple rooms with shared bath and communal kitchen/sitting rooms. Hosts Bob and Kathleen Sherburn (whose family has been renting rooms since 1899) have an assortment of cattle, chickens, ducks and horses. If you come in March or April, you can watch maple sugaring.

Two miles from Franconia is *Sugar Hill Inn* (☎ 603-823-5621, 800-548-4748, fax 603-823-5639, ☒ www.sugarhillinn.com, NH 117) Rooms $90-150, suites $175-225, cottages $140-165 with full breakfast. Atop a hill with panoramic mountain views and lined with sugar maples ablaze in autumn, this restored 1789 farmhouse offers lots of activities, a fine dining room and 16 bright and cheery guest rooms. Put it on your short list of places to stay.

Franconia Inn (☎ 603-823-5542, 800-473-5299, fax 603-823-8078, ☒ www.franconia inn.com, NH 116) Doubles $110-190 with full breakfast. This excellent 34-room inn, just 2 miles south of Franconia, is set on a broad, fertile, pine-fringed river valley. You'll find plenty of common space and well-maintained, traditional guest rooms. The 107-acre estate has prime cross-country ski possibilities and summertime hiking and horseback riding. At certain times of the year, rates will be higher and include dinner, too. But don't worry; it's a good dining room.

Lovett's Inn (☎ 603-823-7761, 800-356-3802, ☒ www.lovettsinn.com, NH 18) Doubles $125-235 (plus $40 for foliage) with full breakfast. Two miles south of Franconia, Lovett's offers fine dining, five inn rooms (some with shared bath) and 14 cottages with fireplaces. An outdoor pool is nice in summer.

Places to Eat
Many of Franconia's inns offer fine dining, including the *Franconia Inn*, *Lovett's Inn* and *Sugar Hill Inn*. See Places to Stay, above, for location information.

Polly's Pancake Parlor (☎ 603-823-5575, NH 117, Sugar Hill) Mains $5-15. Open 7am-3pm daily May–mid-Oct. Attached to a 19th-century farmhouse 2 miles west of Franconia, this local institution offers pancakes, pancakes and more pancakes. They're excellent, made with home-ground flour and topped with the farm's own maple syrup, eggs and sausages. Polly's cob-smoked bacon is tasty enough to convert a vegetarian. In case someone in your party doesn't like fluffy griddlecakes (blasphemy!), sandwiches and quiches are also available.

Getting There & Away
Concord Trailways buses (☎ 603-228-3300, 800-639-3317) stop at Kelly's Foodtown (☎ 603-823-7795) in the center of Franconia. The bus from Franconia to Lincoln costs $4 (25 minutes).

From Franconia head west to St Johnsbury, Vermont (25 miles, 40 minutes) via I-93 or head east through Crawford Notch to North Conway (45 miles, 1¼ hours) via US 3 to US 302.

Mt Washington Valley

The valley, stretching north from the eastern end of the Kancamagus Hwy, includes the towns of Bartlett, Conway, Glen, Intervale, Jackson and North Conway (the valley's hub). It harbors a myriad of outdoor sports possibilities.

NORTH CONWAY
The Kancamagus Hwy's eastern terminus is Conway, at the intersection of NH 16, NH 113, NH 153 and US 302. But the region's activities capital is North Conway, 5 miles north along NH 16 and US 302.

North Conway is the center of the Mt Washington Valley, an area that offers great hiking, camping, canoeing and kayaking. Within a few miles' drive of the town are several alpine ski areas including Attitash, Black Mountain and Cranmore. Nearby Jackson and Intervale have miles and miles of cross-country ski trails.

Most of the time, auto traffic on Main St (NH 16 and US 302) moves at a glacial pace. If your aim is to get around North Conway, not into it, take West Side Rd, which follows the Saco River between Conway and Glen. River Rd connects NH 16 to West Side Rd (see map).

Information

The Mt Washington Valley Chamber of Commerce (☎ 603-356-3171, Ⓦ www.mt washingtonvalley.org, PO Box 2300, North Conway, NH 03860) maintains an office on Main St (NH 16 and US 302), just south of the town center.

New Hampshire runs a state information office on NH 16 and US 302 in Intervale, 2 miles north of the center of North Conway.

The outfitter EMS (☎ 603-356-5433), on Main St in North Conway, sells maps and guides to the White Mountain National Forest. EMS also rents camping equipment, cross-country skis and snowshoes. Their climbing school operates year-round (you'll need reservations).

The ski areas – Attitash Bear Peak, Mt Cranmore, Black Mountain, Wildcat – also make lodging reservations. See those sections, later in the chapter, for more contact information.

Conway Scenic Railroad

This train line (☎ 603-356-5251, 800-232-5251), built in 1874 and restored in 1974, offers three different trips, one of which is the most scenic journey in New England. The most spectacular 5½-hour trip covers 50 miles and passes through Crawford Notch (tickets coach/1st-class: adult $37/45, child 4-12 yrs $21/29; trips 11am Tues-Thur & Sat mid-July–mid-Sept; daily mid-Sept–mid-Oct). Make reservations.

A one-hour, 11-mile antique steam train ride through the Mt Washington Valley costs less (tickets coach/1st-class: adult $8.50/11.50, child 4-12 yrs $7/8.50; three trips daily June–mid-October & daily Sat-Sun mid-Oct–mid-Dec). The 21-mile Bartlett trip is slightly longer and more expensive.

Echo Lake State Park

Two miles west of North Conway via River Rd, this placid mountain lake (☎ 603-356-2672, River Rd; entrance $3) lies at the foot of White Horse Ledge, a sheer rock wall. A scenic road leads up to the 700-foot-high Cathedral Ledge with panoramic White Mountains views. You can swim and picnic here, but there's no camping.

Skiing

You can play and stay at **Attitash Bear Peak** (☎ 603-374-2368, 877-677-7669 snow report, ☎ 800-223-7669 lodging reservations, US 302 west of Glen). The hill has a vertical drop of 1750 feet, 12 lifts and 70 ski trails. Half the trails are intermediate level, 25% are beginner and 25% are expert. If need be, the resort can make 98% of its own snow.

Mt Cranmore Resort (☎ 603-356-5543 lodging, ☎ 800-786-6754 snow report, outskirts of North Conway) has a vertical drop of 1200 feet, 39 slopes and trails (40% beginner, 40% intermediate and 20% expert), nine lifts and 100% snowmaking ability.

Summer Activities

Two miles east of Center Conway, the folks at **Saco Bound Inc** (☎ 603-447-2177, US 302) rent canoes and kayaks ($25.50 daily) and organize guided trips from mid-April to mid-October. These range from a few hours to a few days on the Saco River and other nearby rivers and ponds. Inquire at the information center (summer only) set up on Main St in North Conway (across from the Eastern Slope Inn).

Kayak Jack Fun Yak Rentals (☎ 603-447-5571, NH 16), next to Eastern Slope Campground in Conway, also rents kayaks and canoes ($25-30 daily, including the all-important upstream transportation).

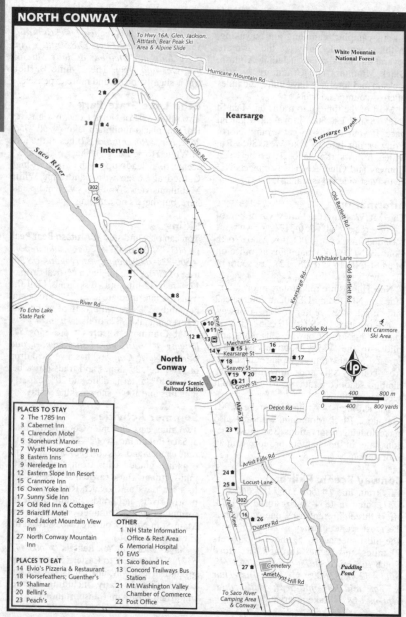

NORTH CONWAY

To Hwy 16A, Glen, Jackson,
Attitash, Bear Peak Ski
Area & Alpine Slide

White Mountain
National Forest

Hurricane Mountain Rd

Kearsarge

Kearsarge Brook

Intervale

Saco River

Intervale Cross Rd

Old Bartlett Rd

Whitaker Lane

Kearsarge Rd

Old Bartlett Rd

To Echo Lake
State Park

River Rd

Skimobile Rd

Mt Cranmore
Ski Area

Pine St

North
Conway

Mechanic St

Kearsarge St

Seavey St

Grove St

Conway Scenic
Railroad Station

Main St

Depot Rd

0   400   800 m
0   400   800 yards

Artist Falls Rd

Locust Lane

Valley View

Duprey Rd

Cemetery

Amethyst Hill Rd

Pudding
Pond

To Saco River
Camping Area
& Conway

PLACES TO STAY
2   The 1785 Inn
3   Cabernet Inn
4   Clarendon Motel
5   Stonehurst Manor
7   Wyatt House Country Inn
8   Eastern Inns
9   Nereledge Inn
12 Eastern Slope Inn Resort
15 Cranmore Inn
16 Oxen Yoke Inn
17 Sunny Side Inn
24 Old Red Inn & Cottages
25 Briarcliff Motel
26 Red Jacket Mountain View
    Inn
27 North Conway Mountain
    Inn

PLACES TO EAT
14 Elvio's Pizzeria & Restaurant
18 Horsefeathers; Guenther's
19 Shalimar
20 Bellini's
23 Peach's

OTHER
1   NH State Information
    Office & Rest Area
6   Memorial Hospital
10 EMS
11 Saco Bound Inc
13 Concord Trailways Bus
    Station
21 Mt Washington Valley
    Chamber of Commerce
22 Post Office

From mid-June to mid-October, the chairlifts at Attitash Bear Peak whisk you to the top of the **Alpine Slide** *(single/double rides for all ages $10/16; all-day pass adult/ child age 2-7 yrs $24/10)*, a long track that you schuss down on a little cart. It's an exhilarating ride safe for all ages.

Attitash Bear Peak also has **mountainbike** rentals and trail access *(adult/child $40/20 daily)* and guided **horseback riding** trips *($40 over age 8)* from mid-June to mid-October.

Places to Stay

Camping Conway, North Conway and Glen are riddled with commercial campgrounds. If these are full, ask at the information booth.

Eastern Slope Camping Area (☎ 603-447-5092, NH 16, Conway) Sites $15-30. Open late May–mid-Oct. Eastern Slope has mountain views, 260 well-kept sites and long beaches on the Saco River; prices depend on location.

Saco River Camping Area (☎ 603-356-3360, NH 16, North Conway) Sites without/ with hookups $19/27. Open May–mid-Oct. This riverside campground, away from the highway, has 140 wooded and open sites.

Beach Camping Area (☎ 603-447-2723, NH 16, Conway) Sites without/with hookups $22/32. Open mid-May–mid-Oct. Many of these 124 forested sites are on the Saco River.

Cove Camping Area (☎ 603-447-6734, off Stark Rd, Conway) Tent/lakeside sites $22/38. Open late May–mid-Oct. These 95 forested sites are right on Conway Lake.

Hostels New Hampshire's only youth hostel (in Conway rather than North Conway!) is the **Albert B Lester Memorial HI-AYH Hostel** *(☎ 603-447-1001, fax 603-447-3346, ⓦ www.angel.net/~hostel, 36 Washington St, Conway)* Dorm beds $19-22, rooms $48-51 with continental breakfast. This 43-bed place off Main St (NH 16) is a 'sustainable living center' focused on environmentally friendly practices and conservation. The hostel is big on recycling and gives out information on how to apply 'green' tech-

nologies to your daily life. More important, the facility offers five bedrooms with bunk beds and four family-size rooms. Prices include linens and free Internet access in their library. Excellent hiking and bicycling opportunities are just outside the door, and canoeists can easily portage to two nearby rivers. Reservations are accepted with a credit card.

Motels Lodging costs are highest from late July to mid-October (when it's still cheaper on weekdays versus weekend) and surprisingly low – less than half of high-season prices – in winter. You may face two- or three-night minimum-stay requirements during high season, at the prices quoted below. Most motels are in a 3-mile stretch along Main St (NH 16 and US 302), south of the town center.

Eastern Inns (☎ 603-356-5447, 800-628-3750, fax 603-356-8936, ⓦ www.eastern inns.com, NH 16) Doubles $59-139. This tidy place with 56 units (including a few suites) offers a good family value.

Clarendon Motel (☎ 603-356-3551, 800-433-3551, ⓦ www.clarendonmotel.com, NH 16) Doubles $59-149. Some of these 17 units (two with kitchen) have nice views of Mt Cranmore.

Junge's Motel (☎ 603-356-2886, ⓦ www .jungesmotel.com, NH 16) Doubles $70-125. This tidy 28-room, family-run hostelry is set back from the busy roadway and boasts a heated outdoor pool.

Briarcliff Motel (☎ 603-356-5584, 800-338-4291, fax 603-383-6076, ⓦ www.briar cliffmotel.com, NH 16) Doubles $100-125. A few of these 31 appealing rooms have mountain views and a few have porches overlooking the heated pool.

North Conway Mountain Inn (☎ 603-356-2803, fax 603-356-3228, NH 16) Doubles $109-169. This comfortably furnished 34-room place features private porches.

Red Jacket Mountain View Inn (☎ 603-356-5411, 800-752-2538, fax 603-356-3842, ⓦ www.redjacketmountainview.com, NH 16) Doubles $109-189. This 164-room motel has resort-style facilities: heated indoor and outdoor swimming pools, saunas, whirlpool baths, tennis courts and a restaurant and lounge.

Inns & B&Bs There are dozens of regional inns and affordable B&Bs, several of which have formed an organization called Country Inns in the White Mountains, with its own reservations line: ☎ 603-356-9460. High-season rates listed below cover mid-July to mid-October. Expect substantial discounts off-season.

Cranmore Inn (☎ 603-356-5502, 800-526-5502, W www.cranmoreinn.com, 80 Kearsarge St) Doubles $69-99 with full breakfast. Among North Conway's most reliable values for decades, Cranmore has 18 guest rooms with traditional country décor.

Oxen Yoke Inn (☎ 603-356-6321, 800-862-1600, fax 603-374-6509, W www.eastern slopeinn.com, Kearsarge St) Doubles $69-99. This complex, with an outdoor pool, has 25 rooms in an old village house and an adjacent motel. Because the inn is administered by the Eastern Slope Inn Resort, Oxen Yoke guests can use the larger inn's many facilities at no additional charge.

Nereledge Inn (☎ 603-356-2831, 888-356-2831, fax 603-356-7085, W www.nereledge inn.com, 94 River Rd) Doubles $69-159 with full breakfast. In addition to 11 nice rooms (some with shared bath), there's a warm, helpful family atmosphere here, thanks to longtime owners. The BYOB English-style pub certainly helps, too.

Wyatt House Country Inn (☎ 603-356-7977, 800-527-7978, fax 603-356-2183, W www.wyatthouseinn.com, NH 16) Doubles $79-199 with full breakfast. You'll be pampered with fresh-baked breakfast goods, afternoon tea, evening sherry and lots of antiques. Rates depend upon views and amenities; the most expensive of the seven rooms have two-person spas.

Cabernet Inn (☎ 603-356-4704, 800-866-4704, fax 603-356-5399, W www.cabernet inn.com, NH 16) Doubles $85-225 with full breakfast. These 11 guest rooms, within a thoroughly renovated 1840 house, have antiques, queen beds and fireplaces or spas.

Stonehurst Manor (☎ 603-356-3113, 800-525-9100, fax 603-356-3217, W www.stone hurstmanor.com, NH 16) Doubles $86-226. Spacious, gracious Stonehurst has 25 luxury rooms (many with fireplaces) in a manor house filled with stained glass and oak paneling. The motel annex is less interesting. All rooms have access to tennis courts and a pool.

The 1785 Inn (☎ 603-356-9025, 800-421-1785, fax 603-356-6081, W www.the1785 inn.com, NH 16) Doubles $89-219 with full breakfast. This colonial hostelry has a deservedly renowned dining room, a swimming pool, readily accessible hiking trails and 17 individually decorated guest rooms. The cheapest rooms ($69-139) share baths.

Eastern Slope Inn Resort (☎ 603-356-6321, 800-862-1600, W www.easternslope inn.com, NH 16) Doubles $120-300. This posh place has a load of facilities like tennis courts, an indoor pool and a play area. The 200-plus rooms are just north of the central business district.

Sunny Side Inn (☎ 603-356-6239, fax 603-356-7622, W www.sunnyside-inn.com, Seavey St) Doubles $144, cottages $199-230 with breakfast. On a quiet back street, this nice old house has nine rooms and five cottages (a few of which have kitchens and a few of which have a fireplace and spa). Cottage prices are for two to seven people.

Places to Eat

Many inns – especially those north of the town center and in Jackson (see below) – have good, elegant dining rooms.

Guenther's (☎ 603-356-5200, Main St) Mains $5-13. Open 7am-3pm. This 2nd-floor cafe is like your mother's kitchen: simple and homey, with big portions of straightforward food such as steak and eggs ($7.50).

Peach's (☎ 603-356-5860, Main St) Average check $6. Open 6am-2:30pm. Away from the in-town bustle, this little house is a good alternative to Guenther's for soup, sandwiches and breakfast dishes.

Shalimar (☎ 603-356-0123, 27 Seavey St) Lunch dishes $5-7, dinner $9-13. Open 11am-2:30pm Tues-Sun & 5pm-10pm daily.

This popular and friendly Indian restaurant has tasteful décor and tasty dishes.

Cafe Noche (☎ 603-447-5050, NH 16, Conway) Mains $8-10. Open 11:30am-9pm. This festive cafe has some of the best Mexican food north of the Massachusetts border.

Horsefeathers (☎ 603-356-2687, Main St) Mains $7-19. Open 11:30am-10:30pm or 11:30pm. The most popular gathering place in town, Horsefeathers has an encyclopedic menu featuring pasta, salads, sandwiches, burgers, bar snacks and main-course platters.

Bellini's (☎ 603-356-7000, 33 Seavey St) Mains $13-24. Open 5pm-10pm Wed-Sun. Come here for classic Italian cuisine served in huge portions at moderate prices, from eggplant parmigiana ($14) to a 13-ounce sirloin steak ($19). Drinks tend to be on the expensive side.

Getting There & Away

Concord Trailways (☎ 603-228-3300, 800-639-3317) runs a daily route between Boston and Berlin, stopping at Conway, Jackson, Pinkham Notch and Gorham. The Boston bus drops you off on Main St across from the Eastern Slope Inn Resort in North Conway. (Note: there is no pickup here.) In Conway the bus station is at the First Stop Convenience Store (☎ 603-447-8444, W Main St).

The 50 miles from Jackson to Franconia takes 1¼ hours, without stopping, via US 302 through the Crawford Notch to US 3.

JACKSON

Seven miles north of North Conway, just east of NH 16 and across the Ellis River via a red covered bridge, Jackson village is Mt Washington Valley's premier cross-country ski center. Jackson has many charming but pricey inns.

NH 16A circles from NH 16 through the center of Jackson and back to NH 16, and NH 16B heads into the hills.

The Jackson Area Chamber of Commerce (☎ 603-383-9356, 800-866-3334, W www.jacksonnh.com, Jackson Falls Marketplace No.3, NH 16B, Jackson, NH 03846) helps with lodging reservations in Jackson, Bartlett, Glen and Intervale. The office, just south of the covered bridge, is open 9am to 4pm weekdays year-round, with additional Saturday hours (9am to 1pm) during the summer, fall and winter.

Concord Trailways (☎ 603-228-3300, 800-639-3317) runs a daily bus between Boston and Berlin, making a stop in Jackson at the Ellis River Grocery Store (☎ 603-383-9041, NH 16).

Storyland

In nearby Glen, Storyland (☎ 603-383-4186, NH 16; adult/child under 4 yrs $18/free; open weekends, then daily, then weekends late May–mid-Oct) is a delightful 30-acre theme and amusement park for children from three to nine years old. The rides, activities and shows are small-scale and well done – a refreshing break from the mega-amusements and crowds in parks such as Walt Disney World and Universal Studios. For the best value, pay and enter after 3pm, and you'll receive a pass good for the next day as well.

Skiing

Jackson is famous for its 93 miles of cross-country trails. Stop at the **Jackson Ski Touring Foundation Center** (☎ 603-383-9355, in the village; day passes adult $12-14, child $6-7) for passes and to inquire about lessons and rentals. They occasionally have organized tours.

Black Mountain Ski Area (☎ 603-383-4490, 800-475-4669 snow report, 800-698-4490 lodging reservations, NH 16B in Jackson) has a vertical drop of 1100 feet, 40 trails (equally divided between beginner, intermediate and expert slopes), four lifts and 98% snowmaking capacity, making this a good place for beginners and families with small children.

NEW HAMPSHIRE

Places to Stay

Motels Just south of Jackson's covered bridge is, yes, the *Covered Bridge Motor Lodge* (☎ 603-383-6630, 800-634-2911, fax 603-383-4146, NH 16) Doubles $58-98 with continental breakfast. This comfortable 32-room motel boasts a heated pool. Some rooms have a kitchenette, or a balcony overlooking the river.

Inns Jackson's inns offer character, charm, lots of activities and substantial price tags. One charming inn quotes prices from $125 to $270, breakfast included, but the small print adds 8% tax and 15% service charge, resulting in a daily price tag of $154 to $332. If you call for reservations, ask that prices be quoted with these extras added.

The Village House (☎ 603-383-6666, 800-972-8343, fax 603-383-6464, Ⓦ www.yellowsnowdoggear.com, NH 16A, Jackson) Doubles $60-100. This large village house and renovated barn has a swimming pool, hot tub and tennis court. Some of the nine comfy rooms have kitchenettes; all are furnished 'country' style.

Wildcat Inn & Tavern (☎ 603-383-4245, 800-228-4245, fax 603-383-6456, Ⓦ www.wildcatinnandtavern, 3 Main St) Doubles $89-149 with full breakfast. This centrally located village lodge has a dozen cozy rooms (most with private bath) and a cottage ($359) that sleeps six.

Whitney's Inn (☎ 603-383-8916, 800-677-5737, fax 603-383-6886, Ⓦ www.whitneys inn.com, NH 16A) Doubles $105-149 with full breakfast. This longtime institution appeals to skiers since there are slopes right out the back door, but it's also a great summertime family destination. The 30 rooms range from family suites (children under age 12 cost $15 additional) to pleasant inn-style rooms and cottages. The renovated barn hosts a rec room for kids and a lunch room during the winter.

Places to Eat

Many of Jackson's inns have excellent (and expensive) dining rooms.

As You Like It (☎ 603-383-6425, NH 16B) Mains $3-6. Open 7am-6pm Wed-Mon.

For a simpler meal or snack in the Jackson Falls Marketplace, try this bakery and deli for hot buffet breakfasts and deli lunches with a salad bar.

Wildcat Inn & Tavern (☎ 603-383-4245, 3 Main St) Breakfast & lunch $5-10, mains $10-15. This popular tavern is fun and serves hearty fare like lasagna and steaks for dinner, lobster Benedict for breakfast and creative sandwiches for lunch.

PINKHAM NOTCH

In the 1820s, a settler named Daniel Pinkham attempted to build a road north from Jackson through the narrow notch on the eastern slope of Mt Washington. Torrential rains in 1826 caused mud slides that buried his best efforts, but not his name. The place is still called Pinkham Notch. It was almost a century later before an auto road was built in the narrow mountain gap and Pinkham's dream of easy transit was finally realized.

Today, the area is still known for its wild beauty even though useful facilities for campers and hikers make it among the most popular activity centers in the White Mountains. Wildcat Mountain and Tuckerman's Ravine offer good skiing, and an excellent system of trails provides access to the natural beauties of the Presidential Range, especially Mt Washington. For the less athletically inclined, the Mt Washington Auto Road provides easy access to the summit.

Concord Trailways (☎ 603-228-3300, 800-639-3317) runs a daily route between Boston and Berlin, stopping at Pinkham Notch. The direct trip from Boston costs $21 (four hours).

Orientation & Information

NH 16 goes north 11 miles from North Conway and Jackson to Pinkham Notch (2032 feet), then past the Wildcat Mountain ski area and Tuckerman's Ravine, through the small settlement of Glen House and past the Dolly Copp Campground to Gorham and Berlin. The Appalachian Mountain Club (AMC) maintains a full-service hikers' kitchen and dormitory bunk facilities at its excellent Pinkham Notch Camp.

Surviving Mt Washington

Mt Washington's summit is at 6288 feet, making it the tallest mountain in the Northeast. The mountain ( www.mountwashington.com) is renowned for its frighteningly bad weather. The average temperature on the summit is 26.5°F. The mercury has fallen as low as -47°F, but only risen as high as 72°F. About 256 inches (more than 21 feet) of snow fall each year. (One year, it was 47 feet.) At times, the climate can mimic Antarctica's, and hurricane-force winds blow every three days or so, on average.

If you attempt the summit, pack warm, windproof clothes and shoes, even in high summer, and always consult with AMC hut personnel. Don't be reluctant to turn back if the weather changes for the worse. On a typical August day, those who set out on Tuckerman Ravine Trail in T-shirts and shorts could suffer hypothermia (and worse) at the summit, where snow, ice and 115mph winds rage in 20°F weather. Dozens of hikers who ignored such warnings and died are commemorated by trailside monuments and crosses. In good weather, the hike is exhilarating. If you're in good physical condition and you start early, you can make it to the top and back down in a day. You can also do several good, short hikes from Pinkham Notch Camp, including the short walk to Crystal Cascade and the equally easy one to Glen Ellis Falls.

The Tuckerman Ravine Trail starts at the Pinkham Notch Camp and continues for 4.2 miles to the summit. It's the shortest hike to the top, taking just over four hours going up and slightly less going down. Other trails to the peak are described in the Crawford Notch section, later in this chapter.

The restored Tip Top House no longer provides overnight lodging, but hikers and patrons of both the Mt Washington Auto Road (see below) and the Mt Washington Cog Railway (described in the Bretton Woods section, later in this chapter) can now find food, souvenirs and great historical exhibits at the top of the mountain.

Pinkham Notch Camp is the intelligence center in these parts; see below. The AMC's main office (☎ 617-523-0636,  www.outdoors.org) is at 5 Joy St, Boston, MA 02108.

Mt Washington Auto Road

The Mt Washington Summit Road Company (☎ 603-466-2222,  www.mtwashington.com) operates an 8-mile-long alpine toll road from Pinkham Notch to the summit of Mt Washington. The entrance is off NH 16, 2½ miles north of Pinkham Notch Camp. Private cars pay a toll ($16 for car and driver; $4-6 for each passenger) which includes an audio cassette tour. Trucks and campers aren't allowed.

If you'd rather not drive, vans will take you up and back (1½ hours) for $22/20/10 adult/senior/child. The auto road is open 8:30am to 5pm, mid-May to mid-October; tours run 8:30am to 5pm. In severe weather, the road may be closed (even in summer).

Pinkham Notch Camp

Guided nature walks, canoe trips, cross-country ski and snowshoe treks and other outdoor adventures out of Pinkham Notch Camp are organized by the **Appalachian Mountain Club** (*AMC;* ☎ *603-466-2727, 800-262-4455,*  *www.amc-nh.org*). They also operate a summer hiker's shuttle that stops at many trailheads along US 302 in Pinkham Notch.

The *AMC White Mountain Guide,* on sale here, includes detailed maps and the vital statistics of each trail: how long and how difficult it is, the vertical rise, the average walking time, reference points along the way and information on what to look at as you walk. Individual trail maps and guides are also available. You can also purchase the guide online from the main AMC site,  www.outdoors.org.

The AMC maintains hikers' 'high huts' providing meals and lodging. Carter Notch

Hut is located on Nineteen-Mile Brook Trail, and Lakes of the Clouds Hut is sited on Crawford Path (for more information, see Crawford Notch, later in this chapter). For those hiking the Appalachian Trail, the Zealand and Carter huts are open year-round.

For lodging and meals at the camp, see Places to Stay, below.

Skiing

With a vertical drop of 2112 feet, **Wildcat Mountain** (☎ 603-466-3326, 800-255-6439, 800-754-9453 snow report, NH 16, Pinkham Notch) tops off at 4415 feet. It's situated north of Jackson. Its downhill skiing facilities include 44 ski trails (30% beginner, 40% intermediate, 30% expert), four lifts and 90% snowmaking capacity.

The cirque at **Tuckerman Ravine** has several ski trails for ski purists. What's pure about it? No lifts. You climb up the mountain, then ski down. Purists posit that if you climb up, you will have strong legs that won't break easily in a fall on the way down. Tuckerman is perhaps best in spring, when most ski resorts are struggling to keep their snow cover, since nature conspires to keep the ravine in shadow much of the time. Park in the Wildcat Mountain lot for the climb up the ravine.

Gondola

Wildcat Mountain's summertime **Gondola Skyride** (adult/child 6-12 yrs $9/4.50; 10am to 5pm daily, mid-May to mid-October) was the first of its kind in the USA. It operates in summer just for the fun of the ride and the view.

Places to Stay

Call for reservations during the summer and autumn at *Dolly Copp Campground* (☎ 603-466-3984, NH 16) Sites $14. Open mid-May–mid-Oct. This USFS campground is 6 miles north of the AMC camp and has 176 primitive sites.

Pinkham Notch Camp (☎ 603-466-2727, 800-262-4455, NH 16) Nonmember dorm beds $31/21 adult/child under 13 yrs; nonmember dorm beds with breakfast and supper $51/35 adult/child. Open year-round. This AMC camp also incorporates the Joe Dodge Lodge, with dorms housing more than 100 beds. Reserve bunks in advance. The camp also has a few private doubles and triples ($63-89).

CRAWFORD NOTCH

US 302 travels west from Glen, then north to Crawford Notch (1773 feet), through some beautiful mountain scenery. Crawford Notch State Park has a system of shorter trails (half-mile to 3 miles) for hikes to the summit of Mt Washington.

Crawford Notch State Park

In 1826, torrential rains in this steep valley caused massive mud slides that descended on the home of the Willey family. The house was spared, but the family was not – they were outside at the fatal moment and were swept away by the mud. The dramatic incident made the newspapers and fired the imaginations of painter Thomas Cole and author Nathaniel Hawthorne. Both men used the incident for inspiration, thus unwittingly putting Crawford Notch on the tourist maps. Soon, visitors arrived to visit the tragic spot, and they stayed for the bracing mountain air and healthy exercise.

In 1859, the Crawford family opened the Crawford House hotel and began cutting mountain trails so their guests could penetrate the previously trackless wilderness. Their work was the basis for today's excellent system of trails. (The hotel was razed in 1977.) Crawford Notch State Park now occupies this beautiful, historic valley.

From the Willey House site, now used as a state park visitor center (☎ 603-374-2272), you can walk the easy half-mile Pond Loop Trail, the 1-mile Sam Willey Trail and the Ripley Falls Trail, a 1-mile hike from US 302 via the Ethan Pond Trail. A half-mile south of the Dry River Campground on US 302 is the trailhead for Arethusa Falls, a 1.3-mile hike.

Mt Washington Hiking Trails

Please read the warnings about severe weather (see the boxed text 'Surviving Mt

Washington') and consult with Appalachian Mountain Club (AMC) personnel before attempting to climb Mt Washington. If you're in shape and properly equipped, try the trails below.

Ammonoosuc Ravine Trail This trail, via the AMC's Lakes of the Clouds Hut (elevation 5000 feet), is one of the shortest hiking routes to the summit. It's also one of the best routes during inclement weather because it is protected from the worst winds, and, if the weather turns very nasty, you can take shelter in the AMC hut. For overnight lodging and meals, see Places to Stay, below.

The trail starts at a parking lot on Base Station Rd, near the entrance to the Mount Washington Cog Railway (elevation 2560 feet), and climbs easily for 2 miles up the dramatic ravine to Gem Pool. From Gem Pool, however, the climb is far more strenuous and demanding, with a sharp vertical rise to the AMC hut.

From the Lakes of the Clouds Hut, other trails ascend to the summit where there are some services.

Jewell Trail This trail is more exposed than the Ammonoosuc Ravine Trail and should be used only in good conditions. The last 0.7 mile is above the tree line and very windy. The Jewell Trail starts at the same parking lot as the Ammonoosuc Ravine Trail but follows a more northeasterly course up a ridge. At 2.8 miles, the trail rises above the timberline and climbs 3½ miles by a series of switchbacks to meet the Gulfside Trail. The Gulfside continues to the summit.

Places to Stay & Eat

It's nice and quiet at *Dry River Campground* (☎ 603-374-2272, US 302) Sites $13. Open late May–mid-Oct. Near the southern end of Crawford Notch State Park, this campground has 31 tent sites with a spanking new bathhouse, showers and even laundry facilities.

Crawford Notch General Store & Campground (☎ 603-374-2779, US 302) Sites $20-25. Open May–mid-Oct. This handy all-purpose place sells camping supplies and groceries to use at its wonderfully wooded sites. You'll probably welcome the hot showers.

AMC's *Lakes of the Clouds Hut* (☎ 603-466-2727, 800-262-4455) Open June–mid-Sept. Nonmembers pay $20 for a dorm bed. Breakfast and dinner is $32 more – a steal, when you remember that everything including cooking gear would have to be packed in. Advance reservations are essential. See the Ammonoosuc Ravine Trail section, above, for details.

BRETTON WOODS

Before 1944, Bretton Woods was known only to locals and wealthy summer visitors who patronized the grand Mount Washington Hotel. When President Roosevelt chose the hotel as the site of the conference to establish a new global economic order after WWII, the whole world learned about Bretton Woods.

The mountainous countryside is still as stunning now as it was during those historic times, the hotel is almost as grand and the name still rings with history. At the very least, stop to admire the view of the great hotel set against the mountains. You may want to stay a night or two. Ascending Mt Washington on a cog railway powered by a steam locomotive is dramatic fun for all, and a must for railroad buffs.

History

WWII devastated both Europe and Asia, causing the world economy to go into an economic tailspin. World leaders realized that rebuilding these war-torn areas and restoring the world economy would be a principal concern once the fighting stopped.

For three weeks in July of 1944 world leaders and financial experts gathered in Bretton Woods for the United Nations Monetary and Financial Conference. Their purpose was to develop a model for the world's postwar economy. The conference's results included the creation of the International Monetary Fund and the World Bank. The experts also formulated plans for stable currency-exchange rates and temporary assistance to member nations with balance-of-payments problems.

The Bretton Woods conference paved the way for the conference at Dumbarton Oaks in Washington, DC, in September and October 1944, at which time a prototype for the United Nations charter was written. At Yalta, in February 1945, the shape of the new organization was refined, setting the stage for the United Nations' founding conference, held in San Francisco from April to June of 1945.

Though some elements of the economic world order that emerged at Bretton Woods – such as the gold standard – have been superseded, much of the conference's work has proven remarkably durable.

Mt Washington Cog Railway

Purists walk, the out-of-shape drive, but certainly the quaintest way to reach the summit of Mt Washington is to take this cog railway (☎ 603-846-5404, 800-922-8825; adult/senior/child 6-12 yrs $44/40/30, child under 6 yrs free; open 8:30am-4:30pm Sat & Sun early May-early June; 8:30am-4:30pm daily early June-late Oct). Since 1869, coal-fired steam-powered locomotives have followed a 3½-mile track up a steep mountainside trestle for a three-hour, roundtrip scenic ride. To secure a seat and to avoid a long wait, make reservations by phone. Also, remember that the average temperature at the summit is 40°F in summer (which means it might be lower) and the wind is always blowing, so bring a sweater and windbreaker.

Instead of having drive wheels, a cog locomotive applies power to a cogwheel, or gear wheel, on its undercarriage. The gears engage pins mounted between the rails to pull the locomotive and a single passenger car up the mountainside, burning a ton of coal and blowing a thousand gallons of water into steam along the way. Up to seven locomotives may be huffing and puffing at one time here, all with boilers tilted to accommodate the grade, which at the 'Jacob's Ladder' trestle is a 37% grade – the second-steepest railway track in the world.

The base station is 6 miles east of US 302. Turn east in Fabyan, just northwest of

the Mount Washington Hotel and between Bretton Woods and Twin Mountain.

Places to Stay & Eat

In addition to being recommended lodgings, the **Mount Washington Hotel** offers extensive breakfast buffets and dress-up dinners, and both the **Bretton Arms Inn** and **Bretton Woods Motor Inn** have dining rooms.

Camping Great tent sites can be found at **Cherry Mountain KOA** (☎ 603-846-5559, 800-743-5819, NH 115, Twin Mountain) Sites without/with hookups $25/32. Open mid-May–mid-Oct. Two miles north of the junction of US 3 and NH 115, this 70-site campground has lots of facilities. The wooded and private tent sites are excellent.

Motels Each of these properties is nice in its own way.

Boulder Motor Court (☎ 603-846-5437, 866-846-5437, W www.bouldermotorcourt.com, US 302, Twin Mountain) Doubles $60-80. This pleasant cottage complex has 10 one- and two-bedroom units with kitchens; a few have fireplaces. The latter are a bargain for four people ($105-114).

Carlson's Lodge (☎ 603-846-5501, 800-348-5502, W www.carlsonslodge.com, US 302, Twin Mountain) Doubles $57-95. Open late May–mid-Oct & Dec–mid-Apr. This chalet-like lodge has 27 country-style rooms set far enough from the highway for noise not to be a problem. Choose from two-room suites and corner rooms with a kitchen.

The Bretton Woods Motor Inn (☎ 603-278-1000, 800-258-0330, fax 603-278-8838, W www.mtwashington.com, US 302) Doubles $99-149. Operated by the Mount Washington Resort, this modern place (with 50 large-ish rooms) actually enjoys the best view of the Mount Washington Hotel and its mountain backdrop. It's also the least expensive of the resort's four accommodations, despite having a pool and sauna.

Hotels & Inns They don't make 'em anymore like the **Mount Washington Hotel** (☎ 603-278-1000, 800-258-0330, fax 603-278-

8838, W *www.mtwashington.com, US 302)*
Doubles $269-329 with breakfast & dinner.
Arguably the *grande dame* of New England
lodging, this 200-room hotel has imposing
public rooms, thousands of acres of grounds,
27 holes of golf, 12 clay tennis courts, an
equestrian center, indoor and outdoor
heated pools and other amenities. Don't
forget to add 15% for service.

For a century, people have been staying
at *The Bretton Arms Inn* (☎ *603-278-1000,
800-258-0330, fax 603-278-8838,* W *www. mt
washington.com, US 302)* Doubles $149-219
with full breakfast. On the same estate as
the Mt Washington resort, this 34-room
manse was built as a grand 'summer cottage' in 1896, but it has been an inn since
1907. It was restored extensively in 1986.

GREAT NORTH WOODS

These woods – north of Berlin – are less
populated and have fewer tourists than the
rest of the state, with one exception, The
Balsams Resort. There are two scenic routes
north of the Notches and Bretton Woods. If
you've been feeling like you can't see the
forest for the trees, nothing beats US 2 from
the Vermont/New Hampshire state line to
the Maine/New Hampshire state line. The
expansive but looming mountain views are
unparalleled. If you really want to get
remote, or are heading to the outposts of
Maine, take NH 16 north from Gorham to
Erol. This route runs parallel to the birch-
lined Androscoggin River.

Rather like coastal whale watching,
Moose Tours *(☎ 603-466-3103, 800-992-
7480, Main St, Gorham)* go in search of
huge land-roaming behemoths frolicking in
their natural habitat, muddy marshes at the
edge of thick forests. From late May to mid-
October, the 2½-hour van tours depart daily
at about dusk from the information center
on NH 16 and US 2 in the middle of town.

Places to Stay

*The Balsams (☎ 603-255-3400, 800-255-0800
in New Hampshire, 800-255-0600 in US and
Canada, fax 603-255-4221,* W *www.the
balsams.com, NH 26, Dixville Notch)* Singles
$260-390, doubles $370-500 with all meals

in summer; singles $155-287, doubles $230-
494 with breakfast and dinner in winter.
Open late May–mid-Oct & mid-Dec–late
Mar. Nestled in a dramatic and narrow
valley, this elegant, 15,000-acre resort with
212 rooms has been hosting guests since
1866. The all-inclusive price gives unlimited
use of two golf courses, putting greens,
tennis courts, a swimming pool and lake,
boats, hiking and mountain-biking trails
and all other resort services. Other activities include shuffleboard, badminton,
croquet, horseshoes, table tennis and billiards. Even if you don't stay, it's worth a
drive to check out this rare bird.

*The Jefferson Inn (☎ 603-586-7998, 800-
729-7908,* W *www.thejeffersoninn.com, US 2,
Jefferson)* Doubles $95-185 with full break-
fast. If you've been wandering the northern
White Mountains and can't afford the
Balsams, this inn serves as a very good base
for exploration. The nine guest rooms and
common areas are freshly renovated and
decorated.

Upper Connecticut River Valley

Hanover is part of the larger community of
the Upper Connecticut River Valley, which
includes Lyme and Lebanon, New Hampshire, as well as Norwich, White River Junction and Woodstock, in Vermont. When
looking for services (including accommodations and dining possibilities), consider all
of these places, not just Hanover.

HANOVER

Chartered in 1761 and settled in 1765,
Hanover was named after Britain's reigning
dynasty. It was a frontier farming outpost
with little to set it apart from others. But
Hanover's future was determined when
Reverend Eleazar Wheelock moved his
Christian school for Native American youth
from Connecticut to Hanover. The new
school was funded with money raised in
England by one of Wheelock's former students, and the Earl of Dartmouth, King

George III's colonial secretary, lent it his noble patronage and name.

Dartmouth College was chartered in 1769 primarily 'for the education and instruction of Youth of the Indian Tribes.' The school was located deep in the forests where its prospective students lived. Although teaching 'English Youth and others' was only its secondary purpose, in fact, Dartmouth graduated few Indian youths and was soon attended almost exclusively by colonists. Daniel Webster (1782–1852), who graduated in 1801 and went on to become a prominent lawyer, US senator, secretary of state and, perhaps, the USA's most esteemed orator, is the college's most illustrious alumnus.

Though it declines to call itself a university, Dartmouth is far more than a New England liberal arts college. It has well-regarded schools of medicine, engineering and business administration. The BASIC computer language was developed in its mathematics department. Today, despite its graceful Georgian buildings and ivy-covered campus, Dartmouth is very high-tech.

Orientation & Information

Hanover is fairly easily to negotiate. Many services are along Main St. The central reference for everything is the green, the broad lawn bounded by Wheelock, N Main, Wentworth and College Sts. To visit Hanover is to visit Dartmouth College, for the college dominates the town.

The Hanover Area Chamber of Commerce (☎ 603-643-3115, Ⓦ www.hanover chamber.org, 216 Nugget Building, Main St, PO Box 5105, Hanover, NH 03755) answers questions about Hanover and adjoining Norwich, Vermont. The chamber also maintains an information booth on the village green, staffed from July to mid-September.

Across the river in Vermont, the Norwich Bookstore (☎ 802-649-1114), Main St, Norwich, is one of New England's most

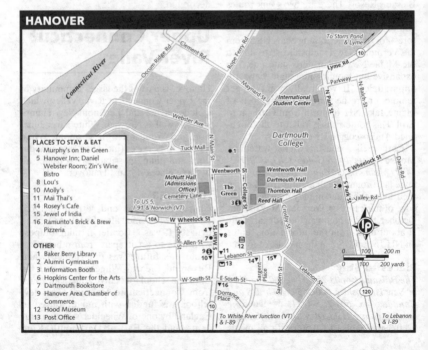

HANOVER

PLACES TO STAY & EAT
4 Murphy's on the Green
5 Hanover Inn; Daniel Webster Room; Zin's Wine Bistro
8 Lou's
10 Molly's
11 Mai Thai's
14 Rosey's Cafe
15 Jewel of India
16 Ramunto's Brick & Brew Pizzeria

OTHER
1 Baker Berry Library
2 Alumni Gymnasium
3 Information Booth
6 Hopkins Center for the Arts
7 Dartmouth Bookstore
9 Hanover Area Chamber of Commerce
12 Hood Museum
13 Post Office

exceptional bookstores. The Dartmouth Bookstore (☎ 603-643-3616, 33 S Main St), with a large selection, is also recommended.

Dartmouth College

Free guided walking tours of the campus are offered throughout the year; call the admissions office (☎ 603-646-2875) for details.

For a look at Dartmouth's prettiest and most historic buildings, start on the green. To the north is the college's central library, **Baker Berry Library** *(☎ 603-646-2560; open 8am-8pm when school is in session)*. The basement reading room houses a series of murals painted by José Clemente Orozco (1883–1949), the renowned Mexican muralist who taught and painted at Dartmouth from 1932 to 1934. The murals follow the course of civilization in North America from the time of the Aztecs to the present.

Along the east side of the green on College St, picturesque **Dartmouth Row** consists of four harmonious Georgian buildings: Wentworth, Dartmouth, Thornton and Reed. Dartmouth Hall was the original college building, constructed in 1791. After it burned in 1904, it was wisely rebuilt using brick.

Hopkins Center for the Arts *(☎ 603-646-2422)* is Dartmouth's outstanding venue for the performing arts on the south side of the green. A long way from such cosmopolitan centers as Boston, New York and Montreal, Dartmouth must make its own entertainment to fill the long winter nights. Look for playbills promoting everything from movies to live performances by international companies.

Hood Museum of Art *(☎ 603-646-2808; admission free; open 10am-5pm Tues & Thur-Sat, 10am-9pm Wed, noon-5pm Sun)*, behind the Hopkins Center, has a collection ranging from ancient Greece and Rome through the European Renaissance and up to modern times.

Special Events

Each February, Dartmouth celebrates its weeklong Winter Carnival. The winter's major fun-and-social event features special art shows, drama productions, concerts, an ice sculpture contest and other amusements. Call the chamber of commerce (☎ 603-643-3115) for dates and details.

Places to Stay

Hanover's economy has a split personality: Eating places are designed and priced for students, while lodgings are designed for the (mostly) well-heeled parents who come to visit. Thus, meals are cheap, but beds are not.

Regional accommodations (in Hanover, Lebanon and White River Junction) are in greatest demand during foliage season, when virtually all the rooms are reserved. There is also high demand in summer and for special college events. Unless otherwise noted, rates below are for June to mid-October. Sometimes visitors find themselves driving for hours to find a room, so it's a good idea to make reservations if you can.

Camping There's plenty of swimming at *Storrs Pond Recreation Area (☎ 603-643-2134, NH 10)* Sites without/with hookups $15/20. Open mid-May–mid-Oct. In addition to 37 sites on a 15-acre pond, this private campground has an Olympic-size pool, tennis courts and two sandy beaches for swimming. From I-89 exit 13, take NH 10 north and look for signs.

Mascoma Lake Camping Area (☎ 603-448-5076, NH 4A) Sites without/with hookups $20/26. Open mid-May–mid-Oct. These 90 sites, in nearby Lebanon, are mostly shaded and overlook a lake.

Motels The 56 rooms are well-priced at *Airport Economy Inn (☎ 603-298-8888, 800-433-3466, 45 Airport Rd, West Lebanon)* Doubles $65-85 July-Oct. All it's missing is a country setting.

Chieftain Motor Inn (☎ 603-643-2550, 800-845-3557, ⓦ www.chieftaininn.com, 84 Lyme Rd) Doubles $101 with continental breakfast. In a country setting along NH 10 North, this 22-room inn has large, clean, comfortable rooms.

Inns & B&Bs Sink a pint. *Norwich Inn (☎ 802-649-1143, ⓦ www.norwichinn.com, Main St)* Doubles $69-149. Just across the

Connecticut River in Norwich, Vermont, this well-run establishment has 16 attractive inn rooms, seven motel rooms, four vestry apartments and a good traditional dining room. Their brewpub, Jasper Murdock's Alehouse, is the really fun draw, though.

Alden Country Inn (☎ 603-795-2222, fax 603-795-9436, W www.aldencountryinn.com, 1 Market St, Lyme) Doubles $105-145 with full breakfast. Ten miles north of Hanover via NH 10 and facing the Lyme Town Common, this 1809 inn has 15 colonial guest rooms with modern facilities, as well as a very good restaurant and tavern.

Trumbull House B&B (☎ 603-643-2370, 800-651-5141, fax 603-643-2430, W www .trumbullhouse.com, 40 Etna Rd) Doubles $125-250 with full breakfast. Four miles east of Dartmouth, this B&B is a wonderful alternative to staying in town. It's a family-friendly colonial house, built in 1919, with five luxurious guest rooms and a tranquil pond. A hiking trail links it to the Appalachian Trail.

Hanover Inn (☎ 603-643-4300, 800-443-7024, fax 603-643-4433, W www.hanoverinn .com, cnr Wheelock & Main Sts) Doubles $257-297. Hanover's most prominent lodging is, not surprisingly, owned by Dartmouth College. The hotel-style décor is colonial reproduction and the ambience upscale, with prices to match.

Places to Eat & Drink

Hanover's eateries are constantly competing to invent new ways of preparing student classics – sandwiches, burgers, pizza, pasta – while keeping prices low. There's not a lot of fancy food in town, but there aren't fancy prices either.

Lou's (☎ 603-643-3321, 30 S Main St) Mains $5-7. Open for breakfast and lunch. Hanover's oldest establishment dates to 1947 and the place is always packed. From the retro tables or Formica-topped counter, order typical diner food like eggs, sandwiches and burgers. Or just grab something from the bakery.

Rosey's Cafe (☎ 603-643-5282, 15 Lebanon St) Sandwiches $6. Open 8:30am-

6pm Mon-Sat & 10am-5pm Sun. Rosey's serves up excellent panini sandwiches with, perhaps, eggplant, feta, pesto, tomato and basil. It's also a cool place to hang out with a cup of robust espresso. The outdoor patio is prime.

Ramunto's Brick & Brew Pizzeria (☎ 603-643-9500, 68 S Main St) Slices $1.50, large cheese $10.75. Open 11am-midnight. Every college town has one, and this is it: Hanover's best pizza joint.

Molly's (☎ 603-643-2570, 43 S Main St) Lunch $5-10, dinner $10-15. Open 11am-10pm. Molly's has gourmet burgers, salads and pastas at lunchtime. The evening menu goes upscale a bit with pepper chicken linguine and similarly trendy fare.

Mai Thai's (☎ 603-643-9980, 44 S Main St) Mains $5-14.50. Open 11:30am-10pm Mon-Sat. This popular 2nd-floor place has five different types of the ubiquitous pad thai, a popular lunch buffet ($8.50) and pleasantly upscale environs.

Jewel of India (☎ 603-643-2217, 27 Lebanon St) Mains $6-11. Open 11:30am-3pm & 4:30pm-10pm. A whiff of curry adds some variety as the gustatory map is expanded to cover the Punjab. Sunday brunch ($8) features lots of curry and 10 kinds of bread.

Murphy's on the Green (☎ 603-643-4075, 11 S Main St) Lunch dishes $6-10, dinner dishes $13-18. Open 11am-10pm; last call at 12:30am. This is classic collegiate tavern, where students and faculty meet over pints of ale ($4) and big, satisfying plates of hearty bar food.

Zin's Wine Bistro (☎ 603-643-4300, Hanover Inn, cnr Main & Wheelock Sts) Mains $7-18. Open 11:30am-10pm Mon-Sat & 1:30pm-10pm Sun. Zin's is cheaper, more relaxing and has lighter fare than its sister restaurant below. The outer section of the Hanover Inn's outdoor patio features Zin's menu.

Daniel Webster Room (☎ 603-643-4300, Hanover Inn) Mains $19-30. Open for breakfast daily, lunch Mon-Fri & dinner Tues-Sat. This conservative dining room is Hanover's most elegant dining place.

Getting There & Away

The short-haul 'commuter' subsidiaries of some major airlines link Lebanon Municipal Airport (☎ 603-298-8878), 6 miles south of Hanover, with Boston, New York (La Guardia) and Philadelphia.

Vermont Transit (☎ 802-864-6811, 800-552-8737) has direct buses from Boston's South Station, Logan International Airport ($38.50; three hours) and Springfield, MA. There's also connecting service from New York, Hartford and Montreal to White River Junction, VT. Advance Transit bus (☎ 802-295-1824) travels from White River Junction to Hanover for free. Bus stops are indicated by a blue-and-yellow AT symbol. Dartmouth Coach (☎ 603-448-2800) operates seven daily shuttles between Lebanon and Boston's Logan International Airport. The one-way fare is $35.

It takes three hours to reach Hanover from Boston; take I-93 to I-89 to I-91. From Hanover to Burlington, VT, it's an additional 2½ hours north via I-89.

Maine

Far from the madding crowd. That's Maine's reputation. To be sure, a few sections of Maine struggle amid shopping malls and coastal resorts beset with summer vacationers. But with the largest land area of the six New England states, 781 sq miles of state and national parks and the sparsest population (1.2 million) of any state east of the Mississippi River, Maine offers travelers wilderness adventures of the first magnitude.

The rockbound coast of Maine is about 228 miles long as the crow flies, but a boat sailing its tortuous course would cover almost 3500 miles. Bays, islands, inlets, peninsulas, isthmuses and coves make up the granite-strewn coast, along with a few stretches of sandy beach.

When European explorers discovered Maine, it was home to an Algonquian people known as the Abenaki, many of whom belonged to the Penobscot and Passamaquoddy tribes.

John and Sebastian Cabot, a father and son from England (John was originally from Italy), sailed the coast of Maine at the end of the 15th century. It was not until 1607 that a permanent English colony was founded at Popham Beach, but it was short-lived. Many of the first European settlers were French who came south from Quebec. English, Scots-Irish and German colonists from Europe followed. In 1614, British explorer John Smith (famous as the man whose life was saved by Pocahontas) charted the Maine coast, and in less than a decade there were settlements at Monhegan (1622), Saco (1623) and York (1624). In 1641, York became the first chartered city in English America.

In the 17th century, a series of wars raged on between Maine's English colonists and Quebec's French colonists, who were aided by Native American tribes. The first war was King Philip's War (1675–78); next was King William's War (1689–97); Queen Anne's War (1702–13) followed; and last was King George's War (1744–48). In 1759, when the British defeated the French on the Plains of

Highlights

- Biking the carriage roads in Acadia National Park
- Taking a windjammer cruise out of Camden's rockbound harbor
- Dining on lobsters and steamers at a lobster pound
- Hiking the Appalachian Trail all the way to Mt Katahdin
- Admiring the stately old homes of Kennebunkport and Castine
- Canoeing in the remote ponds and lakes of Baxter State Park
- Picnicking at the Portland Head Light

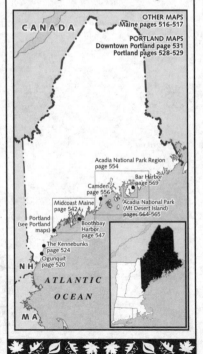

OTHER MAPS
Maine pages 516–517

PORTLAND MAPS
Downtown Portland page 531
Portland pages 528–529

CANADA

Acadia National Park Region
page 554

Bar Harbor
page 569

Camden
page 556

Acadia National Park
(Mt Desert Island)
pages 564–565

Midcoast Maine
page 542

Portland
(see Portland
maps)

Boothbay
Harbor
page 547

The Kennebunks
page 524

Ogunquit
page 520

NH

MA

ATLANTIC
OCEAN

Abraham at Quebec, there was finally peace among Maine's English, French and Native American inhabitants.

During the Revolutionary War, Benedict Arnold started out from Augusta on his expedition to capture Quebec. In 1775, British forces burned Portland.

Maine was governed from Boston, Massachusetts, until 1820. At that time, as part of the Missouri Compromise, Maine became the 23rd state admitted to the union. Portland was the original capital, but the capital was moved to Augusta in 1827, and its state house was completed in 1832.

In 1783, the St Croix River became the border between Maine and the Canadian province of New Brunswick, but both sides were unhappy. By 1838, the dispute flared into the Aroostook War – a war of words, not bullets. The Webster-Ashburton Treaty settled the dispute in 1842.

Today, southern coastal Maine is thickly settled. The settlements vary from well-preserved historic towns to strip malls and 'factory outlet' stores. There are genteel summer resorts and honky-tonk beach towns. In July and August, 'summer people' and tourists invade popular pockets of Maine's south and central coast, and city accents and attitudes can crowd out the simpler speech and ways of local folk until you get east of Bar Harbor. But during the other 10 months of the year, almost all of Maine feels isolated and distant from cosmopolitan USA.

Northern inland Maine is New England's wilderness, with vast (for New England) areas of trackless forest and thousands of glacial lakes inhabited only by fish and fowl. About 89% of Maine stands in forests of white pine, fir and hardwood trees. See the North Woods section, later in this chapter, for more information.

Information

The Maine Office of Tourism (☎ 207-287-5711, 888-624-6345, fax 207-623-0388, Ⓦ www.visitmaine.com, 59 State House Station, Augusta, ME 04330) maintains information centers on the principal routes into the state (these are at Calais, Fryeburg,

Hampden, Houlton, Kittery and Yarmouth). Each facility is open 9am to 5pm daily, with extended hours in the summer.

In an emergency, call ☎ 800-482-0730 for the Maine State Police.

Getting There & Around

Air Portland International Jetport is the state's main airport, but a number of airlines also serve Bangor International Airport.

Commuter or charter aircraft serve the Augusta Airport, Bar Harbor Airport, Caribou, Fort Kent, Houlton, Knox County Regional Airport, Northern Aroostook Airport and the Northern Maine Regional Airport in Presque Isle.

At the time of writing, the airlines serving these airports included US Airways Express, run by Colgan Air (☎ 800-272-5488), and Delta Express Airlines (☎ 800-221-1212) also operating as Business Express. In addition to the above, American Airlines, Continental Airlines, Delta Air Lines, Northwest Airlines, and United Airlines serve Portland and Bangor.

Bus Concord Trailways (☎ 800-639-3317, Ⓦ www.concordtrailways.com) operates daily buses between Logan International Airport in Boston and numerous towns in Maine (Bangor, Bar Harbor, Bath, Belfast, Brunswick, Camden/Rockport, Damariscotta, Ellsworth, Lincolnville, Portland, Rockland, Searsport, Waldoboro and Wiscasset). Some Concord Trailways buses connect with the Maine State Ferry Service to islands off the coast.

SMT (☎ 207-945-3000, Ⓦ www.smtbus .com) buses carry passengers from Bangor to St Stephen, New Brunswick, Canada.

Cyr Bus Lines (☎ 800-244-2335, Ⓦ www .cyrbustours.com) runs from Bangor to Caribou via Orono, Houlton, Presque Isle and other towns in between.

Train The *Downeaster* makes three trips daily between Boston, MA, and Portland, ME, with stops in Dover and Durham (University of New Hampshire), NH; see the Portland section, later in this chapter, for more information.

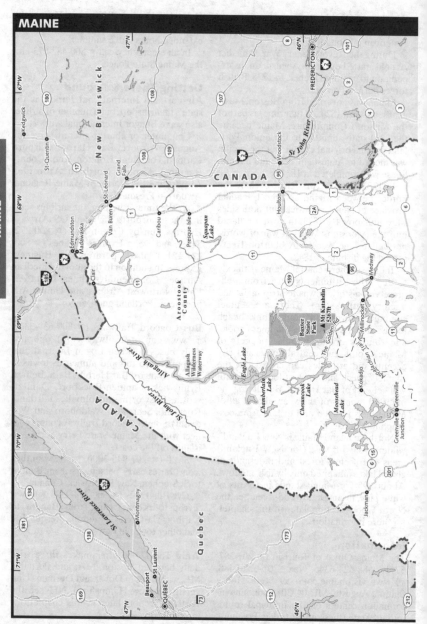

MAINE

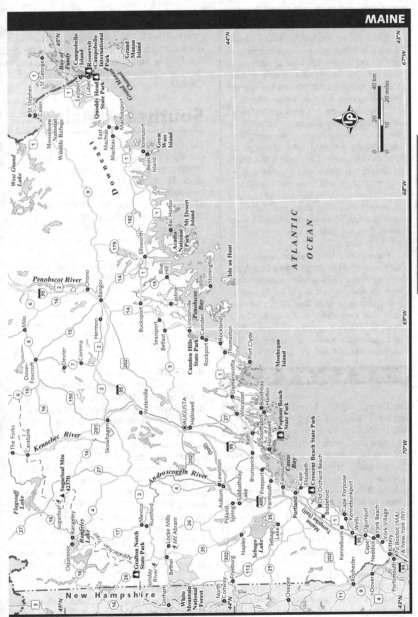

MAINE

I've Got Moxie

In most corner markets in Maine, you'll notice a soft drink with a strange orange label on the shelf: Moxie. This obscure bittersweet soda is Maine's unofficial state drink. In fact, Moxie is so revered that Mainers have named their pets, boats, and even a town after it.

Originally touted as a medicine that cured everything from impotence to 'softening of the brain,' Moxie became America's first mass-marketed soda in 1884. It was so big that an amusement park, built in the 1920s in Boston, was aptly called Moxieland; it remained until it closed in the mid-'40s. (Coca-Cola surpassed Moxie in sales and stamped its presence out of all states but Maine and certain parts of Massachusetts.) Mainers either love this soda or hate it; there's no middle ground.

Every year, during the first weekend of July, Lisbon Falls hosts the Moxie Days festival, where you can buy Moxie paraphernalia from generations past or just knock back as many cans as possible. Year-round, you can stop in at *Kennebec's* (☎ 207-353-8173, 2 Main St, Lisbon Falls), the US's only store and ice-cream parlor dedicated to this obscure taste of America's past.

Car Except for the Maine Turnpike (I-95 and I-495) and part of I-295, Maine has no fast, limited-access highways. Roads along the coast flood with traffic during the summer tourist season. As a result, you must plan for more driving time when traveling in Maine.

Note: Moose are a particular danger to drivers in Maine, even as far south as Portland – they've been known to cripple a bus and walk away. Be especially watchful in spring and fall and around dusk and dawn, when the animals are most active.

Boat Maine State Ferry Service (☎ 207-596-2202, W www.state.me.us/mdot/opt/ferry/ferry.htm) operates boats between the mainland and several of the state's larger islands. Bay Ferries (☎ 207-288-3395, W www.catferry.com) and M/S Scotia Prince (☎ 800-845-4073, W www.scotiaprince.com) offer car and passenger ferry service from Bar Harbor and Portland, respectively (see those sections), to Yarmouth, Nova Scotia, Canada.

Southeast Maine

Many people associate the Maine coast with the works of the American artist Winslow Homer, who spent his summers in Prout's Neck. His powerful watercolors depict the boulder-strewn coastline, the battering surf of the North Atlantic and the merciless Maine climate, complete with dense fog and forceful gales. Well, that Maine coast does exist – to the north of Prout's Neck (just south of Portland).

South of Prout's Neck are long stretches of beach inundated with tourists, taffy and T-shirt shops. This is especially true in towns like the Yorks, Ogunquit, Wells, and Old Orchard Beach, where the commercialism can be daunting. Kennebunkport, former president George Bush's hideaway, is far more serene.

KITTERY

Entering Kittery from New Hampshire via US 1 or I-95 can be less than thrilling – unless you're going shopping. Kittery is famous for its shopping malls and outlet stores, all of which claim to offer deep discounts on everything from apparel to china to camping gear.

If shopping is not your bag, you can head straight past Kittery, quickly on I-95, or much more slowly on US 1. Keep in mind that US 1 from Kittery to Portland is the Maine coast's commercial artery, lined with motels, campgrounds, gas stations, restaurants and shops. If you need a room, tent site, meal or any other service or product, just get on US 1 and cruise until you find it.

THE YORKS

York Village, York Harbor, and York Beach make up the Yorks. York Village, the first city chartered in English North America, has a long and interesting history and well-preserved colonial buildings in the village center. York Harbor was developed more than a century ago as a posh summer resort, and it maintains some of that feeling today. York Beach was where the masses came in summer, and its working-class roots still show in its large number of RV parks and humdrum commercial development.

Historic York was called Agamenticus by precolonial Indian inhabitants. British colonials settled York in 1624, and it was chartered as a city in 1641. The Old York Historical Society (☎ 207-363-4974; family/adult/child $15/7/3; open 10am-5pm Tues-Sat, 1pm-5pm Sun mid-June–Sept) is proud of the town's historic buildings and has preserved several of them as a museum of town history. Admission tickets for the museum are sold at Jefferds' Tavern Visitor Center, off US 1A, on Lindsay Rd.

The **School House** is a mid-18th-century school building. The **Old Gaol** (jail) gives a vivid impression of crime and punishment two centuries ago. The **Emerson-Wilcox House** is a museum of New England decorative arts and the **Elizabeth Perkins House** is a wealthy family's summer home. The **John Hancock** warehouse preserves the town's industrial and commercial history; the **George Marshall Store** now houses a research library.

If you have children, you may want to visit the state's largest zoo, **York's Wild Kingdom** (☎ 207-363-4911, 800-456-4911, US 1; adult/child 4-10 yrs $15.25/11.75; open Memorial Day–mid-Sept).

OGUNQUIT & WELLS
Ogunquit ('Beautiful Place by the Sea') is a small town famous for its 3-mile-long sand beach that affords swimmers the choice of chilly, pounding surf or warm, peaceful back-cove waters. The beach is special enough to draw hordes of visitors from as far away as New York City, Montreal and Quebec City, increasing the town's population exponentially in summer. It is also the USA's northeasternmost gay and lesbian mecca, adding a touch of open San Francisco culture to a more conservative Maine one. For more information, have a look at Ⓦ www.gayogunquit.com.

Many visitors come to stay for a week or more in efficiency units (rooms with kitchens). Many accommodations require minimum two- or three-night stays in summer, particularly on weekends.

Neighboring Wells, to the northeast, has the eastward continuation of Ogunquit Beach and several camping areas. To drive US 1 through Wells is to subject yourself to the usual visual assault perpetrated by American commercial strip development. But for all its commercial tawdriness, Wells has good beaches, as well as lots of useful and relatively inexpensive motels and campgrounds.

Orientation & Information
The center of Ogunquit, called Ogunquit Square, is the intersection of Main St (US 1), Shore Rd and Beach St. The town, which comprises mostly tourist services, stretches southeast down Shore Rd to Perkins Cove, and northeast to the neighboring town of Wells. Parking in town lots costs $6 per day during the busy summer months.

You'll find the Ogunquit Welcome Center (☎ 207-646-5533, Ⓦ www.ogunquit.org) on US 1, near the Ogunquit Playhouse and a third of a mile south of the town's center. It's open 9am to 5pm daily, until 8pm Friday and Saturday.

Marginal Way
Marginal Way, Ogunquit's well-known coastline footpath, starts southeast of Beach St at Shore Rd and ends near Perkins Cove.

It follows the 'margin' of the sea, hence its name. The path and right-of-way were ceded to the town in the 1920s after its owner, Josiah Chase, sold off his valuable sea-view property. The scenic walk is slightly more than a mile. If you don't want to walk back, you can take the trolley that runs in the summer.

Wells Auto Museum
In 1946, a resident of Wells was given a Stanley Steamer that his uncle found in his

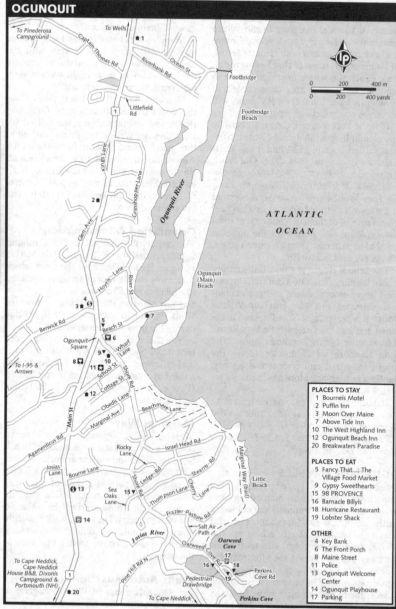

OGUNQUIT

To Pinederosa Campground
To Wells
Captain Thomas Rd
Riverbank Rd
Ocean St
Footbridge
Littlefield Rd
Footbridge Beach
King's Lane
Grasshopper Lane
Glen Ave
Ogunquit River
ATLANTIC OCEAN
Hoyt's Lane
River St
Ogunquit (Main) Beach
Berwick Rd
Beach St
Ogunquit Square
Wharf Lane
To I-95 & Arrows
School St
Shore Rd
Cottage St
Obeds Lane
Beachmere Lane
Marginal Ave
Rocky Lane
Israel Head Rd
Agamenticus Rd
Main St
Ledge Rd
Shore Rd
Stearns Rd
Cherry Lane
Marginal Way (trail)
Little Beach
Josias Lane
Bourne Lane
Sea Oaks Lane
Thompson Lane
Frazier-Pasture Rd
Salt Air Path
Josias River
Oarweed Cove Rd
Oarweed Cove
To Cape Neddick, Cape Neddick House B&B, Dixonis Campground & Portsmouth (NH)
Pine Hill Rd N
Pedestrian Drawbridge
Perkins Cove Rd
Perkins Cove
To Cape Neddick

0   200   400 m
0   200   400 yards

PLACES TO STAY
1   Bourneis Motel
2   Puffin Inn
3   Moon Over Maine
7   Above Tide Inn
10 The West Highland Inn
12 Ogunquit Beach Inn
20 Breakwaters Paradise

PLACES TO EAT
5   Fancy That...; The Village Food Market
9   Gypsy Sweethearts
15 98 PROVENCE
16 Barnacle Billyis
18 Hurricane Restaurant
19 Lobster Shack

OTHER
4   Key Bank
6   The Front Porch
8   Maine Street
11 Police
13 Ogunquit Welcome Center
14 Ogunquit Playhouse
17 Parking

barn in Vermont. The new owner restored the antique car, built early in the century, and soon had a burgeoning collection of restored classic cars powered by steam, electricity and gasoline. The Wells Auto Museum (☎ 207-646-9064, Post Rd/US 1; adult/child 6-12 yrs $5/2, child under 6 yrs free; open 10am-5pm daily Memorial Day-Columbus Day) now has 70 cars of 45 different makes, including Rolls-Royce, Stutz, Cadillac, Packard, Pierce Arrow and Knox.

Ogunquit Playhouse

Ogunquit Playhouse (☎ 207-646-5511, 10 Main St) lit up for the first time in 1933. It has been at its present site, south of the town center, since 1937. The season begins in late June and offers three musicals and two plays each year in the 750-seat theater. Occasionally, there are well-known performers in the cast or in the audience. Call the box office for schedules (usually available in mid-May) and ticket prices.

Beaches

Ogunquit Beach (or Main Beach to the locals) is only a five-minute walk along aptly named Beach St, east of US 1. Walking to the beach is a good idea in the summer, because it costs $2 per hour to park and the lot fills up early. The 3-mile-long beach fronts Ogunquit Bay to the south; on the west side of the beach are the warmer waters of the tidal Ogunquit River. There are toilets, changing rooms, restaurants and snack shops.

Footbridge Beach, 2 miles to the north near Wells, is actually the northern extension of Ogunquit Beach. It's reached from US 1 by Ocean St and a footbridge across the Ogunquit River. There's yet another way to access the beach via Eldridge Rd in Wells – follow the sign for Moody Beach.

Little Beach is near the lighthouse on Marginal Way and is best reached on foot.

Cruises

Finestkind (☎ 207-646-5227, Perkins Cove; adult/child $9/7; 9am-3pm daily), a lobster boat, takes passengers on a 50-minute voyage to pull up the traps and collect the delicious critters. Trips leave every hour on the hour. There are also 90-minute cruises, cocktail cruises in the late afternoon and evening, and even a 9pm starlight cruise as well.

Silverlining (☎ 207-646-9800, Perkins Cove; adult $32) is a 42-foot Hinckley sloop offering two-hour sails four times daily.

The Cricket (☎ 207-646-5227, Barnacle Billy's dock, Perkins Cove; adult $20) is a locally built catboat (a sailboat). It sails on 1¾-hour cruises that depart three times daily.

Places to Stay

Few places stay open year-round; most open in mid-May and close by mid-October.

Footbridge Beach beckons from the other side of the river.

JON DAVISON

MAINE

Room rates, which are low at the start of the season, double in July and August and on holiday weekends (see the Public Holidays and Special Events sections in the Facts for the Visitor chapter).

Camping As you might imagine, the campgrounds fill up early in the day in July and August.

Pinederosa Camping Area (☎ 207-646-2492, ᴡ www.pinederosa.com, Captain Thomas Rd, Wells) Sites $20. Captain Thomas Rd goes north from US 1 a mile northwest of Ogunquit center (turn just south of the Falls at Ogunquit). A bit of a trip from Ogunquit, this secluded campground has 162 sites, most of which are heavily wooded. A shuttle ($1) runs to/from the beach 9am to 5pm daily.

Ocean View Cottages & Campground (☎ 207-646-3308, 84 Harbor Rd) Sites $22-28. This place, with over 100 wooded sites, is just west of exit 2 off the Maine Turnpike. Call for prices for weekly cottage rental.

Dixon's Campground (☎ 207-363-3626, ᴡ www.dixonscampground.com, 1740 US 1, Cape Neddick) Tents/RVs $24/28 per 2 people. South of Ogunquit, this 40-acre campground has 100 sites for tents and RVs. There's free transport to Ogunquit Beach from late June to early September.

Wells has several other campgrounds off exit 2 (mostly on US 1), including the following:

Beach Acres	☎ 207-646-5612
Gregoire's Campground	☎ 207-646-3711
Ocean Overlook	☎ 207-646-3075
Riverside Park Campground	☎ 207-646-3145
Sea Breeze Campground	☎ 207-646-4301
Sea-Vu Campground	☎ 207-646-7732
Stadig Campground	☎ 207-646-2298
Wells Beach Resort	☎ 207-646-7570

Motels There are a couple of simple hotels along US 1.

Breakwaters Paradise (☎ 207-361-1128, 1931 US 1) Rooms $45-95. Just south of Ogunquit, this motel has nine spartan rooms with air con and a pool.

Bourne's Motel (☎ 207-646-2823, 646-9093, ᴡ www.bournesmotel.com, 676 Main St/US 1) Rooms $95-118. North of the town's center, Bourne's has 38 bland rooms close to Footbridge Beach.

Inns & B&Bs Ogunquit has a handful of inns and B&Bs near the beach.

Puffin Inn (☎ 207-646-5496, ᴡ www.puffininn.com, 433 Main St) Rooms $65-145 with continental breakfast. Just north of the center of town, this big Victorian has cheesy decor but a convenient location and 10 rooms.

The West Highland Inn (☎ 207-646-2181, ᴡ www.westhighlandinn.com, 38 Shore Rd) Rooms $70-145 with breakfast. This centrally located Victorian summer house has 14 rooms.

Above Tide Inn (☎ 207-646-7454, 66 Beach St) Rooms $90-195. This aptly named inn is perched on piles above the Ogunquit River, literally a stone's throw from Ogunquit Beach. It has 10 rooms and advertises 'spectacular views.' There is a three-night minimum stay during high season.

Cape Neddick House B&B (☎ 207-363-2500, ᴡ www.capeneddickhouse.com, 1300 US 1, Cape Neddick) Rooms with bath $135-195 with full breakfast. This is a late-19th-century Victorian with five rooms.

For gay- and lesbian-friendly guesthouses try the following:

Ogunquit Beach Inn (☎ 207-646-1112, ᴡ www.ogunquitbeachinn.com, 67 School St) Rooms $69-119 with breakfast. This B&B has nice rooms with refrigerator, TV and private bath and is located near the fire station.

Moon Over Maine (☎ 207-646-6666, 800-851-6837, ᴡ www.moonovermaine.com, 22 Berwick Rd) Rooms $79-129 with continental breakfast. Up the hill from Key Bank, Moon Over Maine, an 1839 Cape-style house, has nine rooms and an outdoor hot tub.

Places to Eat

Our Ogunquit restaurants picks, listed here, are open for lunch and dinner unless otherwise noted.

Fancy That... (☎ *207-646-4118, Ogunquit Square*) Prices $3-6. In Ogunquit Square, this eatery serves pastries, sandwiches and wonderful ice cream, which you can eat on the terrace at umbrella-shaded tables right next to the busy intersection. This is Ogunquit's prime place to people-watch.

The Village Food Market (☎ *207-646-2122, Ogunquit Square*) Sandwiches $3-6. Abutting Fancy That..., this is also a good bet for sandwiches, especially if you want to take them to the beach.

Lobster Shack (☎ *207-646-2941, 110 Perkins Cove Rd*) Mains $6-18. For the cheapest lobster ($15) and steamers ($8) in town head to Lobster Shack, which has been in business since 1947.

Hurricane Restaurant (☎ *207-646-6348, 111 Perkins Cove Rd*) Mains $12-28. For lunch or dinner with a gorgeous view, try this place. It features Maine lobster chowder, but the menu always includes special items like lobster spring rolls ($10) and chocolate martinis. Expect to spend $25 to $45 for dinner with wine.

Barnacle Billy's (☎ *207-646-4711, 70 Oarweed Cove Rd*) Mains $15-35. Another perennial favorite in Perkins Cove, this place was once a rough-and-ready eatery, but is now more refined, with prices to match. Lobsters are priced according to market prices, but a big lunch or dinner usually costs $20 to $40 with wine or beer.

Gypsy Sweethearts (☎ *207-646-7021, 30 Shore Rd*) Mains $17-25. Gypsy Sweethearts serves the catch of the day and other seafood at moderate prices. Dinner with wine costs around $20 to $35 per person. Breakfast includes freshly ground coffee and just-baked bread.

98 PROVENCE (☎ *207-646-9898, 104 Shore Rd*) Mains $21-28. For authentic French cuisine, try this newcomer for dinner. Try the grilled venison on a ragout of artichokes ($28).

Arrows (☎ *207-361-1100, Berwick Rd, York*) Mains $37-42. This is one of the two most expensive restaurants in this part of Maine (the other being White Barn Inn in Kennebunkport). It's located in a wonderfully restored 18th-century farmhouse, and the two owners are chefs from San Francisco, where they picked up Asian culinary influences. One of their signature dishes is grilled lobster stewed in a Thai-style curry sauce. Expect to spend more than $100 per couple. It's 4 miles west of Ogunquit on Berwick Rd. Make reservations.

Entertainment
The Front Porch (☎ *207-646-4005, Ogunquit Square*) This classic piano bar has tons of off-key sing-alongs that you can join while sipping a cosmopolitan.

Maine Street (☎ *207-646-5101, 195 Main St*) If you want to boogie, Maine Street is Ogunquit's hoppin' gay dance club.

Getting There & Around
Ogunquit lies 70 miles northeast of Boston off I-95 on US 1. Portsmouth, New Hampshire, is just 17 miles farther west along the coast. Portland is 35 miles to the east.

'Trolleys' (really just buses disguised as trolleys, $1) circulate through Ogunquit every 10 minutes, 8am to midnight in the summer months. They take you from the center of town to the beach or Perkins Cove.

THE KENNEBUNKS
Together, the towns of Kennebunk, Kennebunkport and Kennebunk Beach make up the Kennebunks. Kennebunkport, the most famous of the three towns, is beautiful, historical and absolutely packed in the summer. Walk anywhere in the town to see the pristine 100- and 200-year-old houses and mansions, manicured lawns and sea views. Even in the autumn, when beach resorts such as Old Orchard Beach have closed down, visitors throng to Kennebunkport to shop in its boutiques, stay in its gracious inns and drive along the ocean to admire the view.

Ocean Ave presents the most dramatic vistas, but the back streets, inland from the Kennebunk River and the sea, are less busy.

Orientation
The epicenter of Kennebunkport activity is Dock Square, just over the bridge on the east side of the Kennebunk River. South of

THE KENNEBUNKS

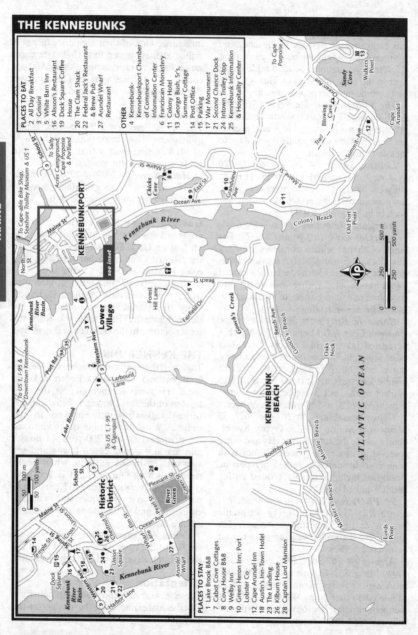

PLACES TO EAT
2   All Day Breakfast
3   Grissini
5   White Barn Inn
16 Alisson's Restaurant
19 Dock Square Coffee
    House
20 The Clam Shack
22 Federal Jack's Restaurant
    & Brew Pub
27 Arundel Wharf
    Restaurant

OTHER
4   Kennebunk-
    Kennebunkport Chamber
    of Commerce
    Information Center
6   Franciscan Monastery
11 Colony Hotel
13 George Bush, Sr's,
    Summer Cottage
14 Post Office
15 War Monument
17 Parking
21 Second Chance Dock
24 Intown Trolley Stop
25 Kennebunk Information
    & Hospitality Center

PLACES TO STAY
1   Lake Brook B&B
7   Cabot Cove Cottages
8   Cove House B&B
9   Welby Inn
10 Green Heron Inn; Port
    Lobster Co
12 Cape Arundel Inn
18 Austin's Inn-Town Hotel
23 The Landing
26 Kilburn House
28 Captain Lord Mansion

Dock Square is the historic district, with many fine old mansions, some of which are now inns. Ocean Ave goes south from Dock Square to the sea, then northeast to Walkers Point and the Bush compound (the vacation residence of former president George Bush). It's not all that exciting, but every visitor to Kennebunkport makes the drive to stare at black Secret Service vehicles. Continue northeast on Ocean Ave to reach Cape Porpoise, a charming hamlet.

Kennebunk Lower Village lies on the west side of the Kennebunk River Bridge.

Information

The Kennebunkport Information & Hospitality Center (☎ 207-967-8600), at Union Square, has toilets, brochures and maps; the staff can help you find accommodations for the same night. It's open daily 10am to 6pm in summer only, weekends only in fall.

The Kennebunk-Kennebunkport Chamber of Commerce Information Center (☎ 207-967-0857, Ⓦ www.kkcc.maine.org, 17 Western Ave/ME 9) in Kennebunk Lower Village, is in the yellow building adjacent to the Sunoco station. It's open 9am to 5pm Monday to Thursday (to 6pm on Friday) and 11am to 3pm weekends in summer; in September and October, it's open 9am to 5pm weekdays only.

Seashore Trolley Museum

Trolleys, the light-rail systems that provided most urban transport a century ago, are the focus of the Seashore Trolley Museum (☎ 207-967-2800, Log Cabin Rd; adult/child 6-16 yrs $7.25/$4.75; open 10am-5pm daily May-Oct). Founded as the Seashore Electric Railway, the museum now holds 255 streetcars (including one named Desire), as well as antique buses and public transit paraphernalia. The museum has a complicated schedule of business hours, so call before you go.

Take North St north from Dock Square to reach Log Cabin Rd.

Beaches

Kennebunkport proper has only **Colony Beach**, dominated by the Colony Hotel. But Beach St and Sea Rd (west of Kennebunk River and then south of Kennebunk Lower Village) lead to three good public beaches: **Gooch's Beach**, **Middle Beach** and **Mother's Beach**, known collectively as **Kennebunk Beach**. Beach use is free, but parking costs $3 per hour.

Bicycling

Bicycling is a good way to get around Kennebunkport. The **Cape-able Bike Shop** (☎ 207-967-4382, 800-220-0907, 83 Arundel Rd) rents bikes; follow North St from Dock Square. Fees range from $8 for a three-speed or child's bike to $25 for a new 21-speed.

Cruises

Second Chance (☎ 207-967-5507, 800-767-2628, 4-A Western Ave; adult/child 6-12 yrs $15/7.50; trips 11am, 1pm, 3pm, 5pm), a lobster boat, makes a 1½-hour cruise. Board the boat in Kennebunk Lower Village, next to the Kennebunk River Bridge.

Eleanor (☎ 207-967-8809, Arundel Wharf; tickets $38) is a schooner carrying passengers on two-hour sailing cruises in the waters off Kennebunkport. Call Capt Rich Woodman or stop by Arundel Wharf for schedules and reservations, and feel free to bring a picnic.

Places to Stay

Accommodations in Kennebunkport are not cheap, but there are many beautiful inns.

Camping Unfortunately all campgrounds but one around the Kennebunks have closed.

Salty Acres Campground (☎ 207-967-2483, ME 9) Open mid-May–mid-October. Sites $18-26. This campground is 3 miles northeast of Kennebunkport, near Cape Porpoise, and has 225 sites.

Motels Most of the Kennebunks' motels lie just outside town.

Turnpike Motel (☎ 207-985-4404, 77 Old Alewife Rd) Rooms $45-70. The 24-room Turnpike Motel is off I-95 precisely at exit 3 in Kennebunk.

Beachwood Resort (☎ 207-967-2483, W *www.beachwoodmotel.com, 272 Mills Rd/ ME 9)* Rooms $50-100. Facing Salty Acres Campground, this motel has 112 rooms (some are efficiencies). There's a swimming pool, children's pool, shuffleboard and tennis court. Not all rooms are air-conditioned.

Cabot Cove Cottages (☎ 207-967-5424, 800-962-5424, W *www.cabotcovecottages .com, 7 S Maine St)* Cabins $95-150. Abutting the Kennebunk River, Cabot Cove Cottages has 15 rustic cabin-efficiencies. Call for weekly rates.

Hotels Just steps from Dock Square is **Austin's Inn-Town Hotel** (☎ 207-967-4241, 888-228-0548, 28 Dock Square) Rooms $54-199. This place couldn't be more centrally located. It's modern, but done in traditional style.

The Landing (☎ 207-967-4221, 21 Ocean Ave) Rooms $85-128. This big, old, wooden summer hotel overlooks the water in the high-rent district. It's most famous for its restaurant, but there are 12 guest rooms.

Inns & B&Bs The Kennebunks offer some exceptional accommodations.

Lake Brook B&B (☎ 207-967-4069, W *www.lakebrookbb.com, 57 Western Ave, Kennebunk)* Rooms $70-115 with full breakfast, suite $130 with full breakfast. On the edge of a salt marsh and tidal brook, this nice, early-20th-century farmhouse has three rooms and one suite.

Green Heron Inn (☎ 207-967-3315, W *www.greenheroninn.com, 126 Ocean Ave)* Rooms $80-135 with full breakfast. This is a dependably comfy inn and all 11 rooms have TV and air-conditioning.

Cove House B&B (☎ 207-967-3704, W *www.covehouse.com, 11 S Maine St)* Rooms $85-110 with full breakfast. A young local fireman runs this converted farmhouse (1793) with four guestrooms.

Welby Inn (☎ 207-967-4655, 92 Ocean Ave) Rooms with bath $85-140 with full breakfast. Thanks to owner Mike McGrath, who's a master woodworker, this large gambrel-roofed house has seven gorgeous guest rooms with period furnishings.

Kilburn House (☎ 207-967-4762, 877-710-4762, fax 207-967-1065, W *www.kilburn house.com, 6 Chestnut St)* Rooms $99-135, suite $195-295. Situated in the historic district, Kilburn House is a B&B with four rooms on the 2nd floor and a suite on the 3rd floor.

Cape Arundel Inn (☎ 207-967-2125, fax 207-967-1199, W *www.capearundelinn.com, 208 Ocean Ave)* Rooms $110-285 with full breakfast. Built in 1895, Cape Arundel Inn boasts 'very bold ocean views' for all of its 14 rooms, which all have porches. Rooms are bright and sunny. The inn's restaurant is one of the finest in the Kennebunks.

The **Captain Lord Mansion** (☎ 207-967-3141, fax 207-967-3172, W *www.captain lord.com, 6 Pleasant St)* Rooms $175-400 with full breakfast. If cost is no object, this is the place for you. This great sea captain's house has been meticulously restored and is, if anything, more plush and beautiful than when lived in by its original occupants. On weekends, you must stay at least two nights.

Places to Eat

Seafood rules Kennebunk's lunch and dinner menus, but the town has some cheap exceptions.

Dock Square Coffee House (☎ 207-967-4422, 18 Dock Square) Pastries $2-4. Open 8am-5pm. This tiny place is usually packed and serves coffees, teas and pastries.

All Day Breakfast (☎ 207-967-5132, 55 Western Ave/ME 9) Mains $5-9. As the name (sort of) implies, this place serves breakfast 'til it closes in the early afternoon. The blueberry pancakes are $5.50.

The Clam Shack (☎ 207-967-2560, 3 Western Ave) Mains $2.50-13. Next to the bridge in Kennebunk Lower Village, this white shack has hamburgers for $2.75 as well as fried-clam and fish plates for $8. You can eat standing up on their deck over the water, but beware of seagulls that will snatch your food.

The Wayfarer (☎ 207-967-8961, 1 Pier Rd, Cape Porpoise center) Mains $5-10. This is a casual and affordable place to head for lunch. A large bowl of haddock chowder costs $5.25.

Port Lobster Co *(☎ 207-967-5411, 122 Ocean Ave)* Mains $5-12. This is simply a lobster pound and fish market that also sells crab ($7) and lobster rolls ($8), as well as boiled lobster (market price). However, there's nowhere to sit.

Alisson's Restaurant *(☎ 207-967-4841, 5 Dock Square)* Lunch $6-12. At the center of town, Alisson's is crowded all day because of its decent pub food at good prices. Lunch selections include a fried shrimp basket ($8), charbroiled swordfish sandwich ($9) and crab cakes ($9).

Federal Jack's Restaurant & Brew Pub *(☎ 207-967-4322, 8 Western Ave)* Mains $6-15. Federal Jack's is in the Shipyard complex in Kennebunk Lower Village, above the Kennebunkport Brewing Co. It has a good menu of pub grub, salads, sandwiches, pizzas and some heartier main courses to go with its selection of 'handcrafted' ales from downstairs on draft. The microbrews here are excellent. Free tours of the brewery leave at 4pm daily.

Arundel Wharf Restaurant *(☎ 207-967-3444, Arundel Wharf)* Lunch $7-15, mains $18-38. Just south of Dock Square, this is a moderately priced place for lunch while a full dinner is much more expensive. Try the steamer clams, mussels and lobster combination ($25). The location, overlooking the Kennebunk River, is pleasant.

Grissini *(☎ 207-967-2211, 27 Western Ave)* Mains $8-14. Grissini serves Northern Italian fare in an informal and very airy room with dishes including fresh fish and homemade pastas.

The Landing *(☎ 207-967-4221, 21 Ocean Ave)* Mains $13-35. In the motel by the same name, this is a comfy old favorite among longtime residents of Kennebunkport. Seafood is the specialty, of course, and prices are moderate during lunch.

White Barn Inn *(☎ 207-967-2321, 37 Beach St)* Four-course meal $77. Open 6pm-9pm daily. This is Kennebunkport's most renowned restaurant. The decor and ambience are 'country-elegant,' and the cuisine is New American. The menu changes weekly and features local seafood complemented by locally grown herbs, fruits and vegetables and California greens. Make reservations and dress well.

Getting There & Around

The Kennebunks lie halfway between Portsmouth, NH, and Portland, ME (28 miles from each city), just off I-95 on ME 9. Ogunquit is 11 miles to the southwest.

The Intown Trolley (☎ 207-967-3686) circulates through Kennebunkport all day. Daily tickets cost $8/4 per adult/child. You can stay on for the 45-minute narrated tour of the entire route, or hop on and off as you like at the designated stops, including along Beach Ave.

OLD ORCHARD BEACH

This is the quintessential New England beach playground, saturated with lights, music and noise. Skimpily clad crowds of fun-loving sun worshippers make the rounds of fast-food emporiums, mechanical amusements and gimcrack shops selling trinkets. Palace Playland, on the beach at the very center of town, is a fitting symbol, with its carousel, Ferris wheel, children's rides, fried-clam and pizza stands, and T-shirt and souvenir shops.

Old Orchard Beach has long been a favorite summer resort of Quebecois, who flock south in July and August. Many signs are bilingual, English and French, to accommodate the friendly Canadians.

Dozens of little motels and guesthouses line the beaches to the north and south of town center, and all are full from late June through Labor Day. Before and after that, Old Orchard Beach slumbers.

PORTLAND

Portland is a small, manageable, safe, prosperous and clean city of 65,000 people. It is Maine's largest city, largest port and largest commercial center. If you include the suburbs, Greater Portland has a population of about 241,000.

Like London, Portland offers many surprising urban perspectives: Turn a corner, look down a street and a grand building or view is framed neatly at the end of it. Walk down the old cobblestones of Portland's

MAINE

narrow Wharf St at twilight and you'll feel as if a tough fisherman might pop out of nowhere to shanghai somebody.

The city center's architectural unity stems in part from tragedy. The city was ravaged by fire several times in its history, the latest and worst being the conflagration of 1866. Built mostly of wood, many of the port area's buildings were reduced to ashes.

Portlanders resolved not to let it happen again, so they rebuilt their city in the style of the time, using red brick and stone. A providential lack of booming prosperity kept its old buildings from being torn down and replaced by sterile modern structures. Today, the Old Port section of Portland begs for exploration.

Orientation

Portland is set on a ridge of hills along a peninsula surrounded by Fore River, Casco Bay and Back Cove. Portland Harbor, where Fore River empties into Casco Bay, is its historical heart, and is where you'll spend most of your time. Known as the Old Port, it holds most of the city's good restaurants, bars, galleries and shops. Atop the hills at the southwestern end of the peninsula is the Western Promenade, a long stretch of green park framing a neighborhood of grand red-brick houses. At the opposite end of the peninsula, the Eastern Promenade, which rings Munjoy Hill, serves the same function, with much finer views of Casco Bay and its islands, though the neighborhood is not nearly as posh.

Downtown Portland, with its business district, museums, shops and galleries, rises between the promenades. Congress St is the main thoroughfare along the top of the ridge, passing Portland's most imposing buildings: city hall, banks, churches and hotels. Commercial St is a fitting name for the main business street that runs the length of the peninsula.

I-95 skirts the city to the west, while I-295 makes a detour into the city and hooks back up with I-95 north of Back Cove. Approaching Portland from the south, follow I-95 to exit 6A, then take I-295 to exit 4, then take US 1 to US 1A North, which is

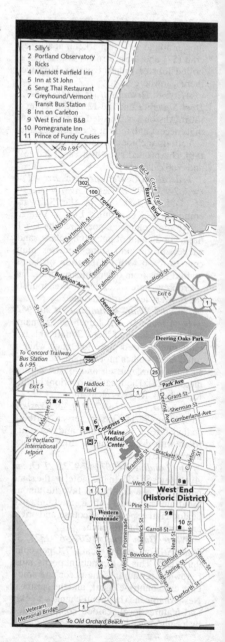

1 Silly's
2 Portland Observatory
3 Ricks
4 Marriott Fairfield Inn
5 Inn at St John
6 Seng Thai Restaurant
7 Greyhound/Vermont
  Transit Bus Station
8 Inn on Carleton
9 West End Inn B&B
10 Pomegranate Inn
11 Prince of Fundy Cruises

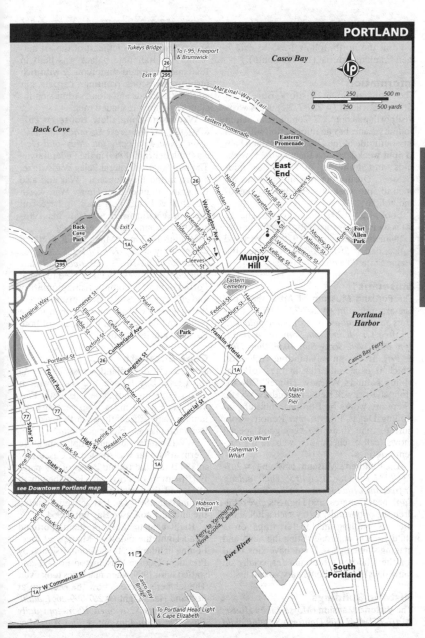

Commercial St. Stay on Commercial St and it will take you directly to the Old Port.

From the north, follow I-295 to exit 7, then Franklin Arterial (US 1A South).

Information

The Convention & Visitors Bureau of Greater Portland (☎ 207-772-5800, W www .visitportland.com, 305 Commercial St), at Foundry Lane, has an information office on the south side of the Old Port. It's open 8am to 5pm weekdays and 10am to 6pm weekends and holidays, mid-May to mid-October. During the rest of the year, it's open to 5pm weekdays and 3pm weekends and holidays.

Books Etc (☎ 207-774-0626, 38 Exchange St) is an inviting store to browse for books.

In an emergency, call ☎ 911; for Portland police, call ☎ 207-874-8300; to reach the Maine State Police, call ☎ 207-624-7076.

Museums

The **Portland Museum of Art** is the city's fine-arts museum (☎ 207-775-6418, 7 Congress Square; admission $6/1 adult/child 6-12 yrs, free for all Fri 5pm-9pm; open 10am-5pm Mon-Wed, Sat & Sun, 10am-9pm Thur & Fri). It has an outstanding collection which is especially rich in the works of Maine painters Winslow Homer, Edward Hopper, Rockwell Kent and Andrew Wyeth. There are works by European masters, including Degas, Picasso and Renoir. From time to time, there are very good special shows (call or check their website for current offerings).

The **Children's Museum of Maine** (☎ 207-828-1234, 142 Free St; adult $5, child under 1 yr free; open 10am-5pm Mon-Sat, noon-5pm Sun), near Congress and High Sts, gives children the opportunity to try such adult activities as hauling in lobster traps on a child-sized boat, broadcasting the news and making stained glass. If you have kids, head for the Children's Museum (especially on rainy days). Winter hours vary, so call first.

Historic Buildings

The **Victoria Mansion** (Morse-Libby House; ☎ 207-772-4841, 109 Danforth St; adult/child 6-17 yrs $7.50/3; open 10am-4pm Tues-Sat, 1pm-5pm Sun late May–early Oct), at Park St, is a few blocks southeast of the art museum. This Italianate palace was built in 1860 and decorated sumptuously with rich furniture, frescoes, paintings, carpets, gilt and exotic woods and stone. Admission includes a 45-minute guided tour.

Wadsworth-Longfellow House (☎ 207-879-0427, 485 Congress St; adult/child $5/1; open 10am-4pm daily late May–mid-Oct) was built of brick (1786) in the Federal style. The builder was General Peleg Wadsworth, a hero in the Revolutionary War and also the grandfather of poet Henry Wadsworth Longfellow. Longfellow grew up here, and the house's furnishings recall his 19th-century surroundings.

Built in 1807 atop Munjoy Hill, **Portland Observatory** (☎ 207-774-5561, 138 Congress St; adult/child 6-16 yrs $3/2; open daily late May-early Oct) was originally used to signal Portlanders of incoming fishing, military and merchant vessels. Recently restored, the seven-story observatory is open to the public and boasts panoramic views of both Portland and its harbor.

Cape Elizabeth

Southeast from Portland, across the bay via the Casco Bay Bridge, are the towns of South Portland and Cape Elizabeth. Fort Williams Park, 4 miles from central Portland in Cape Elizabeth, is worth a visit for its panoramas and picnic possibilities.

WWII bunkers and gun emplacements (a German U-boat was spotted in Casco Bay in 1942) dot the rolling lawns of the park. Fortification of Portland Head began in 1873, and the installation was named Fort Williams in 1899. The fort actively guarded the entrance to Casco Bay until 1964.

Right next to the park stands **Portland Head Light**, the oldest of Maine's 52 functioning lighthouses. It was commissioned by President George Washington in 1791 and staffed until 1989, when machines took over. The keeper's house is now the **Museum at Portland Head Light** (☎ 207-799-2661; adult/ child 6-18 yrs $2/1; open 10am-4pm daily June-Oct; 10am-4pm Sat & Sun Apr, May,

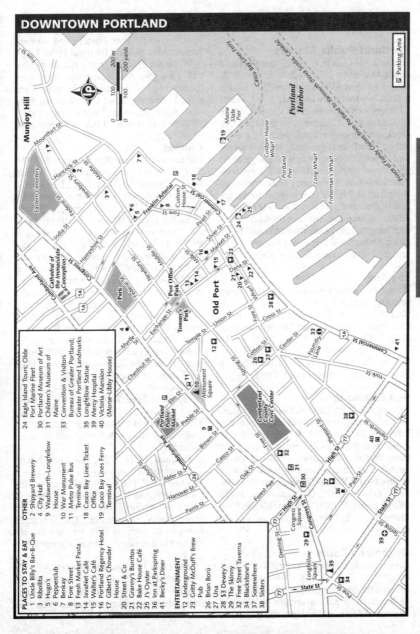

DOWNTOWN PORTLAND

MAINE

PLACES TO STAY & EAT
1 Uncle Billy's Bar-B-Que
3 Ribollita
5 Hugo's
6 Pepperclub
7 Benkay
8 Fore Street
13 Fresh Market Pasta
14 JavaNet Café
15 Walter's Café
16 Portland Regency Hotel
17 Gilbert's Chowder
    House
20 Street & Co
21 Granny's Burritos
22 Bake House Café
25 J's Oyster
36 Inn at Parkspring
41 Becky's Diner

ENTERTAINMENT
12 Underground
23 Gritty McDuff's Brew
    Pub
26 Brian Ború
27 Una
28 $3 Dewey's
29 The Skinny
32 Free Street Taverna
34 Blackstone's
37 Somewhere
38 Sisters

OTHER
2 Shipyard Brewery
4 City Hall
9 Wadsworth-Longfellow
   House
10 War Monument
11 Metro Pulse Bus
    Terminal
18 Casco Bay Lines Ticket
    Office
19 Casco Bay Lines Ferry
    Terminal
24 Eagle Island Tours; Olde
    Port Marine Fleet
30 Portland Museum of Art
31 Children's Museum of
    Maine
33 Convention & Visitors
    Bureau of Greater Portland;
    Greater Portland Landmarks
35 Mercy Hospital
39 Mercy Hospital
40 Victoria Mansion
    (Morse-Libby House)

Nov–mid-Dec), which traces the maritime and military history of the region.

Portland Public Market

Opened in October 1998, the **Portland Public Market** (☎ 207-228-2000, 25 Preble St; open 9am-7pm Mon-Sat; 10am-5pm Sun) is a 37,000-sq-foot open food hall that features 22 locally owned businesses, a half-block from Monument Square. It's a great place to stock up on picnic food, such as freshly baked bread, local produce, Maine cheeses and regional wines. Several of the vendors also serve lunch, and there are numerous tables to sit at. *The Pantry* sells a wide assortment of Maine salsas, salad dressings, honey, jams and granolas. *The New England Bison Company* serves ground bison (buffalo), a daily bison stew ($5) and bison jerky. *Stone Soup* features a variety of hot and cold soups to enjoy at the market.

Jogging

Back Cove, northwest of the city's center on the other side of I-295, is surrounded by a 4-mile gravel jogging trail that extends 3 miles farther around the **Eastern Promenade**. Take I-295 exit 6 and follow US 1 North; or take bus No 2 to Forest Ave Plaza, bus No 6 to Payson Park or bus No 8 to the Shop 'n Save and you'll be near Back Cove.

Sea Kayaking

Just outside of Portland, the islands in Casco Bay are ideal for sea kayaking. **Casco Bay Lines** (☎ 207-774-7871, 56 Commercial St; adult/child $6/3) leaves every hour in the summer for a 15-minute cruise to Peaks Island. Once there, you can hook up with **Maine Island Kayak Company** (☎ 207-766-2373, 800-796-2373, 70 Luther St, Peaks Island; prices $55-95), a reputable outfitter that offers daily instruction and tours of the area.

Organized Tours

Greater Portland Landmarks (☎ 207-774-5561, adult/child $8/free) has daily 90-minute tours of the city that depart at 10:30am from in front of the Convention & Visitors Bureau of Greater Portland, 305 Commercial St. The fun trip gives you an overview of the city's history as you make your way around the Old Port, Eastern and Western Promenades, and the Portland Head Light.

While not exactly a tour, a ride on bus No 1 ($1) is a good and inexpensive way to see the Eastern and Western Promenades, Congress St and the heart of downtown Portland. You can ride until you've had enough. You can catch the No 1 bus on Congress St.

Cruises

The ferries of *Casco Bay Lines* (☎ 207-774-7871, 56 Commercial St; adult $3-4.60, child $6-9.25) cruise the Casco Bay islands delivering mail, freight and visitors. These are working boats, but they're comfortably outfitted. The cruises vary: A roundtrip cruise to the Diamond Islands (1¾ hours) costs $9.50/8/4 adult/senior/child five to nine years old; a roundtrip nature cruise, complete with lecture, to Bailey Island (5¾ hours) is $15.50/14/7.50; a weekly summer sunset-cruise of the bay with live jazz or chamber music (2½ hours) costs $10.75/9.50/5. Five of the six cruises operate daily year-round. All cruises depart from the Casco Bay Lines Ferry Terminal on Maine State Pier.

Bay View Cruises (☎ 207-761-0496, Fisherman's Wharf, 184 Commercial St; adult/child $10/7) offers 1½-hour seal-watches six times per day.

Eagle Island Tours (☎ 207-774-6498, Long Wharf, Commercial St; adult/child $10/8) runs boat trips around Casco Bay, including trips to Eagle Island and Portland Head Light.

Palawan (☎ 207-773-2163, Long Wharf, Commercial St; tours $20-35) cruises Casco Bay under sail. This is a 58-foot ocean racing yacht designed by Sparkman & Stevens. There are cruises in the morning ($20 for three hours), afternoon ($30 for three hours) and evening ($20 for two hours). Seniors and children 12 and under pay half price.

The Olde Port Marine Fleet (☎ 207-775-0727, 800-437-3270) has three boats departing from Long Wharf for deep-sea fishing trips, whale watching, lobstering trips and two-hour sunset harbor music cruises. Call for details, or stop by the blue ticket booth next to the Key Bank on Commercial St.

Places to Stay

There are no camping places in Portland, but there are several near Freeport, only 16 miles to the northeast. See the Freeport section for details.

Motels Outside the city's center, motels are moderately priced. There are several at I-95 exit 8, near the Maine Mall, including Comfort Inn (☎ 800-228-5150), Portland Marriott (☎ 207-871-8000) and Days Inn (☎ 800-329-7466).

Susse Chalet Portland/Westbrook (☎ 207-774-6101, 800-258-1980, fax 207-772-8697, 1200 Brighton Ave) Weekday/weekend $99/109. This motel is off I-95 exit 8 and rooms can accommodate up to four people. Rates are even less if you call and ask for the same-day rate.

Holiday Inn West (☎ 207-774-5601, 800-465-4329, fax 207-774-2103, W www.sixcontinentshotels.com, 81 Riverside St) Rooms $123. This motel, off I-95 exit 8, has 200 rooms.

Hotels Portland's hotels are near the bus station and in the Old Port.

Inn at St John (☎ 207-773-6481, 800-636-9127, fax 207-756-7629, W www.innatstjohn.com, 939 Congress St) Rooms $40-190 with continental breakfast. Built in 1897 to house passengers arriving at Union Station, this inn advertises itself as Portland's 'low-fat' hotel. It's somewhat noisy, but its labyrinth of 37 rooms is right across the street from the Greyhound/Vermont Transit bus station, and on the route of city bus Nos 1 and 3.

Marriott Fairfield Inn (☎ 207-871-0611, 800-228-2880, fax 207-871-8243, W www.marriott.com, 340 Park Ave) Weekday/weekend rates $100/120. Rooms with two double beds sleep up to four. From I-95, take exit 6A to I-295 exit 5A (Congress St); at the end of the ramp turn right, then left at the signs for Stroudwater/Westbrook.

Portland Regency Hotel (☎ 207-774-4200, 800-727-3436, fax 207-775-2150, 20 Milk St) Rooms $129-219. Portland's most upscale hotel is smack in the middle of the Old Port, a block from the waterfront. The inn has 95 very comfortable rooms and a fitness center, which are housed in the Port's substantial redbrick armory.

Inns & B&Bs Portland's West End, near the Western Promenade, is a quiet, mostly redbrick residential neighborhood with many grand Victorian houses, some of which have been converted to inns.

Inn at Parkspring (☎ 207-774-1059, W www.innatparkspring.com, 135 Spring St) Rooms $95-145 with full breakfast. This wooden B&B (1845), at the corner of Park and Spring Sts, is very centrally located.

West End Inn B&B (☎ 207-772-1377, 800-338-1377, fax 207-828-0984, W www.westendbb.com, 146 Pine St) Rooms with bath $100-180. Built in 1871, this inn has six rooms, all with TV.

Pomegranate Inn (☎ 207-772-1006, 800-356-0408, W www.pomegranateinn.com, 49 Neal St) Rooms $115-225 with full breakfast. Few innkeepers can mix modern art with antiques as skillfully as Isabel Smiles has done here. An antiques dealer and interior designer, Smiles' eclectic taste runs the gamut from faux marble columns in the living room to hand-painted walls and century-old dressers in the eight guest rooms. Large contemporary sculpture and collages are displayed in the hallways. Remarkably, they all seem to fit together.

Inn on Carleton (☎ 207-775-1910, 800-639-1779, W www.innoncarleton.com, 46 Carleton St) Rooms with bath $159-199. This is a restored 1869 Victorian house with six grandiose rooms, all with massive antique headboards and period furniture.

Places to Eat

Bostonians think little of making the two-hour drive to Portland for an exceptional meal. Many of these fine dining establishments focus on Maine's abundant goodies – treasures from the sea, as well as locally farmed chickens, venison and organically grown produce. Most of the best restaurants are along Middle St and in the Old Port section of town on Wharf, Exchange and Fore

MAINE

Sts. Restaurants listed here are open for lunch and dinner unless otherwise specified.

JavaNet Café (☎ 207-773-2469, 37 Exchange St) Prices 85¢-$3. In the Old Port, this is a great place to surf the net while nursing a hot mug of chai. They serve a selection of cookies and pastries as well. There are a handful of Macs ($8/hour) and 30 Ethernet connections ($6/hour) for you to plug into.

Becky's Diner (☎ 207-773-7070, 390 Commercial St) Prices $3-12. Open 4am-9pm daily. If you want to meet working fisherfolk, opt for breakfast or lunch at this diner on the waterfront. Sit at the counter and hobnob with the salty dogs and order one of the cheapest meals in town. The diner offers fresh muffins in the morning and sandwiches ($5) in the afternoon.

Granny's Burritos (☎ 207-761-0751, 420 Fore St) Burritos $4.25-5.75. Stop here for some quick, healthful fill-up. Have a burrito with your choice of wrap and whatever fillers you like.

Gilbert's Chowder House (☎ 207-871-5636, 92 Commercial St) Prices $4-13. At Pearl St, Gilbert's is a simple diner with a lunch counter and tables on a pier, good for a load of fish-and-chips ($9) or a big bowl of its renowned thick clam chowder ($5).

Silly's (☎ 207-772-0360, 40 Washington Ave) Mains $3-9. Away from the Old Port area, but worth the walk or short drive, is this funky little place. Locals travel across town to gobble one of the tasty abdullahs (sandwiches rolled in bakery-fresh tortillas) for lunch ($3 to $6). Dinners, such as jerk chicken ($7.50) or fish-and-chips ($5.75), are also cheap.

Seng Thai Restaurant (☎ 207-828-0458, 921 Congress St) Mains $5.25-7.75. Although your food is served on Styrofoam plates, this hole-in-the-wall near the Greyhound bus station has the best bang for your buck in Thai food. Its pad thai ($5.75) is fabulous.

J's Oyster (☎ 207-772-4828, 5 Portland Pier) Prices $6-18. Although it's a total dive, J's Oyster has the cheapest raw bar in town, with a baker's dozen of oysters costing only

$10. It's also the only place in Portland that serves meals ($12 to $18) until midnight.

Bake House Café (☎ 207-773-2217, 233 Commercial St) Prices $6-12. This cafe at Commercial St is good for baked goods, pastries, sandwiches, soups and salads.

Fresh Market Pasta (☎ 207-773-7146, 43 Exchange St) Mains $5-6.25. For affordable and tasty pasta, head here. You can have a large bowl of pasta with any sauce you want, from marinara to bolognese to pesto. There's a children's menu ($2.50).

Ricks (☎ 207-775-7772, 100 Congress St) Lunch $6-10, dinner $12-18. A newcomer to the scene, Ricks, on Munjoy Hill past the Portland Observatory, serves gorgeous brunches and dinners. The cuisine is Californian and the dress is casual. Although this is away from most of the other restaurants in Portland, it's well worth the walk up the hill.

Uncle Billy's Bar-B-Que (☎ 207-871-5631, 69 Newbury St) Mains $7-15. Off the beaten path near the **Shipyard Brewery**, Uncle Billy's serves the best barbecue and jambalaya in Maine. Owner Jonny St Laurent has decorated this unmarked restaurant with as many photos and velvet portraits of Elvis Presley as he could find. If the décor doesn't scare you off, start with catfish fingers ($5) and feast on a rack of pork spareribs ($12). It's open only for dinner and has live music nightly. There's also a good children's menu ($4.65).

Pepperclub (☎ 207-772-0531, 78 Middle St) Mains $8-10. For the best selection of veggie fare, head to Pepperclub, just northeast of Franklin Arterial. The place is usually packed shortly after 6pm. The reason is the eclectic menu – a Middle Eastern *meze* plate for starters, then Thai lime vegetables with udon noodles and sesame tofu, or mushroom and fresh basil lasagna. Most main courses are under $12, making possible an excellent, interesting dinner, with wine, for about $20 per person. Service is friendly and good.

Walter's Café (☎ 207-871-9258, 15 Exchange St) Lunches $8-12, dinners $17-22. Walter's is one of Portland's best-loved bistros, a narrow storefront dining room with a high ceiling and even higher culinary aspirations. Try the Madeira chicken with prosciutto over linguine ($9.50). Vegetarians should try the Thai bulgur salad, a combination of greens plus pecans with a miso-chili vinaigrette ($10). This is a good place for a hot lunch.

Benkay (☎ 207-773-5555, 2 India St) Prices $10-40. You will find the freshest sushi in town here, across from the Casco Bay Wharf. The specialty is lobster sashimi, the whole tail, for $19.50.

Ribollita (☎ 207-774-2972, 41 Middle St) Mains $11-16. This local favorite is one of Portland's best-kept secrets. The tiny restaurant serves fabulous Northern Italian cuisine and prides itself on its handmade pastas. Start with the caramelized onion tart ($5.75) and then move on to shrimp carbonara ($15). Make sure to reserve a table in advance, as this place fills up quickly.

Fore Street (☎ 207-775-2717, 288 Fore St) Mains $15-25. If you have just one night in Portland to dine, head to Fore Street. The airy, exposed-brick and pine-panel room – a former wartime storage area – features an open-air kitchen that practically the entire restaurant can view. Chefs busily sauté food and finish plates on three long tables, but the real spectacle is the food itself. Owner and chef Sam Hayward has made applewood grilling and roasting his forte, and, whenever possible, he uses local meats. Start with roasted Blue Hill bay mussels with pistachios, served in a broth that will leave you craving more ($8). Then choose the incredibly tender roasted pork loin ($16) or the creole curry conch stew ($20). To complete this memorable meal, finish with the maple crème brûlée ($5.50).

Street & Co (☎ 207-775-0887, 33 Wharf St) Mains $16-19. The menu here might be simple – chalked on a blackboard that's carted from table to table – but you can rest assured that the seafood is the freshest in town. There's grilled, broiled or Cajun-style fish (tuna, salmon, swordfish), plus various sea critters like mussels, clams and calamari that are steamed or sautéed. You can have your choice served over pasta or in a broth that's perfect for dipping with a hunk of fresh bread. The cramped but congenial dining rooms are usually packed for dinner, so reserve in advance.

Hugo's (☎ 207-774-8538, 88 Middle St) Mains $19-24. Owned by chef Rob Evans, former sous-chef of California's elite restaurant French Laundry in Napa Valley, Hugo's serves fine European dinners. You could start with the Scottish salmon tartare ($8) and then move on to the luscious Burgundy braised beef ribs ($23). With advance notice, you can also pay a fixed rate for six- and 10-course (!) meals; call for prices.

Entertainment

Fore St, between Union and Exchange Sts, is lined with restaurants and bars.

$3 Dewey's (☎ 207-772-3310, 241 Commercial St) This bar is typical of most bars around Union St; sports bars with large-screen TVs and pinball machines or billiard tables clicking nearby.

Gritty McDuff's Brew Pub (☎ 207-772-2739, 396 Fore St) Here's the most popular spot for a pint of award-winning beer. The half-dozen ales, porters and stouts served here are all brewed downstairs.

Brian Ború (☎ 207-780-1506, 57 Center St) A favorite hangout for the under-30 crowd is this Irish pub, between Spring and Fore Sts.

Una (☎ 207-828-0300, 505 Fore St) If you want to sip martinis and act hip, head to Una.

Free Street Taverna (☎ 207-774-1114, 128 Free St) This bar attracts Portland's bohemian crowd. Local bands also play here nightly.

The Skinny (☎ 207-772-8274, 625 Congress St) For live music, there's no better choice than the Skinny. This small and very popular bar often attracts widely known bands.

Gay & Lesbian Venues

Somewhere (☎ 207-871-9169, 117 Spring St) If you're in a singing mood, head over to Somewhere, a piano bar that also features karaoke.

MAINE

Sisters (☎ 207-774-1505, 45 Danforth St) This is the most popular lesbian bar in Maine.

Blackstone's (☎ 207-775-2885, 6 Pine St) Blackstone's is Sisters' other half, a hot spot for boys.

Underground (☎ 207-773-3315, 3 Spring St) Underground, with a huge dance floor, is Portland's largest gay bar.

Getting There & Away

Air Portland International Jetport (☎ 207-774-7301) is Maine's largest and busiest air terminal. The 'International' in the airport's name refers only to flights to and from Canada. For long-distance international flights, you must connect through Boston or New York City (JFK or Newark).

Airlines serving the airport include Continental, Delta, Northwest, United and US Airways (see the Getting There & Away chapter for contact information).

City buses can take you from Continental Airlines' doors to the center of town for $1 (see Getting Around, below). Take bus No 5 and transfer to bus No 8 to get to the Old Port.

Bus Vermont Transit (☎ 207-772-6587, 802-864-6811, 800-451-3292), in the Greyhound terminal, 950 Congress St at St John St, is near I-295 exit 5. It runs nine buses daily to and from Boston (two hours), connecting with buses to Hartford (3¼ hours more) and New York City (4½ hours more).

Vermont Transit also runs three buses northeastward to Brunswick, and four up the Maine Turnpike to Lewiston, Augusta, Waterville and Bangor (3¼ hours), with one bus continuing to Bar Harbor (four hours from Portland).

Concord Trailways (☎ 207-828-1151, 800-639-3317) has its terminal on Thompson Point Connector Rd at exit 5A off I-295. It runs 11 nonstop buses daily between Portland, Boston and Boston's Logan Airport.

From Portland, two Concord Trailways buses provide local service to towns northeast as far as Bangor (four hours); one bus connects at Bangor with a Cyr bus headed north to Medway, Sherman, Houlton, Presque Isle and Caribou. This local service

goes to Brunswick, Bath, Wiscasset, Damariscotta, Waldoboro, Rockland, Camden/Rockport, Lincolnville, Belfast, Searsport and Bangor.

Train Train service between Boston and Portland, ME, has resumed after a decades-long hiatus. The *Downeaster* makes three trips daily in each direction. The ride lasts about 2½ hours; there are brief stops in Dover and Durham (University of New Hampshire), NH.

Boat For passenger ferry cruises between Portland and Bailey Island, see Cruises, earlier.

Prince of Fundy Cruises' *M/S Scotia Prince* (☎ 207-775-5616, 800-845-4073, Ⓦ www .princeoffundy.com) departs Portland for Yarmouth, Nova Scotia, Canada, each evening at 9pm. It arrives the next morning at breakfast time after cruising for 11 hours. The return trip departs Yarmouth at 10am for Portland, arriving after dinner. You must have proof of citizenship (US citizens may use a passport or US citizen's birth certificate; non-US citizens need a passport or alien registration – green – card; travelers may be asked to present a driver's license) to enter Canada at Yarmouth.

The cruises operate daily (with some exceptions) from early May through late October. From mid-June to mid-September, the one-way Portland-to-Yarmouth overnight fare for adults in an economy cabin is $315, including shipment of a car. The day trip from Portland to Yarmouth costs $86/43 for each adult/child (plus $105 for a car); off-season rates are $66/33 ($85 for your car). Children under five sail free. If you'd like a day-use cabin on the Portland-to-Yarmouth run, prices start at $22. Meals and port tax ($3) are not included in the price.

You get half-price fare on cars certain days (mostly Tuesday and Wednesday); call for details. Thus, for a couple with two children ages five to 14, with a car, traveling in-season in two moderately priced cabins (at night, Portland to Yarmouth), the roundtrip cost can reach about $1000, with meals, taxes and tips included. Off-season, the same family, staying in the least expensive cabin, sailing at night and bringing their own food, can go roundtrip for about $400 minimum.

Getting Around

Portland's Metro (☎ 207-774-0351, W www .gpmetrobus.com) is the local bus company, with its main terminus, 'Metro Pulse,' at Monument Square (Elm St at Congress St). The fare is $1.

Buses run a number of useful routes serving the city center.

destination	bus routes
Airport	No 5
Back Cove	No 2, 3, 6
Casco Bay Municipal Ferry Terminal	No 8
Concord Trailways Bus Terminal	No 8
Eastern Promenade/Munjoy Hill	No 1
International Ferry Terminal	No 8
Old Port	No 8
Portland Museum of Art	No 1, 3, 8
Vermont Transit-Greyhound Bus Terminal	No 1, 3, 5
Western Promenade	No 1, 8

FREEPORT

Here, amid the natural beauties of Maine's rockbound coast, is a town devoted almost entirely to city-style shopping. Tony luggage, expensive china, trendy clothes and perfumed soaps are all available in more than 100 shops that are backed by a maze of parking lots. The town's mile-long Main St (US 1) is a perpetual traffic jam of cars from all over the country and Canada – all visiting Freeport in the name of nature.

Freeport's fame and fortune began a century ago when Leon Leonwood Bean opened a shop to sell equipment and provisions to hunters and fishermen heading north into the Maine woods. LL Bean gave good value for money and his customers were loyal. One foundation of their loyalty was his Maine Hunting Shoe, a rugged rubber bottom molded to a leather upper. It kept hunter's feet dry and warm as they crouched in their duck blinds at dawn.

Over the years, the store added lots of other no-nonsense, good-quality outdoor gear and some engaging retail practices: a catalog operation, 24/7/365 open hours (the store *never* closes) and an iron-clad returns policy that allows shoppers to send items back any time they prove unsatisfactory. Though the store fell on hard times in the 1960s, a shot of big-city marketing expertise soon boosted it to nationwide fame.

In summer, LL Bean (☎ 800-341-4341 ext 7801), and indeed most of Freeport's shops, are busy with shoppers all day and into the night. Don't miss a visit to the DeLorme Mapping Co (☎ 207-846-7100) and its giant 5300-sq-foot rotating globe, *Eartha,* in Yarmouth at exit 17 off I-95. Maker of the essential *Maine Atlas and Gazetteer,* DeLorme also creates maps and software for every destination in the United States.

For the nearest bus transport, see the Portland section, earlier; buses do not stop in Freeport.

Orientation

Take I-95 exit 19 or 20 to reach downtown Freeport. The downtown shopping district along Main St (US 1) is easily negotiated on foot, but you might have to drive a short distance to your lodgings if you plan to stay the night.

The epicenter of Freeport shopping is the big LL Bean store that made Freeport what it is today. It is right on Main St.

South Freeport, south along US 1, is a sleepy residential community, but its town dock has a good local eatery and bay cruises.

Information

The State of Maine has a large information center facing the DeLorme Mapping Co at I-95 exit 17. It can provide you with information on Freeport and all of Maine. The Freeport Chamber of Commerce (☎ 207-865-1212, W www.freeportusa.com) maintains information centers on Main St at Mallet St, and on Mill St a block south of Main St. Both of the centers are open 9am to 5pm weekdays.

Hiking

Bradbury Mountain State Park on ME 9, 6 miles west of Freeport in northern Pownal, has several miles of forested hiking trails, including an instant-gratification 10-minute hike from the picnic area uphill to the summit for a spectacular view that reaches all the way to the ocean. There's camping as well (see below). Surprisingly, one sees very few Freeport shoppers testing their new outdoor gear in this pretty park.

Take ME 125 and ME 136 north from Freeport, but turn left just after crossing I-95, following the state park signs.

Cruises

In South Freeport, a few miles southeast of the shopping frenzy, is the Freeport Town Wharf, the departure point for several boats offering cruises around Casco Bay. To get there, follow US 1 to the well-known 40-foot-high statue of a Native American, and follow the unmarked road in front of it (South Freeport Rd) until you get to the four-way stop sign. Hang a right onto Main Street, which you should follow to the end.

Atlantic Seal Cruises (☎ 207-865-6112; *adult/child $20/15).* Atlantic Seal Cruises offers three-hour cruises. Remember to pack a picnic lunch or ask about catered picnics when you make reservations.

Desert of Maine

Desert of Maine (☎ 207-865-6962, 95 Desert Rd; adult/teen/child 6-12 yrs $7.50/5/4; open daily 9am-5pm May-Oct) William Tuttle came here in 1797 to farm potatoes. But the deadly combination of not rotating his crops and overgrazing caused enough erosion to create Maine's only desert. The shifting dunes, which are 70 feet deep in some areas, cover entire trees and the old farm's buildings. To get there, take I-95 exit 19 and head west of the highway for 2 miles.

Places to Stay

Camping You'll find a handful of campgrounds within a 6-mile radius of Freeport.

Winslow Memorial Park (☎ 207-865-4198, end of Staples Point Rd) Sites $17/19 no-view/water-view. Open Memorial Day weekend-early Sept. This choice pick is a town park right on the ocean. There are no hookups. Head south from Freeport along

US 1, take a left at the towering Native American statue and go toward South Freeport, then right onto Staples Point Rd (there's a park sign); it's about 2 miles more to the park.

Flying Point Campground (☎ 207-865-4569, 10 Lower Flying Point Rd) Sites $17-23. Flying Point is 3½ miles southeast of LL Bean via Bow St and has 38 sites right on the water.

Sandy Cedar Haven Campground (☎ 207-865-6254, W www.campmaine.com/cedarhaven, 39 Baker Rd/ME 125 North) Sites $18-24. Closest to Freeport's center (2½ miles away), this place has 58 mostly wooded sites.

Bradbury Mountain State Park (☎ 207-688-4712, 528 Hallowell Rd/ME 9, Pownal) Sites $10. This place has 41 forested sites. It is north of downtown Pownal. See Hiking (above) for details.

Blueberry Pond Campground (☎ 207-688-4421, 218 Poland Range Rd, Pownal) Sites $19-24. Between ME 9 and ME 136, 4 miles northeast of Freeport and Bradbury Mountain (head for Bradbury Mountain, then follow the signs), this campground is a good alternative.

Motels Many chains (like Super 8 Motel) are south of the city center along US 1 near I-95 exit 19.

Casco Bay Inn (☎ 207-865-4925, 107 US 1) Rooms $55-99 with breakfast. The best of the motels is this newly renovated place, a few minutes' drive south of the town center.

Eagle Motel (☎ 207-865-4088, 800-334-4088, 215 US 1) Rooms $80-97 with breakfast. This is a handsome, classic American motel.

Inns & B&Bs Several B&Bs are on Main St just north of the big Harraseeket Inn. Others are within an easy walk of the city center. In summer, most charge from $95 to $150 for a double room with bath and full breakfast.

Captain Briggs House Inn (☎ 207-865-1868, 800-217-2477, 8 Maple Ave) Rooms $75-120. This house dating from the mid-19th century has four rooms and friendly owners.

The James Place Inn (☎ 207-8865-4486, 800-964-8086, W www.jamesplaceinn.com, 11 Holbrook St) Rooms $95-145. Built in 1880, this B&B has six rooms – three of them with spas. The young owner is a fifth-generation Freeport citizen who knows the area quite well.

The Bagley House Inn (☎ 207-865-6566, 800-765-1772, W www.bagleyhouse.com, 1290 Royalsborough Rd, Durham) Rooms $95-150. Only a 10-minute drive from downtown Freeport, in rural Durham, Bagley House dates from pre–Revolutionary War times. The owners, two former nurses from Boston, definitely know how to cater to the whims of tired shoppers, who are often found lounging in the acres of open fields and gardens.

Harraseeket Inn (☎ 207-865-9377, 800-342-6423, W www.stayfreeport.com, 162 Main St) Rooms $140-275. After shopping all day in town, it's wonderful to know that you have to walk only a block back to Harraseeket Inn with its 84 elegant rooms, where you can enjoy afternoon tea and cakes and then soak your weary bones in an oversized spa or take a swim in their indoor pool. Owner Nancy Gray is a native Mainer who grew up on a sporting camp. When she was 12 years old, her father bought her a gun, just in case she got caught on the way home from school between a mother bear and her cub.

Atlantic Seal B&B (☎ 207-865-6112, 877-285-7325, 25 Main St, South Freeport) Rooms $105-175. Situated near South Freeport's town dock, this quiet B&B features three rooms with harbor views; it offers boat cruises, as well.

Places to Eat

Freeport's Main St (US 1) has a dozen places to eat, including mobile sausage stands. Unfortunately, most restaurants serve standard tourist fare.

The Village Store (☎ 207-865-4230, 97 South Freeport Rd, South Freeport) Sandwiches $3.75-7. Hidden away from the throngs of shoppers is this deli, where workers in the area have their lunch. The nondescript storefront serves large sandwiches. There are several tables if you want to eat on the premises.

Lobster Cooker (☎ 207-865-4349, 39 Main St) Mains $5-20. This fast-food place, which abuts LL Bean, has excellent clam chowder ($5), good coleslaw and boiled lobster lunches ($17). Dine inside or on the deck.

Gritty McDuff's (☎ 207-865-4321, 187 Lower Main St) Mains $6-13. Two miles south of LL Bean, this is a popular place for pub grub and a pint.

Harraseeket Lunch & Lobster Co (☎ 207-865-4888, 36 Main St, South Freeport) Mains $8-18. On the Town Dock, this place serves a full menu of lunch items to be eaten at shaded picnic tables overlooking the bay. Get a clambake ($15) or excellent fish-and-chips ($8). Live and cooked lobsters are sold for take-out as well.

Broad Arrow Tavern (☎ 800-342-6423, 162 Main St) Mains $14-23. Situated in the Harraseeket Inn, this tavern has a good selection of microbrews and moderately priced brick-oven specialties. A bowl of hearty lobster stew costs $10.

Maine Dining Room (☎ 207-865-1085, 162 Main St) Mains $21-36. This upscale dining room, also in the Harraseeket Inn, is far more upscale than the tavern. Fresh tuna ($24), ostrich filet ($28), porterhouse ($34) and Maine coast bouillabaisse are but a few of their tempting offers. Dessert crêpes, made at the table, provide the perfect ending. The restaurant is also known for its extravagant Sunday brunch buffet.

AUGUSTA

Maine's capital city is small (population 21,000). Founded as a trading post in 1628, it was later abandoned, then resettled in 1724 at Fort Western (later Hallowell). Lumber, shingles, furs and fish were its early exports to the world, sent down the Kennebec River in sloops built right here. Augusta became Maine's capital in 1827, but was only chartered as a city in 1849. Aside from its museum and some monumental public buildings there isn't really any reason to come to this depressed New England city (locals call it 'Disgusta'). But if you're passing by, stop at the Maine State Museum, admire the capitol and browse the antique shops in neighboring, rustic Hallowell.

Augusta, 23 miles north of Wiscasset, is best visited on a day excursion, or while passing through along I-95. US Airways Express/Colgan Air (☎ 800-272-5488) flies between Augusta and Boston. Greyhound buses (☎ 207-622-1601) stop at 312 Water St (US 201/ME 27).

Orientation & Information

Memorial Circle, near the state capitol, is this city's traffic nexus. (US 202, US 201, ME 8, ME 11, ME 17, ME 27 and ME 100 all intersect in this large traffic circle.)

Augusta's traditional commercial district is just across the Kennebec River, on its east bank. Western Ave goes from Memorial Circle due west 1½ miles to I-95 exit 30; most of Augusta's motels are on Western Ave or west of the interstate exit. Three miles northwest of the center, at I-95 exit 31, you'll find the University of Maine at Augusta, the Augusta Civic Center, the Mall at Augusta, the Kennebec Valley Chamber of Commerce and a couple more chain motels. Water St (US 201/ME 27) runs south from Memorial Circle, past the capitol, to Hallowell. With attractive shops, cafes and restaurants, Hallowell is the pretty appendage of Augusta.

You can call the office of the Kennebec Valley Chamber of Commerce (☎ 207-623-4559, W www.augustamaine.com), University Dr (I-95 exit 31), Augusta, ME 04332-0676, with questions.

Things to See & Do

The granite **State House** (☎ 207-287-2301, cnr State & Capitol Sts; admission free; open 9am-1pm Mon-Fri) was designed, as was Boston's, by Charles Bulfinch. It was built in 1832 and enlarged in 1909 under the direction of another Boston architect, C Henri Desmond. Park in the lot on the southwest side of the building, near the Department of Education and Maine State Museum, and enter the capitol through the southwest door. You can pick up a leaflet for a self-guided tour or pick up a red courtesy phone and request a free guided tour.

You should have a look at the **Maine State Museum** (☎ 207-287-2301, State St; admission free; open 9am-5pm Mon-Fri, 10am-4pm Sat, 1pm-4pm Sun), in the Maine State Library and Archives next to the State House. The museum traces Maine's history through an astounding 12,000 years and includes prehistoric arrowheads and tools, as well as artifacts from more recent centuries.

Located in its own riverside park, **Old Fort Western** (☎ 207-626-2385, 16 Cony St; adult/child 6-16 yrs $4.75/2.75; open 1pm-4pm daily early May-July 3; 10am-4pm Mon-Fri, 1pm-4pm weekends July 4-Labor Day; 1pm-4pm weekends Labor Day-Columbus Day) is across the river. Originally built as a frontier outpost in 1754, the restored 16-room structure is now a museum and is New England's oldest surviving wooden fort.

The **Blaine House** (☎ 207-287-2121, 192 State St; admission free; open 2pm-4pm, Tues-Thurs), at Capitol St in the city center, was once the family home of US presidential candidate James G Blaine. It's now Maine's governors' mansion and is worth a look. Call for tour times.

Places to Stay

Lodging prices are wonderfully low in this non-touristy town.

Motel 6 (☎ 207-622-0000, W www.motel6 .com, 18 Edison Dr) Singles $40, doubles $46-56. This place is the best value; children 17 and under stay for free with their parents.

Super 8 Motel (☎ 207-626-2888, fax 623-8468, W www.super8.com, 395 Western Ave) Rooms $45-85. Close to Motel 6, this motel is similar, though the rooms are a few dollars more expensive.

Best Inn (☎ 207-622-3776, fax 622-3778, 65 Whitten Rd) Rooms $70-110. Just up from the Sears shopping center, Best Inn offers similar prices and amenities. It even has a small swimming pool.

Best Western Senator Inn & Conference Center (☎ 207-622-5804, 800-528-1234, fax 207-622-8803, W www.bestwestern.com, 284 Western Ave) Singles $110-130, doubles $120-140. This classy place to stay has big, comfortable, luxurious rooms (there's even a TV and refrigerator – in the bathroom).

Maple Hill Farm B&B (☎ 207-622-2708, 800-622-2708, 🆆 *www.maplebb.com, Outlet Rd, Hallowell*) Rooms $55-175 with full breakfast. For more attractive surroundings, take I-95 exit 30 for US 202 West, then immediately turn left onto Whitten Rd and follow the signs to this place. Run by Maine State Representative Scott Cowger, this late-Victorian B&B is set upon 130 acres of rolling hayfields with marked trails you can explore. All rooms have private baths.

Places to Eat

There's a cluster of fast-food chain restaurants at I-95 exit 30, and the motels here have restaurants serving formula food (except for the dining room at the Senator Inn). For more interesting food, cruise Water St (US 201/ME 27), south of the capitol in Hallowell.

Billie's Bakery & Cafe (☎ 207-623-9850, 345 Water St) Prices 50¢-$7. Situated in downtown Augusta, Billie's serves good baked goods and interesting soups and salads.

CJ's Pizza (☎ 207-626-2906, 339 Water St) Prices $1.35-16. CJ's serves the cheapest sandwiches, pasta plates and pizzas in town.

Thai Riverview Restaurant (☎ 207-622-2638, 272 Water St, Hallowell) Mains $8-12. A very decent Thai restaurant, this is a nice place to dine as it overlooks the Kennebec River.

Midcoast Maine

The English first settled this region in 1607 (the same time as the Jamestown settlement in Virginia). The early settlers, however, returned to England within a year. British colonization resumed in 1620. After suffering the long years of the French and Indian wars, the area became home to a thriving shipbuilding industry, a tradition that continues today.

Midcoast Maine is a region celebrated for its exceptional natural beauty and down-to-earth residents. You will find a dramatic coastline dotted with friendly seaside villages, thick pine forests and numerous opportunities for biking, hiking, sailing, kayaking and other adventures.

BRUNSWICK

Settled in 1628 and incorporated in 1738, Brunswick was named in honor of the British royal house. Today, the town is most famous as the home of highly regarded Bowdoin College.

A short drive through the city center reveals stately Federal and Greek mansions built by wealthy sea captains. At 63 Federal St, Harriet Beecher Stowe wrote *Uncle Tom's Cabin*. This story of a runaway slave, published in 1852, was hugely popular. The poignant story fired the imagination of people in the northern states, who saw the book as a powerful indictment against slavery. It was translated into many languages.

Brunswick's green, called the Town Mall, is along Main St. Farmers markets are set up Tuesday and Friday and there are band concerts Wednesday evening in summer. In early August, the four-day Maine Arts Festival is held a short distance east of Brunswick in Cooks Corner at Thomas Point Beach.

Orientation & Information

To someone driving along US 1, the commercial center of Brunswick does not present a very attractive prospect. But in fact, as the home of Bowdoin College, the town is the cultural center for this part of the state. Turn off of US 1 onto aptly named Pleasant St for a completely different view of Brunswick.

The folks at Brunswick Area Chamber of Commerce (☎ 207-725-8797, 🆆 www.midcoastmaine.com, 59 Pleasant St) can provide you with a map and help you with a room reservation if you need one.

Bowdoin College

Founded in 1794 and now one of the oldest colleges in the USA, Bowdoin is the alma mater of Henry Wadsworth Longfellow, Nathaniel Hawthorne and US president Franklin Pierce. For general campus information, call ☎ 207-725-3375. For a campus tour, follow the signs from Main St to Moulton Union.

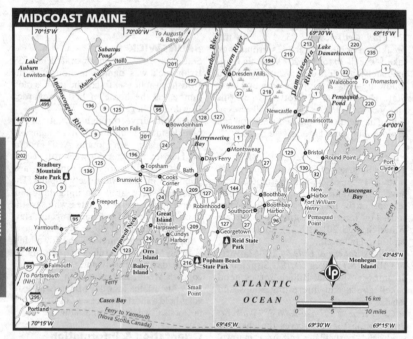

MIDCOAST MAINE

Smith Union is the student center, with an information desk on the mezzanine level, as well as a cafe, pub, small convenience store, lounge and small art gallery. There's also the requisite bookstore where you can buy a sweatshirt, a mailroom where you can get stamps and send letters, and a bulletin board with information on local events and concerts.

Among the sites to visit on campus is the **Bowdoin College Museum of Art** (☎ 207-725-3275; admission free; open 10am-5pm Tues-Sat, 2pm-5pm Sun), strong in the works of 19th- and 20th-century European and American painters.

The **Peary-MacMillan Arctic Museum** (☎ 207-725-3416, Hubbard Hall; admission free; open 10am-5pm Tues-Sat, 2pm-5pm Sun) holds memorabilia from the expeditions of Robert Edwin Peary and Donald Baxter MacMillan, Bowdoin alumni who were among the first explorers to reach the North Pole.

Pejepscot Museums

Local history is preserved in the museums of the Pejepscot Historical Society on the Bowdoin campus.

The **Pejepscot Museum** (☎ 207-729-6606, 159 Park Row; admission free; open 9am-5pm Tues, Wed & Fri, 9am-8pm Thur, 9am-4pm Sat) has displays of old photographs of Brunswick, Topsham and Harpswell. The **Skolfield-Whittier House** (☎ 207-729-6606, 161 Park Row; tour $4), a 17-room brick mansion next to the museum, is a virtual time capsule; it was closed from 1925 to 1982. Even the receipts for the building's construction and the spices in the kitchen racks are authentic. They offer four tours per day.

The **Joshua L Chamberlain Museum** (☎ 207-725-6958, 226 Maine St; tour $4; open 10am-4pm Tues-Sat June 1-Columbus Day) holds artifacts from the late owner's eventful life as college professor, Civil War hero, president of Bowdoin College and four-term governor of Maine.

Entertainment

Bowdoin's Pickard Theater (☎ 207-725-8769, cnr Park Row & Bath Rd, Bowdoin campus) During the summer months this theater hosts the Maine State Music Theater series, a summer musical comedy series that runs eight performances a week, June through August.

Getting There & Away

Brunswick, off I-95 exit 22, is the point at which I-95 heads north and inland toward Augusta, Waterville and Bangor, and US 1 heads northeast along the coast. It's about 9 miles away from Freeport, and 8 miles from Bath. For bus information, see the Portland section, earlier in this chapter.

HARPSWELL

Several narrow, wooded peninsulas dotted with fishing villages jut southward into Casco Bay from Brunswick. Together these settlements comprise the township of Harpswell. If you have a few hours and want to get away from the mad traffic on US 1, venture south for a meal or even a night. There are several B&Bs, inns and motels and enough restaurants to provide dependable sustenance.

Want to go the distance? Head all the way south on ME 24 (I-95 exits 22 and 24) to Bailey Island, reached from Great Island and Orrs Island over three bridges that allow the tides to flow right through them.

The village dock on Bailey Island is a stop on the Casco Bay cruise circuit. It can be more crowded than one would expect when the cruise boats are tied up for their lobster bakes. If you want a lobster lunch, try *Cook's Lobster House (☎ 207-833-2818, 68 Garrison Cove Rd), off ME 24.*

BATH & AROUND

In colonial times, the forested coasts of Maine were thick with tall trees just right for making masts for the king's navy. Indeed, for a time the king forbade anyone to cut Maine's trees for anything else.

In 1607, the pinnace *Virginia*, one of the earliest vessels built by Europeans on this coast, was launched into the Kennebec River at Phippsburg, south of Bath. Later, the shipyards on the Kennebec turned to building coastal freighters, then tall clipper ships and grand multimasted schooners.

Today, Bath continues the tradition by building steel frigates, cruisers and other navy craft at Bath Iron Works (BIW), one of the largest and most active shipyards in the USA. The Maine Maritime Museum, south of the shipyard, is Bath's biggest attraction. The other half of town is the picturesque Historic District, with long stretches of 19th-century Victorian homes.

For bus information, see the Portland Getting There & Away section, earlier in this chapter.

Orientation & Information

Bath is 8 miles east of Brunswick and 10 miles southwest of Wiscasset on US 1. The ironworks sprawls to the south of US 1. At 3:30pm on weekdays, when the work-shift changes at the ironworks, US 1 chokes with cars, and traffic throughout the town comes to a virtual halt. It's best to prepare for this and be on your way past Bath by 3:15pm, or to be parked downtown for a walk around.

Bath has an attractive, small commercial district north of US 1, centered on Front St.

The Chamber of Commerce to the Bath-Brunswick Region (☎ 207-443-9751, W www.midcoastmaine.com, 45 Front St) is next to City Hall. Open 8:30am to 5pm weekdays.

Maine Maritime Museum & Shipyard

The Maine Maritime Museum *(☎ 207-443-1316, 243 Washington St; adult/child/family 6-17 yrs $9/6/25; open 9:30am-5pm daily),* south of the ironworks on the western bank of the Kennebec, preserves the Kennebec's long shipbuilding tradition.

In summer, the 19th-century Percy & Small Shipyard still has boatwrights hard at work building wooden craft. The Maritime History Building holds paintings, models and hands-on exhibits that tell the tale of the last 400 years of seafaring. In the apprentice shop, boat builders restore and construct wooden boats using traditional tools and methods.

In summer, the cruise boat *Schoodic II* takes visitors for a 50-minute ride on the Kennebec, although this is not included in the museum entrance price.

There's a play ship and picnic area, as well as the working **fishing schooner** *Sherman Zwicker*, which is docked here July through August.

Places to Stay

Ocean View Park Campground (☎ 207-389-2564, 817 Popham Rd/ME 209, Popham Beach) RV sites $28. This ugly, beach-front RV park is south of Bath at the end of the peninsula near Popham Beach State Park.

Bath has a number of reasonably priced B&Bs, all with full breakfasts, in nice 19th-century houses.

The Fairhaven Inn (☎ 207-443-4391, 888-443-4391 ⓦ www.mainecoast.com/fairhaven inn, 118 North Bath Rd) Doubles $60-90. Near the Bath Country Club, this early-1800s inn is a few miles north of the city center and set on spacious grounds.

Benjamin F Packard House (☎ 207-443-6069, 800-516-4578, ⓦ www.mainecoast .com/packardhouse, 45 Pearl St) Rooms $90, suite $130. This is a Georgian house (1830) with eight rooms and one suite with private bath.

The 1774 Inn (☎ 207-389-1774, ⓦ www .virtualcities.com/me/1774inn.htm, 44 Parker Head Rd, Phippsburg) Rooms with bath $95-150. This gorgeous Federal-style house (1774) was the home of Mark Hill, the first US congressman from Maine. It is 4 miles south of Bath and overlooks the ocean.

The Inn at Bath (☎ 207-443-4294, 800-423-0964, ⓦ www.innatbath.com, 969 Washington St, Bath) Rooms $99-185. Bath's most splendid B&B is simply named. The early-19th-century Greek home is in the heart of Bath's Historic District. Owner Nick Bayard, a former Wall St broker, has poured all of his profits into the nine elegant rooms and common spaces. Maybe it's his ancestry – the Bayards have been in America since the days of George Washington – that gives rise to Nick's impeccable taste for antiques. The higher-priced rooms have spas.

Popham Beach B&B (☎ 207-389-2409, ⓦ www.pophambeachbandb.com, 4 Riverview Ave, Phippsburg) Rooms $100-185. Formerly a US Coast Guard station, this upscale B&B has five bright rooms directly on the sands of Popham Beach.

Places to Eat

The Cabin (☎ 207-443-6224, 522 Washington St) Mains $2-10. Facing BIW, this is a longtime favorite of the navy personnel who work there. Sit down in one of the small wooden booths or outdoors at picnic tables during the summer, and order pizzas, pastas and affordably priced subs ($2.50 to $4.50).

Beale Street Grill (☎ 207-442-9514, 215 Water St) Mains $8-14. Gnaw on some baby back ribs ($11) and sip a Maine microbrew at this restaurant in downtown Bath.

Kristina's (☎ 207-442-8577, 160 Centre St) Lunch $5-8, dinner $12-17. For fine dining, head to Kristina's, at the corner of Centre and High Sts. Once known only for its baked goods, the restaurant has expanded to offer reasonably priced seafood and steak dishes. This is also a popular destination for Sunday brunch.

WISCASSET

'Welcome to Wiscasset, the Prettiest Village in Maine.' That's what the sign says as you enter Wiscasset from the west along US 1.

Other villages may dispute this claim, but certainly Wiscasset's history as a major shipbuilding port in the 19th century has left it with a legacy of exceptionally grand and beautiful houses.

Like Bath, Wiscasset was a shipbuilding and maritime trading center. Great four-masted schooners sailed down the Sheepscot River bound for England and the West Indies – a route known as the Triangle Trade. They carried items such as timber, molasses, rum, salt and salt fish. Two relics of Wiscasset's vanished maritime importance are the wrecked and weather-beaten hulks of the schooners *Hesper* and *Luther Little*. Built to haul lumber to Boston and bring coal back to Wiscasset, they ran aground in 1932 and have been slowly dissolving in the mud along the Sheepscot's west bank ever since.

Any town with lots of old houses is also bound to have a thriving antiques trade, and Wiscasset does. You can admire the houses and shops as you pass through along US 1, or better, stop for a meal or the night.

Straddling US 1, Wiscasset is 10 miles northeast of Bath, 7 miles west of Damariscotta, 13 miles north of Boothbay Harbor and 23 miles south of Augusta. For bus transportation, see the Portland section.

Orientation & Information

Wiscasset is on the wide Sheepscot River, straddling Main St/US 1. Most of it is easily accessible on foot. If you're just passing through by car, you'll still get to see quite a bit of the village; traffic inches along in summer.

The Wiscasset Regional Business Association (☎ 207-882-4600, PO Box 150, Wiscasset, ME 04578), centered at the Wiscasset Motor Lodge on US 1, serves as the local chamber of commerce.

Things to See & Do

The **Old Jail Museum** (☎ 207-882-6817, 133 Federal St (ME 218); admission free; open 11am-4pm Tues-Sun July & Aug), about a half-mile north of US 1, is a hilltop structure of granite, brick and wood built in 1811 to house Wiscasset's rowdier citizens. It's now a museum.

Wiscasset's grandest and best-situated mansion is **Castle Tucker** (☎ 207-882-7364, cnr High & Lee Sts; admission $5; open 11am-5pm Tues-Sun June 1-Oct 15), reached by a five-minute uphill walk that starts opposite the Bailey Inn. Judge Silas Lee had the house built to resemble a mansion in Dunbar, Scotland. He moved into it in 1807, then moved on to that great mansion in the sky a mere seven years later. Acquired by Capt Richard Tucker in 1858, it's still owned by his descendants. The house commands beautiful views that you can enjoy whether you tour it or not.

On the way to Castle Tucker, stop at the **Musical Wonder House** (☎ 207-882-7163, 18 High St; admission free; open 10am-5pm daily May 25-Oct 15). An outstanding collection of antique music boxes, player pianos and early talking machines are displayed in period rooms. Guided tours are given during opening hours and the gift shop open until 6pm.

The **Nickels-Sortwell House** (☎ 207-882-6218, cnr US 1 & Federal St/ME 218; admission $5; open 11pm-5pm Wed-Sun June 1-Oct 15), just downhill from the Bailey Inn, is one of the town's finest Federal mansions (1807). Tours, given on the hour, start at 11am; the last tour is at 4pm.

Fort Edgecomb (☎ 207-882-7777, 66 Fort Rd, North Edgecomb) is an octagonal wooden blockhouse built in 1808 to protect the valuable shipbuilding trade of Wiscasset. It sits a half-mile south of the eastern end of the bridge that spans the Sheepscot River. Commanding the riverine approach to the town, the fort is now the area's prime picnic site ($1).

Places to Stay

Down East Family Camping (☎ 207-882-5431, ME 27) Sites $16-22. Forty-three wooded campsites are available at this campground, 4 miles north of Wiscasset.

Wiscasset Motor Lodge (☎ 207-882-7137, 800-732-8168, Ⓦ www.wiscassetmotorlodge.com, US 1) Cottages $37-41 with light breakfast, rooms $38-70 with light breakfast. Southwest of the city center, this motel's comfy rooms and cottages are an excellent value.

Highnote B&B (☎ 207-882-9628, Ⓦ www.wiscasset.net/highnote, 26 Lee St) Rooms with shared bath $65 with breakfast. At the Highnote you get a spacious room in a Victorian home (1876). The price also includes a European-style breakfast with fruits, meats, bread and homemade scones. It's within walking distance of all the major sites, antique shops and restaurants in Wiscasset. The name of the inn, by the way, was inspired by the owner's occupation – opera singer.

The Marston House (☎ 207-882-6010, 101 Main St) Rooms $90 with breakfast. Behind an antique shop, the Marston House has two classy rooms in a late-19th-century carriage house that are tastefully styled with a hint of New England simplicity. It's a romantic setting; they even set up the fire-place for your use. A gorgeous breakfast – which is brought to your room in antique jars and a wicker basket – includes fruit, homemade granola and freshly squeezed orange juice. The proprietors also own Treat's, which faces this B&B.

The Sheepscot River Inn (☎ 207-882-6343, 800-427-5503, 306 Eddy Rd, Edgecomb) Rooms $80-110, cottages $90-120, suites $110-140. This place is on the east side of the bridge and has inn rooms, motor lodge suites and tidy little frame cottages in a pine grove overlooking the river.

Places to Eat

Red's Eats (☎ 207-882-6128, Main St) Mains $1-13. Since the '40s, this red shack at Water St has remained a simple take-out stand serving some of the tastiest clam ($8) and whole-lobster ($12.50) rolls in Maine.

Treat's (☎ 207-882-6192, 80 Main St) Prices $3-12. Treat's offers homemade pastries, fresh bread, tasty soups and cheeses. If you're not in the mood for tourist fare, this is a great place for lunch.

Sarah's Café (☎ 207-882-7504, 2 Main St) Mains $5-17. At Water St in the center of town, Sarah's is a family-oriented place offering mostly Tex-Mex food. It's known for its large sandwiches, soups and burritos.

Le Garage (☎ 207-882-5409, 15 Water St) Lunch $8-11, dinner $10-25. Overlooking the wrecks of the wooden schooners *Hesper* and *Luther Little,* Le Garage is perched at the end of Water St. This is the place for a filling, reasonably priced lunch or dinner. Try the sautéd Maine shrimp with herbs and garlic ($14) or the 'finnan haddie' (smoked haddock; $12).

BOOTHBAY HARBOR

Once a beautiful little seafarers' village on a broad fjord-like harbor, Boothbay Harbor is now fully commercialized and overrun by tourists. Large, well-kept Victorian houses crown its many knolls, and a wooden footbridge ambles across the harbor.

Boothbay Harbor is a small town built on and around two hills overlooking the Atlantic Ocean, which is why in summer its narrow, winding streets are choked with cars and its sidewalks are thronged with visitors boarding boats for coastal cruises or browsing Boothbay's boutiques.

It's definitely a walking town. After you've strolled the waterfront along Commercial St and the business district along Todd and Townsend Aves, walk along McKown St to the top of McKown Hill for a fine view. Then, take the footbridge across the harbor to the town's East Side, where there are several huge, dockside seafood restaurants.

From Wiscasset, cross the Sheepscot River on US 1, turn right onto ME 27 and head south to reach Boothbay Harbor.

Boothbay Harbor is a real walking town and having a car here could drive you crazy as the roads are narrow, often one-way, and parking is scarce. There's also a trolley that makes the rounds ($1).

Orientation

There are several towns with similar names, for example, Boothbay and East Boothbay. Boothbay Harbor is the largest and busiest. Follow ME 27 south to the town, which you will enter along Oak St (one-way). Oak St runs into Commercial St, the main street.

Parking can be impossible in the summer months. It's best to park farther out and shuttle (free) into the city center rather than get caught in the slow-moving river of cars flooding the narrow, hilly streets. Catch the shuttle at the small mall on Townsend Ave.

Information

The Boothbay Chamber of Commerce (☎ 207-633-4743, ME 27, Boothbay, ME 04537) maintains an information office on ME 27 in the town of Boothbay. A short distance to the south, along ME 27, is another office that's run by the Boothbay Harbor Region Chamber of Commerce (☎ 207-633-2353, Ⓦ www.boothbayharbor.com, 192 Townsend Ave, Boothbay Harbor, ME 04538). It's open daily during the summer.

Boothbay Railway Village

The Railway Village (☎ 207-633-4727, ME 27; adult/child 3-12 yrs $7/3; open 9:30am-

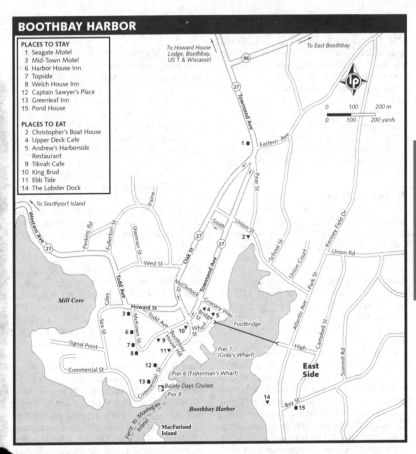

BOOTHBAY HARBOR

PLACES TO STAY
1 Seagate Motel
3 Mid-Town Motel
6 Harbor House Inn
7 Topside
8 Welch House Inn
12 Captain Sawyer's Place
13 Greenleaf Inn
15 Pond House

PLACES TO EAT
2 Christopher's Boat House
4 Upper Deck Cafe
5 Andrew's Harborside
    Restaurant
9 Tikvah Cafe
10 King Brud
11 Ebb Tide
14 The Lobster Dock

MAINE

daily mid-June–Columbus Day) is a
historical replica of a New England village.
It has 27 buildings and a narrow-gauge (2-
foot) steam-train line running through it.
This nonprofit educational park also has a
collection of more than 55 antique steam-
and gasoline-powered motor vehicles.

Cruises

Boothbay's busy natural harbor features
many possibilities for maritime excursions.

Bay Lady (☎ *207-633-2284, 800-298-2284;
tickets $18)* is a 31-foot friendship sloop, the
kind of small sailboat that was once favored
by lobstermen. The *Bay Lady* departs five
times daily from Pier 8 and is operated by
Balmy Days Cruises.

Eastwind (☎ *207-633-6598; tickets $200)*
can take you on a 2½-hour sail-powered
cruise around the harbor; it's a 64-foot windjammer. There are three trips daily in
summer, departing from Fisherman's Wharf.

Sylvina W Beal (☎ *207-633-1109; adult/
child $22/14)* is an 84-foot schooner built in
Boothbay Harbor in 1911. It offers two-
hour trips.

Cap'n Fish's Boat Trips (☎ *207-633-3244,
800-636-3244, Pier 1)* travel a variety of

routes along the coast and among the islands in search of whales (adult/child $28/15), puffins (adult/child $20/10) and seals (adult/child $12/6). Voyages last from one to three hours. And yes, the owner's name really is Cap'n Bob Fish.

Balmy Days Cruises (☎ 207-633-2284, 800-298-2284, Pier 8; adult/child $30/18) takes you out to Monhegan Island (see Monhegan Island, later in this chapter) for a day's visit, leaving after breakfast and returning before supper. It also runs one-hour harbor and nighttime lights tours (adult/child $9/4.50).

Places to Stay

The Boothbays have campgrounds, motels, inns & B&Bs for every taste. Many are open only from early May through mid-October, so call in advance at other times of the year.

Camping Several large campgrounds are north of Boothbay Harbor along ME 27. Most places in the area cater to gigantic land yachts in need of 30-amp electricity and metered LP gas hookups, but all accept tent campers as well.

Little Ponderosa Campground (☎ 207-633-2700, ME 27, Boothbay) Sites $17-23. This campground is 6 miles north of Boothbay Harbor, and has big open fields for games and 97 campsites among tall pine trees, as well as 30 sites along the shore. There's a shuttle bus ($1) from the campground into Boothbay Harbor.

Camper's Cove Campground (☎ 207-633-0050, 286 Back River Rd, Boothbay) Sites $18. Smaller and quieter, this campground has 56 gorgeous waterfront sites. To get there, take ME 27 south from Boothbay to the foreign wars monument (in the middle of the traffic rotary just after the Texaco gas station) and make a right on Back River Rd. Follow it west for 3¼ miles to reach the campground.

Gray Homestead (☎ 207-633-4612, Ⓦ www.graysoceancamping.com, 21 Homestead Rd, West Boothbay Harbor) Sites $19-27. South of Boothbay Harbor on Southport Island, Gray Homestead has 40 wooded, oceanfront sites.

Motels Boothbay and Boothbay Harbor also have many comfortable motels. Those on Townsend Ave (ME 27) north of Boothbay Harbor are less expensive than the elaborate places on Atlantic Ave on the east side of the harbor and are usually open from Memorial Day to late October.

Mid-Town Motel (☎ 207-633-2751, 96 McKown St) Rooms $50-76. Run by a jolly local, this tidy motel is in the very center of town, with 11 simple but adequate rooms.

The Howard House Lodge (☎ 207-633-3933, 800-466-6697, 347 Townsend Ave) Rooms $67-86 with breakfast. This modern, attractive, comfortable and reasonably priced motel is about a mile north of the city center.

Seagate Motel (☎ 207-633-3900, 800-633-1707, 138 Townsend Ave) Rooms $80-90. At the north entrance to Boothbay Harbor, Seagate Motel is well kept. Rooms have all the comforts, including refrigerators. The town trolley ($1) stops here and is available to shuttle you to the city center, so you don't have to deal with the frightful parking.

Inns & B&Bs Boothbay Harbor has dozens of small inns and B&Bs, all of which serve full breakfasts. Some have only two or three rooms, others have up to a dozen. From mid-July through early September, reservations are a must. The chamber of commerce (☎ 207-633-4743) will help you with same-day reservations if you have trouble finding a room.

Pond House (☎ 207-633-5842, Ⓦ ww .gwi.net/~7bayst, 7 Bay St) Rooms $65-85. Situated on the East Side, Pond House is an artists' retreat with an art studio in a detached barn. The five guest rooms are simple and spacious. There is a two-night minimum stay here.

Captain Sawyer's Place (☎ 207-633-2290, 800-434-9657, Ⓦ www.captainsawyersplace .com, 55 Commercial St) Rooms with bath $65-95, suite $115. Captain Sawyer's Place is the big yellow house overlooking the harbor, right in the midst of everything. The captain's suite has its own deck. Rooms in the back without the sea view cost less than those in front.

Harbor House Inn (☎ 207-633-2941, Ⓦ *www.harborhouse-me.com, 80 McKown St)* Rooms $65-115. Near the top of McKown Hill, this homey Victorian, with its wraparound porch, rents nine simple rooms.

Topside (☎ 207-633-5404, Ⓦ *http://home .gwi.net/topside, 60 McKown St)* Rooms with bath $70-155. Atop McKown Hill, Topside has unparalleled views of the town and the harbor. The 22 rooms are in the original sea captain's house or the adjoining motel, and all have refrigerators.

Welch House Inn (☎ 207-633-3431, *56 McKown St)* Rooms with bath $85-165. Despite its extremely tacky wallpaper and decorations, this hilltop inn has harbor views and superb breakfasts.

Greenleaf Inn (☎ 207-633-7346, 888-950-5524, fax 207-633-7346, *65 Commercial St)* Rooms $95-195. Right next to Captain Sawyer's Place, this breezy inn has five well-lit rooms and good breakfasts.

If you don't mind staying outside of town, there are several good choices. The surrounding villages of East Boothbay and West Boothbay Harbor (on Southport Island) are not as touristy or commercialized as Boothbay Harbor. They're a lot more like the real Maine.

Linekin Bay B&B (☎ 207-633-9900, 800-596-7420, Ⓦ *www.linekinbaybb.com, 531 Ocean Point Rd/ME 96)* Rooms $105-175. Right on the water, this B&B has four spacious rooms and is owned by an extremely amicable former police officer who cooks and bakes in his retirement.

Five Gables Inn (☎ 207-633-4551, 800-451-5048, Ⓦ *www.fivegablesinn.com, Murray Hill Rd)* Rooms $120-185. Run by a retired merchant marine (this guy's been everywhere), Five Gables is a grand 125-year-old hotel with wraparound porch on a hill, with 15 rooms and a large parlor.

Lawnmeer Inn (☎ 207-633-2544, 800-633-7645, Ⓦ *www.lawnmeerinn.com, 65 Hendricks Hill Rd/ME 27)* Rooms with bath $80-195. Lawnmeer Inn is on Southport Island, southwest of Boothbay Harbor, via ME 27. It's a nice old 35-room inn, set on spacious lawns at the water's edge, far away from the hustle and bustle of town. Prices vary according to view.

Places to Eat
Most Boothbay Harbor restaurants are open from early May through mid-October and serve lunch and dinner (unless noted here).

The first spot to tempt you on the road into town is ***MacNab's Tea Room*** (☎ 207-633-0572, *812 Back River Rd, Boothbay)* Prices $3.50-10. On the same road as Camper's Cove Campground, MacNab's is a great place to stop for lunch and a pot of tea ($2.50). MacNab's serves Scottish soups, sandwiches and desserts. It also packages and sells 50 tea combinations.

King Brud (cnr *McKown & Oak Sts, Boothbay Harbor)* King Brud has been selling hot dogs ($1) here for more than 50 years. In summer, you'll see his cart every day. Veterans, ladies and others who ask politely may get a free autographed King Brud color picture postcard.

Ebb Tide (☎ 207-633-5692, *43 Commercial St)* Mains $3-12. This funky grease pit is always packed in summer. Its wooden booths are oddly shaped so they'll fit together in the cramped space. It's popular for breakfast, fish chowder ($6) and fresh peach shortcake ($4).

Tikvah Cafe (☎ 207-633-6700, *34A McKown St)* Lunch $3.50-7. This new, environmentally conscious restaurant (even the cutlery is biodegradable!) serves the best veggie and vegan fare in Maine. Try its Middle Eastern plate ($7) and desserts ($1 to $6).

Andrew's Harborside Restaurant (☎ 207-633-4074, *12 Bridge St)* Mains $9-22. Down toward the footbridge, Andrew's serves award-winning seafood chowder ($7), country-style chicken pie ($10), scallops ($14), lots of sandwiches and great views of who's on the footbridge.

Upper Deck Cafe Mains $6-10. If you'd rather have something lighter and cheaper, this cafe adjoining Andrew's has a long sandwich and salad menu and some water views.

Christopher's Boat House *(☎ 207-633-6565, 25 Union St)* Dinner $14-24. This is Boothbay's best bistro, serving innovative seafood and meat dishes.

The Lobster Dock *(☎ 207-633-7120, 49 Atlantic Ave)* Mains $12-20. Of all the lobster joints in Boothbay Harbor, this one is the best and the cheapest. It serves traditional shore dinners (steamed clams, boiled lobster and corn on the cob) as well as other seafood. Prices depend on availability and season.

Lobsterman's Wharf *(☎ 207-633-3443, ME 96, East Boothbay)* Dinner $14-22. For a full sit-down restaurant, also with outdoor tables, try this place.

Cabbage Island Clambakes *(☎ 207-633-7200, 800-628-6872, Pier 6, Fisherman's Wharf)* Prix-fixe $40, transportation included. To experience the full nautical ambience, try this tour. You sail out of Boothbay Harbor from Pier 6 at Fisherman's Wharf aboard the motor vessel *Argo.* When you arrive at Cabbage Island, the captain and crew prepare a traditional clambake with seaweed-baked clams, steamed lobsters, clam chowder, corn on the cob, and Maine potatoes and onions, followed by Maine blueberry cake and coffee. The two- and four-hour voyages depart at 12:30pm Monday through Friday, 12:30pm and 5pm Saturday, and 11:30am and 2:45pm Sunday from late June through early September.

DAMARISCOTTA

Damariscotta is a pretty Maine town with numerous churches and an attractive downtown commercial district that serves the smaller communities of the Pemaquid Peninsula to the south. West of the town center, on US 1, is a tourist information center operated by the Damariscotta Region Information Bureau (☎ 207-563-3176). Follow US 1B ('Business') to reach the center of town. There's another tourism information office run by the Damariscotta Region Chamber of Commerce (☎ 207-563-

8340, Ⓦ www.drcc.org) at the southern end of the town, just after ME 129/130 veers off to the right.

Also try the Maine Coast Book Shop & Café (☎ 207-563-3207, 158 Main St) for additional information on the area.

PEMAQUID PENINSULA

ME 130 goes south from Damariscotta through the heart of the Pemaquid Peninsula to Pemaquid Neck, the southernmost part of the peninsula. Pemaquid – Abenaki for 'Longest Finger' – is the longest peninsula on the Maine coast. On the west side of Pemaquid Neck are Pemaquid Beach and Fort William Henry, a relic of the colonial period. At the southern tip of Pemaquid Neck is Pemaquid Point, one of the most picturesque locales in Maine. Artists from all over the world flock here to capture the beauty of this area in drawings, paintings and photographs.

Pemaquid Beach & Trail

Yes! There are a few stretches of sand beach along this rockbound coast, and Pemaquid Beach is one of them. As ME 130 approaches Pemaquid Neck, watch for signs on the right (west) for Pemaquid Beach and make a right onto Huddle Rd (which turns into Snowball Hill Rd). The Pemaquid Trail, a paved dead-end road, heads south from Snowball Hill Rd just east of the Pemaquid Beach access road.

The beach is set in a park, and both are open in summer for a small fee. The water is usually very cold for swimming (this *is* Maine!).

Fort William Henry

A quarter-mile south of Pemaquid Beach are the remains of Fort William Henry *(☎ 207-677-2423; adult $1, child under 12 yrs & senior free; open 9am-5pm daily Memorial Day-Labor Day).* The reconstructed circular stone fort has commanding views (off to the left as you enter), many old foundations, an old burial ground with interesting tombstones, an archaeological dig and a small museum.

This area was well explored in the early 17th century. English explorers set foot on the Pemaquid Peninsula early in the 1600s, then Weymouth in 1605 and Popham in 1607. But France claimed the land as well, because the great Samuel de Champlain came here in 1605. Capt John Smith (English) came for a look in 1614. By the 1620s, this was a thriving settlement with a customhouse.

The first fortress built, Fort Pemaquid, was overcome and looted by pirates in 1632. In 1689, its replacement, Fort Charles, fell to the allied French and Indians. The fort was later restored and renamed Fort Frederick (1729). During the Revolutionary War it was torn down. In 1908, it was partially rebuilt as a historic site and called Fort William Henry. The nearby Old Fort House was built about this time and still stands.

Pemaquid Point

Along a 3500-mile coastline famed for its natural beauty, Pemaquid Point stands out because of its tortuous, grainy igneous rock formations pounded by restless, treacherous seas.

Perched atop the rocks in **Lighthouse Park** *(adult $2, child under 12 yrs & senior free)* is the 11,000-candlepower Pemaquid Light, built in 1827. It's one of the 61 surviving lighthouses along the Maine coast, 52 of which are still in operation. The keeper's house now serves as the **Fishermen's Museum** *(3115B Bristol Rd, Pemaquid Point; donations accepted; open 10am-5pm Mon-Sat, 11am-5pm Sun)*. Lighthouse and fishing paraphernalia and photos are on display, as well as a nautical chart of the entire Maine coast with all the lighthouses marked.

By all means, take photographs here at Pemaquid. But also take a few minutes to fix the view in your mind, because no photo can do justice to this wild vista. If you clamber over the rocks beneath the light, do so with great care. Big waves sweep in unexpectedly, and periodically, tourists are swept back out with them, ending their Maine vacations in a sudden, dramatic and fearfully permanent manner.

Places to Stay & Eat

Pemaquid Point Campground *(☎ 207-677-2267,* W *www.midcoast.com/~ed, 9 Pemaquid Point Campground Rd, New Harbor)* Sites $22-26. Toward Pemaquid Point off ME 130, this basic campground has 20 tent and 30 RV sites.

Hotel Pemaquid *(☎ 207-677-2312,* W *www.hotelpemaquid.com, 3098 Bristol Rd/ ME 130, New Harbor)* Rooms & cottages $55-140. On Pemaquid Point, this 1870s wood-frame hotel has a grand front porch with 37 period guest rooms and housekeeping cottages. It has a 1920s feel to it and is just 100 yards from Lighthouse Park.

Bradley Inn *(☎ 207-677-2105, 800-942-5560, fax 207-677-3367,* W *www.bradleyinn .com, 3063 Bristol Rd, New Harbor)* Rooms $135-195 with full breakfast. Two hundred yards inland, this place has 16 luxury rooms decorated with Victorian and nautical antiques. The restaurant is pricey, but superb.

The Sea Gull Shop *(☎ 207-677-2374, 3119 Bristol Rd)* Breakfast $7.50, lunch $7-12, dinner $15-20. If you need refreshments, this place abutting Lighthouse Park offers those beautiful views.

THOMASTON & PORT CLYDE

Once among the wealthiest communities in New England, Thomaston's wood shipbuilding business faded away with the coming of iron vessels. The town's stately homes, dating from the mid-19th century, have fallen into dowdiness, though it's still possible to imagine their former glory. Thomaston now houses Maine's largest prison and a huge cement plant.

Just east of Thomaston, ME 131 goes south from US 1 to St George, Tenants Harbor and Port Clyde.

The village of Port Clyde is the mainland port for the Monhegan Thomaston Boat Line vessels out to Monhegan Island (see below).

MONHEGAN ISLAND

This rocky outcrop off the Maine coast, due south of Port Clyde, is a popular destination for summer excursions. The small island

MAINE

(just 1½ miles long by a half-mile wide) was known to Basque and Portuguese fishers and mariners before the English cruised these waters, but it came into its own as a summer resort in the early 19th century. When the cities of the eastern seaboard were sweltering in summer's heat, cool sea breezes bathed Monhegan and those fortunate enough to have taken refuge here. (Be sure to bring a sweater and windbreaker, as the voyage and the coast can be chilly even in August.)

Early in its history as a resort, Monhegan became popular with artists who admired its dramatic views and agreeable isolation. The island village is small and very limited in its services. The few unpaved roads are lined with stacks of lobster traps. This is definitely not a cutesy and overdeveloped celebrities' island like Nantucket; rather, plain living, high thinking and traditional village life are the attractions here. Unfortunately, due to the high volume of day-tourists, Monhegan's year-round residents can often be unfriendly.

You'll notice there are hardly any motor vehicles on little Monhegan. The ones it has for essential jobs are few and old. Thus, Monhegan is laid out for walking, with 17 miles of trails. Children, in particular, enjoy the southern tip of the island, with its wrecked ship rusting away, lots of rocks to climb and cairn-art (stacks of stones and driftwood made into fantasy sculptures). The views from the lighthouse are excellent and its little museum ($2) is amusing.

The island's environments – natural, social and commercial – are fragile and thus subject to strict rules: Smoking and fires are prohibited outside the village and mountain biking is not allowed. In addition, all telephones require credit cards (there are no coin phones).

Unless you've made reservations well in advance at one of the island's few lodgings, you should not plan on finding a room upon arrival. Plan to take a day excursion from Port Clyde or Boothbay Harbor, and allow yourself at least a half-day (four hours or more) to walk the trails over the rocks and around the shore. Stop at the **lighthouse**

(1824) for a look at the museum in the keeper's former house.

Browse Ⓦ www.monhegan.com for more information.

Places to Stay

Accommodations are simple and basic on the island; few rooms have private baths. To reserve by mail, send your letter to the lodging, Monhegan, ME 04852, and it'll get there.

Trailing Yew (☎ 207-596-0440, 800-592-2520, fax 207-596-7636) Rates $62/person with breakfast & dinner. This place has been hosting guests in pretty much the same manner since 1926: Forty spartan guest rooms are illuminated by kerosene lamps, and simple but nutritious meals are served family style.

Monhegan House (☎ 207-594-7983, 800-599-7983, fax 207-596-6472, Ⓦ *www.monheganhouse.com*) Rooms $60-125. This has been a guesthouse since 1870. Its 32 rooms share the common bathroom facilities on the 2nd floor. The *Monhegan House Café* serves three meals, featuring baked goods made fresh in the inn's kitchen. Meals are not included in the rates, so you can dine as you wish.

Hitchcock House (☎ 207-594-8137, Ⓦ *www.midcoast.com/~hhouse*) Efficiency rooms/apartments $65/95. Atop Horn's Hill, the secluded Hitchcock House has five efficiency units (room with kitchen and bath) and apartments.

Tribler Cottage (☎ 207-594-2445, fax 207-594-4714) Doubles $65-110. Tribler has one room with bath and four efficiency apartments. No meals are served.

Shining Sails (☎ 207-596-0041, fax 207-596-7166, Ⓦ *www.shiningsails.com, PO Box 346*) Rooms with bath $90-150 with breakfast. Shining Sails has fine ocean views from several of its seven rooms and kitchen-equipped apartments.

Island Inn (☎ 207-596-0371, fax 207-594-5517, Ⓦ *www.islandinnmonhegan.com*) Rooms $110-250 with full breakfast. This is a typical Victorian mansard-roofed summer hotel with 45 small, simple rooms, eight of them with private bath. The big front porch offers marvelous views, and the dining room serves three meals a day. Reserve early in the spring for dates in July and August.

Places to Eat

Barnacle Café & Bakery (☎ 207-594-7995) Mains $3-7. Right by the wharf, this cafe is on your left as you leave the boat. The pasta and veggie salads are good here, as are the pies and pastries.

North End Market (☎ 207-594-5546) Prices $3-14. Monhegan Island's only convenience store, North End Market also sells good homemade soups, salads, sandwiches and pizzas.

Monhegan House Café (☎ 207-594-7983) Lunch $10-15, dinner mains $20-25. This cafe features a daily blue plate special for about $15, including dessert and coffee; and huge sandwiches, such as their half-pound hamburger ($7).

Island Inn Dining Room (☎ 207-596-0371) Mains $12-22. Housed on the 1st floor of the Island Inn, this restaurant is, by far, the fanciest on the island.

Getting There & Away

Monhegan Thomaston Boat Line (☎ 207-372-8848) vessels to Monhegan Island depart Port Clyde, south of Thomaston, year-round, with schedules and fares varying according to the season. You must make advance reservations to journey on these boats.

In high summer, boats depart Port Clyde at 7am, 10:30am and 3pm. Return trips depart Monhegan at 9am, 12:30pm and 4:30pm daily. The first voyage of the day, in the *Laura B*, takes 70 minutes; the later ones, aboard the *Elizabeth Ann*, take 50 minutes. The roundtrip fare is $27 for adults, $14 for children 12 and under. Parking in Port Clyde costs $4 per day.

Departing New Harbor from Shaw's Fish & Lobster Wharf on ME 32 on the east side of the Pemaquid Peninsula, the motor vessel *Hardy III* (☎ 207-677-2026) leaves at 9am and 2pm daily bound for Monhegan. It returns to New Harbor at 10:15am and 3:15pm. The roundtrip fare is $27 for adults, $15 for children under 12; parking is free.

You can also visit Monhegan on a day excursion from Boothbay Harbor aboard one of the boats run by Balmy Days Cruises (☎ 207-633-2284, 800-298-2284). See Cruises in the Boothbay Harbor section, earlier in this chapter.

Acadia National Park Region

The best-known feature of the coastal area south of Bangor is Acadia National Park, the only US national park in New England. Acadia is the centerpiece of the 'Downeast' region, and is quintessential Maine.

Penobscot Bay, to the west of Acadia, is world famous for its yachting ports: Camden, Rockport and Rockland, from which tall-masted windjammers take passengers on cruises of the jagged coast. Blue Hill Bay and Frenchman Bay frame Mt Desert Island, a choice summer resort area for a century, and now the center of Acadia National Park.

To the northeast of Acadia, the coast of Downeast Maine is less traveled, but more scenic and unspoiled, all the way to the towns of Lubec and Eastport, where the USA meets New Brunswick, Canada.

ROCKLAND

Rockland is the birthplace of poet Edna St Vincent Millay (1892–1950), who grew up in neighboring Camden. Today, Rockland is, along with Camden, at the center of Maine's very busy windjammer sailing business. In the summer, windjammers, the tall-masted sailing ships descended from those long built on these shores, cruise up and down the Maine coast to the delight of their paying passengers. For information on windjammer cruises and places to stay in the area, see the Camden section, later.

Farnsworth Art Museum & Wyeth Center

Rockland is also famous for its Farnsworth Art Museum & Wyeth Center (☎ 207-596-6457, 16 Museum St; adult/student $9/5, child

MAINE

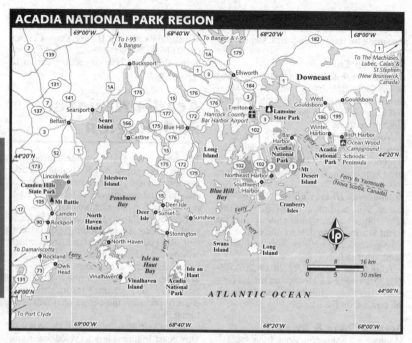

ACADIA NATIONAL PARK REGION

under 18 yrs free; open 9am-5pm daily Memorial Day-Columbus Day, 10am-5pm Tues-Sat, 1pm-5pm Sun Columbus Day-Memorial Day), one of the best small regional museums in the country. Its collection of 5000 works is especially strong in landscape and marine artists who have worked in Maine, such as Andrew, NC and Jamie Wyeth; Louise Nevelson; Rockwell Kent; John Marin and others.

Owls Head Transportation Museum

Two miles south of Rockland on ME 73 is the Owls Head Transportation Museum (☎ 207-594-4418, W www.ohtm.org, ME 73, Owls Head; adult/child 5-12 yrs/family $6/4/16; open 10am-5pm daily April-Oct, 10am-4pm daily Nov-March). The museum collects, preserves (yes, everything works!) and exhibits pioneer (pre-1920) aircraft, vehicles and engines that were instrumental in the evolution of transportation as we know

it today. Besides its year-round exhibits, the transportation museum also has WWI air shows and various specialty vehicle shows (provided by private collectors) throughout the year.

Places to Stay & Eat

LimeRock Inn (☎ 207-594-2257, 800-546-3762, W www.limerockinn.com, 96 Limerock St) Rooms $100-185 with breakfast. This is an eight-room mansion built in 1890 for a local congressman. Now it is decorated with the finest mahogany furniture, rugs and king-size beds the owners could find.

Primo (☎ 207-596-0770, W www.primo restaurant.com, 2 S Main St/ME 73) Mains $12-22. This is what happens when an award-winning chef (Melissa Kelly) marries an award-winning baker and pastry chef (Price Kushner). Primo, set in a Victorian home, is one of the *top* restaurants in the Northeast *region* – which means Washington, DC, through Maine. Set in a Victorian home, this bistro features creative veal, lamb and seafood dishes (for dinner only). Its pastries are among the finest baked in Maine. It's on ME 73 just before the welcome sign to Owls Head. Casual dress is fine, but make reservations a month in advance.

Getting There & Away
US Airways Express, operated by Colgan Air (☎ 207-596-7604, 800-428-4322), serves Rockland via its route from Boston to Bar Harbor.

Concord Trailways (☎ 207-596-2202, 800-639-3317, 517A Main St) runs buses from Boston and Logan Airport to Rockland via Portland (terminating at the Maine State Ferry Terminal for boats to Vinalhaven). The trip from Boston to Rockland takes 4½ hours.

Rockland is the port for the Maine State Ferry Service (☎ 207-596-2202, Ⓦ www.state.me.us/mdot/opt/ferry/ferry.htm) to the islands of Vinalhaven and North Haven. Ferries depart Rockland three times daily year-round on the 70-minute trip to North Haven. For Vinalhaven, boats depart six times daily, April through October, with at least three boats daily during the rest of the year.

CAMDEN
Camden and its picture-perfect harbor, shadowed by the mountains of Camden Hills State Park, is one of the prettiest sites in the state. Home to Maine's large and justly famed fleet of windjammers (multi-masted sailing ships), Camden continues its historic close links with the sea. Most vacationers come to sail on their boats, or on somebody else's boats, or just to look at boats. But Camden is popular with land-lubbers too, who come into town to shop and dine at its seafood restaurants. Camden does have a conservative, preppie feel to it; you'll find that most people here are would-be models for the J Crew catalog. The adjoining state park offers hiking, picnicking and camping.

Like many communities along the Maine coast, Camden has a long history of ship-

Windjammers

The word 'windjammer' is a 19th-century journalist's concoction to describe a sailing ship laboring under a full press of canvas. But in 21st-century Maine, the term describes one of a fleet of traditional wooden sailing craft, 60 to 150 feet in length, with two or three masts (usually schooner-rigged). These graceful vessels evoke the days before good highways and trucks, when so-called coasting schooners were the dominant means of travel and shipping on the Maine coast. Today, both historic and recently built windjammers gather in the coves and harbors around Rockland, Rockport and Camden in summer to ply a new trade. Now, nicknamed 'dude schooners,' they carry vacationers on multiday sailing adventures around Penobscot Bay.

A windjammer normally sleeps between 20 and 45 passengers in rustic single, double, triple and quad cabins. Many have sinks with hot and cold water. Showers are usually shared. Passengers dine aboard, and the prices for cruises usually include meals like a traditional clambake or lobster bake on a coastal island. Windjammers cruise weekly during the summer and welcome passengers of all ages, except for young children.

building. The mammoth six-masted schooner *George W Wells* was built here, setting the world record for the most masts on a sailing ship.

Alas, beauty comes at a price. The cost of Camden's lodgings and food during the summer are higher than in less posh Maine communities.

South of Bangor (53 miles) on US 1, Camden is 85 miles north of Portland and 77 miles southwest of Bar Harbor.

Orientation & Information
US 1 snakes its way through Camden, and is the town's main street, named Elm St to the south, Main St in the center and High St to the north. Though the downtown section is

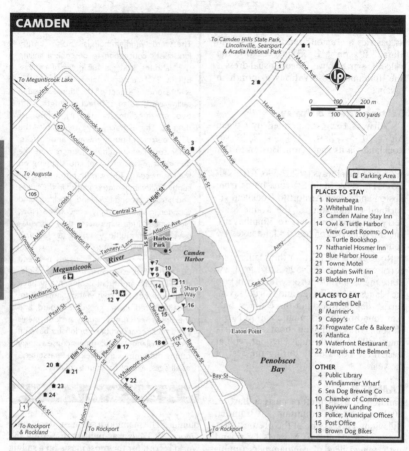

CAMDEN

To Camden Hills State Park,
Lincolnville, Searsport
& Acadia National Park

To Megunticook Lake

To Augusta

Spring St
Trim St
Megunticook St
Mountain St
Hardin Ave
Rock-Brook Dr
Marine Ave
Harbor Rd
Eaton Ave

Cross St
Central St
Alden St
Washington St
Knowlton St
Mechanic St
Pearl St
Free St
Elm St
School St
Pleasant St
Whitmore Ave
Belmont Ave
Union St
Park St
High St
Main St
Chestnut St
Bayview St
Frye St
Sea St
Arey St
Bay St

Tannery Lane
Megunticook River

To Rockport
& Rockland

To Rockport

To Rockport

PLACES TO STAY
1 Norumbega
2 Whitehall Inn
3 Camden Maine Stay Inn
14 Owl & Turtle Harbor
   View Guest Rooms; Owl
   & Turtle Bookshop
17 Nathaniel Hosmer Inn
20 Blue Harbor House
21 Towne Motel
23 Captain Swift Inn
24 Blackberry Inn

PLACES TO EAT
7 Camden Deli
8 Marriner's
9 Cappy's
12 Frogwater Cafe & Bakery
16 Atlantica
19 Waterfront Restaurant
22 Marquis at the Belmont

OTHER
4 Public Library
5 Windjammer Wharf
6 Sea Dog Brewing Co
10 Chamber of Commerce
11 Bayview Landing
13 Police; Municipal Offices
15 Post Office
18 Brown Dog Bikes

Harbor Park
Camden Harbor
Sharp's Way
Megunticook River
Eaton Point
Penobscot Bay

Parking Area

0   100   200 m
0   100   200 yards

easily covered on foot, it is several miles from one end of town to the other. Some accommodations are up to a 15-minute walk from the center of town.

The Rockport, Camden & Lincolnville Chamber of Commerce (☎ 207-236-4404, ⓦ www.camdenme.org, PO Box 919, Camden, ME 04843) has an information office on the waterfront at the public landing in Camden, behind Cappy's.

The Owl & Turtle Bookshop (☎ 207-236-4769, 8 Bayview St) is the place to stop for books.

Camden Hills State Park
Far less crowded than Acadia National Park, Camden Hills State Park (☎ 207-236-3109; *adult/child 5-11 yrs $2/50¢*) has its own set of mountains along the sea, offering some exquisite views of Penobscot Bay. The entrance is just over 1½ miles northeast of Camden center on US 1. The park has an extensive system of well-marked hiking trails, from the half-mile, 45-minute climb up Mt Battie to the 3-mile, two-hour Ski Shelter Trail.

Simple trail maps are available at the park entrance. The picnic area is on the south side of US 1, with short trails down to the shore.

Sea Kayaking

To cruise the coast at your own speed, contact **Maine Sport Outfitters** (☎ *800-722-0826, US 1, Rockport; $45/60 per day per single/tandem)*. This outfit, also at Harbor Park in Camden, offers two-hour tours of Camden Harbor ($35) as well.

Ducktrap Sea Kayak Tours (☎ *207-236-8608, US 1, Lincolnville; 2-hr/half-day tours $25/50)* will take you on a coastal tour. It also offers custom-tailored full-day trips. Call for reservations.

Bicycling

From Camden, it's a five-minute drive to Lincolnville Beach from where you take a 20-minute ferry ride to the island of Islesboro (for Islesboro ferry schedule, call ☎ 207-789-5611). You'll want to bring your bike, because Islesboro is one of the finest places to ride in Maine. Rentals are available at **Brown Dog Bikes** (☎ *207-236-6664, 53 Chestnut St, Camden; $17 per day)*.

The island is relatively flat, yet hilly enough to offer majestic vistas of Penobscot Bay and long enough to feature a 28-mile bike loop. Picnic at Pendleton Point, where harbor seals and loons often lounge on the long, striated rocks.

Cruises

Camden is at the center of windjammer cruise country. Many boats dock at Rockport and Rockland as well. Cruise itineraries vary with the ship, the weather and the length of the cruise.

Daysailers are windjammers that take passengers out for two- to four-hour cruises in Penobscot Bay. Usually you can book your place on a daysailer the same day, even the same hour. The following boats depart from Camden's Town Landing or adjoining Sharp's Wharf (across from the chamber of commerce):

Appledore (☎ 207-236-8353) $25 per adult for two-hour cruise

Olad (☎ 207-236-2323) $25 per adult, $10 per child six to 12, for a two-hour sail

Surprise (☎ 207-236-4687) $28 per adult, includes snacks; no children under 12 accepted

Lively Lady Too (☎ *207-236-6672, Sharp's Wharf; adult/child under 15 yrs $20/5)* is a powerboat that will take you on a two-hour lobstering trip.

The schooner **Wendameen** (☎ *207-594-1751; $170 per person)* takes passengers cruising for a day and a night. The cost includes all meals, and you get a good taste of a Maine coastal cruise.

Longer cruises last from three to six days. Many six-day cruises visit points along the Maine coast from Boothbay Harbor in the southwest to Mt Desert Island (Acadia National Park) in the northeast. Stops may be made at Stonington, at the tip of Deer Isle; at the village of Castine; at various small islands offshore and at points in and around Acadia National Park.

Three-day cruises cover less of the coast, but are still delightful. Many three- to six-day cruises cost $350 to $835 per person, including accommodations. All meals on board are included.

Reservations are a must for overnight cruises. For information on the vessels available, contact the following organizations.

Maine Windjammer Association
(☎ 207-374-2955, 800-807-9463, fax 207-374-5272, W www.midcoast.com/~sailmwa, PO Box 1144, Blue Hill, ME 04614)

North End Shipyard Schooners
(☎ 207-594-8007, 800-648-4544, fax 207-594-8015, W www.midcoast.com/~schooner, PO Box 482, Rockland, ME 04841)

Windjammer Wharf
(☎ 800-999-7352, PO Box 1050, Rockland, ME 04841)

Places to Stay

Camping Camden has a couple of good, scenic camping options.

Camden Hills State Park (☎ *207-236-3109, W www.state.me.us/doc/prkslnds/camden .htm, US 1)* Sites $17. This camping area has hot showers, flush toilets and 107 forested tent and RV sites (no hookups). Reservations are advised for high summer. A few sites cannot be reserved and are held on a first-come, first-served basis. Plan to arrive by noon to claim one.

Megunticook by the Sea (☎ 207-594-2428, 800-884-2428, W www.campground bythesea.com, 620 Commercial St (US 1), Rockport) Sites $19-35. This area, 3 miles south of Camden, has sites on the coast.

Motels & Hotels Most of the area's motels are along US 1. There's a large concentration in Lincolnville, the next town to the north of Camden. Rates range from $40 for the cheapest places off-season to about $100 for the choicest rooms in-season.

High Tide Inn (☎ 207-236-3724, 800-778-7068, W www.hightideinn.com, US 1) Rooms $65-185 with breakfast. Between Camden and Lincolnville, High Tide Inn has an assortment of basic accommodations from cottages to hotel units to a house. Rates include use of the beach.

Birchwood Motel & Cottages (☎ 207-236-4204, Belfast Rd/US 1) Rooms $77 with breakfast. Also north of Camden, this place has 15 motel rooms.

Towne Motel (☎ 207-236-3377, 800-656-4999, W www.midcoast.com/townemotel, 68 Elm St) Rooms $80-100 with light breakfast. Towne Motel has 19 rooms, right in the center of town.

Strawberry Hill Motor Inn (☎ 207-594-5462, 800-589-4009, W www.midcoast.com/~sberyhil, US 1, Rockport) Rooms $80-140. Three miles north of Rockland, this place has 21 rooms set on a hillside overlooking the sea.

Inns & B&Bs Camden has more than 100 places to stay, most of them small inns or B&Bs, with prices ranging from $75 to over $300 for a double room. If you want help making reservations, call Camden Accommodations & Reservations (☎ 207-236-6090, 800-236-1920, PO Box 858, Camden, ME 04843). Like travel agents, they don't charge you for this service; the inns and hotels pay a commission to Camden Accommodations.

For more information and links, see W www.camdeninns.com.

Owl & Turtle Harbor View Guest Rooms (☎ 207-236-8759, 8 Bayview St) Rooms with bath $90-105. Above the Owl & Turtle Bookstore, this place has three rooms overlooking the harbor. They only rent by the week.

Both the Elm St and High St stretches of US 1 have a number of nice B&Bs.

Whitehall Inn (☎ 207-236-3391, 800-789-6565, 52 High St) Rooms $80-165. You'll find traditional, proper New England ambience behind the Ionic columns on the broad front porch here. Most of the 50 rooms in the main inn, the Maine House and the Wicker House have private baths. Breakfast and dinner are served in the elegant dining room.

Captain Swift Inn (☎ 207-236-8113, 800-251-0865, 72 Elm St) Rooms with bath $95-120 with breakfast. This is an 1810 Federal house with four rooms. The fireplace is original and still has a beehive oven.

Nathaniel Hosmer Inn (☎ 207-236-4012, 800-423-4012, W www.nathanielhosmerinn .com, 4 Pleasant St) Rooms with bath $95-125 with full breakfast. This simple Federal house is a block off Elm St in a quiet residential neighborhood and has seven rooms.

Blue Harbor House (☎ 207-236-3196, 800-248-3196, 67 Elm St) Rooms with bath $95-165 with breakfast. This is a cozy New England Cape Cod–style house (1810) with 10 guest rooms and amicable owners.

Blackberry Inn (☎ 207-236-6060, W www .blackberryinn.com, 82 Elm St) Rooms $95-185 with breakfast. Blackberry Inn is a gorgeous Victorian with high ceilings even on the 2nd floor. Most of the fully restored eight rooms have vintage tin ceilings and fireplaces. There's also a spacious efficiency for families.

Camden Maine Stay Inn (☎ 207-236-9636, W www.camdenmainestay.com, 22 High St/US 1) Rooms $115-165 with full breakfast. This fine Greek house (1802) is at the base of Mt Battie. Six of the eight guest rooms have private bath.

Norumbega (☎ 207-236-4646, 877-363-4646, W www.norumbegainn.com, 63 High

St) Rooms $125-340, suites $295-475. A listing of Camden lodgings would not be complete without a mention of Norumbega, a fantastic, castle-like stone Victorian mansion with 13 rooms. The inn's brochure uses such words as 'exceptional,' 'sumptuous' and 'magnificent,' which, for the prices, it should be – and is.

Places to Eat

As with its lodgings, so it is with its restaurants: Camden prices tend to be higher than in most other towns. Restaurants listed here are open for lunch and dinner unless otherwise noted.

Marriner's (☎ 207-236-2647, 35 Main St) Dishes $5-10. Just up the street from Cappy's, in the midst of the shopping district, is Marriner's. It's an old-fashioned, inexpensive restaurant serving egg breakfasts ($4 to $5.50), big plates of fish-and-chips ($10) and huge plates of fried clams with potato, coleslaw and bread and butter ($10).

Camden Deli (☎ 207-236-8343, 37 Main St) Sandwiches $4-10. For a picnic down by the water or atop Mt Battie, pick up a substantial sandwich here. There are several vegetarian choices and a wide range of wines to choose from.

Cappy's (☎ 207-236-2254, 1 Main St) Prices $5-15. Many places in Maine bill themselves as 'the place for chowder,' but this one, smack in the middle of town, is probably telling the truth. A huge mug of thick, creamy chowder – chock-full of clams and potatoes – is served with a buttermilk biscuit for $7. The long menu lists just about everything from sandwiches and light meals to hearty tuck-ins, but stick with the chowder.

Frogwater Cafe & Bakery (☎ 207-236-8998, 31 Elm St) Mains $5-18. Frogwater serves great vegetarian fare and desserts. Try the vegetarian shepherd's pie ($14) and cinnamon bread pudding ($5.25).

Atlantica (☎ 207-236-6011, Bay View Landing) Lunch $7-14, dinner $15-24. Chef-owned, Atlantica serves the best seafood in town and offers good views of the bay. Try the pan-seared peppered tuna ($22) or the sautéed gingered scallops ($19.50).

Waterfront Restaurant (☎ 207-236-3747, Bay View Landing) Lunch $7-17, dinner $15-25. Waterfront Restaurant has atmospheric dining rooms and a spacious deck right next to the boats. Try the summer salad with blueberry cake ($8) for a light lunch, or the shore dinner ($25) – with clam chowder, steamers, mussels and lobster. There's also a raw bar serving clams and oysters.

Lobster Pound Restaurant (☎ 207-789-5550, US 1, Lincolnville) Mains $15-35. For every type of lobster imaginable, steamers, shrimp and fish, head to this restaurant standing alone on Lincolnville's beach. Locals love the blackened swordfish ($18).

Several of Camden's inns have fine dining rooms serving fancy fare in the evenings.

Whitehall Inn (☎ 207-236-3391, 800-789-6565, 52 High St) Mains $15-22. Try the Whitehall for an excellent dinner in formal surroundings. Meals cost $35 to $70 per person.

Marquis at the Belmont (☎ 207-238-8053, 6 Belmont Ave) Mains $16-24. This is chef Scott Marquis' restaurant, serving 'late-20th-century cuisine in late-19th-century surroundings.' Try the Japanese breadcrumb crab cakes ($9) and the very succulent horseradish pork tenderloin ($19).

Entertainment

Sea Dog Brewing Co (☎ 207-236-6863, 43 Mechanic St) Inside the Knox Mill, this is a spacious restaurant/pub/nightspot serving sophisticated pub food ($6 to $12) and locally made brews. One lofty wall, all glass, looks out on the crashing waterfall of the old millrace. This is the most relaxed pub in Camden.

BELFAST & SEARSPORT

Just north of Camden near Belfast and Searsport, motels, campgrounds, restaurants, antique shops and flea markets line the roadside, providing dining, lodging and shopping opportunities. The establishments along here are considerably cheaper, and more likely to have vacancies in the summer high season, than are those in comparable tourist meccas such as Camden, Blue Hill and Bar Harbor.

MAINE

You can also explore Sears Island either by kayak from Searsport Shores Camping (half/full day $25/40) or via the pedestrian causeway. Sears Island is the largest uninhabited island on the USA's eastern seaboard. Hike around and appreciate ospreys, bald eagles and bears (careful!) in their natural habitat.

Searsport Shores Camping (*☎/fax 207-548-6059,* Ⓦ *www.campocean.com, 216 W Main St/US 1, Searsport*) Sites $21-38. This prime campground is a mile south of downtown Searsport. It has 35 tent and 65 RV sites in a pine-forested waterfront location.

Darby's (*☎ 207-338-2339, 105 High St, Belfast*) Mains $6-13. If you're looking for a bite to eat in Belfast, you won't be disappointed with Darby's. The eclectic menu at this reasonably priced restaurant and pub features everything from pad thai to fish-and-chips to Moroccan lamb. Wash it down with a local microbrew beer.

BUCKSPORT

A crossroads for highways and rail lines, Bucksport is a workaday town with light industry and a big Champion paper mill. Look a little closer and you'll also find an artsy community, somewhat similar to that of Brattleboro in Vermont. There are numerous motels, restaurants and other services. The Bucksport Chamber of Commerce has an information office (*☎ 207-469-6818*) next to the municipal offices in the center of town.

Just out of town and north of the bridge on ME 174 is the **Fort Knox State Historic Site** (*☎ 207-469-7719, ME 174; adult/child 5-11 yrs $2/50¢, senior & toddler free; open 9am-sunset summer, 9am-6:30pm spring & fall*). This huge granite fortress dominating the Penobscot River Narrows comes as a surprise in peaceable rural Maine, but only until you learn the spot's history.

This part of the Penobscot River Valley was the riverine gateway to Bangor, the commercial heart of Maine's rich timber industry. It was held by the British in the Revolutionary War and the War of 1812.

In 1839, it appeared that the US and UK might once again go to war over the disputed boundary between Maine and New Brunswick, and the US government feared that Bangor might once again fall into British hands. To protect the river approach to the city, construction was begun on Fort Knox in July 1844. Work continued for almost a decade.

The elaborate fortress mounted 64 cannons, with an additional 69 guns defending the outer perimeter. Though it was garrisoned from 1863 to 1866 during the Civil War, and again in 1898 during the Spanish-American War, it never saw any action. Fort Knox was either a great waste of money or an effective military deterrent, depending on your point of view.

Like so many of the world's elaborate military constructions, it is now a tourist attraction. Bring a flashlight if you plan a close examination, as the fort's granite chambers are unlit. There's a nice picnic area outside the admissions gate.

CASTINE

From Orland, a few miles east of Bucksport along US 1, ME 175/166 goes south to the dignified and historic seaside village of Castine. Following an eventful history, today's Castine is charming, quiet and refreshingly off the beaten track. Almost all of its houses were built before 1900, so you get a feel for how this seaside New England town would have been back then. It's also the home of the Maine Maritime Academy and its big training ship, the *State of Maine* (1952), which you can visit.

Both Castine and Blue Hill are good places to get a feel for the pre–tourist boom Maine; these are gorgeous villages with none of the kitsch you'd stumble across in Boothbay Harbor, Bar Harbor or Camden. For whatever reason, Castine attracts the Washington, DC, bigwig crowd.

Castine, at the southern end of ME 166, is small enough to be easily traversed on foot. A free map entitled *A Walking Tour of Castine* is readily available at establishments in town. The village is 18 miles south of US 1 at Orland, 56 miles northeast of Camden, 23 miles west of Blue Hill and 56 miles west of Bar Harbor.

History

In 1613, nine years before the Pilgrims landed at Plymouth, the French founded Fort Pentagöet – which later became Castine – to serve as a trading post. It was the site of battle after battle through the American Revolution, the War of 1812 and the French and Indian Wars. The French, English, Dutch and Americans all fought for a niche on this bulge of land that extends into Penobscot Bay.

Castine's Forts

After such an embattled history, you'd expect Castine to have old forts, but there are no great stone citadels like Fort Knox at Bucksport. Rather, the forts in Castine are low earthworks, now parklike and grass-covered.

Close to the Maine Maritime Academy campus, **Fort George** is near the upper (northern) end of Main St where it meets Battle Ave and Wadsworth Cove Rd. **Fort Pentagöet** is on Perkins Rd at Tarratine St. The American **Fort Madison** (earlier Fort Porter, 1808) is farther west along Perkins St, opposite Madockawando St.

Take a look also at the **Wilson Museum & John Perkins House** (☎ 207-326-9247, 107 Perkins St; admission free; open 2pm-5pm Tues-Sun July-August) near Fort Pentagöet. It holds a good collection of Native American artifacts, historic tools and farm equipment and other relics from Maine's past.

Places to Stay & Eat

There are only four places to stay in little Castine. Save the Village Inn, they all have excellent restaurants with entrées ranging from $12 to $24.

The Village Inn (☎ 207-326-9510, 26 Water St) Rooms $75-95. At the bottom of the hill, the Village Inn has four rooms. More expensive rooms are those with private bath.

Pentagöet Inn (☎ 207-326-8616, 800-845-1701, W www.pentagoet.com, 26 Main St) Rooms with bath $75-150. Owners Jack Burke, whose many years working in Africa are reflected in the décor, and Julie Van de Graaf, an award-winning pastry chef, run this classy Queen Anne Victorian. Their striking pub is covered with rare photos of eccentric world leaders.

Castine Inn (☎ 207-326-4365, W www.castineinn.com, 33 Main St) Rooms with bath $85-135 with full breakfast. This is a beautifully maintained grand 19-room Victorian summer hotel. From July through early September, you must stay at least two nights.

The Castine Harbor Lodge (☎ 207-326-4335, W www.castinemaine.com, 147 Perkins St) Rooms $85-195. This gracious ocean-front inn has 15 rooms and a good bar.

Pain de Famille (☎ 207-326-4455, 5 Castine Rd) Prices $3-8. At the entrance to town, facing the golf course at the Mobil gas station, is this fantastic bakery. It offers lots of vegetarian sandwiches ($3 to $5), calzones ($5) and pizzas ($7.50).

BLUE HILL

Blue Hill is a dignified, small Maine coastal town with tall trees, old houses and lots of culture. Many outstanding handicrafts artisans live and work here, and a summer chamber music series draws fine musicians.

At the junction of ME 15, ME 172 (Main St), ME 175, ME 176 and ME 177, Blue Hill is small enough for easy walking, with a few inns, a few restaurants, a few antique stores and lots of lofty trees. You can tour the town on foot in 1½ or two hours, as you wish, though a few inns and restaurants are on the outskirts.

The Blue Hill Chamber of Commerce (PO Box 520, Blue Hill, ME 04614) issues a free map at establishments in town.

Blue Hill is 23 miles east of Castine, 13 miles southwest of Ellsworth and 18 miles southeast of Bucksport.

Special Events

From early July through mid-August, the annual **Kneisel Hall Chamber Music Festival** (☎ 207-374-2811) attracts visitors from Portland, Bar Harbor and beyond. Concerts are held in Kneisel Hall on Pleasant St (ME 15) on Friday evening and Sunday afternoon.

The Blue Hill Fair (first week in September), held at the fairgrounds northeast of the town center on ME 172, has oxen and horse pulls, sheepdog trials, livestock shows, fireworks, auto-thrill shows, a petting zoo and other countrylike things to do.

Places to Stay
Gatherings Family Campground (☎ 207-667-8826, ME 172) Tent sites $15-40, RV sites $35-45. Northeast of Blue Hill, this campground has tent sites and RV hookups on a wooded lakefront. You can also rent cabins and cottages by the week.

Blue Hill Farm Country Inn (☎ 207-374-5166, W www.bluehillfarminn.com, ME 15) Rooms $90-105 with breakfast. Set on 48 acres of land with trails, this 1903 farmhouse, with its 14 rooms, is a classic. It is 2 miles north of the village.

Captain Isaac Merrill Inn (☎ 207-374-2555, W www.captainmerrillinn.com, 1 Union St) Rooms $95-125 with breakfast. This inn is right in the center of things. Though open only in 1994, it has the feel of a 19th-century hostelry.

Blue Hill Inn (☎ 207-374-2844, W www.bluehillinn.com, ME 177) Rooms $138-255 with breakfast & dinner. This is the longtime favorite lodging place in the region. It is a few steps from the village center and faces the George Stevens Academy. It has 10 rooms and two suites dating from 1840. Reduce the price by $40 if you don't want dinner.

Places to Eat
Blue Hill Co-op (☎ 207-374-8999, cnr ME 172 & ME 176) Prices $2-10. A great place to pick up organic meat and produce, this co-op also has a restaurant serving sandwiches ($4) and salads ($4 to $8).

Jean-Paul's Bistro (☎ 207-374-5852, Main St) Prices $2-12. Sit on the harborfront terrace of this early-19th-century Federal house and take in the views as you dine on light French food and sip tea.

Blue Hill's top restaurants are very busy at dinner; reservations are necessary.

Arborvine (☎ 207-374-2119, 33 Main St) Mains $16-22. Up Tenney Hill, Arborvine serves meat and fish endemic to the area in an 1823 Cape-style house. Chef John

Hikade manages to incorporate various fruits into almost all of his exquisite dishes. Start with Damariscotta River oysters ($9.50) and try either the tournedos ($22) or a shellfish specialty such as Maine crab cakes ($22). This is Blue Hill's place to see and be seen.

Jonathan's (☎ 207-374-5226, Main St) Mains $16-22. Right in the town's center, Jonathan's menu is as interesting as Arborvine's and similarly priced, featuring Maine fish cakes and lamb shanks braised in maple and ale barbecue sauce ($17).

DEER ISLE & STONINGTON
Travel south along ME 15 for views of pristine farms and stretches of rocky Maine coast with sailboats moored offshore. Deer Isle is a collection of islands joined by causeways and connected to the mainland by a picturesque, tall and narrow suspension bridge near Sargentville.

The Deer Isle–Stonington Chamber of Commerce (☎ 207-348-6124, W www.deerislemaine.com/members.asp) maintains an information booth a quarter-mile south of the suspension bridge, open 10am to 4pm (from 11am Sunday) in summer.

Deer Isle and Stonington are just about 5 miles apart. Stonington is 23 miles south of Blue Hill, 36 miles southwest of Ellsworth and 78 miles east of Camden.

Boats depart Stonington for Isle au Haut. See below.

Deer Isle Village
This small village is a collection of shops and services near the Pilgrim Inn. Seven miles to the east, secluded at the end of Sunshine Rd, is the **Haystack Mountain School of Crafts** (☎ 207-348-2306, 89 Haystack School Dr, Sunrise; admission $2; tour 1pm Wed June-Aug), founded in 1950 and now open for one public tour per week. The several galleries in Deer Isle and neighboring Stonington testify to the fascination this beautiful seaside area holds for fine artists.

Stonington
At the southern tip of Deer Isle, Stonington is a granite-quarrying, fishing and tourist

town, the three industries thriving closely together but separately. Signs warn tourists not to park on the town dock, because it is reserved for pickups hauling lobster traps and refrigerated trucks laden with fish. On the main street, art galleries and other shops alternate with auto parts stores and ship chandleries.

Stonington got its name and its early prosperity from the pink granite quarried here. The rocky islets in the harbor show you the color of the stone, and small-scale quarrying continues today. Stonington calls itself 'the ideal coastal Maine village,' and is proud that it is 'a real place, with a real working harbor,' rather than a fantasy tourist village.

There's not much to do in Stonington but enjoy Stonington, which is easy enough, as a short walk around town will prove.

Places to Stay
Sunshine Campground (☎ 207-348-2663, 877-770-9804, 1181 Sunshine Rd, Sunrise) Tent/RV sites $17/20. This heavily wooded campground with water access is nearly 6 miles east of Deer Isle off ME 15. It has 22 sites and rent kayaks.

Boyce's Motel (☎ 207-367-2421, 800-224-2421, ⓦ www.boycesmotel.com, Main St, Stonington) Rooms $49, apartments $99. This is a cedar shake–covered hostelry that looks more like an inn. It rents simple but suitable rooms and apartments.

Près du Port (☎ 207-367-5007, W Main St) Rooms $85 with breakfast. Just up the hill at the west end of Main St, this B&B has three harbor-view rooms, two with shared bath.

Inn on the Harbor (☎ 207-367-2420, 800-942-2420, ⓦ www.innontheharbor.com, Main St) Rooms with bath $105-135. Right in the center of Stonington, this inn has 13 rooms. The cheaper rooms face the street. The seaside terrace, which serves breakfast, coffee and snacks, has the best harbor view in town.

Goose Cove Lodge (☎ 207-348-2508, 800-728-1963, ⓦ www.goosecovelodge.com, Goose Cove Rd, Sunset) Rooms $150-260 per person with breakfast. Well off the beaten path, on a spruce-clad, granite-ledge cliff, Goose Cove is a tranquil hideaway where the sea rolls in over the ledges and the sounds of foghorns wake you up in the morning. The modern lodge has rooms spread out over 20 acres. Rates include guided nature walks and bike and kayak usage. It also serves fine dinners from $18 to $25 per entrée. Proper dress is required.

Places to Eat
Harbor Café (☎ 207-367-5099, Main St, Stonington) Mains $1.50-10. A local fishermen's favorite, this diner serves breakfast and features a welcome list of sandwiches for around $2.

Lily's Café (☎ 207-367-5936, cnr ME 15 & Airport Rd, Deer Isle) Prices $6-11. This is a good place to dine for lunch, or grab sandwiches, salads and homemade soups for a picnic.

Cafe Atlantic (☎ 207-367-2420, Main St, Stonington) Mains $9-16. This cafe, in the Inn on the Harbor, features broiled and grilled seafood for lunch and dinner. The view here is the cafe's redeeming quality.

Fisherman's Friend Restaurant (☎ 207-367-2442, School St, Stonington) Mains $9-16. Up the hill (away from the water) from Stonington village, Fisherman's Friend serves good, basic Maine seafood.

Pilgrim's Inn (☎ 207-348-6615, Main St, Deer Isle) Prix-fixe $33.50. This inn has a barn that has been converted to a rustic dining room. Nonguests are welcome for dinner.

ISLE AU HAUT
Much of Isle au Haut (that's 'aisle-a-ho'), a rocky island 6 miles long, is in the keeping of Acadia National Park. More remote than the parklands near Bar Harbor, it is not flooded with visitors in summer. Serious hikers can tramp the island's miles of trails and camp for the night in one of the five shelters maintained by the National Park Service.

For information on hiking and camping on Isle au Haut, contact Acadia National Park (☎ 207-288-3338, ⓦ www.nps.gov/acad, PO Box 177, Bar Harbor, ME 04609).

MAINE

Reservations for shelters must be accompanied by a payment; reservations for the summer season are not accepted before April 1.

The Isle au Haut Company (☎ 207-367-5193, 367-6516, Ⓦ www.isleauhaut.com) operates daily mail-boat trips from Stonington's Atlantic Ave Hardware Dock to the village of Isle au Haut year-round. In summer, except for Sunday and major holidays, there are at least three trips a day on the 45-minute crossing, for $30 per adult, $14 per child under 12. On Sunday and major holidays, there is only one boat a day. Bicycles, motorcycles, boats and canoes (no cars) can be carried to the village of Isle au Haut for a fee. Parking costs $9 per day.

From late June through mid-September, the company also makes the one-hour crossing to Duck Harbor, the entrance to the Isle au Haut territory of Acadia National Park. No bicycles, canoes or kayaks are transported on this run; no dogs are allowed in the Acadia campground.

MT DESERT ISLAND

Samuel de Champlain, the intrepid French explorer, sailed along this coast in the early 17th century. Seeing the bare, windswept granite summit of Cadillac Mountain, he called the island on which it stood *l'Île des Monts Déserts*. The name is still pronounced duh-ZERT almost 400 years later.

Mt Desert Island holds Bar Harbor, Maine's oldest summer resort, and most of Acadia National Park, the only national park in New England. Because of its dramatic Maine scenery and outdoor sports possibilities, it's one of the state's most popular and busiest summer resorts. Acadia is among the most heavily visited national parks in the country; see the boxed text in this chapter.

Visitors come, first and foremost, for the coastal vistas and spruce forests. They hike the island's 120 miles of trails, bike the 58 miles of unpaved carriage roads, camp in the park's 500-plus campsites or stay in country inns and seek out the 200 species of plants, 80 species of mammals and 273 kinds of birds that live here.

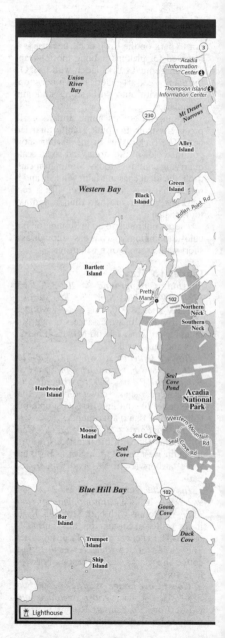

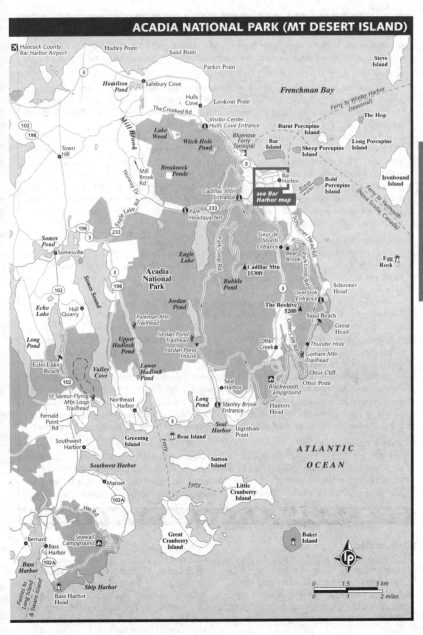

ACADIA NATIONAL PARK (MT DESERT ISLAND)

MAINE

Hancock County-
Bar Harbor Airport

Hadley Point

Sand Point

Parker Point

Steve
Island

Hamilton
Pond

Salisbury Cove

Hulls
Cove

Lookout Point

Frenchman Bay

Ferry to Winter Harbor
(seasonal)

The Hop

102
198

The Crooked Rd

Visitor Center;
Hulls Cove Entrance

Burnt Porcupine
Island

Long Porcupine
Island

Town
Hill

Lake
Wood

Witch Hole
Pond

Bluenose
Ferry Terminal

Bar
Island

Sheep Porcupine
Island

Ironbound
Island

Mill Brook

Mill
Brook
Rd

Norway Dr

Breakneck
Ponds

Bar
Harbor

see Bar
Harbor map

Breakwater

Bold
Porcupine
Island

Cadillac Mtn
Entrance

Eagle Lake Rd

3

Park
Headquarters

233

Somes
Pond

198
3

233

Somesville

Eagle
Lake

Sieur de
Monts
Entrance

Bear
Brook

Egg
Rock

102

198
3

Acadia
National
Park

Bubble
Pond

Cadillac Mtn
1530ft

Park Loop Rd

Schooner Head Rd

Schooner
Head

Echo
Lake

Hall
Quarry

Jordan
Pond

Overlook
Entrance

The Beehive
520ft

Sand Beach

Great
Head

Parkman Mtn
Trailhead

Long Pond

Jordan Pond
Trailhead

Jordan Pond
House

Otter Cliff Rd

Thunder Hole

Gorham Mtn
Trailhead

Echo Lake
Beach

Valley
Cove

102

Upper
Hadlock
Pond

Otter
Creek

Lower
Hadlock
Pond

Seal
Harbor

Blackwoods
Campground

Otter Cliff

Otter Point

St Saveur-Flying
Mtn Loop
Trailhead

Fernald
Point
Rd

Northeast
Harbor

3

Long
Pond

Stanley Brook
Entrance

Hunters
Head

Southwest
Harbor

Greening
Island

Ferry

Bear Island

Seal
Harbor

Ingraham
Point

ATLANTIC
OCEAN

Southwest Harbor

Manset

102A

Ferry

Sutton
Island

Little
Cranberry
Island

Hio Rd

Bernard

Seawall
Campground

Bass
Harbor

102A

Great
Cranberry
Island

Baker
Island

Bass
Harbor

102A

Ferries to
Long Island
& Swans Island

Ship Harbor

Bass Harbor
Head

0   1.5   3 km

0   1   2 miles

Acadia National Park

Acadia National Park, the only national park in all of New England, covers more than 62 sq miles and offers activities for everyone from the couch potato to the hyperactive sports enthusiast.

History

Mt Desert Island was a booming summer resort for the wealthy by the late 19th century, but it was a more industrial development that caused the creation of Acadia National Park. The invention of the 'portable sawmill' meant that the forests of the region could be stripped of trees for cheap lumber.

In 1901, as a result of this threat, summer residents, led by Harvard University president Charles W Eliot, formed a land trust. Wealthy landowners donated land to the trust, and Acadia's extents grew. By 1916, the trust was a national monument, and in 1919, it became a national park.

John D Rockefeller donated 10,000 acres of land to the park. Alarmed at the prospect of its being overrun with automobiles (as it now is), he ordered construction of 58 miles of one-lane, gravel-topped carriage roads throughout the park. The carriage roads, laid between 1918 and 1940, were to provide access to the park's more remote areas by horse-drawn carriage rather than automobile. Today, they're popular with hikers and mountain bikers.

Orientation & Information

The park's main entrance is at Hulls Cove, northwest of Bar Harbor via ME 3. The visitor center (☎ 207-288-3338) is here and opens at 8am in summer. From the visitor center, the 20-mile-long Park Loop Rd circumnavigates the northeastern section of the island. It is a one-way road for much of its length.

The admission fee to the park is $10 per vehicle and is good for seven consecutive days. The fee is collected at a booth on the Park Loop Rd, just north of Sand Beach. If you enter the park by bike or on foot, the fee is $2 per person.

Other entrances to the park and the Park Loop Rd are the Cadillac Mountain entrance just west of Bar Harbor; the Overlook Entrance that is south of the town; and the Stanley Brook Entrance that is east of Northeast Harbor.

Cadillac Mountain (1530 feet), the highest point in the park, is a few miles southwest of Bar Harbor. The summit can be reached by auto road, which is a pity. Most of the carriage roads (closed to motor vehicles) are between Bubble Pond and Somes Sound, to the west of Cadillac Mountain.

Call the visitor center for camping, road and weather information. For park emergencies, call ☎ 207-288-3369. See the Southwest Harbor section for information on the Island Explorer shuttle service.

Maps & Guides

Free NPS maps of the park are available at the information and visitor centers. The AMC Guide to Mt Desert Island & Acadia National Park by the Appalachian Mountain Club (available from Globe Pequot Publishers) has descriptions of all the trails, as well as a good trail map. Acadia Revealed, by Jay Kaiser, is perhaps the most comprehensive guidebook to the park on the market. These guides

Orientation

The resort area of Bar Harbor and Acadia extends from the town of Ellsworth, on US 1, to the southern tip of the large mountainous island of Mt Desert. The island's major town, Bar Harbor, is situated on its northeast side, 20 miles southeast of Ellsworth.

Acadia National Park covers the majority (but not all) of the land on the island. It includes tracts of land on the Schoodic Peninsula south of Winter Harbor, across the water to the east and on Isle au Haut, far to the southwest. You can reach Winter Harbor by ferry from Bar Harbor in summer;

Acadia National Park

and others, as well as a variety of maps, are sold at the Hulls Cove Visitor Center and at bookshops in Bar Harbor.

Touring Highlights

Start your tour with a drive along the Park Loop Rd. On the portion called Ocean Drive, stop at Thunder Hole, south of the Overlook Entrance, for a look at the surf crashing into a cleft in the granite (the effect is best with a strong incoming tide). Otter Cliffs, not far south of Thunder Hole, is a wall of pink granite rising right from the sea.

At Jordan Pond, there's a self-guided nature trail. Here, you're in the midst of the trail and carriage road systems. Stop for tea and popovers at *Jordan Pond House* (☎ 207-276-3116); see Places to Eat in the Bar Harbor section.

For a nice, easy hike, consider making the quick (20 minutes) ascent up The Beehive near the Overlook entrance; for a slightly longer walk on the more-secluded 'backside' of the island, try the St Saveur-Flying Mountain Loop Trail, off Fernald Point Rd, just north of Southwest Harbor. Make sure you use proper shoes (not sandals!) to avoid an injury.

For swimming, try either Sand Beach or Seal Harbor for chilly salt water, or Echo Lake for fresh water.

Bikers should park near Eagle Lake, off ME 233, and pedal on the carriage paths around this body of water.

Finish your first explorations with a stop at the windy summit of Cadillac Mountain.

Outfitters

Acadia is great for all sorts of outdoor activities, including hiking, rock climbing, mountain biking, canoeing and sea kayaking. Numerous outfitters in Bar Harbor provide guide service, equipment for rent or sale and sports lessons. Many are found at the west end of Cottage St near ME 3, including Acadia Bike & Coastal Kayaking (☎ 207-288-9605, 800-526-8615, 48 Cottage St), across from the post office; Acadia Outfitters (☎ 207-288-8118, 106 Cottage St), facing the Irving station; Island Adventures (☎ 207-288-3886, 137 Cottage St); National Park Kayak Center (☎ 207-288-0342, 39 Cottage St); and Acadia Mountain Guides (☎ 207-288-8186, 137 Cottage St).

Campgrounds

There are three campgrounds in the park: Blackwoods Campground (☎ 207-288-3338, 800-365-2267), open all year, requires reservations in summer; Seawall Campground, open May through September, rents sites on a first-come, first-served basis; Duck Harbor, on Isle au Haut, requires a special permit and is open May through October. No backcountry camping is allowed. There are private campgrounds outside the park. See the Places to Stay section in Bar Harbor for details.

Getting Around

Thanks to massive contributions from the Rockefeller family, a new, free shuttle system, 'Island Explorer,' makes the rounds along seven different routes that cover the entire island. Route maps are available at local establishments.

however, the Isle au Haut portion of the park is not easily accessible from Mt Desert Island.

Information

From early May to the end of October, the Acadia Information Center (☎ 207-667-8550, 800-358-8550, Ⓦ www.acadiainfo.com) is your best bet for information. They're located on your right (ME 3) just before you cross the bridge to Mt Desert Island. They'll also make lodging arrangements for you. Acadia National Park's Hulls Cove Visitor Center (☎ 207-288-3338) is 16 miles south of Ellsworth and 3 miles north of Bar Harbor; it is open May through October. Follow the signs. In the off-season, go to Park Headquarters for information. It is 3 miles west of Bar Harbor on ME 233.

The Bar Harbor Chamber of Commerce (☎ 207-288-5103, 800-345-4617, Ⓦ www .barharborinfo.com, PO Box 158, Bar Harbor, ME 04609) maintains a small information office at the Bar Harbor Town Pier.

For strictly walk-in service, there's a new Acadia National Park Information Office, run by rangers, in Bar Harbor (no ☎, Firefly Lane) facing the Town Green.

The Acadia Area Association has an 'official lodging office' at 55 West St in Bar Harbor, open 10am to 6pm weekdays.

In Somesville, west of Bar Harbor, you can browse in a tranquil atmosphere at the Port in the Storm bookstore (☎ 207-244-4114, 1112 Main St).

For information regarding Nova Scotia, stop by the Nova Scotia Visitor Information Center next to the Criterion Theatre in Bar Harbor.

BAR HARBOR

Bar Harbor, on Mt Desert Island, is Maine's most popular summer resort. It's a pleasant town of big old houses, some of which have been converted into inns and restaurants, creating a relaxed, but purposeful, way of life.

Bar Harbor's busiest season is late June through August. There's a bit of a lull just before and just after Labor Day, but then it gets busy again from foliage season through mid-October.

History

Bar Harbor was chartered as a town in 1796, while Maine was part of the Commonwealth of Massachusetts. In 1844, landscape painters Thomas Cole and Frederick Church came to Mt Desert and liked what they saw. They sketched the landscape and later returned with their art students. Naturally, the wealthy families who purchased their paintings asked Cole and Church about the beautiful land depicted in their paintings, and soon the families began to spend summers on Mt Desert.

In a short time, Bar Harbor rivaled Newport, RI, for the stature of its summer-colony guests. A rail line from Boston and regular steamboat service brought even more visitors. By the end of the 19th century, Bar Harbor was one of the eastern seaboard's most desirable summer resorts.

WWII damaged the tourist trade, but worse damage was to come. In 1947, a vast forest fire torched 17,000 acres of park land, along with 60 palatial 'summer cottages' of wealthy summer residents, putting an end to Bar Harbor's gilded age. But the town recovered as a destination for the new car-equipped, mobile middle class of the postwar years.

Although Mt Desert Island still has a number of wealthy summer residents, they are far outnumbered by common folk. There is an especially large contingent of outdoor-sports lovers.

Orientation & Information

ME 3 approaches Bar Harbor from the north and the west, and it passes right through the town. Main St is the town's principal commercial thoroughfare, along with Cottage St. Mt Desert St has many of the town's inns, just a few minutes' walk from the town green.

See Information under Mt Desert Island for tourist facilities.

Rock Climbing

With all that granite, Acadia National Park is a mecca for rock climbers. If you'd like to learn the sport, **Atlantic Climbing** (☎ 207-288-2521, 24 Cottage St; prices half/full day $95/160) offers guide and instruction services. **Acadia Mountain Guides** (☎ 207-288-8186, 198 Main St; half/full day $95/160) also gives instruction and can guide you to the best climbs. These companies have lower prices for groups of two or more.

Soaring

Island Soaring (☎ 207-667-7627, Hancock County-Bar Harbor Airport, ME 3; $110-200 per couple), north of the Trenton Bridge, will take you in a glider for a soar above Mt Desert Island. Call for reservations.

BAR HARBOR

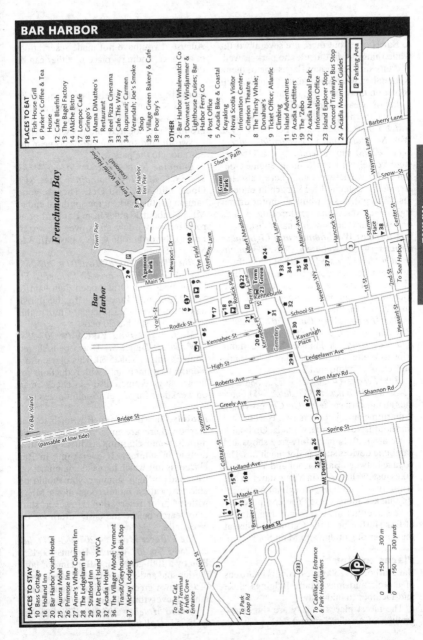

PLACES TO STAY
10 Bass Cottage
16 Holland Inn
20 Bar Harbor Youth Hostel
25 Aurora Motel
26 Primrose Inn
27 Anne's White Columns Inn
28 The Ledgelawn Inn
29 Stratford Inn
30 Mt Desert Island YWCA
32 Acadia Hotel
36 The Villager Motel; Vermont
     Transit/Greyhound Bus Stop
37 McKay Lodging

PLACES TO EAT
1   Fish House Grill
6   Parker's Coffee & Tea
     House
12 Cafe Bluefish
13 The Bagel Factory
14 Mâche Bistro
17 Lompoc Cafe
18 Gringo's
21 Mama DiMatteo's
     Restaurant
31 Reel Pizza Cinerama
33 Cafe This Way
34 Rupununi; Carmen
     Verandah; Joe's Smoke
     Shop
35 Village Green Bakery & Cafe
38 Poor Boy's

OTHER
2   Bar Harbor Whalewatch Co
3   Downeast Windjammer &
     Lighthouse Cruises; Bar
     Harbor Ferry Co
4   Post Office
5   Acadia Bike & Coastal
     Kayaking
7   Nova Scotia Visitor
     Information Center;
     Criterion Theatre
8   The Thirsty Whale;
     Donahue's
9   Ticket Office; Atlantic
     Climbing
11 Island Adventures
15 Acadia Outfitters
19 The Zebo
22 Acadia National Park
     Information Office
23 Island Explorer Stop;
     Concord Trailways Bus Stop
24 Acadia Mountain Guides

Cruises

Acadia National Park is what lures visitors to Bar Harbor, but there are several worthwhile things to do outside the park as well. A cruise on Frenchman Bay is one of them. Remember, when you cruise, it is often 20°F cooler on the water than on land, so bring a jacket or sweater and windbreaker.

Next to the pier *Bar Harbor Whalewatch Co* (☎ 207-288-2386, 800-508-1499, 1 West St; adult/child 5-15 yrs/child under 5 yrs $39/25/8) runs *Friendship V*, a 116-foot steel vessel with three main engines, designed for whale watching. There's also the *Acadian* (adult/child 5-15 yrs/child under 5 yrs $22/15/5), a steel-hulled, motor-driven sightseeing vessel that explores the islands on two-hour cruises with a naturalist.

Downeast Windjammer and Lighthouse Cruises (☎ 207-288-4585, 288-2373; adult/child under 12 yrs $27.50/18.50) has three two-hour cruises departing from the Bar Harbor Inn Pier on the majestic 151-foot, four-masted schooner *Margaret Todd*. Buy your tickets on the pier.

Bar Harbor Ferry Co (☎ 207-288-2984, Bar Harbor Inn Pier; adult/child $24/12; mid-May to mid-Oct) makes three one-hour trips to Winter Harbor per day. Bike transport costs an additional $5.

Bay Ferries (☎ 207-288-3395, 888-249-7245; roundtrip tickets $55, autos $95) operates an ultrafast car ferry *The Cat*, providing a maritime link between Bar Harbor and Yarmouth, Nova Scotia, Canada. On board, there are buffets, bars, duty-free shops and gambling devices such as slot machines. The voyage between Bar Harbor and Yarmouth takes just 2½ hours, so in a long day, you can cruise there and back, though an overnight stay makes more sense. You can purchase tickets at either the Cat ferry terminal west of Bar Harbor or at the Cat ticket office at the corner of Cottage and Main Sts.

Places to Stay

Bar Harbor has 2500 guest rooms in dozens of motels and inns. Many lodgings close mid-October to mid-May.

The nicest places to stay are the campgrounds of Acadia National Park, or in one of Bar Harbor's Victorian inns. The first is cheap, the second expensive, and in July and August, if you have not made reservations in advance, finding a place in either can be difficult.

Camping & Hostels For camping in Acadia National Park, see the 'Acadia National Park' boxed text. Commercial campgrounds are located along ME 3 from Ellsworth, and they are clustered near the entrances to the park.

Lamoine State Park (☎ 207-667-4778, 287-3824, ME 184, Lamoine) Sites $19. Open mid-May–mid-Oct. There's good camping at this park, at the southern end of ME 184, about 30 miles from Bar Harbor by road but only a few miles over the water. From Ellsworth, follow US 1 past ME 3 to ME 184 South.

Bar Harbor Youth Hostel (☎ 207-288-5587, ⓦ www.hiayh.org, 27 Kennebec St) Dorm beds $12. Office open 7am-9am & 5pm-11pm, mid-June–Aug. In the parish hall of St Saviour's Episcopal Church, this safe, clean hostel has 20 beds.

Mt Desert Island YWCA (☎ 207-288-5008, 36 Mt Desert St) Dorm beds/shared doubles/singles $20/25/30. This place offers lodging to women only, with reductions for longer stays. Women also can check email on weekdays for $2 per 15-minute session.

Motels On ME 3 from Ellsworth to Bar Harbor, there are numerous inexpensive motels, some charging as little as $40 a double in summer. If everything in Bar Harbor is full, which happens sometimes on weekends in high summer, you should be able to locate a motel room along ME 3 without prior reservation. However, start your search before the early afternoon on weekends.

The Villager Motel (☎ 207-288-3211, fax 207-288-2270, 207 Main St) Rooms $60-128. Run by a 10th-generation Bar Harbor family, this spic-and-span motel is a block south of the town green and within walking distance of everything. Rates drop August 25.

Aurora Motel (☎ 207-288-3771, 800-841-8925, 51 Holland Ave) Rooms $90-129.

Close to the Primrose Inn, this place is small, simple and well located.

Also, check out the cheap cottages (some are efficiencies) right on the water north of Bar Harbor between Salisbury Cove and Hulls Cove. The best ones are: *Emery's* (☎ 207-288-3432, 888-240-3432, ⓦ *www .emeryscottages.com, Sand Point Rd, Salisbury Cove)*, off ME 3; and *The Colony* (☎ 207-288-3383, 800-524-1159, ⓦ *www .acadia.net/thecolony, ME 3, Hulls Cove)*. All rent cottages by the day (average price $87) or week (average price $620) in summer.

Inns Most of the huge old 'summer cottages' in Bar Harbor along Mt Desert St have been converted to inns. Prices are usually the same for one or two persons and most include full breakfasts.

McKay Lodging (☎ 207-288-5226, 888-766-2529, ⓦ *www.mckaylodging.com, 243 Main St)* Rooms $50-120. With 23 rooms, some with shared bath, this Bar Harbor house is a short hop south of the town green.

Bass Cottage (☎ 207-288-3705, 14 The Field) Rooms $60-100. Hidden from the masses, Bass Cottage has 10 simple rooms, some with shared bath, on a 113-year-old Victorian estate.

Stratford Inn (☎ 207-288-5189, ⓦ *www .stratfordinn.com, 45 Mt Desert St)* Rooms $75-175 with continental breakfast. This aptly named inn, built by a wealthy Boston publisher in 1900, is a Tudor fantasy in the midst of Bar Harbor. It has big, airy rooms.

Acadia Hotel (☎ 207-288-5721, ⓦ *www .acadiahotel.com, 20 Mt Desert St)* Rooms $90-140. Just off the green, rooms in this well-kept old house are usually all reserved in advance; call early.

Anne's White Columns Inn (☎ 207-288-5357, 800-321-6379, 57 Mt Desert St)* Rooms $90-135. This Georgian house with Greek-style columns has 10 tasteful rooms. Afternoon wine and cheese is included in the cost.

Holland Inn (☎ 207-288-4804, ⓦ *www .hollandinn.com, 35 Holland Ave)* Rooms with bath $90-145. This restored 1895 farmhouse is just as affordable as Acadia Hotel, and is also within walking distance of town. The young and extremely personable inn-keepers offer five rooms and serve a large breakfast.

Primrose Inn (☎ 207-288-4031, 877-846-3424, ⓦ *www.primroseinn.com, 73 Mt Desert St)* Rooms $95-175, efficiencies $600-1000 weekly. This 1878 inn, with 11 rooms and four efficiencies, is particularly well kept.

The Ledgelawn Inn (☎ 207-288-4596, ⓦ *www.barharborvacations.com, 66 Mt Desert St)* Rooms $95-250, suites $275-295. Bar Harbor's most magnificent downtown inn is this vast colonial-revival 'summer cottage,' built in 1904 for a Boston shoe magnate. Well kept to this day, it exudes charm and grandeur, yours for a price (which varies depending on the day and the room). Rates include afternoon tea.

There are also good B&B alternatives outside Bar Harbor proper. Among them are the following accommodations.

Coach Stop Inn (☎ 207-288-9886, ⓦ *www .coachstopinn.com, ME 3)* Rooms $79-135. Five miles out of downtown and just 2 miles from the main entrance to Acadia National Park in Hulls Cove, these are the oldest surviving lodgings in the area. The five-room, 1804 inn is set on 3 acres of gardens.

Mill Brook House (☎ 207-288-3860, 877-288-3860, 87 Mill Brook Rd)* Rooms with bath $95-125 with breakfast. In the woods west of Bar Harbor, away from the crowds, lies this traditional New England salt box with three rooms. There are trails, a swimming hole and two small waterfalls nearby.

Places to Eat

Bar Harbor has its share of places serving typical tourist fare; however, some local restaurants serve food of a quality paralleling that served in Portland. Unless noted, the eateries listed here are open for lunch and dinner.

Parker's Coffee & Tea House (☎ 207-288-2882, 37½ Cottage St)* Prices $1-3. Next to the Criterion Theatre, Parker's is good for a cappuccino, latte or mocha and pastries.

The Bagel Factory (☎ 207-288-3903, 116 Cottage St)* Prices $2-7. This hole-in-the-wall is the place to finagle a bagel in Bar Harbor. Several kinds of homemade bagels are served with interesting toppings until 2pm.

MAINE

MAINE

Cafe This Way (☎ 207-288-4483, 14½ Mt Desert St) Breakfast $4-12, lunch $6-12, dinner mains $9-15. This casual, quirky place is *the* place for breakfast, according to locals. Try the Maine blueberry pancakes ($4) or eggs Benedict with smoked trout ($6). Sit back, listen to smooth jazz, peruse one of the many books and chow down. It also serves hefty, healthful lunches and fresh seafood dinners.

Village Green Bakery & Cafe (☎ 207-288-9450, 195 Main St) Prices $5-15. This cafe has fresh baked goods, sandwiches, salads, pasta and, as the menu says, 'lobster, of course.'

The best place for a lobster picnic is one of the lobster pounds clustered north of Trenton Bridge on ME 3, about 6½ miles south of Ellsworth on the road to Bar Harbor. At these places, a lobster dinner with steamed clams and corn or coleslaw should cost only $12 or so. Prices are usually posted on highway signboards.

Trenton Bridge Lobster Pound (☎ 207-667-2977, ME 3, Ellsworth) Prices $9-20. This is the oldest and best of the lobster pounds, and has a pretty water-view picnic area at the north end of the causeway that leads to Mt Desert Island.

Bar Harbor's most interesting dining possibilities are along Rodick, Kennebec and Cottage Sts.

Gringo's (☎ 207-288-2326, 30 Rodick St) Burritos $5-6, smoothies $3.50. If you're in the mood for a quick, healthful burrito, then stop by this new kid on the block. It also serves an array of refreshing smoothies.

Rupununi (☎ 207-288-2886, 119 Main St) Prices $5-16. Rupununi is a good spot for families, serving standard American fare, such as burgers and pasta, at affordable prices. It also has the hottest bar in town upstairs, a cigar den downstairs, pool tables and dancing with live music (see Entertainment, below).

Lompoc Cafe (☎ 207-288-9392, 36 Rodick St) Dishes $6-13. South of Cottage, this cafe has a short but eclectic, international menu – Indonesian peanut chicken, shrimp étouffée ($10 to $13) and ingenious pizzas (Greek, goat cheese, etc, $6 to $8). You can also have a glass of Bar Harbor Real Ale. There's also blueberry ale for the intrepid. On most evenings, there's live entertainment (see Entertainment, below).

Poor Boy's (☎ 207-288-4148, 300 Main St) Mains $8-23. If you're really not sure what you want to eat, head here (there are 65 entrées to choose from!). Don't let the low prices fool you at Poor Boy's. You get huge servings of tasty dishes such as chicken marsala ($13) or a five-course lobster dinner ($18). It also has an extensive early-bird menu (4:30pm to 6pm) for only $8.

Fish House Grill (☎ 207-288-3070, 1 West St) Mains $8-24. Down by the harbor, this seafood restaurant is usually busy because of its pier location, which commands a spectacular sunset view of the water and the pine-fringed coast. A pound of steamed mussels ($8) or salmon oscar (grilled salmon with crabmeat and asparagus) are two of many good choices.

Reel Pizza Cinerama (☎ 207-288-3828, 33B Kennebec St) Pizza $9-15. Reel Pizza caters to those of us who like munching on good pizza and drinking local beer on couches while watching a nightly flick ($5) on the silver screen.

Mama DiMatteo's Restaurant (☎ 207-288-3666, 34 Kennebec Place) Mains $14-23. This restaurant serves nouvelle Italian cuisine: sausage mushroom lasagne; shrimp sautéd with prosciutto, capers and olives and the like. Early-bird specials (slightly smaller portions) are served from 4:30pm to 6pm. If you're in a drinking mood, a pitcher of peach daiquiris is only $10.

Cafe Bluefish (☎ 207-288-3696, 122 Cottage St) Mains $14-21. This is an intimate storefront bistro offering tasty seafood choices such as pecan-crusted salmon ($18) and Cajun-crusted swordfish ($10). Strangely, bluefish isn't on the menu.

Mâche Bistro (☎ 207-288-0447, 135 Cottage St) Mains $17-24. Bar Harbor's premier restaurant, Mâche Bistro, serves cuisine that can best be described as New England–eclectic. Young chef Chris Jelbert, veteran line cook of Portland's Fore St, has been dazzling the palates of everyone who comes through his doors. He and his wife and baker, Maureen Cosgrove, incorporate mushrooms into most of the dishes. Start with an appetizer such as the mushroom *gougère* (cheese puff with chanterelles topped with truffle oil – $10) and don't miss his signature dish, the luscious breast of duck with orange and ginger ($18).

Jordan Pond House (☎ 207-276-3316, *Park Loop Rd, Seal Harbor)* Afternoon tea $7, dinner prix-fixe $19. This is the only restaurant *inside* Acadia National Park. It carries on the long tradition of teahouses, serving tea and delectable popovers with strawberry jam. They also serve a fixed-price three-course dinner.

Entertainment

Carmen Verandah (☎ 207-288-2886, *119 Main St)* The 2nd-floor terrace of Rupununi, with its festive atmosphere, is the place to dance and grab a drink in Bar Harbor. It has pool tables, darts and a large dance floor to groove to the live music. Downstairs, there's *Joe's Smoke Shop*, an upscale cigar bar that often can be just as crowded.

Lompoc Cafe (☎ 207-288-9392, *36 Rodick St)* This is a homey place with a variety of performers playing jazz, blues and folk on a patio. Check the signboard at the corner of Rodick and Cottage Sts for who's on and when. The cover charge varies.

The 'Zebo (☎ 207-288-3070, *5 Rodick Pl)* This laid-back watering hole, a local haunt for both College of the Atlantic students and local wait-staff, serves Maine microbrews both indoors and on its outdoor gazebo.

Other good choices for a pint and live music are the *Thirsty Whale* (☎ 207-288-9335, *40 Cottage St)* and *Donahue's* (☎ 207-288-3030, *30 Cottage St)*.

Getting There & Away

US Airways Express, operated by Colgan Air (☎ 207-667-7171, 800-428-4322), connects Bar Harbor and Boston with daily flights year-round. The Hancock County Airport is in Trenton, off ME 3, just north of the Trenton Bridge.

Vermont Transit/Greyhound (☎ 207-288-3366, 802-864-6811, 800-451-3292) runs an early morning bus daily from Bar Harbor to Boston and New York City via Bangor and Portland. (Buses stop at the Villager Motel, 207 Main St.) Likewise, a bus starts out from New York at breakfast time, reaches Boston by lunchtime and arrives in Bar Harbor by dinnertime.

Also, Concord Trailways (☎ 888-741-8686) has an airport shuttle, four times daily, from Bangor to Bar Harbor (serving both the Bay Ferries terminal and the Village Green). Make advance reservations.

The Bar Harbor bus stop is at Fox Run Travel, 4 Kennebec St at Cottage St. You can also flag the bus down in the parking lot of the McDonald's at the junction of US 1 and ME 3 in Ellsworth.

For details on the Bay Ferries to Yarmouth, Nova Scotia, see Cruises, above.

NORTHEAST HARBOR

The aptly named Northeast Harbor, another of Mt Desert Island's vacation villages, has a marina full of yachts, a main street populated with art galleries and boutiques and back streets dotted with comfortable summer hideaways that are good for a short stay.

Information (☎ 207-276-5040) is available on the hill facing the marina.

Docksider (☎ 207-276-3965, *14 Sea St)* Mains $3-15. This is a beloved lobster shack, especially known for its crab cakes and crab sandwiches.

151 Main St (☎ 207-276-9898, *151 Main St)* Mains $8-12. Open for lunch and dinner, this bistro serves the island's best food outside of Bar Harbor. Try the white clam pizza ($9) or griddled beef and pork meatloaf ($12). And don't skip dessert!

SOUTHWEST HARBOR

More laid-back and less affluent than Northeast Harbor, the island's Southwest Harbor also offers lots of things to do.

From the Upper Town Dock – a quarter-mile along Clark Point Rd from the flashing light in the center of town – boats venture out into Frenchman Bay to the Cranberry Isles and on whale-watching expeditions. Parking costs $4 per day.

MAINE

Cranberry Cove Boating Co (☎ *207-244-5882; adult/child 3-12 yrs $12/8*) carries passengers to and from the Cranberry Isles aboard the 47-passenger *Island Queen*, which cruises four times daily in summer.

Penury Hall (☎ *207-244-7102, 374 Main St,* Ⓦ *www.penuryhall.com*) Rooms $95 with breakfast. This B&B rents three rooms in an 1865 schoolhouse. There is a two-night minimum stay in summer.

Heron House (☎ *207-244-0221,* Ⓦ *www .acadias-heronhouse.com, cnr ME 102 & Fernald Point Rd*) Rooms $95-105 with breakfast. The down-to-earth owners of this homey B&B facing the golf course rent three rooms.

Beal's Lobster Pound (☎ *207-244-3202, 1 Clark Point Rd*) Mains $3-15. For sustenance, everyone heads to Beal's. Grab a picnic table and dine on chowder, crabmeat rolls and, what else, lobster.

Restaurant XYZ (☎ *207-244-5221, Shore Rd, Manset*) Mains $10-17. Across from the town dock, this eatery serves authentic Mexican dinners (not Tex-Mex!) in a fabulous waterfront setting. Order dishes such as chicken in a mole sauce and Yucatan-style pork (both $16), washed down with margaritas ($6.50). Upstairs, the owners rent out six spacious rooms for $65 to $80. The restaurant and the rooms have a fabulous view.

BANGOR

Though Bangor figures prominently in present-day Maine, it's off the normal tourist routes. A boomtown during Maine's 19th-century lumbering heyday, Bangor was largely destroyed by a disastrous fire in 1911. Today it's mostly a modern, working-class town, famous as the hometown of best-selling novelist Stephen King (look for his appropriately spooky mansion – complete with bat-and-cobweb fence – among the grand houses along W Broadway).

The Bangor Historical Society (☎ 207-942-5766) has a Civil War museum in the **Thomas A Hill House** (*159 Union St; adult/senior/child under 18 yrs $4/3/free; open 10am-4pm Tues-Sat*). The **Cole Land Transportation Museum** (☎ *207-990-3600, 405 Perry Rd; adult/senior/child under 19 yrs*

$5/3/free; open 9am-5pm early-May–mid-Nov) has exhibits of antique vehicles and photographs.

The Bangor Mall, off I-95 exit 49, is the shopping mecca for this part of the Penobscot River Valley.

Information

The Bangor Region Chamber of Commerce (☎ 207-947-0307, Ⓦ www.bangorregion.com, 519 Main St, Bangor, ME 04402) and the Bangor Convention & Visitors Bureau (☎ 207-947-5205, Ⓦ www.bangorcvb.org, 115 Main St) can answer questions and provide information. Both are open 8am to 5pm weekdays.

Places to Stay

Paul Bunyan Campground (☎ *207-941-1177,* Ⓦ *www.paulbunyancampground.com, 1862 Union St, Bangor*) Sites $14-18.50. On the outskirts of Bangor, this basic campground has 52 sites.

Pleasant Hill Campground (☎ *207-848-5127, cnr Mansell Rd & Union St/ME 222, Hermon*) Sites $17-26. With 105 spaces for everything from tents to giant motor homes, Pleasant Hill is 5½ miles northwest of I-95 exit 47, along Union St (ME 222).

There are lots of motels off I-95, close to the Maine Mall. You'll save money if you drive beyond the obvious places that are right by the exit.

Bangor Motor Inn (☎ *207-947-0355, 800-244-0355 in Maine and Canada, 701 Hogan Rd*) Rooms $50-68 with continental breakfast. Of the places near the highway, this one with 102 rooms, opposite the Bangor Mall, offers the best value. It'll even grant discounts if business is slow.

Country Inn (☎ *207-941-0200, 800-244-3961, 936 Stillwater Ave*) Rooms $60-80. The fanciest modern hotel is the Country Inn, at Hogan Rd, up on the hill above Crossroads Plaza and the Comfort Inn. The inn's location is convenient, yet quietish, and the price reasonable.

Bangor's other motels charge about the same or a bit more. All the major chains are here (just off the I-95 exits), including ***Best Western White House Inn*** (☎ *207-862-3737*),

Super 8 Motel (☎ *207-945-5681), Comfort Inn* (☎ *207-942-7899), Econo Lodge* (☎ *207-945-0111)* and *Days Inn* (☎ *207-942-8272).*

Phenix Inn at West Market Square (☎ *207-947-0411, 20 Broad St)* Rooms $96-101 with buffet breakfast. This 35-room inn is in the city center in the West Market Square Historic District, a row of buildings dating from 1873, when Bangor was Maine's lumber capital. Rooms in the charming, renovated hotel are tidy. To find the hotel, look for the little park with the fountain and stainless steel sculpture at the intersection of Maine St at Broad and Hammond Sts.

Places to Eat

Dining options are limited. There are numerous national chain restaurants near I-95 exit 49 as well as a few family-owned places in the city center.

Intown Internet Cafe (☎ *207-942-0999, 56 Main St)* Snacks $1-7. Near Broad and Hammond Sts, this cafe serves up java, as well as surprisingly cheap pastries, sandwiches and sausages for you to munch while you surf the net. Web access is $2/3/5 per 15 minutes/half-hour/hour.

Whig & Courier (☎ *207-947-4095, 18 Broad St)* Mains $4-8. This restaurant, adjacent to the Phenix Inn, serves good, cheap pub grub and good pints.

Bangor Wine & Cheese Co (☎ *207-942-3336, 84 Hammond St)* Dishes $8-13. Mostly a wine bar, this new place serves excellent tapas-style dishes such as lime and cilantro salmon ($10) and duck breast with honey, ginger and lavender ($12).

Getting There & Away

Bangor International Airport (☎ 207-947-0384) is the air transportation hub of the region. It is served by regional carriers associated with Continental, Delta and US Airways.

For bus routes, see Getting There & Away in the Portland section. Vermont Transit (☎ 207-945-3000, 802-864-6811, 800-451-3292), at the Bangor Bus Terminal, 158 Main St, runs four direct buses daily between Bangor and Boston via Portland and Portsmouth, New Hampshire. Concord

Trailways (☎ 800-639-3317), Trailways Transportation Center, 1039 Union St, has three more, as well as service south along the Maine coast to Portland, and connecting service north and east to Calais and St Stephen, New Brunswick, Canada.

Downeast Maine

The 'Sunrise Coast' is the name given by Maine's tourism promoters to the area east of Ellsworth to Lubec and Eastport. To Mainers, this is Downeast Maine, the area downwind and east of the rest of the state. It's sparsely populated, and is slower-paced and more traditional than the Maine to the south and west. It also has more frequent and denser coastal fog.

If you seek quiet walks away from the tourist throngs, coastal villages with little impact from tourism, and lower travel prices, explore the 900-plus miles of coastline east of Bar Harbor. But be mindful of the weather.

SCHOODIC PENINSULA

Surrounded by islands, the Schoodic Peninsula juts south into the Atlantic Ocean. At its southern tip is a portion of Acadia National Park, with a 7.2-mile shore drive called Schoodic Point Loop Rd, offering splendid views of Mt Desert Island and Cadillac Mountain. The loop road is one-way, with a smooth surface and relatively gentle hills, and is excellent for biking. At the Fraser's Point entrance to the park is a picnic area. Farther along the loop, at the end of a short walk from the road, you'll find Schoodic Head, a 400-foot-high promontory with fine ocean views.

North of the peninsula, the little towns of Gouldsboro and Winter Harbor provide the area with stores, restaurants and other businesses.

This is the quieter part of Acadia, with fewer crowds – but also fewer activities. For information on local businesses, contact the Schoodic Peninsula Chamber of Commerce (☎ 207-963-7658, 800-231-3008, Ⓦ www .acadia-schoodic.org).

Ocean Wood Campground (☎ 207-963-7194, *Schoodic Point Loop Rd*) Sites $15-30. This pine-filled campground is south of Birch Harbor and ME 186 and has ocean access.

GREAT WASS ISLAND

At the southern tip of the peninsula, just over 4 miles from Jonesport, Great Wass Island is a 1540-acre nature reserve under the control of the Nature Conservancy (☎ 207-729-5181, W www.tnc.org). In order to keep the reserve for those who appreciate it most, the way to it is not well marked, and parking at the trailhead is limited – but the cars parked there bear license plates from many different states. This is a bird-watching reserve for the cognoscenti.

To find it, follow ME 187 into Jonesport. Look for the Union Trust Bank on the left and Tall Barney's Restaurant on the right. Turn left here onto Bridge St, cross the bridge and turn left. A little more than a mile farther on, cross the small, inconspicuous bridge that connects Beals Island to Great Wass Island and turn right; a small sign ('Nature Conservancy') points the way. A mile later, the paved road ends, and after another 1½ miles on an unpaved road, you come to the Great Wass Island parking lot. It is capable of holding about a dozen cars. A sign advises that if the parking lot is full, you should not park on the road, but go away and come back some other time.

The reserve's attraction is its rocky coastal scenery, peat bogs, a large stand of jack pines, and bird life, including the amusing puffins. If time permits, take the 2-mile hike to Little Cape Point (about 1½ to two hours roundtrip).

Jonesport and **Beals Island** are traditional Maine fishing and lobstering villages. Even the street signs show it: Each one is topped with a carving of a Maine lobster boat.

The towns get a smattering of the more discerning tourists during the season, most of whom come to take photographs, paint pictures and walk on Great Wass Island. Follow ME 187 to find most of these towns' services, including restaurants and lodgings.

Henry Point Campground (☎ 207-497-5926, *Campground Rd*) Tent/RV sites $12/15.

On the point in Jonesport, this is a simple campground, with only portable toilets, picnic tables and one big stone fireplace, but it's surrounded by water and the semi-shaded sites have fine Maine coast views. To find it, from ME 187 go southeast on Kelley Point Rd, and thereafter, when in doubt, bear right.

Jonesport By-the-Sea B&B (☎ 207-497-2590, W www.jonesportbythesea.bigstep.com, *Main St/ME 187*) Rooms $60-75. Across from the post office, this B&B has five homey, comfortable rooms, some with private bath.

Raspberry Shores B&B (☎ 207-497-2463, W www.jonesportmaine.com, *ME 187, Jonesport*) Doubles $75 with breakfast. This is a private home with two rooms. You can also rent kayaks ($48) and bikes ($25) by the day.

Harbor House on Sawyer Cove (☎ 207-497-5417, W www.harborhs.com, *Sawyer Square, Jonesport*) Rooms $95-110. This is an oldtime-Maine cafe and antique shop with two rooms overlooking the harbor.

THE MACHIASES

Although Machias prime hosts a branch of the University of Maine, it's an ugly, dead place. However, its beautiful neighbors, East Machias and Machiasport, comprised the location where the first naval engagement of the Revolutionary War took place. When the king received the Declaration of Independence from the colonies, he decided to send a frigate to Machiasport to monitor the timely collection and transportation of lumber to Portland to build his majesty's ships. A few drunken American colonists at **Burnham Tavern**, which is now a museum (☎ 207-255-4432, *Main St, East Machias; open 9am-5pm Mon-Fri May-August*), decided to pay the frigate a visit on their sloop and ended up killing the English captain with a single shot to the head. They then emptied the ship and burned it on the shores of Jonesport. The king's reaction to this act of rebellion was to have his troops torch Portland.

Also worth seeing is the **Jasper Beach**, one of two in the world (the other one is in

Japan). Down Machias Rd toward the village of Starboard lies this bizarre mile-long beach consisting entirely of polished red jasper stones. Listen to their strange song as the tide comes in.

The Machias Bay Area Chamber of Commerce (☎ 207-255-4402, ⓦ www.nemaine .com/mbacc, PO Box 606, US 1, Machias, ME 04654-0606) provides information. It is next to Moore's Restaurant on the western edge of town.

In Machias, numerous basic motels line US 1. East Machias and Machiasport have some nice B&Bs, as those towns are a lot more serene.

Margaretta Motel (☎ *207-255-6671, US 1*) Singles/doubles $40/56. This basic motel with 14 rooms is on US 1.

Machias Motor Inn (☎ *207-255-4861, 26 E Maine St/US 1*) Singles/doubles $62/66. Next to the landmark Helen's Restaurant, this place has 35 rooms overlooking the Machias River and has an indoor heated pool.

Captain Cates B&B (☎ *207-255-8812,* ⓦ *www.captaincates.com, Phinney Lane/ ME 92, Machiasport*) Rooms $60-110 with breakfast. Overlooking Machias Bay, this 1850s B&B has six comfortable rooms with period antiques and shared bath.

Riverside Inn & Restaurant (☎ *207-255-4134,* ⓦ *www.riversideinn-maine.com, US 1, East Machias*) Rooms with bath $69-95. Includes breakfast. Situated less than 5 miles east of Machias' center, this is a large inn comprising four guest rooms. The inn's *restaurant* has a good dinner menu. Full dinners cost $17 to $22; bring your own wine or beer.

Joyce's Lobster House (☎ *207-255-3015, US 1, East Machias*) Mains $6-18. This tidy place is popular, with brisk, friendly service. Lobster is served boiled, sautéd or stuffed. Simpler dishes, such as spaghetti with home-made meat sauce, are cheaper, but in any case, a dinner need cost only $10 to $20. Bring your own wine or beer.

LUBEC

Perched upon a hill overlooking four (!) lighthouses and Canada, the small fishing village of Lubec makes its living off the transborder traffic and a bit of tourism. Away from the crowds and traffic of Acadia National Park and points south, this is the real Downeast Maine. There's an informal **information office** in the foyer of the Eastland Motel, which is on the left-hand side of ME 189 as you roll into town.

Lubec is about as far east as you can go and still be in the USA. People like to watch the sun rise at **Quoddy Head State Park** ($1 per person) so they can say they were the first in the country to see it. The 531-acre park's trademark red-and-white-banded West Quoddy Light (1858) is its most photographed feature, but the volcanic bedrock, the subarctic bogland and extreme tides – almost 16 feet in six hours – are really more interesting. The four hiking trails vary in length from a few hundred feet to 4 miles. Also, you can usually spot finback, minke, humpback and right whales as they migrate here in summer.

In the 1930s, Lubec was the fish-canning capital of the eastern USA. The canneries are now long gone; to see how it was done, drop by **The Old Sardine Village Museum** (*no* ☎ *; adult/teenager/child $5/4/free; open from 1pm to 5pm Tues-Sat, Sun from 1pm to 4pm June-Sept*).

Once beyond Lubec, you're in Canada, specifically on Campobello Island, home to **Roosevelt Campobello International Park** (☎ *506-752-2922, admission free; open 9am-5pm daily*). Franklin Roosevelt's father, James, bought land here in 1883 and built a palatial summer 'cottage.' The future US president spent many boyhood summers here, and he was later given the 34-room cottage. Franklin and Eleanor made brief, but well-publicized, visits during his long tenure as president.

The park hours are given in Maine time (10am to 6pm New Brunswick time). Border formalities are quick and easy for American citizens in cars with US license plates who are crossing into Canada just to visit the park. Travelers from other countries should have their passports (and may need visas) to cross into Canada. The Campobello Island Chamber of Commerce

MAINE

(☎ 506-752-2233) can provide information on island services.

Off US 1 at the end of ME 189, Lubec is on the US's easternmost border with Canada. Lubec is 60 miles south of Calais and 88 miles northeast of Mount Desert Island. If you're going farther in Canada, pick up Lonely Planet's *Canada*.

South Bay Campground (☎ *207-733-2150,* Ⓦ *www.nemaine.com/southbay, ME 189*) Tent sites $15/20, RV sites $25. Just 7½ miles off US 1, this campground has 80 wooded and open field sites as well as a sea-kayak landing.

Eastland Motel (☎ *207-733-5501, ME 189*) Rooms $54-64. A mile west of Lubec on ME 189, this motel has simple but serviceable rooms with two double beds or a queen bed.

Peacock House (☎ *207-733-2403,* Ⓦ *www .peacockhouse.com, 27 Summer St*) Singles $60-70 with breakfast, doubles $70-80 with breakfast. Peacock House was built in 1860 by an English sea captain. Restored in 1989, it's now a fine B&B with five rooms.

Home Port Inn (☎ *207-733-2077, 800-457-2077,* Ⓦ *www.homeportinn.com, 45 Main St*) Doubles with bath $75-95 with breakfast. This hilltop inn was constructed in 1880 and it has been an inn since 1982. It has seven excellent rooms. The ***dining room*** serves fine dinners for $20 to $30.

Murphy's (☎ *207-733-2400, ME 189*) Mains $3-10. If you're up early, this local favorite is the place to go for breakfast.

Phinney Seaview Restaurant (☎ *207-733-0941, ME 189*) Mains $6-17. For lunch and dinner, try the Phinney Seaview for great, fresh seafood.

CALAIS

Farther north of Lubec along US 1, Calais (pronounced 'callous') is a twin town to St Stephen, New Brunswick, Canada. During the War of 1812, when the USA and Britain (including Canada) were at war, these two remote outposts of nationalism ignored the distant battles. Their citizens were so closely linked by blood and strong family ties that politics – even war – was ignored.

The town has some interesting houses – some of them in a 'gingerbread' style – along a pink US 1 (pink granite was mined in Calais). For more information, contact the tourist information office (☎ 207-454-2211, Ⓦ www.visitcalais.com, 7 Union St).

St Stephen is the gateway to Atlantic Canada, which is covered in Lonely Planet's *Canada*.

Southwest of Calais, **Moosehorn National Wildlife Refuge** (☎ *207-454-7161, US 1, Baring; open every day during daylight; admission free*) is America's easternmost breeding ground for migratory fowl – including America's national bird, the bald eagle. With binoculars you can spot numerous nests of these white-headed birds of prey.

Western Lakes & Mountains

Western Maine is far less visited than is coastal Maine. This suits the outdoorsy types who love western Maine the way it is. The fine old town of Bethel and the outdoor pleasures of the Rangeley Lakes are relatively accessible to city-dwellers in Boston, Providence and New York, and even closer to the outdoor playground of the White Mountain National Forest in New Hampshire and in Maine.

The mountains of western Maine yield an abundance of gemstones, such as amethyst, aquamarine and tourmaline. Keep your eye open for **gem shops**, or pick up their brochures at the chamber of commerce information office.

SEBAGO LAKE

Sebago, a mere 15 miles northwest of Portland, is among Maine's largest and most accessible lakes. There are some small settlements along the eastern shore of the lake, best reached by US 302 from Portland. The town of Sebago Lake, at the lake's southern end, is small and sleepy. Along the western shore, at East Sebago, are a few inns and cabins for rent.

At the northern tip of the lake, southeast of Naples, is *Sebago Lake State Park* (☎ *207-693-6613)*, which offers camping, picnicking, swimming, boating and fishing.

SABBATHDAY LAKE

Take I-495 exit 11, then ME 26 to reach the town of Sabbathday Lake, 30 miles north of Portland, near the lake of the same name. Sabbathday has the nation's only active Shaker community. It was founded in the 18th century, and a small number of devotees (perhaps four or five) keep the Shaker tradition of prayer, simple living, hard work and fine artistry alive.

Among the plain white, well-kept buildings of the community are a welcome center, museum and a shop selling the community's crafts. Most other buildings, including the impressive Brick Dwelling House, are not open to visitors.

A few miles to the north is the village of Poland Spring, famous for its mineral water, which is now sold throughout the USA. In the early 19th century, a visitor was miraculously cured by drinking water from Poland Spring. Not known to miss a good thing, the locals opened hotels to cater to those wanting to take the waters.

BETHEL

For a small farm town surrounded by Maine woods, Bethel, 63 miles northwest of Portland via ME 26, is surprisingly beautiful and refined. It's a prime spot to be during Maine's colorful fall foliage season (mid-September to mid-October) and during ski season (winter). Part of its backwoods sophistication comes from its being the home of Gould Academy, a well-regarded prep school founded in 1836.

The town is small enough that you can find your way around easily. The Bethel Area Chamber of Commerce (☎ 207-824-2282, W www.bethelmaine.com, 30 Cross St) maintains an information office in the Bethel Station building near the big Norway Savings Bank. The Maine Information Office and the White Mountain National Forest Information Office (both ☎ 207-824-2134, 18 Mayville Rd/US 2) are opposite the Norway Savings Bank.

Dr Moses Mason House

Stop by the Dr Moses Mason House (☎ *207-824-2908, 14 Broad St; admission $3; open 1pm-4pm Tues-Sun July & Aug)* for a look at the house of Dr Mason (1789–1866), a prominent local physician and state representative. The house is now the museum and research library of the Bethel Historical Society.

Summer Activities

There's golf at the Bethel Inn (see below) and scenic drives and hiking in the nearby forests. The **Mt Will Trail** starts from US 2, east of Bethel, and ascends to mountain ledges with fine views of the Androscoggin Valley. **Grafton Notch State Park**, north of Bethel via ME 26, has hiking trails and pretty waterfalls, but no camping. Try the 1½-mile trail up to Table Rock Overlook, or the walk to Eyebrow Loop and Cascade Falls, with excellent picnic possibilities right by the falls.

If you head west on US 2 toward New Hampshire, be sure to admire the **Shelburne birches**, a high concentration of the white-barked trees that grow between Gilead and Shelburne.

At **Bethel Outdoor Adventure & Campground** (☎ *207-824-4224, 800-533-3607, 121 Mayville Rd/US 2)* you can rent a canoe, kayak or bicycle and arrange lessons, guided trips and shuttles to and from the Androscoggin River. **Wild River Adventures** (☎ *207-824-2608, 288 Vernon St)* offers similar services.

Mahoosuc Mountain Sports (☎ *207-875-3786, ME 26, Locke Mills)* rents mountain bikes and road bikes for excursions into the nearby countryside.

Skiing

The mountains near Bethel are home to several major New England ski resorts. For information on cross-country skiing opportunities, contact the Maine Nordic Ski Council (☎ 800-754-9263, W www.mnsc .com).

Mt Abram (☎ 207-875-5003, W *www .skimtabram.com, Howe Hill Rd, Locke Mills)* is a small, reasonably priced ski area (35 trails) just southeast of Bethel. It is good for families.

Sunday River Ski Resort (☎ 207-824-3000, W *www.sundayriver.com, Sunday River Rd, Bethel),* 6 miles north of Bethel along ME 5/26, boasts eight mountain peaks and 120 trails. It's regarded as one of the best family ski destinations in the region.

Places to Stay

For its small size, Bethel has a surprising number of places to stay, which testifies to its importance as a crossroads town at the junction of routes between the Maine coast, northern Maine and New Hampshire. The Bethel Chamber of Commerce operates the Bethel Area Reservations Service (☎ 800-442-5826), which will help you find a room if you need one. Lists of accommodations and links to their websites can be found at W www.bethelmaine.com/staySet.shtml.

Camping There are five simple public campgrounds, with well water and toilets, in the Maine portion of the White Mountains National Forest: *Basin Pond*, *Cold River*, *Crocker Pond*, *Hastings* and *Wild River*. Site prices vary. For information, contact the Evans Notch Visitor Center (☎ 207-824-2134, 18 Mayville Rd/US 2).

Pleasant River Campground (☎ 207-836-2000, fax 207-836-2058, US 2, West Bethel) Sites $16-22. Pleasant River has 75 sites beneath fragrant pines.

Stony Brook Recreation (☎ 207-824-2836, US 2, Hanover) Sites $16-22. With 100 acres of forest along the Androscoggin River, this great site is north of Bethel and just east of Newry.

Motels Bethel has one motel in the town center, but most are along US 2 to the north.

Bethel Spa Motel (☎ 207-824-2989, 800-882-0293, 88 Main St) Rooms $50. In the center of town, this motel has basic, inexpensive rooms.

Norseman Inn & Motel (☎ 207-824-2002, fax 207-824-0640, 134 Mayville Rd/US 2)

Motel rooms $40-89, inn rooms $68-149. Here you can choose between rooms in a 200-year-old inn and a renovated century-old barn, or rooms in the more modern (and air-conditioned) motel.

Inn at the Rostay (☎ 207-824-3111, US 2) Doubles $45-108. Just north of Bethel, this spartan motel has 18 simple rooms.

Inns & B&Bs Breakfast is included at the following places, and the prices given are for the summer. In winter during the ski season, prices are higher; ask about ski and meal packages when you call to make winter reservations.

The Chapman Inn (☎ 207-824-2657, 877-359-1498, 1 Mill Hill Rd) Dorm beds $25, rooms $49-59. Among the nicest, most economical and best-located lodgings, the Chapman Inn is on the common. It has a 24-bed dormitory and nine rooms for singles, couples and families; the cheaper rooms have shared baths.

Douglass Place (☎ 207-824-2229, 162 Mayville Rd/US 2) Singles/doubles $60/70. This 1813 farm, run by a sweet old lady, has four guest rooms that share 2½ baths.

Sudbury Inn & Suds Pub (☎ 207-824-2174, 800-395-7837, 151 Main St) Rooms with bath $69-99. This is the town's unofficial social center, with 16 guest rooms, a restaurant and pub in a late-19th-century Victorian house. The simple but attractive rooms are in the inn and adjacent carriage house.

Abbott House (☎ 207-824-7600, 800-240-2377, 170 Walkers Mills Rd/ME 26) Rooms without bath $69-132 with full breakfast. On ME 26, and more than two centuries old, Abbott House has five rooms, sharing two baths.

Briar Lea B&B (☎ 207-824-4717, 877-311-1299, 150 Mayville Rd/US 2) Rooms $73-83 with breakfast. Briar Lea is a 150-year-old Georgian farmhouse with a variety of rooms and a full gourmet breakfast.

Holidae House B&B (☎ 207-824-3400, 800-882-3306, 85 Main St) Rooms $90-100. This Victorian has two intimate rooms with private bath; a studio apartment and a three-bedroom apartment.

Resorts At *River View Resort* (☎ *207-824-2808, 357 Mayville Rd)*, suites are $93-200 for 2 people ($10 each additional person). The River View has 32 very comfortable, modern, two-bedroom suites with fully equipped kitchens, a tennis court, spa, sauna and game room. The suites can sleep up to five people.

Bethel Inn & Country Club (☎ *207-824-2175, 800-654-0125, Broad St)* Inn rooms $259-379, luxury suites $359-419. This establishment dominates the town common. It has full resort facilities, including an 18-hole golf course designed by Geoffrey Cornish, a golf school, tennis, an outdoor heated swimming pool, saunas, workout and game rooms, a lake boathouse and numerous other facilities, all set on manicured grounds. Rates depend on when you come, how long you stay and which of the several degrees of luxury you choose, but all rates include breakfast and dinner. The 57 inn rooms are the lowest in price, the luxury suites the most expensive, with a variety of choices in between these.

Places to Eat
Bethel doesn't have a lot of restaurants, but surprisingly good vegetarian dishes are available at most of them for lunch and dinner.

Briar Lea B&B (☎ *207-824-4717, 150 Mayville Rd/US 2)* Breakfast $4-10. For a formal crystal-and-linen breakfast, head here, where breakfast is the main event as far as meals are concerned.

Cafe DiCocoa (☎ *207-824-5282, 125 Main St)* Lunch $7-11. This cafe features good coffee (and espresso), whole-grain baked goods and vegetarian lunches that are also available to go. It opens early for breakfast.

Mother's (☎ *207-824-2589, 43 Main St)* Lunch $7-12, dinner $8-14. Mother's is a local favorite, with an innovative menu, decent prices and even nice outdoor seating in good weather.

Sunday River Brewing Company (☎ *207-824-4253, cnr US 2 & Sunday River Rd)* Lunch $8-12, dinner $14-25. This is Bethel's brewpub, featuring a half -dozen of its own brews (from a light golden lager to a black

porter), as well as a variety of sandwiches, steaks, barbecued meats and vegetarian plates for lunch and dinner.

Sudbury Inn (☎ *207-824-2174, 151 Main St)* Mains $14-21. This inn has a cozy dining room and an excellent menu. Expect to pay $20 to $40 for dinner. The *Suds Pub*, downstairs from the dining room, has a tavern menu (with great pizzas!), a huge selection of draft and bottled beers (many from Maine microbreweries) and live entertainment some nights.

Getting There & Away
Bethel has a small airport (☎ 207-824-4321) with a paved 3150-foot runway, if you want to fly in with your own plane.

From either the Bethel Airport or the Portland International Jetport, you can drive or use the Bethel Express Corporation (☎ 207-824-4646). Its 11-passenger vans will take you to or from Bethel for $6 or Portland for $75.

RANGELEY LAKES
Along the 67 miles from Bethel via US 2 and ME 17 to Rangeley Lake, the road climbs through country that's exceptionally beautiful – even for Maine. During the early 20th century, the lakes in this region were dotted with vast frame hotels and peopled with vacationers from Boston, New York and Philadelphia. Though most of the great hotels are gone – victims of changed economics and vacation preferences – the reasons for spending time here remain.

The staff at Rangeley Lakes Chamber of Commerce (☎ 207-864-5571, 800-685-2537, W www.rangeleymaine.com, Main St, Rangeley) can answer questions.

Skiing
The mountains around Rangeley offer a few skiing and snowboarding options.

Sugarloaf/USA (☎ *207-237-2000, 800-843-5623,* W *www.sugarloaf.com, ME 16, Kingfield)* is good for downhill skiing and snowboarding. It has lifts that take you above tree line.

Sugarloaf Ski Touring Center (☎ *207-237-6830), ME 27/ME 16, Carrabassett Valley)*,

MAINE

near Sugarloaf/USA, has 136 miles of groomed trails.

Saddleback Ski Area (☎ 207-864-5671, Ⓦ www.saddlebackskiarea.com, Rangeley), at 4120 feet, has 40 alpine ski trails with seven lifts and three T-bars. Call for lodging information.

Places to Stay
In the village of Rangeley proper, a few vestiges of the region's early-20th-century heyday remain.

Rangeley Inn & Motor Lodge (☎ 207-864-3341, 800-666-3687, Ⓦ www.rangeley inn.com, 51 Main St) Rooms $84-119. Built in 1907, this spacious motel still hosts guests in its 35 inn rooms and 15 motel rooms.

Country Club Inn (☎ 207-864-3831, Ⓦ www.countryclubinn.com, 1 Country Club Dr) Rooms $108 with breakfast. Off ME 4, the Country Club Inn, which has 20 rooms with views of Rangeley Lake, is right next to the public golf course.

North Country B&B (☎ 207-864-2440, Ⓦ www.northcountrybb.com, Main St) Rooms $85-95 with breakfast. Constructed by Rangeley's first multimillionaire, this gorgeous 1912 house – which faces the town park and lake – was a speakeasy during America's Prohibition days (such sad days, they were…).

North Woods

On a map, it appears as though the farther north you go in Maine, the fewer roads there are. You'd think this is trackless wilderness. In fact, this vast area is owned by large paper companies that harvest timber for their paper mills. The land is crisscrossed by a matrix of rough logging roads. Logs used to be floated down the region's many rivers, but this practice increased the tannin levels in the rivers and threatened the ecological balance. Roads came with the advent of the internal combustion engine.

Now that the logs are out of the rivers, white-water rafters are in them. The **Kennebec River**, below the Harris Hydroelectric

Station, passes through a dramatic 12-mile gorge that's among the US's prime rafting places. Outflow from the hydroelectric station is controlled, which means that there is always water, and the periodic big releases make for more exciting rafting.

The Kennebec Valley Tourism Council (☎ 800-393-8629, Ⓦ www.kennebecvalley .org, 179 Main St, Waterville, ME 04901) will help with information.

Maine sporting camps, those remote forest outposts for hunters, fishers and other deep-woods types, still flourish in the most remote regions. For information, contact the Maine Sporting Camp Association (ⓔ msca @midmaine.com, Ⓦ www.mainesporting camps.com, PO Box 119, Millinocket, ME 04462).

CARATUNK & THE FORKS
These villages, south of Jackman via US 201, are both at the center of the Kennebec rafting area. White-water rafting trips down the Kennebec and nearby rivers are wonderful adventures. Trips cost from $80 to $115 per person and are suitable for everyone from children (ages eight and older) to seniors in their '70s. No experience is necessary for many trips.

Reserve your rafting trip in advance and bring a bathing suit, wool or polar fleece sweater, windbreaker or rain suit. Avoid cotton clothing (such as T-shirts and jeans), because cotton dries slowly and will make you feel cold; synthetics are better. Wear more clothing than you think you'll need, and bring a towel to dry off with and a dry change of clothes for the end of the trip. Sneakers or other soft-soled footwear are required in the inflatable rafts. Before June 30th and after September 1st, you may be required to have a wetsuit for the trip because of the cold water temperature. Rafting companies often rent the suits and booties.

The rafting company supplies the raft, paddles, life vest, helmet, life preserver and first-aid kit. There will be a pre-trip orientation meeting with instruction about rafting and white-water safety. Your rafting company usually provides lunch (often grilled on the riverbank) as well.

Numerous companies will make arrangements for your rafting trip and for lodging on the Kennebec, Dead or Penobscot Rivers. Trips range in difficulty from Class II (easy enough for children ages eight and older) to Class V (intense, difficult rapids, minimum age 15).

Most rafting companies have agreements with local lodgings (inns, dormitories and campgrounds) for your accommodations. Ask about their inclusive rafting packages.

Here are some rafting companies to contact:

Crab Apple Whitewater
(☎ 207-663-4491, 800-553-7238, W www.crab appleinc.com, HC 63, Box 25, The Forks, ME 04985)
Runs trips on rivers in western Massachusetts as well.

Maine Whitewater
(☎ 800-345-6246, W www.mainewhitewater.com, PO Box 633, Bingham, ME 04920)

New England Outdoor Center
(☎ 207-723-5438, 800-766-7238, W www.neoc.com, PO Box 669, Millinocket, ME 04462)
Runs canoe trips on the Allagash Wilderness Waterway as well.

Northern Outdoors
(☎ 207-663-4466, 800-765-7238, W www.northern outdoors.com, PO Box 100, The Forks, ME 04985)
Runs rafting, mountain-biking, fishing and sea-kayaking trips in Maine and other areas.

Professional River Runners of Maine
(☎ 207-663-2229, 800-325-3911, W www.proriver runners.com, PO Box 92, West Forks, ME 04985)
Runs rafting trips on these and other rivers in the eastern US as well.

Three Rivers Whitewater, Inc, The Forks
(☎ 800-786-6878, W www.threeriverswhite water.com, PO Box 10, West Forks, ME 04985)
Runs rafting trips on the Rapid River as well.

Inn by the River (☎ 207-663-2181, W *www .innbytheriver.com, US 201; HCR 63, Box 24, West Forks, ME 04985)* Rooms with bath $65-120 with breakfast. This modern lodge overlooks the river and has very comfortable rooms.

ONWARD TO QUEBEC CITY

North of the Kennebec Valley, US 201 heads through Jackman to the Canadian border. Continuing as QC 173, the road makes its way directly through the lush farm country of the St Lawrence Valley to Quebec City, 111 miles from Jackman and 280 miles from Portland.

Moose Point Tavern (☎ 207-668-4012, W *www.moosepointtavern.com, Jackman)* Cabins $45 per person, canoe rental included. If you want to stay on a lake 'way the hell up there' and canoe on your way to Canada, then this is the place. Run by the president of the Maine Tourism Association, Carolann Oulette, Moose Point Tavern rents log cabin efficiencies with unsurpassed views of Big Wood Lake and has a superb restaurant. Reserve in advance and inquire about weekly rates. For information on travel in Canada, get a copy of Lonely Planet's *Canada*.

MOOSEHEAD LAKE

North of the town of Greenville, Moosehead Lake is huge. In fact, it is the largest lake completely contained within any one New England state (Lake Champlain is bigger, but is split between Vermont, New York and Canada). This is lumber and backwoods country, which is what makes Greenville the region's largest seaplane station. The pontoon planes will take you even deeper into the Maine woods for fishing trips or on lumber company business.

For information about the region, contact the Moosehead Lake Region Chamber of Commerce (☎ 207-695-2702, W www .mooseheadlake.org, 1029 Central St/ME 157, Greenville). Though once a bustling summer resort, Greenville has reverted to a backwoods outpost. A few of the old summer hotels survive, but most of the visitors today are camping or heading through on their way to Baxter State Park and Mt Katahdin.

Make a brief visit to the *SS Katahdin* (☎ 207-695-2716, W *www.katahdincruises .com)* Adult/senior/child $20/18/12. This is a 115-foot steamboat built in 1914, owned and

MAINE

maintained by the Moosehead Marine Museum. It still makes the rounds (three-hour cruise) of the lake from Greenville's center in summer, just as it did in Greenville's heyday. The lake's colorful history is preserved in the museum. Call for schedules as they're quite complicated.

BAXTER STATE PARK

Mt Katahdin (5267 feet), Maine's tallest mountain and the northern end of the 2000-mile-long **Appalachian Trail**, is the centerpiece of Baxter State Park, which has 46 other mountain peaks, 1200 campsites and 180 miles of hiking trails as well. It offers the wildest, most unspoiled wilderness adventures in New England, and Katahdin has a reputation for being a real rock climber's mountain.

Despite its relative inaccessibility – deep in the Maine woods over unpaved roads – Baxter hosts over 100,000 visitors annually, mostly during its summer season from mid-May through mid-October. It's open December through March for winter activities as well.

To fully enjoy Baxter State Park, you must arrive at the park entrance early in the day (only so many visitors are allowed in on any given day), and you should be well equipped for camping and perhaps for hiking and canoeing. *Campsites* ($6 per person per night) in the park must be reserved well in advance by contacting Baxter State Park (☎ *207-723-5140*, ☒ *www .mainerec.com/baxter1.html, 64 Balsam Dr, Millinocket, ME 04462)*. You might also want to get some information from the Maine Appalachian Trail Club (☒ www .matc.org, PO Box 283, Augusta, ME 04330) and the Katahdin Area Chamber of Commerce (☎ 207-723-4443, 1029 Central St, Millinocket, ME 04462). It costs $8 per day per person to be in the park.

If you are unable to get a reservation at one of the park's campsites, you can usually find a site at one of the private campgrounds just outside the Togue Ponds and Matagamon gates into the park. There are several in Medway (just off I-95 exit 56), in Millinocket and in Greenville.

Medway is at I-95 exit 56, Millinocket is about 11 miles northwest, and the southern border of Baxter State Park is about 20 miles northwest from Millinocket. From Greenville, if you have 4WD, take Lily Bay Rd to Kokadjo, where the road becomes a dirt logging one (Sias Hill Rd). Take this until you get to the end and make a right on paved Golden Road. This is a gorgeous drive, and you're likely to see moose in streams if you're on Golden Road toward dusk. However, be careful; these are logging roads! Humongous log trucks can be dangerous when coming around those bends.

AROOSTOOK COUNTY

Home to the original Acadians, for whom the national park was named, Aroostook County is huge, covering more than 6400 sq miles, which makes it larger than the states of Connecticut and Rhode Island combined. 'The county,' as it's called, has more than 2000 lakes, ponds, streams and rivers. The western half of the county is mostly deep forest owned by the timber and paper companies; it's also home to the Allagash Wilderness Waterway (☎ 207-941-4014, ☒ www.state.me.us/doc/prkslnds/alla.htm), a protected natural area with 92 miles of ponds, lakes and north-flowing rivers, which makes it a prime site for canoe trips. The long eastern half, however, is good farming country, though the growing season is short – perfect for raising potatoes. The people of Aroostook County take advantage of this fact by producing 1½ million tons of potatoes every year.

If you're into potatoes or forests, Aroostook is heaven. Sit down at a restaurant in Houlton, Presque Isle or Madawaska and you'll find potatoes on the menu in all sorts of original ways. The names of the many varieties of the noble spud *(Solanum tuberosum)* – Kennebec, Katahdin, Norchip, Superior, Ontario, Russet Burbank, Norgold Russet – are bandied about by the locals over breakfast.

Unless you're in the business, the fascination provided by tubers fades fast. You may well find Aroostook to be a pretty place to pass through on your way elsewhere.

I-95 ends at Houlton, on the border with the Canadian province of New Brunswick. NB 95 continues on the other side and links you to CN 2, the Trans-Canada Highway.

From Houlton, US 1 goes north to Presque Isle, Caribou and Van Buren before crossing into New Brunswick. You can continue on NB 17 to Campbellton and Quebec's beautiful Gaspé Peninsula, or head northwest on CN 185 (the Trans-Canada), to Rivière-du-Loup, Quebec, then southwest up the St Lawrence to Quebec City. The fastest route from Maine to Quebec City is I-95 to Fairfield, just north of Winslow, then US 201 north via Skowhegan, Bingham, the Kennebec Valley and Jack-

man. But this way you don't get to see several thousand square miles of potatoes.

There are various local information offices, including Aroostook County Tourism ( www.nmtc.net/thecounty.htm). Area chambers of commerce include the following:

Caribou
 (☎ 207-498-6156, http://cariboumaine.org)

Houlton
 (☎ 207-532-4216, W www.houlton.com)

Presque Isle
 (☎ 207-764-6561, W www.presqueisle.net)

Van Buren
 (☎ 207-868-5059, W www.vanburenmaine.com)

MAINE

Glossary

For a hilarious and informative look at Boston dialect, browse Adam Gaffin's site at Ⓦ www.boston-online.com/wickedv.html.

Abenaki – a New England Native American tribe

alpine slide – a concrete chute navigated for fun on a simple wheeled cart or, if it's a water slide, on an inflatable cushion

AMC – Appalachian Mountain Club

ayuh – locution pronounced by some people in New Hampshire and Maine during pauses in conversation; perhaps a distant variant of 'yes'; vaguely positive in meaning

Back Bay – a district of Boston west of Beacon Hill and Boston Common developed during the 19th century by filling in a bay in the Charles River

batholith – a mass of rock formed deep in the earth, later perhaps thrust to the surface; they are customarily of large-crystalled rock (such as granite) and appear as mountainous domes of rock above surrounding terrain of softer material (as Mt Monadnock in southern New Hampshire)

boondocks or **boonies** – a city-dweller's derogatory term for the countryside, especially a remote rural place, as in 'The inn is nice, but it's way out in the boonies'

Brahmin – member of Boston's wealthy, well-educated, 19th-century class; now, any wealthy, cultured Bostonian

BYO or **BYOB** – 'bring your own' or 'bring your own bottle'; designates a restaurant that allows patrons to bring their own wine or beer; see *dry town*

Cape, the – Cape Cod

CCC – Civilian Conservation Corps, the Depression-era federal program established in 1933 to employ unskilled young workers, mainly on projects aimed at the conservation of US wildlands

CCNS – Cape Cod National Seashore

chandlery – retail shop specializing in yachting equipment

cobble – a high rocky knoll of limestone, marble or quartzite that is found in western Massachusetts

cod cheeks – soft oyster-like bits of meat found on the sides of a codfish's 'face'; a delicacy, along with cod tongues, in some parts of New England and Atlantic Canada

common – see *green*

DAR – Daughters of the American Revolution, a patriotic service organization for women

Downeast – the Maine coast, especially its more easterly reaches, roughly from Mt Desert Island to Eastport

drumlin – a low, elongated hill formed of glacial till (earth and rock debris) during the most recent Ice Age; a common feature of the terrain in New England

dry town – a town in which municipal ordinances prohibit the sale (but usually not the possession, consumption or service) of alcoholic beverages

efficiency (unit) – a hotel or motel room with cooking and dining facilities (hot plate or range, refrigerator, sink, utensils, crockery and cutlery); see also *housekeeping cabin/unit, kitchenette*

Equity playhouse – 'Actors' Equity' is the US actors' union; Equity actors are professionals, members of the union

gap – mountain pass with steep sides; called a 'notch' in New Hampshire

gimcrack – a small item of uncertain use, perhaps frivolous; a gizmo

glacial pond – a deep, round freshwater pond formed by glacial gouging action during the Ice Age; a common feature of the New England terrain (such as Walden Pond in Concord, Massachusetts)

green – the grass-covered open space typically found at the center of a traditional New England village or town, originally used as common pastureland ('the common'), but now serving as a central park;

often surrounded by community service buildings such as the town hall, library, court house and churches

grinder – a large sandwich of meat, cheese, lettuce, tomato, dressing, etc, in a long bread roll; also called a 'sporkie' or, in other parts of the US, a 'submarine,' 'po' boy,' 'Cuban' or 'hoagie'

hidden drive – a driveway entering a road in such a way that visibility for approaching drivers is impaired; signs warn of them

hookup – a facility at an RV camping site for connecting (hooking up) a vehicle to electricity, water, sewer or even cable TV

housekeeping cabin/unit – a hotel or motel room or detached housing unit equipped with kitchen facilities, rented by the day, week or month; see *efficiency, kitchenette*

Indian summer – a brief warm period, usually in late autumn, before the cold weather sets in for the winter

ironclad – a 19th-century wooden warship with iron sheathing

Islands, the – Martha's Vineyard and Nantucket off Cape Cod

kitchenette – a small, but adequately equipped, food preparation area in an efficiency or housekeeping unit; see *efficiency, housekeeping cabin/unit*

leaf-peeping – recreational touring (by 'leaf-peepers') to enjoy autumn foliage colors

lean-to – a simple shelter for camping, usually without walls, windows or doors, with a steeply slanting roof touching the ground on one side

lobster roll – a hot dog bun or other bread roll filled with lobster meat in a mayonnaise sauce and sometimes dressed with celery and lettuce

Lower (or Outer) Cape – the long, narrow extension of Cape Cod north and east from Orleans to Provincetown

maple – a tree of the genus *Acer* having lobed leaves, winged seeds borne in pairs and close-grained wood, well suited to making furniture and flooring; the sap of the sugar maple *(Acer saccharum)* is gathered, boiled and reduced to make maple syrup; see *sugar bush, sugaring off*

Mid-Cape – region of Cape Cod roughly from Barnstable and Hyannis eastward to Orleans

minuteman – a colonial militiaman pledged to be ready at a moment's notice to defend his home and village; originally organized against Native American attacks, the minutemen provided the first organized American military force in the Revolutionary War against British troops

mud time – springtime in New England when the snow melts and the earth thaws

NPS – National Park Service, a division of the Dept of the Interior that administers US national parks and monuments

OSV – Old Sturbridge Village, Massachusetts

P-Town – Provincetown, on Cape Cod, Massachusetts

package store – liquor store

raw bar – a counter where fresh uncooked shellfish (clams, oysters, etc) is served

rush tickets – sometimes called 'student rush' or 'rush seats,' these are discounted tickets bought at a theater or concert hall box office usually no more than an hour or two before a performance

sachem – Native American chieftain; Massasoit was sachem of the Wampanoag tribe

sagamon – similar to *sachem*

shire town – county seat, town holding county government buildings

shopping center – a collection of stores bordering a huge parking lot; stores usually include a large department or food store, plus smaller ones such as hairdressers, laundromat/dry cleaners and fast-food restaurants

shopping mall – or just 'mall,' a large, climate-controlled building surrounded by parking lots or built above a parking garage and sheltering several large stores, many small shops and a few restaurants

soaring – term for glider (sailplane) rides
Southie – South Boston, a neighborhood inhabited largely by Bostonians of Irish descent with a strong sense of Irish identity
sugar bush – a grove of sugar maple trees; see *maple*
sugaring off – the springtime (March) harvest of sap from maple trees, which is collected and boiled to reduce it to maple syrup

T, the – official nickname for the Massachusetts Bay Transportation Authority (MBTA) Rapid Transit System
tall ships – tall-masted sailing vessels
tin ceiling – late-19th- to early-20th-century decorative feature consisting of thin steel sheets ('tinplates') embossed with decorative patterns, painted and used to cover ceilings
tuck-in – a substantial, sandwich-like meal

UMass – University of Massachusetts
Upper Cape – Cape Cod region near the Cape Cod Canal and the mainland
USFS – United States Forest Service, a division of the Dept of Agriculture that implements policies on federal forest lands on the principles of 'multiple use,' including timber cutting, wildlife management, camping and recreation
USGS – United States Geological Survey, an agency of the Dept of the Interior responsible for, among other things, detailed topographic maps of the entire country (particularly popular with hikers and backpackers)
UVM – University of Vermont

Vineyard, the – (pronounced 'VIN-yerd'), the island of Martha's Vineyard

weir – fishnet of string, bark strips, twigs, etc, placed in a river current to catch fish; using weirs is the oldest known method of fishing in the world
windjammer – a tall-masted sailing ship

Yankee – perhaps from *Jan Kees* (John Cheese), a derogatory term for English settlers in Connecticut used by 17th-century Dutch colonists in New York; an inhabitant or native of New England; one from the northeastern USA; a person or soldier from the northern states during the Civil War; an American

Thanks

Many thanks to the readers who wrote to us with helpful anecdotes, tips and advice:

Elizabeth Arbiter, Glen Armstrong, Christy Bennett, Dianne Bevan, Eimar Burke, Keith & Brenda Burton, Jenny Carlile, Caroline Clayton, Matthew Clough, Mr & Mrs M Copping, Marueen Fuda, Paul Fuller, Jochen Gerlach, Peter Glennon, Ingrid Hecht, Peter & Joyce Hewitt, Andrew Hindmarch, Johannes Kottl, David Lacey, Eric Lacy, Ed Long, Stephanie Lynn Carta, Nicholas Mace, Phil MacIver, Garry Mareels, Emer McCourt, Natasha McCready, Christoph Meyer, CP Millard, Stephanie Minns, Tim Mobbs, Dodd Mohr, Gabriel Moner, Tom Murtha, Katherine Ogburn, Hilary & Ian Potts, Torsten Remmert, Robin & Jean Roberts, Scott Robertson, Sheila M Rumble, John Sabo, John Sleigh, Ken Sommers, Martin Spacek, Kevin Spillane, Mark Stevenson, Dimitri Straub, Michael Terborg, Andrew Thompson, Kendal von Sydow, Naomi Wall, Fran & Mike Wallace, Charles Weedon, Anna-Lisa Wolters, Fenella Woodward

LONELY PLANET

You already know that Lonely Planet produces more than this one guidebook, but you might not be aware of the other products we have on this region. Here is a selection of titles which you may want to check out as well:

Boston
ISBN 0 86442 642 9
US$15.99 • UK£9.99

New York City
ISBN 1 86450 180 4
US$16.99 • UK£10.99

USA
ISBN 1 86450 308 4
US$24.99 • UK£14.99

Hiking in the USA
ISBN 0 86442 600 3
US$24.99 • UK£14.99

Canada's Maritime Provinces
ISBN 1 74059 023 6
US$16.99 • UK£10.99

Québec
ISBN 1 74059 024 4
US$16.99 • UK£10.99

Available wherever books are sold.

Index

Abbreviations

Text

Bold indicates maps.

Boxed Text

MAP LEGEND

ROUTES

City   Regional

.............Freeway
.............Tollway
.............Primary Road
.............Secondary Road
.............Tertiary Road
.............Dirt Road

.............Pedestrian Mall
.............Steps
.............Tunnel
.............Trail
.............Walking Tour
.............Path

ROUTE SHIELDS

(80) Interstate Freeway   (95) State Highway   (55) Canadian Highway
(101) US Highway   (G4) County Road   (40) Trans-Canada Highway

HYDROGRAPHY

.............River; Creek
.............Canal
.............Lake

.............Spring; Rapids
.............Waterfalls
.............Dry; Salt Lake

TRANSPORTATION

.............Train
.............MBTA Commuter Rail
.............MBTA Subway Stop
.............Ferry

BOUNDARIES

.............International
.............State

.............County
.............Disputed

AREAS

.............Beach
.............Building
.............Campus

.............Cemetery
.............Forest
.............Garden; Zoo

.............Golf Course
.............Park
.............Plaza

.............Reservation
.............Sports Field
.............Swamp; Mangrove

POPULATION SYMBOLS

✪ NATIONAL CAPITAL   National Capital
◉ STATE CAPITAL   State Capital

● Large City   Large City
● Medium City   Medium City

● Small City   Small City
○ Town; Village   Town; Village

MAP SYMBOLS

■ ....Place to Stay
▼ ....Place to Eat
● ....Point of Interest

.............Airfield
.............Airport
.............Archeological Site; Ruin
.............Bank
.............Baseball Diamond
.............Battlefield
.............Bike Trail
.............Border Crossing
.............Buddhist Temple
.............Bus Station; Terminal
.............Cable Car; Chairlift
.............Campground
.............Castle
.............Cathedral
.............Cave

.............Church
.............Cinema
.............Dive Site
.............Embassy; Consulate
.............Footbridge
.............Gas Station
.............Hospital
.............Information
.............Internet Access
.............Lighthouse
.............Lookout
.............Mine
.............Mission
.............Monument
.............Mountain

.............Museum
.............Observatory
.............Park
.............Parking Area
.............Pass
.............Picnic Area
.............Police Station
.............Pool
.............Post Office
.............Pub; Bar
.............RV Park
.............Shelter
.............Shipwreck
.............Shopping Mall
.............Skiing - Cross Country

.............Skiing - Downhill
.............Stately Home
.............Surfing
.............Synagogue
.............Tao Temple
.............Taxi
.............Telephone
.............Theater
.............Toilet - Public
.............Tomb
.............Trailhead
.............Tram Stop
.............Transportation
.............Volcano
.............Winery

Note: Not all symbols displayed above appear in this book.

LONELY PLANET OFFICES

Australia
Locked Bag 1, Footscray, Victoria 3011
☎ 03 8379 8000   fax 03 8379 8111
email talk2us@lonelyplanet.com.au

UK
10a Spring Place, London NW5 3BH
☎ 020 7428 4800 fax 020 7428 4828
email go@lonelyplanet.co.uk

USA
150 Linden Street, Oakland, CA 94607
☎ 510 893 8555, TOLL FREE 800 275 8555
fax 510 893 8572
email info@lonelyplanet.com

France
1 rue du Dahomey, 75011 Paris
☎ 01 55 25 33 00 fax 01 55 25 33 01
email bip@lonelyplanet.fr
www.lonelyplanet.fr

World Wide Web: www.lonelyplanet.com or AOL keyword: lp
Lonely Planet Images: lpi@lonelyplanet.com.au